1777 – 1779

1795 – 1818

1914

1861

Development of the Flag

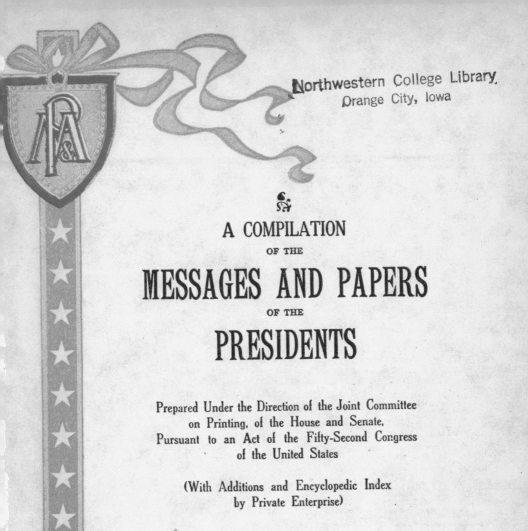

A COMPILATION

OF THE

MESSAGES AND PAPERS

OF THE

PRESIDENTS

Prepared Under the Direction of the Joint Committee
on Printing, of the House and Senate,
Pursuant to an Act of the Fifty-Second Congress
of the United States

(With Additions and Encyclopedic Index
by Private Enterprise)

VOLUME XIX
ENCYCLOPEDIC INDEX
A—M

PUBLISHED BY
BUREAU OF NATIONAL LITERATURE, Inc.
NEW YORK

10973

Government
Is Man's Most Exalted Work.

Republican Government
Is the Supreme Type of Organization.

The United States Government
Is of All Governments the Best.

Therefore, the men who performed that most difficult of human undertakings—the establishment of law—and who performed that task with a success without parallel,—the men who constructed the American Republic are leaders whose works have proved their wisdom consummate. . . . .

That Wisdom is concretely bodied forth in the MESSAGES AND PAPERS OF THE PRESIDENTS. In these Papers our Chief Magistrates and the statesmen, jurists, financiers, warriors who composed their Cabinets discuss questions perpetually before the voter, and define the fundamental policies on which is based this greatest human achievement. Their Doctrines form our Governmental Gospel.

THE ENCYCLOPEDIC INDEX

CONTAINS

More than 25,000 page references to the official utterances of the Presidents, interspersed with some eight hundred encyclopedic articles on American history and politics, elaborating and going into the details of every subject discussed by the executives.

A summary history and description of every branch of the Government—Executive, Legislative and Judicial—outlining the development of each department from its beginning to the present time, together with all bureaus and special commissions.

An analysis of each administration written by competent contemporaneous authority.

Definition and summary of the treaties between the United States and all foreign countries.

The growth of the Army and Navy, with the latest official facts of organization, strength and equipment.

History of each State from original territory to present time.

A brief description and history of every country in the world, and the trade and treaty relations of each with the United States.

Synopsis of all political parties, their platforms, growth and achievements. Leaders in all the great political movements since the organization of the government, together with their votes, are given in detail, as well as the origin of popular nicknames and campaign cries.

Accounts of the wars engaged in by the United States, together with a recital of the causes thereof and a brief account of each battle fought by American soldiers; also important foreign wars.

List of Federal courts and commissions and digests of such leading supreme court decisions as tend to interpret the constitution.

Discussions of public questions of national policy, such as Monroe Doctrine, Panama Canal, Interstate Commerce, Banking, Agriculture, Exports, Imports, Mining, Slavery, Woman Suffrage, Trusts, Prohibition, Labor, Tariff, etc.

Aboriginal inhabitants, characteristics and early home of each tribe and nation, their wars with the white settlers and decline before advancing civilization.

More than a thousand selected biographical sketches of eminent American statesmen and leaders in the country's development.

THE ENCYCLOPEDIC INDEX TO THE

MESSAGES AND PAPERS OF THE PRESIDENTS

SERVES A DOUBLE PURPOSE.

FIRST:

Assuming that the reader desires to investigate a specific subject,—the Index provides him with a succinct digest on that subject and underneath cites the numbers of pages where Presidential references thereto may be found. Thus, after reviewing the fundamental facts involved as presented by the digest, the reader is aided in forming his own opinion on the question by the arguments advanced by the Executives.

SECOND:

Assuming that the user is reading a Presidential Message,—the Index provides him with data on every question mentioned, and, by the page citations, enables him to compare the views of various Chief Magistrates on the same subject. .   .   .   .

See the analysis of each Administration under the name of the Executive. These analyses are paragraphed under subheadings (such as " Slavery "), so that one may readily trace the development of a question through many Administrations, and find the narrative continuous.

See the biographies of men famous in American Statecraft, Warfare and Diplomacy, as well as the biographies of present Cabinet Ministers, Senators, and Congressmen, which appear under their respective names.

SEE THE ARTICLES:

" United States, Government of."

" Constitution, Supreme Court Decisions on."

State, Treasury, War, Justice, Postoffice, Navy, Interior, Agriculture, Commerce and Labor, Departments of.

" Parties, American Political."

" Wars of, or Affecting, the United States."

" Battles by United States Forces."

" United States, History of."

" Foreign Relations."

" Nations."

" States and Territories."

" Banks and Banking."

" Laws."

" Law, Terms of."

" Indian Tribes."

" Geography."

ILLUSTRATIONS

PORTRAITS OF PRESIDENTS FROM
OFFICIAL WHITE HOUSE PAINTINGS,
PUBLIC BUILDINGS, MONUMENTS,
PLACES OF PATRIOTIC INTEREST,
HISTORICAL PAINTINGS AND
CONTEMPORARY CARTOONS,
PRESIDING LADIES OF THE WHITE HOUSE

¶ The collection of pictures appearing in the several volumes of this set can safely be said to be the best ever collected for the purpose of illustrating the history and progress of our country from every viewpoint.

¶ The pictures themselves almost tell the story of the development of this Nation. They appear in about equal number in each volume, and in direct connection with the text matter, therefore in chronological order.

¶ On the back of each of the historical illustration plates there is found descriptive matter which adds value to the illustrations and important historical data supplementing the messages themselves.

¶ In the forepart of each volume will be found a list of the illustrations therein.

FACSIMILE REPRODUCTIONS OF STATE PAPERS

Adams, John, Coinage Proclamation, 256.

Adams, John Quincy, Proclamation of Tonnage Duties (first and last pages), 948.

Buchanan's Note to Senate Relating to Mormon Troubles, 3135.

Clayton-Bulwer Treaty, of Taylor's Administration (final page), 2567.

Cleveland's Proclamation on Utah's Admission to Union, 6154.

Cleveland's Signature to Proclamation Admitting Utah into Union, 6155.

Declaration of Independence (Original Draft of), 4.

Declaration of War against Spain, 6295.

Declaration of War with Mexico, 2312.

Fillmore's Fugitive Slave Proclamation (first page), 2692.

Fillmore's Fugitive Slave Proclamation (last page), 2693.

Garfield's Note to the Senate, 4602.

Grant's Centennial Proclamation, 4376.

Grant's Signature to Centennial Proclamation, 4367.

Grant's Proclamation Calling for an Extra Session of the Senate, 3976.

Harrison's (Benjamin) Proclamation Admitting Washington to Union, 5375.

Harrison's (Benjamin) Signature to Proclamation Admitting Washington to Union, 5376.

Hay-Pauncefote Treaty, 7762.

Hayes' Proclamation, Maryland Railroad Strike (first page), 4470.

Hayes' Signature to Proclamation, Maryland Railroad Strike (last page), 4471.

Jackson's Proclamation about the Public Lands in Alabama, 1041.

Jackson's Signature on a State Document, 1201.

Jefferson's Neutrality Proclamation, 414.

Johnson's Thanksgiving Proclamation, 3530.

Johnson's Signature to Thanksgiving Proclamation, 3531.

Lincoln's Emancipation Proclamation (first, last, and intermediate pages), 3261.

Lincoln's Gettysburg Address, 3373.

Lincoln's Letter to Mrs. Bixby, 3341.

Lincoln's Signature to Emancipation Proclamation, 3262.

Lincoln's Proclamation Admitting West Virginia into the Union, 3389.

Lincoln's Signature to Proclamation Admitting West Virginia into Union, 3390.

Monroe Doctrine (page from Monroe's Seventh Annual Message), 791.

Monroe's Letter to a Friend Explaining National Policy, 759.

Pierce's Proclamation against Cuban Filibusters (first page), 2769.

Pierce's Proclamation against Cuban Filibusters (second page), 2770.

Roosevelt's Proclamation of Special Holiday for Celebration of Centennial of Lincoln's Birth, 6964.

Roosevelt's Announcement of Centennial of Lincoln's Birth, Last Page and Signature, 6965.

South Carolina's Secession Ordinance, 3151.

Taft's Proclamation of the Death of Vice-President Sherman, 7730.

Taft's and Secretary Knox's Signature to Announcement of Death of Vice-President Sherman, 7731.

Taylor's Signature on a State Document, 2566.

Tyler's Signature on the Ratification of the Webster-Ashburton Treaty, 2026.

Van Buren's Proclamation Revoking Tonnage Duties, 1549.

Washington's First Thanksgiving Proclamation, 66.

Webster-Ashburton Treaty, Ratified in Tyler's Administration, 2025.

Wilson's Engagement Book, Page from, 8016.

Wilson's Neutrality Proclamation at the Outbreak of the European War of 1914, 7968.

Wilson's Neutrality Proclamation, Last Page, with Signature of Secretary Bryan, 7969.

ENCYCLOPEDIC INDEX

to the

Messages and Papers of the Presidents

NOTE.—The pages of the MESSAGES AND PAPERS OF THE PRESIDENTS are consecutively numbered from Page 1 to the last page of the last message received before going to press, without regard to the division into volumes. The index numbers therefore refer to pages only. The page numbers in each volume are indicated on the back to assure quick and handy reference.

When a word or group of words is followed by the symbol *(q. v.)*, (which see), an article under that word or group of words is listed in the Index, and should be consulted.

A. B. C. Arbitration.—During the Mexican revolution of 1913-14, citizens of the United States suffered many insults and abuses, as well as loss of life and property, at the hands of the warring factions. Insolent aggression culminated on the 9th of April, 1914, when a paymaster of the U. S. S. *Dolphin* was arrested at Tampico, and the delivery of United States mail was interfered with. Admiral Mayo, commanding the fleet in the harbor, demanded a salute to the United States flag as partial reparation for the injuries sustained by the Americans. This was refused by President Huerta, and President Wilson backed Admiral Mayo's demand with an order for the occupation of Vera Cruz by American land and naval forces. (Page 8314.)

Before these were ready to begin the journey overland to Mexico City Senor Naon, the Argentine minister at Washington, Senhor da Gama, Brazilian ambassador, and Senor Suarez, the Chilean minister, proffered their services as mediators to settle the differences between the two republics. President Wilson accepted the good offices of the diplomats and appointed Justice Joseph R. Lamar, of the Supreme Court, and Frederick W. Lehman, an attorney, of St. Louis, to represent the United States. Huerta also appointed delegates. The mediators met at Niagara Falls, Canada, May 20, and by June 12, had agreed upon a plan for a provisional government for Mexico to consist of a president and a cabinet of four leading Mexicans, who should have been neutral during the revolution. President Wilson demanded that a Constitutionalist should be chosen as provisional president, but the mediators refused to sanction this. June 22, peace protocols were signed whereby the United States abandoned its claim for a salute to the flag and waived the question of a war indemnity from Mexico, as well as claims for damages due American citizens, with the understanding that these would be taken up and adjusted by the provisional government.

Meanwhile the revolutionists were closing in on Mexico City, and Carranza, the Constitutionalist leader, was asked to participate in the arbitration proceedings on condition that he agree to an armistice. This he refused. July 5, a federal election was held in Mexico and Huerta was re-elected President and Senor Blanquet Vice-President. Few of the populace participated in the voting, and ten days later Huerta resigned and boarded the German cruiser *Dresden* at Vera Cruz and departed for Jamaica. Don Francisco Carbajal, minister of foreign relations, was placed in charge of the government at Mexico City, and invited Carranza to come into the city and form a provisional government granting a general amnesty to those who had supported the Huerta administration.

_1_ B. Plot.—William H. Crawford, of Georgia, was a prominent Democratic-Republican candidate for the Presidency in 1824. During the early part of that year a series of letters signed "A. B." appeared in a Washington newspaper charging him with malfeasance in office as Secretary of the Treasury. They were written by Ninian Edwards, of Illinois, who had just been appointed minister to Mexico, and who acknowledged their authorship. Apr. 19, 1824, Edwards presented a memorial to the House of Representatives making specific charges. These he failed to sustain, and Crawford was exonerated.

Abaco Island (Bahamas), negotiations for cession of lands on, for erection of light-houses, 845.

Abandoned Farms.—The reasons given for farm abandonment are the impoverishment of the soil, through lack of fertilizer and rotation of crops, the meager financial rewards of ordinary farm labor, and the disinclination of country-bred men and women to remain on farms when the conveniences and luxuries of life are to be found in the cities, and enjoyed with greater comfort. The city man who takes his family to the country is usually actuated by two motives—sentiment and the high cost of living in the city. When a man only one generation from the farm finds eggs selling at 60 cents a dozen, broiled chickens at a dollar, and the kind of apples he formerly fed to hogs bringing a cent apiece in city markets he is apt to long for the abundant food of his boyhood days.

In his "Altruria," a novel, printed in 1894, William Dean Howells, an American novelist, predicted that soon the railroads would be imploring men to go from the cities and till the soil. Mr. W. C. Brown, President of the New York Central Railroad, in a speech in New York City in 1910, declared that there are 16,000 square miles of practically abandoned farms in New York, New England, the south and middle Southern States, and that there are 2,700 acres of abandoned tillable land within two hours' journey from New York City which can be purchased for $20 an acre. Mr. Brown declared himself willing to head a million-dollar syndicate to buy and reclaim these abandoned farms in a practical effort to decrease the cost of foodstuffs to the consumer.

Many men with city experience and modern industrial and business ideas have made farming profitable where the country-bred farmer with only the conventional methods has failed. The back-to-the-farm movement was given considerable impetus by the development of intensive farming in the West, by irrigation, by the railroads, the Department of Agriculture and the high price of foodstuffs in the cities.

President Roosevelt appointed a commission to investigate the conditions of farm life in America, and he discusses the question fully in a special message (page 7253). (See also Country Life Commission.)

Abelman vs. Booth.—An important Supreme Court case maintaining the constitutionality of the fugitive-slave law of 1850. Booth was tried before a commissioner appointed by the United States district court of Wisconsin for violation of the fugitive-slave law, and ordered to appear before the district court. Failing to do so, he was imprisoned by Abelman, the United States marshal for the district, but was released by the supreme court of the State on a writ of *habeas corpus*. Later he was indicted before the United States district court, but was again released by the State supreme court. In 1858 the case came before the United States Supreme Court. Booth had pleaded the unconstitutionality of the law. The court upheld the law and reversed the decision of the State supreme court.

Abolition Party.—An anti-slavery party organized in 1839, which later absorbed the Liberty Party (q. v.), and the National Anti-Slavery Society (q. v.). Its mission having been fulfilled by the emancipation of the slaves, the party did not continue in existence after the Civil War. (See Abolitionists.)

Abolitionists.—A term applied during and preceding the Civil War to the members of the New England Anti-Slavery Society and those who held with them that "immediate unconditional emancipation without expatriation was the right of every slave and that he could not be withheld by his master an hour without sin." The first society for the abolition of slavery was formed in Pennsylvania in 1774; New York

followed in 1785, Rhode Island in 1786, Maryland in 1789, and Connecticut, Virginia and New Jersey before 1792. Among the presidents of the New York society were John Jay and Alexander Hamilton.

Jan. 1, 1831, William Lloyd Garrison began the publication in Boston of a paper called *The Liberator,* which advocated the immediate liberation of slaves, regardless of all laws or constitutional provisions to the contrary. At the beginning of the following year he organized the above-named society, with the foregoing as its chief doctrine. Near the close of 1833 a similar society was formed in Philadelphia.

From this time forward the question became one of national importance. In consequence of his uncompromising utterances Garrison was indicted by grand juries in several Southern States and rewards were offered for his conviction. The New York *Weekly Emancipator* was another organ of the Abolitionists. Some strong pamphlets on the subject were: "Justice and Expediency; or, Slavery Considered with a View to Its Rightful and Effectual Remedy"; "Abolition," by John G. Whittier, Haverhill, Mass.; "Appeal in Behalf of that Class of Americans Called Africans," by Lydia Maria Child; and "The Sin of Slavery and Its Remedy," by Elizur Wright, a professor in the Western Reserve College. Abolition sentiments were not confined solely to the Northern States. The feeling against the abolitionists ran high and riots were frequent. At Alton, Illinois, in 1837, Elijah P. Lovejoy, an abolition editor, was mobbed and killed, and in 1838, Pennsylvania Hall, in Philadelphia, was burned. In 1838 many of the party desiring to nominate candidates for office, a proceeding to which the "Garrisonians" objected, withdrew. (See Abolition Party and illustrations opposite 1423, 2628.)

Aborigines.—A word used to designate the earliest inhabitants of a country. In America the term is applied generally to the Indians found by the early settlers.

Abrogation.—In international law, the act of breaking or discontinuing, as the abrogation of a treaty.

Absentee Shawnee Indians. (See Indian Tribes.)

Abyssinia (Ethiopia).—The total area of the Ethiopian Empire is estimated at 350,-000 to 400,000 English square miles, with a total population of from 7,000,000 to 8,000,000, of whom about half are Abyssinians, the remainder being Gallas, negro tribes on the west and south frontiers, and Danakils and Somalis on the east. About one-third of the whole area is covered by Abyssinian Somaliland. The boundaries of the empire are defined on the west, north, and northeast, where they touch, in order, the Sudan; the Italian colony of Massowah (Eritrea); the French colony of Djibuti; and the British Somaliland Protectorate. Northwards the boundary is about 15° 30′ N. lat., falling just south of Kassala.

Physical Features.—Western Abyssinia is a plateau, with peaks rising to 13,-000-15,000 feet; Eastern Abyssinia consists of the Danakil and Somali lowlands.

Natural Resources.—Western Abyssinia contains some mineral wealth; iron and coal are not uncommon, and gold is washed in various streams, while salt, saltpetre, and sulphur are also procurable. The lower country and deep valley gorges are very hot; the higher plateaus are well watered, with a genial climate. In the hotter regions, sugar cane, cotton, coffee, rubber, etc., flourish; in the middle zone maize, wheat, barley, wild oranges and other fruit trees, tobacco, potatoes, etc., are cultivated; and above 9,000 feet are excellent pastures with some corn cultivation. There are two seasons in the year, a dry winter and a rainy summer from June to September. The chief river is the Blue Nile. Horses, mules, donkeys, oxen, goats and sheep, and camels in the lowlands, form a large portion of the wealth of the people.

History.—It was visited by the Portuguese in 1492. The various small monarchies were united into one kingdom in 1855. In 1872 Kassai, of Tigre, who had assumed the title Negus Negust (King of Kings), was crowned as Johannes II, Emperor of Ethiopia. At his death in 1889, Menelik II (born 1842) became supreme ruler. Oct. 13, 1889, the Italian Government assumed a protectorate over Abyssinia, and by a subsequent treaty with King Menelik, the country came wholly under Italian influence. By an agreement signed Dec. 13, 1906, Italy, France and Great Britain undertook to preserve the integrity of Abyssinia.

Government.—Negus Negust or King of Kings Menelik II (King of Shoa). The Empire is a federation of the Kingdoms of Shoa, Godjam, Jimma, Kaffa and Wollo, and of the territories conquered by the dominant Kingdom of Shoa; the outward and visible sign of their allegiance to the Emperor being a contribution to the Imperial revenue. In 1908 a Council of Ministers was constituted by the Emperor with Lij Eyassu, grandson of Menelik, President of the Council.

Sept. 30, 1916, Lidj, then only 22 years old, was deposed and his aunt, Ouizero-Zeoditu, succeeded to the regency.

The Judicial System is based upon the code of Justinian, and there is an appeal from the courts to the Emperor. Private property in land being little known and the marriage tie being easily dissolved by either party, there is little social coherence.

Education and Religion.—The Abyssinians are Christian and the Emperor claims descent from Menelek, the son of Solomon and the Queen of Sheba. The Metropolitan (Abuna Mattheos) and the priests and monks are in some degree subject to the Coptic Patriarch of Alexandria, and have combined religious, judicial and educational offices.

Production and Industry.—The principal pursuits are agriculture, cattle breeding and hunting. The chief exports are coffee, civet, wax, hides, rubber, ivory and gold; the chief imports being cottons, hardware, provisions, arms and ammunition, petroleum and glass. External trade is increasing. The import duty on all goods is 8 per cent. *ad valorem.*

Abyssinia is the home of the coffee plant, which furnishes one of the chief exports. Cotton, sugar cane and vines flourish. Iron is abundant. Cattle, sheep and horses are raised. American gray shirting, hardware, ammunition, petroleum are imported. It was announced on May 18, 1911, that Lij Yasu has been proclaimed Emperor after an effort by his cousin to wrest the government from him. The chief exports are coffee, gum, wax, gold, ivory and civet. Pastoral interests dominate; large herds of cattle, sheep and goats are raised; excellent horses and long-wooled sheep in higher elevations. Manufactures primitive; some cloth, and working of leather and metals, etc. Caravan trade important; hides, skins, ivory, wax, gum, coffee, gold, ostrich feathers, etc., exchanged for manufactured articles.

Transportation is generally carried on by mules, donkeys and pack-horses in the west and by camels in the lowlands. A railway has just been built under French auspices. The posts and telegraphs are under French management, and Abyssinia has been admitted to the Postal Union. Telegraphs and telephones have been constructed, and admission to the International Telegraph Convention has been sought.

Army.—The active army consists of the Imperial Troops, numbering about 200,-000 men, armed with rifles, with some artillery and troops of Galla horsemen. The Feudatory States maintain local armies, available for Imperial purposes in time of war.

Towns.—The Capital, Adis Ababa, in Shoa, has a population of about 50,000; Harrar contains about 40,000; and Dire Dawa from 6,000 to 7,000. There are ancient architectural remains at Aksum, Gondar, and Ankober; modern architecture is very poor, while drainage and sanitation are unknown.

Foreign Relations.—Great Britain, France and Italy possess territory bordering the Abyssinian Empire and have entered into an agreement to respect the integrity of the Empire. The United States, Austria-Hungary and Germany have signed commercial treaties with the Empire. There are representatives of France, Germany, Great Britain, Italy, Russia and the U. S. A. at the capital. (See also Africa.)

Academy, Military. (See Military Academy.)

Academy, Naval. (See Naval Academy.)

Academy of Sciences, National, commission from membership of, to formulate plans for forestry system, 6167. (See also National Academy of Science.)

Acapulco, Mexico:

Controversies between American consul at, and Mexican authorities, 2695.

Imprisonment of American citizens in, 2720, 2834, 2837.

Acapulco, The, seizure and killing of Gen. Barrundia on, and action of American minister to Guatemala, discussed, 5544.

Conduct of commander Reiter regarding, referred to, 5569.

Papers regarding, transmitted, 5565.

Accessory.—In law one who is guilty of a felony, not by committing the offense in person or as a principal, nor by being present at its commission, but by being in some other way concerned therein, as by advising or inciting another to commit the crime or by concealing the offender or in any way helping him to escape punishment. An accessory *before the fact* is one who counsels or incites another to commit a felony and who is not present when the act is done; *after the fact,* one who receives and conceals or in any way assists the offender, knowing him to have committed a felony. The laws of different States vary as to the punishment of accessories.

Acclamation.—In legislative bodies, the act of voting by ayes and nays; also called voting *viva voce.*

Accounts and Disbursements, Division of, Agriculture Department.—An important division of the Bureau of Agriculture. It has complete charge and supervision over the fiscal affairs of the Department. It audits and pays all accounts and adjusts claims against the Department; decides questions involving the expenditure of public funds; prepares advertisements, schedules and contracts for annual supplies, leases, agreements, letters of authority, and all letters to the Treasury Department and Department of Justice; issues requisitions for the purchase of supplies and requests for transportation; prepares the annual estimates for appropriations, etc.

An idea of the work of the division may be had from the statement of its chief that in a recent year there were received, audited and paid 118,921 accounts, amounting to $15,736,198.02. More than 4,200 of these accounts, moreover, were so-called combined accounts. There were also audited and sent to the Treasury for payment 4,368 accounts. In the payment of the 118,921 accounts mentioned above it was necessary to draw 244 requisitions on the Treasury and issue 225,019 checks. To carry on the work of the Department of Agriculture for this year Congress appropriated $13,487,636 for ordinary expenses, in addition to permanent annual appropriations amounting to $6,329,-000, and special appropriations of $1,874,-614, making a total of $21,691,250. The cost of maintaining the Department of Agriculture has grown from $7,643,688 in 1906 to $29,019,703.98 for 1916.

Accounts, Public, system of, should be improved, 1120.

Acheen, native Kingdom of North Sumatra, war with Netherlands, neutrality preserved by United States in, 4192.

Acknowledgment.—An acknowledgment is the act of declaring the execution of an instrument before an officer authorized to certify to such declaration. The officer certifies to the fact of such declaration, and to his knowledge of the person so declaring. Conveyances or deeds of land to be entitled to be recorded must first be acknowledged before a proper officer. Most of the States have forms of acknowledgments, which should be followed.

Acknowledgments may be taken in general by notaries public, justices of the peace, Judges or Clerks of Courts of the higher grades, Registers, Masters in Chancery, Court Commissioners, town clerks, Mayor and Clerks of incorporated cities, within their respective jurisdictions.

Seals or their equivalent (or whatever is intended as such) are necessary in Alaska, Connecticut, Delaware, District of Columbia, Florida, Idaho, Illinois, Maine, Maryland, Massachusetts, Michigan, Minnesota, Missouri, New Hampshire New Jersey, New York, North Carolina, Oregon, Pennsylvania, South Carolina, Vermont, Virginia, West Virginia, Wisconsin, Wyoming. In almost all the States deeds by corporations must be under seal. Forms are prescribed or indicated by the statutes of most of the States except Connecticut, Florida, Louisiana. Separate acknowledgment by wife is required in Alaska, Arkansas, Delaware, District of Columbia, Florida, Georgia, Idaho, Kentucky, Louisiana, Montana, Nevada, New Jersey, North Carolina, Oregon, Pennsylvania, South Carolina, Tennessee, Texas. One witness to the execution of deeds is required in District of Columbia, Maine (customary), Maryland, Nebraska, New Jersey (usual), Oklahoma, Utah, Wyoming. Two witnesses to the execution of deeds are required in Arkansas, Connecticut, Florida, Georgia, Louisiana, Michigan, Minnesota, New Hampshire, Ohio, Oregon, South Carolina, Texas, Vermont, Wisconsin.

Acre Right.—The share of a citizen of a New England town in the common lands. The value of the acre right was a fixed quantity in each town, but varied in different towns. A ten-acre lot or right in a certain town was equivalent to 113 acres of upland and twelve acres of meadow, and a certain exact proportion was maintained between the acre right and salable lands.

Act of Hostility.—An unfriendly representation calculated to provoke war; or conduct of a war-like nature on the part of one country toward another. When the unfriendly, or war-like act is of such a nature as to preclude or make undesirable any attempt at adjustment by arbitration or diplomatic protest and representations, it becomes an overt act (q. v.), and is tantamount to a declaration of war on the part of the offender.

Acts of Congress. (See Bills and Acts.)

Acts, Public.—Public acts are the laws of a State and of the United States. State records are the registered deeds of property, journals of legislatures, etc. Judicial proceedings are the records of courts. Under the Constitution each State must give full faith and credit to the public acts, records, and judicial proceedings of every other State (twenty-four). The chief value of this provision is that it prevents endless lawsuits. When a case has been decided in one State, it cannot be opened in the courts of another State.

Ad valorem.—Duty on imported goods, based on the value thereof, rather than on their quantity or quality.

Adams, John.—1797-1801.
> Third Administration—Federal.
> *Vice-President*—Thomas Jefferson.
> *Secretary of State*—
> Timothy Pickering (continued).
> John Marshall, from May 13, 1800.
> *Secretary of the Treasury*—
> Oliver Wolcott (continued).
> Samuel Dexter, from Jan. 1, 1801.
> *Secretary of War*—
> James McHenry (continued).
> Samuel Dexter, from May 13, 1800.
> Roger Griswold, acting from Feb. 3, 1801.
> *Secretary of the Navy*—
> George Cabot appointed. Declined May 3, 1798.
> Benjamin Stoddert, from May 3, 1798.
> *Attorney-General*—
> Charles Lee (continued).
> *Postmaster-General*—
> Joseph Habersham (continued).

Party Affiliation.—Adams was essentially a Federalist and in common with his party, distrusted the self-governing power of the masses. He believed in strong central government by a class, not hereditary, but fitted by merit. He was democratic to the extent of believing that equality meant that all men should have equal rights in the eyes of the law; but that in hereditary rights, capacity, advantages, and position, all men are by no means equal. While vice-president and presiding officer in the Senate he was frequently called upon to decide by his casting vote questions of vital importance in the maintenance of the policy of

EXTENT OF THE UNITED STATES DURING THE ADMINISTRATION OF PRESIDENT J. ADAMS, 1797-1801.

(NOT INCLUDING TERRITORIES)

TENNESSEE 1796

KENTUCKY 1792

GEORGIA 1788

SOUTH CAROLINA 1788

NORTH CAROLINA 1789

VIRGINIA 1788

PENNSYLVANIA 1787

NEW YORK 1788

MD. 1788

DEL. 1787

N.J. 1788

CONN. 1788

VT. 1791

N.H. 1788

R.I. 1790

MASSACHUSETTS 1788

Washington. This occurred no fewer than twenty times in one session of Congress.

The Fifth Congress first met in extra session at Philadelphia, May 15, 1797, to consider the threatening relations with France. Jonathan Dayton, Federalist, of New Jersey, was elected Speaker of the House. The use of the three frigates already built was authorized and 80,000 militia were called for. An act was passed punishing privateering on a friendly nation by a fine of $10,000, and imprisonment for ten years. The House Committee on Ways and Means was first organized at this session.

War with France Threatened. — Adams appointed John Marshall, Elbridge Gerry and C. C. Pinckney commissioners to treat with France. They met in Paris Oct. 4, 1797, and were approached with a proposition to bribe members of the French Directory. They refused with indignation, implicating Talleyrand, the French Minister of Foreign Affairs, and were ordered out of France. It was on this occasion that Mr. Pinckney is reported to have given utterance to the famous sentence declaring that the United States had "Millions for defense; not one cent for tribute." Partisan feeling was general and bitter throughout the country and diplomacy was strained to the utmost to avert actual hostilities with France.

Congress organized the Navy Department and authorized a provisional army of 10,-000 men. Harper's Ferry was selected as a site for a government armory and manufactory. Washington was appointed commander-in-chief of the army with the rank of Lieutenant-General. The patriotic song "Hail, Columbia," was first sung in May, 1798. Commanders of ships of war were instructed to seize French armed vessels attacking American merchant-men or hovering about the coast for that purpose. Commercial intercourse with France was suspended and in July all treaties with that country were declared void. Although several naval engagements took place, a state of war did not exist according to international judicial opinion. The passage of the Alien and Sedition laws (*q. v.*) was one of the notable acts of the Fifth Congress.

March 30, 1799, upon assurance from France that a representative from the United States would be received with the "respect due a powerful nation" Adams sent William Vans Murray as Minister and associated with him Chief Justice Ellsworth, of Connecticut, and Gov. Davie, of North Carolina. All were received by Napoleon, first Consul.

Foreign Policy.—Party lines and party strife during the Adams administration were more largely influenced by foreign than by domestic political issues. Despite the humiliation inflicted upon the young Republic by both France and Great Britain, Adams resolutely followed Washington's policy of strict neutrality. It was difficult to steer safely between the bitter feeling against Great Britain which the Democrats displayed, and the dislike for France manifested by the Federalists. The decrees issued by France against American commerce caused Adams to convene Congress in special session soon after his inauguration. In his message on this occasion he reviews the situation and asks Congress to consider how war with France may be averted. He said: (page 226) "I shall institute a fresh attempt at negotiation and shall not fail to promote and accelerate an accommodation on terms compatible with the rights, duties, interests, and honor of the nation." The special commission composed of Pinckney, Marshall, and Gerry was sent to France, but was not openly received.

Then followed the X. Y. Z. affair (*q. v.*),

and the publicity of the despatches relating to it aroused great excitement in Europe and a storm of indignation in America. From all parts of the United States came the war-cry. "Millions for defense; not one cent for tribute." It was then that the nucleus of the navy was formed, and the army strengthened and commanded by Washington, who accepted the rank of lieutenant general. Then the French directory saw the error they had committed and made overtures to the United States. Adams met them, though his manner of doing so by appointing Vans Murray to negotiate peace antagonized Hamilton and his friends and brought about a rupture in the Cabinet. Adams always stoutly maintained that this was the most meritorious act of his life; and later generations have so testified. "I desire," he said, "no other inscription over my gravestone than this: 'Here lies John Adams, who took upon himself the responsibility of peace with France in 1800.'" The stringent alien and sedition acts, passed later in this administration, greatly increased the unpopularity of Adams.

Finances.—Adams very closely followed Washington's policy of paying off the national debt as rapidly as possible, so far as the exigencies of war would permit. He, however, deprecated doing so by means of loans. In his First Annual Address (page 253) he said: "The national defense must be provided for as well as the support of Government; but both should be accomplished as much as possible by immediate taxes, and as little as possible by loans." Feb. 12, 1798, in a special message (page 252) he reports a balance on hand at the beginning of the year of $15,494.24. In his Fourth Annual Message (page 297) he is able to report to Congress a greater revenue during the year than ever before, and says: "This result affords conclusive evidence of the great resources of this country and of the wisdom and efficiency of the measures adopted by Congress for the protection of commerce and preservation of public credit." In his reply to the Senate (page 302) he fully agrees "that the great increase in revenue is a proof that the measures of maritime defense were founded in wisdom. This policy has raised us in the esteem of nations." By proclamation of July 22, 1797 (page 239) all foreign silver coins, except Spanish milled dollars and parts of such dollars, shall cease to pass current or to be legal tender within the United States after Oct. 15, 1797; and all foreign gold coins shall cease to be legal tender after July 31, 1798. It also records the fact that coinage of silver began at the Mint of the United States on Oct. 15, 1794; and of gold on July 31, 1795.

Tariff.—July 8, 1797, an act was passed "laying additional duty on salt imported into the United States and for other purposes."

Public Debt.—During the administration of John Adams the public debt of the United States stood as follows: January 1, 1798, $79,228,529.12; 1799, $78,408,669.77; 1800, $82,976,294.35; 1801, $83,038,050.80.

Commerce.—The retaliatory prohibition of trade with certain of the French West Indies was removed by proclamations in 1799. These applied to ports in the Island of Santo Domingo. The defensive measures adopted by Congress for the protection of merchant vessels under convoy of an armed frigate, together with the renewal of amity and friendship with France, caused a rapid recuperation in commercial circles. Commercial transactions in the country for the year 1800 are represented as follows:

Total money in circulation, $26,500,000; Revenues, $10,848,749; Expenditures, $7,-

411,370; Imports, $91,252,768; Exports, $70,971,780

Political Complexion of Congress.—In the Fifth Congress the Senate of thirty-two members was made up of twenty-one Federalists and eleven Democrats; the House, of 105 members, was made up of fifty-one Federalists and fifty-four Democrats. In the Sixth Congress the Senate, of thirty-two members, was made up of nineteen Federalists and thirteen Democrats; the House, of 105 members, was made up of fifty-seven Federalists and forty-eight Democrats.

The Sixth Congress, the last to assemble in Philadelphia, met Dec. 2, 1799, and Theodore Sedgwick, of Massachusetts, was elected Speaker of the House. The death of Washington (Dec. 14) was announced to Congress Dec. 19 (page 287), and in his eulogy Henry Lee of Virginia used the memorable phrase, "First in war, first in peace and first in the hearts of his countrymen." At this session a gold medal was awarded to Thomas Truxtun, who, in command of the *Constellation*, had captured the French ship of war *L'Insurgente* and the frigate *La Vengeance.* The frigate *George Washington* carried tribute money from the United States to the Dey of Algiers and was required to carry the Dey's ambassador to Constantinople.

Successor Elected.—When the electoral votes were counted in February it was found that Jefferson and Burr, Democratic-Republican candidates, had each 73 votes; John Adams, Federalist, 65, and C. C. Pinckney, Federalist, 64, and John Jay, 1. The tie between Jefferson and Burr was sent to the House to decide, and after seven days, in which thirty-six ballots were taken, Jefferson and Burr were elected.

Adams, John:

Annual addresses of, 240, 261, 279, 295.

Addresses of Senate in reply, 244, 265, 282, 298.

Replies of President, 246, 267, 283, 299.

Addresses of House in reply, 247, 267, 283, 300.

Replies of President, 248, 270, 286, 302.

Biographical sketch of, 217.

Constitutional amendment relative to postponement of meeting of Congress suggested by, 240.

Death of, announced and honors to be paid memory of, 914.

Referred to, 930.

Death of Washington announced by, 287.

Address and replies, 288, 289, 290.

Division between people and government discouraged by, 229.

Exequaturs issued consuls of France revoked by, 260.

Finances discussed by, 228, 243, 252, 265, 281, 297.

Foreign policy discussed by, 228.

Hostile policy of France discussed by, 262.

Inaugural address of, 218.

Oath of office, notifies Congress of time and place of taking, 1220.

Pardons granted insurgents in Pennsylvania by, 293.

Portrait of, 216.

Proclamations of—

Commerce with France, restraints on, removed, 278, 292, 294.

Exequaturs of French consuls revoked, 260.

Extraordinary session of—
Congress, 222.
Senate, 306, 1220.

Foreign coins, legal tender of, 239.

Insurrection in Pennsylvania, 276.

Land for light-house designated, 1221.

Pardons to insurgents in Pennsylvania, 293.

Restraints on commerce with France removed by proclamation, 278, 292, 294.

Thanksgiving, 258, 274.

Property of United States in possession of, discussed by, 305.

Senate requested by, to postpone adjournment, 257.

Special session message of, 223.
Address of Senate in reply, 229.
Reply of President, 232.
Address of House in reply, 232.
Reply by President, 234.

Thanksgiving proclamations of, 258, 274.

Adams, John Quincy.—1825-1829.

Tenth Administration—Democratic-Republican.

Vice-President—John C. Calhoun.

Secretary of State—
Henry Clay.

Secretary of the Treasury—
Richard Rush.

Secretary of War—
James Barbour.
Peter B. Porter, from May 26, 1828.

Secretary of the Navy—
Samuel L. Southard (continued).

Attorney-General—
William Wirt (continued).

Postmaster-General—
John McLean (continued).

Party Affiliation.—Though trained in politics and diplomacy by his father, John Quincy Adams soon manifested independence of political thought and action. He broke with the Federalists when he gave unqualified support to Jefferson on the Louisiana Purchase, and, later, on the embargo. Speaking of the Federalists defending the *Leopard* affair, he said: "This was the cause which alienated me from that day and forever from the councils of the Federalist party." It was not long until he became active in Republican circles, both as a diplomat and as a Cabinet officer. During his administration, he was Whig so far as favoring internal improvements, the national bank, and high tariff on importations. As ex-President, he was elected to Congress (1831) by the anti-Masonic party, but he there maintained a perfectly independent attitude. When he left Congress he supported the Abolitionists, and from 1836 until 1845 he was fierce in his denunciation of gag-rule.

John Quincy Adams became Chief Magistrate by popular choice in an election where personality was concerned more than party affiliation. The election of 1824 was not regulated by Congressional caucus, which had lost its importance with the waning of

EXTENT OF THE UNITED STATES DURING THE ADMINISTRATION OF PRESIDENT J. Q. ADAMS, 1825-1829.

(NOT INCLUDING TERRITORIES)

MAINE 1820

VT 1791

N H 1788

MASS 1788

CONN 1788

R. I. 1790

N. J. 1787

DEL 1787

NEW YORK 1788

PENNSYLVANIA 1787

MD. 1788

VIRGINIA 1788

NORTH CAROLINA 1789

SOUTH CAROLINA 1788

GEORGIA 1788

OHIO 1803

INDIANA 1816

KENTUCKY 1792

TENNESSEE 1796

ALABAMA 1819

ILLINOIS 1818

MISSISSIPPI 1817

LOUISIANA 1812

MISSOURI 1821

FLAG OF 1829

COPYRIGHT. BY BUREAU OF NATIONAL LITERATURE (INC.)

the Federalists, nor by national convention, which mode of nomination did not originate until formed by the Anti-Masons in 1830.

Vote.—The contest was free for all, and narrowed down to four candidates: Adams, Jackson, Crawford, and Clay. Twenty-four States took part in the election, which was held Nov. 2. This is the earliest election in which there appears a record of the popular vote, as most of the electors were chosen by that means. That record shows that Andrew Jackson received 155,872 votes; John Quincy Adams, 105,321; William H. Crawford, 44,282; and Henry Clay, 46,587. The electoral vote, counted on Feb. 9, 1825, gave Andrew Jackson, 99; John Quincy Adams, 84; William H. Crawford, 41; and Henry Clay, 37.

Vote in House.—As no one received a majority, the House proceeded on the same day to elect a President from the three highest candidates. This excluded Clay, the most popular of the candidates in the House. John Quincy Adams was elected by the votes of thirteen States; Jackson received seven, and Crawford four. The electoral college had elected John C. Calhoun Vice-President, with 182 votes. In the electoral college, had three New York men, who were returned as Clay men, voted in accordance with their instructions, Clay would have been one of the three to go to the House, and the result might have been very different. This was the second time that the House was called upon to choose a President.

Political Complexion of Congress.—In the Nineteenth Congress (1825-1827) the Senate, of forty-eight members, was made up of thirty-eight Democrats and ten Whigs; and the House, of 213 members, was made up of seventy-nine Federalists and 134 Democrats. In the Twentieth Congress (1827-1829) the Senate, of forty-eight members, was made up of thirty-seven Federalists and eleven Whigs; and the House, of 213 members, was made up of eighty-five Federalists and 128 Democrats.

John W. Taylor, of New York, was elected Speaker of the House in the Nineteenth Congress, which numbered among its members Edward Everett, of Massachusetts, and James K. Polk, of Tennessee.

In 1826 the South American States called a general congress to meet in Panama and invited the United States to be represented (page 884). During the debate on the subject in the Senate John Randolph referred to the association of Adams and Clay as that of the Puritan and the blackleg. A duel followed between Clay and Randolph. The disappearance of William Morgan from Canandaigua, N. Y., Sept. 12, 1826, gave rise to the Anti-Masonic party.

Indian Affairs.—Numerous treaties were made with Indians during Adams' administration, among them the cession of the lands of most of the tribes inhabiting territory east of the Mississippi River and their removal to the Indian Territory. The refusal of the Creeks to be bound by a treaty signed by their chiefs formed the subject of special message by Mr. Adams (page 890).

Tariff.—Two acts relating to the tariff were passed in this administration—that of May 22, 1824, and of May 19, 1828. Speaking of the latter in his Fourth Annual Message (page 980) President Adams said: "The tariff of the last session was in its details not acceptable to the great interests of any portion of the Union, not even to the interests which it was specially intended to serve. Its object was to balance the burdens upon native industry imposed by the operation of foreign laws, but not to aggravate the burdens of one section of the Union by the relief afforded to another. . . . But if any of the duties imposed by

the act only relieve the manufacturer by aggravating the burden of the planter, let a careful revisal of its provisions, enlightened by the practical experience of its effects, be directed to retain those which impart protection to native industry and remove or supply the place of those which only alleviate one great national interest by the depression of another."

Internal Improvements.—The policy of President Adams differed materially in regard to internal improvement from those of his immediate predecessors. In his Inaugural Address (page 864) he said: "To pursue to their consummation those purposes of improvement in our common condition instituted or recommended by him [Monroe] will embrace the whole sphere of my obligations. To the topic of internal improvement emphatically urged by him at his inauguration, I recur with peculiar satisfaction. It is that from which, I am satisfied, the unborn millions of our posterity who are in future ages to people this continent will derive their most fervent gratitude to the founders of the Union; that in which the beneficent action of its Government will be most deeply felt and acknowledged. . . . The extent and limitation of the powers of the General Government in relation to this transcendently important subject will be settled and acknowledged to the common satisfaction of all, and every speculative scruple will be solved by a practical public blessing."

Public Debt.—The public debt of the United States during the administration of President Adams stood as follows: January 1, 1826, $81,054,059.99; 1827, $73,-987,357.20; 1828, $67,475,043.87; 1829, $58,421,413.67.

In his Second Annual Message (page 924) the President says: "It is well for us, however, to be admonished of the necessity of abiding by the maxims of the most vigilant economy, and of resorting to all honorable and useful expedients for pursuing with steady and inflexible perseverance the total discharge of the debt." In his Third Annual Message (page 952) he says: "The deep solicitude felt by our citizens of all classes throughout the Union for the total discharge of the public debt will apologize for the earnestness with which I deem it my duty to urge this topic upon the consideration of Congress—of recommending to them again the observance of the strictest economy in the application of the public funds."

Finance.—In his Fourth Annual Message (page 977), at the close of his administration, President Adams was able to say: "The condition and prospects of the revenue are more favorable than our most sanguine expectations had anticipated." He reported a balance in the Treasury, Jan. 1, 1828, of $5,861,972.83; with a prospect of a balance of over $5,000,000 on the first of the coming year. "The receipts for the present year have amounted to near two millions more than was anticipated at the commencement of the last session of Congress."

Slavery.—"The African Slave Trade," said President Adams in his First Annual Message (page 875), "has long been excluded from the use of our flag, and if some few citizens of our country have continued to set the laws of the Union, as well as those of nature and humanity, at defiance by persevering in that abominable traffic, it has been only by sheltering themselves under the banners of other nations less earnest for the total extinction of the trade than ours." But the intensity of feeling with which the President loathed slavery came out in its fullest force when, as ex-President, he returned to Congress and, single-handed, fought the pro-slavery forces and brought about the repeal of the "gag-law" which the House tried to enforce against the Abolitionists.

Adams, John Quincy:

Annual messages of, 865, 916, 944, 973.

Astronomical observatory, establishment of, recommended by, 789.

Biographical sketch of, 857.

Commissioner to negotiate treaty with Sweden, nomination of, 254.

Death of, announced and honors to be paid memory of, 2477.

Election of, notification of, 858.
Reply of, 858.

Finances discussed by, 869, 923, 952, 977.

Foreign Policy discussed by, 862, 868, 884, 895, 903, 922, 950.

Inaugural address of, 860.

Internal Improvements discussed by, 982.

International Congress at Panama discussed by. (See Panama, Isthmus of.)

Minister plenipotentiary of the United States to the court of Russia at St. Petersburg appointed by President Madison, June 26, 1809, 456.

Oath of office, notifies Congress of time and place of taking, 859.

Portrait of, 856.

Private secretary of, assaulted while delivering message to Congress, 966.

Proclamations of—

Commercial intercourse with British colonial ports suspended, 941.

Discriminating duties suspended on vessels of—

Hanover, 970.

Italy, 942.

Extraordinary session of Senate, 997.

Facsimile of, opposite 948.

Reward for apprehension of Willis Anderson, 943.

Secretary of State, 604.

Correspondence in regard to claims against France, 834.

State of the Union, discussed by, 865, 916, 944, 978.

Tariff discussed by, 979.

Tribute paid memory of Jefferson and Adams by, 930.

Adamson Law. (See Railroads, *Eight-hour Day*.)

Addison, The, impressment of seamen from, 2772.

Adelaide, international exhibition at, discussed, 5116.

Adjutant General. (See War Department and Army.)

Administration.—This term is generally applied to the President and his Cabinet.

The President as chief executive officer of the nation may direct, without consultation, the acts of any departmental chief, guided solely by the Constitution. He is authorized, however, to consult the heads of Departments. Washington consulted with his Attorney-General and Secretaries of State, War, and the Treasury. When in 1798 the Navy Department was established, Benjamin Stoddert, its chief executive officer, was admitted to the President's council. The Postmasters-General were not called into council until 1829, during William T. Barry's incumbency. Secretaries of the Interior, of Agriculture and of Commerce and Labor were invited to seats at the council table immediately upon the establishment of their Departments.

Admiral.—The highest rank in the United States Navy. The word is derived from the Arabic amir-al, and means "chief of the." It was early used in England as the title of the commander of the navy. In the United States the rank was first created especially to confer honor upon David G. Farragut.

July 11, 1862, upon recommendation of President Lincoln, Farragut, then referred to courteously but unofficially as Commodore, received the thanks of Congress for his distinguished services in capturing New Orleans and opening the lower Mississippi to the Union forces. Upon the reorganization of the navy in the same month he was placed first on the list of rear-admirals. Further successes on the lower Mississippi and in Mobile Bay induced Congress to express the gratitude of the country by creating another and higher grade for Farragut —that of Vice Admiral—in which office he was confirmed Dec. 21, 1864. After the war between the States Congress created the office of Admiral and conferred it upon Farragut July 25, 1866. Vice Admiral David D. Porter succeeded to the title in 1870, and upon his death in 1891, the title became extinct. For distinguished services in the battle of Manila Bay, May 1, 1898, George Dewey was promoted by Congress to be Admiral of the Navy, a grade above admiral and corresponding to admiral of the fleet in the British navy and a similar one in other navies.

The naval appropriation bill of 1915 contained a provision that after June 1 of that year the commanding officer of the Atlantic fleet, the Pacific fleet and the Asiatic fleet, while serving as such, should have the rank of Admiral, and the officer serving as second in command of those fleets should have the rank of Vice Admiral. Under that law Frank F. Fletcher, Thomas B. Howard and Walter Cowles were named as Admirals. The Admiral's flag has a navy blue background, on which four stars are arranged like the points of a diamond in the middle of the pennant. The rank of Admiral in the navy corresponds to that of General in the army; that of Vice Admiral to Lieutenant General, Rear Admiral (first nine class) to Major General and Rear Admiral (second nine class) to Brigadier General.

Admiral, revival of grade of, recommended, 6345.

Admiral P. Tordenskiold, The, appropriation in behalf of owners of, recommended, 3328.

Admission of States.—The Declaration of Independence declares "that these United Colonies are, and of right ought to be, free and independent States" (page 4). Its adoption on July 4, 1775, created as such the original thirteen States of the Union, viz.: Delaware, Pennsylvania, New Jersey,

Georgia, Connecticut, Massachusetts, Maryland, South Carolina, New Hampshire, Virginia, New York, North Carolina, and Rhode Island. Shortly before this date several of the Colonies had modified their original charters and established independent local governments. Oct. 10, 1780, the Continental Congress passed a resolution providing that western territory which might be "ceded to the United States by any particular State shall be disposed of for the common benefit of the United States and be settled and formed into distinct republican States, which shall become members of the Federal Union and have the same rights of sovereignty, freedom, and independence as the other States"; and in 1789 the Constitution made its provision for the admission of new States (page 24).

Most of the States that have been admitted since the formation of the original Union have achieved statehood from a condition of territorial organization prescribed by Congress, although some have not gone through this process. Such territorial organization was first established by Congress in July, 1787, when it passed the ordinance providing a government for the Northwest Territory (*q. v.*). The method of direct admission is illustrated by Vermont, which was formed out of territory claimed by New York and New Hampshire; Texas, which was annexed; and California, which was admitted soon after the Mexican war, without waiting to be organized as a Territory. The usual steps by which a Territory becomes a State are: (1) A petition to Congress expressing the desire of the people for admission; (2) an enabling act passed by Congress stating the conditions of admission; (3) the adoption of a constitution and a form of State government by a convention of delegates chosen by the people; (4) the ratification of the constitution and the election of State officers by the people; and (5) a proclamation by the President announcing that the Territory has become a State.

The question of the admission of Kansas under a constitution which permitted slavery or one which forbade it became a national political question between 1856 and 1859. Pro-slavery and anti-slavery partisans sent colonists into the territory to help form a constitution, and the animosities between these became so bitter as to cause riot and bloodshed. (See Kansas; Lecompton Constitution; Wyandotte Constitution.)

Provisions for the admission of New Mexico and Arizona into the Union as States were made by Chapter 310 of the acts of the Second Session of the sixty-first Congress, approved June 20, 1910. Constitutional conventions were held in both Territories under the provisions of the above-mentioned act. State Constitutions were framed and submitted to the people for ratification and were adopted. The Constitution of Arizona having contained a provision providing for the recall of the judiciary by the electors and the Constitution of New Mexico having contained a clause "attempting to annul and set aside the boundary lines heretofore legally run" between the Territory of New Mexico and the State of Texas, said Constitutions failed to receive the approval of the President and Congress.

At the First Session of the sixty-second Congress, a joint resolution "to admit the Territories of New Mexico and Arizona upon an equal footing with the original States" was adopted, which admitted both Territories to statehood conditionally; the condition being the elimination of the objectionable provisions from the State Constitutions adopted by the people of the re-

spective Territories. The first State to be joined to the original Union of thirteen States was Vermont, in 1791, and the last, Arizona, in 1912.

The following table shows the order and date of admission to the Union of the several states, as well as the order and date of ratification of the Constitution by the original states:

ORIGINAL STATES States	Ratified the Constitution
1—Delaware	Dec. 7, 1787
2—Pennsylvania	Dec. 12, 1787
3—New Jersey	Dec. 18, 1787
4—Georgia	Jan. 2, 1788
5—Connecticut	Jan. 9, 1788
6—Massachusetts	Feb. 6, 1788
7—Maryland	April 28, 1788
8—South Carolina	May 23, 1788
9—New Hampshire	June 21, 1788
10—Virginia	June 26, 1788
11—New York	July 26, 1788
12—North Carolina	Nov. 21, 1789
13—Rhode Island	May 29, 1790

STATES ADMITTED TO THE UNION States	Admitted
1—Vermont	Mar. 4, 1791
2—Kentucky	June 1, 1792
3—Tennessee	June 1, 1796
4—Ohio	Feb. 19, 1803
5—Louisiana	April 30, 1812
6—Indiana	Dec. 11, 1816
7—Mississippi	Dec. 10, 1817
8—Illinois	Dec. 3, 1818
9—Alabama	Dec. 14, 1819
10—Maine	Mar. 15, 1820
11—Missouri	Aug. 10, 1821
12—Arkansas	June 15, 1836
13—Michigan	Jan. 26, 1837
14—Florida	Mar. 3, 1845
15—Texas	Dec. 29, 1845
16—Iowa	Dec. 28, 1846
17—Wisconsin	May 29, 1848
18—California	Sept. 9, 1850
19—Minnesota	May 11, 1858
20—Oregon	Feb. 14, 1859
21—Kansas	Jan. 29, 1861
22—West Virginia	June 19, 1863
23—Nevada	Oct. 31, 1864
24—Nebraska	Mar. 1, 1867
25—Colorado	Aug. 1, 1876
26—North Dakota	Nov. 2, 1889
27—South Dakota	Nov. 2, 1889
28—Montana	Nov. 8, 1889
29—Washington	Nov. 11, 1889
30—Idaho	July 3, 1890
31—Wyoming	July 11, 1890
32—Utah	Jan. 4, 1896
33—Oklahoma	Nov. 16, 1907
34—New Mexico	Jan. 6, 1912
35—Arizona	Feb. 14, 1912

Admission of States (see also the several States; Reconstruction; Restoration):

Acts for admission of certain Southern States vetoed, 3846, 3848.

Recommendations regarding, 3033, 3086.

Admittance, The, seizure of, on coast of California, 2456.

Adobe State.—A nickname for New Mexico (q. v.). (See also States.)

Aeronautics.—The science of navigating the air has an authentic history dating back to A. D. 67. The free flying balloon or aerostat is a spherical bag filled with gas whose specific gravity is lighter than the air near the surface of the earth; it cannot be steered, and is at the mercy of the air currents.

A dirigible balloon has an elongated envelope, and is equipped with a motor, propellers and a rudder, and can be steered in a moderate wind.

Flying machines which are not lifted into the air by gas bags are generally known as aeroplanes. They are respectively classified as monoplanes, biplanes, triplanes, etc., according as they consist of one or a number of plane surfaces.

The French army, in a battle with the Austrians at Mauberge, June 13, 1794, used an aerial vessel for reconnoitering the position of the enemy, and balloons were used during the civil war in the United States and by the French at the siege of Paris.

Experiments with plane surfaces driven at high speed were first successful in 1843, when the English inventor Henson flew the first aeroplane. In America the pioneers in mechanical flight were Octave Chanute, of Chicago, and A. M. Herring.

The first substantial advance in flying machines was made by Lilienthal in Germany, in the seventies and eighties. His researches, followed by practical demonstration of aeroplanes, have formed the basis of all subsequent achievement. Professor Langley, of the Smithsonian Institution in Washington, began experimenting in 1885, and flew across the Potomac River in 1896. The Wright brothers, Wilbur and Orville, following the lines of Langley and Lilienthal, made their first flights under motor power in 1903. July 4, 1908, Glenn H. Curtiss flew in a biplane at the rate of forty miles an hour.

International meetings, the possibility of securing government contracts and offers of prizes by newspapers and aviation societies gave great impetus to the development of aeroplanes in 1909, 1910 and 1911. The Wright brothers and Glenn H. Curtiss continued to be the foremost experimenters in America, as well as winning fame and prizes abroad. In September, 1908, Orville Wright had almost met the government requirements for a practical aeroplane for use in the army, when one of his propeller blades broke during a flight at Fort Myer, Va., and the machine fell to earth, killing Lieut. Selfridge, U. S. A., who was a passenger, and seriously injuring Wright. In July, 1909, Orville Wright fulfilled all the specifications laid down by the government and won a bonus of $25,000 for exceeding the stipulated speed, and the Wright machine was purchased by the government for the use of the Signal Corps.

The American aviator, Curtiss, was the most conspicuous winner at the Rheims, France, meeting in 1909, winning the James Gordon Bennett Cup and $5,000. A few weeks previous he had won the *Scientific American* Cup for the second time. The New York *World* offered a prize of $10,000 for the first aviator to fly from Albany to New York or vice versa. Curtiss made this trip, winning the prize, May 29, 1910. He covered the distance in 2 hours, 46 minutes on the wing, an average of 54 miles an hour. June 30, 1910, Charles K. Hamilton won a prize offered by the New York *Times* and the Philadelphia *Ledger* by flying from New York to Philadelphia carrying a message from the Mayor of New York to the Governor of Pennsylvania, and returning. Nov. 7, 1910, Philip P. Parmalee flew from Dayton to Columbus, O., a distance of 62 miles, in 57 minutes, carrying 200 pounds of merchandise. Charles T. Weymann, an American, won the James Gordon Bennett Cup at Eastchurch, England, July 1, 1911.

The use of flying machines as engines of war has attracted the attention of military men of all countries, particularly in Europe where huge armaments are the rule. Their chief uses, it has been determined, have been for scouting and dropping explosives or combustibles. The most successful experiments at bomb-dropping made in America were those of Clifford B. Harmon, at Mineola, L. I., N. Y. Guns to bring down aeroplanes have been given some attention, and the Krupp works, at Essen, Germany, have produced a gun capable of shooting from 20,000 to 35,000 feet into the air, whereas air craft are scarcely discernible beyond 10,000 feet. (See European War, *Aerial Warfare.*)

At the close of 1910 France had thirty aeroplanes building and in commission for military service. The first use of the aeroplane under conditions of actual warfare occurred at Ciudad. Juarez, Mexico, in February, 1911, when Charles K. Hamilton crossed the Mexican border from the United States, made a circuit over the territory supposed to be occupied by the insurgent army and discovered that the insurgents had retired to distant mountain fastnesses. As a naval auxiliary the aeroplane promises to be of great value in rising to a height of a mile or more to inspect the wide expanse of ocean visible from such an elevation. The use of the aeroplane in war may revolutionize military tactics by discovering the exact location, armament and numbers of the enemy, and might prove destructive by dropping explosives upon battleships in the enemy's lines.

During 1911 and 1912 a number of flights were undertaken to show the possibility of carrying mail by aeroplane. In connection with the aviation meet at the Nassau Boulevard Aerodrome on Long Island, N. Y., in September, 1911, an aerial post was maintained and letters carried to Mineola, and delivered to the postmaster. On one occasion Postmaster-General Hitchcock was a passenger on a biplane and personally carried a mail sack.

All world records for cross-country flying were broken during the New York to Los Angeles flight of Calbraith P. Rodgers, who left Sheepshead Bay, N. Y., on Sunday, Sept. 17, 1911, and completed his flight to the Pacific coast on Sunday, Nov. 5, at Pasadena, Cal. Rodgers flew a Wright biplane, and during his long trip the machine was repeatedly repaired, so great was the strain of the long journey in the air. Rodgers is estimated to have covered 4,231 miles, although the actual route as mapped out was but 4,017 miles.

Jan. 18, 1911, E. Ely flew from aviation field near San Francisco to deck of U. S. Cruiser *Pennsylvania*, anchored in San Francisco Bay, in flight of sixteen minutes' duration. Ely, flying a Curtiss biplane, landed on a specially built platform at the stern of the vessel. Later he successfully arose from the deck and returned to the aviation field. This was the first aeroplane to land upon the deck of a vessel.

Stephen McGordon established a new cross country passenger-carrying flight record, Apr. 1, 1916, when he flew from Newport News to Washington and return, about 300 miles, in 4½ hours.

(See also Army, *Signal Corps;* Navy, *Flying Corps,* and for practical uses in war, see European War, *Aerial Warfare.*)

Aeroplane.—An airship which is heavier than air, as distinguished from lighter-than-air machines, such as balloons or Zeppelins (q. v.). (See Aeronautics; European War, *Aerial Warfare.*)

Affairs, Foreign. (See Foreign Affairs, Foreign Policy of United States, and also the several powers.)

Expense incurred in, for which no provision was made by law, 108. Report on, transmitted, 5200.

Afghanistan (called Khorassan by the natives) is an independent Asiatic state on the northwest frontier of India. Its area is estimated at 246,000 English square miles and its population at 5,000,-000. It is bounded on the west by Persia, on the south by British Baluchistan, on the north by Russia in Asia, and on the east by the Punjaub and northwest Frontier Provinces of British India.

Ethnography.—The population is mixed. The Afghans (or Duranis) have been predominant since 1747, especially in Kandahar. Next came the Ghilzais (military and commercial) and the Tajiks (aboriginals, who are cultivators or retail traders). On the Indo-Afghan frontier are many Pathan tribes, who are much influenced by the mullahs. All are Sunni Mohammedans, except the Hazaras and Kizilbashes, who belong to the Shiite sect. The national tongue is Pushtu. Recently steps have been taken to develop education, hitherto controlled by the Mullahs.

Physical Features.—Mountains, chief among which are the Hindu Kush, cover three-fourths of the country, the elevation being generally over 4,000 feet. There are three great river basins, the Oxus, the Helmand, and the Kabul. The climate is dry, with extreme temperatures in winter and summer.

Government.—Amir of Afghanistan and its Dependencies. Habibullah Kahn ("Lamp of the National Religion") succeeded his father (Abdur Rahman Khan) Oct. 3, 1901. The Amir (Abdur Rahman Khan) established a strong central government and introduced a regular civil and military organization, including officers for public works, posts, police, finance and trade, etc. For the purposes of local government, the country is divided into six provinces, Kabul, Kandahar, Herat, Turkestan, Farrar and Badakshan (with Kafristan and Wakhan), which are under governors (hakim), with subordinate nobles and judges, police and revenue officers. The Afghan laws are Islamic sacred laws, tribal laws, and those of the Amir, who is the Court of Appeal. The law is bulky and the crim' al law severe.

Foreign Relations.—By agreement with the Amir, the "buffer State" of Afghanistan has no foreign relations with any Power except the Government of India. The modern history of Afghanistan dates from 1881, when Abdurrahan was recognized as ruler. The British Government engaged to preserve the safety and integrity of Afghanistan against any unprovoked attack, provided that the Amir acted as a friend and ally. By the Anglo-Russian convention of August, 1907, Russia declared Afghanistan outside the Russian sphere of influence, and engaged to conduct all her political relations with Afghanistan through Great Britain, and that Great Britain and Russia should enjoy equality of commercial facilities.

Production and Industry and Commerce.—Most of the people are industrious cultivators, and the country has become fairly settled, peaceful and prosperous. There is excellent irrigation and all profitable soil is utilized. There are generally two crops a year, one of wheat (the staple food), barley, or lentils; the other of rice, millet, maize and *dal*, while the country is rich in fruits. Sheep and transport animals are bred. The manufactures include silk, woolen and hair cloths, and carpets. Salt, silver, copper, coal, iron, lead, rubies and gold are found. The exports to India are mainly fruits and nuts, raw wool, and *ghi;* while the imports therefrom are chiefly cotton yarn and piece goods, metals, leather goods, tea and sugar. The Afghan customs duties are heavy. There is a large export of wool to Persia and Russia, cotton and silk goods, sugar, etc., being taken in exchange.

Transportation.—The roads are generally unsuitable for wheeled traffic, but are being improved. Goods are conveyed by pack-animals. The chief trade routes to India are the Khaibar Pass, from Kabul to Peshawar (191 miles), along which a motor service has been established by the Amir, and the road from Kandahar to Quetta (125 miles). The Sind-Pishin railway terminates at Chaman, on the frontier, 65 miles from Kandahar, from which a fine road of 318 miles runs to Kabul.

Towns.—Capital, Kabul, about 150,000). The chief commercial center is Kandahar (30,000). (See also Asia.)

Afognak Island (in Gulf of Alaska, separated from Alaskan Peninsula by Shelikof Strait), lands in, set apart as public reservation by proclamation, 5795.

Africa.—The area of Africa is 11¾ million square miles, about three times that of Europe. Its extreme longitudes are 17° W. at Cape Verde and 51° E. at Cape Guardafui. The extreme latitudes are Cape Blanco in 37° N. and Cape Agulhas in 35° S., at a distance of about 5,000 miles. It is surrounded by seas on all sides, except in the narrow isthmus through which is cut the Suez Canal, and may be considered as a great peninsula of the Eurasian continent.

The nations of Africa, with the form of government and the capital of each, follow:

	Area Sq. Miles	Population
Abyssinia (Empire), Adis Ababa	350,000	7,000,000
Egypt (Con-dominium), Cairo.	363,200	11,400,000
Liberia (Republic), Monrovia.	48,000	1,500,000
Morocco (Empire), Fez	220,000	5,000,000
Sudan (Con-dominium), Khartum	950,000	2,750,000
Union of South Africa (British), Pretoria	470,000	6,000,000

Area and Population.—Islands adjacent to the continent of Africa, their size and the government to which they belong are:

Name and Government	Area Sq. Miles	Population
Ascension, British	38	150
Azores, Portuguese	920	260,000
Canary Islands, Spanish	2,800	300,000
Cape Verde Islands, Portuguese	1,500	150,000
Comoro Islands, French	750	60,000
Madagascar, French	228,000	3,000,000
Madeira, Portuguese	310	150,000
Mauritius, British	720	370,000
Reunion, French	970	180,000
Rodriguez, British	90	3,000
St. Helena, British	50	3,500
Seychelles, British	150	23,000
Socotra, British	1,400	12,000

Physical Features.—Africa is broadly a tableland with few mountain ranges, except the Atlas, though isolated peaks rise to a considerable elevation in Abyssinia, in East Africa (Kenya, Kilimanjaro and Ruwenzori), and in West Africa (Kamerun Peak). If an irregular line is drawn from a point on the West Coast, a little south of the Equator, to a point near the middle of the Red Sea, Africa can be divided into two nearly equal parts which differ considerably in character. The northwestern part comprises two regions of comparative lowland separated by the Atlas and the plateaus of Tibesti and Tasili. The southeastern part consists of great masses of highlands and plateaus broken up by river valleys. The rivers of Africa drain into the Atlantic, the Mediterranean, and the Indian Ocean. Both the Senegal and Gambia are navigable for some distance in the rainy season. The most important river which flows into the Gulf of Guinea is the Niger. The Congo rises in the plateau southwest of Lake Tanganyika. From Stanley Falls to Stanley Pool, a broad, navigable river flows for 1,000 miles. As these are themselves great rivers, an enormous amount of water is carried down to the mouth. Owing to the depth of the ocean, the sediment deposited does not reach the surface in the form of a delta, but forms submarine ridges 5,000 feet in height for over 300 miles on each side of its ocean channel. The Orange River rises in the Drakensberg Mountains not far from the East Coast and receives the Vaal and other large rivers. The Nile rises in the south of Victoria Nyanza, the largest lake in Africa, of about the area of Scotland, and breaks through the plateau to the north by the Murchison Falls into the Albert Nyanza, some 1,600 fe t below the level of the larger lake. Owing to the flat character of the country and the large amount of water which has no sufficient outlet, an extensive swamp vegetation, the "sudd," has been formed in this part of its course. At Khartum it receives the Blue Nile, which, with the other Abyssinian rivers, is largely the source of the Nile floods, due to the monsoon rains of the Abyssinian Plateau, and further north the Atbara, which brings down the alluvium which has helped to fertilize Egypt. From this point it receives no permanent tributaries and navigation is hindered by six cataracts, of which the first is at Assuan. The extensive delta formed north of Cairo, where the Nile leaves its long narrow valley, is the most fertile area in North Africa. Between the Nile and Tunis the Sahara reaches the Mediterranean and there are no permanent streams. The Sahara is partly occupied by plateaus and mountains and partly by steppes and deserts which contain oases. Africa is cut by the Equator nearly halfway between its extreme points, so that rather more than three-quarters of the continent lies within the Tropics and receives the sun's rays vertically at least once a year. Except on the more lofty mountains, Africa has no areas with cold winters, where the temperature is 32° F. or less for one month, or cool summers, which are less than 50° F. in any month. It is, therefore, typical generally of tropical rather than temperate conditions, in which there is no resting season for vegetation, except in consequence of want of rain.

Ethnography.—Four main groups of native races may be distinguished in Africa, the Semitic and Hamitic, belonging to the Caucasic type in the north, the Negro, and the Hottentot and Bushmen in the south.

Political Divisions.—Africa is apportioned among the powers of Europe as follows:

Great Britain—Basutoland, Bechuanaland Protectorate, Cape Colony, Central Africa, East Africa Protectorate, Uganda Protectorate, Zanzibar Protectorate, Mauritius, Natal, Niger Coast Protectorate, Territory of the Royal Niger Co., South Africa, West Africa, Zululand and Islands, and the Boer colonies.

France—Algeria, Senegal, French Soudan and the Niger Gaboon and Guinea Coast, Congo Region, Somali Coast, Madagascar and Islands.

Germany—Togoland, Cameroons, South West Africa, East Africa.

Italy—Eritrea, Somaliland, Tripoli.

Portugal—Angola, the Congo, Guinea, East Africa and islands.

Spain—Rio de Oro, Adrar, Fernando Po and islands.

Turkey—Egypt.

Belgium—The Congo State.

Summary	Area Sq. Miles	Population
Independent	1,700,000	20,000,000
Belgian	800,000	15,000,000
British	2,132,840	40,000,000
French	4,300,000	36,000,000
German	930,000	15,000,000
Italian	591,000	1,750,000
Portuguese	800,000	9,000,000
Spanish	86,000	250,000

(See Union of South Africa.)

BRITISH EAST AFRICA comprises the main portion of the highlands of eastern equatorial Africa. The surface in east slopes gradually to lowlands of coast; west and northwest to valley of Upper Nile. The principal river is the Nile; Tana and Juba chief rivers entering Indian Ocean. Has many interesting lakes; embraces northern half of Victoria Nyanza. Politically the district is divided among the protectorates of East Africa, Uganda, and Zanzibar.

East Africa Protectorate includes the coast from Juba River to German East Africa and inland to Uganda borders. Higher plateaus, clothed with luxuriant grasses, especially adapted to stock raising. Mombasa, capital and chief city, has a fine harbor; population, 30,000. Lamu and Kismayu, chief ports in the north; Vanga and Takaungu, south.

Uganda Protectorate came under sphere of British influence 1890; includes Uganda proper, Usoga to the east, and Unyoro and other countries west.

Zanzibar Protectorate.—Zanzibar, an important Mohammedan power under Imans of Maskat 1698-1807; independence confirmed 1861; placed under British protection 1890. Zanzibar, free port; chief trade centers in this region; Mohammedism prevails; Christian missions established.

GERMAN POSSESSIONS.—German East Africa.—German possessions in East Africa were acquired 1885 to 1890. Sphere of influence embraces a coast line of about 620 miles, stretches south from British East Africa to Portuguese possessions and westward to Lakes Nyasa and Tanganyika. Chief products: Millet, bananas, sisal, cocoanuts, cloves, castor oil, sugar cane, and vegetables. Natives have large banana plantations, also cultivate Indian corn and pulse. On coast lands are German plantations of cacao, coco palms, vanilla, tobacco, and India rubber; in more elevated districts coffee is grown. Among natives the goat is the most common domestic animal; cattle and sheep also raised. Exports, ivory, sisal, India rubber, coffee. Chief seaports: Dar-es-Salaam, Bagamoyo, Kilwa. Protestant mission societies, 7; Roman Catholic, 3.

Kameruff extends between British Nigeria and French Equatorial Africa. Became German protectorate, 1884; in 1911, France ceded over 100,000 square miles to Germany, giving colony outlets to Congo Basin. Value of imports, $6,065,000;

chiefly cottons, salt, rice, spirits, wood, and tobacco; exports, $4,740,000; rubber exported, $1,800,000; palm oil, $261,000; palm kernels, $622,000; ivory, $270,000; cacao, $680,000. Duala is the chief town, population, 22,000; Buea, seat of government.

BELGIAN CONGO.—This grew out of the Congo International Association, founded 1835 by Leopold II, King of Belgians, and organized by Stanley, first Governor-General. Boundaries of state defined by neutrality declarations 1885; state placed under sovereignty of the King, who, 1889, bequeathed his sovereign rights to Belgium. Annexed to Belgium in 1907. The Congo River and its many tributaries are the great natural features of the country. Chief products: rubber, ivory, palm nuts, and palm oil; coffee and tobacco thrive. Boma, capital and port on Congo River. Banana, seaport on Congo River.

ANGOLA.—Discovered by Portuguese in 1486. Possessions extend from mouth of Congo to Cunene River, over 1,000 miles; surrounded inland by Belgian Congo, British South Africa, and German Southwest Africa. Oil palm not found below 10° south; coffee grows wild in nearly all hilly districts, chief export from Ambriz; cotton is grown in district of Mossamedes, sugar in lowlands; other productions are rubber, wax, vegetable oils, cocoanuts, oxen, fish, and ivory. Trade is largely with Portugal. In 1908 1,741 vessels of 1,005,004 tons entered the four ports. Malachite, copper, salt, petroleum, and iron found in large quantities; gold also exists. S. Paulo de Loanda, capital and seaport. Port Alexander, seat of fish salting industry.

FRENCH EQUATORIAL AFRICA.— The first trading post on Gabun was established by the French in 1842; authority extended to Cape Lopez and Ogowe River in 1862; interior between Ogowe and Congo explored by de Grazza 1878-80, large tract of country annexed; French claims recognized by Berlin Conference 1885. Region east of Kamerun and north to Lake Tchad conceded to French 1894. Since then growth by exploration and military occupation. In 1906 three autonomous colonies formed: Gabun, Middle Congo, and Ubangi-Shari-Chad. The country is well watered and covered with extensive forests. Cotton, tobacco, cinnamon, pepper, gums, resins, and dyewoods are produced. Libreville, capital of Gabun and seaport.

NYASALAND PROTECTORATE (British).—Includes the region on south and west shores of Lake Nyasa. Imports, cotton goods, provisions, hardware, etc.; exports, coffee, cotton, tobacco. Blantyre, chief town; Zomba, seat of administration.

BECHUANALAND PROTECTORATE.— The territory lying between the Molopo and Zambesi rivers and extending from the South African Republic and Matabeleland west to German Southwest Africa. Railway extends from Buluwayo to the Cape.

RHODESIA.—The territory within the British sphere of influence to the north of Bechuanaland and the Union of South Africa. Divided into Northern and Southern Rhodesia by the Zambesi. Forests of hardwood timber abound. India rubber, indigo, and cotton indigenous. Country rich in minerals; gold, silver, copper, tin, lead, coal, and antimony exist. Salisbury, capital of Southern Rhodesia.

PORTUGUESE EAST AFRICA.—First Portuguese settlements made on west coast 1505; colony formed 1569. Possessions divided into five districts: Mozambique, Lourenco Marques, Inhambane, Quilimane, and Tete.

REUNION, or BOURBON.—Island about 110 miles southwest of Mauritius. French possession since 1767.

ST. HELENA, in South Atlantic about 1,200 miles from west coast of Africa. Discovered by Portuguese 1502; belonged to East India Company 1651 to 1834. Now a British colony. Napoleon I imprisoned here 1815 to 1821. Area, 47 square miles. Population, 3,250. Climate mild and agreeable. Capital, Jamestown.

MADAGASCAR.—An island known to the ancients and early Arabs; first described by Marco Polo; rediscovered by Portuguese in 1506; France laid claim to the island in 1642. Christianity was introduced in 1810-1828; war between French and natives in 1882-1884 and 1895, resulted in French protectorate. The island and its dependencies were declared a French colony in 1896.

MAURITIUS.—Island in Indian Ocean, 500 miles east of Madagascar. Discovered by Portuguese, 1505; confirmed as British possession, 1814. Chief export raw sugar. Spoken language French; official English. Port Louis, capital.

FRENCH POSSESSIONS. — Algeria.— Original inhabitants were Numidians or Berbers, conquered by Romans and Vandals. Turkish possession 1519 to 1710. Piratical power sixteenth to nineteenth centuries; defeated by the United States in 1815. Algiers taken by France 1815; Constantine, 1837. The Kabyles were subdued and Abd-el-Kader was captured in 1847.

Tunis.—Invaded by French 1270; by Spanish, 1535; became a Turkish province 1575; ruled by beys and long noted as a piratical state. It was occupied by France 1881.

Senegal colony consists of four municipal communes of St. Louis, the capital of the colony; Dakar, a fortified naval station and seat of Government General of French West Africa; Rufisque; and Goree, area 438 square miles; territory of direct administration, area 74,000 square miles.

French Guinea was detached from Senegal in 1890 and first known as Rivieres du Sud Colony. The coast territory extends inland between Sierra Leone and Portuguese Guinea.

Ivory Coast.—Annexed by France 1892-93. The colony extends inland between Liberia and British Gold Coast, embracing Kong and other states on northeast.

Dahomey stretches inland between Togoland and British Lagos; and northward to the French Military Territories.

Mauretania, formed into a protectorate in 1909, consists of five districts, Trarza, Brakna, Gorgol, Guidimaka and Tagant.

Upper Senegal and Niger, extends between Ivory Coast on the south and Algerian sphere on the north.

MOROCCO, the Mauritania of the ancients; conquered by the Arabs about 700. Present dynasty, Scheriffs, pretended descendants of Mohammed, established 1516. Most flourishing period of country 1579-1603. Slavery of Christians abolished 1814; piracy prohibited 1817. The southern frontier toward Sahara unsettled. The country comprises a "Tell" or fertile region opening upon the Atlantic, an elevated region beyond traversed by ranges of Atlas Mountains (Ayashlu 14,500 feet), and the eastern or desert region of Sahara. Coast district interesected by numerous short rivers. The climate is warm and generally healthful. The northwest has sufficient rain from October to March; droughts not uncommon in southwest. Soil of coast region and mountain valleys fertile; yields abundantly under rudest cultivation. Products: Wheat, barley, Indian corn, hemp, henna, and tropical and subtropical fruits; dates a regular crop in south. Wealth of Arabs consists of cattle, horses, sheep, and ostriches. Manufactures comprise carpets, fezzes, leather, woolens, silks, jewelry, saddlery, earthenware, etc. Mineral deposits—undeveloped —include iron, gold, silver, manganese, antimony, lead, etc.; fine amethysts found. Fez is the northern capital and leading commercial city; Morocco southern capital and has manufactures of morocco leather. Tangier, seaport and chief center of trade. Education is limited to teachings from Koran. Mohammedanism predominant religion. The Sultan is the head of the religion. The army comprises about 12,000 men under European discipline and an additional force of 8,000 militia and 10,000 infantry.

SPANISH POSSESSIONS.—Canary Islands.—Became a Spanish possession, 1493. Administratively part of Spain. Surface mountainous, diversified by plains and valleys. Chief products, sugar, cochineal, and wine; other products, tobacco, silk, oil, wheat, barley, and tropical fruits. Capital, Santa Cruz de Teneriffe; chief port, Palmas. Religion, Roman Catholic. Rio de Oro and Adrar—area, 73,000 square miles; population, 12,000—under Governorship of Canary Islands with Subgovernor at Rio de Oro. Fernando Po and Annabon, fertile, mountainous islands in Gulf of Guinea.

PORTUGUESE POSSESSIONS.—Cape Verde Islands discovered and colonized by Portuguese 1460. Has flourishing cinchona plantations. Other products include coffee, cacao, tobacco, sugar, brandy, palm oil, fruits. Cattle, goats, pigs, numerous. Manufactures: Salt, soap, linens, pottery, and leather. Iron and amber in southern islands. Capital, Praia.

Portuguese Guinea.—On Senegambia coast, surrounded on land side by French possessions, includes Bissagos Archipelago and Bolama Island. Chief products: India rubber, wax, oil, seeds, ivory, and hides. Capital, Bolama.

St. Thomas and Prince Islands.—St. Thomas (Sao Thomé) discovered by Portuguese, 1470; with Prince Island (Ilha do Principe), its dependent, forms province of Portugal. Volcanic and mountainous (Pico de Sao Thomé, 7,028 feet) with luxuriant vegetation. Climate unhealthful; more rain than on mainland. Chief products, coffee, cacao, cinchona; sugar and vanilla also produced. Capital, Cidade de Sao Thomé. Chief town and port (Prince Island) Sao Antonio.

Madeira Islands.—Islands known to ancients and visited by Arabs in the twelfth century; rediscovered and colonized by Portuguese, 1420. Very mountainous (Pico Ruivo, 6,060 feet). Notable health resort for European invalids. Mean temperature, 65 deg.; highest, 85 deg.; lowest, 54 deg. Sugar cane, tobacco, and all tropical and European fruits grown; wines famous. Funchal, capital, 20,844.

BRITISH POSSESSIONS.—Gold Coast.—Danish settlements transferred to England, 1850; Dutch claims, 1872; colonial government established, 1874; Ashantee placed under British protection, 1895-96. Coast regions level; interior hilly. Soil fertile. Products: Palm oil and kernels. India rubber, kola nuts, and timber. Gold widely distributed. Akra, capital and chief city. Cape Coast Castle. Railways, 168 miles. Telegraph, 1,363 miles. Education mainly in hands of religious bodies.

Gambia.—Territory discovered by Portuguese, 1447; fort established by English,

1686; became British possession, 1783; annexed to Sierra Leone, 1841; independent colony, 1888. Products and exports: Ground nuts, hides, beeswax, rice, cotton, corn, and India rubber. Bathurst, capital and chief city.

Sierra Leone.—Northwest of Liberia. Unsuccessful attempt made to colonize liberated slaves, 1787; territory annexed by England, 1791; became Crown colony, 1807. Coast an undulating plain; interior elevated plateaus. Forests extensive. Soil fertile, rice yielding abundantly in interior; cotton plentiful; indigo practically wild. Exports include palm oil and palm kernels, ginger, ground and kola nuts, tropical fruits, India rubber, copal, and hides. Cocoanut oil is produced; workers in gold and silver are numerous and skilful. Freetown, capital; most important seaport (fortified) of West Africa.

Nigeria, bounded on the east by Kamerun, west by Dahomey, and divided into two divisions, Northern and Southern Nigeria. About nine-tenths of the area was formerly within the territories of the Royal Niger Company. In 1884-87 whole of Nigeria was declared to be under British protection; in 1900 it was transferred to direct imperial administration.

Northern Nigeria.—Products of the lowcountry, palm oil; inland region, rubber, ground nuts, sheabutter, ivory, hides, live stock, ostrich feathers. Cotton growing is carried on; tobacco also grown. Minerals: Tin ore is in rich deposits, silver also found. Protestant missionary societies have industrial schools.

Southern Nigeria, colony and protectorate of Southern Nigeria and Lagos. The chief products are palm-oil, cotton, cocoa, coffee, ivory, hides, earthnuts and fruits. Minerals: Manganese ore, tin ore, lignite, and monazite. Lagos is the capital and important port. Railways, in all Nigeria over 700 miles, connecting Lagos, Jebba, Zungeru, and Kano; telegraph mileage, 3,000.

British Somaliland.—Became a protectorate 1884. Region extends from Lahadu to Zilyada, with an area of 68,000 square miles. Imports: chiefly rice, textiles, and dates; exports: skins, hides, ostrich feathers, cattle, sheep, and gum. Berbera, chief town. (See also Union of South Africa.)

LIBERIA.—Country settled 1822 by free negroes, sent out under American Colonization Society; declared independent, 1847. The coast lands are generally low and sandy; interior hills and mountains are covered with beautiful forests, diversified by well-watered, fertile valleys: the largest rivers are St. Johns and St. Pauls. Climate unhealthful, seasons wet and dry: hottest month January; heat mitigated by almost constant land and sea breezes. Coffee—renowned for its excellence—and ginger are chief products. Maize, rice, cotton, arrowroot, sugar cane, cereals, and vegetables readily produced. Fruits are abundant and finely flavored. Exports—Leading articles, coffee, palm oil and palm kernels, rubber, cocoa, sugar, arrowroot, ivory, hides, and piassava. Imports—textiles, clothing, provisions, hardware, tobacco, furniture, etc. Monrovia, capital.

GERMAN SOUTHWEST AFRICA.—Region annexed by Germany in 1884. Possessions extend along the coast 930 miles.

EGYPT.—One of earliest seats of civilization renowned alike for its great antiquity and former splendor. Modern history begins with the conquest by Mohammedans, 638 A.D.; taken by Mamelukes, 1250; came Turkish province, 1517; invaded by Napoleon, 1798; restored to Turkey, 1801. The New era began with Mehemet Ali, founder of present dynasty; reigned, 1805-49. The Suez Canal was opened in 1869. A native revolt under Arabi Pasha, 1881, suppressed by British; English financial adviser appointed. Mahdists in Sudan revolted 1881-85; conquered, 1899. The great natural features are the River Nile and the desert. The Nile has its source in Victoria Nyanza; by its annual inundation and deposit of loam is great fertilizer of Egypt.

Climate of Upper Egypt continuously hot and dry; farther north hot season is April-November; temperate, December-March. Rainfall scanty, except in delta. Vast reservoir for flood waters of Nile at Assuan; irrigated area constantly increasing. Perennial irrigation assures two or three crops annually; in winter, cereals; summer, cotton, sugar, and rice; autumn, rice, maize, and vegetables. The Nile Valley and delta are densely peopled. The Copts, descendants of ancient Egyptians, dwell chiefly in Upper Egypt. Arabic language is spoken. Cairo, capital, on Nile; founded by Saracens, 970; contains museum of antiquities, mosques. Alexandria, founded 332 B.C., commercial center and chief seaport. Port Said, at mouth of Suez Canal. Railways belonging to state, 1910, 1,449 miles. Government telegraphs, 1910, 3,450 miles. Suez Canal, 87 miles long, connects Mediterranean with Red Sea. Government, principality tributary to Turkey. Power nominally in hands of Khedive and Ministry, supported since 1882 by British advisers.

Anglo-Egyptian Soudan extends from Egyptian frontier to Uganda and Belgian Congo and from Red Sea to confines of Wadai. Chief towns: Khartum, Omdurman (capital, formerly Dervish capital), Wady Halfa. Convention of 1899 provides for Governor-General appointed by Egypt with consent of Great Britain.

TRIPOLI, conquered, successively by Arabs and Turks, formed one of Barbary States; independence secured, 1714; reconquered by Turkey, 1835. Attempted annexation by Italy, and Turco-Italian war, 1911. Surface mostly desert; mountainous in west and south. Coast line 800 miles; chief harbor Tripoli. Imports: Cloth, tobacco, provisions, etc.; exports: ostrich feathers, skins, hides, cauls, etc.

ABYSSINIA.—An independent empire, bounded on the north by Eritrea, on the east by Danakil country and Somaliland, on the south and west by British East Africa, and on the northwest by the Sudan. It is the direct descendant of the ancient Ethiopia, possesses an ancient and interesting national Christian church which owes allegiance to the Coptic Patriarch of Alexandria,

ITALIAN POSSESSIONS. — Eritrea.— Colony of Eritrea constituted 1890. Assab occupied 1880, town and island of Massaua 1885. Colony now embraces coast of Red Sea from Ras Kasar to Strait of Bab-el-Mandeb, 670 miles, extending inland about 200 miles. Pearl fisheries at Massaua and Dahlak Archipelago; industry in hands of Banians (Indians). Massaua, fortified seaport and important center of commercial exchange. Asmara, seat of government.

Italian Somaliland.—Sultanate of Obbia placed under Italian protection, 1889; protectorate extended in 1892 and 1896. By treaty of Adis Ababa, 1896, Italian dominion restricted to strip of coast extending from Ras Alula to mouth of Juba River.

FRENCH POSSESSIONS. — Obock and Somali Coast Protectorate acquired by France 1864. Situated on Gulf of Aden, surrounded by Eritrea, Abyssinia, and British Somaliland, extends inland about forty miles. Trade chiefly with interior countries. Chief cities, Obock and Tajurah

Africa:

Agents sent to, to receive slaves taken from vessels, 633.

Citizens of United States must not violate rights of inhabitants of, 396.

Natives of, in slavery. (See African Slave Trade.)

Naval force of United States stationed on coast of, referred to, 2173, 3071.

Repressing liquor trade in, suggestions made by Belgium, 6363, 6425.

Slavery on coast of, 4160.

Vessels of United States seized on coast of, 1857, 3017.

Africa, The, attempted seizure of Mr. Fauchet by commander of, 3344.

African Slave Trade.—Prior to the discovery of America negroes, like other savage races, either enslaved or put to death the captives taken in war. The deportation of the captives to the mines and plantations of the New World increased the value of the African and made slavery rather than death the prisoner's fate. This disposition of captives also led many petty chiefs to wage war for the prospective gain in human chattels. The aborigines of America having proved too weak for the work required of them, the Portuguese, who possessed a large part of the African coast, began the exportation of negroes, in which they were imitated by other nations of the Old World. Sir John Hawkins was the first Englishman to engage in slave traffic. The first importation of negro slaves was authorized in 1517. Extreme cruelty and inhuman treatment characterized their transportation. They were landed at Haiti and Santo Domingo and placed in the mines. In 1619 a Dutch vessel brought a cargo of slaves into the James River. Twenty negroes were sold to Virginia settlers. In 1713, by the treaty of Utrecht, Great Britain obtained the contract for supplying slaves to the Spanish West Indies. This stimulated the slave trade generally. Several of the Colonies attempted to prohibit the importation of slaves, but Great Britain forced the trade upon them. Virginia passed several acts forbidding the traffic, but they were vetoed by the British Government, as were also those passed by Pennsylvania in 1712, 1714, and 1717, and by Massachusetts in 1774.

Slavery was prohibited by Rhode Island and Connecticut in 1774, and by all the Colonies under the non-importation covenant of Oct. 24, 1774, and forbidden by nearly all the States during the Revolution. The slave-trade question was an important one in the formation of the Constitution. The Southern States, except Virginia and Maryland, insisted that no restriction should be imposed upon the traffic.

A compromise was finally effected allowing Congress to prohibit it after 1808. The act of March 22, 1794, prohibited the carrying of slaves from one foreign country to another by American citizens; that of May 10, 1800, allowed United States war ships to seize vessels engaged in such traffic; that of Feb. 28, 1803, prohibited the introduction of slaves into States which had forbidden slavery. In 1808 the importation of slaves into the United States was forbidden. The acts of April 20, 1818, and March 3, 1819, authorized the President to send cruisers to the coast of Africa to stop the slave trade. As no restrictions were ever placed upon domestic slave trading before its abolition in 1865, the surreptitious trade in imported slaves was not entirely given up until that time.

African Slave Trade. (See also Compromise of 1850; Kansas-Nebraska Act; Missouri Compromise; Negroes; Slavery.)

Abuses of United States flag referred to, 2134.

Act for suppression of, referred to, 5621.

Agents sent to Africa to receive slaves, 663.

American citizens engaged in, 2215.

Information regarding, requested, 2907.

Cargo of African negroes—

Captured on coast of Cuba, and return of to Africa, discussed, 3058, 3124, 3126.

Landed on coast of Georgia, referred to, 3065, 3069, 3086.

Stranded on coast of Florida, and removal of, discussed, 967.

Ceased in United States, 3779.

Correspondence regarding—

Referred to, 2268, 2287, 2426, 2428, 2538, 2765.

Surrender of slaves to United States consul referred to, 1944.

Discussed by President—

Adams, J. Q., 875, 967.

Buchanan, 3086, 3124, 3126, 3180.

Lincoln, 3254.

Madison, 470, 562.

Monroe, 583, 631, 783, 812, 819.

Taylor, 2553.

Tyler, 2215.

Van Buren, 1836.

Excluded from use of United States flag, 875.

Foreign slave traders discussed, 3446.

International congress at Brussels for abolition of, 5471, 5543, 6363.

Interpretation given act prohibiting, 632.

Laws for suppression of—

Amendments recommended, 2553.

Should be more severe, 1903, 1931.

Liberation of slaves by authorities of Nassau, New Providence, 2064.

Proposition to Great Britain to abolish mixed courts created for suppression of, 3989.

Treaty regarding, 4055.

Punishment for engaging in, should be same as for piracy, 779, 812.

Referred to, 1755, 2064, 2173, 2202, 2219, 2268, 2587, 2630, 3015, 3071, 3121, 3185, 3413.

Removal of negroes—

Captured by American vessels, to Liberia, recommended, 3058, 3124.

Captured on coast of Cuba, 3058, 3124, 3126.

Stranded on coast of Florida recommended, 967.

Seizure of slaves on board the *Encomium* and *Enterprise*, 1499.

Suppression of and suggestions that Great Britain be asked to discontinue the naval force maintained for its suppression, 3779.

Desired by Government, 631, 1836, 1930, 2082, 2215, 3086, 3254.

But interpolations into maritime code not permitted, 1930.

Referred to, 649, 650, 651, 678, 827, 958, 1857, 2048, 2082, 2553, 3180.

Squadron kept on coast of Africa for, 2173.

Treaty between five powers of Europe for, 2011.

Inquiry of Senate respecting, and reply of President, 2068.

Protest of American minister to France regarding, 2011, 2048, 2297.

Treaty with Great Britain regarding, referred to, 810, 812, 819, 886, 2016, 2048, 2071, 2082, 3272, 3281, 3328, 3366, 3380, 4017.

Vessels transporting slaves should be seized, 632, 783.

African Squadron, instruction to commanding officers of, referred to, 2173, 3071.

Agents, Indian. (See Indian Agents.)

Agitator.—A person who, either by speech or action, endeavors to change existing conditions. The term may be employed in a complimentary sense as synonymous with "reformer" (q. v.), but is often restricted to a person who endeavors to disturb conditions from ulterior or anti-constructive motives.

Agricultural Census recommended, 5982.

Agricultural Colleges and Experiment Stations. (See Agriculture, Department of.)

Agricultural Experiment Stations discussed, 5384, 5888, 5980, 6347.

Agricultural Implements.—From the earliest times and in all countries until the beginning of the Nineteenth century agriculture was distinctly manual labor. Horses and oxen were used for plowing and harrowing, but the labor of planting, cultivating and harvesting was all performed by hand. Grain was sown broadcast by hand, cut with a sickle, gathered with a fork and thrashed out on the barn floor with a club. Corn was cultivated with a hoe and its husking was made a social event of rural communities. By these primitive methods the farmer was unable to produce much of a surplus to exchange for the fabrics of the cities or for export. The only part of America where farming proved a commercial success was in the South, where slave labor was employed in the cultivation of cotton and tobacco. The invention of the cotton gin, though not strictly a farm implement, made a commercial crop of a plant theretofore of only ordinary domestic value.

From the first turning of the soil to the gathering of the crops American inventive genius has lightened the labor and increased the profits of agriculture so that the farmers today enjoy a greater amount of comfort and wealth than any other class of citizens.

Prior to 1850 the manufacture of agricultural implements could hardly be considered as more than a hand trade, and in no sense as a factory industry, as the term is at present understood. Ideas had been evolved, and, on a small scale, executed, which contained much that the improved processes and facilities of the latter part of the century brought to complete fruition. Implements were made in small shops with an average capital of $2,674 per establishment. The evolution of the manufacture from the small shops of the blacksmith and wheelwright to the immense establishments of the present day embodies all the phases of the development of the modern factory system. In a large western plant 600 men, by the aid of machinery, do the work that, without machinery would require 2,145 men.

The McCormick reaper was first put on the market as a successful machine for the harvest of 1845. In 1847 the exports of wheat and flour jumped to $32,178,161, about five times the average of the preceding forty years, and increased rapidly to 1860. The wheat crop, which had not kept pace with the growth of population from 1839 to 1849, gained more than 70 per cent in the decade between 1849 and 1859, and from a total crop of 84,823,272 bushels in 1845 increased to nearly a billion bushels in 1915. Cyrus H. McCormick inherited the idea of making a grain reaper from his father, who had patented an imperfect revolving scythe in 1816. The essential elements which made the reaper finally successful were the reel, the divider, the reciprocating knife, and the platform. Later a self-raking attachment took the place of the man who had raked the grain by hand from the platform.

The Marsh harvesting machine had toothed belts which carried the grain from the platform over the master wheel to two men who stood on a footboard and bound the sheaves on tables attached to the machine. By 1875 twine binding attachments had been patented.

The automatic self binder, invented by John F. Appleby, seems to have been the culminating improvement made in grain harvesting machines, and is used in one form or another as an attachment to the harvester to bind by far the largest part of the grain harvested in this and other countries. Now a million binders are in use on American farms and a large export business has grown up. Through the use of American harvesting machines Argentina, Australia and Russia have become large exporters of wheat, and single cargoes shipped to Europe contain more of these machines than the entire output of any European manufacturer in this line. In Kansas, Nebraska and other Western States, headers are used, which cut off the stalk just below the head, elevate the wheat into a wagon ready to be hauled to the thrasher, and leave the straw standing. In California, Oregon and Washington the combined harvester carries a thrashing attachment, which is operated by the traction wheel, so that a wide swath is cut and thrashed and delivered in bags as the machine is drawn across the field by horses or a traction engine.

The mowing machine, the corn planter and the two-horse cultivator, distinctively American inventions, have served the same purpose in promoting the production of corn and hay as the reaper in the cereal fields. Farmers were unable to produce live stock, poultry and dairy products on a commercial scale until they had labor saving machinery for the cheap production of hay and corn.

The principal steps in the development of the harvesting machine are recorded in the Patent Office as follows:

Reapers—Harvester, handraker, 1855; self-raker, 1856; dropper, 1861; adjustable switch reel rakes, 1865, 1875, 1879 and 1884.

Harvester Binders—Cord knotter, 1853; wire twister, 1856; straw braid twister, 1857; gleaner and binder, 1862; self-tripping cord knotter, 1867; wire twister, 1868; automatic trip, 1870; straw looper, 1870; vibrating binder, 1875; low-down binder, 1878; compressor automatic trip, 1879; low-down oblique delivery, 1884.

Bean and Clover Harvesters—Clover harvester, 1849; clover stripping drum harvester, 1854; clover head cutter and breaker, 1856; bean stalk cutter and bundler, 1859; clover spiral drum harvester, 1861; bean underground cutter, 1865; clover head stripper, 1877; bean stalk puller, 1879.

Corn Harvesters—Cutter, 1844; ear stripper, 1850; ear stripper, husker and sheller, 1850; cutter and shocker, 1852, 1854, 1856; high and low cutter, 1859; cutter and shocker, 1866; picker and husker, 1867; picker, husker and shocker, 1869; cutter, husker and shocker, 1875.

Cotton Harvesters — Toothed picking disks and cylinders, 1850; hand picker, 1855; brush stripper, 1859; exhaust flexible pipe, 1859; fan blower, 1868; saw and stripper brush, 1870; electric belt, 1870; picker stem, 1872; toothed cylinder, 1874, 1883; revolving picker stems, 1878, 1901.

Hemp and Flax Harvesters—Revolving pulling drum and band, 1838; roller, 1852; reciprocating, pulling jaw, 1863; stalk puller, 1866; side delivery, 1870, 1871; stalk cutter, 1872.

Combined Reapers and Thrashers—Reaper and thrasher, 1836; thrasher, separator and sacker, 1846; head cutter and side deliverer, 1849; harvester and thrasher, 1877; steam harvester, 1879; header, thrasher and separator, 1883.

Horse Rakes—Flopover, 1822; spring tooth, 1839; dumping sulky, 1848; draft dumping, 1850; self dumping, 1852; spring tooth self dumping, 1856; draft dumping, 1856, 1859, 1866, 1876, 1884; drag dumping, 1866, 1870.

Horse Hay Forks—Spiral fork, 1867; harpoon, 1867, 1884. 1881; tilting, 1870; grapple, 1880; handfork, 1882.

Hay Rackers and Loaders—1848, 1850, 1858, 1860, 1861, 1864, 1865, 1867, 1868, 1870, 1876, 1883.

Hay Tedders—1855, 1861, 1862, 1865, 1867, 1870, 1883.

Next to harvesting machines the thrashing machine is the most important feature of the equipment of modern agriculture. The "ground hog" thrasher came into use early in the nineteenth century. Thrashing mills, with fanning and screening devices, were set up in England in 1800, but these were stationed at some central point, and the grain had to be hauled to them. The first portable thrashing machine with cleaning devices was made by Hiram A. and John A. Pitts, of Winthrop, Me., in 1830, and George Westinghouse began making thrashing machines in Fonda, N. Y., about 1840. He later removed to Schenectady, N. Y., and patented a number of useful improvements in separating and cleaning devices. A notable improvement is the "wind stacker," by which the straw is blown by a revolving fan through a large steel pipe to the straw stack, thus saving the labor of several men. Automatic band cutting and feeding attachments and automatic grain weighers have also come into general use, and traction engines to replace horses in the field have gained new impetus from the use of the internal combustion engine and wider knowledge of the auto truck.

The grain drill is a recent implement of economy on the farm. The first patent for a force feed grain drill was issued to Foster, Jessup & Brown, of Palmyra, N. Y., in 1851, and their general use came with the use of commercial fertilizer.

The first patent on a practical corn planter was issued to George W. Brown, of Illinois, in 1853, and improved by George D. Haworth, of the same State.

Corn cultivators are made in a great variety of forms, but the essential feature of all is an arched axle which straddles the row, is drawn by two horses, and has two gangs, or frames, one on each side of the row, which swing freely under direction of the operator, who may ride or walk. Corn binders and pickers are also manufactured, as well as portable huskers and fodder shredders. Power corn shellers have been in use since 1860, and are indispensable wherever corn is grown for shipment to market. The first successful machine of this type was invented by Augustus Adams, of Sandwich, Ill.

The plow in primitive form antedates history, and, while it appears to be a simple implement, the improved American plow of today is the product of slow evolution, careful study and much mechanical skill. Efforts at improvement have been largely directed toward establishing upon a mathematical basis the proper lines of the moldboard which raises and turns the furrow slice. President Thomas Jefferson published his views on this subject in 1798. Jethro Wood, of Scipio, N. Y., took out a patent in 1819 for a plow with a moldboard in three separate pieces, so they could be replaced by new parts when worn.

Among the names that will ever be associated with the plow in America are John Deere, pioneer inventor and manufacturer, whose establishment at Moline, Ill., supplied the West for many years, and James Oliver, whose perfection of the chilled steel plowshare was an important step in advanced manufacture.

The history of steam plowing dates from the inventions of Fowler and Smith in 1854. The plows are in gangs of twelve to eighteen and are drawn by traction engines of from 40 to 80 horsepower.

Machinery for shelling, sorting, sifting or grading according to size the various vegetable and root crops forms an extensive industry in itself.

Agricultural implements in general are divided into four groups—those of cultivation, seeding and planting, harvesting, and seed separating. These groups in turn are subdivided into numerous classes, as indicated in the accompanying table. At the census of 1849, 1,333 establishments were reported as engaged in the manufacture of agricultural implements, the number of hands employed being 7,220, and the value of their products amounted to $6,842,611. In 1869 the number of factories had increased to 2,076. These were comparatively small establishments, their aggregate capital amounting to only $34,834,600, and their output being valued at little more

than $52,000,000. In 1909 through combining shops and capital the number of establishments had fallen to 640, the capital had increased to $256,281,086, and the value of the output to $146,329,268.

Of the 772 establishments engaged in the industry in 1914, 86 were located in Illinois, 67 in Ohio, 61 in Wisconsin, 58 in New York, 49 in Pennsylvania, 45 in California, 42 in Indiana, 40 each in Iowa and Michigan, 35 in Minnesota, 27 in Missouri, 25 in Tennessee, 22 each in North Carolina and Virginia, 18 in Georgia, 14 in Vermont, 12 in Kansas, 11 in Maine, 10 each in Alabama and New Jersey, 7 each in Kentucky, Massachusetts, Nebraska, and Washington, 6 each in Connecticut and Mississippi, 5 in Texas, 4 in Colorado, 3 each in Arkansas, Florida, Maryland, New Hampshire, Oregon, South Carolina, and South Dakota, 2 each in Idaho, Oklahoma, and West Virginia, and 1 each in Louisiana and Montana.

The statistics for 1914 are summarized in the following table:

Number of establishments	772
Total value of products	$168,120,632
Implements of cultivation	39,632,903
Planters and seeders	12,268,156
Harvesting implements	40,561,472
Seed separators	13,980,184
All other products, including parts for all classes of agricultural implements	60,211,327
Amount received for repair work	1,460,590

IMPLEMENTS OF CULTIVATION.

Cultivators—		Land Rollers	22,942
Beet	2,184	Listers	37,953
Small (horse		Plows—	
and hand)	495,407	Disk	15,830
Wheeled	382,189	Gang	75,839
Cotton Scrapers	17,537	Shovel	181,802
Fertilizing Ma-		Engine	3,285
chines	185,990	Sulky (single)	108,248
Harrows—		Walking	913,385
Disk	212,133	Pulverizers	12,795
Spring-tooth	188,247	Other	80,269
Spike-tooth	382,141		

PLANTERS AND SEEDERS.

Seeders (broad-		Cotton planters	101,256
cast and wagon		Potato planters	37,276
or endgate) and		Drills	199,805
seeder at-		Seed Sowers,	
tachments	61,954	hand, field	12,608
Corn planters—		Other planters or	
Hand	102,850	seeders	4,124
Horse	115,053		

HARVESTING IMPLEMENTS.

Grain cradles	38,821	Hay loaders	29,059
Harvesters—		Hayrakes, horse	185,081
Bean	3,605	Hay stackers	7,567
Corn	52,087	Hay tedders	9,796
Grain	215,386	Mowers	274,521
Harvesters and		Other haying tools	42,344
thrashers		Potato diggers	
combined	284	horse	25,923
Other	2,758	Reapers	56,982
Hay carriers	69,199	Other	13,774
Hayforks, horse	75,202		

SEED SEPARATORS.

Clover hullers	1,166	Power	12,075
Corn huskers	453	Fanning mills	27,504
Corn huskers and		Thrashers—	
shredders	4,338	Horsepower	302
Corn Shellers—		Engine	13,386
Hand	74,405	Other	7,174

Agricultural Products.—The agricultural products of the United States are so diversified that it would be useless to attempt to describe all in a single article or even in an ordinary sized volume. The Department of Agriculture publishes annual reports covering the field in general and frequent special reports and bulletins on agricultural products.

The accompanying table gives the quantity and value of the principal products as reported in the latest census.

Poultry and Eggs.—The Census of 1910 gave the production of poultry in the United States, in 1909, as 488,468,354. The enumeration covered chickens, guinea fowls, turkeys, geese, ducks, pigeons and peafowls. The total value of fowls raised during 1909 was reported at the Census of 1910 to be $202,506,272, or an increase of 47.9 per cent. over the total value reported ten years earlier.

According to the Census of 1910, Illinois was the leading state in the number of fowls raised during 1909, the number being 32,-352,888. Missouri ranked second in this re-

spect, reporting the number of fowls raised in 1909 as 31,913,210. Iowa ranked third and reported the production of 29,990,147 fowls in 1909.

AGRICULTURAL PRODUCTS OF THE UNITED STATES

Crop	Unit of Measure	Quantity	Value
Animals*........	Number	206,643,069	$5,296,421,619
Apples†.........	Bush.	253,200,000	(a) 145,084,000
Apricots*.......	Bush.	4,150,263	2,884,119
Beans, Castor*...	Bush.	2,077	3,432
Beans, Dry*.....	Bush.	11,251,160	21,771,482
Bees*..........	Swarms	3,445,006	10,373,615
Broom Corn*.....	Pounds	78,959,958	5,134,434
Butter:			
Made on farms*.	Pounds	994,650,610	222,861,440
Made in factor's*	Pounds	624,764,653	179,510,619
Cereals (b)†.....	Bush.	4,959,494,000	(c)3,255,994,000
Cheese:			
Made on farms*.	Pounds	9,405,864	1,148,708
Made in factor's*	Pounds	311,126,317	43,239,924
Chicory*........	Pounds	19,284,000	70,460
Cider*..........	Gallons	32,583,998	(d)
Cotton†.........	Pounds	8,067,465,000	(e) 588,925,000
Cotton Seed†....	S. Tons	7,186,000	(a) 100,676,000
Flaxseed †......	Bush.	15,559,000	(c) 19,540,000
Flowers, Plants*.	....		34,872,329
Forest products*.	....		195,306,283
Fruits, small*...	Quarts	426,565,863	29,974,481
Fruits, sub-trop'l*	....		24,706,753
Grapes*.........	Pounds	2,571,065,205	22,027,961
Hay (tame)†.....	S. Tons	70,071,000	(c) 779,068,000
Hemp*..........	Pounds	7,483,295	412,699
Honey (f)*.......	Pounds	55,719,757	5,992,083
Hops*..........	Pounds	40,718,748	7,844,745
Milk (g)*.......	Gallons	7,466,406,384	....
Molasses (h)*....	Gallons	46,093,630	4,018,502
Nursery products*	....		21,050,822
Nuts (i)*........	Pounds	62,328,010	4,447,674
Onions*.........	....		6,709,047
Orchard products*	Bush.	214,683,695	140,867,347
Peaches†........	Bush.	54,109,000	(j) 56,814,000
Peanuts*........	Bush.	19,415,816	18,271,929
Pears†..........	Bush.	12,086,000	(j) 11,941,000
Peas, dry*.......	Bush.	7,129,294	10,963,739
Plums & Prunes*.	Bush.	15,480,170	10,299,495
Potatoes, Irish†..	Bush.	405,921,000	(c) 198,609,000
Potatoes, Sweet†..	Bush.	56,574,000	(c) 41,294,000
Rice (rough)†....	Bush.	23,649,000	(c) 21,849,000
Seeds, Clover*....	Bush.	1,025,816	6,925,122
Seeds, Grass*....	Bush.	6,671,348	15,137,683
Sugar, Beet†....	S. Tons	722,000	(k) 67,378,000
Sugar, Cane (l)†.	S. Tons	243,000	(k) 22,647,000
Sugar, Maple*...	Pounds	14,060,206	1,380,492
Syrup, Cane*....	Gallons	21,633,579	9,642,312
Syrup, Maple*...	Gallons	4,106,418	3,797,317
Syrup, Sorghum*.	Gallons	16,532,382	7,963,499
Tobacco†........	Pounds	1,034,679,000	(c)101,411,000
Vegetables, Misc..	....	....	209,548,021
Wool (unwashed)†	Pounds	290,192,000	(m) 53,395,000

* Figures reported for the Census of 1910. † Figures for 1914. (a) Farm price Nov. 15, 1914. (b) Not including rice. (c) Farm price Dec. 1, 1914. (d) Included in orchard products. (e) Average price for the year. (f) Including wax. (g) $656,301,246 was the aggregate value of milk, butter and cheese by the Census of 1910. (h) Made in factories: the product on farms and plantations in 1909 was 4,153 gallons, valued at $1,710. (i) Not including peanuts. (j) Farm price Aug. 15, 1914. (k) Based on the export value of refined, for year ending June 30, 1915. (l) Louisiana only. (m) Farm price June 15, 1914.

PRINCIPAL CEREAL CROPS BY STATES IN 1915
(From Report of the Bureau of Crop Estimates of the Dept. of Agricult.)

States	Oats * Bushels	Corn (a) Bushels	Wheat * Bushels
Maine.........	6,080,000	630,000	112,000
New Hampshire	444,000	940,000	......
Vermont.......	3,483,000	2,181,000	30,000
Massachusetts.	324,000	2,130,000	......
Rhode Island...	66,000	451,000	......
Connecticut...	352,000	2,977,000	......
New York.....	54,080,000	21,740,000	8,671,000
New Jersey....	2,240,000	10,257,000	1,443,000
Pennsylvania...	43,624,000	63,650,000	22,732,000
Delaware......	136,000	6,414,000	1,812,000
Maryland.....	1,530,000	24,626,000	10,208,000
Virginia.......	4,728,000	61,900,000	16,674,000
West Virginia..	3,219,000	29,540,000	3,990,000
North Carolina.	5,500,000	59,210,000	11,267,000
South Carolina.	9,712,000	38,323,000	2,547,000
Georgia........	17,100,000	64,122,000	3,129,000
Florida........	1,218,000	11,644,000	......
Ohio..........	69,003,000	154,330,000	40,228,000
Indiana........	65,520,000	197,629,000	46,712,000
Illinois........	195,435,000	372,402,000	56,062,000
Michigan......	64,260,000	53,742,000	18,774,000
Wisconsin.....	109,181,000	40,392,000	4,436,000
Minnesota.....	133,343,000	53,560,000	73,900,000
Iowa..........	200,475,000	288,858,000	16,465,000
Missouri.......	30,888,000	217,282,000	34,108,000
North Dakota..	92,470,000	7,800,000	142,782,000
South Dakota..	68,124,000	76,398,000	62,520,000
Nebraska......	69,600,000	212,915,000	75,035,000
Kansas........	44,382,000	165,227,000	119,463,000
Kentucky......	4,539,000	119,088,000	8,620,000
Tennessee.....	8,390,000	94,670,000	8,163,000
Alabama......	9,828,000	69,918,000	1,076,000
Mississippi....	4,300,000	64,970,000	44,000
Louisiana......	2,730,000	50,578,000	......
Texas.........	39,060,000	175,893,000	21,080,000
Oklahoma.....	35,640,000	125,885,000	38,770,000
Arkansas......	8,450,000	61,393,000	2,160,000
Montana......	25,968,000	1,428,000	30,697,000
Wyoming......	9,307,000	515,000	2,944,000
Colorado......	12,675,000	11,706,000	12,160,000
New Mexico....	2,160,000	2,809,000	2,020,000
Arizona.......	342,000	635,000	1,162,000
Utah..........	4,600,000	391,000	8,220,000
Nevada.......	559,000	31,000	1,595,000
Idaho.........	15,594,000	652,000	16,914,000
Washington....	14,400,000	1,158,000	51,238,000
Oregon.......	15,456,000	729,000	17,364,000
California.....	6,963,000	2,440,000	7,040,000
Total bushels..	1,517,478,000	3,026,159,000	1,004,277,000
Total acres....	40,193,000	109,273,000	59,417,000
Total farm val., Oct. 1.......	$523,529,910	$2,133,442,095	$912,887,793
Yield per acre..	37.8	27.7	16.9
Farm price per bush. Oct. 1.	$.345	$.705	$.909

* Preliminary estimate. (a) Forecast from condition on Oct. 1, 1915.

DOMESTIC ANIMALS, 1913

	Number	Value
Milch cows and other cattle...........	56,527,000	$1,827,428,000
Horses.............	20,567,000	2,278,222,000
Mules.............	4,386,000	545,245,000
Sheep and lambs....	51,482,000	202,779,000
Swine.............	61,178,000	603,109,000
All domestic animals..	194,140,000	$5,501,783,000

By the Census of 1910 there were on farms and ranges in United States 61,803,866 neat cattle, cows, bulls, etc., valued at $1,499,523,607; horses and colts, 19,833,113, valued at $2,083,588,195; mules, 4,209,769, valued at $525,391,863; asses and burros, 105,698, valued at $13,200,112; sheep and lambs, 52,447,861, valued at $232,841,585; swine, 58,185,676, valued at $399,338,308; goats, 2,915,125, valued at $6,176,423.

TOTAL ANNUAL YIELD OF CEREAL CROPS IN RECENT YEARS. (Reported by the Department of Agriculture)

Years	Indian Corn	Wheat	Oats	Barley	Rye	Buckwheat
	Bushels	Bushels	Bushels	Bushels	Bushels	Bushels
1897	1,902,967,933	530,149,168	698,737,809	66,685,127	27,363,324	14,997,451
1898	1,924,185,000	675,149,000	730,905,000	55,792,000	25,657,000	11,722,000
1899	2,078,143,933	547,303,846	796,177,713	73,381,563	23,961,741	11,094,471
1900	2,105,102,516	522,229,505	809,125,989	58,925,833	23,995,927	9,566,966
1901	1,522,519,891	748,460,218	736,808,724	109,932,924	30,344,830	15,125,939
1902	2,523,648,312	670,063,008	987,842,712	134,954,023	33,630,592	14,529,770
1903	2,244,176,925	637,821,835	784,094,199	131,861,391	29,363,416	14,243,644
1904	2,467,480,934	552,399,517	894,595,552	130,748,958	27,241,515	15,008,336
1905	2,707,993,540	692,979,489	953,216,197	136,651,020	28,485,952	14,585,082
1906	2,927,416,091	735,260,970	964,904,522	178,916,484	33,374,833	14,641,937
1907	2,592,320,000	634,087,000	754,443,000	153,597,000	31,566,000	14,290,000
1908	2,668,651,000	664,602,000	807,156,000	166,756,000	31,851,000	15,874,000
1909	2,552,189,630	683,379,259	1,007,142,980	173,344,212	29,520,457	14,849,339
1910	2,886,260,000	635,121,000	1,186,341,000	173,832,000	34,897,000	17,598,000
1911	2,531,488,000	621,338,000	922,298,000	160,240,000	33,119,000	17,549,000
1912	3,124,746,000	730,267,000	1,418,337,000	223,824,000	35,664,000	19,249,000
1913	2,463,000,000	753,233,000	1,122,139,000	178,189,000	41,381,000	13,833,000
1914	2,672,804,000	891,017,000	1,141,060,000	194,953,000	42,779,000	16,881,000
1915	3,026,159,000	1,004,277,000	1,517,478,000	237,009,000	49,190,000	15,769,000
1916	2,583,241,000	639,886,000	1,251,992,000	180,927,000	47,383,000	11,840,000

The Census of 1910 gives the following farm statistics for the United States: Farms, total number, 6,361,502; total acres in farms, 878,798,325; improved acres in farms, 478,451,750; value of land in farms, $28,475,674,169; value of buildings on farms, $6,325,451,528; value of implements and machinery on farms, $1,265,149,783; value per acre of land and buildings, $39.60; value per acre of land alone, $32.40. Value of wealth produced on farms in 1915, estimated by Secretary of Agriculture, $10,501,686,000.

Dairy Products.—The Thirteenth Census presented the following condensed analysis of the dairy industry of the United States for the census year 1909:

Total number of cows kept for milk 21,795,770
Milk produced on farms, gals. 5,813,699,474
Total pounds of butter made. 1,619,415,263
Total pounds of cheese made. 320,532,181
Condensed milk produced, lbs. 494,796,544

The quantity of milk reported was produced on farms reporting 16,069,298 dairy cows and does not include estimates for 4,556,134 cows reported as dairy cows by farmers but for which no statement was given of quantity of milk produced. In many cases the reason for not giving the quantity of milk produced was that the farmers were unable to make even a rough estimate. Generally speaking, however, these cows were on farms in the western and southern parts of the United States where the production is likely to be less than the average for other parts of the country. Also, many cows reported as dairy cows are as a matter of fact milked only a very small part of the year. No estimate is included for the "cows kept for milk" *not* on farms.

Agricultural Products:

Beet Sugar—
  Culture of, 6865.
Coffee—
  Production of, 6731.
  Commerce with foreign countries in, 4973.
Corn—
  Commerce in, restrained by Great Britain, 138.
  Introduction of products of, into Europe discussed, 5764.
Cotton—
  Captured and forfeited referred to, 3666.

Commerce in, referred to, 4973.
Culture of, in—
  African possessions of Portugal, 3864.
  Brazil, 4711.
Discriminating duties on, from British North American colonies discussed, 996.
Duty on, Lord Aberdeen's letter regarding, 1134.
Persons engaged in bringing out, order regarding, 3439.
Exportation of, discussed, 5887, 5979, 6171.
Hay, exportation of, prohibited, 3476.
  Order rescinding, 3532.
Referred to, 4800.
Rice—
  Duties on, discussed and referred to, 1243, 1931, 2112, 2181, 2274, 2419.
  Production of, in U. S., 6727, 6906.
Tobacco—
  Duties on, in foreign ports, 1648, 1738, 1909, 2167, 2192, 2909, 3120.
  Exportation of, to countries at peace with United States, orders regarding, 3379, 3434.
  From Netherlands and Dutch colonies, tax on, discussed, 4979, 4986, 5088.
  Growth, production, and trade of, referred to, 2133.
  Internal tax on, removal of, recommended, 5474.
  Trade with foreign countries to be promoted, 1588, 1713, 1822, 2167.
  Referred to, 1806.
  Value of annual production of, discussed, 5642, 5744, 5764, 5978.
Agricultural Land Grants. (See Agricultural Colleges.)
Agriculture:
  Advancement of, recommended, 58, 60, 61, 77, 78, 194, 197, 318, 361, 3776, 4457, 4530, 4947, 5112.

Prosperous state of, 978, 1747.
Reference to, 95, 175, 240, 3353.

Agriculture, Bureau of:

Appropriations for, recommended, 3996.

Discussed, 3334, 3452, 3564, 4066, 4106, 4364, 4645, 4947, 5112, 5383.

Employees in—
To participate in decoration of graves of soldiers, 4753, 4818, 4899, 5078, 5350.
To participate in dedication of Washington Monument, 4879.
To witness inauguration of President Cleveland, 4881.

Enlargement of facilities of, recommended, 4530.

Establishment of, 3334.
Recommended, 2556, 2622, 2663, 2714, 3253.
Referred to, 4066, 4947.

Experiment stations, recommendations regarding, 5384, 5888, 5980.

Food adulteration discussed, 5384.

Seed distribution. (See Seed Distribution.)

Agriculture, Commissioner of:

Reply of, to Senate resolution regarding diseases prevailing among swine, 4435.

Reports of, referred to, 4158, 4364, 4428, 4432, 4462, 4578.

Agriculture, Department of.—

This Department of the Executive Branch of the Government had its origin in the recommendation of Washington. As early as Dec. 7, 1796, in his eighth annual address (page 194) he said that "with reference either to individual or national welfare agriculture is of primary importance," and at the same time urged the importance of the "establishment of boards . . . charged with collecting and diffusing information, and enabled by premiums and small pecuniary aids to encourage and assist a spirit of discovery and improvement." The sentiments expressed by Washington were reiterated and enlarged upon by all or nearly all of his successors (pages 3776, 4457, 4530, 4947, 5112).

From the very beginning of the Government its foreign representatives had sent home seeds and cuttings of agricultural products to be tried in the United States, and in 1839 Congress made an appropriation of $1,000 for the distribution of material thus collected and for the publication of agricultural statistics. This work was entrusted to the Patent Office, which belonged to the Department of State until 1840, when the Department of the Interior was established and the Patent office became a part of it. Up to 1849 the agricultural work was carried on by the Commissioner of Patents, Henry L. Ellsworth, but from that time until 1861, a special official, under the direction of the Commissioner, was employed for the work.

May 15, 1862, an act was approved which created the Department of Agriculture, the duties of which were to "diffuse useful information on subjects connected with agriculture in the most general and comprehensive sense of the word, and to procure, propagate, and distribute among the people new and valuable seeds and plants." It was provided that the head of this bureau should be a Commissioner of Agriculture, to hold office by a tenure similar to that of other civil officers appointed by the President.

The bureau was made a full executive department by an act of Congress approved Feb. 9, 1889, and placed under a Secretary, who was made a member of the President's Cabinet. To promote the agricultural interests of the country in the most thorough manner an act of Congress approved March 2, 1887, provided for the establishment of agricultural experiment stations (see Agricultural Colleges and Experimental Stations), in connection with the agricultural colleges in the several states and territories, and placed the Commissioner of Agriculture over these stations in an advisory and administrative capacity.

To represent the Department of Agriculture in its relation with these experiment stations, the Office of Experiment Stations was established in the same year.

The Agricultural colleges established in the several states and territories in accordance with the land grant act of Congress of July 2, 1862, have no organic relation to the Department of Agriculture further than that the agricultural experiment stations are generally departments of the agricultural colleges, and that the president of each of these colleges is obliged to make an annual report to the Secretary of Agriculture.

The Weather Bureau (q. v.), an important branch of the Department, was authorized by Congress Feb. 4, 1870, under the direction of the War Department, but by an act of Oct. 1, 1890, it was transferred to the Department of Agriculture.

Some other important bureaus are:

Bureau of Animal Industry (established in 1884), which, besides its investigations to improve the condition of the animal industries of the country, has wide powers of inspection and supervision as to the health of live stock. (See Animal Industry, Bureau of.)

Bureau of Forestry (1881), which has charge of the administration of the national forest reserves. (See Forest Service.)

Bureau of Entomology (1863), which obtains and disseminates information regarding injurious insects and their relation to plant and animal life.

Bureau of Chemistry (1862), whose work includes the investigation of food products imported into the United States, analysis of adulterated products, and experiments to determine the effect of adulterants upon the human system.

Bureau of Statistics, organized as the Division of Statistics in 1863 and made a bureau in 1903. This bureau is the oldest distinctively statistical agency of the Government, its work being the fathering of material of interest to the agriculturist, from all parts of the world.

Agricultural Colleges.—Large tracts of land in the northwest territory were granted to the states formed therefrom, to be sold by the legislatures or by the Federal Government for educational purposes. As early as 1785 Congress, foreshadowing the permanent policy of the nation in encouraging education, enacted that one thirty-sixth of all the public lands should be set apart for and dedicated to the cause of education, and by the act of July 23, 1787, this reservation was made perpetual. The further to encourage and dignify the science of husbandry, Congress, by the Morrill Act of July 2, 1862, provided "that there be granted to the several states . . .

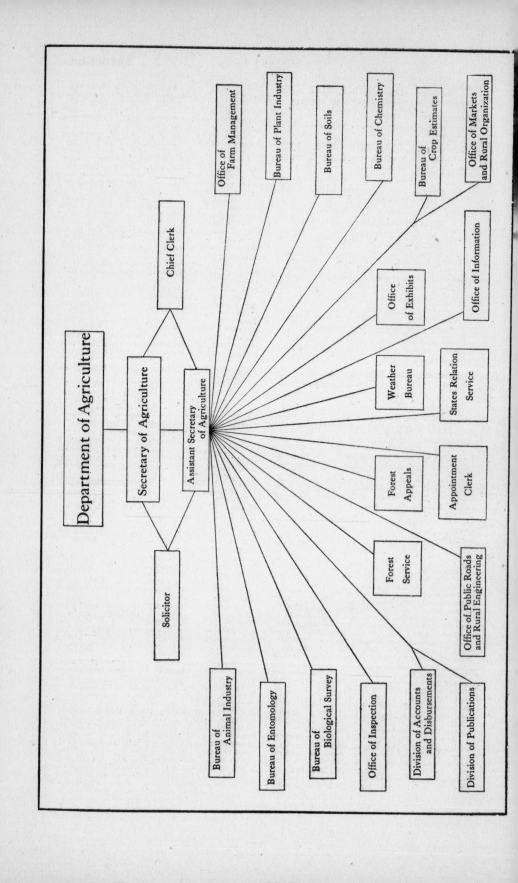

Department of Agriculture

Secretary of Agriculture

Chief Clerk

Solicitor

Assistant Secretary
of Agriculture

Office of
Farm Management

Bureau of Plant Industry

Bureau of Soils

Bureau of Chemistry

Bureau of
Crop Estimates

Office of Markets
and Rural Organization

Office of Information

Office
of Exhibits

Weather
Bureau

States Relation
Service

Forest
Appeals

Appointment
Clerk

Forest
Service

Office of Public Roads
and Rural Engineering

Bureau of
Animal Industry

Bureau of Entomology

Bureau of
Biological Survey

Office of Inspection

Division of Accounts
and Disbursements

Division of Publications

an amount of public land, to be apportioned to each state a quantity equal to 30,000 acres for each Senator and Representative in Congress to which the states are respectively entitled by the apportionment under the census of 1860," but excepting mineral lands, to found colleges of agriculture and the mechanical arts. This act was amended by an act of March 3, 1833, which provided that all money derived by the states from the sale of land apportioned by the general Government must be invested in stocks of the United States or in the several states, or in some safe manner to be prescribed by the legislature of the several states in such a manner as to yield not less than five per cent., the principal to remain forever inviolate and undiminished.

College instruction in agriculture is given in the colleges and universities receiving the benefits of the acts of Congress of July 2, 1862, August 30, 1890, and March 4, 1907, which are now in operation in all the states and territories except Alaska. The total number of these institutions is sixty-eight, of which sixty-five maintain courses of instruction in agriculture. In twenty-three states the agricultural colleges are departments of the state universities. In sixteen states and territories separate institutions having courses in agriculture are maintained for the colored race. All of the agricultural colleges for white persons and several of those for negroes offer four-year courses in agriculture and its related sciences leading to bachelors' degrees, and many provide for graduate study. About sixty of these institutions also provide special short, or correspondence, courses in the different branches of agriculture, including agronomy, horticulture, animal husbandry, poultry raising, cheese making, dairying, sugar making, rural engineering, farm mechanics, and other technical subjects. Officers of the agricultural colleges engage quite largely in conducting farmers' institutes and various other forms of college extension.

Location of agricultural colleges (including only institutions established under the land-grant act of July 2, 1862) :

Alabama—Alabama Polytechnic Institute, Auburn.
Agricultural School of the Tuskegee Normal Industrial Institute, Tuskegee Institute.
Agricultural and Mechanical College for Negroes, Normal.
Arizona—University of Arizona, Tucson.
Arkansas—College of Agriculture of the University of Arkansas, Fayetteville.
Branch Normal College, Pine Bluff.
California—College of Agriculture of the University of California, Berkeley.
Colorado—The State Agricultural College of Colorado, Fort Collins.
Connecticut—Connecticut Agricultural College, Storrs.
Delaware—Delaware College, Newark.
State College for Colored Students, Dover.
Florida—College of Agriculture of the University of Florida, Gainesville.
Florida Agricultural and Mechanical College for Negroes, Tallahassee.
Georgia—Georgia State College of Agriculture, Athens.
Georgia State Industrial College, Savannah.
Hawaii—College of Hawaii, Honolulu.
Idaho—College of Agriculture of the University of Idaho, Moscow.
Illinois—College of Agriculture of the University of Illinois, Urbana.
Indiana—School of Agriculture of Purdue University, La Fayette.

Iowa—Iowa State College of Agriculture and Mechanic Arts, Ames.
Kansas—Kansas State Agricultural College, Manhattan.
Kentucky—The College af Agriculture of the State University, Lexington.
The Kentucky Normal and Industrial Institute for Colored Persons, Frankfort.
Louisiana—Louisiana State University and Agricultural and Mechanical College, Baton Rouge.
Southern University and Agricultural and Mechanical College of the State of Louisiana, Scotland Heights, Baton Rouge.
Maine—College of Agriculture of the University of Maine, Orono.
Maryland—Maryland Agricultural College, College Park.
Princess Anne Academy, Eastern Branch of the Maryland Agricultural College, Princess Anne.
Massachusetts—Massachusetts Agricultural College, Amherst.
Michigan—Michigan Agricultural College, East Lansing.
Minnesota—College of Agriculture of the University of Minnesota, University Farm, St. Paul.
Mississippi—Mississippi Agricultural and Mechanical College, Agricultural College.
Alcorn Agricultural and Mechanical College, Alcorn.
Missouri—College of Agriculture of the University of Missouri, Columbia.
Lincoln Institute, Jefferson City.
Montana—Montana State College of Agriculture and Mechanic Arts, Bozeman.
Nebraska—College of Agriculture of the University of Nebraska, Lincoln.
Nevada—College of Agriculture of the University of Nevada, Reno.
New Hampshire—New Hampshire College of Agriculture and the Mechanic Arts, Durham.
New Jersey—Rutgers Scientific School (the New Jersey State College for the Benefit of Agriculture and the Mechanic Arts), New Brunswick.
New Mexico—New Mexico College of Agriculture and Mechanic Arts, State College.
New York—New York State College of Agriculture, Ithaca.
North Carolina—The North Carolina College of Agriculture and Mechanic Arts, West Raleigh.
The Agricultural and Mechanical College for the Colored Race, Greensboro.
North Dakota—North Dakota Agricultural College, Agricultural College.
Ohio—College of Agriculture of Ohio State University, Columbus.
Oklahoma—Oklahoma Agricultural and Mechanical College, Stillwater.
Agricultural and Normal University, Langston.
Oregon—Oregon State Agricultural College, Corvallis.
Pennsylvania—The Pennsylvania State College, State College.
Porto Rico—College of Agriculture of the University of Porto Rico, Mayaguez.
Rhode Island—Rhode Island State College, Kingston.
South Carolina—The Clemson Agricultural College of South Carolina, Clemson College.
The Colored Normal, Industrial, Agricultural, and Mechanical College of South Carolina, Orangeburg.
South Dakota—South Dakota State College of Agriculture and Mechanic Arts, Brookings.

Tennessee—College of Agriculture, University of Tennessee, Knoxville.

Texas—Agricultural and Mechanical College of Texas, College Station.

Prairie View State Normal and Industrial College, Prairie View.

Utah—The Agricultural College of Utah, Logan.

Vermont—College of Agriculture of the University of Vermont, Burlington.

Virginia—The Virginia Agricultural and Mechanical College and Polytechnic Institute, Blacksburg.

The Hampton Normal and Agricultural Institute, Hampton.

Washington—State College of Washington, Pullman.

West Virginia—College of Agriculture of West Virginia University, Morgantown.

The West Virginia Colored Institute, Institute.

Wisconsin—College of Agriculture of the University of Wisconsin, Madison.

Wyoming—College of Agriculture, University of Wyoming, Laramie.

Experiment Stations.—A law approved March 2, 1887, provided for the establishment—under the direction of the agricultural colleges, or agricultural departments of colleges, established in each state or territory in accordance with the law of July 2, 1862, mentioned above—of departments to be known as Agricultural Experiment Stations. It was provided that the duties of these stations should consist in conducting original research as to the physiology of plants and animals; the diseases to which they are subject and their remedies; the chemical composition of useful plants; the comparative advantages of rotative croppings as pursued under varying series of crops; the analysis of soils and water; the chemical compositions of natural and artificial fertilizers; the scientific and economic questions involved in the production of butter and cheese; and such other matters bearing directly upon the agricultural industries of the United States as might be deemed advisable by the directors of the several stations. For carrying on this work the act provided $15,000 a year to each state and territory out of funds proceeding from the sale of public lands.

Agricultural experiment stations are now maintained in whole or in part by the federal government, and exist in every state and territory. The total amount expended in one recent year was $3,053,446, of which nearly half was received from the National government. Agricultural experiment stations represent one of the most important institutions in the United States, doing much to promote intensive farming and to show farmers how to reduce costs and derive the greatest benefit from their crops.

Following is a list of the secretaries of agriculture and the Presidents under whom they served:

President	Secretary of Agriculture	Appointed
Cleveland..	Norman J. Colman, Missouri....	1889
B. Harrison	Jeremiah M. Rusk, Wisconsin...	1889
Cleveland..	J. Sterling Morton, Nebraska....	1893
McKinley .	James Wilson, Iowa............	1897
Roosevelt..	" " "	1901
Taft......	" " "	1909
Wilson....	David F. Houston, Missouri....	1913

The following persons have held the office of Commissioner of Agriculture in the order named: Isaac Newton, Pennsylvania;

Horace Capron, Illinois; Frederick Watts, Pennsylvania; William G. Le Duc, Minnesota; George B. Loring, Massachusetts; and Norman J. Colman, Missouri.

For more detailed information as to the scope of the activities of the Department of Agriculture consult the index references to the Presidents' Messages and Encyclopedic articles under the following headings:

Accounts and Disbursements, Division of.

Animal Industry, Bureau of.

Biological Survey, Bureau of.

Chemistry, Bureau of.

Crop Estimates, Bureau of.

Entomology, Bureau of.

Exhibits, Office of.

Experiment Stations.

Farm Management, Office of.

Food and Drug Inspection, Board of.

Forest Reserve.

Forest Service.

Horticultural Board.

Insecticide and Fungicide Board.

Inspection, Office of.

Markets and Rural Organization, Office of.

National Forests.

Plant Industry, Bureau of.

Public Roads and Rural Engineering, Office of.

Publications, Division of.

Referee Board of Consulting Scientific Experts.

Soils, Bureau of.

States Relation Service.

Weather Bureau.

Agriculture, Department of:

Creation of, discussed, 5486.

Discussed, 5554, 5641, 5763, 5886, 5978, 6169, 6346, 6390, 6455, 6655.

Educational work of, 6905, 6906.

Efforts of, in behalf of farmers, 7909.

Expenditures of, 5886, 5981.

Experiment Stations of, 6733, 6905.

Forest Service recommended, 6910.

Land reserved for use of, 6709.

Law officer for, recommended, 5487.

Statistical division of, 5982.

Sugar-beet culture, 4534, 5554, 6280, 6347, 6356, 6415, 6455, 6865.

Sugar cane experiments, 6849.

Transfer of Weather Service to, 5487.

Usefulness vindicated, 7091.

Works of, 6655, 6727, 6906, 6927.

Aircraft Board.—By act of Congress approved October 1, 1917, a board was created to expand and coordinate the industrial activities pertaining to aircraft and their parts and to facilitate the development of air service. The board consists of not more than nine members, including a civilian chairman, the Chief Signal Officer of the Army, two other Army officers to be appointed by the Secretary of War, the Chief Constructor of the Navy, two other Navy officers to be appointed by the Secretary of the Navy, and two additional civilian employees. The civilian employees are appointed by the President, by and with the consent of the Senate. The Board continues in existence at the pleasure of the President, but not more than six months after the end of the European War, and the civilian members serve without compensation.

Aircraft Production, War, in United States.—A report of the Senate Military Affairs Committee published on April 10, 1918, revealed the following facts regarding the production of aircraft for the military purposes of the United States during the first year of the war with the Central Powers:

Twenty aviation training schools were established and conducted, with 4 more in process of construction, to be finished about June 1. The capacity of the schools in operation was about 3,000 cadets. 1,926 had already been graduated from this primary training course and commissioned as reserve military aviators. Very few of these received their advanced training in the United States.

In addition, the Signal Corps dispatched some 1,200 cadets to England, at the invitation of the Entente Allies. Only some 500 of these, however, by the time of the committee report had received their preliminary training.

On April 1, 1918, 3,458 primary training planes had been completed. The planes were of two standard types developed for the purpose, and were equipped with Curtiss and Hall-Scott motors, respectively. Of advanced training planes, 342 had been manufactured, of four different types and three different types of engines, of which 965 had been completed, of foreign design, but American manufacture. The Liberty motor was not suitable for use in these planes.

The Liberty motor, of twelve cylinders, was first set up in July, 1917, but changes had been made in it up to the very time of the committee's report. It was not designed for the single-seated, swift fighting machine. It was of the direct driven type. 22,500 Liberty motors had been ordered, of which 122 had been completed for the Army and 142 for the Navy. Four had been shipped overseas.

Of the combat planes, five types had been adopted at one time or another, two of which had been abandoned. Of one, the Handley-Page, a heavy bombing machine, none had been completed. Of another, the De Haviland, 15 had been completed. The third, the Bristol Fighter, was under construction.

To aid in the foreign manufacture of planes for American purposes, the Signal Corps had shipped to France 11,000 tons of material and 7,000 mechanics.

By act of Congress approved July 24, 1917, $640,000,000 was appropriated for airplane production. For the national service, the leading airplane producers in the United States pooled their patent interests under the Manufacturers' Aircraft Association, organized for that purpose.

On May 31, 1918, the House Committee on Military Affairs authorized the publication of the following facts concerning the status of aircraft production for war purposes at that time:—In the Aviation Corps there were 12,107 officers and 136,761 enlisted men. In Europe there were 1,316 planes, of which 321 were battleplanes; and in the United States there were 3,760 planes, most of which were training planes. None of the former was made entirely in the United States, but they were constructed in British and French factories, chiefly by American mechanics, and almost entirely of raw materials furnished by the United States. 561 Liberty motors had been delivered to the Army and 480 to the Navy; and the Chief of Staff of the Army was authority for the statement that the United States forces abroad were furnished with all the aircraft they needed for offense and defense.

Insignia used for United States airplanes are a white star, with red centre, upon a blue circumscribed field. These are placed on the upper surface of the upper wings of the aeroplane and on the lower surface of the lower. The rudders are marked with three bands of blue, white and red, looking from the rudder post.

Alabama.—One of the southern group of states; nicknamed, the "Land of Flowers." The name is Indian and means "Here we rest," and has been adopted as the motto of the State. Alabama is bounded on the north by Tennessee, on the east by Georgia, and on the west by Mississippi. It is about 330 miles in length from north to south and its greatest width is 200 miles. It contains 51,998 square miles of area, or about 33,000,000 acres. The State was admitted into the Union Dec. 14, 1819, seceded Jan. 11, 1861, and was readmitted by act of Congress June 25, 1868 (pages 3521, 3857). The population in 1910 was 2,138,093, of which 45 per cent. are negroes.

The staple production of Alabama is cotton, though corn, oats, wheat, and all kinds of vegetables are produced in abundance, besides butter, cheese, and lumber. Alabama is particularly rich in mineral deposits. A vein of bituminous coal runs eastward from Tuscaloosa into Georgia. The statuary granite of Alabama is among the best in the United States. The chief industries of the State are farming and the manufacture of iron and cotton fabrics.

Cotton is grown on about 3,436,000 acres, and the yield in 1915 was 1,050,000 bales. Other field crops were: corn, 3,000,000 acres, 54,000,000 bushels, valued at $42,120,000; oats, 283,000 acres, 5,434,000 bushels, $3,586,000; hay, 120,000 acres, 168,000 tons, $2,150,000. There are more than 171,000 horses in the State, worth about $22,525,000; 253,000 mules, 817,000 cattle, worth $11,399,000; 178,000 sheep, $325,000, and 1,176,000 pigs, $7,056,000. The wool clip of 1909 weighed about 552,250 pounds and sold for $185,650. About 96,000,000 gallons of milk are yearly produced, from which are made twenty million pounds of butter and 40,000 pounds of cheese.

The iron ores of Alabama, though inferior to those of Lake Superior, have a compensating advantage in lying near beds of good coking coal and of limestone suitable for fluxing, so that Birmingham, the Pittsburgh of the South, can manufacture pig iron cheaper than any other place in the world. Before 1882, when the boom began, the coal production of Alabama had not amounted to as much as half a million tons in any one year; in 1913 it was 17,678,522 tons. The value of the coal product of Alabama is approximately two-thirds that of the total mineral output, amounting in 1913 to $23,083,724.

The number of manufacturing establishments in Alabama having an annual output valued at $500 or more at the beginning of 1915 was 3,240. The amount of capital invested was $218,062,000 giving occupation to 87,916 persons, using material valued at $105,632,000, and turning out finished goods worth $175,897,000. Salaries and wages paid amounted to $80,000,000.

Alabama (see also Confederate States; Tuscaloosa, Ala.):

Act prescribing number of district attorneys and marshals in, vetoed, 5785.

Direct tax due from, request of United States for payment of, 3579.

Fifteenth amendment ratified by, 3998.

Fourteenth amendment ratified by, 3843.

Proclaimed, 3837.

Indian depredations in, 1645.

Indians attempt to establish government in, 1020.

Lands granted to, in aid of railroads referred to, 3580.

Memorial from colored citizens of Montgomery asking rights of citizenship referred to, 4258.

Property owners in, should be compensated for losses sustained, 1474.

Provisional governor for, appointed and restoration of, into Union, 3521.

Railroads in, memorial from legislature of, asking extension of time to complete, 3579.

Alabama Claims.—During the Civil War in the United States the Queen of England issued a proclamation of neutrality, May 13, 1861, granting belligerent rights to both combatants and forbidding her subjects to take part with either. Great Britain's laws prohibited the equipment of any land or naval forces within her dominions to act against any friendly power. Notwithstanding this prohibition, the *Alabama, Florida, Georgia, Shenandoah,* and other vessels were built in Great Britain for the Confederate States, and, regardless of the remonstrances of the American ministry, were allowed to escape from British ports fitted out as commerce destroyers. In less than two months the *Alabama* had taken twenty-seven prizes. After a long cruise among islands of the East and West Indies and along the coast of Brazil the *Alabama* came to anchor at Cherbourg, France. Off this harbor she was sunk by the U. S. S. *Kearsarge,* after having destroyed 58 vessels and about $6,550,000 worth of property. After the war the United States pressed a claim for damages against Great Britain. After much discussion it was agreed to submit the matter to a court of arbitration composed of Charles Francis Adams, appointed by the President of the United States; Sir Alexander Cockburn, by the Queen of England; Count Federigo Sclopis, by the King of Italy; M. Jacques Staempfli, by the President of Switzerland, and Viscount d'Itajuba, by the Emperor of Brazil. The commissioners met at Geneva, Switzerland, Dec. 15, 1871, Count Sclopis presiding. The United States was awarded $15,500,000 in gold in satisfaction for all claims. All claims to indirect damages were rejected, and Great Britain was held culpable for not doing more to prevent the sailing and success of the cruisers. The award was paid. (See Geneva Tribunal and illustration opposite 4056.)

Alabama Claims:

Arbitration of, proposed by United States, and reply of Great Britain discussed, 3565.

Commission to take proof on, recommended, 4056.

Correspondence regarding mode of settling, 4075.

Court of Commissioners of—
Discussed, 4244, 4296, 4356, 4372.
Time of duration of, extended, 4278, 4296.

Discussed, 3565, 3655, 3777, 3987, 4056, 4321.

Transfer of indemnity to United States referred to, 4312.

Tribunal at Geneva for settlement of, award of, 4138.

Commissioners to report on distribution of, appointment of, recommended, 4139, 4190.

Payment of, 4190.

Case of United States and counter case referred to, 4115, 4118, 4119.

Difference of opinion regarding powers of, 4120, 4122.

Discussed, 4097, 4138.

Legislation in connection with, urged, 4164.

Referred to, 4161.

Alabama Indians. (See Indian Tribes.)

Alabama, The, destruction of, by the *Kearsarge* referred to, 3457. (See also Alabama Claims.)

Alamo.—Originally built as a church, situated on the San Antonio River, near San Antonio, Texas, it was converted into a fort. In February, 1836, it was occupied by Colonel W. B. Travis with 140 men who were in arms against the government of Mexico. The party was besieged by some 2,000 Mexicans under Santa Ana from February 23 until March 6, when the place was surrendered to Santa Ana under the promise of his protection. At the command of that general, however, the six survivors, including David Crockett and Colonel Bowie, famous frontiersmen, were massacred, and the bodies of their comrades were mutilated. Thereafter Texans were roused to fury by the cry, "Remember the Alamo!" In allusion to the heroic defense made by the Greeks of antiquity at Thermopylæ, this struggle was sometimes referred to as the Thermopylæ of Texas.

Alaska. — *History.* — Alaska derives its name from an English corruption of the native word "Al-ay-ek-sa," probably meaning "The great land" or "Mainland."

The region now known as Alaska was first explored by the Russian officers Bering and Chirikov in 1741. Russian traders and trappers soon entered the country and through their activity other nations became interested in this region. Spanish expeditions in 1774 and 1775 visited the southeastern shore and in 1778 the English Explorer, Capt. James Cook, made extensive surveys of the coast for the British Government. The first settlement was made by the Russians at Three Saints on Kodiak Island in 1784, and in 1804 the Russian-American Co. founded Sitka, making it the seat of government in the following year.

In 1799 the trade and regulation of the Russian possessions in America were given over to the Russian-American Co. for a term of 20 years, which was afterwards twice renewed for similar periods.

In 1821 Russia attempted by ukase to exclude foreign navigators from Bering Sea and the Pacific coast of her possessions, which caused a controversy with the United States and Great Britain. The question was settled by a treaty with the United States in 1824 and one with Great Britain in 1825, by which the boundaries of the Russian possessions in America were permanently fixed.

In March, 1867, Alaska was purchased by the United States for the sum of $7,-200,000 in gold, and in October of the same year the formal transfer was made at Sitka. From 1867 to 1877 Alaska was governed by the War Department, although the customs were from the beginning collected by the Treasury Department, and with the latter the control rested from 1877 until the passage of the act of 1884. This act extended over Alaska the laws of the State of Oregon so far as they were applicable, created a judicial district and a land district, put in force the mining laws of the United States, and gave the country an administrative system.

The influx of settlers after the discovery of gold in the Klondike in 1896 rendered more adequate laws necessary. In 1899 and 1900 Congress made provisions for a code of civil and criminal law, and in 1903 passed a homestead act. In the meantime a serious boundary dispute had arisen between the United States and Canada regarding the interpretation of the treaty of 1825. This was settled in 1903 by an agreement whereby the seacoast of Canada extended no farther north than 54° 40′. By the act of May 7, 1906, Alaska was given power to elect a Delegate to Congress. The act of August 24, 1912, provided for the creation of a Territorial legislature.

Geography.—Alaska in its greatest extent is included between the meridians of 130° west longitude and 173° east longitude and between the parallels of 51° and 72° north latitude. It is bounded on the north by the Arctic Ocean, on the west by the Arctic Ocean, Bering Strait, and Bering Sea, on the south and southwest by the Gulf of Alaska and the Pacific Ocean, and on the east by the Yukon Territory and British Columbia. The eastern boundary from the Arctic Ocean to the neighborhood of Mount St. Elias is the one hundred and forty-first meridian; thence southeastward to Portland Canal it is irregular and cannot be described in general terms.

Alaska is in approximately the same latitude as the Scandinavian Peninsula; Point Barrow, its northernmost point, is in about the same latitude as North Cape; Dixon Entrance, which marks its southern boundary, is nearly on the same parallel as Copenhagen; St. Elias is in the latitude of Christiania and St. Petersburg; and Sitka is in the latitude of Edinburgh. The longitude of the western terminal of the Aleutian Islands is almost identical with that of the New Hebrides Islands and is the same as that of New Zealand, and Cape Prince of Wales, the most westerly point of the mainland, is nearly as far west as the Samoan Islands. Thus a person traveling from New York to Attu Island, the westernmost of the Aleutian chain, on reaching San Francisco will have accomplished less than half the journey from east to west.

The area of Alaska is about 586,400 square miles, one-fifth that of the United States. The popular conception of the size of Alaska is based on maps of North America, which always distort it. The map of Alaska, superimposed on a map of the United States of the same scale, demonstrates that the distance from the easternmost to the westernmost point in Alaska is equal to the distance from the Atlantic to the Pacific in the latitude of Los Angeles, and that its northernmost and southernmost points are nearly as far apart as the Mexican and the Canadian boundaries of the United States.

The main mass of Alaska is nearly rectangular and is carved out from the continent by Mackenzie Bay on the north and the Gulf of Alaska on the south. An extension to the southeast is furnished by the so-called panhandle of southeastern Alaska, and to the southwest by the Alaska Peninsula and the Aleutian Islands.

Topography.—The main topographic features of Alaska are similar to those of the western United States. The highlands of Alaska, like those of the United States and Canada, are in general parallel to the coast line, and the four topographic provinces of the United States are fairly well defined throughout western Canada and continue into Alaska. Along the Pacific coast of Alaska and British Columbia is a mountainous belt 50 to 200 miles in width, which is the westernmost of the four provinces, and may be designated the "Pacific Mountain system." It properly includes the mountainous Alexander Archipelago and Aleutian Islands, as well as a number of other island groups. While this region is in the main rugged and mountainous, its ranges are distinct and often separated by broad valleys or indentations of the coast line, forming in several cases large basins, like that of the Copper River. Except for a section of the inner slope which drains into the Yukon and Kuskokwim, its waters reach the Pacific through streams flowing transverse to the axis of the mountains.

East and north of the Pacific Mountains is the Central Plateau region, corresponding in a broad way with the Central Plateau of the western United States and Canada. This belt is drained largely by the Yukon and Kuskokwim Rivers into Bering Sea, and includes a number of lowland areas of considerable extent. East and north of the plateau province, a broad cordillera forms the northern extension of the Rocky Mountain system. The drainage of the southern slopes of the mountains is chiefly tributary to the Yukon, while the northern slope drains into the Arctic Ocean.

The Great Plains east and north of the Rockies form an area of low relief which lies between the western extension of the Rocky Mountains and the Arctic Ocean and is designated the "Arctic slope region."

Climate.—Though Alaska is often loosely referred to as an Arctic province, yet nearly three-quarters of its area lies within the North Temperate Zone. Geographic position and extent relative to oceanic bodies, together with relief, have brought about physical conditions producing strong contrasts in climate between different parts of the Territory. Three general climatic provinces, each of which in turn includes a number of subordinate provinces, are recognized.

The climate of the coastal province is comparable with that of Scotland and the Scandinavian Peninsula, in Europe, but is somewhat warmer. That of the inland region is not unlike the climate of Alberta, Saskatchewan, and Manitoba, in Canada. The northerly province bordering the Polar Sea is the only one in which Arctic conditions prevail.

The precipitation of southeastern Alaska varies from about 147 inches at Ketchikan to less than 30 inches at Skagway. While there is but little snow near sea level, there is a very heavy fall in the mountains. At White Pass the winter snowfall is about 25 to 30 feet, but is probably less than 4 feet on the Chilkat summit. The highest recorded summer temperature in southeastern Alaska is 92° F.; the lowest winter temperature — 4° F.

In the coastal region, stretching from Katalla to Seward, the average temperature for the three summer months is about 51° F.; of the three winter months from 20° to 30° F. The lowest temperature recorded in this region is — 14° F.; the highest 82° F. The total snowfall is about 5-8 feet at Seward, 12 feet at Valdez, about 6 feet on Trail Creek along the Alaska Northern Railroad, about 30 feet at Childs Glacier on the Copper River Railroad, and about 15 feet at Thompson Pass, crossed by the Military Road from Valdez.

Some of the most important climatic features of the coast of Alaska to shipping are the severe winds which blow in and out of the valleys that traverse the coast ranges and their connecting fiords. These blow toward the land in summer and toward the sea in winter. The severest are the outward winds, which are most common during January, February, and March, when velocities of 60 and 70 miles an hour are said to be not infrequent.

The Aleutian Islands and the Alaska Peninsula have a climate characterized by comparatively moderate temperature and less humidity than that of the Pacific coast to the east. Cook Inlet has quite a different climate from that of the outer coast line. The highest recorded summer temperature is 87° F.; the lowest winter temperature, — 40° F. The climate of the lower Susitna and of the Matanuska Valleys differs again both from that of Cook Inlet and of the outer coast line. Here the summers are known to be warmer than on Cook Inlet and the winters are probably milder. The lowest temperature recorded at this locality during the same period was — 12° F.; the highest 84° F. The lower Copper River Valley has much the same climate as that of the coast. At Kennicott, the inland terminal of the Copper River & Northwestern Railroad, the snowfall is about 4 feet, and the extremes of temperatures recorded are — 31° and 76° F. This station is 2,000 feet above sea level and close to a glacier. At Copper Center the total precipitation is about 10 inches and the snowfall about 3 feet. Extremes of temperatures of — 50° and 85° have been recorded. The total annual precipitation in the upper Yukon Basin varies locally from 10 to 16 inches. The mean temperature for the three summer months at Fairbanks is about 56° F.; the mean temperature for the three winter months about — 12° F. The precipitation on the lower Yukon and Kuskokwim is about 17 to 20 inches. Along the shores of Bering Sea the mean summer temperature varies from 40° to 50°. The climate of the northern half of Bering Sea is comparable with that of the Province of Archangel, in northern Russia, a region which supports some agricultural population. The arctic province, which includes the littoral of the Polar Sea, as well as the drainage basins of the tributary rivers, is similar to that of the Bering Sea, but colder.

One effect of climate is the frozen condition of the ground which prevails in much of the inland region. At Fairbanks the alluvium is in many places frozen to bedrock, ground frost having been met with to a depth of over 300 feet. It is to be noted that unless the cover of moss and vegetation is stripped, only about 18 to 24 inches of the surface thaws during the summer. On removal of the vegetative covering the ground thaws, so that the frozen subsoil is no detriment to agriculture. The ground is, however, not everywhere frozen in the inland region. The beds of the larger watercourses are usually unfrozen, and this also holds true of the gravel benches along the valley walls and other deposits of alluvium which are drained. No permanent ground frost occurs along the Pacific littoral, and the same probably holds true of most of the Susitna and Matanuska Basins. There is considerable permanently frozen ground in the Copper River Valley, especially along the foothills and slopes of the Alaska Range. The experience of those long resident in Alaska has shown the climate to be very healthful. No extremes of cold or heat occur along the Pacific seaboard. The excessive rains characteristic of many parts of this district are, to be sure, disagreeable, but experience demonstrates the fact that they have no adverse effect on health.

Of the Yukon it may be said that the summers are cool and that bright clear weather prevails most of the time. The aridity of the climate makes the extreme temperatures of winter easy to resist. All who have lived in this inland region are agreed that the winter climate is far more healthful than in many parts of the States where the temperature is higher, but where there is an excess of humidity. Residents of the interior have no fear of the extreme cold that often prevails during the winter months. The winter journey between Fairbanks and Valdez is made by men, women, and children and offers no serious hardships except when storms are encountered. On the other hand, the more humid climate of Seward Peninsula is much more trying. Here the winter storms are severe and the absence of timber gives no shelter. The summer climate at Nome is delightful.

Population.—According to the census of 1910 the total population of Alaska was 63,700, of which about 36,000 were whites. The census was taken in winter, when only permanent residents could be enumerated, and these figures should therefore be augmented by many thousands, representing the annual summer migration to Alaska of miners, cannery employes, and others, but of course not including tourists. Skagway had a population of 872 (1910). It is also estimated that there are 2,000 or 3,000 more in the Klondike and other Canadian mining districts of the Yukon. The town of Haines, on Lynn Canal, had a population of 445 (1910), and the total of the tributary district was about 1,000. The coastal towns of Prince William Sound and adjacent regions had populations in 1910 as follows: Katalla, 188; Cordova, 1,152; Seward, 534. The incorporated town of Valdez had 810, to which should be added some 600 or 700 more, representing the population of a settlement immediately adjacent, not included within the city limits. There are no facts available regarding the population of the Copper River Valley, as the census was taken before the influx of people, due to the completion of the railroad. The population of the Kenai Peninsula, including Seward, is about 1,700, and there are between 600 and 700 in the Cook Inlet region, including the Susitna Valley. In 1910 there were nearly 17,000 residents in the Alaska part of the Yukon and in the Kuskokwim Basins. Of these nearly 8,000 were in Fairbanks and the adjacent region. The population of Fairbanks was 3,541 (1910); Chena, 138; Tanana, at the mouth of the river of the same name, 398; Rampart, 83; Hotsprings, 101.

Government.—The executive power is vested in the governor, who is appointed by the President for a term of four years by and with the advice and consent of the Senate. The governor may veto any bill passed by the Territorial legislature within three days after it is presented to him. The legislature may override the veto by a two-thirds vote of all the members to which each house is entitled.

The legislative power is vested in a Territorial legislature consisting of a Senate and a House of Representatives. The Senate consists of 8 members, 2 from each of the four judicial divisions into which Alaska is now divided. The House of Representatives consists of 16 members, 4 from each of the four judicial divisions. The term of each member of the Senate is four years, one member from each judicial division being elected every two years. The term of each member of the House of Representatives is two years.

The legislature convenes biennially at Juneau, the capital, on the first Monday in March in odd years, and the length of the session is limited to 60 days, but the governor is empowered to call a special session, which shall not continue longer than 15 days. Elections for members of the legislature are held every two years on the first Tuesday after the first Monday in November of each even year.

The judicial power of the Territory is vested in the United States District Court for Alaska, which has the same jurisdiction as the district courts of the United States and has general jurisdiction in civil, criminal, equity, and admiralty causes. This court is divided into four divisions, presided over by four judges appointed by the President, by and with the advice and consent of the Senate, for a term of four years.

The Territory elects a Delegate to Congress, who may participate in debate, but who has no vote. Beginning in 1914 this Delegate is elected on the same date as members of the legislature.

Public Lands.—Local land offices are located at Nome, Fairbanks, and Juneau, where entries for public lands should be filed. The surveyor general for the Territory is located at Juneau.

By the act of August 24, 1912, the general laws of the United States not locally inapplicable were extended to Alaska. The homestead law, however, had been previously extended with certain liberal modifications.

Surveys by the rectangular system are being extended from three separate bases and principal meridians, distinguished as the Copper River, the Fairbanks, and the Seward Meridian.

A qualified person may make a homestead entry in Alaska for not more than 320 acres of surveyed or unsurveyed land. No such entry may, however, be allowed for land extending more than 160 rods along the shore of any navigable water, and along such shore a space of at least 80 rods is reserved between all claims. If any of the land settled upon is unsurveyed, then the claim must be located in a rectangular form not more than 1 mile in length by north and south lines, run according to the true meridian.

National Forests.—The coast forests, which comprise the most heavily timbered areas in Alaska, are nearly all included in the Tongass and Chugach National Forests. These are under the jurisdiction of the Forest Service of the United States Department of Agriculture.

The best estimates available place the total stand of merchantable timber on the Tongass National Forest at 70,000,000,000 board feet, and on the Chugach at 8,000,-000,000 board feet. This timber consists largely of hemlock and Sitka spruce, although there is considerable western red cedar and some yellow cypress, chiefly on the Tongass. The timber is suitable for construction material, finish, and a very large amount is suitable for paper pulp. The conditions for the manufacture of pulp are very favorable. Logging distances are short, since the great bulk of the timber is situated within a short distance of the shore line. Transportation to the point of manufacture is comparatively cheap. Unlimited water power for purposes of manufacture is available and may be used without charge for manufacture of national forest products. From points of manufacture, all of which must be situated on tide

water, deep-sea transportation is available to the great world markets.

The best data available indicate that at least 700,000,000 board feet per annum can be cut indefinitely from the Tongass National Forest and at least 80,000,000 from the Chugach. This will leave a very large surplus for export after supplying local needs.

Mature timber on either forest may be purchased on reasonable terms. A sufficient amount of timber will be included in any sale to justify fully the investment required for logging and manufacture. Reasonable cutting periods will be allowed, based upon market demands and the capacity of the plant. Payment is required on the basis of actual or scale measurement in comparatively small amounts immediately in advance of cutting, thus doing away very largely with carrying charges. Sales in which the value of the timber exceeds $100 must be advertised at least 30 days. Settlers, farmers, prospectors, fishermen, and others may take timber from these forests for personal use free of charge and without permit in amounts not exceeding 20,000 board feet, or 25 cords of wood in any one year.

Postal Service.—The domestic rates of postage and conditions apply to matter mailed at any point in Alaska to any other point in that Territory, or in the United States or its possessions, with the following exceptions:

The graduated zone rates on fourth-class or domestic parcel-post matter do not apply, the postage rate on such matter between any point in Alaska and the United States and between any two points in Alaska being 12 cents for each pound or fraction thereof on parcels exceeding 4 ounces in weight, regardless of distance.

The rate of postage on gold coin, gold bullion, and gold dust offered for mailing between any two points in Alaska or between any point in Alaska and any point in the United States or its possessions shall be 2 cents an ounce or fraction thereof, regardless of distance. Such gold coin, gold bullion, or gold dust shall be inclosed in sealed packages not exceeding 11 pounds in weight and sent by registered mail.

Resources.—The mineral wealth of Alaska is at present its most important resource, but the Territory also includes extensive tracts of farming and grazing lands and many water powers. Excellent timber occurs in southeastern Alaska, while the inland forests are valuable for local use. There are also valuable fisheries along the Pacific seaboard.

The developed mineral resources of Alaska include gold lodes and placers, copper, tin, and silver deposits, together with petroleum, marble, and gypsum. There are also extensive fields of bituminous and lignitic coal and some iron ores, which are practically undeveloped. In addition to these, silver-lead, zinc, antimony, quicksilver, and other ores, and peat, graphite, asbestos, and mica have been found.

Gold lode mining has been carried on in southeastern Alaska since 1882, and is a large and well-developed industry. The value of the total lode production is about $57,000,000, of which $4,600,000 should be credited to 1912. Copper mining began in 1900 and has made rapid strides during the past few years. The total copper production is about 90,000,000 pounds, valued at $13,145,000. Of this, 28,940,000 pounds, valued at about $4,630,000, represents the output of 1912.

Placer mining, begun at Juneau in 1880, was extended to the Yukon Basin in 1886. No very important discoveries of placer gold were, however, made in Alaska until after the Klondike rush of 1898. This brought a large number of people into the Territory and led to the finding of gold at Nome in 1898, at Fairbanks in 1901, and in the Innoko-Iditarod region in 1908. Meanwhile the other smaller districts were developed, notably those of the Yukon, the Copper, and the Susitna Basins. The total gold output of all the placer mines has a value of $145,000,000, while the placer-mine output of 1912 has an estimated value of $12,000,000. Silver has been recovered, incidental to gold and copper mining, to the total value of about $1,800,-000. The value of the output of tin, marble, gypsum, petroleum, lead, etc., to the close of 1912, is about $1,000,000.

The exploitation of coal deposits on Cook Inlet in 1854 by the Russians was the first attempt at any form of mining within the Territory. The output of coal in the Territory up to the close of 1912 is insignificant, being less than 40,000 tons. During this period upward of 1,-500,000 tons of coal have been imported into the Territory.

To sum up, Alaska has produced to date mineral wealth having an aggregate value of $229,000,000, of which about $22,000,000 is to be credited to the year 1912. This output is remarkable, considering that large mining operations are practically confined to the coastal region, easily accessible to ocean transportation, and that the vast mineral wealth of the interior, except the richest of the gold placers, is almost untouched.

Gold placers, copper, and gold lode mines have been operated in central Alaska, and silver has been recovered incidentally to gold mining. There has also been a small output of coal and petroleum. Of the kinds of mineral deposits which are practically undeveloped, there are extensive coal fields, silver-lead ores, tin and antimony deposits, etc. In addition to these, some iron-ore deposits have been found, but their commercial value remains to be proven.

Auriferous gravels are very widely distributed in central Alaska, and their exploitation has yielded gold to the value of nearly $90,000,000. Most of this has been taken from deposits which were very rich, for the high cost of operating here prevented the exploitation of the more extensive deposits of lesser gold tenor.

The high cost of mining in the interior has in a large measure deterred the prospector from searching for auriferous lodes, as only the richest and most favorably situated of such deposits could be profitably exploited under present conditions. Gold lodes have, however, been found in many parts of the province and have been successfully mined in the Kenai Peninsula, in Willow Creek district of the Susitna Basin, and in the Fairbanks district.

The copper deposits of central Alaska are among its most important resources. The only developed copper district is that of the Chitina Valley, from which one mine began shipments in 1911.

The coal fields of central Alaska are extensive and include some of the best coal of the Territory. High-grade steaming and coking bituminous coals as well as some anthracite are found in the Bering River and Matanuska coal fields. Much of this coal is crushed and will furnish a large percentage of slack, and in many instances the coal beds have been so deformed as to prevent their profitable mining. While the percentage of the coal beds that can be profitably mined can

only be determined by actual exploitation, yet the fact remains that these two fields contain much workable coal of a higher grade than any now known in that part of the North American Continent tributary to the Pacific Ocean.

Commerce.—Up to the close of 1912 Alaska produced minerals, fishery products, and furs to the value of about $460,000,000. Alaska's commerce includes northward shipments of food products, merchandise, machinery, lumber, coal, etc., and return shipments of gold, silver, copper, salmon, halibut, etc. The average annual value of this growing commerce during the five years ending with 1912 is nearly $50,000,000.

The average value of the merchandise shipped annually from the United States to Alaska, during the five years ending with 1911, is $16,740,256. The highest value during this period for any one year (1909) was $17,705,330, the lowest (1911), $15,170,109. An average of about 22 per cent of the above annual value is made up of the shipments made to St. Michael and Yukon Basin. This includes some shipments to the Canadian Yukon.

It is estimated that during this five-year period an average of some 42,000 tons of merchandise were shipped into the Yukon region. This includes the traffic into the Iditarod-Innoko region, into the Tanana region, and into the Canadian Yukon. The greatest average for any one year was 50,000 (1909), and the lowest 40,500 (1910). It has been estimated that of this freight an average of 24,000 tons is shipped into the Fairbanks-Rampart region, the highest being 33,000 tons for 1909 and the lowest 15,000 tons for 1911. The information at hand indicates that about 8,500 tons have been annually shipped into the Innoko-Iditarod region during the years 1910 and 1911. A small amount of freight is also carried into Fairbanks over the military road during the winter months, and some also reaches the Kuskokwim Valley by direct shipments to the mouth of that stream.

The in and out bound passenger traffic to and from Alaska, not including tourists or cannery employees bound to remote places, amounted to 50,916 in 1910 and 43,293 in 1911. A part of this represents the travel into the Klondike and other districts of the Canadian Yukon. Most of this travel was to and from coastal points. The average annual passenger travel to the Fairbanks region by steamboat route for 1910-11 is estimated to be about 2,000, and 1,000 to the Iditarod-Innoko region. About 800, in addition, travel in and out of Fairbanks by a stage during the winter months, and probably 1,000 go in and out on foot. In addition to these there are also several hundred who travel in and out of the Iditarod-Innoko region by the Kuskokwim River or by the winter trail to Seward.

The average value of the outbound shipments from Alaska for the five years ending in 1911, and including mineral products, fish, furs, etc., is $32,200,392. The highest value for any one year was $35,-910,701 (1911), and the lowest $29,151,-404 (1910). The only outbound shipments from the Yukon and Kuskokwim Basins are gold and silver. The same is true of the Susitna Basin and a large part of the Copper River Basin, where there is, however, one which which has been shipping copper ore for two years. While much of the value of the outbound shipments is represented by gold, silver, and copper, the greater part of the actual tonnage is made up of the fishery products which are not dependent on inland transportation.

This commerce is carried on by vessels which ply between Alaska and west coast ports. Its importance is indicated by the records of clearances and entrances of vessels. In 1910 a total of 451 domestic vessels, with a total tonnage of 396,740, entered, and 419, aggregating 384,967 tons, cleared Alaska ports; 1911 the entrances were 514 vessels, with an aggregate tonnage of 426,986, and clearances, 495 vessels, with an aggregate tonnage of 421,905. Trade in foreign bottoms was as follows: In 1910, 393 vessels, with an aggregate of 244,694 tons, entered, and 366 vessels, with an aggregate of 183,284 tons, cleared. In 1911, 367 vessels, with an aggregate of 187,849 tons, entered, and 331 vessels, with an aggregate of 156,-647 tons, cleared. These figures for foreign bottoms include the clearances of the Canadian steamers on the Yukon.

The traffic on the Yukon and its tributaries is carried on by 58 river steamers varying in capacity from 6 to 588 net tons, and with an aggregate net tonnage of 14,081. There are also 12 steamers on the Kuskokwim, with a net tonnage of 1,568. About 60 vessels clearing from Puget Sound are regularly engaged in Alaska traffic. This does not include the whaling ships, cannery tenders, or small gasoline boats.

Transportation.—Alaska is a Territory of great size, about one-fifth that of the total area of the United States. About a quarter of its area lies north of the Endicott Range, which is itself north of the Arctic Circle. This portion of the Territory is Arctic, and it alone presents the bleak and frozen aspect popularly associated with Alaska. South of this range in Alaska there is an area greater than that of all the States east of the Mississippi and north of the Ohio River and Mason and Dixon's line, which is as capable of high development as many well-settled and rich countries.

The Pacific mountain system fronts the coast, extending from British Columbia in a huge arc and tailing out in the Alaska Peninsula. This system is widest in the several ranges which divide central Alaska from southern Alaska, just north of Prince William Sound, and stands as a barrier separating the comparatively small coastal valleys from the two great inland valleys of the Yukon and the Kuskokwim, which themselves are separated by a comparatively low divide. Both these great valleys may be described as regions characterized by broad, open bottom lands and gently, rolling uplands.

The Yukon River enters the Bering Sea at a latitude which prohibits the use of the stream as a connection with ocean-borne commerce excepting during three summer months. The same may be said of the Kuskokwim, though ocean commerce may reach its mouth for an additional month. Both of these rivers have difficult entrances, that of the Yukon being a shifting channel of little depth across mud flats, and the entrance to the Kuskokwim, while deep enough for the smaller ocean steamers, is extremely tortuous and not well known. Once inside, however, each presents a long stretch of navigable water for the ordinary river boat. The Yukon is navigable up to White Horse in Canada, about 2,200 miles, and its greatest tributary, the Tanana, is navigable without difficulty to Chena, near Fairbanks, and at times has been navigated much farther, though with difficulty. The Kuskokwim is navigable to the Forks, about

50 miles above the Takotna, or about 650 miles from the mouth. Both of these streams have navigable tributaries which extend their scope as transportation routes and together provide about 5,000 miles of navigable waters in the two systems. The open season is about three to three and a half months.

There are other lesser valleys with navigable waters. Of these the Copper and Susitna are the most important. These two rivers are more important as offering the best possibilities of penetrating the coastal range by rail lines than for purposes of navigation. The Copper River breaks through the Chugach Range, but with a slope so steep as to make navigation difficult and hazardous, though not impossible.

A number of good harbors along the Pacific seaboard of Alaska are now connected with near-by inland points by railroads and trails, or by wagon roads and trails only. All these harbors as far west as Cook Inlet are open throughout the year, and are from 1,000 to 1,400 statute miles from Puget Sound ports. At present a summer steamboat service of about six trips a month is maintained with the more important of these ports, and in addition some freighters carry coal and other supplies north and bring back cargoes of fish and ore. During the summer, of about three and a half months, ocean steamers make the trip between Puget Sound and St. Michael and Nome. There is also an occasional steamer to the mouth of the Kuskokwim and other points in Bering Sea.

Railroads.—The following table gives in concise form the data as to mileage, terminals, and gauge of existing railroads in Alaska:

	Miles.
Southeastern Alaska:	
White Pass and Yukon route, Skagway to White Pass (narrow gauge). Terminal at White Horse, Yukon Territory—total mileage, 102 miles	20.4
Yakutat Southern Railway, Yakutat to Situk River (narrow gauge)	9.0
Copper River: Copper River & Northwestern Railway, Cordova to Kennicott (standard gauge)	
(The same company has built a few miles of track at Katalla, where the Alaska Pacific Railway & Terminal Co. has also done some work. At Valdez a few miles of track of the Alaska Home Railway were laid in 1907, and some work was previously done on the Copper River & Northwestern Railway and on the Valdez & Yukon Railway.)	
Kenai Peninsula: Alaska Northern Railway, Seward to a point near head of Turnagain Arm (standard gauge)	71.6
Yukon Basin: Tanana Valley Railway, Fairbanks and Chena to Chatanika (narrow gauge)	46.0
Seward Peninsula:	
Seward Peninsula Railway, Nome to Shelton (narrow gauge)	80.0
Paystreak Branch, Seward Peninsula Railway (narrow gauge)	6.5
Council City & Solomon River Railway, Council to Penelope Creek (standard gauge)	32.5
Wild Goose Railway, Council to Ophir Creek (narrow gauge)	5.0
	466.0

The act approved August 24, 1912, provided for the appointment by the President of a railroad commission consisting of an officer of the Engineer Corps of the Army, a geologist in charge of Alaskan surveys, an officer of the Engineer Corps of the Navy, and a civil engineer who has had practical experience in railroad construction.

This body was authorized and instructed to conduct an examination into the transportation question in the Territory of Alaska; to examine railroad routes from the seaboard to the coal fields and to the interior and navigable waterways; to secure surveys and other information with respect to railroads, including cost of construction and operation; to obtain information in respect to the coal fields and their proximity to railroad routes; and to make report to Congress, together with their conclusions and recommendations in respect to the best and most available routes for railroads in Alaska which will develop the country and the resources thereof for the use of the people of the United States. A public act based upon the Report of the Alaska Railway Commission, approved March 12, 1914, authorizes the President of the United States to locate, construct, and operate railroads in the Territory of Alaska. The cost of the work authorized by this act is not to exceed $35,000,000.

Wagon roads and trails are being constructed by the Board of Road Commissioners for Alaska, which is under the supervision of the Secretary of War. The mileage of road and trail constructed and maintained is as follows: Wagon road, 862; winter sled road, 617; trail, 2,167

Probably the most important road constructed by the Board of Road Commissioners is the one that connects Fairbanks with Valdez on the coast and with Chitina on the Copper River Railroad, and forms the present winter route between Fairbanks and the outside world. On this route throughout the winter months a regular stage company operates a line carrying freight, passengers, and mail. In the early winter and in the spring wheel stages are used, but through most of the winter season horse sleds carry the traffic. As the service is expensive, the freight and passenger rates are high.

The Kuskokwim Valley and the Iditarod section, immediately adjacent thereto, are much more poorly provided with transportation than the Yukon and Tanana Valleys. A winter sled road has been built from the end of the Alaska Northern Railroad at Kern Creek, on Turnagain Arm, up the Susitna Valley, and across the divide into the Iditarod region.

At the present time the interior of Alaska is most conveniently accessible during the three or four summer months, June to September, inclusive. Fairbanks, the center of the Yukon-Tanana Basin, may be reached by two routes. The first involves a 1,000-mile steamer trip, through the inland passage, to Skagway, then 110 miles of rail over the White Pass to White Horse, the head of Yukon navigation. A transfer is here made to a Canadian river steamer which reaches Dawson, 460 miles downstream. From Dawson an American steamer is used to Fairbanks, a further distance of 1,000 miles. At the best this journey consumes two weeks going in, but ordinarily connections cannot be made promptly and more time is required. The outward trip by this route would require much longer. This route is used chiefly for high-class freight and passengers.

Most of the freight, however, for Fairbanks is shipped to St. Michael by ocean vessels. Here it is transshipped to river steamers which are exposed to the open sea before entering the mouth of the river. These steamers carry the freight up the Yukon and Tanana Rivers. The mileage of this route is about 2,700 miles of ocean travel and about 1,100 miles of river travel, and usually occupies about a month. This route is open for a shorter summer season than the other. All rates are high, which is accounted for by the short season, ex-

pensive fuel, and cost of transshipping on both routes. In addition to having to bear the high rates, all goods have their sale price increased by the necessity of financing the nine months' storage.

The valley of the Kuskokwim is not so well served. Small steamers reach Bethel, and a few river steamers distribute freight to river points nearest the camps, whence they are hauled, usually during the winter season.

Telegraph and Cable Lines.—Telegraph and cable lines and a wireless system are constructed and operated by the War Department. The military cable line has its southern terminus at Seattle, Wash., where connection is made with the commercial telegraph companies.

Agriculture. — The economic conditions which prevail in Alaska have prevented speedy settlement of the Territory by farmers. The only markets available are local ones and transportation has so far been too expensive to seek outside or distant markets. Farm labor is scarce and in many places very high. The cost of clearing land of trees and the removal of moss is so great as to seem almost prohibitive.

Education and Reindeer Service.—The schools for the education of natives and the reindeer industry are under the supervision of the Commissioner of Education. In the schools instruction in carpentry, cooking, and sewing is emphasized.

The importation of reindeer from Siberia into Alaska began in 1892 in order to furnish material for food and clothing for the Eskimo in the vicinity of Bering Strait.

There had long been a disagreement with Great Britain over the location of the boundary line between Canada and Alaska, owing to a difference in the interpretation of a treaty made between Russia and Great Britain in 1825, defining this boundary; and on the discovery of gold in Alaska, in 1895-96, this matter reached a serious stage. The main point of difference was whether the boundary line should be thirty marine leagues (mentioned in the Russia-Great Britain treaty of 1825) east from the western boundary of the islands off the Alaska coast, or that distance east of the mainland coast. In 1899 a provisionary boundary was agreed upon, and on Jan. 24, 1903, a treaty was signed between Great Britain and the United States providing for a tribunal of three British and three American commissioners to settle the dispute. The treaty was ratified by the United States Senate on Feb. 11, 1903, and on March 3 ratifications were exchanged between the two governments. The commission sat in London and on Oct. 17, 1903, made a decision mainly in favor of the United States, granting Canada access to the Pacific only near the southern end of the boundary and giving her Wales and Pease islands, in Portland Canal. In June, 1904, a survey of the boundary thus determined was begun by engineers of the United States and Canada.

The general question of the public lands was opened up by President Taft in throwing open to private entry in July, 1911, a tract containing 12,800 acres of land on Controller Bay, near the Bering coal fields. Mr. Taft on July 26, 1911, sent a special message to Congress for the purpose of reassuring the American people that the alleged danger of monopoly was not a real danger (page 7599). In this message (*q. v.*) he set forth at considerable length his reasons for throwing open this tract of land for private entry.

The Sixty-second Congress on Aug. 24, 1912, passed a law creating a territorial government for Alaska and establishing Juneau as the capital. In order to develop the mineral possibilities and prevent a threatened monopoly of the coal fields a railroad commission was appointed to conduct an examination into the transportation question in the Territory of Alaska. Upon the report of this committee was based legislation providing for purchase or construction of railroads and the leasing of the coal lands. The act of March 12, 1914, authorized the President to purchase or construct 1,000 miles of railroad at a cost not to exceed $35,000,000 to connect one or more of the open Pacific harbors on the southern coast of Alaska with the navigable rivers of the interior, and with one or more of the known coal fields. This railroad may be leased or operated by the government, as Congress may see fit. The act of Oct. 22 provided for the lease of coal lands at two cents a ton for the coal mined.

On June 30, 1917, there were 82,151 reindeer in 76 herds.

Prohibition and a general 8-hour working day become effective in 1918.

The total mineral production amounted in value in 1914 to $19,065,666; in 1915, to $32,854,000; in 1916, to $50,900,000.

According to figures of the United States Geological Survey, Alaska produced in 1917 minerals valued at $41,760,000. The copper production was 88,200,000 pounds, valued at $24,000,000, as compared with 119,600,-000 pounds and $29,480,000 in 1916. (1916 was the banner year for mineral production in Alaska, and the 1917 figures surpass the figures for all previous years, except those of 1916.) The value of the gold produced was $15,450,000, as compared with $17,240,-000 in 1916. The silver production was valued at $1,050,000 in 1917; the coal production at $300,000; the lead at $160,000; the tin at $160,000; the antimony at $40,-000; and other minerals at $600,000.

During 33 years of mining, Alaska has produced minerals valued at $391,000,000, of which $293,000,000 represents the value of the gold and $88,200,000, the copper produced.

In 1917, the coal production was 61,000 tons, valued at $300,000.

The following table summarizes by leading articles the shipments of Alaskan products into the United States during the last three fiscal years:

Classes	1916	1915	1914
Copper in ore, matte and regulus	$26,488,000	$ 5,182,000	$ 3,876,000
Canned salmon	18,307,000	17,590,000	13,264,000
Other salmon	550,000	785,000	955,000
Other fish and fish products	773,000	850,000	982,000
Furs and skins, except seal	468,000	564,000	610,000
Seal skins	105,000	115,000	92,000
Animal oils	371,000	298,000	211,000
Antimony	189,000	No data	No data
Tin ore and concentrates	79,000	71,000	73,000
Lead in ore, etc	72,000	No data	No data
Marble and stone	59,000	117,000	127,000
Gypsum	51,000	110,000	101,000
Total domestic merchandise	$48,966,000	$27,039,000	$21,480,000

In the fiscal year ending June 30, 1917, the movement of merchandise between Alaska and the United States equalled $99,-765,908, as compared with the 1916 figures (the previous high ones) of $76,500,000 and the 1915 figures of $48,702,387. The shipments from the United States to Alaska amounted to $38,992,049, and the shipments to the United States amounted to $60,773,-850. The value of total shipments to and from Alaska in 1917 was $121,265,947.

The value of the 231,372,337 pounds of canned salmon shipped in the fiscal year 1917 was $21,195,612. In 1916 there were 100 salmon canneries in operation.

In 1917, the value of the fishery products of Alaska was $42,000,000, as compared with $22,000,000 in 1916. In that year, Alaska shipped to the United States almost 250,000,000 pounds of canned salmon alone. The exports of dried fish in 1917 were 6,500,000 pounds, an increase of 1,000,-000 pounds over 1916; and the exports of fresh fish other than salmon were nearly 12,000,000 pounds, an increase of more than 2,000,000 pounds over the exports of 1916. Altogether, Alaska exported in 1917 more than 286,500,000 pounds of fish food, an increase of more than 25,000,000 pounds above the 1916 figures.

Alaska:

Alaska-Yukon-Pacific Exposition commended, 7052, 7103.

Attempted occupation of portion of, by Great Britain and Canada, 6097.

Attempts of Great Britain and Canada to establish post routes in, 6097.

Boundary line with British possessions—

Commission to determine, recommended, 4141, 4918.

Discussed, 4141, 4917, 4985, 5366, 5400, 5958, 6063, 6370, 6430, 6792, 6826.

Report regarding, referred to, 4985.

Cession of, to United States—

Discussed, 3778, 3886.

Referred to, 3798.

Treaty regarding, referred to, 3719, 3722.

Appropriation for payment under, recommended, 3719, 3778.

Chinamen in, cruel treatment of, 5083.

Coal fields of, 7561, 7564, 7720.

Coast line charts for, 8019.

Collection district established at Sitka, 3865.

Commission government suggested for, 7436, 7535, 7722.

Conditions of, 6725, 6792, 6799, 6918, 6919, 7019.

Controller Bay, opening to settlement of land on, discussed, 7599.

Delegate to Congress from, discussed, 6920, 7019.

Development of, discussed by President—

Roosevelt, 6920.

Taft, 7616.

Wilson, 7912.

Education in, appropriation for, recommended, 4667, 5483, 6453.

Encroachments of Hudsons Bay Company upon trade of, 3898.

Fur Seal Service, supervision of Bureau of Fisheries over, 7230.

Government for—
Act providing for, 4879.
By commission, 7436, 7535, 7722.
Discussed by President Benj. Harrison, 5760.
Municipal governments recommended by President Benj. Harrison, 5483, 5641.
Recommended by President—
Arthur, 4651, 4731, 4771.
Hayes, 4522, 4573.
Taft, 7436, 7535.
Government railroad for, proposed by President—
Roosevelt, 6920, 7019.
Taft, 7535, 7721.
Wilson, 7911, 8101.
Importation of breech-loading rifles and fixed ammunition into, forbidden, 4282.
Instructions regarding, modified, 4711.
Indians of, nature of, discussed, 7020.
Lands in—
Discussed, 6799.
Proclamation modifying order reserving, 612.
Set apart, 5795, 8215.
System of regulations for sale of, 8171.
Legislation recommended for, 3722, 6269, 6400, 6725, 6799, 6919, 7436, 7535, 7722.
Light-house on coast of, point to be selected for, 3902.
Local government for, 7103.
Military arrests in, 4312, 4313, 4314.
Military Department of, 3830, 6269.
Mineral wealth in, discussed, 6063.
Naval radio station in, 8215.
Necessity for development of, 7616.
Needs of people of, 6920, 6941, 7103.
Pictures of, 4769, 7458.
Port of entry in, establishment of, recommended, 5484.
Privileges of hunting, trading, and fishing in, referred to, 3829, 3830.
Property rights of natives, 6920, 6921.
Public lands of. (See Lands of.)
Railroads in. (See Government Railroad for.)
Referred to, 3818, 3829, 6269, 6352, 6453.
Reorganization needed in government of, 7052.
Report of governor of, 4975.
Report of Lieut. Emmons, 6941.
Resources of—
Discussed, 6918.
Must be used, not wasted or monopolized, 7912.
Opened up, 8152.
Roads in, government, 6920.
Seal fisheries within limits of. (See Bering Sea.)

Seal islands in, sale of, recommended, 3990.
Settlement in, importance of, 6793.
Survey of coast of, urged, 8019.
Territorial Government recommended for, 7911.
Townsite in, withdrawal of, 8005.
Transportation problem in, discussed, 7842.
Wealth and needs of, discussed, 6799.

Alaskan Engineering Commission.—The chief task of this body is the construction and supervision of the Government railroad in Alaska. It is under the control of the Department of the Interior.

Alaska Salmon Commission, mentioned, 6860.

Alaska-Yukon-Pacific Exposition. — For the purpose of exploiting the resources and potentialities of the Alaska and Yukon territories and to demonstrate the progress of the western parts of the United States and Canada, as well as to foster the trade of the countries bordering on the Pacific, an international exposition was held at Seattle, Wash., from June 1, to Oct. 15, 1909. Eleven exhibition palaces were built on the Campus of the University of Washington (a tract of 225 acres). The expenses preliminary to opening were $10,-000,000. The funds were raised by appropriations by the federal government, the State of Washington and the City of Seattle.

Alaska-Yukon-Pacific Exposition, object of, 7052, 7103.

Alaskan Railroad Townsite Regulations, amended, 8300.

Albania.—An extensive tract of the western littoral of the Balkan Peninsula, from the southern frontier of Montenegro to the northern frontier of Greece. Within these limits are included an area of close on 22,000 square miles, with a population of three to three and a half million persons. Of this area about 12,000 square miles have been absorbed by Servia, Greece, and Montenegro, leaving the area of the autonomous portion at about 10,000 square miles, with a population of 2,000,000, of whom about 1,200,000 are Albanians and the remainder principally Serbs, Bulgars and Greeks.

History.—Albania was governed by native rulers until the close of the thirteenth century, when the Kingdom of Albania was formed by the Sicilian House of Anjou. This kingdom was perpetually at war with Servia, and for many years with Venice, until the advance of the Mohammedan forces extinguished the independence of the kingdom in the fifteenth and sixteenth centuries. From 1571 to 1913 Albania was under Turkish rule, forming the vilayets of Scutari and Jannina and the western portions of the vilayets of Kossovo and Monastir. The Balkan Wars of 1912-13 were nominally caused by the desire of the Allied States (Bulgaria, Servia, Montenegro and Greece) to free the Albanians from Turkish misrule, and one of the pretexts of the first war was the inability of Turkey to cope with the Albanian risings.

By the Treaty of London (May 30, 1913), the Ambassadors of the assembled Powers agreed upon the principle of an autonomous Albania, and the throne was accepted by Prince William of Wied. Since the date of the treaty the claims of Servia to additional Albanian territory led to desultory fighting between Serbo-Albanian forces, and to a threat of interference on the part of other Powers. Servia finally withdrew from the disputed territory in October, 1913, owing to pressure from Austria-Hungary, but the new country is still a prey to internal dissensions.

On March 10, 1917, announcement was made that Albania had been granted autonomy under an Austrian protectorate. Before that date, it had been overrun by Austrian, Bulgarian, Italian and Greek forces during the European War. On April 20, 1917, the French proclaimed the independence of Albania. Before the Italian retreat in 1917 (see European War), Italy declared the southern portion of Albania autonomous under Italian protection, declaring that Italy would annex only Valona.

Transportation.—Albania is traversed from Scutari (in the north) to Valona (in the southwest) by a railway from Montenegro, and lines from Servia cross the eastern frontier at Pizrend, Dibra, and Struga. The principal ports are Durazzo and Valona.

The capital is Scutari, population 30,000.

Albany Convention.—One of the important predecessors of the Continental Congress and among the first definite steps taken toward national union. Upon a call issued by the Lords of Trade, commissioners from the Colonies of New Hampshire, Massachusetts, Rhode Island, Connecticut, New York, Pennsylvania, and Maryland, met at Albany, N. Y., on June 19, 1754, to arrange a treaty with the Six Nations of Indians. Benjamin Franklin proposed and the convention adopted a plan for colonial union. It provided for a president-general of all the Colonies, with veto power, and a grand council to be composed of from two to seven delegates from each Colony, chosen by assembly for a term of three years each. This grand council was to be authorized to equip forces for the common defense of the Colonies and to levy taxes for their maintenance and have control of all Indian affairs. The plan was rejected by the Crown because it gave too much power to the Colonies.

Albany Regency.—A combination of politicians of the Democratic party. Prominent among these were Martin Van Buren, William L. Marcy, John A. Dix, and Silas Wright. This combination was, it was charged, organized to manage and control that party in New York State from about 1820 to 1855. Their organization was quite thorough and complete, and its success was mainly due to this fact. A majority of those in the combination resided in Albany or operated from that city. The name arose from this circumstance.

Albemarle, The.—A Confederate iron-clad ram built on the Roanoke River, below Weldon, N. C., in 1863. She was destroyed with a torpedo by Lieut. W. B. Cushing on the night of Oct. 27, 1864 (3457). Before her destruction she did much damage to vessels of the United States. In 1867, she was raised, towed to Norfolk, and sold.

Albemarle, The:

Destruction of, 3457.

Referred to, 6306.

Engagement of, with the *Sassacus* referred to, 3411.

Alcohol, Denatured, freedom from tax, 7224.

Alcoholic Content of Liquors, limited, 8415.

Aldrich-Vreeland Currency Law. — A measure passed by Congress May 30, 1908, to render the currency of the United States more elastic by placing it within the power of the national banks to transform all suitable available assets into money in response to any financial emergency. The purpose of the law was to prevent panics, and was the direct result of the financial stringency of 1907. The law provided that the Comptroller of the Currency, who has governmental supervision over the national banks, shall cause to be printed and kept on hand at all times a special issue of currency amounting to 50 per cent. of the combined capital stock of all the national banks. To secure a portion of this emergency bank note issue a bank must be a member of a currency association formed by at least ten banks having a combined capital of not less than $5,000,000. State, county or municipal bonds, commercial paper or other valuable and readily convertible assets may be used as security, provided it first secures the approval of the association and the government. If the securities are acceptable the currency is immediately forwarded to the bank. It was superseded by the Glass-Owen currency law of 1913 (*q. v.*).

Aleutian Islands.—A chain of about 150 islands extending from the western extremity of Alaska near the continent of Asia. The area is about 6,000 square miles. The inhabitants, a half-civilized and declining race, about 2,000 in number, are variously regarded as of Asiatic or American origin. Their trade is chiefly in fish and furs. The islands belong to the United States by reason of the acquisition of Alaska. They were discovered by the Russians about the middle of the eighteenth century.

Alert, The, convention, between Nicaragua and Costa Rica signed on, 6325. (See also Greely, A. W.)

Alexander Archipelago Forest Reserve, proclaimed, 6697.

Alexandria, Va.:

Act incorporating church in, vetoed, 474.

Blockade of port of, removed by proclamation, 3371.

British retreat from, 582.

Property in, destroyed by British forces, 530, 532.

Alexandria County, D. C.:

Court-house in, unsafe and new one recommended, 1621.

Jail erected in, 930.

Retrocession of, to Virginia by proclamation, 2320.

Alfalfa.—A leguminous fodder plant, native to the valleys of Central Asia. It has been cultivated in Europe for more than 2,000 years, and was introduced into Mexico and South America at the time of the Spanish conquest. In 1854 it was brought from Chile to California, whence it spread rapidly over the Pacific and Rocky Mountain states, where it is now more extensively grown than any other forage crop. The word alfalfa is derived from the Arabian and comes to us through the Spanish language. It is interpreted to mean "the best feed." It is also known as lucerne. The plant is an upright branching perennial, one to three feet high, with triple parted leaves and irregular purple flowers, which grow in loose clusters like pea flowers. On loose, permeable soils the roots frequently descend to ten or twelve feet. It grows best on rich, sandy, well-drained loams of a calcareous nature, and does not succeed on damp soil or tenacious clay. Two years are required thoroughly to establish a field, but when once established the plant endures many years. The crop is cut when the plants are coming into bloom, and again from two to six times, according to the length of the season. The ordinary annual yield varies from three to eight tons of dry hay per acre. Green or cured hay is relished by all farm animals, and is used both for fattening and milk production.

Statistics of production gathered by the Census Bureau show that in 1909 there were 4,702,202 acres devoted to alfalfa in the United States, from which 11,849,998 tons of hay was cut and 259,586 bushels of seed gathered.

On Sept. 15, 1916, the average value of alfalfa was $17.59 ton, as compared with $10.25 ton the year previously. The estimated product in 1916 was 23,000,000 short tons. In 1917 more than 6,000,000 acres were devoted to raising alfalfa in the United States.

Algeciras Convention.—At a conference of the Powers at Algeciras, Spain, Jan. 16 to April 7, 1906, France and Spain were commissioned to maintain order on the Moroccan coast. The town lies on the west side of the Bay of Gibraltar, seven miles from Europa Point. The convention was called in response to many complaints by Europeans and Americans that treaty rights were not respected by the Moors, and that life and property of foreigners were unsafe in Morocco. It was participated in by United States, Germany, Austria-Hungary, Belgium, Spain, France, Great Britain, Italy, the Netherlands, Portugal, Russia and Sweden. The treaty was published Jan. 22, 1907. (See Treaties.) Before the end of the year French troops were landed at Ujda and Casablanca. Jan. 11, 1908, the religous authorities of Morocco deposed Abdel Aziz and proclaimed his brother Mulai Hafid Sultan. His embassy to Berlin was refused recognition without consent of the Powers. (See Morocco.)

Algeciras Convention, ratification urged, 7062.

Algeria.—A French possession on the north coast of Africa, about 342,500 miles in area and containing a population of about 5,600,000. This includes the acquisition since 1901 of some 250,000 square miles of territory on the south. The chief native people are Berbers and Arabs. Its capital and principal city is Algiers. It comprises the ancient country of Numidia and a portion of Mauritania. For many centuries it harbored a band of corsairs, who haunted the coasts of the Mediterranean Sea and the Atlantic Ocean as far as the North Sea, preying upon the commerce of all nations which refused to pay them tribute. To pay this tribute was deemed wiser by many European powers than to wage war against them. Following the examples of other nations, the United States signed a treaty in 1795, agreeing to pay the Dey $1,000,000 for the ransom of American captives and promising an annual tribute (see pages 115, 174).

Algeria made war against the United States in 1815. Commodore Decatur, with ten vessels, sailed against the Dey and met with such success that he was enabled to exact indemnity from the Dey himself, and also a treaty renouncing all claim to trib-

ute, presents, or ransoms, and a promise not to reduce prisoners of war to slavery (see page 547). France has since reduced Algeria to the dominion of her Government, organizing it as a colonial possession in 1834, of which it is now the most important. The chief resource of the country is agriculture. Since 1870 there have been a number of extended revolts; and in recent years the country has suffered from serious anti-Jewish agitations. (See also Africa.)

Algeria:

Consuls of United States in, 169, 380, 506.

  Banished, 503.

  Change in pay of, 1318.

  Powers of, should be increased, 238.

  Salary of, should be increased, 238.

  Unjustifiable proceedings toward, by Dey of, 441.

Declaration of war against, recommended, 539.

Hostile attitude of toward United States, 42, 539, 560.

Imprisonment of American citizens in, 80, 90, 115, 140, 169, 192, 197, 199, 539.

Referred to, 144, 145, 202.

Treaty of peace with, 554, 679.

Treaty with, transmitted and discussed, 115, 174, 178, 184, 197, 554, 679.

  Annulled by Algeria, with alternative of war or renewal of former treaty, 560.

Tribute to be paid by United States to, 115, 174.

  Payment of, 325.

Vessels sold to, 237.

War with United States. (See Algerine War.)

Algerine War.—The countries on the Mediterranean coast of Africa, from Egypt to the Atlantic, namely, Morocco, Algeria, Tunis and Tripoli (which are known collectively as the Barbary Powers) had been in the habit of preying on the commerce of nations that refused to pay a tribute to them. Shortly after the Revolution the operations of these pirates were directed against our commerce, to protect which treaties purchasing immunity by the payment of yearly tribute were negotiated with the Barbary States—in 1786-1787 with Morocco, in 1795 with Algiers, in 1796 with Tripoli, and in 1799 with Tunis. In 1812 Algiers declared war against the United States. As soon as the war then commencing against England had been brought to an end, our government turned its attention to Algiers. The Algerian war was short and decisive. In the spring of 1815 Commodore Decatur was sent with nine or ten vessels to chastise the pirates. In June he captured the largest of their frigates, and soon after took another vessel. He then dictated a treaty to the Dey of Algiers, which was signed June 30, 1815, relinquishing all claims to tribute in the future.

Algerine War (see also Algeria):

Declaration of war by Congress recommended, 539.

Dey of Algiers begins war against United States, 428.

Information of amicable settlement, 428.

Termination of, 547.

Threatened by Algiers, 560.

Treaty of peace concluded, 554, 679.

Alien and Sedition Laws.—Two important acts of Congress passed by the Federalists in 1798. Their importance consists not so much in their essential character and the fact that they largely caused the downfall of the Federalist party as in their position in American history as a landmark beyond which it is unsafe for the law-making power to go. During the French Revolution American feeling was high and bitter. Many public speakers and writers openly advocated intervention by the United States in favor of the one side or the other, denounced the neutral attitude of the Government as cowardly and ungrateful, and heaped invectives upon the Administration. The fact that many of the newspapers in which the Government was so bitterly assailed were in the hands of foreigners, had much to do with the passage of the alien act. This law authorized the President to order out of this country all such aliens as he might judge to be dangerous to the peace and safety of the United States or engaged in plotting against them. The sedition act provided heavy fines and imprisonment for any person who should conspire to oppose the United States Government or laws, or who should print or publish any false, scandalous or malicious writings against the Government, Congress, or the President .intended to bring disrepute or hatred upon them or to stir up sedition. These laws were regarded by the Republican party of that day as unconstitutional and were denounced by the Kentucky and Virginia resolutions as subversive of the liberty of speech and the press. They expired in 1800 and 1801 respectively. (See also Kentucky and Virginia Resolutions.)

Alien Contract Law, amendment of, recommended, 6348, 6455.

Alien Enemies.—Under section 4067 of the Revised Statutes of the United States, an enemy alien is defined as follows: Any native, citizen, denizen, or subject of a hostile government being a male of the age of fourteen years and upwards and not actually naturalized in the United States.

Amplifications of the definition are as follows:

(a) Children of naturalized enemies, even though born in the enemy country, are not enemy aliens providing naturalization of their parents is completed before the children have reached maturity. Otherwise, such children are enemy aliens until they are naturalized themselves.

(b) Children born in the United States of enemy aliens residing in the United States are not alien enemies unless after maturity they become naturalized in the enemy country.

(c) Naturalization of enemy aliens cannot be completed during the period of war with the enemy country.

(d) Children born in an enemy country of American citizens temporarily residing in that enemy country are not alien enemies. However, if the residence of the parents in the enemy country is permanent, the children are alien enemies unless they have established by suitable action citizenship in the United States.

(e) A native, citizen, denizen or subject of an enemy country remains an alien enemy even though he has taken out his first naturalization papers or has been naturalized in a country other than the United States.

Various regulations for and discussion of enemy aliens by the Presidents are noted below.

During the first year of the war between the United States and the Central Powers, 2,040 alien enemies and war prisoners were confined in war prison barracks at Fort McPherson, Ga., Fort Oglethorpe, Ga., Fort Douglas, Utah.

During the struggle of the United States with the Central Powers, Attorney-General Gregory estimated the number of unnaturalized male alien enemies upward of 14 years of age as follows : Germans, 450,000; Austrians, 600,000; Hungarians, 400,000. Estimating 3 to a family, there were accordingly more than 4,000,000 persons in the United States during the war who were either male unnaturalized alien enemies or members of the families of such.

By act of Congress approved April 16, 1918, the term "alien enemies" was made to include women as well as men.

In February, 1918, all male alien enemies were required to register with the government and in June of the same year, female alien enemies.

Alien Enemies. (See Aliens in United States.)

Alien Laborers discussed, 6065.

Alien Land Law of California, 7873.

Changes in wording of, to avoid offense, 7876.

Protest against, 7875.

Alien Land Laws, Federal and State, discussed by Governor Johnson of California, 7874.

Alien Property Custodian.—The Powers of the Alien Property Custodian during the war of the United States against the Central Powers are set forth in the executive orders of President Wilson under date of Oct. 12 and 29, 1917 (see pages 8372 and 8380). The word "enemy' for the purposes of the work of the Alien Property Custodian covers all persons within the military or naval lines of the Central Powers, and all persons residing outside the United States transacting business with any one within such military or naval lines. A German citizen in the United States (unless interested) is not an enemy under the Trading-with-the-Enemy Act, whereas an American citizen in Germany may be so considered.

All who hold enemy property or any interest therein, by knowledge or by suspicion, must report on the same through blanks furnished by the Alien Property Custodian, under penalty of not more than ten years' imprisonment or a fine of $10,000 or both.

The purpose of the work of the Alien Property Custodian is to make available for war financing any funds in the United States belonging to enemies, to prevent such funds being used so as to give aid and comfort to the enemy, and to safeguard property of enemies for such disposition after the war as Congress might make.

For all property which comes into his hands, the Custodian acts as a common law trustee, depositing all money with the Treasurer of the United States, to be invested in United States bonds or certificates of indebtedness. In the discretion of the Custodian, enemy property may be used or supervised, without confiscation. In certain cases licenses are issued to permit the property of enemies to be carried on, especially to enemy insurance companies.

On May 1, 1918, the Alien Property Custodian's trust accounts comprised $282,-067,927, of which $115,824,409 represented stocks; $46,016,434, bonds; $51,325,434, accounts receivable; $27,965,975, cash; $6,-522,279, mortgages; $4,267,618, notes receivable; $4,503,142, real estate; and $25,-612,633, miscellaneous.

Alien Property Custodian:

Administration of certain portions of Trading with the Enemy Act vested in, 8462.

Office of, created and explained, 8372, 8380.

Sales to be conducted by, rules for, 8479.

Aliens. (See Naturalization.)

Aliens in United States (see also Naturalized Citizens):

Abduction of foreigners claiming protection of United States should be made a crime, 2550.

Allegiance of, to Government discussed and orders regarding, 3318.

Appointment of, under Civil Service, when no citizens are available, 8175.

Claims of, court to try, recommended, 4191, 4243, 4297, 4360.

Enemy—

Directions for, during European War, 8243, 8407.

Germans and Austro-Hungarians included in term under Trading with the Enemy Act, 8445.

Legislation regarding, further, needed, 8404.

Listing of, for International Red Cross, 8243.

Registration of, 8394.

Regulations for conduct of, 8243, 8392.

Women included in, 8491.

Intrigues of, denounced, 8154.

Jurisdiction over, should belong only to Federal government, 7373, 7504.

Liability of, to perform military duty—

Discussed, 3381.

Proclaimed, 3369.

Loyalty and disloyalty of, discussed, 8066, 8080, 8086, 8114, 8154.

Number of, employed in Executive Departments, report on, transmitted, 6102.

Offenses against treaty rights of, should be cognizable in Federal courts, 5618.

Property of, to be taken over during war, 8372, 8380.

Rights of under treaties, enforcement of, 7055.

Allatoona (Ga.), Battle of.—In the hope of drawing Gen. Sherman's army out of Georgia, the Confederates, 36,000 strong,

under Gen. Hood, threatened his railroad communications with Nashville. Oct. 5, 1864, a division of Hood's infantry appeared before Allatoona Pass, where were stored about 1,500,000 rations. The post was held by Col. Tourtelotte, who was re-enforced by Gen. Corse, thus increasing the Union force to 1,944 men. The attack was made on the 6th. The conflict lasted from 8:30 A. M. until night, when the Confederates withdrew, leaving 231 dead and 411 prisoners. Corse lost 707 men and was himself wounded. Hood crossed the Coosa Oct. 10, and Sherman's army followed him to Gaylesville by way of Rome, and then returned to Atlanta.

Allegiance.—According to Blackstone, allegiance signifies "the tie which binds the subject to the sovereign in return for that protection which the sovereign affords the subject." Natural or implied allegiance is that obligation which one owes to the nation of which he is a natural-born citizen or subject so long as he remains such, and it does not arise from any express promise. Express allegiance is that obligation which arises from an expressed oath or promise. Local allegiance is that obedience and temporary aid due by an alien to the State or community in which he resides. Local allegiance is temporary and expires with residence.

Allegiance, American, meaning of, 7952, 8066, 8087.

Allegiance, Oath of, army officers directed to subscribe anew, 3219.

Allentown, Pa., act for erection of public building at, vetoed, 5243.

Allianca, The, firing upon, by Spanish vessel disavowed by Spain, discussed, 6068.

Allies. (See Entente Allies and European War.)

Alsace-Lorraine.—The two French provinces which Germany annexed in 1870 as part of the indemnity from the Franco-Prussian war. The use of the French language was officially forbidden, German colonists were imported by the thousands, and other methods were used to make the land forget its French associations. Alsace and Lorraine are on the French side of the Rhine, and Germany utilized within them two of her strongest fortresses, Metz and Strassburg. The French people, however, kept the memory of their lost provinces ever fresh in their minds, and much of their determination in the later war with Germany arose from their resolve to re-gain their lost land. Proposals for the disposition of Alsace and Lorraine played an important part in all the discussions of peace terms. Alsace and Lorraine were made independent members of the German Empire, and were known as the Reichsland. (See Germany.)

The area of Alsace-Lorraine is 5,607 square miles. In 1871 the population was 1,549,738; in 1910, it was 1,828,522. According to the German figures, of the latter number, 1,624,260 were German-speaking and 204,262 were French-speaking. More than 75% of the inhabitants are Roman Catholics.

Alsace-Lorraine is administered by a governor appointed by and responsible to the Emperor, the legislative power being in the hands of the Emperor and a parliament of two chambers, of which only the lower is elected by the people.

Alsace-Lorraine, wrong of, must be righted, 8424.

Alsop Case.—The Alsop case, which was settled by King George V of England, as arbitrator, was a dispute with the Republic of Chile of forty years' standing. It grew out of a debt incurred by a Brazilian to the firm of Alsop & Co., of Valparaiso, a chartered Chilean concern with American members. In settlement of the debt the Brazilian made over to the Chilean firm certain claims from Bolivia lying in territory which was afterward, as a result of the war of 1879, ceded to Chile. In 1909 Secretary Knox demanded the reference of the claim to The Hague, but Chile objected to this unless her government was allowed to use the argument that Alsop & Co. had been expressly excluded from the rights of American nationals by the Chilean-American Claims Tribunal in 1900, the American Government having insisted on this exclusion. Then Secretary Knox issued an ultimatum demanding reference of the case to The Hague or payment of a million dollars to the United States. Finally an alternative was offered of reference of the claim to King Edward as arbitrator, and Chile was induced to accept this, Dec. 1, 1909. King Edward died, and his son and successor on July 10, 1910, rendered his award in the Alsop claim. It assigned £187,000 to the Alsop firm in full settlement, and Chile paid this amount through the United States Government Nov. 18, 1910. The original amount of the claim was £600,000 with interest. The award was received with satisfaction in the United States.

Alta Vela Island (Santo Domingo), claim of citizens of United States to guano on, 3827.

Amazon River. (See also Brazil. *Physical Features.*)

Explorations of, by officers of Navy, 2712, 2724, 2762, 4449.

Appropriation for, recommended, 4201.

Free navigation of, desired, 2744.

Attempts to secure, unsuccessful, 2813.

Opened to commerce, 3776.

Ambassador.—This term was long erroneously used in reference to our envoys to foreign countries. The United States did not appoint diplomatic representatives of higher rank than envoy or minister until the year 1893, when by act of March 3 of that year the higher grade was established. Thomas F. Bayard was raised to the rank of ambassador to Great Britain, being the first to hold that rank. Ambassadors are now duly accredited to Argentina, Great Britain, France, Italy, Germany, Russia, Mexico, Japan, Turkey, Brazil, and Austria-Hungary (5874, 6335) and receive salaries of $17,500 per annum. In ancient times ambassadors were appointed on special occasions. Mediæval republics, like Venice, both received and sent ambassadors.

Ambassadors extraordinary and plenipotentiary of foreign countries to the United States in 1918 were as follows:

Argentina................Romulo S. Naon
Austria-Hungary.............
Brazil...............Dominicio da Gama
Chile.............Don Santiago Aldunate
France................Jean J. Jusserand
Germany..................

Great Britain....Sir Rufus Isaacs, Earl Reading
Italy...........Count V. Macchi di Celieri
Japan....................Viscount Ishii
Mexico...............I. Ignacio Bonillas
Russia...............Boris Bakhmeteff
Spain..........Don Juan R. y. Gayangos
Turkey....................

Envoys extraordinary and ministers plenipotentiary in the same year were as follows:

Belgium......E. de Cartier de Marchienne
Bolivia..........Don Ignacio Calderon
Bulgaria............Stephen Panaretoff
China.........V. K. Wellington Koo
Colombia................Carlos A. Urueta
Costa Rica........Don Manuel C. Quesada
Cuba............Carlos M. de Cespedes
Denmark................Constantin Brun
Dominican Republic.........Louis Galvan
Ecuador.........Don Raphael H. Eliziade
Greece................Georges Roussos
Guatemala.........Don Joaquin Mendez
Hayti................Solon Menoz
Honduras............Alberto Membreno
Netherlands...............August Phillips
Nicaragua....................
Norway..................H. H. Bryn
Panama..........Don Belisario Porras
Paraguay..............Hector Velasquez
Persia................Mehdi Khan
Peru....................
Portugal.............Viscount de Alte
Salvador............Don Rafael Zaldivar
Servia...........Lioubomir Michailovitch
Siam................Phya P. Karavongse
Sweden............W. A. F. Ekengren
Switzerland................Hanz Sulzer
Uruguay............Carlos M. de Pena
Venezuela.........Don Santos A. Dominici

Ambassadors (see also Ministers):

Elevation of missions of—

Great Britain, France, Italy, and Germany to grade of, and like action of United States, 5874.

Russia to grade of, and like action of United States, 6335.

Official residences for, recommended, 6072, 6155.

Amelia Island.—A small island off the northeast coast of Florida, between the St. Mary's and Nassau rivers. During Spain's nominal occupation of Florida it became the rendezvous of pirates, smugglers, fugitive slaves and other outlaws. These not only preyed upon the commerce of friendly nations, but extended their operations inland, robbing and murdering American settlers in Georgia and Florida. General Matthews with a small force, in March, 1812, took possession of the country under a misinterpretation of his orders to protect American property in East Florida, and President Monroe promptly disavowed the act as unfriendly to Spain, with which country negotiations were at the time under way for cession. It was later occupied by a band of adventurers organized by General McGregor in Philadelphia. These set up an independent government and claimed recognition by the United States and other powers. They entered upon a career of privateering and smuggling, and were finally suppressed by the United States forces. The island came into possession of the United States with the cession of Florida. The island and its inhabitants were a source of serious annoyance to Monroe, and formed the subject of several communications to Congress.

Amelia Island.—A coast island, N. E. of Florida, between St. Mary's and Nassau rivers.

Colonial governments not responsible for unlawful conduct of persons in, 601.

Governor Mitchell ordered to restore, to the Spanish, 493.

Possession of—

Inquired into, 620.

Taken by Gen. Matthews, 492.

Unlawful expeditions to, discussed, 582, 590, 592, 601, 609, 620.

Amendments.—One of the chief defects of the original Articles of Confederation was that they could only be amended by the unanimous consent of the thirteen States. Three needful changes having failed of ratification, a convention was called in 1787 to consider amendments. The result of the deliberations of this convention is the present Constitution, which provides for amendments in the following words: "The Congress, whenever two-thirds of both Houses shall deem it necessary, shall propose amendments to this Constitution, or, on the application of the legislatures of two-thirds of the several States, shall call a convention for proposing amendments, which in either case shall be valid, to all intents and purposes, as part of this Constitution when ratified by the legislatures of three-fourths of the several States or by conventions in three-fourths thereof, as the one or the other mode of ratification may be proposed by the Congress; provided," etc. (Art. V. 25.)

Many amendments to the Constitution have been proposed, but only seventeen have been ratified. They relate to (1) freedom of speech, the press, and religion; (2) right to establish State militia; (3) quartering of troops in private houses; (4) security against unreasonable search and seizure; (5) capital crime; (6) criminal prosecutions; (7) trial by jury under common law; (8) forbidding excessive bail or fines and cruel and unusual punishment; (9) relation of constitutional to natural rights; (10) powers reserved to the States; (11) suits of non-residents against States in Federal courts; (12) election of President and Vice-President; (13) slavery; (14 and 15) abridgment of the franchise, etc., by States; (16) taxes on incomes; (17) election of senator by direct vote.

The first ten of these amendments were submitted to the several State legislatures by a resolution of Congress which passed on Sept. 25, 1789, at the first session of the First Congress, and were ratified by a sufficient number of States on or before Dec. 15, 1791. The eleventh amendment was declared adopted Jan. 8, 1798; the twelfth Sept. 25, 1804; the thirteenth Dec. 18, 1865; the fourteenth July 28, 1868; the fifteenth March 30, 1870; the sixteenth, Feb. 25, 1913; the seventeenth, May 31, 1913.

The sixteenth amendment is as follows:

The Congress shall have power to lay and collect taxes on incomes, from whatever source derived, without apportionment among the several States, and without regard to any census or enumeration.

The seventeenth amendment is as follows:

1. The Senate of the United States shall be composed of two Senators from each State, elected by the people thereof, for six years; and each Senator shall have one vote. The electors in each State shall have the qualifications requisite for electors of the most numerous branch of the State Legislatures.

2. When vacancies happen in the representation of any State in the Senate, the executive authority of such State shall issue writs of election to fill such vacancies: Provided, That the Legislature of any State may empower the executive thereof to make temporary appointment until the people fill the vacancies by election as the Legislature may direct.

3. This amendment shall not be so construed as to effect the election or term of any Senator chosen before it becomes valid as part of the Constitution.

Amendment, Constitutional:

Proposed by Johnson, 3840, 3889.

By Taft, 7390, 7391.

America.—The entire Western Continent or grand division of the world, including North, Central, and South America and the adjacent islands. It was named in honor of Amerigo Vespucci, an early explorer, whose accounts of the country received wide publicity. It was visited by Norse navigators as early as about 1000 A. D., and there are myths of Chinese and Irish discoveries, but it was not until after its discovery by Columbus in 1492 that it became generally known to Europeans. In a treatise on the new country published in 1507, called Cosmographiæ Introductio, by Waldseemüller, a teacher of geography in the college of St. Die in the Vosges, the name of American was proposed. (See North America and South America.)

America, Four Hundredth Anniversary of Discovery of:

Celebration of. (See Madrid, Spain; World's Columbian Exposition.)

Observance of, enjoined by proclamation, 5724.

American Committee on War Finance. (See Peace Societies.)

American Continentals.—Uniformed patriotic corps composed of descendants of officers and soldiers of the War of the Revolution. The staff headquarters and offices of the Adjutant are Drexel Building, Wall and Broad Streets, New York.

American Cross of Honor.—This life-saving order was organized A. D. 1898, and is composed of persons upon whom the United States Government has conferred the life-saving medal of honor. May 1, 1906, Congress incorporated the order, and the following officers were elected: Thomas H. Herndon, President; John J. Delaney, Vice-President; Harry A. George, Secretary, and Richard Stockton, Treasurer. All persons who have received the life-saving medal of honor under any act of Congress are eligible to membership in the order. No membership fees or annual dues are collected from any member of this order, only voluntary contributions being received to assist in paying the current expenses.

The cross of the order will be conferred annually upon the person who has rendered the most heroic service in saving life and who, also, has received the medal of honor of the United States Government.

American Federation of Labor. (See Trade Unions.)

American Flag Association.—Organized Feb. 17, 1898, its motto being, "One Flag, One Country, God over all." Its object is to secure National and State legislation for the protection of the flag from degrading and desecrating uses, and to secure a general observance of June 14 as "Flag

Day," because on that day in 1777 Congress adopted the United States flag. The Association is composed of individual members and also the members of the Flag Committees of patriotic societies for the purpose of fostering public sentiment in favor of honoring the flag of our country and preserving it from desecration.

American Legion. — An organization formed in 1915 to enroll the names of citizens of the United States qualified either by previous military or technical experience who express their willingness to respond in case the government should at any time need their services. The membership consists of men of experience in the army, navy or marine corps or in the National Guard or naval militia of any state; men especially trained in any of the numerous vocations drawn upon to meet the conditions of modern warfare, such as aviation, navigation, operation of motor cars or cycles, and trades in which technical and skilled manual labor is employed; also those trained in surgery, medicine and nursing. The form of application carries about seventy such vocations. The dues are 25 cents per year, and members are entitled to wear a button consisting of a blue star in a white field surrounded by a red circle.

American Merchant Marine, need for, 7674.

American National Red Cross. (See Red Cross, American National.)

American Party.—From the beginning of the government, movements against aliens have been common. In New York City, a center of foreign population, this subject had, from time to time, been agitated, and after a period of success in 1844, it had again sunk out of view. About 1852, when the Whig Party was breaking asunder, a secret, oath-bound organization, said to have been called "The Sons of '76," or "The Order of the Star-Spangled Banner," was formed. Those of its members that had not been admitted to the higher degrees were kept in ignorance of the aims and name of the organization, and their constant answer of "I don't know" to questions regarding the society gave them the title of "Know-Nothings." All meetings of the party were secret. It carefully avoided the subject of slavery, and attempted to draw the voters that were tired of agitation on that subject by confining itself to vigorous opposition to Catholics and aliens. Its principle was "Americans must rule America."

The first national convention of the party met in February, 1856. It favored more stringent naturalization laws; opposed foreign immigration suffrage and office-holding by foreign-born citizens; opposed the withdrawal of the Bible from the public schools. Millard Fillmore, of New York, was nominated for President and Andrew Jackson Donelson for Vice-President. These nominations were endorsed by a Whig convention in September. Fillmore carried but one state, Maryland, while his total popular vote was about 850,000.

In 1860 Presidential candidates were again nominated, but under another name. (*See Constitutional Union Party.*) After Fillmore's defeat, the party in 1857 carried the State elections in Rhode Island and Maryland, and in 1859 it was still represented by a few members in Congress. (*See Anti-Masonic Party.*)

The second party of this name was founded on opposition to secret societies, unlike the first, which had itself been such a society. The name was adopted by the members of the National Christian Association when that body began in politics. Its platform demanded prohibition of the sale of liquor, recognition of the Sabbath, the withdrawal of the charters of secret societies and legislative prohibition of their oaths, arbitration of international disputes, the introduction of the Bible into schools, the restriction of land monopolies, resumption of specie payments, justice to the Indians and a direct popular vote for President and Vice-President. James B. Walker, of Illinois, was nominated for President and D. Kirkpatrick for Vice-President. In 1880 nominations were again made; in 1884 the nominee, S. C. Pomeroy, withdrew in favor of St. John, the Prohibition candidate, on his assurance that he "stood on every plank of the American platform."

A third American party was organized by a convention held in Philadelphia, Sept. 16-17, 1887. Its platform declares the "present system of immigration and naturalization of foreigners detrimental to the welfare of the United States; demands amendment of the naturalization laws so as to make fourteen years' residence a prerequisite to citizenship; excludes from citizenship all anarchists, socialists, and other dangerous characters; condemns alien proprietorship in land; grants of land to corporations; reasserts American principles of absolute freedom of religious worship and belief and the permanent separation of Church and State and declares in favor of the enforcement of the Monroe Doctrine.

American Patriotism, Chair of. (See Chair of American Patriotism.)

American Peace Society.—National Headquarters, Colorado Building, Washington, D. C. Organized in New York City, May 8, 1828, and formed by the merging of many State and local societies, the oldest of which, the New York, dated back to 1815. Located in Boston from 1837 to 1911. Moved headquarters to Washington, D. C., May 1, 1911. (See Peace Societies.)

American Protective Association.—While disclaiming to be a political party, this association, popularly known as the A. P. A., has influenced results in many localities. Its principles, as set forth in a platform adopted at Des Moines, Iowa, in 1894, are (1) protection of our nonsectarian free public-school system; (2) no public funds or property to be used for sectarian purposes; (3) preserving and maintaining the Constitution and Government of the United States; (4) restriction of immigration, and (5) extension of time required for naturalization. The association was organized in 1887, and soon had well-attended councils in nearly every State of the Union.

American Republics, Bureau of the International Union of. (See also Pan-American Union, International American Conference.)

American Republics, Bureau of:
Buildings of, 6824.
Bulletins of, transmitted, 5678, 5785.
Discussed, 6338, 6349, 6381, 6436.
Report of, transmitted, 5647, 5769, 5907, 6001, 6099, 6183, 6349.
Collection by governments of debts due their citizens, from other countries, by force of arms, referred to The Hague Tribunal by, 7061.

Conference at Rio Janeiro, visited by Secretary of State Root, 7058.

American Rights Committee. (See Preparedness Societies.)

American Seamen. (See Seamen, American.)

American Society of Mechanical Engineers, memorial of, relating to Ericsson transmitted, 5565.

American System.—In his annual message, December, 1848, President Polk discussed what its authors and advocates called the "American system" (2504). He insisted that this so-called system was founded on a departure from the earliest policy of the Government; that it depended on an enlargement of the powers of the Federal Government by construction and was not warranted by a just interpretation of the Constitution. One branch of the new system, it was claimed, was the establishment of a large national bank. The next branch was a high protective tariff, levied not to raise the revenue needed, but for protection merely; the next was a comprehensive scheme of internal improvements, and finally a plan for the distribution of the proceeds of the sales of the public lands among the States. But the term "American system," as most generally understood, is used to denote the policy of protection to home industries by means of high duties on imports. The term was probably first used by Henry Clay in the debates which preceded the enactment of the tariff law of 1824, when he called his plan of protective duties and internal improvements the "American system."

American Union Against Militarism. (See Peace Societies.)

American Wood Preserving Co., purchase of machinery from, referred to, 4676.

Americanism, President Roosevelt defines, 6915.

Americans in Europe:
Board of relief established for, 7962.
Relief, protection and transportation home of, 7961.

Amistad Case.—The case of the United States against the Spanish vessel, *Amistad.* A cargo of kidnapped Africans who had been landed near Havana, Cuba, by a Portuguese slaver, was shortly afterwards placed aboard the Spanish vessel *Amistad* for shipment to Puerto Principe. On the voyage the negroes took possession of the vessel and ordered the crew to return to Africa; but the sailors brought her into American waters, where, off the coast of Long Island, she was captured by a United States war vessel and carried into New London, Conn., Aug. 29, 1839. On a libel for salvage the Supreme Court of the United States held on appeal that the negroes, having been kidnapped from a foreign country, were free men, and not bound by treaties with Spain.

Amistad, The:
Appropriations for claimants in case of, recommended, 2401, 2742, 2977, 3042, 3092.
Claims arising out of, 2634, 2720.
Negroes taken on board, referred to, 1856.
Reference to, 2128, 3172.
Release of, demanded by Spanish minister, 1805.

Amity.—From the literal meaning, "friendship," the word is employed in international relations to indicate friendly understanding and co-operation; applied especially in connection with treaties, as a treaty of amity, or a treaty of amity and commerce.

Ammunition. (See Arms and Ammunition.)

Amnesty.—An act of pardon for political offenses. The effect of it is that the crimes and offenses against the State specified in the act are so obliterated that they can never again be charged against the guilty parties. When amnesty is proclaimed without restriction as to persons or localities it is called absolute. Numerous instances of qualified amnesty are found in ancient and modern history. When Thrasybulus overthrew the oligarchy at Athens he proclaimed an amnesty, excepting thirty tyrants and a few of their followers. President Lincoln's first amnesty proclamation excepted all officers or agents of the Confederate government, all army officers above the rank of colonel, all naval officers above the rank of lieutenant, all persons who left the service of the United States to participate in the insurrection, and all those who had resigned from the military or naval service and afterwards participated in rebellion; also all those who had treated colored persons or those in charge of them otherwise than as prisoners of war (3414). Dec. 25, 1868, President Johnson proclaimed absolute amnesty (3906).

Amnesty (see also Pardons):
Proclamation of President Lincoln, 3414.
Discussed, 3390, 3455.
Persons entitled to benefits of, defined, 3419.
Referred to, 3508.
Proclamation of President Roosevelt, 6718.
Proclamations of President Johnson, 3508, 3745, 3853, 3906.
Authority for, discussed, 3895.
Circular regarding, 3539.
Persons worth more than $20,000 to whom special pardons issued, referred to, 3583.
Referred to, 3659, 3669, 3722, 3779.
Recommendations of President Grant regarding, 4107, 4209.

Amphion, H. R. M. S., protects American interests, 6809.

Amphitrite, The, mentioned, 6318.

Amsterdam, Netherlands:
Accounts of bankers of United States in, rendered, 113.
Loan contracted with, 120.

Anarchy, legislation for suppressing, recommended, 6643, 6644.

Anatolia College (Marsovan, Turkey), partial destruction of by mob, and indemnity paid for, discussed, 5872.

Ancona, note on sinking of, 8117.

Andorra.—A neutral, autonomous and semi-independent state on the frontier of France and Spain in the Eastern Pyrenees. Area 175 English square miles. Population 6,000.

Government and People.—The State is divided into the six communes or parishes of Andorra Vicilla, Canillo, Encamp, Massana, Orvino and San Julian de Loria, which are sub-divided into fifty-two *pueblos;* and is under the joint suzerainty of France and the Spanish Bishop of Urgel. The Andorrans are all Roman Catholics. The people are virile and independent, engaged mainly in pastoral pursuits and agriculture. France has agreed to extend a branch line of railway (from Toulouse to Ax), from Ax southwards to Andorra Vicilla, and Spain to continue the Barcelona-Ripoll line to Andorra Vicilla, which would thus become a station on a Toulouse-Barcelona line across the Pyrenees. The central government is administered by a General Council of twenty-four members (four from each commune), the executive power residing in the Syndic and Vice-Syndic of the Council. The French Republic (through the *préfet* of the Eastern Pyrenees) and the Bishop of Urgel receive a tribute of 960 fr. and 460 fr. respectively. Every alternate year two delegates visit the *préfet* of the Eastern Pyrenees to pay the tribute and renew the bond of fidelity. The capital is Andorro Vicilla, population 600.

Anglo-American.—An American of English birth or descent. Loosely, any such person who maintains a divided allegiance between England and the United States, with preference for the former.

Animal Industry, Bureau of.—This bureau of the Department of Agriculture (q. v.) makes a study of diseases of animals, including chemical, bacteriological, and zoological investigations. Its activities include dairying and animal breeding and feeding.

The administrative work of the bureau consists of the inspection of import and export animals and of vessels for their transportation; supervision of the interstate movements of cattle and inspection of live stock and their products after slaughter for food consumption; eradication of animal diseases; supervision of serums for use with animals; and management of experimental farms at Beltsville and Bethesda, Md.

Fighting diseases among domestic animals is the important task of this bureau, and some idea of the magnitude of the work may be gained from the statement conservatively made by the officials, estimated on the basis of data for thirty years, that the annual direct losses from animal diseases are approximately $212,000,000. Some of the most virulent diseases are hog cholera, Texas fever and cattle ticks, tuberculosis, contagious abortion, blackleg, anthrax, foot and mouth disease, glanders, scabies of sheep and cattle, parasites, and poultry diseases. The efforts of the bureau have materially lessened all of these.

Inspection of meats by the agents of the Bureau of Animal Industry in one recent year covered a total of 896 establishments, situated in 247 cities and towns in the United States. The number of animals inspected at the time of slaughter was approximately 58,000,000, divided as follows: Cattle, 6,964,000; calves, 1,735,000; goats, 165,000; sheep, 12,900,000; swine, 36,247,-000. The carcasses condemned on this inspection and destroyed to prevent their use for human food numbered 290,600.

This bureau co-operates with the state colleges in the formation of boys' pig clubs, and under its patronage these clubs now exist in thirteen states and have a membership of about 10,000. The dairy division of the bureau has for its object the improvement of dairy herds. In this connection co-operative bull associations are formed, and farmers are assisted in the organization of co-operative creameries and furnished advice regarding buildings, equipment, operation and management. When a sufficient number of patrons is reported, with enough cows to make the establishment of a creamery practicable, the department furnishes blue-print plans for a building and machinery with estimates of cost. Practical assistance is given also in creamery management.

Animal Industry, Bureau of:

Appropriation for, 5887, 5979.

Inspector and assistant inspector in, recommendation that diplomas and examinations be required of applicants for, 5887.

Report of, 6734, 6857.

(See also Agriculture, Department of.)

Animals and Animal Products. (See also Agricultural Products.)

Commission appointed to report on unhealthfulness of, discussed and recommendations regarding, 4793.

Contagious diseases among animals discussed, 4578, 4580, 4771, 5112, 5383, 5764, 5887.

Exportation of, discussed, 4578, 5554, 5763, 5887, 5978.

Importation of, into United States—

Discussed, 5887.

Laws prohibiting, in certain cases recommended, 5197.

Proclamation removing prohibition on, 6025.

Preserves for native animals, recommended, 6911.

Restrictions upon importation of, into foreign countries—

Austria, 4916.

Belgium, 5956, 6325.

France, 4693, 4758, 4789, 4916, 5194, 5545.

Germany, 4758, 4789, 4916, 5957, 6061, 6330.

Great Britain, 4519, 5764, 6178.

Correspondence regarding, referred to, 4979.

Decrees of—

France regarding, 5517.

Germany, France, Belgium, and Denmark regarding, 6100.

Discussed, 4947, 5554, 5641.

Removed, 5616, 5641, 5763.

Annals of Congress.—A record of the debates and proceedings of Congress from the commencement of the First Congress, March 4, 1789, to the close of the first session of the Eighteenth Congress, May 27, 1824. The Annals also contain many valuable State papers, public documents, laws, and much correspondence. (See Congressional Globe; Congressional Record; Register of Debates.)

Annapolis, Md.:

Act for erection of public building at, reasons for applying pocket veto to, 5071.

Naval Academy at. (See Naval Academy.)

Annexation.—After the adoption of the Federal Constitution the individual states ceded to the United States all territory west of the lines they established as their western boundaries. In the original charters this territory extended nominally to the Pacific Ocean, but really only to the Mississippi River, for Louisiana and Florida were Spanish possessions. In 1800 Louisiana was retroceded by Spain to France, and was acquired by the United States from the latter April 30, 1803, by payment of $15,000,000. The territory embraced all of the present State of Louisiana lying west of the Mississippi River, together with New Orleans and the adjacent district east; Arkansas, Missouri, Iowa, a portion of Idaho and Minnesota, all of the Dakotas, most of Kansas, all of Nebraska and Indian Territory, part of Colorado, most of Wyoming, and the whole of Montana, and contained 1,171,931 square miles. Feb. 22, 1819, Florida was ceded to the United States by Spain for $5,000,000. Texas, which had for nine years existed as an independent Republic, was added to the United States as a State Dec. 29, 1845. As a result of the Mexican War and the payment of $18,-250,000 to Mexico and $10,000,000 to Texas, territory including what are now California and Utah and portions of New Mexico, Nevada, Arizona, Wyoming and Colorado was added, and later the southern part of Arizona and New Mexico were by the Gadsden Treaty purchased from Mexico. Alaska was acquired in 1867 by purchase, the price being $7,200,000, and Hawaii in 1898 by treaty. By the Treaty of Paris, between the United States and Spain at the close of the Spanish-American War, Dec. 10, 1898, the Philippine Islands; Guam, of the Ladrone Islands, Puerto Rico, and the Isle of Pines were ceded to the United States. Tutuila, Tau, Onesinga and Ofu, of the Samoan group, were acquired in 1899 by treaty with Great Britain and Germany. Wake and other small islands in the Pacific were taken in 1899. The Panama Canal Zone (see Panama Canal) was acquired in 1903.

Annual Addresses of President—
Adams, John, 240, 261, 279, 295.
Washington, 57, 73, 95, 117, 130, 154, 174, 191.
Wilson, 8286.

Annual Messages of President—
Adams, John (addresses), 240, 261, 279, 295.
Adams, J. Q., 865, 916, 944, 973.
Arthur, 4624, 4713, 4757, 4822.
Buchanan, 2967, 3028, 3083, 3157.
Cleveland, 4909, 5082, 5165, 5358, 5866, 5955, 6058, 6146.
Fillmore, 2613, 2649, 2699.
Grant, 3981, 4050, 4096, 4138, 4189, 4238, 4286, 4353.
Harrison, Benj., 5467, 5542, 5615, 5741.
Hayes, 4410, 4444, 4509, 4553.
Jackson, 1005, 1063, 1107, 1154, 1238, 1316, 1366, 1455.
Jefferson, 314, 330, 345, 357, 370, 393, 413, 439.
Johnson, 3551, 3643, 3756, 3870.
Lincoln, 3245, 3327, 3380, 3444.
McKinley, 6251, 6307, 6356, 6416.

Madison, 458, 467, 476, 499, 519, 532, 547, 558.
Monroe, 580, 608, 623, 642, 667, 754, 776, 817.
Pierce, 2740, 2806, 2860, 2930.
Polk, 2235, 2321, 2382, 2479.
Roosevelt, 6641, 6709, 6784, 6894, 6973, 7023, 7070, 7198.
Taft, 7409, 7492, 7644, 7766.
Taylor, 2547.
Tyler, 1927, 2047, 2110, 2187.
Van Buren, 1590, 1700, 1746, 1819.
Washington (addresses), 57, 73, 95, 117, 130, 154, 174, 191.
Wilson (addresses), 7906, 8015, 8102.

Antarctic Regions.—Lands discovered within Antarctic regions are almost everywhere inaccessible. Recent explorations have determined the character of the polar region as an elevated land-mass of continental proportions, containing beds of coal and other mineral wealth. Antarctic regions as compared with Arctic are remarkable for low temperature. While icebergs from Arctic Ocean are carried south as far as the 40th parallel, bergs and floes from Antarctic are found, even in summer, 10 or 15 degrees nearer the equator. In the warmest part of midsummer the temperature is practically at freezing point. The entire region is within the snow line.
Explorations—Cook (1772) reached lat. 71° 10' S.; Weddell (1823) lat. 74° S.; Ross (1841-42) lat. 78° 10' S.; sighted a land with mountain ranges 7,000 to 15,000 feet high; traced coast from 72d parallel 800 miles S. and W.; named it Victoria Land; on it observed an active volcano, Mt. Erebus (13,300 feet). A Belgian expedition, De Gerlache commandant (1899), reached lat. 71° 36' 5". Borchgrevink (1898-1900) reached lat. 78° 34'; Scott (1902) lat. 82° 17'; Shackleton (1909) lat. 88° 23', expedition located S. Magnetic Pole at 72° 25' S. 155° 16' E. Amundsen discovered the south pole in 1912.

Anthracite Coal Strike Commission, referred to, 6737.

Anti-Federalists.—A political party which opposed the adoption and ratification of the Constitution. Its fundamental principle was opposition to the strengthening of the National Government at the expense of the States. George Clinton, George Mason, and Patrick Henry were its leaders. Their strength was shown in the First and Second Congresses. They opposed Hamilton and his followers and championed a strict construction of the Constitution as against monarchial federalism. They later became merged into the Republican party, under the leadership of Jefferson. There have been many political parties, termed "antis." As their names imply, they have opposed some specific measure, organization, or person. Though acting as political parties, they are not such in the strict sense of the word, for they have no affirmative policy and their claims are negative. Organized with specific purpose to oppose, they disappear with the issue. Prominent among quasi parties have been the Anti-Lecompton, Anti-Masonic, Anti-Monopoly, Anti-Nebraska, and Anti-Renters.

Anti-Masonic Party.—In 1826 William Morgan and David C. Miller, of Batavia, N. Y., announced that they were about to publish an exposé of Free-masonry. Before the book was produced Morgan was arrested for debt and confined in the jail at Canandaigua, whence he disappeared on the night of Sept. 12, 1826. It was charged, but never shown to be true, that he had been foully dealt with by members of the Masonic order, as all attempts to discover his whereabouts were unavailing. The oft-reiterated charges aroused a bitter opposition to the order, and Thurlow Weed began the publication of the Anti-Masonic *Enquirer* at Rochester.

In 1827 a convention was held by the Anti-Masons of Genesee County at Le Roy, N. Y., and a political party organized. It was claimed that many of the State officials were Masons and regarded their fraternal obligations as more binding than their civil oaths. The Anti-Masonic feeling grew rapidly. The party cast 33,000 votes in New York State in 1828, 70,000 in 1829, and 128,-000 in 1830, though many of the latter were anti-Jackson men regardless of Masonry.

In September, 1830, a national convention met at Philadelphia, Francis Granger, of New York, presiding. In 1831 they nominated William Wirt for President, but carried only the State of Vermont. In 1835, through a Democratic split, they elected Joseph Ritner governor of Pennsylvania. After this date the Anti-Masonic party declined as rapidly as it had arisen.

Anti-Monarchical.—Opposed to a monarchial form of government.

Anti-Monopoly Party.—The Anti-Monopoly Organization of the United States met at Chicago, May 14, 1884, and nominated Benjamin F. Butler, of Massachusetts, for the Presidency. It adopted a platform demanding economical government, and the enactment and enforcement of equitable laws, including an Interstate Commerce Law (one has since been enacted), establishing Labor Bureaus, providing Industrial Arbitration, a direct vote for Senators, a graduated income tax, payment of the national debt as it matures, and "fostering care" for agriculture; while it denounced the tariff and the grant of land to corporations. Their nominee was also selected by the Greenback Labor party, the joint ticket being known as the People's party. It polled 130,000 votes.

Anti-Nebraska.—Opposed to the Kansas-Nebraska act (q. v.).

Anti-Saloon League.—Founded in 1890, and is installed in practically every State of the Union. The League throughout the nation employs 500 persons, who give their entire time to the work of this institution, and it has over 100 offices from which were distributed during the year 100,000,000 pages of anti-saloon literature. The annual income is about $400,000.

Anti-Trust Law.—In 1887 Congress enacted the Interstate Commerce Law, having for its purpose the regulation and control of the business of common carriers engaged in commerce between the States. The main object of this law was to prevent favoritism and unfair discrimination in freight rates, which had, it was claimed, contributed largely to the upbuilding of trusts and monopolistic enterprises and worked to the disadvantage of smaller competing concerns. This was amended and passed in 1890 as the Sherman Anti-Trust Law. It provides that all contracts, combinations in form of trusts or otherwise, or conspiracies in restraint of interstate or international commerce are illegal, and that all persons participating in such agreement, combination or conspiracy are guilty of a misdemeanor and subject to a penalty for violation of the act. The statute also provides that all goods in transportation in violation of the act may be seized and

forfeited by the Government, and that injunction proceedings may be brought by the Attorney-General under the act. Although supplemental acts were passed in 1903, on the recommendation of the Attorney-General, the Sherman law was found ineffectual in the purposes for which it was intended, *i. e.*, restraining the growth of monopolies or trusts, so-called, and that it operated against both reasonable and unreasonable restraints of trade, and prohibited all combinations, both good and bad. Further criticism of the law was invoked when the Supreme Court decided that a trade union boycott was a conspiracy in restraint of trade.

The law creating the Department of Commerce and Labor provided for a Bureau of Corporations, whose duty it should be to collect data regarding trusts, which might be used in shaping further legislation.

The decisions of the Supreme Court and of the United States Circuit Court indicate that the government has the power to prevent combinations among railroads or manufacturing corporations engaged in interstate business, even when such combination only tends toward monopoly. (See Northern Securities Case.)

While the law seems effective against railroads, it was set at defiance by the Addyston Pipe and Steel Company, which pending the decision of a case brought against it by the Attorney-General, sold out the six defendant companies to a New Jersey corporation and continued the alleged unlawful practices. (See Addyston Case.)

Commissioner Garfield, of the Bureau of Corporations, recommended, and President Roosevelt has urged upon Congress the necessity of a federal incorporation law. (6943, 7074.) To compel a corporation doing business in any State to secure a federal franchise to transact business in another State is of doubtful constitutionality.

Commissioner H. K. Smith of the Bureau of Corporations in 1908 said: "Corporate combination seems to be not only an economic necessity but also largely an accomplished fact. It is not the existence of industrial power, but rather its misuse, that is the real problem." Senator Beveridge said the most urgent legislation needed by honest business was a law legalizing capitalistic corporations for honest purposes. President Roosevelt declared it to be "profoundly immoral to keep on the statute books a law, nominally in the interest of public morality, that really puts a premium upon public immorality by undertaking to forbid honest men from doing what must be done under modern business conditions." (7075.)

The entire status of anti-trust legislation in the United States was altered by the passage of a bill, approved on Sept. 26, 1914, establishing the Federal Trade Commission; and by the passage of the bill, approved on Oct. 15, 1914, known as the Clayton Anti-Trust Law. The articles in the Index under the head of Federal Trade Commission and Clayton Anti-Trust Law must be read carefully for an adequate understanding of the anti-trust situation in the country at the present time.

Following is a complete list of suits brought and prosecutions instituted by the United States under the Sherman Anti-Trust Law. A complete index to the various cases will be found at the end of the article.

PRESIDENT HARRISON'S ADMINISTRATION.—Seven Cases.

[William H. H. Miller, Attorney-General, March 5, 1889, to March 6, 1893.]

1. *United States v. Jellico Mountain Coal Company.* Suit against the members of the "Nashville Coal Exchange," composed of various coal-mining companies operating mines in Kentucky and Tennessee, and of persons and firms dealing in coal in Nashville, formed for the purpose of fixing prices and regulating the output of coal. A preliminary injunction was denied on Oct. 13, 1890. Upon full hearing the court, on June 4, 1891, held the combination to be in violation of the anti-trust law and enjoined the further carrying out of the agreement.

2. *United States v. Greenhut et al.* A proceeding by indictment against the officers of the Distilling and Cattle Feeding Co. (Whisky Trust) for an alleged violation of the anti-trust law. Indictment quashed, as allegations were held not to constitute an offense under the statute.

2a. *In re Corning.* Application for a warrant of removal from Ohio to Massachusetts to answer to the indictment found in the Greenhut case. Application denied and prisoner discharged.

2b. *In re Terrell.* Application for a writ of habeas corpus to secure a discharge from arrest and detention upon a warrant for removal from New York to Massachusetts to answer to the indictment found in the Greenhut case. Petitioner discharged.

2c. *In re Greene.* Petition for writ of habeas corpus to secure release from the custody of the marshal, by whom he was held awaiting an order for the removal of Greene to Massachusetts to answer to the indictment in the Greenhut case. Prisoner discharged.

3. *United States v. Nelson.* Indictment of a number of lumber dealers for conspiring together to raise the price of lumber in violation of the anti-trust law. Demurrer to indictment sustained, the court holding that an agreement between a number of dealers to raise prices, unless they controlled nearly the entire commodity, could not operate as a restraint of trade under the act.

4. *United States v. Trans-Missouri Freight Association.* Bill filed Jan. 6, 1892, to enjoin the operations of a combination of railroads engaged in interstate commerce, formed for the purpose of maintaining "just and reasonable rates," etc. Bill dismissed by Circuit Court; decree of dismissal affirmed by Circuit Court of Appeals, and reversed by the United States Supreme Court on March 22, 1897. Final decree entered on June 7, 1897.

5. *United States v. Workingmen's Amalgamated Council of New Orleans et al.* Suit to restrain defendants, a combination of workmen, from interfering with interstate and foreign commerce, in violation of the anti-trust law. The injunction was granted and the law held to apply to combinations of laborers as well as capitalists. This decree was affirmed by the Circuit Court of Appeals.

6. *United States v. Patterson et al.* Cash register case. Indictment of members of a combination formed for the purpose of controlling the price of cash registers. A demurrer was sustained as to certain counts of the indictment and overruled as to others and leave granted to file special demurrers to the counts which were sustained. The special demurrers were heard on June 1, 1893, and the demurrers overruled, the court adhering to its former ruling. Letter of Attorney-General dated Oct. 16, 1893, shows case was allowed to lapse because of reconciliation of complaining witness with defendants.

7. *United States v. E. C. Knight Company* (Sugar Trust). Bill in equity to enjoin the operations of the Sugar Trust, charged with a violation of the anti-trust law. The bill was dismissed Jan. 30, 1894. Appeal was taken to the Circuit Court of Appeals and the decree affirmed. From this decision an appeal was taken to the Supreme Court of the United States, where the decree of dismissal was affirmed.

PRESIDENT CLEVELAND'S SECOND ADMINISTRATION.—Eight cases.

[Richard Olney, Attorney-General, March 6, 1893, to June 7, 1895; Judson Harmon, Attorney-General, June 8, 1895, to March 5, 1897.]

1. *United States v. Eugene V. Debs et al.* Petition filed on July 3, 1894, in the United States Circuit Court for the District of Indiana, seeking to restrain interference by American Railway Union and forty-nine individual defendants with mails and interstate commerce carried by all railroads operating in Indiana. An injunction was issued on July 3, 1894, which was continued in force until September 19, 1898, when the case was dismissed at the instance of the Government.

1a. *United States v. Agler.* Information charging contempt of court in disobeying in injunction restraining Agler and others from interfering with interstate commerce and obstructing the mails. Information quashed. It was charged that Agler was a member of the American Railway Union, the members of which order were on a strike and had been enjoined under the anti-trust law from interfering with the carrying of the mails and from obstructing interstate commerce. Information quashed. This is one of the "Debs" cases.

2. *United States v. Elliott.* Suit to restrain Elliott, Debs, and other members of the American Railway Union, from carrying out their unlawful conspiracy to interfere with interstate commerce and to obstruct the carrying of the mails, in violation of the anti-trust law. Preliminary injunction granted. A demurrer to this bill was overruled. Final decree entered April 6, 1896, against 295 defendants, and temporary injunction made permanent.

3. *United States v. Debs et al.* Petition filed on July 2, 1894, in the Circuit Court for the Northern District of Illinois, alleging conspiracy to obstruct the mails and to interfere with interstate commerce. A temporary injunction was issued on July 2, 1894, for violation of which contempt proceedings were instituted. Original petition dismissed on July 28, 1899, at the instance of the Government.

3a. *United States v. Debs et al.* Proceedings in contempt to punish Debs and others for disobeying an injunction restraining them from interfering with interstate commerce and with obstructing the mails, by means of a conspiracy, in violation of the anti-trust law. Defendants found guilty and punished.

3b. *In re Debs, petitioner.* Proceedings instituted July 2, 1894. Application for a writ of habeas corpus to secure a discharge from imprisonment for disobeying an injunction of the Circuit Court for the Northern District of Illinois, restraining Debs and others from conspiring to interfere with interstate commerce, in violation of the anti-trust law. Petition for the writ denied.

4. *United States v. Cassidy.* Cassidy and others were indicted under section 5440, United States Revised Statutes, for conspiring to commit offenses against the United States, which acts consisted in a combining and conspiring to restrain trade and commerce between the States, in violation of the anti-trust law, and grew out of the Pullman strike in California. The trial

lasted five months and resulted in a disagreement of the jury. A *nolle prosequi* entered July 1, 1895.

5. *Moore v. United States.* Indictment of the members of an association of dealers in coal at Salt Lake City for entering into a conspiracy to regulate the price of coal. Indictment returned Nov. 4, 1895. Moore was tried and convicted in the District Court of Utah upon this indictment. The Circuit Court of Appeals reversed the judgment of conviction, for the reason that upon the admission of Utah as a State it was no longer a "Territory" within the meaning of the anti-trust act, and the combination was not in restraint of interstate commerce, and the court therefore had no jurisdiction of the offense.

6. *United States v. Joint Traffic Association.* Suit instituted Jan. 8, 1896. Bill in equity to enjoin the alleged violation of the anti-trust law by a combination of railroads. The Circuit Court dismissed the bill, and the Court of Appeals affirmed the action of the Circuit Court. These judgments were reversed by the United States Supreme Court. On March 3, 1899, a decree was entered enjoining the defendants from observing the agreement or articles of organization entered into.

7. *United States v. Addyston Pipe and Steel Company.* Suit instituted Dec. 10, 1896. Bill in equity to enjoin the operations of the Cast-Iron Pipe Trust, which attempted to control the price of cast-iron pipe. The bill was dismissed by the Circuit Court. The Circuit Court of Appeals reversed the decree of the Circuit Court and remanded the case, with instructions to enter a decree for the Government. On appeal to the Supreme Court the action of the Circuit Court of Appeals was affirmed.

8. *United States v. Hopkins et al.* Suit instituted Dec. 31, 1896. Bill to restrain the operations of the "Kansas City Live Stock Exchange," organized to control the shipments of live stock. The injunction was granted, but on appeal the Supreme Court reversed the decree of the Circuit Court and remanded the case, with instructions to dismiss the bill.

PRESIDENT MCKINLEY'S ADMINISTRATION. —Three cases.

[Joseph McKenna, Attorney-General, March 5, 1897, to June 25, 1898; John W. Griggs, Attorney-General, June 25, 1898, to March 29, 1901; Philander C. Knox, Attorney-General, April 5, 1901, to June 30, 1904.]

1. *Anderson v. United States.* Bill in equity to restrain the operations of "The Traders' Live Stock Exchange," of Kansas City, an association formed for the purpose of buying cattle on the market. This suit was instituted June 7, 1897, in the Circuit Court of the United States for the Western District of Missouri. Decree of temporary injunction was granted and the case appealed to the Circuit Court of Appeals for the Eighth Circuit. From there it was certified to the Supreme Court of the United States for instructions upon certain questions, under the provisions of section 6 of the act of March 3, 1891 (26 Stat., 828). The Supreme Court reversed the decree of the Circuit Court and remanded the case, with directions to dismiss the bill, holding that the acts complained of were not a violation of the anti-trust law.

2. *United States v. Coal Dealers' Association.* Suit brought Dec. 16, 1897. Bill for injunction to restrain the operations of a combination of coal dealers known as the "Coal Dealers' Association of California." A temporary injunction was granted from which no appeal was taken and

final decree ordered May 2, 1899, granting relief prayed for.

3. *United States v. Chesapeake and Ohio Fuel Company et al.* Bill filed May 8, 1899, to annul a contract and dissolve a combination of producers and shippers of coal in Ohio and West Virginia, engaged in mining coal and making coke intended for "Western shipment," under agreement to sell the same at not less than a memorandum price, to be fixed by an executive committee appointed by the producers. Defendants enjoined, contract declared void and illegal, and the combination dissolved. Affirmed by Circuit Court of Appeals. No appeal taken.

PRESIDENT ROOSEVELT'S ADMINISTRATION. —Forty-four cases.

[Philander C. Knox, Attorney-General, April 5, 1901, to June 30, 1904; William H. Moody, Attorney-General, July 1, 1904, to Dec. 16, 1906; Charles J. Bonaparte, Attorney-General, Dec. 17, 1906, to March 4, 1909.]

1. *United States v. Northern Securities Co., Great Northern R'y Co., Northern Pacific R'y Co. et al.* This suit was brought on March 10, 1902, in the Circuit Court of the United States for the District of Minnesota, to enjoin the defendant, the Northern Securities Co., from purchasing, acquiring, receiving, holding, voting, or in any manner acting as the owner of any of the shares of the capital stock of the two defendant railway companies, and to restrain the defendant railway companies from permitting the securities company to vote any of the stock of said railways, or from exercising any control whatsoever over the corporate acts of either of said railway companies, it being charged that the securities company was formed for the purpose of acquiring a majority of the capital stock of the two railway companies in order that it might in that way effect practically a consolidation of the two companies by controlling rates and restricting and destroying competition, in violation of the Sherman Anti-Trust Law. The Circuit Court on April 9, 1903, entered a decree in favor of the Government as prayed for in the petition, and this decree was, on March 14, 1904, affirmed by the Supreme Court of the United States.

2. *United States v. Swift & Co. et al.* Suit brought on May 10, 1902, in the Circuit Court of the United States for the Northern District of Illinois to restrain the defendants (commonly known as the Beef Trust), who are engaged in the buying of live stock and the selling of dressed meats, from carrying out an unlawful conspiracy entered into between themselves and with the various railway companies, to suppress competition and to obtain a monopoly in the purchase of live stock and in the selling of dressed meats. A preliminary restraining order was granted on May 20, 1902. The defendants having demurred to the bill, the court, after hearing, on April 18, 1903, overruled the demurrers and granted a preliminary injunction. The defendants having failed to answer, the court, on May 26, 1903, entered an order making the decree final and perpetually enjoining the further operations of the trust. The defendants, on Aug. 14, 1903, appealed from the final decree of the Circuit Court to the Supreme Court of the United States, where decree was affirmed Jan. 30, 1905.

3. *United States v. The Federal Salt Company et al.* Suit brought in the Circuit Court of the United States for the Northern District of California, on Oct. 15, 1902, to restrain the defendants (known

as the Salt Trust) from unlawfully combining and conspiring to suppress competition in the manufacture and sale of salt in the States west of the Rocky Mountains, in violation of the Sherman Anti-Trust Law. A temporary restraining order was issued on that date, and the cause coming on for hearing, the court, on Nov. 10, 1902, granted an injunction *pendente lite,* thus, in effect, making the restraining order perpetual. No appeal was taken from this order.

4. *United States v. The Federal Salt Company.* On Feb. 28, 1903, the grand jury for the United States District Court for the Northern District of California returned an indictment against the Salt Trust for having violated the anti-trust law. On May 12, 1903, the trust pleaded guilty, and the court sentenced it to pay a fine of $1,000, which was paid.

5. *United States v. Jacksonville Wholesale Grocers' Association.* A proceeding in equity, instituted on Sept. 12, 1903, in the United States Circuit Court for the Southern District of Florida, for the purpose of dissolving a combination of wholesale grocers operating in violation of the anti-trust law, Nov. 1, 1907, dismissed.

6. *United States v. General Paper Co. et al.* Dec. 27, 1904, a bill in equity was filed in the Circuit Court of the United States for the District of Minnesota against the General Paper Co. and twenty-three other corporations engaged in the manufacture and sale of paper, alleging that they had entered into combination and conspiracy to restrain trade and commerce in the manufacture of news print, manila, fiber, and other papers by making the General Paper Co. their common sales agent. On May 11, 1906, the court ordered judgment in favor of the Government, dissolving the combination and affording all relief prayed for in the bill.

7. *United States v. Armour & Co. et al.* After the affirmance by the Supreme Court of the decree of the Circuit Court in United States v. Swift & Company (above referred to) complaints from various quarters were made to the department that the combination still continued. The department thereupon began an exhaustive inquiry before the grand jury for the northern district of Illinois, which resulted in the return of an indictment on July 1, 1905, against Armour & Co., J. Ogden Armour, president; Patrick A. Valentine, treasurer; Arthur Neekler, general manager; Thomas J. Connors, superintendent, and Samuel A. McRobert, assistant treasurer, of Armour & Co.; the Armour Packing Co., and Charles W. Armour, president; Swift & Co., and Louis F. Swift, president; Lawrence A. Carton, treasurer; D. Edwin Hartwell, secretary, and Albert H. Veeder and Robert C. McManus and Arthur F. Evans, agents of Swift & Co.; the Fairbank Canning Co., and Edward Morris, vice-president; Ira N. Morris, secretary of the Fairbank Canning Co.; the Cudahy Packing Co., and Edward A. Cudahy, vice-president and general manager of the Cudahy Packing Co.

Against this indictment many preliminary objections were urged. All were disposed of in favor of the Government, except certain special pleas of immunity in bar, based upon information concerning the matters for which the defendants were indicted, which they had given to the Department of Commerce and Labor. The court sustained the pleas so far as the individual defendants were concerned and overruled them with respect to the corporations. Dismissed Feb. 5, 1913.

8. *United States v. MacAndrews & Forbes Company et al.* In June, 1906, the grand jury returned an indictment against the MacAndrews & Forbes Co., the J. S. Young Co., a corporation of Maine, and Karl Jungbluth and Howard E. Young, their respective presidents, for illegally combining and conspiring to regulate the interstate trade and sale in licorice paste, an article used in the manufacture of plug and smoking tobacco, snuff, and cigars. Defendants entered pleas of not guilty, with leave to withdraw or demur on or before July 9, 1906. July 9, 1906, demurrers filed by all of the defendants. Dec. 4, 1906, demurrers overruled. Dec. 19, 1906, trial commenced. Jan. 10, 1907, MacAndrews & Forbes Co. was found guilty on first and third counts of indictment, the J. S. Young Co. guilty on first and third counts; verdict of acquittal as to individual defendants. MacAndrews & Forbes Co. fined $10,000. J. S. Young Co. fined $8,000.

8a. *The Tobacco Trust Cases.* (*Hale v. Henkel; McAlister v. Henkel.*) These cases grew out of an investigation by a Federal grand jury in the Southern District of New York of the American Tobacco Co. and the MacAndrews & Forbes Co., believed to be violating the anti-trust laws, the matter having been brought to the attention of the grand jury by the officers of the Department of Justice, special counsel having been appointed for the purpose of investigation and prosecution. Subpoenas *duces tecum* were served upon the officers of the companies directing them to produce papers and other documentary evidence belonging to the corporations. They refused to obey the subpoena to answer questions propounded to them. The Circuit Court adjudged them in contempt and committed them until they should produce the books and answer the questions. They applied to another judge of the same court for writs of habeas corpus, which, upon hearing, were discharged. Upon appeal the Supreme Court affirmed the orders denying the writs.

9. *United States v. Metropolitan Meat Company et al.* Bill filed in equity in October, 1905, in the United States Circuit Court for Hawaii, to restrain the operation of alleged unlawful combinations in restraint of the trade in beef and beef products. Demurrer to bill overruled Oct. 2, 1906. Pending, 1917.

10. *United States v. Nome Retail Grocers' Association.* Nov. 4, 1905, the department directed the United States attorney for the Second Division of Alaska to file a bill in equity against the Nome Retail Grocers' Association, alleging a combination to fix prices and to suppress competition. Suit was promptly instituted, whereupon the defendants agreed to the entry of a decree granting all the relief prayed for in the petition. A decree dissolving the combination was entered accordingly.

11. *United States v. Terminal Railroad Association of St. Louis et al.* Petition filed in Circuit Court of United States for the Eastern District of Missouri on Dec. 1, 1905, to enjoin the defendant railroads from continuing an unlawful combination entered into between them to operate Eads Bridge and Merchants Bridge as a common agency of interstate commerce. Upon disagreement of Circuit Judges case was carried to the Supreme Court and was remanded by that court for further proceedings. The petition was then dismissed by the Circuit Court, and an appeal was taken to the Supreme Court, where, on April 22, 1912, the decree of the Circuit Court was reversed, and the case remanded with directions to enter a decree in conformity with the opinion of the Supreme

Court. A controversy having arisen as to whether the district judge or the three circuit judges had jurisdiction a writ of prohibition was filed against the district judge, which was sustained by the Supreme Court. The form of final decree to be entered is now under consideration by the circuit judges, the respective parties having submitted their views on December 6, 1913. The circuit judges entered a final decree on March 2, 1914. The government, believing that the decree did not carry out the mandate and opinion of the Supreme Court, appealed, and the appeal was argued in October, 1914. The decree entered by the circuit judges was affirmed.

12. *United States v. Allen & Robinson et al.* Bill filed in October in United States Circuit Court for the District of Hawaii, alleging unlawful combination to control the trade in lumber in that Territory. Answers filed Jan. 2, 1906. Decision adverse to Government and petition ordered dismissed March 30, 1911.

13. *United States v. Otis Elevator Co. et al.* Bill filed March 7, 1906, in the United States Circuit Court for the Northern District of California against the Otis Elevator Co. and a number of other corporations and individuals, in which it was alleged that they were maintaining a combination in restraint of trade in the matter of the manufacture and sale of elevators. June 1, 1906, a decree was entered by consent dissolving the combination and granting the relief prayed.

14. *United States v. F. A. Amsden Lumber Company et al.* Indictment returned in the District Court of Oklahoma May 4, 1906, for violation of the Sherman Act in restricting competition and maintaining prices in the sale of lumber. May 13, 1907, change of venue granted to Grant County. Sept. 25, 1907, pleas of guilty and fines imposed aggregating $2,000, which were paid.

15. *United States v. National Association of Retail Druggists et al.* Bill in equity filed May 9, 1906, in the United States Circuit Court for the District of Indiana against the National Association of Retail Druggists, alleging a combination in restraint of interstate trade in the sale of drugs and proprietary medicines. May 9, 1907, final decree entered by agreement, giving the Government all the relief prayed for in the petition.

16. *United States v. Virginia-Carolina Chemical Company et al.* May 25, 1906, the Federal grand jury for the Middle District of Tennessee, upon information furnished by the Department of Justice, returned an indictment against thirty-one corporations and twenty-five individuals engaged in the fertilizer business in the States of North Carolina, South Carolina, Georgia, Florida, Alabama, Mississippi, Arkansas, and Tennessee, charging them with engaging in a conspiracy in violation of the Federal anti-trust act and with conspiring to commit an offense against the United States, viz., the aforesaid conspiracy, in violation of section 5440 of the Revised Statutes. The fertilizer manufacturers combined to fix the price of fertilizers in the territory mentioned and to apportion the trade among themselves according to an agreed percentage. July 11, 1906, all the defendants appealed to the Supreme Court of the United States from an order of the Circuit Court of the Eastern District of Virginia denying the right of habeas corpus and remanding them to the custody of the marshal for removal to the Middle District of Tennessee for trial. The case before the Supreme Court was argued on Dec. 3, 1906, and on March

4, 1907, the judgment of the Circuit Court for the Eastern District of Virginia was reversed and the case remanded to that court for further proceedings in accordance with the opinion of the Supreme Court. April 17, 1908, various motions, pleas in abatement, and demurrers filed. July 3, 1908, certain motions and demurrers overruled, plea in abatement allowed, and indictment quashed.

17. *United States v. American Ice Company et al.* July 12, 1906, indictment returned in the Supreme Court of the District of Columbia, charging an unlawful agreement to control prices and restrict competition in the sale of ice. No further action taken.

18. *United States v. Chandler Ice and Cold Storage Plant et al.* Sept. 19, 1906, indictment returned in the District Court for the territory of Oklahoma against the Chandler Ice and Cold Storage Plant and others, charging a combination to apportion territory in the matter of the sale of ice. May 5, 1907, demurrer filed by defendant Groves and overruled. May 20, 1907, demurrer filed by Chandler Ice and Cold Storage Plant. Dismissed.

19. *United States v. Alfred M. Gloyd et al.* Sept. 21, 1906, indictment returned against Alfred M. Gloyd and others in the District Court for the Territory of Oklahoma, charging a combination to maintain prices and restrict competition in the sale of lumber. Dismissed.

20. *United States v. People's Ice and Fuel Company, a corporation, and W. B. Lount.* Oct. 23, 1906, indictment returned in the District Court for the Territory of Arizona, charging a combination to control prices and restrict competition in the sale of ice. Jan. 5, 1907, trial commenced. Verdict not guilty as to People's Ice and Fuel Co. and company held to next grand jury. Trial of W. B. Lount continued over term. Oct. 16, 1907, plea in bar filed. Oct. 17, 1907, plea in bar sustained.

21. *United States v. Demund Lumber Company et al.* Oct. 23, 1906, indictment returned in the District Court for the Territory of Arizona, charging a combination to control prices and restrict competition in the sale of lumber. Jan. 2, 1907, trial commenced. Verdict of not guilty as to Demund Lumber Co. Jan. 7, 1907, cases against Chamberlain Lumber Co. and Valley Lumber Co. continued over term. May 8, 1907, motion made to court to instruct for acquittal. Motion argued and taken under advisement. May 9, 1907, motion sustained and verdict of acquittal returned.

22. *United States v. Phœnix Wholesale Meat and Produce Company, a corporation, P. T. Hurley, and S. J. Tribolet.* Oct. 23, 1906, indictment returned in the District Court for the Territory of Arizona, charging a combination to control prices and restrict competition in the sale of meats. Jan. 7, 1907, trial commenced. Verdict of not guilty as to Phœnix Wholesale Meat & Produce Co. Jan. 8, 1907, indictment against Hurley dismissed. Verdict of guilty as to defendant S. J. Tribolet, Jan. 12, 1907. Tribolet sentenced to pay fine of $1,000. Jan. 9, 1907, case against Phœnix Wholesale Meat & Produce Co. dismissed. Appeal to the Supreme Court of the Territory of Arizona. Supreme Court affirmed decision of lower court. Fine paid.

23. *United States v. Standard Oil Company of N. J. et al.* Nov. 15, 1906, bill in equity filed in United States Circuit Court for the Eastern District of Missouri against the Standard Oil Co. and others, in which it is alleged that they are maintaining a

combination in restraint of trade in the manufacture and sale of petroleum. Case argued in Circuit Court April, 1909; decision by unanimous court in favor of the Government Nov. 20, 1909. Appealed to Supreme Court; argued March, 1910, reargued January, 1911, and judgment affirmed May 15, 1911.

24. *United States v. T. B. Hogg et al.* Dec. 8, 1906, indictment returned in the District Court for the Territory of Oklahoma, charging a combination and conspiracy in restraint of trade and commerce in the sale of lumber. March 25, 1907, plea of not guilty. Change of judge granted on application of defendants. Dismissed.

25. *United States v. Atlantic Investment Company et al.* Feb. 11, 1907, indictment returned in the United States District Court for the Southern District of Georgia against the Atlantic Investment Co. and others, charging a combination in restraint of trade and commerce in the matter of the manufacture and sale of turpentine. Feb. 18, 1907, four corporations and two individuals, defendants to this indictment, entered pleas of guilty, and the court imposed a fine of $5,000 upon each of the six defendants, making a total of $30,000.

26. *United States v. American Seating Company et al.* March 12, 1907, indictment returned to the District Court of the Northern District of Illinois charging a violation of the Sherman Anti-Trust Law by engaging in a combination in restraint of trade in the manufacture and sale of school and church furniture. April 1, 1907, defendant corporations entered pleas of guilty, with one exception. May 20, 1907, fines imposed aggregating $43,000. Defendant E. H. Stafford Manufacturing Co. filed demurrer April 3, 1907. May 31, 1907, demurrer overruled and plea of not guilty entered. Dismissed Jan. 27, 1913.

27. *United States v. American Seating Company et al.* March 12, 1907, bill in equity filed in the United States Circuit Court for the Northern District of Illinois against the American Seating Co. and others, in which it is alleged that they are maintaining a combination in restraint of trade in the manufacture and sale of school and church furniture. Aug. 15, 1907, decree entered granted perpetual injunction against all defendants, except E. H. Stafford Manufacturing Co., E. H. Stafford, E. M. Stafford, and E. G. Bentley. As to these defendants the case was dismissed Jan. 27, 1913.

28. *United States v. Santa Rita Mining Company and Santa Rita Store Company.* April 4, 1907, indictment returned in the district of New Mexico charging a violation of section 3 of the Sherman Anti-Trust Law for engaging in a combination in restraint of trade. Demurrer filed and overruled. Fine of $1,000 imposed on each defendant; total, $2,000. Appeal taken to the Supreme Court of the Territory of New Mexico, where judgment of the lower court was reversed, and the case was subsequently dismissed.

29. *United States v. The Reading Company et al.* Petition filed June 12, 1907, in the Circuit Court for the Eastern District of Pennsylvania, to dissolve a combination among the anthracite coal-carrying roads and others. December 8, 1910, a decision was handed down by the Circuit Court adjudging that defendants were joined in a combination in restraint of trade through the instrumentality of the Temple Iron Co., but dismissing the charge of the petition as to the so-called 65 per cent. contracts whereby it was alleged the independent output was controlled, and also the charges as to certain so-called minor combinations. Cross appeals were taken to the Supreme Court, where the decree of the Government lower court, in so far as it adjudged the defendants parties to a combination in restraint of trade through the instrumentality of the Temple Iron Co., was affirmed, but was reversed as to the so-called 65 per cent. contracts with instructions to cancel them, and was further modified by dismissing the petition in other respects without prejudice, instead of absolutely.

30. *United States v. National Umbrella Frame Company et al.* July 1, 1907, indictment returned in the District Court for the Eastern District of Pennsylvania charging a conspiracy to restrain interstate trade and commerce in the manufacture and sale of umbrella material in violation of the Sherman Anti-Trust Law and section 5440, R. S. Pleas of guilty entered and fines aggregating $3,000 imposed and collected.

31. *United States v. American Tobacco Company et al.* Bill in equity filed July 10, 1907, by the United States against the American Tobacco Co. and others, in which it was alleged that they were maintaining a combination in restraint of trade and commerce in the manufacture and sale of tobacco. Nov. 7, 1908, decision rendered in favor of the Government, except as to individual defendants and certain foreign and other corporations. Cross appeals were taken to the Supreme Court, where case was argued March, 1910, and reargued January, 1911. May 29, 1911, a decision was rendered sustaining the Government on every point, and the case was remanded to the Circuit Court and the unlawful combination was dissolved in accordance with the decision of the Supreme Court.

32. *United States v. E. H. Stafford Manufacturing Company et al.* July 10, 1907, indictment returned in the District Court for the Northern District of Illinois charging a violation of the Sherman Anti-Trust Law by engaging in a combination in restraint of trade in the manufacture and sale of school and church furniture. Dismissed Jan. 27, 1913.

33. *United States v. E. I. du Pont de Nemours & Co. et al.* July 30, 1907, bill in equity filed in the Circuit Court for the District of Delaware against E. I. du Pont de Nemours & Co. and others, in which it is alleged that they are maintaining a combination in restraint of trade in the manufacture and sale of gunpowder and other high explosives. June 21, 1911, a decision was rendered holding combination illegal and ordering its dissolution. Final decree dissolving the combination was approved by the court June 13, 1912.

34. *United States v. One Hundred and Seventy-five Cases of Cigarettes.* Oct. 28, 1907, information filed in the District Court for the Eastern District of Virginia covering the seizure of 175 cases of cigarettes under Section 6 of the Sherman Anti-Trust Act. Cigarettes subsequently released under bond. Decree of dismissal entered Jan. 31, 1913.

35. *United States v. H. D. Corbett Stationery Company et al.* Nov. 1, 1907, indictment returned in the District Court for the District of Arizona charging a combination in restraint of trade. Nov. 4, 1907, demurrer filed. Nov. 14, 1907, demurrers sustained and defendants referred to next grand jury. Oct. 28, 1908, reindicted. Nov. 6, 1908, verdict not guilty.

36. *United States v. Union Pacific Coal Company et al.* Nov. 20, 1907, indictment returned in the District Court for the District of Utah, charging a conspiracy to

violate and a violation of the Sherman Act. Jan. 6, 1908, demurrer filed. March 2, 1908, demurrer sustained as to first count and overruled as to second count. Dec. 3, 1908, verdict guilty. March 29, 1909, fines aggregating $13,000 imposed. November, 1909, judgment reversed by the Circuit Court of Appeals, and the suit was dismissed March 21, 1910.

37. *United States v. Chas. L. Simmons et al.* Jan. 20, 1908, indictment returned in the District Court for the Southern District of Alabama charging a combination in restraint of trade and commerce in the matter of the manufacture and sale of plumbers' supplies. Dec. 1, 1910, pleas of guilty, and fines aggregating $265 imposed.

38. *United States v. Union Pacific Railroad Company et al.* Feb. 1, 1908, a bill in equity was filed in the Circuit Court of the United States for the District of Utah, charging a combination and conspiracy in violation of the Sherman Act on the part of the so-called Harriman lines. June 23, 1911, decision by Circuit Court to the effect that the roads involved were not competing lines and hence the combination was not a violation of law, Hook, J., dissenting. An appeal was taken to Supreme Court, which handed down a decision reversing the lower court on December 2, 1912. Final decree entered at St. Paul, Minn., on June 30, 1913.

39. *United States v. E. J. Ray et al.* Feb. 14, 1908, indictment returned in the Circuit Court for the Eastern District of Louisiana against seventy-two laborers, charging a combination and conspiracy in restraint of foreign trade and commerce, in violation of the Sherman Act. See note under following case.

40. *United States v. E. J. Ray et al.* Feb. 15, 1908, indictment returned in the Circuit Court for the Eastern District of Louisiana against seventy-two laborers, charging a combination and conspiracy in restraint of interstate trade and commerce, in violation of the Sherman Act.

NOTE.—Jan. 26, 1911, cases consolidated for trial. Verdict of guilty as to three defendants and fines amounting to $110 imposed. Appeal granted and judgment of the lower court was affirmed.

41. *United States v. Joseph Stiefvater et al.* Feb. 15, 1908, indictment returned in the United States Circuit Court for the Eastern District of Louisiana, charging a combination in restraint of trade and commerce in the matter of the manufacture and sale of plumbers' supplies. June 25, 1910, dismissed.

42. *United States v. American Naval Stores Company et al.* April 11, 1908, indictment returned in the United States Circuit Court for the Southern District of Georgia, charging a combination in restraint of trade and commerce in the matter of the manufacture and sale of turpentine. May 10, 1909, verdict guilty as to five individual defendants. Fines aggregating $17,500 imposed and two defendants sentenced to three months in jail. Appealed to Circuit Court of Appeals and judgment affirmed. Certiorari granted by Supreme Court. Judgment of lower Court reversed June 9, 1913, on ground of error in judge's charge to jury. A verdict of not guilty was handed down in June, 1914.

43. *United States v. New York, New Haven, and Hartford Railroad Company et al.* May 22, 1908, a bill in equity was filed in the Circuit Court of the United States for the District of Massachusetts, charging the New Haven Co. with combining and attempting to combine and attempting to combine under one common control the various railroad and electric railway systems in New England in violation of the Sherman Act. Dismissed June 26, 1909.

44. *United States v. John H. Parks et al.* June 16, 1908, indictment returned in the Circuit Court of the United States for the Southern District of New York, charging a combination in restraint of trade in the matter of the manufacture and sale of papers. June 19, 1908, defendants plead guilty and sentenced to pay fines aggregating $50,000, which were paid.

PRESIDENT TAFT'S ADMINISTRATION.— Eighty-nine cases.

[Geo. W. Wickersham, Attorney-General, March 4, 1909, to March 4, 1913.]

1. *United States v. American Sugar Refining Company et al.* Indictment under Sherman law July 1, 1909. A plea of the statute of limitations was interposed by the defendant Kissell, which was taken to the Supreme Court, where it was decided in favor of the Government. March 31, 1912, trial of the case resulted in disagreement of the jury.

2. *United States v. Albia Box & Paper Company et al.* Dec. 7, 1909, indictment returned in Southern District of New York charging combination in restraint of trade in paper board. Feb, 7, 1910, all defendants plead guilty and fines aggregating $57,000 were assessed and collected.

3. *United States v. John S. Steers et al.* Indictment returned in Eastern District of Kentucky Feb. 17, 1910, charging conspiracy to restrain trade. This is the so-called "Night Rider" case where the restraint consisted in preventing the shipment of tobacco in interstate commerce by means of violence and intimidation. After the overruling of demurrers and various pleas in abatement a trial was had, and on April 16, 1910, a verdict of guilty was returned as to eight of twelve defendants and fines aggregating $3,500 imposed. Appealed to Circuit Court of Appeals, argued November, 1911, and the judgment was affirmed May 11, 1912. The sentences were commuted by the President to payment of costs of suit.

4. *United States v. Imperial Window Glass Company et al.* Indictment found in western Pennsylvania April 7, 1910, charging combination and conspiracy to enhance the price of window glass. Demurrers to the indictment were overruled, and on Nov. 10, 1910, pleas of nolo contendere were entered and fines aggregating $10,000 and costs were imposed and collected.

5. *United States v. National Packing Company et al.* Indictment returned in Northern District of Illinois, March 2, 1910, charging combination to restrain trade in fresh meats. Demurrer to indictment sustained June 23, 1910.

6. *United States v. National Packing Company et al.* Northern Illinois. Bill in equity charging combination in restraint of trade in fresh meats and praying for dissolution filed March 21, 1910. Dismissed in order to facilitate the prosecution of later criminal case.

7. *United States v. Armour Packing Company et al.* Indictment returned at Savannah, Ga., in April, 1910, charging combination to control prices and restrict competition. Demurrer sustained as to second count on May 21, 1914. *Nolle prosequi* entered March 9, 1915.

8. *United States v. Missouri Pacific Railroad Company and twenty-four other railroads.* Petition to restrain violation of Sherman law filed May 31, 1910, and temporary restraining order issued on that day enjoining advances in freight rates in western trunk-line territory, which would have become effective June 1, 1910. Thereupon

the railroads, after consultation with the President, withdrew their proposed advances in freight rates, and after the passage of the act of June 18, 1910, the matter was referred to the Interstate Commerce Commission. Thereafter the Interstate Commerce Commission enjoined the rate advances which the temporary restraining order obtained by the department on May 31, 1910, had prevented from going into effect and the petition was dismissed.

9. *United States v. Southern Wholesale Grocers' Association.* Bill in equity charging combination to regulate prices of necessities of life, filed at Birmingham, Ala., June 9, 1910. An agreement was reached between the Government and defendant's counsel, and a decree prepared, submitted to, and passed by the court Oct. 17, 1911, perpetually restraining the association, its officers and members, from doing any and all of the acts complained of. Some of the grocers violated the agreement with the Court and contempt proceedings were brought on a petition for rule to show cause why an attachment for criminal contempt of court for alleged violation of decree entered Oct. 17, 1911, should not issue was filed in the District Court at Birmingham, Ala., Feb. 10, 1913. The association and three of its members were found guilty of contempt and fines aggregating $5,500 were imposed.

10. *United States v. Great Lakes Towing Company et al.* Petition filed in Northern District of Ohio on June 19, 1910, against an alleged combination of towing facilities on the Great Lakes. A decision in favor of the Government was handed down Feb. 11, 1913. The plan of dissolution is now under consideration by the court. A decree concerning the dissolution was entered on Feb. 13, 1915, but the government believed that the decree would not afford adequate relief, and appealed to the Supreme Court. On Oct. 12, 1917, the suit was dismissed by the petition of the government.

11. *United States v. Chicago Butter & Egg Board.* Bill asking for dissolution filed at Chicago, June 13, 1910. A demurrer to the petition was sustained with leave to amend, and an amended petition was filed. Set for hearing on master's report on Jan. 8, 1914. The case was decided favorably to the government and a decree to that effect was entered on Oct. 12, 1914.

12. *United States v. Frank Hayne, James A. Patten et al.* Indictments returned, New York City, against alleged cotton-pool conspirators, Aug. 4, 1910. Demurrers were sustained as to certain counts of indictment and overruled as to others, and the Government appealed to the Supreme Court, where case was argued November, 1911, and reargued at the October term, 1912. Decision by Supreme Court Jan. 6, 1913, sustaining indictments. Patten entered plea of guilty Feb. 11, 1913, and was fined $4,000. Indictment dismissed as to other defendants, and another indictment was returned July 1, 1913. See case 6, under the first administration of President Wilson.

13. *United States v. Standard Sanitary Manufacturing Company et al.* Petition filed at Baltimore July 22, 1910, charging a combination, under cover of a patent licensing arrangement, to restrain competition and enhance prices of enamel ware. Four volumes of testimony were taken and case set for argument at Richmond on June 15, 16, and 17, 1911. In a decision rendered Oct. 13, 1911, the court sustained all the Government's contentions, and a decree was entered Nov. 25, 1911, from which an appeal was taken to the Supreme Court. Decision of lower court affirmed Nov. 8, 1913. Judgment compelled dissolution.

14. *United States v. Louis F. Swift et al.* Indictment returned by the grand jury at Chicago, in September, 1910, against ten prominent individuals engaged in the meat-packing industry. Defendants have filed numerous pleas in bar, demurrers, etc., all of which were decided in favor of the Government. Defendants applied to Circuit Judge Kohlsaat for writ of certiorari based on contention that anti-trust law was unconstitutional. Petition dismissed. Defendants appealed to Supreme Court and gave notice of motion Dec. 4, 1911, for stay of trial pending appeal. March 27, 1912, after a trial lasting over three months the jury returned a verdict of acquittal.

15. *United States v. John Reardon & Sons Company and Consolidated Rendering Co.* Indicted jointly by Federal grand jury at Boston in October, 1910. Demurrer to indictment sustained June 23, 1911.

15, 16, and 17 A. See at the end of 70.

16. *United States v. Ferdinand Sulzberger,* doing business under the name of *John Reardon & Sons Company, and Horatio W. Heath,* of Boston, doing business as the *Consolidated Rendering Company.* Jointly indicted at Boston in October, 1910, for violation of the Sherman law. Demurrer to indictment sustained June 23, 1911.

16 A. See at the end of 70.

17. *United States v. Horatio W. Heath and Cyrus S. Hapgood.* Indictment returned in October, at Boston, charging violation of the Sherman law. Demurrer to indictment sustained June 23, 1911.

17 A. See at the end of 70.

(Note.—In the last three indictments, which were found simultaneously, the Government charges that the defendants have attempted to divide territory between themselves throughout New England, so as to avoid competition and drive out competitors in the hide and rendering business.)

18. *United States v. Standard Sanitary Manufacturing Company et al.* In addition to the above suit in equity (No. 13, supra), indictments were returned by grand jury at Detroit on Dec. 6, 1910, against the same corporations and individuals charging the same acts. Various demurrers and dilatory pleas have been filed, argued, and overruled. After a trial lasting six weeks the jury reported a disagreement on March 14, 1912. Retrial in February, 1913, resulted in a verdict of guilty and fines aggregating $51,006 were imposed.

19. *United States v. American Sugar Refining Company et al.* A suit in equity was filed at New York on Nov. 28, 1910, against this corporation, its officers and agents, and its owned and controlled corporations, attacking it as a combination in restraint of trade and praying for its dissolution. The case was ready for trial in Oct., 1915, but the presiding judge suggested postponement to await the decision of the Supreme Court in the Harvester and Steel cases. The case was still pending in 1917.

20. *United States v. General Electric Company et al.* Bill in equity filed at Cleveland, Ohio, on March 3, 1911, charging a combination in incandescent electric lamps. This suit is the outcome of an extensive investigation into the electrical industry. Like the enameled-ware combination, it is founded on a cross-licensing arrangement under patents. A formal decree has been agreed upon between counsel for the Government and the defendant companies, and was submitted to and passed by the Circuit Court Oct. 12, 1911.

21. *United States v. Purrington et al.* Indictment returned in the Northern District of Illinois Sept. 14, 1910, charging combination to restrain trade in paving bricks and paving blocks. Demurrer overruled Nov. 9, 1911. Nolle prosequi entered June 3, 1913.

22. *United States v. Hamburg-Amerikanische Packetfahrt Actien Gesellschaft and others.* (Trans-Atlantic steamship pool.) Combination of steamship lines regulating steerage traffic on the Atlantic Ocean. Suit filed Jan. 4, 1911, at New York City. Testimony complete and case set for argument, April 17, 1914. On Oct. 12, 1914, a decision unfavorable to the government was handed down, and an appeal to the Supreme Court was taken. On Jan. 10, 1916, the Supreme Court reversed the decision of the lower court. However, the Supreme Court refused to decide the questions in issue on the ground that the European War had rendered them moot.

23. *United States v. William C. Geer, president Albia Box and Paper Company, et al.* Indictment returned April 28, 1911, in the Southern District of New York, alleging a combination and conspiracy in restraint of interstate commerce in paper board. Demurrer overruled May 9, 1913. In Feb., 1915, the defendants withdrew their pleas of not guilty and offered pleas of *nolo contendere*, which the court accepted and fined them $16,000.

24. *United States v. Eastern States Retail Lumber Dealers' Association.* Suit in equity filed at New York on May 19, 1911, charging the Eastern States Lumber Dealers' Association, its officers and members, with a conspiracy, in restraint of trade through the instrumentality of black lists and trade agreements. Decision by lower court in favor of Government Jan. 9, 1913, and decree entered March 1, from which appeal was taken to Supreme Court. Argued at October term. Decided June 22, 1914, sustaining the decree of the district court.

25. *United States v. Isaac Whiting, John K. Whiting, Charles H. Hood, Edward J. Hood, and William A. Grautstein.* Indictment returned by the grand jury at Boston, Mass., on May 26, 1911, charging a combination to restrain trade in milk throughout the New England States. Pending, 1914. A demurrer was sustained concerning conspiracy and monopoly in restraint of trade, but overruled concerning combinations in restraint of trade, to which the defendants entered a plea of not guilty on May 4, 1914. Certain of the defendants entered pleas of *nolo contendere*, and the case is being prosecuted against the others.

26. *United States v. Isaac Whiting, John K. Whiting, Charles H. Hood, Edward J. Hood, and William A. Grautstein, and William A. Hunter, Secretary of Producers' Co.* May 26, 1911, indictment returned by the grand jury at Boston, Mass., charging a conspiracy to restrain trade in milk throughout the New England States. Pending, 1914. A demurrer was sustained concerning conspiracy and monopoly in restraint of trade, but overruled concerning combinations in restraint of trade, to which charge the defendants pleaded not guilty on May 4, 1914. Certain of the defendants entered pleas of *nolo contendere*, and the case is being prosecuted against the others.

27. *United States v. Lumber Secretaries' Bureau of Information et al.* Indictment returned June 23, 1911, in the Northern District of Illinois, charging that the secretaries of fourteen retail lumbermen's associations, covering twenty-three States

from Pennsylvania to the Pacific coast, were in a conspiracy by means of a central controlling bureau to control the marketing of lumber by forcing the product through the retailer to the consumer, and restraining the trade of the manufacturer, wholesaler, and consumer, and eliminating competition for the trade of the consumer. Demurrer filed. Nolle prosequi entered June 6, 1913.

28 to 36. *United States v. Philip H. W. Smith et al.* Indictments returned at New York City, June 29, 1911, against various individuals charging violations of Sections 1 and 2 of the anti-trust law through the conduct and operation of the Underground Power Cable Association, Telephone Cable Association, Fine Magnet Wire Association, Wire Rope Manufacturers, Horseshoe Manufacturers' Association, Lead-encased Rubber Cable Association, and the Rubber-covered Wire Association.
Defendants appeared and pleaded, and fines aggregating $128,700 have been imposed.

37. *United States v. Periodical Publishing Company.* Bill in equity filed in New York in June, 1911, against the members of the so-called Magazine Trust. The trial resulted in an equally divided court, and an order of dismissal was entered May 29, 1913.

38. *United States v. Jay B. Pearce et al.* Indictment returned against certain manufacturers and jobbers at Cleveland, Ohio, July 19, 1911, for combination and conspiracy in the manufacture and sale of wall paper. Demurrer overruled May 13, 1912. Verdict of not guilty May 24, 1912.

39. *United States v. Lake Shore & Michigan Southern R. R., Chesapeake & Ohio R. R., Hocking Valley R. R., Toledo & Ohio Central Ry., Kanawha & Michigan Ry., Zanesville & Western R. R. and others.* Bill in equity filed at Columbus, Ohio, Aug 4, 1911, to enjoin combination and conspiracy in restraint of trade. Decision of lower court in favor of Government Dec. 28, 1912. Proposed plan of dissolution being considered by court. On Nov. 10, 1913, a supplemental decision concerning the relief to be granted was entered, and on Mar. 14, 1914, a final decree was entered, awarding in the main the relief prayed for by the government.

40. *United States v. Edward E. Hartwick et al.* Petition filed at Detroit, Mich., Aug. 31, 1911, alleging conspiracy and unlawful restraint of trade on the part of members of the Michigan Retail Lumber Dealers' Association, The Scout Publishing Co., and the Lumbermen's Secretaries' Bureau of Information. Issues joined and testimony complete.

41. *United States v. Standard Wood Company et al.* Petition filed in the Circuit Court at New York City in September, 1911, against the members of the so-called Kindling Wood Trust, praying for injunction against the further carrying into effect of trade agreements and combination and conspiracy to monopolize trade. On default of answer, decree was entered against defendants March 11, 1912.

42. *United States v. Hunter Milling Company, Blackwell Milling and Elevator Company, and Frank Foltz.* Indictment returned by grand jury to District Court for the Western District of Oklahoma, Sept. 10, 1911, on one count, charging violation of Section 1 of the Sherman Act. Demurrer overruled Dec. 16, 1912, and verdict of guilty rendered. Fines aggregating $2,000 were imposed.

43. *United States v. S. W. Winslow, Wm. Barbour, E. P. Howe, Ed. P. Hurd,*

Geo. W. Brown, and Jas. J. Storrow. Two indictments returned by the grand jury at Boston, Mass., Sept. 19, 1911, charging combination, conspiracy, and monopoly in trade in shoe machinery. One indictment sustained and one partially overruled. Appeal taken by government. The petition was dismissed.

44. *United States v. The Colorado and Wyoming Lumber Dealers' Association and the Lumbermen's Secretaries' Bureau of Information.* Bill in equity filed at Denver, Colo., Sept. 25, 1911, for injunction against defendants for conspiracy to restrain trade in lumber and its products. Testimony complete. Further action deferred awaiting decision of Eastern States Lumber Dealers' case.

45. *United States v. Willard G. Hollis et al.* Petition filed in October, 1911, at St. Paul, Minn., in the United States Circuit Court, against the Lumbermen's Secretaries' Bureau of Information, The Lumberman Publishing Company, and certain individuals, alleging conspiracy and combination in the lumber trade. Testimony complete. Further action deferred awaiting decision of Eastern States Lumber Dealers' case. The case was finally argued in Dec., 1914.

46. *United States v. United States Steel Corporation and others.* Petition for injunction and dissolution filed at Trenton, N. J., Oct. 27, 1911. Thirty-seven cases. Issues joined and testimony on behalf of Government has been taken. The case was argued during Oct., 1914. On June 3, 1915, a decision adverse to the government was handed down, and on Sept. 10, 1915, a decree was entered dismissing the petition. An appeal has been taken to the Supreme Court.

47. *United States v. Joe Cotton et al.* Defendants were, on Nov. 15, 1911, indicted in the Southern District of Mississippi for conspiring to restrain interstate commerce during course of a strike on the Illinois Central Railroad. The strike having been terminated, no further action has been taken.

48. *United States v. National Cash Register Co. et al.* Petition filed December 4, 1911, in Circuit Court, Southern District of Ohio, alleging conspiracy and monopoly in the manufacture, sale, and shipment of cash registers and other registering devices. Issue joined and taking of testimony will shortly be commenced. Delay due to prosecution of criminal case. The verdict was against 29 of the 30 defendants. Fines aggregating $135,000 and jail sentences varying in length between nine months and a year were imposed by the court. The defendants appealed, and the appeal was argued before the Circuit Court in October, 1914. The civil case awaits the disposition of the appeal in the criminal case. In March, 1915, the court of appeals reversed the judgment of the lower court. The government made application to the Supreme Court for a writ of certiorari, which was denied on June 14, 1915.

In the civil case, a decree was entered on Feb. 1, 1916, finding that the defendants had violated the provisions of the anti-trust act. The decree forbids the use of any of the means to that end which it enumerates—the defendants consenting to the entry of the decree. The criminal proceedings were dropped, after a decision unfavorable to the government had been handed down by the Court of Appeals.

49. *United States v. United Shoe Machinery Co. et al.* Petition in equity filed Dec. 12, 1911, in Circuit Court, District of Massachusetts, alleging combinations and conspiracies in restraint of interstate and foreign trade in shoe machinery, and praying for perpetual restraining order, dissolution of company, and restoration of normal conditions. Testimony now being taken in open court. The trial was completed in June, 1914, on the result of which will depend the criminal action to be taken. In March, 1915, a decision adverse to the government was handed down, and an appeal was taken to the Supreme Court.

50. *United States v. A. Haines et al.* Two indictments returned Dec. 16, 1911, in the Southern District of Florida against members of Longshoremen's Association for combining, conspiring, and agreeing to interfere with interstate operations of the Mason Forwarding Company which had declined to recognize one of the conspirators known as the "walking delegate." See note to following case.

51. *United States v. A. Haines et al.* Two indictments returned Dec. 16, 1911, in the Southern District of Florida for combining, conspiring, and agreeing upon rules, regulations, requirements, etc., with reference to the employment of workmen to load vessels with lumber for interstate shipment.

NOTE.—Two above cases consolidated for trial. Defendants entered pleas of guilty and were sentenced each to four hours' confinement.

52. *United States v. Pacific Coast Plumbing Supply Association et al.* Petition filed Dec. 18, 1911, in Circuit Court, Southern District of California, alleging unlawful restraint of trade and commerce in plumbing supplies on the Pacific coast. Decree enjoining defendants from further committing the acts complained of was entered Jan. 6, 1912.

53. *United States v. The Keystone Watch Case Company et al.* Petition filed Dec. 20, 1911, in the Circuit Court, Eastern District of Pennsylvania, alleging unlawful contracts, combinations, and conspiracies to monopolize trade in filled watch cases and watches, and praying for a permanent decree ordering the dissolution of the company and enjoining defendants from further committing the unlawful acts complained of. Issues joined, taking of testimony completed, and the case is now ready for trial. The case was argued in June, 1914. In January, 1915, a decision was handed down, partly favorable and partly unfavorable to the government, and a decree in conformity thereto was entered in June, 1915, from which both the government and the defendants have appealed to the Supreme Court.

54. *United States v. American Naval Stores Company et al.* Petition filed Jan. 8, 1912, in the District Court, Southern District of Georgia, alleging unlawful combination and conspiracy in restraint of interstate and foreign commerce in turpentine and resin. Demurrer overruled Jan. 2, 1913. Defendant suspended business in March, 1913, on account of financial difficulties, and since then no further action has been taken.

55. *United States v. New Departure Manufacturing Company et al.* Indictment returned Jan. 8, 1912, in the Western District of New York against six corporations and eighteen individual defendants, charging unlawful combination and conspiracy for the purpose of monopolizing the coaster-brake business, and fixing and maintaining prices for coaster brakes. Plea in abatement overruled April 2, 1912. Demurrer overruled March 12, 1913. Defendants entered pleas of guilty and nolo contendere and fines aggregating $81,500 were imposed in May, 1913.

56. *United States v. The North Pacific Wharves & Trading Co. et al.* Indictment

returned Feb. 12, 1912, in the First Division, District of Alaska, charging defendants with conspiring to monopolize and monopolizing the coal business at Skagway. Demurrer sustained May 3, 1912.

57. *United States v. Pacific & Arctic Railway & Navigation Co. et al.* Indictment returned Feb. 12, 1912, in the First Division, District of Alaska, charging defendants with engaging in a conspiracy to monopolize and monopolizing the transportation business between the head of Lynn Canal and the headwaters of the Yukon River. Demurrer sustained on May 3, 1912.

58. *United States v. The North Pacific Wharves & Trading Co. et al.* Indictment returned Feb. 12, 1912, in the First Division, District of Alaska, charging defendants (1) with engaging in a conspiracy and combination in restraint of trade and commerce by way of combining the four wharves at Skagway under one management, and (2) with monopolizing the wharfinger business at Skagway. Demurrer overruled on May 3, 1912. First trial resulted in disagreement of jury on Jan. 27, 1913. In February, 1914, the defendant corporations entered pleas of guilty and paid fines aggregating $19,500. Indictments dismissed as to individual defendants.

59. *United States v. Pacific & Arctic Railway & Navigation Co. et al.* Indictment returned Feb. 13, 1912, in the First Division, District of Alaska, charging defendants with engaging in a conspiracy to monopolize and monopolizing the steamship transportation between Puget Sound and British Columbia ports in the south and Skagway in the north. Demurrer sustained, except as to corporation defendants to count No. 6. Upon appeal to the Supreme Court the judgment was reversed and the case remanded for further proceedings. In Feb., 1914, the defendant corporations entered pleas of guilty and paid fines aggregating $8,500. Indictment dismissed as to individual defendants.

60. *United States v. John H. Patterson et al.* Indictment returned Feb. 22, 1912, in the Southern District of Ohio, against John H. Patterson, president, and twenty-nine other officials and employees of the National Cash Register Company, alleging a conspiracy in restraint of interstate trade and commerce in cash registers, resulting in an unlawful monopoly of the industry. Demurrer overruled June 26, 1912. Trial resulted in a verdict of guilty as to twenty-nine of the thirty defendants and fines aggregating $135,000 and jail sentences ranging from nine months to one year were imposed. The defendants appealed, and the Court of Appeals annulling two of the three counts of the indictment and restricting the third very narrowly, the prosecution was dropped.

61. *United States v. American-Asiatic Steamship Company et al.* Petition in equity filed March 30, 1912, in Southern District of New York, charging defendants with combining and conspiring, entering into unlawful contracts and pooling agreements, and allowing rebates, for the purpose of securing a monopoly of the business of transporting freight between ports on the Atlantic coast of the United States and ports in the Philippine Islands, Japan, China, and the Far East. Issue joined. Taking of testimony on behalf of Government nearing completion. In Feb., 1915, a decision unfavorable to the government was handed down, and an appeal was taken to the Supreme Court.

62. *United States v. Julius F. Miller, Secretary, New York Charcoal Company et al.* Indictment returned April 2, 1912, in the Eastern District of New York charg-

ing defendants with restraining interstate trade and commerce in charcoal. Demurrer sustained Oct. 17, 1912.

63. *United States v. International Harvester Company et al.* Petition filed April 30, 1912, in the District Court, District of Minnesota, alleging the acquisition and maintenance of a monopoly in harvesting and agricultural machinery and implements and twine. Testimony taken, expediting certificate filed, and case argued before three circuit judges at St. Paul during November, 1913. On August 12, 1914, the court decided in favor of the government and a dissolution was ordered. The defendants appealed to the Supreme Court. The appeal was argued in April, 1915, and on June 2, 1915, the Supreme Court ordered the case restored to the docket for re-argument at the fall term, 1915, when a decision favorable to the government was handed down. An appeal was taken to the Supreme Court.

64. *United States v. Aluminum Company of America.* Petition filed May 16, 1912, in the District Court, Western District of Pennsylvania, to prevent a further monopoly of and restraint upon the interstate and foreign trade and commerce in aluminum and aluminum wares. Consent decree granting relief substantially as prayed for was entered at Pittsburgh on June 7, 1912.

65. *United States v. Herman Sielcken et al.* Petition filed May 18, 1912, in the District Court, Southern District of New York, alleging conspiracy to reduce the production of coffee, especially in the State of São Paulo, Brazil, and to withdraw a large per cent. of coffee from the market by purchase. Motion for preliminary injunction denied. Upon the advice of the State Department that representations had been made by the Brazilian Government that the entire quantity of coffee which was being withheld from market had been sold to a large number of dealers throughout the United States, an order of dismissal was entered May 29, 1913.

66. *United States v. Prince Line (Limited) et al.* Petition filed June 5, 1912, in the District Court, Southern District of New York, charging defendants, as common carriers of freight and passengers between ports of the United States and ports in the Republic of Brazil, with acquiring and maintaining a substantial monopoly by means of contracts, rebates, and other unlawful acts, and praying for an annulment of said contracts, agreements, etc. Issue joined and testimony in chief on behalf of Government has been introduced. In Feb., 1915, a decision unfavorable to the government was handed down, and an appeal was taken to the Supreme Court.

67. *United States v. Central-West Publishing Co. et al.* Petition filed August 3, 1912, in the District Court, Northern District of Illinois, charging defendants with engaging in unfair competition against each other and against others engaged in competing industries, with the intent to restrain and monopolize interstate trade and commerce in plate and ready-print matter. Consent decree granting relief as prayed for entered at Chicago on Aug. 3, 1912.

68. *United States v. Associated Billposters and Distributors of the United States and Canada et al.* Petition filed Aug. 3, 1912, in the District Court, Northern District of Illinois, charging defendants with engaging in a combination and conspiracy to place unlawful restraints upon interstate and foreign trade and commerce in posters. Hearing on demurrer set for Jan. 30, 1914. The demurrer was over-

ruled, the case tried, a decision favorable to the government handed down in March, 1916, and a decree granting the relief prayed for entered in July, 1916.

69. *United States v. Motion Picture Patents Company et al.* Petition filed Aug. 15, 1912, in the District Court, Eastern District of Pennsylvania, to remove the restraints which defendants have imposed upon interstate and foreign trade and commerce in machines, appliances, and apparatus relating to the motion-picture art, and upon persons engaged in such trade and commerce. The taking of testimony in chief on behalf of Government has been completed. The case was argued in Nov., 1914, and a decision favorable to the government was handed down on Oct. 1, 1915. A decree granting the relief prayed for was entered in January, 1916, from which the defendants have appealed to the Supreme Court.

70. *United States v. Calvin N. Payne et al.* Indictment returned August 29, 1912, in the Northern District of Texas, charging defendants with engaging in a conspiracy in restraint of interstate and foreign trade and commerce in oils and oil products. Nolle prosequi entered Feb. 25, 1913.

(15, 16, and 17 A.) *United States v. Consolidated Rendering Co.* Indictment returned Oct. 31, 1912, in the District of Massachusetts, charging monopoly of interstate trade and commerce in rendering materials. Dec. 1, 1913, plea of nolo contendere by defendant and fine of $5,000 imposed.

United States v. Consolidated Rendering Company et al. Indictment returned October 31, 1912, in the District of Massachusetts, charging monopoly of interstate trade and commerce in rendering materials. Dec. 1, 1913, plea of nolo contendere by corporation and fine of $3,000 imposed. Indictment nolle prossed as to individual defendants.

NOTE.—These actions were instituted as a result of demurrers having been sustained in cases 15, 16, and 17, and are therefore not counted as additional cases.

71. *United States v. The Master Horseshoers' National Protective Association of America and others.* Petition filed Dec. 12, 1912, in the Eastern District of Michigan, charging defendants with engaging in a combination and conspiracy in restraint of trade and commerce in drilled horseshoes, adjustable calks, and rubber hoof pads. Some of the defendants did not contest, and decrees were entered against them. Demurrers of the others were overruled, whereupon they consented to the entry of a decree against them, which was filed in Jan., 1916, ordering a dissolution of the combination, and granting the relief sought by the government as to the several defendants.

72. *United States v. Philadelphia Jobbing Confectioners' Association et al.* Petition filed Dec. 13, 1912, in the Eastern District of Pennsylvania, charging defendants with unlawfully interfering with interstate commerce in candies and confections. Consent decree entered Feb. 17, 1913.

73. *United States v. Elgin Board of Trade et al.* Petition filed December 14, 1912, in the Northern District of Illinois, charging defendants with combining and conspiring in the interest of a number of large centralizing concerns to restrain interstate commerce in butter and butter fat, and arbitrarily fixing the price thereof to obtain throughout the United States. Issue joined and taking of testimony in open courts will be commenced on Jan. 8, 1914. On April 27, 1914, a decree was entered enjoining the defendants from continuing certain practises by which prices of butter over a large area were arbitrarily fixed.

74. *United States v. Charles S. Mellen, Edson J. Chamberlin, and Alfred W. Smithers.* Indictment returned December 23, 1912, in the Southern District of New York, charging a combination and conspiracy to restrain interstate commerce by preventing the construction of subsidiary lines of the Central Vermont Railway Company (itself a subsidiary of the Grand Trunk Railway Company) from Palmer, Mass., to Providence, R. I.; from White River Junction, Vt., to Boston; and from Boston to Blackstone, connecting there with the Palmer-Providence line. Case at issue awaiting trial.

75. *United States v. Kellogg Toasted Corn Flake Company et al.* Petition filed Dec. 26, 1912, in the Eastern District of Michigan, alleging that the business policy of the defendant company in fixing and enforcing resale prices on Kellogg's Toasted Corn Flakes is unlawful and tends to restrain and monopolize interstate commerce in said product. A motion to dismiss the petition on grounds involving the merits of the case was argued in July, 1914. In a decision handed down on April 14, 1915, the contention of the government was maintained and on Sept. 20, 1915, a decree was entered in accordance with the decision.

76. *United States v. Page et al.* Indictment returned Feb. 5, 1913, at Portland, District of Oregon, charging fifteen individuals, through the medium of the Produce Merchants' Exchange, of Portland, with unlawfully controlling the purchase, distribution, and sale of approximately 90 per cent. of the produce, fruit, and vegetables shipped into the State of Oregon. The defendants entered pleas of guilty on Feb. 21, 1913, and fines aggregating $8,450 were imposed and collected.

77. *United States v. Krentler-Arnold Hinge Last Company et al.* Petition filed Feb. 7, 1913, in the District Court, Eastern District of Michigan, alleging the unlawful control by defendant of the interstate trade and commerce in shoe and boot lasts, both patented and unpatented. Consent decree was entered at Detroit, Mich., on Feb. 7, 1913.

78. *United States v. United Shoe Machinery Company of New Jersey et al.* Petition filed Feb. 8, 1913, in the District Court at Trenton, N. J., seeking to have annulled an alleged unlawful contract involving "inseam trimming machines." The disposition of the case is awaiting the decision of the civil case in 49 (q. v.).

79. See No. 9.

80. *United States v. Board of Trade of the City of Chicago et al.* Petition filed Feb. 11, 1913, in the District Court at Chicago, Ill., attacking rule 33 of the Chicago Board of Trade, by virtue of which it is alleged the price of all corn, oats, wheat, and rye arriving in Chicago at times when the board of trade is not in session is arbitrarily determined. Motion to strike out certain portions of defendants' answer has been argued, and the ruling of the court is awaited. The ruling of the court was favorable, and a decision favorable to the government was handed down on Sept. 8, 1915. An appropriate decree was entered in December of the same year. An appeal has been taken to the Supreme Court.

81. *United States v. The Cleveland Stone Company et al.* Petition filed Feb. 12, 1913, in the District Court at Cleveland, Northern District of Ohio, charging defendants with establishing and maintaining a practical monopoly of the stone busi-

ness. Without contest, the case was disposed of by the entry of a decree on Feb. 11, 1916, granting the relief prayed for by the government.

82. *United States v. The Delaware, Lackawanna & Western Railroad Company and The Delaware, Lackawanna & Western Coal Company.* Petition filed February 13, 1913, in the District Court at Trenton, N. J., charging defendants with transporting coal in which it had an interest in violation of the commodities clause of the interstate-commerce act, and with entering into an unlawful contract whereby the Coal Company acquired a monopoly of the sale of anthracite coal produced along the line of the Railroad Company, in violation of the anti-trust act. The taking of testimony has been completed and brief is being prepared. Expediting certificate filed and case set for hearing on Jan. 27, 1914. On April 7, 1914, a decision adverse to the government was handed down and an appeal was taken to the Supreme Court. The Supreme Court unanimously reversed the decision of the lower court; and in pursuance to the Supreme Court mandate, the district court entered a decree on August 11, 1915, forbidding the railroad from further transporting in interstate commerce coal mined or purchased by it and purported to have been sold to the coal company under contract, and forbidding both the railroad and the coal company from further carrying out or enforcing the contract between them.

83. *United States v. The McCaskey Register Company et al.* Petition filed Feb. 20, 1913, in the District Court at Cleveland, Northern District of Ohio, charging defendants with conspiring to restrain and monopolize the manufacture and sale of account registers and appliances. The government concluded that the case was not well founded and the petition was dismissed without prejudice on January 7, 1915.

84. *United States v. International Brotherhood of Electrical Workers, Local Unions Nos. 9 and 134, et al.* Petition filed Feb. 24, 1913, in the District Court at Chicago, Northern District of Illinois, seeking to enjoin defendants from interfering with the interstate business of the Postal Telegraph-Cable Company. A temporary injunction was granted and was made permanent on February 27, 1914.

85. *United States v. Corn Products Refining Company et al.* Petition filed March 1, 1913, in the District Court at New York City, charging defendants with monopolizing interstate trade and commerce in corn products, and praying for the dissolution of the combination. A decision favorable to the government was handed down on June 24, 1916, and a final decree entered on Nov. 13, 1916.

86. *United States v. The American Thread Company et al.* Petition filed March 3, 1913, in the District Court at Trenton, N. J., charging defendants with monopolizing the thread industry. Answers of defendants filed Sept. 10, 1913. On June 2, 1914, a decree was entered dissolving the combination between the American Thread Company and J. and P. Coats, Lim., and affiliated corporations, and enjoining them from engaging in certain unfair trade practises against independent manufacturers of threads.

87. *United States v. The Burroughs Adding Machine Company et al.* Petition filed March 3, 1913, in the District Court at Detroit, Mich., alleging that defendants were engaged in a conspiracy to monopolize interstate trade and commerce in adding machines. A consent decree was entered at Detroit on March 3, 1913.

88. *United States v. American Coal Products Company et al.* Petition filed March 3, 1913, in the District Court at New York City, charging defendants with monopolizing the supply of coal tar and restraining the trade of competitors in the purchase of coal tar and in the manufacture and sale of tarred roofing felts, coal-tar pitch, and other coal-tar products. A consent decree was entered on March 4, 1913.

89. *United States v. Terminal Railroad Association of St. Louis et al.* Petition filed March 4, 1913, in the District Court at St. Louis, Eastern District of Missouri, alleging a conspiracy on the part of the members of the St. Louis Coal Traffic Bureau to suppress and eliminate competition in various rates for the transportation of soft coal from the State of Illinois to the city of St. Louis, Mo. The new rates imposed by the carriers were upheld by the Interstate Commerce Commission on Jan. 29, 1915, and the case hence was dismissed without prejudice on Sept. 20, 1915, without going into the question of the existence of a combination.

90 *United States v. Allen Brothers Company et al.* Petition filed April 16, 1909, in the Circuit Court, Southern district of New York, against a number of paper manufacturers for entering into a combination in restraint of trade and commerce (known as the F. & M. Association) with respect to the manufacture, price, sale, shipment and distribution of fibre, manila and other papers. A decree ordering the dissolution of the Association, enjoining the members from further participation therein, was entered May 10, 1909.

PRESIDENT WILSON'S ADMINISTRATION

[James C. McReynolds, Attorney-General, March 4, 1913—Aug. 19, 1914; Thomas W. Gregory, Aug. 19, 1914—.]

1. *United States v. The New Departure Manufacturing Company et al.* Petition filed May 27, 1913, in the District Court at Rochester, Western District of New York, alleging that defendants entered into a conspiracy and combination and devised a license agreement for the purpose of restraining and monopolizing the manufacture and sale of bicycle and motorcycle parts and coaster brakes. An agreed decree was entered at Rochester on May 27, 1913.

2. *United States v. White et al.* Indictment returned June 7, 1913, in the District Court for the Southern District of West Virginia, against nineteen members of the United Mine Workers of America, alleging a conspiracy to interfere with interstate commerce in coal mined in West Virginia. The case was *nolle prossed* on June 20, 1914, it having been instituted by a district attorney without authority and being without foundation.

3. *United States v. Eastman Kodak Company et al.* Petition filed June 9, 1913, in the District Court at Buffalo, Western District of New York, alleging that defendants have acquired a monopoly of the business of manufacturing, selling, and distributing photographic supplies. A decision favorable to the government was handed down on Aug. 24, 1915, and a decree granting the relief sought was entered in Jan., 1916. An appeal was taken to the Supreme Court.

4. *United States v. The Quaker Oats Company et al.* Petition filed June 11, 1913, in the District Court at Chicago, Ill., alleging combination to restrain and monopolize interstate trade and commerce in oatmeal products and by-products. By a two to one vote of the three circuit judges sitting for the case under the expediting

act, a decision unfavorable to the government was rendered, and an appeal has been taken to the Supreme Court.

5. *United States v. Hippen et al.* Indictment returned June 25, 1913, in the District Court for the Western District of Oklahoma against The Oklahoma Brokerage Company and two other corporations and the officers thereof, alleging a conspiracy to restrain and monopolize interstate trade and commerce in fruits and vegetables. Demurrer sustained Oct. 1, 1913.

6. *United States v. Thompson et al.* Indictment returned July 1, 1913, in the District Court for the Southern District of New York alleging that the defendants conspired to run a corner in cotton on the New York Cotton Exchange. Defendants entered pleas of nolo contendere in December, 1913, and fines aggregating $18,000 were assessed.

7. *United States v. American Telephone & Telegraph Company et al.* Petition filed July 24, 1913, in the District Court at Portland, Ore., seeking to destroy a monopoly of the telephone business on the Pacific Coast. Issue joined and taking of testimony on behalf of Government is nearing completion. The defendants agreed to meet the demands of the government and a decree sustaining the petition was entered on March 26, 1914.

By the terms of the decree, the defendant disposes of its holdings in the Western Union Telegraph Company so as to make the control of the latter quite independent. The defendant agrees not to make any further direct or indirect acquisition of competing telephone companies. And the defendant agrees to connect its long-distance wires with the local exchanges of independent companies.

8. *United States v. Reading Company et al.* (Anthracite coal combination.) Petition in equity filed Sept. 2, 1913, in the District Court at Philadelphia, Pa., against a combination consisting of Reading Company and affiliated corporations, charging it with restraining and monopolizing trade in anthracite coal. The case was argued in June, 1914. On July 3, 1915, a decision partly favorable and partly unfavorable to the government was handed down, and an appeal to the Supreme Court was taken.

9. *United States v. The National Wholesale Jewelers' Association et al.* Petition filed Nov. 18, 1913, in the District Court at New York City, charging defendants with conspiring to eliminate all competition—except as between wholesalers or jobbers—for the trade of all classes of retail dealers in jewelry and jewelry products. A decree favorable to the government was granted Jan. 30, 1914.

10. *United States v. American Can Company et al.* Petition filed Nov. 29, 1913, in the District Court at Baltimore, Md., alleging monopolization of the business of making tin cans. On July 7, 1916, the district court entered a decree adjudging that the American Can Company was a combination in restraint of trade, but since the only relief granted by the court was the retention of the bill (i. e., keeping the combination under the supervision of the court), an appeal was taken to the Supreme Court.

11. *United States v. John P. White et al.* Indictment returned Dec. 1, 1913, in the District Court, Pueblo, Colo., charging officials and members of the United Mine Workers of America with monopolizing all diggers of coal and mine laborers and with restraining interstate commerce in coal. The case was nolle prossed on Jan. 8, 1916.

12. *United States v. Frank J. Hayes et al.* Indictment returned Dec. 1, 1913, in the District Court, Pueblo, Colo., charging a combination and conspiracy by mine workers to interfere with the mining of coal in Colorado and its transportation to and sale in other states. The case was nolle prossed on Jan. 8, 1916.

13. *United States v. Southern Pacific Company, Central Pacific Railway Company et al.* Petition in equity filed Feb. 11, 1914, in the District Court at Salt Lake City, Utah, to compel the Southern Pacific to relinquish its control of the Central Pacific. The case was argued in Dec., 1915.

14. *United States v. Lehigh Valley Railroad Company et al.* Petition filed March 18, 1914, in the District Court at New York City, N. Y., charging the defendants with having monopolized the production, transportation and sale of anthracite coal from mines tributary to Lehigh Valley Railroad Company in violation of the Anti-Trust Act, and charging the said Railroad Company with transporting in interstate commerce coal in which it has an interest, in violation of the Commodity Clause of the Act to Regulate Commerce. A decision adverse to the government was handed down in Dec., 1914, and an appeal to the Supreme Court was taken.

15. *United States v. Knauer et al.* Indictment returned June 4, 1914, at Des Moines, Southern District of Iowa, charging defendants with having entered into a combination in restraint of trade in plumbing supplies.

In Feb., 1915, a verdict of guilty was handed down. The defendants made a motion for a new trial. The judge imposed fines aggregating $4,000 against 4 of the defendants and granted a writ of error as to them; and pending a decision by the Court of Appeals, ordered the case to stand in the motion for a new trial as to the remaining 31 defendants. In an opinion filed Sept. 16, 1916, the Circuit Court of Appeals for the Eighth District sustained the conviction.

16. *United States v. The American Wringer Company et al.* Indictment returned May 22, 1914, in the District Court for the Western District of Pennsylvania, charging defendants with unlawfully engaging in a combination in restraint of interstate trade and commerce in clothes wringers. On Nov. 13, 1914, the defendants entered pleas of nolo contendere and were fined $6,000.

17. *United States v. Booth Fisheries Company et al.* Indictment returned July 20, 1914, in the District Court at Seattle, Wash., charging defendants with entering into a combination and conspiracy in restraint of interstate trade and commerce in fresh fish.

18. *United States v. The New York, New Haven & Hartford Railroad Company et al.* Petition filed July 23, 1914, in the District Court for the Southern District of New York, alleging monopolization of transportation facilities in New England and praying for a dissolution thereof. Because of the shaky financial condition of the railroad affected, and of the consequent danger to the investment markets and to the business conditions of New England, litigation was avoided and the following plan of voluntary dissolution was incorporated in a final decree entered Oct. 17, 1914.

1—The agreement between the New Haven Company and the New York Central Railroad for the joint operation of the Boston and Albany Railroad was canceled. 2—The New Haven Company gave up control of the Boston and Maine Railroad. 3—The New Haven Company disposed of its interests in trolley lines of New England.

4—The New Haven Company disposed of its interests in steamship lines between New England ports and New York, Philadelphia, Baltimore and other Atlantic sea-ports. 5— The question of the retention of control by the New Haven Company over steamship lines on Long Island Sound was submitted for determination to the Interstate Commerce Commission according to the provisions of the Panama Canal Act.

The criminal aspects of the case were not neglected and indictments were returned against 21 officers and directors of the New Haven Company. (See 23.)

19. *United States v. Western Cantaloupe Exchange et al.* Indictment returned Aug. 7, 1914, in the District Court at Chicago, Northern District of Illinois, charging defendants with having entered into a combination to restrain and monopolize interstate trade in cantaloupes.

20. *United States v. Collins et al.* An indictment was returned in the district court for the District of Columbia on Sept. 4, 1914, against 31 commission merchants, charging them with engaging in a combination to fix arbitrarily and without competition the prices at which country produce is bought and sold in the District of Columbia. A demurrer was overruled on May 1, 1915. In December of the same year, the defendants entered pleas of *nolo contendere*, and were fined $650.00 by the court.

21. *United States v. McCoach et al.* An indictment was returned Oct. 5, 1914, in the district court for the western district of Pennsylvania, charging 33 individuals, each a master plumber and a retail dealer in plumbing supplies, with entering into a combination to secure a monopoly of the business of selling and installing plumbing supplies.

22. *United States v. Irving et al.* An indictment was returned on Oct. 31, 1914, in the district court for the district of Utah, charging 14 individuals, each a master plumber and a retail dealer in plumbing supplies, with entering into a combination to restrain trade in plumbing supplies. A demurrer and motion to quash were denied in January, 1915. In September, 1916, the jury returned a verdict of guilty against 12 of the defendants, who paid the fines aggregating $7,250 which were imposed by the Court.

23. *United States v. Rockefeller et al.* (See 18.) An indictment was returned on November 2, 1914, in the district court for the southern district of New York, charging 21 defendants, each at some time a director or an officer of the New York, New Haven and Hartford Railroad, with conspiring to monopolize the transportation facilitise of New England. After numerous demurrers and pleas in abatement had been disposed of, the case went to a trial, and on Jan. 9, 1916, the jury returned a verdict of not guilty against 6 of the defendants and disagreed concerning the 5 others.

24. *United States v. Isaac E. Chapman et al.* An indictment was returned on Jan. 27, 1915, in the district court for the southern district of New York, charging the defendants with combining and conspiring to monopolize interstate trade and commerce in the derrick, lighterage and wrecking business in New York harbor and its environs and along the Atlantic coast of the United States. A demurrer was sustained on April 13, 1915.

25. *United States v. Carl C. King et al.* (Aroostook Potato Shippers Association.) An indictment was returned on March 4, 1915, in the district court for the district of Massachusetts, charging the defendants with entering into a combination and conspiracy in restraint of trade in potatoes. A demurrer was overruled and a verdict of guilty was returned on Oct. 10, 1916.

26. *United States v. Michael Artery et al.* Eight indictments were returned in the district court for the northern district of Illinois in Jan. and Apr., 1915, against certain so-called business agents of Chicago labor unions, charging them with combining and conspiring to prevent in Chicago the unloading of goods shipped from other states. Demurrers were overruled.

27. *United States v. Michael Boyle et al.* On Apr. 27, 1915, two indictments were returned in the district court for the northern district of Illinois, charging a conspiracy among labor unions and certain manufacturers in Chicago to prevent the installation in Chicago of electrical appliances and lighting fixtures manufactured elsewhere. Demurrers were argued and overruled.

28. *United States v. S. F. Bowser & Co. (Inc.) et al.* A petition was filed June 10, 1915, in the district court for the district of Indiana, charging the defendants with combining to restrain and attempting to monopolize interstate trade and commerce in pumps, tanks and outfits for the storage and handling of gasoline and other inflammable materials. A decree granting the relief sought by the government was entered simultaneously with the decree, the defendants not contesting.

29. *United States v. United Shoe Manufacturing Company et al.* A petition was filed Oct. 18, 1915, in the district court for the eastern district of Missouri, charging that the so-called tying clauses in the series of leases used by the defendants in the conduct of their business violated section 3 of the Clayton Act. A temporary restraining order was granted at the time the petition was filed, and an application for a preliminary injunction was argued Oct. 27 and granted Nov. 12, 1915. A motion to dismiss the petition, on grounds largely involving the merits of the case, was overruled.

30. *United States v. Rintelen, Buchanan et al.* An indictment was returned on Dec. 28, 1915, in the district court for the southern district of New York, charging the defendants with conspiring to restrain, prevent and hinder foreign commerce in military supplies and stores. A motion to quash was overruled on June 29, 1915. Certain of the defendants residing in the District of Columbia instituted proceedings to resist their removal to New York.

31. *United States v. Franz Bopp et al.* On Feb. 11, 1916, an indictment was returned against the defendants in the district court for the northern district of California, charging them with conspiring to restrain and destroy interstate and foreign commerce of the United States in munitions of war, etc. Demurrers and motions to quash were denied on March 30, 1916.

32. *United States v. Cowell et al.* An indictment was returned on October 27, 1916, in the district court for the district of Oregon, charging officers and agents of nine cement manufacturing companies with engaging in a combination to restrain and with monopolizing interstate trade and commerce in cement on the Pacific coast. The indictment charges the defendants with apportioning territory and maintaining uniform prices.

INDEX TO ANTI-TRUST CASES

President Harrison's Administration

Name   Number of case
Cash Register Case 6
Corning, in re ....2 A
Distilling and Cattle Feeding Co........2
Greene, in re ....2 C
Greenhut et al..........................2
Jellicoe Mountain Coal Co.............1
Knight Company, E. C................7
Nashville Coal Exchange 1
Nelson 3
Patterson et al 6
Sugar Trust 7
Terrell, in re.........................2 B
Trans-Missouri Freight Association.....4
Whisky Trust 2
Workingmen's Amalgamated Council of
  New Orleans 5

President Cleveland's Administration.

Name   Number of case
Addystone Pipe and Steel Company 7
Agler ....1 A
Cassidy 4
Cast Iron Pipe Trust 7
Debs et al ....1, 3, 3 A, 3 B
Elliott 2
Hopkins et al 8
Joint Traffic Association 6
Kansas City Live Stock Exchange......8
Moore 5

President McKinley's Administration.

Name   Number of case
Anderson 1
Chesapeake and Ohio Fuel Co.........3
Coal Dealers' Association 2
Traders' Live Stock Exchange 1

President Roosevelt's Administration.

Name   Number of case
Allen and Robinson et al..............12
American Ice Co. et al...............17
American Naval Stores Co. et al......42
American Seating Co. et al........26, 27
American Tobacco Co. et al............32
Amsden, F. A., Lumber Co. et al......14
Armour & Co. et al....................7
Atlantic Investment Co. et al.........25
Beef Packers (Beef Trust) 2, 7, 9, 22
Chandler Ice and Cold Storage Plant....18
Cigarettes Case 34
Coal Cases 29, 36
Corbett, H. D., Stationery Co. et al...35
Demund Lumber Co. et al..............21
Druggists Cases 15
du Pont de Nemours Co................33
Eads Bridge Case 11
Elevator Trust 13
Federal Salt Co. et al..............3, 4
Fertilizer Case 16
Furniture Cases 26, 27, 32
General Paper Co. et al...............6
Gloyd, Alfred M., et al...............19
Great Northern Railroad 1
Hale v. Henkel ....8 A
Harriman Railroad Lines 38
Hogg, T. B., et al...................24
Ice Trust 17, 18, 20
Jacksonville Wholesale Grocers' Asso-
  ciation 5
Licorice Paste Case 8
Lumber Cases 12, 14, 19, 21, 24
MacAndrews and Forbes Co. et al......8
McAlister v. Henkel ....8 A
Meat Packers 2, 7, 9, 22
Merchants' Bridge Case 11
Metropolitan Meat Co. et al..........9
National Association of Retail Druggists.15
National Umbrella Frame Co..........30

New York, New Haven & Hartford R. R.
  et al 43
Nome Retail Grocers Association 10
Northern Pacific R. R. 1
Northern Securities Co...............1
Otis Elevator Co. et al..............13
Papers Cases 6, 44
Parks, John H., et al................44
People's Ice & Fuel Co..............20
Phoenix Wholesale Meat and Produce Co.22
Plumbers Supplies Cases...........37, 41
Powder Trust 33
Railroad Cases 38, 43
Ray, E. J., et al................39, 40
Reading Company et al...............29
Retail Druggists Case 15
Salt Trust 3
Santa Rita Mining Co. and Santa Rita
  Store Co. 28
Simmons, Chas. L., et al. 37
Stafford, E. H., Manufacturing Co. et al..32
Standard Oil Company 23
Stationery Case 35
Stiefvater, Joseph, et al............41
Swift and Co. et al..................2
Terminal Railroad Association of St.
  Louis 11
Tobacco Trust ....8 A, 31
Turpentine Cases 25, 42
Umbrella Case 30
Union Pacific R. R. Co. et al........38
Virginia-Carolina Chemical Co. et al...16

President Taft's Administration.

Name   Number of case
Adding Machine Cases................87
Albia Box and Paper Co............2, 23
Allen Brothers Co. et all 90
Aluminum Company of America........64
American-Asiatic Steamship Co. ....\..61
American Coal Products Co...........88
American Naval Stores Co............54
American Sugar Refining Co........1, 19
American Thread Co..................86
Armour Packing Co...................7
Associated Billposters and Distributors
  of the U. S. and Canada 68
Blackwell Milling and Elevator Co.....42
Burroughs Adding Machine Co.......87
Cash Register Case 60
Central-West Publishing Co...........67
Charcoal Case 62
Chesapeake and Ohio R. R. et al......39
Chicago Board of Trade 80
Chicago Butter and Egg Board........11
Cleveland Stone Co..................81
Coal Cases 56, 82, 89
Coal Tar Case 88
Coaster-Brake Case 55
Coffee Case 65
Colorado and Wyoming Lumber Dealers'
  Association 44
Confections Case 72
Consolidated Rendering Co. .15, 15-17 A, 17
Corn Products Refining Co...........85
Cotton, Joe, et al...................47
Cotton Pool Case.....................12
Delaware and Lackawanna Railroad and
  Delaware and Lackawanna Coal Co...82
Eastern States Retail Lumber Dealers' As-
  sociation 24
Electrical Workers' Union 84
Elgin Board of Trade 73
Enamel Ware Case 13, 18
F. and M. Association 90
Fine Magnet Wire Association 28-36
Folz, Frank 42
Freight Rate Cases 8, 57, 61
Geer, Wm. C., et al.................23
General Electric Co..................20
Great Lakes Towing Company.........10
Haines, A., et al..............50, 51
Hamburg-Amerikanische Packetfahrt Ac-
  tien Gesellschaft 22
Hapgood, Cyrus S...................17

Hayne, Frank; Patten, James A.; et al.12
Hartwick, Edward E., et al..........40
Heath, Horatio W...............16, 17
Hide and Rendering Cases......15, 16, 17
Hocking Valley Railroad et al........39
Hollis, Willard G..................45
Horseshoe Manufacturers Association.28-36
Hunter Milling Co..................42
Imperial Window Glass Co............ 4
International Brotherhood of Electrical
    Workers 84
International Harvester Co..........63
Kanawha & Michigan Railroad.........39
Kellogg Toasted Corn Flake Co.......75
Keystone Watch Case Co.............53
Kindling Wood Trust 41
Krentler-Arnold Hinge Last Co......77
Lake Shore & Michigan Southern R. R.
    et al......................39
Lead Encased Rubber Cable Associa-
    tion 28-36
Lumber Cases 40, 44, 45
Lumber Secretaries' Bureau of Informa-
    tion 27, 44, 45
Lumberman Publishing Co. 27
Magazine Trust 37
Master Horse-shoers National Protective
    Association of America 72
McCaskey Register Co...............83
Meat Packers Cases..........5, 6, 7, 14
Mellen, Charles S., et al...........74
Milk Cases 25, 26
Miller, Julius F..................62
Missouri Pacific and other railroads.... 8
Motion Picture Patents Co..........69
National Cash Register Co...........48
National Packing Co..............5, 6
New Departure Manufacturing Co......55
New York Charcoal Co..............62
Night Rider Case 3
North Pacific Wharves and Trading
    Co. 56, 58
Oil Case 70
Pacific and Arctic R. R. and Navigation
    Co. 57, 59
Pacific Coast Plumbing Supply Associa-
    tion 52
Page et al......................76
Paper Manufacturers Case 90
Parrington et al..................21
Patten, James A., et al............12
Patterson, John H., et al...........60
Payne, Calvin N..................70
Paving Brick & Stone Case..........21
Periodical Publishing Co...........37
Philadelphia Jobbing Confectioners 72
Pierce, J. B., et al...............38
Plumbing Supplies Case............52
Posters Case 68
Prince Line, Lim. 66
Railroad Cases 8, 39, 57, 66, 74, 89
Reardon, John and Sons Co.........15, 16
Rubber Covered Wire Association....28-36
St. Louis Terminal R. R. Association...89
Shoe Machinery Cases 43, 49, 78
Sielcken, Herman, et al............65
Smith, Philip H. W.............28-36
Southern Wholesale Grocers' Associa-
    tion 9, 79
Standard Sanitary Manufacturing Co. 13, 18
Standard Wood Co. et al............41
Steel Trust 46
Steers, John S., et al.............. 3
Stone Case 81
Sugar Trust 1, 19
Sulzberger, Ferdinand 16
Swift, Louis E., et al.............14
Telephone Cable Association 28-36
Terminal R. R. Association of St. Louis.89
Thread Cases 86
Toledo & Ohio Central R. R.........39
Trans-Atlantic Steamship Pool Case....22
Turpentine and Resin Case..........54
Underground Power Cable Association.28-36
United Shoe Machinery Co.........49, 78
United States Steel Corporation 46

Wall Paper Case 38
Watch Case Case 53
Whiting et al 25, 26
Window Glass Case 4
Winslow et al 43
Wire Rope Manufacturers 28-36
Zanesville and Western Railroad........39

President Wilson's Administration.

Name   Number of case
American Can Co..................10
American Telephone and Telegraph Co.. 7
American Wringer Co..............16
Anthracite Coal Cases 8, 14
Aroostook Potato Shippers Association..25
Artery, Michael, et al.............26
Booth Fisheries Co...............17
Bopp, Franz, et al...............31
Bowser, S. F., et al..............28
Boyle, Michael, et al.............27
Buchanan et al..................30
Camera Trust 3
Canteloupe Case 19
Cement Case 32
Central Pacific Railroad 13
Chapman, Isaac E., et al...........24
Clothes Wringer Case.............16
Collins et al...................20
Cotton Corner Case 6
Country Produce Case.............20
Cowell et al...................32
Eastman Kodak Co............... 3
Fish Case 17
Hayes, Frank J., et al............12
Hippen et al................... 5
Irving et al...................22
Jewelry Trust 9
King, Carl C., et al 25
Knauer et al...................15
Lehigh Valley Railroad et al........14
McCoach et al..................21
National Wholesale Jewelers Association 9
New Departure Manufacturing Co. et al.. 1
Oklahoma Brokerage Co............ 5
Plumbing Supplies Cases........15, 21, 22
Potatoes Case 25
Quaker Oats Co.................. 4
Reading Co. et al................ 8
Rintelen, Buchanan et al...........30
Rockefeller et al..............18, 23
Shoe Machinery Case 29
Southern Pacific Co. et al..........13
Telephone Trust 7
Thompson et al.................. 6
Tin Can Trust 10
United Mine Workers Cases.... 2, 11, 12
United Shoe Manufacturing Co........29
Western Canteloupe Exchange........19
White, John P., et al.............2, 11

Anti-Trust Law (see also Sherman
    Act, and Assistant to the Attorney-
    General.)

Amendment of, would control trusts
    and monopolies, 7916.

Amendments suggested, 7131, 7343.

Appropriations for enforcement of,
    needed, 6712.

Common stock ownership, 7650.

Confiscation not the purpose of the
    statute, 7649.

Definition of, to clarify, 8151.

Effectiveness of the decree, 7649.

Enforcement of, 6712, 6790, 6975,
    7073.

Explicit legislation under, 7910.

Federal corporation commission pro-
    posed, 7654.

Federal incorporation recommended,
    7652.

Force and effectiveness of statute a matter of growth, 7646.

Futile provisions of, pointed out, 7131.

Government administrative experts needed to aid courts in trust dissolutions, 7654.

Importaɪce of the Anti-Trust Act, 7655.

Incorporation voluntary, 7655.

Interlocking directorates, discussed, 7915.

Lack of definiteness in the statute, 7651.

Labor organizations should be exempt from, 7194.

Legislation needed to clarify, 7910.

Legislation urged, 7193.

Modifications of, needed, 7078.

Movement for repeal of, 7650.

New remedies suggested, 7651.

No change necessary in rule of decision, merely in the form of expression, 7645.

Opinion by Judge Hough cited, 7131.

Regulation of trusts by, need not hamper business interests, 7914.

Remedy in equity by dissolution, 7647.

Should be made clearer and fairer, 7910.

Situation after readjustment, 7647.

Size of new companies, 7648.

Strengthening of, 7191.

Supreme Court decisions on, cited by Taft, 7644.

Supplemental legislation needed, not repeal or amendment, 7652.

Taft message on, 7644.

Trust heads' attitude toward, 7126.

Uncertainty of, hampers business, 7916.

Voluntary reorganization of other trusts at hand, 7650.

Anti-Trust Legislation. (See also Roosevelt, Taft and Wilson, and Assistant to the Attorney-General.)

Advice and guidance of trade commission desired, 7916.

Co-operative groups of individuals, 7917.

Effect of uncertainty regarding, 7916.

Holding companies should be prohibited, 7917.

Individual punishment for business irregularities, 7917.

Individual suits should be based on government findings, 7918.

Individuals put out of business, 7918.

Industrial management usurped by investment bankers, 7915.

Interlocking directorates of corporations, 7915.

Monopoly indefensible and intolerable, 7915.

Not to unsettle business, 7914.

Principles of, discussed, 8040.

Production and transportation businesses, separation of, 7916.

Railroads, financing under Interstate Commerce Commission, 7915.

Railroads, harm done to, by financiers, 7915.

Statute of Limitations should run from conclusion of government suits, 7916.

Trade Commissions needed as guide to justice, 7916.

Trade Commission to direct corrective processes, 7917.

Trusts and monopolies, control of, 7913.

Antietam (Md.), Battle of.—After the severe engagement at South Mountain, Lee's army concentrated to the west of Antietam Creek, a small stream flowing into the Potomac River, eight miles above Harpers Ferry. Here, near the town of Sharpsburg, between the Potomac and the creek, Lee awaited the return of Jackson, who had been sent to capture Harpers Ferry. According to Federal accounts, Lee had not more than 25,000 men until Jackson's two divisions came up. Later he was joined by D. H. Hill's, McLaw's and Anderson's divisions. This raised the strength of Lee's command to over 45,000 combatants. Sept. 16, 1862, McClellan's army, about 70,000 strong, was re-enforced to 87,164, of which 4,320 were cavalry. About 60,000 of this force bore the brunt of the battle. On the evening of the 16th Hooker's division crossed the creek and began an attack, which darkness ended. Fighting was resumed at daylight on the 17th and continued all day, with varying success and terrific slaughter. Darkness again put an end to the carnage. McClellan did not renew the attack on the 18th, but orders were issued to resume fighting on the 19th. During the night of the 18th, however, the Confederates withdrew to the west of the Potomac and proceeded toward Martinsburg. A few days later McClellan occupied Martinsburg. The total loss of the Union army was 12,469 (2,010 killed) ; of the Confederates, 25,899. Other estimates of the Confederate loss are 9,000 to 12,000. The official Confederate accounts claim that this was a drawn battle, and that the total effective force of Lee was a little more than 35,000. This was called by the Confederates the battle of Sharpsburg. (See illustration opposite 3277.)

Antiquities, American, Preservation of.—Under the act of Congress approved June 8, 1906, interdepartmental regulations governing the excavation, appropriation, etc., of prehistoric ruins or objects of antiquity have been promulgated by the Secretaries of the Interior, Agriculture, and War. Applications for permits to make excavations on the public lands, Indian reservations, or the national monuments named below should be addressed to the Secretary of the Interior. The following have been reserved from entry and set aside as national monuments : Devils Tower, Wyoming ; Montezuma Castle, Arizona ; Petrified Forest, Arizona ; El Morro, New Mexico ; Chaco Canyon, New Mexico ; Muir Woods, California ;

Natural Bridges, Utah; Lewis and Clark Cavern, Montana; Tumacacori, Arizona; Navajo, Arizona; Mukuntuweap, Utah; Shoshone Cavern, Wyoming; Gran Quivira, New Mexico; Sitka National Monument, Alaska; Rainbow Bridge, Utah; Pinnacles, California; Colorado, Colorado. Eleven other national monuments within national forests have also been set aside under this act and placed under the jurisdiction of the Secretary of Agriculture, to whom inquiries in regard thereto should be addressed.

Antipodes.—Peoples living on the extreme opposite sides of the earth; so-called from the Greek words which mean "with feet opposite." Also, the opposite portions of the earth.

Apache Indians. (See Indian Tribes.)

Apalachicola Indians. (See Indian Tribes.)

Apollo, The, seizure of, by American Government referred to, 669.

Appeals, Courts of. (See Courts of Appeals.)

Appeals to a People Over the Head of Its Government.—Even in times of peace, there is precedent in American history for reaching the people of a foreign government in a matter where the United States has not been satisfied with its negotiations with that government itself. During the Civil War, President Lincoln, alarmed by the hostility of both the government of England and the English people to the cause of the North, sent Henry Ward Beecher to plead the cause of the North to popular meetings in England, with great success. In 1870, during the war between Germany and France, General Burnside made an offer to carry a suggestion from Bismarck to the French Government, although the offer was not accepted by the French.

Appointing Power of President. (See Executive Nominations.)

Appointment to Office. (See Executive Nominations.)

Appointments, Division of Postmasters, Post-Office Department.—This division falls under the supervision of the First Assistant Postmaster-General (q. v.). By order of President Wilson, effective April 1, 1917, all postmasterships in the Department of the Post-Office are placed under Civil Service. (See Civil Service; Civil Service Commission; Post-Office Department.)

Appomattox (Va.), Battle of.—After the battle of Farmville, April 7, 1865, Lee moved off toward the west, closely followed by Meade on the north side of the Appomattox. Sherman learning of the arrival of supply trains for Lee's Army at Appomattox Station, pushed forward for that place with all the cavalry. Lee's hopeless condition being now apparent, Grant sent him a note inviting surrender. Lee replied, asking for terms, and Grant insisted upon the unconditional surrender of the Confederate Army of Northern Virginia. On the night of April 8 Custer, who was in Sheridan's advance, reached Appomattox Station, where the Confederate advance had just arrived. He attacked the forces and captured 25 guns and 4 supply trains, a hospital train, and a park of wagons. During the night Sheridan came up, and by daylight was joined by Gen. Ord's command and the Fifth Corps. Lee was now only

20 miles from Lynchburg, his objective point. At first, underestimating the opposing forces, he ordered Gen. Gordon to make a reconnoissance and attack. Sheridan's cavalry withdrew to one side and revealed the lines of Ord's and Griffin's commands in line of battle. Gordon sent forward a white flag. Gen. Lee then dispatched a note to Gen. Grant requesting an interview, which being allowed closed with the signing of articles of surrender of Lee's army and camp followers, about 27,000 men. The officers and men were paroled April 12, and allowed to return to their homes. All public property was turned over, but the officers were allowed to keep their side arms and both officers and men to retain their private horses and baggage.

Apportionment.—The distribution of representation in the Federal House of Representatives and in the general assemblies of the various States. In the Continental Congress each State had but one vote. Long contention over the matter of representation finally led to the establishment of two Houses of Congress—the Senate, wherein all States should have equal representation regardless of area or population, and the House, in which each State should have representation in proportion to its population. President Washington vetoed a bill on this subject (116). A census was taken and 1 Representative was allowed for every 30,000 inhabitants. This rule governed apportionments for 70 years, though the ratio was changed from time to time as the population increased.

In order to keep the number of members of the House a fixed quantity, the Thirty-first Congress decided to divide the representative population by 233 after each census, and by the quotient thus obtained divide the representative population of each State. This gave the number of Representatives to which each State was entitled, and when the total number fell short of 233, Representatives were allowed the States having the largest fractions after division. According to the apportionment act of Jan. 16, 1901, it was provided that after March 3, 1903, the House should be composed of 386 members, to be chosen in districts composed of contiguous and compact territory and containing as nearly as practicable an equal number of inhabitants, each district electing one Representative. It was also provided that in case of an increase allowed any State, such additional ones shall be elected by the State at large until the State shall be redistricted; and that whenever a new State is admitted to the Union the Representative or Representatives assigned to it shall be in addition to the number 386. According to the census of 1900 the ratio of apportionment was 194,182, and as this gave only 384 Representatives, Nebraska and Virginia were each allowed one additional, making a total of 386 Representatives. (See also Gerrymander.)

By an act of Congress approved Aug. 8, 1911, the ratio of representation under the thirteenth census was fixed at one for each 212,407 of population, increasing the number of representatives to 435. The accompanying table shows the ratio of representation in each Congress under the Constitution:

Apportionment:

According to census of 1890 necessary, 5553.

Approved and reasons therefor, 2012. Vetoed, 116.

APPORTIONMENT OF CONGRESSIONAL REPRESENTATION

Ratios under Constitution and at each Census, 1790 to 1910, by States

State	Constitution	1790	1800	1810	1820	1830	1840	1850	1860	1870	1880	1890	1900	1910
(ratio)	30,000	33,000	33,000	35,000	40,000	47,700	70,680	93,423	127,381	131,425	151,911	173,901	194,182	212,407
							Representation							
Alabama				1	3	5	7	7	6	8	8	9	9	10
Arizona														1
Arkansas						1	1	2	3	4	5	6	7	7
California							2	2	3	4	6	7	8	11
Colorado										1	1	2	3	4
Connecticut	5	7	7	7	6	6	4	4	4	4	4	4	5	5
Delaware	1	1	1	2	1	1	1	1	1	1	1	1	1	1
Florida							1	1	1	2	2	2	3	4
Georgia	3	2	4	6	7	9	8	8	7	9	10	11	11	12
Idaho											1	1	1	2
Illinois				1	1	3	7	9	14	19	20	22	25	27
Indiana				1	3	7	10	11	11	13	13	13	13	13
Iowa							2	2	6	9	11	11	11	11
Kansas									1	3	7	8	8	8
Kentucky		2	6	10	12	13	10	10	9	10	11	11	11	11
Louisiana				1	3	3	4	4	5	6	6	6	7	8
Maine				*7	7	8	7	6	5	5	4	4	4	4
Maryland	6	8	9	9	9	8	6	6	5	6	6	6	6	6
Massachusetts	8	14	17	13	13	12	10	11	10	11	12	13	14	16
Michigan						1	3	4	6	9	11	12	12	13
Minnesota								2	2	3	5	7	9	10
Mississippi				1	1	2	4	5	5	6	7	7	8	8
Missouri					1	2	5	7	9	13	14	15	16	16
Montana											1	1	1	2
Nebraska									1	1	3	6	6	6
Nevada									1	1	1	1	1	1
N. Hampshire	3	4	5	6	6	5	4	3	3	3	2	2	2	2
New Jersey	4	5	6	6	6	6	5	5	5	7	7	8	10	12
New Mexico														1
New York	6	10	17	27	34	40	34	33	31	33	34	34	37	43
North Carolina	5	10	12	13	13	13	9	8	7	8	9	9	10	10
North Dakota											1	1	2	3
Ohio			1	6	14	19	21	21	19	20	21	21	21	22
Oklahoma														8
Oregon									1	1	1	2	2	3
Pennsylvania	8	13	18	23	26	28	24	25	24	27	28	30	32	36
Rhode Island	1	2	2	2	2	2	2	2	2	2	2	2	2	3
South Carolina	5	6	8	9	9	9	7	6	4	5	7	7	7	7
South Dakota											2	2	2	3
Tennessee		1	3	6	9	13	11	10	8	10	10	10	10	10
Texas							2	2	4	6	11	13	16	18
Utah												1	1	2
Vermont		2	4	6	5	5	4	3	3	3	2	2	2	2
Virginia	10	19	22	23	22	21	15	13	11	9	10	10	10	10
Washington											1	2	3	5
West Virginia										3	4	4	5	6
Wisconsin							2	3	6	8	9	10	11	11
Wyoming											1	1	1	1
Total	65	106	142	186	213	242	232	237	243	293	332	357	386	435

* Included in the 20 members originally assigned to Massachusetts, but credited to Maine after its admission as a State March 15, 1820.

Note—The following representation included in the table was added after the several census apportionments indicated: First—Tennessee, 1. Second—Ohio, 1. Third—Alabama, 1; Illinois, 1; Indiana, 1; Louisiana, 1; Maine, 7; Mississippi, 1. Fifth—Arkansas, 1; Michigan, 1. Sixth—California, 2; Florida, 1; Iowa, 2; Texas, 2; Wisconsin, 2. Seventh—Massachusetts, 1; Minnesota, 2; Oregon, 2. Eighth—Illinois, 1; Iowa, 1; Kentucky, 1; Minnesota, 1; Nebraska, 1; Nevada, 1; Ohio, 1; Pennsylvania, 1; Rhode Island, 1; Vermont, 1. Ninth—Colorado, 1. Tenth—Idaho, 1; Montana, 1; North Dakota, 1; South Dakota, 2; Washington, 1; Wyoming, 1. Eleventh—Utah, 1. Thirteenth—Alabama, 1; Arizona, 1; California, 3; Colorado, 1; Florida, 2; Georgia, 1; Idaho, 1; Illinois, 2; Louisiana, 1; Massachusetts, 2; Michigan, 1; Minnesota, 1; Montana, 1; New Jersey, 2; New Mexico, 1; New York, 6; North Dakota, 1; Ohio, 1; Oklahoma, 8; Oregon, 1; Pennsylvania, 4; Rhode Island, 1; South Dakota, 1; Texas, 2; Utah, 1; Washington, 2; West Virginia, 1.

Appropriations.—Article 1, section 7, clause 1, of the Constitution provides that "All bills for raising revenue shall originate in the House of Representatives"; a similar privilege has been claimed by the House in the case of appropriations of public money, but in this case the claim has not been insisted on. Previous to 1865 the appropriation bills were, in the House, considered by the Committee of Ways and Means, but in that year the Committee on Appropriations was formed. By a rule of the House and Senate, appropriation bills must include only items authorized by existing laws, and they cannot contain provisions changing existing laws. But this rule is frequently disregarded. These bills must be reported to the Committee of the Whole, and may be reported at any time, taking precedence of any other measures. This rule puts vast power into the hands of the chairman of the committee, and of late years this power has been used to choke discussion on the subject of the tariff, by withholding the report of the appropriation bills until the end of the session and then introducing them at a time when, the most urgent duties of Congress having been performed, that topic is most likely to come up for discussion. In the House the yeas and nays on the passage of these bills must be recorded. But bills are frequently passed under a suspension of this rule. In the Senate this is not necessary. The Appropriation Committee in that body was organized in 1867, the Finance Committee having previously had that matter in charge. The appropriation bills are made up from estimates furnished by the heads of the executive departments; these are usually much reduced in the House, and these estimates are again usually raised by the Senate (which body has less political capital to make out of a claim of economy) ; a compromise between the two usually results in appropriations considerably lower than the amount asked for by the department officers. This necessitates the passage, at the beginning of every session, of a bill to supply the deficiency of the previous appropriations; this bill is known as the Deficiency Bill.

Besides the appropriations there are "permanent annual appropriations," or money expended by the treasury by virtue of laws whose operation involves the expenditure without a specific appropriation renewed each year, as interest on the public debt. (See Riders.)

Arbitration (International) and Disarmament.

—The movement in behalf of universal peace between the nations has made great progress in recent years in the interest it has created and in the number and character of its advocates.

An International Peace Congress meets annually. Its eighteenth annual meeting, held at Stockholm in August, 1910, was attended by about 700 representatives of various countries. A "Palace of Peace" has been erected at The Hague through the munificence of Andrew Carnegie, and contributions to the adornment of this splendid building have come from all the principal countries. More recently Mr. Carnegie has donated a fund of $10,000,000, the revenue of which is to be used in the interests of peace.

A Permanent International Court of Arbitration was established at The Hague by a treaty of July, 1899, which was signed and later ratified by twenty-four powers. Representation in the court by non-signatory powers was provided for by protocol of June, 1907. The permanent court consists of men of recognized authority on in-

ternational law. The members on the part of the United States are Senator Elihu Root, John Bassett Moore, Judge George Gray and Hon. Oscar S. Straus. (See Hague Peace Conference.) A number of cases have been tried by this court—one of the most important being the Atlantic Fisheries Dispute, which threatened the friendly relations of Great Britain and Canada with the United States, and in which a satisfactory settlement was reached. (See Great Britain, Treaties with. Here, under the heading Arbitration, will be found the essential principles of all international arbitration treaties.)

The movement for disarmament, or the limitation of armaments, has made little material progress. It was opposed by Germany at The Hague Conference in 1907. Great Britain is willing to join the other powers in a plan to reduce armaments, provided they shall all agree to it, not otherwise. The Balkan Crisis in 1908, and the Italian-Turkish war have discouraged, if not, for the time being, destroyed, all hopes of any agreement between the powers to disarm, or reduce armaments, in the near future. The principle that to be prepared for war is the surest way to preserve peace is likely to be adhered to. The road to universal peace is evidently not yet in sight. What progress the movement for disarmament had made in the United States was completely nullified by the European war of 1914, and millions were spent to increase both army and navy. (See also Hague Peace Conference ; Peace, International.)

Between August 7, 1913, and September 15, 1914, the United States, through Secretary of State Bryan, signed peace treaties with the following 26 nations : Argentina, Bolivia, Brazil, Chile, China, Costa Rica, Denmark, Dominican Republic, England, France, Guatemala, Honduras, Italy, Netherlands, Nicaragua, Norway, Panama, Paraguay, Persia, Peru, Portugal, Salvador, Spain, Switerland, Uruguay, Venezuela.

The following text of the treaty with The Netherlands will serve to show the nature of all the "Bryan" treaties :

The President of the United States of America and her Majesty the Queen of The Netherlands, being desirous to strengthen the bonds of amity that bind them together and also to advance the cause of general peace, have resolved to enter into a treaty for that purpose, and to that end have appointed as their plenipotentiaries :

The President of the United States, the Honorable William Jennings Bryan, Secretary of State ; and

Her Majesty the Queen of The Netherlands, Chevalier W. L. F. C. Van Rappard, Envoy Extraordinary and Minister Plenipotentiary of The Netherlands to the United States ;

Who, after having communicated to each other their respective full powers, found to be in proper form, have agreed upon and concluded the following articles :

ARTICLE I

The High Contracting Parties agree that all disputes between them, of every nature whatsoever, to the settlement of which previous arbitration treaties or agreements do not apply in their terms or are not applied in fact, shall, when diplomatic methods of adjustment have failed, be referred for investigation and report to a permanent International Commission, to be constituted in the manner prescribed in the next succeeding article ; and they agree not to declare war or begin hostilities during such investigation and before the report is submitted.

ARTICLE II

The International Commission shall be composed of five members, to be appointed as follows: One member shall be chosen from each country, by the Government thereof; one member shall be chosen by each Government from some third country; the fifth member shall be chosen by common agreement between the two Governments, it being understood that he shall not be a citizen of either country. The expense of the Commission shall be paid by the two Governments in equal proportion.

The International Commission shall be appointed within six months after the exchange of the ratifications of this treaty; and vacancies shall be filled according to the manner of the original appointment.

ARTICLE III

In case the High Contracting Parties shall have failed to adjust a dispute by diplomatic methods, they shall at once refer it to the International Commission for investigation and report. The International Commission may, however, spontaneously offer its services to that effect, and in such case it shall notify both Governments and request their co-operation in the investigation.

The High Contracting Parties agree to furnish the Permanent International Commission with all the means and facilities required for its investigation and report.

The report of the International Commission shall be completed within one year after the date on which it shall declare its investigation to have begun, unless the High Contracting Parties shall limit or extend the time by mutual agreement. The report shall be prepared in triplicate; one copy shall be presented to each Government, and the third retained by the Commission for its files.

The High Contracting Parties reserve the right to act independently on the subject-matter of the dispute after the report of the Commission shall have been submitted.

ARTICLE IV

The present treaty shall be ratified by the President of the United States of America, by and with the advice and consent of the Senate thereof; and by her Majesty the Queen of The Netherlands; and the ratifications shall be exchanged as soon as possible. It shall take effect immediately after the exchange of ratifications, and shall continue in force for a period of five years; and it shall thereafter remain in force until twelve months after one of the High Contracting Parties have given notice to the other of an intention to terminate it.

In witness whereof, the respective plenipotentiaries have signed the present treaty and have affixed thereunto their seals. Done in Washington on the eighteenth day of December, in the year of our Lord nineteen hundred and thirteen.

As will be seen, when any dispute arises between the United States and one of the signatory nations which cannot be settled by diplomacy, it goes before a permanent international commission. This commission investigates and reports, having a year in which to accomplish its work. During this year, the nations are not allowed to declare war. When the report is made, the nations may disregard it, if they so desire; but the delay and the investigation, with their consequent sobering of international and national thought, should make a resort to arms extremely unlikely.

By Dec. 15, 1916, the following countries had been added to those listed above which have signed the peace treaties: Ecuador, Greece, Sweden and Russia.

According to La Fontaine, between 1821 and 1900, 281 treaties of arbitration had been signed by nations of the globe. According to Moch, of such treaties there were 194 in effect in 1909. In 1908, there were 80 treaties between nations making arbitration compulsory, and over 100 by the time of the European War.

According to Moch, from 1800 to 1904, 243 formal arbitrations took place, all of them successful; and Darby gives 297 other instances during this period in which the principle of arbitration was applied. The most important case of arbitration in United States history is that concerned with the *Alabama* claims (q. v.).

Among the treaties providing for unlimited and unqualified arbitration are those between Argentine and Chile, 1902; Denmark and Netherland, 1906; Denmark and Italy, 1906; Denmark and Portugal, 1907; Costa Rica, Honduras, Guatemala, Nicaragua, Salvador, 1907; Italy and Netherlands, 1909.

Arbitration, International:

Arbitration Court at Hague, United States and Mexico first to use, 6718.

Arbitration treaties, ratification asked, 7906.

Armaments, limitation of, discussed by President Taft, 7494.

Armaments, limitation of, necessary to perpetual peace, 8203.

Attitude of Great Britain and the United States discussed, 5874, 6154, 6178, 6241, 6267, 6432.

Convention with republics of South and Central America for arbitration of pecuniary claims, 7982.

Disarmament, naval, impossibility of, 7113.

Discussed by President—Roosevelt, 6923, 6993.

Interparliamentary union for, 6796.

Limitations of naval armaments, hopelessness of, 7113.

Failure of treaty of, referred to, 5623.

Movement for, among Powers, 7656.

Of Pecuniary Claims, convention with South and Central American Republics for, 7982.

Panama and Costa Rica, Colombia and Haiti, 7657.

Points of, agreed upon at Hague conference, 7118.

Ratification of treaties asked, 7906.

Relation of United States to movement for, 8285.

Reports adopted by International American Conference regarding, transmitted, 5518.

Referred to, 5623, 5874.

Treaty for, with Great Britain and France, transmitted, 7617.

Treaty of, with Germany, lack of, deplored, 8289.

Treaty with Great Britain regarding, discussed, 6178, 6242, 6380.

United States vs. Mexico, report of Hague Tribunal on, 6731.

Venezuelan claims submitted to Hague Tribunal, 6717, 6731, 6993.

World Court long the hope and ideal of America, 8285.

Arbitration (Labor).—Submitting disputed points of agreement between employers and employees to a joint committee, composed of representatives of both parties, has been found effective in reducing the number of costly strikes and lockouts, so frequent a few years ago. An equal number of arbitrators is usually selected by each of the parties to the dispute, these in turn selecting an odd member of the commission. The method of procedure is usually prescribed by trade agreements between labor organizations and employers. Arbitration and conciliation are usually brought about by the interference of State or National labor bureaus in the interest of the public, who often suffer through the interruption of services on which they have come to depend for the supply of commodities necessary to life or health. The federal labor law of 1898, known as the Erdman law, provides for the mediation and arbitration, by the labor bureau of the Department of Commerce and Labor, in cases of disputes between interstate common carriers and their employees. There is no power but public opinion to compel resort to arbitration, but this has been found effective in many cases; but when agreed to by both parties to a dispute the decision of the arbitration is final. In 1908, a bill was introduced in Congress favoring compulsory investigations of labor disputes. It was opposed by organized labor, and failed of passage. England, Canada, New Zealand and New South Wales have established boards of arbitration for trade disputes.

So far as is known, the first strike to occur in the United States took place in New York among the journeymen bakers in 1741. The journeymen shoemakers of Philadelphia struck in 1796, 1798, 1799 and 1805. In New York sailors organized a strike in 1802. From 1830 to 1840 occurred a number of strikes for the ten-hour day, and by that time strikes had become common phenomena.

The first instance of arbitration in the United States occurred early in the nineteenth century, among the copper miners of Connecticut. In 1865 the first trade agreement resulted—in the iron industry; and was followed by another in 1867. In 1870, at Lynn, Mass., in the centre of the shoe manufacturing district, a board of industrial arbitration was established.

The board consisted of five representatives of the Knights of St. Crispin, the union powerful in that industry, and five representatives of the manufacturers. It represented chiefly an agreement concerning wages; but the agreement was abrogated in 1872, after which time the manufacturers were able to maintain the upper hand.

In 1877, the occurrence of the great railroad strikes awoke the country for the first time to the serious problem presented by the antagonism between capital and labor and to the fact that the strength of labor organizations could no longer be disregarded.

It has been estimated that in the United States from 1881 to 1905 there occurred about 37,000 strikes. In the latter year, figures showed that the record of the United States in this respect was as follows:

United States, one strike to every 5,705 workers.

Germany (1907), one strike to every 6,502 workers.

France (1906), one strike to every 6,990 workers.

Great Britain (1911), one to every 14,608 workers.

The first state law providing for industrial arbitration was passed in Maryland, the home of the great railroad strikes in the period around 1877, on April 1, 1878; but seems never to have been used. It provided for local arbitration only. New Jersey passed a more comprehensive law in 1880. By 1916, two-thirds of the states in the Union had passed laws providing for some form of industrial arbitration. Of the sixteen states which have no such laws, eight are in the South, where capital is still able to preserve much of a paternalistic attitude towards labor.

There are two chief forms of arbitration in the United States. One provides for a permanent state board of arbitration, always on hand to render its services. The other provides for voluntary arbitration by local boards when the need for it arises. Seventeen states have permanent boards, nine states have local boards, and nine states have both forms.

Owing to the opposition of organized labor to compulsory arbitration, in which respect it is often supported by employers, all this arbitration is voluntary—and there is no compulsion to accept the awards and decisions of the various arbitrating agencies.

Since 1894, New Zealand has had compulsory arbitration, although the awards are not legally binding.

About 70% of strikes are ordered by unions. Half of all strikes seem to be successful, 16% partly successful, and 34% unsuccessful. Strikes are much more successful when organized by unions than without union control and support. Thirty-two per cent of strikes are for higher wages, 19% for recognition of the union and 11% against reduction in wages.

The state boards in five of the states having permanent boards of arbitration intervened in 23% of the strikes, and successfully in 55% of this number. In New York state, from 1886 to 1911, there were 8,265 strikes, in 35% of which the Bureau of Mediation and Arbitration intervened—successfully in about 30% of this number, representing about 10% of the whole number of strikes.

Since 1898, the bituminous coal workers have had an agreement with the operators, and since 1902 the anthracite workers.

In July, 1910, occurred the great International Garment Workers Strike in New York City, which was finally terminated by the adoption of a protocol providing for concessions from both sides. The union was recognized, and preference was to be paid its members, but there was to be no closed shop. There is an arbitration board of three, a board of sanitary control composed of seven, and a grievance committee of four. There is a fifty-four hour week and a nine-hour day, with double pay for overtime and a definite minimum wage scale.

Very similar is the agreement between Hart, Schaffner and Marx, of Chicago, and their employees, except for the fact that by the terms of a new agreement adopted in 1916, the workers obtained even more liberal terms than those mentioned above. There is a preferential union agreement similar to that mentioned above, a trade board composed of one representative ·of labor and one of capital, with a neutral chairman, and an arbitration board as a kind of court of last resort. There is a forty-nine hour week and a minimum wage scale for apprentices—in the case of women, $9.00 a week; and of men, $12.00 a week. The 1916 agreement granted a 10% increase in wages over the agreement of 1911, in which the interesting feature is the fact that, by request of the workers themselves, this increase is so distributed as to provide a 20% increase for those receiving the lower wages, and a 5% increase for those receiving the higher wages.

The Newlands Act (q. v.), passed in 1913, created the United States Board of Mediation and Conciliation. (See Mediation and Conciliation, Board of). It consists of a commissioner, assistant commissioner, and two other officials, all appointed by the President to offer arbitration in disputes between capital and labor. Some idea of its services may be gained from the fact that in three years (1913-1916) it applied mediation successfully in 45 of 56 controversies between railroad employers and employees, and arbitration successfully in the 11 other cases. The Board, however, may play the part merely of a voluntary mediator, organized labor resisting bitterly all attempts at compulsory arbitration, under the plea that such procedure deprives employees of their right to strike and in other ways obtain their ends. In September, 1916, when the Railroad Brotherhoods threatened to strike in order to obtain an eight-hour day, mediation failed; and a strike was averted only by act of Congress, called the Adamson Law (see Railroads, *Eight Hour Day*).

In spite of the fact that the American Federation of Labor was on record as unqualifiedly supporting the administration of President Wilson in the war against Germany, from the outbreak of the war on April 6, 1917, to November 15 of the same year approximately 500 large strikes had been called in American industry, as against 144 for the same period of the preceding year. In addition to the efforts of the Board of Mediation, the Council of National Defence had a special committee working for labor arbitration, and President Wilson appointed another committee for the same end.

The entire principle of labor arbitration is to destroy the feeling that industrial quarrels must be settled according to the strength of the elements concerned, and to substitute a democratic and orderly arrangement, in which industry is recognized as belonging neither to capital nor to labor, but to both and that the relations between employers and employees must be based on a kind of partnership agreement according to justice and needs.

See also Labor, Bureau of; Labor Statistics; Labor Question; and Strike Commission.

Arbitration (Labor):

Arbitration (compulsory) of disputes between employees and employers urged, 7089.

Failure of, in railroad disputes, 8145, 8184.

Machinery for compulsory investigation of controversies between employers and employees recommended, 7036.

Steps for, during war with Germany, 8359.

Arbor Day.—The first suggestion of tree planting under the direction of state authority was made by B. G. Northrop, then Secretary of the Connecticut Board of Education, about 1865, in an official state report. In 1876 this same gentleman endeavored to stimulate "centennial tree planting" by the offer of prizes to the children of Connecticut. But the idea of setting apart a day for the work had originated with ex-Governor J. Sterling Morton, of Nebraska, who, about 1872, induced the Governor of that state to issue a proclamation appointing a day for the planting of trees throughout the state. In honor of Mr. Morton his birthday, April 22, was made a legal holiday by the Legislature, and provision was made for awarding premiums to those who put out the most trees. It is said that nearly 700,000,000 Arbor Day trees are now in thriving condition on the prairie tracts of the state.

The example of Nebraska was soon followed by Kansas, and with grand results. Arbor Day in Minnesota, first observed in 1876, resulted, it is said, in planting over a million and a half of trees. In Michigan the Arbor Day law was passed in 1881, and in Ohio in 1882. Since then Arbor Day has been observed in Colorado, Wisconsin, West Virginia, Indiana, Vermont, New Hampshire, Massachusetts, New Jersey, Pennsylvania, Florida, Alabama, Missouri, California, Kentucky, Maine and Georgia. In several other states its observance has been secured by the recommendation of the Grange, the Grand Army of the Republic, or by state agricultural societies. On the first Ohio Arbor Day the children of Cincinnati joined in an attractive celebration, in the form of planting memorial trees and dedicating them to authors, statesmen, and other distinguished citizens. The date is not uniform, but is usually late in April or early in May, varying from January to March.

Archives, public building for, recommended, 7728.

Arctic Circle.—Known lands of the arctic regions are estimated at 1,233,000 square miles in area. The most important is Greenland, discovered by Eric the Red in 986. Later explorers were Davis (1585), Kane, Hall, Nares, Greely, Nansen, and Peary. It is regarded as a Danish possession. The islands of the Arctic Archipelago of North America belong to Great Britain. Spitzbergen was visited by Dutch navigators in 1596. It belongs to Russia, and affords a base for Swedish explorers of the arctic regions. Nova Zembla and Kolguev also belong to Russia. Franz Josef Land was discovered by Austrian explorers. It is uninhabited. The productions of these frigid lands are sealskins, blubber, cod liver oil, furs and ivory.

Arctic Explorations.—Arctic explorations to the north of the American continent begin with Frobisher (1576), Davis (1585-88), and Baffin (1616) who discovered the straits and bay which bear their names. In 1612 Henry Hudson entered Hudsons Bay and wintered there, but was abandoned by his men the next spring and perished.

In 1845 Sir John Franklin sailed on another expedition from which he never returned. In the course of the expeditions to rescue his party or learn their fate the islands and channels north of the continent were pretty thoroughly explored and mapped. From the west, McClure (1850) reached Parry Sound, discovered by Parry;

his crew, joining by sledge the eastern squadron under Sir Edward Belcher, was the only party to accomplish the Northwest Passage ; Collinson, sailing at the same time, coasted the northern shore of the continent, reaching, without knowing it, the scene of Franklin's death on King William Land. From the east between 1849 and 1855, eight expeditions, fitted out by the British Government, by private parties, and by Lady Franklin, searched in vain for Franklin and his men.

The work of American explorers begins with the Grinnell expedition under De Haven and Kane, in 1850. Information obtained by Dr. Rae, in a land journey in 1854, had already made evident the loss of Franklin and his men ; but Lady Franklin determined to make one last effort, sent out, in 1859, the *Little Fox*, under the command of McClintock, who obtained a record (the only one found) stating the abandonment of the ships and Franklin's death. But little has been done in this field since 1855, although in 1898-99, Sverdrup (Norwegian) visited Jones Sound, traced the west coast of Grinnell Land, and discovered several islands. Two American expeditions, those of Kane in 1853, and Hayes in 1860, undertaken with the object of exploring Smith Sound, discovered Kane Sea and Kennedy Channel, and reached 80° 35′ and 81° 35′ respectively. In 1870, C. F. Hall, an American, who had already spent several years among the Hudson Bay Eskimos, searching for traces of the Franklin expedition, reached 82° 11′ in the sea north of Kennedy Channel ; a record which was surpassed five years later by the British expedition under Nares, with 83° 20′.

In 1881 an American expedition under Lieut. A. W. Greely was sent to establish one of the International Circumpolar Stations at Lady Franklin Bay. It secured valuable scientific data, made extensive explorations, and a party under Lieutenant Lockwood reached the farthest north up to that time attained, 83° 24′. In the fall of 1883 the party was forced to retreat to Cape Sabine, where they were rescued the next spring, after much suffering and the loss of several lives.

In the interior of Greenland, important explorations have been made by Nordenskjöld in 1870 and 1883 : Nansen in 1888 ; and especially by the American expeditions commanded by Lieut. Peary in 1886, 1891-92, and 1893-95. In these expeditions, and in a longer and still more successful visit in 1898-1902 Peary determined the northern limits of Greenland, besides exploring Grinnell Land and reaching 84° 17′.

July 17, 1905, Lieut. Peary sailed in the new ship *Roosevelt* on another expedition, intending to push his ship as far north as possible through Smith Sound and make a dash for the Pole by sledges.

This trip proving fruitless, a second voyage was made by the *Roosevelt*, leaving New York, July 6, 1908, and arriving at Etah, Greenland, Aug. 18. Proceeding thence overland, Lieut. Peary arrived at 90° N. Lat. (the north pole) April 6, 1909.

The history of hoaxes and human gullibility contains no more amusing episode than the claims of Dr. Frederick A. Cook, of Brooklyn, N. Y., that he reached the north pole, April 21st, 1908, one year before Peary. The denunciations of Peary, who was being cheated of his just reward, merely heightened popular interest. Very few were sufficiently conversant with conditions in the arctic zone to pass intelligent judgment, but sympathy went out to the haggard doctor, when he related his odyssey of days and nights of suffering and danger.

Spitzbergen and the seas north of Asia have been the field of many expeditions. The exploration of Spitzbergen, discovered by Barents (1596), was carried on by Nordenskjöld in 1863-64, and 1872 ; the islands served as a starting point for André's ill-fated balloon (1897), and were visited by Wellman (American), 1894. Franz Josef Land, discovered by the Austrian expedition under Weyprecht and Payer in 1873, was chosen as a base for the Harmsworth-Jackson expedition in 1893, and the two expeditions sent out by William Ziegler of Brooklyn, under Baldwin (1901), and Fiala (1903), neither of which succeeded in reaching its objective point, the north pole. The Duke of Abruzzi's expedition from the same quarter in 1902 was more successful, reaching 86° 34′, the farthest north ever attained. A French expedition led by the Duke of Orleans was, at the beginning of 1906, somewhere north of Franz Josef Land. In 1893, Frithiof Nansen, a Norwegian, entering the ice north of Asia, allowed himself to be carried by the currents until, leaving his ship, he reached by a sledge journey 86° 14′.

The Northeast Passage, long an object of English and Russian exploration, was accomplished by Nordenskjöld in 1878-79. The westernmost of the Asiatic islands were discovered by the American expedition under G. W. DeLong in the *Jeannette*, which, setting out from San Francisco in 1879, was crushed in the ice, DeLong and the larger part of the crew perishing during the retreat. Late in 1905 the Amundsen expedition returned with valuable discoveries concerning the position of the North Magnetic Pole.

Argentina.—A republic occupying the greater portion of the southern part of the South American Continent, and extending from Bolivia to Cape Horn, a total distance of nearly 2,300 miles ; its greatest breadth is about 930 miles. It is bounded on the north by Bolivia, on the northeast by Paraguay, Brazil, and Uruguay, on the southeast and south by the Atlantic, and on the west by Chile, from which Republic it is separated by the Cordillera de los Andes.

Physical Features.—On the west the mountainous Cordilleras, with their plateaus, extend from the northern to the southern boundaries ; on the east are the great plains (known as El Gran Chaco) and the treeless pampas, which together constitute La Plata, extending from the Bolivian boundary in the north to the Rio Negro ; and south of the Rio Negro are the vast plains of Patagonia. Argentina thus contains a succession of level plains, broken only in Cordoba by the San Luis and Cordoba ranges, and in the northwestern states by the eastern spurs of the Andes. The Paraná River, formed by the junction of the Upper Paraná with the Uruguay River, flows through the northeastern states into the Atlantic, and is navigable throughout its course ; the Pilcomayo, Bermejo, and Salado del Norte are also navigable for some distance from their confluence with the Paraná. In Buenos Aires the Salado del Sud flows southeast for some 300 miles into Samborombon Bay (Atlantic). In the south the Colorado and Rio Negro rise in the extreme west and flow across the pampas into the Atlantic, many similar streams in Patagonia traversing the country from the Andes to the Atlantic.

History.—The Argentine was discovered in 1516 by Juan Diaz de' Solis and the capital, Buenos Aires, was founded in 1580 ; it remained a Spanish colony until 1817, when it gained its independence under the leadership of Jose de San Martin. The official designation of the country is

Argentine Nation. Patagonia and Tierra del Fuego were divided between Argentina and Chile in 1881.

From 1835 to 1852 the country was under the dictatorship of Rosas. Brazil and Argentina were allied in a war with Paraguay from 1865 to 1870. In 1902 a dispute of considerable bitterness arose with Chile, respecting the armaments and size of their respective navies. It was eventually settled by treaty in January, 1903, by which it was agreed that both navies were to be maintained at identical strength and that certain ships, then being built for both parties in various European yards, were to be sold.

AREA AND POPULATION

PROVINCES	Area Sq. Miles	*Population, 1912
Buenos Aires	117,778	1,670,660
Catamarca	47,531	108,755
Cordoba	62,160	480,185
Corrientes	32,580	332,144
Entre Rios	28,784	428,387
Jujuy	18,977	62,477
Mendoza	34,546	225,530
Rioja	56,502	93,900
Salta	62,184	152,087
San Juan	33,715	112,487
San Luis	28,535	112,898
Santa Fé	50,916	823,269
Santiago del Estero	39,764	201,404
Tucuman	8,926	306,183
Total Provinces	618,898	5,110,366
TERRITORIES		
Chaco	52,741	26,379
Chubut	93,427	29,500
Formosa	41,402	10,408
Los Andes	21,989	2,500
Misiones	11,282	40,321
Neuquen	42,345	29,746
Pampa	56,320	50,546
Rio Negro	75,924	25,498
Santa Cruz	109,142	5,198
Tierra del Fuego	8,299	1,822
Indian Nomads	......	46,518
Total Territories	512,871	267,436
Capital:—Buenos Aires	72	1,358,979
Grand Total	1,131,841	6,736,781

* The population figures are the estimates of the National Statistical Society, no census having been taken for 20 years. The language of the people is Spanish and their religion Roman Catholic, the foreign element (1,750,000) being composed of 850,000 Italians, 450,000 Spanish, and 100,000 French, with 30,000 English, 25,000 Austrians, 22,000 Germans, 17,000 Swiss, and 256,000 of various nationalities.

Government.—The constitution is that of a Federal Republic modelled upon that of the United States of America, and embodied in the fundamental law of May 25, 1853 (with amendment of Nov. 11, 1859). The President and Vice-President are elected for six years by an electoral college. *President* (Oct. 12, 1916-1920), Hippolite Irigoyen.

There is a responsible Ministry, appointed by the President, consisting of eight Secretaries of State.

Congress sits annually from May 1 to September 30, and consists of a Senate of thirty members (two from each of the fourteen Provinces, and two from the capital), elected (by an electoral college) for nine years, one-third being renewable every three years; and of a Chamber of Deputies of 120 members, elected by the people for four years, and one-half renewable every two years.

The Judicial System consists, like that of the United States, of a Federal Supreme Court and the Courts of Appeal, with Provincial Courts in each State for non-national or single state causes.

Production and Industry.—Of the total area about one-third is suitable for agriculture and cattle raising, and vast tracts are held by the Federal Government for sale or lease to colonists. In 1911 close on 50,000,000 acres were under cultivation, wheat, maize, oats, linseed, cotton, sugar, wine and tobacco being grown, while the surplus wheat exported in 1910 exceeded 2,500,000 metric tons. The live stock in 1910 included 30,000,000 cattle, 7,500,000 horses, 67,000,000 sheep, 4,000,000 goats, and 1,500,000 pigs; the total value of the live stock is estimated at $1,650,000,000. There is a large export trade in frozen and chilled meats, seven factories being in operation with American and British capital. There are 32,000 industrial establishments, employing close on 330,000 persons, the output including cottons and woolens, but at present failing to supply the demand for home consumption. The mineral output includes gold, silver and copper, and coal, petroleum, manganese, wolfram, and salt.

Army.—Service in the Army is universal and compulsory on all citizens between the ages of 20 and 45: for 10 years in the Active Army; then 10 years in the National Guard; 5 years in the Territorial Guard. The Peace Establishment is 2,000 officers and 19,000 others. The War Establishment of the Active Army is 125,000. (See Armies of the World.)

Navy.—Two Dreadnought battleships (*Moreno* and *Rivaldavia*) of 28,000 tons (22½ knots, 12 12-inch guns), 12 torpedo-boat destroyers, and 12 torpedo-boats were laid down under a recent naval programme, the remaining ships being five small battleships, seven cruisers, and seventeen units of torpedo craft; the navy is manned by about 5,000 men. The naval port is Bahia Blanca. (See Navies of the World.)

Education.—Primary Education is secular, free and nominally compulsory from the ages of six to fourteen, but Schools are maintained by provincial taxation, and controlled by provincial boards. Secondary Education is controlled by the Federal Government. There are also naval, military, mining, and agricultural schools. There are National Universities at Cordoba and Buenos Aires, and Provincial Universities at La Plata, Santa Fé, and Paraná.

Railways.—On Dec. 31, 1912, there were 33,029 kilometres of railway (31,049 kilometres open and working). Of the total length open, 3,971 kilometres (2,220 miles) were the property of the State, the remainder being owned by Companies with a total capital of over £170,000,000, of which over £150,000,000 was supplied by British investors. The capital has an efficient service of electric trams.

Post Offices and Telegraphs.—In 1912 there were 2,655 post offices. In 1911 there were 2,628 telegraph offices and 12 radio-telegraph stations; the former possessed 69,603 kilometres of line, with 212,237 kilometres of telegraph wire.

Shipping.—The mercantile marine in 1912 numbered 228 steam (171,631 tons) and 66 sailing vessels (32,720 tons). The number of ocean-going vessels entered in cargo and in ballast at Argentine ports in 1912 was 4,655 steam vessels (11,220,540 tons), and 255 sailing vessels.

The principal ports are Buenos Aires, Rosario, La Plata, and Bahia Blanca.

Towns.—Capital, Buenos Aires, estimated population (1910), 1,300,000; other towns are Bahia Blanca, Barracas al Sud, Chivilcoy, Concordia, Cordoba, Corrientes, Gualeguaychu, La Plata, Mendoza, Paraná, Rio

Cuarto, Rosario, Salta, San Juan, San Luis, San Nicolas, Santa Fé, Tucuman.

The Metric System of Weights, Measures, and Currency is compulsory.

The currency unit is the Peso of 100 Centavos, equal to $0.964 American money, but the circulating medium is paper. By a Conversion Law of 1899 a gold standard has been adopted and the paper peso is convertible at .44 gold.

Argentina depends entirely upon the outside world for its machinery and related products and before the European war the United States ran a poor third to Germany and England in supplying this fine market. The opportunity is now before American manufacturers to take over permanently an important part of this trade. German houses supplied leading technical and industrial schools with machinery and machine tools free of charge so that the future engineers and shop officials would naturally favor the German makes.

Previous to the war Germany furnished 46.5 per cent of the miscellaneous machinery imported by Argentina, England 21.8 per cent, and the United States 13.6 per cent. The United States was first in supplying spare parts for machinery with 29.1 per cent, Germany was second with 25.5 per cent, and England third with 21.7 per cent. It is a curious fact that 46.9 per cent of the agricultural machinery was imported from Australia, the United States standing second in the list with 34.8 per cent and Canada third with 16.6 per cent. The United States furnished 63.1 per cent of the thrashing machinery and England 33.4 per cent. The dominant position of England in the supply of railway plant and rolling stock is very apparent, as that country furnished 75.6 per cent of the locomotives, 89.07 per cent of the passenger coaches, and 47.8 per cent of the freight cars. Of the steel-rail business, England held 31.8 per cent, Germany 29.6 per cent, and the United States 26.1 per cent. Of wheels and miscellaneous railway material, England supplied over 70 per cent. The Germans led in miscellaneous electric-railway material, and supplied 45.1 per cent of the dynamos and electric motors, England being second in the latter line with 41.4 per cent. France furnished 36.8 per cent of the automobiles, the United States 19.3 per cent, and Germany 16.3 per cent.

The following are the most important reasons for this state of affairs. The very few American houses that tried to do business in Argentina failed to succeed because, in great measure, of their failure to adapt themselves to the business practice of the country. The American manufacturer was content to send out traveling salesmen with little or no knowledge of the country's language or customs—selling, or endeavoring to sell, mainly from catalogues and price lists printed in English. In general he demanded payment for his goods cash against shipping documents in New York. The fact that Europe has immensely superior shipping facilities has been an important factor. Europe, also, has made large investments of capital in Argentina and practically all of the important industries, the railroads, power plants, etc., are in the hands of Europeans. The fact that Argentina has a large and free market in Europe for its products is not without its influence. And, finally, it must be confessed that the Europeans have had the incentive of really needing the market, while many Americans have been only mildly interested.

Argentine Republic:
Agricultural exhibition in, 7414.

Battleships for, constructed by Americans, 7501, 7599.

Boundary question with—
Brazil submitted to President of United States, 5867.
Award of, discussed, 6058.
Chile referred to, 4629, 6323.
Paraguay submitted to President of United States, 4449.

Cables of American company, questions regarding rate charges imposed upon by, 6323.

Claims of, against United States, 4910.

Claims of United States against, 1246, 1594, 4806.
Adjusted, 6324.

Coined silver, and products of, referred to, 5908.

Consul at Buenos Aires, recommendation regarding salary of, 4849.

Cordiality of relations with, 7498.

Diplomatic relations with Buenos Aires discussed, 2116.

Imprisonment of American citizens in, 632.

Independence of Buenos Aires asserted, 612, 627.

Internal disorders in, 4563.

Joint resolution relating to congratulations from, vetoed, 4384.

Minister of United States in Buenos Aires, return of, 1171.

Minister to be sent to United States, 1370.
Received, 1706, 4718.

Outrages upon American vessels in Falkland Islands discussed, 1116, 1246.

Revolution in Buenos Aires discussed, 2702.

Tariff laws of, modifications in, discussed, 6058.

Treaty with, 2759, 2813, 4852, 5115, 6425.
Return of, requested, 4888.

War between Buenos Aires and Brazil—
Peace concluded, 977.
Questions between United States and Brazil arising out of, 929, 951.

Argentina, Treaties with.—In 1853 a treaty was concluded with the Argentine Confederation granting the United States free navigation of the rivers Paraná and Uruguay. This was followed by another of friendship, commerce and navigation, and provided for the exchange of diplomatic and consular agents. An extradition convention was signed in 1896 providing for the extradition of prisoners accused of the following crimes: Homicide, or attempted homicide; arson; burglary; housebreaking; robbery with violence, actual, attempted or threatened; larceny of property of the value of $200; forgery, or the utterance of the thing forged; counterfeiting; embezzlement of public or private money in excess of $200; fraud, or breach of trust committed by a bailee, banker, agent, factor, trustee, director, member or public officer of any company, when such act is punishable by the laws of both countries; perjury; rape; abduction; kidnapping or childstealing; any act committed with criminal intent, the object of which is to endanger the safety of any person traveling or being upon a railway; crimes committed at sea, and trading in slaves when the offense is criminal under the laws of both countries.

Arid Lands. (See Lands, Public; also Irrigation.)

Reclamation of, 6801, 7004.

Arizona.—One of the southwestern states of the Union; motto, "Ditat Deus." It is separated from the Pacific Ocean on the west by California and Nevada, and bounded on the north by Utah and Nevada, on the east by New Mexico, and on the south by the Republic of Mexico. It lies between the parallels 31° 20' and 37° north lat. and the meridians of 109° and 114° 45' west long., including an area of 113,956 square miles. In addition to whites there are Apache, Moqui, Pueblo, Arivaipa, Chemehuevi, Cohahuila, Cocopa, Walapai, Maricopa, Mohave, Navajo, Papago, Pima, and Paiute Indians. The chief industry is mining gold, silver, and copper. In the northern portion of the State there are large pine forests and the lumber trade is rapidly progressing. The surface is much broken by the erosion of the streams, which cut deep gorges in the rocks, the Grand Canyon of the Colorado at some points being more than a mile deep.

The greater portion of the State was acquired by treaty with Mexico in 1848, the remainder by the Gadsden Purchase of 1853.

Statistics of agriculture collected for the last Federal census place the number of farms in the State at 9,227, comprising 1,246,613 acres, valued with stock and improvements at $75,123,970. The cattle numbered 824,970, valued at $14,624,708; horses, 99,578, $4,209,726; mules, 3,963, $399,447; swine, 17,208, $113,714; sheep, 1,226,723, $4,400,513. The acreage, production and value of the principal field crops for 1911 were: corn, 15,000 acres, 495,000 bushels, $480,000; wheat, 27,000 acres, 800,000 bushels, $760,000; oats, 6,000 acres, 252,000 bushels, $151,000; hay, 130,000 acres, 502,000 tons, $6,024,000. The State ranks first in the production of copper. The production in 1910 was 297,481,151 pounds, valued at $37,781,376, a decrease from the figures of 1909, and the reports for 1911 show a still further decline in the production. The largest producer in 1911 was the Bisbee district, with 133,000,000 pounds; the Globe-Miami district produced 40,000,000 pounds. The United Verde mine, in the Jerome district, showed a decrease from the 38,600,000 pounds produced in 1910. Extensive pasture lands are favorable for the rearing of cattle and sheep. The federal Reclamation act provided for the irrigation of 210,000 acres of land in the Salt River region of Arizona by the end of the year 1911, at a cost of $6,300,000. The population in 1910 was 204,354.

Arizona Territory:

Act to authorize leasing of lands for educational purposes in, vetoed, 6102.

Admission to Statehood—
Joint act for, vetoed, 7636.

Proposed, 7020.

Recommended, 7229.

Appropriation for, recommended, 4691.

Barracks, etc., within limits of Military Department of, construction of, recommended, 4696.

Bill to authorize issuance of bonds in aid of railroads in, vetoed, 5523.

Indian outrages in, discussed, 4933, 4943.

Lands in—
Claims under Spanish and Mexican grants, discussed, 5484, 5510, 5561.

Records of Mexican Government regarding, 4257.

Set apart as public reservation by proclamation, 5811, 6702.

Lawlessness prevailing in, and means for suppressing, discussed, 4640, 4663, 4688.

Proclamation against, 4709.

Population of, 3045, 3099.

Territorial government for, recommended, 2987, 3045, 3100.

Arkansas.—One of the southern states of the Union; nickname, the "Bear State"; motto, "Regnant Populi" (The people rule). It is bounded by Missouri on the north, on the east by Tennessee and Mississippi (from both of which it is separated by the Mississippi River), on the south by Louisiana, and on the west by Texas and Indian Territory. It extends from lat. 33° to 36° 30' north and from long. 89° 40' to 94° 42' west. It contains 53,335 square miles, and in 1910 the population was 1,750,000. By legislative enactment the name of the State is pronounced Ar'kansaw. The State contains rich forests of oak, pine, walnut, hickory, cypress, cedar, and other lumberproducing timber. Coal, iron, and building stone exist in abundance. The Mississippi River bottom lands are a fine cotton region. One of the curiosities of the State is the large number of medicinal springs, the most popular of which—the Hot Springs—is visited annually by thousands of people. One spring in Fulton County discharges 15,000 barrels of water per day, at a temperature of 60°. The State was first settled by the French in 1685, and formed part of the Louisiana Purchase of 1803. It was organized as a Territory March 2, 1819, admitted as a State into the Union June 15, 1836, seceded May 6, 1861, and was readmitted June 22, 1868. Population (1912) 1,574,449.

National forests cover an area of 3,189,781 acres in the State. The original homestead entries in 1909 covered 153,568 acres. The live stock reported for the last federal census consisted of 505,000 horses and mules, 961,000 cattle, 233,000 sheep, and 978,000 swine. According to the last statistics the annual production of butter was 21,585,250 pounds; cheese, 18,375 pounds, and milk, 109,861,393 gallons.

The number of manufacturing establishments in Arkansas having an annual output valued at $500 or more at the beginning of 1915 was 2,604. The amount of capital invested was $76,866,000, giving employment to 48,440 persons, using material valued at $44,907,000, and turning out finished goods worth $83,941,000. Salaries and wages paid amounted to $24,915,000.

Arkansas is first among the states in the production of two minerals—bauxite and novaculite, the former being the ore of aluminum and the latter the source of the larger part of the oilstones produced in the United States. The principal mineral product of Arkansas, however, is coal, the annual value of which constituted over fifty per cent of the state's total. The total value of all the mineral products of Arkansas in 1913 was $6,780,760, according to the United States Geological Survey, compared with $6,258,726 in 1912. The coal production was 2,234,107 short tons, valued at $3,923,701, in 1913, against 2,100,-819 tons, valued at $3,582,789, in 1912. The coals of Arkansas are generally of high grade, particularly in the eastern part of the coal field, where they approach anthracite in character. The semianthracite of Arkansas is an excellent domestic fuel and reaches markets as far north as Kansas City.

Bauxite, from which aluminum is derived, is second among the mineral products of the state. It is mined near Benton, in Saline County, and in Pulaski County.

In 1913 the stone quarries of Arkansas furnished products valued at $525,050, exclusive of novaculite and of limestone burned for lime. In 1912 the quarry products were valued at $513,844. The clay-working industries, while not highly developed, take third place and in 1913 produced an output valued at $529,624, an increase of $67,019 over 1912. The sand and gravel pits yielded $320,639 in 1913 and $393,639 in 1912. The only metalliferous products of Arkansas besides bauxite are lead, zinc, and manganiferous ores. Other commercial mineral products are fuller's earth, gems and precious stones, lime, mineral waters, natural gas, phosphate rock, and slate.

Arkansas (see also Confederate States):

Act for admission of, into Union vetoed, 3846.

Acts of governor should be legalized, 801.

Admission of, into Union, constitution adopted, 1444.

Boundary of, 795.

Constitution of, referred to, 3830.

Defalcation of officers in, 941.

Election disturbances in, and claims of persons to governorship discussed, 4218, 4219, 4252, 4273.

Proclamation regarding, 4226.

Lands granted to, in aid of railroads referred to. 3580.

Marshal of United States in, advance of public moneys to, referred to, 2835.

Military governor of, office of, abolished, 3377.

Public lands in, proclamation regarding unlawful possession of, 1106.

Restoration of, into Union, discussed, 3423, 3452.

Road in, from Little Rock to Cantonment Gibson, 932.

Secretary of, appointment of, revoked, 3377.

Arkansas Northwestern Railway Co., act authorizing construction of railroad by, through Indian Territory, vetoed, 6012.

Arkansas Post (Ark.), Battle of.—Jan. 10, 1863, an expedition under command of Gen. McClernand and convoyed by Admiral Porter's fleet of gunboats, moved against Fort Hindman, at Arkansas Post, on the Arkansas River. Jan. 11 a combined attack was begun, which was maintained until 4 o'clock in the afternoon, when the post, with 5,000 prisoners, was surrendered to the Union forces. The Federal loss in the action was 977 killed, wounded, and missing.

Arlington Cemetery:

Appropriation for memorial amphitheatre recommended, 7048.

Memorial amphitheatre at, recommended, 7686.

President Wilson's address at, 7948.

Arlington Confederate Monument Association. — During the administration of President McKinley the Confederate dead buried in the City of Washington, D. C., and vicinity were removed to the National Cemetery at Arlington, Va., the old home of Robert E. Lee, where they were reinterred in a plot of ground set apart by the President for that purpose, and designated "The Confederate Section."

The Arlington Confederate Monument Association was formed for the purpose of erecting in this section a suitable monument to the dead there buried, and to stand, in a larger sense, as a memorial to all those who lost their lives in defense of the Confederacy, as well as to the cause they represented.

The Association was formed as a committee of the United Daughters of the Confederacy, the President-General of which is the President of the association. The monument was completed and unveiled by President Wilson, June 4, 1914. (Page 7948.)

Armada.—A group of war vessels maneuvering, or in action.

Armageddon.—In the peroration of his speech on the eve of the National Republican Convention at Chicago, June 17, 1912, Mr. Roosevelt, after denouncing what he termed fraudulent practices of corrupt politicians, called upon his hearers to take the side of the people against the dishonest party managers, saying at the close: "We stand at Armageddon and we battle for the Lord." The expression is not a quotation, but is based on several passages in the book of Revelations, Chapter XVI, notably in the 16th and following verses. The word Armageddon is used in an apocalyptic sense as a synonym for the battlefield—whether above the earth or in the underworld—on which the final victory over evil was to be won by the forces of righteousness. It was here that the kings of the lower world were to be gathered by the Dragon, the Beast, and the False Prophet to make war on the Lord. Revelations xvii, 14, reads: "These shall make war with the Lamb and the Lamb shall overcome them; for he is Lord of Lords and King of Kings, and they that are with him are called and chosen and faithful." Specifically Armageddon is a corruption of the Hebrew words Har Mageddon, signifying the mountains of Megiddo. The reference in the passage in Revelations is probably to Megiddo, but some authorities refer it to the plain of Esdraelon, or Jezreel, in Galilee and Samaria, famous as a battlefield from the time Gideon overcame the Midianites to Napoleon's victory over the Turks.

Armament.—1.—Soldiers or sailors on a war footing. 2.—Equipment and munitions for war purposes.

Armed Neutrality.—In 1780 the powers of northern Europe—Russia, Sweden, and Denmark—formed a confederacy against England, then at war with the United States, and proclaimed the doctrine that neutral ships had the right to visit the ports of belligerents, that free ships make free goods, and that blockades to be recognized must be effectual. These countries assumed a threatening position and armed themselves to repel aggression. By treaty, ratified in 1800, the flags of these nations were to be respected by belligerents. Great Britain rejected the principle, and Nelson and Parker destroyed the Danish fleet at Copenhagen, April 2, 1801. This led to the dissolution of the armed neutrality.

For months before the United States finally entered the European War on April 6, 1917, there was much discussion in the United States concerning the advisability of adopting a policy of armed neutrality towards Germany and Austria. As the term was used in those days, it was understood to mean a situation where American merchant ships would be supplied with guns and gunners, in order to protect themselves in case they were attacked by a submarine of the Central Powers. When Germany announced that, beginning with February 1, 1917, she would sink on sight all ships found within the blockade zone she had drawn around the British Isles, France and Italy, the term "armed neutrality' was broadened to mean that armed merchantmen might fire at sight upon a submarine, without waiting to be attacked, as the hostile intentions of the submarine might be postulated. Despite opposition from a small group of Senators, who prevented passage of the bill authorizing President Wilson to adopt armed neutrality, in the closing days of the Sixty-fourth Congress (Feb. 27-Mar. 5, 1917), the policy was put into effect by the United States Government. It did not prove to be practicable, however, as President Wilson himself admitted in his message to Congress on April 2, 1917, in which he asked for a declaration of the existence of a state of war with the Imperial German Government.

Armed Neutrality:

Confederacy of, discussed, 2808.

In Middle States, discussed, 3225.

Armenians.—Inhabitants of Armenia. They belong to the Aryan family of nations. Armenia is the classical name of the Hebrew Ararat, Assyrian Urartu, the country which extends from the shores of Lake Van, between the Upper Euphrates and Media, forming the juncture between the high plateau of Iran and the table-land of Asia Minor. It is the original seat of one of the old civilized peoples in the world. According to their records they were governed in ancient times by independent kings, but afterwards became tributary to the Assyrians. After the Assyrian period Armenia became a dependency of Persia and Media. Subsequently it was conquered by Alexander the Great, and later it passed under the nominal supremacy of Parthia and Rome. Then it was ruled by Persian, Byzantine, and Arabic governors until the dynasty of the Bagratides, which came to an end in 1045. The last vestige of Armenian independence was destroyed by the Mameiukes in 1375. Since that date they have been without an independent state, their country being divided between Persia, Turkey, and Russia. They still have an independent church, with the seat of government at Constantinople.

In 1894 the greatest cruelties were visited upon Armenians in Turkey, in part because they were Christians. It was claimed that some of those upon whom outrages were committed were persons who had declared their intention to become citizens of the United States. Our consuls were sent there to make investigation of these atrocities and cruelties, and in the diplomatic correspondence which followed assurances were given by Turkey that our countrymen should be secured and protected in all their rights (pages 5989, 6069, 6095, 6147).

It was learned, however, that an Armenian journal published in this country in the Armenian language openly counseled its readers to engage in rebellion against Turkish authority in the Asiatic provinces. Turkey complained that Armenians sought American citizenship with the intention of claiming the protection of the United States when convicted of seditious practices in the land of their birth.

The Ottoman government announced its intention to expel from its dominions Armenians who have obtained naturalization in the United States later than 1868.

Armenians:

Cruelties and atrocities committed upon, in Turkey, discussed, 5989, 6069, 6147.

   Investigation of, by American consul discussed, 5989, 6069.

   Referred to, 6090.

Obtaining citizenship in United States and returning to Turkey expelled, discussed, 5872, 6435.

Treatment of naturalized citizens of United States of Armenian origin by Turkey, 6095.

Armies, Cost of.—The United States Army appropriations for 1916-1917 amount to *$232,831,043, not including the expenditure by the several States on their National Guard or the sums paid for pensions to ex-volunteers. The Navy appropriations for 1915-16 amount to †$149,661,865, an increase of $46,853,801 over the previous year, but a later appropriation in 1916 for enlarging the Navy swelled this increase to $139,345,287. The cost of the British Army, according to estimates for 1913-14, amounted to $224,300,000. The estimates for the Navy for 1913-14 are placed at $224,140,000. The estimated military expenditure of the German Empire in the budget for 1912-13 amounted to $183,090,000, excluding expenditures on Colonial troops. The German Naval estimates for 1913-14 amounted to $111,300,000. The military budget of France for 1913 showed an estimated expenditure of ‡$191,431,580 for the military establishment. Italy during 1913-14 expected to spend about $51,000,000 on her Navy, and about $82,928,000 on her Army. The military budget of Russia, ordinary and extraordinary, for 1913-14 called for $317,800,000, and the Navy expenditures in 1913-14 would have amounted to about $122,500,000. The Army estimate of Austro-Hungary for 1913 was $82,300,000, and for the Navy $42,000,000. The military expenditure of Japan

*This does not include cost of fortifications, Military Academy, etc., but only for the Army. †This includes construction of ships, Naval Academy, Navy Yards, etc. ‡Excluding cost of Colonial troops not serving in France.

for 1913-14 were about $49,000,000. All estimates for foreign Armies and Navies have been largely exceeded, owing to the general war in Europe.

Armor and Armor Plate:

Discussed, 5759, 5882, 5972.

Manufacture of, in United States recommended, 5100.

Tests of, discussed, 5552, 5635.

Armories. (See Arms and Ammunition; Arsenals.)

Armies of the World.—The following table shows the peace footing of the land forces of the principal states of Europe, and of Japan; also of the secondary States of Europe, Asia and America, compiled from the latest available data before the general European war of 1914:

Countries	Peace Strength	Reserves*	Total War Strength
Germany	870,000	4,430,000	5,200,000
France	720,000a	3,280,000	4,000,000
Russia	1,290,000	3,300,000	5,500,000
Austria-Hungary	390,000	1,610,000	2,000,000
Italy	250,000	950,000	1,200,000
Great Britain	254,500b	476,500c	730,000
Japan	250,000	950,000	1,200,000
Spain	115,000	235,000	350,000
Belgium	42,000	180,000	222,000
Netherlands	35,000d	145,000	180,000
Denmark	14,000	56,000	70,000
Sweden	50,000	400,000	450,000
Norway	35,000	80,000	115,000
Portugal	30,000e	120,000	150,000
Bulgaria	60,500	320,500	380,000
Servia	32,000	208,000	240,000
Rumania	95,000	100,000	500,000
Switzerland	22,300f	252,700	275,000
Turkey	400,000	300,000	700,000
Greece	25,000	125,000	150,000
China	212,000g	100,000h	312,000
Mexico	31,000k	80,000i	101,000
Brazil	21,000	500,000i	521,000
Argentina	21,500	250,000i	271,500
Chile	28,000	57,000i	85,000
Peru	10,000	50,000i	60,000
Venezuela	11,600	49,000i	60,600
Bolivia	3,000	90,000i	93,000
Colombia	6,000	44,000i	50,000
Guatemala	6,000	76,000i	82,000
Ecuador	7,000	75,000i	82,000
Salvador	3,000	18,000i	21,000
Nicaragua	3,000	27,000i	30,000
Uruguay	4,000	75,000i	79,000
Haiti	6,000j	.....	6,000

* Except as to some of the principal and a few of the minor States, it is doubtful whether the numbers given of the reserves or auxiliary forces could be mobilized and made effective within a considerable period of time. In some States, all men of military age are enrolled in national militia and are partly trained. aIncluding Colonial troops. bIncluding regular forces at home, in the Colonies, and 76,000 men in India and excluding the native Indian army of about 175,000. cIncludes army reserves and territorial force. dExclusive of Colonial army of about 36,000. eExclusive of troops in Colonies. fTrained National militia. gOrganization of army under present government incomplete. There were about 212,000 men under arms in the recent revolution. hProvincial troops available in case of war. iNational guard, or militia partly trained. jNominal strength. Population nearly all negroes. kStrength previous to present revolution. The Provisional Government claims to have an army of 80,-000, and proposes to increase it to 150,000.

Arms and Ammunition.—The use of firearms followed close upon the invention (about 1320) of gunpowder. The use of gunpowder in military operations in England dates from 1346. Gibbon writes of a

cannon used at the siege of Adrianople by Mahomet II in 1543. During that year the first English cannon was cast at Uckfield, Sussex. The arquebuse and musket were evolved by successive improvements on the large guns. The Swiss are said to have had 10,000 arquebusiers in 1471. At the battle of Pavia, in 1525, the Spaniards, under Emperor Charles V, with a force of 2,000 arquebusiers and 800 musketeers, defeated Francis I of France, the effectiveness of the firearms turning the tide of battle. The flintlock came into use in 1630, was introduced into England under William III, and was effectively used as late as 1840 in the British army. The Landgrave of Hesse armed his followers with rifles in 1631. The Fergusson breech-loading rifle was in use throughout the entire Revolutionary War, though the flintlock was the principal weapon used.

The first practical breech-loading firearm made in the United States was that patented by Hall in 1811. About 10,000 were made for the Government, the inventor superintending their manufacture at the Harpers Ferry Arsenal until his death in 1844. In 1854 Congress made an appropriation for breech-loading rifles, and experiments in this arm were conducted until the breaking out of the Civil War, during the progress of which the Government manufactured and purchased at home and abroad over 4,000,000 small arms of between 25 and 30 different patterns. Among these were breech-loading rifles and carbines and a magazine gun—the Henry.

In 1866, 1869, and 1872 boards of officers were appointed to report upon a desirable small arm, and their investigations led to the adoption in 1873 of the Springfield rifle, which remained in use for twenty years.

The decade between 1880 and 1890 witnessed a further development in small arms in the substitution of magazines for the single breech-loading apparatus, a decrease in the calibre of the ball, and the adoption of smokeless powder.

The forms of gunpowder used in military operations in America as well as in foreign countries until within the last few years were essentially the same as those used a century or more ago. Ever since the invention of gun cotton by Schönbein in 1845 scientific attention has been directed to the manufacture of smokeless powder. The French seem to have been the first to compound a successful smokeless powder for use in small arms. The material used is a form of melinite and belongs to the nitrocellulose or nitro-gun-cotton preparations. The powder is not absolutely smokeless, but the film of smoke arising from individual rifle firing is not visible from more than 300 yards.

Among the latest explosives produced in the United States are cannonite, fulgurite, progressite, Americanite, and Schnebelite. The Army has several depots for the storage of powder, the principal one of which is near Dover, N. J. Powder for both branches of the service is supplied by private firms. Projectiles for the naval guns are made at the Naval Gun Foundry at Washington, D. C. The armor-piercing shells are carefully machined and tempered, and much more expensive to make than ordinary projectiles. In 1892 the United States adopted the Krag-Jörgensen cut-off model magazine rifle. The rifle adopted in 1903 and still in use is the United States (Springfield) magazine rifle; its calibre is 7.62 millimetres or .30 in., its velocity 2,-300 ft. per second, its penetration power at 53 ft. being 54.7 in white pine, and it carries five rounds of ammunition. These rifles are made chiefly at the Springfield and Rock Island Arsenals.

The appended table of military rifles in use by the principal countries of the world is compiled from the latest available data. Changes are frequently made, however, and it is difficult, if not impossible, to present accurate statistics up to date.

Countries	Name or Model of Gun	Year of Introduction	Calibre. In.	Length. Feet.	Weight. Lbs.	Cartridges in Magazine	Covering or Jacket of Bullets	Weight of Entire Cartridge Grains	Gun Sighted to — Yards	Muzzle Velocity Ft. Second	Kind of Powder
United States	Springfield	1903	.30	3.6	8.6	5	Cupro Nickel	395	2,850	2,700	Pyrocellulose
Argentina	Mauser	1909	.301	4.1	8.9	5	Nickel Coated Steel	371	2,187	2,788	Nitrocellulose
Austria-Hung	Mannlicher	1895	.315	4.1	8.0	5	Lubricated Steel	454	2,132	2,840	Nitrocellulose
Belgium	Mauser	1889	.301	4.1	8.6	5	Cupro Nickel	432	2,187	1,975	Nitrocellulose
Bolivia	Mauser	1899	.28	4.0	9.0	5	Cupro Nickel	382	2,187	2,280	Nitrocellulose
Brazil	Mauser	1894	.301	4.1	9.1	5	Cupro Nickel	417	2,187	2,035	Nitrocellulose
Bulgaria	Mannlicher	1895	.315	4.2	9.8	5	Nickel Coated Steel	458	2,132	2,034	Nitrocellulose
Chile	Mauser	1895	.276	4.0	8.6	5	Cupro Nickel	386	2,187	1,910	Nitrocellulose
China	Mauser	1895	.28	4.0	9.0	5	Cupro Nickel	382	2,187	2,280	Nitrocellulose
Colombia	Mauser	1894	.28	4.0	9.0	5	Cupro Nickel	382	2,187	2,280	Nitrocellulose
Denmark	Krag-Jörgensen	1889	.315	4.3	9.3	5	Cupro Nickel	448	2,295	2,535	Nitrocellulose
England ... {	Lee-Enfield	1907	.303	4.1	9.2	10	Cupro Nickel	415	2,800	2,060	Cordite
	Mark I. & III.	1907	.303	3.7	8.6	10	Cupro Nickel	415	2,800	2,060	Cordite
France	Lebel	1893	.315	4.3	9.2	8	Copper Zinc	452	2,620	2,310	Nitrocellulose
Germany	Mauser	1898	.311	4.1	8.3	5	Nickel Coated Steel	363	2,187	2,960	Nitrocellulose
Greece	Mannlicher-Sch'n'r	1903	.256	4.0	8.1	5	Nickel Coated Steel	345	2,187	2,400	Nitrocellulose
Italy	Paravicino-Carcano	1891	.256	4.2	8.3	6	Cupro Nickel	340	2,187	2,300	Balistite
Japan	Arisakae	1905	.264	4.2	8.6	5	Copper	346	2,187	2,420	Nitrocellulose
Mexico	Mauser	1902	.276	4.0	9.0	5	Cupro Nickel	336	2,187	2,295	Nitrocellulose
Netherlands	Mannlicher	1895	.256	4.2	9.0	5	Nickel Coated Steel	346	2,187	2,370	Nitrocellulose
Norway	Krag-Jörgensen	1894	.256	4.1	8.8	5	Nickel Coated Steel	364	2,405	2,370	Nitrocellulose
Peru	Mauser	1910	.301	4.1	9.1	5	Cupro Nickel	384	2,187	2,780	Karlsruhe s'less
Portugal	Mauser-Verguiero	1904	.256	3.6	8.1	5	Nickel Coated Steel	372	1,968	2,347	Nitrocellulose
Rumania	Mannlicher	1893	.256	4.0	8.8	5	Nickel Coated Steel	347	2,187	2,430	Nitrocellulose
Russia	Three line rifle	1891	.30	4.2	8.8	5	Nickel German Silver	348	2,660	2,886	Pyroxilin
Servia	Mauser	1899	.276	3.7	8.8	5	Cupro Nickel	374	2,187	2,450	Nitrocellulose
Spain	Mauser	1893	.276	4.0	8.8	5	Cupro Nickel	380	2,187	2,330	Nitrocellulose
Sweden	Mauser	1896	.256	4.1	8.6	5	Cupro Nickel	340	2,187	2,400	Nitrocellulose
Switzerland	Schmidt-Rubin	1906	.295	4.4	9.9	6	Nickel Coated Steel	425	2,187	2,705	Grafiled powder
Turkey	Mauser	1903	.301	4.0	9.0	5	Nickel Coated Steel	417	2,187	2,140	Nitrocellulose
Uruguay	Mauser	1908	.275	4.1	8.8	5	Nickeled Copper	365	4,370(30°)	2,740	Smokeless flakes

In 1908, the entire army and the national guard, with the exception of the States of Florida and Nevada, had been supplied with the United States magazine rifle, model of 1903, chambered for model of 1906 ammunition. This rifle has proved to be more powerful, accurate, and rapid than the rifle of the Krag-Jörgensen type which it replaced. The introduction of the ammunition of the model of 1906, with its sharp-pointed bullet of flat trajectory, represents the latest advance in fighting material of the civilized world.

At the present time no great difference exists in the effectiveness of the kinds of rifles with which the armies of the great powers are supplied with regard to their ranges and shooting qualities. It is well known that the effectiveness of any arm depends greatly on the experience and skill of the men who use it, and that, other things being equal, the troops most thoroughly instructed and drilled in the use of the rifle are the most efficient in battle. While the wounds inflicted by the modern small calibre high velocity rifles are less fatal and yield more readily to treatment than those made by the guns of large calibre using slow-burning black powder formerly in use, yet it is claimed that men hit by the smaller bullet, even if not killed or mortally wounded, are as completely put out of action as if struck by the larger.

The automatic rifle is, beyond question, the military weapon of the near future. Nearly all of the principal countries of Europe have been experimenting with rifles of this type, as well as the United States.

Germany adopted an automatic pistol for military use in 1908. The United States has recently adopted for the army, in place of the service revolver, the Colt automatic pistol, after extended and rigid experiments and tests by a board of army officers. This is regarded as a remarkably effective weap-on. Its length is 8.5 inches; length of barrel, 4.8 inches; weight, 2 lbs. 8 oz.; calibre, .45; cartridges in magazine, 7. The German automatic pistol has a length of 8.54 inches; length of barrel, 4.02 inches; weight 1 lb. 13½ oz.; calibre, .35; cartridges in magazine, 8.

Arms and Ammunition:

Contract for, referred to, 3795.

Delivery of, to—

State arsenals referred to, 2839.

Exportation of, order prohibiting, 3326, 8469.

Extended, 3436.

Modified, 3379.

Recommended, 373.

Rescinded, 3533.

Gunpowder, manufactory, erection of, recommended, 1608, 1714.

Loans of, to private citizens inquired into, 636.

Manufactory for small arms recommended, 1608, 1714.

Manufacture of—

Progress made in, 301, 471.

Should be encouraged, 255, 297, 443.

Statement of, 597.

Patent rifle, expenditures relating to procurement and properties of, 936.

Statement of, 767, 770, 790.

Supply of, 461.

Territories and District of Columbia to receive supplies not to exceed the quota of a State with least representation in Congress, 5159, 5462.

Army.—The earliest American military establishment consisted of two parts, the continental army, organized by the Continental Congress June 15, 1775, and the militia (*q. v.*) organized by the States, averaging between the years 1775 and 1781 about 60,000 men, though often not more than half that number were in active service. The War Department (*q. v.*) was established by act of Congress Aug. 7, 1789. Nov. 5, 1783, the army was disbanded and 1,000 men retained until the peace establishment could be organized. Though temporarily increased by Indian wars and troubles with France, the federal forces numbered only from 3,000 to 5,000 men at the outbreak of the War of 1812. During that war the number of regular troops was more than 85,000, and 470,000 militia were enlisted. Up to the time of the Mexican War the army averaged 9,000 men. During that war the regular troops enrolled numbered 30,000 and the volunteers 74,000. With the return of peace the regular forces were reduced to 10,000, and later increased to 12,000.

During the first year of the Civil War the regular army was increased to 35,000 by the addition of eleven regiments, viz.: One of cavalry, 1,189 officers and men; one of artillery, twelve batteries, six pieces each, 1,909 men; nine of infantry, consisting of three battalions of eight companies each, 22,068 officers and men; but the number of militia and volunteers was very much larger. President Lincoln's first call, issued April 15, 1861, was for 75,000 men for three months' service (3214). Later enlistments were mostly for three years. At the beginning of 1862 the number of volunteers in the army was 550,000, and during the next three years it was 900,000. At the close of the war the Federal army numbered 1,000,000. The total number of enlistments was 2,213,363 (4156).

In 1867 the "peace establishment" of the United States army was fixed at 54,641 men. It was then reduced by successive enactments to 25,000 enlisted men in 1875. At the beginning of 1898 the peace establishment of the army consisted of ten regiments cavalry, 8,410; five regiments artillery, 2,900; twenty-five regiments infantry, 13,525; one engineer battalion, 216; total, 25,051. This did not include brigade and staff officers. At the outbreak of the Spanish-American War two additional regiments of artillery were added to the regular forces and the line of the army was reorganized on the basis of two battalions of four companies each to the regiment, and two skeleton companies. In case of a declaration of war these skeleton companies were to be manned, and, with two other companies for which authority to raise was granted, were to form the third battalion in each infantry regiment.

Under the provisions of a law approved March 2, 1899, the regular army establishment was fixed at about 27,700 officers and men. To meet the exigencies of the service in the newly acquired possessions, the President was authorized to maintain the regular army at a strength of 65,000 enlisted men and to raise a force of 35,000 volunteers, to be recruited from the country at large or from the localities where their services are needed, "without restriction as to citizenship or educational qualifications."

An act of February, 1901, abolished the "canteen" from the army, that is, prohibited the sale of beer or any intoxicating liquors at the army posts. The organization of the army was further modified by an act of Congress approved Feb. 14, 1903, which created the General Staff Corps. This consists of the Chief of Staff, who

AUTHORIZED STRENGTH OF THE ARMY IN 1916.

Source—Report of Chief of Staff to Secretary of War.—The strength of the entire Military Establishment authorized by the President, under the statutory limitation of 100,000 enlisted men, on June 30, 1915, by branches of service, is shown in the following table:

BRANCHES OF SERVICE.	Officers.	Enlisted men.	Total.
General officers.....................	25	......	25
Adjutant General's Dep't..........	23	......	23
Inspector General's Dep't........	17	......	17
Judge Advocate General's Dep't...	13	......	13
Quartermaster Dep't.............	183	[1]6,403	[1]6,586
Medical Dep't....................	[2]601	[3]4,012	[2][3]4,613
Corps of Engineers...............	248	1,942	2,190
Ordnance Dep't..................	85	745	830
Signal Corps.....................	106	1,472	1,578
Bureau of Insular Affairs.........	3	......	3
Professors, U.S. Military Academy.	7	......	7
Chaplains........................	67	......	67
Cavalry..........................	809	14,148	14,957
Field Artillery...................	262	5,541	5,803
Coast Artillery Corps.............	748	19,019	19,767
Infantry.........................	1,606	35,339	36,945
Porto Rico Regiment of Infantry..	31	599	630
U.S. Military Academy............	......	632	632
Recruiting parties, etc...........	......	6,125	6,125
U.S. Disciplinary Barracks guards.	......	350	350
Service-school detachments.......	......	729	729
With disciplinary organizations....	......	110	110
Mounted orderlies................	......	7	7
Indian scouts....................	......	75	75
Total Regular Army......	**4,834**	**97,248**	**102,082**
Philippine Scouts................	182	5,733	5,915
Aggregate...............	**5,016**	**102,981**	**107,997**
Actual Aggregate.........	4,798	101,195	105,993

[1] Includes the enlisted strength (6,000 men) of the Quartermaster Corps, which men, under the provisions of the act of Congress approved Aug. 24, 1912 (37 Stat. L., 593), are "not to be counted as a part of the enlisted force provided by law."

[2] Includes 97 officers of the Medical Reserve Corps assigned to active duty under the provisions of the act of Congress approved Apr. 23, 1908 (35 Stat. L., 66).

[3] Authorized strength of the Hospital Corps, which, under the act of Congress approved Mar. 1, 1887 (24 Stat. L., 435), is not to be counted as a part of the enlisted strength of the Army.

Table showing the actual strength of the Army prior to the passage of the army law of 1916.

ORGANIZATIONS.	Strength June 30, 1915.	
	Officers.	Enlisted men.
General officers....................	25	....
Adjutant General's Department....	23	....
Inspector General's Department...	17	....
Judge Advocate General's Department................	12	....
Quartermaster Corps [1]............	185	4,792
Medical Corps [2]..................	422	3,993
Medical Reserve Corps.............	97	....
Dental Surgeons...................	34	....
Corps of Engineers................	207	1,948
Ordnance Department.............	85	740
Signal Corps......................	63	1,371
Bureau of Insular Affairs..........	3	....
Chaplains........................	64	....
Professors........................	7	....
Total.................	**1,244**	**12,844**

ORGANIZATIONS.	Strength June 30, 1915.	
	Officers.	Enlisted men.
First Cavalry	47	950
Second Cavalry	44	985
Third Cavalry	48	1,000
Fourth Cavalry	50	977
Fifth Cavalry	46	1,049
Sixth Cavalry	46	952
Seventh Cavalry	49	960
Eighth Cavalry	48	960
Ninth Cavalry	46	1,038
Tenth Cavalry	47	968
Eleventh Cavalry	44	1,001
Twelfth Cavalry	46	936
Thirteenth Cavalry	47	963
Fourteenth Cavalry	43	919
Fifteenth Cavalry [3]	47	988
Additional Officers [3]	12	....
Detached Officers [4]	47	....
Unassigned	21	....
Total	778	14,646
First Field Artillery	41	889
Second Field Artillery	37	885
Third Field Artillery	40	955
Fourth Field Artillery	38	904
Fifth Field Artillery	40	1,031
Sixth Field Artillery	39	1,000
Additional officers [3]	1	....
Detached officers [4]	15	....
Unassigned	11	....
Total	262	5,664
Coast Artillery Corps	728	19,185
First Infantry	48	1,804
Second Infantry	47	1,802
Third Infantry	47	887
Fourth Infantry	47	956
Fifth Infantry	48	1,736
Sixth Infantry	47	850
Seventh Infantry	46	927
Eighth Infantry	47	1,835
Ninth Infantry	48	851
Tenth Infantry	48	1,744
Eleventh Infantry	46	886
Twelfth Infantry	46	856
Thirteenth Infantry	48	1,835
Fourteenth Infantry	47	1,100
Fifteenth Infantry	47	1,823
Sixteenth Infantry	46	918
Seventeenth Infantry	46	886
Eighteenth Infantry	46	922
Nineteenth Infantry	46	820
Twentieth Infantry	45	894
Twenty-first Infantry	44	858
Twenty-second Infantry	47	928
Twenty-third Infantry	48	859
Twenty-fourth Infantry	44	1,849
Twenty-fifth Infantry	49	1,808
Twenty-sixth Infantry	45	922
Twenty-seventh Infantry	43	918
Twenty-eighth Infantry	46	937
Twenty-ninth Infantry	49	1,177
Thirtieth Infantry	49	949
Porto Rico Regiment of Infantry	31	586
Additional officers [3]	12	....
Detached officers [4]	94	....
Unassigned	67	....
Total	1,604	36,123
West Point detachments	......	623
Indian Scouts	......	24
Casuals and recruits at depots and en route		6,656
Total	......	7,303
Total, Regular Army	4,616	95,765
Philippine Scouts	182	5,430
Aggregate	4,798	101,195

takes the place of the Commanding General of the Army, two general officers detailed by the President from the regular army not below the grade of brigadier-general, and forty-two officers of minor grade similarly detailed by the President. It is the duty of the General Staff Corps to prepare plans for the national defense and for the mobilization of the military forces in time of war; to assist the Secretary of War in increasing the efficiency of the military establishment; and in case of war to act as a Board of Strategy. The Chief of Staff has supervision of all troops of the line, the Military Secretary's Office, the Inspector-General's, Judge-Advocate-General's, Quartermaster's, Subsistence, Medical, Pay, and Ordnance Departments, the Corps of Engineers and Signal Corps.

The army reorganization law of 1916, approved June 3, provides that the Army of the United States shall consist of the Regular Army, the Volunteer Army, the Officers' Reserve Corps, the Enlisted Reserve Corps, the National Guard while in the service of the United States, and such other land forces as were then or might thereafter be authorized by law.

Composition of the Regular Army.—The Regular Army of the United States, including existing organizations, was made to consist of 64 regiments of Infantry, 25 regiments of Cavalry, 21 regiments of Field Artillery, a Coast Artillery Corps, the brigade, division, army corps, and army headquarters, with their detachments and troops, a General Staff Corps, an Adjutant General's Department, an Inspector General's Department, Judge Advocate General's Department, Quartermaster Corps, Medical Department, Corps of Engineers, Ordnance Department, Signal Corps, the officers of the Bureau of Insular Affairs, the Militia Bureau, the detached officers, detached non-commissioned officers, chaplains, the Regular Army Reserve, as well as the officers and enlisted men on the retired list; the additional officers; also the professors, Corps of Cadets, general Army service detachment, and detachments of Cavalry, Field Artillery, Engineers, and band of the United States Military Academy; the post non-commissioned staff officers; recruiting parties, recruit depot detachments, and unassigned recruits; service school detachments; disciplinary guards; disciplinary organizations; Indian Scouts; and such other officers and enlisted men as may be provided for.

The law fixes a minimum of 160,000 fighting regulars, below which it will be the duty of the War Department to see that the Army never falls. This may be increased to a peace maximum of 175,000. Besides this in peace there will be 5,733 Philippine scouts, 6,409 of the Quartermaster Corps, 7,299 of the Medical Corps, 3,387 of the Signal Corps, and 8,750 unassigned enlisted men, a total of 206,169 men in peace. The force may be increased by executive order without Congressional action to about 293,-000 men and 12,000 officers.

The National Guard, when raised to full war strength, numbers almost 330,000 men. The first draft army authorized by the Sixty-fifth Congress in May, 1917, provides for 547,197 officers and men in addition to the above.

Draft Bill of 1917.—Section 5 of the bill for the increase of the army passed by Congress and approved by the President on May 18, 1917, made provision for a draft army of 500,000 men, which, with the addition of officers and other military units, brought the total of the force thus provided to 687,000. All citizens between the ages of 21 and 30, inclusive, were subject to the draft, which, according to figures given out by the Census Bureau, would thus select for military service about 1 in every 20 men included in these age limits. The draft was arranged according to the quotas of the several states, and from compulsory universal registration taken upon June 5. The bill also provided for the selection of a second similar force in case of necessity. (See Drafts.)

Those exempted from the draft were officers and officials of the several states and of the Federal Government, those in industry whom the President might deem it wise to withhold from military service, ministers and theological students, those belonging to a well-established religious body whose tenets forbid participation in war, and those found upon examination to be morally or physically unfit for service. No provision is made for the so-called "conscientious objectors" (q. v.), but all cases of those claiming exemption other than that provided for under the law were to be tried before local civil boards, with the right of appeal to the higher courts. Refusal to register was pronounced a misdemeanor by the provisions of the act, and made those found guilty of such misdemeanor subject to not more than a year's imprisonment. Furthermore, such persons became automatically registered upon release from imprisonment, as though they had been registered at the first conscription registration.

The remaining sections of the act increased the regular army to full war strength; drafted into the national service all Federal Guard units; allowed the raising of four divisions of volunteer infantry, if the President deemed such action advisable; increased the pay of all enlisted men from $15 monthly for those receiving less than $21 monthly at the time of the passage of the act to $6 monthly for those receiving at that time more than $45 monthly; and prohibited the sale of liquor at or near army training camps, with other provision for safeguarding the morals of army and camp life.

Secretary of War Baker reported that on December 31, 1917 there were in the United States Army 110,865 officers and 1,428,650 enlisted men. By April 6, 1918, there were 123,801 officers and 1,528,924 men, as compared with 9,524 officers and 202,510 men on April 6, 1917, the date upon which war with Germany was officially declared.

General Officers of the Line.—Officers commissioned to and holding in the Army the office of a general officer shall hereafter be known as general officers of the line; officers commissioned to and holding in the Army an office other than that of a general officer, but to which the rank of a general officer is attached, shall be known as general officers of the staff. The number of general officers of the line now authorized by law is hereby increased by four major generals and nineteen brigadier generals: *Provided,* That hereafter in time of peace major generals of the line shall be appointed from officers of the grade of brigadier general of the line, and brigadier generals of the line shall be appointed from officers of the grade of colonel of the line of the Regular Army.

General Staff Corps.—The General Staff Corps shall consist of 1 Chief of Staff, detailed in time of peace from major generals of the line; 2 Assistants to the Chief of Staff, who shall be general officers of the line, one of whom, not above the grade of brigadier general, shall be the president of the Army War College; 10 colonels; 10 lieutenant colonels; 15 majors; and 17 captains, to be detailed from corresponding grades in the Army. All officers detailed in the General Staff Corps shall be detailed

therein for period of four years, unless sooner relieved. While serving in the General Staff Corps officers may be temporarily assigned to duty with any branch of the Army.

Adjutant General's Department is made to consist of the Adjutant General with the rank of brigadier general; 7 adjutants-general with the rank of colonel; 13 adjutants-general with the rank of lieutenant colonel; and 30 adjutants-general with the rank of major.

The Inspector General's Department.—One Inspector General with the rank of brigadier general; 4 inspectors-general with the rank of colonel; 8 inspectors-general with the rank of lieutenant colonel; and 16 inspectors-general with the rank of major.

Judge Advocate General's Department.—One Judge Advocate General with the rank of brigadier general; 4 judge advocates with the rank of colonel; 7 judge advocates with the rank of lieutenant colonel; and 20 judge advocates with the rank of major.

Quartermaster Corps.—One Quartermaster General with the rank of major general; 2 assistants with the rank of brigadier general; 21 colonels; 24 lieutenant colonels; 68 majors; 180 captains; and the pay clerks now in active service, who shall hereafter have the rank, pay, and allowances of a second lieutenant, and the President is authorized to appoint and commission them, by and with the advice and consent of the Senate, second lieutenants in the Quartermaster Corps, United States Army. The total enlisted strength of the Quartermaster Corps and the number in each grade shall be limited and fixed from time to time by the President in accordance with the needs of the Army, and shall consist of quartermaster sergeants, senior grade; quartermaster sergeants; sergeants, first class; sergeants; corporals; cooks; privates, first class; and privates. The number in the various grades shall not exceed the following percentages of the total authorized enlisted strength of the Quartermaster Corps, namely: Quartermaster sergeants, senior grade, ½ of 1 per cent; quartermaster sergeants, 6 per cent; sergeants, first class, 2½ per cent; sergeants, 25 per cent; corporals, 10 per cent; privates, first class, 45 per cent; privates, 9 per cent; cooks, 2 per cent. Master electricians now authorized by law for the Quartermaster Corps shall be known as quartermaster sergeants, senior grade, and shall be included in the number of quartermaster sergeants, senior grade, herein authorized. All work pertaining to construction and repair that has heretofore been done by or under the direction of officers of the Quartermaster Corps shall, except as otherwise now provided by laws or regulations, be done by or under the direction of officers of said corps.

Medical Department.—One Surgeon General, with the rank of major general during the active service of the present incumbent of that office, and thereafter with the rank of brigadier general, who shall be chief of said department, a Medical Corps, a Medical Reserve Corps within the limit of time fixed by this Act, a Dental Corps, a Veterinary Corps, an enlisted force, the Nurse Corps and contract surgeons as now authorized by law, the commissioned officers of which shall be citizens of the United States.

Medical Corps.—Commissioned officers below the grade of brigadier general, proportionally distributed among the several grades as in the Medical Corps now established by law. The total number of such officers shall approximately be equal to, but not exceed, 7 for every 1,000 of the total enlisted strength of the Regular Army authorized from time to time by law. When in time of war the Regular Army shall have been increased by virtue of the provisions of this or any other Act, the medical officers appointed to meet such increase shall be honorably discharged from the service of the United States when the reduction of the enlisted strength of the Army shall take place; persons commissioned in the Medical Corps shall be citizens of the United States between the ages of twenty-two and thirty years and shall be promoted to the grade of captain upon the completion of five years' service in the Medical Corps and upon passing the examinations prescribed by the President for promotion to the grade of captain in the Medical Corps; the President is authorized to detail not to exceed five officers of the Medical Department of the Army for duty with the military relief division of the American National Red Cross.

The enlisted force of the Medical Department shall consist of the following personnel (in the proportions stated), who shall not be included in the effective strength of the Army nor counted as a part of the enlisted force provided by law: Master hospital sergeants, ½ of 1 per cent of the total authorized strength of the Medical Department; hospital sergeants, ½ of 1 per cent; sergeants, first class, 7 per cent; sergeants, 11 per cent; corporals, 5 per cent; and cooks, 6 per cent; the number of horseshoers, saddlers, farriers, and mechanics shall not exceed 1 each to each authorized ambulance company or like organization; the number of privates, first class, shall not exceed 25 per cent of the number of privates. Privates, first class, of the Medical Department are eligible for ratings for additional pay as follows: As dispensary assistant, $2 a month; as nurse, $3 a month; as surgical assistant, $5 a month.

The President is authorized to appoint dental surgeons, who are citizens of the United States between the ages of 21 and 27 years, at the rate of 1 for each 1,000 enlisted men of the line of the Army. Dental surgeons shall have the rank, pay, and allowances of first lieutenants until they have completed 8 years' service; of more than 8 but less than 24 years' service (subject to examination), may have the rank, pay, and allowances of captains; after more than 24 years' service shall have the rank, pay, and allowances of major. The total number of dental surgeons with rank, pay, and allowances of major shall not at any time exceed 15.

Authority is given the Secretary of War to grant permission, by revocable license, to the American National Red Cross to erect and maintain on any military reservations within the jurisdiction of the United States buildings suitable for the storage of supplies, or to occupy for that purpose buildings erected by the United States, under such regulations as the Secretary of War may prescribe, such supplies to be available for the aid of the civilian population in case of serious national disaster.

Corps of Engineers.—One Chief of Engineers, with the rank of brigadier general; 23 colonels; 30 lieutenant colonels; 72 majors; 152 captains; 148 first lieutenants; 79 second lieutenants; and the enlisted men hereinafter enumerated. The Engineer troops of the Corps of Engineers shall consist of 1 band, 7 regiments, and 2 mounted battalions.

Each regiment of Engineers shall consist of 1 colonel; 1 lieutenant colonel; 2 majors; 11 captains; 12 first lieutenants; 6 second lieutenants; 2 master engineers, senior grade; 1 regimental sergeant major; 2

regimental supply sergeants; 2 color sergeants; 1 sergeant bugler; 1 cook; 1 wagoner for each authorized wagon of the field and combat train, and 2 battalions.

Each battalion of a regiment of Engineers shall consist of 1 major, 1 captain, 1 battalion sergeant major; 3 master engineers, junior grade; and 3 companies. Each Engineer company (regimental) shall consist of 1 captain; 2 first lieutenants; 1 second lieutenant; 1 first sergeant; 3 sergeants, first class; 1 mess sergeant; 1 supply sergeant; 1 stable sergeant; 6 sergeants; 12 corporals; 1 horseshoer; 2 buglers; 1 saddler; 2 cooks; 19 privates, first class; and 59 privates, with provision for increase.

The Engineer band shall consist of 1 band leader; 1 assistant band leader; 1 first sergeant; 2 band sergeants; four band corporals; 2 musicians, first class; 4 musicians, second class; 13 musicians, third class; and two cooks.

Each battalion of mounted Engineers shall consist of 1 major; 5 captains; 7 first lieutenants; 3 second lieutenants; 1 master engineer, senior grade; 1 battalion sergeant major; 1 battalion supply sergeant; 3 master engineers, junior grade; 1 corporal; 1 wagoner for each authorized wagon of the field and combat train; and 3 mounted companies. Each mounted Engineer company shall consist of 1 captain; 2 first lieutenants; 1 second lieutenant; 1 first sergeant; 2 sergeants, first class; 1 mess sergeant; 1 supply sergeant; 1 stable sergeant; 4 sergeants; 8 corporals; 2 horseshoers; 1 saddler; 2 cooks; 2 buglers; 12 privates, first class; and 37 privates, with provisions for increase. The enlisted force of the Corps of Engineers and the officers serving therewith shall constitute a part of the line of the Army.

Ordnance Department.—One Chief of Ordnance, with the rank of brigadier general; 10 colonels; 15 lieutenant colonels; 32 majors; 42 captains; 42 first lieutenants; the ordnance sergeants, as now authorized by law, and such other enlisted men of grades now authorized by law as the President may direct. The Secretary of War is authorized to detail not to exceed 30 lieutenants from the Army at large for duty as student officers in the establishments of the Ordnance Department for a period of 2 years; and the completion of the prescribed course of instruction shall constitute the examination for detail in the Ordnance Department.

Signal Corps.—One Chief Signal Officer, with the rank of brigadier general; 3 colonels; 8 lieutenant colonels; 10 majors; 30 captains; 75 first lieutenants; and the aviation section, which shall consist of 1 colonel; 1 lieutenant colonel; 8 majors; 24 captains; and 114 first lieutenants, who shall be selected from among officers of the Army at large of corresponding grades or from among officers of the grade below, exclusive of those serving by detail in staff corps or departments, who are qualified as military aviators, and shall be detailed to serve as aviation officers for periods of 4 years unless sooner relieved; and the provisions of section 27 of the Act of Congress approved Feb. 2, 1901, are hereby extended to apply to said aviation officers and to vacancies created in any arm, corps, or department of the Army by the detail of said officers therefrom.

Aviation officers may, when qualified therefor, be rated as junior military aviators or as military aviators. Each aviation officer shall, while on duty that requires him to participate regularly and frequently in aerial flights, receive an increase of 25 to

75 per cent in the pay of his grade and length of service under his commission. Married officers of the line of the Army shall be eligible equally with unmarried officers, and subject to the same conditions, for detail to aviation duty; and the Secretary of War shall have authority to cause as many enlisted men of the aviation section to be instructed in the art of flying as he may deem necessary; the age of officers shall not be a bar to their first detail in the aviation section of the Signal Corps, and neither their age nor their rank shall be a bar to their subsequent details in said section. When it shall be impracticable to obtain from the Army officers suitable for the aviation section of the Signal Corps in the number allowed by law the difference between that number and the number of suitable officers actually available for duty in said section may be made up by appointments in the grade of aviator, Signal Corps, and that grade is hereby created. The personnel for said grade shall be obtained from especially qualified civilians who shall be appointed and commissioned in said grade. The base pay of an aviator, Signal Corps, shall be $150 per month, and he shall have the allowances of a master signal electrician and the same percentage of increase in pay for length of service as is allowed to a master signal electrician.

The total enlisted strength of the Signal Corps shall be limited and fixed from time to time by the President in accordance with the needs of the Army, and shall consist of: Master signal electricians, 2 per cent of the total authorized enlisted strength of the Signal Corps; sergeants, first class, 7 per cent; sergeants, 10 per cent; corporals, 20 per cent. The number of privates, first class, shall not exceed 25 per cent of the number of privates. Authority is hereby given the President to organize, in his discretion, such part of the commissioned and enlisted personnel of the Signal Corps into such number of companies, battalions, and aero squadrons as the necessities of the service may demand.

Chaplains.—The President is authorized to appoint chaplains in the Army at the rate of not to exceed, including chaplains now in service, one for each regiment of Cavalry, Infantry, Field Artillery, and Engineers, and one for each 1,200 officers and men of the Coast Artillery Corps.

Veterinarians.—The President is authorized to appoint veterinarians and assistant veterinarians in the Army, not to exceed, including veterinarians now in service, 2 such officers for each regiment of Cavalry, 1 for every 3 batteries of Field Artillery, 1 for each mounted battalion of Engineers, 17 as inspectors of horses and mules and as veterinarians in the Quartermaster Corps, and 7 as inspectors of meats for the Quartermaster Corps; and said veterinarians and assistant veterinarians shall be citizens of the United States and shall constitute the Veterinary Corps and shall be a part of the Medical Department of the Army. The Secretary of War shall from time to time appoint boards of examiners to conduct the veterinary examinations hereinbefore prescribed, each of said boards to consist of 3 medical officers and 2 veterinarians.

Coast Artillery Corps.—1 Chief of Coast Artillery, with the rank of brigadier general; 24 colonels; 24 lieutenant colonels; 72 majors; 360 captains; 360 first lieutenants; 360 second lieutenants; 31 sergeants major, senior grade; 64 sergeants major, junior grade; 41 master electricians; 72 engineers; 99 electrician sergeants (first class); 275 assistant engineers; 99 electrician sergeants (second class); 106 firemen; 93 radio sergeants; 62 master gunners; 263 first sergeants; 263 supply sergeants; 263 mess sergeants; 2,104 sergeants; 3,156 corporals; 526 cooks; 526 mechanics; 526 buglers; 5,225 privates (first class); 15,675 privates; and 18 bands, organized as hereinbefore provided for the Engineer band. The rated men of the Coast Artillery Corps shall consist of casemate electricians; observers (first class); plotters; chief planters; coxswains; chief loaders; observers (second class); gun commanders and gun pointers. The total number of rated men shall not exceed 1,784. Coxswains shall receive $9 per month in addition to the pay of their grade.

Porto Rico Regiment of Infantry.—The same organization, and the same grades and numbers of commissioned officers and enlisted men, as are prescribed by law for other regiments of Infantry of the Army. The colonel of said regiment shall be detailed by the President, from among officers of Infantry of the Army not below the grade of lieutenant colonel, for a period of 4 years.

All men hereafter enlisting in said regiment shall be natives of Porto Rico. All enlistments in the regiment shall hereafter be the same as is provided herein for the Regular Army, and the regiment, or any part thereof, may be ordered for service outside the island of Porto Rico. The pay and allowances of members of said regiment shall be the same as provided by law for officers and enlisted men of like grades in the Regular Army.

Officers of the Porto Rico Regiment of Infantry, United States Army, who held commissions in the Porto Rico Provisional Regiment of Infantry on June 30, 1908, shall now and hereafter take rank in their grades in the same relative order held by them in said Porto Rico Provisional Regiment of Infantry on June 30, 1908, subject to any loss in rank due to failure to pass examinations for promotion or to sentence of court-martial.

Pay of Officers.—Yearly pay for the following grades in the Army is as follows:

General $10,000
Lieutenant General 9,000
Major General 8,000
Brigadier General 6,000

These officers receive no increase for continuous service.

Monthly pay for the following grades is as follows:

Colonel $333.33
Lieutenant Colonel 291.67
Major 250.00
Captain 200.00
First Lieutenant 166.67
Second Lieutenant 141.67

These amounts are increased 10% for each period of five years' service, provided that the sum total of such increase shall not exceed 40%.

All officers are furnished living quarters with fuel and light. If these cannot be furnished, the officers receive a commuted value for them. A second lieutenant's quarters consist of two rooms, and the figure is increased by one for each grade, the general's allowance being eleven rooms. Commutation is at the rate of $12.00 monthly per room. The allowance for heat and light depends upon locality.

There is an additional 10% of base pay and longevity pay for foreign service.

Aviation officers while in regular aerial service receive 25% additional of their pay; junior military aviators, 50%; and military aviators, 75%. If the ranks are not higher than that of captain, each junior military aviator and each military aviator qualified and serving gets the rank, pay and allowance of one grade higher than that of his commission.

Officers are not furnished clothing or equipment or subsistence.

Pay of Enlisted Men.—Monthly pay of enlisted men is as follows according to the different grades:

Privates, the entering grade, $30.

Privates of the first class, $33.

Corporals, saddlers, mechanics, farriers, wagoners, musicians of the third class, $36.

Sergeants of Infantry, Field and Coast Artillery, Cavalry; cooks, horseshoers, band corporals, musicians of the second class, $38.

Sergeants of Engineers Corps, Ordnance, Signal and Quartermaster Corps, and Medical Department; band sergeants, and musicians of the first class, $44.

Battalion sergeant majors, squadron sergeant majors, sergeant majors of the junior grade, sergeant buglers, master gunners, assistant band leaders of the line, $48.

Regimental sergeant majors, regimental supply sergeants, sergeant majors of the senior grade, quartermaster sergeants of the Quartermaster Corps, ordnance and first sergeants, electrician sergeants of the first class, assistant engineers and battalion sergeant majors and battalion supply sergeants of the engineers, $51.

Sergeants of the Medical Department (first class), $56.

Hospital sergeants, engineers and master engineers of the junior grade, $71.

Senior grade quartermaster sergeants of the Quartermaster Corps, band leaders, master signal electricians, master electricians, master engineers (senior grade), master hospital sergeants, $81.

Increased pay for continuous service is as follows: For privates, $3 per month for the second enlistment period, $3 per month for the third enlistment period, and $1 per month for further enlistment periods up to the seventh. The same provision applies to men between the $30 and $38 grades except that the additional monthly pay from the second to the seventh enlistment period is $3. Men above the $38 grade are entitled to $4 additional monthly pay for each enlistment period from the second to the seventh.

Enlisted men of the Coast Artillery below the grade of mess sergeant are granted additional pay in accordance with especial qualifications which they may possess.

Enlisted men of the Signal Corps who have the rating of aviation mechanics receive 50% additional of their monthly pay while they participate regularly in aerial flights.

Enlisted men are furnished subsistence, or if located where it cannot be furnished, are given $15 monthly for housing and an additional suitable allowance for subsistence and heat and light.

Enlisted men attached to the Military Academy are entitled to the same pay as enlisted men of the Regular Army of the same grade.

All enlisted men serving in a foreign country or beyond the continental limits of the United States (Porto Rico, Hawaii and the Canal Zone excepted) receive 20% increase over their base pay and service pay prevailing prior to June 1, 1917, on which day an act of Congress increased the pay of all enlisted men, in amounts ranging from 8% to 50%, during the existing emergency.

Enlisted men in active service have no standing expense except for barber and laundry services. Uniforms, underclothing, hats, shoes, medical attendance, living quarters and subsistence are supplied free by the Government. Other supplies, such as tobacco and sweets, are furnished at cost.

All enlisted men must contribute not more than 50% of their pay for the support of their immediate families. On application, the Government will add to this allotment an allowance of its own of from $5 to $50 per month, according to the size of the family. The amount that the Government gives to an enlisted man's immediate family is fixed by law as follows: $15 monthly for a wife, $25 for a wife and one child, $32.50 for a wife and two children, with $5 additional for each child. The minimum of the contribution from the enlisted man, deducted from his pay, is $15 monthly and the maximum is half his pay; but otherwise such contribution must equal the amount of the Government allowance.

See also Soldiers' and Sailors' Insurance.

Retirement.—Officers are retired for disability or after the age of 64, and then receive 75% of the pay of the grade held at the time of retirement.

Enlisted men may apply for retirement after 30 years of service. They then receive 75% of the pay drawn at the time of retirement with $15.75 monthly additional pay in lieu of allowances.

Original Appointments to Be Provisional. —Hereafter all appointments of persons other than graduates of the United States Military Academy to the grade of second lieutenant in the Regular Army shall be provisional for a period of two years, at the close of which period such appointments shall be made, permanent if the appointees shall have demonstrated, under such regulations as the President may prescribe, their suitability and moral, professional, and physical fitness for such permanent appointment.

Increase to Be Made in Five Increments. —Except as otherwise specifically provided, the increases in the commissioned and enlisted personnel of the Regular Army shall be made in five annual increments, each of which shall be, in each grade of each arm, corps, and department, as nearly as practicable, one-fifth of the total increase authorized for each arm, corps, and department.

Detached Officers.—That on July 1, 1916, the line of the Army shall be increased by 822 extra officers of the Cavalry, Field Artillery, Coast Artillery Corps, and Infantry arms of the service, of grades from first lieutenant to colonel, inclusive, lawfully available for detachment from their proper arms for duty with the National Guard, or other duty, the usual period of which exceeds one year. Said extra officers, together with the 200 detached officers provided for by the Act of Congress approved March 3, 1911, shall, on and after July 1, 1916, constitute the Detached Officers' List, and all positions vacated by officers assigned to said list, and the officers so assigned, shall be subject to the provisions of section 27 of the Act of Congress approved Feb. 2, 1901, with reference to details to the staff corps.

Enlistments in the Regular Army.—On and after Nov. 1, 1916, all enlistments in the Regular Army shall be for a term of 7 years, the first 3 years to be in the active service with the organizations of which those enlisted form a part and, except as otherwise provided herein, the last 4 years in the Regular Army Reserve hereinafter provided for; at the expiration of 3 years' continuous service with such organizations, either under a first or any subsequent enlistment, any soldier may be re-enlisted for another period of 7 years, as above provided for, in which event he shall receive his final discharge from his prior enlistment; after the expiration of 1 year's honorable service any enlisted man serving within the continental limits of the United States whose company, troop, battery, or detachment commander shall report him as proficient and sufficiently trained may, in the discretion of the Secretary of War, be furloughed to the Regular Army Reserve under such regulations as the Secretary of War may prescribe, but no man furloughed to the reserve shall be eligible to re-enlist in the service until the expiration of his term of 7 years; in all enlistments accomplished under the provisions of this Act 3 years shall be counted as an enlistment period in computing continuous-service pay; any noncommissioned officer discharged with an excellent character shall be permitted, at the expiration of 3 years in the active service, to re-enlist in the organization from which discharged with the rank and grade held by him at the time of his discharge if he re-enlists within 20 days after the date of such discharge; no person under the age of 18 years shall be enlisted or mustered into the military service of the United States without the written consent of his parents or guardians, provided that such minor has such parents or guardians entitled to his custody and control; the President is authorized in his discretion to utilize the services of postmasters of the second, third, and fourth classes in procuring the enlistments of recruits for the Army, and for each recruit accepted for enlistment in the Army, the postmaster procuring his enlistment shall receive the sum of $5.

In addition to military training, soldiers while in the active service shall hereafter be given the opportunity to study and receive instruction upon educational lines of such character as to increase their military efficiency and enable them to return to civil life better equipped for industrial, commercial, and general business occupations. Civilian teachers may be employed to aid the Army officers in giving such instruction, and part of this instruction may consist of vocational education either in agriculture or the mechanic arts.

Final Discharge of Enlisted Men.—No enlisted man in the Regular Army shall receive his final discharge until the termination of his 7-year term of enlistment except upon re-enlistment as provided for in this Act or as provided by law for discharge prior to expiration of term of enlistment, but when an enlisted man is furloughed to the Regular Army Reserve his account shall be closed and he shall be paid in full to the date such furlough becomes effective, including allowances provided by law for discharged soldiers; when by reason of death or disability of a member of the family of an enlisted man occurring after his enlistment members of his family become dependent upon him for support, he may, in the discretion of the Secretary of War, be discharged from the service of the United States or be furloughed to the Regular Army Reserve, upon due proof being made of such condition; when an enlisted man is discharged by purchase while in active service he shall be furloughed to the Regular Army Reserve.

Regular Army Reserve.—The Regular Army Reserve shall consist of, first, all enlisted men now in the Army Reserve or who shall hereafter become members of the Army Reserve under the provisions of existing law; second, all enlisted men furloughed to or enlisted in the Regular Army Reserve under the provisions of this Act; and, third, any person holding an honorable discharge from the Regular Army with character reported at least good who is physically qualified for the duties of a soldier and not over

45 years of age who enlists in the Regular Army Reserve for a period of 4 years.

The President is authorized to assign members of the Regular Army Reserve as reserves to particular organizations of the Regular Army, or to organize the Regular Army Reserve, or any part thereof, into units or detachments of any arm, corps, or department in such manner as he may prescribe, and to assign to such units and detachments officers of the Regular Army or of the Officers' Reserve Corps, and he may summon the Regular Army Reserve or any part thereof for field training for a period not exceeding 15 days in each year, the reservists to receive travel expenses and pay at the rate of their respective grades in the Regular Army during such periods of training; and in the event of actual or threatened hostilities he may mobilize the Regular Army Reserve in such manner as he may determine, and thereafter retain it, or any part thereof, in active service for such period as he may determine the conditions demand; all enlistments in the Regular Army, including those in the Regular Army Reserve, which are in force on the date of the outbreak of war shall continue in force for one year, unless sooner terminated by order of the Secretary of War, but nothing herein shall be construed to shorten the time of enlistment prescribed; subject to such regulations as the President may prescribe for their proper identification, and location, and physical condition, the members of the Regular Army Reserve shall be paid semi-annually at the rate of $24 a year while in the reserve.

Regular Army Reserve in Time of War.— When mobilized by order of the President, the members of the Regular Army Reserve shall, so long as they may remain in active service, receive the pay and allowances of enlisted men of the Regular Army of like grades; upon reporting for duty, and being found physically fit for service, members of the Regular Army Reserve shall receive a sum equal to $3 per month for each month during which they shall have belonged to the Reserve, as well as the actual necessary cost of transportation and subsistence from their homes to the places at which they may be ordered to report for duty under such summons; service in the Regular Army Reserve shall confer no right to retirement or retired pay, and members of the Regular Army Reserve shall become entitled to pension only through disability incurred while on active duty in the service of the United States.

Use of Other Departments of the Government.—The President may utilize the services of members and employees of all departments of the Government of the United States, without expense to the individual reservist, for keeping in touch with, paying, and mobilizing the Regular Army Reserve, the Enlisted Reserve Corps, and other reserve organizations.

Re-enlistment in Time of War.—For the purpose of utilizing as an auxiliary to the Regular Army Reserves the services of men who have had experience and training in the Regular Army, or in the United States Volunteers, outside of the continental limits of the United States, in time of actual or threatened hostilities, and after the President shall, by proclamation, have called upon honorably discharged soldiers of the Regular Army to present themselves for re-enlistment therein within a specified period, subject to such conditions as may be prescribed, any person who shall have been discharged honorably from said Army, with character reported as at least good, and who, having been found physically qualified for the duties of a soldier, if not over 50 years of age, shall re-enlist in the line of said Army, or in the Signal, Quartermaster, or Medical Department thereof, within the period that shall be specified in said proclamation, shall receive on so re-enlisting a bounty which shall be computed at the rate of $8 for each month for the first year of the period that shall have elapsed since his last discharge from the Regular Army and the date of his re-enlistment therein under the terms of said proclamation ; at the rate of $6 per month for the second year of such period ; at the rate of $4 per month for the third year of such period ; and at the rate of $2 per month for any subsequent year of such period ; but no bounty in excess of $300 shall be paid to any person under the terms of this section.

Enlisted Men Prohibited from Civil Employment.—No enlisted man in the active service of the United States in the Army, Navy, and Marine Corps, respectively, whether a noncommissioned officer, musician, or private, shall be detailed, ordered, or permitted to leave his post to engage in any pursuit, business, or performance in civil life, for emolument, hire, or otherwise, when the same shall interfere with the customary employment and regular engagement of local civilians in the respective arts, trades, or professions.

Sergeants for Duty with the National Guard.—For the purpose of assisting in the instruction of the personnel and care of property in the hands of the National Guard the Secretary of War is authorized to detail from the Infantry, Cavalry, Field Artillery, Corps of Engineers, Coast Artillery Corps, Medical Department, and Signal Corps of the Regular Army not to exceed 1,000 sergeants for duty with corresponding organizations of the National Guard and not to exceed 100 sergeants for duty with the disciplinary organizations at the United States Disciplinary Barracks, who shall be additional to the sergeants authorized by this Act for the corps, companies, troops, batteries, and detachments from which they may be detailed.

Officers' Reserve Corps.—For the purpose of securing a reserve of officers available for service as temporary officers in the Regular Army, as officers of the Quartermaster Corps and other staff corps and departments, as officers for recruit rendezvous and depots, and as officers of volunteers, there shall be organized, an Officers' Reserve Corps of the Regular Army. Said corps shall consist of sections corresponding to the various arms, staff corps, and departments of the Regular Army. A member of the Officers' Reserve Corps shall not be subject to call for service in time of peace, and whenever called upon for service shall not, without his consent, be so called in a lower grade than that held by him in said reserve corps.

The President alone shall be authorized to appoint and commission as reserve officers in the Officers' Reserve Corps, in all grades up to and including that of major, such citizens as, upon examination shall be found physically, mentally, and morally qualified to hold such commissions ; the proportion of officers in any section of the Officers' Reserve Corps shall not exceed the proportion for the same grade in the corresponding arm, corps, or department of the Regular Army, except that the number commissioned in the lowest authorized grade in any section of the Officers' Reserve Corps shall not be limited.

No person shall be appointed or reappointed a second lieutenant in the Officers' Reserve Corps after he shall have reached the age of 32 years, a first lieutenant after he shall have reached the age of 36 years, a captain after he shall have reached the age of 40 years, or a major after he shall have reached the age of 45. When an officer of the Reserve Corps shall reach the age limit fixed for appointment or reappointment in the grade in which commissioned he shall be honorably discharged from the service of the United States, and be entitled to retain his official title and, on occasions of ceremony, to wear the uniform of the highest grade he shall have held in the Officers' Reserve Corps ; nothing in the provisions as to the ages of officers shall apply to the appointment or reappointment of officers of the Quartermaster, Engineer, Ordnance, Signal, Judge Advocate, and Medical sections of said Reserve Corps. One year after the passage of this Act the Medical Reserve Corps, as now constituted by law, shall cease to exist. Members thereof may be commissioned in the Officers' Reserve Corps, or may be honorably discharged from the service.

Officers' Reserve Corps in War.—In time of actual or threatened hostilities the President may order officers of the Officers' Reserve Corps, to temporary duty with the Regular Army in grades thereof which can not, for the time being, be filled by promotion, or as officers in volunteer or other organizations that may be authorized by law, or as officers at recruit rendezvous and depots, or on such other duty as the President may prescribe. While such reserve officers are on such service they shall, by virtue of their commissions as reserve officers, exercise command appropriate to their grade and rank in the organizations to which they may be assigned, and shall be entitled to the pay and allowances of the corresponding grades in the Regular Army, with increase of pay for length of active service, as allowed by law for officers of the Regular Army, from the date upon which they shall be required by the terms of their orders to obey the same ; officers so ordered to active service shall take temporary rank among themselves, and in their grades in the organizations to which assigned, according to the dates of orders placing them on active service ; and they may be promoted, in accordance with such rank, to vacancies in volunteer organizations or to temporary vacancies in the Regular Army thereafter occurring in the organizations in which they shall be serving ; officers of the Officers' Reserve Corps shall not be entitled to retirement or retired pay, and shall be entitled to pension only for disability incurred in the line of duty and while in active service.

Instruction of Officers of the Officers' Reserve Corps.—To the extent provided for from time to time by appropriations for this specific purpose, the Secretary of War is authorized to order reserve officers to duty with troops or at field exercises, or for instruction, for periods not to exceed 15 days in any one calendar year, and while so serving such officers shall receive the pay and allowances of their respective grades in the Regular Army ; with the consent of the reserve officers concerned, and within the limit of funds available for the purpose, such periods of duty may be extended for reserve officers as the Secretary of War may direct ; in time of actual or threatened hostilities, after all available officers of any section of the Officers' Reserve Corps shall have been ordered into active service, officers of Volunteers may be appointed in such arm, corps, or department as may be authorized by law.

Reserve Officers' Training Corps.—The President is hereby authorized to establish and maintain in civil educational institutions a Reserve Officers' Training Corps, which shall consist of a senior division organized at universities and colleges requiring four years of collegiate study for a degree, including State universities and those State institutions that are required to provide instruction in military tactics under the provisions of the Act of Congress of July 2, 1862, donating lands for the establishment of colleges where the leading object shall be practical instruction in agriculture and the mechanic arts, including military tactics, and a junior division organized at all other public or private educational institutions, except that units of the senior division may be organized at those essentially military schools which do not confer an academic degree but which, as a result of the annual inspection of such institutions by the War Department, are specially designated by the Secretary of War as qualified for units of the senior division, and each division shall consist of units of the several arms or corps in such number and of such strength as the President may prescribe.

The President may, upon the application of any State institution described in this Act, establish and maintain at such institution one or more units of the Reserve Officers' Training Corps: *Provided,* That no such unit shall be established or maintained at any such institution until an officer of the Army shall have been detailed as professor of military science and tactics, nor until such institution shall maintain under military instruction at least 100 physically fit male students.

The President may, upon the application of any established educational institution in the United States other than a State institution described above the authorities of which agree to establish and maintain a two years' elective or compulsory course of military training as a minimum for its physically fit male students, which course when entered upon by any student shall, as regards such student, be a prerequisite for graduation, establish and maintain at such institution one or more units of the Reserve Officers' Training Corps.

The Secretary of War is authorized to prescribe standard courses of theoretical and practical military training for units of the Reserve Officers' Training Corps, and no unit of the senior division shall be organized or maintained at any educational institution the authorities of which fail or neglect to adopt into their curriculum the prescribed courses of military training for the senior division or to devote at least an average of three hours per week per academic year to such military training; and no unit of the junior division shall be organized or maintained at any educational institution the authorities of which fail or neglect to adopt into their curriculum the prescribed courses of military training for the junior division, or to devote at least an average of three hours per week per academic year to such military training.

Eligibility to membership in the Reserve Officers' Training Corps shall be limited to students of institutions in which units of such corps may be established who are citizens of the United States, who are not less than 14 years of age, and whose bodily condition indicates that they are physically fit to perform military duty, or will be so upon arrival at military age.

The President is hereby authorized to detail such numbers of officers of the Army, either active or retired, not above the grade of colonel, as may be necessary, for duty as professors and assistant professors of military science and tactics at institutions where one or more units of the Reserve Officers' Training Corps are maintained; but the total number of active officers so detailed at educational institutions shall not exceed 300.

The President is authorized to detail for duty at institutions where one or more units of the Reserve Officers' Training Corps are maintained such number of enlisted men, either active or retired or of the Regular Army Reserve, as he may deem necessary, but the number of active noncommissioned officers so detailed shall not exceed 500.

The Secretary of War is authorized to issue to institutions at which one or more units of the Reserve Officers' Training Corps are maintained such public animals, arms, uniforms, equipment, and means of transportation as he may deem necessary, and to forage at the expense of the United States public animals so issued. He shall require from each institution to which property of the United States is issued a bond in the value of the property issued for the care and safe-keeping thereof, and for its return when required.

The Secretary of War is authorized to maintain camps for the further practical instruction of the members of the Reserve Officers' Training Corps, no such camps to be maintained for a period longer than six weeks in any one year, except in time of actual or threatened hostilities; to transport members of such corps to and from such camps at the expense of the United States so far as appropriations will permit; to subsist them at the expense of the United States while traveling to and from such camps and while remaining therein so far as appropriations will permit; to use the Regular Army, such other military forces as Congress from time to time authorizes, and such Government property as he may deem necessary for the military training of the members of such corps while in attendance at such camps; to prescribe regulations for the government of such corps; and to authorize, in his discretion, the formation of company units thereof into battalion and regimental units.

The President alone, under such regulations as he may prescribe, is authorized to appoint in the Officers' Reserve Corps any graduate of the senior division of the Reserve Officers' Training Corps who shall have satisfactorily completed the further training provided for below, or any graduate of the junior division who shall have satisfactorily completed the courses of military training prescribed for the senior division and the further training provided for below, and shall have participated in such practical instruction subsequent to graduation as the Secretary of War shall prescribe, who shall have arrived at the age of 21 years and who shall agree, under oath in writing, to serve the United States in the capacity of a reserve officer of the Army during a period of at least 10 years from the date of his appointment as such reserve officer, but the total number of reserve officers so appointed shall not exceed 50,000; any qualified graduate undergoing a postgraduate course at any institution shall not be eligible for appointment as a reserve officer while undergoing such postgraduate course.

When any member of the senior division of the Reserve Officers' Training Corps has completed two academic years of service in that division, and has been selected for further training by the president of the institution and by its professor of military science and tactics, and has agreed in writing to continue in the Reserve Officers' Training Corps for the remainder of his course in the institution, devoting five hours per week to the military training prescribed by the Secretary of War, and has agreed in writing to pursue the courses in camp training prescribed by the Secretary of War, he may be furnished, at the expense of the United States, with commutation of subsistence at such rate, not exceeding the cost of the garrison ration prescribed for the Army, as may be fixed by the Secretary of War, during the remainder of his service in the Reserve Officers' Training Corps.

Any physically fit male citizen of the United States, between the ages of 21 and 27 years, who shall have graduated prior to the date of this Act from any educational institution at which an officer of the Army was detailed as professor of military science and tactics, and who, while a student at such institution, completed courses of military training under the direction of such professor of military science and tactics substantially equivalent to those prescribed pursuant to this Act for the senior division, shall, after satisfactorily completing such additional practical military training as the Secretary of War shall prescribe, be eligible for appointment to the Officers' Reserve Corps and as a temporary additional second lieutenant.

The President alone is hereby authorized to appoint and commission as a temporary second lieutenant of the Regular Army in time of peace for purposes of instruction, for a period not exceeding six months, with the allowances now provided by law for that grade, but with pay at the rate of $100 per month, any reserve officer appointed pursuant to this Act and to attach him to a unit of the Regular Army for duty and training during the period covered by his appointment as such temporary second lieutenant, and upon the expiration of such service with the Regular Army such officer shall revert to his status as a reserve officer.

No reserve officer or temporary second lieutenant appointed pursuant to this Act shall be entitled to retirement or to retired pay and shall be eligible for pension only for disability incurred in line of duty in active service or while serving with the Regular Army.

The Adjutant General of the Army shall, under the direction and supervision of the Secretary of War, obtain, compile, and keep continually up to date all obtainable information as to the names, ages, addresses, occupations, and qualifications for appointment as commissioned officers of the Army, in time of war or other emergency, of men of suitable ages who, by reason of having received military training in civilian educational institutions or elsewhere, may be regarded as qualified and available for appointment as such commissioned officers.

Training Camps.—The Secretary of War is hereby authorized to maintain camps for the military instruction and training of such citizens as may be selected for such instruction and training, upon their application and under such terms of enlistment and regulations as may be prescribed by the Secretary of War; to use, for the purpose of maintaining said camps and imparting military instruction and training thereat, such arms, ammunition, accouterments, equipments, tentage, field equipage, and transportation belonging to the United States as he may deem necessary; to furnish, at the expense of the United States, uniforms, subsistence, transportation by the most usual and direct route within such limits as to territory as the Secretary of War may prescribe, and medical supplies to persons receiving instruction at said camps during the period of their attendance thereat, to authorize such expenditures, from proper Army appropriations, as he may deem necessary for water, fuel, light, temporary structures, not including quarters for officers nor barracks for men, screening, and damages resulting from field exercises, and other expenses incidental to the maintenance of said camps, and the theoretical winter instruction in connection therewith; and to sell to persons receiving instruction at said camps, for cash and at cost price plus 10 per centum quartermaster and ordnance property, the amount of such property sold to any one person t. be limited to that which is required for his proper equipment. The Secretary of War is authorized further to prescribe the courses of theoretical and practical instruction to be pursued by persons attending the camps authorized by this section; to fix the periods during which such camps shall be maintained; to prescribe rules and regulations for the government thereof; and to employ thereat officers and enlisted men of the Regular Army in such numbers and upon such duties as he may designate.

Two series of officers' training camps were held in 1917 and a third series early in 1918. The training camps for the first series, lasting three months from May 15, 1917, were located at Plattsburgh, N. Y.; Madison Barracks, N. Y.; Fort Niagara, N. Y.; Fort Myer, Va.; Fort Oglethorpe, Ga.; Fort McPherson, Ga.; Fort Benjamin Harrison, Ind.; Fort Sheridan, Ill.; Fort Logan H. Roots, Ark.; Fort Snelling, Minn.; Fort Riley, Kan.; Leon Springs, Tex.; The Presidio, San Francisco, Cal.; Fort Des Moines, Ia.

In the first series commissions were issued to 2 colonels; 1 lieutenant-colonel; 235 majors; 3,722 captains; 4,452 first lieutenants; 18,929 second lieutenants; making a total of 27,341. There were 40,203 in attendance. The attendance at the second series of camps was approximately 23,000. They were held from August 27 to November 26, 1917. Commissions were awarded to 17,237.

A third series of training camps was inaugurated on January 5, 1918, to create an officers' reserve force. Only enlisted men and a limited number of students who had received military training in schools under army officers during the past ten years were admitted. About 18,000 were in attendance.

The location of the camps at which the draft army, called the National Army, was trained for service in Europe will be found under the heading Cantonments.

Enlisted Reserve Corps.—For the purpose of securing an additional reserve of enlisted men for military service with the Engineer, Signal, and Quartermaster Corps and the Ordnance and Medical Departments of the Regular Army, an Enlisted Reserve Corps, to consist of such number of enlisted men of such grade or grades as may be designated by the President from time to time, is hereby authorized, such authorization to be effective on and after July 1, 1916.

There may be enlisted in the grade or grades specified, for a period of four years, under such rules as may be prescribed by the President, citizens of the United States, or persons who have declared their intentions to become citizens of the United States, subject to such physical, educational, and practical examination as may be prescribed in said rules. For men enlisting in said grade or grades certificates of enlistment in the Enlisted Reserve Corps shall be issued by The Adjutant General of the Army, but no such man shall be enlisted in said corps unless he shall be found physically, mentally, and morally qualified to hold such certificate and unless he shall be between the ages of 18 and 45 years. The certificates so given shall confer upon the holders when called into active service or for purposes of instruction and training, and during the period of such active service, instruction, or training, all the authority, rights, and privileges of like grades of the Regular Army; the Secretary of War is hereby authorizeɪ to issue to members of the Enlisted Reserve Corps and to persons who have participated in at least one encampment for the military instruction of citizens, conducted under the auspices of the War Department, distinctive rosettes or knots designed for wear with civilian clothing.

The uniform to be worn by enlisted men of the Enlisted Reserve Corps, except corps insignia, shall be the same as prescribed for enlisted men of the Regular Army Reserve, and that in lieu of any money allowance for clothing there shall be issued to each enlisted man of the Enlisted Reserve Corps in time of peace such articles of clothing and equipment as the President may direct.

Upon a call by the President for a volunteer force the members of the Enlisted Reserve Corps may be mustered into the service of the United States as volunteers for duty with the Army in the grades held by them in the said corps, and shall be entitled to the pay and allowances of the corresponding grades in the Regular Army, with increase of pay for length of service, as now provided by law for the Regular Army.

Military Equipment and Instructors at Other Schools and Colleges.—Such arms, tentage, and equipment as the Secretary of War shall deem necessary for proper military training shall be supplied by the Government to schools and colleges, having a course of military training prescribed by the Secretary of War and having not less than 100 physically fit male students above the age of 14 years, under such rules and regulations as he may prescribe; and the Secretary of War authorized to detail such commissioned and noncommissioned officers of the Army to said schools and colleges.

Composition of the Militia.—The militia of the United States shall consist of all able-bodied male citizens of the United States and all other able-bodied males who have or shall have declared their intention to become citizens of the United States, who shall be more than 18 years of age and, not more than 45 years of age, and said militia shall be divided into three classes, the National Guard, the Naval Militia, and the Unorganized Militia.

Composition of the National Guard.—The National Guard shall consist of the regularly enlisted militia between the ages of 18 and 45 years organized, armed, and equipped, and of commissioned officers between the ages of 21 and 64 years.

Exemptions from Militia Duty.—The Vice President of the United States; the officers, judicial and executive, of the Government of the United States and of the several States and Territories; persons in the military or naval service of the United States; customhouse clerks; persons employed by the United States in the transmission of the mail; artificers and workmen employed in the armories, arsenals, and navy yards of the United States; pilots; mariners actually employed in the sea service of any citizen or merchant within the United States, shall be exempt from militia duty without regard to age, and all persons who because of religious belief shall claim exemption from military service, if the conscientious holding of such belief by such person shall be established under such regulations as the President shall prescribe, shall be exempted from militia service in a combatant capacity; but no person so exempted shall be exempt from militia service in any capacity that the President shall declare to be noncombatant.

Number of the National Guard.—The number of enlisted men of the National Guard to be organized under this act within one year from its passage shall be for each State in the proportion of 200 such men for each Senator and Representative in Congress from such State, and a number to be determined by the President for each Territory and the District of Columbia, and shall be increased each year thereafter in the proportion of   less than ⴄ0 per cent until a total peace strength of not less than 800 enlisted men for each Senator and Representative in Congress shall have been reached.   When increased to full war strength, the National Militia includes 433,-800 men.

Chiefs of Staff of National Guard Divisions.—The President may detail one officer of the Regular Army as chief of staff and one officer of the Regular Army or the National Guard as assistant to the chief of staff of any division of the National Guard in the service of the United States.

Adjutants General of States, Etc.—Adjutants general of the States, Territories, and the District of Columbia and the officers of the National Guard shall make reports to the Secretary of War, as he may prescribe.

Appropriation, Apportionment, and Disbursement of Funds for the National Guard.—Money shall be appropriated annually for the support of the National Guard, including the expense of providing arms, ordnance stores, quartermaster stores, and camp equipage, and all other military supplies for issue to the National Guard, apportioned among the several States and Territories in direct ratio to the number of enlisted men in active service in the National Guard in such States and Territories at the date of apportionment.

Enlistments in the National Guard.—The period of enlistment in the National Guard shall be for six years, the first three years of which shall be in an active organization and the remaining three years in the National Guard Reserve.

Federal Enlistment Contract.—Enlisted men in the National Guard of the several States, Territories, and the District of Columbia now serving under enlistment contracts which contain an obligation to defend the Constitution of the United States and to obey the orders of the President of the United States shall be recognized as members of the National Guard under the provisions of this Act for the unexpired portion of their present enlistment contracts. When any such enlistment contract does not contain such obligation, the enlisted man shall not be recognized as a member of the National Guard until he shall have signed an enlistment contract and taken and subscribed to the following oath of enlistment, upon signing which credit shall be given for the period already served under the old enlistment contract: "I do hereby acknowledge to have voluntarily enlisted this ———— day of ————, 19—, as a soldier in the National Guard of the United States and of the State of ————, for the period of three years in service and three years in the reserve, under the conditions prescribed by law, unless sooner discharged by proper authority. And I do solemnly swear that I will bear true faith and allegiance to the United States of America and to the State of ———, and that I will serve them honestly and faithfully against all their enemies whomsoever, and that I will obey the orders of the President of the United States and of the governor of the State of ———, and of the officers appointed over me according to law and the rules and articles of war."

Hereafter all men enlisting for service in the National Guard shall sign an enlistment contract and take and subscribe to the oath prescribed in the preceding section of this Act.

Discharge of Enlisted Men from the National Guard.—An enlisted man discharged from service in the National Guard shall receive a discharge in writing in such form and with such classification as is prescribed for the Regular Army.

Federal Oath for National Guard Officers.—Commissioned officers of the National Guard of the several States, Territories, and the District of Columbia now serving under commissions regularly issued shall continue in office, as officers of the National Guard, without the issuance of new commissions: *Provided,* That said officers have taken, or shall take and subscribe to the following oath of office:

"I, ———, do solemnly swear that I will support and defend the Constitution of the United States and the constitution of the State of ———, against all enemies, foreign and domestic; that I will bear true faith and allegiance to the same; that I will obey the orders of the President of the United States and of the governor of the State of ———; that I make this obligation freely, without any mental reservation or purpose of evasion, and that I will well and faithfully discharge the duties of the office of ——— in the National Guard of the United States and of the State of ——— upon which I am about to enter, so help me God."

Armament, Equipment, and Uniform of the National Guard.—The National Guard of the United States shall be uniformed, armed, and equipped with the same type of uniforms, arms, and equipments as the Regular Army.

The Secretary of War is authorized to procure, by purchase or manufacture, and to issue to the National Guard, upon requisition of the governors of the States and Territories or the commanding general of the National Guard of the District of Columbia, such number of United States service arms, with all accessories, field-artillery, matériel, engineer, coast artillery, signal, and sanitary matériel, accoutrements, field uniforms, clothing, equipage, publications, and military stores of all kinds, including public animals, as are necessary to arm, uniform, and equip them for field service.

Training of the National Guard.—Each company, troop, battery, and detachment in the National Guard shall assemble for drill and instruction, including indoor target practice, not less than forty-eight times each year, and shall, in addition thereto, participate in encampments, maneuvers, or other exercises, including outdoor target practice, at least fifteen days in training each year, including target practice.

Inspection of the National Guard.—The Secretary of War shall cause an inspection to be made at least once each year by inspectors general, and if necessary by other officers, of the Regular Army, detailed by him for that purpose, to determine whether the amount and condition of the property in the hands of the National Guard is satisfactory; whether the National Guard is organized as hereinbefore prescribed; whether the officers and enlisted men possess the physical and other qualifications prescribed; whether the organization and the officers and enlisted men thereof are sufficiently armed, uniformed, equipped, and being trained and instructed for active duty in the field or coast defense, and whether the records are being kept in accordance with the requirements of law.

Encampments and Maneuvers.—The Secretary of War is authorized to provide for the participation of the whole or any part of the National Guard in encampments, maneuvers, or other exercises, including outdoor target practice, for field or coast-defense instruction, either independently or in conjunction with any part of the Regular Army, and the officers and enlisted men of such National Guard while so engaged shall be entitled to the same pay, subsistence, and transportation as officers and enlisted men of corresponding grades of the Regular Army.

National Guard, When Subject to Laws Governing Regular Army.—The National Guard when called as such into the service of the United States shall, from the time they are required by the terms of the call to respond thereto, to be subject to the laws and regulations governing the Regular Army, so far as such laws and regulations are applicable to officers and enlisted men whose permanent retention in the military service, either on the active list or on the retired list, is not contemplated by existing law.

National Guard When Drafted into Federal Service.—When Congress shall have authorized the use of the armed land forces of the United States, for any purpose requiring the use of troops in excess of those of the Regular Army, the President may draft into the military service of the United States, to serve therein for the period of the war unless sooner discharged, any or all members of the National Guard and of the National Guard Reserve, with the same pay and allowances as officers and enlisted men of the Regular Army of the same grades and the same prior service.

Protection of the Uniform.—It shall be unlawful for any person not an officer or enlisted man of the United States Army, Navy, or Marine Corps, to wear the duly prescribed uniform of the United States Army, Navy, or Marine Corps, or any distinctive part of such uniform, or a uniform any part of which is similar to a distinctive part of the duly prescribed uniform of the United States Army, Navy, or Marine Corps, excepting Boy Scouts and honorably discharged soldiers.

Any person who offends against the provisions of this section shall, on conviction, be punished by a fine not exceeding $300, or by imprisonment not exceeding six months, or by both such fine and imprisonment.

A soldier after four years' continuous service, either under a first or any subsequent enlistment, may be re-enlisted for seven years and receive a final discharge from his prior enlistment, or after three years' continuous service may, upon his written request, be furloughed and transferred to the Reserve. Enlistment periods for service pay are counted as four years. First enlistments are confined to men between the ages of 18 and 35 years. All soldiers receive, in addition to their pay, rations, clothing, bedding, and medical attendance while with the colors.

Insignia.—Insignia denoting rank of officers of the Military Service consist of

CHEVRONS WORN ON SLEEVES BETWEEN SHOULDER AND ELBOW

REG. SGT. MAJOR | BAT. SGT. MAJOR | REG. SUPPLY SGT. | BAT. SUPPLY SGT. | COLOR SGT. | FIRST CLASS SGT. SIGNAL CORPS | FIRST CLASS ORDNANCE SGT. | FIRST CLASS SGT. MED. CORPS

BAND LEADER | CHIEF TRUMPETER | MESS SGT. | FIRST SGT. | CO. SUPPLY SGT. | SERGEANT | CORPORAL | LANCE CORPORAL

STABLE SGT. | QUARTERMASTER SGT. | MASTER ELEC. C. A. C. | ENGINEER C. A. C. | MASTER GUNNER C. A. C. | MASTER ELECTRICIAN Q. M. C. | MASTER SIGNAL ELEC. | CHIEF MECHANIC

SLEEVE BADGES DESIGNATING MEN ASSIGNED TO SPECIAL DUTY

GUN COMMANDER | GUN POINTER | CASEMATE ELECTRICIAN | CHIEF PLANTER | FIRST CLASS GUNNER | SECOND CLASS GUNNER | FIRST CLASS OBSERVER | SECOND CLASS OBSERVER

WAGONER | FARRIER | FIRST CLASS PRIVATE ENG'R CORPS | FIRST CLASS PRIVATE HOSPITAL CORPS | SADDLER | HORSESHOER | COOK | EXCELLENCE, TARGET PRACTICE C. A. C.

ENLISTED MEN, COLLAR INSIGNIA, INDICATING BRANCH OF SERVICE

WORN RIGHT SIDE BY ALL | CAVALRY | INFANTRY | FIELD ARTILLERY | COAST ARTILLERY | ENGINEER CORPS | QUARTERMASTER CORPS | SIGNAL CORPS

HOSPITAL CORPS | ORDNANCE CORPS | BAND MUSICIAN | ELECTRICIAN | INF. PORTO RICO | INF. PHILIPPINES | RECRUITING SERVICE | AVIATION SECTION

ENLISTED AVIATOR

AVIATION MECHANIC

ENLISTED MEN

OFFICERS' AVIATION SECTION

AVIATION

HAT CORDS

ALL GOLD, GENERAL OFFICERS
GOLD AND BLACK, FIELD AND LINE OFFICERS
RED, WHITE AND BLUE, RESERVE OFFICERS TRAINING CAMP
LIGHT BLUE, INFANTRY
ORANGE AND WHITE, SIGNAL CORPS
MAROON AND WHITE, MEDICAL DEPT.
GREEN AND BLACK, AVIATION SECTION

SCARLET, ARTILLERY
GREEN, SERVICE SCHOOL
YELLOW, CAVALRY
SCARLET AND WHITE, ENGINEER
BUFF, QUARTERMASTER CORPS

BLACK AND SCARLET, ORDNANCE
BLACK, STAFF DEPTS.
SILVER AND BLACK, FIELD CLERK
BLUE AND WHITE, V. T. C. & R. M.
STEEL BLUE, Y. M. C. A.

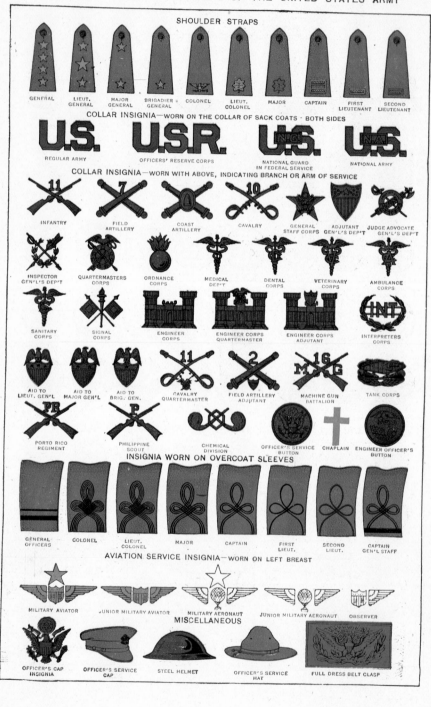

shoulder, sleeve and collar devices, chevrons, hat cords and special insignia. (See colored plate: Insignia of Rank U. S. Army.)

Medals.—Strips of a prescribed length of 1⅝ inches are army service ribbons, standing for medals and campaign badges which the bearer is entitled to wear, as follows:

Congressional medal of honor—White stars on a field of light blue.

Certificate of merit badge—Two red, white and blue bands, separated by a thin band of white, the blue being outermost.

Philippines Congressional Medal—Blue band in centre flanked by bands of white, red, white and blue, the latter outermost.

Civil War—Campaign ribbon of equal-sized bands of grey and blue.

Indian Wars—Bright red, with narrow edges of deeper red.

Spanish Campaign—Alternating stripes of yellow and blue.

Philippine Campaign—Blue band in centre, flanked by narrower bands of red, blue edges.

Cuban Occupation—Blue in centre, flanked by narrow yellow, then broader red and blue borders.

Cuban Pacification—Broad olive drab centre, flanked by three narrow stripes of blue, white and red, the latter outermost.

China Campaign—Broad band of yellow with narrow border of blue.

Ribbons for gallantry are worn farthest to the left, followed by campaign ribbons in order of chronology.

Following is a complete list of the commanders of the army since 1775, together with their respective ranks and the period of command:

Gen. George Washington, June 17, 1775, to Dec. 23, 1783.

Maj.-Gen. Henry Knox, Dec. 23, 1783, to June 20, 1784.

Capt. John Doughty (artillery), June 20, 1784, to Aug. 12, 1784.

Lieut.-Col. Josiah Harmar (infantry), Aug. 12, 1784, to March 4, 1791.

Maj.-Gen. Arthur St. Clair, March 4, 1791, to March 5, 1792.

Maj.-Gen. Anthony Wayne, April 13, 1792, to Dec. 15, 1796.

Brig.-Gen. James Wilkinson, Dec. 15, 1796, to July 13, 1798.

Lieut.-Gen. George Washington, July 13, 1798, to Dec. 14, 1799.

Maj.-Gen. Alexander Hamilton, Dec. 14, 1799, to June 15, 1800.

Brig.-Gen. James Wilkinson, June 15, 1800, to Jan. 27, 1812.

Maj.-Gen. Henry Dearborn, Jan. 27, 1812, to June 15, 1815.

Maj.-Gen. Jacob Brown, June 15, 1815, to Feb. 24, 1828.

Maj.-Gen. Alexander Macomb, May 29, 1828, to June 25, 1841.

Maj.-Gen. Winfield Scott, July 5, 1841, to Nov. 1, 1861.

Maj.-Gen. George Brinton McClellan, Nov. 1, 1861, to March 11, 1862.

Maj.-Gen. Henry Wager Halleck, July 23, 1862, to March 9, 1864.

Gen. Ulysses Simpson Grant, March 9, 1864, to March 4, 1869.

Gen. William Tecumseh Sherman, March 8, 1869, to November 1, 1883.

Gen. Philip Henry Sheridan, Nov. 1, 1883, to Aug. 5, 1888.

Lieut-Gen. John McAllister Schofield, Aug. 14, 1888, to Sept. 29, 1895.

Lieut.-Gen. Nelson Appleton Miles, Oct. 5, 1895, to Aug. 8, 1903.

Lieut.-Gen. Samuel B. M. Young, Aug. 8, 1903, to Jan. 9, 1904.

Lieut.-Gen. Adna R. Chaffee, Jan. 9, 1904, to Feb. 1, 1906.

Lieut. Gen. John C. Bates, Feb. 1, 1906, to Sept. 15, 1906.

Lieut.-Gen. Arthur McArthur, Sept. 15, 1906, to June 2, 1909, when he was retired under the operation of the law, and the rank became extinct.

Re-adjustment of Army for War against Germany.—The announcement of the War Department concerning the re-adjustment of American forces sent to Europe to fight against Germany was as follows:

"The ratio of artillery strength to infantry is greatly increased. A division will hereafter include only four infantry regiments in two brigades in place of the old division of three brigades, each comprising three regiments of infantry. There will still be three regiments of field artillery in each division. Thus, in the new organization, there will be three regiments of field artillery to every four regiments of infantry instead of the ratio of three to nine. In addition, a trench mortar battery is attached to each division.

"The machine gun arm is also materially enlarged. A machine gun battalion of four companies has been made a unit of each division, in addition to the three machine gun companies included in each regiment.

"The American division will be made by this order to conform practically to the units utilized by the Entente Allies, among whom a division numbers approximately 19,000 men. The reason for the change is that the division as heretofore made up of about 28,000 men is too unwieldy for the demands of trench warfare. With so large a unit, sure and swift communication with all parts is difficult. The problem to be met was basically one of mobility for the peculiar needs of fighting on the western front.

"The smaller sized units call for maintenance of all units at full fighting strength. For this purpose reserve battalions will be provided. These will consist of 612 men each and are listed in the general order as 'separate training battalions.' The number of these battalions has not been made public. Details of regimental organization are also withheld for military reasons.

"The new order provides for army corps and armies, units which have practically existed only on paper since the Civil War. Corps were organized during the Spanish war, but were not actually operated as such to any great extent.

"Each army corps will consist of three infantry divisions, corps headquarters, and certain army corps troops not specified. Each army will normally consist of three or more army corps, army headquarters, and certain army troops not specified.

"Under the new order each infantry division will be composed as follows, the changes from the present organization being as indicated:

"One division headquarters (same as at present).

"One machine gun battalion of four companies (new).

"Two infantry brigades of two regiments and one machine gun battalion (four companies) each. (The present division is three infantry brigades of three regiments each.)

"One field artillery brigade of three regiments and one trench mortar battery (same, except trench mortar battery is new).

"One field signal battalion (same).

"One train headquarters and military police (same).

"One ammunition train (same).

"One supply train (same).

"One engineer train (same, except that pontoon and searchlights sections are not included in new plan).

"One sanitary train of four field hospital companies and four ambulance companies (same).

"The new organization provides for no cavalry in the division. The division as at present constituted calls for one regiment of cavalry. The present division also calls for one aero squadron, while the new plan calls for none, the aircraft units being otherwise provided for.

"The order specifies sixteen divisions of the national army to be organized and numbered from 76 to 91, both inclusive, and states the numbers to be given to each of the different units in each division. It provides that the sixteen divisions of the National Guard now organized shall be reorganized to conform to the new plan as soon as practicable after their arrival in the training camps.

"The regular army, the National Guard, and the national army will all conform to the same plan."

At maximum strength, an Infantry division will comprise 103 officers and 3,652 men, as follows:

	Officers and Men
1 headquarters and headquarters company	303
3 battalions of four rifle companies each	3,078
1 supply company	140
1 machine gun company	178
1 medical detachment	56
	3,755

Each rifle company has a strength of 250 men and 6 officers. It is composed of a company headquarters (2 officers and 18 men) and four platoons. Each platoon comprises:

	Officers and Men
1 headquarters	2
1 section bombers and rifle grenadiers	22
2 sections riflemen, 12 each	24
1 section auto riflemen (4 guns)	11
	59

The machine gun company has 6 officers and 172 men. It consists of the headquarters (3 officers and 21 men), 3 platoons (each with 1 officer and 46 men), and a train (13 men). Its armament is 12 machine guns of heavy type and 4 spare guns.

The number of men and officers in the infantry division is as follows:

1 division headquarters	164
1 machine-gun battalion of 4 companies	768
2 Infantry brigades, each composed of 2 Infantry regiments and 1 machine-gun battalion of 3 companies	16,420
1 Field Artillery brigade composed of 3 Field Artillery regiments and 1 trench-mortar battery	5,068
1 field signal battalion	262
1 regiment of Engineers	1,666
1 train headquarters and military police	337
1 ammunition train	962
1 supply train	472
1 engineer train	84
1 sanitary train composed of 4 field hospital companies and 4 ambulance companies	949
	27,152

The transportation equipment of the regiment is: 22 combat wagons, 16 rolling kitchens, 22 baggage and ration wagons, 16 ration carts, 15 water carts, 3 medical carts, 24 machine gun carts, 59 riding horses, 8 riding mules, 332 draft mules, 2 motor cycles with side cars, 1 motor car, 42 bicycles.

For more detailed information as to the scope and activities of the Army as well as equipment consult the index references to the Presidents' Messages and the Encyclopedic articles under the following headings: Arms and Ammunition.

Arsenals.   Artillery.
Battles fought by United States troops, which are arranged alphabetically.
Civil War.   Military Education.
Fortifications.   Revolutionary War.
Indian Wars.   Spanish-American
Mexican War.   War.
Military Academy.   War Department.
Military Departments.   Wars, Foreign.

War activities of the bureaus within the War Department will be found under the latter head, together with their history.

Army (see also Arms and Ammunition; Arsenals; Militia; War Department.)

Absence of soldiers of, orders and proclamation regarding, 3320, 3364.

Act—
Depriving President of command of, discussed, 3670.
Repeal of, recommended, 3871.
Fixing military establishment vetoed, 203.
Making certain debts of soldiers, lien against pay, 4672.
Providing for additional medical officers in volunteer service vetoed, 3289.

Aero squadron for, 8106.

Annuities for families of deceased soldiers recommended, 4425.

Appointments in, 2134.

Appropriations for. (See War Department.)

Artillery tactics for, prepared, 927.

Asylum for aged and disabled members of. (See Soldiers' Home.)

Barracks, permanent, for, 1754.

Battalion formation in, recommendations regarding, 5631, 5878, 5967.

Brevet appointments in, 3582.

Brevet rank—
Conferred for services in Indian wars, 2008.
Discussed, 1002, 2559.

Brownsville, trouble with civilians at, 7329, 7347.

Care of, in Philippines, 6947.

Cavalry regiments wisely decreased, 6669.

Cavalry tactics for, prepared, 927.

Certificate of merit granted enlisted men, additional pay to, 4735.

Changes in, 6669, 6670, 6804.

Chaplains for hospitals, 3249.

Clothing accounts of enlisted men in, referred to, 4660.
Manufactured in United States, referred to, 635, 685.

Command and rank in. (See Officers of, *post.*)

Commanders of. (See Encyclopedic Index article, Army.)

Commanding officers a n d m e n praised by Roosevelt, 6693.

Commission to define and maintain permanent policy regarding, urged, 7515.

Conduct of, in Mexican War, discussed, 2481.

Constitutional provisions concerning, 19, 22.

Courts-martial in. (See Courts-Martial; Courts, Military.)

Deserters from—
Efficiency of, 667, 6671, 6805.
Pardons granted. (See Pardons.)
Shot, referred to, 2287.

Desertions in—
Discussed, 4933, 6684.
Legislation regarding military Statute of limitations as applied to, recommended, 4524.
Portion of pay withheld so as to prevent, 871.
Reduction in, 5550, 5631.

Discharge of troops of 25th Infantry, 7329.

Discipline of companies for acts of individuals, discussed, 7329.

Discussed by President—
Adams, J. Q., 871, 925, 953.
Arthur, 4636, 4724, 4832.
Cleveland, 4932, 5099, 5373, 5877, 5966, 6158.
Grant, 4062, 4147, 4202, 4248, 4304, 4360.
Harrison, Benj., 5550, 5631, 5754.
Hayes, 4424, 4451, 4524, 4569.
Jackson, 1166, 1251, 1332, 1387.
Jefferson, 317, 333, 373, 394.
Johnson, 3561, 3649, 3773, 3881.
Lincoln, 3249.
McKinley, 6320, 6341, 6385, 6449.
Madison, 461, 471, 479, 490, 513, 533, 538, 549.
Monroe, 619, 680, 757, 780, 823.
Pierce, 2748, 2819, 2941.
Polk, 2260, 2276, 2481.
Roosevelt, 6669, 6693, 6721, 6999, 7068, 7110, 7234.
Taft, 7371, 7428, 7513, 7515.
Tyler, 1942, 2121.
Van Buren, 1607, 1754.
Washington, 52, 57, 75, 114, 118, 176.
Wilson, 8106, 8172.

Dismissal without honor of three companies, 7337.

Division of, sent abroad, 8260.

Education in, 4570, 5879, 6669.

Efficiency of, discussed, 6721, 6805, 6999, 7069.

Elections, interference in, by, inquired into, 1315.
Prohibited, 3866.

Engineers Corps, service in, defined as non-combatant, 8475.

Enlisted men in, limits of punishment for, 5602, 6034.

Eulogy on the army of the United States by President Roosevelt, won by their gallantry and efficiency in the Cuban and Philippine campaigns, 6693, 6921.

European War activities of. (See European War.)

Executions in, contrary to law, referred to, 635.

Expenditures for, in Philippines, 6740.

Expenditures of. (See Finances; War Department.)

Field maneuvers for, 6670, 6927, 6999, 7113.

General Staff of, 6670, 6805, 7069.

Imprisonment of American citizens by officers in, referred to, 4009.

Improvement noted in, 6671, 6805.

Increase in, 1714, 2553.
Recommended, 429, 534, 538, 1473, 1606, 2276, 2354, 2559, 2623, 2666, 2714, 2748, 2819, 2830, 2941, 2987, 2989, 3249, 4330, 4424, 4637, 5476, 6341, 6721, 7515, 8106, 8172.

Increase should be in efficiency, not in size, 6669.

Increased pay for officers and men of, urged, 7492.

Indian campaigns. (See Indian Wars.)

Indians enlisted in, discussed, 5631.

Insane asylum for. (See Government Hospital for Insane.)

Inspector-General of. (See Inspector-General of Army.)

Intoxicating liquors, order prohibiting sale of, in, 4592.

Lands granted persons who have served in. (See Lands, Bounty.)

Large standing, unnecessary in time of peace, 317, 1389, 1607, 1901, 2263, 2733.

Legislation for, referred to, 3585.

Maneuvers—
Effect of, 6805.
Necessity for, 6670.

Measures for efficiency of, recommended, 4148, 4248, 4304.

Medical Corps—
Improvement of, urged, 7111.
Recommended, 4148.
Needs of, 6935, 7000.
Service in, defined as non-combatant, 8475.

Medical Department of, reorganization of, referred to, 3282.

Mexico, authority for use in, asked, 7934.

Mileage system, repeal of law abolishing, recommended, 4304.

Military establishment act vetoed, 203.

Military peace establishment discussed, 680, 2453, 3561, 3881.

Military statute of limitations against deserters, 4524.

Militia—
Called into national service, 8306.
Qualifications of, 6671.
Volunteer act regarding, passage of, 7514.

Modern rifles for, recommended, 5631.

Nominations—
Correspondence regarding, 2269, 2367, 2368, 2436.
Reasons therefor, 1773, 2296, 2367, 2368, 2370.
Withdrawn, 695.

Non-combatant service in, defined, 8475.

Northwestern, referred to, 602.

Number of men and officers in, referred to, 3578.

Office of Inspector-General in. (See Inspector-General of Army.)

Officers and soldiers of temporary, discharged, 296.

Officers of—
Absence of, orders and proclamation regarding, 3320, 3364.
Accounts of, referred to, 806.
Additional grades of, 2632.
Annuities for families of deceased, recommended, 4304, 4362, 4451.
Appointments and promotions, brevet rank discussed, 1002, 2559.
Appointments and promotions of, 1773, 2269, 2296, 2367, 2368, 2437.
Recommendations r e g a r d i n g, 5099, 5374.
Assignments of, to duty referred to, 3268.
Brevet rank conferred upon, for service in Indian wars, 2008.
Brevetted, 811.
Commissions of brevet and staff, referred to, 2559.
Details of, to colleges and universities, from retired list recommended, 4570.
Increase in number of, recommended, 114, 490, 504.
Law authorizing retirement of, when incompetent, 2624.
Letter of John Randolph, jr., demanding that certain, be punished for insulting, 291.
Pay of—
Equalization of, with naval officers discussed, 1254.
Inequality in, between naval officers and, discussed, 1023.
Question of restraining, from usurping powers of civil functionaries, referred to, 2632.

Relative rank of—
Referred to, 1773, 2633.
With officers of Navy referred to, 2624, 2633, 2669, 2714, 3240.

Retired list of—
Details for colleges and universities from, recommended, 4570.
Recommended, 2624, 2714, 2871, 4724.
Repeal of act limiting numbers on, recommended, 4425.

Ordnance Corps of, needs of, 6936, 7000.
Increase in, discussed, 2819, 6671, 7112.

Organization of, report relating to, transmitted, 995.

Pardons granted deserters. (See Pardons.)

Partial reorganization of, 2872.

Pay of—
In depreciated paper, 1315.
Increase in, discussed, 2819, 7492.
Revision of, recommended, 1475.

Payment of, resolution providing for, approved, 3350.

Promotion in, and basis for, discussed, 6670, 6999, 7000, 7234, 7428.

Provision for aged horses, 6722.

Provision for support of. (See War Department.)

Punishment for enlisted men in, limits of, 5602, 6034.

Quartermaster Corps established, 7800.
Service in, defined as non-combatant, 8475.

Quartermaster-General of, fireproof building for records in office of, recommended, 4524.

Quartermaster's Department, appointments in, referred to, 1773.

Rank and command in. (See officers of, *ante.*)

Reading matter for, recommendations, regarding, 4425, 4451.

Reduction in, referred to and discussed, 549, 698, 705, 3561, 3881.

Re-enlistment after 10 years, repeal of law forbidding, recommended, 5878.

Referred to, 631, 3578, 3585, 7371.

Regulations—
Compiled by General Scott, 795.
Orders promulgating, 5602, 6034.

Reorganization of, 6671, 7796.
Commission to report upon—
Appointed, 4352.
Referred to, 4376.
Time to report, extension of, recommended, 4361.
Recommended, 2872.
Report regarding, transmitted and investigation into referred to with a view to proper action in the matter, 291.

Repeal or amendment of act forbidding use of, as *posse comitatus* recommended, 4452.

Retirement for seniority discussed, 6670.

Retirement of retrogressive officers of, urged, 7428.

Revision of laws respecting, urged, 7428.

Rifle for use of, 6159.

Adoption of, recommended, 5631.

Selected, 5878.

Rules and regulations compiled by General Scott, 595.

Sabbath observance enjoined upon, 8433.

School buildings for posts of, recommended, 4451.

Service Corps established in, 7800.

Size of, 6669, 6671, 6721, 6927, 6994.

Skeleton in peace, expansion in war theory of, 7514.

Smokeless powder recommended, 5631.

Staff corps of, recommendations regarding, 1606, 1754, 3994, 4102, 4202, 4248.

Subsistence Department, appropriation for, recommended, 4304.

Subsistence of, referred to, 594, 706.

Sunday, observance of, by, enjoined by President Lincoln, 3326.

Surgeon-General of. (See Surgeon-General of Army.)

Thanks of President to, for Cuba and Philippines service, 6693.

Trained riflemen and riders needed for, 6669.

Volunteers for, acceptance of, encouraged, 416, 429.

Army and Navy Forces, mobilized on borders of Mexico to protect interests of citizens of United States during uprising, 7659.

Army List and Register.—An o f f i c i a l pamphlet, published monthly by the War Department, containing the names of all active and retired officers of the United States Army, with their addresses; the names and locations of all organizations connected with the Army, including both voluntary bodies and official army posts and camps; and the ranks of all men on the active list, with an account of all changes in the army organization since the previous monthly issue.

Army Medical Department.

Enlargement of, 6935, 6936, 7000.

Rank of officers in, 7000.

Army Medical Museum, building for, recommended, 4572, 4780, 4833.

Army of the Republic, Grand. (See Grand Army of the Republic.)

Army Ordnance Department.—Enlargement of, 6936.

Arnold's Treason.— Up to the time when he betrayed the cause of the United States, there had been few officers in the colonial army who had rendered more valuable service than had Benedict Arnold. In 1775,

he assisted Ethan Allen to capture Fort Ticonderoga, and showed his devotion to the rebels' cause on that occasion by yielding command of the expedition to Allen, although he had better claims to it. He next played a prominent part in the colonial campaign against Canada, in which he was severely wounded. Indeed, the retreat from Canada, fought almost step by step, was engineered under Arnold's direction; and he revealed remarkable skill and persistence in going to the support of Fort Ticonderoga and preventing its re-capture by the British forces.

His exploits clearly entitled him to be raised to the command of major-general, but the jealousy of the several states in the Continental Congress blocked his appointment. Arnold seems to have been of a high-strung temperament, the kind of man who broods over real or fancied slights. And although he prevented in 1777 the capture of the important American position on Bemis Heights, which commanded the Hudson, Congress persisted, not only in refusing him just recognition, but also in making him subject to baseless trials and charges.

In 1778, Arnold was fulfilling his duties in Philadelphia, and there fell under the influence of the Tory society of that city, marrying a Philadelphia matron whose chief associations were with the Tory party. The last straw came when Congress refused to allow his claims for expenses which he had incurred in the colonial expedition against Canada, and by that action rendered Arnold a bankrupt. These circumstances, combined with a realization of the unprepossessing nature of the American cause at that time, with a change in the colonials' war aims and with disgust at the petty jealousies which were disrupting the colonies, proved too much for Arnold's patriotism, and he entered into treasonable negotiations with the British commanding officer.

Arnold asked for the command of the American position at West Point, meaning to betray it to the British; and although this position was the key to the whole war situation, so great was the confidence placed in Arnold by Washington that the command was granted him unquestioningly. Major André, of the British forces, was sent secretly to communicate with Arnold at West Point, and it was his chance capture as a spy which first revealed the treachery which Arnold had contemplated. Arnold, however, learned of André's capture, and made good his escape to a British warship. He later served in the British army in the South, and died, neglected and scorned, in England.

It was not so much the direct treason of Arnold which was so culpable, for his wrongs were many and undeniable and there were many in the American army deserting to England at that time, as was his betrayal of the implicit trust placed in him, and the consequent discouragement to the whole American cause, well expressed in Washington's comment on hearing the news of Arnold's treason—"Whom can we trust now?"

Aroostook War.—Between 1837 and 1839 the settled boundary between Maine and New Brunswick came near leading to active hostilities on the Aroostook River. The governor of Maine sent troops to drive off the intruders and erect fortifications, and Congress authorized the President to resist the encroachments of the British. President Van Buren sent Gen. Scott to the scene, who arranged a truce, and it was agreed that the country should be occupied jointly, as before, pending adjustment of the boundary, which was definitely settled

Aug. 9, 1842, by the Ashburton treaty (pages 1733, 1738, 1747).

Aroostook, The, claim of owners of, for compensation in searching for bodies and property lost in steamer *Oneida*, 4119.

Arsenals.—Armories and arsenals were not established in the United States until the beginning of the Revolutionary War. In 1776 powder was manufactured in Virginia and brass cannon were cast in Philadelphia. An arsenal was established at Carlisle, Pa., the same year. Washington in 1777 chose Springfield, Mass., as a suitable location for an arsenal, and small arms were manufactured there in 1787. This establishment, now the chief small arms manufactory, has a capacity of 1,000 rifles per day. The arsenal at Harpers Ferry, W. Va., was begun in 1795, and from that time the number was gradually increased until 1860, when there were 23 arsenals scattered over the country. The principal ones at present in use are at Augusta, Ga.; Benicia, Cal.; Frankford, Pa.; Springfield, Mass.; Governors Island, N. Y.; Rock Island, Ill.; San Antonio, Tex.; Dover, N. J.; Watertown, Mass., and Watervliet, N. Y. Ordnance, arms, ammunition, and accouterments are manufactured at many of these places, the idea being to devote each to a special line of fabrication. Thus the establishment at Watervliet is devoted to the manufacture of heavy ordnance. Casting and assembling of guns are carried on at Rock Island and Benicia, as well as the making of leather goods. Naval guns and projectiles are made at Washington, D. C.

Arsenals:

Augusta, Ga., referred to, 893.

Erection of, and armories on Western waters referred to, 705, 781, 808, 2079.

Establishment of, recommended to utilize the iron mines and works at Berkeley and in the State of Virginia, 99.

In the South, 323.

Frankford, Pa., arsenal at, referred to, 4661.

Location for magazines, referred to, 3844.

Replenishment of, recommended, 255.

Rock Island Arsenal, appropriation for, recommended, 4680, 4738.

Sale of, not used by Government recommended, 3994, 4149, 4362.

Schuylkill Arsenal, appropriation for, recommended, 4785.

Sites for—

Appropriation for, 772.

Referred to, 178, 2896, 4148.

Art. (See Science and Art.)

Art Exhibition. (See International Exhibition of Fine Arts.)

Arthur, Chester A.—Sept. 20, 1881-March 3, 1885.

Twenty-fourth Administration (continued)—Republican.

Secretary of State—
   James G. Blaine (continued).
   F. T. Frelinghuysen.

Secretary of the Treasury—
   William Windom (continued).
   Charles J. Folger.
   Walter Q. Gresham.
   Hugh McCulloch.
Secretary of War—
   Robert T. Lincoln (continued).
Secretary of the Navy—
   William H. Hunt (continued).
   William E. Chandler.
Secretary of the Interior—
   Samuel J. Kirkwood.
   Henry M. Teller.
Postmaster-General—
   Thomas L. James (continued).
   Timothy O. Howe.
   Walter Q. Gresham.
   Frank Hatton.
Attorney-General—
   Wayne MacVeagh (continued).
   Benjamin H. Brewster.

Arthur was the fourth vice-president to succeed to the office of President through the death of the incumbent; and the second to succeed through death by assassination. He took the oath of office in New York city Sept. 20, 1881. Arthur continued most of Garfield's appointees as heads of departments.

Party Affiliation.—President Arthur early received strong anti-slavery sentiments from his father, who took part in the organization, at Utica in 1835, of the anti-slavery society. Mr. Arthur in his law practice took an active part as counsel in several cases in which the rights of colored people were concerned. He became a Henry Clay Whig and cast his first vote for General Scott in 1852. He was present at the Republican convention at Saratoga and, in 1856, took an active part in the Fremont campaign. From 1862 to 1872, while engaged in his law practice, General Arthur took an active part in politics.

Public Debt.—The public debt of the United States during the administration of President Arthur stood as follows: July 1, 1881, $1,819,650,154.23; 1882, $1,675,023,474.25; 1883, $1,538,781,825.15; 1884, $1,438,542,995.39.

In his First Annual Message (page 4635) the President said: "In view, however, of the heavy load of taxation which our people have already borne, we may well consider whether it is not the part of wisdom to reduce the revenues, even if we delay a little the payment of the debt." In his Second Annual Message (page 4721) he says: "But I renew the expression of my conviction that such rapid extinguishment of the national indebtedness as is now taking place is by no means a cause of congratulation; it is a cause rather for serious apprehension. If it continues it must speedily be followed by one of the evils so clearly set forth in the report of the Secretary. Either the surplus must lie idle in the Treasury or the Government will be forced to buy at market rates its bonds not then redeemable, and which under such circumstances can not fail to command an enormous premium, or the swollen revenues will be devoted to extravagant expenditure, which, as experience has taught, is ever the bane of an overflowing treasury." In his Third Annual Message (page 4765) he said: "There are cogent reasons, however, why the national indebtedness should not be thus rapidly extinguished. Chief among them is the fact that only by excessive taxation is such rapidity attainable."

Tariff.—In his First Annual Message (page 4636) the President says: "The tariff laws also need revision; but, that a due regard may be paid to the conflicting interests of our citizens, important changes should be made with caution. If a careful

revision can not be made at this session, a
commission such as was lately approved by
the Senate and is now recommended by
the Secretary of the Treasury, would doubtless lighten the labors of Congress whenever
this subject shall be brought to its consideration." In his Second Annual Message
(page 4722) he says: "The present tariff
system is in many respects unjust. It makes
unequal distribution both of its burdens and
its benefits. This fact was practically recognized by a majority of each House of
Congress in the passage of the act creating
the Tariff Commission. . . . If a general revision of the tariff shall be found to
be impracticable at this session, I express
the hope that at least some of the more conspicuous inequalities of the present law
may be corrected before your final adjournment. One of them . . . . the necessity of amending the law by which the
Dutch standard of color is adopted as the
test of the saccharine strength of sugars is
too obvious to require comment." In his
Fourth Annual Message (page 4839) he
says: "The healthful enlargement of our
trade with Europe, Asia, and Africa should
be sought by reducing tariff burdens on such
of their wares as neither we nor the other
American States are fitted to produce, and
thus enabling ourselves to obtain in return
a better market for our supplies of feed, of
raw materials, and of the manufactures in
which we excel. It seems to me that many
of the embarrassing elements in the great
national conflict between protection and
free trade may thus be turned to good account; that the revenue may be reduced so
as no longer to overtax the people; that protective duties may be retained without becoming burdensome; that our shipping interests may be judiciously encouraged, the
currency fixed on firm bases, and, above all,
such a unity of interests established among
the States of the American system as will
be of great and ever-increasing advantage
to them all."

Standard Time.—President Arthur called
an international conference to establish a
universal meridian from which to reckon
time throughout the world. Twenty-five
nations participated in the conference, which
was held at Washington in October, 1884,
and the meridian of Greenwich was agreed
upon (pages 4718, 4800, 4827, 4841, 5180).
This followed the division of the United
States into four time sections.

Civil Service.—In his First Annual Message (page 4648) the President fully discusses the Civil Service. He repeats his
views as set forth in his letter of acceptance
of the nomination of the Vice-Presidency;
describes the salient features of the English
system; and selects from it such elements
as he deems applicable to American conditions. Among these are: A practically
life-tenure of office; limitation of age below
middle life; and a retiring allowance. Competitive examination before appointment for
fitness, and promotion on efficiency, are
corner-stones of his plan. In his Second
Annual Message (page 4733), in urging action by Congress, he said: "In the judgment of not a few who have given study
and reflection to this matter, the nation has
outgrown the provisions which the Constitution has established for filling the minor
offices in the public service." Full and
careful statistics of removals and appointments are here also given. A code of rules
regulating the conduct of civil service employees was promulgated by Executive order
(page 4748) under authority of the civil
service act of 1883. This code was further
supplemented and amended by another order
(page 4754) under the same authority.
These rules and the report of the Civil

Service Commission are referred to (page
4773) in the President's Third Annual Message. In speaking of the effects of the
Civil Service reform, the President says
(page 4839) in his Fourth Annual Message:
"The system has fully answered the expectations of its friends in securing competent and faithful public servants and in
protecting the appointing officers of the
Government from the pressure of personal
importunity and from the labor of exam-
ining the claims and pretensions of rival
candidates for public employment."

Star Route Trials.—Early in Arthur's
administration public attention was directed
to the indictment in Washington of John W.
Dorsey, John M. Peck, John R. Miner,
Stephen Dorsey, M. C. Rerdell, Thomas J.
Brady, William H. Turner and J. L. Sander-
son for conspiracy to defraud the government in bids for mail service. (See Star
Routes.)

Internal Improvements.—President Arthur's attitude toward this great question is
shown by his First Annual Message (page
4646) where he said: "I advise appropriations for such internal improvements as the
wisdom of Congress may deem to be of
public importance. The necessity of improving the navigation of the Mississippi
River justifies a special allusion to the subject. I suggest the adoption of some
measure for the removal of obstructions
which now impede the navigation of that
great channel of commerce." On Aug. 1,
1882, the President withheld his signature
from a river-and-harbor bill appropriating
the sum of $18,743,875. In doing so he
said (page 4707): "My principal objection
to the bill is that it contains appropriations
for purposes not for the common defense or
general welfare, and which do not promote
commerce among the States. These provisions, on the contrary, are entirely for
the benefit of the particular localities in
which it is proposed to make the improvements. I regard such appropriation of
the public money as beyond the powers
given by the Constitution to Congress and
the President." On Aug. 2, 1882, this bill
was passed by Congress over the President's
veto. In this connection it is worthy of
note that in three of his annual messages
(pages 4725, 4774, and 4839) the President
recommended the provision of a Constitutional amendment which would permit the
President to assent to parts of a bill and
to veto other parts, without being obliged
to veto the entire bill on account of one or
two objectionable points.

Arthur, Chester A.:

Annual messages of, 4624, 4713, 4757,
4822.

Biographical sketch of, 4618.

Bland-Allison Act discussed by, and
recommendations regarding, 4633,
4720, 4830.

Civil service discussed by, 4647, 4732,
4748, 4754, 4773, 4839, 4863.

Collector of port of New York, suspension of, discussed, 4463.

Constitutional amendment regarding
approval of separate items of bill
and veto of others recommended
by, 4725, 4774, 4840.

Death of, announced and honors to be
paid memory of, 5081, 5082.

Death of President Garfield—
Announced to, and reply of, 4604.
Discussed by, 4620, 4624.

EXTENT OF THE UNITED STATES DURING THE ADMINISTRATION OF PRESIDENT ARTHUR, 1881-1885.

(NOT INCLUDING TERRITORIES)

MAINE 1820

VT. 1791

N.H. 1788

MASS. 1788

CONN. 1788

R.I. 1790

NEW YORK 1788

N.J. 1787

PENNSYLVANIA 1787

DEL. 1787

MD. 1788

WEST VIRGINIA 1863

VIRGINIA 1788

NORTH CAROLINA 1789

SOUTH CAROLINA 1788

GEORGIA 1788

FLORIDA 1845

OHIO 1803

MICHIGAN 1837

INDIANA 1816

KENTUCKY 1792

TENNESSEE 1796

ALABAMA 1819

MISSISSIPPI 1817

WISCONSIN 1848

ILLINOIS 1818

MISSOURI 1821

ARKANSAS 1836

LOUISIANA 1812

MINNESOTA 1858

IOWA 1846

NEBRASKA 1867

KANSAS 1861

COLORADO 1876

TEXAS 1845

OREGON 1859

NEVADA 1864

CALIFORNIA 1850

FLAG OF 1885

Finances discussed by, 4632, 4719, 4763, 4829.

Inaugural address of, 4620.

Internal improvements discussed by, 4646.

Oath of office administered to, 4615.

Portrait of, 4617.

Powers of Federal and State Governments discussed by, 4707, 4771, 4808.

Proclamations of—
Day of mourning in memory of President Garfield, 4621.
Discriminating duties on vessels from Cuba and Puerto Rico suspended, 4810.
Duties on foreign vessels suspended, 4871, 4872.
Extraordinary session of Senate, 4621, 4873.
Hundredth anniversary of surrender by Washington of commission as Commander-in-Chief, 4810.
Quarantine regulations, 4812.
Thanksgiving, 4623, 4710, 4746, 4812.
Treaty with Great Britain, termination of, 4867.
Unauthorized occupancy of lands in Indian Territory, 4811.
Unlawful combination in Utah, 4709.
World's Industrial and Cotton Centennial Exposition, 4746.

State of the Union discussed by, 4822.

Tariff discussed by, 4636, 4721, 4839.

Thanksgiving proclamations of, 4623, 4710, 4746, 4812.

Veto messages of—
Chinese immigration, 4699.
Passengers by sea, 4705.
Relief of Fitz-John Porter, 4808.
Rivers and Harbors, 4707.
Discussed, 4724.

Articles of Confederation, 5.
Signers of, 13.

Articles of War.—Rules and regulations for the guidance of the Army and Navy. In addition to the set rules, general orders of a special nature are issued by the War Department as occasion requires.

Artillery.—The history of artillery begins shortly after the invention of gunpowder. It was used by the Moors of Algeciras, in Spain, in 1343, and Edward III had four cannons at Crecy in 1346. During the sixteenth century brass guns and cast-iron projectiles were adopted throughout Europe. Gustavus Adolphus, Sweden's greatest warrior, introduced the battalion system and reduced the use of artillery to a science in Europe. Napoleon owed much of his military success to his skill in the manipulation of artillery. In his wars was seen the first important effects of the concentration of fire, which in those days could only be produced by the massing of guns. Napoleon III made a special study

of the subject of artillery, and the treatise begun and mainly written by him is a standard work on the subject. During the Civil War Gen. William F. Barry did much to improve the organization of the artillery of the Union Army. The aggregate of field guns was about 15,000 with 40,000 horses and 48,000 men. According to the army reorganization act of Feb. 2, 1901, the regimental organization of the artillery arm was discontinued and the arm constituted and designated as the artillery corps. This consists of 30 batteries of field artillery and 126 batteries of coast artillery. The officers of the artillery corps are a Chief of Artillery, to serve on the staff of the general officer commanding the army; fourteen colonels; thirteen lieutenant-colonels; thirty-nine majors; 195 captains; 195 first lieutenants; 195 second lieutenants; twenty-one sergeants-major with rank and pay of regimental sergeants-major of infantry; and twenty-seven sergeants-major with rank, pay and allowance of battalion sergeants-major of infantry. The aggregate of enlisted men must not exceed 5,416 for the field artillery and 18,471 for the coast artillery. (See also Army; Arsenals; Arms and Ammunition.)

Artillery School of Practice at Fortress Monroe, Va., 940.

Artists, Foreign, tariff discriminations against, 4794, 4824, 4924, 5091, 5501.

Arundel Manuscripts, copy of, placed in Library of Congress, 1445.

Arve, The, seizure of, by Haitian authorities, 2680.

Ashburton Treaty.—A treaty concluded at Washington, Aug. 9, 1842, between Great Britain and the United States. It was negotiated by Lord Ashburton and Daniel Webster. It settled the long-disputed boundary line between the United States and Canada. The former secured about seven-twelfths of the territory which had been claimed by both countries. Provision was also made by the treaty for the suppression of the slave trade and the mutual extradition of fugitives from justice (pages 2015, 2047, 2082). (See Great Britain, Treaties with.)

Ashburton Treaty:
Reference to, 2134, 2273, 2760, 3071.

Asheville, N. C., act for erection of public building in, vetoed, 5060.

Asia.—The area of Asia is 17¼ million square miles, and it extends over nearly one-third of the land surface of the globe. The distance between its extreme longitudes, the west coast of Asia Minor (26° E.) and the East Cape (170° W.) is 6,000 miles. The extreme latitudes, Cape Chelyuskin (78° 30″ N.) and Cape Buru (90 miles north of the Equator), are 5,350 miles apart. Asia is bounded by the ocean on all sides except the west. The Isthmus of Suez (cut by a canal) connects it with Africa. The boundary between Europe and Asia is formed on the west mainly by the Ural Mountains and the Ural River. In the southwest the valley of the Manych, which stretches from the Caspian Sea to the mouth of the Don, is now taken as the line between the two continents, although the Caucasus was formerly considered as belonging to Europe. The islands of the archipelago which lies in the southeast, between the continents of Asia and Australia, may be divided into two groups by a line passing east of Timor, Timor Laut, the Kei Islands, and the

Moluccas. Asia is assumed to be the birth-place of mankind. It has certainly been the scene of many highly developed civilizations and notable conquests. In it also originated the great religions of the world.

The Nations of Asia, with the form of government and capital of each, follow :

Afghanistan (Monarchy), Kabul.
Bhutan (Monarchy), Punakha.
China (Republic), Peking.
India (Empire), Delhi.
Japan (Empire), Tokyo.
Nepal (Monarchy), Khatmandu.
Oman (Monarchy), Muscat.
Persia (Monarchy), Teheran.
Russia in Asia (Empire).
Siam (Kingdom), Bangkok.
Turkey in Asia (Monarchy).

The East India Islands, the government to which they belong, the area in square miles and population are :

		Area Sq. Miles	Population
Borneo	British	85,000	850,000
	Netherlands	200,000	1,200,000
Celebes, Netherlands		72,000	900,000
Java, Netherlands		48,400	28,000,000
Lesser Sundas	Netherlands	22,000	800,000
	Portuguese	7,000	280,000
Moluccas, Netherlands		43,000	400,000
Philippines Sulus	United States	115,000	8,300,000
Sumatra, Netherlands		160,000	3,200,000

Physical Features.—The northern coast is almost entirely within the Arctic Circle. The subsoil is permanently frozen, only a few inches of the upper surface thawing in summer, when extensive marshes are formed. The main islands are the New Siberian Islands and Wrangel Island. In the northeast, Asia reaches to within thirty-six miles of the northwest peninsula of North America, from which it is separated by the shallow Bering Strait, which divides the Arctic from the Pacific Ocean. The east coast is fringed by numerous peninsulas and islands, both of which are usually mountainous. The peninsula of Kamchatka, Sakhalin Island, and the Kuriles mark off the Sea of Okhotsk, and to the south the Islands of Japan and the peninsula of Korea form the boundaries of the Sea of Japan. The largest island off this coast is the mountainous island of Formosa. The South China Sea is separated from the Pacific by the Philippines and Borneo. Indo-China forms a huge peninsula stretching far to the south with one long arm, the Malay Peninsula, which nearly reaches the Equator, and two lesser projections, the growing deltas of the Mekong and Irawaddy. Sumatra is separated by the Malacca Strait, the eastern gate between the Indian Ocean and the China Sea, to which Singapore owes its importance. The Deccan and Arabia project as large peninsulas into the Indian Ocean. The island of Ceylon is the only large island and is nearly joined to the mainland by Adam's Bridge. The Strait of Ormuz and the Strait of Bab-el-Mandeb lead to the Persian Gulf and Red Sea respectively. To the north of the Red Sea the Gulfs of Suez and Akaba form openings to the north. The former is separated from the Mediterranean by the Isthmus of Suez, through which is cut the Suez Canal, while the latter leads to the rift valley of the Dead Sea. The Sea of Marmora between the Black Sea and the Ægean is bounded by narrow channels, the Dardanelles and the Bosphorus. Constantinople has a unique position at the west of the strait on the European side. Asia may be divided into three main natural divisions :

The Northern Lowlands, an extensive plain rising gradually to the south and east.

Plateaus and Folded Ranges.—More than one-twelfth of Asia lies above 10,000 feet. A series of lofty plateaus extends from Asia Minor to Eastern Asia at varying elevations.

The Tablelands.—The Deccan, Ceylon, and Arabia form tablelands of old rock without the folded mountains which are characteristic of the rest of Asia. The Deccan of Peninsular India is a fragment of old land smoothed and worn by river erosion.

Five areas may be distinguished in Asia in which there is marked difference in climate : The Arctic Area, where the temperature in no month exeeds 50° F. The Siberian Area, where there is great winter cold but where the hardier cereals can be grown in summer. The Central Area, mostly a region of inland drainage. The Monson Area, comprising the most densely cultivated and populated regions of Asia. This includes China, Indo-China, and India. The Equatorial Area, which has two rainy seasons and a high annual rainfall. This includes the island grounds of Borneo, Sumatra, Java, etc., to the southeast of Asia.

Political Divisions.—The republic of China, the monarchies of Japan, Siam, Afghanistan, Persia, Nepal, Bhutan, and Oman are organized ; Arabian tribes are independent, and there are Russian, British, Dutch, French, German, Turkish, American, and Portuguese possessions.

Asia:

Commerce with, extension of, recommended, 2624, 2703.

Coolie trade with, referred to, 3261.

Immigrants from, should be protected against lawless assault, 7372.

Asphalt.—A general term applied to several varieties of hydrocarbons of a bituminous nature, varying in hardness from semi-fluid to solid. It is used for paving purposes in the United States. Most of the asphalt used in the United States is brought from the island of Trinidad, off the coast of Venezuela. Other imports are from Bermudez, Venezuela. It is also found in Southern California. The supply in Trinidad is obtained from Pitch Lake, a name given to the crater of an extinct volcano, 138 feet above sea level. This crater covers an area of about 114 acres and is 135 feet deep at the center. The supply is gradually renewed by the constant exudation of soft pitch from subterranean sources to the extent of about one-fourth of that removed. Surrounding the crater is a deposit of land pitch, the overflow of past times. The Bermudez supply comes from a morass on the main land consisting of numerous small lakes. The California deposit exists in the form of large banks of bituminous sandstone (sand saturated with asphalt). These deposits are controlled by the American Asphalt Company, which holds a concession from the British government to work Pitch Lake on Trinidad.

Although there was a decrease in the production of natural asphalt in the United States in 1913, including all the varieties of natural asphalt and asphaltic sandstone and limestone, there was a far greater corresponding increase in the output of manufactured or oil asphalt, according to the United States Geological Survey. Oil asphalt obtained as a residue from the distillation of Mexican, Gulf, and California asphaltic oils, and even from those of the Middle West, is becoming more and more available. There is correspondingly less interest in the development of new sources of natural asphalt.

The production of natural asphalt in 1913 amounted to 92,604 short tons, valued at $750,713, a decrease from 95,166 short tons, valued at $865,225, in 1912. On the other hand, the output of manufactured or oil asphalt in 1913 was 436,586 short tons, valued at $4,531,657, against 354,344 short tons in 1912, valued at $3,755,506. The total quantity of asphalt imported into the United States for consumption in 1913 was 228,178 short tons, valued at $910,611. The island of Trinidad furnished the greater part of this—125,273 short tons.

Asphaltum, disposition of lands in Utah containing, discussed, 6168.

Aspinwall, United States of Colombia:
  Claims arising out of destruction of, 4912, 5122.
  Imprisonment of American citizens in, 4798.
  Maltreatment of passengers and seamen on ships plying between New York and, 3413.
  Vessels from, duties on, suspended, 4871.

Assassination of American Presidents, discussed, 6639. (See also under Lincoln; Garfield; McKinley.)

Assay Offices are establishments maintained by the government in which gold and silver bullion may be deposited by citizens, they receiving its value, less charges, in return. There are six, namely, at New York City; Helena, Mont.; Charlotte, N. C.; St. Louis, Mo.; Deadwood, S. Dak., and Seattle, Wash. The New York Assay Office is the largest, and more than half the gold and silver refined by the mint service is handled there.

Assembly.—The lower house of the State Legislature, in many States corresponding to the House of Representatives in the National Congress.

Assistant Attorneys-General.—There are eight in number, each receiving a salary of $5,000 yearly. They assist in preparing opinions, and in arguing cases before the Supreme Court; they defend suits in the Court of Claims; and they represent the Government in the classification, etc., of imports. (See Attorney-General and Justice Department.)

Assistant Postmasters-General. — There are four of these, designated as first, second, third, and fourth assistant postmasters-general. They are appointed by the President, and their salaries are $5,000 a year each. The administration of the postal system is actively in their hands as follows:

First Assistant Postmaster-General—Has charge of appointments, salaries and allowances, dead letters (q. v.), and of the post-office service, including delivery of mail within cities. (See City Delivery, Divison of; Division Miscellaneous Transportation.)

Second Assistant Postmaster-General—Has charge of the railway mail service (q. v.), of foreign mails (q. v.), and of general mail transportation matters. (See Division of Miscellaneous Transportation.)

Third Assistant Postmaster-General—Has charge of stamps (q. v.), money orders (q. v.), registered mail (q. v.), postal savings (q. v.). and other financial responsibilities of the Department.

Fourth Assistant Postmaster-General—

Has charge of the rural mail service (q. v.) and supplies.

(See Post-Office Department; Postmaster-General; Postal Service.)

Assistant Secretaries of the Treasury. —There are three assistant secretaries in the Treasury Department, who are theoretically of equal rank, and who are distinguished in the administration of the Department as Secretaries A, B, and C. They are appointed by the President, by and with the consent of the Senate, and their yearly salaries are $5,000 each. Under one assistant secretary falls the supervision of the departments of the life saving service (q. v.), the public health service (see Health Service), and the work of the supervising architect (q. v.). Under another assistant secretary falls the administration of the work of the Treasurer of the United States (q. v.), the Comptroller of the Currency (q. v.), the Register of the Treasury (q. v.), the Public Monies (see Revenue, Public), the Comptroller of the Treasury (q. v.), the Director of the Bureau of Engraving and Printing (see Engraving and Printing, Bureau of), the Director of the Mint (q. v.), the Commissioner of Internal Revenue (q. v.), the Secret Service (q. v.), and the auditors (q. v.). Another assistant secretary of the treasury supervises the administration of the customs (q. v.), the Bureau of War Risk Insurance (q. v.), and the investigations of special agents (q. v.). (See Treasury Department.)

Assistant Secretary of the Interior.— This officer was authorized by act of Congress approved March 14, 1862, and is appointed by the President, by and with the consent of the Senate, with a yearly salary of $4,500. He has no stated duties, but assists the Secretary of the Interior in the administration of the Department. (See Interior Department; Secretary of the Interior.)

Assistant Secretary of State, State Department.—This officer evolved from the chief clerk, who was the only other officer authorized to serve under the Secretary of State, when that office was created in 1789. It was not until 1853 that the office of assistant secretary of state was established by law. The assistant secretary of state is appointed by the President, by and with the consent of the Senate, and his yearly salary is $5,000. He has both general and direct supervision over the activities of the entire department, and puts into active operation the policy of the department. (See State Department; Secretary of State.)

Assistant Secretary of the Navy. — An assistant secretary of the Navy was appointed by act of Congress in 1882, but the act was repealed the following year. The present office of assistant secretary in the Navy Department was created on July 11, 1890. The incumbent is appointed by the President, by and with the consent of the Senate, and his yearly salary is $5,000. He acts as general assistant to the Secretary of Navy in the administration of the Department, but in addition has particular jurisdiction over naval yards and docks (q. v.), and over the Marine Corps (q. v.). (See Navy Department; Navy.)

Assistant Secretary of War.—The office of assistant secretary of war was created on March 5, 1890. The assistant secretary of war is appointed by the President, by and with the consent of the Senate, and receives a yearly salary of $5,000. His duties are the assistance of the Secretary of War in the administration of the War Department, and he exercises direct supervision only over those matters which do not determine or effect the policy of the department, and which will not serve to establish a precedent for it. (See War Department.)

Assistant to the Attorney-General.—The appropriations for the Department of Justice made by Congress in 1913 carried an item of $9,000 as yearly salary for an assistant to the Attorney-General. This officer was created by act of March 3, 1903, and is in charge of the work of the Department of Justice covering the application of the Anti-trust and Interstate Commerce laws. (See Department of Justice; Attorney-General; Anti-trust Law; Anti-trust Legislation; Interstate Commerce; Interstate Commerce Act; Interstate Commerce Commission.)

Assumption of State Debts.—Early in the second session of the First Congress Alexander Hamilton, Secretary of the Treasury, recommended that in order to restore public credit the Federal Government should fund and pay the foreign debt of the Confederation ($13,000,000), the domestic debt ($42,000,000) and also that it assume and pay the unpaid debt of the States. Massachusetts, Connecticut, New York, New Jersey, and South Carolina favored the plan. Virginia strongly opposed the latter clause. She was sustained in her opposition by Maryland, Georgia, and New Hampshire. The influence of North Carolina thrown against the measure defeated it for the time, but it was revived later, and passed Aug. 4, 1790, it was claimed, by a combination of its friends with those of the measure locating the Federal capital on the Potomac. The amount authorized to be assumed by the Government in the liquidation of the State debts was $21,500,-000, but the amount actually assumed was $3,250,000 less than that sum.

Astronomical Observatory. (See Meteorological Observatory; Naval Observatory.)

Establishment of, recommended, 879.
Report of Simon Newcomb on improvements for, 4790.

Asylum.—In its poetico-political use, the term characterizing America as a place of refuge to which down-trodden people from other countries may flee, as "The Asylum for Every Land."

Asylum, Military. (See Soldiers' Homes.)

Asylum, Right of, discussed, 3883, 5961.

Atchison and Pikes Peak Railroad Co. referred to, 3658.

Atlanta, The. (See *Weehawken*, The.)

Atlanta, Ga.:

Capture of, and orders regarding celebration of, 3439.

Collection of remains of officers and soldiers around, referred to, 3581.

Cotton Exposition at, 4631.

Atlanta (Ga.), Battle of.—On the night of July 21, 1864, Gen. Hood transferred his forces before Atlanta to a point near Decatur, about five miles east of Atlanta. Sherman came up and, finding the works on Peach Tree Creek abandoned, proceeded to invest the city. At 11 A. M. of the 22d, Hood surprised the left wing of Sherman's

army, under McPherson, by a sudden movement from Decatur. The whole line was soon engaged. Gen. McPherson was killed in the action, and the command of the Army of the Tennessee devolved upon Gen. Logan. After four hours of fighting the Confederates retired into their main works about Atlanta, leaving their dead and wounded on the field. The total Confederate loss was estimated at about 8,000. The Federal loss was 3,722 killed, wounded and missing. Sherman now drew his lines closely around Atlanta and prepared for a siege, but was unable to cut off Confederate supplies from Macon. Aug. 25 he gave up the idea of a direct siege. Sept. 1, however, a part of Hood's forces under Hardee having been repulsed at Jonesboro, Hood blew up his magazines and evacuated the city.

Atlanta, U. S. S., mentioned, 6806, 6909.

Atlantic Islands.—The Atlantic Ocean has a large number of bordering islands—the British Isles and West Indies are most important; Islands in the deep ocean like the Bermudian group are few.

Iceland.—Settled by Norsemen about 870. United with Norway 1262. Passed to Denmark 1380. Area, 39,756 square miles. It contains many hot springs and volcanoes, the largest of which is Mt. Hekla. It is subject to earthquakes.

Bermuda is a group of 360 coral islands 580 miles east of North Carolina. They were discovered by Bermudez, 1522; colonized 1612. They form a British colony.

Bahamas are noted as the first point of discovery by Columbus, 1492, San Salvador (Watling I.) Settled by British, 1629; ceded to England, 1783; British Crown Colony. The group comprises 20 inhabited and many uninhabited islands.

Atlantic Ocean:

Canal from—

Great Lakes to, commission to consider construction of, 6179.

Gulf of Mexico to, discussed, 995.

Junction between Pacific and, referred to, 2128, 2676.

Desired, 2813, 2988.

Atlantic Telegraph:

Discussed, 3653.

Illustration of laying of, opposite 3802.

Referred to, 3329, 3382, 3445.

Atlixco (Mexico), Battle of.—Immediately after the battle of Humantla Gen. Lane pressed forward to relieve the garrison at Puebla, Oct. 18, 1847; he learned that Rea, with a body of guerillas, was at Atlixco, a town about 10 leagues from Perote. The enemy was encountered on the afternoon of the 19th outside of the city, driven into and through the city, and dispersed. The Mexican loss was very severe, no less than 519 having been killed and wounded, while the Americans lost only two men.

Atrocities, Belgian, Bryce Report on. (See Bryce Report on Belgian Atrocities.)

Attainder.—The extinction of civil rights and privileges in an individual, and the forfeiture of his property to the government. In England, under the common law, it followed as a matter of course on a conviction and sentence to death for treason, and to some extent on sentence for other crimes. A Bill of Attainder is a legislative conviction of crime, with a sentence of death. The accused may or may not be given a trial. Foreign governments have employed this method of disposing of political offenders without giving them the opportunity of a regular judicial trial. The crime against which Bills of Attainder are usually directed is treason. Attainder following on sentence of death for treason formerly worked forfeiture of the condemned person's estate to the government, and by corruption of blood, as it is called, prevented his heirs from inheriting. Legislative convictions which impose punishments less than death are called Bills of Pains and Penalties; they are included in the meaning of the words, "Bill of Attainder," used in the Constitution of the United States. That Document prohibits the passage of Bills of Attainder by Congress or any State (Article 1, section 9, clause 3), and further provides, concerning judicial convictions of treason (Article 3, section 9, clause 2), that "no attainder of treason shall work corruption of blood or forfeiture except during the life of the person attained." The Supreme Court has decided unconstitutional as coming within the prohibitions of the Constitution, an act of Congress aimed at those who had engaged on the Confederate side in the Civil War, requiring all persons to take an oath negativing any such disloyal action before they should be allowed to practice in the United States Courts. (See Treason.)

Attorney-General.—The office of attorney-general was created by an act of Sept. 24, 1789. He is appointed by the President with the confirmation of the Senate. He is a member of the Cabinet, and receives a salary of $12,000 per year. All United States district attorneys and marshals are under his control. He seldom argues cases, this work being assigned to subordinates. He is assisted by a solicitor general and eight assistant attorneys general, besides one for the Post Office and one for the Interior Department. (See Justice, Department of.)

Attorney-General (see also Judiciary System; Justice, Department of):

Compensation to, referred to, 697, 1091.

Duties of, 2265.

Duty to prosecute and conduct all cases in the Supreme Court in which the United States should be concerned or interested, 697.

Member of board to examine quotas of States under call for troops, 3476.

Modifications in office of, recommended, 1090, 2265.

Opinion of—

Concerning treaty of Ghent, 966.

Regarding delivery of persons charged with crimes referred to, 1808.

Opinions of, compiled, 1856, 2632, 2643.

Recommendation that he be placed on footing with heads of other Executive Departments, 562, 880, 1016, 2265.

Attorney in Charge of Titles, Justice Department.—This officer renders opinions relating to purchase and condemnation of land by the United States. (See Justice Department, Public Lands.)

Attorneys, District:

Compensation of, discussed, 189, 2666, 2714, 4770, 4836, 4939, 5103.

Necessity of a uniform fee bill for guidance of, referred to, 2666.

Auditors, Treasury Department. —There are six auditors in the Department of the Treasury—one supervising accounts in the department itself, one the accounts in the War Department (q. v.), one the accounts in the Interior Department (q. v.), one the accounts in the Navy Department (q. v.), one those in the Post-Office Department (q. v.), and one those in the State and other departments (q. v.). The auditors determine the proper form of all accounts in the various departments of the Government, as well as investigate them thoroughly. (See Treasury Department, and illustration, frontispiece, Vol. XVII.)

Augusta (Ga.), Siege of.—In the autumn of 1780, Cornwallis stationed Lieut.-Col. Brown, with a Loyalist force, at Augusta, Ga. Col. Clark threatened the place for two days, inflicting some loss upon the garrison. The British loss was principally of their Indian auxiliaries. In the spring of the following year, while Gen. Greene besieged Fort Ninety-Six, Lee, Pickens, Clark, and other Southern partisans laid siege to Augusta, beginning May 23. June 5, 1781, Brown surrendered. The American loss was fifty-one killed and wounded. The British lost fifty-two killed. The wounded and prisoners on the British side amounted to 334.

Austin-Topolovampo Railroad, survey of, correspondence with Mexico regarding, referred to, 4475.

Australasia.—One of the two divisions of Oceania. It is subdivided by geographers into Australia proper (q. v.) and Melanesia. The latter includes New Guinea, Bismarck Archipelago, New Caledonia, Solomon, Santa Cruz, New Hebrides, and Loyalty Islands. (See also Australia and Oceania.)

Australia.—The territory of the Commonwealth of Australia includes the Continent of Australia, the Island of Tasmania and part of the island of New Guinea (Papua).

Australia (mainland) is probably the oldest of all land surfaces in either hemisphere. It is surrounded by the following waters: North, the Timor and Arafura Seas and Torres Strait; East, Pacific Ocean; South, Bass Strait (which separates Tasmania from the Continent) and Southern Ocean, and West, Indian Ocean. The coast-line of Australia is approximately 8,805 miles, and the geographical position of the Continent is between 10° 39′ – 39° 11′ South latitude and 113° 5′ – 153° 16′ East longitude; the greatest distance East to West is 2,400 miles, and from North to South 1,971 miles.

Physical Features.—Nearly all round the coast and in eastern and southeastern Australia, stretching far inland from the coastal range, is a rich grazing country, admirably adapted to the rearing of sheep. The most extensive mountain system takes its rise near the southeast point, and includes a number of ranges known by different names in different places, none of them being of any great height. The principal rivers are the Murray, with its tributaries, the Murrumbidge, Lachlan, and Darling, in the southeastern part of the island, which fall into the sea on the south coast; on the east coast, the Hawkesbury, Hunter, Clarence, Richmond, Brisbane, Mary, Burnett, Fitzroy, and Burdekin; on the west, the Swan, Murchison, Gascoyne, Ashburton, Fortescue, De Grey, and Fitzroy; on the north, the Drysdale, Ord, Victoria, and Daly; and the Roper, the Flinders, and Mitchell, which debouch into the Gulf of Carpentaria. Lakes are numerous, but nearly all are salt; the scarcity of the natural water supply has been, however, mitigated by successful borings.

Minerals.—Minerals comprise gold, silver, copper, iron, and coal in large quantities, antimony, mercury, tin, zinc, etc.

The seasons commence about March 21 (Autumn), June 21 (Winter), Sept. 22 (Spring), and Dec. 22 (Summer). The climate is extremely dry, but, except in the tropical coast-land of the north, the Continent is everywhere highly beneficial to Europeans, the range of temperature being smaller than that of other countries similarly situated.

Government.—The Government is that of a Federal Commonwealth within the British Empire, the executive power being vested in the Sovereign (through the Governor-General), assisted by a Federal Executive Council of seven Ministers of State and such honorary Ministers who may be appointed thereto. The Constitution rests on the fundamental law of March 16, 1898, ratified by the Imperial Parliament on July 9, 1900; and the Commonwealth was inaugurated on Jan. 1, 1901. Under the Constitution the Federal Government possesses limited and enumerated powers as surrendered by the federating States, the residuum of legislative power being in the Governments of the various States. Briefly stated, the enumerated powers include authority over commerce and navigation, finance, defense, post offices and telegraphs, census and statistics, and conciliation and arbitration in extra-State industrial disputes; with authority to assume the control of railways and lighthouses, marriage and divorce, emigration and immigration, currency and banking, and weights and measures.

AREA AND POPULATION

States and Capitals	Area in English Sq. Miles	Population Dec. 30, 1912
New South Wales (Sydney)	309,460	1,777,534
Victoria (Melbourne)	87,884	1,380,561
South Australia (Adelaide)	380,070	430,090
Queensland (Brisbane)	670,500	636,425
Tasmania (Hobart)	26,215	197,205
Western Australia (Perth)	975,920	306,129
Northern Territory (Darwin)	523,620	3,475
Papua (Port Moresby)	88,460	350,000
Federal District (Canberra)	912	1,940
Total	3,063,041	5,083,359

The Federal Parliament consists of a Senate and a House of Representatives. The Senate contains thirty-six members, six from each of the Original States, elected for six years by universal suffrage. The House of Representatives, similarly elected for a maximum of three years, contains members proportionate to the population, with a minimum of five Representatives for each State. The House of Representatives, 1913-1916, is made up of twenty-seven for New South Wales, twenty-one for Victoria, ten from Queensland, seven from South Australia, and five each from Tas-

mania and Western Australia, and consists of thirty-eight Liberals and thirty-seven members of the Labor Party.

There is a Federal High Court with a Chief Justice and six Judges, having original and appellate jurisdiction, subordinate to the final Appeal Court of the Empire, the Judicial Committee of the Privy Council.

Army and Navy.—In 1913 there was a total membership of the Defense Force of 240,065, of whom 281 officers and 7,507 men were serving in the Navy and 4,885 officers and 227,422 others in the Army. The latter figure includes 50,000 riflemen and 146,000 cadets.

An agreement was entered into (1902) by the Commonwealth and Imperial Governments under which a naval force was to be maintained (for ten years, 1903-13) in Australasian waters by the British Board of Admiralty, in return for annual contributions from Australia (£200,000) and New Zealand (£40,000), a third party to the agreement. This agreement provided also for the maintenance of Sydney as a first-class naval station, and for the nomination of naval cadets in the Royal Navy by the Australian and New Zealand Governments. This agreement is merged into an Australian Defense scheme, under which the Commonwealth provides and maintains certain ships of war, which form an Australian squadron of the Royal Navy, under the command of a Commonwealth officer in time of peace, and an integral part of the Eastern Fleet of the Royal Navy in time of war. Ships of the Royal Australian Navy are known as *H.M.A.S.* (His Majesty's Australian Ship).

Debt.—The Commonwealth has now undertaken responsibility for the Northern Territory Debt and the Port Augusta-Coodnadatta Railway Debt, whose combined amounts are £5,671,847. The other State Debts remain at the charge of the State Governments. The total of the Public Debts of the several States on June 30, 1912, was £277,124,095 (N.S.W. £100,052,-635; Victoria £60,737,216; South Australia £31,680,124; Queensland £47,068,186; Tasmania £11,302,411, and Western Australia £26,283,523).

Production and Industry.—The estimated value of the products of the Commonwealth in 1911 was: Agricultural, £38,774,000; Pastoral, £50,725,000; Dairying, etc., £19,-107,000; Forests and Fisheries, £5,728,000; Mining, £23,480,000; Manufacturing, £50,-767,000, a total of £188,581,000.

The land area of the Commonwealth is estimated at 1,903,731,840 acres, of which 15,642,000 were under cultivation in 1911-12.

In 1912 the Commonwealth produced 734,000,000 lbs. of wool (as in the grease), against 768,572,000 lbs. in 1911; 187,260,-000 lbs. of butter, against 211,578,000 lbs. in 1911; 16,147,000 lbs. of cheese, against 15,887,000 lbs. in 1911, and 54,370,000 lbs. of bacon and hams, against 53,265,000 lbs. in 1911.

In 1912 the value of gold produced was £9,880,000; silver and lead, £4,217,000; copper, £3,304,000; tin, £1,344,000; coal, £4,418,000; the value of all minerals produced in 1912 being £25,849,000.

Manufactures.—In 1912 there were in the Commonwealth 14.878 industrial establishments, employing 327,516 hands; wages paid amounted to £31,295,876; the value of plant and machinery £34,460,895; of materials used £88,317,749; value added by manufacture £60,427,360, and total value of final output £148,745,109.

Railways.—The total length of Government (and private) railways open at June 30, 1912, is stated as follows:

State	State Owned	Private
New South Wales	4,098	266
Victoria	3,673	51
Queensland	4,633	367
Western Australia	3,430	832
South Australia	1,973	34
Tasmania	701	205
Northern Territory	145	...
Total	18,653	1,755

The gross earnings of all Government lines in 1911-12 were £19,100,995, working expenses £12,471,004, and net earnings £6,-629,991, being at the rate of 2s. 5d. per train mile, and representing a return on the total cost (£160,557,000) of 4.13 per cent., as against 4.45 per cent. in 1910-11.

Shipping.—The Australian mercantile marine consists of 1,171 steamers (311,059 tons) and 1,316 sailing vessels (66,243 tons), other vessels not self-propelled, 276 vessels (63,065 tons), a total of 2,793 vessels (440,367 tons). The entrances and clearances of vessels engaged in oversea trade at the various Australian ports in the five years 1908-1912 were as follows (tonnage in parentheses):

Year	Entered	Cleared
1908	2,022 (4,295,679)	2,029 (4,285,472)
1909	2,000 (4,361,194)	1,910 (4,155,557)
1910	1,988 (4,607,820)	2,060 (4,725,326)
1911	2,081 (4,993,220)	2,093 (4,991,581)
1912	2,035 (5,163,357)	2,017 (5,111,957)

The weights, measures and coinage are identical with those used in the United Kingdom.

Towns.—Capital, Canberra, in the Federal District, purchased in 1911 from the State of N.S.W., is to be laid out as the capital of the Commonwealth. Meanwhile the seat of government is Melbourne.

There were sixteen cities and towns with a population exceeding 20,000 at the census of 1911, viz.:

Sydney (N.S.W.), 637,102; Melbourne (Vic.), 591,830; Adelaide (S.A.), 192,294; Brisbane (Q.), 141,342; Perth (W.A.), 84,-580; Newcastle (N.S.W.), 65,500; Ballarat (Vic.), 44,000; Bendigo (Vic.), 42,000; Hobart (Tas.), 38,055; Broken Hill (N.S.W.), 31,000; Geelong (Vic.), 28,880; Charters Towers (Q.), 25,000; Launceston (Tas.), 24,556; Ipswich (Q.), 23,000; Rockhampton (Q.), 21,033; Fremantle (W.A.), 20,-000. (See also Oceania.)

History.—The continent of Australia was known in the sixteenth century. It was visited by the Dutch in 1606. New South Wales was visited and named by Captain Cook in 1770. A British penal colony was established at Sydney in 1788, and at Brisbane, Queensland, in 1825. Settlements were made in Western Australia in 1826, Victoria in 1834, and at Adelaide in 1836. The discovery of gold near Bathurst, New South Wales, in 1851, gave strong impetus to immigration. The Commonwealth of Australia was created in 1900 by the federation of the States of New South Wales, Victoria, Queensland, South Australia, Western Australia, and Tasmania. The Governor-General is appointed by the Crown.

New South Wales is the oldest state. Sydney, the capital and principal port, has a population of 621,000. Forests cover one-quarter of the surface, and the cultivated area was reported in 1911 at 3,-381,000 acres. Besides wheat, corn, and tobacco 20,000 acres were under citrus fruit, mostly oranges, the yield being reported as 687,283 cases. In 1910 45,561,000 sheep were reported, from which were clipped 415,338,000 pounds of wool.

Victoria was originally a part of New South Wales but was made a separate colony in 1851. The imports in 1910 were valued at $97,350,000, and exports $88,-700,000, of which $11,790,000 was gold. Melbourne, the chief city, has a population of 591,830.

Queensland was visited by Captain Cook in 1770 and settlements were made in 1825. The staple production of the state is wool, the production in 1910 being 139,-250,000 pounds. Sugar is the principal manufactured article.

South Australia was proclaimed a British province in 1836, and the northern territory was transferred to the Commonwealth in 1911. The area of South Australia was 380,070 square miles, to which the northern territory added 523,620 square miles. The climate resembles that of southern France or Italy. The wine product of 1910 was more than three million gallons. Sugar cane and fruits are also grown. Adelaide is the capital and commercial center, having a population of 192,000 in 1911.

Western Australia is the largest Australian state. It has an area of 975,920 square miles. The forest area is estimated at twenty million acres, the timber (including eucalyptus) is especially valuable for shipbuilding and bridgework, owing to its durability.

Australian Ballot. (See Ballot.)

Australian System of Military Training. —Australia (q. v.) has had universal service since 1903. At the age of 12, the Australian boy enters a voluntary Cadet Corps as a junior cadet. Until the age of 14, he spends 90 hours a year in gymnastics, "setting up" exercises, and easy military maneuvers. He receives a uniform from the Government, but no musket. From the age of 14-18, he is enrolled as a senior cadet, when he receives a cadet rifle, later changed to the regulation army rifle when he shows sufficient progress to handle it. He now obtains careful drill in marching, in guard duty, and in military tactics, with especial attention to marksmanship. During these four years, he must receive at least 24 drills of 1 hour each, 12 drills of 2 hours each, and 4 drills of 4 hours each. At the age of 18, he joins the citizen army, and remains in it until he is 26, although he is liable to service until he reaches the age of 60. During his 8 years in the regular army, he devotes to training 16 days of 6 hours each yearly. It is estimated that this system has provided Australia with a citizen army of 120,000, with 150,000 cadets. The forces can be sent to foreign lands only by a referendum vote of the citizens of Australia, and the first referendum taken to allow conscription for service in Germany during the European war was voted down on October 29, 1916. (See Swiss System of Military Training; Compulsory Military Service.)

Austria *(Austro-Hungarian Monarchy).* —The largest empire, next to Russia, on the Continent of Europe, situated between 42° 51′ N. latitude and 9° 30′-26° 20′ E. longitude, with a total area of 676,077 square kilometres (260,695 square miles), and a total population (1910) of 51,340,378.

AREA AND POPULATION

States	Area, English Sq. Miles	Estimated Population
Austrian Empire	115,874	28,567,898
Kingdom of Hungary	125,395	20,840,678
Territories		
Bosnia and Herzegovina	19,760	1,931,802
Total	261,029	51,340,378

Government.—The Austro-Hungarian Monarchy consists of two states, the Empire of Austria and the Kingdom of Hungary, and of the Provinces Bosnia and Herzegovina. Each of the States has its own Constitution and Parliament, and for most branches of State affairs its own Ministry and Administration; but they are closely bound together by the identity of the Ruler and by a permanent Constitutional Union, which, upon the common principle of possession and defense, was first proclaimed by the Pragmatic Sanction of 1723, and has since been regulated by the so-called "Compromise" (Ausgleich-Kiegyezés) of 1867. According to the Constitutional Union foreign affairs and the greater part of war affairs (Army and Navy), together with the finances concerning them, and the administration of the Territories, are dealt with by common ministries. The control of the official actions of these ministers and the voting of the common budget is exercised by two delegations, each consisting of 60 members, of whom 20 are chosen from the Upper House of Austria and of Hungary, and 40 from the Lower House of Austria and of Hungary. The delegations are elected for one year, meet alternately at Vienna and Buda Pesth, and appoint their own President and Vice-President. In every other respect legislation concerning the common affairs belongs to the two Parliaments, and each State provides separately for its contribution to the common expenses. The proportion to be contributed by each State is fixed by mutual agreement, renewable every ten years.

History.—In connection with the Ausgleich-Kiegyezés the two States entered into a commercial and customs union in 1867, by which the two States form one commercial and customs territory; and possess the same system of coinage, weights and measures, and a joint bank of issue. In the same way as the quota agreement, this union is renewable every ten years.

Following the assassination of Archduke Ferdinand and his wife at Serajevo by a student, said to have been incited by Servian societies, and with Servian official connivance, Austria, on July 28, 1914, declared war against Servia, and an army was immediately sent to occupy Belgrade. The Servian government fled to Nish and prepared for resistance. (See European War.)

Reigning Sovereign.—Karl Franz Joseph (Charles I), Emperor of Austria, Apostolic King of Hungary (King of Bohemia, Dalmatia, Croatia, Slavonia, Galicia, Lodomeria and Illyria, King of Jerusalem, etc.), succeeded his grand uncle, the aged Franz Josef, who died Nov. 21, 1916, after a reign of sixty-eight years.

Army.—The Common Army of the Austro-Hungarian Monarchy is recruited by universal compulsory service for all male subjects between the ages of 19 and 42 in Austria, Hungary, and Bosnia-Herzegovina. The available military force also includes the Austrian Landwehr and Landsturm and the Hungarian Honvédség (Landwehr) and Nepfolkeles (Landsturm).

The Peace Establishment of the Active Army is 17,840 officers, 4,700 officials, and 290,000 others.

The Austrian Landwehr consists of 3,680 officers and 37,000 others.

The Hungarian Landwehr consists of 3,000 officers and 26,000 others.

The War Establishment of the Mobilized Field Army is 895,000 all ranks, with about 1,000,000 from the other formations. (See Armies of the World.)

Navy.—The Navy is administered by a department of the War Ministry, and manned by 1,500 officers and 13,500 men in

1912. (For the latest reports as to present establishment, see Navies of the World.)

Common Finance.—The Expenditure on Common Affairs (Defense, Foreign Affairs, Finance Ministry, and Board of Control) is met from the Common Revenue, derived from the net proceeds of the Customs, and from the matricular contributions of Austria (63.6 per cent.) and Hungary (36.4 per cent). The customs receipts for 1913 were 197,694,000 crowns. The contributions from Austria were 255,352,000, while Hungary's share amounted to 146,146,000 crowns. (5 crowns equal to $1 United States money.)

There is no Common Debt, but the Kingdom of Hungary sets aside a certain sum annually for the service of the Debt of Austria contracted before the year 1867. (See Hungary, Finance.)

AUSTRIA.—The Austrian Empire comprises the following provinces: Lower Austria, Upper Austria, Bohemia, Bukovina, Carinthia, Carniola, Dalmatia, Galicia, Görz and Gradiska, Istria, Moravia, Salzburg, Silesia, Styria, Trieste and District, Tyrol, Vorarlberg.

Physical Features.—Nearly three-fourths of Austria is high ground above the 600 foot level, with three main mountain systems—the Alps, Carpathians and Bohemia-Moravian mountains. The Central Alps traverse the country, while the Eastern Alps lie entirely within its boundaries; the Carpathians form a frontier with Hungary; the Bohemia-Moravian mountains enclose these countries and link up the Austrian mountain system with the Mittelgebirge of Central Europe. The remaining fourth part is occupied by fertile plains, of which the largest is in Galicia. The capital is on the Danube-drained Wiener Becken. The Danube, joined by the Inn, enters Austria from Bavaria at the gorge of Passau. The Dniester rises in eastern Galicia, and enters Russia at Chotin. The Vistula rises in Silesia, and forms the boundary of Russian Poland. The Oder has its source in Moravia. The Elbe, after a winding course of 185 miles in Bohemia, enters Saxony. The Adige (or Etch) rises in the mountains of Tyrol, and flows into the Adriatic.

Government.—The Government is that of a constitutional monarchy, the Sovereign bearing the title of Emperor, and the succession hereditary (in the order of primogeniture) in the male line of the House of Habsburg-Lothringen, and after the failure of the male, in the female line of that house. (See Austria-Hungary.)

The Reichsrath (Council of the Empire) consists of two houses, the Herrenhaus (House of Lords) and the Abgeordnetenhaus (House of Deputies).

The Herrenhaus consists of the 15 Archdukes of the Imperial family; of 82 of the landed nobility, in whose families the dignity is hereditary; of 5 prince-archbishops, 7 prince bishops, and 5 archbishops; and of 158 members nominated by the Emperor for life, for public service—a total of 272 members in 1912.

The Abgeordnetenhaus is composed of 516 deputies, elected by universal manhood suffrage (twenty-four years) and by secret ballot.

The courts of first instance are the 969 *Bezirksgerichte* (District Courts) and the 75 Superior District Courts with Jury Courts attached. Supervision of, and appeals from, these courts are conducted in nine Provincial Appeal Courts at Vienna, Graz, Trieste, Innsbruck, Zara, Prague, Brünn, Cracow, and Lemberg. The Supreme Court and Court of Cassation at Vienna is the Supreme Court of the Empire. Cases of conflict between different authorities are decided by the Tribunal of the Empire at Vienna.

All the kingdoms and countries represented in the Austrian Reichsrath possess self-government for matters not expressly reserved by the central government of the Empire. In addition, there are communal councils with executive committees, the council of the town of Trieste having the functions of a provincial diet. The diets meet annually, are elected for six years, and consist of a single chamber, with an executive council.

Finance.—The revenue of Austria for the year 1913 was 3,147,473,000 crowns, and the expenditure was 3,137,196,000 crowns.

To the General Debt of Austria, contracted before the year 1867, the kingdom of Hungary contributes over $12,000,000 annually (60,619,340 crowns in 1912), for amortization and interest. This General Debt. on Dec. 31. 1912. was 5.158.396.399 crowns. and the special debt was 7,377,033,-325 crowns.

Education.—Primary education is free and compulsory between the ages of 6 and 14 and about 96 per cent. of the attendances is secured. The schools are maintained by local taxation almost exclusively. Secondary education is controlled by the central government, including the private schools. Gymnasia and Realschulen prepare for the Universities and technical high schools.

Production and Industry.—Agriculture is the most important industry of the inhabitants, and more than one-half of the people are occupied therein. Of the total area about 94 per cent. is productive, 36 per cent. being arable land and 24 per cent. pastures and meadows, and 32 per cent. woodlands. The arable land produces wheat, rye, barley, oats. maize, potatoes, sugar beet, turnip and miscellaneous crops, but wheat and maize have also to be imported from Hungary. The gardens produce a variety of fruit and the vineyards produce excellent wine. The meadows and pastures support horses, cattle, sheep, etc.

Forestry is conducted on scientific principles and the periodic denudations are met by systematic afforestation. Oak, pine, beech, ash, elm, etc., form a valuable source of wealth.

Mines and Minerals.—In addition to gold, silver, iron, copper, lead and tin ores in profusion, there are rich deposits of coal and petroleum. While the salt mines of the Carpathians are the richest in the world, the mines of Wieliczka, in Galicia, and of Salzkammergut, in Upper Austria, are the most famous.

Austria is noted for its medicinal waters, notably the alkaline springs of Carlsbad. Marienbad, Franzenbad, Giesshübel, Bilin, and Gastein, where are the most frequented watering places in the world.

About 8,000,000 are dependent on the various industrial establishments, and Austria is abundantly equipped for industrial activity on account of its richness in raw materials, while its rivers offer both power and transport. In addition to the iron and steel industries, textiles and glass (particularly in Bohemia), leather, furniture, and woodwork, brewing and distilling, chemicals, printing and stationery, and tobacco trades are of great importance.

The sea fisheries of the Adriatic coast (about 1,000 miles) employ about 20,000 persons. The river and lake fisheries are also important, especially in Bohemia.

Transportation and Communication.—In 1910 23,000 kilometres (14,300 miles) of railway were open and working, of which 11,000 were owned or worked by the State, and 3.300 owned and worked by companies. In 1910 the length of navigable rivers and canals exceeded 4,000 miles for vessels and rafts, 900 miles being navigable for steamers, which ply to the number of about 340 on the Danube and Elbe.

There were 9,655 post offices in Austria (1911). There were 7,039 telegraph offices with 47,076 kilometres of line and 237,847 kilometres of wire. Telephones are in full operation and are extensively used.

In 1910 the mercantile marine of Austria consisted of 360 steamers of 368,000 tons, and 15,114 sailing vessels of 47,000 tons.

Towns.—Capital, Vienna, on the Danube. Population, 1910, 2,031,498. Other towns are: Trieste, 161,653; Prague, 223,741; Lemberg, 206,113; Graz, 151,781; Cracow, 151,886; Brünn, 125,737; Czernowitz, 87,-128; Pilsen, 80,343.

HUNGARY is a great lowland, encircled by the Carpathians and the Alps, and occupying the basin of the Danube from the gorge of Pozsony to the "Iron Gates" of Orsova. The eastern portion is known as Transylvania (Királyhágóntúl, or Land beyond the Forests; the German name being Siebenbürgen, from the seven castles of the Saxon invaders of the eighth century), and lies in the angle formed by the Carpathians and the Transylvanian Alps. Croatia and Slavonia, which form an annex of the Hungarian crown, extend eastwards from the Adriatic to the confluence of the Save with the Danube.

Rivers and Lakes.—The Danube (Duna) enters Hungary from a gorge in the Little Carpathians and flows eastwards and southwards to its confluence with the Drave; thence eastwards, until it is met at Zimony by the Save and flows in a mile-wide stream between Hungary and Servia to the Iron Gate on the Wallachia (Rumanian) boundary. The Danube is navigable throughout its course in Hungary and is the great highway and the outlet into the Black Sea. Its tributaries. the Save and Drave, are also navigable to the base of the Alps in the west. The Tisza, which divides Hungary almost equally into a western and eastern portion, flows in a winding but navigable course southward. Of the northern tributaries the March (with the Leitha in the south) divides Hungary from Austria.

Government.—The constitution is based on the Pragmatic Sanction of 1723 and on the fundamental law of 1867, and is that of a Constitutional Monarchy hereditary in the male line by primogeniture of the Habsburg-Lorraine dynasty. and after the extinction of the male, in the female line of that house.

The Hungarian Parliament consists of a House of Magnates and a House of Representatives. The House of Magnates consisted (in the Session of 1911-12) of 15 Archdukes, 50 Ecclesiastical Dignitaries, the 12 Bannerets, 5 official members, 3 Delegates from Croatia-Slavonia, the Governor of Fiume, 229 hereditary nobles and 60 life members appointed by the sovereign or elected by the House—a total of 375. The House of Representatives consists of 453 members, of whom 413 are elected by an electoral college in Hungary and 40 by the Diet of Croatia-Slavonia. Parliament meets annually. and has a maximum duration of five years.

The courts of first instance are the 76 County Courts, and 458 District Courts. controlled and supervised by the 12 Királyi Táblák. There is a Supreme Court of Hungary at Budapest and one of Croatia-Slavonia at Zágráb.

Production and Industry.—The fertile soil of Hungary and its magnificent forests provide employment for nearly 70 per cent. of the entire population, only 15 per cent. being engaged in the various industries.

The agricultural holdings are stated to number about 3,000,000, of which 1,500,-000 were less than 7 acres, and 14,000,000 under 150 acres each. All the great plains produce grain of excellent quality.

The mountainous regions which envelop Hungary, the western basin of the Danube, and the basins of the Drave and Save, are covered with forests which contain oak, beech, pine, and other valuable trees, which enable Hungary to export timber and forest products. The total area of the forests in 1911 was 8,885,042 hectares. (1 hectare= 2½ acres.)

Lignite, iron and coal are won, in addition to gold and silver, some 80,000 persons being employed in the mining and smelting industries. Salt is also largely produced.

Weaving, metal, stone, glass, wood, brewing, and tobacco industries employ most of the industrial population, but manufactures are of small importance compared with agriculture.

Inland Fisheries are of great importance. The river Tisza (Theiss) is stated to be "one part fish to two parts water."

Education.—Primary education is compulsory and free, and is maintained by local taxation. There are numerous Infant Schools with nursing staffs for 3 to 6 years, with Lower Elementary Schools 6 to 12 years (and Repetition courses 12 to 15). The average attendance is over 78 per cent.

Finance.—The Austro-Hungarian Monarchy has no Common Debt, but in the expenditure of the Kingdom of Hungary the sum of 60,621,984 crowns is set aside annually as a contribution to the service of the General Debt of Austria, contracted before 1867. The special debt of Hungary for 1911 was stated at 6,304,558,000 crowns.

Transportation and Communication.—The total length of lines open and working in 1911 was 13,033 miles, of which 10,942 were owned and worked, or leased and worked, by the State. Over 3,000 miles of rivers and canals are available for transport. There were 6,331 post offices and 4,765 telegraph offices. The sea-going mercantile marine amounts only to some 120,-000 tons. The chief port is Fiume, on the Adriatic coast of Croatia.

Towns.—Capital, Budapest, on the Danube. Population (1910), 880,371. Twenty towns have over 40,000, 15 exceed 30,000, and 27 exceed 20,000 inhabitants.

Trade with the United States.—The value of merchandise imported into Austria-Hungary from the United States for the year 1913 was $23,320,696 and goods to the value of $19,192,414 were sent thither, a balance of $4,128,282 in favor of the United States.

BOSNIA AND HERZEGOVINA comprise six districts, covering an area of 19,760 square miles, with a population, by the census of 1910, of 1,898,044, besides the military garrison of 33,758. The inhabitants are Slavs and the language is Servian.

Government.—The administration of Bosnia-Herzegovina was handed over to the Austro-Hungarian Monarchy by the Treaty of Berlin (1878), and in 1908 the Emperor-King extended his sovereignty over the provinces by autograph letter.

The Diet of 92 members (72 elected and 20 nominated) deals with home affairs, justice, finance, and public works. The local revenue was estimated at 79,129,475 crowns in 1911, the expenditure at 79,535,-715 crowns.

Capital, Serajevo (Bosna-Seral), on the Bosna River. Population (1910) 51,872. Other towns are Mostar 16,385, Banjaluka 14,793, and Tuzla 11,333.

Austria (see also Austria-Hungary):
Chargé d'affaires of, to United States, withdrawal of, referred to, 2690.
Commercial relations with, 1114,2004.
Confederate envoys sent to Great Britain and France referred to. (See Mason and Slidell.)
Consul of United States to Vienna, referred to, 2583.
Consular convention with, 4023.
Fugitive criminals, convention with, for surrender of, 2911.
Importation of American products to, legislation against, discussed, 4916.
Imprisonment of American citizens by, 2689, 2742.
Minister of United States to be sent to, 1592.
Relations opened with, 1706.
Statement of, regarding peace offer, 8189.
Reply of Entente Allies to, 8193.
Treaty with, transmitted and discussed, 975, 1008, 1026, 1097, 1105, 1157, 2434, 2911.
Correspondence regarding, referred to, 2564.
Referred to, 1070, 1114.
Troops of, departing to Mexico, referred to, 3588, 3589.
Vessels of, discriminating duties on, suspended by proclamation, 1003, 1004.
War with Hungary, sympathy of American Government with latter, 2550, 2579.
Wines from, duties on. (See Wines.)
Austria-Hungary (see also Austria; Hungary):
Claims of, regarding subjects killed in conflict in Pennsylvania,6324,6363.
Consular convention with, 4098.
Empress-queen of, assassination of, 6324.
Expulsion of American citizens, 6425.
Minister of, to United States, received, 4718.
Minister of United States to, appointment of A. M. Kelley as, and refusal to receive, discussed, 4910.
Naturalization treaty with, 4069, 4098, 4142.
Neutrality of United States in war with—
Belgium, 7977.
France, 7975.
Great Britain, 7975.
Italy, 8065.
Japan, 7977.
Russia, 7974.
Servia, 7969.
Tariff laws of, evidence of modification of, proclaimed, 5718.
Discussed, 5747.
Trade-marks, treaty, regarding, 4114.

Austria-Hungary, Treaties with.—The treaty of commerce and navigation of 1829 was proclaimed Feb. 10, 1831. It was made originally for the space of ten years, with renewal from year to year thereafter. It provides for liberty of commerce and navigation between the two countries under protection of person, property, and the equitable imposition of fees, charges, and taxes; lawful importation and re-exportation of products in vessels of the one party or the other under reciprocally equitable terms, except coastwise trade, which is excepted from the operation of this treaty. The establishment of consular representatives and agents is agreed upon under conditions of the most favored nation; but such consular agents who engage in trade on their own account shall derive from their official position no advantage or privilege not accorded to private citizens in similar transactions.

Extradition.—An extradition convention was proclaimed Dec. 15, 1856. It covers extradition of criminals and fugitives from justice accused or convicted of murder, assault with intent to kill, piracy, arson, robbery, forgery, making or circulating counterfeit money, or embezzlement of public money. The offence is to be regarded in the light of the laws of the country in which an asylum is sought, and not of those where the offence was committed. The provisions of the treaty are not retroactive, nor do they apply to political offenders or citizens of the country. All expense is to be borne by the country asking extradition. If the refugee commits a new crime in the country of asylum, such offence must be disposed of before extradition is permitted. The treaty extends from year to year, subject to six months' notice of intention to terminate.

Naturalization.—To regulate the citizenship of immigrants a naturalization convention was proclaimed Aug. 1, 1871. The government of Austria-Hungary agrees to recognize as American citizens those of its people who have resided in the United States for a period of five years, and who have become its citizens by regular and legal naturalization processes; and reciprocally the United States recognizes one of its own people who has similarly conformed to the naturalization laws of Austria-Hungary; but the declaration of intention is not in either country regarded as naturalization. Naturalization in one country does not grant to the person immunity from the consequences of a crime committed prior to immigration, subject, of course, to limitation; especially does this apply to those who have sought to escape military duty in Austria-Hungary. A naturalized subject may renounce his foreign citizenship, if he desire, without a fixed period of residence. This treaty was designed to endure for a period of ten years, and thereafter from year to year, subject to six months' notice of termination.

Trade-marks.—The reproduction of trade-marks by other than the owner is prohibited and legal redress is accorded to the owner on the same terms and conditions as to citizens of both countries under the provisions of a trade-mark convention proclaimed June 1, 1872. The life of a trade-mark shall be that provided by law in the country in which it originated, and when it becomes public property at home it is then public property in the country of the other contracting power. To acquire trade-mark protection, duplicate copies must be deposited in the Patent Office at Washington and in the Chamber of Commerce and Trade at Vienna and Pesth. This treaty, originally of ten years' duration, now lives from year to year, subject to one year's notice of termination. It was interpreted to apply also to copyrights.

Arbitration.—Differences of a legal nature or as to the interpretation of treaties impossible of settlement by diplomacy are to be referred to the Permanent Court of Arbitration at The Hague according to a convention signed Jan. 15, 1909.

Austro-American.—An American of Austrian birth or descent.

Automobile Trade.—Early experimenters in motor vehicles were hampered by the lack of engines which used a fuel less heavy and bulky than coal. Light vehicle motors were made possible by the successful production of liquid or volatile fuels and the internal combustion engine. The motive power in these gas or gasoline engines is furnished by a succession of explosions which take place within the cylinder itself, thereby doing away with the cumbersome boiler and furnace.

In 1886 two Germans, Gottlieb Daimler and Carl Benz, working independently, first applied the gas engine successfully to road vehicles. Daimler, who was manager of the Otto Gas Engine Works, at Deutz, Prussia, fitted his small air-cooled motor to a bicycle by placing it vertically between the front and rear wheels, the rear wheel being driven by means of a belt. In 1889 he constructed a two-cylinder engine, which attracted the attention of Messrs. Panhard and Levassor, of Paris, who acquired the necessary rights and immediately began the construction of the essentially modern motor car, the first of which was brought out in 1891.

Carl Benz first applied his single horizontal cylinder, water-jacketed engine to a three-wheel carriage. It was placed over the rear axle and drove a vertical crankshaft, thus giving the flywheel a horizontal position. This arrangement insured stability in the steering of the car. The crank-shaft was connected by bevel gearing to a short horizontal shaft, which was in turn coupled to a counter-shaft by a belt. The ends of this countershaft were connected to the road wheels by chains.

The early attempts by American inventors to build horseless carriages were confined to steam motors. An omnibus built in 1878 by a Mr. Fawcett, of Pittsburg, employed a Brayton motor of unknown design. During the eighties a Mr. Copeland brought out a bicycle equipped with a steam motor, followed by two tricycles similarly equipped, which were the predecessors of the light steam vehicles.

The distinction of early experiments in this line is also claimed by R. E. Olds, of Michigan, who in 1886 began the construction of a horseless carriage. This vehicle, completed in 1887, was first fitted with a steam engine geared to the rear axle. The boiler was of the porcupine type and gasoline was the fuel. Later this machine was remodeled, using a flash boiler, that is, the steam was generated only as required by the engines. In 1893 Mr. Olds began building gasoline motors for horseless carriages, which, since their perfection in 1895, have proved practical and successful.

Charles and J. F. Duryea completed their first automobile in 1892. Their second car, completed in 1893, embodied all the essential features of the modern automobile. The Duryea Motor Wagon Company was organized, and the thirteen automobiles, finished in the summer of 1896, were the first manufactured for sale in the United States. The price of these vehicles, $1,500, was considered too high for an untried substitute for the horse and carriage, and prevented the immediate acceptance of the gasoline automobile in America. A large majority of plants reporting for the industry to the census of 1900, commenced operations in 1899, the date of the substantial beginning of the automobile business in America.

Automobile Engine—There are three types of automobiles—the steam, the electric, and the gasoline. Of these, the steam is used the least, and the electric is used chiefly in cities and thickly-populated sections, because of the necessity of having a charging station handy where the batteries can be re-charged—although the increase in the number of charging stations has served to increase the number of electrics. The gasoline engine, on the other hand, finds gasoline obtainable almost everywhere, and has less weight in proportion to horsepower than the other forms.

Fuel—Many attempts have been made and are still being made to use other forms of fuel in the automobile, but up to the present time without marked success. In particular, ether, kerosene, alcohol, and naphthalene have been tried. The objections to kerosene are the difficulty of inducing vaporization and the clogging of the machinery by the residue. The chief objection to alcohol is its costliness.

Gasoline Engine—The principle of the gasoline engine used in automobiles is that of internal combustion. A quantity of gasoline is sprayed into an air-current in the carbureter, the resultant combination of air and gasoline being then compressed in the engine-chamber. At one end of the cylinder is located the spark plug, which ignites the mixture by an electric spark and causes it to explode. The expansion of the explosion drives out the piston, and power is generated.

Horsepower—The horsepower of the engine is found by multiplying the diameter of the cylinders by itself, multiplying this product by the number of cylinders, and dividing by 2½.

Mechanics of the four-cycle engine—The cycle in the gasoline engine must be started by moving the piston. Until the last several years, this was accomplished by turning a crank by hand, but now an electric *Starting apparatus* is in general use. This is operated by a storage battery, which is re-charged by the engine after the lat-

ter gets into motion; and is usually utilized also to provide the current for ignition, lighting, etc.

The down-stroke of the piston sucks in the mixture of air and gasoline through the inlet valve, and the up-stroke automatically closes this valve, and thus compresses the mixture. Ignition then occurs through the medium of the spark plug, the force of which sends down the piston on its second down stroke. Just before the completion of this stroke, the exhaust valve opens and releases the burnt gases, any of which may remain being driven out by the second up-stroke of the piston, which completes the cycle.

The *carbureter* has separate openings for the admission of gasoline and air. The air is forced in by the suction stroke of the engine, the amount being controlled by a valve. The gasoline is forced in by the force of gravity or pressure, another valve regulating its quantity. The mixture is let into the cylinder by the inlet manifold. The *vacuum feed system* is now in general use, whereby the main gasoline tank may be removed far from the engine, the gasoline being pumped from it into a smaller feed tank near the engine, from which it is forced into the carbureter.

Ignition may occur through either the make-and-break or the jump-spark system, although the latter is now almost universal. A high tension current, arising from storage batteries and a spark coil, causes an electric spark to jump between two electrodes in the spark plug, which are about ¼ inch apart. The current may come also from a magneto.

The *muffler* is a drum of sheet steel used to deaden the noise which would otherwise occur when the exhaust gases are emitted. The exhaust gases are passed through it, and are reduced gradually to atmospheric pressure by being passed through chambers of increasing size.

A *cooling system* is imperative, as the rapid explosions would otherwise make the engine red-hot. The water-cooling system is the more common. In this system, the cylinders are constructed of two walls, and are cooled by having water flow in the space between. The water itself, naturally, is thereby heated, and is in turn cooled by the radiator (see below). Under the air cooling system, a fan blows air over the cylinder, which is covered with short rods to facilitate the conduction of heat into the air.

STATEMENT ON THE MANUFACTURE OF AUTOMOBILES, AND AUTOMOBILE BODIES AND PARTS

	Automobiles	Automobile bodies and parts	Total
Number of establishments [1]	300	971	1,271
Persons engaged in manufacture	91,997	53,954	145,951
Proprietors and firm members	60	700	760
Salaried employees	12,630	5,469	18,099
Wage earners (average number)	79,307	47,785	127,092
Primary horsepower	104,983	68,701	173,684
Capital	$312,876,000	$94,854,000	$407,730,000
Services	84,901,000	54,552,000	139,453,000
Salaries	17,966,000	19,560,000	37,526,000
Wages	66,935,000	34,992,000	101,927,000
Materials	292,598,000	63,610,000	356,208,000
Value of products	503,230,000	129,601,000	632,831,000
Value added by manufacture (value of products less cost of materials)	210,632,000	65,991,000	276,623,000

[1] In addition, in 1914, 33 establishments primarily engaged in other lines of manufacture, produced automobiles to the value of $6,636,920, and 434 establishments of this character manufactured automobile bodies and parts to the value of $10,515,070; in 1909, similar establishments produced automobiles valued at $830,080 and automobile bodies and parts valued at $4,415,266.

The *radiators* may function by either the water-tube or the air-tube process. In the former, the water is cooled by passing through thin metal pipes, over which a constant current of air passes. In the latter, the tubes are inserted into the water. When the automobile is in rapid motion, a breeze comes naturally through the radiator. When the automobile is driven slowly, the current of air is obtained by the revolution of a fan, which is driven from the engine-shaft.

Lubrication is necessary to keep the various parts of the engine well-oiled. The splash system has a pool of oil at the bottom of the crank case, into which the crank-pin splashes at each revolution of the engine—the oil being driven to all parts which need it. The direct system of lubrication pumps the oil directly to each part needing lubrication. A combination of the two systems is common.

Transmission connection between the shaft and the driving machinery is effected by means of a friction clutch. The clutch is mounted close to the fly-wheel. A variety of speed ratios may be obtained, and the transmission includes also gearing for backward driving, as the engine cannot be driven backwards. Differential gearing is a device to carry power from the drive shaft to both halves of the axle at all times.

Tires on automobiles follow the pneumatic tube principle of the bicycle tire, although trucks are equipped with solid rubber tires. An outer tube takes the wear and tear, the air being contained in an inner tube. Detachable rims, held to the wheels by bolts, may be easily removed and applied with the tire already in place upon them.

Service brakes are usually operated by foot; emergency brakes by hand.

Trucks may be operated, according to the latest figures, at a cost of about ten cents per ton mile. In cities, where charging is readily available, electric trucks are coming into general use.

The latest steps in automobile building have been the armored gun-carrying machine and the farm tractor.

The rapid growth of the business is shown by the fact that the number of establishments making automobiles and parts jumped from 57 in 1900 to 743 in 1909, and the value of output during the same time from $4,748,011 to $249,202,075.

Continued demand for automobiles and trucks in this country and abroad has brought a remarkable increase in sales, the statistics for the year ending with June 30, 1915, as compiled by Alfred Reeves, general manager of the National Automobile Chamber of Commerce, Inc., showing the production to have been 703,527 cars, valued wholesale at $523,463,803, which is an advance of 36 per cent in the number of cars and more than 10 per cent in value over the previous twelve months.

Sales of passenger cars of all types to June 30, which is the end of the year in the industry, were 665,826, for which the manufacturers received $450,941,131, while the sales of commercial vehicles of all types are estimated at 37,700, valued at $72,522,-692. The figures for twelve months ending June 30, 1914, were 515,101 cars, passenger and commercial, valued at slightly more than $485,000,000.

It will be noted that while the number of cars increased 36 per cent, the value increased only 10 per cent, indicating the greater value the makers have been giving purchasers as manufacturing costs were brought down and fewer changes were made in chassis construction.

Exports of automobiles and motor trucks reached a total in the year ending with June, 1915, far in excess of any previous twelve months. They totalled $60,254,635, made up of motor trucks to the value of $39,140,682 and automobiles valued at $21,-113,953. This value represented 37,876 vehicles made up of 13,996 motor trucks and 23,880 passenger cars. To this can be added parts to the value of $7,853,183, giving a total of $68,107,818.

	1916	1915
Motor vehicles produced ..	1,617,708	892,618
Passenger cars sold	1,525,578	842,249
Motor trucks sold	92,130	50,369
Retail value of sales ..	$1,088,028,273	$691,778,950
Retail value of passenger cars sold ..	921,378,000	565,856,450
Retail value of trucks sold	166,650,273	125,922,500
Average retail price passenger cars ...	605	672
Average retail price trucks	1,809	2,500

No. cylinders in cars	Companies manufacturing in 1916
4	58
6	43
8	12
12	5
4 or 6	16
4 or 8	6
6 or 8	5
6 or 12	2
4, 6, or 8	3
Total	150

In 1916, there were 2,445,664 cars and trucks in the United States, of which some 2,300,000 were non-commercial in their uses. This number represents approximately 80% of the total number in the world.

Autonomous Government for Cuba discussed, 6152, 6261, 6284, 6308, 6660. (See also Cuba.)

Autonomy.—The right to representative government in any form; not subject to any laws other than self-made laws.

Auxiliary Navy in Spanish-American War, 6313.

Averysboro (N. C.), Battle of.—March 16, 1865, Gen. Slocum, in the advance of the Union Army, encountered the Confederates under Gen. Hardee near Averysboro, in the narrow, swampy neck between Cape Fear and South rivers. Hardee hoped to hold Sherman in check until Johnston could concentrate his army at some point in his rear. Incessant rains had made the ground so soft that men and horses sank deep in the mud. A severe fight took place amid showers of rain and gusts of wind. The whole line advanced late in the afternoon and the Confederates retreated to Smithfield, leaving 108 dead upon the field. The Federal loss was seventy-seven killed and 477 wounded.

Aves Islands.—A group of small islands in the Caribbean Sea, belonging to Venezuela.

Aviation. (See Aeronautics, also Army, *Signal Corps,* Navy, *Flying Corps,* and for application to military uses see European War, *Zeppelins.*)

Back-Stair Policy.—A term used in derision against several of the Presidents for the purpose of insinuating that their policy was dictated by secret friends, who were figuratively admitted by way of the back stairs.

Bacon's Rebellion.—An insurrection in 1676 of the people of Virginia, led by Nathaniel Bacon. In 1673 the Crown assigned the entire Province of Virginia for thirty-one years to Lords Arlington and Culpeper, with power to collect for their own use all quit rents, escheats, and duties; to name sheriffs and other officers; to make new counties, and in general to exercise the authority of absolute rulers. Sir William Berkeley, the English governor of the Colony, was very unpopular on account of his opposition to free education and a free press. He seemed to think that the function of a governor was to get as much as possible from the colonists for himself and his masters at the least possible cost. He also proved inefficient in protecting the settlers against the ravages of the Indians. He laid heavy taxes upon the people and restricted the franchise. An Indian uprising having occurred in the state, a force of 500 men gathered to march against them. Berkeley ordered them to disband. The colonists chose Bacon, who was a popular lawyer, as their leader, and despite the refusal of the governor to commission him, he led his men against and defeated the Indians. Berkeley thereupon proclaimed Bacon a rebel, notwithstanding which the people chose him a member of the new assembly. On his way to Jamestown he was arrested and tried by the governor and his council, but was released on parole and left the capital. He soon returned with 600 men and again demanded a commission, which was granted. While Bacon was successfully engaged in another campaign against the Indians, Berkeley again proclaimed him a rebel and a traitor. Bacon then burned Jamestown, the governor taking refuge on an English vessel in the harbor. The rebellion was carried on in a desultory way until the death of Bacon in 1677, when it collapsed for want of a leader. The English executed twenty-three of the participants in this rebellion. It is notable as the first formidable resistance to colonial authority in British America. The significance of its occurrence just 100 years before independence has often been remarked. One of Bacon's lieutenants put to death for his part in the rebellion was William Drummond, who had served for a few years as the first governor of North Carolina.

Baden.—A German grand duchy, of southern Germany and a state of the German Empire. The reigning duke is Frederick II. It is bounded by Hesse and Bavaria on the north, Bavaria on the northeast, Württemberg on the east, Switzerland (separated mainly by Lake Constance and the Rhine) on the south, and Alsace and the Rhine Palatinate (separated by the Rhine) on the west. Its capital is Carlsruhe. It produces grain, wine, tobacco, hemp, potatoes, hops and chicory, manufactures silk goods, chemicals, clocks, machinery, woodenware, brushes, paper, etc.

Government.—The government is a constitutional hereditary monarchy under a grand duke and a Landtag with an Upper House and a Chamber of sixty-three Representatives. It sends three representatives to the German Bundesrath and fourteen to the Reichstag. It entered the German confederation in 1815, received a Constitution in 1818, and became a member of the German Empire in 1871. It has an area of 5,823 sq. miles and a population (1910) of 2,141,832. (See also Germany).

Baden, fugitive criminals, convention with, for surrender of, 2898.

Baden, Treaties with.—The extradition treaty of 1857 and the naturalization convention of 1868 were not affected by the formation of the German Empire in 1871. The extradition treaty of 1857 was proclaimed on May 19 of that year. The extraditable crimes are: Murder, assault with intent to kill, piracy, arson, robbery, forgery, making or circulating counterfeit money, and embezzlement of public monies. Evidence of guilt sufficient to convict within the country of asylum must be supplied. The expense must be borne by the country asking surrender. The treaty does not apply to political offenders, nor is either nation bound to deliver up its own citizens. Commission of a new crime within the country of asylum causes the offender to be tried and, if guilty, to be punished there before surrender. The treaty remained in force until Jan. 1, 1860, and thereafter from year to year, subject to one year's notice of intention to terminate.

The treaty of 1868 is a naturalization treaty designed to regulate the recognition of naturalized citizens by their native country, and was proclaimed Jan. 10, 1870. Each country agrees to recognize as citizens those of its former subjects who have legally conformed to the naturalization laws of the other country. No immunity from punishment for crimes committed before emigration, saving the limitation established by the laws of the original country. Especially does this refer to the liability of a former citizen of Baden for non-fulfillment of military duty. But he shall not be subject to punishment for this offence unless he shall have emigrated while drafted or in actual military service. Provision is made whereby a former citizen may, if he desire, easily resume his citizenship. This treaty was made to run ten years and thereafter from year to year, subject to twelve months' notice of intention to terminate. A protocol was signed in Munich on May 26, 1868, in further explanation of the several causes. (See German Empire.)

Badger State.—A nickname for Wisconsin (q. v.). (See also States.)

Bahama Banks, negotiations with Great Britain regarding cession of keys on, to United States, 913.

Bahama Islands, formerly Lucayos.—A chain of islands stretching from near the north coast of Haiti to the east coast of Florida. They are separated from Florida by the Gulf Stream and from Cuba by the Old Bahama channel. There are some 3,000 of these islands but only about 30 of any size. The principal ones, beginning at the northwest, are Great Bahama, The Abacos, Eleuthera, New Providence, Andros, Guanahani or Cat Island or San Salvador, Watling Island, Exuma, Long Island, Crooked Islands, Mariguana, Inagua, Little Inagua, Caicos, and Turks Island. The climate of these islands is very mild and salubrious, even in winter. The soil is thin, but produces cotton, maize, pineapples, oranges, etc.

History.—The Bahamas were Columbus's earliest discovery, but there is some doubt as to which of the islands he called San Salvador. The islands were occupied by the English in 1629 and finally secured to them by the treaty of 1783. Area, about 5,450 sq. miles; population (1909), 61,277.

Government.—The capital is Nassau, New Providence. A Governor, an executive council, and a legislative council of nine members each and a representative assembly of twenty-nine members constitute the government.

During the Civil War in United States blockade runners made their headquarters in the Bahamas, especially in New Providence. The islands have some reputation as a winter resort, the thermometer, from November to May, varies from 60° to 75°, and during the remainder of the year from 75° to 85°.

Bahama Islands, postal convention with, 5377.

Bail.—A legal term representing money, or other valuable security, risked to guarantee the appearance of a person released from the custody of the law.

Baking Business.—The baking industry, according to the last federal census, stands thirteenth in the list of American industries in point of value of products. Bread is regularly shipped by a large number of bakeries throughout the country a distance of a hundred and fifty miles, and in a few instances it is shipped a thousand miles. This last is exceptional, however, and only peculiar conditions make it possible. Length of shipments depends entirely on the local bread market and on the express rates. The margin of profit on bread generally is small. Shipments of bread will not stand an exorbitant express rate, and when sent long distances always goes to a market where the demand for a superior article to that baked locally is equal to a somewhat increased price. The capitalization of the baking industry is given in the last federal census (1909) at $212,910,000. The largest producers of bread in the United States operate a number of plants in one or more cities. The Ward Baking Company and the General Baking Company of New York and other cities, the Shults Bread Company of New York City, the City Baking Company of Baltimore, Md., the Schulze Baking Company of Chicago, the American Bakery Company of St. Louis, and the Consumers' Bread Company of Kansas City are among the largest in the country.

The baking industry is growing by leaps and bounds and very likely by this time stands twelfth or even higher in the list of American industries. At the time of the last census report it ranked fourth in value of the product in a list of industries with annual products valued at over a hundred million. The per cent of increase for ten years covered in the report was 126.3 per cent in value of products, exceeded in the same period only by such products as women's clothing, automobiles, electrical machinery, fertilizers, wire, beet sugar, manufactured ice, photographic apparatus, etc.

The history of biscuit baking in the United States is a record of the development of a small and obscure business to an industry of national importance. The word biscuit, derived through French from the Latin, means twice baked, and had its origin in the fact that the military bread of the Romans was twice prepared in the oven. In Europe all small cakes made of flour, with sweetening and flavoring added, are called biscuits. In the United States the word "cracker" was used to describe the early productions of crisp unsweetened dough, and later extended to include those with both sweetening and flavor. When these American crackers were sent to Europe they were included

under the general name of biscuits, and the term is coming into a wider use in America.

The first cracker bakery recorded in the United States was that of Theodore Pearson, of Newburyport, Mass., who as early as 1792 made a large round crisp wheat loaf, or cracker, which, unlike ordinary bread would keep for a long time. For this reason it was favored among the supplies of sailing vessels.

Joshua Bent built an oven in Milton, Mass., in 1801, and began the manufacture of his water crackers, which later achieved a national reputation, and Artemas Kennedy followed at Menotomy (now Arlington), Mass., in 1805. In Boston the Austins carried on the business successfully for many years. Other noted New England firms were Thurston, Hall & Co., of Cambridgeport; J. S. Carr, of Springfield; C. D. Boss of New London, Conn., and Parks & Savage, of Hartford. The earliest New York cracker baker was Ephraim Treadwell, who began business in 1825, and the Brinckerhoffs started in 1850. The Larrabee Company, of Albany, established in 1860, made an enviable reputation. Some of the other bakers engaged in interstate trade in the early history of the industry, and who contributed to its national importance were J. R. Vanderveer, of New York; Wilson & Medlar, of Philadelphia; Skillman, of Baltimore; Haste & Harris, of Detroit; The Margaret Bakery, of New Orleans; The Dake Bakery, of Chicago; S. S. Marvin, of Pittsburg; and Dozier & Weyl, of St. Louis. These and many others joined in the race for recognition throughout the country, sending their representatives from Maine to Oregon, and from the lakes to the gulf, besides exporting to South America, Africa and Australia.

Until about 1840 machinery in the biscuit business was almost unknown. A machine was then invented which rolled the dough into a thin sheet, which, passing along on an endless belt or apron, was cut into the required shape by a stamp rising and falling automatically. In this way about a dozen crackers were cut at a time and it became possible to bake five or six barrels of flour a day—an important increase over the preceding average rate of one barrel.

In 1849 the discovery of gold in California and the consequent demand for crackers as a suitable article of pioneer food proved a marked stimulus to the biscuit trade. Plants were enlarged and steam power was introduced to work the machines. The civil war gave a second great impetus to the industry and the old-time flat-tile ovens being taxed beyond their capacity to meet the increased demand for hard bread for army and navy rations, a mechanical reel oven, consisting of a series of long iron pans revolving in a framework, similar in action to a Ferris wheel, the whole enclosed in a large brick oven chamber, was invented, and this again revolutionized the biscuit baking business. With this device the capacity of a single oven leaped from the average rate of six barrels to twenty-five or thirty barrels of flour per day. The size of these reel ovens has been increased until now all the large plants have a daily capacity of from forty to fifty barrels per day per oven.

The biscuit baking business has not escaped the national tendency toward concentration. Four holding companies now control nearly all the larger plants in the country. The first of these, the New York Biscuit Company, includes the leading houses in New England and New York, with an immense factory in New York City, baking a thousand barrels of flour a day. The American Biscuit Company runs one large factory in New York, and the United States Biscuit Company controls the principal factories in Ohio, Indiana and Pennsylvania. The National owns bakeries in Denver, Colo.; Cedar Rapids and Des Moines, Iowa; Rock Island, Ill., and New Orleans, La.

Statistics of the baking business as a whole, including bread, crackers, pies, cakes, pastry, pretzels, etc., collected for 1914 show 25,963 establishments in the United States, employing 124,052 wage-earners, and producing goods to the value of $491,893,000 for the year. The cost of materials used in these bakeries was given as $274,257,000, and the amount distributed in wages as $96,634,000. Besides these 183 factories reported biscuits and crackers as subsidiary products. All these figures show substantial increases over the census of 1909.

Balance of Power.—The term used to describe the organization of the various great nations of the world into alliances so that one group will equalize the other group, hence preventing a strong nation from preying upon a weaker. Practically all peace terms after modern wars have been so drawn up as to provide for a balance of power. Thus, before the outbreak of the European War, Russia was allied with Servia to protect the latter country against the stronger forces of Austria, while England was allied with France, along with Russia thus forming the Triple Entente (q. v.), against Germany and her associates in the Triple Alliance (q. v.). It was thought that the organization of the great countries of Europe into these two alliances would preserve the balance of power between them.

Balance of Trade.—The difference in value between the exports and imports of a country is called its balance of trade.

Balkan States.—A general term referring to those states or parts of states in the Balkan peninsula in the southeastern part of Europe, including the country south of the Save and Danube rivers. It comprises Dalmatia, parts of Croatia and Kustenland, Albania, Bosnia, Herzegovina, Montenegro, Servia, Bulgaria, European Turkey, Greece, and part of Rumania. In the political sense it usually applies to Bulgaria, Servia, Montenegro, Rumania, Turkey in Europe and Greece.

Balkan Question.—Situated as it is, guarding the coveted Ægean Sea and the Strait of Dardanelles, and composed of nations holding variant political and religious views, this group of states is looked upon as a constant menace to the peace of Europe. Political troubles in the peninsula are generally referred to as the Balkan Question.

The Congress of Berlin, which attempted to alter the map of Europe after the Russian victory of 1878, in failing to recognize the just claims of the different nationalities in the Balkans, is responsible for all the years of subsequent restlessness and rebellion, and the ultimate general European war, begun in 1914, in which Russia, France, England, Italy and Servia were allied against Austria-Hungary, Germany, Turkey and Bulgaria.

The great powers of Europe in 1903 ordered these three reforms in Turkey: (1) The Turkish Inspector-General must have two civil agents appointed by the Powers; (2) there shall be international gendarmes in Turkey; (3) the three Macedonian villayets shall be specifically restricted in power.

The Prime Minister of Bulgaria was as-

sassinated March 11, 1907. Then the peasant Rumanians demanded much needed land reforms. During the summer of 1907 Greco-Bulgarian fights in the district of Florina resulted in 135 deaths and many afflictions. Dissatisfaction in the contiguous realms of the peninsula was so widespread and pronounced as to frighten Turkey and attract the attention of all Europe. This condition of affairs continued until late in the year 1908. In September of that year Bulgaria declared herself free from the Turks and all others, and proceeded to take possession of the Novi-Bazar railway, which though in Bulgaria was owned by Turkey. The Turkish government complained to the signatory powers of the Treaty of Berlin, which had left the Bulgarians vassals to Turkey.

Oct. 5, 1909, Prince Ferdinand read his manifesto of independence and union for Bulgaria and eastern Rumelia. Next Austria, on Oct. 7, proclaimed to the world that the provinces of Bosnia and Herzegovina were hers of right to annex. The Treaty of Berlin had authorized their occupation and Austria chose the moment for annexation when Turkey was wholly unprepared to hold her protectorates. Diplomatic Europe seemed to see in this act the insincerity of Austria's desire for the liberty of the provinces and a premeditated plan for the prevention of a possible Slavic coalition of the future. The Turkish government appealed to the powers. Servia and Montenegro were ready to unite against Austria in the event of a war. Great Britain refused to recognize Austria's infringement of the Treaty of Berlin. Oct. 7, Crete proclaimed itself a dependency of Greece. Turkey again protested, and Great Britain, France, Russia and Italy agreed to take the demands of Crete under consideration and negotiate with the Turkish government. Late in October, 1908, Great Britain, France and Russia advised Bulgaria to negotiate with Turkey with a view to compensating the latter power for acceding to Bulgarian independence. The culmination of the Austro-Turkish difficulties was effected in a protocol signed in February, 1909, whereby Turkish customs duties were increased 15 per cent, Turkish monopolies in matches, cigarette paper and some other articles were established, all Moslems of Bosnia and Herzegovina were to enjoy political and religious freedom, and Turkey received an indemnity of $12,500,000 from Austria. In May, 1910, the Cretan assembly was opened in the manner of the Greek parliament and an oath of allegiance was taken to the King of the Hellenes.

As early as February, 1912, the governments of Bulgaria, Serbia, Montenegro and Greece had come to a complete understanding and formed an alliance for the purpose of securing the freedom of their compatriots and co-religionists from Turkish domination, and the aggrandizement of each state through the division of Turkey in Europe. Alleged massacres in Macedonia and a revolt in Albania had almost brought matters to a crisis, when Count Berchtold, Austrian Minister of Foreign Affairs, proposed to the powers that they should co-operate to restrain the Balkan States from upsetting the *status quo* in European Turkey, and encourage the Porte in a policy of moderate decentralization on ethnic lines. Austria's purpose was to prevent war. By the Balkan allies the proposal seemed favorable to their claims. The Turks looked upon it as a threat of European intervention for the ulterior purpose of taking the Macedonian provinces from the control of the Sultan.

Turko-Bulgarian War.—During the peace negotiations between Italy and Turkey in Sept., 1912, Turkey mobilized a large force on the Bulgarian frontier, and the incensed Bulgarians also began a mobilization of forces, and demanded that the promises made by Turkey in the Treaty of Berlin be guaranted, declaring that the powers of Europe had temporized too long. Bulgaria called upon Servia, Greece, Macedonia, Montenegro and Herzegovina to rise against Turkey, and by Oct. 10, 1912, 600,000 bayonets surrounded European Turkey.

The Powers in the meanwhile had been endeavoring to concert measures to prevent actual war. Representatives of Austria-Hungary and Russia at Sofia, Belgrade, Cettinge and Athens announced to the Balkan allies the attitude of the Powers as follows:

The governments of Russia and Austria declare to the Balkan States:

First—That the Powers energetically reprove any measure susceptible of causing a rupture of the peace.

Second—That, leaning on Article XXIII of the Treaty of Berlin, they will take in hand, in the interest of the Balkan peoples, the realization of reforms in the administration of European Turkey, it being understood that these reforms shall not affect the sovereignty of the Sultan or the territorial integrity of the Ottoman Empire. The Powers reserve to themselves liberty of action for a collective ulterior study of these reforms.

Third—That if nevertheless war breaks out between the Balkan States and the Ottoman Empire, they will permit at the end of the conflict no modification of the territorial *status quo* in European Turkey. The Powers will make collectively to the Sublime Porte representations similar to the above declaration.

Montenegro had previously (Oct. 6, 1912) declared war on Turkey and the other Balkan allies made demands which Turkey considered offensive.

M. Pasitch, Servian Minister of Foreign Affairs, and President of the Council of Ministers, issued a statement saying: "Since the arrival of the Turks in Europe, Christian populations under their rule have never ceased to suffer. The relations between them have never been other than those between conqueror and conquered. Servia is not recognized as a nation; she has neither church nor school.

"Servia, like other Balkan nations, has peaceably waited for the putting into effect of reforms which would assure the safety of the lives of the Christian populations in the Ottoman Empire, but all has been in vain. We are convinced that war is now the only means of attaining autonomy for Old Servia, where a majority of the population are Serbs. I consider that these people merit our effort all the more because they were altogether abandoned even in the attempts at reforms undertaken by the great Powers. Old Servia must include the vilayet of Kossovo with the Sandjak of Novi-Bazar, the northern portion of the vilayet of Scutari, with the shores of the Adriatic, where there are ancient Servian forts; also the northwestern portion of the vilayet of Monastir, including Lake Ochrida.

"Besides Old Servia, autonomy must be given to Macedonia, Albania, Thessaly and Epira. At the head of these autonomous provinces there must be Christian governors, each province naving an Assembly, with representatives whose authority will be drawn proportionately from the various nationalities."

Fighting began on Oct. 10, 1912, and was prosecuted with the utmost vigor by Bulgaria, assisted by Servia, Montenegro and Greece. After investing Adrianople and advancing almost to the Black Sea, peace was concluded at London, May 30, 1913, and all Thrace to the Enos-Midia line fell to the share of Bulgaria, as well as parts of Macedonia to the west of Bulgaria.

In a campaign of eight weeks the Balkan allies had swept the Turks from Albania, Epirus, Macedonia and the greater part of Thrace. The Turks were in possession of only five important positions. By the terms of the treaty of peace signed in London, Turkey relinquished her European territory west of the Enos-Midia line, all of which, except Albania, she ceded to the allies. Crete was also ceded to the allies, and the disposition of the Ægean Islands, the financial settlements and exact delimitation of boundaries was left to the Powers.

Two bitter controversies now broke out among the Balkan allies. They both related to frontier delimitations. National feeling ran so high that a settlement through the ordinary diplomatic channels failed, and each was finally determined by military action. They grew out of the problem of new frontier lines made necessary by the elimination of the Turk from Macedonia and the greater part of Thrace. Bulgaria, a party to both disputes, was worsted in each controversy.

Having brought the war against theb common enemy to an issue successful beyond their most sanguine hopes, the Balkan allies fell out over a division of the spoils. Their original plans contemplated a joint campaign for the liberation of Macedonia, and at the outset their expectations did not go beyond the expulsion of Turkey from this one province. The unexpected successes of the Bulgarians in Thrace, however, extended the prospect of conquest and altered the concert of the allies. While the Bulgarians concentrated most of their troops before Adrianople and Tchataldja, the Servians overran northern Macedonia and occupied territory far beyond the limits laid down in the treaty of alliance. In southern Macedonia the Greeks were determined at all costs to hold their conquest of Salonika. Thus the Servians and Greeks were united in a common interest against their dominant partner. In a bloody struggle in Macedonia in July, 1913, the Bulgarians were beaten at all points and driven within their own frontiers. Here they were attacked on the north by Rumania. In this emergency Russia was appealed to for mediation, which ended with the treaty of Bucharest, August 6, 1913, by which Bulgaria was stripped of her newly acquired western possessions and ceded a part of her former territory to Rumania. During this second war, in which Bulgaria was worsted by her former allies, Turkey reoccupied Adrianople and the adjacent territory.

Bulgaria was unable to endure a third war, and on Sept. 29, 1913, signed a treaty at Constantinople by which the Turko-Bulgarian line was traced up the Maritza River from its mouth to a point near Mandra, and thence, passing west of Demotika, left both that town and Adrianople to Turkey; close to Mustapha Pasha the line bent eastward, and, passing north of Kirkkilisse and south of Malko Tirnova, terminated on the Black Sea at Sveti Stefan. Thus the territory in Europe allotted to Turkey by the Treaty of London was practically doubled in extent by the Treaty of Constantinople.

Such matters as were left to international arbitration or to settlement by the Powers were never satisfactorily adjusted.

Servia nursed a grievance against Austria-Hungary on account of being deprived of a seaport on the Adriatic. Servia took possession of Albania, but was ordered out by Austria-Hungary. The growing hatred between the two countries culminated in the assassination at Sarajevo, June 28, 1914, of Crown Prince Francis Ferdinand of Austria and his wife. Austria charged that the murder was part of a widespread political plot known and perhaps instigated by the Servian Government, and demanded a voice in the investigation and punishment of the crime. Austria's determination was opposed by Russia, and when the latter began mobilizing her forces in August, 1914, after Austrian armies had landed in Belgrade, Germany took up the cause of Austria, and France came to the aid of Russia.

The immediate cause of the European war of 1914-16 may be traced to the political situation in the Balkans, and the general war really grew out of the Balkan wars of 1912 and 1913. The result of those wars was to bring Russia and Austria-Hungary into direct opposition. Both had been striving for years for mastery of the peninsula. The growth of Austria-Hungary east and south to the Ægean Sea, taking in Bosnia, Herzegovina and Servia, was the aim of Austria. Hungaria had been permanently attached. Bosnia and Herzegovina were recent acquisitions. Servia was still necessary and Greece desirable to the culmination of the Austrian ambitions.

Russia, meanwhile, was equally desirous of obtaining a southern port open to the Mediterranean without passing through the Dardanelles by consent of Turkey. Russia, therefore, encouraged the Pan-Slav idea in the Balkans to block Austria's ambitions to southern extension. The collapse of the Turkish empire in Europe, as a result of the Balkan league, said to be a creation of Russian diplomacy, scored a point in favor of Russia. The second Balkan war, in which the allies fought among themselves, was reputed to be a counter diplomatic play of Austria. For a time it ruptured Slavic solidarity.

During the general European war of 1914-16, the attitude of the Balkan States was closely watched by the belligerents. After early attacks on Belgrade by Austrians, in 1914, no military operations were carried on in Servia for nearly a year. Rumania, Bulgaria and Greece maintained strict neutrality until in October, 1915, when a Teuton army began to assemble in southern Hungary, with the evident intention of proceeding into Servia. King Ferdinand of Bulgaria mobilized his armies on the frontier and declared his action to be for the preservation of neutrality. Russia immediately demanded the demobilization of the forces and the dismissal of the German officers who it was said were in command. French and English troops, which had been operating in the Dardanelles, were landed at Salonika in the northern part of Greece coveted by Bulgaria. The Grecian government protested against this violation of neutral territory.

By the middle of December, 1915, the Austro-German and Bulgarian armies had occupied all of Servia, Montenegro and part of Albania. Greece, in maintaining her neutrality, permitted the belligerents to cross her territory in pursuance of their military operations. Roumania joined the entente allies August 27, 1916.

Ballinger, R. A., Controversy Concerning. (See Pinchot-Ballinger Controversy.)

Ballot.—Literally a little ball. The term is applied to all methods of secret voting,

because formerly all such votes were taken by black and white balls placed in the same box, or balls of only one color were deposited in different boxes so arranged that none but the voter could see which box received his ball. The Greeks used marked shells (*ostrakon*), whence the term ostracism. The Romans used tickets for secret voting as early as 139 B. C. The first use of the ballot in the United States was in the selection of a pastor by the Salem Church, July 20, 1629. During the same year it was used in ecclesiastical and municipal elections in the Netherlands, but in England the custom was not established until 1872, though secret voting was actually employed in the parliament of Scotland in cases of ostracism two centuries earlier. In 1634 it began to be used in elections for governor of Massachusetts. The constitutions of Pennsylvania, New Jersey, and North Carolina, which were adopted in 1776, made voting by ballot obligatory. Some of the southern states were slow to adopt the ballot system of voting, the *viva voce* method having prevailed in Kentucky local and state elections up to a late date. In Alabama, Florida, Indiana, Kansas, Kentucky, Louisiana, Nevada, North Carolina, Pennsylvania, Tennessee, Texas, and possibly other states, the constitutions require the legislatures to vote *viva voce*. In 1875 Congress passed a law requiring all Congressmen to be elected by ballot.

Australian Ballot.—Bills embodying the Australian ballot system were introduced in the legislatures of Michigan and New York in 1887, but failed of passage until 1889, when the system was adopted in a slightly modified form. In 1888, the system was adopted at Louisville, Ky., and in Massachusetts. This method requires the names of all the candidates for all the offices to be placed on one ticket. The voter retires to a private booth and indicates his choice by making a mark opposite a party emblem or a candidate's name. This system of voting was first proposed by Francis S. Dutton, a member of the legislature of South Australia, in 1851. Its use in the United States was first advocated in 1882 by Henry George in a pamphlet entitled "English Elections." The Australian ballot has been adopted in some form in all the states except North Carolina, South Carolina, Georgia and Nevada. Delaware adopted it, but later returned to the old system. A modification of the ballot, used in some localities, is the so-called voting machine in which the voter indicates his choice by pressing knobs which record his vote upon slips of paper and record also the number of votes cast for each candidate.

Short Ballots.—The short ballot is an attempt to simplify elections by placing a few officers in nomination at one time and providing that only important officers be elective. Two short ballot amendments were submitted at the special election held in California, Oct. 10, 1911, and both were adopted.

Baltic Provinces.—The three Russian governments of Courland, Livonia and Esthonia, bordering on the Baltic Sea. The area of the three is 35,614 square miles and the population about 1,700,000. Livonia, which is the largest of the three, and Esthonia were ceded to Russia by Sweden in 1721. Courland came into the incorporation of Poland in the sixteenth century, was the scene of bitter strife between the Polish and Russian factions for the ensuing several hundred years, came definitely under Russian influence in 1737, and was formally annexed to Russia in 1795.

The population is mostly Letts and Esths, the former akin to the Lithuanian race and the latter to the Finnish. There are few Russians. The upper classes, comprising less than 7% of the population, are Teutonic, and there are strong commercial and other German affiliations. The provinces enjoyed practical autonomy under Russia until 1880, after which stringent attempts were made to Russianize them. The Baltic provinces were the scene of a violent revolutionary outbreak in 1905.

During 1917, after the Russian military collapse, the Baltic provinces were occupied by the German forces; and negotiations looking toward peace between the Central Powers and the Bolsheviki (q. v.) government of Russia hinged largely upon the question of the evacuation of those provinces from official and unofficial German authority.

Baltic Sea.—A European inland sea washing the shores of Sweden, Germany, and Russia. It terminates in the Gulfs of Bothnia, Finland, and Riga.

Free transit into and from, discussed, 2867, 2944.

Sound dues on commerce to, imposition of, 2774.

Baltimore, The:

Mentioned, 6297.

Sailors of, assaulted at Valparaiso, and action of Government discussed, 5620, 5650, 5662.

Indemnity for, paid by Chile, 5747, 5750.

Baltimore, Md.:

British retreat from, referred to, 533.

Courts of United States in, provision for accommodation of, referred to, 2898.

Duties at port of, referred to, 80.

Insurrection in, on day of election, measures to prevent, 2975.

Memorial from merchants in, transmitted, 384.

Military police to be established in, 3313.

National convention at, for prevention of cruelties to animals, 4458.

National Prison Congress at, referred to, 4162.

Police commissioners of, arrested, referred to, 3234.

Post-office building for, referred to, 2898.

Bank Bill. (Same as Bank Note, q. v.)

Bank Bills less than $20 should be suppressed, 1385.

Bank, International American:

Charter for, recommended by President Benj. Harrison, 5560.

Establishment of, recommended by International American Conference, 5505.

Discussed, 5560.

Bank, Manufactory.—A banking scheme which originated in Massachusetts in 1740. The idea was to secure the issues by mortgage on the real estate of each subscriber to the amount of his subscription. Though opposed by a strong party, it passed the House of Representatives. The bank failed after issuing notes to the extent of £50,000.

Bank Note.—A promise to pay made by a legally authorized bank and circulated as money.

Bank Notes. (See Banks and Banking and Finances discussed.)

Bank of Missouri, measures taken by Government to enforce payment of sums due from directors of, 941.

Bank of Pennsylvania:

Payment of bonds of, held by United States, referred to, 1726.

Suspension of, referred to, 1768.

Bank of the United States.—Feb. 25, 1791, Congress issued a charter authorizing the Bank of the United States to do business for twenty years. Its capital stock was $10,000,000, of which Congress subscribed $2,000,000, partly in coin and partly in government securities. It was made the fiscal agent of the government and the depository for the public moneys. It was also authorized to issue its notes, payable in specie, and was made in every way possible the agent of the United States Treasury, and a strong power in the financial affairs of the country. Its capital was divided into 25,000 shares of $400 each, payable one-fourth in specie and three-fourths in six per cent stock of the United States. It was allowed to hold property of all kinds up to the value of $15,000,000, inclusive of its capital stock, and further to establish branch banks in the various cities. In accordance with this last provision a branch was at once opened in New York City and called an office of discount and deposit. During its entire career the Bank of the United States averaged annual dividends of 8 per cent. (See illustration opposite 1137.)

Bank of United States:

Act to extend charter of, vetoed, 1139.

Referred to, 1225.

Act to incorporate, vetoed, 540.

Agent should be appointed to take charge of books of, 1382.

Attempts to impair credit of Government, 1232, 1250.

Bills of exchange discounted at, for benefit of Senators inquired into, 1346.

No report on subject of, 1347.

Bills of, should not be received for taxes, 1382.

Charter obtained by officers of, from Pennsylvania for new bank, 1471.

Charter of, not to be renewed, 1226, 1250.

Expiration of, discussed, 1025, 1897.

Chartered rights of, should be terminated, 1250.

Claims of, and course pursued by, 1329.

Constitutionality of law creating, questioned, 1025, 1092, 1225.

Dangers from, apprehended, 1091, 1224, 1249.

Deposits in, removal of, 1249.
  President Jackson's paper to Cabinet on, 1224.
    Refuses to transmit, to Senate, 1255.
  Recommended, 1163, 1236.
  Referred to, 1386.
  Views of President Tyler on, 1897.

Directors of, nomination of, and reasons therefor, 1260.

Discussed by President—
  Jackson, 1121, 1382, 1470.
  Polk, 2504.
  Tyler, 1897.

Distresses caused by, needlessly produced, 1328.
  Reference to, 1383.

Flagrant misconduct of, commented on, 1229, 1249, 1330.

Government must be separated from, 1329.

Judicial power, attempts to usurp functions of, 1259.

Money in, not accounted for, 1259.

Notes of, cannot be reissued after expiration of charter, 1471.

Organization of, referred to, 564.

Panic, attempts to bring about, 1250.

Papers and funds in possession of, refusal to deliver, 1258.

Pension money retained by, 1328.

Political power of, fund employed by, to sustain, 1249.

President of, funds at disposal of for electioneering purposes, 1249.

Recharter of, a leading question in election of President, 1225, 1249.

Sound currency, failure of, to establish, 1025.

Stock in—
  Government should be notified regarding, 1382.
  Should be sold, 1330.

Subscriptions to, 96.

Substitute for, must be adopted by Congress, 1228.

Successor of, cannot issue notes of, 1471, 1600.

With limited powers, recommended, 1092.

Bank of United States vs. Halstead.—
An important Supreme Court case on appeal from the circuit court of Kentucky in 1825. Property, including real estate, was offered for sale for debt. The highest bid being less than three-fourths of its appraised value, the property was not sold. The Supreme Court held that it had jurisdiction in a case to which the Bank of the United States was a party, and that a law which forbade the sale of land under execution for less than three-fourths of its appraised value did not apply to writs of execution issued by Federal courts.

Bank of United States vs. Planters' Bank of Georgia.—A suit brought by the Bank of the United States for payment of a promissory note which had been indorsed to it by the Planters' Bank of Georgia. The State of Georgia had stock in this bank. The action was brought against the Planters' Bank and also against the State. The Supreme Court in 1824 decided that if a State became a party to a banking or a commercial enterprise the State could be sued in the course of business, on the principle that when a government becomes a partner in any trading company it divests itself, so far as concerns the transactions of that company, of its sovereign character and takes that of a private citizen. The State, said the court through Chief Justice Marshall, is not a party—that is, an entire party—in the cause. It was also held that the circuit court had jurisdiction in such matters.

Banking, extension of, to foreign countries recommended, 7674.

Banking System. (See Banks and Banking.)

Bankrupt.—A person who, being insolvent, is by legal process relieved from paying indebtedness. (See Bankruptcy.)

Bankruptcy.—The Constitution gives Congress the power to establish uniform bankruptcy laws throughout the United States. Bankruptcy is a state of inability to pay all debts. It is also the process by which an individual may secure a discharge of his indebtedness by surrendering his property and complying with the law. April 4, 1800, a bankruptcy act was passed by Congress and was repealed in December, 1803. In May, 1837, a commercial crisis occurred in the United States, causing failures to the amount of $100,000,000. On account of the heavy losses incurred during the financial panic which ensued, another act was passed Aug. 19, 1841, and repealed in 1843. Another financial panic occurred in 1857, and most of the banks suspended specie payments. A third (the Lowell) act was passed March 2, 1867, and repealed in 1878 (4204). The present law was passed July 1, 1898, and amended June 25, 1910. During the years of our history when no national bankrupt law existed all matters relating to insolvencies have been under the control of State laws.

  *Bankruptcy Law.—*Extracts from the United States Bankruptcy Act of July 1, 1898, as amended by Act of June 25, 1910:

  Who may become bankrupts.—(a) Any person except a municipal railroad, insurance or banking corporation shall be entitled to the benefits of this act as a voluntary bankrupt. The bankruptcy of a corporation shall not release its officers, directors, or stockholders, as such, from any liability under the laws of a state or territory or of the United States. (b) Any natural person, except a wage-earner or a person engaged chiefly in farming or the tillage of the soil, any unincorporated company and any moneyed business, or commercial corporation, except a municipal railroad, insurance or banking corporation, owing debts to the amount of one thousand dollars or over, may be adjudged an involuntary bankrupt upon default or an impartial trial and shall be subject to the provisions and entitled to the benefits of this act.

  Duties of Bankrupts.—(a) The bankrupt shall (1) attend the first meeting of his creditors, if directed by the court or a judge thereof to do so, and the hearing upon his application for a discharge, if filed; (2) comply with all lawful orders of the court; (3) examine the correctness of all proofs of claims filed against his estate; (4) execute and deliver such papers as shall be ordered by the court; (5) execute to his trustee transfers of all his property in foreign countries; (6) immediately inform his trustee of any attempt by his creditors or other persons to evade the provisions of this act, coming to his knowledge; (7) in case of any person having to his knowledge proved a false claim against his estate, disclose that fact immediately to his trustee; (8) prepare, make oath to, and file in court within ten days, unless further time is granted, after the adjudication if an involuntary bankrupt, and with the petition if a voluntary bankrupt, a schedule of his property, showing the amount and kind of property, the location thereof, its money value in detail, and a list of his creditors, showing their residences, if known (if unknown that fact to be stated), the amount due each of them, the consideration thereof, the security held by them, if any, and a claim for such exemptions as he may be entitled to, all in triplicate, one copy of each for the clerk, one for the referee, and one for the trustee; and (9) when present at the first meeting of his creditors, and at such other times as the court shall order, submit to an examination concerning the conducting of his business, the cause of his bankruptcy, his dealings with his creditors and other persons, the amount, kind, and whereabouts of his property, and, in addition, all matters which may affect the administration and settlement of his estate; but no testimony given by him shall be offered in evidence against him in any criminal proceedings.

Provided, however, that he shall not be required to attend a meeting of his creditors or at or for an examination at a place more than one hundred and fifty miles distant from his home or principal place of business or to examine claims except when presented to him, unless ordered by the court, or a judge thereof, for cause shown, and the bankrupt shall be paid his actual expenses from the estate when examined or required to attend at any place other than the city, town, or village of his residence.

Bankruptcy, Laws of:
Modifications regarding involuntary bankruptcy recommended, 4204.
Passage of, recommended, 1907, 2972, 3052, 4730, 4840, 5478, 5561.
Memorial favoring, presented, 1907.
Power to make, vested in Congress, 869, 2972.
Uniform system of, act to establish, referred to, 683.

Banks and Banking:
Banking and currency reform urged, 7908.
Banking system—
Control of, must be public, 7881.
Should be instruments and not masters of enterprise, 7881.
Discussed by President—
Lincoln, 3331, 3350, 3449.
Madison, 550.
Polk, 2257.
Van Buren, 1541, 1707, 1757.
Wilson, 7879, 7908.
Reforms in, recommended, 1380.
Discussed by President—
Buchanan, 2968.
Grant, 4241.

Van Buren, 1541, 1707, 1757.
Wilson, 7879, 7908.
Laws, must not permit concentration of funds for speculative purposes, 7881.
Special commission to make suggestions concerning, recommended, 6654.
Specie payments discussed. (See Specie Payments.)

Banks.—A bank is an institution for receiving and lending money. The banking institutes of the United States may be classed as National and State banks, private banks or bankers, savings banks, and loan and trust companies. In 1781 the Congress of the Confederation chartered the Bank of North America with a capital of $400,000, with a view to providing through its notes a circulating medium for the country. Doubts as to the power of Congress caused the bank to be rechartered by Pennsylvania in 1782. By 1791 two more banks had been established, one in New York, the other in Boston. In that year Congress established the Bank of the United States. The charter authorized an existence of 20 years and a capital of $10,000,000, one-fifth to be supplied by the United States. In 1811 Congress refused to renew the charter. During the trying times of the War of 1812 only State banks existed, and these largely increased in number. In 1816 the second United States Bank was chartered to run 20 years with a capital of $35,000,000, of which the Federal Government subscribed one-fifth. The bank was to have custody of the public funds, and 5 of its 25 directors were to be appointed by the United States. Congress passed an act renewing the charter in 1832, but President Jackson vetoed it (1139). After a Presidential election in which his fight with the bank was made an issue President Jackson ordered the public funds to be removed from the Bank of the United States and placed in State banks (1224). In 1836 the bank's charter expired. In 1841 President Tyler vetoed two bills to revive it (1916, 1921). In 1846 the Independent Treasury system was established providing that all public funds of the United States should be received and paid out without the intervention of the bank. Between 1836 and 1863 only State banks existed. Feb. 25, 1863, the National bank act was passed. This act proving defective, it was superseded by the act of June 3, 1864, which forms the basis of the present system.

Banks.—See Encyclopedic Index articles and page references under headings:

Bank, Manufactory.	Clearing House.
Bank Notes.	Currency Law.
Bank of Missouri.	Deposits, Public, Removal of.
Bank of Pennsylvania.	
Bank of United States.	Fiscal Bank of United States.
Bank of United States vs. Halstead.	Free Banking System.
Bank of United States vs. Planters' Bank of Georgia.	Funding. National Bank Circulation.
Banks, National.	National Bank Examiners.
Banks, Pet.	National Banks.
Banks, Postal Sav'gs.	Postal Savings Banks.
Banks, Savings.	Safety Fund.
Banks, State.	Specie Payments.
Briscoe vs. Bank of Commonwealth of Kentucky.	United States Notes. United States Bank of Pennsylvania.

Banks, National. — Dissatisfaction and losses in connection with the State banking system in vogue in the first half of the nineteenth century led to the passage of laws by the Federal Government for the protection of holders of the circulating medium. The first National bank act of the new and comprehensive series was suggested to Congress by Secretary Chase in 1861 and passed in 1863. It was amended by a law passed June 3, 1864. These acts form the basis of the present law. It is patterned after the New York State banking law, which in 1849 required circulating notes of all banks of that state to be secured by a deposit of stocks and bonds, one-half in issues of that state. The circulating notes were redeemable at agencies within the state. This latter feature of the New York law was adapted from the Suffolk system in vogue in New England.

Under the National banking law, as amended by the act of March 14, 1900, any five persons with a combined capital of $25,000 may open a bank and receive circulating notes to the amount of the par value of their capital invested in United States bonds, but not to exceed the par value of the bonds. In cities of more than 3,000 and less than 6,000 inhabitants the capital required is $50,000, while a capital of $100,000 is required in cities having a population of over 6,000, and double this amount where the population exceeds 50,000. The ratio of circulating medium to capital remains the same in all places. The law also established the National Bank Bureau in the Treasury Department and created the office of Comptroller of the Currency. This act added some $350,000,000 to the currency of the country.

The annual report of the Comptroller of the Currency for the year 1913 showed 7,488 National banks, with a capital of $1,056,919,792, a total surplus of $725,272,182, reporting net earnings of $160,980,084, paying in dividends $119,906,051, a ratio of dividends to capital of 11.40 per cent. The circulation outstanding Sept. 1, 1913, was $724,500,000; individual deposits, $5,761,350,000; principal resources, loans and discounts, $6,186,800,000; United States bonds on deposit to secure circulation, $735,800,000; United States bonds on hand and with the Treasurer to secure public deposits, $103,200,000; specie, $728,300,000; legal tender notes, $170,900,000; aggregate resources, $10,876,800,000. Sept. 1, 1914, the number of banks was 7,551, and the authorized capital was $1,073,524,175. The outstanding circulation was $877,540,281, of which $126,241,760 was secured by other than United States bonds. (See also Currency.)

Banks, National:

Circulation of. (See National Banks.)

Discussed by President—

Arthur, 4720, 4766, 4832.

Cleveland, 4926, 5876, 5965, 5986, 6079, 6156.

Grant, 4199.

Johnson, 3563, 3770.

Lincoln, 3331, 3350, 3384, 3449.

McKinley, 6254, 6358.

Roosevelt, 6654.

Van Buren, 1541, 1707, 1757, 1828.

Wilson, 7980.

Organization of, discussed, 4720, 4926, 5876, 5965, 6156.

Reports of examiners of, 4655.

Should engage attention of Congress, 551, 1025.

Tax on capital and deposits of, repeal of, recommended, 4636, 4766.

Treasury balance deposited in, 7980.

Banks, Pet.—When President Jackson ordered the public funds withdrawn from the United States Bank in 1833, it became necessary for the Administration to find some other place of deposit for the Federal moneys. Certain State banks were chosen, and the allegation was made that the selection was determined not so much on the ground of fitness as on that of party fidelity, a principle also much in vogue in the granting of bank charters before the system of free banking came into use. The banks selected by Jackson as public depositors were in derision called "pet banks."

Banks, Postal Savings. (See also Postal Savings Banks.)

Recommended by President—

Arthur, 4639.

Grant, 4152, 4204.

Hayes, 4574.

Roosevelt, 7102, 7226.

Taft, 7373.

Banks, Savings.—The first savings bank in the United States was the Boston Provident Savings Institution, incorporated Dec. 13, 1816. The Philadelphia Savings Fund Society began business the same year, but was not incorporated until 1819. In 1818 banks for savings were incorporated in Baltimore, Md., and Salem, Mass., and in 1819 in New York, Hartford, Conn., and Newport and Providence, R. I. There were in 1905 some 1,237 savings banks in the United States in which 7,696,229 persons had deposited $3,261,263,119. These figures are the highest reached in the history of this country both with regard to the number and the amount of depositors and the amount of deposits. Statistics of the savings banks of the world, obtained by the Department of Commerce and Labor, show that the United States, with about 9¼ per cent of the total population considered, has more than 29 per cent of the savings banks deposits. These institutions are for the encouragement of the practice of saving money among people of slender means and for the secure investment of savings, the profits thereof being paid as interest to the depositors.

In 1913 there were 1,978 savings banks in the United States, having 10,766,936 depositors and deposits of $4,727,403,950.79, an average of $439.07 to each depositor. New York has the largest number of depositors and the largest total of deposits, 3,114,240 persons having $1,700,063,766.36 to their credit, an average of $545.90 to each person. The 1,710 depositors in the savings banks of Montana have an average of $781.39 to their credit, nearly double the average for the entire country.

Banks, State.—A State bank is an institution chartered by a State legislature for banking purposes. It performs similar functions of National banks. After the expiration of the charter of the Bank of the United States in 1836, and the refusal of Congress to recharter it, State banks sprang up in large numbers throughout the Union. Each state passed its own law for their government or control. In many states these laws were not carefully drawn and the holders of their circulating notes not sufficiently protected against loss from suspensions and failures. Between 1836 and 1863 there were no United States banks or National banks, and only State banks existed. Being allowed to issue notes to circulate as currency, they availed themselves of the privilege, and in many instances the privilege was much abused. By act of Congress passed March 3, 1865, all circulating notes of banks other than National banks were taxed 10 per cent. The result of this law was to speedily cause the retirement of all such notes. There are in all some 14,000 State banks at present in operation.

Banks, State:
Deposits in should be regulated by law, 1331, 1385.
Discussed by President—
Buchanan, 2968.
Cleveland, 5986.
Jackson, 1469.
Tyler, 1899.
Van Buren, 1541, 1548, 1711, 1757.
Measures should be adopted to correct unlimited creation of, 1899.
Number of, 6157.
Paper to Cabinet concerning, 1224.
President Jackson refuses to transmit to Senate, 1255.
Practicability of, commented on, 1236, 1250, 1330, 1384.
Public deposits should be placed in, 1236.
Order regarding, 1249.
Reference to, 551.

Banner.—A decorated cloth, as the flag or insignia of a country, or of an army, or of any organized group.

Bannock Indians. (See Indian Tribes.)

Baptist Church in Mississippi Territory, act for relief of, vetoed, 475.

Bar Harbor, Me., acts for erection of public buildings at, vetoed, 5257, 5571.

Barbados Island (West Indies), postal convention with, 5277.

Barbara Frietchie. (See illustration opposite 3486 and description.

Barbarian.—A savage; originally used to describe a person of foreign language or customs.

Barbary States.—The region on the north coast of Africa bordering on the Mediterranean Sea. It is capable of high cultivation. In early times the soil was made to yield richly. Barbary was known in ancient times as Mauritania, Numidia, Africa Propria, and Cyrenaica. It now comprises the countries of Barca, Tripoli, Fezzan, Tunis, Algeria and Morocco. Besides Europeans, seven distinct races inhabit the Barbary States—Berbers, Moors, Bedouins, Jews, Turks, Kuluglis, and Negroes. The population is about 11,000,000 Mohammedans and a floating population of Jews and Christians not enumerated. The language of commerce is Arabic, except in Tunis and Tripoli, where the Turkish language and government dominate.
During the latter part of the Eighteenth Century most of the European States were compelled to pay tribute to the pirates of the Barbary States. Tribute was also levied upon the United States as the price

of safety in the Mediterranean, and for a time was paid, but in the early part of the nineteenth century, after subjugating Tripoli and Algiers, the United States exacted terms of peace from the pirates. The action of America was followed by Germany, France, and other European powers, and the pirates were completely subjugated. (See also Africa, Algerian War, Tripolitan War, and the several States of northern Africa and illustration opposite 382.)

Barbary States (see also the several States; Algerine War; Tripolitan War.)
Consuls of United States in, referred to, 169.
Disbursements in intercourse with, 464.
Friendly disposition of, toward United States, 395, 460, 469, 649, 677.
Friendly intercourse with, 415, 503, 649.
Reference to, 321, 324, 325.
Relations with which, through unreasonable demands of Tripoli, led to a declaration of war against the United States, 314.

Barbecue.—A picnic, usually of political character, where animals are roasted whole for the repast.

Barcelona, Spain, International exposition of Labor at, discussed, 5177, 5399.

Baring Brothers & Co., funds of United States on deposit with, 3828.

Barnburner and Hunker.—In 1845 the Democratic party in New York State, owing to internal squabbling, became divided into two pronounced factions. These were the administration Democrats, calling themselves Conservatives, and the sore-heads of those days, stigmatized as Radicals, because, among other things, they were affected with anti-slavery, or "free soil" (*which see*) sentiments; whereas, the administration party was strongly pro-slavery. In the Democratic State Convention held at Syracuse early in 1847 the latter faction, by political manipulation, secured the organization of that body, and decided nearly all the contested seats in their own favor, and made the State ticket and the State committee to suit themselves; in other words, "carried off the hunk," and fairly won the name of "Hunkers." The other faction refused to support the ticket, and, as a consequence, the Whigs carried the State by over 30,000 majority in the gubernatorial election. One of the Hunker orators likened the other faction to the Dutch farmer who burned his barn to rid himself of rats, and thenceforward the name of Barnburners was fastened on them, and the two nicknames, Barnburner and Hunker, were bandied back and forth until after the former joined with the Liberty party (*which see*), in 1852, to support Mr. Van Buren as the Free-Soil candidate for the Presidency. Hunk is evidently a corruption of the Dutch *honk*, or *home*, and was used to signify that the administration faction had reached their goal, or home.

Barracks.—Lodging houses or tents for soldiers.

Barrataria, Island of, pardon granted lawless inhabitants of, who aided in defense of New Orleans, 543.

Bataan, Province of, Ph. I., mentioned, 6701.

Baton Rouge (La.), Battle of.—Early in May, 1862, after the fall of New Orleans, Admiral Farragut passed up the river and raised the American flag over the public buildings in Baton Rouge, the capital of Louisiana. Gen. Thomas Williams was placed in command of the place with a small garrison. Aug. 5, 1862, he was attacked by Gen. Breckenridge, who was to have been assisted by the ironclad gunboat *Arkansas*. The *Arkansas* exploded her boilers and failed to reach the scene of action. The Confederates were repulsed. The Union loss was 200, including Gen. Williams, who was killed.

Battalion.—An organized part of an army; as a regiment, or two or more companies of a regiment.

Battery.—A number of cannon with wagons and other equipment, including the artillerymen; also the armament of a warship; also a protection for gunners defending a fort.

Battleship.—An armored ship equipped for war.

Battleships, construction of four urged, 7147.

Battle State.—Alternative nickname for Nevada.

Batture Cases.—Before the cession of Louisiana to the United States, a man named Gravier had purchased a plantation on the Mississippi River near New Orleans. Part of it afterwards became the village of St. Mary. An alluvial deposit or river beach formed in front of the village and was used as a landing place for the citizens of St. Mary. Under the law it was a part of the Gravier estate, which was purchased by Edward Livingston, of New York, who began improving it for his own use. The people protested on the ground of an old French law giving alluvions to the government. President Jefferson dispossessed Livingston of the Batture, and the latter immediately began suit against Jefferson and the United States marshal. The Supreme Court refused to entertain the suit against the President, but decided to restore the Batture to Livingston.

Bavaria.—A kingdom of southern Germany, and one of the States of the German Empire. It consists of two unequal and disconnected parts, the larger eastern and the smaller western. The country produces wheat, rye, oats, and other cereals, tobacco, potatoes, hops, ax, wine, etc. The most important manufactures are textiles, beer, machinery, iron-ware and porcelain.

Government.—Its government is a constitutional hereditary monarchy, with a king, an upper house, and a chamber of 159 deputies. The reigning king is Louis III. It made a treaty with the North German Confederation in 1870 and entered the German Empire in 1871. Area, 29,286 sq. miles; population in 1900 was 6,524,372.

The army consists of three corps of the Imperial army, but is numbered separately and administered independently, and on a peace footing has about 60,000 men. About 70½ per cent of the population are Roman Catholics and some 28 per cent Protestants.

Bavaria (see also Munich):
Convention with, 2218, 2760.

Fugitive criminals, convention with, for surrender of, 2760.
Immigration treaty with, 3834.
Naturalization treaty with, 3888.

Bavaria, Treaties with.—These include the treaty of 1845, treaty of 1853, and the treaty of 1868. They were not affected by the formation of the German Empire in 1871. The treaty of 1845 abolished the *droit d'aubaine* and taxes on emigration. In France the *droit d'aubaine* was the right of the king to the goods of an unnaturalized foreigner (*aubain*) dying within his kingdom. The king stood in place of the heirs. In France this right was abolished in 1819. This treaty declared that the *droit d'aubaine, droit de retraite,* and *droit de tractioner* tax or taxes on emigration be abolished. When any person holding real property dies, the person to whom it would descend, were he not disqualified by alienage under the laws of the land, shall be allowed two or more years, if necessary, in which to dispose of it, and may withdraw the proceeds from the country without paying detraction duties. Power of transfer by will, donation, or otherwise, is conferred upon alien residents equal to those enjoyed by citizens or subjects. When no heirs exist the property of the deceased is to receive the same care as that of a native or citizen. Disputes regarding possession are to be decided according to the laws, and by the courts in which the property is situated. For extradition terms of the treaty of 1854, see Extradition Treaties. The treaty of 1868 was a naturalization treaty. (See Germany.)

Bayard vs. Singleton.—This is one of the earliest instances of a court passing upon the constitutionality of an act of the legislature. Suit was brought before the court of appeals of North Carolina in 1787 for the recovery of certain property that had been confiscated and sold to the defendant under an act of the legislature passed during the Revolution which authorized the confiscation of the property of aliens. Counsel for defendant moved the dismissal of the case in accordance with an act of the legislature passed in 1785, which "required the courts, in all cases where the defendant makes affidavit that he holds the disputed property under a sale from a commissioner of forfeited estates, to dismiss the case on motion." Judge Ashe refused to dismiss the case, declaring the act of the legislature "unconstitutional and void." Judgment was, however, found for the defendant on the ground that aliens cannot hold land, and if they purchase it the land is forfeited to the sovereign.

Bayonet.—A detachable sharp instrument for stabbing, for use on the muzzle of a gun.

Bayonne Decree.—April 17, 1808, Napoleon decreed that all American vessels which should enter the ports of France, Italy, and the Hanse Towns should be seized, "because no vessels of the United States can now navigate the seas without violating the law of said States." In his attempts to subdue England, Napoleon sought to destroy her commerce with all neutral powers, including the United States.

Bayou State.—A nickname for Mississippi (q. v.). (See also States.)

Beacon.—A warning light or other conspicuous object.

Bear, The, sent to relief of whaling fleet, 6350.

Bear Flag War.—An insurrection against the Mexican Government in June, 1846, supposed to have been instigated by John C. Frémont, then a captain of United States troops in California. A body of American settlers seized some Mexican horses and then captured the town of Sonoma. They raised a flag, having on it the figure of a bear. In July, the Mexican War having begun, the Stars and Stripes were raised at Monterey, and the Bear Flag War became a factor in the American conquest of California. A battalion called the Bear Flag battalion was active in expelling the Mexicans.

Bear State.—A nickname for Arkansas (q. v.). (See also States.)

Beaufort, N. C., blockade of, removed by proclamation, 3290.

Beaver Dam (Canada), Battle of.—After the retreat of the American army from the Niagara River they rendezvoused near the western end of Lake Ontario. Gen. Dearborn sent Lieut.-Col. Charles G. Boerstler with 540 men to capture Beaver Dam. A British lieutenant, on June 24, 1813, with forty or fifty men, but claiming to be the advance guard of 1,500 troops and 700 Indians, demanded of him to surrender. Boerstler surrendered 542 men, one 12-pounder and one 6-pounder cannon, and a stand of colors.

Beaver State.—Alternative nickname for Oregon. (See Web-Foot Country.)

Bedloes Island. (See Liberty Enlightening the World.)

Beef Products. (See Animals and Animal Products; also Meat Packing and Slaughtering.)

Beer. (See Liquors—Malt, Vinous and Distilled.)

Beet Sugar.—Although the manufacture of sugar from cane antedates its production from beets by several centuries, the latter were put to practical use fourteen centuries before refined sugar was produced from the "sweetsticks" of the East. In the first century, Pliny the Elder wrote: "Next to grain and beans there is no more serviceable plant than the white beet, the root of which is used for human and animal food, the young sprouts as a vegetable, and the leaves as an accessory fodder. * * * Beets should not be grown continuously on the same soil, but a rotation should be observed."

Europe follows this **advice** religiously, though it has not been accepted generally by American farmers, which accounts for their inferior yields of both beets and cereal crops.

The first to suspect the presence of sugar in the beet was the famous French agronomist, Olivier de Serres, in 1600, but this discovery led to no immediate results. A century and a half later, in 1747, the distinguished German chemist, Andreas Marggraf, Professor of Physics in the Academy of Science of Berlin, succeeded in producing a few crystals of sugar from beet roots. The French claim that de Serres' writings conveyed the idea to Marggraf, while the Germans assert that the idea was original with their countryman.

Marggraf's pupil and successor, Franz Carl Achard, devoted his scientific career to applying Marggraf's discovery to industrial purposes. Through the liberal assistance of Frederic the Great, Achard carried on experiments near Berlin for a number of years, but on the death of his Sovereign he was compelled to abandon the work until Friederich Wilhelm III interested himself in it and made him a grant of 9,000 thalers ($25,000). In 1799, Achard was able to present his Sovereign with beet sugar loaves which in every respect were comparable to the best cane sugar. The King then loaned him 50,000 thalers, and in 1802, Achard erected at Cunern, Lower Silesia, the first beet sugar factory in the world. It was a primitive affair, with a capacity of but a few hundred pounds of beets per day, the beets being rasped and the juice pressed out, as with the cane. The beets contained but 3 to 4 per cent of sugar, and it cost sixteen cents per pound to produce.

Achard's enterprise attracted the attention of Napoleon Bonaparte, and he sent French scientists to Silesia to investigate the new industry. Upon their return two factories were established near Paris. These were unsuccessful, but the French made the discovery then which was destined to revolutionize methods of tillage, establish modern scientific agriculture, and, by doubling the acreage yield of cereals, add more to the wealth of the world and its ability to maintain population than has any other discovery before or since. At that time the cereal crop yields of the continent were but twelve bushels per acre, and starvation threatened the rapidly increasing population. In alternating beets with cereal crops the French scientists discovered that he yield of cereals was increased nearly twofold. When Napoleon became convinced of this fact he ordered during 1811 and 1812 thousands of acres to be planted in beets, and technical schools and factories to be built. As a result the industry was firmly established in France and the yield of cereal crops increased.

German and French scientists then began developing the sugar content of the beet plant, and most wonderful results have been obtained. By careful selection of seed and scientific tillage the sugar in the beet has been increased from 7 per cent to 20 per cent. The beet of today weighs from two to three pounds, and from one-sixth to one-fifth of its entire weight is pure sugar. The factory beet contains more pure sugar than the total weight of the original beet, and the tonnage secured from a single acre is more than originally could be secured from a good sized farm.

In answer to the criticisms that beet sugar has less sweetening power than cane sugar the assertion is made that even a chemist, surrounded with all his scientific laboratory equipment, can not distinguish one from the other. Although derived from different species of plants, the refined product from the juice of the cane and beet is the same in composition, in sweetening power, in dietetic effect, in chemical reaction, in all other respects. Furthermore, if maple sugar were reboiled and passed through the process of refining, it would lose its aroma and flavor, which are wholly in the impurities, and the white crystals would be identical with those derived from sugar cane and sugar beets.

Pure sugar, whether derived from beet or cane, is as identical as is pure gold, whether mined in the Rocky Mountains or in the Transvaal.

The earliest attempt to produce sugar

from beets in the United States was made in Philadelphia in 1830 by Vaughan and Ronaldson, but their efforts were unsuccessful. Eight years later David Lee Child erected a small factory at Northampton, Mass., and succeeded in producing a small quantity of sugar, for which he was awarded a silver medal by the Massachusetts Charitable Mechanic Association in 1839. Due to lack of technical knowledge in both field and factory, the Northampton plant operated but one season.

In 1852 Bishop Tyler, of the Mormon Church, purchased in France the machinery for a factory, shipped it to Fort Leavenworth, Kans., by water and by ox teams hauled it from there to Salt Lake City. This effort also was a failure.

During the next few years, attempts were made to produce beet sugar in the United States as follows: Illinois, 1863-71; Wisconsin, 1868-71; New Jersey, 1870-76; Maine, 1876; but all these efforts ended in failure, absorbed some two and a quarter million dollars, and ruined most of the men who attempted to establish the industry in America.

The first American to wrest success from failure was E. H. Dyer, who erected a small plant at Alvarado, Cal., in 1879. Although a failure for many years, much of which time the plant was idle, it finally became a success. Several times it has been rebuilt and re-equipped with machinery and while running today, it never will pay interest on more than a mere fraction of the amount actually invested in it.

In 1883 our federal treasury needed money and as our national legislators had become enthusiastic about the possibilities of producing our sugar supply at home, Congress enacted a tariff bill which carried a duty of 3½ cents a pound on refined sugar and 2¼ cents on raw. But no one knew what soil or climate were required for producing high grade beets nor how to grow them nor how to operate a factory, and the string of dismal failures which had reached from ocean to ocean made capitalists cautious. While the duty levied was more than generous, the acquirement and dissemination of field and factory technical knowledge was lost sight of and capital held aloof. When in 1890, our federal treasury was overflowing and sugar was placed on the free list, the bounty of two cents per pound which was placed on domestic production, failed to attract capital, as did the Wilson 40 per cent ad valorem bill of 1894.

When the Dingley bill of 1897 was passed and President McKinley made James Wilson Secretary of Agriculture, a new order of affairs was established. While the duty fixed on sugar imports was but 52 per cent of what it had been under the bill of 1883 and but six factories were in existence, the Department of Agriculture set to work to determine where favorable natural conditions existed, to learn and to teach the farmers cultural methods and to exploit the industry generally. It was deemed wise that a great industry, destined to supply a large portion of the $400,000,000 worth of sugar which we annually consume, should not be confined to a few States, where localized unpropitious weather conditions might seriously interfere with our supply of a staple food product. On the contrary, it was considered desirable that the factories should be scattered as much as possible, even though one State or one group of States could produce for a fraction less than could other States. To this end, the department issued a wall map, on which was traced the theoretical beet sugar area of

the United States and from time to time as it was demonstrated that favorable conditions existed in other territory, that fact was made known. The last statement of the department concerning this subject shows that we have in the United States 274,000,000 acres, the soil and climate of which are adapted to sugar beet culture, and if but a fraction of one per cent of this area were planted to sugar beets, it would furnish all the sugar we consume.

Roughly speaking, this territory extends from ocean to ocean and from the Canadian boundary to and including portions of Virginia, West Virginia, Ohio, Indiana, Illinois, Missouri, Oklahoma, Texas and to the Mexican boundary. Sugar beets can be grown on a variety of soils, clay loams and sandy loams being preferred. Dr. Wiley and the Bureau of Chemistry and Dr. Galloway and the Bureau of Plant Industry were set to work; a field agent was placed on the road to investigate conditions throughout the country and experiments were conducted in various States. As a result of the information and the inviting conditions set forth in the numerous bulletins and reports of the department, in 14 years, $84,000,000 had been coaxed into the industry, the number of factories increased from six in two States to 76 in 16 States, and the annual output has grown from 40,000 to 700,000 tons or one-fifth of the total sugar consumption of the United States, enough to supply all the people living west of the Mississippi River. As a result of the Newlands bill, great areas of desert land have been reclaimed where sugar beets can be raised more profitably than can any other crop, and upon the expansion of this industry largely depends the success of the great irrigating works which the Government has constructed at an expense of $80,000,000.

When on June 17, 1902, President Roosevelt laid down his pen after signing the Reclamation Act, his Secretary of Agriculture remarked to him: "Mr. President, today you have solved the sugar problem of the United States. Not only will that legislation reclaim an empire, but the most natural enterprise to be established at the foot of those huge dams will be beet sugar factories."

Secretary Wilson knew that the necessary long haul freight charges ate up the profits of the far western farmers on low priced cereal products when shipped to the east. But with alfalfa and beet pulp with which to fatten stock, they obtain two crops—sugar and live stock—on which the freight charges are small in proportion to the value of the product. Sugar beets reach their greatest perfection when grown under irrigation, and our farmers, especially in the irrigated west, have found the crop to be one of the most profitable if also the most difficult which they can grow. Due to rotating them with sugar beets one year in four, thousands of farms are producing greater yields of all other crops than ever before.

This industry now distributes $63,000,000 annually to American farmers, to laborers in the sugar factories and to labor in coal mines and other American industries which furnish it with supplies, all of which money would be sent to foreign countries in payment for imported sugar, but for this domestic industry.

Since this industry was established, it has distributed $400,000,000 to American toilers, and when fully developed it will distribute $200,000,000 annually to American industry.

During the 15 years in which the domestic beet sugar industry has grown from

40,000 to 700,000 tons, the average wholesale price of sugar has declined from $4.97 per 100 to $3.17 per 100, the present wholesale price, or 17 per cent despite the fact that during the same period the price of practically all other food commodities has increased from 33½ to 100 per cent. When fully developed, this industry will still further reduce not only the price of sugar, but of all other food products, through increasing the yield per acre.

The German increase in yield per acre of wheat, rye, barley and oats has been 80 per cent during the past thirty years, as compared with an increase of but 6.6 per cent in the United States. German economists are a unit in attributing Germany's increase in yield to the introduction of sugar beet culture which taught their farmers to grow a root crop one year in four in rotation with cereals and thus of the $986,000,000 worth of these crops which Germany annually produces, $438,-000,000 is due to the introduction of sugar beet culture. Even greater results than those obtained in Germany have been secured wherever sugar beet culture has been introduced in this country, and should the further expansion of the industry result in duplicating Germany's experience throughout the United States, our yield of these four crops, at present farm prices, would be worth $2,000,000,000 instead of $1,124,000,000, as at present.

In 1912 there were 555,300 acres of beets harvested, yielding a little less than 9½ tons per acre, and 5,224,377 tons of beets were worked into 692,556 tons of sugar. The buildings and machinery were valued at $84,000,000, and 120,000 persons were engaged in cultivation; 57,021 farmers, of whom 93 per cent were independent, contracted to raise beets. These were paid $30,000,000 for their product. More than $10,000,000 was paid in wages. Of the 65 factories reported in 1914, 15 were located in Michigan, 13 in Colorado, 12 in California, 7 in Utah, 4 in Idaho, 3 in Wisconsin, 2 in Nebraska, 3 in Ohio, and 1 each in Kansas, Montana, Illinois, Indiana, Iowa, and Minnesota.

Belantse-Etva Indians. (See Minnetaree Indians.)

Belden, S. A., & Co., claim of, against Mexico, 2687.
  Distribution of award in case of, referred to, 4988.

Beleaguer.—To blockade or to surround by siege.

Belgian Atrocities, Bryce Report on. (See Bryce Report on Belgian Atrocities.)

Belgian Relief.—When the German armies swept through Belgium and northern France in August, 1914, they created a situation for the non-combatant population of those districts which soon became desperate in the extreme. Belgium was a country with a density of population twenty times as great as that of the United States, with a population largely industrial, and producing itself less than 40 per cent of the food it consumed. The able-bodied men of the country had flocked to the armies opposing the Teutonic forces, and Belgium was helpless. Germany would not divert food from its own inhabitants to feed the inhabitants of the land which it had invaded; and it seemed as though 7,000,000 persons would slowly starve. For the estimated population of 7,800,000 in Belgium in 1914, only 800,000 were refugees or were out of the

occupied territory; and in addition there were 2,250,000 residents left in that portion of northern France occupied by the Germans, whose plight was similar to that of the Belgians, altogether representing more than 9,000,000 persons in a district of 19,-455 miles.

It was America who came to the rescue. In October, 1914, Brand Whitlock, the Minister from the United States to Belgium, brought the situaton before Ambassador Page in London, and as a result the Commission for the Relief of Belgium was founded. Ambassador Page placed at the head of the Commission Herbert C. Hoover (q. v. in Biographical Index), an American mining engineer who had rendered efficient service in behalf of Americans stranded in London by the outbreak of the great European struggle; and under his direction Belgium and northern France were rescued.

From the beginning of the War to April, 1917, when the entrance of the United States compelled the withdrawal of the American relief administrators, the Commission expended in the neighborhood of $250,000,000. Even the official loans made by the governments of England and France to the Belgian Government were administered by the Commission. For Belgium $148,000,000 was loaned by the English Government, $16,000,000 came in private subscriptions from the British Empire, $11,-000,000 was contributed in money and in merchandise by the United States, and $6,000,000 came from other sources. For northern France, French banks and institutions contributed $90,000,000. The United States Government in May, 1917, lent the sum of $75,000,000 to the Belgian Government for the relief of that country. This sum was payable in monthly instalments of $12,500,000, with the understanding that the loan would be renewed in case of necessity.

New York was the chief purchasing and shipping branch for the Commission, particularly as to pork and wheat shipments. Although probably three-fourths of the inhabitants of the destitute district were able to pay to some extent for the assistance they received, yet all their food, clothing, and other necessities had to be shipped into Belgium and France through the channels of the Commission. By November 1, 1916, there had arrived in Rotterdam for the Commission 2,164,218 tons of supplies. There were about 50 trained American administrators volunteering their services in Belgium and France for the Commission, and they were assisted by thousands of Belgians. The Commission appealed to the whole world for support, and was assisted by more than 4,000 committees all over the globe engaged in the solicitation of charity and the mobilization of food supplies. The relief work itself was carried on by committees in each of the 4,000 communes which were in the destitute district. With the withdrawal of the officials of the Commission in April, 1917, the administration of the relief went into the hands of the Dutch and Spanish. (See Belgium; France; European War.)

Belgium.—Belgium has a frontier of 831 miles, and is bounded on the north and northeast by the Netherlands (268 miles), on the south by France (381 miles), on the east by Rhenish Prussia (60 miles) and the Grand Duchy of Luxemburg (80 miles), with a low unbroken seaboard (North Sea) of 42 miles. The "polders" near the coast, which are protected by dikes against floods, cover an area of 193 square miles.

Physical Features.—The Meuse (Maas) and its tributary the Sambre divide the country into two distinct regions, that of the north and west being generally a low fertile plain, while the forest-covered table-land of the Ardennes in the south and east has for the most part a poor soil. The highest hill (Baraque Michel) rises to a height of 2,230 feet, but the mean elevation of the country does not exceed 536 feet. The principal rivers are the Meuse (Maas) and its tributary the Sambre, which flow from France to the Netherlands, and are navigable streams throughout their course in Belgium. The Ourthe is also a tributary from the frontier of Luxemburg, and is partly navigable. The river of the western plains is the Schelde (Escaut). These waterways have an auxiliary network of canals for the purposes of transport. The principal harbor and commercial entrepôt is Antwerp, a strongly fortified city on the Schelde. Other harbors on the western coast are Ostend, Nieuport, Blankenberg and Zeebrugge.

AREA AND POPULATION

Provinces	Area in English Sq. Miles	Population Census of 1910
Antwerp	1,093	968,677
Brabant	1,267	1,469,677
Flanders, East	1,158	1,120,335
Flanders, West	1,248	874,135
Hainaut	1,437	1,232,867
Liège	1,117	888,341
Limburg	931	275,691
Luxemburg	1,705	231,215
Namur	1,414	362,846
Total	11,370	7,423,784

History and Government.—Belgium, the country of the ancient Belgae, and known as Flanders and Brabant in the "Low Countries," was joined to the Kingdom of the Netherlands in 1815, an arrangement which was upset by the Revolution of 1830. On Oct. 14, 1830, a National Congress proclaimed its independence, and on June 4, 1831, Prince Leopold of Saxe-Coburg was chosen Hereditary King. Reigning Sovereign Albert Leopold Clement Marie Meinrad, King of the Belgians, Duke of Saxony, Prince of Saxe-Coburg and Gotha, born at Brussels, April 8, 1875, son of Prince Philippe, Count of Flanders, succeeded his uncle, King Leopold II., Dec. 23, 1909.

After Germany had declared war against Russia in August, 1914, German armies started for the French border through Belgian territory. Belgian permission being refused Germany declared war and the King of England was appealed to to support the neutrality of Belgium. (See European War of 1914-17 and Belgian Relief.)

The Senate, elected for eight years, consists of 120 members, of whom twenty-seven are elected by the Provincial Councils and ninety-three by the people. The Chamber of Representatives consists of 186 members (one for each 40,000 of the inhabitants), elected by the people. The electoral law of 1894 introduced universal male suffrage at the age of twenty-five, with plural voting up to three votes by property and educational qualification. Failure to vote is punishable by law. The Legislature meets annually in November.

There is a justice of the peace in each of the Cantons (227), twenty-six District Courts, a Criminal Assize Court in each Province and three Courts of Appeal at Brussels, Ghent, and Liège. There is a Court of Cassation at Brussels.

In each of the nine Provinces, and in each of the 2,632 Communes, there is an elected Council. These Provincial and Communal Councils are elected for eight

years (one-half retiring every four years), and meet annually.

The Army is recruited by yearly calls and voluntary enlistments. The yearly calls include, according to the number fixed by the contingent bill, all the young men of the levy fit for military service who are not exempted. The Peace Establishment was, in 1913, 3,499 officers and 40,073 men, including a Gendarmerie of 74 officers and 8,629 men. There are Military Governors of the fortresses of Antwerp, Liège, and Namur. The neutrality of Belgium is guaranteed by Austria, Russia, Prussia, and the United Kingdom by the Treaty of London (Nov. 15, 1831).

Education.—Primary education is universal although not legally compulsory, and it is free to the necessitous, schools being maintained by communal taxation with provincial and state grants; in addition, many schools are under ecclesiastical control—Roman Catholic predominating. Special schools, communal and private, abound, music and fine art schools are a special feature, the Conservatoires of Brussels and Liège and the Académies of Brussels and Antwerp being justly famous; there are thirty-five Royal Atheneums. There are State Universities at Ghent and Liège, and free Universities at Brussels and Louvain.

Production and Industry.—Of the 7,277,- 000 acres, 4,660,000 are under cultivation, 1,289,000 are under forest, 495,000 are fallow or uncultivated, and 833,000 are marshes, rivers and canals, roads, etc. The principal crops are wheat, oats, barley, rye, potatoes, beet, flax, tobacco and hops, and although great quantities of cereals are produced, wheat, maize and barley are largely imported. About 500,000 persons are employed in agriculture. The Live Stock in 1912 included 232,709 horses, 1,830,747 cattle, and 1,348,514 pigs. The total value of the Forest products exceeds 20,000,000 francs annually.

There are two great coal fields (125 mines working) along the valleys of the Meuse and Sambre, the annual output being about 24,000,000 English tons. Iron is obtained in large quantities, and the steel industry (ingots and rails) is of great importance. The principal iron towns are Liège, Seraing and Charleroi. There are also 1,780 stone quarries. The mineral springs of Spa are still famous. About 450,000 persons are engaged in the mining and metallic industries.

Belgium is essentially a manufacturing country. Some 800,000 persons are employed in the various factories; the chief industries are glass making at Charleroi, the quarries of the southern counties, wool-spinning at Verviers and linen weaving, particularly in Ghent, Aalst, Tourney, Courtrai, Rousselaire, and Bruges. Cotton manufactures center at Ghent, lace at Brussels, Mechlin and Bruges, and textiles at Verviers.

Transportation and Communication.—In 1912 there were 4,369 kilometres of railway worked by the State, of which 4,110 were State owned. There were also 350 kilometres of privately owned and worked line and 4,038 kilometres of branch lines, while there were 9,757 kilometres of public roads. The gross receipts from railways worked by the State in 1912 were 331,339.666 francs, the working expenses being 229,672,818 francs; the passengers carried numbered 191,814,188. The private lines amount to less than one-fourteenth of the total mileage.

The navigable rivers and canals have a total length of 2,179 kilometres and are very greatly used. The Meuse and Sambre traverse the coal fields, and the Schelde is the waterway of the western agricultural district.

In 1911 there were 1,594 post offices. There is also a Marconi installation.

Towns.—Capital, Brussels (Bruxelles). Population, Dec. 31, 1910, 195,630 (with suburbs 720,347). Other large cities are Antwerp, 320,650; Liège, 175,000; Ghent, 165,000; St. Nicolas, 34,000; Namur, 32,-000; Berchem, 31,000.

In 1914 the country was invaded by the Germans in their progress toward Paris. The principal cities were occupied by the German armies, the country was laid waste, and the inhabitants reduced to starvation.

Trade with the United States.—The value of merchandise imported into Belgium from the United States for the year 1913 was $66,845,462 and goods to the value of $41,-941,014 were sent thither—a balance of $24,904,448 in favor of the United States.

CONGO COLONY—The territory of the Congo includes the right bank of the Congo River from Manyanga to the sea, and sixteen miles of seacoast north of the estuary; the left bank from Noki (eighty miles from the sea); and thenceforth both banks. The total area amounts to 802,000 square miles, with a native population estimated at not more than 15,000,-000. The total European population (January, 1912) was 5,465, of whom 379 were British, 48 Americans, 278 Italians, 303 Portuguese, 177 Swedes, 150 Germans, and 3,307 Belgians. A terrible disease, called "Sleeping Sickness," for which no remedy has yet been discovered, has of late years made increasing ravages upon the native population, and threatens to depopulate large districts (especially along the banks of the Congo River and its principal tributaries) of a country in other respects capable of supporting with ease a large population. However, the disease seems to have attained its highest point of severity, and in several districts is decreasing.

Government.—By law of Oct. 18, 1908, the Independent State of the Congo (founded in 1882 by the late King Leopold II.) was annexed by Belgium, and is administered by a Colonial Council of fourteen members, over which the Minister for the Colonies presides.

Trade and Finances.—There are many fertile tracts, especially along the rivers; but barren mountain-land shuts out the coast from the more productive interior. The exports consist mainly of rubber (three-fifths of whole), palm-kernels, palm-oil, ivory and a few minor articles. The coffee plant and cotton grow wild, and coffee, cocoa, and tobacco have been planted with success. Iron, copper, and other minerals have been found. Revenue (1912), 45,-367,640 francs; expenditure (1912), 68,957,-370 francs; imports (1912), 53,867,847 francs; exports (1912), 59,125,394 francs.

The river is navigable (for 15,000 kilometres) for large vessels from its mouth at Banana to Matadi (95 miles), where the European steamers discharge and recharge their cargo; but between that place and Leopoldville, on Stanley Pool, there occur rapids and falls which have been avoided by a railroad 240 miles in length. There is also a second line, 60-centimetre gauge, from Boma to the Mayumbe country. The Great Lakes Railway has a line from Stanleyville to Ponthierville, 125 kilometres, and another line from Kindu to Kongolo, 355 kilometres (total length of railways open in 1911, 1,239 kilometres). There is telegraphic communication with Europe (total length of telegraph lines in 1911, 2,881 kilometres).

Towns.—The capital is Boma (pop. 3,500), other towns being Matadi (4,000), Banana, Elizabethville, Stanleyville, and Leopoldville.

Local Administration.—There is a Governor-General at Boma with six Vice-Governors-General, and a General Directorate of five departments. For local administrative purposes the colony is divided into two districts. (See also Congo; Africa.)

Belgium (see also Brussels and European War of 1914-16):

Chargé d'affaires to, 1130.

Claims of United States against, 1456.

Commercial relations with, 2193.

Consular convention with, 3888, 3893, 3997, 4539, 4561.

Consuls of, in United States, exequaturs to, revoked, 3420.

Convention with, for regulating right of inheriting and acquiring property, 2697, 4822, 4841, 4864.

Convention with, on slave trade, 6363.

Convention with, regarding Scheldt dues, 3395.

Copyright privilege extended, 5582. Referred to, 5625.

Difference of France and, with Venezuela, 6070.

Fugitive criminals, convention with, for surrender of, 2724, 4124, 4216, 4247, 4695, 4715.

Importations of American products to, restrictions upon, discussed, 5956, 6325, 6363.

Decrees regarding, referred to, 6100.

King of, arbiter in cases of the *Georgiana* and *Lizzie Thompson*, 3353.

Loan contracted by United States with Antwerp, 120.

Monetary convention of Latin Union, adhesion to, declared by, 4957.

Naturalization treaty with, 3892.

Neutrality of United States in war with—

Austria-Hungary, 7977.

Germany, 7976.

Postal convention with, 3775, 3883, 4203.

Reply to Germany's peace overtures, 8196.

Trade-marks, treaty with, regarding, 4799, 4822, 6425.

Treaties with, transmitted and discussed by President—

Arthur, 4695, 4715.

Buchanan, 3063.

Fillmore, 2697, 2704.

Grant, 4124, 4216, 4247, 4275, 4296.

Jackson, 1196.

Johnson, 3893.

Lincoln, 3395, 3459.

Polk, 2272, 2479.

Van Buren, 1821, 1839.

Approbation of Belgian Chambers not received, 1932.

Delay in exchange of ratifications, 1244, 2004.

Disavowal of, by Belgium, discussed, 1317.

Termination of, referred to, 4242.

Belgium, Treaties with.—The history of the diplomatic relations of the United States with the kingdom of Belgium displays very amicable sentiment on both sides. The treaty of 1845, on commerce and navigation, was terminated by the Belgian government in 1858. The treaty on commerce and navigation which replaced it in the same year was also terminated by that power in 1875. The treaty on import duties of 1863 was in part superseded by the treaty of 1875.

By a treaty of May 12, 1863, between Belgium and the Netherlands, it was agreed that in consideration of the payment of the sum of 17,141,640 florins (at 47.25 cents of the Netherlands) by the government of the Netherlands, the king of the Belgians renounced forever the duties levied upon the navigation of the Scheldt and its mouths. By treaty with the United States it was agreed that this renunciation applied to all flags and the duty should never be reestablished in any form; also that the pilotage dues and local taxes, reduced 20 per cent for sailing vessels, 25 per cent for towed vessels, and 30 per cent for steam vessels, should never be increased.

The treaty of 1868 on naturalization was proclaimed July 30, 1899. It agreed to the recognition by each country of such emigrants from the respective countries as should by legal naturalization become citizens of the other. Provision was made for the punishment, subject to the statute of limitations, of those guilty of misdemeanor committed prior to emigration, should they return. Freedom from military service in Belgium is accorded to legally naturalized citizens of the United States; and provision is made for restoration to former citizenship, if desired. The treaty remains in force from year to year, subject to six months' notice.

The consular convention treaty of 1868 was terminated on notice by Belgium on Jan. 1, 1880. The trade-mark convention of 1868 expired, with the treaty of 1858, of which it was a part, on July 1, 1875. The extradition convention of 1874 was terminated by substitution of clauses in the treaty of 1882.

The treaty of commerce and navigation of June 29, 1875, provides for full and entire freedom of commerce and navigation. No higher or other taxes shall be imposed upon inhabitants of the one state residing in the other; nor other or higher duties, fees, or imposts of any kind upon ships of the one country in the ports of the other. Coasting trade privileges shall be in both cases those of the most favored nation. In transshipment of goods from other countries the duties and formalities shall be not otherwise than in the case of direct importation and exportation under the national flag.

A consular convention was concluded in 1880, and an extradition convention, made in 1882, was succeeded by one of more breadth in 1901. A trade-mark convention concluded in 1884 was extended to cover copyrights in 1891, and specifically extended to the protection of trade-marks of both countries in China in 1905.

Bellicose.—War-like.

Belligerent.—1.—A country or individual at war. 2.—A citizen of a country in a state of war. (See Belligerent Rights.)

Belligerent Rights.—Rights granted by neutral governments to nations at war with each other, as distinguished from the unrecognizable rebellious subjects of a friendly power. Belligerent rights were accorded the Confederate States by Great Britain in a proclamation by the Queen recognizing the existence of war between the United States and the Confederate States and the right of each to exercise belligerent powers on the ocean, but not recognizing the national independence of the latter. It also enjoined neutrality upon British subjects. Such recognition of rights was also made by France and other leading commercial powers of Europe and by Brazil.

Belligerent Rights:

Accordance of, to Cuban insurgents deemed unwise by President—
Cleveland, 6068, 6151.
Grant, 3985, 4018, 4292.
McKinley, 6258.

Accorded Confederate States by foreign powers, discussed, 3259, 3327, 3565.

Recognition and aid of foreign powers invoked by Confederate States, 3221, 3246.

Belmont (Mo.), Battle of.—Nov. 1, 1861, Gen. Grant, who had been in command of posts in eastern Missouri and southern Illinois under Frémont, had a force of 20,-000 men at Cairo. A Confederate force under Gen. Polk held Columbus, Ky., on the east bank of the Mississippi River. This position commanded the navigation of the river, and was eventually made very strong, being defended by more than 120 heavy guns. On the Missouri bank opposite Columbus the Confederates had established a camp at Belmont, under Gen. Pillow. Grant learned that re-enforcements were to be sent by way of this camp in November to join Price. He thereupon left Cairo and, sending a force to occupy Paducah, Ky., conveyed 3,000 men down the river in transports, accompanied by gunboats to attack Belmont. The battle was fought Nov. 7, 1861. Few of the men had been under fire before. Grant's men took the camp, but were compelled to abandon it and return to their transports. The Federal loss was 485 killed, wounded and missing. The Confederate loss was 642, including prisoners.

Bemis Heights (N. Y.), Battles of.—Also called battles of Saratoga and Stillwater. In the autumn of 1777 the condition of Burgoyne's army in the upper Hudson Valley began to grow serious. Provisions were running short and the likelihood of effecting a junction with Howe at New York was remote. Gen. Gates had been sent by Congress to succeed Schuyler in command. The American army was daily increasing. Sept. 19, the two armies met at Bemis Heights, between Saratoga Lake and the Hudson River. An engagement took place between about 3,000 British and 2,500 Americans. Of the British about 500 were killed, wounded or captured; the Americans lost 319. This fight, sometimes called the battle of Freeman's Farm, was not decisive, as the British held their ground. The Americans showed, however, that Burgoyne could not break through their lines. The two armies remained almost within cannon shot of each other for some three weeks. Oct. 7, Burgoyne, despairing of re-enforcements, made a second attack, but was forced to retire to the heights near Saratoga. The numerical strength of the Americans was now greater than that of the British. Burgoyne was completely surrounded by Gates's army, which refused to engage him, but held him until famine forced his capitulation Oct. 17, 1777. The number of troops surrendered was 5,791, of whom 2,412 were Riedesel's Hessians. The battle of Saratoga is often treated by historians as the decisive conflict of the Revolution. Arnold, who subsequently turned traitor, was the hero of these engagements.

Ben Franklin, The. (See Butterfield, Carlos, & Co.)

Beneficence Congress at Milan, 4626.

Benevolent Assimilation.—A catch-phrase used by President McKinley in outlining the proposed treatment of the Filipinos. The term was used in derision by Democratic campaigners in 1900.

Bennett Law. (See White Slavery.)

Bennington (Vt.), Battle of.—An important conflict of the Revolutionary War. Aug. 11, 1777, Burgoyne sent Lieut.-Col. Baum with about 800 British and some Indians from Fort Edward to forage for cattle and supplies in Vermont. On the road to Bennington they were opposed by Col. John Stark, Aug. 16, with a force of some 2,000 men, mostly militia from New Hampshire and Vermont. The engagement began about 3 o'clock in the afternoon. At the outset the Indians deserted, and the remainder of Baum's brigade was soon overcome. Col. Breyman with 500 men, who had been sent to re-enforce Baum, was also defeated. The British loss was about 200 killed, and the American is variously estimated at from 550 to 900. Four pieces of artillery, 1,000 stand of arms, and many swords were also captured. Americans lost about 40 killed and as many wounded.

Bennington, The, refuge on, sought by Salvadorean insurgents, discussed, 5961.

Bentonville (N. C.), Battle of.—After the engagement at Averysboro Sherman's army continued its march toward Goldsboro. When near Bentonville, March 18, 1865, Slocum's advance encountered the Confederates in force. Johnston had hastily collected Stewart's and Cheatham's corps, Hardee's force, and Hampton's cavalry, aggregating something like 24,000 men. The attack of the Confederates was directed mainly against the corps of Jeff. C. Davis. A strong line of battle confronted Johnston, with Mill Creek and a single bridge in his rear. March 20 a general attack was made by Sherman's skirmish line. During the night Johnston retreated, as it was not his purpose to bring on with his small force a general battle with the large army of Sherman. The battle was not a distinct victory for either side.

Berceau, the allowance made for, 328.

Bergen, Norway, international exhibition to be held in, 3470.

Bering Sea (between Alaska and Asiatic Russia; 850,000 sq. miles); American vessels seized by Russian cruisers in, discussed, 6336.

Bering Sea Fisheries.—In 1886 the American Government set up the claim that Bering Sea was *mare clausum*, and claimed jurisdiction over the eastern half of it. In July, 1889, the British Columbian sealer

Black Diamond was seized for trespassing. Russia pretended to grant such rights when ceding Alaska in 1867, though in 1822 the United States had disputed Russia's claim to sovereignty over the sea beyond the usual three-mile limit of territorial jurisdiction. In consequence of this new doctrine many Canadian and American vessels were seized by a United States naval vessel for taking seal about the Pribyloff Islands and in the open sea in violation of the laws of the United States, which had leased a monopoly of seal killing to the Alaska Commercial Company (afterwards to the North American Company, in 1890). The British government claimed damages for the Canadian vessels seized.

Secretary Blaine and Sir Julian Pauncefote, the British ambassador, held many long consultations over the affair, but could arrive at no conclusion. After a *modus vivendi* had been agreed upon in 1891 the matter was finally left to a board of arbitration to consist of two members appointed by the United States, two by Great Britain, and one each by the President of France, the King of Italy, and the King of Norway and Sweden. The members appointed were, respectively, Justice John M. Harlan, of the Supreme Court, and Senator John T. Morgan; Lord Hannen and Sir John S. D. Thompson; Baron de Courcel; the Marquis Emilio Visconti-Venosta, and Gregers W. Gram. The Tribunal began its sessions at Paris, March 23, 1893, and August 15 following rendered its decision denying the right of American jurisdiction outside the usual three-mile limit. In order, however, to prevent extermination of the seals, the commission stipulated that seal fishing could be engaged in by licensed vessels only, established a closed season for seals in those waters from May 1 to August 1 and forbade pelagic sealing within sixty miles of the Pribyloff Islands, sealing with firearms or in steam vessels. These restrictions were made binding for five years but proved wholly ineffective. Another meeting of English, American and Canadian commissioners was held on Nov. 18, 1897, which unanimously upheld the attitude of the United States. In addition the United States agreed to prohibit all sealing even on the Pribyloff Islands for one year. To this Canada did not agree. Finally another mixed commission met at Quebec August, 1898, transferred its session to Washington, D. C., in November of the same year, and adjourned in February, 1899. It has never reassembled and the matter has remained *in statu quo.* (See also Paris Tribunal of Arbitration.)

Bering Sea Fisheries (see also Fisheries):

Claims against Russia, 6375.

Measures to prevent the extermination of seals discussed, 5366, 6155.

Proclamations regarding, 5449, 5476, 5533, 5578, 5581, 5697, 5826, 5926, 6015, 6123.

Modus vivendi—

To embrace Great Britain and Japan referred to, 6067.

With Russia restricting sealing in, 5961, 6067.

Questions with Great Britain regarding, 5545, 5616, 6062, 6266.

Adjustment of, referred to, 5747.

Agreement for *modus vivendi* proclaimed, 5581.

Discussed, 5616.

Arbitration of—

Agreed upon, 5616.

Proposed by Great Britain, declined by United States, 5545.

Treaty regarding, 5671, 5746, 6063.

Correspondence regarding, transmitted, 5515, 5567.

Discussed by President Cleveland, 5958.

Tribunal of Arbitration—

Acts to give effect to award of, proclaimed, 5926, 6123.

Award of, discussed and recommendations regarding, 5958, 6062.

Case of United States at, prepared by John W. Foster, 5748.

Convention for settlement of claims under, 6097.

Discussed by President Cleveland, 5869.

Enforcement of regulations in accordance with decision of, referred to, 6000.

Failure of negotiations of, to protect fur seals of Alaska, 6182.

Reports of Agents of United States to, transmitted, 5909.

Pelagic sealing complained of, 7443.

Recommendation that President be given power to prohibit taking of seals, 5748.

Report on, transmitted, 5396.

Berlin Decree.—An edict issued from Berlin Nov. 21, 1806, by Napoleon I. It declared a blockade of the British Islands and ordered all Englishmen in countries occupied by French troops to be treated as prisoners of war. All trade in English merchandise was forbidden, and no letters in the English language were to be allowed to pass through French post-offices. No vessel directly from England or the English colonies was to be admitted into any French port, and by a later interpretation all merchandise derived from England or her colonies, by whomsoever owned, was liable to seizure even on board neutral vessels. The decree reserved for future consideration the question whether vessels carrying English merchandise might not themselves be liable to seizure and confiscation. The object of this decree was to destroy the foreign trade of England, as well as to retaliate against the British for an order in council issued May 16, 1806, declaring a blockade of the coasts of Germany, Holland, Belgium, and France, from Brest to the Elbe, a distance of about 800 miles. No commendations took place under the Berlin Decree. (See Embargo; Milan Decree; Orders in Council.)

Berlin and Milan Decrees discussed and referred to by President—

Jefferson, 409, 415, 430, 432, 434, 441, 446.

Madison, 467, 476, 503, 513, 522.

Proclamations regarding, by President Madison, 457, 466.

Berlin (Capital of German Empire):

International Exhibition of Fish and Fisheries at, discussed, 4560.

Kongo conference at, 4855, 4865.

Bermuda (Group of 360 islands; British; 580 miles east of North Carolina; area, 20 sq. miles): slaves seized on board brigs by authorities of, 4867.

Berne, Switzerland:

International Copyright Convention at, discussed, 4919, 5090.

International Postal Congress at, discussed, 4250.

Bernstorff, Ambassador von. (See Diplomatic Negotiations, Breaking of.)

Betsy Ross House. (See Flag.)

Bhutan.—A native state in the southeastern Himalayas, between 26° 42'-28° N. latitude and 89°-92° E. longitude, and is bounded on the north and east by Tibet, and on the south and west by British India. The total area is estimated at 20,000 English square miles, with a population variously stated at 200,000 to 400,000 persons, mainly Buddhists, and consisting of an idle priestly class and struggling cultivators.

Government.—From the middle ages until 1907 the country was under the dual government of a spiritual chief and a temporal sovereign. In 1907 this dual government came to an end and the Tongsa Pelop (the chief councillor and virtual ruler) was chosen hereditary Raja. In 1863, owing to outrages on British subjects, portions of Bhutan were annexed to British India, an allowance being paid annually by the Indian Government as compensation. Bhutan agreed to be guided in its external relations by the advice of the British, who undertook not to interfere in its internal affairs.

Biennial Register, distribution of:

Act providing for, reasons for applying pocket veto to, 5072.

Referred to, 1783.

Big Bear State.—Alternative nickname for Tennessee. (See Volunteer State.)

Big Bethel (Va.), Battle of.—One of the preliminary skirmishes of the Civil War. In June, 1861, Maj.-Gen. B. F. Butler, of Massachusetts, was placed in command of the Federal forces in eastern Virginia. He established headquarters at Fortress Monroe and was soon in command of 10,000 men. June 9, Butler sent Brig.-Gen. E. W. Pierce with a detachment of 3,500 (composed of New York, Massachusetts, and Vermont infantry and a battery of artillery) to dislodge the Confederates at Big and Little Bethel under Gen. J. B. Magruder's command. Magruder's force (1,400) had made frequent raids upon the Federal lines. The attack, which was intended as a surprise, was made by the Union forces on the morning of June 10 and was repulsed. The Union loss was seventy-six. Among the killed was Maj. Theodore Winthrop. The Confederate loss was one killed and four wounded. Big Bethel was the first real battle of the war.

Big Black (Miss.), Battle of.—May 17, 1863, the day after the battle of Champion Hills, Grant's army pushed on toward Vicksburg. McClernand's corps, in advance, soon came upon Pemberton's army, strongly intrenched on both sides of the Big Black River. The Confederate batteries posted on the high bluffs were carried after a sharp engagement, the Federal assault being led by Lawler's brigade. The Confederates retreated. Seventeen pieces of artillery and about 1,200 prisoners were here taken. A portion of Pemberton's outposts crossed the river on temporary bridges, which they destroyed behind them, and joined the main body of the army in the retreat into the fortifications at Vicksburg. The Federal loss was 279.

Big Wichitaw River, exploration of, referred to, 2897.

Bigamy.—The state of having two or more husbands or wives at the same time. (See Mormon Church; Polygamy.)

Bill of Rights.—The earliest colonial or State declaration of American rights after the "Body of Laws" of Massachusetts, in 1640, was that which accompanied the Virginia constitution of 1776. It was based upon the English Bill of Rights of 1689. The latter was an instrument signed by William and Mary when accepting the crown of England from the Convention of Parliament. It asserted the right of subjects to petition, the right of Parliament to freedom of debate, the right of electors to choose representatives freely, and other privileges. This Bill of Rights, which contained the fundamental principles of political liberty, was not extended to the colonies. Other State constitutions in defining the rights of the citizen as against the scope of the State largely followed the phraseology of this famous instrument. The National Constitution was harshly criticised on account of the omission of some such guaranty of personal rights, and might have failed of ratification had not the Federalists promised to incorporate such a set of statements. The first ten amendments stand as the partial fulfillment of their promises. (See also Amendments.)

Bills and Acts:

Acts to be published in certain newspapers, 4116.

Approved but not signed, whether in force, discussed, 856.

Consideration by President, time allowed for, discussed, 2993, 3060.

Constitutional amendment regarding approval of separate items of bill and veto of others recommended, 4196, 4725, 4774, 4840.

Duly certified and approved which had not passed, discussed, 1353.

Effect on, of adjournment of Congress before expiration of ten days after presentation to President discussed, 3797.

List of acts transmitted, 3963.

Bimetallic Conference. (See International Monetary Conference.)

Bimetallism.—The use of two metals as money at relative values set by legislative enactment; the doctrine that two metals can and ought, at the same time and in the same country, to be adopted as standards of value and bear to each other a fixed ratio established by the Government. As used in this country, the term usually refers to the use of gold and silver at a fixed relative value established by law. Monometallism is the doctrine that only one metal ought to be so used. (See Silver.)

Biographical Sketches of President—
Adams, John, 217.
Adams, J. Q., 857.
Arthur, 4618.
Buchanan, 2960.
Cleveland, 4882.
Fillmore, 2599.
Garfield, 4593.
Grant, 3957.
Harrison, Benj., 5438.
Harrison, W. H., 1858.
Hayes, 4391.
Jackson, 998.
Jefferson, 307.
Johnson, 3499.
Lincoln, 3204.
McKinley, 5234.
Madison, 450.
Monroe, 572.
Pierce, 2728.
Polk, 2221.
Roosevelt, 6637.
Taft, 7367.
Taylor, 2541.
Tyler, 1888.
Van Buren, 1528.
Washington, 33.
Wilson, 7867.

Biological Survey, Bureau of, Agriculture Department.—A bureau of the Department of Agriculture which studies the geographic distribution of animals and plants, makes maps of life zones, and studies the food and habits of birds and mammals. It enforces the laws regulating the importation of foreign birds and animals. It looks after the protection of game by control of interstate trade; also the protection of migratory and insectivorous game birds.

An important fact established by this bureau is that the dreaded bubonic plague is a disease of rats and that it is transmitted to human beings chiefly through the agency of fleas which infest rats and then convey the poisonous germ to human beings.

A careful study of birds in relation to fruit raising engaged the attention of this bureau for several years. The result was a report informing orchardists how to discriminate between friends and foes—that they might encourage the one class and prevent or lessen losses from the other. Bird reservations (sanctuaries where flocks may breed safely or take refuge during the migration) have also been set aside upon recommendation of this bureau.

Biological Survey, work of, reviewed and commended, 7486. (See also Agriculture, Department of.)

Biplane. (See Aeronautics.)

Birds:

(Migratory), regulations for protection, 7895, 7986.

(Native), reservation established for, 7959.

Bivouac.—An out-door encampment of soldiers held in prime readiness for action.

Bixby Letter. (See illustration opposite 3341 and description on back.)

Black Cockades.—A badge first worn by the American soldiers during the Revolution and later, during the hostility toward

France (about 1797) occasioned by the X. Y. Z. dispatches, adopted by the Federalists as a patriotic emblem and as a rejoinder to the tri-colored cockade worn by the Republicans as a mark of affection toward France. Its significance in some degree lay in the fact that it had been a part of the Continental uniform.

Black Code.—A systematized set of rules for the guidance of the colored people before slavery was abolished.

Black Friday.—There have been several Black Fridays. The term is often used to designate a dark financial day. In England it has special reference to Friday, Dec. 6, 1745, the day on which news came to London that the young Pretender, Charles Edward, had reached Derby; and also to Friday, May 11, 1866, which was the height of the commercial panic in London through the failure of Overend, Guerney & Co. Sept. 24, 1869, is sometimes referred to as Black Friday in the United States. On this day a syndicate of New York bankers advanced the price of gold to 162½, causing a panic. It sold at 143⅛ the previous evening. Another such day was Friday, Sept. 19, 1873, when Jay Cooke & Co., leading American bankers, failed. A great crash ensued in Wall Street, the center of financial operations in America, and the historic panic of 1873 began. Credit generally was impaired and many financial institutions were forced into bankruptcy.

Black Hand.—An Italian secret society, often resorting to violence to obtain its demands for blackmail. Prominent Italian-Americans have organized as a counteracting force the White Hand, which has aided the Secret Service to suppress the activities of the Black Hand, which derives its name from the fact that the communications of the society are often signed with a black hand, as its official emblem.

Black Hawk War.—By a treaty signed at Prairie du Chien, Wis., July 15, 1830, the Sac and Fox Indians ceded all their lands in Illinois and Wisconsin to the United States. Black Hawk, a noted chief of the tribe, refused to abide by the treaty and made war upon the whites. He resisted the survey of the land at Rock Island, Ill., although most of the Sacs and Foxes were west of the Mississippi. In 1831 he attacked some Illinois villages, but was driven off by the militia under Gen. Gaines in June of that year. The next spring he returned with a strong force and began to massacre the whites. Gen. Scott was sent against him with a force of United States troops. Black Hawk was defeated at the Wisconsin River July 21, 1832, by a detachment of troops under Gen. Dodge, and again at Bad Axe River, Aug. 2 of the same year, by Gen. Atkinson. After these successive defeats Black Hawk was compelled to surrender.

Black Hawk War, discussed, 1166, 1251.

Black Hills:
Emigration to, 4276, 4306, 4355.
Gold discovered in, referred to, 4306, 4355.

Black Horse Cavalry.—A political term applied to those legislators (more or less numerous in every legislative body) that act together for the purpose of exacting money from friends of any measure under consideration and threaten its defeat in case of non-compliance. Their number is

frequently great enough to be of considerable influence.

Black Laws.—Laws passed in many of the northern states before the abolition of slavery requiring certain acts to be performed by free negroes, as a condition to their residing in those states, or prescribing disabilities under which they labored. Such were laws requiring them to file certificates of their freedom; forbidding them to testify in cases in which a white man was interested; excluding them from the militia and from the public schools, and requiring them to give bonds for their good behavior.

Black-List.—A list of persons considered objectionable—used in attacking public and private persons; also by organized capital to prevent certain classes of labor from obtaining employment, and by organized labor to prevent certain classes of capital from securing patronage. (See Boycott.)

Black-Mail.—The act of attempting to extort money or other valuable objects by threats of exposure.

Black Mesa Forest Reserve proclaimed, 6700.

Black Rock (N. Y.), Battles of.—Lieut.-Col. Bishop, with about 400 men from the British camp at Lundys Lane, crossed the Niagara River July 11, 1813, and attacked the blockhouse at Black Rock, where the Americans had a considerable quantity of naval stores and ammunition. The blockhouse was in charge of Gen. Peter B. Porter, with less than a dozen artillerists. About 300 militia and a small band of Indians were scattered about in the neighborhood. The militia fled at Bishop's approach and Porter narrowly escaped capture. On his way to Buffalo, meeting re-enforcements of 100 regulars, he returned and attacked the invaders. After a short struggle the British were driven with loss to their boats. Lieut.-Col. Bishop was mortally wounded. In August, 1814, Black Rock was again attacked by the British and successfully defended by the Americans. After the battle of Lundys Lane the American army retired to Fort Erie and vicinity. Gen. Drummond, having received re-enforcements, went in pursuit. As a preliminary step toward attacking Fort Erie, the British general resolved to take possession of Black Rock. About 1,200 men under Lieut.-Col. Tucker crossed the river on Aug. 3, 1814, and were met and driven back by 300 Americans under Lieutenants Ryan, Smith, and Armstrong. The British lost a considerable number; the American loss was slight.

Black Rock, N. Y., works at, referred to, 1563.

Black Sea:
Navigation of, unlocked, 1008.
Vessels of United States excluded from, discussed, 1065.
Free passage for, secured by treaty with Turkey, 1067, 1157.

Black Warrior, The.—The American merchant vessel which was seized at Havana by Cuban customs officials Feb. 28, 1854, and with its cargo was declared confiscated (2767, 2778). The proceedings aroused a bitter feeling against Spain, and a special messenger was dispatched instructing the American minister at Madrid to demand, as immediate redress, indemnification to the owners in the sum of $300,000. The reluctance of Spain to accede led to the Ostend manifesto. Spain afterwards made compensation for the seizure (2869), but the incident was used as a pretext for later filibustering expeditions into Cuba.

Black Warrior, The, seizure of, by Spanish authorities discussed, 2767, 2778.

Disavowal of, by Spain, and payment of indemnity, 2869.

Reparation for, refused, 2779.

Black Water State.—A nickname for Nebraska (q. v.). (See also States.)

Blackfeet Indians. (See Indian Tribes.)

Blackstock's (S. C.), Battle of.—In November, 1780, Gen. Sumter started for Fort Ninety-Six to attempt its capture. He was pursued by Col. Tarleton. A skirmish took place Nov. 20 at Blackstock's plantation, on the Tyger River, Union District, S. C. Tarleton fled, leaving nearly 200 dead and wounded upon the field. The American loss was only three killed and five wounded.

Bladensburg (Md.), Battle of.—As early as January, 1814, intelligence was received at Washington that 4,000 British troops had landed at Bermuda, destined for the United States. The British Admiral Cockburn arrived at Lynnhaven Bay, Va., in March with 1 ship, 2 frigates, and 1 brig. Early in August he was joined by Vice-Admiral Cochrane, who took command, and was later joined in the Chesapeake by 4,000 veterans of Wellington's army, under Gen. Ross. The civil government at Washington was apathetic in the face of impending danger. Washington, with its public buildings and records, was entirely unprotected. At the suggestion of Gen. Winder the President called a Cabinet council in July and proposed raising an army for the defense of the Federal capital. This comprehended a requisition on the States for militia aggregating 93,000 men. The naval defenses were intrusted to Commodore Barney, with a small flotilla of gun-boats carrying 400 men. By Aug. 1 Gen. Winder, who was assigned to the defense of the capital, had 1,000 regulars and almost 4,000 militia under his command for the defense of Washington and Baltimore. The remainder of the army was on paper. The British moved up the Patuxent by land and water to Upper Marlboro. Barney destroyed his flotilla at Pig Point and crossed toward the Eastern Branch of the Potomac, forming a junction with Winder's advance, which had proceeded to Bladensburg, about five miles from Washington, on the post road to Baltimore. Here at noon, Aug. 24, 1814, the two armies faced each other, the British, under Gen. Ross, nearly 5,000 strong, 4,000 of them seasoned by service in continental Europe, while the defenders of the capital consisted mainly of undisciplined, untried militia, many of them only three days from their homes. The battle lasted from about half-past twelve till four o'clock and resulted in the utter rout of the Americans. The British lost upward of 500 men in the engagement. The Americans had only 26 killed and 51 wounded. After this battle the invaders marched to the capital, seized it, and burned the public buildings.

Bland-Allison Act:

Discussed by President—

Arthur, 4633, 4720, 4830.

Cleveland, 4927, 5097, 5373.

Harrison, Benj., 5475.

Hayes, 4511, 4568.

Vetoed by President Hayes, 4438.

Bland Dollar.—A name sometimes applied to the silver dollar of the United States, the coinage of which began in 1878. During that year Congress passed the act providing for such coinage. A bill was introduced in the House of Representatives by Richard P. Bland, of Missouri, July 25, 1876, providing for the free and unlimited coinage of silver, which had been suspended since 1873. Mr. Bland's bill passed the House providing for free coinage, but was modified in the Senate by the Allison amendment. As the bill became a law it provided that instead of free coinage the Secretary of the Treasury should purchase each month not less than $2,000,000 nor more than $4,000,000 worth of silver bullion to be coined into silver dollars of 412½ grains each. President Hayes returned the bill with his veto Feb. 28, 1878 (4438), but on the same day both House and Senate passed the bill over his veto. The effects of the law were discussed by the Chief Executives from time to time. (See Bland-Allison Act.) This act was repealed in 1890 by the act of Congress known as the Sherman act (q. v.).

Blizzard State.—Alternative nickname for South Dakota. (See Coyote State.)

Blockade.—A well-defined principle of international law which secures to any nation the right in time of war to render intercourse with the enemy's ports unlawful, hazardous, or impossible on the part of neutrals. It was introduced by the Dutch about 1584. The principle recognized by European powers is that a blockade to be binding must be effective. It is carried into effect by a force of war ships, which patrol the sea outside the enemy's harbor and arrest any vessels of any power attempting to enter. Should any arrested vessel contain goods or persons contraband of war, it is condemned by a prize court and sold, the proceeds being divided among the blockade squadron. This right is incontrovertible, having its origin in the soundest principles of maritime jurisprudence, sanctioned by the practice of the best nations of enlightened times. The Elbe was blockaded by Great Britain in 1803; the Baltic by Denmark in 1848-49 and in 1864; the Gulf of Finland by the Allies in 1854. At the outbreak of the Civil War in America the Confederate government required every English vessel that entered its ports to bring arms and ammunition as part of its cargo. Plymouth, Newbern, Wilmington and other North Carolina ports were much used by these vessels, as also the port of Charleston, S. C. United States cruisers blockaded these ports, and under the established rules of international law seized, searched and confiscated foreign vessels attempting to run the blockade, as well as enemy's ships in transit. At the commencement of the Spanish-American War in 1898 the United States maintained a strict blockade of Cuban ports for several weeks under the direction of Acting Rear-Admiral Sampson, which finally resulted in the battle of July 3, when the American squadron under the immediate command of Commodore Schley entirely destroyed the Spanish fleet under Admiral Cervera. In the Russo-Japanese War (see Japan), the Japanese maintained a strict blockade of Port Arthur from Feb. 10, 1904, when the first attack was made, until the fall of the city, Jan. 2, 1905.

Blockades:

Correspondence regarding, referred to, 3259.

During War of 1812 discussed, 486.

Established by—

Portugal, claims of United States growing out of, 1098, 1113, 1243.

Spain, claims of United States growing out of, 1112.

In order to be binding, must be effective, 2945.

Maximilian's decrees declaring, proclaimed void, 3631.

Of Cuban ports, proclaimed, 6472, 6481.

Discussed, 6296, 6312.

Removal of, referred to, 6321.

Of Mexican ports, and effect of, on United States, 1705, 1733.

Of Southern ports proclaimed, 3215, 3216, 3481.

Claims of foreign powers arising out of, discussed, 3328.

Nonresident foreigners engaged in violating, order regarding 3483.

Referred to, 3225, 3385.

Removed, 3523.

From certain ports, or relaxed in the South in the interests of trade and commerce, both home and foreign, 3290, 3372, 3417, 3431, 3482, 3507.

Of Spanish Main, referred to, 776.

Of Tripoli, questions between United States and Tunis growing out of, 388, 389.

Blockhouse.—A structure in which soldiers shelter themselves from attack, and from which they attack the enemy through suitable openings in the walls.

Bloody Shirt.—A term used to describe the utterances of impassioned speakers and writers who after the close of the Civil War endeavored to revive its memories and to agitate the minds of their hearers for political effect. Reviving war animosities was said to be waving the bloody shirt.

Blue Book. (See Biennial Register.)

Blue Grass State.—Alternative nickname for Kentucky. (See Corn-Cracker State.)

Blue Hen State.—Alternative nickname for Delaware. (See Diamond State.)

Blue Laws.—A name applied to the early laws of some of the American Colonies. The general court of New Haven, Conn., in April, 1644, ordered that the "judicial laws of God as they were delivered to Moses," should be binding on all offenders and a rule to all the courts of the jurisdiction "till they be branched out into particulars hereafter." New Haven's criminal code was developed along these lines. It is doubtful, however, if some of the rigid rules of conduct often quoted as Blue Laws were ever enforced. Some of them are as follows: "No one shall run on the Sabbath day, or walk in his garden or elsewhere, except reverently to and from meeting." "No woman shall kiss her child on the Sabbath or fasting day." "No one shall read common prayer, keep Christmas or saints' days, make minced pies, dance, play cards, or play on any instrument of music except the drum, trumpet and jews-harp." As early as 1649 a law of Massachusetts provided for the prohibition of labor, play or travel on the Lord's Day, beginning on Saturday evening. The "Duke's Laws" of New York also forbade the profanation of the day by travel or labor. The Pennsylvania laws of 1682 forbade labor. Those of South Carolina in 1684 forbade profanation of the Sabbath. Virginia in 1692 forbade travel or profanation. Remnants of these laws still survive in state legislation.

Blue Licks (Ky.), Battle of.—Aug. 19, 1782, a body of 182 Kentucky pioneers were drawn into an ambuscade at Blue Licks, Nicholas County, Ky., by Indians under Simon Girty. The settlers were defeated with the loss of sixty-two, including a son of Daniel Boone.

Blue Lights.—During the summer and autumn of 1813, while the British commander, Sir Thomas Hardy, with his fleet, had the port of New London, Conn., blockaded, Commodore Decatur made several futile attempts to escape therefrom with his fleet, consisting of the frigates *United States* and *Macedonian* and the sloop-of-war *Hornet*. Decatur claimed that his failure was due to the fact that blue signal lights were flashed from the shore toward the British. The friends of the British and the opponents of the war became known as Blue-Light Federalists.

Blue Sky Laws.—A popular designation applied to the several state laws regulating the sale of securities of industrial or railroad companies to the public. The first act of the kind was passed by Kansas in 1911 and amended in many particulars in 1913. Those of the other states are based upon the Kansas law and follow its general outline. The definite objects are (1) to define and provide for the registration, regulation and supervision of foreign and domestic investment companies and their agents and representatives; (2) to regulate corporations and associations selling the stocks, bonds or other securities issued by such investment companies; (3) to protect the purchasers of securities issued by such concerns; (4) to prevent fraud in the selling of such securities; and (5) to create some governmental authority to supervise such companies and otherwise administer the provisions of the law. The Kansas law applies to every person, corporation, copartnership, or association (with the exception of banks and trust companies and building and loan associations) which offers or negotiates for the sale of or to take subscriptions for, or to sell, any stocks, bonds, or other securities (except government, state and municipal bonds, national bank stock, building and loan stock, or shares in corporations not organized for profit) to any person in the State. Brokers and investment companies must obtain licenses or permits from the Bank Commissioner and file (1) an itemized statement of their financial condition; (2) a copy of all contracts, stocks and bonds or other securities which they propose to make or sell; (3) sample copies of all literature or advertising matter to be used in the sale of securities; (4) a copy of any charter or constitution and by-laws under which they do business. Any misrepresentation of the condition of the corporations whose securities are offered for sale is made a felony, punishable by $10,000 fine and ten years in prison. In some states brokers are required to furnish evidence of their good character and financial standing, and permission to do business may be revoked if the official in charge of enforcing the law decides that unsound securities are being offered for sale.

Besides Kansas the following states have enacted Blue Sky Laws: Arizona, Arkansas, California, Florida, Idaho, Iowa, Maine, Michigan, Missouri, Montana, Nebraska, North Carolina, North Dakota, Ohio, Oregon, South Dakota, Vermont and West Virginia. A similar law was defeated in the New York legislature in 1912-13, and Minnesota has a statute applicable only to the securities of insurance companies.

Bluefields. (See Mosquito Indian Strip.)

Board of Food and Drug Inspection. (See Food and Drug Inspection, Board of.)

Board of Health. (See National Board of Health.)

Board of Ordnance and Fortification. (See Ordnance and Fortification, Board of.)

Board of Trade and Plantations.—In 1660 Charles II. established two separate councils, one for trade and the other for foreign plantations. For a time these were united (from 1672 to 1675). The charter of Rhode Island and Providence Plantations was secured from Charles II., July 8, 1663, by John Clarke, who acted as agent for the Colony. This charter continued in force 180 years. In 1695 the Board of Trade and Plantations was established and given charge of the English Colonies in America. In 1768 a Secretary of State for America was established, and the duties of the board were transferred to him.

Boatswain.—A minor ship officer having charge of ship equipment.

Boca del Toro, United States of Colombia, vessels from, tonnage duty on, suspended, 4895.

Boche.—A term of uncertain origin, applied contemptuously in the European War to the German soldiers.

Body of Liberties.—A bill of rights consisting of a code of 100 fundamental laws setting forth the sacredness of life, liberty, property and reputation. The Body of Liberties was compiled by Nathaniel Ward, pastor of the church at Ipswich, Mass., from drafts submitted. A copy of these laws was sent to every town within the jurisdiction of Massachusetts to be first considered by the magistrates and elders, and then to be published by the constables, "that if any man saw anything to be altered he might communicate his thoughts to some of the deputies." In December, 1641, the General Court of Massachusetts adopted this fundamental code as the basis of common law, there having been up to that time no written law in the Colony.

Boer War.—The conflict between Great Britain and the South African republics of Transvaal and the Orange Free State. Following the organization of the Transvaal Republic the British claimed suzerainty over the country, and sent a governor and a military force to support their claims in 1879. The Boers, who were descendants of Dutch colonists, offered military resistance and defeated the British troops in several engagements, notably at Laing's Neck, Jan. 28, 1881, and at Majuba

Hill, Feb. 27, 1881. In March, the independence of the Republic was acknowledged by a British treaty, and the Boers acknowledged the suzerainty of the Queen of England.

During the following years British settlers, or uitlanders, protested to their home government that they were harshly treated by the local authorities. British military forces were increased and the incensed Boers demanded the instant withdrawal of all troops. The Orange Free State supported the Transvaal in opposing British authority.

In October, 1899, 10,000 British forces were concentrated at Ladysmith, in Natal, at the junction of two railroads, one running into the Transvaal, the other into the Orange Free State. Here they were besieged by the Boers until they were relieved by the British General Buller, Feb. 28, 1900. Other British forces were besieged in Kimberley, in Cape Colony, from Oct. 20, 1899 to Feb. 15, 1900, and in Mafeking, Bechuanaland, from October, 1899, to May 16, 1900. Attempts to relieve these positions occasioned the principal battles of the war. In 1899 General Sir Redvers Buller had 54,000 troops in the country. He made three futile attempts to relieve Ladysmith, and was severely defeated while attempting to force the Tugela river near Colenso, Dec. 15, 1899. In January, 1900, Lord Roberts was ordered to South Africa with the whole Seventh Army Division, of 100,000 men, with Lord Kitchener as chief of staff. Under his direction Gen. French, with 5,000 British, relieved Kimberley. The Boer general Cronje, with 5,000 men, surrendered at Paardeeberg, in the bed of the Modder River, Feb. 27, 1900. Bloemfontein surrendered to Lord Roberts March 15, Presidents Steyn and Kruger escaping to the north. General DeWet continued to harass the British, and cut off the water supply of Bloemfontein. The Boer general, Joubert, died March 27th and was succeeded by Louis Botha. June 5th, Roberts occupied Pretoria. By establishing a system of block signal houses throughout the country and driving the inhabitants into concentration camps the British finally succeeded in forcing the Boers to surrender. Peace was signed May 31, 1902.

American interest in the Boer War is shown by the fact that the Senate vote on Mr. Pettigrew's resolution of sympathy with the Boers was 20 in favor of to 29 against. The South African republics officially appealed to the United States to intervene, with a view to the cessation of hostilities early in 1900. President McKinley, however, refused to interfere.

The Boer force during the war was about 75,000. The total British force sent to South Africa from Aug. 1, 1899, to May 31, 1902, was 396,000. The cost of the war to England was more than a billion dollars and 20,000 men. (See illustration opposite 6503.)

Boer War, attitude of the United States in, 6371, 6410, 6429.

Bohemian Independence, Struggle for. (See Czecho-Slovaks and Jugo Slavs; and Austria-Hungary.)

Boisé City, Idaho, mentioned, 6816.

Bokhara.—A Russian dependency in central Asia. It lies between latitude 41° 30′ and 36° 40′ north and between longitude 61° 40′ and 73° east, and is bounded on the north by the Russian provinces of Syr-Daria and Samarkand, on the east by the province of Ferghana, on the south by

Afghanistan and on the southwest by the Russian transcaspian province and the Khanat of Khiva. It has an area of 92,000 square miles and a population of 2,500,000.

History.—The modern State of Bokhara was founded by the Uzbegs in the fifteenth century. The dynasty of Manguts, to which the present ruler belongs, dates from the eighteenth century. Mir Muzaffar-eddin in 1866 proclaimed a holy war against the Russians, who thereupon invaded his dominions and forced him to sign a treaty ceding the territory now forming the Russian district of Syr-Daria, to consent to a war indemnity, and to permit Russian trade. In 1873 a further treaty was signed by virtue of which no foreigner is admitted to Bokhara without a Russian passport, making the State practically a Russian dependency. By this treaty also merchandise belonging to Russian traders, whether imported or exported, pays a duty of 2½ per cent *ad valorem,* and no other duty can be levied on Russian goods, which are also exempt from transit duty.

Bolivia.—A republic of South America. It extends between 10° and 22° S. lat. and 58° and 69° W. longitude in the west centre of South America. It has no seaboard and is bounded on the north and east by Brazil, on the west by Peru and Chile, and on the south by Argentina and Paraguay. The boundaries have been settled by treaties with its territorial neighbors. Of the total population about one-half are Indians and 500,000 of mixed Spanish-Indian, Spanish-Negro or Negro-Indian descent.

Physical Features.—Bolivia slopes eastwards from the Andes, which form the western boundary with Peru, and occupy the greater portion of the south and west of the republic. In the north and east are plains, that of the south-east being a portion of the Gran Chaco of Argentina.

The waters rising in the eastern slopes of the Andes are divided into a northern and southern system by a lofty plateau in Chuquisaca. Those of the north form the rivers Grande-Mamoré and Beni. Those of the south form the upper waters of the Pilcomayo. The western boundary crosses Lake Titicaca (nearly 13,000 feet above sea level), which is joined by the river Desaguadero to a chain of salt lakes in the Pampa Aullagas further south.

AREA AND POPULATION

Departments and Capitals	Area in English Sq. Miles	Estimated Population 1911
Chuquisaca (Sucre)	26,410	250,000
Cochabamba (Cochabamba)	23,321	420,000
El Beni (Trinidad)	102,080	40,000
La Paz (La Paz)	53,762	550,000
Oruro (Oruro)	18,973	120,000
Potosi (Potosi)	48,903	380,000
Santa Cruz (Santa Cruz)	141,660	260,000
Tarija (Tarija)	33,027	130,000
Territories (Riberalta)	119,362	50,000
Total	567,498	2,200,000

History.—Bolivia was formerly a Spanish possession. It became independent in 1825 and united with Peru from 1836 to 1839. The country consists of 10 departments and territories, governed by a President and two Houses of Congress, with a constitution modeled after that of the United States. Revolutions have frequently occurred. From 1879 to 1883 Bolivia and Peru were united in a war against Chile. The result was disastrous to the allies, and Chile became possessed of all the western seacoast, including the niter districts of Bolivia.

Government.—The government is that of a democratic Republic under a modification (dated Oct. 28, 1880) of the fundamental law of Aug. 6, 1825, at which date Bolivia declared its independence of Spain. The Republic was previously comprised in the Spanish Vice-Royalty of Alto-Peru, and derives its present name from its liberator, Simon Bolivar.

The Executive is entrusted to a President (elected for four years by direct popular vote and ineligible for re-election), aided by two Vice-Presidents, and a Cabinet of six members.

President of the Republic (1913-1917) Dr. Ismael Montes, assumed office Aug. 14, 1913.

Congress consists of the Senate and Chamber of Deputies. The Senate of sixteen members, two from each province, is elected by direct vote for six years, one-third retiring every two years. The Chamber of Deputies, of seventy-five members, is elected by direct vote for four years, one-half retiring every two years. Congress meets annually on August 6th, for 60 to 90 days.

There is a Supreme Court at the capital, with seven judges appointed by Congress for ten years, and eight district courts at the provincial capitals.

Each of the eight Departments is administered by a Prefect, under whom are sub-prefects, corregidores and alcaldes. The larger municipalities are governed by councils, the smaller by boards or appointed agents. The Territories are administered by a national delegation of two.

Army.—By a law of Jan., 1907, service in the Army (militia) is universal and compulsory between the ages of 20 and 50. Service in the Active Militia is for five years with five years in the Reserve, and ten years in the Territorial Guard. The Peace Establishment is (Aug. 6, 1913) about 350 officers and 4,650 others. The War Establishment is stated to be about 90,000.

Education.—Primary education is free and nominally compulsory, but is confined to the municipalities, who are the controlling authorities; 81,336 pupils were enrolled in 1912. Secondary education reaches only about 1,500 pupils; for higher education there are university colleges, special schools and technical institutes.

Debt.—The Public Debt on June 30, 1913, stood as follows:—

Sterling Loan of 1908, 6%	$2,250,000
Sterling Loan of 1910, 5½%	7,287,000
Railway Loan of 1913, 5%	5,000,000
Internal Debt	900,000
Floating Debt	3,000,000

Production and Industry.—About 500,000 (one-fourth of the population) live by agriculture and pastoral pursuits, the total area under cultivation being about 5,000,000 acres. The *puñas* provide excellent grazing for large herds of llama vicuña, and alpaca, and cinchona bark is produced from the trees in that region. The forest-clad plains and the lowest slopes of the Andes produce rubber, cotton, indigo, tropical fruits, and medicinal herbs.

Rubber is now the most important agricultural industry, the exports in 1912 amounting to 4,080 tons, valued at $5,200,000.

The mineral productions are very valuable, tin being the principal product of the mines, the exports in 1912 being valued at $24,000,000; and the silver mines of Potosi are regarded as inexhaustible; gold, partly dug and partly washed, is obtained on the Eastern Cordillera of the Andes, and copper, lead, antimony, wolfram, bismuth, salt, and sulphur are also found.

Towns.—Capital, Sucre, in Chuquisaca, situated about 10,000 feet above sea level, named after a victorious general in the War of Independence of 1824. Population, 24,-000. The great trading centre and seat of government is La Paz, population 80,000. Other towns are Cochabamba, Potosi, Oruro, Santa Cruz, and Tarija.

The Unit of Currency is the *boliviano* of 100 *centavos,* worth (legal value) $0.38.9.

Trade with the United States.—The value of merchandise imported into Bolivia from the United States for the year 1913 was $940,744, and goods to the value of $350 were sent thither—a balance of $940,394 in favor of the United States.

Bolivia (see also Peru-Bolivia Confederation):

Diplomatic relations with, 5468, 6364, Resumed, 4449, 4562.

Insurrection in, discussed, 6364.

Treaty with (3111).

Ratification of amendments to, recommendation regarding, 3260.

War between Chile, Peru, and, 4522, 4563, 4628, 4717.

Claims of United States arising out of, 4913, 5083, 5369, 5544.

Conditions of peace presented by Chile discussed, 4662, 4717, 4760.

Efforts of United States to bring about peace, discussed, 4522, 4563, 4582, 4662, 4717.

Negotiations for restoration of peace, 4676.

Terminated, 4822, 6364.

Treaty of peace discussed, 4760.

Bolivia, Treaties with.—May 13, 1858, a treaty of peace, friendship, commerce and navigation was concluded with Bolivia. This contained the favored-nation clause, defined neutral rights, contraband of war, rights of citizens in case of war, forbade confiscation or the granting of letters of marque, and opened the Amazon River and its tributaries to navigation by ships of the United States. A previous convention with the Peru-Bolivian confederacy was terminated by the alliance in 1839. An extradition convention was concluded in 1900. (See Extradition.)

Bollman Case.—An important Supreme Court case in which treason is defined and the authority of the Supreme Court to issue writs of *habeas corpus ad subjiciendum* is maintained. Bollman was charged with being implicated in a treasonable attempt to levy war upon the United States, in that he had joined Aaron Burr in a scheme to establish an independent State in the southwest in 1805. It was decided that a mere conspiracy to subvert the Government by force is not treason, an actual levying of war being necessary. The court held that the crime with which the prisoners Bollman and Swartwout stood charged had not been committed, and they were discharged.

Bolsheviki.—The radical, or "Left," wing of the Russian Socialists. The name comes from a Russian root meaning "more" and seems to have been generally applied first in 1906. At that time an important convention of the revolutionary elements in Russia was held, and the Bolsheviki represented that branch of the Social Revolutionaries who refused to sanction a program for a more moderate immediate program and a more radical ultimate program, but insisted upon making the ultimate So-

cialist demands the goal for immediate action. Since the Bolsheviki at that time were outvoted on most questions, the term was hardly applied to them in the sense of "majority," but rather in the sense of "those who want more." The Bolsheviki were known also, for the same reason, as the Maximalists, their opponents of the more moderate type being known as the Mensheviki or Minimalists.

After the Russian revolution (q. v.), the Bolsheviki represented an element hostile both to the liberal elements of the Miliukoff regime and to the moderate Socialist elements of the Kerensky regime. Under the leadership of Lenine and Trotzky, with a program calling for immediate steps to negotiate a general peace and the inauguration of the social revolution in all lands, the exclusion from power of all elements not included in the proletariate, the abolition of private ownership and management in the socially-necessary factors of production, they succeeded to power in November, 1917. The details of their rule in Russia will be found under the head of Russian Revolution.

Bonded Debt. (See Debt, Public.)

Bonds.—In a legal sense an obligation in writing and under seal whereby one party binds himself to pay a sum of money to another at a certain time, and usually bearing a specified rate of interest. The security for the payment of the bonded indebtedness is generally a mortgage on productive property. The mortgage is placed in the hands of a third party as trustee to whom the bondholders may apply for foreclosure in the event of failure to pay interest or principal. The entire mortgage is then divided into separate bonds of (usually) $1,000 each and sold to separate investors. When issued to creditors named they are registered on the books of the company issuing them and their ownership is a matter of record. When made payable to bearer, coupons are attached in the form of notes falling due at the several interest periods, and are made payable at the company's offices or at a bank or by the trustee.

Bonds issued by governments are not based upon any mortgage, but upon the integrity of the government and its ability to collect sufficient funds from its subjects to pay interest and principal. In case of default by a government in the payment of its bonds recourse may be had to the attachment of the revenues. This course has been followed in the case of some of the smaller republics of South and Central America. (See Debt, Public.)

Bonds of United States (see also Debt, Public; Loans):

Authority vested in Secretary of Treasury to issue, recommendations regarding, 5877.

Discussed. (See Debt, Public, discussed.)

Issuance of, discussed and recommendations regarding, 5877, 5985, 5993, 5999, 6074, 6076, 6077, 6175.

Purchase of, with Treasury surplus recommended, 3985.

Bonhomme Richard, The.—An old East India merchantman fitted up as a man-of-war by the French at L'Orient in 1779. It was one of five fitted out by the French at the suggestion of Benjamin Franklin, and christened in his honor *Bonhomme*

Richard, or Good-Man Richard. She was commanded by John Paul Jones, an American officer, and carried American colors. She was accompanied by two French vessels. They attempted to enter the harbor of Leith, Scotland, but storms prevented. Off Flamborough Head, Sept. 23, 1779, the fleet encountered a British merchant fleet convoyed by the *Serapis* and *Countess of Scarborough.* The larger war ship, the *Serapis,* though much superior in every respect to the *Bonhomme Richard,* was fiercely attacked by the latter. The conflict took place by moonlight, in the presence of thousands of spectators. Jones lashed the *Serapis's* bowsprit to the *Richard's* mizzenmast and raked her deck with musketry. Broadside answered broadside in one of the most stubbornly contested battles in the history of naval warfare. The engagement lasted three hours. Finally a bucketful of hand grenades thrown down the hatchway of the *Serapis* caused her commander to surrender. Jones transferred his crew to the conquered ship, and the *Bonhomme Richard* sank in a few hours.

For picture of the conflict, see opposite 366.

Boodle.—Money obtained by graft or bribery; especially used with reference to public officials.

Boom.—A term used in politics to signify a systematic candidacy for office; also a synonym for "prosperous."

Boomer State.—A nickname for Oklahoma (q. v.). (See also States.)

Boomerang.—A South African missile which, being hurled, returns to the hand of the thrower; hence a campaign hoax which has proved false in time to prevent harm to the intended victim, but which returns to the perpetrator and works injury to him.

Boonville (Mo.), Battle of.—When President Lincoln's call for troops, April 15, 1861, reached Governor Jackson, of Missouri, he refused to furnish the four regiments forming the quota of the state. Francis P. Blair, Jr., had, however, organized, under the military command of Nathaniel Lyon, five regiments, and these were mustered in immediately, Lyon being made brigadier-general. When another Missouri brigade had been formed, May 8, Lyon was put in command of the department. Meantime Governor Jackson ordered the state militia to camp at St. Louis. May 10 Gen. Lyon surrounded the camp, and on its surrender by Gen. Frost paroled the men, 700 in number. June 15 he occupied Jefferson City, the governor fleeing to Boonville. Lyon followed. On June 17 he dispersed the state troops collected there.

Bootleggers, misdeeds of, 7014.

Booty.—Goods captured from the enemy.

Border.—A boundary line; especially the neighborhood of the boundary line between countries, as the Mexican Border—formerly the Indian Border.

Border States.—A designation for the several slave states of Delaware, Maryland, Virginia, Kentucky and Missouri, lying next to the free states, and sometimes including Arkansas, North Carolina and Tennessee. Many people of these states were anxious, both during and before the Civil War, for an amicable adjustment of the slavery question. They originated the Peace Conference of 1861.

Borneo.—A large island in Malaysia. It is situated in the Indian Archipelago, bounded on the east by the Sea of Celebes and the Macassar Strait, on the south by the Sea of Java, and on the west and north by the China Sea.

History.—It was first visited by the Portuguese in 1518. Borneo has an area of about 213,000 square miles and a population of 1,250,000.

Physical Features.—Two chains of mountains traverse the island in a nearly parallel direction from northeast to southwest.

Natural Products.—Vegetation grows luxuriantly and choice woods and spices are exported. The mineral wealth is great, gold, antimony, salt, petroleum, tin, copper, iron, and coal exist, but are not, as yet, largely worked.

Borneo, treaty with, 2688.

Borough.—A political division incorporated for municipal purposes, now prevailing in some of the states, as Connecticut, Minnesota, New Jersey and Pennsylvania. (See Pocket-Borough.)

Bosphorus, The, restrictions on passage of Straits of the Dardanelles and, by ships of other nations, 4078.

Boss.—In politics a leader who dominates a political party in his district, ward, state or other political division.

Boston:

Execution of laws for return of fugitive slaves forcibly resisted in, 2637.

Proclamation regarding, 2548.

Reference to, 2673.

Fire in, referred to by President Grant, 4138.

Industrial exposition at, discussed, 4773.

Navy-yard at, referred to, 4676.

Title of United States to land occupied as, referred to, 4698.

Unlawful assemblages in, and proclamation against and authorization to employ force in suppressing, 2637, 2645.

Boston Case.—The case of a fugitive slave who escaped from his owner in Georgia and took passage on the *Boston,* a vessel bound for the coast of Maine. The governor of Georgia charged the captain of the ship with stealing the slave and demanded that the governor of Maine restore the fugitive. This was refused. The legislature of Georgia then called upon Congress to pass a law compelling the governor of Maine to comply with such demand. No action was taken by Congress.

Boston, Evacuation of.—During the winter of 1776 Washington, having received some ordnance captured at Ticonderoga and a supply of ammunition taken by privateers at sea, determined to attack Boston, then occupied by the British. In pursuance of this plan he occupied Nooks Hill (an eminence at the extremity of Dorchester Neck) and Dorchester Heights, which commanded Nooks Hill, and the town itself. On the night of March 4, 1776, the heights were covered with breastworks, and the British were forced to risk a general action to dislodge them or abandon the town. They chose the latter alternative, and on March 17 the town and harbor were evacuated by the British army and navy without firing a gun.

Boston Fire referred to, 4138.

Boston Massacre.—The British navigation acts were a source of great annoyance and loss to the American colonists, and their execution was resisted at all points. Great Britain attempted to coerce the people into a compliance with the laws by sending Gen. Gage with three regiments to Boston in 1768. The presence of the troops further aggravated the people of Boston. During 1769 and the early part of 1770 numerous quarrels occurred between the citizens of Boston and British soldiers charged with the enforcement of the laws. In February, 1770, a press gang from the British frigate *Rose* boarded a ship belonging to a Mr. Hooper, of Marblehead, whereupon a riot ensued. On the night of March 5 following a large crowd responded to the ringing of the fire bells and came into collision with the soldiers. The latter fired, killing three persons and wounding several others. The soldiers were tried and acquitted, but the news of the Boston massacre spread rapidly and did much to strengthen the spirit of revolution among the people.

Boston Port Act.—An act of Parliament introduced by Lord North and passed March 7, 1774, in retaliation for the destruction of cargoes of tea in Boston Harbor. It provided for the discontinuance of lauding and discharging, loading or shipp'ng of merchandise to or from the city of Boston or in Boston Harbor. Commerce was transferred to Salem and Marblehead, and Gen. Gage arrived in Boston, June 1, 1774, to enforce the law. The Boston people were indignant. Much sympathy was expressed for them throughout the Colonies. In many places people refused to buy British goods. Oct. 20, 1774, the American Association was formed, pledging the members to non-consumption and nonintercourse with Great Britain, Ireland and the British West Indies. The Association included 52 members of the Continental Congress.

Boston Tea Party.—In 1767 Great Britain imposed a duty on tea sold in the American Colonies. The East India Company prevailed upon the ministry in 1773 to amend the act so as to relieve the company from paying the duty, thereby forcing the consumers to pay it. The colonists were indignant at this transfer of the tax from the company to themselves, and adopted various methods to evade payment. Nov. 28, 1773, a ship arrived in Boston harbor carrying 114 chests of tea, and early in December two others arrived. On the evening of December 16th an enthusiastic meeting was held at Faneuil Hall, and at its close between 50 and 60 men disguised as Indians took possession of the three ships and threw overboard the cargoes of tea, amounting in all to 342 chests. Seventeen chests were also destroyed in New York harbor about the same time. These events resulted in the passage of the Boston Port Act (*q. v.*) and were an important part of the train of causes of the American Revolution.

Boston, The, mentioned, 6297, 6367.

Boston, U. S. S., mentioned, 6766, 6767, 6769, 6771, 6835, 6836.

Boundaries.—The colonial boundaries of the United States were indefinite and often the subject of much dispute. The grants of territory in America were made by European rulers, who were careless or ignorant of the geography of the country. The Wyoming dispute between Connecticut and Pennsylvania, and the Western Reserve of the former in Ohio, are in evidence of the interminable wrangles created by these royal grants. The boundaries of the United States were agreed upon in 1783 at the treaty of Versailles. Congress then took up the question of the border lines between states and provided an elaborate mode of procedure, modeled after the Grenville Act of Great Britain. Since 1789 such cases, as well as all other matters between states, have been under the jurisdiction of the Supreme Court. In 1783 the northeast boundary of the United States was defined as extending from the source of the St. Croix River due north to the watershed between the St. Lawrence and the Atlantic, thence along the watershed to the northwesternmost head of the Connecticut River. After long and irritating disputes over the line, the Webster-Ashburton treaty was negotiated in 1842, fixing the boundary between the United States and British possessions on the present lines. The territory bounded on the north by latitude 54° 40', on the east by the Rocky Mountains, on the south by latitude 42°, and on the west by the Pacific Ocean, has been variously claimed by Russia, Spain, Great Britain and the United States. By treaty with Russia Jan. 11, 1825, the United States were to make no settlements north of 54° 40' and Russia none south of that line. By the treaty which ceded Florida in 1819 Spain relinquished all claims to anything north of latitude 42°. Though Great Britain had little claim to the territory, joint occupation was agreed upon by the treaty of Oct. 20, 1818, and this becoming unsatisfactory Great Britain was induced in 1846 to accept latitude 49° as the boundary between her possessions and the United States from the Rocky Mountains to the channel between Vancouver Island and the mainland. (For boundary disputes after 1846, see articles on Alaska, Gadsden Purchase and Mexican War.)

Botanic Gardens.—West of the Capital in Washington is a broad stretch of land known as the Mall, extending to the Potomac River. The part of the Mall nearest the Capitol is called the Botanic Gardens. These contain great conservatories stored with rare plants. There is also a beautiful fountain, designed by Bartholdi. Further west along the Mall are the grounds of the National Museum, the Smithsonian Institution and the Department of Agriculture, under whose charge are the great propagating gardens. The Mall further extends to the Washington Monument.

Bounty.—A reward offered by a government to its citizens for enlistment in the Army or Navy; also for industrial or other achievements, as for building and operating ships. (See Sugar Bounty.)

Bounty-Jumper.—A soldier who deserts after enlisting for bounty.

Bounty Lands. (See Lands, Bounty.)

Bourbons.—The house of Bourbon is the family of kings that ruled France for over two hundred years, from 1589 to the time of the French revolution, 1791. One of their characteristics was an obstinate refusal to keep pace with events. Experience taught them nothing. This trait in their character has caused their name to be applied (in American political parlance) to any statesman or politician that clings to dead issues and refuses to accommodate himself to changes.

Boxer Rebellion. (See Boxers.)

Boxers.—The name popularly given to the Chinese anti-foreign secret society, Ih-hwo-Ch'uan, "Volunteer United Fists," who were largely responsible for the disturbances in that country in 1900. Excited by the progress of European civilization and Christianity in China they caused anti-foreign riots in various parts of the empire and massacred many missionaries, native converts and European merchants. On June 20th, they murdered the German minister, Baron Ketteler, and being joined by the Imperial troops besieged the foreigners and foreign ministers in the British legation in Peking until Aug. 13, when the siege was raised by a relief expedition from the allied fleets—Japanese, Russian, British, American and French. On May 29, 1901, China agreed to pay to the injured powers, Austria-Hungary, Belgium, France, Germany, Great Britain, Italy, Japan, The Netherlands, Russia and the United States, an indemnity amounting to 450,000,000 taels ($333,000,-000) for injuries inflicted by the Boxers. This indemnity is to constitute a gold debt repayable in thirty-nine annual installments, due on Jan. 1 of each year up to 1941, interest at 4 per cent. to be payable half-yearly. The securities for the debt are the Imperial Maritime Customs, otherwise unappropriated, increased to 5 per cent., *ad valorem*, the Navy Customs, and the Salt Tax otherwise unappropriated.

See illustration opposite 6391.

Boy Scouts of America.—The Boy Scout movement can be traced back to widely separated sources where constructive ideas came to boy workers and were tested with varying degrees of success. In America there were a number of originators of methods, plans and principles that have proved effective. In Great Britain, Lieut.-Gen. Sir Robert S. S. Baden-Powell became active in organization work based largely on the ideas and methods of American workers. He did this so successfully that the enrollment of British Boy Scouts soon grew into the hundred thousands, with the emphasis, not on the military note, but on peace virtues and learning practical trades. Then the movement spread to Germany, France, Italy, Australia and New Zealand, to Canada and the United States; to South American republics; in short, almost the world over, since it is already established in twenty-seven countries. Everywhere it has shown adaptation to new fields and nationalities.

In Germany the boys have engaged in the work with such enthusiasm and in such numbers that the Prussian and Bavarian authorities are giving the movement financial aid. But it has been left to the United States to show what the system of scouting can accomplish, when it returns to the lands in which the larger number of its working ideas and principles originated. While the number of the Boy Scouts enrolled throughout the world is estimated as not less than two million, one-sixth of the whole number are in the United States. The emphasis and ideals of the movement belong here also to the highest plans—that of efficient citizenship, service and character-building.

"The Boy Scouts of America," the name under which the movement in the United States was incorporated, February 8, 1910, has as its Honorary President, the Hon. Woodrow Wilson, President of the United States, and Hon. William H. Taft and Col. Theodore Roosevelt as its Honorary Vice-

Presidents. Associated with these in approval and promotion of the movement are eminent citizens from all walks of public life, who are members of the National Council and of the local councils in the cities and towns of the whole country, and a host of others who earnestly co-operate in the work.

A group of men, representing the various religious and civic organizations of the community that are engaged in boys' work, are brought together as a local council for the promotion of Scout work. This local council receives a charter from the national organization, giving them full authority to deal with all questions relating to scouting in that district and to pass upon all Scout Masters' applications. In many cases this council engages a boys' work director, to be known as the Scout Commissioner, to take charge of the work in that community. He is responsible to the local council for the direction and promotion of the work. He is the leader of the Scout Masters, and as such, gives such instructions and help as may be necessary, arranges inter-troop meets, games, camps, and in general, makes uniform the plan of work conducted in that community. The Scouts are organized in patrols and troops. Eight boys constitute a patrol, one of whom is chosen as the Patrol Leader. Three patrols make up a troop. The Scout Master is the adult leader of the troop. Already there are about 700 local councils in as many cities throughout the United States and under the direction of each there are from five to one hundred and fifty Scout Masters in charge of troops.

The Scout programme is proving practicable as a civic enterprise. There are many cities so thoroughly organized that every phase of boy life in the community is being reached by Scout activities. The movement is adapting itself not only to the wealthy classes, but to the boys of the slums, to the newsboys and to foreign boys alike.

Scouting means outdoor life and so health, strength, happiness and practical education. By combining wholesome, attractive, outdoor activities with the influence of the Scout oath and law, the movement develops character and worth-while ability.

Scoutcraft includes instruction in first aid, life saving, tracking, signalling, cycling, nature study, seamanship, campcraft, woodcraft, chivalry and all the handicrafts.

The national organization is largely maintained by public subscriptions. Sustaining and Contributing Memberships are issued to men and women throughout the country who are financially assisting in the development and promotion of this organization among boys. National Headquarters, No. 200 Fifth Avenue, New York City. Officers of the National Council: Honorary President, Woodrow Wilson; Honorary Vice-Presidents, William H. Taft, Col. Theodore Roosevelt; President, C. H. Livingston, Washington, D. C.; Vice-Presidents, B. L. Dulaney, Bristol, Tenn.; Milton A. McRae, Detroit, Mich.; David Starr Jordan, Stanford University, Cal.; F. L. Seely, Asheville, N. C.; A. Stamford White, Chicago, Ill.; Chief Scout, Ernest Thompson Seton, Greenwich, Ct.; National Scout Commissioner, Daniel Carter Beard, Flushing, N. Y.; Treasurer, George D. Pratt, Brooklyn, N. Y.

Boycott.—In November, 1880, during the Land League agitation in Ireland, Capt. James Boycott, agent of Lough Mask farm, an estate of Lord Erne, having evicted many of the tenants of the estate for refusing to pay rent, was besieged on his premises. The neighboring tradesmen refused to supply him with their goods at any price. His servants left and no others could be induced to take their places. To gather his crops it became necessary to bring in immigrant laborers and to protect them while at work by the presence of armed constabulary. This method of coercion became popular among the land leaguers and was soon put into operation against shopkeepers as well as landlords.

This policy of non-intercourse and efforts to commercially isolate business opponents was introduced into the United States by the Knights of Labor and Trade Unions about 1885. In 1886 two women bakers of New York were boycotted by the labor unions and their friends. Persons without grievances against the women were induced to withdraw their patronage. The business of the women was seriously injured, until they were relieved by receiving large orders for bread for charity hospitals. During the same year one man was convicted of attempting to extort money under a threat of boycotting. One man was boycotted for giving testimony against conspirators.

Boycotting has been defined by an American judge as a "combination of many to cause a loss to one person by coercing others against their will to withdraw from him their beneficial business intercourse, through threats that unless those others do so, the many will cause a similar loss to them." A boycott, even when not accompanied by violence or intimidation, has been pronounced unlawful by many courts. When accompanied by violence it is a criminal offence at common law.

President Taft, when judge of an Ohio court, decided that while the employees of any person or company had a right to refuse to work at any time, they had no right to prevent the work being done by others, the attempt at the latter action being characterized as a secondary boycott.

Decisions of the United States Courts in boycotting cases have been contradictory. In the case of the Danbury (Conn.) hatters, the employers were adjudged injured to the extent of $80,000, and authorized to bring suit against the boycotting organization for thrice the amount. In Montana, the Supreme Court held that the boycotted company did not have a property right in the trade of any particular person: hence, any one person may rightfully withdraw his patronage. The judge disagrees with the doctrine that an act perfectly lawful when done by one person becomes criminal when done by two or more acting in concert, and rules that if the boycotters violated no law in withdrawing their patronage they could not be enjoined from continuing the boycott in force, so long as the means employed to make it effective were not illegal. (See Lindsay & Co. *vs.* Montana Federation of Labor *et al.;* Loewe *vs.* Lawlor *et al.*) Other indictments against members of labor unions charged with boycotting have been prosecuted in the United States Supreme Court and the results will be found under Anti-Trust Laws; Bucks Stove Case, etc.

The states having laws prohibiting boycotting in terms are Alabama, Colorado, Illinois, Indiana and Texas. The states having laws prohibiting blacklisting in terms are Alabama, Arkansas, Colorado, Connecticut, Florida, Illinois, Indiana, Iowa, Kansas, Minnesota, Mississippi (applies to telegraph operators only), Missouri, Montana, Nevada, North Carolina, North Dakota, Oklahoma, Oregon, Texas, Utah, Virginia, Washington and Wisconsin. A number of states have enacted laws concerning intimidation, conspiracy against workingmen and interference with employment, viz.: Alabama, Connecticut, Delaware, Florida, Georgia, Idaho (applies to mine employees only), Illinois, Kansas, Kentucky, Louisiana, Maine, Massachusetts, Michigan, Minnesota, Mississippi, Missouri, New Hampshire, New Jersey, New York, North Dakota, Oklahoma, Oregon, Pennsylvania, Porto Rico, Rhode Island, South Dakota, Texas, Utah, Vermont, Washington, West Virginia and Wisconsin. In the following states it is unlawful for an employer to exact any agreement, either written or verbal, from an employee not to join or become a member of a labor organization, as a condition of employment: California, Colorado, Connecticut, Idaho, Indiana, Kansas, Massachusetts, Minnesota, Mississippi (applies to telegraph operators only), Nevada, New Jersey, Ohio, Oklahoma, Oregon, Pennsylvania, Porto Rico, South Carolina and Wisconsin. (See Loewe *vs.* Lawlor et al.)

Boycott (secondary) denounced as at variance with American instinct, 7378.

Brakes and Couplers, legislation for increased safety in use of, recommended, 5486, 5561, 5642, 5766.

Brandy Station, or Fleetwood (Va.), Battle of.—After the battle of Chancellorsville Hooker's army remained inactive on the north side of the Rappahannock for about a month. June 9, 1863, two divisions of cavalry, supported by two brigades of infantry, were sent across the river to reconnoiter the Confederate position. Gen. Pleasonton was in charge of the expedition and the cavalry was commanded by Generals Buford and Gregg. They were driven back after the loss of 500 men in one of the most important cavalry fights of the Civil War. The only practical result of the expedition was the discovery that Lee's infantry was moving north by way of Culpeper. Here, also, on Aug. 1, Gen. Buford with his division of cavalry met the Confederate General Stuart and compelled him to retreat until re-enforced, when Buford in turn retreated. Between Oct. 10 and 16 desultory fighting with both cavalry and infantry occurred in the vicinity of Brandy Station.

Brandywine (Pa.), Battle of.—In the latter part of May, 1777, Washington left Morristown, N. J., where he had been in winter quarters, and took up a strong position behind the Raritan. Howe left his quarters at New Brunswick and embarked his troops for Philadelphia, landing about 18,000 men at Elk Ferry, fifty miles from the city, Aug. 25. Washington, having been joined by Lafayette, DeKalb, and Pulaski, drew near to defend the city. The nominal strength of the American army was 14,000 men, though only 11,000 were considered effective. Howe's advance was slow, and it was not until Sept. 11 that he encountered the Americans at Chadds Ford, on Brandywine Creek, about thirty miles southwest of Philadelphia. In the battle which occurred that day the British gained a clear victory through a successful flank movement, executed by Cornwallis. The American loss was about 1,000 killed, wounded, and missing, while that of the British was somewhat more.

Brazil.—The most extensive State of South America. It was discovered in 1500 by Pedro Alvarez Cabral, Portuguese navigator. It is bounded on the north by the Atlantic Ocean, Guiana, and Venezuela; on the west by Ecuador, Peru, Bolivia, Paraguay, and Argentina; on the south by Uruguay; and on the east by the Atlantic Ocean; and extends between lat. 4° 22' N.

and 33° 45′ S. and long. 34° 40′ and 73° 15′ W., being 2,600 miles from north to south, and 2,500 from west to east; with a coast-line on the Atlantic of 3,700 miles.

History.—It was claimed and colonized by the Portuguese both by right of discovery and the dictum of the Pope. It became the residence of the exiled Portuguese royal family during the Napoleonic period. Its independence was proclaimed in 1822. An empire was formed and Dom Pedro, son of the Portuguese King, became the first emperor. He resigned in 1831 in favor of his son Pedro II. In November, 1889, the empire was overthrown and a republic organized under President Fonseca. He was succeeded two years later by Peixoto, and he by De Moraes. Wenceslau Braz is now president.

The bloodless revolution of 1889 transformed the provinces of the Empire into States of a Federal Union. The States have their own laws and considerable fiscal autonomy, being administered at their own expense, and controlling the outward (but not inward) customs. National defence, police, finance, currency, and national or inter-State justice are reserved to the central government. Each State has an elected President or Governor and a bicameral legislature, raises its necessary revenue, floats loans, and controls its indebtedness. The External Debts of the various States of the Union amounted in the aggregate to $220,-000,000 at the end of 1910; their Internal Debts to over $65,000,000; and their Floating Debts to over $40,000,000. The territory of Acré (Aquiry) was purchased for $10,000,000 from Bolivia by treaty of Nov. 17, 1903, thus terminating a dispute with that republic through the incursion in north-western Bolivia of large numbers of Brazilian settlers. Acré has petitioned to be received into the States of the Union.

Physical Features.—The northern States of Amazones and Pará and the central State of Matto Grosso (which together constitute more than one-half of Brazil) are mainly wide, low-lying, forest-clad plains. The eastern and southern States are traversed by successive mountain ranges interspersed with fertile valleys. The principal ranges are the Serra do Maro, the Serra do Mantequeira (Itatiaiassu, 9,000 feet), and the Serra do Espinhaço (Itacolumi, 6,000 feet), in the southeast of Minas Geraes; the Serra do Paranan, the Serra dos Aymores and the Serra da Gurgueia, Branca, and Araripe. Brazil is unequalled for the number and extent of its rivers. The Amazon, the largest river in the world, has tributaries which are themselves great rivers, and flows from the Peruvian Andes to the Atlantic, with a total length of some 4,000 miles. Its northern tributaries are the Rio Branco, Rio Negro and Japura; its southern tributaries are the Jurua, Purus, Madeira and Tapajos, while the Xingu meets it within 100 miles of its outflow into the Atlantic.

January 6, 1914, a Brazilian commission, headed by Col. Theodore Roosevelt, ex-President of the United States, and Col. Rondon, started to explore the Duvida River, which turned out to be a tributary of the Madeira, the lower part of which was known to rubber men but not to cartographers, as the Castanha. Embarking February 27, after traveling 542 miles from San Luis de Caceres, the party descended the Duvida, or River of Doubt, as its headwaters had been called by an expedition surveying for a telegraph line in 1909. Descending the river 469 miles directly north from 12° 1′ S. lat. and 60° 18′ W. long, the Aripauna was reached April 26, 1914, in lat. 7° 34′. Here the rapids ended and the Aripauna discharged into the Madeira at 5° 30′ S. lat.

and 60° 32′ W. long. In honor of the distinguished American the indefinite Castanha, including its newly explored upper half, was named the Rio Theodoro, and thereby put upon the map; it had never appeared previously on any map.

The Tocantins and Araguaya flow northwards from the plateau of Matto Grosso and the mountains of Goyaz to the Gulf of Pará. The Paranahyba flows from the encircling mountains of Piauhý into the Atlantic. The Sao Francisco rises in the south of Minas Geraes and traverses Bahia on its way to the Eastern coast, between Alagoas and Bolivia on its way through Paraguay to its confluence with the *Paraná*, which rises in the mountains of that name and divides the Brazilian State from the Paraguay. The Paraguay and Paraná, from their confluence, become the principal river of Argentina and flow into the Atlantic at the estuary of La Plata.

AREA AND POPULATION

States and Capitals	Area in English Sq. Miles	Estimated Population 1910
Federal District..........	470	900,000
Acré (Nova York)........	73,720	70,000
Alagoas (Maceio).........	10,230	800,000
Amazonas (Manáos)......	714,000	380,000
Bahia (Sao Salvador).....	216,000	2,300,000
Ceara (Fortaleza).........	61,750	800,000
Espirito Santo (Victoria)..	17,000	300,000
Goyaz (Goyaz)..........	266,000	290,000
Maranhão (Sao Luiz).....	131,000	550,000
Matto Grosso (Cuyabá)...	580,000	140,000
Minas Geraes (Bello Horizonte)................	231,000	4,000,000
Pará (Belem)...........	482,500	600,000
Parahyba (Parahyba)....	21,600	500,000
Paraná (Curityba).......	67,500	420,000
Pernambuco (Recif).....	38,600	1,500,000
Piauhý (Therezina)......	92,600	400,000
Rio de Janeiro (Nictheroy).	16,800	1,000,000
Rio Grande de Norte(Natal)	20,000	280,000
Rio Grande do Sul (Porto Alegre)...............	109,000	1,500,000
Santa Catharina (Florianopolis)...............	43,000	350,000
Sao Paulo (Sao Paulo)....	96,500	4,000,000
Sergipe (Aracaju)........	9,600	500,000
Total...............	3,298,870	21,580,000

Of the total number about 1,000,000 are "wild" Indians.

Ethnography.—There are five distinct elements in the population: the Portuguese settlers, the aboriginal Indians, imported African negro slaves, mixed descendants of these three races, and European immigrants of all nationalities, principally Italians, Portuguese and Spanish. The descendants of the Portuguese settlers are the true Brazilians, the aboriginal Indians are now mainly tribes in the forests and plains of the interior. The slaves were freed between 1871 and 1888, their importation having ceased in 1855. The modern trend of Teutonic immigration is towards the southern states, particularly Rio Grande do Sul. The official language of Brazil is Portuguese.

Government.—Brazil was colonized by Portugal in the early part of the sixteenth century, and in 1822 became an independent empire under Dom Pedro, son of the exiled King João VI. of Portugal. On Nov. 15, 1889, Dom Pedro II. second of the line, was dethroned and a republic was proclaimed. The constitution rests on the fundamental law of Feb. 24, 1891, which established a federal republic under the name of Estados Unidos do Brazil.

The President and Vice-President are elected for four years by the direct votes of all male Brazilians over twenty-one years who can read and write, and are ineligible for the succeeding terms. They are aided, as executives, by a Council of Ministers, who do not attend Congress.

The National Congress consists of a Senate and Chamber of Deputies, which meet annually, on May 3, for four months. The Senate is composed of sixty-three members elected for nine, six and three years in accordance with their place in the ballot, those for lesser periods being renewed in due course. The Chamber of Deputies consists of 212 members elected for three years. The electors for both houses are all male Brazilians over twenty-one years who can read and write.

There is a Supreme Federal Tribunal and a Federal Court of Appeal at the capital, and judges sit in each State for Federal causes. Except in the federal district justice is administered by State Courts for State causes, from the lowest to the highest courts.

Army.—By a law of Jan. 1, 1908, military service is obligatory on all male Brazilians from twenty-one to forty-four years. The Peace Effective is 2,200 officers and 28,000 others. (See Armies of the World.)

Navy.—The Navy is manned by about 750 officers and 9,000 seamen, etc. (See Navies of the World.)

Primary education is secular and free, but is not as yet compulsory; it is maintained and controlled by the governments of the various States. Public instruction is progressing and reading and writing are the qualifications for the franchise for males at twenty-one. About 600,000 children attended the primary schools in 1911.

Production and Industry.—Agriculture is encouraged by all the State governments, and is the principal industry, the produce being varied and abundant. In the extreme south towards the interior European fruits and grain are reared, while other parts are found extremely favorable for the raising of coffee, sugar, cotton, cocoa, india-rubber, tobacco, and tropical products, many of which are indigenous. Maize, beans, cassava-root, and nuts are very generally cultivated. Three-fourths of the world's supply of coffee comes from Brazil, being grown chiefly in Rio de Janeiro, Minas Geraes, Sao Paulo, and Espirito Santo, and in a smaller degree in the north. Cotton is largely cultivated for export, and is being raised for home manufactures. Sugarcane is grown in large and increasing quantities in the northern provinces, Pernambuco being the centre of the sugar-producing zone. India-rubber comes from the more northern provinces, especially the valley of the Amazon, and is shipped from Pará and Manãos. Tobacco and cocoa are grown largely, especially in Bahia. The Live Stock included 18,000,000 cattle in 1910, cattle and stock raising being an important industry.

Brazilian forests are immense, and abound in the greatest variety of useful and beautiful woods adapted for dyeing, cabinet work, or shipbuilding; among them are mahogany, logwood, rosewood, brazilwood, cinchona, etc.

The mineral products are considerable, and comprise gold, silver, iron, quicksilver, copper, and coal. In the Province of Minas Geraes there are vast iron ore deposits, which are expected to be worked in the near future; there are believed to be hundreds of millions of tons of ore, much of it containing 69 per cent. of iron. Among non-metallic minerals are the world-famous Brazilian diamonds, and emeralds, rubies, topazes, beryls, garnets, etc. The black diamonds (*carbonatos*) are very highly prized.

Manufactures.—In 1908 there were 1,541 industrial establishments employing 46,000 hands, and representing an invested capital of over £14,000,000. The establishments are protected by enormous import duties on manufactured articles. Cottons, woollens, and silks are produced, but the output is considerably below the demand. Flour mills, for imported Argentine wheat, and brewing are important industries.

The imports consist of every description of manufactured article, in spite of a high protective tariff. There is a heavy duty on coffee exports in excess of 9,000,000 bags, but the annual despatches far exceed that number, being nearly 17,000,000 bags in 1909.

Transportation and Communication.—Each State has its railway system, but the central government is developing intercommunication and opening up new routes. On Dec. 31, 1910, there were 13,611 English miles open and working, with 1,683 miles under construction, the Federal Government owning 6,300 miles of the whole. There were 3,250 post offices in 1910. There were 2,125 telegraph offices (and 12 wireless installations) with 35,873 miles of line and 74,327 miles of wire, in 1910.

The sea-going mercantile marine of Brazil in 1911 included 313 steamers (223,358 tons) and 70 sailing vessels (18,395 tons), a total of 383 vessels (over 100 tons each) of 251,753 tons. Coasting and river traffic is confined to Brazilian vessels. In 1909, 5,016 foreign vessels entered at Brazilian ports, their total tonnage being 12,247,013. The principal harbors are Rio de Janeiro, Sao Paulo, Bahia, Pernambuco, Pará, Maranhão, Rio Grande and Santos.

Towns.—Rio de Janeiro, the capital, is the second largest city in South America and possesses one of the finest harbors in the world. Population, 1912, estimated at 1,000,000. Other towns and their population are:

Sao Paulo	380,000	Santos	40,000
Bahia	250,000	Maceio	40,000
Pará (Belem)	200,000	Cuyabá	36,000
Pernambuco	160,000	Nictheroy	35,000
Porto Alegre	90,000	Florianapolis	33,000
Manaes	70,000	Parahyba	30,000
Ceará	50,000	Sao Luiz	30,000
Therezina	50,000	Aracaju	22,000
Curityba	50,000	Natal	17,000

Money.—The Currency is nominally metallic, but almost entirely paper, in denominations of milreis. The gold milreis is equal to $0.546 United States money and government paper is convertible at $0.324 to the milreis.

The national debt in 1912 was stated at $663,667,000. The revenue in 1913 was $192,729,000, and expenditures were $203,860,000. Interest, etc., amounted to $29,637,000.

Trade with the United States.—The value of merchandise imported into Brazil from the United States for the year 1913 was $42,638,467, and goods to the value of $120,155,855 were sent thither, a balance of $77,517,388 in favor of Brazil.

Brazil:

Blockade by naval forces of, referred to, 970.

Boundary question with Argentine Republic submitted to President of United States, 5867, 6058.

With Bolivia, 6426.

Chargé d'affaires received from, 820.

Correspondence with, referred to, 2430.

Claims of United States against, 929, 951, 962, 1009, 1115, 1245, 1594, 1933, 2051, 3050, 3899, 4220.

Convention for satisfaction of, negotiated, 2553, 2562, 2568,2618.

Payment of, 1009, 1245, 2116, 2618.

Commercial relations with, 3049, 4078, 4629, 5570, 5663.

Commission of United States sent to, 952.

Convention with, referred to, 2681.

Cotton culture in, 4078.

Disturbances in, 1158, 2051.

Duties on American goods reduced, 968.

Imprisonment of American citizens in, 970, 2779.

Mail steamship service between United States and, 3565, 3586.

Minister of, to United States received, 2553, 4718.

Minister of United States in, official functions of, terminated, 951.

Phosphates discovered in coast of, 4795.

Political disturbances in, discussed, 5617.

Relations with, 2399, 6364.

Revolution in—

　Action of American commander in saluting revolted Brazilian admiral disavowed, 5867.

　Policy of United States regarding, 5472, 5867, 5956.

　Questions with Portugal respecting escape of insurgent Admiral Da Gama, 5956.

　Republican form of government established and recognition of, by United States, 5543.

Slavery in, 4100.

　Abolished, 5369.

Tariff laws of, evidence of modifications of, proclaimed, 5576.

　Notice of intention of Brazil to terminate, discussed, 5956.

　Referred to, 5615, 5747.

Trade-marks, treaty with, regarding, 4460.

Treaty with, 996.

　Obligations of, to cease, 1822.

　Reference to, 1009.

Vessels of—

　Discriminating duties on, suspended by proclamation, 2372.

　United States seized or interfered with by, 962, 2779. (See also *Caroline*, The.)

War with—

　Buenos Ayres—

　　Peace concluded, 977.

　　Questions between United States and Brazil growing out of, 929, 951.

　Paraguay, 4078.

　　Good offices of United States tendered, 3776, 3883.

Brazil Steamship Co. referred to, 5634.

Brazil, Treaties with.—Diplomatic negotiations with Brazil are embodied in five treaties: Treaty of 1828 on amity, commerce, and navigation; Treaties of 1849 on claims in general and a protocol submitting to arbitration the claim of George C. Benner *et al.*, signed in 1902. Treaty of 1878 on trade-marks (see Trade-marks, Treaties on); and extradition convention and protocol of 1898 (see Extradition, Treaties of).

The treaty of 1828 accords reciprocal freedom of commerce and navigation upon equal terms and conditions to those by which they are enjoined by any and every other nation; the citizens of the respective countries are privileged to conduct commercial and professional transactions in the country of the other nation upon the same terms and under like conditions as citizens and subjects. Coastwise trade is, however, excluded from this agreement. Freedom of, and equality in, carrying trade of export or reexport or import of goods is permitted without payment of higher or other duties, imposts, taxes, or fees, than those to which citizens and subjects are liable. If subjected to embargo or detention for military purposes, proper indemnification is to be paid in all cases. Refuge, asylum, and protection is accorded to vessels in all ports, rivers, or dominions of the other country. All reasonable assistance is to be rendered to vessels sustaining shipwreck or damage in the waters of the other country; and protection from pirates, with restitution of property, if possible. Freedom of sale, disposition, and succession, in the case of personal goods is granted to individual citizens and subjects within the other country. Protection of the person and of the property of citizens and subjects of each other is to be the special care of each contracting party. Entire freedom of conscience is accorded to individuals, together with protection of the dead.

In event of war of one of the parties with a third it is agreed that full recognition of the principle that the flag covers property be accorded when the property belongs to a nation which recognizes this principle, but to none other. But where the neutral flag shall cover the property of an enemy of one of the parties, such property shall be confiscated unless put on board before the declaration of war; an excuse of ignorance of declaration of war shall not be valid after a period of four months shall have elapsed. Liberty of commerce and navigation shall not extend to arms and instruments or materials designed for making war by sea or land, and vessels carrying such contraband goods shall be detained for the confiscation of such contraband. At such times the examination of vessels shall be conducted by all means calculated to minimize vexation or abuse. When one of the parties shall be at war with a third State, no citizen or subject of the other contracting party shall accept letters of marque or reprisal to act against the other contracting party under pain of punishment for piracy. In the event of war between the United States and Brazil, a period of six months shall be granted to residents to close up their affairs and transport their effects; in the case of residents in the interior of the country this period shall be increased to one year from the time of declaration of war. Sequestration and confiscation of public and private debts by reason of war is forbidden. The favors, immunities, and exemptions to consular officers shall be those of the most favored nation. These officials shall be exempt from all public service, taxes, imposts, and duties, except such as they shall pay on account of commerce or property, and these shall be the same as those paid by citizens of the country. The consular papers, records, and archives, shall at all times and under all circumstances be inviolably respected, and may not be seized or interfered with by any magistrate. Consuls shall have full authority to arrest and detain for a period not to exceed two months all deserters from public and private vessels of their country.

This treaty was drawn to endure for a period of twelve years, with a renewal from year to year, with one year's notice of intention to terminate. Infringement of its conditions by individuals renders the individual and not the State liable for such infringement and the State pledges itself to surrender the offender. The State shall not countenance any reprisal for infringement of the conditions nor declare war until a statement of the injuries, with competent proof, shall have been forwarded to the offending State and a reasonable time allowed for reparation.

Brazil also became a party to the convention between the United States and the several republics of South and Central America for the arbitration of pecuniary claims and the protection of inventions, etc., which was signed in Buenos Aires in 1910 and proclaimed in Washington, July 29, 1914. (See South and Central America, Treaties with.)

Brazito (Mexico), Battle of.—In June, 1846, the Army of the West was organized at Fort Leavenworth, on the Missouri. It consisted of 1,658 men and sixteen pieces of ordnance, under command of Col. Phil. Kearny, of the First United States Dragoons. He was ordered to proceed to New Mexico and take possession of Santa Fé and proclaim the entire Territory to be under the jurisdiction of the United States. His orders were later amended to include California. In fifty days the army marched 883 miles, and on Aug. 18, 1846, the American flag was floating over the citadel at Santa Fé. Not a blow had been struck. After establishing a civil government at Santa Fé, Kearny started for California Sept. 25, with 300 United States dragoons and a small corps of topographical engineers. The main supply train and 200 dragoons were left at Albuquerque. Col. Doniphan, with his own regiment and Weightman's battery of artillery, was ordered to proceed southward and join Wool in Chihuahua. The whole force under Doniphan consisted of 856 effective men. Dec. 25, 1846, the advance of 500 men halted at the Brazito, an arm of the Rio Grande. Here they were surprised by Gen. Ponce de Leon with 1,220 Mexicans, of whom 537 were well mounted and equipped. The assailants were utterly routed, with heavy loss, including Gen. Ponce de Leon, while the American loss was only seven men wounded.

Brazos River, explorations of, referred to, 2897.

Brazos Santiago, Tex., commerce of district of, referred to, 2610.

Bread. (See Baking Business.)

Bread-Line.—The line of men who assemble, usually around midnight, to receive bread at a mission or other alms-giving institution. (See Soup-Houses.)

Bread Riots.—During a period of general financial depression in 1837 the poor of New York held frequent riotous meetings, which culminated in violent assaults upon flour warehouses. Employment was meager, rents were exorbitant, and flour was $12 per barrel. In many instances stores were broken open and pillaged by the mobs. The rioters were suppressed by the militia.

Breadstuffs, importation of, into foreign countries, and rates of duty on, 5503.

Breaking Diplomatic Negotiations. (See Diplomatic Negotiations, Breaking of.)

Breakwaters, expenditures on, 1126.

Bremen: Submarine. (See Deutschland.)

Bremen:
Ministers of, received, 949.
Postal arrangements with, 2412.
Treaty with, 988, 991, 2686.
Vessels of—
Application for rights, 621.
Discriminating duties on, suspended, 606.

Brevet.—The promotion, without advance in pay, of a military officer.

Brevet Commissions. (See Army.)

Breweries. (See Liquors—Malt, Vinous and Distilled.)

Bribery.—The giving or receiving of money or other valuable consideration in return for unethical conduct.

Bribery:
Proposal to class campaign contributions by corporations as, 6990.
Proposed extraditional offense, 6791.
Severer laws advocated, 6917.

Bridges:
Construction of, over navigable waters, 4303.
Pictures of, 2185.
Referred to, 1171, 1257.

Bridgewater, The, correspondence regarding case of, transmitted, 5396.

Brier Creek (Ga.), Battle of.—March 3, 1779, Gen. Lincoln sent a detachment of his army, consisting of 1,500 North Carolina militia and some Georgia Continentals under Gen. Ashe, to the junction of Brier Creek with the Savannah River. In this position they were attacked by Lieut.-Col. Prevost with some 2,000 men and completely routed. Gen. Elbert, Col. McIntosh, several other officers, and nearly 200 men were captured. Nearly an equal number are supposed to have been killed in action or met death in their flight through the swamps. The remainder, with the exception of 400 or 500, retired to their homes. The British loss was only sixteen killed and wounded.

Brigade.—A body of soldiers made up of a number of smaller units. In cavalry there are usually from eight to ten squadrons to a brigade; in infantry a brigade consists of from four to six battalions or regiments.

Brigadier.—The commander of a brigade; a brigadier-general.

Brigand. (See Bandit.)

Briscoe vs. Bank of Commonwealth of Kentucky.—A suit brought by the Bank of the Commonwealth of Kentucky against Briscoe et al. as holders of a promissory note for which the notes of the bank had been given as a loan to the drawers of the note. The defendants claimed that their note was void, since those given in return by the bank were nothing else than bills of credit and issued contrary to the clause of the Constitution which forbids States issuing such bills. The circuit court and the court of appeals of Kentucky gave judgment for the bank on the ground that the act incorporating the Bank of the Commonwealth of Kentucky was constitutional and that the notes issued were not bills of credit within the meaning of the National Constitution. The Supreme Court in 1837 decided the case in favor of the bank, the notes not being deemed bills of credit.

Bristow Station (Va.), Battle of.— Hooker's and Heintzelman's divisions of McClellan's army had been sent to reinforce Pope, who had taken a position west of the Rappahannock. Stonewall Jackson made a forced march from the Shenandoah Valley by way of Thoroughfare Gap and passing by the battlefield of Bull Run, Aug. 26, 1862, destroyed Pope's stores at Bristow Station, and then advanced to Manassas. Hooker's division the next day came upon the Confederates under Ewell at Bristow Station and drove them from the field. Each side suffered a loss of about 300 men.

British America:

Commercial relations with, 1130, 1131.

Consul-general of United States to, arrest of, referred to, 3399.

Insurrection in Red River settlement referred to, 4001.

Military expedition against, proclamation regarding, 3631.

Discussed, 3655.

Reciprocity relations with, referred to, 3665.

Treaty regarding, not favorably considered by United States, 3988.

British Colonies:

Commercial relations with, 652, 5688, 5748, 6332.

Tariff laws of, evidence of modifications of, proclaimed, 5688, 6381, Discussed, 5747.

British Columbia:

Agent sent to, referred to, 3068, 3072.

Boundary line with Alaska. (See Alaska.)

British Debts. (See Debts, British.)

British Empire.—The British Empire occupies about one-quarter of the known surface of the globe, and its population exceeds one-quarter of the estimated number of the human race. The total area is distributed almost equally over the Northern and Southern Hemispheres, but more than two-thirds lie in the Eastern and less than one-third in the Western Hemisphere. The greatest area of the empire lies in America, but the largest subject population lives in Asia.

Ethnography.—By far the greater portion of the Empire lies within the temperate zones, the tropical areas being Southern India, West and Central Africa, parts of the West Indies, British Guiana and Honduras, Northern Australia, Borneo, and the various settlements in the Malay Peninsula. The estimated white population of

AREA AND POPULATION

Continental Divisions and Capitals	Area in English Sq. Miles	Population in 1911
Europe—		
United Kingdom (London).	121,090	45,500,000
Isle of Man (Douglas).....	230	50,500
Channel Islands..........	70	97,000
Malta and Gozo (Valletta).	120	211,500
Gibraltar (Gibraltar)......	2	20,000
Total, Europe........	121,512	45,878,500
Asia—		
Indian Empire (Delhi).	1,900,000	315,000,000
Ceylon (Colombo)........	25,500	4,100,000
Straits Settlements (Singapore).................	1,660	700,000
Federated Malay States (Kuala Lumpor)........	28,000	1,000,000
Feudatory Malay States...	13,000	620,000
Hong Kong (Victoria).....	390	440,000
Weihaiwei...............	300	160,000
North Borneo (Sandakan).	31,100	204,000
Brunei (Brunei)..........	4,000	30,000
Sarawak (Kuching).......	50,000	650,000
Cyprus (Nikosia)........	3,600	274,000
Total, Asia..........	2,187,550	323,158,000
Africa—		
Union of South Africa (Pretoria and Cape Town)..	470,000	5,100,000
Basutoland (Maseru)......	10,300	350,000
Bechuanaland (Mafeking).	275,000	126,000
Swaziland (Mbabane).....	6,540	90,000
Rhodesia (Salisbury)......	450,000	1,750,000
Gambia (Bathurst).......	4,000	146,000
Gold Coast (Accra).......	120,000	1,400,000
Sierra Leone (Freetown)...	34,000	1,100,000
Northern Nigeria (Zungeru)	256,000	10,000,000
Southern Nigeria (Lagos)..	77,300	7,000,000
Somaliland (Berbera).....	68,000	300,000
East Africa Protectorate (Nairobi)..............	180,000	4,000,000
Uganda (Kampala)........	225,000	2,500,000
Zanzibar (Zanzibar).......	1,000	200,000
Nyasaland (Blantyre).....	40,000	1,000,000
Egypt (see pp. 223–230)....	400,000	12,000,000
Sudan Provinces (see pp. 231–234).............	1,000,000	2,000,000
Mauritius (Port Louis)....	830	370,000
Seychelles (Victoria)......	150	23,000
Ascension (Georgetown)...	78	150
St. Helena (Jamestown)...	47	3,500
Total, Africa, etc.....	3,618,245	49,458,150
America—		
Canada (Ottawa).........	3,730,000	7,200,000
Newfoundland and Labrador (St. Johns).........	163,000	240,000
Bermuda (Hamilton)......	20	18,000
British Honduras (Belize)..	8,600	50,000
West Indies..............	12,300	1,730,000
British Guiana (Georgetown)...............	90,300	310,000
Falkland Islands (Port Stanley)...............	6,500	4,000
South Georgia, etc........	1,000	......
Total, America.......	4,011,720	9,552,000
Australasia—		
Australia (Yass Canberra).	3,000,000	4,500,000
New Zealand (Wellington).	104,750	1,050,000
Fiji (Suva)...............	7,435	130,000
Papua (Port Moresby)....	90,000	360,000
Pacific Islands............	12,500	200,000
Total, Oceania.......	3,214,685	6,240,000
Navy, Army, and Seamen abroad.................	......	400,000
Grand Total.........	13,123,712	434,686,650

the Empire in 1911 was sixty millions, mainly Anglo-Saxon but partly French, Dutch, and Spanish. The remaining 370 millions include 315 millions of the native races of India and Ceylon, forty million black races, six million Arabs, six million Malays, a million Chinese, and a million Polynesians, with various other elements, including 100,000 Red Indians in Canada.

Of the total population over 210 millions are Hindus, 100 millions Muhammadans, 70 millions Christians (63 millions Protestants, seven millions Catholics), twelve millions Buddhists, twelve millions Animists, four millions Sikhs, Jains and Parsees, 750,000 Jews, and the remainder Polytheists and Idol worshippers.

Government.—There is no fundamental law upon which the Constitution of the Empire rests, but there are three main principles underlying its administration, viz., self-government, self-support, and self-defence. The first of these principles has been applied for many years, and is fully developed in the case of Canada, Newfoundland, Australia, New Zealand, and the Union of South Africa. The second principle is equally developed, almost every unit being financially self-supporting. The third principle is of modern growth, and may be said to be the outcome of the Imperial Conference, which has gradually become recognized as the Cabinet of the Empire. Its origin may be traced to the presence in London (in 1887) of the Premiers of the various self-governing Dominions, representing their countries at the celebrations of the Jubilee of Queen Victoria. Similar gatherings took place in 1897, 1902, 1907 and 1911, and in 1907 the title of "Colonial" Conference was changed to Imperial Conference. At the earlier meeting the Colonial Secretary presided, but with the change of title additional importance was given to the assembly by the assumption of the Presidency by the Prime Minister of the United Kingdom.

Ruler.—His Most Excellent Majesty George the Fifth, by the Grace of God King of the United Kingdom of Great Britain and Ireland, and of the British Dominions beyond the Seas, Defender of the Faith, Emperor of India.

Legislature.—The Parliament of the United Kingdom is the supreme legislative authority of the Empire. This parliament has, with the consent of the King-Emperor, delegated its legislative authority to other parliaments constituted by itself, while retaining a general supervision of Imperial affairs through the medium of the Colonial Office.

Judiciary.—The Supreme Judicial Authority of the Empire is the Judicial Committee of the Privy Council, before which appeals may be brought (in the form of a petition to the Crown) from Consular Courts and Courts of Vice-Admiralty, and from the Courts of India and every British Dominion.

Defence.—The general defence of the Empire is undertaken by the Imperial Government, aided in an increasing degree by the governments of India and the self-governing Dominions (see Canada, Australia, New Zealand, and South Africa). The "first line of defence" is the Royal Navy (see United Kingdom), the "second line" being the Regular and Auxiliary troops of the British Army (see United Kingdom).

The United Kingdom.—The Constitution recognizes certain great principles, including the fair administration of justice, the prohibition of taxation without the consent of the people, and a limited monarchy, the power of the monarch being, in effect, wielded by a ministry supported by a majority of the House of Commons. The component parts of the British Government are the King; the Legislature (House of

Lords and House of Commons) ; the Executive Ministry appointed by the Sovereign and responsible to Parliament; and the Judicature.

The Indian Empire.—India is governed by the King as Emperor, acting on the advice of the Secretary of State for India, who is assisted by a council whose members are appointed by the Secretary of State. (See Indian Empire.)

Imperial Dominions.—All British dominions are subject (except as regards taxation) to the legislation of the British Parliament, but no Act of Parliament affects a dominion unless that dominion is specially mentioned. If the legislature of a dominion enacts a law which is repugnant to an imperial law affecting the dominion, it is to the extent to which it is repugnant absolutely void. (See Australia, Canada, etc.) The Imperial Dominions may be divided into several classes, according to the way in which they are governed :

(a) Those having responsible government:—The principal government departments are administered by political chiefs who are responsible, not merely or mainly to the Crown, but to the elected legislature. The Dominions thus governed are Canada, Newfoundland, Australia, New Zealand, and the Union of South Africa.

(b) Where there is government by legislative assembly wholly or partly elected, and an executive council nominated by the Crown or the governor representing the Crown;—In this class may be placed the Bahamas, Barbadoes, Bermuda, British Guiana, Jamaica, Leeward Islands, Mauritius, and Malta.

(c) Where there is government by a governor acting with an executive and a legislative council, the councils being nominated by the Crown or a governor representing the Crown :—Dominions so governed include Ceylon, Falkland Islands, Fiji, Gambia, St. Vincent, Sierra Leone, Straits Settlements, Trinidad.

(d) Wherein both legislative and executive powers are vested in the governor alone :—In this class are Gibraltar, Labuan, and St. Helena, where power is also reserved to the Crown to legislate by Order in Council. In South Africa, Bechuanaland, Basutoland, and Zululand are governed in substantially the same way, but no power is reserved to the Crown.

(e) Protectorates.—The protectorates are countries which, as regards their foreign relations, are under the exclusive control of the King-Emperor. The protectorates of the British Empire include British East Africa, Somaliland, Nyasaland, Uganda, Swaziland, and Nigeria.

(f) Spheres of Influence.—A sphere of influence may be described as an area wherein other Powers undertake not to attempt to acquire influence, or territory by treaty or annexation.

Education.—Educational systems on a more or less uniform plan, are developed throughout the Empire under the control of the respective governments. University Colleges and Universities have been established and degrees are conferred. Under the will of Cecil Rhodes scholarships were founded at various colleges of Oxford University. These Rhodes Scholarships are tenable for three years, are of the annual value of $1,500, and are open to scholars of each Province of Canada, of each State of Australia, of New Zealand, Newfoundland, Natal, Cape of Good Hope (4), Jamaica and Bermuda. (Each State of the United States has a similar nomination, and fifteen scholarships of $1,250 are in the nomination of the German Emperor.)

History.—The most recent historical event of interest was the declaration of war against Germany, Aug. 4, 1914, in support of the neutrality of Belgium, through which country Germany was sending troops for an invasion of France.

Shipping.—In 1912 there were 11,444 vessels (over 100 tons) flying the British flag, of which total 9,279 were registered in the United Kingdom and 2,165 in other parts of the Empire.

Towns.—Capital, London (England). Population (1911), 4,522,961 (with suburbs, 7,252,963).

At the Census of 1911 there were 94 towns in the British Empire exceeding 100,000 inhabitants. (See Great Britain.)

UNITED KINGDOM.—England, Scotland, Ireland and Wales.—The inhabitants of the United Kingdom are almost entirely Christians, and mainly Protestants, the exceptions being five million Roman Catholics, 250,000 Jews, and a small number of non-Christian immigrants. The language of the people is English, with a large proportion of Welsh-speaking people in Wales.

The climate of the British Isles is influenced by the prevailing southwest winds and by the existence of the Gulf Stream. The prevailing winds cause a plentiful rainfall in the western region, the average fall being highest in Ireland. The *Gulf Stream,* from the Gulf of Mexico, is a belt of temperate water, which divides at the southwestern extremity of Ireland and at the Land's End (Cornwall), the former current skirting the north of Scotland, and reuniting with the southern arm in the North Sea. The climate of the British Isles is thus warmer and far more equable than that of other lands between the same parallels, and its harbors are free from ice all the year round.

AREA AND POPULATION

Divisions and Capitals	Area Sq. Miles	Population 1911
England and Wales (London)	58,324	36,070,492
Scotland (Edinburgh)	29,796	4,760,904
Ireland (Dublin)	32,531	4,390,219
Islands	302	148,915
Total	120,953	45,370,530

Government.—The British Constitution is mainly unwritten and customary, but its development is marked by certain outstanding and fundamental laws, of which the principal are Magna Charta (1215), the Habeas Corpus Act (1679), the Act of Settlement (1701), the Act of Union with Scotland (1707), the Act of Union with Ireland (1800), and the Parliament Act (1911). The first secured annual parliaments and the equal administration of justice; the second established the liberty of the person; the third provided for the Protestant succession to the throne; the fourth and fifth created the United Kingdom; and the last enabled the Commons to pass certain Acts without the adherence of the other Chamber. The constituent parts of the British Constitution may be thus briefly described.

The throne is hereditary in the English house of Saxe-Coburg-Gotha with mixed succession, the sons of the Sovereign and their descendants having precedence of daughters, but daughters and their descendants preference over lateral lines. The Monarchy is constitutional and limited. The King has a right to veto bills passed by both Houses of Parliament, but in practice his veto is almost obsolete.

Parliament of the United Kingdom consists of two Houses. The House of Lords consists of Spiritual and Temporal Peers, the former by virtue of their office, the latter by hereditary right, by election or by appointment. It contains 3 Princes of the Blood, 2 Archbishops, 22 Dukes, 24 Marquesses, 123 Earls, 46 Viscounts, 24 Bishops, 344 Barons, 16 Scottish Representative Peers elected for the duration of Parliament, and 28 Irish Representative Peers elected for life—total 632. The House of Commons consists of 670 members, elected for a maximum of five years by direct vote of registered male electors, the qualification being ownership or occupation and registration. The total number of registered voters in the United Kingdom is just over 8,000,000.

The laws in England and Wales are administered by judges appointed by the Crown, who hold office for life, and cannot be removed save on petition presented by both Houses of Parliament. The High Court comprises the King's Bench, Chancery, and Probate, Divorce and Admiralty Divisions. Two Courts of Appeal hear appeals from these divisions, the ultimate Court of Appeal from all the courts in the United Kingdom being the House of Lords.

Scots civil law, which is entirely different from that of England, is administered by the Court of Session, which is a court of law and equity. The High Court of Justiciary is the supreme criminal court in Scotland. It consists of all the judges, and as a rule it is confined to the trial of serious cases. The Sheriff of each county is the proper criminal judge in all crimes occurring within the county which merit only an arbitrary punishment. (For the British Army, see Armies of the World; and for the Navy, see Navies of the World).

Education.—Elementary Education is compulsory for all children between five and fourteen years of age, and is provided free at Public Elementary Schools maintained by Local Authorities and aided by State Grants.

There are 18 Universities in the United Kingdom, of which 10 are in England, 4 in Scotland, 1 in Wales, and 3 in Ireland. These, with dates of foundation, are Oxford (1249), Cambridge (1257), Durham (1831), London (1836), Manchester (1850), Birmingham (1900), Liverpool (1903), Leeds (1904), Sheffield (1905), and Bristol (1909), in England; University of Wales (1893), in Wales; St. Andrews (1411), Glasgow (1450), Aberdeen (1494), and Edinburgh (1582), in Scotland; and Dublin (1591), National (1910), and Belfast (1909), in Ireland.

Production and Industry.—In 1901 the total number of occupied persons in the United Kingdom was 15,388,501 (12,134,259 males and 3,254,242 females). Of this total the largest percentage, or 12.66, were employed in agriculture, 11.39 in commerce, 8.2 in conveyance, 5.0 in mines and quarries, 7.89 in metals and machinery, 6.77 in building and construction, 6.92 in textile fabrics, and 7.23 in dress.

Manufactures.—The United Kingdom imports annually (for home consumption) about 2,000,000,000 lbs. of cotton and 400,000,000 to 450,000,000 lbs. of wool (in addition to 150,000,000 lbs. produced at home), the former principally from the United States, the latter principally from Australasia.

England and Wales.—The southern and larger portion of the Island of Great Britain, is situated in western Europe, between latitude 50° and 55° 46′ north and longitude 1° 46′ and 5° 42′ west. It is bounded by Scotland on the north, on all other sides by the sea—on the east by the North Sea or German Ocean, on the south by the English Channel, and on the west by St. George's Channel and the Irish Sea. Its length measured on a meridian from Ber-

wick to St. Albin's Head, is 365 miles.
Its breadth, between St. David's Head in
South Wales and the Naze in Essex, is 280
miles. Wales was called by the early Romans Britannica Secunda. It was brought
under the dominion of the English by Kings
Henry II. and Edward I. The independence
of Wales died with Prince Llewellyn, who
was murdered in 1283. In 1284 Queen
Eleanor gave birth to a son in Caernarvon
Castle, whom Edward I., his father, called
Prince of Wales. This title has ever since
been given to the heir apparent to the
throne of Great Britain. Wales was incorporated with England by an act of Parliament in 1536.

Ireland.—An island west of Great Britain, forming with it the United Kingdom
of Great Britain and Ireland. It is bounded
by the Atlantic Ocean on the north, west
and south and on the east by Great Britain,
separated by the Irish Sea and St. George's
and North Channels. It extends from lat.
51° 26' to 55° 21' north, and from long.
5° 23' to 10° 28' west. The leading occupation is agriculture, and the chief manufactures are linen, woolens, spirits, etc.
Government is administered by a Lord
Lieutenant appointed by the British Crown,
together with a privy council at Dublin
and a Chief Secretary in Parliament. Ireland is represented by 103 members in the
House of Commons, and the peerage, consisting of 172 members, appoints twenty-
eight representative peers to sit in the
House of Lords. The country is divided
into four provinces, Ulster, Munster, Leinster and Connaught. By the Local Government Act of 1898 provision was made for
popularly elected councils for counties and
rural districts. These councils are elected
for three years and take the place of the
old grand juries and presentment sessions.
The principal cities are Dublin, Belfast,
Cork, Limerick, Londonderry and Waterford.
These have Borough Councils. Women are
eligible for election in borough and county
councils. (See Home Rule.)

Trade with the United States.—The value
of merchandise imported into the United
Kingdom from the United States for the
year of 1913 was $597,149,059, and goods
to the value of $295,564,940, were sent
thither—a balance of $301,584,119 in favor
of the United States.

British Empire. (See Great Britain.)

British Guiana:

Boundary dispute between Great Britain and Venezuela regarding, discussed, 5204, 5471, 5616, 5873,
5958, 6064, 6087, 6154.

Arbitration of, discussed, 6337, 6380.

Recommended by President Cleveland, 6064.

Treaty for, 6154.

Monroe doctrine reasserted and attitude of United States respecting, discussed by President Cleveland, 6064, 6087.

Tariff laws of, evidence of modifications of, proclaimed, 5688, 6381.

Discussed, 5747.

British Hudsons Bay Co. (See Hudsons Bay Co.)

British North America. (See British
America.)

British North American Fisheries. (See
Fisheries.)

British West Indies:

Employment of colored laborers from
United States in, 2678, 2683.

Tariff laws of, evidence of modifications of, proclaimed, 5688.

Discussed, 5747.

Vessels from Trinidad, tonnage duty
on, suspended, 4889.

Broad-Seal.—The official seal of a state or
nation.

Broad Seal War.—The clerk of Middlesex
County, N. J., threw out the vote of South
Amboy in the Congressional election of 1838
on account of defects in the returns. The
Democrats protested, but the Whig representatives were declared elected and given
certificates under the broad seal of the
state. When Congress met, Dec. 2, 1839,
the House contained 119 Democrats and
118 Whigs outside of the New Jersey contestants. The Clerk of the House refused
to recognize the New Jersey delegation. Great
confusion followed. Dec. 5 John Quincy
Adams was elected Speaker pro tempore.
Dec. 17, after much wrangling, R. M. T.
Hunter, of Virginia, was elected Speaker.
The Democratic contestants were finally
seated.

Broadside.—1. A concerted discharge of
fire-arms or cannon. 2. A speech or a communication which is presumed to have great
effect on opponents.

Brooklyn (N. Y.), Battle of.—July 2,
1776, Gen. Howe arrived from Halifax and
took possession of Staten Island, N. Y.
He was soon joined by Sir Henry Clinton
from the south and Admiral Lord Howe,
his brother, from England, with a fleet and
a large land force. By Aug. 1, arrivals
of Hessian troops had increased the force
under Howe to nearly 30,000. Gen. Charles
Lee entered New York the same day that
Clinton arrived at Sandy Hook. Washington placed Boston in a state of security
and proceeded to the Highlands of the
Hudson, 50 miles above New York. The
combined American forces numbered about
17,000, under the immediate command of
Sullivan, Stirling (Sir William Alexander)
(who had succeeded Lee), and Putnam.
Aug. 22, 1776, 10,000 men and 40 cannon
were landed by the British on Long Island
between the present Fort Hamilton and
Gravesend villages. American troops to
the number of 5,000 under Sullivan guarded a range of hills extending from The
Narrows to Jamaica village. On the morning of Aug. 27 a desperate battle was
fought. Stirling was taken prisoner and
Sullivan was forced to surrender. The
American loss was 500 killed and wounded
and 1,100 made prisoners. The British loss
was 367 killed, wounded, and taken prisoners. Putnam's division of the army was
silently withdrawn by Washington under
cover of a fog on the night of the 29th.

Brooklyn, The, mentioned, 6317.

Brooklyn, N. Y., site for dry dock at,
934.

Brother Jonathan.—A general name applied to the people of the United States.
Its origin is said to be as follows: General
Washington found soon after having taken
command of the Continental army that it
was sadly in need of many articles. Jonathan Trumbull, the elder, at that time
Governor of Connecticut, was a friend of
Washington and one in whose judgment
Washington had great confidence. During
a consultation on the state of the army,

Washington suggested that they consult "Brother Jonathan," meaning Trumbull. This advice was followed, and Trumbull devised the means of procuring what was desired. The story was told in the army, and the reply to a demand for any article was invariably advice to ask "Brother Jonathan." The phrase became proverbial and has lived to the present time.

Brown's Insurrection.—During the year 1859 John Brown, with a few companions, rented a farm in Maryland, near Harpers Ferry, Va. (now W. Va.), to which he smuggled arms. He had designed a plan for the seizure of the United States armory at Harpers Ferry in which over 100,000 stand of small arms were stored. His object was to free the negro slaves. Sunday evening, Oct. 16, 1859, Brown, with a force of 22 men, seized the armory. The telegraph wires were cut, trains were stopped, and about 60 prisoners taken. It was said he intended after taking the armory to flee to the mountains, where he expected to be joined by the negroes, who were to rise and fight under his leadership. Brown abandoned this plan, however, and remained at the Ferry. The militia was summoned and surrounded him, and, together with some marines and artillery, captured him and his party after a desperate fight, in which he was wounded. John Brown was tried, was condemned to death, and on Dec. 2 was executed by hanging. This incident created tremendous excitement and intensified the growing bitterness between the North and the South. President Buchanan, in his annual message, December, 1859, referred to this insurrection as "the recent sad and bloody occurrences at Harpers Ferry." (3084.) See illustration opposite 3071.

Brownstown (Mich.), Battle of.—In July, 1812, Governor Meigs, of Ohio, sent Capt. Brush with men, cattle, and provisions to the relief of General Hull, who had crossed the Detroit River into Canada. Learning that a body of British and Indians were lying in wait at Brownstown, at the mouth of the Huron River, to intercept his supplies, Hull sent Major Thomas B. Van Horne with 200 men from Findlays Ohio regiment to act as an escort from the River Raisin to the destination in Canada. Van Horne's detachment had crossed the Ecorces River and was approaching Brownstown Aug. 5 when it found itself in an ambush and almost surrounded by Indians under Tecumseh. The party retreated in disorder with loss, having been pursued part of the way by the Indians.

Brownsville.—On the night of Aug. 13-14, 1906, a riot occurred in Brownsville, Texas, in which one citizen was killed and another wounded and the chief of police seriously injured. (Page 7338.) Bitter feelings had for some time existed between the townspeople and the soldiers of the Twenty-fifth infantry (colored), who were stationed at Fort Brown. According to the theory of the Secretary of War, from nine to twenty men from a battalion of 170 formed a plan of revenge upon some of the people of the town for some real or fancied slight. About midnight they secretly left the barracks and fired through certain houses of the town, with the result noted above. An investigation was at once begun by the inspector-general, who reported that he was unable to obtain any evidence from the troops that they had any knowledge of the affair.

On receiving this report President Roosevelt issued an order dismissing "without honor" the entire battalion, on the ground that there had been formed a "conspiracy of silence" to protect the offenders. (Page 7329.) He assumed that it was impossible that such an affray should have happened without the knowledge of a part or all of the battalion. This action of the President was severely criticised by his opponents, and the Senate passed resolutions calling for all the facts in the case. Senator Lodge defended the President.

Feb. 25, 1908, a committee of the Senate, after investigation, reported that the "shooting up" of Brownsville was done by "some of the soldiers of the Twenty-fifth infantry." (Page 7347.) The action of the President was not passed upon. Two resolutions were introduced in the Senate —one to restore the discharged soldiers with back pay, and the other, authorized by the President, permitting the re-enlistment of such as could satisfactorily show the President that they had not participated in, and had no guilty knowledge of, the shooting in Brownsville.

President Roosevelt recommended that the Secretary of War be allowed to reinstate any soldiers found innocent within a fixed time. (Page 7348.) Senator Lodge denounced a bill to compel the President to reinstate the discharged soldiers as an unconstitutional usurpation of executive authority.

Judge Hough, of the United States Circuit Court for New York, on May 15, 1908, decided in the case of Oscar M. Reid, one of the discharged soldiers, that the President's action was legal, and that the authority therefor was found in the articles of war. The action was brought under an act which allows the Government to be sued in certain cases, and was to recover the pay and emoluments accruing from the date of his discharge to the end of his enlistment. The case was appealed to the Supreme Court.

Brownsville, Tex., blockade of port of, removed by proclamation, 3417.

Brunswick Harbor, Ga., improvement of, referred to, 1496.

Brussels, Belgium:

International congress at, for abolition of African slave trade, 5471, 5543.

International Exhibition of Sciences and Industry at, 5187, 5399.

Report of Commissioners to, referred to, 5400.

International Monetary Conference at, in 1892, 5752.

Postponement of, discussed, 5876.

Reports of, transmitted, 5784.

Universal Exposition at, American exhibits at, discussed, 6324.

Bryce Report on Belgian Atrocities.—A report of an English committee headed by Viscount Bryce, formerly ambassador to the United States from Great Britain, investigating and confirming reports that the German troops in their invasion of Belgium, and afterwards during their occupation of that country during the European War (q. v.), had committed wide-spread and horrible atrocities upon male and female noncombatants.

Buchanan, James.—1857-1861.

Eighteenth Administration—Democratic.

Vice-President—John C. Breckinridge.

Secretary of State—

Lewis Cass.

Jeremiah S. Black.

Secretary of the Treasury—
  Howell Cobb.
  Philip F. Thomas.
  John A. Dix.
Secretary of War—
  John B. Floyd.
  Joseph Holt.
Secretary of the Navy—
  Isaac Toucey.
Secretary of the Interior—
  Jacob Thompson.
Postmaster General—
  Aaron V. Brown.
  Joseph Holt.
  Horatio King.
Attorney General—
  Jeremiah S. Black.
  Edwin M. Stanton.

Buchanan was elected by the Democratic party, Nov. 4, 1856. The National Convention, at Cincinnati, June 2-6, 1856, nominated him for President and John C. Breckinridge for Vice-President. Pierce, Douglas, and Cass were the other possibilities for candidates, but in the seventeen ballots taken, Buchanan always led.

Platform.—The platform reiterated many of the elements of the platforms of 1840 and 1844, including such topics as the public lands ; opposing the national bank ; advocating the sub-treasury system ; supporting the veto power ; and objecting to further restrictions upon naturalization. To these were added, in 1856, sections denouncing opposition to Catholics ; contending for State authority only on the slavery question and non-interference by Congress in this matter ; supporting the compromises of 1850 ; giving emphatic announcement to States Rights ; supporting the Monroe Doctrine ; advocating the establishment, by government aid, of good communication between the Atlantic and Pacific coasts ; and endorsing the administration of President Pierce.

Opposition.—The American (Know Nothing) National Convention, held at Philadelphia, Feb. 22-25, 1856, nominated Millard Fillmore for President and Andrew Jackson Donelson for Vice-President, on a platform advocating the government of America by American-born citizens ; refusal to accord office-holding rights to any who recognized allegiance to foreign potentates ; raising the period of residence qualification for naturalization to twenty-one years ; opposing any union between Church and States ; enforcement of all laws. The Republican National Convention, held at Philadelphia, June 17, 1856, nominated John C. Fremont and William L. Dayton on a platform upholding the tenets of the Declaration and the Constitution ; condemning slavery ; prohibition by Congress within the Territories of polygamy and slavery ; sympathy with Kansas ; condemnation of the doctrine that "might makes right" ; imperatively demanding a transcontinental railroad ; acknowledging the constitutionality of the internal improvements policy. The Whig National Convention, held at Baltimore, Sept. 17-18, 1856, endorsed the nominations of Fillmore and Donelson, made by the American party on a platform announcing adherence to the old time Whig doctrines ; denouncing sectional antagonism and the formation of geographical parties ; and endorsing the administration of Millard Fillmore.

Vote.—The popular vote cast by thirty-one States gave Buchanan 1,838,169 ; Fremont, 1,341,264 ; and Fillmore, 874,534. The electoral vote counted Feb. 11, 1857, gave Buchanan, 174 ; Fremont, 114 ; and Fillmore, 8.

Party Affiliation.—In his early career, Buchanan sided with the Federalists in disapproving of the War of 1812. Yet he felt it a patriot's duty always to defend his country, and spoke of the war as "glorious

in the highest degree to the American character, but disgraceful in the extreme to the administration." During the "era of good feeling," when party and sectional lines were not closely drawn, Buchanan's political views underwent a change. In Congress, during Adams' administration, he became one of the Democratic leaders against the friends of the administration who called themselves National Republicans ; and he was always a zealous supporter of General Jackson.

Political Complexion of Congress.—In the Thirty-fifth Congress (1857-1859) the Senate of sixty-four members was composed of thirty-nine Democrats, twenty Republicans, and five Americans ; and the House of 237 members was made up of 131 Democrats, ninety-two Republicans, and fourteen Americans. In the Thirty-sixth Congress (1859-1861) the Senate of sixty-six members was composed of thirty-eight Democrats, twenty-six Republicans, and two Americans ; and the House of 237 members was made up of 101 Democrats, 113 Republicans, and twenty-three Independents.

Tariff.—In speaking of the revenue, President Buchanan in his Inaugural Address (page 2964) said : "It is beyond all question the true principle that no more revenue ought to be collected from the people than the amount necessary to defray the expenses of a wise, economical, and efficient administration of the Government. . . . Any discrimination against a particular branch for the purpose of benefiting favored corporations, individuals or interests would have been unjust to the rest of the community and inconsistent with that spirit of fairness and equality which ought to govern in the adjustment of a revenue tariff." In his Second Annual Message (page 3052) in discussing the sort of duties, he said : "In regard to the mode of assessing and collecting duties under a strictly revenue tariff, I have long entertained and expressed the opinion that sound policy requires that this should be done by specific duties in cases to which these can be properly applied. . . . The present system is a sliding scale to his (the manufacturer's) disadvantage. Under it, when prices are high and business prosperous, the duties rise in amount when he least requires their aid. On the contrary, when prices fall and he is struggling against adversity, the duties are diminished in the same proportion, greatly to his injury." In his Fourth Annual Message (page 3183) on the same subject, he said : "An impression strangely enough prevails to some extent that specific duties are necessarily protective duties. Nothing can be more fallacious. Great Britain glories in free trade, and yet her whole revenue from imports is at the present moment collected under a system of specific duties."

Foreign Policy.—Domestic affairs were so disturbed during President Buchanan's administration that the foreign policy has been to some extent unappreciated. In his Inaugural Address (page 2966) the President points out that all of the acquisition of territory by the United States has been conducted by purchase or by the voluntary impulse of the people, never by conquest,— even in the case of Mexico, after the war, no advantage was taken of her conquered state, but a fair price was paid to her for the ceded territory. In his Second Annual Address (page 3037) he announces the conclusion of the Perry treaty with Japan. In the same message he discusses the differences with Great Britain, conditions which led to the settlement by President Buchanan of the long standing "right of search."

Internal Improvements.—In vetoing "An act making an appropriation for deepening the channel over the St. Clair flats, in the

EXTENT OF THE UNITED STATES DURING THE ADMINISTRATION OF PRESIDENT BUCHANAN, 1857-1861.

(NOT INCLUDING TERRITORIES)

MAINE
1820

OHIO

VT.
1791

N. H.
1788

MASS
1788

CONN
1788

R. I.
1790

N. J.
1787

DEL.
1787

NEW YORK
1788

PENNSYLVANIA
1787

MD.
1788

VIRGINIA
1788

NORTH CAROLINA
1789

SOUTH CAROLINA
1788

FLORIDA
1845

MICHIGAN
1837

OHIO
1803

INDIANA
1816

KENTUCKY
1792

TENNESSEE
1796

GEORGIA
1788

ALABAMA
1819

MISSISSIPPI
1817

WISCONSIN
1848

ILLINOIS
1818

MISSOURI
1821

ARKANSAS
1836

LOUISIANA
1812

MINNESOTA
1858

IOWA
1846

KANSAS
1861

TEXAS
1845

OREGON
1859

CALIFORNIA
1850

FLAG OF 1861

COPYRIGHT BY BUREAU OF...

State of Michigan," the President, in his
Veto Message (page 3130) clearly expresses
his views upon the question: "What a vast
field would the exercise of this power open
for jobbing and corruption! Members of
Congress from an honest desire to promote
the interest of their constituents would
struggle for improvements within their own
districts, and the body itself must necessarily be converted into an arena where each
would endeavor to obtain from the Treasury
as much money as possible for his own
locality. The temptation would prove irresistible. A system of 'log-rolling' (I know
no word so expressive) would be inaugurated under which the Treasury would be
exhausted and the Federal Government
would be deprived of the means necessary
to execute those great powers clearly confided to it by the Constitution for the purpose of promoting the interests and vindi-
cating the honor of the country."

Slavery.—In his Inaugural Address (page
2962) President Buchanan treats the whole
question of slavery as being settled by the
regulations of Congress. "The whole Territorial question," he says, "being thus settled upon the principle of popular sovereignty—a principle as ancient as free government itself—everything of a practical nature
has been decided." This is the keynote to
all of the President's acts in connection with
this subject. The onus rested upon Congress, and it was for him to carry out the
laws which Congress had made on the subject. There was no option in his case. He
did what the Constitution obliged him to
do. The legislature of his administration
was in the hands of the pro-slavery party,
and the President's conduct in enforcing
the laws formulated by them made it appear
as though he endorsed their policy. President Buchanan was opposed to slavery; his
messages teem with suggestions for conciliatory measures; but he did object to the
interference of unsympathetic abolitionists
in the affairs of other States. He says
(page 2963): "But this question of domestic slavery is of far graver importance
than any mere political question, because
should the agitation continue it may eventually endanger the personal safety of a large
portion of our countrymen where the institution exists. Let every Union-loving men,
therefore, exert his best influence to suppress this agitation, which since the recent
legislation of Congress is without any legitimate object." In his Third Annual Message (page 3084) the President makes an
impassioned appeal to his countrymen to
"cultivate the ancient feelings of mutual
forbearance and good will toward each other
and strive to allay the demon spirit of sectional hatred and strife now alive in the
land." While he warns the people of the
danger of disruption of the Union, which
he professes to believe impossible, yet the
happenings at Harper's Ferry serve as the
text for a lesson of what may happen. In
his Fourth Annual Message (page 3157)
the President announces that "The long-
continued and intemperate interference of
the Northern people with the question of
slavery in the Southern States has at length
produced its natural effect. The different
sections of the Union are now arrayed
against each other, and the time has arrived, so much dreaded by the Father of his
Country, when hostile geographical parties
have been formed. . . . How easy would
it be for the American people to settle the
slavery question forever and to restore peace
and harmony to this distracted country!
They, and they alone, can do it. All that is
necessary to accomplish the object, and all
for which the slave States have ever contended, is to be let alone and permitted to
manage their domestic institutions in their
own way. As sovereign States, they, and
they alone, are responsible before God and
the world for the slavery existing among
them. For this the people of the North
are not more responsible and have no more
right to interfere than with similar institutions in Russia or Brazil." Speaking of
the President's responsibility and duty in
the premises, he says: "After all, he is no
more than the Chief Executive of the Government. His province is not to make but
to execute laws." Following South Carolina's ordinance of secession of Dec. 20,
1860, the President in a special message to
Congress (page 3186) discussed the right
of any State to secede.

Buchanan, James:

Admission of states discussed and
recommendations of, regarding,
3033, 3086.

Annual messages of, 2967, 3028, 3083,
3157.

Biographical sketch of, 2960.

Constitutional amendment regarding
slavery, recommended by, 3169.

Correspondence of, while minister at
St. Petersburg, referred to, 3967.

Correspondence of, with Lewis Cass,
referred to, 3964.

Cuba, acquisition of, discussed by,
3040, 3066.

Recommended by, 3041, 3092, 3173.

Death of, announced and honors to be
paid memory of, 3862, 3863.

Duties on vessels of Italy suspended
by proclamation, 2824.

Finances discussed by, 2967, 2988,
3019, 3052, 3073, 3104, 3179.

Foreign policy discussed by, 2966,
2998, 3037, 3041, 3066, 3089, 3092,
3173, 3177.

Inauguration, see illustration opposite 2975.

Instructions to, while minister to
England, regarding free ships, etc.,
referred to, 2910.

Internal improvements discussed by,
3130.

Monroe doctrine reasserted by, 3043,
3177.

Official conduct of, investigated, 3145,
3150.

"Pocket vetoes of," 3073, 3130, 3138.

Portrait of, 2959.

Powers of Federal and state governments discussed by, 2962, 2981,
3028, 3074, 3084, 3130, 3139, 3145,
3150, 3157, 3168, 3186.

Proclamations of—

Day for voting on adoption of code
in District of Columbia, 3021.

Duties on vessels of Italy suspended, 3022.

Extraordinary session of Senate, to
act upon Executive communications, 3026, 3081, 3156, 3203.

Military expedition to Nicaragua,
3027.

Rebellion in Utah, 3024.

Protests of, against procedings of House of Representatives, 3145, 3150.

Secession discussed by, 3159, 3186.

Secretary of State, 2319.

Slavery discussed by, 2962, 2981, 3028, 3084, 3157, 3186.

State of the Union discussed by, 2967, 3028, 3051, 3063, 3157, 3192, 3200.

Tariff discussed by, 2964, 3052, 3181.

Time allowed President for consideration of bills discussed by, 2993, 3060.

Veto messages of—

Deepening channel over St. Clair Flats, r e a s o n s for applying pocket veto, 3130.

Donating lands for benefit of agricultural colleges, 3074.

Relief of—

Edwards & Co., 3138.

Hockaday & Leggit, 3201.

Removal of obstructions in Mississippi River, reasons for applying pocket veto, 3138.

Securing homesteads to settlers, 3139.

Transportation of mail from St. Joseph, Mo., to Placerville, Cal., reasons for applying pocket veto, 3073.

Buck, The, seizure of, and claims arising out of, 4114, 5198, 5547, 5673, 5873, 5962.

Award in case of, 5673.

Bucket-Shop.—A concern dealing in stocks, bonds, etc.; but, unlike the stock exchange, bucket-shops provide no means for transfer or delivery of certificates; therefore they are simply gambling places where wagers are made on the fluctuations of the market.

Buckeye State.—The nickname given to Ohio because the buckeye tree was indigenous to the soil, and was found in great abundance throughout the state. (See Ohio.)

Bucks Stove Case.—In August, 1907, the Bucks Stove and Range Company of St. Louis brought proceedings in the Supreme Court of the District of Columbia against the officers of the American Federation of Labor to enjoin them from conducting a boycott against the company by advertising that the concern was on the "unfair" and "We-don't-patronize" lists published in the federations official organ. The injunction asked for was issued by Judge Gould Dec. 23, 1907. On the plea that the terms of the injunction were being violated proceedings for contempt of court were brought against Samuel Gompers, president of the American Federation of Labor; John Mitchell, vice-president; and Frank Morrison, secretary. Justice Wright, of the Supreme Court of the District of Columbia, before whom the case was tried, decided Dec. 23, 1908, that the defendants were guilty. Mr. Gompers was sentenced to one year's imprisonment, and Messrs. Mitchell and Morrison to nine months and six months, respectively. They were admitted to bail and the case was appealed to the Court of Appeals of the Dis-

trict of Columbia. This tribunal in a decision rendered Nov. 2, 1909, affirmed the decree of the Supreme Court of the District of Columbia. An appeal was then taken to the Supreme Court of the United States, which on May 15, 1911, handed down a decision reversing the judgments of the Court of Appeals and the Supreme Court of the District of Columbia, and remanding the case, with the direction that the contempt proceedings instituted by the Bucks Stove and Range Company be dismissed, but without prejudice to the power and right of the Supreme Court of the District of Columbia to punish by a proper proceeding any contempt committed against it. The basis of the opinion was that the proceedings brought against the labor union officers was for civil contempt, which could be punished only by a fine. The sentence of the lower court to imprisonment was the penalty for criminal contempt, and therefore it was not a legal punishment in this case. The Supreme Court held that the published or spoken utterance of organized labor could be enjoined or attacked legally, because organized labor is a combination, and, as such, relinquishes the rights of individuals. It also establishes the fact that legal prosecution could be levelled not only at the union itself, but at the officers as well. (See also Boycott.)

Buckshot War.—The election in Philadelphia Oct. 9, 1838, was of considerable importance because upon it hinged the control of the legislature which was to elect a United States Senator. The Democratic candidates for the legislature were elected by small majorities, but their Congressional candidate was defeated. The Democratic return judges thereupon cast out 5,000 Whig votes, claiming fraud. The Whig judges then issued certificates of election to both their Congressional and legislative candidates, and these returns were accepted by the Whig secretary of state. Dec. 4, 1838, the date for the meeting of the legislature, armed partisans of both sets of contestants met at Harrisburg. The Senate, which was Whig, met and adjourned because of the mob. Two warring bodies met in the house (1724, 1725). The Whig governor called upon the militia and tried without effect to obtain Federal aid. The Democratic house was recognized Dec. 25. A remark made during the height of the excitement, that the mob would feel the effect of "ball and buckshot before night," gave the episode the name of the Buckshot War.

Buckshot War, documents regarding, transmitted, 1724, 1725.

Bucktails.—A name applied to the Tammany Society of New York City from the fact that the members of the organization wore buck's tails in their hats as a badge instead of a feather. Between 1812 and 1828 the Bucktails were anti-Clintonian New York Democrats. They were the most vigorous opponents of Clinton's canal policy from its inception in 1817, and the name was later applied to all who opposed this policy throughout the State.

Buena Vista (Mexico), Battle of.—After part of his army had been sent to Gen. Scott, Gen. Taylor, with less than 5,000 men, mostly raw militia, was attacked at Buena Vista by Santa Anna's army of 21,000, Feb. 22, 1847. Taylor intrenched himself in the pass of Angostura, in the Sierra Madre Mountains, on the road leading to San Luis Potosi. The engagement began at 3 o'clock in the afternoon and was suspended at dark, the loss to the Americans being but 4 men wounded, while the enemy lost more than 300 killed and wounded. Fighting was renewed at dawn of the 23d and continued until sunset. The Mexicans retired during the night to Agua Nueva. The American loss in killed, wounded and missing amounted to 745 : that of the Mexicans upward of 2,000. Jefferson Davis in this battle commanded a Mississippi regiment as its colonel, and saved the army by receiving the charge of the Mexican lancers. His troops were formed in the shape of a V. (See illustration opposite 2121.)

Buena Vista, Mexico:

Battle of, referred to, 2385.

Mutiny in camp of, referred to, 2443.

Buenos Ayres (see also Argentine Republic):

Convention with, ratified, 7672.

Diplomatic relations with, discussed, 2116.

Imprisonment of American citizens in, 632.

Independence of, asserted, 612, 627.

Minister of United States in, returns, 1171.

Revolution in, 2702.

War with Brazil—

Peace concluded, 977.

Questions between United States and Brazil growing out of, 929, 951.

Buffalo (N. Y.), Destruction of.—During the winter of 1813 the British regained Forts George and Niagara. The British and Indians, under the command of Lieut.-Gen. Drummond, Maj.-Gen. Riall, and Col. Murray, overran and laid waste the valley of the Niagara and pressed hard upon Buffalo. Gen. Amos Hall succeeded Gen. McClure at Buffalo Dec. 26, in the command of 2,000 badly organized American troops. On the night of Dec. 29 Riall crossed the river at Black Rock with 1,450 men, largely regulars, and a body of Indians. At sight of the enemy 800 of Hall's troops deserted. He, however, made a gallant defense with the Chautauqua troops and Canadian refugees until he was forced to retreat, keeping the enemy in check and covering the flight of the inhabitants. The British and Indians took possession of Buffalo and proceeded to burn, plunder, and massacre. Only 4 buildings were left standing in the town and only 1 at Black Rock.

Buffalo in 1815. (See illustration opposite 553.

Buffalo, Pan-American Exposition at, 6382, 6436.

Buffalo Exposition. (See Pan-American Exposition.)

Bugle.—An instrument used by military forces for sounding various orders.

Building and Loan Associations.—Corporations organized primarily to enable persons of limited means to secure homes, and, secondarily, to enable such persons to put aside a certain fixed sum at stated intervals, so that the investment may be safe and remunerative. In the beginning the home-building or home-buying fund came entirely from the periodic payments of the members (shareholders). At present prepaid, full-paid and permanent shares are sold by the association, payable in full or in large part on subscription. Special deposits in any amount are received. Shares partly paid are brought to their par value

by adding to payments made dividends apportioned thereto. Special deposits are generally withdrawable by the depositor at pleasure. Installment shares and prepaid shares remain in until they reach their par value. Full-paid shares remain in a certain fixed time. Permanent shares remain in until the dissolution of the corporation. These associations came into existence in England nearly 100 years ago, but were not made the subject of legislative enactment until 1836. The first association established in the United States was the Oxford Provident Building Association, of Frankford, Pa., organized in 1831. There are according to the official report made to the National League of Building Associations, in 1911, in the United States 5,869 associations with assets of $931,867,175. The estimated membership is 2,169,893.

Building and Loan Associations, report on, transmitted, 5909.

Buildings, Public:

Acts for erection of, vetoed, discussed, 5553.

Architects for, authority for employing, referred to, 2954.

At Washington destroyed by Great Britain, 530.

Commission appointed to determine extent of security of, against fire referred to, 4432.

Construction of—

Recommended, 4577.

Referred to, 399, 436, 1483, 1911, 2281.

Expenditures for, 985.

Discussed, 4197.

Heating and ventilating referred to, 3110, 3112.

Illustrations of the principal governmental, and most important in Washington, D. C. (See the frontispieces of various Volumes.)

Improvement of, recommended, 831.

Bulgaria. — Bulgaria is an independent kingdom in the northeast of the Balkan Peninsula, bounded on the north by Rumania, on the south by Turkey and the Aegean Sea, on the east by the Black Sea, and on the west by Servia and Greece.

Physical Features.—The Balkan range runs parallel with the Danube, about sixty miles to the north. The Rhodope mountains extend along the southern boundary of Eastern Rumelia. The western portion of Bulgaria is occupied by extensive plateaus which connect the Balkan and Rhodope ranges.

All the rivers of Northern Bulgaria rise in the Balkans and flow northwards into the Danube, the fall being often precipitous.

AREA AND POPULATION

Provinces	Area in Square Miles	Population in 1910
Burgas	4,576	351,500
Kiustendil	1,825	231,522
Plevna	2,957	365,868
Philippopolis	3,907	447,309
Rustchuk	2,948	406,309
Shumla	2,316	282,601
Sofia	3,734	481,598
Stara-Zagora	4,095	442,969
Tirnovo	2,989	448,197
Varna	3,485	329,612
Vidin	1,701	237,571
Vratza	2,669	312,460
Total	37,202	4,337,516

Bulgarian, a language of the Slavonic group, is the national language.

History.—The Bulgarian kingdom was originally founded in the seventh century by an incursion of Bulgars across the Danube, and their settlement in a district of the Roman (Byzantine) Empire. At the close of the fourteenth century the kingdom fell under the sway of the Turks, from whose dominion Bulgaria was separated by the Treaties of San Stefano and Berlin (1878) after an armed revolt against Turkish misrule, many heroic engagements marking the course of the struggle. The Treaty of Berlin (July 13, 1878) created the Principality of Bulgaria as a tributary State of the Turkish Empire. In 1886 war broke out between Bulgaria and her western neighbor, the outcome of the Servo-Bulgarian War being the political union of Eastern Rumelia and Bulgaria.

Oct. 5, 1908, the principality of United Bulgaria was declared an independent kingdom, and the present ruler declared himself Tsar (King) of the Bulgarians. The independence was recognized by all the Powers, April 20-29, 1909, the tribute to Turkey being capitalized and the annual payments cancelled. In 1912 Bulgaria (in conjunction with Servia, Montenegro, and Greece) declared war against the Ottoman Empire. The war was prosecuted with the utmost vigor and the town of Adrianople and all Thrace to the Enos-Midia line fell to the share of Bulgaria at the Treaty of London of May 30, 1913, together with parts of Macedonia to the west of Bulgaria. But the second war of Bulgaria against her former allies, who were aided by Rumania, resulted in the treaty of Bucharest (Aug. 6, 1913), by which Bulgaria was shorn of much of the westward extension, and ceded a part of her former territory to Rumania. Turkey also took advantage of Bulgaria's difficulties and reoccupied Adrianople and the adjacent territory. (See also Balkan States and European War of 1914-16.)

Government.—A Constitutional monarchy, hereditary in the male line of a prince, "freely elected by the population and confirmed by the Sublime Porte with the assent of the Powers." The Constitution was adopted April 29, 1879.

Ruler—Ferdinand I. (Ferdinand Maximilian Charles Leopold Marie, Duke of Saxony) born at Vienna, Feb. 26, 1861.

The National Assembly (Sobranje) consists of 213 representatives (1 for 20,000 inhabitants), elected by direct manhood suffrage for a maximum duration of four years. Certain matters are reserved for the *Grand Sobranje*, which is similarly elected (when occasion demands) with twice the number of representatives. There are departmental courts and courts of appeal (Sofia, Rustchuk,, and Philippopolis). The supreme court of appeal is the Court of Cassation at Sofia. The Greeks, Muhammedans and Jews have special spiritual courts for family law and the law of inheritance.

Service in the Army is universal and compulsory on all males between the ages of 20 and 46. The Peace Effective is 3.844 officers, 54,037 others. War Effective, Field Army, 275,000; Territorial Army, 55,000.

Production and Industry.—Over 70 per cent. of the population live by agriculture, and more than one-third of the land is under cultivation, one-third being woods and forests and the remainder barren mountain. The principal crop is wheat, but wine, tobacco, silk, cotton, and rice are also largely cultivated, while attar of roses is produced in large quantities from the rose fields of the sheltered valleys. Bulgarian homespuns and embroidery are unrivalled in their excellence but suffer from the competition of heap and inferior imports from Europe.

Railways.—In 1912 there were 2,000 kilomètres of railway open, all belonging t the State, with 260 kilomètres under construction.

Trade with the United States.—The valu of merchandise imported into Bulgaria fror the United States for the year 1913 wa $103,749, and goods to the value of $440 537 were sent thither—a balance of $336, 608 in favor of Bulgaria.

Bulgaria:

Diplomatic relations with, establish ment of, recommended, 4759.

Massacre by Turks in, referred to 4376.

Bull Moose.—An emblem of the Progressiv Party.

Bull Run (Va.), Battle of, or First Battle of Manassas.—For the double purpos of menacing Washington and preventin an advance of the Federal troops into Vir ginia, the Confederates during the summe of 1861 collected a large body of troops i the vicinity of Manassas Junction, Va The position was 33 miles southwest o Washington. The troops here assemble numbered, including all reenforcements re ceived during the battle, about 32,000, un der command of Gen. Beauregard. Th senior officer, Gen. J. E. Johnston, afte his arrival on the field, did not take th actual command. The aggregate force o Union soldiers in and around Washingto was 34,160 men. Both armies were com posed mostly of undisciplined volunteers July 16, 1861, Maj.-Gen. McDowell bega a general forward movement. Lieut.-Gen Scott advised postponement until the force should be better prepared for servic but his warning was disregarded. Th Federal army was divided into 5 divisions Leaving 5,700 men under Brig.-Gen. Run yon to guard the approaches to Washing ton, the other 4 divisions, aggregating 28, 500 men, under Brigadier-Generals Tyle Hunter, Heintzelman and Miles, advance to Bull Run, a tributary of the Potoma River, about 30 miles from Washington on the way to Manassas Junction. Hunt er's and Heintzelman's divisions crossed th run July 21 and attacked the Confeder ate left, slowly forcing it back. Beaure gard's army, when the action began, con sisted of about 24,000 available men. H was reenforced at intervals during the da; by 8,000 men under Johnston, who ha been encamped in the Shenandoah Valle and whose junction with the main army was thought would be prevented by Ger Patterson. The latter had been statione at Martinsburg with 18,000 men. Be tween 3 and 4 o'clock in the afternoon when everything seemed favorable to th Federals, the last 3,000 of Johnston's men under Gen. Kirby Smith, arrived and fel upon the Federals, forcing a retreat. Thi attack was followed by another by Early' brigade, and the Federal retreat became rout. Men threw away their arms an equipments; artillery horses were cut fron their traces and guns abandoned on th road; soldiers, civilians, and camp follow ers fled panic-stricken toward Washingto afoot, astride, and in carriages. The re treating army and followers reached Wash ington July 23. The casualties of the bat tle were: Federal losses—killed, 481 wounded, 1,011; missing, 1,216; tota 2,708. Confederate losses—killed, 387 wounded, 1,582; missing, 13; total, 1,982 This battle was the first very importan engagement of the war. (See also Grove ton (Va.), Battle of; Manassas (Va.), o Bull Run, Second Battle of.)

Bullion.—Gold, silver, or other metals en masse, or undefined state, as distinguished from coin.

Bullion State.—A nickname for Missouri (q. v.). (See also States.)

Buncombe.—To talk buncombe is to speak for effect on persons at a distance, without regard to the audience present. The phrase originated near the close of the debate on the famous "Missouri Question," in the Sixteenth Congress. It was then used by Felix Walker, a naïve old mountaineer who resided at Waynesville, in Haywood, a western county of North Carolina, near the border of the adjacent county of Buncombe, which was in his district. The old gentleman rose to speak while the House was impatiently calling "Question," and several members gathered around him, begging him to desist. He persevered, however, for a while, declaring that the people of his district expected it, and that he was bound to make a speech for Buncombe.

Bunker Hill, or Breeds Hill (Mass.), Battle of.—After the battles of Lexington and Concord the British force under Gen. Gage was increased to 10,000 men by the arrival of Generals Howe, Clinton, and Burgoyne from England. These officers occupied the town of Boston, on a peninsula extending into the harbor. On the surrounding hills were encamped some 20,000 undisciplined Americans. On the night of June 16, 1775, 1,000 of them under Col. Prescott were sent to fortify Bunker Hill, on another peninsula lying north of Boston. Through some misapprehension they seized Breeds Hill, near Boston, and threw up a line of fortifications. In the morning of the 17th, about 3,000 (possibly 3,500) British crossed the harbor in boats and charged the hill, which was defended by about half that number of raw recruits. After three bloody charges the Americans were driven from their position, having defended themselves with gunstocks and stones when their ammunition was exhausted. The British loss was about 1,050; that of the Americans about 450, including Gen. Warren. The statistics of this battle show the number of killed and wounded to have been more than 30 per cent of the number engaged, thus placing it among the bloodiest battles known to history. At Gettysburg after three days' fighting, the Union army lost 25 per cent while 30 per cent of those who fought at Bunker Hill fell in an hour and a half.

Bunting.—A collective mass of flags, especially on ships.

Burchardism.—A term of reproach applying to indiscreet utterances by political promoters, due to the unfortunate reference by Reverend Samuel Dickinson Burchard to the Democratic Party as a party of "Rum, Romanism and Rebellion" (q. v.).

Bureau.—From the meaning in general use, —namely, a place where business is transacted,—the word "Bureau" has come into use as descriptive of a department of the government, like the Bureau of Education, Bureau of Engraving and Printing, etc.

Bureau of Accounts, State Department. —The Bureau of Accounts was first organized in the re-adjustment of the Department of State in 1870. It directs the finances of the department, controls all its receipts and expenditures, and supervises its funds and accounts. (See State Department.)

Bureau of Animal Industry. (See Animal Industry, Bureau of.)

Bureau of Biological Survey. (See Biological Survey, Bureau of.)

Bureau of Chemistry. (See Chemistry, Bureau of.)

Bureau of Construction and Repair, Navy Department.—This bureau plans the construction of new vessels and of necessary changes on old vessels, both those under construction in United States Naval Yards and those under contract in private yards. Under its supervision come also the construction of and repairs on submarines and aircraft. It maintains a staff which periodically examines all ships of the United States Navy for repairs and alterations. (See Navy; Navy Department.)

Bureau of Corporations. (See sub-heading Corporations under article Commerce Department.)

Bureau of Crop Estimates. (See Crop Estimates, Bureau of.)

Bureau of Education.—(See Interior Department and Education, Bureau of.) Provision was made for a Commissioner of Education by enactment approved March 2, 1867. He is appointed by the President, by and with the consent of the Senate, and his yearly salary is $5,000. He administers and distributes the collection of facts and statistics showing the condition of education in the various states. He diffuses such educational information, particularly information concerning the organization and the management of schools and methods of teaching, as shall promote the cause of education throughout the country. The Bureau of Education also issues bulletins on the condition of the higher education in the United States, on the advance of technical and industrial education, and on the enactment and enforcement of compulsory school attendance laws. The Commissioner of Education has charge of the education, support, and medical condition of the Alaskan natives.

In addition, the Bureau of Education serves as a kind of education clearing-house for the country. It advises educational authorities in all localities, and maintains a corps of experts whose services are available for all manner of educational institutions. But the Bureau goes further—it encourages to the limit of its ability what seem to it to be desirable trends in education, as the payment of more adequate salaries to teachers; and the establishment of public school systems organized into six years of primary and six years of secondary education (the so-called "Six-and-six plan"), instead of the customary system of eight years of primary and four years of secondary education. The Commissioner of Education also pays particular attention to the encouragement of education after the student has left school, and supports this endeavor extensively by the promotion of the establishment of country libraries. He inspects, surveys and grades colleges, universities, and professional schools; and helps in standardizing and modernizing school plants and provision for school sanitation. In recent years the Bureau has expended much of its energy in the stimulation and organization of industrial education and education for home-making; in the encouragement of gardening; and in the general improvement of negro education. It is actively helping to establish new kindergartens and to make more available the various opportunities for education in the home. It also is co-operating with other departments of the Government and with public and private civic and social welfare organizations in promoting education for citizenship, better facilities for educating and Americanizing immigrants, and in extending night schools.

Bureau of Entomology. (See Entomology, Bureau of.)

Bureau of Fisheries. (See Fisheries.)

Bureau of Foreign and Domestic Commerce, Commerce Department.—This bureau was organized in 1912, combining the activities and functions of the Bureau of Statistics (see Statistics, Bureau of) and the Bureau of Manufactures (see sub-heading Manufactures under Commerce Department). It is charged with the encouragement and development of United States manufacturing interests both at home and abroad. It collects, supervises, and distributes reports from the 10 commercial attachés and 19 commercial agents of the Department, as well as the trade reports of the United States consuls (q. v.). It provides general statistical information which will enable American manufacturers and merchants to invest capital abroad with the most beneficial results. It also issues authentic statistics of exports, and reports on the costs of production in various industries. The Bureau's reports and criticisms of commercial conditions aim to be constructive so well as informing, and for this purpose it has divided the country into commercial districts, over each of which presides an officer of the Bureau. (See Commerce; Commerce Department.)

Bureau of Immigration. (See Commissioner of Immigration.)

Bureau of Insular Affairs. (See Insular Affairs, Bureau of.)

Bureau of Investigations, Department of Justice.—This bureau aids in detecting violation of Federal laws, among which may be mentioned the Federal White Slave Act (q. v.), the Anti-trust law (q. v.), the United States Neutrality laws (see Neutrality), the Bankruptcy acts (q. v.), and the acts prohibiting peonage. The Bureau, through its division of accountants, enforces the national banking laws, investigates mail-frauds and offenses against the bankruptcy enactments. Another division is charged with the examination of the offices of United States court officials, looks into the conduct of the court officials, and investigates the characters of applicants for appointments. (See Justice Department.)

Bureau of Labor Statistics. (See Commissioner of Labor Statistics.)

Bureau of Lighthouses. (See Lighthouses.)

Bureau of Medicine and Surgery, Navy Department.—This bureau is under the direction of the Surgeon-general of the Navy. It is charged with supervision over the health and sanitary conditions of the Navy, Naval Stations (q. v.), and Naval Academy (q. v.). It maintains naval hospitals, a naval medical school, and hospital and medical corps. (See Navy; Navy Department.)

Bureau of Naturalization. (See Commissioner of Naturalization.)

Bureau of Navigation, Commerce Department.—A Bureau of Navigation was constituted in the Treasury Department in 1884, transferred to the Department of Commerce and Labor when that department was organized in 1903, and was kept in that department when the Department of Labor was separated from it in 1913. The Bureau of Navigation is directed by the Commissioner of Navigation, who superintends conditions surrounding the commercial marine and merchant seamen of the United States over whom jurisdiction is not definitely assigned to some other authority. The Commissioner of Navigation decides all questions concerning the registers and licenses of vessels, superintends the laws relating to navigation, and prepares and publishes annually a list of United States vessels in the commercial marine, with full data thereon. He also investigates the working of the laws of navigation and recommends new laws when they seem to be advisable. He is appointed by the President, by and with the consent of the Senate, and his yearly salary is $4,000. (See Merchant Marine; Commerce Department.)

Bureau of Navigation, Navy Department.—This bureau is charged with the manning of all vessels in the Navy, and the determination of the personnel of the Navy, under which head fall the recruiting of sailors and the commissioning of officers. It also conducts the Naval Training Stations (see Naval Stations) and the Naval Observatory (q. v.). Through the Hydrographic Office (q. v.), it controls the issuance of charts for use in the Navy, and it superintends the publication of the "Nautical Almanac" (q. v.). It has charge of the enlistment of the Naval Reserve, of the establishment and the administration of the various naval districts into which the country is divided, of the courses in naval warfare in the War College (q. v.) and elsewhere, and of the naval service trade schools. (See Navy; Navy Department; Navigation.)

Bureau of Ordnance, Navy Department.—This bureau has charge of the construction and design of all guns, shells, armor, powder, torpedoes, mines, magazines, and other pieces of ordnance used in the Navy. It also manages the United States Naval Gun Factory and the Naval Torpedo Station. (See Navy Department; Navy.)

Bureau of Pensions. (See Pensions and Interior Department.)

Bureau of Plant Industry. (See Plant Industry, Bureau of.)

Bureau of Soils. (See Soils, Bureau of.)

Bureau of Standards, Commerce Department.—This bureau is charged with the examination of all manner of standards of measurements, of quality, and of mechanical performance and practice, to see that they conform to the official standards at Washington, which are in the custody of the Bureau. The Bureau is charged also with the solution of problems concerning standards, either for the Government, a state, a city, or any society, institution, or firm in the United States, although it charges a fee for such service, except that rendered to the Government or to any State. It serves as a testing bureau for all governmental departments at Washington. Its work is divided into examinations of standards falling under the following divisions: 1, Weights and measures; 2, Heat and thermometry; 3, Electricity; 4, Light and optical instruments; 5, Chemistry; 6, Engineering, research and testing; 7, Metallurgy; 8, Miscellaneous materials. The Bureau is administered by a Director, whose yearly salary is $5,000.

Bureau of Steam Engineering, Navy Department.—This bureau plans all machinery repairs to United States vessels, and also has charge of the machinery in use at the United States Navy Yards. It maintains an engineering station at Washington. It also inspects the radio equipment at the United States naval stations and wireless stations, examines engineering material used in the Navy Yards and on vessels, and has charge of other engineering supplies. (See Navy; Navy Department; Naval Stations.)

Bureau of the Census. (See Census.)

Bureau of War Risk Insurance.—The Bureau of War Risk Insurance was created on September 2, 1914, in order to assist commerce in American vessels and to grant war risk insurance, but not maritime insurance, on the hulls or on the cargoes of American vessels. From the creation of the Bureau to June 30, 1917, it had issued 6,883 policies, amounting to $646,717,912. It had to cover losses amounting to $11,-649,697, but received premiums amounting to $15,208,730. The Bureau is under the supervision of the Treasury Department (q. v.).

In 1917, the Sixty-fifth Congress provided further for the insurance of the personal effects of masters, officers and crews of American ships, and against their loss of life or injury. It provided also for compensation for detention after capture by the enemy. The Secretary of the Treasury is authorized, in his discretion, to compel the owners of such vessels to insure their masters, officers and crews against loss of life, personal injury, and capture for a principal sum ranging from $1,500 to $5,000, of which percentages are to be paid for various losses. The Bureau of War Risk Insurance was authorized also to reinsure vessels flying foreign friendly flags, or their cargo insured by any ally of the United States, and to reinsure with any such government American vessels and their cargoes.

For the work of the Bureau of War Risk Insurance in insuring American soldiers and sailors, see the article Soldiers' and Sailors' Insurance.

Bureau of Yards and Docks, Navy Department.—The Bureau of Yards and Docks supervises the United States navy yards, navy stations, dry docks, and other naval depots; and also has control over the construction of naval hospitals and naval barracks. (See Navy Department; Navy; Navy Stations; Navy Yards.)

Bureaucracy.—A government conducted through the instrumentality of bureaus; also used to characterize the office-holders so conducting the government.

Burnt Corn Creek (Ala.), Battle of.—As a result of Tecumseh's efforts to induce all the Southern Indians to join in a war of extermination against the whites, the Creeks were divided into two factions—one for war, the other for peace. In 1813 Peter McQueen, a half-breed of Tallahassee, one of the leaders of the war party, was furnished by British agents at Pensacola with large quantities of supplies, under sanction of the Spanish governor. On learning of this Col. James Caller, of Washington, set out July 25, 1813, to disperse the Indians McQueen had collected and intercepted the supplies. On the morning of July 27 Caller's command, increased by re-

enforcements to 180 men, came upon McQueen's party at their camp on Burnt Corn Creek. The Indians were surprised and fled into the woods, leaving their pack horses to the whites. They soon returned, however, and fiercely attacked 100 of Caller's men. Overwhelming numbers compelled Caller's men to retreat after a brave resistance. Two of Caller's command were killed and 15 wounded.

Burr Conspiracy.—In consequence of Burr's duel with Hamilton, in which the latter met his death, Burr was indicted in New York and New Jersey for murder. (See illustration opposite 430.) He went west and made an extensive tour, in the course of which he made preparations for a gigantic but mysterious scheme. The real object of this is unknown. It was either to separate the Mississippi Valley from the rest of the Union and erect it into a new nation, or to conquer Mexico. In 1806 he gathered a number of reckless persons about him and started for the region of Texas, ostensibly on a colonizing expedition. President Jefferson issued a proclamation warning citizens against joining the expedition. Burr was arrested by Jefferson's order, brought back to Virginia, and indicted there by a United States Grand Jury for treason and for a misdemeanor, based on his course in levying war within this country on a friendly nation; but it was hoped that Burr could also be shown to have had treasonable designs against the unity of his country. He was acquitted of treason for want of jurisdiction, on the failure of the evidence required by Article 3, section 3, clause 1 of the Constitution; he was also acquitted for misdemeanor. He was bound over to present himself for trial in Ohio, but the matter was pressed no further. One of Burr's dupes in this scheme was Harman Blennerhasset, who was also arrested, but who was discharged after Burr's acquittal. Among the witnesses against Burr were Gen. Wilkinson, commander of the United States army, and Commodore Truxtun, of the navy. Washington Irving was one of his attorneys.

Burr Conspiracy:
Mentioned by President, 394.
Proclamation against, 392.
Progress of, 400.

Bushwhacking.—A term which came into use during the Civil War as indicating irregular warfare, particularly that of fighting from behind bushes,—and therefore from any hiding place.

Business (See also Anti-trust law, Monopolies, Commerce, Trusts, Incorporations, Injunctions, Interstate Commerce, Manufactures):
Advantages of Chambers of Commerce, 8036.
And diplomacy go hand in hand, 7771.
Antagonism of government ended, 7914.
Capital, foreign employment of, discussed, 7415.
Conditions in 1912, 7791.
Conditions in December, 1910, 7440.
Conditions of, should be best possible, 8036.
Co-operation necessary in, 8036.

Cost and economy not properly studied, 7870.

Credit extension necessary, 7880.

Crop of 1910, effect of, on, 7536.

Department of Agriculture's influence on, 7374.

Dishonesty in, denounced, 7140.

Export, control of, by government, during European War, 8301.

Foreign, importance of fostering, 7374.

Government supervision over big business, benefits of, 7079.

Government's assistance to, 8151.

Hampered by uncertainty of antitrust law, 7916.

Importance of diplomatic service to, 7421.

Incorporation, Federal—
  Arguments against, refuted, 7456.
  Constitutionality of, discussed, 7457.

Discussed and recommended, 7522.

Interference with, 8038.

Investigation of industrial companies by Department of Justice, recommended by President Taft, 7453.

Legislation on abuses of, should be ended and existing statutes enforced, 7555.

Men should be relieved of uncertainties, 7910.

Monopolies, attempted, more failures than successes in, 7451.

Not to be kept in suspense, 7871.

Of Germany, how controlled by German government, 8387.

Price-fixing during European War, 8311.

Private management of, the American tradition, 8418.

Profits and patriotism should not be mentioned in the same breath, 8312.

Programme of regulation of, by 63d Congress commended, 8015.

Restraint of trade, legal or illegal according to extent of monopoly and methods, 7450.

Risk of trade a legitimate charge upon society, 7036.

Safe maxim for, 8033.

Secured for United States by official conduct, 7778.

Shippers' right to choose transfer routes for goods, 7446.

Trade agreements, encouragement of, 7345.

Butter, act defining and imposing tax on, and regulating manufacture of oleomargarine, discussed, 4992.

Butter, Cheese, and Condensed Milk.—
Of the 8,479 establishments in the dairy industry in the United States in 1909 56.4 per cent. reported butter as their product of chief value, 42 per cent. cheese, and 1.6

per cent. condensed milk. Of the value of products shown for the combined industry the butter factories contributed $194,999,-198, or 71 per cent.; the cheese factories $44,263,177, or 16.1 per cent.; and the condensed milk factories $35,295,343, or 12.9 per cent. The combined production of butter in the factories and on farms in United States amounted to 1,619,415,263 pounds, an increase of 127,662,661 pounds, or 8.6 per cent., over the production in 1899.

The quantity of cheese produced in the United States in the factories of the industry and on farms during 1909 amounted to 320,532,181 pounds, an increase of 22,187,-539 pounds, or 7.4 per cent., over the production in 1899.

In the quantity of butter manufactured in the factories of the industry, there was an increase of 204,638,107 pounds, or 48.7 per cent., during the decade 1899-1909. Wisconsin ranked first in the production of butter in 1909, with 103,884,684 pounds; Minnesota was second, with 88,842,846 pounds; and Iowa was third, with 88,582,-187 pounds. Although the manufacture of butter was reported from 43 states in 1909, the combined product of six states—Wisconsin, Minnesota, Iowa, New York, California and Michigan—amounting to 400,-002,143 pounds, represented 64 per cent.

Detailed figures for the combined industry in the leading states follow:

States	Number of Establishments	Value of Product	Per Cent. of Total
Wisconsin......	2,630	$53,843,249	19.6
New York.....	1,552	42,458,345	15.5
Iowa..........	512	25,849,866	9.4
Minnesota.....	784	25,287,462	9.2
Illinois........	295	17,798,278	6.5
Michigan......	435	14,287,499	5.2
Pennsylvania...	536	13,544,065	4.9
California......	161	12,760,670	4.6
Ohio..........	325	9,689,670	3.5
Vermont.......	186	8,112,239	3.0
Nebraska......	37	7,681,272	2.8
Washington....	97	7,271,047	2.7
Kansas........	60	6,070,634	2.2
Oregon........	95	4,920,462	1.8
Indiana.......	132	3,958,600	1.4
Missouri......	56	2,958,818	1.1
South Dakota..	95	2,685,511	1.0
Colorado......	39	2,339,765	0.9
Utah..........	37	1,971,031	0.7
Maine.........	29	1,301,027	0.5
United States..	8,479	$274,557,718	100.0

Condensed milk shows an increase in production for the decade 1899-1909 amounting to 307,874,757 pounds, or 164.7 per cent. The bulk of this product was reported by a small number of states. New York produced 24.4 per cent. of the total quantity in 1909, Illinois 23.1 per cent., and Washington 10.8 per cent., the combined output of these three states representing 58.4 per cent. (See also Dairying and Cattle Raising.)

Butterfield, Carlos & Co., claim of against Denmark for seizure of the *Ben Franklin* and *Catherine Augusta*, 4462, 5369.

Agreement to submit to arbitration, 5388.

Award of arbitrator, 5545.

By Chance, claim for, adjusted, 3464.

By-Law.—A rule laid down for the regulation of a legislative body.

Cabal.—Originally used in the reign of King Charles II., because of intrigue charged against five men, the initials of whose names spelled the word,—namely, Clifford, Ashley, Buckingham, Arlington, and Lauderdale. In American politics the word has come to mean a conspiracy to achieve private ends at the expense of the Government.

Cabinet.—Specifically, a body of counselors, usually composed of heads of departments, meeting in a private room or cabinet. In the United States the term is applied to the council composed of the heads of some of the Executive Departments of the Government, with whom the President confers on matters of administrative policy. Their meeting as advisers of the President is unknown to law or the Constitution and their conclusions have no binding force. The Constitution does not provide for a Cabinet, but it authorizes the President to "require the opinion in writing of the principal officer in each of the Executive Departments upon any subject relating to the duties of their respective offices." Washington required such opinions frequently. Cabinet officers receive a yearly salary of $12,000. (See State Department, Treasury Department, War Department, Justice Department, Post-Office Department, Navy Department, Interior Department, Agriculture Department, Commerce Department, Labor Department.)

Changes have taken place in the method pursued, and the Cabinet is now regarded as an advisory board with which the President holds regular consultations. From being merely the heads of the Executive Departments certain of its members have come to be recognized as an essential part of the Government. (See also Presidential Succession and Administration.)

Cabinet:
Official conduct of, complimented, 2203.

Cables.—Pacific cable, 6663, 6719. (See also Ocean Cables.)

Caddo Indians. (See Indian Tribes.)

Cadet.—A private in the army preparing to qualify for a commission; a student in a military school, especially West Point, preparing for the rank of officer; also a candidate for admission as cadet on the nomination of the President, or a United States Senator, or a Member of Congress. By act of Congress in 1902, the title "midshipman" superseded the title "naval cadet." (See Military Academy.)

Cadets, Military. (See Military Academy.)
Enlistment of, time of, should be extended, 1607.
Increase in corps of, recommended, 3249.
Promotion of, referred to, 2422.
Referred to, 621.

Cadre.—A military term applied to the force of 500,000 men first to be raised and trained by the selective draft under the draft (q. v.) law of 1916. The word comes from France, where it had been applied to the various groups of soldiers called to the colors under the different classes.

Cahokia Indians. (See Indian Tribes.)

Cairo and Tennessee Railroad Co., act to authorize construction of bridges by, returned, 5505.

Calapona Indians. (See Indian Tribes.)

Calaveras Big Tree Grove, preservation of, 6859.

Calebee Creek (Ala.), Battle of.—In his expedition against the Creek Indians Gen. Floyd, with more than 1,200 Georgia volunteers, one company of cavalry, and 400 friendly Indians, arrived at Calebee Creek on the night of Jan. 26, 1814, and established a camp on the highland bordering on the swamp of that name in Macon County, Ala., 50 miles west of Fort Mitchell. Before dawn of the following morning the camp was suddenly attacked by Indians. The assailants were received with grapeshot, followed by a bayonet charge, and fled in dismay. They left 37 dead. The whites lost 17 killed and 132 wounded. Of the friendly Indians 5 were killed and 15 wounded. Floyd retired to Fort Mitchell, where most of his men were discharged. No other expedition against the Creeks was organized in Georgia.

California.—One of the Pacific Coast states; nickname, "The Golden State"; motto, "Eureka" (I have found). California is named, it is said, after a fictitious island in the Spanish romance "Las Sergas de Esplandian." Other authorities derive the name from the Spanish words "caliente" (hot) and "fornalla" (furnace). The State extends from lat. 32° 30' to 42° north and from long. 114° to 124° 25' west, an area of 158,297 square miles. It is bounded on the north by Oregon, on the east by Nevada and Arizona, and on the south by lower California, and on the west by the Pacific Ocean. Its capital is Sacramento, and San Francisco is the chief city. The State is famous for its beautiful scenery, its salubrious climate, and its wealth of precious metals and choice fruits. (See illustration opposite 2488.)

From the time of its discovery to 1846 it was practically a part of Mexico. July 5, 1846, Col. John C. Frémont assumed command of the insurgents at Sonoma and on July 7 the Star and Stripes were hoisted over Monterey by order of John D. Sloat, commanding the U. S. Pacific squadron. Gold was discovered Jan. 19, 1848. Feb. 2, of the same year, California and New Mexico were ceded to the United States by the treaty of Guadaloupe Hidalgo. It was admitted to the Union Sept. 9, 1850, as a result of the famous Clay compromise resolutions passed by Congress. (See Compromise of 1850). Statistics of agriculture collected for the last Federal Census place the number of farms in the State at 88,197, comprising 27,931,444 acres, valued, with stock and improvements, at $1,614,694,584. The value of domestic animals, poultry, etc., was $127,599,938, including 2,017,025 cattle, valued at $52,785,068; 468,886 horses, $47,099,196; 69,761 mules, $9,016,444; 166,551 swine, $5,106,883; 2,417,477 sheep, $8,348,997; poultry, $3,844,526. The yield and value of the field crops for 1911 was: corn, 51,000 acres, 1,836,000 bushels, $1,-652,000; wheat, 480,000 acres, 8,640,000 bushels, $7,603,000; oats, 210,000 acres, 7,140,000 bushels, $4,213,000; rye, 8,000 acres, 136,000 bushels, $116,000; potatoes, 72,000 acres, 9,720,000 bushels, $8,748,000; hay, 700,000 acres, 1,225,000 tons, $13,-352,000. The total value of the mineral products in 1910 was $86,688,347.

The political occurrences in the state during 1913 are of national importance owing to the passage by the legislature of a law limiting ownership of land by aliens, directed primarily against the Japanese. The subject is discussed in detail in the correspondence between Governor Johnson and President Wilson. (Page 7873.)

Since 1906, when the Japanese began to arrive in California in large numbers the labor element has maintained opposition, which manifested itself in riots and public meetings of protest. An attempt was made to exclude Japanese children from the public schools. President Rosevelt's attention was directed to the troubles and in his message of Dec. 18, 1906 (page 7744), declares his purpose to maintain the integrity of our treaty obligations to Japan.

The state also passed a civil service law, a "blue sky" law, intended to safeguard the people in the purchase of securities of corporations, a mothers' pension law, a commission to fix minimum wages and hours of labor, and a commission to assist the legislature in framing laws.

The number of manufacturing establishments in California having an annual output valued at $500 or more at the beginning of 1915 was 10,057. The amount of capital invested was $736,105,000, giving employment to 176,548 persons, using material valued at $447,475,000, and turning out finished goods worth $712,801,000. Salaries and wages paid amounted to $140,843,000.

California:

Admission of, into Union discussed, 2556, 2564.

Affairs of, report of, transmitted, 2579, 2584.

Alien land law discussed, 8253, 8255.

Census of, delay in taking, 2665.

Cession of New Mexico and, to United States of Mexico—
Area and value of, 2449, 2484.
Discussions and recommendations regarding, 2306, 2309, 2344, 2356, 2386, 2426, 2437, 2444, 2484.
Treaty for, transmitted, 2437.

Cession of, to Great Britain by Mexico, negotiations regarding, referred to, 2078.

Circuit court of United States in, referred to, 3282.

Claims of citizens of, against United States, 2679.

Constitution adopted by, 2570.

Constitutional convention in, referred to, 2556, 2584.

Cuartel lot in Monterey, survey and disposal of, discussed, 5504.

Customs collected in, 2586.

Difficulty between consul of France and authorities of, 2835.
Satisfactorily settled, 2868.

Elections in, national military forces to be used at, referred to, 4076.

Expeditions organized in, for invasion of Mexico, 2770.
Proclamation against, 2804.

Forces to be employed in, 2454.

Fraudulent claims to lands in, defeated by Attorney-General, 3184.

Geological and mineralogical exploration in, recommended, 2558.

Gold in, production of, 2660.

Gold mines discovered in, 2486, 2493.

Government of, discussed, 2556, 2564.

Indians in—
Claims of persons for supplies furnished, 2777.
Colonization of, referred to, 2834.
Hostilities of, referred to, 2668, 2894.
Number of, 2453.
Removal of, referred to, 2833.
Irrigation of valleys in, 4217.

Land grants in, appointment of commissioners to settle claims under, recommended, 2622.
Compensation of Commissioners, inadequate, 2662.

Land laws, extension of, over, recommended, 2623.

Land office in, recommended, 2663, 2714.

Lands in, set apart as public reservation by proclamation, 5792, 5804, 5814, 5815, 6207, 6211, 6701, 6706.

Light-houses on coast of, sites for, referred to, 2557.

Line of communication with eastern section of United States recommended, 2558, 2622.

Mail facilities should be afforded citizens of, 2489, 2560.

Mail route from Mississippi River to, recommended, 2992.

Mineral lands in, disposition of, discussed, 2493, 2558, 2623, 2663.

Miners' strike, proclamation against violence in, 8317.

Mines in, referred to, 2486, 2493.

Mine, branch of, in recommended, 2486, 2557, 2621.
Construction of, discussed, 2747.

National military forces to be used at election in, referred to, 4076.

Payment of settlers for improvements on Round Valley Reservation is recommended, 4692, 4781.

Private land claims in, referred to, 3127.

Public lands in—
Modifications in laws regarding, recommended, 2623.
Referred to, 2558, 2662.

Revenue laws, extension of, over, recommended, 2493.
Referred to, 2557.

Slavery in, right to introduce, discussed, 2490.

Surveyor-General's offices in, recommended, 2493, 2558.

Territorial government, for, recommended, 2392, 2439, 2488.

Unlawful combinations in, proclamation against, 5932.

Vigilance committee in, application of governor to maintain law against usurped authority of, 2916.

California and Oregon Railroad, commissioners appointed to report upon, referred to, 4865.

Cambrai, Battle of. (See European War.)

Cambrian, The, ordered from and forbidden to re-enter waters of United States, 391.

Camden (S. C.), Battle of. (See Sanders Creek (S. C.), Battle of.)

Camouflage.—Officially, the art of military concealment; in common connotation, "faking."

Camoufleur.—One who practices camouflage (q. v.).

Camp Alger, Va., mentioned, 6774.

Campaign Contributions.—At the extra session of the Sixty-second Congress an act was passed to provide for the publicity of contributions for the purpose of influencing elections at which representatives in Congress are elected. This act forbids any candidate for representative from giving, contributing, expending, using or promising any sums in the aggregate exceeding $5,000 in any campaign for his nomination and election. A candidate for Senator is limited to $10,000. Sworn statements of all expenditures must be filed in Washington not less than ten nor more than fifteen days before the time for holding any primary election or nominating convention, and not less than ten nor more than fifteen days before the day of the election at which the person is to be balloted for.

Campaign Contributions, publication of, discussed, 7015, 7439.

Canada.—The Dominion of Canada occupies the whole of the northern part of the North American Continent (with the exception of Alaska and part of the coast of Labrador), from 49° north latitude to the Arctic seas, and from the Pacific to the Atlantic Ocean.

AREA AND POPULATION

Provinces	Area (English Sq. Miles)	Population 1911*
Alberta	255,285	374,663
British Columbia	355,855	392,480
Manitoba	251,832	455,614
New Brunswick	27,985	351,889
Nova Scotia	21,428	492,338
Ontario	407,262	2,523,274
Prince Edward Island	2,184	93,728
Quebec	706,834	2,003,232
Saskatchewan	251,700	492,432
Yukon	207,076	8,512
North-West Territories	1,242,224	18,481
Total	3,729,665	7,206,643

*The rural population, in 1911, was 3,-925,679, and the urban population, 3,280,-964. Of the immigrants in 1911-12, 108,082 were from England, 2,019 from Wales, 30,-735 from Scotland, and 9,706 from Ireland, total 150,542; and 139,009 came from the United States and 112,881 from other countries. In 1912-13 the immigrants numbered 402,432.

On Jan. 1, 1916, the population was estimated at 8,361,000. In the census of 1911, 78% of the population was reported as Canadian-born and 11% as born in other English territory.

The 1911 census reported the population of the largest cities as follows: Montreal, 470,480; Toronto, 376,538; Winnipeg, 136,-035; Vancouver, 100,041.

There are only 886 women to every 1,000 men in Canada. The density of the population is 1.93 to the square mile. 55% of the population is rural and 45% urban.

The census taken in 1911 showed that 34% of the people are engaged in agriculture; 9% in building trades; 8% in domestic and personal service; 18% in manufacturing pursuits; 10% in trade and merchandise; 3% in hunting, fishing and lumbering; and 8% in transportation.

Except in certain rural parts of Quebec, where the French-Canadians have preserved their old French *patois*, English is generally understood in the Dominion. The French-Canadians inhabit mostly the eastern parts of Ontario and Quebec. Both French and English are official languages —for instance, in the Quebec legislature, French is usually spoken, whereas in the Canadian Parliament, English is the rule. However, a person resident in Canada needs both languages.

In 1911, the distribution of the various denominations was as follows:

Roman Catholic	2,833,041
Presbyterian	1,115,324
Methodist	1,079,892
Episcopalian	1,043,017
Baptist	382,666
Mennonites	44,611

The percentage of illiteracy among the population over the age of 6 is 8½. Quebec is the only province without a compulsory education law.

The following are the immigration figures for Canada of recent years:

	United Kingdom	United States	Others	Total
1912	138,121	133,710	82,406	354,237
1913	150,542	139,009	112,881	402,432
1914	142,622	107,530	134,726	384,876
1915	43,276	59,779	41,734	144,789
1916	8,664	36,937	2,936	48,537
1917	8,282	61,389	5,703	75,374

History.—Canada was originally discovered by Cabot in 1497, but its history dates only from 1534, when the French took possession of the country. The first settlement (Quebec) was founded by them in 1608. In 1759 Quebec succumbed to the British forces under General Wolfe, and in 1763 the whole territory of Canada became a possession of Great Britain by the Treaty of Paris of that year. Nova Scotia was ceded in 1713 by the Treaty of Utrecht, the Provinces of New Brunswick and Prince Edward Island being subsequently formed out of it. British Columbia was formed into a Crown colony in 1858, having previously been a part of the Hudson Bay Territory, and was united to Vancouver Island in 1866. By the British North America Act, passed in 1867, the Provinces of Canada (Ontario and Quebec), Nova Scotia, and New Brunswick were united under the title of The Dominion of Canada, and provision was made in the Act for the admission at any subsequent period of the other provinces and territories of British North America.

Physical Features.—From a physical point of view Canada may be divided into an eastern and a western division, the Red River Valley, in long. 97°, forming the separating line. The eastern division comprises three areas: (1) The southeastern area, which is generally hilly, and sometimes mountainous, with many fine stretches of agricultural and pastoral lands. (2) The southern and western area, presenting in the main, a broad, level, and slightly undulating expanse of generally fertile country, with occasional step-like ridges or rocky escarpments. The main hydrographical feature is the chain of lakes, with an area of 150,000 square miles, contributing to the great river system of the St.

Lawrence. (3) The northern area, embracing nearly two-thirds of the Dominion, with an average elevation of 1,000 feet above the level of the sea, pre-eminently a region of waterways, and including the great Laurentian mountain range. In this area are found the other great river systems, the Nelson and the Mackenzie. The western division referred to may also be said to possess two areas equally distinct in character. The first stretches from the Red River Valley to the Rocky Mountains. Here, between lat. 49° and 54°, is the great Prairie Region, rising to the west in three terrace-like elevations. North of the 54th parallel the country passes again into forest. The second area, from the western edge of the Prairie to the Pacific coast, is a distance of 400 miles, and contains the Rocky Mountains (Mount Hooker, 15,700 feet) and the Gold and Cascade Ranges, whose summits are from 4,000 to 16,000 feet high, the country being on the whole densely wooded.

Government.—Canada is a self-governing Dominion within the British Empire, its constitution resting on the British North America Act of 1867, under which the Dominion of Canada came into being on July 1, 1867 (Dominion Day.) The Executive power is vested in a Governor-General appointed by the Sovereign and aided by a Privy Council. Governor-General and Commander-in-Chief—The Duke of Devonshire, who succeeded the Duke of Connaught (appointed in 1911) on Aug. 19, 1916. The prime minister in 1917 was Sir Robert Laird Borden (Conservative) who succeeded in 1911 the Liberal, Sir Wilfrid Laurier.

Parliament consists of a Senate and a House of Commons. The Senate consists of 87 members, nominated for life by the Governor-General, distributed between the various provinces. The House of Commons is chosen every five years at longest, and the 1911-16 Parliament consists of 221 members.

By act of the English Parliament, the life of the Canadian Parliament which would have terminated in 1916 was lengthened to Oct. 7, 1917.

Justice is administered, as in England, by judges, police magistrates, and justices of the peace, of whom the first-named are appointed by the Governor-General, for life, from among the foremost men at the Bar in the several provinces. The highest court is the Supreme Court of Canada, composed of a Chief Justice and five puisne judges, and holding three sessions in the year at Ottawa. The only other Dominion Court, viz., the Exchequer Court of Canada, is presided over by a separate judge, and its sittings may be held anywhere in Canada.

Women have the right of suffrage in Manitoba and Alberta. Manitoba, British Columbia and Ontario forbid the sale of intoxicating liquors.

Army.—Service in the Militia is universal and compulsory on all male citizens from 18 to 60. The Peace Effective consists of a Permanent Staff of 3,520 officers and men, and 74,000 undergoing service. The War Effective consists of four classes: the unmarried men 18 to 30; the unmarried men 30 to 40; the married men 18 to 45; and, finally, the remaining male citizens of 18 to 60, a total of 2,153,000.

Canada rallied to the support of the mother country in the European War, and it was estimated that on May 1, 1917, about 500,000 Canadians had volunteered for war service. 316,400 had been actually sent overseas, 136,400 to France, while the others were being trained in Canada. Some of the greatest victories of English arms were due to Canadian valor, and it was estimated that by May, 1917, almost 100,000

Canadians had been reported killed, wounded or missing. This number, however, came almost entirely from the English-speaking element of the country; and the feeling that the French-Canadians were not upholding their end of the burdens of war compelled conscription.

Education is under the control of the provincial governments, the cost being met by local taxation, aided by grants from the several Provincial Governments. There are some 25,000 elementary and secondary schools (attendance at the former being compulsory), with over 1,137,000 pupils; and sixty universities and university colleges with 40,000 students. The twenty universities had about 10,000 students in 1912.

Production and Industry.—According to the census of 1911, there were 6,328 butter and cheese factories and 5 factories for preserved milk and cream, the total value of all dairy products being $39,143,089 in 1911. The fisheries are an important source of wealth and include salmon, cod, herrings, mackerel and lobsters, the total value of the catch in 1912-3 being $32,973,179; in 1913-4, $33,207,-748; in 1914-5, $31,264,631; 1915-6, $35,-860,708; 1916-7, $39,208,378. The lumber lath and shingles produced in Canada in 1911 had a total value of $81,555,258. The forests have a total estimated area of nearly 568,500,000 acres. The industrial establishments of all kinds numbered 19,218 in 1911, with a total capital of $1,247,583,-609, the value of the products being $1,-165,975,639; 515,203 persons were employed. The metals produced in 1912 were valued as follows'—Gold, $12,559,443; silver, $19,425,656; copper, $12,709,311; nickel, $13,452,463. In 1916, the figures had risen as follows: Gold, $19,162,000; silver, $16,855,000; copper, $32,580,000; and nickel, $29,035,000. The total value of the minerals produced in 1913 was $145,-634,812; in 1914, $128,863,075; in 1915, $138,513,750; in 1916, $177,357,454.

The imports of Canada for recent years have been as follows:

1913	$692,032,392
1914	650,746,797
1915	629,444,894
1916	564,505,796
1917	892,585,566

They were distributed chiefly as follows:

	1913	1917
United States	$419,143,000	$677,632,000
United Kingdom	138,749,000	121,738,000
South America	10,529,000	4,000,000
Germany	14,215,000	14,000

The exports for recent years have been as follows:

1913	$393,232,057
1914	478,997,928
1915	490,808,877
1916	882,872,502
1917	1,300,000,000

They were distributed chiefly as follows:

	1913	1917
United States	$167,110,000	$486,871,000
United Kingdom	177,982,000	756,071,000
South America	4,352,000	2,000,000
Germany	3,402,000	

In 1915, there were 21.306 manufacturing establishments, of a capital of $1,994,103,-272, employing 514,883 persons, paying out yearly in wages and salaries $290,000,000, and producing annually goods to the value of $1,407,137,140. The value of the objects of chief output in 1915 was as follows:

Food products	$388,815,362
Textiles	144,686,605
Lumber and timber	123,396,686
Iron and steel	120,422,420

Paper and printing 74,038,398
Leather 71,036,644
Metals other than iron and steel 90,943,278

In 1917, Canada, like the United States, fixed the prices of wheat.

The estimates for the live stock in 1917 and 1916 follow:

	1916	1917
Horses	3,258,342	3,412,749
Cows	2,833,433	3,202,283
Cattle	3,760,718	4,718,657
Sheep	2,022,941	2,369,358
Swine	3,474,840	3,619,382

In 1916, the total area under crops in Canada was reported at 38,930,333 acres, with the crops valued at $886,494,900. In that year, the records of the principle crops were as follows:

	Acreage	Bushels
Wheat	15,370,000	262,781,000
Oats	11,000,000	410,200,000
Barley	1,800,000	42,775,000
Rye	148,000	2,875,000L
Potatoes	473,000	64,000,000
Hay	7,775,000	14,525,000*

* Tons.

Transportation.—The total length of railways in operation on June 30, 1912, was 26,727 miles, the total capital involved being $1,588,937,526, the earnings being $219,403,753, and the working expenses $150,736,540, in 1911-12; there were also 1,308 miles of electric railways. The sea-going and lake mercantile marine of Canada on Dec. 31, 1912, consisted of 4,713 sailing vessels and 3,667 steamers (total net tonnage 836,278 tons).

On June 30, 1916, there were 37,434 miles of railroad in operation, a considerable amount of which represented Government undertaking. The Government also operates much of the telegraph system.

Banking.—There were 27 incorporate banks of issue in 1912 with liabilities $1,240,124,354 and average assets $1,470,065,478. The balance of undrawn deposits in Post Office and Government savings banks on March 31, 1913, amounted to $57,140,484, the depositors numbering 180,796. The deposits in special savings banks on March 31, 1913, amounted to $40,133,551.

Trade with the United States.—The value of merchandise imported into Canada from the United States for the year 1913 was $415,449,457, and goods to the value of $120,571,180 were sent thither—a balance of $294,878,277 in favor of the United States.

The system of weights and measures is the same as used in England, but the unit of value is the dollar of the United States.

Canada has fifty cities with a population in excess of 10,000, Montreal approaching 500,000.

Canada, Dominion of:

Abduction of Allan Macdonald from, referred to, 3826.

Admission of into United States, cause providing for, in Articles of Confederation, 12.

Armed men from, seize American citizen, 1928.

Attempted occupation of portions of Alaska by Great Britain and, referred to, 6097.

Attempts of Great Britain and, to establish post routes in Alaska, 6097.

Boundary dispute with, arbitration of, discussed, 7409.

Boundary line with, discussed, 5470, 5616, 6064.

Canal tolls charged by, negotiations regarding. (See Welland Canal.)

Chief justice of, arbitrator in claim of United States against Peru, 6335. (See also 5988, 6092.)

Chinese entering United States through, 5476, 5632.

Civil war in, neutrality of United States in, discussed, 1702, 1748. Proclaimed, 1698, 1699.

Commercial relations with, 2582, 2654, 3989, 3999, 5748, 6332. (See also Welland Canal.)

Conference on subject of, discussed, 5675, 5678, 5748.

Commission, Joint High, 6370.

Fenians in. (See Fenians.)

Fisheries, questions regarding. (See Fisheries.)

Hostile disposition of people of, toward United States, 1749.

Illegal expeditions against, proclamation against, 4039.

Incursions from, discussed, 3447.

Jurisdictions of United States and, in Great Lakes discussed, 6064.

Merchandise transported from one port in United States, over Canadian territory, to another port therein, discussed, 5770.

Natural products, reciprocal arrangements regarding importation of, 2582.

Outrages committed on American frontier by inhabitants of, discussed, 1260, 1676, 1695, 1840.

Parliament of. (See Canadian Parliament.)

Postal arrangements with, referred to, 2175.

Postal convention with, 4203, 5377.

St. Lawrence, navigation of. (See St. Lawrence River.)

Trade with, effect of 1909 tariff on, 7502.

Trials in, of citizens of United States for complicity in Fenian invasion of, 3718.

Vessels of United States seized by revenue cutter of, 4070.

Vessels from Ontario, duties on, suspended by proclamation, 4871.

Vessels of, permission to aid disabled vessels in waters of United States proclaimed, 5828.

Vessels of United States in Great Lakes granted facilities for returning, 6331.

Welland Canal tolls discussed. (See Welland Canal.)

Canada, Reciprocity with:

Annexation not foreshadowed by, 7593.

Effect on cost of living, 7583.

Effect on trade conditions forecasted, 7582.

Farmers not injured by, 7589.

Good effect of, on future relations, 7592.

Manufacturers least benefited by, 7591.

National scope of, 7584.

Proclamation convening extra session of Congress for consideration of, 7586.

Special message of, 7587.

Speech of Taft on, 7588.

Treaty providing for, transmitted, 7581.

Canada, The, claims arising from wreck of, on coast of Brazil and award discussed, 4052, 4069.

Canadian Parliament, expression of thanks from legislative council of Canada for donations for library of, 2677.

Canadian Volunteers, bounty lands to, proclamation regarding, 558.

Canals.—Before the days of railroads overland transportation was a serious problem. Water seemed to present the cheapest and most available medium. The natural water courses were extensively navigated, but as the necessities of transportation between commercial centers increased canals were projected in many parts of the country. The oldest works of the kind in the United States are the South Hadley and Montague canals, in Massachusetts, built by companies chartered in 1792. The Middlesex Canal, connecting Boston harbor with the Merrimac River, was completed in 1808. The Erie Canal, the largest and most important in this country, was projected by De Witt Clinton, begun in 1817, and completed in 1825. It extends from the Hudson River at Albany to Lake Erie at Buffalo. It is 387 miles long and cost $52,-540,800. In 1903 the legislature of the State of New York voted $101,000,000 to improve the canal system of the state, the chief improvement being the deepening and widening of the Erie Canal to permit its use by boats of 1,000 to 1,200 tons.

The Ohio and Lake Erie Canal, from Cleveland, on Lake Erie, south through the State of Ohio, to the Ohio River at Portsmouth, a distance of 317 miles, was formally begun July 4, 1825, by Gov. Clinton, of New York, removing the first shovelful of earth. The work was completed in 1832 at a cost of $4,695,204. Another canal across the State of Ohio was completed in 1834, extending from Cincinnati to Defiance, 178 miles, where it joined the Wabash and Erie, forming another water route between the river and lake, of 265 miles. The cost of this canal was $3,700,000. The Morris Canal, from Jersey City to Phillipsburg, N. J., 102 miles in length, connecting Newark Bay with the Delaware River, was begun in 1825 and finished in 1836. With the development of railroads these canals fell into neglect and were finally wholly or partly abandoned or taken over by the railroads.

The Illinois and Michigan Canal extends from Chicago to LaSalle, on the Illinois River, a distance of 102 miles. It cost $7,357,787. A later extension of this waterway is the Hennepin Canal, from Hennepin, Ill., fifty miles through the Rock River and twenty-seven miles through land to the Mississippi River, at Rock Island. The Chesapeake and Ohio Canal, the outcome of a project of Washington to improve navigation of the Potomac River, was begun in 1828 by the board of public works of Virginia and completed in 1850. It cost $11,000,000. It extends from Georgetown, D. C., to Cumberland, Md., a distance of 184 miles. By means of seventy-four locks an elevation of 609 feet is attained. The Delaware and Hudson Canal, extending from Rondout, N. Y., to Honesdale, Pa., 108 miles, was completed in 1829. The Schuylkill Coal and Navigation Canal, also 108 miles long, from Mill Creek to Philadelphia, Pa., was begun in 1816 and completed in 1825. The Lehigh Coal and Navigation Company have a canal from Easton to Coalport, Pa. An important ship canal is the Sault Sainte Marie, connecting Lakes Superior and Huron, which was built in 1855 at the cost of $6,033,533. (See illustration opposite 932.)

The Panama Canal is described in a separate article. (See also Suez Canal, which is inserted for comparison.)

Following is a complete list of canals in the United States, together with their length and cost of construction:

Albemarle and Chesapeake—From Norfolk, Va., to Currituck Sound, N. C., 44 miles; cost, with improvements, $1,641,363.

Augusta—From Savannah River, Ga., to Augusta, Ga., 9 miles, $1,500,000.

Beaufort—From Beaufort, N. C., to Neuse River, in course of construction.

Black River—From Rome, N. Y., to Lyons Falls, N. Y., 35 miles, $3,581,954.

Cape Cod Canal (Sea Level Ship Canal), about 13 miles long, to connect Massachusetts Bay and Buzzard's Bay, $12,000,000.

Cayuga and Seneca—From Montezuma, N. Y., to Cayuga and Seneca Lakes, N. Y., 25 miles, $2,232,632.

Champlain—From Whitehall, N. Y., to Watervliet, N. Y., 81 miles, $4,044,000.

Chesapeake and Delaware—From Chesapeake City, Md., to Delaware City, Del., 14 miles, $3,730,230.

Chesapeake and Ohio—From Cumberland, Md., to Washington, D. C., 184 miles, $11,290,327.

Companys—From Mississippi River, La., to Bayou Black, La., 22 miles, $90,000.

Delaware and Raritan—From New Brunswick, N. J., to Bordentown, N. J., 66 miles, $4,888,749.

Delaware Division—From Easton, Pa., to Bristol, Pa., 60 miles, $2,433,350.

Des Moines Rapids, at Des Moines Rapids, Mississippi River, 7½ miles, $4,582,009.

Erie—From Albany, N. Y., to Buffalo, N. Y., 387 miles, $52,540,800.

Fairfield—From Alligator River to Lake Mattimuskeet, N. C., 4½ miles.

Galveston and Brazos—From Galveston, Tex., to Brazos River, Tex., 38 miles, $340,000.

Harlem River Ship Canal, connecting the Hudson River and Long Island Sound, by way of Spuyten Duyvil Creek and Harlem River, was opened for traffic on June 17, 1895, and cost about $2,700,000.

Hocking—From Carroll, Ohio, to Nelsonville, Ohio, 42 miles, $975,481.

Illinois and Michigan—From Chicago, Ill., to La Salle, Ill., 102 miles, $7,357,787.

Illinois and Mississippi—Around lower rapids of Rock River, Ill., connected with Mississippi River, 75 miles, $7,250,000.

Lake Drummond—Connects Chesapeake Bay with Albemarle Sound, 22 miles, $2,800,000.

Lake Washington—Through Lake Union, Seattle, Wash., to Puget Sound.

Lehigh Coal and Navigation Co.—From Coalport, Pa., to Easton, Pa., 108 miles, $4,455,000.

Louisville and Portland—Falls of Ohio River, Louisville, Ky., 2½ miles, $5,578,631.

Miami and Erie—From Cincinnati, Ohio, to Toledo, Ohio, 274 miles, $8,062,680.

Morris—From Jersey City to Phillipsburg, N. J., 102 miles ; begun 1825, opened 1836.

Muscle Shoals and Elk River Shoals—From Big Muscle Shoals, Tenn., to Elk River Shoals, Tenn., 16 miles, $3,156,919.

Newberne and Beaufort—From Clubfoot Creek to Harlow Creek, N. C., 3 miles.

Ogeechee—From Savannah River, Ga., to Ogeechee River, Ga., 16 miles, $407,810.

Ohio—From Cleveland, Ohio, to Portsmouth, Ohio, 317 miles, $4,695,204.

Oswego—From Oswego, N. Y., to Syracuse, N. Y., 38 miles, $5,239,526.

Pennsylvania—From Columbia, Northumberland, Wilkes-Barre, Huntingdon, Pa., 193 miles, $7,731,750.

Portage Lake and Lake Superior—From Keweenaw Bay to Lake Superior, 25 miles, $528,892.

Port Arthur—From Port Arthur, Tex., to Gulf of Mexico, 7 miles.

Santa Fé—From Waldo, Fla., to Melrose, Fla., 10 miles, $70,000.

Salt Ste. Marie (Ship Canal)—Connects Lakes Superior and Huron at St. Mary's River, 3 miles, $6,033,533.

Schuylkill Navigation Company—From Mill Creek, Pa., to Philadelphia, Pa., 108 miles, $12,461,600.

Sturgeon Bay and Lake Michigan—Between Green Bay and Lake Michigan, 1¼ miles, $99,661.

St. Mary's Falls—Connects Lake Superior and Huron at Sault. Ste. Marie, Mich., 1½ miles, $7,909,667.

Susquehanna and Tidewater—From Columbia, Pa., to Havre de Grace, Md., 45 miles, $4,931,345.

Walhonding—From Rochester, Ohio, to Roscoe, Ohio, 25 miles, $607,269.

Welland (Ship Canal)—Connects Lake Ontario and Lake Erie, 26¾ miles, $2,080,-366.

Canals (see also the several canals):

Across continent, practicability of construction of, referred to, 4473.

Altamaha River to Tennessee River, referred to, 1027.

Appropriations for, 926.

Atlantic Ocean to Gulf of Mexico, discussed, 995.

Constitutional amendment for improvement of, suggested, 552.

Great Lakes to Hudson River, discussed, 482.

Lands granted to States in aid of, 1029, 1725.

Recommendations regarding aid to, 4149, 4201, 4209.

Surveys for, referred to, 824, 987.

Utility of canal navigation discussed, 482, 552, 586, 785, 877.

Canal Zone.—The Panama Canal act of 1912 provided for the government by the United States of a zone of land and land under water of the width of ten miles extending to the distance of five miles on each side of the center line of the route of the canal, which zone begins in the Caribbean Sea three marine miles from mean low-water mark and extends to and across the

Isthmus of Panama into the Pacific Ocean to the distance of three marine miles from mean low-water mark, excluding therefrom the cities of Panama and Colon and their adjacent harbors located within said zone, as excepted in the treaty with the Republic of Panama dated November 18, 1903, but including all islands within said described zone, and in addition thereto the group of islands in the Bay of Panama named Perico, Naos, Culebra and Flamenco, and any lands and waters outside of said limits above described which are necessary or convenient or from time to time may become necessary or convenient for the construction, maintenance, operation, sanitation, or protection of the said canal or of any auxiliary canals, lakes, or other works necessary or convenient. The President is authorized, by treaty with the Republic of Panama, to acquire any additional land or land under water not already granted, or which was excepted from the grant, that he may deem necessary, and to exchange any land or land under water not deemed necessary for other land or land under water which may be deemed necessary, which additional land or land under water so acquired shall become part of the Canal zone.

When in the judgment of the President the construction of the Panama Canal shall be sufficiently advanced toward completion to render the further services of the Isthmian Canal Commission unnecessary, the President is authorized by executive order to discontinue the Isthmian Canal Commission, which, together with the present organization, shall then cease to exist ; and the President is authorized thereafter to complete, govern, and operate the Panama Canal and govern the Canal zone, through a Governor and such other persons as he may deem competent for the protection of the Canal and Canal zone. The Governor of the Panama Canal shall be appointed by the President, by and with the advice and consent of the Senate, commissioned for a term of four years at $10,-000 per year. President Taft (page 7687) suggested a permanent military government for the zone, but it was later decided that a civil government would be best suited to the colonial policy of the United States. President Wilson by executive order (page 7920) established a permanent civil government for the zone in 1914, and in additional orders enunciated important rules of government. (Pages 7903, 7905, 7918, 7919, 7923. See also Panama Canal.)

Canal Zone:

Alien enemies barred from, 8394.

Arms, bearing of, in, regulated, 7903.

Ceded to United States, 6815.

Chinese excluded from, 8213.

Corruption of government employees in, forbidden, 7918.

Customs service in, order relating to, 7963.

Employees in, appointment and compensation of, 7924.

Employment conditions in, 7923.

Extent of, 7687.

Gambling law in, amended, 7988.

Government of—

Discussed, 7687.

Permanent, established, 7920.

Health department of, 7921.

Hunting in, regulated, 7919.

Interest rates on money fixed in, 7905.

Manifests, fines for dishonest, in, 7963.

Military government for, 7687.

Money orders in, interest on, 8140.

Neutrality of, proclaimed, 8008.

Population of, 7687.

Postal crimes in, order relating to, 7964.

Postal deposits in, interest rates fixed on, 8140.

Quarantine regulations for, 7966.

Sanitation of, 7021.

Security for costs in civil cases in, required, 7964.

Wireless telegraph to be fitted on vessels using, 7958.

Wireless telegraph station for use of Navy established in, 7960.

Workmen's Compensation Act in, 7806.

Order relating to customs service and providing for fines for dishonest manifests in, 7963.

Order relating to Postal Crimes in, 7964.

Quarantine regulations for, 7966.

Regulating bearing of arms in, 7903.

Regulating hunting in, 7909.

Requiring security for costs in civil cases in, 7964.

Wireless telegraph station established in for use of Navy, 7960.

Cancer.—A malignant growth of epidermic, epithelial or glandular tissue, having secondary growths or extensions. The disease is increasing rapidly in all civilized countries. It is essentially a disease of middle life, occurring mostly in persons of more than forty years of age. Senility and the decadence of tissues which have passed the period of their usefulness and are about to undergo physiological rest are predisposing factors. The symptoms often elude trained observers and the causes of the disease have never been accurately determined. Domestic animals as well as man are subject to the disease. The prevalence of cancer in fishes and the coincidence of the geographical distribution of the disease in fish and the human family so impressed President Taft that he recommended to Congress an appropriation of $50,000 for the study of the question. (Page 7481.)

There seems to be no evidence that cancer is either hereditary or contagious. The early indication of the disease is usually a hard spot or lump in the place affected, which should be submitted immediately to a physician for examination. Often the presence of the lump is unaccompanied by any sensation of pain; and in the case of a cancer of the stomach, the only indication may be indigestion.

Operations for cancer remain the only form of treatment; and in case the operation is performed in the earlier stages of the disease, there is little danger connected with it. Before the glands are affected, 85% of all operations for cancer are successful; and even after the glands are affected, almost half of the operations are successful.

In 1910, there were about 75,000 deaths from cancer in the United States. 1 in every 8 women and 1 in every 11 men over the age of 35 die from cancer.

Cancer in Fishes, appropriation recommended for research work subject of, 7480.

Candia. (See Crete.)

Cannon.—A large gun, mounted usually on a frame, movable or stationary, or on a gun carriage. (See also Arms and Ammunition; Arsenals; Artillery, and Encyclopedic Index article on Arms and Ammunition.)

Cannon, foundry for making, recommended, 1607, 1714, 4797.

Canton, China, hostilities in, referred to, 2977.

Cantonment Gibson, Ark., road from Little Rock to, referred to, 932.

Cantonments.—Military establishments intended for lengthy occupation, and distinguished from camps also in that they possess buildings of some pretension.

After the entrance of the United States into the European War, the following cantonments were used for training the troops of the National Army, called together under the selective service system, in addition to the forts (q. v.) of the regular army:

Custer—Battle Creek, Michigan, containing troops from Michigan and Wisconsin, forming the 85th division.

Devens—Ayer, Massachusetts, containing troops from Maine, New Hampshire, Rhode Island, Vermont, Massachusetts, Connecticut, forming the 76th division.

Dix—Wrightstown, New Jersey, containing troops from New York state and northern Pennsylvania, comprising the 78th division.

Dodge—Des Moines, Iowa, containing troops from Minnesota, Iowa, Nebraska, North Dakota, South Dakota, comprising the 88th division.

Funston—Fort Riley, Kansas, containing troops from Kansas, Missouri and Colorado, forming the 89th division.

Gordon—Atlanta, Georgia, containing troops from Georgia and Alabama, and forming the 82d division.

Grant—Rockford, Illinois, containing troops from Illinois and forming the 86th division.

Jackson—Columbia, South Carolina, containing troops from North Carolina, South Carolina, Florida and Tennessee, and forming the 81st division.

Lee—Petersburg, Virginia, containing troops from New Jersey, Delaware, Maryland, Virginia and the District of Columbia, and forming the 80th division.

Lewis—American Lake, Washington, containing troops from Washington, Oregon, California, Utah, Nevada, Idaho, Wyoming and Montana, and comprising the 91st division.

Meade—Annapolis Junction, Maryland, containing troops from southern Pennsylvania and comprising the 79th division.

Pike—Little Rock, Arkansas, containing troops from Arkansas, Mississippi and Louisiana, and comprising the 87th division.

Sherman—Chillicothe, Ohio, containing troops from Ohio and West Virginia, and comprising the 83d division.

Taylor—Louisville, Kentucky, containing troops from Kentucky and Indiana, and comprising the 84th division.

Travis—Fort Sam Houston, Texas, containing troops from Texas, Arizona, Oklahoma and New Mexico, and comprising the 90th division.

Upton—Yaphank, Long Island, New York, containing troops from the metropolitan section of New York and comprising the 77th division.

The encampments for the training of the National Guard of the various states were as follows:

Beauregard—Alexandria, Louisiana, containing troops from Louisiana, Mississippi and Arkansas, and forming the 39th (old 18th) division.

Bowie — Fort Worth, Texas, containing troops from Texas and Oklahoma, and forming the 36th (old 15th) division.

Cody—Deming, New Mexico, containing troops from Minnesota, Iowa, Nebraska, North Dakota and South Dakota and forming the 34th (old 13th) division.

Doniphan—Fort Sill, Oklahoma, containing troops from Missouri and Texas, and comprising the 35th (old 14th) division.

Fremont—Palo Alto, California, containing troops from Washington, Oregon, Montana, Idaho and Wyoming, and forming the 41st (old 20th) division.

Greene—Charlotte, North Carolina, containing troops from Maine, New Hampshire, Vermont, Massachusetts, Rhode Island and Connecticut, and forming the 26th (old 5th) division.

Hancock — Augusta, Georgia, containing troops from Pennsylvania, and forming the 28th (old 7th) division.

Kearny—Linda Vista, California, containing troops from California, Nevada, Utah, Colorado, Arizona, New Mexico, and forming the 40th (old 19th) division.

Logan—Houston, Texas, containing troops from Illinois, and forming the 33d (old 12th) division.

MacArthur.— Waco, Texas, containing troops from Michigan and Wisconsin, and forming the 32d (old 11th) division.

McClellan—Anniston, Alabama, containing troops from New Jersey, Marylnd, Delaware, Virginia, and District of Columbia, and comprising the 29th (old 8th) division.

Sevier—Greenville, South Carolina, containing troops from Tennessee, North Carolina, South Carolina, and comprising the 30th (old 9th) division.

Shelby—Hattiesburg, Mississippi, containing troops from Indiana and Kentucky, and comprising the 38th (old 17th) division.

Sheridan — Montgomery, Alabama, containing troops from Ohio and West Virginia, and comprising the 37th (old 16th) division.

Wadsworth — Spartanburg, South Carolina, containing troops from New York, comprising the 27th (old 6th) division.

Wheeler.— Macon, Georgia, containing troops from Georgia, Alabama and Florida, and comprising the 31st (old 10th) division.

Cape Cod Canal (see Canals).

Cape Fear River, N. C., act for improving, approved and reasons therefor, 2776.

Cape Horn:
Expenditures for freight and passage by way of, referred to, 4072.
Shortening of sea voyage around, discussed, 4601.

Cape Spartel, light-house on, treaty with Morocco regarding, 3582.

Cape Verde Islands. (See Portugal.)

Cape Vincent, N. Y., proclamation granting privileges of other ports to, 2859.

Capital, relation of labor to. (See Labor, discussed.)

Capital:
Combinations of, 6790.
Organized, problem of control over, 6895.

Capital.—The municipality in which is located the seat of government.

Capital Issues Committee. (See War Finance Corporation.)

Capital of United States.—Up to the time of the adoption of the Constitution the Congress had no fixed place for holding its sessions, but met at York, Lancaster, Philadelphia, Baltimore, Princeton, Annapolis, Trenton, and New York. The First Congress under the Constitution met in New York City in 1789. Later it held sessions in Philadelphia from 1790 to 1800. During the second session of the First Congress under the Constitution, after a long and bitter debate in which sectional jealousy ran high, an act was passed, June 28, 1790, selecting the present site of Washington as the permanent seat of Government. The Government removed to its new headquarters in 1800. (See Washington City and District of Columbia.)

Capital of United States, seat of Government removed from Philadelphia to Washington discussed, 281, 295, 298, 299, 300.

Capital Punishment.—In nearly all states the death penalty is specified as punishment for first degree murder: Following are the methods of execution and the exceptions to the rule:

STATES AND METHODS.	STATES AND METHODS.
Alabama—Hanging.	New Hampshire — Hanging.
Alaska—Hanging.	New Jersey — Electrocution.
Arizona—Hanging.	New Mexico—Hanging.
Arkansas — Electrocution.	New York—Electrocution.
California—Hanging.	North Carolina — Electrocution.
Colorado—Hanging.	North Dakota—Hanging.
Connecticut—Hanging.	Ohio—Electrocution.
Delaware—Hanging.	Oklahoma — Hanging.
District of Columbia—Hanging.	Oregon—Hanging.
Florida—Hanging.	Pennsylvania—Electrocution.
Georgia—Hanging.	Porto Rico—Hanging.
Hawaii—Hanging.	Rhode Island—Life Imprisonment.
Idaho—Hanging.	South Carolina — Electrocution.
Illinois—Hanging.	South Dakota — Hanging.
Indiana—Hanging.	Tennessee — Hanging.
Iowa—Hanging.	Texas—Hanging.
Kansas — Life Imprisonment.	Utah—Hanging or Shooting at discretion of murderer.
Kentucky—Electrocution.	Vermont—Hanging.
Louisiana—Hanging.	Virginia — Electrocution.
Maine—Life Imprisonment.	Washington — Life Imprisonment.
Maryland—Hanging.	West Virginia — Hanging.
Massachusetts—Electrocution.	Wisconsin—Life Imprisonment.
Michigan—Life Imprisonment.	Wyoming — Hanging.
Minnesota — Life Imprisonment.	
Mississippi — Hanging.	
Missouri—Hanging.	
Montana—Hanging.	
Nebraska — Electrocution.	
Nevada—Hanging or shooting at discretion of murderer.	

Capitol.—From *Capitolium*, the name of the magnificent temple of Jupiter Capitolinus on the Capitoline Hill in ancient Rome. The *Mons Capitolinus* was so called from the finding of a skull during the excavation for the first building. The name is applied to the magnificent edifice in which the Congress of the United States holds its sessions and to the statehouses which are erected at the capitals of the various states.

The Capitol is situated on a low hill commanding one of the best views of Washington, and dominates the city with its magnificent dome. Its extreme length is 751 feet, and it varies from 121 to 324 feet in width; it consists of a main edifice of sandstone, painted white and crowned with an iron dome, and two wings of white marble. The general style is classic and its columns and detail are Corinthian. As a whole it is one of the most imposing and beautiful governmental buildings in the world. The original dome was a low structure of wood covered with copper, but this was replaced in 1856 by the present iron dome, 287 feet high, designed by Thomas U. Walter, and surmounted by a fine statue of Freedom by the American sculptor Thomas Crawford. The corner stone of the building was laid by President Washington Sept. 18, 1793, with Masonic ceremonies. The north wing was completed Nov. 17, 1800; the south wing in 1811. The interior of both were burned by the British under General Ross Aug. 24, 1814. (See illustration opposite 537, 1693.) The foundation of the main building was laid March 24, 1818, and the whole was completed in 1827, at a cost up to that time of nearly $2,500,000.

An act of Sept. 30, 1850, provided for extensions to the north and south, and President Fillmore laid the corner stone July 4, 1851, Daniel Webster delivering the oration. These extensions were finished in 1867, and added very considerably to the beauty of the building, with their porticoes and columns of white marble, which contain the Senate Chamber and Hall of Representatives.

The former Senate Chamber is now occupied by the Supreme Court, the former Hall of Representatives is now a Statuary Court to which each state contributes statues of her most famous sons. Among the special objects of interest inside are the busts of the Vice-Presidents in the Senate Chamber; a number of historical paintings, some of them colossal in size, in various parts of the building; the Marble Room of the Senate, with its mirrors; the collection of Speakers' portraits in the Representatives' Lobby of the House, and the massive Rotunda, with its historical paintings and frescoes. Outside, on the east is the plaza, near the center of which sits the classic figure of George Washington. On the west side Story's bronze statue of John Marshall, like the Washington, a sitting figure, is encountered by the visitor just before he ascends the stairs over the terrace. It is curious to note that the main façade faces east, as it was anticipated that the city would spread in that direction; the reverse has proved to be the case and the Capitol turns its back toward the main portion of the city.

See illustrations opposite 537, 1693 and frontispiece, Vol. II.

Capitol:

Care of, should be committed to public agent, 596.

Congress recommences its duties in, 623.

Destroyed by British forces, 531, and illustration, opposite 537.

Extension of—

Appropriation of $100,000 to be expended, 2672.

Architect engaged in, referred to, 2680.

Discussed, 2672.

Jurisdiction over, transferred from Interior to War Department, 2737.

Plans submitted unsatisfactory, and combination of same adopted, 2672.

Reference to, 2684, 2915, 2917, 2918.

Heating and ventilating referred to, 3110, 3112.

Improvement of, interest should be taken in, 588.

In 1839, 1693.

Incomplete and not in a state to receive Members of Congress, 588.

Longitude of, 680, 688, 789.

Marble columns for, referred to, 3114.

Secretary of President J. Q. Adams assaulted in, 966.

Washington, statue of, to be placed in, 881.

Appropriation for, recommended, 1170.

Erection of, referred to, 1910.

Wings added to, nearly complete, 2672.

Work of art for, referred to, 2910.

Captive.—One held prisoner, especially in war.

Captured Property:

Cotton captured and forfeited, referred to, 3666.

Should not be adjudged, without regular investigation, 485.

Car Couplers. (See Brakes and Couplers.)

Caracas Commission discussed, 4761, 4826, 4920, 5090.

Caracas, Venezuela:

Centennial celebration of birth of Bolivar to be held at, 4716, 4760.

Statue of Washington to be commenced at, and industrial exhibition to be opened, 4716, 4760.

Carbine.—A short rifle for the use of cavalrymen.

Cardenas Bay, Cuba, conflict in, discussed, 6302, 6316.

The *Winslow* rescued by the *Hudson* in, thanks of Congress, etc., to officers and men of latter recommended, 6302.

Cardinal.—A prince of the Church of Rome, ranking in Catholic countries with princes of the blood royal, a member of the conclave or sacred college, which is the council of the Pope. Since 1179 the cardinals have claimed and exercised the privilege of electing the Pope. The full college consists of seventy cardinals. On March 15, 1875, Archbishop John Mc-Closkey, of New York, was made the first American cardinal. He died Oct. 10, 1885, and on June 7, 1886, Archbishop James Gibbons, of Baltimore, was created cardinal. Nov. 27, 1911, Pope Pius X bestowed the red hat of Cardinal upon John M. Farley, of New York; William H. O'Connell, of Boston, and Diomede Falconio, formerly of Washington, for the United States.

Carlisle Indian School, establishment of, discussed, 4529.

Carmick & Ramsey, claims of, referred to, 3065.

Carnegie Foundation for the Advancement of Teaching.—An institution founded by Andrew Carnegie in 1905, and incorporated by the Congress of the United States in 1906. The institution is endowed with $15,000,000, and its primary purpose is to provide retiring allowances for teachers and officers of colleges, universities, and technical schools in the United States, Canada and Newfoundland. By the seventh annual meeting of the trustees in 1912, 315 allowances were being paid to teachers, and 83 pensions to widows of teachers, at an annual cost of $603,855. The amount of the average retiring allowance is $1,676.66, the average age of retirement being about seventy years.

In the payment of retiring allowances to professors and pensions to widows of professors, the foundation aims to deal with institutions rather than with individuals. It has, therefore, formed an accepted list of institutions, the teachers and officers of which may retire under fixed rules. There were in November, 1913, seventy-three institutions on the accepted list. In addition to being a retiring allowance system for the benefit of higher education, the foundation has become an educational agency national in its influence. Educational problems are discussed in the annual report of the president, and in other bulletins published by the foundation. The president of the foundation is Dr. Henry S. Pritchett; secretary, Clyde Furst; address, 576 Fifth Avenue, New York City.

Carnegie Hero Fund.—In April, 1904, Andrew Carnegie created a fund of $5,000,-000 for the benefit of the dependents of those losing their lives in heroic effort to save their fellow men, or for the heroes themselves if injured only. Provision was also made for medals to be given in commemoration of heroic acts.

The endowment known as "The Hero Fund" was placed in the hands of a commission composed of twenty-one persons, residents of Pittsburg, Pa., of which Charles L. Taylor is president, and F. M. Wilmot, secretary and manager of the fund.

In his letter to the Hero Fund Commission, Mr. Carnegie outlined the general scheme of the fund thus: "To place those following peaceful vocations who have been injured in heroic effort to save human life, in somewhat better positions pecuniarily than before, until able to work again. In case of death, the widow and children or other dependents are to be provided for until she remarries, and the children until they reach a self-supporting age. For exceptional children, exceptional grants may be made for exceptional education. Grants

of sums of money may also be made to heroes or heroines as the commission thinks advisable—each case to be judged on its merits."

The fund applies only to acts performed within the United States of America, the Dominion of Canada, the colony of Newfoundland, and the waters thereof, and such acts must have been performed on or after April 15, 1904.

The commission has awarded 841 medals—506 bronze, 319 silver and 16 gold. In addition to the medals, $835,986 has been awarded for disablement benefits, and for educational and other special purposes, and for the dependents of heroes who lost their lives, including payments made to December 31, 1913, on monthly allowances. Pensions in force as of this date amount to $65,460 annually. The commission has also awarded $169,462 for relief of sufferers from disasters—at Brockton, Mass., $10,000; from the California earthquake, $54,462; at Monongah Mines, Monongah, W. Va., $35,000; at Darr Mine, Jacobs Creek, Pa., $25,000; at Lick Branch Mine, Switchback, W. Va., $10,000; at McCurtain Mine, McCurtain, Okla., $15,-000; at Jed Mine, Jed, W. Va., $10,000, and for relief of Ohio and Indiana flood sufferers, $10,000.

Carnegie Peace Foundation. (See Peace Societies.)

Carnifex Ferry (W. Va.), Battle of.—After McClellan's promotion, July 22, 1861, to the command of the Army of the Potomac, Rosecrans succeeded him in command in West Virginia. Gen. Floyd took a position on the Gauley River, eight miles south of Nicholas, W. Va., at Carnifex Ferry, with 2,000 Confederates, intending to cut off Cox's brigade from Rosecrans's army. Sept. 10 he was attacked in this position by Rosecrans with 10,000 men. Darkness terminated a sharp engagement, and the next morning Floyd was in the mountains, thirty miles away. The Federal loss was 120 killed and wounded. Among the former was Col. Lowe, of the Twelfth Ohio, who fell at the head of his regiment.

Caroline, The.—A steamer in the service of Canadian rebels which was seized on American soil by the British and burned. In 1836-37 a revolutionary spirit developed in Lower Canada. Dec. 12, 1837, the leaders of the insurrection, under one Mackenzie, seized the Canadian Navy Island, in the Niagara River, and set up a provisional government. Dec. 26 the Canadians, crossing the Niagara, after a fight in which several rebels were killed, burned the vessel (1618, 1929). The affair caused great indignation. President Van Buren issued proclamations demanding observance of the neutrality laws (1698, 1699). The New York militia was called out and placed under command of Gen. Scott.

Caroline, The, attacked and destroyed by British forces, 1618.

Claim on Brazil concerning, 4220.

Correspondence regarding, 1618, 1676, 1839, 1840, 2016, 2073.

Discussed, 1929.

Satisfaction demanded of Great Britain for destroying, 1732.

Caroline Islands.—A Pacific archipelago extending from lat. 3° to 11° north and from long. 137° to 163° east. The principal islands are Yap, Ponape, Strong, Babelthouap, and Rouk. The name usually includes the Pelew Islands. The inhabitants are Polynesians. Germany and Spain both claimed Yap Island until 1885, when the dispute was settled in favor of Spain. By treaty of Feb. 12, 1899, these islands, with the exception of Guam, the largest of the Marianne which had been ceded to the United States in 1898, passed on Oct. 1, 1899, from Spain into the hands of Germany. The purchase price paid by Germany was about $4,000,000. They consist of about five hundred coral islets which are small and sparsely peopled. The most important product and export is copra.

Caroline Islands:

Dispute between Germany and Spain relating to domination of, discussed, 4916, 6370.

Questions with Spain touching rights of American citizens in, 5622, 5751, 5872.

Carpenters' Hall.—Building owned by the guild or union of carpenters of Philadelphia. It was similar to the guild halls of London. The First and Second Continental Congresses held their sessions in this hall.

Carpetbaggers.—A term of reproach applied to certain northern politicians who in the days of the reconstruction of the southern states shortly after the close of the Civil War took up temporary residence in the south and sought election to Congress and various state offices. The name arose from the fact that only a few of them intended to settle permanently, and therefore carried, it was said, their effects in carpetbags. Some of them proved to be good and useful citizens, while many were unscrupulous adventurers who sought official positions for the purpose of enriching themselves.

Carriages and Wagons.—Ages of progress have intervened between the luxurious automobile touring car of to-day and the gaudy chariots of ancient kings. American inventive genius has added materially to this progress. Until the advent of the automobile the American buggy represented the highest type of private conveyance, being a modification of the English brougham and the German landau. Before the Revolution very little manufacturing was done in this country. Wealthy Americans imported their coaches, carriages and phaetons from England and France. The number of repair shops, however, increased with the number of vehicles.

The first American vehicle to be manufactured to any extent was the two-wheeled chaise, which became popular in New England. New York and Boston were connected by a stage-coach route in 1770. In 1776, when John Hancock married Dorothy Quincy, he took her by stage-coach to Philadelphia for a honeymoon.

After the Continental Congress had organized the Government, "the importation of coaches, chairs, and carriages of all sorts from England was forbidden." In 1794 Congress, looking upon carriages as articles of luxury, imposed a tax on them.

With the improvement of roads through federal and state aid, the vehicle business grew. The Conestoga wagon, with broad wheels and canvas-covered body, often drawn by several teams of horses, came into general use in New York, New Jersey and Pennsylvania. Troy, N. Y., became famous for its coaches; Salem and Worcester, Mass., were also early noted as manufacturing centers. With the migration westward after the war of 1812, the vehicle business followed the main routes of travel. John Studebaker established a shop at Ashland, Ohio, in 1835, and two of his sons, having learned their father's trade, went to South Bend, Ind., in 1852, and established the business which has since grown to be the largest manufactory of vehicles in the world. The plant covers more than a hundred acres of ground, employs 3,000 workmen, uses annually 50,-000,000 feet of lumber and thousands of tons of iron and steel. The yearly output of the factory exceeds 100,000 vehicles.

In 1872 the Carriage Builders' National Association was founded by the leading manufacturers of the country for training skilled workmen and to standardize the business. Rubber tires came into use in 1890.

In family and pleasure carriages Ohio ranks first. New York leads in the number of public conveyances manufactured, while Indiana heads the list of States turning out farm, government and municipal wagons. Michigan, Minnesota, Wisconsin and New York turn out about three-quarters of the sleighs and sleds.

In the census report for 1900 the statement was made that in the earliest stages of the carriage and wagon industry almost the entire work of manufacturing was done at the establishment, but specialization has wrought a change in this as in many other lines of manufacture, and now few, if any, manufacturers produce all the parts. The making of carriage and wagon materials as a separate industry is growing.

The busy time for the factories is covered by March, April and May, but work is fairly continuous the year round. About 40 per cent of the wage-earners work 60 hours per week.

Carriage and wagon making in its various branches, according to the census of 1910, was carried on in 5,492 establishments in the United States, and gave employment in 1909 to 82,944 persons, of whom 69,928 were wage-earners, and paid $45,555,126 in salaries and wages. The total cost of materials was $81,951,288, which was equal to about half (51.3 per cent.) of the total value of the products ($159,892,547), while the value added to the materials by manufacture was $77,-941,259. Many establishments reported at censuses prior to the thirteenth as manufacturing carriages and wagons have since turned wholly or in part to the manufacture of automobiles.

For the industry as a whole in 1914 there were reported 5,320 establishments, which manufactured 1,187,002 vehicles, valued at $72,283,898. At the 1909 census there were reported 5,613 establishments, with an output of 1,584,571 vehicles, valued at $94,037,900. The number of establishments thus decreased during the five-year period by 293, or 5.2 per cent; the number of vehicles, by 397,569, or 25.1 per cent; and the value, by $21,754,002, or 23.1 per cent.

Carson and Colorado Railroad, right of way of, through Walker River Reservation, Nev., referred to, 4736, 4776, 4953, 5178.

Carsons Valley, Utah, Territorial government over, referred to, 3014.

Cartel.—An agreement between belligerent states relating to the methods of carrying on the war, as for the exchange of prisoners, declaring certain ground neutral, repressing marauders, carrying on postal communication, or the like. A cartel-ship (sometimes simply called a cartel) ls one used in exchanging prisoners or carrying communications to the enemy. Cartels for the exchange of prisoners are perhaps the most common. These are usually concluded by the two governments, but generals may treat with each other directly. An exchange of prisoners is beneficial to each side, which thereby recovers its own men and is saved the trouble and expense of guarding and feeding its captives. In an exchange, the rank of the prisoners is taken into account, and, so far as possible, man is exchanged for man of equal rank.

Carthage (Mo.), Battle of.—After Governor Jackson and his followers had been driven from Boonville by Gen. Lyon they pushed westward into Jasper County, being joined on the way by Gen. Sterling Price. This increased the Confederate forces to 3,600. July 5, 1861, they were confronted near Carthage by Gen. Franz Sigel with a force of 1,500 men, who had been sent to the southwestern part of the State to prevent reenforcements arriving from Arkansas and Texas. Sigel, after a short engagement, retreated through Carthage to Sarcoxie, fifteen miles to the eastward. His loss was 13 killed and 31 wounded. The Confederates reported their loss at 40 to 50 killed and 125 to 150 wounded.

Cartoon.—A caricature used in attacking an individual or a policy, especially public officials or political measures.

Cartoons, Early. (See illustrations opposite 1202, 1456, 1581, 2628, 3034, 3245, 4248, 4280.

Cary's Rebellion.—Thomas Cary, deputy governor of North Carolina, was deposed in 1705 at the solicitation of the Quakers for disfranchising them under the requirements of the test act. For several years Cary endeavored to usurp the government. In 1711 he attempted to capture Governor Hyde by force. Governor Spotswood, of Virginia, sent soldiers to Hyde's assistance and Cady was forced to submit.

Casa Grande Ruin, Arizona. (See Parks, National.)

Casement, Sir Roger. (See Home Rule in Ireland.)

Castle Island, Boston Harbor, joint resolution authorizing use and improvement of, vetoed, 5246.

Casualty.—In war, the loss of life, directly, or as a result of wounds.

Casus-Belli.—Literally a cause of war; as an overt act, or an insult by one nation to the dignity and peace of another nation when the circumstances will not permit of diplomatic adjustment.

Catawba, The, purchased for Peru, detention of, 3831, 3835.

Catchword.—A word or phrase of popular appeal—often one employed by a political party, as "Fifty-Four, Forty or Fight"; "Protection and Prosperity"; "Peace and Prosperity"; "He kept us out of War," etc.

Catherine, The, seizer of, by British cruiser *Dolphin* discussed, 2070.

Catherine Augusta, The, seized by Denmark with the *Ben Franklin*, 4462, 5369. (See Butterfield, Carlos & Co.) Arbitration in case of, 5369.

Cattle:
Contagious diseases among, discussed, 4578, 4580, 4771, 5112, 5383, 5764, 5887.
Convention at Chicago on subject of diseases of, 4771.
Exportation and importation of. (See Animals and Animal Products.)
Inspection of. (See Animal Industry, Bureau of.)
Restrictions on importation of. (See Animals and Animal Products.)
Slaughter of, from United States required by Great Britain, 5764, 6178.

Cattle, Exhibition, International, at Hamburg, Germany, discussed, 4714.

Cattle Plague. (See Pleuro-Pneumonia.)

Caucus.—A meeting of the adherents of a political party to name candidates for office or agree upon lines of party policy. Though the caucus is strictly an American institution, similar meetings are sometimes held in England. Mr. Gladstone held a caucus respecting the ballot bill July 6, 1871. The caucus originated in Boston in the early part of the eighteenth century. It is supposed to have derived its name from the meetings of the calkers connected with the shipping business in the North End. From these local meetings the custom grew and carried the name with it until after the institution of the Federal Government it was applied to the Congressional meetings which nominated candidates for the Presidency and Vice-Presidency of the United States. The custom was pursued until 1824. In 1828 nominations were made by state legislatures, and in 1831 the present system of nominating by conventions came into use. State officers were similarly nominated by legislative caucuses until, somewhat previous to the general party system, nominating conventions took their place. Caucuses of members of Congress are now held regularly by the adherents of the several political parties to discuss and determine upon party policies and to choose the officers of the Senate and House.

Cavalry.—Soldiers on horse-back. (See Army.)

Cavalry, increase in, recommended, 228, 230, 2714, 4961.

Cavite, Philippine Islands, batteries at, silenced by American squadron, 6297, 6315.

Cayuga Indians. (See Indian Tribes.)

Cayuse Indians. (See Indian Tribes.)

Cedar Creek (Va.), Battle of.—One of the most notable actions in the Civil War. After the engagement at Fishers Hill Sheridan posted his army on the north side of Cedar Creek, near Strasburg, and went to Washington to consult as to the return of the Sixth Corps. During his absence Early, who had been reenforced by Lee to his original strength, returned up the valley, crossed Cedar Creek, and on the morning of Oct. 19, 1864, surprised the Federal camp and captured 24 guns and 1,500 prisoners. The Federal army under command of Gen. Wright retired toward Winchester, when Sheridan, who had arrived at the latter place during the forenoon, rejoined the army and ordered the battle renewed. Early's men were in possession of the camp at Cedar Creek when they were attacked about 3 o'clock in the afternoon and defeated, with heavy losses to both sides. The Confederates lost all the guns and camp equipage which they had previously captured, about 24 guns of their own, and some flags. Sheridan's loss in the two engagements, in killed, wounded and prisoners, was 5,990; the Confederate loss was 2,400. This was the last effort of the Confederate forces to occupy the Shenandoah Valley.

Cedar Keys, Fla., interference with collector of customs in, and action of Government discussed, 5507.

Cedar Mountain (Va.), Battle of.—June 26, 1862, Gen. Pope was assigned to the command of the combined forces of Banks, Frémont, and McDowell, known as the army of Virginia. Each of the separate armies had been defeated or forced into retreat by Jackson. The combined forces numbered 45,000, including 5,000 cavalry. Pope established headquarters at Culpeper, about 60 miles southwest of Washington. Gen. Lee sent Jackson and A. P. Hill to occupy Gordonsville, a few miles south of Culpeper. Their united armies, numbering, according to Federal accounts, 25,000 men, advanced toward Culpeper, and on Aug. 9 attacked Gen. Banks, with a force of 8,000 men, at Cedar Mountain, a hill two miles west of Mitchells Station, Culpeper County, Va. Banks was defeated. The Federal losses were 314 killed, 1,445 wounded, and 620 missing. The Confederates lost 229 killed, and 1,047 wounded.

Cedar Rapids, Iowa, act for erection of public buildings in, returned, 5503.

"Celerity, Certainty and Security." (See Star Routes.)

Cemeteries, National.—The army appropriation bill for 1850 contained a clause setting aside $10,000 to purchase a lot near the City of Mexico for the interment of United States soldiers who fell near that place during the Mexican War.

Since the Civil War Congress has established eighty-four cemeteries within the United States. They are mostly in the South, as most of the soldiers fell in that region. In all there are 370,415 graves, each marked with a marble headstone. The name and rank of each occupant is chiseled on the head-stone when known.

The following table shows the number of cemeteries maintained by the Federal Government and the interments of soldiers and sailors therein up to June 30, 1915:

NAME OF CEMETERY	AREA IN ACRES	INTERMENTS	
		Unknown Dead	Total
Alexandria, La.	8.24	2,380	4,539
Alexandria, Va.	5.50	124	3,565
Andersonville, Ga.	125	1,037	13,723
Andrew Johnson (Greenville), Tenn.	15		19
Annapolis, Md.	4.125	205	2,540
Antietam, Md.	11	1,848	4,759
Arlington, Va.	408.33	4,691	23,965
Balls Bluff, Va.	.0057	24	25
Barrancas, Fla.	8.56	741	1,656
Baton Rouge, La.	7.50	536	3,158
Battle Ground, D. C.	1		44
Beaufort, S. C.	29	4,598	9,485
Beverly, N. J.	1	7	199
Camp Butler, Ill.	6	166	1,596
Camp Nelson, Ky.	9.50	1,245	3,659
Cave Hill, Ky.	3.58	593	4,757
Chalmette, La.	13.69	746	12,093

NAME OF CEMETERY	AREA IN ACRES	INTERMENTS	
		Unknown Dead	Total
Chattanooga, Tenn.	129.53	5,058	13,679
City Point, Va.	7.49	1,406	5,159
Cold Harbor, Va.	1.75	1,337	1,963
Corinth, Miss.	20	3,995	5,737
Crown Hill, Ind.	1.37	37	794
Culpeper, Va.	6	912	1,375
Custer Battlefield, Mont.	6.91	274	1,579
Cypress Hills, N. Y.	18.14	384	7,565
Danville, Ky.	.31	9	358
Danville, Va.	3.50	159	1,331
Fayetteville, Ark.	6.63	810	1,311
Finns Point, N. J.	2.50	30	2,631
Florence, S. C.	3.76	2,800	3,013
Fort Donelson, Tenn.	15.34	512	675
Fort Gibson, Okla.	6.90	2,208	2,487
Fort Harrison, Va.	1.55	582	818
Fort Leavenworth, Kans.	15	1,583	4,016
Fort McPherson, Nebr.	107	361	852
Fort Scott, Kans.	10.26	126	827
Fort Smith, Ark.	15	1,466	2,394
Fredericksburg, Va.	12	12,736	15,185
Gettysburg, Pa.	14.87	1,632	3,676
Glendale, Va.	2.12	959	1,197
Grafton, W. Va.	3.40	650	1,273
Hampton, Va.	19.61	634	11,246
Jefferson Barracks, Mo.	50	3,015	12,572
Jefferson City, Mo.	2	446	842
Keokuk, Iowa.	2.75	45	897
Knoxville, Tenn.	9.83	1,163	3,542
Lebanon, Ky.	2.50	277	875
Lexington, Ky.	.75	106	1,130
Little Rock, Ark.	12.12	3,030	6,881
Loudon Park, Md.	5.29	348	3,954
Marietta, Ga.	24	3,094	10,423
Memphis, Tenn.	43.91	8,862	14,424
Mexico City, Mex.	2	751	1,548
Mill Springs, Ky.	3.50	410	727
Mobile, Ala.	2.68	238	1,122
Mound City, Ill.	10.50	2,759	5,424
Nashville, Tenn.	65	4,121	16,767
Natchez, Miss.	11	2,786	3,397
New Albany, Ind.	5.46	732	3,137
Newbern, N. C.	7.60	1,110	3,397
Philadelphia, Pa.	13.26	40	3,404
Poplar Grove, Va.	8.65	4,068	6,216
Port Hudson, La.	8	3,240	3,848
Quincy, Ill.	.459	57	312
Raleigh, N. C.	7.83	550	1,214
Richmond, Va.	9.74	5,678	6,574
Rock Island, Ill.	1	45	424
Salisbury, N. C.	6	12,035	12,148
San Antonio, Tex.	3.63	318	1,932
San Francisco, Cal.	37.50	472	6,976
Santa Fe, N. Mex.	9.35	455	1,089
Seven Pines, Va.	1.55	1,238	1,400
Shiloh, Tenn.	10.55	2,405	3,622
Soldiers' Home, D. C.	16	291	7,737
Springfield, Mo.	5	1,247	2,434
St. Augustine, Fla.	.58	1,553	1,773
Staunton, Va.	1.15	536	766
Stone River, Tenn.	20.10	2,547	6,149
Vicksburg, Miss.	40.	12,910	17,046
Wilmington, N. C.	5	1,609	2,358
Winchester, Va.	4.89	2,435	4,545
Woodlawn, N. Y.	2.36	20	3,270
Yorktown, Va.	3	1,446	2,195
Total	1,564.370	153,095	370,415

Of these interments about 9,847 are those of Confederates, being mainly in the National Cemeteries at Camp Butler, Cypress Hills, Finns Point, Fort Smith, Hampton, Jefferson Barracks, Springfield and Woodlawn.

The national cemetery at Gettysburg, Pa., is peculiarly interesting from its having been dedicated by President Lincoln in 1863. It abounds in numerous memorials of the departed soldiers, including a national monument. It has been the scene of a reunion of the survivors of the great battle fought there July 1-3, 1863. The Government assumed charge of it in 1872.

Cemeteries, National. (See also National Cemeteries.)

Establishment of, and number of Union soldiers buried in, discussed, 3649.

Government employees to be permitted to participate in ceremonies at, 3862, 4120, 4137, 4184, 4237, 4282, 4352, 4402, 4443, 4508, 4552, 4603, 4712, 4753, 4818, 4899, 5078, 5350, 5463, 5540, 5609, 5832, 5949, 6046.

Censors.—Roman magistrates to survey and rate the property and correct the manners of the people were appointed about 443 B. C. The old constitution of Pennsylvania, framed in 1776, provided for a council of censors, to be chosen two from each city or county every seven years, whose duty it should be to investigate the departments of the government and inquire whether the constitution had been violated. A new constitution was framed in 1790 with this provision omitted. The Vermont constitution, modeled after that of Pennsylvania, provided for censors, and this requirement was not abolished till 1870.

Censorship.—Regulation of and control over publications and utterances. Foreign nations, especially during the European War, frequently have resorted to this means of preventing publicity of governmental action and political plans, but in the United States censorship has not yet been resorted to by the Government except in an advisory way, and then only in war times. The first Amendment to the Constitution specifically inhibits the abridgement of the freedom of speech or of the press. (See Espionage Law.)

Censure, Resolutions of.—Two resolutions of censure on the president have been passed, once by the Senate and once by the House, on occasions where the majority passing these resolutions was not sufficiently large either to pass measures over the president's veto or to impeach him. March 28, 1834, after three months' debate over an attempt to impeach Andrew Jackson, Congress resolved that the "president, in the late executive proceedings in relation to the public revenue, has assumed upon himself authority and power not conferred by the Constitution and laws, but in derogation of both." Jackson protested, but without avail. In 1837 the resolutions were expunged from the records. Jan. 10, 1843, John M. Botts, of Virginia, offered a resolution for the impeachment of President Tyler for "gross usurpation of power, wicked and corrupt abuse of the power of appointment, high crimes and misdemeanors," etc. Tyler protested against this as Jackson had done before him, but he had as a member of the Senate voted against the reception of Jackson's protest, and in answer to his protest the House sent him a copy of the Senate resolution on the former occasion. The resolution was rejected by a vote of 83 to 127. (See also Protests.)

Census.—The Constitution requires that a census of the United States shall be taken decennially. The first census was taken in 1790 under the supervision of the president; subsequent censuses, to and including that of 1840, were taken under the supervision of the Secretary of State. In 1849 the supervision of the census was transferred to the newly organized Department of the Interior, and continued under the control of that department until the passage of the act of 1903, creating the Department of Commerce and Labor; by this act the Census Bureau was transferred to the new department. Congress, by act approved March 6, 1902, made the Census Bureau a permanent bureau of the Government.

The work of the Census Bureau is divided into two main branches, namely, the decennial census and special statistical inquiries, the latter mostly made in the intervals between the decennial censuses. The Thirteenth Decennial Census was taken as of date April 15, 1910. It covered the three main subjects—(1) population, (2) agriculture, and (3) manufactures, mines and quarries.

The permanent work of the Census Bureau is provided for by the act of Congress approved March 6, 1902, and amendments thereto. These acts authorize and direct the Bureau to make statistical inquiries regarding the insane, feeble-minded, deaf and dumb, and blind; crime, pauperism, and benevolence; deaths and births in the areas maintaining registration system; social and financial statistics of cities; wealth, debt and taxation; religious bodies; electric light and power, telephones and telegraphs, and street railways; transportation by water; cotton production and distribution; and production of forest products. The statistics of deaths (which now cover a little over half of the country), of cities, and of production of cotton and forest products, are secured annually; the other statistics mentioned are taken usually at intervals of five or ten years, not, however, at the same time as the regular decennial censuses. The act of 1902 also provides for a census of manufactures in the fifth year intervening between the decennial censuses, and the new Thirteenth Census act further provides for a census of agriculture in 1915, as well as in 1910.

The Director of the Census is appointed by the President of the United States and receives a salary of $6,000 *per annum.* The present Director is William J. Harris of Georgia. The permanent office organization includes a chief clerk, four chief statisticians—for population, for manufactures, for finance and municipal statistics, for vital statistics—a geographer, and eight chiefs of division. The entire number of employees in the Bureau at Washington is now about 640; in addition there are about 700 special agents employed intermittently in the southern states for the collection of cotton statistics. The number of employees in Washington was greatly increased during the decennial census: on November 1, 1910, it was 3,565, in addition to field employees. (See Population.)

Census:

Appropriation for expenses of, recommended, 4654, 4664, 4690, 4695, 4737.

Discussed and recommendations regarding, by President—

Adams, J. Q., 880, 985.

Arthur, 4635.

Cleveland, 5978.

Fillmore, 2622, 2665, 2708.

Grant, 3996, 4066, 4156, 4208.

Harrison, Benj., 5553, 5640.

Jackson, 1093, 1367.

Jefferson, 315.

Johnson, 3872.

Lincoln, 3259, 3338.
McKinley, 6345, 6389, 6454.
Monroe, 788, 817.
Pierce, 2756.
Roosevelt, 6676, 7104, 7176, 7228.
Taylor, 2560.
Tyler, 1894, 1934, 1943.
Van Buren, 1714, 1775.
Washington, 98, 175.
Every five years recommended, 4208.
In 1875, recommendation for, 4157, 4208.
Laws regarding time of taking, discussed, 986.
Referred to, 1775.
Pensioners, names and ages of, should be taken with, 1744.
Postage on papers concerning, discussed, 654.
Referred to, 6345, 6389, 6454, 6676.
Supervisors of, removed, referred to, 4543.

Census, Agricultural, recommended, 5982.

Census Board referred to, 2560.

Census Bureau discussed, 4066, 5640.

Cent.—Copper coins stamped with various designs were issued first by the states and later by the Federal Government. Vermont was the first state to issue copper cents, having granted permission in June, 1785, to Reuben Harmon, Jr., to make money for the state for two years. In October, 1785, Connecticut granted the right to coin £10,000 in copper cents, known as the Connecticut cent of 1785. In 1786 Massachusetts established a mint and coined $60,000 in cents and half cents. In the same year New Jersey granted the right to coin £10,000 at 15 coppers to the shilling. In 1781 the Continental Congress directed Robert Morris to look into the matter of governmental coinage. He proposed a standard based on the Spanish dollar, one hundred units to be called a cent. His plan was rejected, and in 1784 Jefferson proposed to Congress that the smallest coin should be of copper, of which 200 should pass for one dollar. In 1876, one hundred was substituted. The act of April 2, 1792, authorized the coinage of copper cents containing 264 grains and half cents in proportion. By the acts of Jan. 14, 1793, and Jan. 26, 1796, their weight was reduced (183). Their coinage commenced in 1793. In 1857 the nickel cent was substituted and the half cent discontinued and in 1864 the bronze cent was introduced, weighing forty-eight grains and consisting of ninety-five per cent of copper and the remainder of tin and zinc. In the calendar year 1910 there were coined 152,846,218 cent pieces worth $1,528,462.18. This was about $20,000 more than the value of five cent pieces coined, and about $100,000 less than the value of dimes coined. A proposition to coin a half-cent piece was introduced in the Sixty-second Congress in 1912, but failed of passage.

Cent. (See Copper Coins.)

Centennial Anniversary of Founding of Washington as Capital to be held in 1900, 6347, 6404, 6456.

Centennial Anniversary of Framing of Constitution, proposition to celebrate, in Philadelphia, 5118.

Centennial Anniversary of Independence, proclamation recommending delivery and filing of historical sketches of counties and towns, 4345.

Centennial Celebration of Inauguration of President Washington to be held in New York, 5371.
Proclamation regarding, 5453.

Centennial Exposition at Philadelphia.—An international exhibition of arts, manufactures, and products of the soil and mines, held at Fairmount Park, Philadelphia, from May 19 to Nov. 10, 1876. It was the first international exhibition of the kind held in this country, and was intended to celebrate the completion of a century of the existence of the United States as an independent nation. The enterprise received President Grant's warmest support (4158, 4216, 4254, 4308). Citizens of Philadelphia subscribed $10,000,000 of capital stock. Congress appropriated $2,000,000 as a loan, Pennsylvania $1,000,000, and the city of Philadelphia $1,500,000. Eight million persons paid admission, and many foreign countries were represented by exhibits.

Centennial Exposition at Philadelphia discussed, 4158, 4216, 4254, 4308.
Appropriation for, recommended, 4270, 4314.
Commission referred to, 4272, 4315.
Correspondence regarding, referred to, 4311.
Executive orders regarding, 4235, 4280.
Government aid to, recommended, 4215.
Proclamation regarding, 4181.
Removal of government exhibit to capital for permanent exhibit recommended, 4364.
Exhibits of foreign nations contributed, 4365.
Report of board on behalf of Executive Departments, printing and distribution of, recommended, 4381, 4429.
Report of commission referred to, 4364, 4465.
Results of, discussed, 4355, 4365, 4465.

Centennial State.—A nickname for Colorado (q. v.). (See also States.)

Central America.—The six Isthmian states have an area which a little exceeds 200,000 square miles. The greatest breadths, approximately along 15° N. lat. from Cape Gracios á Dios to the southwest of Mexico, is about 10°. The republics of Central America are: Costa Rica, Guatemala, Honduras, Nicaragua, Panama, Salvador.
Panama Canal Zone belonging to the United States has an area of 474 square miles.
The uplands of the plateau of Mexico are interrupted by the lowland of the Isthmus of Tehuantepec, but rise again on the southeast. The general formation as far south

as Costa Rica, where the Isthmus narrows and the mountains tend to form a single chain, is that of a plateau sloping gently towards the Atlantic and steeply towards the Pacific. On this are many more or less parallel ranges.

Nicaragua 'has a wide coast plain on the east, the Mosquito Coast, uplands in the interior from 1,000 to 7,000 feet, sloping gently towards the Atlantic and steeply towards the lakes, and volcanic cones, which continue the western volcanic zone. Some of these are active, Coseguina and Masaya have been the scenes of vast eruptions. To the east of this range is a great depression occupied by Lakes Managua and Nicaragua. These are drained by the San Juan River which flows into the Pacific.

To the south the main Cordillera follows the center of the isthmus to Panama, where a relative depression from Limon Bay on the Atlantic to Panama on the Pacific has favored the construction of the canal at the narrowest portion.

Central America (see also the several States):

Affairs of, discussed, 6325.

Civil war in, 977.

Commercial relations with, 1115, 4327, 4826.

Commission to South America and, for improving commercial relations, 4826, 4863, 4864, 4915, 4955, 5116.

Consuls of United States to, increase in number of, recommended, 4760.

Conventions and treaties between Great Britain and United States regarding dominion over, discussed, 2861, 2884, 2901, 2951, 2952.

Complications arising under, 2973, 3039.

Construction of, discussed, 2973.

Correspondence regarding, transmitted, 2722, 2894.

Diplomatic relations with, referred to, 2724.

Diplomatic representation of United States in, discussed, 6325.

Fugitive criminals, convention with, for surrender of, 4055.

Greater Republic of Central America, establishment of, discussed, 6325, 6365.

Greytown, bombardment of. (See Greytown, Nicaragua.)

Minister of United States—

Attacked and wounded by outlaws in, 2814.

Grade of, elevated to plenipotentiary rank, 4717.

Sent to, 2744.

Monarchical government, establishment of, in, referred to, 3402.

New British colony established in, 2719.

Outlaws in—

American minister attacked and wounded by, 2814.

Marauding bands of, destroying property of American citizens, discussed, 2815.

Town occupied by, bombarded, 2816.

Complaint of foreign powers regarding, 2817.

Policy of United States toward, discussed, 5750.

Questions between Great Britain and United States regarding, 2741, 2813, 2901, 2943, 2973, 3039.

Referred to, 2722.

Ship Canal through, discussed, 1115. (See also Nicaragua Canal; Panama Canal.)

Treaty with Great Britain regarding. (See Clayton-Bulwer Treaty.)

Treaty with States formerly composing, referred to, 2553, 2569, 2570.

Transmission of, to House declined, 2601.

Treaty with, transmitted and discussed, 883, 916, 1750, 4055.

War in, discussed, 4911.

Central America, Greater Republic of, establishment of, discussed, 6325, 6365.

Central America.—Honduras and Nicaragua Treaties proposed by President Taft, 7663.

Central American Peace Conference.—On account of the frequent revolutions in the Central American republics, as well as the wars between them, President Diaz, of Mexico, and President Roosevelt appealed to the republics to confer with each other on the question of a general treaty of arbitration and amity. In response to this invitation all the Central American States—Costa Rica, Guatemala, Honduras, Nicaragua, and Salvador—sent delegates to a conference in Washington, lasting from Nov. 14 to Dec. 18, 1907.

As a result of the deliberations of this conference, eight conventions were agreed to as follows and signed by the delegates: General Treaty of Peace and Amity; Additional Conventions to the General Treaty; Establishing a Central American Court of Justice; Extradition; On Future Conferences (monetary); On Communications; Establishing an International Central American Bureau; Establishing a Pedagogical Institute.

These conventions provide for permanent legations in each from all the others; forbid inciting rebellion against any one country within the borders of another; arrest and trial of any person, of whatever nationality, accused of inciting rebellion against any of the republics; refusal of any to recognize revolutionary governments which may come into power in another until acknowledged by the freely elected representatives of the people; non-interference in internal warfare. The Central American Court of Justice was formed, to consist of five justices, one from each republic, to sit at the city of Cartago, in Costa Rica. This court has jurisdiction over international questions between the republics or between citizens of one and the government of another. Other conventions provide for unification of the monetary system of the republics, as well as weights, measures, transportation, education, and the development of the commerce, industries, peace and prosperity of the countries of Central America.

May 26, 1908, the Central American Court of Justice was opened at Cartago, Costa Rica, in the presence of representatives of United States, Mexico, and all the Central American republics. The day was celebrated throughout Central America as a national holiday. The United States commissioner announced the gift of $100,000 from Andrew Carnegie to build a temple for the sittings of the court. In July, Honduras and Nicaragua brought charges against Salvador and Guatemala. President Davilla, of Honduras, charged that a recent revolt in Honduras was organized and supported in the neighboring States of Guatemala and Salvador. President Zelaya, of Nicaragua, made similar charges. The latter's claims were dismissed as lacking foundation. The Honduras claims were examined and decided adversely in the following December. This was taken as an indication of the ultimate utility of the court for the purposes for which it had been created. The differences here peacefully adjusted were of the class that formerly led to hostilities.

Central American Peace Conference, result of efforts of Presidents of United States and Mexico, 7125.

Central Powers.—The term applied during the European War to the opponents of the Entente Allies (q. v.), namely,—Germany, Austria-Hungary, Bulgaria, and Turkey. The term succeeded the previous term, the "Triple Alliance" (q. v.), when that term was rendered void by Italy's refusal to assist Germany and Austria in the European conflict. The term "Quadruple Alliance" was occasionally used to describe the Central Powers. (See European War.)

Centralization.—A term used to indicate the tendency toward greater power and authority in the Federal Government, as distinguished from the power of state governments; and the power of the state government as distinguished from local power. The telegraph, telephone and railroad have made communication so readily available as effectually to shorten the distance between points in the United States and interstate commerce has grown to be the rule, whereas formerly it was the exception. These influences have greatly assisted the present trend toward greater national centralization. An example of centralization is fixing rates and otherwise specifying regulations for railroads on the part of the Federal Government. (See State Rights.)

Centre of Population.—Bishop Berkeley, writing early in the eighteenth century, said in his poem "On the Prospect of Planting Arts and Learning in America":

"Westward the course of empire takes its way;
The four first acts already past,
A fifth shall close the drama with the day;
Time's noblest offspring is the last."

The epigraph to Bancroft's "History of the United States" made the first line of the above read as follows:

"Westward the star of empire takes its way."

The centre of population, the "star of empire," of the United States has moved steadily westward from a point east of Baltimore in 1790 to the city of Bloomington, Ind., in 1910. It has never departed far from the 39th parallel of latitude, and only twice crossed it to the south. The annexed table shows its progress:

Census Year	Approximate Location	Movement in Miles during Preceding Decade
1790	Twenty-three miles East of Baltimore, Md.	....
1800	Eighteen miles West of Baltimore, Md.	40.6
1810	Forty miles Northwest by West of Washington, D. C.	36.9
1820	Sixteen miles North of Woodstock, Va.	50.5
1830	Nineteen miles West-South-west of Moorefield, W. Va.*	40.4
1840	Sixteen miles South of Clarksburg, W. Va.*	55.0
1850	Twenty-three miles Southeast of Parkersburg, W. Va.*.	54.8
1860	Twenty miles South of Chillicothe, Ohio	80.6
1870	Forty-eight miles East by North of Cincinnati, Ohio.	44.1
1880	Eight miles West by South of Cincinnati, Ohio	58.1
1890	Twenty miles East of Columbus, Ind.	48.6
1900	Six miles Southeast of Columbus, Ind.	14.6
1910	In the city of Bloomington, Ind.	39.0

* West Virginia formed part of Virginia until 1860.

Cerro Gordo (Mexico), Battle of.—This battle was fought on April 17 and 18, 1847. Ten days after the surrender of Vera Cruz the vanguards of Scott's army, under Brig.-Gen. Twiggs, took up the march toward the Mexican capital. The distance to be covered was nearly 200 miles. Three days later they arrived at the foot of the Orizaba Mountains, 50 miles to the westward. Here Santa Anna, the Mexican President, had assembled a force of 15,000 men, intrenched on the heights of Cerro Gordo. The American force did not exceed 8,000 men. By cutting a new road around the mountain to the flank of the enemy and simultaneously assaulting front and rear the Mexicans were forced to surrender. Santa Anna escaped with some 6,000 or 7,000 of his army down the road toward Jalapa. The loss to the Americans was 63 killed and 398 wounded. That of the enemy was estimated to be nearly 1,200 killed and wounded. The victors captured 3,000 prisoners (who were paroled), between 3,000 and 4,000 stand of arms, 43 pieces of heavy bronze cannon, and a large quantity of fixed ammunition. (See illustration opposite 2408.)

Cerro Gordo (Mexico), Battle of, referred to, 2386.

Cerruti, claim of, against Colombia discussed, 6328.

Cervera, Admiral, Spanish fleet under command of, in Santiago Harbor, Cuba, 6316.

Destroyed by American squadron while attempting to escape, 6317. (See also Spanish-American War.)

Cession of Lands. (See Lands, Indian.)

Chair of American Patriotism.—An endowment established by a gift of $25,000 from Mayor Thompson, of Chicago, in May, 1917, to assist in the teaching of American patriotism in the Lincoln Memorial University (q. v.).

Chalmette's Plantation (La.), Battle of. —One of the battles near New Orleans.

After the indecisive engagement at Villiere's plantation, Dec. 23, 1814, Sir Edward Pakenham joined the British army with reenforcements. which swelled the invading forces to 8.000. On the morning of the 28th, the British advanced to Chalmette's plantation exposed to the deadly fire of the *Louisiana*. Jackson awaited the movement with 4,000 men and 20 pieces of artillery. The British were led into the engagement in 2 columns under Generals Kean and Gibbs. After facing the heavy fire of the American sharpshooters for a short time, Sir Edward Pakenham ordered a retreat. The British loss in the engagement was about 150. The loss of the Americans was 9 killed and 8 wounded. One man on board the *Louisiana* was killed. More than 800 shots were hurled from her guns with deadly effect. One of them is known to have killed and wounded 15 men.

Chamber of Commerce of the United States.—A national organization formed at a commercial conference called by the President of the United States to meet in Washington, April 22 and 23, 1912. Its published purposes are to encourage and promote the organization of associations of business men in all parts of the country.

When debatable policies affecting our National commerce are advocated by the Federal authorities, there should be a recognized organization capable of expressing the business opinion of the entire country available for conference, alike to the executive and legislative branches of the Government. It is the purpose of the Chamber of Commerce of the United States of America to act in this capacity—not to originate legislation, nor to be unnecessarily critical of legislation proposed by others, but rather to assume that the National Government desires to act in harmony with the commercial interests of the country and will accept its co-operation in an endeavor to make all business legislation constructive.

Organization Membership.—Every commercial or manufacturers' association not organized for private purposes shall be eligible for membership in the Chamber. Such associations shall be of two classes. First—Local or State, commercial or business organizations whose chief purpose is the development of the commercial and industrial interests of a single state, city or locality. Second—Local, state, interstate or National organizations whose membership is confined to one trade, or group of trades.

Representation.—Each member of the Chamber of Commerce of the United States of America shall be entitled to one delegate and one vote for the first twenty-five members, and one delegate and one vote for each additional two hundred members in excess of twenty-five, but no member shall be entitled to more than ten delegates and ten votes.

Individual Membership.—Persons, firms and corporations who are members in good standing of any organization admitted to the Chamber are eligible for election as individual members. Individual members receive the regular publications of the Chamber and they may avail themselves of the facilities of the National headquarters ; may attend all regular and special meetings of the Chamber and, subject to the rules of such meetings, may have the privilege of the floor, but they are not entitled to vote except as duly accredited delegates of organization members. Individual membership is limited to 5,000.

Chambers of Foreign Commerce, suggested, 7674.

Chambers, Talbot, court-martial of, referred to, 912.

Chamizal, arbitration with Mexico of boundary question not satisfactory, 7658.

Champion Hills (Miss.), Battle of.—Sherman was directed to remain at Jackson to destroy everything that could be of value to the Confederates. Grant himself turned toward the west. Pemberton, the Confederate general, with 25,000 men, had left Vicksburg hoping to cut off Grant from his supplies and form a junction with Johnston's forces. Learning the strength and position of the enemy, Grant ordered Sherman and McPherson to leave Jackson and hasten forward. May 16, 1863, Pemberton's army was encountered at Champion Hills, a precipitous, narrow, wooded ridge twenty-five miles west of Jackson and twenty miles east of Vicksburg. The Confederates were strongly posted, and it was necessary for the Federal troops to approach the position across open fields exposed to the fire of 10 batteries of artillery. Hovey's division and McPherson's corps, with the exception of Ramsey's division, which did not arrive till the battle was over, began the attack in front while Logan's division was working to the left and rear. The battle was hotly contested and the Confederates were driven back after they had sustained heavy loss. Grant's losses were 410 killed, 1,844 wounded. and 187 missing—total, 2,441. The Confederate losses were probably nearly the same, and in addition 2,000 prisoners.

Champlain, Lake. (See Lake Champlain.)

Chancellorsville (Va.), Battle of.—Jan. 26, 1863, Maj.-Gen. Joseph Hooker succeeded Maj.-Gen. Burnside in command of the Army of the Potomac. By April 1 that army was in excellent condition, numbering at the beginning of the new operations over 100,000 infantry, 10,000 artillery, 12,000 or 13,000 cavalry, and more than 400 guns. Gen. Lee was at Fredericksburg, Va., with 57,000 Confederates. April 28 (some authorities say the 29th) Hooker began a movement with Lee's left as his objective point. To cover his real design, however, he dispatched Gen. Stoneman with most of the cavalry on a raid to the rear of the Confederate army, stationed Gen. Sedgwick with 30,000 men opposite Fredericksburg, and moved with about 70,000 men toward the United States Ford, on the Rappahannock. By April 30 Hooker had crossed the Rappahannock with the main body of the army and established his headquarters at Chancellorsville, eleven miles west of Fredericksburg. The Confederate accounts say he then had with him 91,000 men. Lee had 48,000.

Fighting began May 2, the Fifth Corps advancing on the road to Fredericksburg and engaging a Confederate advance. The result was the recall of Hooker's advance and a better position for the Confederates. May 2 Lee detached "Stonewall" Jackson, with about 25,000 men, to attack the Eleventh Corps, under Gen. O. O. Howard, at the Federal right. The attack culminated in the evening with a panic in the Federal lines. "Stonewall" Jackson was mortally wounded during the night by the fire of his own men, who in the darkness mistook him for an enemy.

The next day, May 3, the contest was renewed, nearly 14,000 troops under Lee having made a junction with the forces under Stuart, Jackson's immediate successor. It resulted in general Confederate success. Sedgwick in the meantime had crossed the Rappahannock, forced Early out of the Fredericksburg Heights, and threatened the Confederate rear at Chancellorsville. Lee, having defeated the greater wing of the Federal army and driven it away, reenforced on the 3d and 4th of May the troops in front of Sedgwick. The latter was pushed back and recrossed the river at night with a loss of 5,000 men. Hooker also recrossed the river during the night of the 4th. According to Federal accounts their loss was 17,197, of whom 5,000 were prisoners; 13 guns and 20,000 muskets also fell into the hands of the Confederates. Lee's loss was about 13,000, including prisoners. The battle of Chancellorsville was probably the most important victory won and the greatest disaster sustained by the Confederates up to that period. They here defeated the splendid Union Army which attacked them; but the death of Lieut.-Gen. Jackson was a loss from which it was well-nigh impossible to recover.

Chantilly (Va.), Battle of.—Aug. 31, 1862, the day after the second battle of Bull Run, or Manassas, Lee sent Jackson northward for the purpose of turning Pope's right wing toward Washington. Pope's headquarters were at Centerville and he had been reenforced by Sumner's and Franklin's corps. Anticipating the movement of the Confederates, he disposed his forces in position to meet and frustrate it at Chantilly, just north of Centerville, on the evening of Sept.1, by the troops under McDowell, Hooker, and Kearny. In the engagement Generals Kearny and Stevens were killed. Pope was forced to fall back upon the works at Washington. Federal loss, 1,300; Confederate, 800.

Chaplain.—A preacher employed for the religious ceremonies in the Senate, the House of Representatives, and in the Army and Navy.

Chapultepec (Mexico), Battle of.—The reduction of El Molino del Rey and Casa de Mata by Gen. Scott's army left the City of Mexico still protected by the formidable citadel of Chapultepec. This was filled with troops and the approaches were guarded by mines. Sept. 12, 1847, a preliminary fire was opened on the outworks, and on the 13th a strategic assault was made and the walls scaled in the face of a terrible fire. The American force consisted of 7,180 men. Some 25,000 of Santa Anna's men were distributed between Churubusco and the City of Mexico and the causeways connecting them. Between Chapultepec and the City of Mexico proper were two causeways or elevated roads leading to the gates of Belen and San Cosmé. These were crossed under the enemy's fire and the divisions of Worth and Quitman entered the ancient seat of the Montezumas. During the fighting from Sept. 12 to 14 incident to the taking of Chapultepec and the occupation of the city the American loss was 62. The Mexican army, strongly fortified in the vicinity of its capital, numbering at first some 30,000, lost 10,743. Santa Anna, then President and commander in chief of the army, was a fugitive. The trophies included more than 20 colors and standards, 75 pieces of ordnance and 57 wall pieces, 20,000 small arms, and an immense quantity of ammunition. (See illustration opposite 2440.)

Charleston, S. C., foreign vessels at, referred to, 3192.

Charleston, S. C., Exposition, relations of U. S. Government to, 6675.

Charleston (S. C.), Surrender of.—After Sir Henry Clinton had learned of the failure of the attack on Savannah he sent an additional force of 8,500 men to the South under Maj.-Gen. Leslie. The main body of the American army was in winter quarters at Morristown, and reenforcements were sent from there to join Gen. Lincoln, who had command of the Southern army. The entire garrison at Charleston was less than 4,000 regulars and militia. March 20, 1780, the British squadron, having touched at Tybee Island, near Savannah, crossed the bar, and on April 9 passed Fort Moultrie, with a loss of 27 men, and anchored off Fort Johnson, which had been abandoned by the Americans. April 29 Admiral Arbuthnot, with 500 marines, forced the Americans to abandon L'Empries Point, with a loss of nearly 100 men, who were captured by the guard boats on the way to Charleston. May 4, 200 marines took Fort Moultrie, on Sullivans Island. May 12, 1780, Gen. Lincoln was compelled to surrender. The British casualties were 76 killed and 189 wounded. The American casualties were nearly the same; 5,618 men, which included all the male citizens of Charleston, were made prisoners, and 405 pieces of ordnance were captured.

Charlestown, Mass., docks constructed at, 985.

Site for, 934.

Charter.—A name commonly applied to grants of land or special privileges made by governments or individual rulers to companies or bodies of men for a term of years. In American law a charter is a written grant from the sovereign power conferring rights or privileges upon a municipality or other corporation. The term is generally applied to the statute, letters patent, or articles of association sanctioned by statute creating a corporation, as a city, college, stock company, benevolent society, or social club. During the early settlement of America European potentates, claiming sovereignty by right of discovery, issued charters granting land for purposes of colonization. The principal charters granted for this purpose were those of the Virginia Company, 1606, 1609, and 1612; Plymouth, 1620; Massachusetts Bay, 1629; Providence Plantations, 1644; Connecticut, 1662; Rhode Island and Providence Plantations, 1663; Massachusetts, 1691, and Georgia, 1732. The same sort of charters were given to the Dutch West India Company by the States-General of the United Netherlands in 1621 and to the Swedish Company by Gustavus Adolphus in 1624.

Charter Oak.—A tree celebrated in American legend. According to tradition, in 1687 Edmund Andros, the colonial governor of Connecticut, demanded the return of the charter of the Colony. During a meeting held to deliberate upon the action to be taken the lights were suddenly extinguished. When they were relighted the charter was missing. It was said that Capt. Wadsworth prevented the confiscation of the charter by secreting it in the hollow of an oak tree near Hartford. The tree was long held in great veneration. Aug. 20, 1856, it was prostrated by a gale.

Chasta Indians. (See Indian Tribes.)

Chattanooga (Tenn.), Battle of. (See Missionary Ridge.)

Chauvinism.—An unreasoning, exaggerated enthusiasm for war. (See Militarism.)

Chauvinist.—One addicted to chauvinism (q. v.).

Chayenne Indians. (See Indian Tribes.)

Chehalis Reservation, Wash., allotment of lands in severalty to Indians on, referred to, 4779.

Chemicals.—The chemical industry of the United States is but little more than 100 years old, and ranks fourth among the manufacturing businesses. No chemicals were made here before the Revolution. In 1810 copperas was made in Vermont and Maryland, and the latter state produced alum in 1813. The manufacture of chemicals, paints and medicines began in Baltimore in 1816.

Chemical manufacture, as such, can hardly be said to have existed until the continuously working chamber process for sulphuric acid was introduced, about 1810, while the Leblanc soda process, although discovered by him in 1789, failed to get a footing until 1814, when it was introduced into England by Losh. Now we find this great discovery approaching extinction through the contact process.

By 1830 the industry was firmly established in the United States, Philadelphia being the center. There were thirty firms doing business throughout the entire country, with a capital of $1,158,000, producing articles valued at $1,000,000. The list of articles included acetate and nitrate of lead, acetic and oxalic acids, alum, ammonia, aqua fortis, bichromate of potash, borax, camphor, copperas, chrome yellow, chrome green, Glauber's and Rochelle salts, muriatic and nitric acids, oil of vitriol, Prussian blue, prussiate of potash, saltpetre, sulphate of quinine, tartar emetic, tartaric acid and compounds of these.

The chemical industry is divided for purposes of analysis by the Census Bureau into twelve groups as follows: I—Acids, except sulphuric, nitric, and mixed acids, and such as are made by establishments in the wood distillation industry. II—Sodas. III—Potashes. IV—Alums. V—Coal-tar products. VI—Cyanides. VII—Bleaching materials. VIII—Electro-chemicals (substances produced by the aid of electricity, including metals and alloys produced by electrolytic or electrometallurgic processes. IX—Plastics. X—Compressed or liquefied gases. XI—Fine chemicals. XII—Chemicals not otherwise specified.

Besides the exceptions noted in the first group, this classification excludes alcohol, dye stuffs, fertilizers, explosives, oils, paints and others which are considered under appropriate headings. The number of establishments in these twelve groups in 1910 was given as 349. The capital invested was $155,143,739 and 27,791 persons were engaged in the industry, extracting therefrom in salary and wages, $20,221,089. The total value of the products was placed at $117,688,887. The value of the several groups was: Acids, $11,926,389; sodas, $21,417,982; potashes, $88,940; alums, $2,578,842; coal-tar products, $2,675,327; cyanides, $1,941,893; bleaching materials, $1,635,046; chemical substances produced by the aid of electricity, $17,962,277; plastics, $7,180,172; compressed or liquefied gases, $4,969,805; fine chemicals, $10,956,666; chemicals, not elsewhere specified, including glycerin, Epsom salts, blue vitriol, copperas, phosphate

of soda, zinc salts, tin compounds, by-products, etc., $34,349,548.

Besides these groups, the production of sulphuric, nitric, and mixed acids (sulphuric and nitric in various proportions) was carried on in 42 separate establishments, by 2,582 persons using a capital of $18,726,195, and the output was valued at $9,884,057.

There are 120 establishments engaged in wood distillation, not including turpentine and rosin. The chief products of this industry are wood alcohol, acetate of lead, turpentine and charcoal and creosote. The capital invested was reported in 1910 as $13,017,192. Less than 4,000 persons were engaged in the business and their wages and salaries amounted to $1,818,059. The materials used cost $5,875,851, and the value of the products was $9,736,998.

The production of sulphuric acid is a matter of the greatest importance, as it is not only the foundation of the inorganic heavy-chemical industry and is used for many other purposes, but also has lately become a most important material in the organic dye-stuff industry, especially in the production of alizarine colors and of synthetic indigo.

The first manufacturer of sulphuric acid in the United States appears to have been John Harrison, of Philadelphia, who, in 1793, had a lead chamber capable of producing 300 carboys of acid per annum. The business proved very profitable, acid selling as high as 15c. per pound. Powers & Weightman began making sulphuric acid in Philadelphia in 1825, and the Lennig plant, erected in 1829, is said to have been so successful that the then existing New York Chemical Company went into liquidation and put the funds realized therefrom into a banking company, now widely known as the Chemical National Bank.

Nitric acid was manufactured in Philadelphia in 1834 by Carter & Scattergood. The most notable recent advance made in its manufacture is in the form of apparatus employed, which is due to Edward Hart and Oscar Guttman. It is used in the manufacture of nitrates, like silver nitrate, or nitrites, like sodium nitrite; in making "mixed acids" and aqua regia, gun cotton, nitroglycerine, as an oxidizing agent and for etching on metals.

Sulphuric acid ranks first in importance among manufactured chemicals, followed closely by artificial fertilizers. Paints and dyes come next. The conduct of the industry depends more upon skill and knowledge than any other industry, and the growth is so rapid that the skilled worker of twenty years ago would be useless to-day.

Among the manufactures depending upon the chemical industry are the following: cotton, woolen and silk fabrics, oil cloth, paint, glucose, fertilizers, soap, glass, paper, ink, explosives, pyroxylin, electrical, pyrotechnic, pharmaceutic, tanning, oil and sugar refining, artificial ice, bleaching works and the reduction of metals.

Merchandising of many chemicals is handicapped by our inability to compete with the low wages of some foreign countries; but, on the other hand, through natural advantages not enjoyed by foreign manufacturers, considerable exportation of certain chemicals is going on at all times.

For the manufacture of chemicals and allied industries, the census of 1910 reports 2,140 establishments employing 88,097 persons, including proprietors, firm members, wage-earners and salaried attendants. The capital invested in the several branches of the business amounted to $483,729,410, and the value of the products was $425,084,540. The number of establishments manufacturing dye-stuffs and extracts was reported as 107, having a capital of $17,934,545, and turning out finished products valued at $15,954,574, of which $6,270,923 was added in the process of manufactures. More than $50,000,000 was invested in making explosives, which was carried on in eighty-six factories. The fertilizer industry was capitalized at $121,537,451, and the output of the 550 factories was worth $103,960,213.

Of the 111 establishments manufacturing dyestuffs and extracts as chief products in 1914, 23 were located in New York, 18 in New Jersey, 17 in Massachusetts, 13 in Virginia, 9 in Pennsylvania, 6 in Rhode Island, 6 in Tennessee, 4 in North Carolina, 4 in West Virginia, 2 in Georgia, 2 in Illinois, 2 in Wisconsin, and 1 each in Alabama, California, Connecticut, Indiana and Michigan.

Chemistry, Bureau of, Agriculture Department.—A bureau of the Agriculture Department devoted to the inspection of foods and drugs imported or entering interstate commerce. It makes analyses for the department, and tests supplies for other departments. It makes studies in agricultural chemistry; bacteriology and physiology, especially with food, drugs, waters, paper, leather, foodstuffs, insecticides and fungicides; enology and methods of analysis. The bureau especially studies the chemical problems of agriculture relating to soils, fertilizers and irrigation waters.

The Bureau of Chemistry, among its other activities, has studied the composition of thousands of materials used in the home and many processes for converting the raw materials of agriculture into finished products. One has but to remember its extended studies of sugar, of bread and breadstuffs, of commercial food products, etc., to realize how closely the results concern the home. The same could be said of its studies of fruits and their preservation, of storage and its relation to quality and of the extended activities which have resulted in the establishment of food standards and the carrying out of the provisions of the national pure food law. It is through this bureau that the department administers the Food and Drugs act. Samples are collected, analyses are conducted, and hearings are held by this bureau. A compliance with department decisions is secured in many cases without resort to the courts. (See Agriculture, Department of.)

Chemulpo, Korea, agreement respecting foreign settlement at, 5391.

Cherokee Case.—The Indian tribes known as the "Creeks" and the "Cherokees" possessed large tracts of land in what are now the States of Georgia and North Carolina, and the territory to the west of them. From time to time treaties had been made with these Indians by which much of this land had been ceded to the United States. Among these were the Hopewell treaty of 1785 and the Holston treaty of 1791; the first of these instruments had, among other things, recognized the Cherokees as a nation possessing its own laws and all the other attributes of nationality; the second had guaranteed to them all lands not thereby ceded. When Georgia in 1802 ceded her western territory to the United States, the latter agreed to extinguish Indian titles to lands in the state proper as soon as it could peaceably and reasonably be done; but the Cherokees could not be induced to surrender their lands. The state therefore claimed the right to extend its own laws over all its territory, and passed acts depriving the Cherokees of their courts and other machinery of government; these were followed by acts dividing the Cherokee land into counties, and after allotting 160 acres to each head of a Cherokee family, providing for the distribution of the remainder by lot among the people of the state. Notwithstanding the treaties, President Jackson took the ground that as the state was sovereign the United States could not interfere. The question now came up before the United States Supreme Court in the following way. A Cherokee named Tassels was sentenced to be hanged, under the laws of Georgia, for killing another Indian on the Cherokee lands. The United States Supreme Court granted a writ of error requiring the state to show cause why the case should not go to the Cherokee courts. This writ was disregarded, and the Indian was hung. There the matter was dropped. Again, two missionaries were convicted of entering the Cherokee territory without having complied with certain requirements demanded by Georgia enactments regarding these lands. Their case was carried to the United States Supreme Court on a writ of error, and the judgment of the court held the provisions of our Indian treaties as paramount to the state laws. But the decision was never enforced. Jackson is reported to have said: "Well, John Marshall (the Chief Justice) has made his decision; now let him enforce it." The Cherokee case is important as the first instance of successful nullification of United States laws by a state. The Indians were finally persuaded to move to the Indian Territory, and by 1838 the last had left the state.

Cherokee Commission:

Agreement with—

Cherokee Indians, 5671.

Cheyenne and Arapahoe Indians, 5565.

Comanche, Kiowa, and Apache Indians, 5768.

Indians of Pyramid Lake Reservation, Nev., 5649.

Iowa Indians, 5508, 5512.

Proclaimed, 5591.

Kickapoo Indians, 5638, 5649.

Pawnee Indians, 5768.

Pottawatomie and Absentee Shawnee Indians, 5514.

Proclaimed, 5591.

Sac and Fox Indians, 5508, 5510.

Proclaimed, 5591.

Shoshone and Arapahoe Indians, 5649.

Tonkawa Indians, 5638, 5649.

Wichita, Caddo, etc., Indians, memorial regarding, 5671.

Wichita Indians, 5638, 5648.

Appointed and discussed, 5481, 5506, 5508, 5638.

Lands acquired by, opened to settlement. (See Lands, Public, opened.)

Cherokee Indians. (See Indian Tribes.)

Cherokee Outlet:

Cession of, to United States, agreements and propositions regarding, discussed, 5481, 5638, 5760.

Claims of Indians regarding, discussed, 5667.

Contracts and leases for grazing on, proclaimed null and void, 5532.

Time for removal of stock extended by proclamation, 5534.

Fraudulent occupation of, discussed, 5886.

Opened to settlement by proclamation, 5838.

Form of declaration required, 5856.

Cherokee Strip. (See Cherokee Outlet.)

Cherry Valley (N. Y.), Massacre.—Nov. 11, 1778, during a blinding storm of snow and rain, about 800 Indians and Tories surprised the force of Colonial troops under Col. Ichabod Alden at Cherry Valley and massacred 43 persons, including women and children, took some 49 prisoners, burned all the buildings, and drove away the live stock.

Chesapeake, The.—June 22, 1807, as the U. S. S. *Chesapeake* was leaving Hampton Roads, Va., a lieutenant of the British ship *Leopard* boarded her and demanded the return of three negro deserters who had escaped from the British man-of-war *Melampus* and enlisted on the *Chesapeake*. The Government had previously refused the demand of the British admiral for the return of the deserters. Commodore Barron accordingly refused to deliver the men. The officer of the *Leopard* then returned to his ship, which immediately opened fire on the *Chesapeake*. The latter vessel, being entirely unprepared for battle, was forced to surrender without firing a gun (414). President Jefferson at once issued a proclamation (410) and demanded a disavowal of the act, a restoration of the captured men, and the recall of Admiral Berkeley. Only tardy reparation was made for the affair (481), and it served to embitter American opinion against the British and hastened the War of 1812.

Chesapeake, The, attacked by British ship *Leopard*, 410, 414, 420, 454, 460.

Captured by the Shannon. (See illustration opposite 647.

Claims of Peter Shackerly growing out of, 1687.

Indemnity for, demanded, 433, 441.

Paid, 481.

Referred to, 463.

Chesapeake and Delaware Canal Co., shares in, taken by United States, 870.

Chesapeake and Ohio Canal:

Cession of Government interests in, to Maryland considered, 1776.

Incorporation of, referred to, 852.

Legislative acts of Virginia respecting, transmitted, 1037.

Propriety of constructing, discussed, 785.

Subscriptions for, commissioners appointed to receive, 873.

Chesapeake Bay, canal from Delaware River to. (See Chesapeake and Delaware Canal Co.)

Chesnimnus Forest Reserve, proclaimed, 7114.

Cheyenne and Arapahoe Reservation, Ind. T.:

Deed for release of lands in, by Choctaws and Chickasaws, discussed, 5637, 5664, 5761.

Opened to settlement by proclamation, 5710.

Appropriations for, recommended, 5638.

Unauthorized occupancy of, proclamation against, 4892.

Cheyenne Indians. (See Indian Tribes.)

Chicago:

Convention at, on subject of diseases of cattle, 4771.

Fire in, referred to, 4108, 4138.

Government buildings in, destroyed by fire, discussed and recommendations regarding, 4108.

International military encampment to be held at, foreign guests not to pay duties on baggage, 5164.

Memorial of convention at, in respect to enlarging water communication between Mississippi River and Atlantic Ocean, 3388.

Proclamation granting privileges of other ports to, 2859.

Unlawful combinations in, proclamation against, 5931.

World's Columbian Exposition at—

Board of management of Government exhibits designated, 5833.

Chinese artisans, admission of, temporarily to, recommended, 5622.

Military encampment to be held during, discussed, 5458.

Proclamation regarding opening of, 5575.

Proposition to observe four-hundredth anniversary of discovery of America, discussed, 5487.

Referred to, 2040.

Reports of—

Deposited in State Department, 6181.

Discussed and recommendations regarding, 5567, 5669, 5765, 5769, 6184.

Resolution of International American Conference regarding, 77.

Chicago Fire referred to, 4108, 4138.

Chicago Fire.—Oct. 8, 9, and 10, 1871, the City of Chicago, Ill., was visited by the most disastrous fire of modern times. Two thousand one hundred acres of the city, the greater portion of which was covered by costly stores and other business houses, were burned over. The loss was nearly $200,000,000. (See illustration opposite 4136.)

Chicago Indian Massacre.—At the outbreak of the War of 1812 Capt. Nathan Heald commanded fifty men at Fort Dearborn, where now stands the city of Chicago. Ordered by Gen. Hull to abandon the fort and join him at Detroit, Capt. Heald's party were waylaid by Indians on Aug. 15, 1812, among the sand hills along the lake shore. The greater part of them, including twelve children, were massacred and their scalps sold to Col. Proctor, who had offered a premium for American scalps.

Chicago, Milwaukee and St. Paul Railway, agreement with Indians for right of way for, 4780, 4788, 4954, 5178.

Lands granted to, for right of way declared forfeited, 5944.

Proclaimed, 5529.

Chicago Riots, proclamation regarding, 5931.

Chicago Strike, report of commission on, transmitted, 5988.

Chicago, Texas and Mexican Central Railway, application of, for right of way across Indian Territory, 4653.

Chichagof Island, referred to, 6697.

Chickahominy (Va.), Battle of. (See Cold Harbor, Battle of; Gaines Mill, Battle of.)

Chickamauga (Ga.), Battle of.—After the battle of Stone River, or Murfreesboro, Jan. 2, 1863, Bragg retreated to Shelbyville, and then to Tullahoma, Tenn. June 24 Rosecrans advanced from Murfreesboro and gradually forced Bragg to evacuate middle Tennessee and cross Tennessee River to Chattanooga. Aug. 19 Rosecrans's army in 3 corps, under Generals George H. Thomas, Alexander McD. McCook, and Thomas L. Crittenden, made an advance through the Cumberland Mountains. Sept. 7 and 8 the Confederates retired from Chattanooga, Tenn., to Lafayette, Ga. Longstreet having arrived from Virginia with reenforcements for Bragg, Rosecrans concentrated his army near Lee & Gordon's Mill on Chickamauga Creek, a tributary of the Tennessee. On the evening of Sept. 18 the two armies were on opposite sides of Chickamauga Creek.

Rosecrans's army numbered between 55,-000 and 60,000 men; Bragg's army about 50,000. Bragg crossed the creek with a portion of his army during the night, and on the morning of the 19th Gen. Polk in command of the Confederate right wing, attacked the Federal left under Thomas. The battle continued all day without definite results. On the morning of the 20th the Confederates renewed the attack. Longstreet penetrated the center of the Federal line and separated Rosecrans, McCook, and Crittenden from the rest of the army, and the brunt of the battle fell upon Thomas. The Federals retreated at night to Rossville, and on the night of the 21st to Chattanooga. The Federal losses in the battle were 1,687 killed, 9,394 wounded, and 5,255 missing; total, 16,336. The Confederate loss was 18,000.

Chickamauga and Chattanooga National Military Park discussed, 5879.

Chickamauga Indians. (See Indian Tribes.)

Chickasaw Case.—Through the efforts of Northern people in organizing vigilance committees to prevent kidnapping of free colored persons on the charge of being fugitive slaves, a writ of *habeas corpus* was served upon the captain of the brig *Chickasaw* demanding the delivery of two colored women whom, it was charged, he intended to carry South. On exhibiting their free papers the women were liberated.

Chickasaw Indians. (See Indian Tribes.)

Chief Clerk, Department of State.—The chief clerk was the only other officer authorized in the State Department when that department was placed in charge of a secretary of state in 1789. His salary at that time was $800 yearly, which has been increased until it has reached the present figures of $3,000. The chief clerk is under the supervision of the assistant secretary of state, whose own office is a development from the office of the chief clerk in the early days of the Department. The Chief Clerk's Bureau was established by act of Congress in 1870, and has charge of the details of the administration within the department, including the translations, printing office, lithographing, and mail room. (See State Department.)

Chief Magistrate. (See President of United States.)

Chief of Bureau of Insular Affairs. (See Insular Affairs, Bureau of.)

Chief of Engineers. (See War Department, heading Engineer Corps; also Army.)

Chief of Ordnance. (See War Department, heading Ordnance Department; also Army.)

Chief of Staff. (See item under General Staff in article War Department.)

Chief Signal Officer. (See Signal Corps heading under War Department.)

Chief Signal Officer of Army, printing of report of, recommended, 4658, 4737, 4778.

Child Labor.—With the introduction of machinery which requires but slight attention and no highly skilled operatives came the employment of children in factories. The invention of spinning machinery in England and the cotton gin in America transferred the field of youthful industry from the cottage home and farmhouse to crowded mills and shops and factories. Competition between manufacturers gradually resulted in increasing the tasks and lengthening the hours of employment of children, until the Government came to the rescue.

As long ago as 1784 the magistrates of Lancashire, England, found it necessary to pass a resolution that apprentices should no longer "work in the night or more than ten hours in the day." Subsequent legislation culminated in the present code of factory supervision in England, which dates from 1878. It prohibits the employment of children under ten, and those fourteen may only be employed half time. Night work is forbidden and children under sixteen must furnish medical certificates of fitness for employment, and weekly certificate showing a certain amount of school attendance.

In European countries the regulation of child labor is the duty of the central government, while in America it comes within the jurisdiction of the several states. No two of these states have the same code of laws or collect similar statistics on the subject of child labor, and its existence has been shown to be a monstrous evil in some of them.

For this reason President Roosevelt, in his sixth annual message to Congress, Dec. 3, 1906, recommended the enactment of a model child labor law for the District of Columbia, which should be a guide to those states which wished to legislate against the evil (pages 7036, 7090, 7189, 7342). Accordingly, Congress passed such a law May 28, 1908. It had been contended that Washington not being a manufacturing city no child labor existed in the District of Columbia. By Nov. 1, 8,000 applications under the new law had been received, 3,500 of which were denied on account of age or education.

Statistics collected by the general secretary of the National Child Labor Committee show that something like 5,000,000 children of school age have left school to engage in wage work. According to the census of 1910, 186,358 children under fourteen years of age were engaged in industries other than agricultural. The committee believes, however, that more children, in proportion to the population, are attending school to-day than ever before.

Child Labor Law.—The 64th Congress passed, and President Wilson signed, Sept. 1, 1916, a law forbidding the shipment from one state to another of articles made by the labor of children. This as far as the authority of the federal government extends under the Constitution. This law provides that no producer, manufacturer, or dealer shall ship or deliver for shipment in interstate or foreign commerce any article or commodity the product of any mine or quarry, situated in the United States, in which within thirty days prior to the time of the removal of such product therefrom children under the age of 16 years have been employed or permitted to work, or any article or commodity the product of any mill, cannery, workshop, factory, or manufacturing establishment, situated in the United States, in which within thirty days prior to the removal of such product therefrom children under the age of 14 years have been employed or permitted to work, or children between the ages of 14 years and 16 years have been employed or permitted to work more than eight hours in any day, or more than six days in any week, or after the hour of 7 o'clock postmeridian, or before the hour of 6 o'clock antemeridian.

The Attorney General, the Secretary of Commerce, and the Secretary of Labor are constituted a board to make and publish uniform rules and regulations for carrying out the provisions of the act. For the purpose of securing proper enforcement of the act the Secretary of Labor, or any person duly authorized by him, has authority to enter and inspect at any time mines, quarries, mills, canneries, workshops, factories, manufacturing establishments, and other places in which goods are produced or held for interstate commerce.

It is made the duty of each district attorney to whom the Secretary of Labor shall report any violation of this act, or to whom any State factory or mining or quarry inspector, commissioner of labor, State medical inspector, or school-attendance officer, or any other person shall present satisfactory evidence of any such violation to cause appropriate proceedings to be commenced and prosecuted in the proper courts of the United States without delay for the enforcement of the penalties in such cases herein provided: Provided, That nothing in this act shall be construed to apply to bona fide boys' and girls' canning clubs recognized by the Agricultural Department of the several States and of the United States.

Any person who violates any of the provisions of this act, or who refuses or obstructs entry or authorized inspection, shall for each offense prior to the first conviction be punished by a fine or not more than

$200, and for each offense subsequent to such conviction by a fine of not more than $1,000, nor less than $100, or by imprisonment for not more than three months, or by both such fine and imprisonment, in the discretion of the court:

Provided, That no dealer shall be prosecuted under the provisions of this act for a shipment, delivery for shipment, or transportation who establishes a guaranty issued by the person by whom the goods shipped or delivered for shipment or transportation were manufactured or produced, to the effect that such goods were produced or manufactured in a mine or quarry in which within thirty days prior to their removal therefrom no children under the age of sixteen years were employed or permitted to work, or in a mill, cannery, workshop, factory, or manufacturing establishment, in which within thirty days prior to the removal of such goods therefrom no children under the age of fourteen years were employed or permitted to work, nor children between the ages of fourteen years and sixteen years employed or permitted to work more than eight hours in any day or more than six days in any week or after the hour of seven o'clock postmeridian or before the hour of six o'clock antemeridian; and in such event, if the guaranty contains any false statement of a material fact, the guarantor shall be amenable to prosecution and to the fine or imprisonment provided. Said guaranty, to afford the protection above provided, shall contain the name and address of the person giving the same; and no producer, manufacturer, or dealer shall be prosecuted under this act for the shipment, delivery for shipment, or transportation of a product of any mine, quarry, mill, cannery, workshop, factory, or manufacturing establishment, if the only employment therein, within thirty days prior to the removal of such product therefrom, of a child under the age of sixteen years has been that of a child as to whom the producer or manufacturer has in good faith procured, at the time of employing such child, and has since in good faith relied upon and kept on file a certificate, issued in such form, under such conditions, and by such persons as may be prescribed by the board, showing the child to be of such an age that the shipment, delivery for shipment, or transportation was not prohibited by this act.

Any person who knowingly makes a false statement or presents false evidence in or in relation to any such certificate or application therefor shall be amenable to prosecution and to the fine or imprisonment provided. In any State designated by the board, an employment certificate or other similar paper as to the age of the child, issued under the laws of that State and not inconsistent with the provisions of this act, shall have the same force and effect as a certificate herein provided for.

The word "person" as used in this act shall be construed to include any individual or corporation or the members of any partnership or other unincorporated association. The term "ship or deliver for shipment in interstate or foreign commerce" as used in this act means to transport or to ship or deliver for shipment from any State or Territory or the District of Columbia to or through any other State or Territory or the District of Columbia or to any foreign country; and in the case of a dealer means only to transport or to ship or deliver for shipment from the State, Territory, or district of manufacture or production.

Owen R. Lovejoy, chairman of the National Child Labor Committee, said of the law: "The law will reach 150,000, but there are 1,850,000 children in the United States who cannot possibly be touched by any federal legislation. These are wards of the various States: the infant hawkers of news and chewing gum on our city streets; the truck garden conscripts of Pennsylvania, New Jersey, Ohio, Colorado, and Maryland; the sweating cotton pickers of Mississippi, Oklahoma, and Texas; the 90,000 domestic servants under 16 years old who do the menial drudgery in our American homes; and the pallid cashgirls in our department stores."

Child Labor and Labor of Women:

Congress asked to investigate condition of, 7035.

Children's Bureau.—The Children's Bureau of the Department of Labor was created by Congress in 1912 to investigate and report upon all matters pertaining to the welfare of children and child-life among all classes of our people, and especially to investigate the questions of infant mortality, the birth rate, orphanage, juvenile courts, desertion, dangerous occupations, accidents and diseased children, employment and legislation affecting children in the several states and territories. The functions of the bureau are thus largely investigative. It has no power to administer anything or to regulate anything, and the act creating the bureau stipulates that "no official, or agent, or representative of said bureau shall, over the objection of the head of the family, enter any house used exclusively as a family residence." It is to serve as a centre to which people can turn for definite information regarding child welfare movements, so that every individual or organization working for children can learn of and profit from the experience of others.

The bureau has been in active operation since August, 23, 1912. It has already published, in addition to a brief circular containing the law establishing the bureau and a statement of its scope and plans, a monograph entitled "Birth Registration an Aid in Protecting the Lives and Rights of Children. Necessity for Extending the Registration Area," a pamphlet "Baby-Saving Campaigns. What Some American Cities are Doing to Prevent Infant Mortality," and a monograph called "Prenatal Care," designed for the use of the expectant mother.

The publications thus far issued have all been in the field of the work to promote child health. Other pamphlets on the care of children are in the course of preparation, and the results of an investigation into the social causes of infant mortality in Johnstown, Pa., will soon be published. The bureau expects to follow it with reports of the results of other similar investigations in typical cities and rural districts to be conducted in the future.

The bureau has not as yet, published anything on the employment of children, but it has in the course of preparation a thorough digest of all the state laws on child labor. It proposes to undertake in the near future an investigation of the methods employed by the several states in the administration and enforcement of these laws.

A handbook of Federal statistics of children is also being prepared. It will be published in five sections or parts, the first dealing with the number of children in the country and their sex, race, nativity, parentage and geographic distribution; the second with the growth of the child population, including the questions of the birth rate and infant mortality; the third with illiteracy and school attendance; the fourth with the employment of children, and the fifth with statistics of the defective, dependent and delinquent classes.

Chile.—Chile extends down the western coast of South America from the Rio Sama to Cape Horn, and is bounded on the north by Peru and on the east by Bolivia and Argentina. It lies between 18° 28'-56° 35' South latitude and 66° 30'-75° 40' West longitude, with a coast line of 2,485 miles, an extreme length of 2,800 miles, and an average breadth (north of 41°) of 100 miles.

Physical Features.—The great chain of the Andes runs along its eastern limit, with a general elevation of 5,000 to 10,000 feet above the level of the sea; but numerous summits attain the height of 18,000 feet—the highest, Aconcagua, an extinct volcano, being 22,422 feet. The chain, however, lowers considerably toward its southern extremity. There are no rivers of great size.

AREA AND POPULATION

Provinces	Area English Sq. Miles	Population 1912
Aconcagua	5,404	135,558
Antofagasta	46,591	122,354
Arauco	2,188	62,732
Atacama	30,687	65,875
Bio-Bio	5,349	102,170
Cautin	6,377	166,895
Chiloé	8,583	93,684
Colchagua	3,849	159,676
Concepción	3,311	230,442
Coquimbo	14,089	181,242
Curicó	3,041	108,791
Lináres	3,967	113,365
Llanquihué	35,387	118,973
Magallanes	66,176	24,374
Malleco	3,301	115,177
Maule	2,809	119,107
Ñuble	3,497	172,244
O'Higgins	2,168	95,524
Santiago	5,890	566,787
Tacna	9,248	44,291
Talca	3,862	133,235
Tarapacá	18,126	119,714
Valdivia	8,991	141,298
Valparaiso	1,774	311,809
Easter Island, etc.	75	248
Total	294,740	3,505,565

Ethnology.—There are four distinct elements in the racial divisions: the Spanish settlers and their descendants; the indigenous Auracanian Indians, Fuegians, and Changos; mixed Spanish Indians; European immigrants. The latter were represented in 1910 by 20,000 Spaniards, 15,000 Italians, 11,000 Germans, 10,000 British, and 10,000 French. Spanish is the language of the country, and the State religion is Roman Catholic.

History.—It was invaded by the Spanish under Almagro in 1535, and was first settled by Valdivia at Santiago, in 1541. Independence was proclaimed in 1818, though the last stronghold of the Spaniards was not taken until 1826. After gaining its independence Chile made extensive conquests in Patagonia and that country was finally divided between Chile and Argentina with the Andes as the boundary. Wars with Peru and Bolivia from 1879-1883 extended the northern boundaries. Chile has enjoyed greater tranquility, both internal and external, than the majority of South American Republics, but in 1902 the quiet was interrupted by a violent dispute with Argentina over the size and armament of their respective navies. The dispute was satisfactorily settled in 1903 by treaty. (See Argentina.)

Government.—The Constitution rests on the fundamental law of May 25, 1833, and is that of a democratic Republic. The Government (despite a fierce civil war of 1890-91) is far the most stable in South America. The President is elected by indirect vote for five years, the election being held on June 25 and the inauguration on September 18, the anniversary of the Declaration of Independence (1810). The President is ineligible for a succeeding term of office, and receives a salary of $30,000 and an allowance of $22,000.

President (1910-15), Ramon Barros Luce assumed office December 23, 1910.

There is a Council of State of eleven members (five appointed by the President and six chosen by Congress.

The National Congress consists of a Senate and a Chamber of Deputies. The Senate of thirty-seven members (one for every three members of the Chamber) is elected by direct vote of the people for six years. The Chamber of Deputies of 108 members (one per 30,000 inhabitants of each Department, with a minimum fraction of 15,000) is elected by direct vote for three years. There is universal adult male suffrage at twenty-one for those who can read and write.

There is a High Court of Justice at Santiago (with a President elected annually) and Courts of Appeal at Concepción, Santiago, Serena, Tacna, Talca, Valdivia, and Valparaiso. There are Courts of First Instance turoughout the country and District Courts subordinate to the High Court at the capital.

The Provinces are governed by Intendentes under whom are Gobernadores for Departments of each Province and for the Magallanes Territory. The municipalities have popularly elected triennial councils. The police are a national force financed by the Treasury and the Municipalities.

Army.—By law of 1900 all able-bodied male citizens from 18th to 45th year are obliged to serve in the Militia. For the Chilean army see Armies of the World; for navy see Navies of the World.

Primary education is free, but is not compulsory, and reading and writing are the qualifications for adult male suffrage. There were in 1912 2,947 primary schools, with an average attendance of 169,744. There is a State University and a Roman Catholic university at Santiago. The National Library at the capital contains 155,880 volumes.

Production and Industry.—Agriculture and mining are the principal occupations of the people. The central belt enjoys a moderate rainfall, and wheat, maize, barley, oats, beans, peas, lentils, wines, tobacco, ax, hemp, Chile pepper, and potatoes are grown extensively; the vine and all European fruit-trees flourish. In the south the rainfall is excessive and the mountains are covered with dense forests. The mineral wealth is considerable, the country being extremely rich in copper-ore, and some rich gold mines have been discovered. The rainless north yields more, especially nitrate of soda, iodine, borate of soda, gold and silver, a large number of mines yielding both being in actual work in Tarapacá, Guanaco, and Cachinal in Atacama, and Caracoles in Antofagasta; the centre, copper and silver; and the south, iron and coal.

There are smelting works for copper and silver, tanneries, corn and saw mills, starch, soap, biscuit, rope, cloth, cheese, furniture, candle, and paper factories, breweries and distilleries, and the domestic industry furnishes cloth, embroideries, baskets, anu pottery.

Transportation and Communication.—In 1911 there were 3,804 Englisn miles of railway open and working, and 1,878 under construction. In April, 1910, the trans-Andean line was complete, thus connecting Valparaiso with Buenos Aires. A longitudinal railway of 950 miles from Iquique in the north, to connect with the southern provinces, is now under construction by two British syndicates. A line from Arica to La Paz (Bolivia) was opened in 1912.

In 1910 there were 1,096 post offices There were also 1,400 telegraph offices (and four wireless stations), with 21,950. miles of wire. Telephones are highly efficient and general.

The mercantile marine in 1911 consisted of 98 steamers (114,887 tons) and 41 sailing vessels, (36,331 tons), a total of 139 vessels exceeding 100 tons each (151,218 tons). There are ten lines of steamers on the Chilian route to Europe, the total number of vessels entered at Chilian ports in 1910 being 11,482 (16,789,159 tons).

Towns.—The principal port is Valparaiso. Other ports are Arica, Iquique, Cobija and Antofagasta in the north; Caldera and Coquimbo in the centre; and Talcahuano, Conception and Valdivia in the south. The capital is Santiago, in the centre of the country on a plateau amidst magnificent mountain scenery. Population, 1910, 355,000. Other town are: Valparaiso, Concepción, Iquique, Talca, Chilian, Antofagasta, Viña del Mar, and Curico.

The unit of value is the gold peso, equal to $0,365 United States money.

Trade with the United States.—The value of merchandise imported into Chile from the United States for the year 1913 was $16,076,763. and goods to the value of $27,655,420 were sent thither—a balance of $11,578,657 in favor of Chile.

Chile:

American sailors on the *Baltimore* assaulted at Valparaiso. (See *Baltimore*, The.)

American seamen impressed by, 2772.

Boundary question with Argentine Republic, 4629, 6323, 6363.

Church of the Compañia at Santiago, destroyed by fire, 3398.

Claims of, against United States commission to settle, discussed, 5862, 5956, 6058, 6327.

Claims of United States against, 1594, 2051, 2193, 4913, 5083, 5369, 5544. (See also *Baltimore*, The.)

Agreement regarding, referred to, 1822.

Award of arbiter, King of Belgium, referred to, 3381.

Commission to settle, discussed, 5867, 5956, 6058, 6327, 6366.

Convention providing for adjustment of, by arbiter, 3064.

Payment of, 2116, 3485, 4289.

Protocol relative to, transmitted, 4214.

Provision made for, 2051.

Consul of, to United States, exequatur to, revoked, 3625.

Consular convention with, 2057.

Controversy with Bolivia referred to, 3410.

Copyright privilege extended by proclamation, 6125.

Fugitive criminals, convention with, for surrender of, 2912.

Independence of, asserted, 613.

Minister of, to United States, reception of, referred to, 4522, 5416.

Minister of United States in, 821.

Action of, in harboring criminals discussed, 5867.

Naval force of United States on shores of, 875.

Proceeds of cargo by the *Macedonia* seized in Peru by authorities of, 3015.

Award of arbiter referred to, 3381.

Convention regarding, 3064.

Relations of, with Peru referred to, 4662, 4673.

Specie payments, resumption of, by, discussed, 6059.

Treaty with, transmitted and discussed, 1158, 1169, 1246, 1260, 1270, 2912, 2957.

Vessels of, discriminating duties on, suspended by proclamation, 2612.

Referred to, 2618.

Vessels of United States seized or interfered with by, 1822, 2051, 2116, 2193, 3445, 4289. (See also *Good Return*, The.)

War in, and policy of United States respecting, discussed, 5618.

Seizure of the *Itala* by the United States for violation of neutrality laws discussed, 5618. (See also *Baltimore*, The.)

War with Bolivia and Peru, 5422, 4563, 4628, 4717.

Claims of United States arising out of, discussed, 4913, 5083, 5369, 5544.

Conditions of peace presented by Chile, 4662, 4717, 4760.

Efforts of United States to bring about peace, 4522, 4563, 4582, 4662, 4717.

Negotiations for restoration of peace, 4676.

Terminated, 4822.

Treaty of peace discussed, 4760.

Chile, Treaties with.—May 16, 1832, a convention of peace, amity, commerce and navigation was concluded with Chile, and proclaimed by President Jackson April 29, 1834. It included the most favored-nation clause, and provided for freedom of commerce and navigation, reciprocal privileges in business affairs, indemnity for vessels of either country detained in the ports of the other, asylum for vessels disabled by storm or pursued by enemies, special protection and religious freedom to citizens; defined contraband goods, and prescribed rules for trading privileges of neutrals, visitation and search of vessels, blockades, etc. Exchange of consuls was also provided for. An additional convention was concluded Sept. 1, 1833, extending the privileges of the most favored-nation clause to Republics of Bolivia, Colombia, Peru, the United States of Mexico, the Federation of Central America, and the provinces of the Rio de la Plata, and including Uruguay, Paraguay, Buenos Ayres, New Granada, Venezuela, Ecuador, and any new states which may be dismembered from those now existing. (See pages 1158, 1169, 1246, 1260 and 1270). This treaty was terminated Jan. 20, 1850, on notice given by the Chilean Government. In 1858 a convention was concluded for the arbitration of the claims made on behalf of the American owners of the brig *Macedonian*, for goods and silver coin and bars confiscated by order of the Vice Admiral of the Chilean navy. The King of Belgium was appointed arbiter and rendered his award in favor of the United States for damages to the extent of $42,400. (See *Macedonian*, The, also pages 2912 and 2957.)

A general claims convention was agreed to in 1892 by which all United States citizens having °claims against Chile might present them to a special claims commission. The commission provided for in this treaty awarded $240,564.35 in favor of American citizens. (See *Baltimore*, The.)

An exchange of copyright privileges was proclaimed May 25, 1896, and a special claims protocol of 1897 awarded the heirs of Patrick Shields $3,500 for damages.

In 1897 a convention was agreed to reviving the general claims commission. This commission adjourned June 18, 1901, after awarding $28,062.29 gold, without interest, in favor of the United States, and $3,000 gold, without interest, in favor of Chile. An extradition treaty was concluded in 1900.

Chile also became a party to the convention betwten the United States and several republics of South and Central America for the arbitration of pecuniary claims and the protection of inventions, etc., which was signed in Buenos Aires in 1910 and proclaimed in Washington July 29, 1914. (See South and Central America, Treaties with.)

China.—China Proper (or the Eighteen Provinces) occupies the southeastern corner of the continent of Asia, and covers about one-third of the total area of China. Its northern boundary is marked by the Great Wall of China, a rampart of earth, originally reinforced with bricks and masonry, some 12 to 28 feet high, and 1,500 miles in extent, with numerous gates, many of which are now neglected or abandoned. This barrier was erected in the third century B. C. as a defence against the Mongols of the north, and reached from Shang-hai-kwan on the east coast (Gulf of Chih-li) in long. 120° E. to Turkestan in the west (98° E.). It is now broken in many places and the Chinese have themselves advanced beyond its northeastern edge, in the province of Chih-li. The eastern boundary is the China Sea, and on the south the land frontier is coterminous with French Indo-China and the Shan States of British India. In the west the Eighteen Provinces adjoin British India, Tibet and Chinese Turkestan.

History.—Chinese civilization is the oldest in the world, and its government, based upon that of the family, remained unchanged in its root idea until the revolution of 1911-1912, by which the autocracy of the Emperor and the power of the bureaucracy were merged into a Republican form of government. For more than 2,000 years the Emperor was the supreme head of the State, legislating by edict in matters great and small. In the seventeenth century the Ming Dynasty was overcome by the Manchus from the north, who have now become almost entirely absorbed by the conquered race. The conditions and practices of the autocracy were preserved by the Manchus, but for many years the Civil service had become the power in the Empire and the central authority was but loosely exercised over the provincial and district administration.

Government.—Many reforms were initiated or promised in the last few years of the Imperial rule, and an executive body was actually created, while a legislature was promised. At the close of the year 1911 the party of reform forced the Imperial dynasty to a "voluntary" abdication, and a Republic was proclaimed, which was formally recognized by all the Powers on Oct. 6, 1913. President, Yuan Shih-kai, born 1859, elected provisionally Feb. 12, 1912; re-elected Oct. 6, 1913 (for five years), and formally inaugurated Oct. 10, 1913. A national assembly was formed consisting of 64 members, and a House of Representatives of 506 members. Each province was represented in the House.

In December, 1915, the Council of State voted to return to the imperial form of government, and Yuan reluctantly accepted the crown. March 22, 1916, China again became a republic, with Yuan Shih-kai as president. He died June 6, and was succeeded by Li Yuan-hung.

Foreign Relations.—Foreign relations with the Chinese Dominions have existed for many centuries. In the thirteenth century the Ventian merchant-adventurer, Marco Polo, resided in Cambaluc (the present Peking), and was employed by the Mongol Emperor Kublai Khan as adviser. In the seventeenth century Jesuit missionaries had attained considerable influence. The Dutch and Portuguese traders had for centuries maintained commercial dealings with the port of Canton, but toward the end of the eighteenth century were largely replaced by the British East India Company. A treaty was signed at Nanking in 1840 ceding Hong Kong to Great Britain and opening five ports to foreign trade and residence.

On the conclusion of the war between Russia and Japan in 1905 a Treaty and Additional Agreement relating to Manchuria were entered into between Japan and China. April 15, 1911, negotiations with certain international groups of financiers resulted in a loan of $50,000,000, the proceeds of which are to be employed in carrying out a scheme for the unification of the currency on a silver basis.

The continued exclusiveness of the Chinese Government led by a long chain of events to the war of 1860, when British and French troops captured Peking. In 1894 China fought a disastrous war with Japan, resulting in the loss of Formosa and the establishment of Korea as an independent state. An abortive attempt was made, in 1898, by the Emperor to introduce administrative reforms, but his reactionary ministers persuaded the Dowager Empress (his aunt) to reassume the reins of government. Under her rule a plot was hatched to rid the country of foreigners; and in the summer of 1900 the Legations in Peking and the foreign settlements in Tientsin were fiercely attacked and bombarded for many weeks. The situation was relieved at its most critical moment by the arrival of an allied army despatched by nearly all the Treaty Powers, and Tientsin and Peking were captured. The Imperial Court fled, and remained in voluntary exile until early in 1902. Meanwhile, a Peace Protocol was signed between the Envoys of the Treaty Powers

and the Chinese Plenipotentiaries, Prince Ch'ng, and the late Li Hung Chang. This provides for an indemnity of $320,000,000, to be paid within thirty-nine years. Subsequent negotiations resulted in three new commercial treaties—between the United Kingdom and China (Sept. 5, 1902); United States and China (Oct. 8, 1903); and Japan and China (Oct. 9, 1903). Under the two last Mukden, Tatungkow, Chang-sha, and Antung in Manchuria, were made Treaty ports.

During the European war of 1914–15 Japan drove the Germans out of Kiau-Chau, and later made a series of demands on China, which practically amounted to a Japanese protectorate.

The State Council held a special session at Pekin, March 28, and, acting as Parliament, rescinded all monarchial legislation, restored all the laws of the Republic affected by the monarchial movement, and then adjourned permanently.

Thus was given public evidence of an admission of the errors made by Parliament in urging a monarchy upon the President.

The following comprises the list of Japanese demands upon China, so far as they have been made public. At least one other clause has been suppressed. This represents the demands after revision, the original list including many more drastic features, among others the right to propagate Buddhism in China.

Group I.—Transfer complete to Japan of the German lease upon Kiachow; a pledge not to alienate any of the territory of Shantung Province; consent to a Japanese railway joining Kiaochow with Chefoo or Lungkow; the opening of certain treaty ports in Shantung, to be selected later.

Group II.—Extension of the Port Arthur lease to ninety-nine years; freedom of residence and travel and the right to lease or own land or work mining concessions in South Manchuria ad East Mongolia; the consent of the Japanese Government to be obtained before granting any railroad concessions, borrowing any money on the taxes, or appointing any advisers in South Manchuria and East Mongolia; a ninety-nine-year lease of the Kirin-Changchun Railway.

Group III.—The Hanyehping Company (the largest mining and steel-making company in China) to be made a joint concern of the two nations, and none of its property or rights to be alienated without the consent of Japan; the company to be given a monopoly over all mines in its neighborhood. (This company owns the steel works around Hangchow.)

Group IV.—No island, port or harbor on the Chinese coast to be ceded or leased to any foreign power.

Group V. (as amended).—In times of crisis the Chinese Government shall ask Japan to appoint "many Japanese advisers." Japanese shall have the right to rent or lease lands in the interior of China for hospitals, churches and schools.

The police of important places in China to employ Japanese advisers for the purpose of organizing and improving the service. China shall send to Japan a commission to arrange for the purchase of munitions of war and for the administration of Chinese arsenals.

China must agree to permit Japan to build a railway connecting Wuchang with Kiukiang and Nanchang, also a line between Nanchang and Chiaochua. No foreign capital to be employed in the Province of Fukien without Japanese consent.

Japan later withdrew Group V and China submitted to the others by a treaty signed May 25, 1915.

AREA AND POPULATION OF THE EMPIRE

Territories and Capitals	Area English Sq. Miles	Estimated Population
China Proper (Peking)	1,501,000	402,000,000
Manchuria (Mukden)	360,000	11,000,000
Mongolia (Urga)	1,076,000	3,000,000
Tibet (Lhasa)	750,000	3,000,000
Eastern Turkestan (Urumchi)	600,000	2,000,000
Total, China	4,287,000	421,000,000

Races and Religions.—The prevailing race in China is of Mongolian origin, but there are many races in addition to "Chinese" in the aboriginal Lolos, Miaotze, Ikias, Hakka and Hoklos. The Manchus, who ruled China from about the middle of the seventeenth century, although numbering only from 4,000,000 to 5,000,000, are Mongols from Eastern Tartary, whose superior military organization enabled the race to dominate the less warlike Chinese. In addition to the Chinese in the above-mentioned territories, whose numbers are variously estimated at 350,000,000 to 450,-000,000, there are some 10,000,000 Chinese in various quarters of the globe, particularly in the Malay Peninsula, North and South America, and Oceania.

The principal religions are Taoism and Buddhism, which have grown up side by side since the first century of the Christian era, until the older faith, to which no date can be assigned, is difficult to distinguish from the younger. Confucianism is too general a philosophy to be termed a religion and it has no temples or priests. Muhammadanism was introduced in the seventh century of the Christian era and is believed to have some 30,000,000 adherents. Christianity has made little headway, although its missionaries have been protected since 1860. The total number of converts does not exceed 1,500,000, of whom over 1,000,000 are Roman Catholics.

CHINA PROPER, AREA AND POPULATION

Provinces	Area in English Sq. Miles	Estimated Population
Chehiang	35,200	20,000,000
Chihli	120,500	25,000,000
Fukien	43,500	22,000,000
Honan	67,000	34,000,000
Hunan	77,500	22,000,000
Hupeh	73,500	35,000,000
Kansu	135,500	10,000,000
Kiangsi	69,500	20,000,000
Kiangsu	38,600	27,000,000
Kwangsi	84,000	6,000,000
Kwangtung	93,500	30,000,000
Kweichow	61,000	9,000,000
Nganhui	55,200	21,000,000
Shansi	80,000	10,000,000
Shantung	58,000	27,000,000
Shensi	77,000	9,000,000
Szechuan	179,000	65,000,000
Yunnan	153,000	10,000,000
Total	1,501,000	402,000,000

Army.—The land forces cannot yet be regarded as capable of offensive warfare or of withstanding trained European or Japanese troops. Energetic measures of reform aim principally at. (See Armies of the World.)

Navy.—The Navy has not recovered from the effects of the Chino-Japanese War, when more than ten important war vessels were sunk or captured.

Production and Industry.—The Eighteen Provinces are essentially agricultural, the land being held on freehold tenure with a small annual government tax. The richest zone lies between 35° and 27° N.,

and has two rainy and two dry seasons, the principal crops being rice in the low-lying river valleys, and tea, silk, wheat, cotton, mulberry and sugar. The northern zone (about 35° N.), produces wheat, barley, maize, peas and beans; the southern zone (below 27° N.), with its tropical climate, produces oranges, mangoes, bananas, ground nuts, sweet potatoes, yams, and rice, while the poppy is extensively grown. Tea is universally consumed, and very largely exported by land to Russia and Siberia (which absorb nearly five-sixths of the exports), and overseas to the United Kingdom, Hong Kong, the United States, and elsewhere. Cotton has been grown for centuries, and about half the produce is locally absorbed, the exports amounting to about 200,000,000 pounds. Silk is largely grown and about one-third of the world's supply is derived from China, while great quantities are used in home manufactures. Timber, particularly bamboo, is supplied from the forests of the western mountains.

Gold is found in large quantities in the southwestern province of Yunnan, and silver, lead, iron, tin, and cinnabar are found over a wide area. White copper is worked in Yunnan. Iron ore is abundant and is being locally absorbed, and tin is produced for export. The coal fields probably exceed those of any other country in extent and value; jade, lapis lazuli, porcelain clay and petroleum are plentiful, and the latter is now successfully exploited.

Railways.—About 5,900 miles were open in 1912, inclusive of the Manchurian lines, while 2,200 miles more are under construction.

The amount of the Chinese debt outstanding at the end of 1912 excluding interest and provincial loans is roughly estimated at $840,000,000.

The unit of value is the yuan, equal to about 60 cents United States money.

MANCHURIA.—Manchuria lies to the north of China Proper, between 39°-53° N. and 116°-134° E., its northern boundary being the Amur River, with the coast province of Russia and the Japanese dependency of Korea on the east, and the Transbaikal Province of Russia and (Chinese) Mongolia on the west. It is watered by the Sungari River and the climate is similar to that of Northern China.

The administration is under the control of the Central Government at Peking.

The principal agricultural products are indigo and opium, which provide highly profitable crops.

Capital, Mukden (on the Hun-ho). Population, 250,000.

Four of the great Asiatic highways traverse Manchuria: from Peking to Mukden and Kirin and thence to Sansing and Possiet Bay; from Niu-chwang to Mukden and Petuna, and thence to Tsitsihar, Mergen and across the northern boundary; from Niu-chwang southward across the Liaotung peninsula to Kin-chow; and from Niu-chwang eastward to the Korean gate and Antung. These highways are of great importance to the cultivators of the indigo and opium districts of the south, and to the mining districts of the northwest.

The Trans-Siberian Railway enters Manchuria at the western boundary of Heilung-kiang and thence southeast to its termination at Vladivostok.

MONGOLIA.—The total area of Mongolia, which extends from the Great Wall in the south to Siberia in the north, and from the Khingang Mountains in the east to Russian Central Asia in the west, is estimated at 1,076,000 English square miles, with a nomadic Mongol and Kalmuck population variously computed at 1,750,000 to 3,250,000.

History.—In the thirteenth century of the Christian era, the Mongolian ruler, Jenghiz Khan, held sway over an empire "from the China Sea to the banks of the Dneiper," and the vast area of the Chinese dominions is but a portion of the former Mongolian Empire.

Physical Features.—The country is rugged and mountainous in the northwest, where the Altai range runs from northwest to southeast almost to the center of Mongolia. In the extreme east the Khingan range crosses the southern and northern boundaries. The greater part of Mongolia is occupied by a high tableland, known as the Desert of Gobi or Shamo, about 3,000 feet above sea level, 2,000 miles from east to west and 500 miles from north to south, an arid, rocky waste with no vegetation.

Government.—The administration of Mongolia was the subject of a Russo-Chinese Agreement signed Nov. 5, 1913. Russia recognizes Chinese suzerainty over Outer Mongolia and China recognizes the autonomy of that region.

TIBET.—Tibet (or Bod) occupies more than half the western area of the Chinese dominions, with the Eighteen Provinces on the east, Nepal, Bhutan and British India on the south, British India on the west, and Chinese Turkestan on the north.

Physical Features.—The country is mainly a lofty plateau, part of the Great Asiatic Tableland, the highest country in the world, with the Himalaya Mountains as a western and southern boundary. The great hydrographic feature is the chain of lakes, all 15,000 feet or more above the mean level of the sea.

CHINESE TURKESTAN.—Eastern Turkestan occupies the northwestern corner of the Chinese dominions, between Mongolia, Russian Central Asia and Tibet.

Recent discoveries show that numerous towns have been covered by the moving sands of the desert, the date of the inundations being early in the Christian era. Towns now exist mainly as stations on the various caravan routes between China, Russia and India.

Trade with the United States.—The value of merchandise imported into China from the United States for the year 1913 was $21,326,834, and goods to the value of $39,010,800 were sent thither.

China (see also Canton):

American citizens in—
  Property of, destroyed, 4823.
  Protection for, discussed, 4006, 4055, 5544, 5621, 6059, 6328, 6366.

American manufactures in, 4762.

Artisans from, admission of, to World's Fair temporarily, recommended, 5622.

Boxer uprising in, 6417, 6678. (See also Boxers.)

Cable connection with, 6719.

Claims of United States against, 4436, 4761, 4801.
  Convention for adjustment of, 3071, 3090, 3173.
    Referred to, 3818.
  Indemnities received, discussed and recommendations regarding, 3173, 3247, 4520, 4561, 4630, 4715, 4762, 4823.
  Payment of, 3173, 4761, 4823.

Commercial relations with, 1114, 1790, 2066, 2743, 2977, 3446, 4060, 6328, 6366, 6914, 7010.
  Interruption of, by Great Britain referred to, 1839.

Commercial treaty with, 6797.

Commission to study conditions in, recommended, 6328, 6366.

Commissioner of United States to—
  Appointment of, recommended and compensation to, discussed, 2067, 2658.
  Correspondence of, transmitted, 2894, 2911, 2994, 3062.
  Instruction to, referred to, 3015, 3113.
  Report of, referred to, 2610.

Conditions in, discussed, 2066, 6327, 6367.

Consular courts of United States in—
  Jurisdiction of, 2951.
  Regulations for, referred to, 4675, 5388, 5432.
    Revision of, referred to, 3111.
  Treaty regarding, 4581.

Consular premises in, rent of, referred to, 4806.

Controversy between Japan and, regarding Lew Chew Islands, 4521.

Cooley trade, referred to, 2907, 3127, 3261, 3837, 3991, 4034, 4190.

Disturbances in, discussed, 6418, 6678.

Emperor of, accession of, referred to, 5469.

Expenditures from appropriation for providing for intercourse with, referred to, 2268.

Immigration of Chinese. (See Chinese Immigration.)

Import duties of, 6700.

Japanese citizens in, treatment of, and action of officers of United States regarding, inquired into, 5992, 7053.

Judicial tribunal in, for trial of American citizens recommended. 2400.

Maritime provinces of, passing under control of European powers discussed, 6327.

Massacre of French and Russian residents in, discussed, 4055.

Military operations of Great Britain against, terminated by treaty, 2066.

Minister of, to United States—
  Establishment of legation discussed, 4448.
  Received, 4718.

Minister of United States to—
  Appointment of, to mission by Emperor referred to, 3796, 3825.
  Appropriation for support of American youths to serve as part of official family of, recommended, 4101, 4145.
  Instruction to, referred to, 3113.

Letter of, transmitted, 3064.
Reception of, discussed, 3090, 4190.
Mr. Ward declines to submit to humiliating ceremonies attending, 3090.
Referred to, 2218, 3122.
Refusal to receive, 5621, 5673, 5679.
Return of, on account of illness, 2251.
Sent to, 2116, 2977, 3090.
Mission to, recommendation that it be raised to first class, 3991.
Missionaries in. (See American citizens in, *ante*.)
Monetary system of, improved, 6941.
Open Door in, 6679, 6797.
Opium traffic, treaty for repression of, referred to, 4629, 4986.
  Legislation regarding, recommended, 5083.
Outbreaks against foreigners in, 5621.
Political relations with, referred to, 1845.
Population of, 2066.
Postal convention with, 3775.
Rebellion in, 3446.
Relations with, 2977, 3991.
Revenue laws of, rules regarding fines for breaches of, etc., referred to, 3892.
Rules for seamen of American vessels in ports of, referred to, 2682.
Slavery in, referred to, 4539.
Straw Shoe Channel, vessels sailing under American flag prohibited from passing through, 3896, 3902.
Subjects of, in United States—
  Outrages committed on, discussed, 4914, 4968, 5083, 6419, 6678.
  Indemnity to, recommended, 5219.
  Appropriations for, 5367.
  Registration of. (See Chinese Immigration.)
Troops sent to protect, 4933, 6419.
Swedish missionaries murdered in, 5868.
Tariff of, 6679.
Treaty with, transmitted and discussed, 2205, 2211, 2251, 3037, 3061, 3071, 3089, 3108, 3836, 4629.
  Modification of article of, 3398.
  Proposed modification of, 3781.
  Referred to, 2610, 2977, 3090, 3113.
Vessels of, discriminating duties on, repealed by proclamation, 4552.
War with—
  France, 4823.
  Great Britain and France, neutrality preserved by United States, in, 3037, 3089, 3174.
  Japan—
    Action taken by United States regarding, 5957, 6059, 6417.
    Agents of United States requested to protect subjects of contestants, 5957, 6059.
Women imported into United States from, for dishonorable purposes, 4309.

China, Treaties with.—The treaty of peace, amity, and commerce concluded with China in 1844 was in part superseded by the treaty of 1858. Several articles, however, were not changed. Passenger boats plying with mail and baggage between the five ports are exempt from duty if the vessels are owned by citizens of the United States. Cargo boats owned by citizens of the United States and not hired from Chinese subjects, pay the regular duty of one mace (58 ounces of pure silver) per ton. Each of the consuls at the five ports to be supplied with standard, stamped, and sealed weights and measures, according to the standard at the custom house at Canton. Citizens of the United States are admitted to trade with Chinese subjects without distinction. Detailed reports of all vessels and cargoes belonging to the United States are to be made annually to the governor-general of each of the five ports by the consuls at these ports, such reports for use and examination for revenue purposes. The vessels, property, and persons of citizens of the United States are not subject to embargo and cannot be prevented from pursuing their transactions without molestation or embarrassment.

The treaty of peace, amity, and commerce, of 1858, after the customary declaration of friendship between the two countries, makes provision for communication at all times directly between the highest United States minister in China and the officers of the privy council at the capital or with the governors-general of the two provinces of Fuh-Kien and Cheh-Kiang; the minister is also privileged to make one visit a year to the capital of the Emperor of China, and there to confer with a high official, deputed for the purpose, upon matters of common interest. If at any time the privilege of residence be granted by the Emperor of China to the representative of any other foreign country, that privilege, without further notice or formal permission, shall become a right of the minister of the United States. The form in which communications may pass between representatives of the two governments is prescribed in terms of the Chinese court ritual. National vessels of the United States cruising near Chinese coasts are to be accorded courtesy and hospitality in token of the friendly relations of their respective nations. These national vessels have the right to pursue and capture pirates who pillage United States vessels, but the offenders must be handed over to the Chinese authorities for punishment.

Consuls.—The United States is granted the right to appoint consuls and commercial agents in such parts of the Chinese dominions as shall be agreed upon as being open to them. Citizens of the United States may reside or sojourn in any of the ports open, may rent houses and places of business, and build houses, churches, hospitals, and cemeteries; they shall not be subjected to exorbitant demands or unreasonable conditions. The customary provisions are made in cases of shipwreck, and the onus of arrest, trial, and punishment of robbers and pirates who plunder vessels belonging to the United States rests upon Chinese authorities. But if for any reason these cannot be apprehended, the Chinese authorities shall not be called upon to indemnify for lost goods or damage. If, however, it be shown that local authorities were in collusion with the robbers or pirates, their goods shall be confiscated to indemnify for loss or damage.

Open Ports.—The ports of China opened by this treaty to the citizens of the United States for commerce, residence, or trade are: The cities and ports of Canton and Chau-Chau or Swatau, in the provinces of Kwang-tung; Amoy, Fuh-Chau, and Tai-wan in Formosa, in the province of Fuh-Kien; Ning-po, in the province of Cheh-Ki-ang; and Shanghai, in the province of Ki-ang-su, and any other port hereafter opened by treaty to any other power or to the United States. Trade may be freely carried on in these ports, and vessels may proceed from one to the other of them; but no fraudulent or clandestine trade may be carried on with any other port under penalty of confiscation of vessel and cargo. Any citizen of the United States carrying on trade in contraband goods shall be punished by the Chinese authorities without protection or countenance of the United States. The tariff of duties to be paid shall in all cases be the same as that under which the most favored nation shall conduct importation and exportation.

Tonnage Dues.—Vessels of over 150 tons burden shall pay tonnage duties of four mace per ton of 40 cubic feet; those of 150 tons or under, one mace per ton of 40 cubic feet. The tonnage in all cases to be that of the ship's register, which with her other papers must, on her arrival, be lodged with the consul for examination by the commissioner of customs. (See Treaty of 1880.) If a vessel pay tonnage duties at one port and proceed for a part or the whole of her cargo to another port, she shall not pay duties a second time on her tonnage, but only upon her cargo or part of it. Pilots and all other assistants may be hired as required upon terms agreed upon by the parties, or determined by the consul.

Supervision of Ships and Cargoes.—The Chinese customs officials may exercise control over vessels of the United States while in Chinese ports to the extent of putting subordinate officers on board of same, to live on board during the stay in port. Mutineers or deserters are, upon information from the consul, to be arrested by the Chinese authorities and handed over to the consuls for punishment. Criminals taking refuge in the houses or on ships of citizens of the United States are to be handed over to Chinese officials on demand and shall not be harbored or concealed. Public peace is to be preserved by the officers of both nations, who must exert themselves to maintain order by dispensing impartial justice. Within forty-eight hours after a merchant vessel of the United States shall cast anchor in either of the ports, the ship's papers must be deposited with the consul, and from them a true report of necessary details shall be communicated to the superintendent of customs. Upon receipt of this information he shall grant a permit for her discharge. If cargo be discharged without such permit, the goods shall be confiscated, and a fine of $500 be imposed upon the master or consignee. If the master determine within forty-eight hours to proceed to another port without breaking bulk, he may do so without the payment of tonnage, duties, or other charges until he shall reach the other port. In the absence of the consul or proper representative, the master may call upon the consul of a friendly power to act for him in the premises. Disputes in the adjustment of duties are to be settled within twenty-four hours by the consul and the superintendent of customs. Duty paid goods imported into a Chinese port by citizens of the United States may be reexported after due examination by the customs authorities to guard against fraud; in the event of detection of fraudulent proceedings, the goods are subject to confiscation. Foreign grain or rice brought to a Chinese port in United States bottoms and not landed may be reexported without hindrance.

Tonnage duties on vessels are to be paid on entry; import duties, on the landing of the goods; a port clearance is given only when all charges have been paid and the consul then returns the ship's papers. The consul is held responsible for the departure of a ship without the payment of charges. Goods may be transshipped on application to the consul, who shall certify to the superintendent of customs the cause of such transshipment, and at his discretion permit the transshipment. Goods transshipped without such permission are subject to confiscation.

Personal Relations.—Citizens of the United States may sue Chinese debtors in local courts, and Chinese creditors may sue United States debtors before the consul or in the consular court. Citizens of the United States may employ scholars in any part of the empire to teach any of the languages and may buy books of any kind. In the event of the exclusion of the vessels of another country from Chinese ports because of war with that country, the vessels of the United States shall have free and friendly access to Chinese ports so long as her vessels do not engage in work of assistance to the unfriendly power. Disputes between United States citizens in China are to be settled in the courts of their own country. All disputes between citizens of the United States and citizens of another power resident in China are to be settled according to the treaties in force between those countries. Citizens of the United States desiring to address a Chinese official must transmit their communications through the consul, who shall see to it that the communication conforms to the prescribed court ritual and is respectfully addressed. A Chinese citizen may address the consul directly, at the same time informing his own proper officials fully in the premises. Disputes between citizens of the United States and Chinese citizens are to be adjusted when otherwise impossible by public officers of the two countries acting together. Those who quietly profess and teach the doctrines and principles of the Christian religion shall not be harassed or persecuted on account of their faith. Any favors, rights, and privileges, not conferred by this treaty, and which at a future time shall be granted to any other country, shall at once freely accrue to the citizens of the United States.

Tariff.—Another treaty of 1858, concluded on Nov. 8, established the tariff and regulations of trade, specifying fully the taxes on imports and exports in detail, the duty-free goods, and contraband goods, and established weights and measures in United States equivalents. By this treaty citizens of the United States were excluded from entering the capital city of Peking for purposes of trade.

Claims.—A claims convention was concluded on the same date, Nov. 8, 1858, whereby $735,238.97 was paid by China to the United States in liquidation of claims of citizens of the United States against China. Of this sum, $489,187.95 was paid out by a commission to claimants, and as the Chinese government declined to accept the surplus the amount was sent to the United States and invested in government bonds. Out of this investment, $281,-319.64 was paid to claimants against China, and on April 24, 1885, the sum of $453,-400.90 was returned to the Chinese minister at Washington.

Immigration and Emigration.—The treaty of trade, consuls, and emigration of 1868 was proclaimed Feb. 5, 1870, and supplements and explains that of 1858. The Emperor of China asserts his right of eminent domain to all of the land opened to trade by citizens of the United States, and stipulates that any and all concessions to them do not give an enemy the right to make war upon the United States within his waters nor to permit the United States to make attacks upon enemies therein; and further that the jurisdiction of the Emperor of China over his lands and subjects is in no wise impaired by any concession made. Any further rights of trade which are not provided for by treaty are to be adjusted at the discretion of the Emperor in a spirit compatible with treaty stipulations. The right of the Emperor of China to appoint consuls in the several ports is affirmed upon the same conditions as those to which Russia and Great Britain are subject. United States citizens in China and Chinese citizens in the United States are to suffer no disability or persecution by reason of their religious belief, and due respect is to be paid to burial places of all religious denominations and beliefs. Emigration from and immigration into both countries must be wholly voluntary and with entire free will of the subjects. The mutual enjoyment of rights, privileges, and immunities of the citizens of both countries within the territories of the other, is fully assured. Especially is this affirmed regarding education and the establishment of schools. No interference by the United States in matters of internal administration is to be attempted, particularly in matters of railroad, telegraph, and other internal construction and improvement.

Immigration.—The immigration treaty of 1880 provides that at any time that the United States decides that the immigration of Chinese laborers tends to disturb economic conditions, the United States may limit, or suspend, but may not wholly prohibit, the coming or the residence of such laborers; this provision applies only to laborers. Teachers, students, merchants, or travelers from curiosity, as well as laborers residing within the United States at the time of the proclamation of this treaty, may come and go at will and enjoy all the rights, privileges, and immunities formerly prescribed by treaty. Such legislation on the subject as may be meditated at any time is to be submitted to the Chinese legation at Washington for consideration, discussion, and regulation, that no hardship may be inflicted upon Chinese subjects.

Traffic in Opium: Judicial Procedure.—Nov. 17, 1880, another treaty of commercial intercourse and judicial procedure was concluded which prohibits the importation of opium into United States ports by Chinese, or into Chinese ports by citizens of the United States, in vessels owned by citizens or subjects of either power, in foreign vessels employed by them, or in any vessels operated by others. It is also mutually and reciprocally agreed between the two countries that no duties, tolls, or imposts, be levied upon the ships or trade of the respective countries, other than are levied upon ships or trade of other foreign countries or upon the citizens of such countries. In cases of controversy between citizens of the United States and subjects of China, which call for judicial intervention, it is agreed that the presiding officer shall be of the nationality of the defendant. All privileges, courtesies, and facilities are to be accorded to the representative of the plaintiff, and protest will be permitted against any decision reached in the proceedings conducted according to the judicial procedure of the country of the presiding officer.

Immigration.—The convention of 1894, regulating Chinese immigration, prohibited the immigration of Chinese laborers for ten years, except in the case of the return of a registered Chinese laborer who had a lawful wife, child, or parent in the United States, or property therein worth one thousand dollars, or debts of that amount due to him or pending settlement. Such returning Chinese laborer must, before his departure from the United States, deposit with the collector of customs of his district a full description in writing of his family, his property, and his debts, as a condition precedent to his return. A false return in such cases shall prevent his return. In all such cases the return must be made within a period of one year, unless the time shall be extended by reason of sickness or valid disability, such extenuating facts being reported to the Chinese consul at the point of departure, and by him transmitted to the collector of the port at which he shall land in the United States. These prohibitory restrictions shall in nowise extend to teachers, students, merchants, or travelers for pleasure and curiosity, other than laborers, who must be provided with a certificate from their government or from the government of the last place of residence, and properly viséd by the consular representative of the United States at the point of departure. Resident laborers in the United States shall have all rights, privileges, and immunities enjoyed by others, except the right of naturalization, and their persons and property shall be protected by the government of the United States. The Chinese government agrees to the enforcement of the acts of 1892 and 1893, which require all resident Chinese laborers to be registered for the assurance of their better protection, and the United States recognizes the right of the Chinese government to enact similar legislation to apply to laborers of the United States within the Emperor's dominions. The government of the United States engages by this treaty to supply annually to the government of China a list of all citizens of the United States (other than the diplomatic corps) including missionaries, resident or traveling in China, together with the names, addresses, and full particulars of themselves and suites. The life of this treaty was ten years, with a renewal period of another ten years.

Commercial.—The treaty of 1903, on commercial relations, was made in further extension of the commercial intercourse between the two countries. It confers upon the United States minister to China the right to reside at the city of Peking, to have audience with the Emperor whenever necessary to present his credentials or a message from the President, and to enjoy all the honors, prerogatives, and privileges of the representatives of the most favored nation. The authoritative texts of all documents shall be English for all documents from the United States, and Chinese for all documents from China. Freedom of intercourse with Chinese officials is granted to consular officers, such intercourse is restricted to the officials within their own jurisdiction. The extension of commercial freedom to citizens of the United States is again confirmed. The tax known as likin was abolished. This was a tax of one cash per tael imposed upon all sales throughout China as a war tax to meet the deficiency caused by the Tai-ping rebellion (1850-1864). In its place, the United States agreed to the imposition of a surtax, in addition to the current tariff rates on all foreign goods imported by citizens of the United States, and on Chinese produce intended for foreign export; this surtax never to exceed one and a half times the tariff established by the final protocol of China with the Powers, Sept. 7, 1901, and the total taxes of all kinds upon such goods must never exceed seven and a half per cent *ad valorem.* The likin collecting stations are abolished in all parts of the nineteen provinces of China and in three eastern provinces, but the customs stations within these districts are retained. The abolition of likin is further compensated for by a special surtax on foreign goods not to exceed one and a half times the five per cent import duty established by the protocol of 1901. It is permitted to the Chinese government to recast the foreign export tariff on a scale not exceeding five per cent *ad valorem,* and all existing tariff rates which exceed the last named limit are to be reduced. In place of all internal taxation of every kind, China may add an export duty of one half the existing rate as a special surtax. Provision is made within the treaty for the adjustment of all matters of controversy.

Arbitration.—In 1908 an arbitration convention was signed with China providing that all differences which may arise relating to the interpretation of treaties and which may be impossible to settle by diplomacy shall be referred to the Permanent Court of Arbitration at The Hague, provided they do not affect the vital interests, the independence or the honor of the contracting parties.

The establishment of bonded warehouses at the several open ports is provided for and permitted. China agrees to revise the mining regulations of the empire within one year, with a view to the encouragement of the investment of foreign capital in that industry. China agrees to establish a Patent Office and to permit and to protect the patenting of inventions by citizens of the United States. Copyright protection within certain limits is granted to citizens of the United States. The navigable inland waters of the Empire are opened to steam navigation by firms, companies, and individuals. Mukden and Antung, in the province of Sheng-king, are added to the list of open ports. China agrees to provide a uniform coinage throughout the Empire to be recognized as legal tender, though the payment of customs duties is to be made in terms of the Haikwan tael. The practice of the Christian religion is permitted with several privileges and certain restrictions upon missionaries. The United States agrees to help China remodel her judiciary upon western lines. China prohibits the importation of morphia and instruments for its injection, except for medicinal or surgical uses. Conditions of the treaty of 1900 not at variance with the terms of this treaty are reaffirmed. A schedule of tariff duties upon imported goods is appended to the treaty.

Chinese Immigration.—In 1844, under a treaty negotiated by Caleb Cushing, five Chinese ports were opened to American trade and protection of life and property was guaranteed American citizens. By the Burlingame treaty of 1868 the right of Chinese immigration was admitted, and the promise was made that the subjects of China should enjoy the same privileges, exemptions, and immunities respecting travel and residence in the United States as the subjects of the most favored nation. The Chinese came to this country in consider-

able numbers until their presence began to cause opposition on the Pacific Coast and agitation was begun for their exclusion. They were obnoxious to many Americans on account of their increasing numbers and their habits of life which rendered their assimilation with Americans impossible. In 1879 after a Congressional investigation a bill restricting their immigration passed Congress but was vetoed by President Hayes (4466). The continued opposition to the Chinese, however, led to the framing of a new treaty with China in 1880. This treaty conceded to the Government of the United States the right to regulate, limit or suspend, but not absolutely to prohibit the coming of Chinese laborers, whenever their presence should be deemed injurious. Chinese students, teachers, merchants, and travelers were to be admitted freely as before. In 1882 an act was passed by Congress suspending the immigration of Chinese laborers for ten years. This act was amended several times in the direction of greater stringency. In 1892 the Geary Act was passed extending the operation of previous acts for ten years and providing that any Chinaman not lawfully entitled to remain in the United States should be removed to China and all Chinese laborers should be obliged to procure certificates of residence from the collector of internal revenue, failure to do so within a year to be followed by deportation. This act was modified considerably by a law passed in 1893. A new treaty was agreed upon by the United States and China in 1894 absolutely prohibiting the coming of Chinese laborers for ten years. This treaty, in accordance with the terms of one of its articles, was terminated by China at the expiration of the ten years' period, in December, 1904. By an act approved April 29, 1902, all laws in force prohibiting and regulating Chinese immigration were reenacted as far as not inconsistent with treaty obligations until otherwise provided by law, and their operation extended to the island territory of the United States. The number of Chinese in the United States, proper, as reported by the census of 1910 was 71,531, as compared with 89,863 in 1900, showing a decrease of 18,332 in the decade. Of the total number in 1910, 66,-856 were males and 4,675 were females; 53 per cent of the males were single and 23 per cent of the women. More than one-half resided in California. There were 760 farms operated by Chinese, of which 512 were in California, and only 57 were owned by Chinese, the others being worked by Chinese cash tenants.

Chinese Immigration:

Act—
  Regarding, vetoed, 4466, 4699.
  To execute certain treaty stipulations approved and discussed, 5215.
Conventional regulation of passage of laborers across borders proposed to Mexico and Great Britain, 5544.
Conventions regarding. (See Treaty regarding, *post.*)
Discussed by President—
  Arthur, 4716.
  Cleveland, 4914, 4968, 4975, 5083, 5194, 5215, 5868.
  Grant, 4242, 4309.
  Harrison, Benj., 5469, 5476, 5632.
  Hayes, 4521, 4540.
  Roosevelt, 7008, 7010.

Execution of acts regarding, referred to, 5495.

Head tax collected from Chinamen entering Canada, 5476, 5632.

Registration of Chinese laborers—
Extension of time for, 5838, 5868.
Law regarding, sustained by Supreme Court, 5868.
Reports on, referred to, 4973, 4975.
Through Canada and Mexico, discussed, 5476, 5632.
Treaty regarding, 4561, 4581, 5195, 5908, 5956.
Discussed, 4629, 4823, 5194, 5386.
Referred to, 4691, 5212, 5215.
Rejected by China discussed, 5367, 5386, 5387, 5469.
Violation of laws, restricting, discussed and recommendations regarding, 4762, 5632.

Chinese Indemnity.—In May, 1900, a secret society, known as the Boxers, arose in the provinces of Shan Tung and Pe-chi-Li, China, and massacred native Christians and European missionaries. In June the Boxers destroyed the Tien Tsin railway, isolating the foreigners in Peking, and shortly after murdered the German minister and the Japanese chancellor of legation. It was not until the middle of August that a relief force composed of 12,000 American, British, French, German, Russian and Japanese troops was enabled to rescue the besieged legations in Peking. The Empress Dowager and the court had fled, and it was impossible to apprehend the leaders in the anti-foreign uprising.

Peace negotiations were opened, and on Dec. 4, the Powers sent a joint note to the Chinese peace commissioners, demanding, among other things, the execution of the leaders in the massacre of foreigners and the payment of an indemnity; forbade the importation of arms and ammunition or the materials for their manufacture; the conversion of *ad valorem* into specific duties, the improvement of certain rivers, prohibited Chinese membership in anti-foreign secret societies under pain of death, ordered the dismissal of governors who should hereafter permit anti-foreign agitation. A legation district in Peking which might be fortified and guarded was defined, and certain points were indicated that might be occupied by the foreign powers to keep communication open between the capital and the sea.

In October, 1901, the amount of the indemnity was fixed at $735,000,000. Later, through the good offices of the United States, this was reduced to $387,500,000. The share of the United States in this indemnity was fixed at $24,440,778.81. In 1905 it was decided by the powers that this debt was payable in gold. The principal is payable in thirty-nine annual installments, ending in 1941. The interest, payable semi-annually, at four per cent, is about $12,-800,000; the securities for the indemnity are the maritime customs and the salt monopoly and the native customs or transit dues within sixteen miles of the ports. Payments are made monthly to a commission in Shanghai. In his seventh annual message to Congress, Dec. 3, 1907, President Roosevelt recommended the remission of a portion of the United States' allotment of this indemnity (7503). In accordance with this recommendation Congress passed a joint

resolution which was approved May 25, 1908, reducing the total amount to $13,-655,492.69, reserving $2,000,000 for the payment of future claims under the treaty and providing for their adjudication by the Court of Claims. This was done purely as an act of friendship toward China.

Chinese Indemnity of 1900:
Authority asked for cancelling part of, 7123.

Chinese Loan.—The construction of extensive railway lines by the government, with the use of foreign capital and the granting of concessions to foreign companies to build railroads is opening up China to influences which the great Powers are not slow to avail themselves of. In June, 1908, work was begun on the Tien Tsin-Pukow railroad, about 700 miles long, connecting the imperial railways in North China with the German transverse line and extending to the Yangtse, opposite Nanking, and connecting three open ports. About $25,000,000 was borrowed to build this road. The road from Nanking to Shanghai, 196 miles, was opened in April, 1908.

The entering wedge of American predominance in the awakening of China was securely put in place in Peking and the door of the Far East firmly opened to American capital, trade and governmental influence in August, 1909. This wedge takes the form of an allotment to New York bankers of one-fourth participation in a loan negotiated by the Chinese government for the construction of the Hankow-Szechuen Railway. This total amount of the loan is $30,000,000, of which $7,500,000 is to be taken by an American syndicate. The sum, so small for Wall Street, is truly a mere wedge, but the principle involved is considered of world-wide importance, and opens the door for things far greater.

The Chinese Government gave assurance that Americans are to have equal opportunity to supply material for both the Canton and Szechuen lines with branches and to appoint subordinate engineers. They are to have one-half of all future loans on the Szechuen Railroad with corresponding advantages.

For years Great Britain, France and Germany have been diplomatically struggling for the controlling influence over China when that vast country should have its awakening to western civilization and exploitation. They have manœuvred in every way to bring about conditions that might result in the partition of the empire so that vast slices of its territory might fall into their imperialistic laps. A brief resumé of the indemnities exacted and loans made to pay the same follows:

After the British had captured several ports in the opium war, in 1840, taken Ching-Kiang in a bloody assault, and threatened Nanking, a treaty was made with China, which, besides opening five ports to foreign trade and ceding the island of Hong Kong to England, exacted a war indemnity of $21,000,000. In 1856-1858 another expensive war was forced upon China by England and France, to end which China was compelled to pay the expenses of her conquerors. By the treaty of Shimonoseki, ending the war between China and Japan, in 1895, China agreed to pay an indemnity of 200,888,200 taels (about $160,000,000). This disclosure of China's weakness aroused the interest of European nations, and Russia, France and Germany, jealous of the growing influences of Japan, protested against the cession of the Liao-tung peninsula to the latter country, and Russia, through the agency of France, placed a loan in 1895 amounting to $77,-200,000 to enable China to meet the payments of the indemnity. In 1896 $80,000,-000 was loaned by German and American capitalists, and in 1898 another $80,000,-000 was advanced by the Hong Kong and Shanghai Banking Corporation, and the Deutsche-Asiatische Bank of English, German and American capital.

In return for these loans valuable railway and trading concessions were exacted, with a view to establishing in the disintegrating empire spheres of influence which would serve as a pretext for military occupation should that become desirable. In 1907, Germany by way of reparation for the murder of two German missionaries, seized the port of Kiao-chau, on the Shantung peninsula, and obtained valuable mining, trading and railway privileges in the rich Shantung province.

Early in 1898, while the British government was endeavoring to secure guarantees that the Yangtsekiang region should not be alienated, Russia obtained a lease of the harbors of Port Arthur and Talien Wan, in the Liao-tung peninsula, with railway concessions in the adjacent territory. As an offset Great Britain obtained a lease of Wei-hai-wei for as long as Russia should retain Port Arthur.

The United States Government has stood by China as her friend. John Hay, as Secretary of State, laid down the policy of this government as insisting on what was called the "open door," meaning thereby that all nations should stand on equal terms with China and that empire should not be exploited exclusively by any other nation to its own material advantage.

This relatively insignificant railway loan proved to be the critical incident to bring to a focus the international diplomatic game that powerful nations have been playing, with the vast, unknown Flowery Kingdom as the most magnificent spoils at stake since the days that Rome was annexing practically all the world to pay it tribute.

Great Britain has been in the Chinese game with her gold. Germany has been working the military end, training and arming the Chinese soldiers. France had been let in as their helpful ally. The United States, standing for fair play, for the open door, for the best interests of China, was not to be let into the game. All the cards had been stacked for a three-handed deal, and this little loan, that practically marked the beginning of China's entrance on railway construction, and all the commercial progress to follow along the lines, was to be held closely between the three European countries.

This was the situation when President Taft instructed the American Ambassadors in Europe and the Chargé d'Affaires in Peking to lodge a protest and to demand this country's participation in whatever affected the welfare of our peaceful ally across the Pacific. The affair at once was lifted above a mere financial transaction into the realms of international diplomacy.

It was an unprecedented act for the Government at Washington to involve itself in the transactions of a group of private bankers, but President Taft held that the conditions warranted the move. The action of the Foreign Board indicates that the Chinese Government has turned toward America as its friend and believes in the disinterested policy of this country.

Peking's announcement that the American share of the loan for constructing the Hankow-Szechuen Railway was allowed by the Foreign Board is most gratifying to the State Department, not that the amount involved is sufficient to justify a spirit of jubilance, but because the American victory is considered the triumph of a principle.

During the summer of 1912 private fiscal agents of the Chinese Government secured pledges of a loan of sufficient size to tide the new Chinese Republic over the period of reorganization, without the aid of the so-called "six power" loan, and without submitting to the conditions of the powers.

Chinese Loans, neutral adviser proposed by the United States, 7664.

Chinook State.—A nickname for Washington (q. v.). (See also States.)

Chippewa Commission, report of, discussed, 5500.

Chippewa Indians. (See Indian Tribes.)

Chippewa Plains (Canada), Battle of.—On the morning of July 4, 1814, the entire American Army of the North advanced northward along the western bank of the Niagara River to a point near the mouth of the Chippewa. Here they were confronted by the British under Gen. Riall, who was reenforced during the night by the King's regiment from Toronto. On the afternoon and evening of the 5th a stubborn battle was fought. The British were defeated with a loss of 604. The American loss was 335. Gen. Scott distinguished himself for bravery and efficiency. Gen. Riall was wounded and taken prisoner. (See illustration opposite 679.)

Chippewa Reservations in Wisconsin, disposition of timber on, 5566.

Chippeway Indians. (See Indian Tribes.)

Chiriqui, Isthmus of, persons sent to, to make required examinations, referred to, 3192.

Chisholm vs. Georgia.—In 1792 Alexander Chisholm, of South Carolina, brought suit in the Supreme Court of the United States against the State of Georgia for the payment of a private claim, Chisholm's counsel claiming that section 2 of Article III. of the Constitution vested the court with jurisdiction in such cases. The court gave judgment to the plaintiff and issued a writ of inquiry, but the writ was never executed, the legislature of Georgia having passed an act making the execution of such a writ punishable by death. This case led to the adoption in 1798 of the eleventh amendment to the Constitution.

Cho-bah-áh-bish Indians. (See Indian Tribes.)

Choctaw Coal and Railway Co., act authorizing Oklahoma City, Okla., to issue bonds to provide right of way for, vetoed, 5571.

Choctaw Commission, proceedings of, referred to, 2129.

Choctaw Indians. (See Indian Tribes.)

Choctaw Nation, Ind. T., right of way for railroads across lands of, 4653, 4655.

Cholera (see also Contagious Diseases; International Sanitary Conference; Quarantine Regulations).

Causes of, report on, referred to, 4259.

International conference on subject of, at Rome, 4918.

International conference to be held at Constantinople upon subject of, referred to, 3576.

Representatives to foreign countries to report on progress, etc., of, appointed, 4898, 4902.

Report of, referred to, 5565.

Christian Indians. (See Indian Tribes.)

Christiana Case.—In 1851 Edward Gorsuch and a party from Maryland attempted to seize a fugitive slave in Christiana, Pa. A riot ensued in which Gorsuch was killed. Castner Hanway, an invalid Quaker, was arrested and charged with treason, riot, and bloodshed for refusing to assist a marshal in quelling the disturbance. No indictments were found, but the case created much excitement.

Christians, massacre of. (See Armenians.)

Christian Socialists. (See Socialism.)

Chrystler's Fields (Canada), Battle of. —Nov. 11, 1813, Gen Wilkinson, with the main body of the American army, here fought a slightly superior force of British. The battle lasted 5 hours, victory alternately favoring one and then the other. Night ended the conflict, with the British in possession of the field. The Americans lost heavily, many officers being either killed or wounded. American loss, 339; British loss, 17 killed, wounded, and missing.

Chugach National Forest (Alaska):

Opening to occupation by railroads of 12,800 acres of, discussed, 7599.

Church and State.—The relation of the state to religious bodies in America differs from all previous relationships in Europe and the Colonies. Rhode Island, Pennsylvania, and Maryland provided for religious freedom early in their respective histories. Most of the Colonies established the Church of England, though Massachusetts and Connecticut maintained the Congregational. The Constitution guarantees religious freedom in all parts of the United States. Article VI. declares that "no religious test shall ever be required as a qualification to any office or public trust under the United States." The first amendment provides that "Congress shall make no law respecting an establishment of religion or prohibiting the free exercise thereof."

Church of Latter-Day Saints. (See Mormon Church; Polygamy; and Utah.)

Churches and Church Property. (See Religious Establishments.)

Churubusco (Mexico), Battle of.—Churubusco was a strongly fortified place near the City of Mexico. The American army, in two divisions, under Generals Worth and Twiggs, attacked the Mexicans under Gen. Santa Anna, Aug. 20, 1847, a few hours after the action at Contreras. The Americans numbered 8,000 and the Mexicans 25,000. Early in the engagement the garrison at San Antonio was routed. The hottest fighting took place along the Rio Churubusco, where for some time the Americans were threatened with defeat, but rallying they drove the Mexicans before them. Simultaneously were taken the tête-du-pont, or bridgehead (the key to Santa Anna's position), and the Pablo de Churubusco. The conflict lasted three hours. Including the casualties, the Mexican loss was 5,877. The Americans lost 1,015.

Churubusco (Mexico), Battle of, referred to, 2386.

Cimarron.—The name originally proposed for the northwestern part of Indian Territory, now Beaver County, Oklahoma. The strip of land lying between 36° 30′ and 37° north latitude and 100° and 103° west longitude was ceded by Texas to the United States in 1850. The name Cimarron is Spanish for "wild," and was applied to a tributary of the Arkansas River which had its source in the country. The strip was sometimes called "No Man's Land." Since between the years 1850, when it was added to the United States, and 1890, when it was made a part of Oklahoma, it was under no form of government and the resort chiefly of outlaws. Recently settlers from Kansas and Colorado have removed thither and taken up their abode.

Cincinnati Industrial Exposition, board on behalf of Executive Departments designated, 4819.

Instructions to, 4820.

Cincinnati, Society of the.—A society originated in 1783 by Revolutionary officers. At the second general meeting in 1787 Washington was chosen president-general and was reelected every three years while he lived. The membership rolls were open only to the officers and their eldest sons, though a number of French officers were included. The hereditary principle aroused popular jealousy. It was denounced by the Governor of South Carolina and the legislatures of Massachusetts, Pennsylvania, and Rhode Island. In 1784, at the solicitation of Washington, the society dropped the requirement of heredity, but the principle has since been reestablished and full membership is restricted to those having the hereditary right. A few distinguished men are admitted to honorary membership, but the number is strictly limited. President Monroe was an original member and President Pierce was a hereditary member. Presidents Jackson, Taylor, Pierce, Buchanan, Grant, Benjamin Harrison, Cleveland, McKinley, Roosevelt and Taft were made honorary members, as were ex-President Loubet of France, and Admiral Dewey, Lieutenant-Generals Miles and Chaffee.

The chief immediate objects of the society were to raise a fund for the relief of the widows and orphans of those who fell in the Revolutionary War and to promote a closer political union between the states. The number of living hereditary members of the Society of the Cincinnati as reported at the Triennial meeting in Newport, R. I., in June, 1911, was 981.

Cipher Dispatches.—The result of the presidential election of 1876 was for several months in doubt. During this period of uncertainty numerous telegraphic dispatches passed between the friends of Samuel J. Tilden, Democratic candidate for the presidency. The dispatches were in cipher and purported to be instructions to party workers in South Carolina, Oregon and Florida. Charges of fraud having been made these dispatches were ordered turned over to the Senate Committee on Privileges and Elections. A large number of them came into the possession of the New York "Tribune," which caused a sensation by publishing transcripts of them. Mr. Tilden in a letter emphatically denied all knowledge of them.

Cities.—Cities have existed since the dawn of civilization, but it is only within the last half-century that industrial developments have increased urban population to such an extent that in many countries more than half of the people may be considered city- or town-dwellers. The cities of ancient Greece were city-states, the boundaries of the city and of the state being identical, but the proportion of free citizens was very small in all Greek cities. In the Roman Empire, cities lost their identity largely as independent units, and became merged within the Empire itself, although they still continued to perform functions of a purely local character.

Through the Dark and the Middle Ages, medieval cities were founded both as centres of commerce and as points of advantageous military defense, but it was not until the medieval system had died that city-growth became marked. For instance, it is estimated that in 1500 Europe had only seven cities with a population above 100,000, whereas by 1600 the number had increased to 14. Nevertheless, it was not until the nineteenth century that the vast bulk of the population could no longer be considered agricultural.

Even in the United States, where natural resources were and are more available than in European countries, the urban population has increased from 30% in 1880 to more than 50% at the present time.

The congestion of the population into the cities as a result of the vastly increased scale of industrial production and commerce has created new problems which are distinctly those of the city, and which have created a demand for the reconstruction of a social and political structure planned originally for a civilization where the cities were outweighed in importance by the country-side. Problems of housing, of tenements, of vivid contrasts in well-being, of crime, of prostitution, of organized recreation, of vocational training, of more socialized and less academic curricula of education, of hours of labor, of opportunity for physical development, all these new problems presented by the increase in city life and the decrease in country life were merely accentuated by the Great War; and merely made more vivid the need for general social, political and industrial reconstruction.

Cities in the United States and Great Britain perform functions assigned to them through the granting of charters from the states or central government, to which they are accordingly subservient; whereas upon the Continent of Europe cities generally perform all fitting functions not otherwise and expressly reserved for the jurisdiction of the central state.

According to the dates indicated, the largest cities of the world are as follows:

London, Greater (1911)	7,251,358
New York, Greater (1917)	5,637,492
Paris (1911)	2,888,000
Chicago (1916)	2,467,285
Berlin (1910)	2,071,000
Tokio, Japan (1914)	2,050,000
Vienna (1910)	2,031,000
Petrograd (1910)	1,908,000
Philadelphia (1916)	1,725,000
Buenos Ayres (1914)	1,594,000
Moscow, Russia (1909)	1,481,000
Rio de Janeiro, Brazil (1913)	1,250,000
Canton, China (1908)	1,250,000
Osaka, Japan (1908)	1,227,000

Calcutta, India (1911)	1,222,000
Peking, China (1908)	1,000,000
Bombay, India (1911)	980,000
Hamburg, Germany (1910)	931,000
Hankow, China (1908)	900,000
Buda-Pest, Hungary (1910)	880,000
Tientsien, China (1908)	850,000
Birmingham, England (1911)	840,000
St. Louis, U. S. A. (1916)	820,000
Glasgow, Scotland (1911)	785,000
Warsaw, Poland (1909)	780,000
Liverpool, England (1911)	750,000
Boston, U. S. A. (1916)	732,000
Naples, Italy (1911)	723,000

Estimates of the population and the area comprised within the city limits of the largest cities in the United States in 1918 are as follows:

City	Population	Sq. Miles
New York, N. Y.	5,670,167	316
Chicago, Ill.	2,521,822	198
Philadelphia, Pa.	1,750,000	129½
St. Louis, Mo.	850,000	61¼
Detroit, Mich.	825,000	76¼
Boston, Mass.	767,000	47¾
Cleveland, O.	750,000	52½
Baltimore, Md.	605,000	31½
Los Angeles, Cal.	600,000	338
Pittsburgh, Pa.	590,000	41½
San Francisco, Cal.	530,000	46
Buffalo, N. Y.	480,000	42
Cincinnati, O.	450,000	75
Milwaukee, Wis.	448,765	25¾
Newark, N. J.	401,000	23¼
New Orleans, La.	400,000	198
Minneapolis, Minn.	370,000	53¼
Washington, D. C.	365,000	69¼
Seattle, Wash.	330,834	58½
Indianapolis, Ind.	300,000	37¼
Kansas City, Mo.	300,000	61
St. Paul, Minn.	290,000	54½
Portland, Ore.	275,000	66¼
Jersey City, N. J.	270,000	19
Louisville, Ky.	265,000	26¾
Rochester, N. Y.	265,000	24
Denver, Colo.	253,000	58¾
Providence, R. I.	251,000	18¼
Oakland, Cal.	250,000	60¼
Toledo, O.	250,000	31¾
Omaha, Neb.	210,000	31¾
Columbus, O.	210,000	22¼
Atlanta, Ga.	200,000	26¾
Birmingham, Ala.	199,000	51
Worcester, Mass.	175,000	38½
Bridgeport, Conn.	170,000	13½
New Haven, Conn.	160,000	22½
Richmond, Va.	160,000	25
Syracuse, N. Y.	150,000	19
Hartford, Conn.	150,000	18
Memphis, Tenn.	150,000	19
Houston, Tex.	148,000	32¾
Scranton, Pa.	145,000	19½
San Antonio, Tex.	140,000	36
Nashville, Tenn.	139,000	18½
Dallas, Tex.	135,000	17½
Dayton, O.	135,000	16½
Grand Rapids, Mich.	132,000	18
Akron, O.	130,000	24
Paterson, N. J.	130,000	8½
Youngstown, O.	125,000	25
Fall River, Mass.	125,000	41
Spokane, Wash.	125,000	39¼

Cities, plan to make Washington the model for, 6902.

Citizen.—One who owes allegiance to a nation or state by reason of the protection and benefits afforded by its government;—a foreign born person in order to become a citizen must be naturalized. (See Naturalization.)

Citizen Genêt.—In 1793, the newly-created French Republic dispatched its ambassador to the United States, who, because his country had abolished all titles of nobility and had dignified all its people by the title of "Citizen," was known as Citizen Genêt. Genêt had previously been minister to Russia.

In 1793, France and England were at war, and Genêt used every possible method to draw the United States into the conflict as the ally of its former ally. It was considered that Spain was about to cast in her lot with that of England, and Genêt would have been successful if he could have stirred up a quarrel between Spain and the United States.

Accordingly, in 1794, he put on foot three expeditions to seize Louisiana and Florida from Spain. In the first two attempts his money did not materialize, and he was discredited.

The third expedition, however, promised to become more serious, as George Rogers Clark, the hero of the Northwest, offered his services to Genêt in the attempt to wrest Louisiana and Florida from Spanish rule. Clark was actually commissioned an officer of the French army. For a time, the government at Washington had winked at these efforts, as it was entering upon negotiations with Spain for the Louisiana Territory, and considered that the negotiations would not be harmed by Spain's realization that her territory was in actual danger of invasion by her enemies. Finally, however, the threat became so serious that President Washington was considering taking steps to thwart Genêt's plans, when the French minister's own home government altered its policy, and gave instructions to Genêt to abandon his plans. But Spain had seen the danger confronting her defenseless territory in North America, and the negotiations for the purchase of Louisiana, were hastened and helped by Genêt's activities.

Genêt's reception in this country in 1793 had been in the nature of an enthusiastic welcome, and had so eclipsed his shrewder sense that he believed that he could defy the President. Washington had laid down certain rules which were to govern the extensive fitting out of privateers in this country by Genêt; but Genêt finally disregarded completely the assurances he had given that Washington's orders would be met. Washington immediately countered, much to the surprise and humiliation of the Frenchman, by informing his home government that his actions had rendered him persona non grata to the American government and requesting his recall. Genêt, in the meantime, had become persona non grata also to the radical revolutionists who by this time had gained control of the French Revolution, so that execution for treason was in all probability awaiting him when he should return to his native country.

Under the circumstances, Washington permitted the dismissed minister to remain in this country, where, completely disillusioned, he settled down to a peaceful existence. He later married a daughter of Governor Clinton, of New York, where he lived to enjoy a ripe old age.

Citizens of United States:

Aid furnished Cubans by, 6284.

Appropriation for relief of, abroad in certain cases recommended, 4145.

Attacked by British forces, 1618.

Militia called forth to protect, 1620.

Captured by army of Mexico, 1944, 2010.

Liberated, 2050.

Claims of, against—
Foreign Powers. (See the several Powers.)

United States. (See P r i v a t e Claims; War Claims.)

Condemned to death in Cuba, 4690.

Death of, in Cuba, 6178, 6184.

Destitute in—
Colombia, order for transportation of, to United States, 5437.
Cuba, appropriation for, 6256.
Recommended, 6248.
Referred to, 6256.

Detained as British prisoners of war, 6681.

Disloyalty among, denounced, 8114, 8120, 8154.

Emigration of, to Turkey for purpose of acquiring lands referred to, 3661.

Estates of deceased, in Cuba referred to, 2893, 2894.

Expelled from—
Jurisdiction of Mexico, 2180, 2198, 3044, 3120.
Prussia, 3123.

Forbidden to sell goods in Mexico, 2115.

Illegally taken from United States by the English, 485.

Impressed into military service of foreign countries. (See Naturalized Citizens.)

Imprisonment of, abroad. (See Imprisonment.)

Imprisonment of, by army officers referred to, 4009.

In Europe, passports for, 7966, 8169.

Injuries inflicted upon, in Turkey discussed, 6090, 6147.

Injuries sustained by, in Mexico 2869, 3043, 3094, 4143.

Interference with rights of naturalized subjects by Austria, 6425.

Legislation for protection of, 4006.

Marriages of, when abroad, recommendations regarding, 4246, 4301, 4360.

Murdered in—
Cuba, 4002, 4004, 4022, 4023, 4196, 6182.
Great Britain, retaliatory measures discussed, 522.
Mexico, 3096.
Quallah Battoo, Sumatra, 1138.

Naturalized, disloyalty among, 8114. 8120, 8154.

Naturalization discussed. (See Aliens; Naturalization.)

Of Hebrew persuasion discriminated against in Switzerland, 3123.

Outrages on, in—
Costa Rica, 3048.
Mexico, 2323, 2383, 3175.
New Granada, 2948, 3049.
Nicaragua, 3048.
Pontifical States, 3110.

Pardons granted. (See Pardons.)

Passports used by, in France referred to, 3902.

Presented at Court of France, 3265.

Privileges accorded, in Turkey discussed, 4920.

Property of—
Confiscated in Cuba, 4019, 4022, 4023.
Destroyed in Spain, 372, 376, 682.
Destroyed in China, 4823.
Protected in South Africa, 6371.
Seized or destroyed in Mexico, 2323, 3044, 3096, 3120.

Protection of, in China discussed, 4006, 4055, 5544, 5621, 6059, 6069.

Qualifications of, 31.

Ransom of, from Mediterranean pirates, urged and discussed, 90, 115, 140.

Registration of, in Europe, 8177.

Relief for, stranded in Europe as result of war, 7961, 7962.

Religious and educational establishments of, in Turkey, treatment of, discussed, 5752.

Rescued by Spanish brig, 1123.
Compensation for services rendered recommended, 1123.

Rights of—
Abroad discussed, 3381, 6917.
In Egypt discussed and proclaimed, 4344, 4357.
Violated by Spanish authorities, 2770.

Selected to serve in offices in Japanese Government, 4099.

Should not wage private war, 358, 392.

Slaughter of, in Hamburg, S. C., referred to, 4329.

Steps taken for protection of, in Turkey referred to, 4321.

Suffrage, irrespective of race, color or previous condition of servitude, guaranteed to, 32.

Trading under false colors, 480.

Training of, in use of arms, 8022.

Treatment of—
By Great Britain referred to, 3718.
In Cuba discussed, 6256.

Trial and conviction of, abroad. (See Imprisonment.)

Citizenship. (See Naturalization.)

Citizenship:
In America, meaning of, analyzed by President Wilson, 8066.
Requirement of, waived in special case, 8175.

Citizenship Bureau, State Department. —This bureau was established by Secretary of State Elihu Root, on order of May 31, 1907, as an expansion of the Passport Bureau (which had been organized in 1870) since its work had outgrown the mere supervision over the issuance of passports. Its Chief is "authorized and empowered to receive and attest all oaths * * * in passport cases." The Bureau also examines applications for passports, issues them, conducts correspondence concerning them, receives and files "duplicates of evidence of registration, or other acts * * * in reference to the expatriation of citizens and their protection abroad," keeps records and conducts correspondence relative to the records. The Citizenship Bureau is also custodian of the seal of the department. (See State Department.)

Civic Federation.—A national organization of prominent representatives of capital, labor, and the general public formed as the direct outgrowth of conventions held in Chicago and New York in 1900-1901. Its purpose is to organize the best brains of the nation in an educational movement seeking the solution of some of the great problems related to social and industrial progress; to provide for study and discussion of questions of national import; to aid thus in the crystallization of the most enlightened public opinion; and when desirable, to promote legislation in accordance therewith.

Civil Law.—The state or national rule of conduct governing civil rights and duties in contradistinction to military rights and duties. Civil law governs persons and property except in time of war, when military rule takes its place.

Civil Rights:
Acts regarding, vetoed, 3603.
Enactment of law to better secure, recommended, 4209.
Supreme Court decision regarding, referred to, 4775.
Violations of, referred to, 3666.

Civil Rights Act.—A law passed by Congress April 9, 1866, over President Johnson's veto, placing the negro on the same civil footing as the white man (page 3603). It provided that all persons born in the United States and not subjects of any foreign power, excluding Indians not taxed, were to be recognized as citizens of the United States. The violation of the law was made a misdemeanor to be considered by the Federal courts alone.

A long controversy ensued over the constitutionality of this law. The fourteenth amendment was framed in accordance with it (page 29), and in 1875 more stringent measures were passed to secure the civil rights of the negro. In June, 1883, a number of cases were brought before the United States Supreme Court on certificates of division from the circuit courts of Kansas, California, Missouri, New York, and Tennessee. They were, respectively, United States vs. Stanley, United States vs. Ryan, United States vs. Nichols, United States vs. Singleton, and Robinson and Wife vs. Memphis and Charleston Railroad Co. The cases against Nichols and Stanley were on indictments for refusing the privileges of a hotel; against Singleton and Ryan for refusing admission to a theater. Robinson brought suit against the railroad company for refusing his wife, a colored woman, the privileges of the ladies' car on the Memphis and Charleston Railroad. In the latter case, as well as that of Ryan, judgment was given for the plaintiff on the ground of violation of the first and second sections of the fourteenth amendment to the Constitution. In the other cases the court declared certain provisions of the civil rights act of 1875 null and void and judgment was rendered for the defendants.

Civil Rights Bill.—An act passed by Congress in 1866 assuring citizenship to all citizens regardless of race or color, or previous condition of servitude.

Civil Rights Bill.—An act of Congress approved March 8, 1918, chiefly providing that—

1—In all actions in all courts, the plaintiff must file an affidavit showing that the defendant is not in the military service of the United States; otherwise, no judgment may be entered without an order of court, which shall not be granted if the defendant is in military service until the court has appointed an attorney to represent the defendant's interests, as the court is required to do on application. No such attorney, however, has the right to waive any rights of such person in such service nor to bind him by the attorney's acts. In the discretion of the court, any action by or against any person in military service, on its own motion, may be delayed; and must be delayed on application, unless the court is satisfied that the interests of such person in the military service will not be injured in such case because of his service. No fines may be assessed for failure to live up to a contract by the terms of that contract if the person to be penalized has been unable to fulfill his obligations because of military service. Similarly, the court may stay the execution of any judgment or attachment, etc., against any person in the military service of the United States.

2—No eviction shall be made during the period of military service for which the agreed rent does not exceed $50 per month occupied chiefly by dependents of such person in service, except upon leave of court granted where right of possession is involved. Except by action of a court, no person shall terminate a contract on which a deposit or partial payment has been made by a person in such service, but the court may void the contract after ordering such deposits or payments to be refunded or may otherwise dispose of the case for the best interests of all concerned.

3—In cases of insurance policies, etc., not exceeding a total face value of $5,000, where the contract was made and a premium paid before September 1, 1917, but only upon application sent to the insurer by the insured on a form furnished according to regulations of the Secretary of the Treasury and of which a copy has been sent to the Bureau of War Risk Insurance, and only when the premium was due and unpaid for less than a year from the date of such application—no policy shall lapse which had not lapsed before the commencement of military service on the part of the insured and this provision shall extend for one year after the end of the war. The United States pays monthly to each insurance company under this act bonds to recompense it for the premiums unpaid by the insured under the provisions of this act, receiving in return a first lien upon such insurance policies to the amount forwarded by the United States, after liens existing at the time of such payment for such unpaid premium. The terms of this section of the act apply for one year after the end of the military service of the United States.

4—When a person in military service, or his agent, shall file an affidavit showing that his ability to pay taxes upon real property has been materially affected by such service, no proceeding against the property may be taken to collect such taxes, except by the leave of the court having jurisdiction. When by law such property may be sold for taxes, such person in military service may institute actions to redeem it within six months after the end of his service. Similar provisions protect settlers and applicants for Lands Public, Desert and Homestead (q. q. v.).

Civil Service.—Jan. 16, 1883, Congress passed what is known as the civil service law. This act established the United States Civil Service Commission, to be composed of three members, not more than two of whom should be adherents of the same political party.

Purpose of the Act.—The act itself is a mere outline of its purposes, but for its amplification it provides for rules to be promulgated by the President, such rules to be equally binding with the statute upon the heads of Departments and offices, as well as upon the Commission. The fundamental purpose of the law and rules is to establish in the parts of the service within their provisions a merit system whereby selection for appointments shall be made upon the basis of demonstrated relative fitness without regard to political considerations.

Classification.—To carry out this purpose a plan of competitive examinations is prescribed. The term "classified service" indicates the parts of the public service within the provisions of the civil service law and rules requiring appointments therein to be made upon examination and certification by the Commission. The term "unclassified service" indicates the parts of the service which are not within those provisions, and therefore in which appointments may be made without examination and certification by the Commission.

The number and location of federal civil service positions on June 30, 1913, was as shown in the adjoining table.

Presidential Appointments.—Under the terms of the law positions outside the executive branch of the Government, positions to which appointment is made by the President and confirmed by the Senate, and positions of mere unskilled manual labor are not required to be classified. With these limitations, the President is authorized to direct from time to time, in his discretion, the heads of Departments and offices to extend the classified service. The civil service law and rules do not give to the Commission any power of appointment and removal; that power is left where it was prior to such law, namely, in the President and heads of Departments.

Department Appointees.—Upon requisition of an appointing officer the Commission provides eligibles secured as the result of competitive examinations; from the eligibles thus provided the appointing officer makes selection and appointment. When the Commission certifies three eligibles for any particular position, the appointing officer has absolute discretion in making selection and appointment from such eligibles, except that the rules require that selection shall be made without regard to political considerations. When certification is made the Commission's duty ends so far as an appointment is concerned, except, of course, it is charged with investigating and reporting any irregularity of appointment or removal. A vacancy in the classified service may be filled either by original appointment upon examination and certification by the Commission, as explained, or by transfer or promotion from certain other positions in the classified service, or by reinstatement of some person within one year from the date of his separation if separated without delinquency or misconduct. For a larger part of the positions in the classified service the Commission holds examinations on regular schedule dates throughout the country. No information can be given prior to their announcements as to when such examinations will be held or as to their scope and character. They are, however, always announced in the public press.

Examinations.—The act requires the rules to provide, as nearly as the conditions of good administration will warrant, for open competitive practical examinations for testing the fitness of applicants for the classified service ; for the filling of all vacancies by selections from among those graded highest ; for the apportionment of appointments at Washington among the states upon the basis of population ; for a period of probation before absolute appointment ; that no person in the public service shall be obliged to contribute service or money for political purposes ; that persons in the competitive service, while retaining the right to vote as they please or to express privately their political opinions, shall take no active part in political campaigns ; and that no person in said service has any right to use his official authority or influence to coerce the political action of any person or body.

Provisions of the Rules.—The act requires the rules to provide, as nearly as the conditions of good administration will warrant, for open competitive practical examinations for testing the fitness of applicants for the classified service ; for the filling of all vacancies by selections from among those graded highest ; for the apportionment of appointments at Washington among the states upon the basis of population ; for a period of probation before absolute appointment ; that no person in the public service shall be obliged to contribute service or money for political purposes ; that persons in the competitive service, while retaining the right to vote as they please or to express privately their political opinions, shall take no active part in political campaigns ; and that no person in said service has any right to use his official authority or influence to coerce the political action of any person or body.

Extent of the Service.—There were on June 30, 1912, over 395,000 positions in the Executive Civil Service, nearly 60 per cent. of which, or about 236,000 were subject to competitive examination. The expenditure for salaries in the Executive Civil Service is over $200,000,000 a year. The Civil Service act does not require the classification of persons appointed by the President and confirmed by the Senate, or of persons employed merely as laborers or workmen. Many positions are excepted in part from the provisions of the rules for various reasons.

Applications.—Persons seeking to be examined must file an application blank. The blank for the Departmental Service at Washington, Railway Mail Service, the Indian School Service, and the Government Printing Service should be requested directly of the Civil Service Commission at Washing. The blank for the Customs, Postal or Internal Revenue Service should be requested of the Civil Service Board of Examiners at the office, where service is sought.

Applicants for examination must be citizens of the United States, and of the proper age. No person using intoxicating liquors to excess may be appointed. No discrimination is made on account of sex, color or political or religious opinions. The limitations of age vary with the different services, but do not apply to any person honorably discharged from the military or naval service of the United States by reason of disability resulting from wounds or sickness incurred in the line of duty.

Examinations.—The examinations are open to all persons qualified in respect to age, citizenship, legal residence, character and health. During the fiscal year ended June 30, 1912, 33,240 persons were appointed. Of those appointed, 2,264 were

rural letter-carriers, 12,807 were mechanics and workmen at navy yards appointed on registration tests of fitness given by a board of labor employment at each yard. Several hundred different kinds of examinations were held, each one of which involved different tests. Three hundred and twenty of these examinations contained educational tests, the others being for mechanical trades or skilled occupations and consisting of certificates of employers or fellow-workmen. Examinations are held twice a year in each state and territory, the places and dates being publicly announced.

Appointments.—In case of a vacancy not filled by promotion, reduction, transfer or reinstatement, the highest three of the sex called for on the appropriate register are certified for appointment, the apportionment being considered in appointments at Washington. In the absence of eligibles, or when the work is of short duration, temporary appointments, without examination, are permitted. The number of women applying for ordinary clerical places is greatly in excess of the calls of appointing officers. The chances of appointment are good for teachers, matrons, seamstresses and physicians in the Indian Service, for male stenographers and typewriters, draughtsmen, patent examiners, civil, mechanical and electrical engineers, and for technical and scientific experts.

Preference Claimants. — Persons who served in the military or naval service of the United States, and were discharged by reason of disabilities resulting from wounds or sickness incurred in the line of duty, are, under the Civil Service rules, given certain preferences. They are released from all maximum age limitations, are eligible for appointment at a grade of 65, while all others are obliged to obtain a grade of 70, and are certified to appointing officers before all others. Subject to the other conditions of the rules, a veteran of the rebellion or of the war with Spain, or the widow of any such person, or any army nurse of either war, may be reinstated without regard to the length of time he or she has been separated from the service.

Insular Possessions.—Examinations are also held for positions in the Philippines, Porto Rico and Hawaii, and also for the Isthmian Canal service.

The Unclassified Service.—Under an executive order unclassified laborers are appointed after open, competitive examination upon their physical condition. This action is outside the Civil Service act.

Publications of the Commission.—The Commission publishes the following :

Manual of Examinations, giving places and dates of examinations, rules by which papers are rated, descriptions of examinations, specimen questions and general information.

The Civil Service act and rules.

The Annual Reports of the Commission, showing its work. These annual reports may be consulted at public libraries.

Civil Service (see also Government Service):

Appointments—

Having relation to, 4990.

Relations of Members of Congress to, discussed, 4557.

Breaches of trust in, 7002.

Appointment of aliens when no citizens are available, 7959.

Board to devise rules and regulations to effect reform in, convened, 4109, 4110.

[This table is based upon the number of positions shown in the Official Register of 1903, and changes in the service since reported by the departments and offices. Some of the reports were not made in such manner as to permit of a definite distinction as to employment in Washington and elsewhere. The figures are, therefore, to be regarded as approximate only. Omissions to report certain changes, as explained in the detailed tables, and neglect of details necessary only for statistical purposes also contribute to making the figures approximate only.]

(Reported by The Civil Service Commission.)

DEPARTMENT AND SUBDIVISION OF THE SERVICE	Classified Competitive	Excepted and Non-Competitive	Un-classified	Presidential[1]	All other	Total
In Washington, D. C.						
White House		34	3	.....	37	37
State Department	184	74	4	5	262	267
Treasury Department	6,930	37	528	25	7,495	7,520
War Department	2,130	25	86	7	2,241	2,248
Navy Department	1,152	10	1	2	1,163	1,165
Post Office Department	1,459	10	137	6	1,606	1,612
Department of the Interior	4,673	120	259	20	5,052	5,072
Government Hospital for the Insane	735	3	.....		738	738
Miscellaneous[2]	122	.....	77	5	199	204
Department of Justice[3]	233	272	33	862	538	1,400
Department of Agriculture	3,124	246	286	3	3,656	3,659
Department of Commerce and Labor[4]	1,908	20	722	10	.....	2,650
Interstate Commerce Commission	623	88	15	10	726	736
Civil Service Commission	174	1	4	5	179	184
Smithsonian Institution and Bureaus	451	3	281	.....	735	735
State, War, and Navy Department Building	129	1	104	.....	234	234
Isthmian Canal Commission	136	14	12	.....	162	162
Government Printing Office	3,647	5	384	1	4,036	4,037
Total	27,810	963	2,936	961	31,709	32,670
Outside Washington, D. C.						
Treasury Department:						
Assistant Custodian and janitor service and contingent force on public buildings	2,096	48	2,457	.....	4,601	4,601
Mint and Assay Service	668	32	133	26	833	859
Sub-Treasury Service	381	.....	1	9	382	391
Public Health Service	1,609	1,240	131	133	2,980	3,113
Life-Saving Service	2,268	1	2	.....	2,271	2,271
Customs Service	6,425	285	705	229	7,415	7,644
Internal Revenue Service	3,523	333	6	67	3,862	3,929
Miscellaneous[5]	176	250	6	242	432	674
War Department:						
Quartermaster Corps	4,415	1,178	2 692	.....	8 285	8,285
Ordnance Department at large	3,027	89	1,181	.....	4,297	4,297
Engineer Department at large	7,516	639	6,087	.....	14,242	14,242
Miscellaneous	961	648	721	.....	2,330	2,330
Navy Department:						
Exclusive of trades and labor positions	2,906	2	1	.....	2,909	2,909
Trades and labor positions[6]	16,000	.....	4,000	.....	20,000	20,000
Post Office Department[7]	535	.....	.....	.....	535	535
Post Offices, except fourth-class postmasters[8]	176,923	.....	.....	.....	168,500	176,923
Fourth-class postmasters[9]	49,598	.....	.....	.....	49,598	49,598
Rural Carrier Service	42,685	.....	1	.....	42,686	42,686
Railway Mail Service	19,620	122	7	.....	19,749	19,749
Department of the Interior:						
Land Service[10]	1,090	49	14	223	1,153	1,376
Pension Agency Service[11]	767	4,612	13	.....	5,392	5,392
Indian Service[12]	2,452	4,132	813	33	7,397	7,430
Reclamation Service	2,158	5	5	.....	2,168	2,168
Miscellaneous[13]	509	142	16	8	667	675
Department of Justice[14]	692	1,481	6	172	2,179	2,351
Department of Agriculture	7,286	3,911	564	.....	11,761	11,761
Department of Commerce and Labor:						
Lighthouse Service	2,992	2,395	1,194	.....	6,581	6,581
Immigration Service[15]	1,386	240	175	7	1,801	1,808
Steamboat Inspection Service[16]	305	6	.....	10	311	321
Miscellaneous[17]	511	658	1,624	.....	2,793	2,793
Interstate Commerce Commission	55	8	.....	.....	63	63
Civil Service Commission	31	.....	.....	.....	31	31
Isthmian Canal Commission	1,116	116	.....	.....	1,232	1,232
Total	254,787	120,841	23,808	9,582	399,436	409,018
Grand Total of table	282,597	121,804	26,744	10,543	431,145	441,688
Isthmian Canal Commission, unclassified and excepted working force on June 30, 1913[18]	.....	.....	.....	.....	.....	28,191
Grand Total	.....	.....	.....	.....	.....	469,879

[1] Figures in this column are principally from Senate Document No. 836, Sixty-first Congress, third session, furnished in response to Senate resolution of Dec. 21, 1910.
[2] Presidential appointments, under the heading "Miscellaneous, Interior" in Washington, consist of the recorder of deeds, register of wills, inspector of gas and meters, and Superintendent of Capitol Building and Grounds.
[3] Under "Presidential Justice" in Washington are 16 department officers, 30 commissioners of deeds, 800 notaries and 16 trustees of Reform School.
[4] Most of the unclassified appointments and separations in the Department of Commerce and Labor were of persons appointed under the Thirteenth Census act outside of the provisions of the Civil Service Act and Rules. Although Congress created the Department of Labor and renamed the Department of Commerce by act of March 4, 1913, it has not been found practicable to separate the statistics for the year ended June 30, 1913.
[5] The presidential appointments under "Miscellaneous, Treasury," are revenue-cutter officers.
[6] By an Executive order of Dec. 7, 1912, all artisan and supervisory artisan positions under the jurisdiction of the Navy Department were included in the competitive classified service; but no occupant of such a position may be classified unless he has established his capacity for efficient service or has been examined and found qualified by the Labor Board. The total number of these employees was estimated by the department at 25 000 on June 30, 1912, and at 20,000 on June 30, 1913, of whom about 4,000, or one-fifth, are mere unskilled laborers.
[7] These positions are in the Post-Office Inspection Service; the stamped-envelope agency at Dayton, Ohio; and the official-envelope agency at Cincinnati, Ohio.

Appropriation to continue services of, recommended, 4111, 4254.

Rules and regulations adopted by, 4111, 4135, 4184.

Abolished, 4281.

Amendments to, 4134, 4183.

Civil War veterans given preference in, 6703.

Competitive tests for laborers in, 6780, 6804.

Consular offices, order regarding, 6056.

Discussed, 6071, 6154.

Defense of, 7753.

Corporation and joint stock companies, order governing inspection of returns of, 7960.

Discussed by President—

Arthur, 4647, 4732, 4773, 4792, 4839, 4863.

Cleveland, 4948, 4974, 5112, 5201, 5348, 5399, 5429, 5882, 5889, 5972, 5974, 5982, 6171.

Garfield, 4601.

Grant, 4063, 4108, 4159, 4177, 4208, 4217, 4254.

Harrison, Benj., 5487, 5555, 5642, 5766.

Hayes, 4396, 4417, 4513, 4527, 4555, 4588.

McKinley, 6241, 6274, 6405, 6455.

Roosevelt, 6673, 6803, 7010, 7102.

Dismissal of employees in, 6970, 6971.

Employees forbidden to instruct candidates, 6970.

Examinations for, 7010.

Executive orders, concerning, 6893.

Extension of, discussed, 5642, 5766.

Fourth-class postmasters, 6172.

Government Printing Office, extended over, 6046, 6055.

Interstate Commerce Commission, extended to include, 6143.

Limitation of term of employment in, opposed, 7753.

Merit system in, 6672, 6673, 7010.

Partisan interference in elections by public officers, order respecting, 4402.

Partisan spoils system in Great Britain, report on, referred to, 4513.

Pensions for age and disability favored, 8134.

President, extended to include employees in office of, 6232.

Railway Mail Service, classification of employees in, 5429.

Amendments to rules regarding, 5465, 5466, 5542, 5610, 5948, 5954, 5955, 6040.

Discussed, 5882.

Recommended, 4527.

Time for, extended, 5462.

Discussed, 5488.

Record of efficiency of persons in, 5642.

Recommended, 5615.

Regulations governing appointments and promotions in customs service and subtreasury in New York City, 4501, 4502, 5157.

Report on, discussed, 4588.

Rules and regulations abolished, 4281.

Rules and regulations revised, 6803, 6892.

Rules for regulation and improvement of, and amendments thereto by President—

Arthur, 4748, 4754, 4813, 4814, 4816, 4818, 4820, 4821, 4873.

Cleveland, 4897, 4899, 4901, 4903, 4906, 5078, 5080, 5157, 5160, 5329, 5350, 5353, 5429, 5831, 5832, 5866, 5945, 5950, 6030, 6040, 6046, 6057, 6131, 6230, 6233.

Grant, 4111, 4134, 4183, 4184.

Harrison, Benj., 5462, 5463, 5464, 5538, 5540, 5541, 5599, 5601, 5607, 5609, 5737, 5740, 5818.

Hayes, 4402, 4501, 4502, 4507.

Rules governing appointment and promotion in New York post-office, 4507.

Salaries in, 8135.

Tenure of office in, 7391, 8135.

Civil Service Commission. (See Civil Service.)

Appointment of, referred to, 4773.

Appropriations for, recommended, 4418, 4517, 4556, 4647, 4669, 4863, 5642.

Chief examiner of, nomination of, and reasons therefor, 4745.

Clerical force of, increase in, recommended, 5488, 5766.

Discussed, 5487.

Report of, transmitted and discussed, 4217, 4588, 4792, 4863, 4948, 4974, 5201, 5399, 6182.

Rules adopted by (see also Civil Service)—

Effect of enforcement of, discussed, 4219.

Extension of, order regarding, 4238.

For government of Light-House Service, referred to, 4238.

Salaries of Commissioners, increase in, recommended, 4949, 5113, 7390.

Civil War.—A four years' military conflict between the United States Government and the states adhering to it, on the one side, and the Confederate States Government (composed of the States of South Carolina, Mississippi, Florida, Alabama, Georgia, Louisiana, Texas, Virginia, Arkansas, North Carolina and Tennessee) on the other. There was behind the war a constitutional struggle between the North and South, beginning nearly at the time of the formation of the Union and involving principles of politics, differences of origin and climate, of soil and social conditions, and the general circumstances of peoples who had been steadily drawing apart from the period when by the sword and self-sacrifice they had achieved a common liberty. The contest was unique among modern civil wars, and no ancient conflict between the members of a confederacy of republics was comparable with it, either in the magnitude of the questions involved or in the extent of the operations in the field and the results finally attained. While slavery was the apparent cause, or rather, it should be stated, the occasion, of the war between the states, the real causes were a combination of things inherent in the population, the nature of their surroundings, the structure of their Government, as well as the conditions of life and the objects and aims of a society not homogeneous but variant in many important respects.

From the beginning of colonization in America these differences appeared. The bond, slender in the colonial wars, was scarcely strengthened at the outset of the Revolution, and had distinctly lessened, except among the more cultivated classes, in the years immediately succeeding the peace of 1783. Jealousies between the New England and some of the Southern States well-nigh prevented a permanent union. In the Federal Convention of 1787 it required much mutual concession to avoid a dissolution of the feeble bonds of union. The Constitution as adopted lacked guaranties of perpetual peace and amity between the sections, but the amendments soon afterwards ratified reasonably satisfied the discontent. Discussions in all the early Congresses after the adoption of the Constitution are full of expressions of doubt as to the perpetuity of the federation, uttered by eminent men from New England as well as from other sections, many of whom had been prominent in the work of establishing the new frame of government.

The assertion of state sovereignty was not confined to any one section or party, though it has been the custom to assign to the old Republican (now the Democratic) party the origination of this doctrine. The two sets of resolutions of Kentucky and Virginia, adopted in the years 1798 and 1799, which were attributed on good evidence to Jefferson and Madison, respectively, declared the fundamental principles of states rights as clearly and as boldly as they were ever proclaimed at any subsequent period. The report written by Madison and presented to the Virginia legislature has often been referred to as the ablest official exposition of the doctrine that the state is the creator and sovereign component of the Union, and that it may on sufficient grounds withdraw from the compact, the latter having already been infracted and made of no binding effect. It is true that Mr. Madison subsequently denied that this construction could be placed upon the argument in the report. From 1803, the date of the acquisition of the Louisiana territory, to 1811, when the State of Louisiana was admitted into the Union, many New England public men and writers, opposed to the extension of the Union, especially on the ground that it seemed to involve the extension of slavery, sometimes avowed secession sentiments. Josiah Quincy, in a speech in Congress in 1811, used the threat that the New England States would withdraw in a certain contingency, "peaceably if they can, forcibly if they must." Again, this doctrine of a separable union was advanced by the Hartford Convention (q. v.) in 1814, called by some of the New England States to protest against the continuance of the War of 1812 with Great Britain. When the question of admitting Missouri into the Union as a slave state (1817-1821) was being discussed, threats of disunion if she were refused admission were heard, this time proceeding from the South. In 1828 Congress passed a stringent tariff measure following the protective act of 1824. This was deemed by South Carolina inimical to her business interests. The state legislature called a convention and passed an ordinance of nullification (q. v.), which, however, she subsequently rescinded. As the question of slavery began to overshadow that of the tariff, Northern extremists, called by some "Abolitionists," contended for the overthrow of human bondage, although the Constitution conferred on Congress no power over the domestic institutions of the states for the admission of new states. The first struggle occurred on the right of petition. Applications for the admission of new states organized from the public domain added fuel to the fire on both sides of the controversy. The occupation of the territories by slavery and anti-slavery partisans kept the people there in a constant state of turmoil bordering on civil war. In the midst of this the John Brown raid (q. v.) occurred.

In 1860, after Lincoln was elected President on a platform of resistance to the extension of slavery, South Carolina, through her legislature, called a state convention which, on Dec. 20, 1860, declared that the state was no longer in the Union. Similar action was taken during that winter and the following months by Mississippi, Florida, Alabama, Georgia, Louisiana, Texas, Virginia, Arkansas, North Carolina and Tennessee. Feb. 4, 1861, delegates from the states that had by that date seceded met at Montgomery, Ala., and organized the government of the Confederate States of America. The forts, military supplies and provisions within the seceded states were seized, generally with little opposition until the attack on Fort Sumter, in Charleston Harbor, S. C. The war began, so far as military operations were concerned, with the effort of the Government at Washington to relieve the garrison at Fort Sumter and the firing upon that fort by order of the Confederate government. This event practically ended with the surrender of Gen. Robert E. Lee, commander of the Confederate forces, at Appomattox, Va., April 9, 1865, and the subsequent surrender of the armies of Gen. Joseph E. Johnston in North Carolina and of Gen. E. Kirby Smith beyond the Mississippi River.

As clear a view of the position and attitude of the United States in the war as could be obtained in a few words from an official document is to be derived from the "memorandum" of Secretary of State William H. Seward in regard to the letter addressed to him by the Confederate Commissioners Forsyth and Crawford. Although filed earlier, it was delivered April 8, 1861. In it the fact was stated that President Lincoln coincided generally with the views expressed by the Secretary of State. Frankly confessing, he said, that his understanding of recent events (meaning the attempted secession of the Southern States) was very different from the aspect in which they were presented to Messrs. Forsyth and Crawford, he proceeded, in the third person, to say that "he saw in them not a rightful and accomplished revolution, and an independent nation, with an established government, but rather a perversion of a temporary and partisan excitement to the inconsiderate purposes of an unjustifiable and unconstitutional aggression upon the rights and the authority vested in the Federal Government, and hitherto benignly exercised, as from their very nature they always must so be exercised, for the maintenance of the Union, the preservation of liberty, and the security, peace, welfare, happiness and aggrandizement of the American people." Disavowing any authority to recognize the commissioners as diplomatic agents, or hold correspondence or other communication with them, Mr. Seward brought the memorandum to a close. President Lincoln in his first inaugural address combated the ideas of the Confederates and held that the states in the Union were in an analogous case with the counties in the states. He believed in the right of coercion, and as to slavery he is quoted as saying that he would save the Union "with or without slavery."

The best official exposition of the views of the Confederate people is perhaps to be collected from the constitution of the Confederate States and from the inaugural address and messages of their President. Their constitution was professedly based on the principles of the Federal Constitution of 1787, with the amendments to the same. Its preamble, however, in order to put at rest all argument or dispute, contained the pregnant words, "each state acting in its sovereign and independent character." It was expressly declared that no duties or taxes on importations from foreign nations should be laid to promote or foster any branch of industry. Export duties were allowed to be levied with the concurrence of two-thirds of both houses of Congress. Any judicial or other federal officer resident and acting solely within the limits of a particular state was impeachable by two-thirds of both branches of the legislature thereof, as well as by two-thirds of the house of representatives in Congress. Internal improvements by the general government were prohibited, except the improvement of harbors and local duties for lights, beacons and buoys, the expenses to be borne by the navigation facilitated. Citizens of the several states were not permitted to sue each other in the federal courts. It required a two-thirds vote of

each house of Congress, the Senate voting by states, to admit new states. A constitutional convention could meet to consider proposed amendments on the call of any three states legally assembled in their several conventions. The vote in convention was to be taken by states and afterwards ratified by the legislatures of two-thirds of the states, or by conventions in them. The power of Congress over territories was settled explicitly, and it was provided that "in all such territory the institution of negro slavery * * * shall be recognized and protected by Congress and by the territorial government," etc. The constitution was adopted March 11, 1861.

In his inaugural address as provisional president, Feb. 18, 1861, Mr. Davis said in part: "Sustained by the consciousness that the transition from the former Union to the present Confederacy has not proceeded from a disregard on our part of just obligations or any failure to perform any constitutional duty; moved by no interest or passion to invade the rights of others; anxious to cultivate peace and commerce with all nations if we may not hope to avoid war we may at least expect that posterity will acquit us of having needlessly engaged in it. We have changed the constituent parts but not the system of our government. The Constitution formed by our fathers is that of these Confederate States in their exposition of it, and in the judicial construction it has received we have a light which reveals its true meaning."

The principal battles of the war were: Bull Run, or First Manassas, July 21, 1861; Shiloh, April 6-7, 1862; Antietam, or Sharpsburg, Sept. 17, 1862; Fredericksburg, Dec. 13, 1862; Stone River, or Murfreesboro, Dec. 31, 1862, to Jan. 2, 1863; the Seven Days' Battles around Richmond, June 25 to July 1, 1862; Chancellorsville, May 1-4, 1863; Gettysburg, July 1-3, 1863; Chickamauga, Sept. 19-20, 1863; Wilderness, May 5-7, 1864; Spottsylvania, May 8-18, 1864; Cold Harbor, June 1-12, 1864; Petersburg, June 15-19, 1864, and Five Forks, April 1, 1865. The total number of enlistments in the Union armies was 2,688,523 (4156). The number of enlistments in the Confederate army was between 650,000 and 700,000. The total number of deaths on the Federal side, including those killed in action, those who died of wounds received in action, and from disease and other causes, 9,584 officers and 349,944 men. The cost of the struggle to the United States during the four years was $6,500,000,000. It is interesting to note in this connection that the cost of the Revolutionary War was $135,193,703; of the War of 1812, $107.159,003, and of the Mexican War, $66,000,000. The public debt of the United States rose from $90.867,828.68 in July, 1861, to $2,682,593,026.53 in July, 1865, an increase in four years of $2,591,725,197.85.

The results of the war were the restoration of the Union, the emancipation of the slaves, and the several amendments to the Constitution regarding the rights of the new citizens under the new conditions established.

For a more detailed account of the causes and history of the war, see the messages of Presidents Buchanan and Lincoln. (See also Abolitionists; Confederate States; Missouri Compromise; Slavery; and the several battles.)

Civil War:

(See also Confederate States; Reconstruction; Restoration; Secession; Slavery; Southern States.)

Act—
Prescribing oath of office to be taken by persons who participated in rebellion discussed, 4076.
To confiscate property used for insurrectionary purposes, 3361.
Attorney-General charged with superintendence of proceedings under, 3361.
To equalize bounties of soldiers of, reasons for applying pocket veto, to, 4274.
To fix status of certain Southern Union troops vetoed, 4035.
To suppress insurrection, punish treason, etc., 3294.
Approved and reasons therefor, 3286.
Attorney-General charged with superintendence of proceedings under 3325.
Joint resolution explanatory of, 3297.
Action taken by the several States in, discussed, 3256.
Aiders and abetters of, proclamation against, 3294, 3299.
Alabama-Kearsarge naval engagement referred to, 3457.
Albemarle, The—
Destruction of, referred to, 3457.
Engagement of, with the *Sassacus*, 3411.
Aliens, liability of to perform military duties, 3381.
Proclaimed, 3369.
Anderson, Robert—
Commander of forts in Charleston Harbor, 3189.
Dispatches of, while in command of Fort Sumter referred to, 3213, 3222.
Empowered to receive volunteers, 3219.
Flag over Fort Sumter at evacuation of, to be raised on ruins of, by, 3484.
Appropriation for prosecuting, recommended, 3226.
Armed neutrality in Middle States discussed, 3225.
Arms and munitions of war, order prohibiting export of, 3326. (See also 373.)
Extended, 3436.
Modified, 3379.
Rescinded, 3533.
Army of Potomac—
Honors achieved by, discussed, 3376.
Organization of, 3311.
Thanks of President tendered, 3360.
Army of United States—
Headquarters of, 3435.

Information regarding operations of, forbidden, 3240.
Joint resolution providing for payment of, approved, 3350.
Army officers and privates, orders regarding absence of, 3320.
Act for enrolling and calling out national forces, etc., 3365.
Proclamation regarding, 3364.
Army officers directed to subscribe a new oath of allegiance, 3219.
Assignments of commands in, and orders regarding, 3241, 3309, 3310, 3311, 3312, 3313, 3314, 3317, 3325, 3379, 3435.
Atlanta, Ga., capture of, and orders regarding celebration of, 3439.
Belligerent rights accorded Confederate States by foreign powers discussed, 3259, 3327, 3565.
Recognition and aid from foreign powers invoked by Confederate States, 3221, 3246.
Blockade of Southern ports proclaimed, 3215, 3216, 3481.
Claims arising therefrom discussed, 3328.
Nonresident foreigners engaged in violating, order regarding, 3483.
Referred to, 3225, 3385.
Removed, 3523.
From certain ports, 3290, 3372, 3417, 3431, 3482, 3507.
British vessels carrying contraband of war for insurgents referred to, 3352.
Burdens imposed upon people, President expresses desire to relieve, 3476.
Burnside, Ambrose E.—
Brigadier-general, thanks of President tendered, 3305.
Major-general, command of Army of Potomac assumed by, 3325.
Chaplains for hospitals, 3249.
Citizens liable to be drafted not permitted to go abroad, order regarding, 3322.
Claims—
Against citizens of insurgent States and means for collecting, discussed, 3251.
Growing out of, discussed by President—
Grant, 4205, 4303.
Harrison, Benj., 5755.
Claims of—
Aliens arising out of, discussed, 4191.
Court to try, recommended, 4243.
Foreign powers growing out of, discussed, 3328, 4086.
France growing out of, paid, 4916.
Great Britain growing out of, 4191.
Payment of, 4243.

Clerks in Departments to be organized into companies for defense of capital, 3323, 3642.
Combinations in Southern States opposing revenue laws, proclamations against, 3215, 3216.
Commerce disturbed by, 3327.
Commercial intercourse of Southern States. (See Confederate States.)
Communication with insurgents under Executive sanction referred to, 3461.
Confederate envoys sent to Great Britain and France. (See Mason and Slidell.)
Confederate flags—
  Captured, presented to Congress, 3309.
  Return of, to States recommended, 5163.
  Proposition withdrawn, 5164.
Confederate States, seat of government of, was first located in Montgomery, Alabama, 3225.
Contraband on British vessels for use of insurgents referred to, 3352.
Contraband trade and protection for neutral vessels, order regarding, 3377.
Corinth, Miss., capture of, 3315.
Correspondence with foreign powers regarding, referred to, 3234.
Courts of justice for insurgent States recommended, 3251.
Craney Island, evacuation of batteries on, 3313.
Cumberland-Merrimac naval engagement discussed, 3345.
Deserters—
  Condemned to death, sentence of, commuted, 3434.
  Returning to duty pardoned, 3364, 3479.
  Act authorizing, 3368.
Discussed, 3221, 3245, 3255, 3278, 3301, 3303, 3305, 3313, 3376, 3389, 3452, 3547, 3477.
Dix, John A.—
  Applications to go south of military lines to be made to, 3302.
  Authority given to, while at Baltimore, 3313.
  Commissioners to examine cases of State prisoners, 3310.
  Prisoners of war released to report to, 3303.
Drafts to be made, orders regarding, 3321, 3433.
  Citizens liable to draft not permitted to go abroad, 3322.
  Deficiency in quota of States referred to, 3412.
Emancipation of slaves discussed. (See Emancipation; Emancipation Proclamation.)

Executive orders regarding, 3218, 3239, 3300, 3360, 3375, 3431, 3474, 3483.
Expenditures incident to, discussed, 3248, 3330.
Fasting and prayer—
  Day of, set apart, 3237, 3365, 3422.
  Recommended, 3437.
Fingal-Weehawken naval engagement referred to, 3392.
Forces of United States in, movements of, and orders regarding, 3301, 3302, 3311, 3312, 3315.
Foreign interference in, discussed, 3246.
  Aid furnished rebellion by British subjects referred to, 3458.
Foreign recruits, enlistment of, in services of United States referred to, 3413.
Fort Gaines, reduction of, and orders regarding celebration of, 3439.
Fort Henry, capture of, referred to, 3305.
Fort Morgan, reduction of, and orders regarding celebration of, 3439.
Fort Powell, reduction of, and orders regarding celebration of, 3439.
Fort Sumter, assault upon and reduction of, discussed, 3222.
Fredericksburg, Va., battle of, referred to, 3360.
Gen. Wadsworth to command the force composed of the clerks in the departments organized for the defense of the Capital, 3323, 3642.
Georgia, campaign in, discussed and orders regarding celebration of, 3439, 3452.
Government of Confederate States first located at Montgomery, Ala., 3225.
  Transferred to Richmond, Va., 3225.
Governments to be reestablished in Confederate States. (See Confederate States.)
Habeas corpus, writ of—
  Authority given to suspend, 3217, 3218, 3219, 3220, 3240, 3300, 3313, 3322.
  Referred to, 3225.
  Suspension of, 3299, 3371, 3420.
  Revoked as to certain States, 3529, 3531.
Halleck, Henry W., assigned to command of—
  Department of Mississippi, 3312.
  Land forces of United States, 3317.
  Relieved from command and orders regarding, 3435.
Hampton Roads, Va., conference and correspondence at, regarding restoration of peace discussed, 3641.

Hooker, Joseph, commander of corps in Army, 3325.
  Military possession of railroads to be taken by, 3379.
Hunter, David—
  Command of corps formerly under Gen. Burnside assumed by, 3325.
  Proclamation of, for freedom of slaves in certain States declared void, 3292.
Illinois volunteers, thanks of President tendered, 3442.
Illustrations of, see opposite 3213, and list of illustrations, Vol. VIII.
Imprisonment of loyal citizens by forces in rebellion referred to, 3235.
Indiana volunteers, thanks of President tendered, 3442.
Indians, attitude of, in, discussed, 3253, 3333.
Injuries to citizens of foreign countries growing out of, discussed, 3383.
Instructions to ministers of United States abroad regarding, referred to, 3234.
Insurgent cruisers infesting h i g h seas, proclamation regarding, 3506.
Insurgent leader and attempts to negotiate with, discussed. (See Davis, Jefferson.)
Insurgent privateers in foreign ports referred to, 3275.
Iowa volunteers, thanks of President tendered, 3442.
Kansas troops, treatment of, when captured, referred to, 3398.
Kearsarge-Alabama naval engagement referred to, 3457.
Leader of the insurgents and attempts to negotiate with, discussed and recommendations made. (See Davis, Jefferson.)
Leaves of absence and furloughs revoked, 3320.
Legislature of Maryland, arrest and dispersion of members of, by Gen. Scott would not be justifiable, 3218.
Live stock order prohibiting export of, 3326.
  Modifications in, order regarding, 3379.
  Order extending, 3436.
  Order rescinding, 3533.
McCallum, D. C., appointed military director and superintendent of railroads, 3302.
McClellan, George B. (See McClellan, George B.)
McPherson, James B., command of Department and Army of the Tennessee assigned to, 3436.

Merrimac-Cumberland naval engagement discussed, 3345.
Merrimac-Monitor naval engagement discussed, 3313.
Military authorities not vested with authority to interfere with contracts between individuals, order regarding, 3548.
Military force—
  Necessary to prosecute, discussed, 3226.
  To be raised by governor of Missouri discussed, 3241.
Military possession of—
  Railroads taken, 3314, 3379.
  Telegraph lines, orders regarding and recommendations, 3309.
Military supplies purchased and frauds in, discussed, 3278.
Mill Springs, Ky., battle of, referred to, 3301.
  Thanks of President tendered officers and soldiers in, 3301.
Missouri troops, order regarding inspection of records of, 3433.
Mobile Harbor, Ala., achievements of Federal forces in, and orders regarding celebration of, 3439.
Monitor-Merrimac naval engagement discussed, 3313.
Navy of United States—
  Discussed, 3385, 3449.
  Joint resolution providing for payment of, approved, 3350.
  Naval engagement of *Kearsarge* and *Alabama*, referred to, 3398.
  Bank in, order regarding, 3240.
  Discussed, 3450.
Negotiations attempted with Jefferson Davis, for the restoration of peace discussed and correspondence concerning, and F. P. Blair's correspondence concerning, 3461.
Negro soldiers—
  Discussed, 3389.
  Enslaved and measures of retaliation discussed, 3378.
  Opinion of Attorney-General on rights of, referred to, 3410.
Negroes to be employed for military purposes, order regarding, 3318.
Neutral rights of foreign powers violated. (See Neutral Rights.)
Neutrality of foreign powers, 3380, 3665.
New Orleans, La., capture of, 3315.
Norfolk, Va., surrender of, referred to, 3313, 3315.
Number of United States soldiers enlisted in, 4156.
Oath of allegiance to United States, army officers directed to subscribe anew, 3219.
Object of, declared by President Lincoln, 3297.

Official Records of. (See War of Rebellion, Official Records of.)

Ohio National Guard, expiration of enlistment of, referred to and thanks of President tendered, 3440.

Pardons granted—

Deserters. (See Deserters, *ante.*)

Persons participating in. (See Pardons.)

Peace—

Negotiations attempted with Jefferson Davis for the restoration of, and correspondence concerning, 3461.

Negotiations for, and correspondence regarding restoration of, discussed, 3461.

Proposition embracing restoration of, etc., would be considered by Government, 3438.

Pensioners of. (See Pensions.)

Persons—

Discouraging enlistments or resisting drafts subject to court-martial, 3299.

In rebellion—

Commanded to disperse, 3214, 3294.

Must return to allegiance under penalty of confiscation of property, 3294.

Trading with insurgents, order prohibiting, 3483.

Pierrepont Edwards, commissioner to examine cases of State prisoners, 3310.

Plymouth, N. C., capture of, referred to, 3458.

Porter, Fitz-John, relieved from command of corps, 3325.

Presidential election of 1864, effects of, discussed, 3453.

Prisoners—

Of war—

Exchange of, referred to, 3399.

Interview between Col. Key and Gen. Cobb on subject of, 3459.

Order for discharge of, 3538.

Paroled, order regarding passports to be furnished. 3547.

Released, to report to Maj.-Gen. Dix, 3303.

Political—

Orders regarding provision for, 3239.

Released on subscribing to parole, etc., 3303.

State, commissioners appointed examine cases of, 3310.

Proclamation of President Lincoln regarding, 3214, 3237, 3289, 3358, 3362, 3364, 3414, 3472, 3479.

Spurious proclamations published in New York *World* and New

York *Journal of Commerce*, orders regarding, 3438.

Property to be seized for military uses, orders regarding, 3318.

Protection for capital, recommendations regarding, 3323, 3642.

Purchasing places in insurgent States designated and orders regarding, 3441.

Quasi armistice of President Buchanan's administration referred to, 3223, 3235.

Railroads—

Construction of, as military measure recommended, 3247.

In Missouri to be made available for military uses, 3317.

Military possession of, taken, 3314, 3379.

Points of commencement of Union Pacific discussed and order regarding, 3401, 3435.

Reconstruction of Southern States. (See Reconstruction; Restoration.)

Records of. (See War of Rebellion, Official Records of.)

Records of association founded for purpose of aiding soldiers of, offered to United States, 4798.

Refugees from Virginia, communication regarding removal of, 3360.

Restoration of Southern States. (See Reconstruction; Restoration.)

Roanoke Island, N. C., capture of, referred to, 3305.

Sanford, Edward S., appointed military superintendent of telegraph messages, 3310.

Sassacus-Albemarle naval engagement referred to, 3411.

Scott, Winfield, retirement from active service in, orders regarding, 3241.

Referred to, 3257.

Successor of, referred to, 3241, 3257.

Secession discussed. (See Secession.)

Sentences of imprisonment by military tribunals remitted and prisoners discharged, 3537.

Sewells Point, Va., evacuation of batteries on, 3313.

Shenandoah, reported surrender of the, 3575.

Sheridan, Philip H. (See Sheridan, Philip H.)

Sherman, William T. (See Sherman, William T.)

Slavery discussed. (See Slavery.)

Stager, Anson, appointed military superintendent of telegraph lines, 3310.

States in which insurrection exists proclaimed, 3238, 3293, 3366.

Sunday, observance of, enjoined, 3326.

Taxes upon real estate in seceded States declared a lien on same, 3293.

Telegraph lines, military possession of, order regarding, 3309.

Termination of—
Mediation of other measures looking to, referred to, 3355.
Proclaimed, 3627.
In Tennessee, 3515.
In Texas, 3632.
Correction of date in, by proclamation, 3747.

Thanks tendered commanders and soldiers in. (See Thanks of Congress; Thanks of President.)

Thanksgiving order of President Lincoln, 3439.

Thanksgiving proclamation of President Lincoln, 3290, 3371, 3373, 3429.
Order regarding day appointed, 3245.
(See also fasting and prayer.)

Threatening aspect of. (See Secession discussed; Slavery discussed.)

Transportation to be furnished refugees and freedmen, order regarding, 3547.

Treason against United States, act to punish, 3286, 3294.

Troops sent through Mexican territory in 1861 referred to, 3574.

Union and Confederate flags, return of to respective States recommended, 5163.
Proposition withdrawn, 5164.

Vessels of United States destroyed by rebel vessels referred to, 3964.

Victories of Federal troops discussed, 3301, 3305, 3313, 3376, 3439, 3442, 3452, 3457, 3477.

Virginia—
Attitude of, in, discussed, 3224.
Persons in, attempting to exercise official powers of civil nature, order regarding, 3245.

Volunteer service—
Act to provide for additional medical officers of, vetoed, 3289.
Officers and men in, 3578.
Officers in, 3357.

Volunteers called for, and orders regarding, 3215, 3216, 3315, 3316, 3321, 3322, 3370, 3374, 3427, 3433, 3436, 3472.
Authority to call for additional volunteers recommended, 3227.
Board constituted to examine quotas of States, 3476.
Bounty and pay to, 3322, 3375, 3436, 3649.

Recommendations regarding, 3396.

Clause, three-hundred-dollar, repeal of, recommended, 3412.

Increase of, letter of President to governors regarding, 3315.

Proposition of governor of Missouri regarding, 3241.

Order of President regarding, 3243.

Proposition of governors of States regarding, and reply of President, 3241, 3316, 3437.

Reenlistment of veterans referred to, 3400.
Referred to, 3225.

Three-hundred-dollar clause, repeal of, recommended, 3412.

Weehawken-Fingal naval engagement referred to, 3392.

Wisconsin volunteers, thanks of President tendered, 3442.

Wool, John E. (See Wool, John E.)

Civil War Veterans:
Roosevelt praises, 6672, 7006.
Their privileges in civil service, 6703.

Claims:
Against citizens of insurgent States and means for collecting, discussed, 3251.
Arbitration of pecuniary, with republics of South and Central America, 7982.
Growing out of War between the States. (See Civil War; War Claims.)
Of aliens. (See Aliens.)
Of foreign powers against United States. (See the several powers.)
Of United States against foreign powers. (See the several powers.)
Referred to, 253.
Surplus remaining after payment of awards, discussed, 3173, 3247.
Private claim against United States. (See Private Claims.)

Claims, Court of. (See Courts.)

Clarksburg, W. Va., act making appropriation to continue construction of public building at, approved and recommendations regarding, 4991.

Classification Bill.—A bill passed during Van Buren's administration, at his request, which provided for the levy of 12,000 men for use by the Government during a period of two years.

Clayton Anti-Trust Law.—To supplement existing laws against monopolies and unlawful restraint of trade, the Clayton bill approved Oct. 15, 1914, defines "Commerce" as trade between the states or territories or with foreign countries, and "Persons" as corporations authorized under law. It forbids persons engaged in commerce to either directly or indirectly discriminate in price between different purchasers of commodities where the effect of such discrimination may be to substantially lessen competition or tend to create a monopoly in any line of commerce, making allowance for difference in cost of selling or transportation, or discrimination in price in the same or different communities made in good faith to meet competition. Persons selling goods may also select their own customers; agreements or understandings, as a condition of trade, that goods of a competitor are not to be handled are declared unlawful. Any person injured in his business by reason of the violation of the anti-trust laws may sue in a United States Court, and recover three fold the damage sustained by him, together with costs and attorney's fees. The final decree in any criminal prosecution under the anti-trust laws is made *prima facie* evidence against the same defendant in subsequent actions, except in consent judgments, and the statute of limitations is suspended.

The labor of a human being is declared not to be a commodity or article of commerce, and labor unions and agricultural associations instituted for mutual benefit having no capital stock and not conducted for profit, are exempt from the operations of all anti-trust laws, and such organizations and their members are not to be construed as illegal combinations or conspiracies in restraint of trade. No corporation may acquire stock in another corporation where the effect of such acquisition may be to lessen competition between the two or create a monopoly. Holding companies are forbidden except for investment purposes, and stock owned by holding companies is allowed neither vote nor proxy; subsidiary corporations may however be organized for carrying on legitimate branches or extensions of business when they will not substantially lessen competition. Railroad companies may build, own, and buy stock in branch lines or acquire control of other lines in extension of their own where the effect will not tend to lessen competition.

Two years after the passage of the act no person shall at the same time be a director or employee of more than one bank having an aggregate capital in excess of $5,000,000; no bank in a town of 200,000 inhabitants shall have as a director or employee any private banker or director or employee of any other bank situated in the same town: no person shall at the same time be a director in two or more corporations either one having a capital in excess of $1,000,000 engaged in commerce other than banking and transportation, if such corporations have theretofore been competitors. Embezzlement of the funds of a common carrier by an officer thereof is made a felony punishable by a fine of $500 and from one to ten years in prison. No common carrier shall deal in securities or supplies or make contracts in excess of $50,000 a year with another corporation when the said common carrier has among its directors or managers any person who is at the same time a director or officer of the firm with which such dealings are made, except when such firm or corporation is the lowest bidder for such supplies, etc., under penalty of a fine of $25,000 for the company and $5,000 for the person, with a year in jail added for the latter.

Authority to enforce compliance with this law is vested in the Interstate Commerce Commission, the Federal Reserve Board and the Federal Trade Commission, and action may be brought in any district where the defendant is known to transact business. Individual directors, officers or agents are held personally responsible for violations of the act and subject to a fine of $5,000 or a year in jail.

United States Courts may issue injunctions to restrain violations of this act upon evidence of danger of irreparable loss pending hearing; no injunction may be granted by a United States judge in a case between employer and employee or between persons employed and persons seeking employment growing out of disputes over terms of employment unless necessary to prevent injury to property or property rights; (and no such injunction shall prohibit persons, whether singly or in concert, from ceasing to perform work or from peacefully persuading others to do so, or from ceasing to patronize or employ any party to such dispute, or from advising others to do so, or from paying or withholding strike benefits, or from peacefully assembling or doing any act which might lawfully be done in the absence of such dispute, and none of these acts shall be considered violations of the United States laws. Disobedience to injunctions is made contempt of court, punishable by a fine of $1,000, payable to the person injured by the contempt.

Clayton-Bulwer Treaty.—John M. Clayton, Secretary of State, in 1850 concluded a treaty with Sir Henry Lytton Bulwer, representing Great Britain, for establishing communication between the Atlantic and Pacific oceans (2580). The treaty provided for a ship canal across Nicaragua and forbade exclusive control of canal communication by either party. It was succeeded by the Hay-Pauncefote Treaty, ratified by the Senate of the United States, Dec. 17, 1901, which made the way clear for the United States to construct, own and operate an isthmian canal. (See Great Britain, Treaties with, and facsimile, 7762.)

Clayton-Bulwer Treaty:

Correspondence respecting, referred to, 2583, 2897, 2908, 4758.

Differences regarding—

Discussed, 3039, 3092.

Final settlement of, 3170.

Proposition to refer, to arbitrament, 2895.

Treaty for settlement of, discussed, 2973.

Discussed, 2580, 2617, 2903, 2943, 3117, 4628.

Proposed modifications of, referred to, 4653, 4662, 4694.

Referred to, 4667, 4698, 4782, 6664, 6849.

Clearance Papers.—A paper certifying that the law has been complied with by a vessel leaving port.

Clearing House.—An institution set up by banking houses, railroad companies, or persons engaged in any department of trade or finance who have credit transactions with each other. In the course of a day's business each bank receives various amounts of commercial paper which must be debited to the acount of other banks, and is itself not unlikely the debtor to one or more other banks. Before the establishment of the clearing house it was customary to have these accounts adjusted every morning, or at least every week. To do this it was necessary for each bank to have a messenger visit every other bank with which it had dealings and pay or receive the difference between the debit and credit sides of the account. The collection and payment

EXTENT OF THE UNITED STATES DURING THE ADMINISTRATION OF PRESIDENT CLEVELAND, 1885-1889.

(NOT INCLUDING TERRITORIES)

MAINE 1820

VT. 1790

N. H. 1788

MASS. 1788

CONN. 1788

R.I. 1790

N. Y. 1787

N. J. 1787

(PA.)

(DEL.) 1787

NEW YORK 1788

PENNSYLVANIA 1787

MD. 1788

WEST VIRGINIA 1863

VIRGINIA 1788

NORTH CAROLINA 1789

SOUTH CAROLINA 1788

GEORGIA 1788

FLORIDA 1845

OHIO 1803

KENTUCKY 1792

TENNESSEE 1796

ALABAMA 1819

MICHIGAN 1837

INDIANA 1816

MISSISSIPPI 1817

ILLINOIS 1818

WISCONSIN 1848

MISSOURI 1821

ARKANSAS 1836

LOUISIANA 1812

MINNESOTA 1858

IOWA 1846

NEBRASKA 1867

KANSAS 1861

TEXAS 1845

COLORADO 1876

OREGON 1859

NEVADA 1864

CALIFORNIA 1850

FLAG OF 1889

of these balances became a laborious and dangerous part of the banking business. To do away with this cumbersome method of squaring accounts the clearing-house system was introduced. It was first established in London about the beginning of the nineteenth century. The banks of New York associated and began doing a clearing-house business Oct. 11, 1853. The New York Clearing House is the largest in the world. The member banks have a capital of $175,300,000, and the average daily clearances for 1914 were $296,238,762, and the clearings for the year were $89,-760,344,971.25. The number of banks in the Clearing House Association varies slightly, the present number being 62. All the accounts of each of these 62 banks with each other are adjusted in just one hour each day—between 10 and 11 A. M. The debtor banks are required to pay the amount of their indebtedness to the clearing house in legal-tender notes or coin by 1.30 P. M. each day, and the creditor banks immediately receive the amounts due them from other banks or certificates of credits for the amounts. Impending financial crises may be averted by all the banks which are members of the clearing house pooling their reserve funds and taking certificates therefor. The associated banks of New York in this way made it possible for the government to secure the necessary funds for carrying on the Civil War. The panic of 1873 was checked in a similar manner, as were also those of 1884, 1890, and 1893. In 1893 the Clearing House Association resolved that any member might present to the loan committee its bills receivable or other securities, together with its own obligation and receive therefor certificates for 75 yer cent. of their par value, which certificates would be accepted in lieu of cash in the payment of balances at the clearing house. Railway companies and the various produce and stock exchanges have introduced the clearing-house system into their business. Similar institutions have been established in most of the large cities of the country.

The clearing house principle has generally been adopted in stock and produce exchanges. A broker may buy or sell stock, and, through the simple clearing house method of adjustment, may drop out of the transaction entirely, except for collecting his commission or paying his loss. Thus if Broker A sell certain securities to Broker B, and Broker B then sell them to Broker C, who later sells them to Broker A, the transactions cancel, except for the difference in price agreed upon at each sale.

Clearing Houses recommended, 4199.

Clermont.—The name of the first steamship invented by Robert Fulton, plying between New York and Albany. (See illustration opposite 350.)

Cleveland, Grover.—1885-89, 1893-97.

(FIRST TERM, 1885-1889.)

Twenty-fifth Administration—Democratic.
Vice-President—Thomas A. Hendricks.

Secretary of State—
Thomas F. Bayard.

Secretary of the Treasury—
Daniel Manning.
Charles S. Fairchild.

Secretary of War—
William C. Endicott.

Attorney-General—
Augustus H. Garland.

Postmaster-General—
William F. Vilas.
Don M. Dickinson.

Secretary of the Navy—
William C. Whitney.

Secretary of the Interior—
Lucius Q. C. Lamar.
William F. Vilas.

Secretary of Agriculture—
Norman J. Coleman.

Cleveland was elected by the Democratic party in 1884 and in 1892. The convention which met at Chicago, July 8-11, 1884, nominated him on the second ballot, despite the bitter opposition of Tammany.

Platform.—The platform of 1884 recited the fundamental principles of Democracy; charged the Republican party with fraud, jobbery, and recklessness, from long possession of power; pledged Democracy to a complete reform, rigid economy, reduction of taxation, and a lower tariff for revenue only; devoted internal revenues to pensions and war expenditures only; favored an American continental policy; believed in honest money of gold, silver, and easily convertible currency; asserted equal justice for all; urged the choosing of Federal officers in Territories from citizens who have been previous residents; favored civil service reform, free education, prevention of monopoly, unrestricted labor, retention of public lands for settlers, pledged government protection to all citizens at home and abroad; opposed Chinese immigration; advocated a measure of internal improvements; upheld Democracy's efforts for commerce and merchant marine; and paid a tribute to Samuel J. Tilden.

Opposition.—The Republican National Convention at Chicago, June 3-6, 1884, nominated James G. Blaine over President Arthur, on the fourth ballot. The Greenback National Convention at Indianapolis, May 28, 1884, nominated Benjamin F. Butler. The Prohibition Convention at Pittsburgh, July 23, 1884, nominated John P. St. John; another branch of the Prohibitionists, under the name of the American Prohibition Convention, met at Chicago, June 19, 1884, and nominated Samuel C. Pomeroy. The Equal Rights party in convention at San Francisco, Sept. 20, 1884, nominated Belva A. Lockwood.

Vote.—The popular vote of thirty-eight States gave Cleveland 4,874,986; Blaine, 4,851,981; Butler, 175,370; and St. John, 150,369. The electoral vote, counted on Feb. 11, 1885, gave Cleveland 219, and Blaine 182.

Party Affiliation.—Cleveland's political career dated from his election as the Democratic mayor of Buffalo, where (1881) he curbed extravagance and violation of the Constitution and charter to such an extent that he became known as the "veto mayor." As governor of New York, his State administration was a continuation of his course as mayor of Buffalo, and it was the conspicuous evidence of his ability, integrity, and consistency, that made him so strong a candidate for the Presidency.

Political Complexion of Congress.—During President Cleveland's first administration, Congress was divided politically as follows: In the Forty-ninth Congress (1885-1887) the Senate, of seventy-six members, was composed of thirty-four Democrats, forty-one Republicans, with one vacancy; and the House, of 325 members, was made up of 182 Democrats, 110 Republicans, two Nationals, with one vacancy. In the Fiftieth Congress (1887-1889) the Senate, of seventy-six members, was composed of thirty-seven Democrats and thirty-nine Republicans; and the House, of 325 members, was made up of 170 Democrats and 151 Republicans.

(SECOND TERM, 1893-1897.)
Twenty-seventh Administration—Democratic.

Vice-President—Adlai E. Stevenson.
Secretary of State—
Walter Q. Gresham.
Richard Olney.
Secretary of the Treasury—
John G. Carlisle.
Secretary of War—
Daniel S. Lamont.
Attorney-General—
Richard Olney.
Judson Harmon.
Postmaster-General—
Wilson S. Bissell.
William L. Wilson.
Secretary of the Navy—
Hilary A. Herbert.
Secretary of the Interior—
Hoke Smith.
David R. Francis.
Secretary of Agriculture—
J. Sterling Morton.

SECOND TERM—Nomination.—Cleveland was a second time elected President of the United States by the Democratic party at the election held in November, 1892. At the Democratic National Convention held at Chicago, June 22, 1892, he was nominated on the first ballot, though he was bitterly opposed by the entire delegation from his own State.

Platform.—The platform of the Democratic party in 1892 denounced the Republican party and its administration; made the tariff the most important issue of the election by a section amended in open convention in which the McKinley Tariff was condemned as class legislation; exposed sham reciprocity; demanded control of the trusts; repeated the public lands policy of former years; reaffirmed civil service reform; favored restriction of Chinese immigration; supported internal improvements; favored the construction of the Nicaragua Canal; endorsed the World's Columbian Exposition, free education, the plan to admit as States, Arizona and New Mexico; condemned the sweating system and convict labor.

Opposition.—The Republican National Convention at Minneapolis, June 7, 1892, nominated Benjamin Harrison, on a platform of protection, reciprocity, free coinage of gold and silver, freedom of the ballot, extension of foreign commerce, freedom of speech, opposition to trusts, free postal delivery, civil service reform, building of Nicaragua Canal, admission of Territories to Statehood, reclamation of arid lands, sympathy with temperance, pledges to veterans, and commendation of Harrison's administration. The Prohibition convention at Cincinnati, in June, 1892, nominated John Bidwell. The National People's Convention at Omaha, in July, 1892, nominated James B. Weaver. The Socialist Labor Convention, at New York, nominated Simon Wing.

Vote.—The popular vote ran: Cleveland, 5,556,543; Harrison, 5,175,582; Weaver, 1,040,886; Bidwell, 255,841; and Wing, 21,164. The electoral vote gave Cleveland 277; Harrison, 145, and Weaver, 22.

Public Debt.—The public debt of the United States during the two administrations of President Cleveland stood as follows: July 1, 1885, $1,375,352.443.91; 1886, $1,282.145,840.44; 1887, $1,175,168,-675.42; 1888, $1,063,004,894.73.
Second Administration: July 1, 1893, $838,969,475.75; 1894, $899,313,380.55; 1895, $901,672,966.74; 1896, $955,297,-253.70.

Tariff.—In his First Annual Message (page 4926) President Cleveland said: "The proposition with which we have to deal is the reduction of the revenue received by the Government. and indirectly paid by the people, from customs duties. The question of free trade is not involved, nor is there now any occasion for the general discussion of the wisdom or expediency of a protective system. These sentiments are expressed and emphasized in his Second Annual Message (page 5095), and in his Third Annual Message (page 5169) the subject is again urged. In his Fourth Annual Message (page 5359) the President paints a picture of the result of economic conditions as he sees them produced by the inequalities of the tariff laws.

In the elections of 1890, Mr. Cleveland championed the cause of tariff reform and made it the issue of the elections. When he accepted the Presidential nomination in 1892, he wrote in his letter of acceptance: "Tariff reform is still our purpose. Though we oppose the theory that tariff laws may be passed having for their object the granting of discriminating and unfair governmental aid to private ventures, we wage no exterminating war against any American interests. We believe a readjustment can be accomplished, in accordance with the principles we profess, without disaster or demolition. We believe that the advantages of freer raw material should be accorded to our manufacturers, and we contemplate a fair and careful distribution of necessary tariff burdens, rather than the precipitation of free trade." In the First Annual Message of his second administration (page 5890) the President said: "While we should stanchly adhere to the principle that only the necessity of revenue justifies the imposition of tariff duties and other Federal taxation and that they should be limited by strict economy, we can not close our eyes to the fact that conditions have grown up among us which in justice and fairness call for discriminating care in the distribution of such duties and taxation as the emergencies of our Government actually demand."

Foreign Policy.—In his First Annual Message (page 4922) President Cleveland recommended increased appropriations for the consular and diplomatic service. At the beginning of his second administration, the President was obliged to confront the grave situation arising out of the proposed annexation of Hawaii to the United States. The queen and her ministers asserted that at the time she yielded to the provisional government she yielded to the force and power of the United States. The President made the matter the subject of a special message to Congress (page 5892) in which he states that "a candid and thorough examination of the facts will force the conviction that the provisional government owes its existence to an armed invasion by the United States," and that the overthrowing of the government was brought about "by a process, every step of which, it may safely be asserted, is directly traceable to and dependent for its success upon the agency of the United States acting through its diplomatic and naval representatives." He declined to submit the treaty of annexation again to the Senate and advised our minister to inform the queen and her advisers of his desire to reestablish in the islands the status which existed before the armed interference of the United States. The Senate, however, recognized the new republic in 1894, and the matter passed beyond the jurisdiction of the President. In 1895, upon the outbreak of the insurrection in Cuba, the President took immediate steps to secure the neutrality of the United States. Though resolutions favoring the recognition of the insurgents as

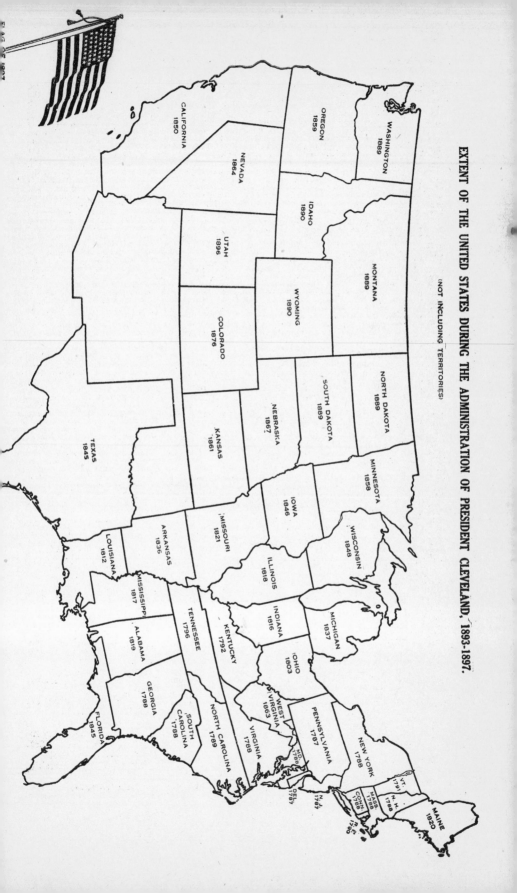

belligerents passed Congress, the President disregarded them, and Secretary Olney made public statement of the fact that they were regarded by the administration only as "an expression of opinion on the part of a number of eminent gentlemen." A second proclamation of neutrality was issued in July, 1896 (page 6126), following the appointment of General Fitzhugh Lee as minister to Cuba. The entire subject required delicate handling of relations with Spain during the rest of the life of the administration. The most notable act of foreign policy during the administration was the Venezuela Message (page 6087) in which the President informed Congress that Great Britain had refused to submit the question of boundary between Venezuela and British Guiana to arbitration; that a commission should be appointed by Congress to examine into the matter of boundary; that appropriations should be made at once for this work; that the Commission should report at once. Then the message reads: "When such report is made and accepted it will, in my opinion, be the duty of the United States to resist by every means in its power, as a wilful aggression upon its rights and interests, the appropriation by Great Britain of any lands or the exercise of governmental jurisdiction over any territory which, after investigation, we have determined of right to belong to Venezuela." The signing of the arbitration treaty at Washington was regarded as the first formal acquiescence by a European power of the principles of the Monroe Doctrine and the accompanying virtual protection of the smaller republics of the New World by the United States.

Finance.—In his First Annual Message (page 4927) the President discussed the Bland-Allison act and said: "The desire to utilize the silver product of the country should not lead to a misuse or the perversion of this power. The necessity for such an addition to the nation as is compelled by the silver-coinage act is negatived by the fact that up to the present time only about 50,000,000 of the silver dollars so coined have actually found their way into circulation, leaving more than 165,000,000 in the possession of the Government, the custody of which has entailed a considerable expense for the construction of vaults for its deposit. Every month two millions of gold dollars in the public Treasury are paid out for two millions or more of silver dollars, to be added to the idle mass already accumulated." He adds that this will lead to the hoarding of gold, and says: "This hoarding of gold has already begun." He recommends the suspension of compulsory coinage. In his Second Annual Message (page 5097) he reports the failure to distribute silver dollars among the people, and again urges the suspension of coinage. In his special message in 1893, the President discusses the working of the Sherman act and reports (page 5834) disappointment in its effects. He said: "Undoubtedly the monthly purchases by the Government of 4,500,000 ounces of silver, enforced under that statute, were regarded by those interested in silver as a certain guaranty of its increase in price. The result, however, has been entirely different, for, immediately following a spasmodic and slight rise, the price of silver began to fall after the passage of the act, and has since reached the lowest point ever known." In his Third Annual Message of his second administration (page 6072), the President gives a résumé of the legislation relating to silver coinage and the attendant train of financial troubles.

Civil Service Reform.—In his First Annual Message (page 4948) President Cleve-

land said: "Civil Service reform enforced by law came none too soon to check the progress of demoralization. One of its effects, not enough regarded, is the freedom it brings to the political action of those conservative and sober men who, in fear of the confusion and risk attending an arbitrary and sudden change in all the public offices with a change of party rule, cast their ballots against such a change." "The civil service law does not prevent the discharge of the indolent or incompetent clerk, and it does prevent supplying his place with the unfit party worker." In his Second Annual Message (page 5113) he says that while the reform may be incomplete and its applications imperfect, "if the people of this country ever submit to the banishment of its underlying principle from the operation of their Government they will abandon the surest guaranty of the safety and the success of American institutions." Statistics regarding the efficacy of the rules laid down by the Commission are given in a special message to Congress on page 5201. Suggested amendments and additional rules were made the subject of a special message (page 5347 *et seq.*). In the First Annual Message of his second administration (page 5888), in speaking of the working of the reform, the President said: "The law embodying this reform found its way to our statute books more from fear of the popular sentiment existing in its favor than from any love for the reform itself on the part of legislators, and it has lived and grown and flourished in spite of the covert as well as open hostility of spoilsmen and notwithstanding the querulous impracticability of many self-constituted guardians." The several Executive Orders relating to amendments of the civil service appear on page 6030. His last official word regarding the success of the reform appears in his Fourth Annual Message of his second administration (page 6170) where the President says: "The progress made in civil service reform furnishes a cause for the utmost congratulation. It has survived the doubts of its friends as well as the rancor of its enemies, and has gained a permanent place among the agencies destined to cleanse our politics and to improve, economize, and elevate the public service."

At the beginning of President Cleveland's administration, he came into serious conflict with many influential men of his own party, who sought the immediate removal of Republican office-holders to make way for Democrats, that the party organization might be thereby strengthened. It was at this time that the expression "offensive partisanship" came into use, though the expression is correctly "obtrusive partisanship" as it appears in his Executvie Order upon the subject (page 5079). His special message (page 4960) refusing on constitutional grounds to accede to the Senate's request for papers regarding appointments and dismissals brought about a struggle with Congress and its refusal to sanction his nominations.

Cleveland, Grover:

Advancement and progress of United States discussed by, 5358.

Annual messages of, 4909, 5082, 5135, 5358, 5866, 5955, 6058, 6146.

Arbitrator—

    In boundary dispute between Argentine Republic and Brazil, 5867.

    Award of, discussed by, 6058.

    Of claim of Italy against Colombia, 6328.

Biographical sketch of, 4882.

Bland-Allison Act discussed by, 4927, 5097, 5373.

British minister's interference in political affairs of United States and action of, respecting, 5365, 5396.

Civil Service discussed by, 4948, 4974, 5112, 5201, 5348, 5399, 5429, 5882, 5889, 5972, 5974, 5982, 6171. (See also Civil Service.)

Congress requested by, not to take recess until enactment of financial legislation, 6092.

Correspondence requested by Senate respecting relations with Spain refused by, 6101.

Cuban insurrection and policy of United States regarding, discussed by, 6068, 6148.
Referred to by President McKinley, 6291.

Currency legislation plan of, indorsed by, 5985.
Discussed by, 5993, 5999, 6072, 6091, 6175.

Death of, announced by Roosevelt, 6961.

Discretionary power of President over nominations, removals, and other acts discussed by, 4960.

Finances discussed by, 4924, 5092, 5097, 5165, 5371, 5833, 5875, 5964, 5985, 5993, 5999, 6072, 6091, 6155, 6175.

Foreign policy discussed by, 4912, 5867, 5871, 5873, 5892, 5955, 5963, 6064, 6068, 6087, 6148.

Inaugural address of—
First, 4884.
Second, 5821.

Inauguration of, see illustration opposite 5039.

Legation asylum discussed by, 5867.

Monroe doctrine reasserted by, 6064, 6087.

Photograph of, last, opposite 7204.

Pocket vetoes of, 5070, 5071, 5072, 5073, 6193.

Portrait of, 4881.

Powers of Federal and State Governments discussed by, 4960, 4992, 4996, 5142, 5363, 5412, 5422, 5924, 6010, 6109.

Proclamations of—
Admission of Utah, 6120, and illustration opposite ——.
Canadian vessels permitted to aid disabled vessels in American waters, 5828.
Chicago riots, 5931.
Copyright privilege to—
Chile, 6125.
Denmark, 5827.
Mexico, 6022.
Portugal, 5830.
Spain, 6024.

Death of—
Grant, 4893.
Gresham, 6022.

Discriminating duties suspended on vessels from—
Cuba and Puerto Rico, 5075, 5155.
Philippine Islands, 5155.

Duties suspended on vessels from—
Boca del Toro, Colombia, 4895.
Cuba and Puerto Rico, suspension of, revoked, 5074.
Germany, 5326.
Revoked, 6129.
Grenada, 5930.
Guadeloupe, 5327.
Netherlands, 5154.
Trinidad, 4889.

Extraordinary session of—
Congress, 5828.
Senate, 5428, 6230.

Importation of cattle, prohibition on, suspended, 6025.

Lands—
Granted Chicago, Milwaukee and St. Paul Railway forfeited, 5944.
In Greer County boundary dispute not to be sold, 5325.
Opened to settlement, 5838, 6016, 6018, 6020, 6026.
Set apart as public reservation, 5859, 5864, 6122, 6205, 6207, 6209, 6211, 6213, 6215, 6216, 6218, 6219, 6221, 6222, 6225, 6227.

Modifying order reserving lands in Alaska, 6128.

Neutrality in insurrection in Cuba, 6023, 6126.

Order restoring Sioux lands to public domain declared void, 4890.

Pardons to polygamists, 5942.

Preventing extermination of seals in Bering Sea, 5826, 5926, 6015, 6123.

Thanksgiving, 4895, 5076, 5156, 5328, 5865, 5943, 6025, 6127.

Unauthorized occupancy of—
Indian reservations, 4892.
Lands in Indian Territory, 4888.

Unlawful combinations in—
Washington Territory, 4896, 5073.
Western States, 5932.

Unlawful inclosures of public lands, 4893.

Removals from office, transmission of papers regarding, refused by, 4960.

Right of asylum discussed by, 5961.

Sherman Act, repeal of purchasing clause of, 5875, 6073, 6074.
Recommended by, 5833.

Special session message of, 5833.

State of the Union discussed by, 4909, 5358, 6146.

Tariff discussed by, 4926, 5093, 5169, 5359, 5890, 5984, 6173.

Thanksgiving proclamations of, 4895, 5076, 5156, 5328, 5865, 5943, 6025, 6127.

Union and Confederate flags, return of, to respective States recommended by, 5163.

Proposition withdrawn, 5164.

Veto of bill, authorizing Arkansas N. W. Ry. Co. to construct railway through Indian Territory, 6012.

Washington's inauguration, celebration of centennial of, 5371.

Wedding of, see illustration opposite 5407.

Closed Shop.—A term used to describe conditions of employment in establishments where only members of trade unions (q. v.) are or may be employed, usually by agreement between the employers and the trade unions, as distinguished from the open shop (q. v.).

Closure.—The practice of shutting off debate on a subject in a deliberative body, usually by applying the "previous question," for which a two-thirds vote is necessary. (See Senatorial Courtesy.)

Clothing Trade.—It is only within recent times that the manufacture of ready-made clothing came to be looked upon as an industry inviting the investment of capital and the energies of trained business men. Prior to 1830 the business seems to have been limited to shipping supply merchants, who kept a small stock of garments adapted to the use of sailors, who found no time between arrival at and departure from ports to have clothes made to their measure, as was the custom among the landsmen. The chief shipping ports, therefore, became the early centers of the ready-made clothing trade. New Bedford, Mass., the home port of the whaling industry, was the early nucleus of the trade. It then spread to Boston and New York. Migration to the West, and especially the hurried departure of gold-seekers for California in 1849, gave an impetus to the business, and factories and stores carrying made-up stocks began to succeed custom tailor shops.

One of the first to engage in the wholesale manufacture of clothing was George Opdyke, once mayor of New York, who began business in 1831. He and his successors opened stores in New Orleans, Memphis and Charleston, which were carried on until the close of the civil war. They supplied mostly the coarser grades of clothing. John T. Martin conducted a prosperous business in St. Louis before the civil war, out of which grew the present firm of Rogers, Peet & Co., of New York. Thomas Chatterton, a merchant of New Haven, began to manufacture ready-made clothing in 1846, and opened a store in New York. In 1848 John H. Browning, of New York, established a branch store in California, and soon began shipping large quantities of the coarser grades of men's clothing to the miners in the gold fields. The business which he founded at that time is still in existence. At the outbreak of the civil war Browning obtained a contract to furnish more than a million dollars' worth of clothing for the Union army.

The invention of the sewing machine concentrated within factory walls much of the work that had previously been done in the homes of work people, and the cutting machine, with a capacity for twenty-four thicknesses of cloth, further cheapened the work. The following figures show the saving of time in the making of 100 suits of clothes under the factory system:

By the use of the sponging machine the cloth for 100 coats is prepared by two persons in 1 hour and 48 minutes, as against 11 hours and 40 minutes by hand; for 100 pairs of trousers the time is 1 hour and 8 minutes, as against 8 hours and 20 minutes by hand; for 100 vests the time is 20 minutes, against 3 hours and 20 minutes. By use of a machine cutting 16 thicknesses of cloth, three persons now consume 4 hours and 32 minutes in cutting out 100 coats, against 33 hours and 20 minutes when cut by hand; for the trousers the machine time is now 2 hours and 58 minutes, against 16 hours and 40 minutes by hand; and for the vests 1 hour and 34 minutes, against 11 hours and 40 minutes. The sewing of the seams shows, of course, the greatest saving. While it took 1,000 hours to sew the coats by hand, it takes only 66 hours and 40 minutes on the power driven sewing machine; for the trousers the hand time was 433 hours and 20 minutes; by machine, 64 hours and 17 minutes. For sewing the vests the hand time was 416 hours and 40 minutes and by machine 64 hours and 35 minutes. Other operations have been correspondingly cheapened.

A peculiar feature of the men's clothing business is that about three-fifths of the establishments make clothing by contract from materials furnished by others. Though the sweat-shop has been partially eliminated many of the factories are small. The total number reported by the last census was 4,830, and of these 3,217 were contract shops. The number of wage-earners was 173,747, of whom 57,651 were employed in the contract shops and 126,196 in the regular factories. In the matter of wages the contract shops paid $33,283,969, and the regular factories paid $56,360,952. The total value of the product was $458,210,985, of which $228,154,926 was added by manufacture. Of this latter sum the contract shops contributed $42,985,415, and the regular factories $190,169,511. These figures do not include shirts and furnishing goods.

Women's Clothing.—The manufacture of women's clothing as a commercial industry did not start until the early sixties. At that time only cloaks and mantillas were made for the trade. Until 1880 the traffic in women's ready-made clothing was confined almost entirely to cloaks. About this time the ladies' suits branch was established. During the last decade all the different articles which are comprised in the collective term lingerie have been put on the market ready made.

The development of the factory has been on lines similar to those of the men's clothing establishments. A greater degree of skill is required of the workers in this branch of the business, and women have almost entirely displaced men.

The last census reported 4,558 factories and shops, employing 153,743 wage-earners, turning out a finished product valued at $384,751,649, of which amount $175,963,423 was added by manufacture. This shows the remarkable increase from 1860 when there were only 188 shops employing 5,739 workers.

Cloture. (See Closure.)

Coal Fields of Alaska, 7720.

Coal Lands.—The United States leads the world, both in the production of coal and the extent of its coal fields. The area of known deposits is nearly 280,000 square miles. The average annual yield for five years ending with 1908 was about 425,-000,000 tons. This is worth about $1.50 per ton at the mines.

The coal fields are grouped for convenience into the following divisions: The Appalachian, extending from near the New York and Pennsylvania State line southwesterly through the western half of Pennsylvania and eastern Ohio, western Maryland, southwest Virginia, all of West Virginia, eastern Kentucky and Tennessee into north central Alabama, and covering about 70,800 square miles. The eastern interior fields cover western Indiana, nearly the whole State of Illinois, and part of Kentucky, and are about 58,000 square miles in extent. The northern interior field covers a large area in the southern peninsula of Michigan, and is about 11,300 square miles in extent. The west central field extends from western Iowa across western Missouri, northwestern Arkansas and eastern Nebraska and Kansas, and through Oklahoma into Texas, and has an area of about 94,000 square miles. The Rocky Mountain field includes the numerous disconnected areas lying in narrow belts along either flank of the range from the Canadian frontier southward for a thousand miles. These occur in Montana, Utah, Wyoming, Colorado and New Mexico, and have a total area of some 43,600 square miles. The Pacific coast coal fields occur in California, Oregon and Washington. Those of Washington are of the most importance, supplying fuel for railroads and steamships, as well as the market of San Francisco.

Owing to the discovery of collusion on the part of the Union Pacific Railroad and subsidiary companies in the acquisition of coal lands, President Roosevelt, through the Interior Department, in December, 1906, withdrew from settlement 64,000,000 acres of mineral lands in North and South Dakota, Montana, Wyoming, Colorado, New Mexico, Utah, Washington and Oregon. Of this land 28,000,000 acres were later opened to entry. In December the President sent a special message to Congress urging the repeal or revision of the timber, stone and desert land acts and the commutation clause of the Homestead act. Then, in February, 1907, President Roosevelt sent a second special message to Congress urging legislation for the preservation of the coal, oil, lumber and grazing lands (page 7418). He especially urged that the Government be authorized to retain title to the coal lands with a system of leasing for mining purposes. He pointed out that some such system has been adopted in every coal mining country of Europe except Great Britain. Among the advantages he pointed out, were the preservation of fuels especially suited to certain industries, increased opportunities for coal miners without capital, the protection of the public against unreasonable and discriminating charges for fuel, the prevention of wholesale land frauds, and the ruthless exploitation of the Nation's resources (page 7418).

Coal Lands:

Withdrawal of, from entry or settlement and government ownership of, recommended, 7038.

Removal of duty on anthracite, recommended, 6714.

Coaling Stations. (See Naval Stations.)

Coalition.—A working understanding effected by opposition parties or factions for the purpose of effecting legislation or accomplishing other purposes mutually desired.

Coal-Tar Products.—Popular interest in coal tar is centered mainly in dyestuffs and the other refined drugs and chemicals derived from it. The United States for commercial reasons has developed little manufacture of these products, and has been dependent upon European nations for the bulk of her supply.

In considering why this condition exists there must be borne in mind the fact that only about 10 per cent of coal tar can be made into drugs and dyes. The other 90 per cent, suited only for the manufacture of pitches and various heavy oils, forms the basis of an industry already well developed in the United States. Coal tar, however, is not the only source of what are commonly known as "coal-tar" dyes and drugs. So-called "gas benzol," or light oil, which is abstracted from coal gas, and is therefore, like tar, a by-product of the carbonization of coal, constitutes an important commercial source of these refined products. "Gas benzol," unlike tar, has no constituents that cannot be utilized in making dyes and refined chemical preparations.

About 25 per cent of the combined yield of tar and "benzol" may be made into the dyes, drugs, and refined chemicals for which America has heretofore practically depended on Germany. The gross market value of these refined products made from the 25 per cent portion is probably at least twice that of the pitch and heavy oils recoverable from the 75 per cent portion.

The United States has the raw material, namely, high-grade coal, in great abundance and of a kind well suited for making all the tar products consumed in the country. In the calendar year 1913 the United States produced about 150,000,000 gallons of coal tar and 7,500,000 gallons of "gas benzol," less than 500,000 gallons of tar being imported. The output of bituminous coal, the source of coal tar, was somewhat more than 475,000,000 tons. Germany, with a coal output of only 295,000,000 tons in the same year, produced more than 250,000,000 gallons of coal tar and about 50,000,000 gallons of benzol, 3,500,000 gallons of tar being imported. Evidently, in the utilization of coal to make tar and "benzol," the United States is far behind Germany. Also, in the utilization of tar and "benzol" to make the most refined and valuable products, the United States lags behind. Germany exported in the fiscal year ending June 30, 1913, coal-tar dyestuffs worth over $55,000,000, whereas the United States in the same year imported dyestuffs worth $10,000,000—practically the entire consumption. Two raw materials are the sources of the so-called "coal-tar products," namely, crude coal tar itself, and light oil or "benzol" stripped from coal gas. The tar and "benzol" produced from American coal need not be in any way inferior to those produced in Europe. This country produces, however, less than one-third of the quantity of tar and about 7 per cent of the quantity of "benzol." In addition to the coal remaining in the great fields of coking coal in western Pennsylvania, which produces over 60 per cent of the coke made in the United States, this country has an entirely adequate source of tar, "benzol," and other by-products in the coking coals of other districts. Coal fields in West Virginia, Virginia, and eastern Kentucky which now supply many by-product coke ovens and gas works may be drawn on for much more coking coal than they now produce.

Oil and water-gas tars formed from the petroleum used in the manufacture of gas were produced in the United States in 1912 to the amount of 33,930,000 gallons. Coal tar is separated by distillation into a number of fractions, each of which serves as the base for the manufacture of certain refined chemical products.

Creosote Oil.—Between 90,000,000 and 100,000,000 gallons of creosote oil, valued at nearly $6,000,000, were consumed in the United States in the year 1913 for the impregnation and preservation of wood. Probably half of this consumption was for the treatment of railroad ties, and most of the remainder for paving blocks, piling, and structural timber. Two-thirds of the entire consumption was imported. Coal tar yields 15 to 30 per cent of creosote oil, according to the kind of tar, grade of oil, and the softness desired in the residual pitch.

Aniline Dyes are made chiefly from benzene, toluene, and phenol. "Aniline oil," the crude intermediate product made by reduction of nitrobenzene, was imported into the United States in 1913 to the amount of 2,000,000 pounds, and aniline salts, also an intermediate product, to the amount of nearly 5,000,000 pounds. The aniline dyes manufactured in this country are made almost entirely from imported intermediate products. The quantity of aniline dyes consumed in this country annually would probably not require over 3,000,000 gallons of "benzol."

Naphthalene is the source of a large number of dyes produced through various intermediate products. The eosin dyes are derived from resorcin, a benzene product, and phthalic acid, a naphthalene product. Artificial indigo, made from naphthalene, was imported into the United States in 1913 to the amount of nearly 8,000,000 pounds, valued at $1,150,000. Naphthalene enough for making the dyes of this class used in America could be obtained from the domestic production of coal tar. Average tar carries between 5 per cent and 10 per cent of naphthalene.

Alizarin Dyes are made from anthracene. An adequate supply of anthracene for these dyes is at hand in American coal tar. Between 1 per cent and 2 per cent crude anthracene is contained in coal tar, and the amount of pure anthracene in the tar produced in the United States in 1913 was probably at least 8,000,000 pounds. In the same year the imports of alizarin dyes were more than 8,000,000 pounds, valued at $1,825,000.

Pure Phenol (or carbolic acid) occurs in the light and middle oils or in the special "carbolic-oil" fraction of coal tar. Between 0.3 and 1.0 per cent of the average crude tar is phenol. It may be manufactured synthetically also from benzene through benzene-sulphonic acid. About 8,300,000 pounds of carbolic acid were imported into the United States in 1913. Phenol is used not only as a drug and antiseptic, but also to a considerable extent in the manufacture of picric acid for explosives and of certain dyestuffs. Another use of growing importance is the manufacture of hard, infusible, amorphous substances resembling celluloid.

Benzoic and Salicylic Acids, the photographic developers, "metol," "rhodol," or "elon," hydroquinone, etc., many drugs, such as acetanilide, phenacetin, saccharin, antipyrine, acetyl salicylic acid (aspirin), and a great variety of other refined chemical products used in comparatively small quantities, are derived from coal tar, chiefly from the light-oil or carbolic-oil fraction. A large part of the amount consumed in the United States has been imported.

Explosives.—The coal-tar products of greatest importance as raw materials in the explosives industry of the United States are benzene, toluene, naphthalene, and phenol (carbolic acid). As explosives the nitrosubstitution products of coal-tar derivatives are used as bursting charges for explosive projectiles, torpedoes, and mines, and also for detonators and primers. The most commonly known blasting explosives used in this country, black blasting powder and "straight" nitroglycerin dynamite, contain no coal-tar derivatives.

The nitrotoluenes are more extensively used in the explosives industry than any other nitrosubstitution compounds. Pure crystalline trinitrotoluene has proved one of the most efficient explosives for use in explosive shells, torpedoes, and mines, and is extensively used by almost every important military service, including that of this country. In recent years it has also come into use as a substitute for a large proportion of the mercury fulminate in detonators (blasting caps) and as a charge for detonating fuse. The nitronaphthalenes are used to some extent, chiefly as sensitizers in the "short-flame" permissible explosives of the ammonium-nitrate type.

Picric Acid and certain of the picrates are highly important as military shell explosives; the acid is also employed in surgical dressings for burns and wounds.

The manufacture of these compounds depends entirely on phenol (carbolic acid) as a raw material.

The possibilities of the use of the nitro-derivatives of coal-tar products in explosives are far greater than is indicated by the above brief summary. Much investigative work on such compounds is being carried on in this country as well as abroad, from which important developments in the explosives art may result. The Bureau of Mines has instituted a systematic research into the preparations and properties of these nitrosubstitution compounds with a view to studying their possibilities in the explosives industry.

Coast and Geodetic Survey.—The Coast and Geodetic Survey of the Department of Commerce is charged with the survey of the coasts of the United States and coasts under the jurisdiction thereof, and the publication of charts covering said coasts. This includes base measure, triangulation, topography and hydrography along said coasts; the survey of rivers to the head of tide water or ship navigation, deep-sea soundings, temperature and current observations along said coasts and throughout the Gulf and Japan streams, magnetic observations and researches and the publication of maps showing the variations of terrestrial magnetism; gravity research, determination of heights, the determination of geographic positions by astronomic observations for latitude, longitude and azimuth, and by triangulation to furnish reference points for state surveys and to co-ordinate governmental surveys.

The results obtained are published in annual reports and in special publications; charts upon various scales, including sailing charts, general charts of the coast and harbor charts; tide tables issued annually in advance; coast pilots with sailing directions covering the navigable waters; notices to mariners issued weekly as a joint publication of the Coast and Geodetic Survey and the Bureau of Lighthouses and containing current information necessary for safe navigation; catalogues of charts and publications, and such other publications as may be required to carry out the organic law governing the survey.

Coast and Geodetic Survey, act respecting printing of report of, in quarto form, returned, 6100.

Coast Artillery.—The Coast Artillery of the United States Army was first organized into a separate division of the Army administration by the Army Re-organization Act of February 2, 1901. At that time, the Coast Artillery consisted of 126 batteries ; in 1916, its complement was 748 officers and 19,019 men. The coast artillery is defined as "the artillery charged with the care and use of the fixed and movable elements of land and coast fortifications, including the submarine mine and torpedo defenses." It constitutes a corps, and provision is made that it shall consist of a chief, 14 colonels, 42 majors, 210 captains, 210 first lieutenants, 210 second lieutenants and subordinate officers in proportion. Each company is commanded by one captain, under whom are one first lieutenant, one second lieutenant, one first sergeant, one quartermaster, and other minor officers, the number of which is fixed by the President. (See War Department and Army.)

Coast Cities, protection for. (See Defenses, Public, provision for.)

Coast Defenses. (See Defenses, Public.)

Coast Guard.—By the act approved Jan. 28, 1915, introduced by Senator Townsend of Michigan the Revenue Cutter Service and the Life Saving Service were combined in a single new body to be known as the Coast Guard. It provides that in times of peace the new arm of the military service shall operate under the Treasury Department, and during war be subject to the Secretary of the Navy. The officers of the Coast Guard were taken from the Revenue Cutter Service and the same ranks and titles were established in the new arm, and the officers and men of the Life Saving Service were transferred to the Coast Guard with their same rank and pay. The administration of the Coast Guard was placed in the hands of two chiefs of division at a salary of $3,000 a year. The laws and regulations governing the discontinued bodies were extended to apply to the Coast Guard. The general superintendent of the Life Saving Service is retired on a pension of 75 per cent. of salary and the office is abolished.

Coast Survey:

Discussed, 636, 680, 1477, 4932, 8019.

Expenses of, 599, 2521.

Light-houses on Pacific coast, sites for, referred to, 2557.

Near completion of, 630, 677.

Transfer of, to Navy Department recommended, 4727.

Vessels employed in prosecuting, 1835, 2537, 4103.

Coasts of United States, survey of, referred to, 4932, 8019.

Cobden Club.—An organization of leading English free traders, formed in 1866 in honor of Richard Cobden. It had for its object the promulgation of those principles with which Mr. Cobden's name as an ardent free trader was so intimately associated. It established headquarters in London and published many tracts, pamphlets and books upon the subject of free trade for free distribution in America, England and her colonies. The Cobden Club held its first dinner in London July 21, 1866, with W. E. Gladstone in the chair. June 27, 1868, a statue of Cobden was unveiled at Camden Town. In July, 1880, 12 out of 14 cabinet ministers were members. It has for honorary members several American economists and statesmen. Recently the Cobden Club has acquired a distinct political character, having become identified with the fortunes of the Liberal and Free-Trade Parties.

Code.—1. A key by which a secret message may be deciphered only by the person familiar with or having access to the code. 2. A systematized set of rules : as the military code for the governing of the Army ; the naval code for the governing of the Navy.

Code of 1650. (See Ludlow's Code.)

Codes. (See Criminal Code; Naval Code.)

Cœur d'Alêne, Idaho, military reservation granted to city, 6953.

Cœur d'Alênes. (See Indian Tribes.)

Coffee:

Consular reports on production of and trade in, among Central and South American states referred to, 5201.

Duties on—

Recommended by President—

Grant, 4303.

Hayes, 4422, 4511.

Polk, 2366, 2405.

Referred to, 2250.

Repeal of, recommended, 4061.

Cohnawagas. (See Indian Tribes.)

Coin.—A piece of metal shaped according to government design with a fixed value for use as money.

Coinage.—A term employed to describe coin in general when used as money ; the process of coining. (See Coins and Coinage Laws.)

Coinage Laws.—The subject of coinage received the early attention of the founders of the Government. Many and varied laws have been passed to regulate the proportion of pure gold, silver, copper and nickel in the various coins and the ratio of one metal to another.

The most important coinage laws, together with their main provisions, are as follows : The act of April 2, 1792, provided that any person could have gold or silver coined at the mint, receiving therefor lawful coins of the same metal in equal weight. The standard of fineness for gold was eleven parts pure to one of alloy, and for silver 1,485 parts pure to 179 of alloy. The ratio of gold to silver was as 1 to 15, and both coins were legal tender. By the law of March 3, 1795, the Treasurer retained 24 cents per ounce for silver below the standard and 4 cents for gold ; and under that law the President by proclamation reduced the weight of the copper coin one pennyweight and sixteen grains in each cent and in like proportion in each half cent (page 183). By the law of April 21, 1800, there was retained for deposits of gold and silver below the standard a sum sufficient to pay for refining. By the law of May 8, 1828, a sum for materials and wastage was retained from silver bullion requiring the test. The law of June 28, 1834, provided that a deduction of one-half of one per cent. should be made from all standard gold and silver deposited for coinage if paid for in coin within five days from deposit. The law of Jan. 18, 1837, required the standard gold and silver coin to be made nine-tenths pure, one-tenth alloy, and to be a legal tender for any sum. By the law of Feb. 21, 1853, the weight of the half dollar was reduced from 206¼ to 192 grains and the lesser silver coins in the same proportion, and were made legal ten-

The weight, fineness and value of the several coins are shown below:

	Gold Coin	Standard Silver Dollars	Subsidiary Silver Coin	Minor Coin
Weight.........	25.8 grains to the dollar.	412.5 grains.	385.8 grains to the dollar.	5c. piece: 77.16 grains, 75 p. c. copper, 25 p. c. nickel.
Fineness........	900-1000.	900-1000.	900-1000.	
Ratio to gold....	....	15.988 to 1.	14.953 to 1.	1c. piece: 48 grains, 95 p. c. copper, 5 p. c. tin and zinc.
Limit of issue...	Unlimited.	Coinage ceased in 1905.	Needs of the people.	Needs of the people.
Denominations..	$20, $10, $5, $2½.	$1.	50 cents,25 cents,10 cents	5 cents, 1 cent.
Legal tender....	Unlimited.	Unlimited, unless otherwise contracted.	Not to exceed $10.	Not to exceed 25 cents.
Receivable......	For all public dues.	For all public dues.	For all dues up to $10.	For all dues up to 25 cents.
Exchangeable...	For gold certificates, as below, and subsidiary and minor coin.	For silver certificates and smaller coin.	For minor coin.	....
Redeemable.....	....	....	In "lawful money" at the Treasury in sums or multiples of $20.	In "lawful money" at the Treasury in sums or multiples of $20.

der to the amount of $5. No private deposits for conversion into these coins were received, and charges of one-half of one per cent. were made for refining. The law of Feb. 12, 1873, provided for the coining of a "trade dollar," the weight of which was made 420 grains, and of the half dollar 193 grains; legal tender to the amount of $5. No provision was made for the coinage of silver dollars of full legal-tender value. Silver bullion could be deposited for coinage into trade dollars only; gold for coinage for the benefit of the depositor. The directors of the mints were authorized to buy silver for coins of less than one dollar. One-fifth of one per cent. was charged for converting standard gold bullion into coin and silver into trade dollars. Silver coins, except trade dollars, were to be exchanged at par for gold coins in sums not exceeding $100. The charges on gold coinage were removed in 1875. July 22, 1877, an act was passed by the provisions of which the trade dollar ceased to be a legal tender. Feb. 28, 1878, an act was passed by the terms of which silver dollars of 412½ grains were made legal tender for all debts, and the Secretary of the Treasury was authorized to purchase at market value and coin not less than $2,000,000 and not more than $4,000,000 worth of silver bullion per month. By the law of June 9, 1879, silver coins of less than one dollar were made legal tender to the amount of $10.

Silver Purchase Act.—June 14, 1890, the law of 1878 was repealed and the Secretary of the Treasury was authorized to purchase 4,500,000 ounces of silver bullion per month, issuing legal-tender notes in payment, and to make a sufficient monthly coinage for the redemption of these notes. In 1893 the silver-purchase clause of this act was repealed.

Gold Standard.—In 1900 a new coinage law was passed which made the gold dollar the standard of value in this country and increased the reserve for the redemption of legal-tender notes. The law also permitted the national banks to issue notes to the amount of the par value of the bonds deposited and reduced the tax upon the circulation of the banks.

The weight, fineness and value of the several coins are shown in the table on the top of page.

Legal Tender.—There are now ten different kinds of money in circulation in the United States, viz.: gold coins, standard silver dollars, subsidiary silver, gold certificates, silver certificates, treasury notes issued under the act of July 14, 1890, United States notes (also called greenbacks and legal tenders), national bank notes, and nickel and bronze coins. Gold coins, treasury notes and silver dollars are legal tender

at face value in any amount. Subsidiary silver is legal tender to the extent of $10 in any one payment. United States notes are not legal tender for duties and imports and interest on the public debt. Gold certificates, silver certificates and national bank notes are not legal tender, but both classes of certificates are receivable for all public dues. All national banks are required by law to receive the notes of other national bank notes at par. The minor coins of nickel and copper are legal tender to the extent of 25 cents. (See also Mints and Assay Offices.)

The following table shows the coinage of the mints from their organization in 1792 to Jan. 1, 1916:

Denomination Gold	Pieces	Values
Fifty dollars..........	3,019	$ 150,950.00
Double eagles.........	121,011,106	2,420,222,120.00
Eagles	51,532,985	515,329,850.00
Half eagles...........	78,009,869	390,049,345.00
Three - dollar pieces (coinage discontinued under act of September 26, 1890).........	539,792	1,619,376.00
Quarter eagles.........	17,866,607	44,666,517.50
Dollars (coinage discontinued under act of September 26, 1890).	19,499,337	19,499,337.00
Dollars, Louisiana Purchase Exposition (act of June 28, 1902)...	250,000	250,000.00
Dollars, Lewis & Clark Exposition	60,000	60,000.00
Dollars, Panama - Pacific Exposition......	25,034	25,034.00
Total gold........	288,794,730	$3,391,872,529.50
Silver		
Dollars (coinage discontinued act of February 12, 1873, resumed act of February 28, 1878).....	578,303,848	$ 578,303,848.00
Trade dollars (discontinued, act of February 19, 1887).....	35,965,924	35,695,924.00
Dollars (Lafayette souvenir, act of March 3, 1899)...........	50,000	50,000.00
Half dollars..........	381,846,472	190,923,236.00
Half dollars (Columbian souvenir).......	5,000,000	2,500,000.00
Quarter dollars.......	417,981,758	104,495,439.50
Quarter dollars (Columbian souvenir)......	40,000	10,000.00
Twenty - cent pieces (coinage discontinued, act of May 2, 1878)	1,355,000	271,000.00
Dimes	739,457,997	73,945,799.70
Half dimes (coinage discontinued, act of February 12, 1873)..	97,604,388	4,880,219.40
Three-cent pieces (coinage discontinued, act of February 12, 1873)	42,736,240	1,282,087.20
Total silver........	2,300,341,627	$ 992,627,553.80

Minor Coin

Five-cent pieces, nickel	861,894,453	$ 43,094,722.65
Three - cent pieces, nickel (coinage discontinued, act of Sept. 21, 1890)......	31,378,316	941,349.38
Two-cent pieces, bronze (coinage discontinued, act of Feb. 12, 1873)	45,601,000	912,020.00
One-cent pieces........	2,739,692,331	27,396,923.31
Half-cent pieces, copper (coinage discontinued, act of Feb. 21, 1857)	7,985,222	39,926.11
Total minor coins.	3,686,461,322	$ 72,384,941.55
Grand total.....	6,275,597,679	$4,456,885,024.85

Silver-dollar coinage under acts of April 2, 1792, $8,031,238; February 28, 1878, $378,166,793; July 14, 1890, $187,027,345; March 3, 1891, $5,078,472—total, $578,-303,848.00.

Coins and Coinage (see also Coinage Laws; Coins, Foreign):

Act—

Authorizing coinage of standard silver dollars vetoed, 4438.

Directing coinage of silver bullion in Treasury vetoed, 5915.

Bland-Allison Act—

Discussed by President—

Arthur, 4633, 4720 4830.

Cleveland, 4927, 5097, 5373.

Harrison, Benj., 5475.

Hayes, 4511, 4568.

Vetoed by President Hayes, 4438.

Copper coins, weight of, reduced to weigh one pennyweight, sixteen grains, 183.

Discretionary authority of President to invite nations to conference on subject of, recommendations regarding, 5877.

Discussed by President—

Arthur, 4633, 4720, 4830.

Cleveland, 4927, 5097, 5372, 5833, 5875, 5965, 5996, 6073, 6156.

Harrison,Benj.,5474,5548,5628,5753.

Hayes, 4413, 4451, 4510, 4568.

Washington, 141.

Gold coinage—

Progress made in, 1331.

Value, laws regulating, referred to, 1382.

International arrangement fixing rates between gold and silver coinage, report on, 5177.

International coinage, referred to, 4113.

International conference at Brussels regarding use of silver, 5752.

Postponement of, discussed, 5876.

Report of, transmitted, 5784.

International conference to consider free coinage of silver, information regarding, refused, 5673.

International movement for reform of system, referred to, 3592.

International ratio, establishment of, referred to, 4955.

Laws connected with, changes in, recommended, 1432.

Opening of more mints recommended, 4201.

Silver coinage—

Act—

Authorizing coinage of standard silver dollars vetoed, 4438.

Directing coinage of silver bullion in Treasury vetoed, 5915.

Discussed by President—

Arthur, 4633, 4720, 4830.

Cleveland, 4927, 5097, 5373, 5833, 5875, 5965, 5996, 6072, 6084.

Harrison, Benj., 5475, 5548, 5628, 5753.

Hayes, 4413, 4511, 4568.

Repeal of act requiring, recommended, 4569, 4633, 4720.

Repeal of purchasing clause of act of 1890 discussed, 5875, 6073, 6074.

Recommended, 5833.

Should not be disparaged, 4414.

Suspension of, recommended, 4830.

Suspension of, at present ratio recommended, 4510.

Suspension of, compulsory, recommended, 4931, 5098, 5373.

Coins, Copper, weight of, reduced, 183.

Value of foreign coins fixed, 6616.

Coins, Foreign:

Assay of, 935.

Ceased to be legal tender, proclaimed, 239.

Counterfeiting of, should be made a crime, 1136, 1268.

Overvaluation of gold in, 1845.

Referred to, 2307.

Spanish milled dollars legal tender, 239.

Spanish milled doubloons referred to, 304.

Cold Harbor (Va.), Battle of.—Finding Lee's position on the North Anna too strong, Grant turned Lee's right wing, crossed the Pamunkey River at Hanover Court-House, and after considerable fighting reached Cold Harbor, to the northeast of Richmond. Lee had arrived there before the Federal army and was well intrenched. On the afternoon of June 1, 1864, an attack on the Confederate lines was made. It resulted in a loss of 2,000 men to the Federals and no advantage in position. June 2 was spent in skirmishing. At daylight June 3 a general assault was made on the Confederate lines, but it was repulsed after half an hour's fighting, with a loss of 7,000 men to Grant and a much smaller number to the Confederates. The strength of the Federal forces was about 150,000 and that of the Confederates about 65,000. For the next ten days the armies lay confronting each other. June 12 Grant decided to approach Richmond from the south. Accordingly the army passed from the Chickahominy to the James River between the 12th and 15th of June and took up the line of march to Petersburg. The Federal losses in the operations at Cold Harbor, including the conflict of Bethesda Church and the march across the Chickahominy and James rivers to the front of Petersburg, were 14,931. The Confederate loss was about 1,700.

Collector of Internal Revenue.—An officer appointed by the government to collect internal taxes levied by the government.

Collector of the Port.—An officer appointed by the President to collect duties on imported goods.

Collectors of Customs, compensation of, recommendations regarding, 4102.

Colleges. (See Education.)

Collisions at Sea. (See also Marine Disasters.)

Acts regarding, and time for taking effect proclaimed, 5537, 5933, 6193.

Discussed, 5962.

Proclamation revoking, 6016.

Discussed, 6063.

Adoption of new code of international rules for prevention of, recommended, 4631, 4683, 4718, 4827, 4848.

Colombia.—Colombia occupies the northwest corner of the South American continent from the Isthmus of Panama to the western boundaries of Venezuela and Brazil and the northern boundaries of Peru and Ecuador.

Physical Features.—The Republic is divisible into two unequal portions, of which the larger (about two-thirds of the whole) consists of the plains of the east and the extreme northwest, and the smaller (about one-third) consists of rugged mountains with three main ranges traversing the country and an isolated group of peaks in the northwest. The southern boundary crosses the Andes where the range consists of a massive series of volcanic peaks, the highest of which are Chiles (15,900 feet), Cumbal (15,900 feet), and Pasto (14,000 feet). The Western and Central Cordilleras run almost parallel with the Pacific coast, the Eastern Cordillera has a north-easterly direction and divides at the Venezuela boundary. In the northwest of Colombia is the Sierra Nevada de Santa Marta, the highest peak being about 17,000 feet above sea level. The mountainous region of the west contains ninety per cent. of the inhabitants.

The principal rivers of Colombia are the Magdalena, Cauca, and Atrato. The Magdalena has a total length of about 1,000 miles. The Cauca flows through a valley between the Western and Central Cordillera, and joins the Magdalena about 200 miles from its mouth at Barranquilla. Its total length is about 800 miles. The Atrato rises in the slopes of the Western Cordillera and flows into the Gulf of Uraba and the Caribbean Sea. The principal rivers of the eastern plains are the Meta and Guaviare, and the Putamayo, Yápuru (or Caqueta) and the Napo.

Colombia lies almost entirely in the north torrid zone, and but for its elevation would possess a completely tropical climate. The middle slopes and the sub-tropical valleys contain the most fertile and productive regions.

History.—The Colombian coast was visited in 1502 by Christopher Columbus, and in 1536 a Spanish expedition under Quesada established a government of certain coastal communities under the name of New Granada, which continued under Spanish rule until the revolt of the Spanish-American colonies of 1811-1824. In 1819 Bolivar established the Republic of Colombia, consisting of the territories now known as Colombia, Panama, Venezuela and Ecuador. In 1829-1830 Venezuela and Ecuador withdrew from the association of provinces, and in 1831 the remaining territories were formed into the Republic of New Granada. From 1853-1861 many of the Colombian Provinces declared their independence and the nineteenth century contained frequent revolutions and internal wars. In 1903 Panama seceded from Colombia, and is now a separate Republic.

AREA AND POPULATION.

Divisions and Capitals	Area in English Sq. Miles	Estimated Population
Departments—		
Antioquia (Medellin)	22,752	740,937
Atlántico (Barranquilla)	1,008	114,887
Bolivar (Cartagena)	22,320	425,975
Boyacá (Tunja)	16,460	586,499
Cáldas (Manizales)	7,380	341,498
Cauca (Popayán)	20,403	211,756
Cundinamarca (Bogotá)	8,046	715,610
Huila (Neiva)	8,100	158,191
Magdalena (Santa Marta)	19,080	140,106
Panamá (Panamá)	29,760	400,000
Nari o (Pasto)	9,360	293,918
Santander (Bucaramanga)	17,865	400,084
Norte de Santander (Cúcuta)	6,255	204,381
Tolima (Ibagué)	10,080	282,426
Valle (Cali)	3,897	217,140
Intendencies—		
Meta (Villavicencio)		29,299
Chocó (Quibdó)	258,840	60,653
Goagira (Guaraguarau)		53,018
Caquetáy demás Comisarias		99,576
Total	461,606	5,475,961

Ethnography.—There are six distinct elements in the population: White descendants of the Spanish settlers in the sixteenth to nineteenth centuries; Indian aboriginals; mestizos, or mixed Spanish-Indians; negroes; mixed Spanish negroes; mixed Indian negroes. The numbers of these elements are roughly estimated at 1,500,000 whites; 600,000 Indians, of whom about 150,000 are wild and uncivilized; 2,000,000 mestizos; and 1,400,000 negroes and mixed Spanish and Indian negroes.

Government.—The government is that of a centralized Republic under a constitution of 1886, by which the practical independence of the Provinces was extinguished. The Executive consists of a President, and there is a Legislature of two houses, with appointed Governors and biennial assemblies in each of the Departments. President of the Republic of Colombia (Aug. 7, 1910-1914), Dr. Carlos E. Rostrepo.

Congress meets annually for ninety days from July 20, and consists of a Senate and a House of Representatives. The Senate contains thirty-four members elected for four years by electoral colleges in each department. The House of Representatives contains ninety-two members, elected for two years by the direct vote of all male Colombians aged twenty-two who can read and write or possess an income of 300 pesos (or land valued at 1,500 pesos).

There are magistrates' courts of first instance with superior district courts and a supreme court, with appellate jurisdiction, at Bogotá.

Army.—The strength of the Army is determined by Congress, and the permanent force consists of about 6,00J of all arms. Every able-bodied male Colombian is liable for service, and a war strength of about 50,000 could be raised. (See Armies of the World.)

Navy.—The Navy consists of five old cruisers of little or no fighting value and a few miscellaneous craft, and is stationed on either side of the Isthmus of Panama, with a gunboat on the Magdalena River.

Education.—Primary education is free, but is not compulsory, although the schools are well attended. The white population retains the literary instincts of the Spaniards. The principal factor is the work of the Catholic corporations, whose secondary schools are State-aided.

Finances.—The revenue and expenditure of Colombia for the five years 1909-1913 are estimated at the following totals in gold pesos:

Year	Revenue	Expenditure
1909	16,600,000	16,600,000
1910	10,831,500	10,831,500
1911	9,779,500	8,937,688
1912	12,000,000	12,000,000
1913	16,500,000	16,115,000

Debt.—The External Debt has been reduced by arrangement with foreign (mainly British) bondholders, and now amounts to $12,400,000. The Internal Debt amounted on July 1, 1912, to about $3,000,000.

Production and Industry.—Maize and wheat are grown on the elevated plateaus of the western regions, but the principal product is coffee, of which excellent qualities are produced and exported through the neighboring republic of Venezuela and through Colombian ports. Cocoa, sugar, and bananas are also cultivated, and the indigenous rubber trees are being brought into commercial use. The grassy plains of the northeast support large herds of cattle and sheep, and considerable developments are possible in the export of the former.

Gold, silver, and platinum are found and worked in large quantities, and there are rich mines of copper, lead, mercury, and cinnabar, which form a great potential asset. Salt, coal, and iron are plentiful, and there are extensive petroleum fields. Concessions for the development of the oil industry, including the right to construct railways, docks, quays and canals, in connection with the transport of the oil have been let to an English company. The Government emerald-mines and pearl fisheries are believed to be valuable.

There is at Pradera a small iron industry in close proximity to the mines, and agricultural machinery is produced. A pottery and earthenware industry has survived the Spanish invasion of the sixteenth century unchanged. Sugar refining is encouraged by the State, and there are Panama hat factories.

Foreign Trade.—The Imports are principally flour and prepared foodstuffs, machinery, and textiles; the Exports being coffee, cattle, hides, and skins, bananas, tobacco, rubber, Panama hats, orchids (the choicest varieties of which are found by adventurous explorers), and gold, silver, and platinum. Textiles are sent principally by the United States and the United Kingdom, and flour by the United States; sugar of a better quality than can be produced by the primitive factories in Colombia is sent by Germany, in addition to rice. Coffee is sent to the United States through Venezuelan and Colombian ports; tobacco principally to Hamburg; and cotton to the United Kingdom and France. The values of the Imports and Exports for

the five years 1908-1912 are stated as follows in gold pesos:

Year	Imports	Exports	Total
1908	13,513,890	14,998,434	28,512,324
1909	11,117,927	16,040,198	28,148,125
1910	17,385,040	17,786,806	35,171,846
1911	18,108,863	22,375,899	40,484,762
1912	23,964,623	32,221,746	56,186,369

Railways.—Only about 620 miles of railroad were open in 1913. Internal communication is mainly carried over the principal rivers and their tributaries, a regular service of river steamers running on the Magdalena and its many auxiliary streams. Mountain tracks only fit for mules, and cart roads some in very good condition, are the principal means of getting about the country.

Shipping.—There are many harbors on the Pacific Coast. The Caribbean Coast (Atlantic) has many ports, of which Barranquilla, Cartagena, Santa Marta, and Rio Hacha are engaged in traffic with Europe and North America, while Villamazar has a coasting trade with Venezuela. The tonnage entered and cleared at Barranquilla (at the mouth of the Magdalena River) exceeded 1,400,000 tons in 1910, that of Cartagena being about 1,200,000 tons.

Towns.—Capital, Bogotá, founded by Quesada in 1538. There are fifteen towns credited with more than 20,000 inhabitants.

The unit of value under the law of 1907 was the gold peso worth about a dollar in United States money. In the later coinage the peso had been superseded by the dollar, but the actual currency is the paper peso, of which it requires 102 to equal $1.

Trade with the United States.—The value of merchandise imported into Colombia from the United States for the year 1913 was $7,397,696, and goods to the value of $15,- 979,912 were sent thither—a balance of $8,582,216 in favor of the United States.

Colombia:

Action of, in Panama, 6807-6815, 6827-6857.

American citizens in, destitute, order for transportation of, to United States, 5437.

American citizens in New Granada, outrages on, 2948, 3049.

Boundary question with Costa Rica discussed, 4627, 5869.

Civil war in, discussed and action of United States regarding, 4911, 6364, 6426.

Claims of American citizens arising out of. (See Aspinwall, Colombia.)

Claim of Italy against, and arbitration of, President of United States discussed, 6328.

Claims of United States against, 292, 1594, 1751, 1822, 4289, 4804, 6364, 6681, 6735.

Allowance of, 1030.

Convention for adjustment of, 3444.

Payment of, 868, 4358.

Claims of United States against New Granada, 2116, 2193, 2948, 3049.

Adjustment of, 2116, 3175.

Commission to settle, extension of time of, recommended, 3268.

Convention for adjustment of, 3329.

Commercial relations with, 1124.
Convention between United States and Granadian Confederation, 3268.
Convention with, 855, 907, 3412, 3444.
Correspondence with, transmitted, 5610.
Demonstration by Congress of, in honor of President Juarez, of Mexico, 3575.
Diplomatic relations with, 1132. Resumed, 4449, 4521, 4562.
Dispute with Haiti settled by arbitration, 7657.
Dissolution of three states composing, 1158. Reunion of, discussed, 1245, 1319.
Flour, duties on, reduced, 1115.
Fugitive criminals, convention with, for surrender of, 4587, 5200.
Import duties imposed upon American products by, 5672. Retaliatory measures proclaimed, 5700.
Imprisonment of American citizens by authorities of, 4798.
Minister of, to United States, arrival of, referred to, 3381, 4521, 4562.
Minister of United States in, 1030. Sent to, 3390. Transferred from Stockholm, Sweden, to, 3665.
Minister of United States to New Granada, reasons for not presenting credentials discussed, 3348.
Postal convention between United States and New Granada, 2168.
President of, delivered from assassins, medal offered President Jackson in commemoration of, declined, 1029.
Relations between United States and New Granada discussed, 2978.
Tonnage duties levied on American vessels by New Granada, discussed, 2948, 3049.
Treaty between United States and New Granada, 2217, 2359, 2361, 2582, 3063, 3122, 3174. Contravention of, by latter, 2948, 3049. Provisions of, discussed, 2361. Referred to, 2576, 2577, 2581, 2902, 3349.
Treaty with, transmitted and discussed, 855, 868, 907, 1115, 1124, 4587, 5200. (See also Panama Canal.)
Vessels from port of Boca del Toro, duties on, suspended, 4895.
Vessels of United States seized or interfered with by, 4289, 4358.
Wars in New Granada, 3349.

Colombia, Treaties with.—In 1824 a treaty of amity, commerce and navigation was concluded with Colombia. This treaty expired by its own terms in 1836. With the division of the republic in 1831, New Granada succeeded Colombia, and a treaty of peace, amity, navigation and commerce was negotiated with this government in 1846. In 1862 the name was changed to the United States of Colombia and in 1886 the states were abolished and the country became the Republic of Colombia. A consular convention was concluded with the existing government in 1850, and claims conventions in 1857 and 1864. In 1888 an extradition treaty was concluded on nearly the same lines with those of other South American republics.

Ship Canal.—In 1903 a ship canal convention was signed in Washington, by John Hay, American Secretary of State, and Thomas Herran, chargé d'affaires of Colombia, providing for the transfer of the property of the New Panama Canal Company to the United States and granting to the United States the right to construct a canal across the isthmus of Panama and maintain jurisdiction over a zone five kilometres wide on each side thereof for a period of one hundred years (page 6901). Colombia's congress adjourned without ratifying this treaty, and its provisions became inoperative. (See Panama Canal.)

Colombia also became a party to the convention between the United States and the several republics of South and Central America for the arbitration of pecuniary claims and the protection of inventions, etc., which was signed in Buenos Aires in 1910 and proclaimed in Washington July 29, 1914. (See South and Central America, Treaties with.)

Colon Fire Claims, mentioned, 6864.

Colonel.—A commander-in-chief of a regiment of infantry or cavalry.

Colonel Lloyd Aspinwall, The, seizure of, by Spain, and award to United States discussed, 4052.

Colonial Dames of America.—The Society of the Colonial Dames of America was organized in the City of New York, May 23, 1890, and was the first society of women for this patriotic purpose founded in this country. It was incorporated April 23, 1891. The Society is purely patriotic and educational in its objects, which are: (1) To collect and reserve relics, manuscripts, traditions and mementoes of the founders and builders of the thirteen original states of the Union, and of the heroes of the War of Independence, that the memory of their deeds and achievements may be perpetuated. (2) To promote celebrations of great historic events of National importance to diffuse information on all subjects concerning American history, particularly among the young, and to cultivate the spirit of patriotism and reverence for the founders of American constitutional history. This Society has a large membership and chapters in many states.

Another society of the same name and having similar purposes is composed of delegates from the state societies. These exist in the thirteen original states and in twenty-one other states and the District of Columbia, and are all incorporated. The aggregate membership is (1909) over 5,000.

Under the constitution of the National Society it is prescribed that the members shall be women "who are descendants in their own right of some ancestor of worthy life who came to reside in an American colony prior to 1750, which ancestor, or some one of his descendants, being a lineal ascendant of the applicant, shall have rendered efficient service to his country during the Colonial period, either in the founding of a commonwealth or of an institution which has survived and developed into importance, or who shall have held an important position in the Colonial Government, and who, by distinguished services, shall have contributed to the founding of this great and powerful nation." Services rendered after 1776 do not entitle to membership, but are accepted for supplemental applications. There is no admission except through Colonial ancestry.

Colonial Society of America.—The object of this society is to advance historic research, and particularly to arouse and sustain widespread interest in the perpetuation of the memory of the chief historic events, places and scenes in the colonial and revolutionary periods of our country. The Society consists of members, patrons and fellows. They are persons interested in American history and the preservation of the historic scenes and places in the colonial and revolutionary periods.

The Society prepares each year etchings of historic scenes, buildings and places of America, and India proofs printed from the etching plates, signed by the artist, are sent to all members, patrons and fellows of the society, together with the Memorial Book of the Society, which contains a complete history of the subjects represented in the etchings. It also issues reproductions of rare documents, relics, etc., of historic value pertaining to the period.

Colonial System.—It was the custom of European countries having colonies in America to manage them solely for the profit and convenience of the mother country. In this Great Britain was no more culpable than other European nations. Great Britain's policy has of late become more liberal, her colonial possessions, wherever capable, being self-governing.

Colonization of Negroes. (See Negroes.)

Colonization Society, American.—A national organization formed at Washington, D. C., Jan. 1, 1817, for the purpose of encouraging the emancipation of slaves by providing a place outside the United States to which they might emigrate when freed. The scheme was also intended to relieve the South of the free black population. Numerous branches of the society were soon organized in many states. Free negroes were first sent to Sierra Leone, then for a short time to Sherbro Island, and in 1821 a permanent location was purchased near Cape Mesurado. In 1847 the colony declared itself an independent republic under the name of Liberia. It was recognized by the United States in 1861.

Colonization Society, American, agreement with, discussed, 3059, 3124, 3180.

Color-Line.—The distinction, social or political, between white and colored people.

Colorado.—One of the western group of states, named from the Colorado River; nickname, "The Centennial State"; motto, "Nil sine numine." It lies between lat. 37° and 41° north and long. 102° and 109° west, an area of 103,948 square miles. It is bounded on the north by Wyoming and Nebraska, on the east by Nebraska and Kansas, on the south by New Mexico and Oklahoma, and on the west by Utah. It is formed partly from territory included in the Louisiana Purchase and partly from that acquired from Mexico in 1848. Colorado is traversed by the Rocky Mountains

and is noted for its beautiful scenery, formed by lofty peaks and deep canyons. Colorado is the chief gold and silver producing State in the Union and its iron, copper, coal and lead mines are also important. Extensive irrigation has contributed largely to the success of its agriculture, and stock-raising is one of the most important industries. The excellent climate has rendered the State noted as a health resort, especially in cases of pulmonary disease. It was organized as a territory in 1861 and admitted as a State in 1876 (4346). President Johnson vetoed two acts on this subject (3611, 3681). Area, 103,925 sq. miles; population in 1910, 799,024.

Statistics of agriculture collected for the last Federal census place the number of farms in the State at 46,170, comprising 13,532,113 acres, valued with stock and improvements at $491,471,806. The average value of land per acre was $26.81 against $9.54 in 1900. The value of domestic animals, poultry, etc., was $70,161,344, including 1,127,737 cattle, valued at $131,017,-303; 294,035 horses, $27,382,926; 14,739 mules, $1,798,935; 179,294 swine, $1,568,-158; 1,426,214 sheep, $6,586,187, and poultry, $1,012,251. The yield and value of the field crops of 1911 was: corn, 373,000 acres, 5,222,000 bushels, $4,073,000; wheat, 438,000 acres, 8,274,000 bushels, $6,950,-000; oats, 290,000 acres, 10,150,000 bushels, $4,872,000; rye, 21,000 acres, 252,000 bushels, $176,000; potatoes, 90,000 acres, 3,150,000 bushels, $3,118,000; hay, 707,000 acres, 1,414,000 tons, $13,150,000.

Though Colorado does not now lead in the production of any important mineral substance, the United States Geological Survey reports that it closely approximates California in the production of gold, of which in former years it has been the leading producer. (See illustration opposite 4344.) It ranks eleventh among the mineral-producing states, and fifth among the states west of the Mississippi River. It is the leading producer of tungsten ores and vanadium minerals, and ranks second in the production of gold, third in the production of zinc and fluorspar, and fourth in lead. On account chiefly of the decreased production of coal the total value of the mineral products of Colorado decreased from $58,167,399 in 1912 to $54,-294,281 in 1913. The product of chief value is gold, the production of which in 1913 was almost exactly one-third the total value of the mineral products of the state. The production decreased from 899,222 fine ounces, valued at $18,588,562 in 1912, to 877,857 fine ounces, valued at $18,146,916. Second in importance among the state's mineral products is coal, but on account of labor troubles in the last quarter of the year the production of the state decreased from 10,977,824 short tons, valued at $16,-345,336, in 1912, to 9,232,510 tons, valued at $14,035,090.

The production of zinc, which showed a marked increase in 1912 over 1911, suffered a decrease in 1913, which was particularly emphasized in the diminished value of the output. The recoverable zinc content of the ores mined in Colorado in 1913 was 59,673 short tons, valued at $6,683,400, against 66,111 tons, valued at $9,123,374, in 1912. The zinc mining operations are third in importance among Colorado's mining industries.

Colorado leads all of the western states in the manufacture of pig iron, but produces only a small quantity of iron ore. Silver ranks fourth in the value of Colorado's mineral product, and, unlike gold, showed an increase of output in 1913. The production of silver in the state increased from 8,212,070 fine ounces, valued at $5,050,-423, in 1912, to 9,325,255 fine ounces, valued at $5,632,454. The recoverable lead content of the ore in 1913 was 43,949 short tons, valued at $3,867,502. The other mineral products which had a total value in excess of $1,000,000 in 1913 were clay products and copper. Other mineral products of the state are cement, ferro-alloys, fluospar, fuller's earth, gems, graphite, gypsum, lime, manganiferous ore, mica, mineral waters, natural gas, petroleum, sand and gravel, sand-lime-brick, sulphuric acid from zinc smelting, tungsten concentrates, and uranium and vanadium ores.

The number of manufacturing establishments in Colorado having an annual output valued at $500 or more at the beginning of 1915 was 2,126. The amount of capital invested was $181,719,000, giving employment to 33,715 persons, using material valued at $89,756,000, and turning out finished goods worth $136,839,000. Salaries and wages paid amounted to $26,568,000.

Colorado:

Admission of, into Union—
  Acts for, vetoed, 3611, 3681.
    Table accompanying veto message, 3687.
  Proclaimed, 4346.
  Recommended, 4209.
  Referred to, 4360.
Boundary of, 6937.
Constitution adopted by, discussed and action of President, 3573.
Creation and organization of, as a Territory, referred to, 3254.
Governor of, absence of, from Territory, referred to, 3721.
Italian laborers lynched in, discussed and recommendations regarding, 6065, 6096.
Labor disturbances in, 6942.
Lands in, set apart as public reservation by proclamation, 5595, 5695, 5705, 5722, 5786, 5797.
Unlawful combinations in, proclamation against, 5932.

Colorado River (Lower), improvement of, 7722.

Colorado Springs, Colo., act granting lands to, for water reservoirs returned, 5501.

Colors of France presented to United States on the occasion of the presentation of an address of amity from the Committee of Public Safety in Paris, 181.

Columbia.—The poetical symbol of the United States, often visualized in the form of a tall and stately female figure. (See Uncle Sam.)

Columbia, The, attacked by Mexican armed vessel, 1684, 1685.

Columbia, The, mentioned, 6318.

Columbia, District of. (See District of Columbia.)

Columbia River:
Exploration of, 396, 831.
Improvement of recommendations regarding, 4571.

Military posts at mouth of, recommended, 831.
Referred to, 705, 768.
Territory of United States on, information regarding occupancy of, 1615.

Columbian Exposition. (See World's Columbian Exposition.)

Columbian Historical Exposition at Madrid:
Acceptance of invitation to participate in, recommended, 5622.
Report of United States commissioners to, transmitted, 5988.

Columbian Institution for the Deaf.—This institution was established in Washington in 1857. Its average population is around 150, for whom it cares in the most modern and scientific methods at an average expenditure of about $125,000. Deaf persons within the District of Columbia are admitted free of charge, but residents of other states may be admitted by the payment of a yearly fee of $350, which includes all expenses except clothing. The institution is administered through the Interior Department, and it is divided into the following departments—Gallaudet College, Department of Articulation and Normal Instruction, The Kendall School, and the Domestic Department.

Columbus, Christopher. (See America.)

Columbus Day. (See Holidays, Legal.)

Columbus and Sandusky Turnpike referred to, 2278.

Columbus Barracks, Ohio, new buildings for recruiting service at, referred to, 4664.

Columbus, Ga., act for erection of public building at, vetoed, 5257.

Columbus, Ohio, establishment of mint at, referred to, 4311.

Colville Reservation, Wash., agreement for cession of lands on, 5648.

Comanche Indians. (See Indian Tribes.)

Combinations, Illegal. (See Illegal Combinations.)

Comet, The, compensations by Great Britain in case of, referred to, 1732, 1784.

Comity of Nations.—A courteous custom, having the force of law, by which one nation holds itself accountable to the laws of another nation in matters of common interest; limitations as to the extent of the courtesy involved are frequently stipulated in treaties.

Command.—As a body of men, an organized force of naval or military troops under a given officer.

Commander.—An officer with authority to direct a body of troops.

Commanders of Army. (See Encyclopedic Article, Army.)

Commerce.—The trade between states, countries and other political or economic units.

The commerce of the United States is reported by the Department of Commerce under two general headings, foreign and domestic. The extent of the foreign commerce is represented in the imports and exports, while the domestic trade is summed up in the freight traffic of the railroads. Besides that carried by the railroads, the rivers and lakes carry a considerable amount of merchandise, which is only partially reported. The data for the river traffic is obtained from a report made by the Inland Waterways Commission and a report of the Chief Engineer of the War Department made in 1910. Reports of lake traffic were discontinued in 1911.

FOREIGN TRADE.—Exports for the fiscal year just ended with June amounted to $4,345,000,000, and the imports were valued at $2,180,000,000, making a total foreign trade for the year of over six and a half billion dollars, which is much larger than any previous total in the history of American commerce. These figures were announced July 12, 1916, by the Bureau of Foreign and Domestic Commerce, of the Department of Commerce, with the explanation that the figures included for June are an estimate based on the final May statistics.

It was in 1872 that our foreign trade first exceeded one billion dollars. By 1900 it had crossed the two billion dollar mark, by 1907 had exceeded three billion, and by 1913 had risen above four billion, remaining around that level until the year just ended, when the six billion mark was exceeded. Imports first exceeded one billion dollars' value in 1903 and are now a little more than twice as much as at that time.

Exports first rose above one billion dollars' value in 1892 and are now four times as much as in that year.

Thirteen great classes of exported articles yield a total estimated at 3,024 million dollars for 1916, as against 1,321 million for all other articles. The following table shows the remarkable increases which have occurred in exports of this group during the last two years:

LEADING ARTICLES OF EXPORT

Classes	*1916	1915	1914	Classes	*1916	1915	1914
	Mil. Dol.	Mil. Dol.	Mil. Dol.		Mil. Dol.	Mil. Dol.	Mil. Dol.
Iron and steel	618	226	251	Railway cars	27	3	11
Explosives...	473	41	6	Paper and mfrs......	29	20	21
Raw cotton.	370	376	610	Vegetable oils	28	26	16
Wheat and flour......	314	428	142	Dairy products......	25	14	3
Meats......	270	206	143	Mules......	23	13	1
Copper mfrs.	170	109	146	Fiber mfrs...	22	12	13
Mineral oils.	165	134	152	Agricultural implements	18	10	32
Brass and mfrs......	126	21	7	Photographic goods......	17	8	9
Autos and parts......	123	68	33	Rye and rye flour......	16	15	13
Chemicals, etc........	123	46	27	Cottonseed oilcake and meal......	16	20	11
Cottonmfrs..	112	72	51	Vegetables..	16	11	7
Refined sugar	80	26	2	Spirits, wines and liquors	14	3	4
Leather......	80	65	37	Lead mfrs...	14	9	3
Horses......	73	64	3	Naval stores.	13	11	20
Leather mfrs.	66	55	21	Paraffin......	13	11	7
Coal........	65	56	60	Glass and glassware..	12	6	4
Wood and mfrs......	61	50	103	Flax seed oilcake and meal......	12	9	10
Oats and oatmeal...	53	60	1	Paints and colors...	11	7	7
Wool mfrs...	54	27	5	Nickel oxide, matte, etc.	10	11	9
Tobacco, unmanufact'd	48	44	54				
Zinc mfrs....	44	21	1				
Rubber mfrs	36	15	12				
Fruits......	36	34	31				
Corn and cornmeal..	32	41	8				
Electrical goods.....	30	20	25				

* Estimated upon basis of 11 months.

Articles exported in values ranging downward from 9 million to 5 million dollars each last year included furs and fur skins, 9; barley, 8; aeroplanes and tobacco manufactures, each, 7; coffee, eggs, starch, soap, aluminum goods, and scientific instruments, each, 6; and fertilizers, silk manufactures, seeds, hides and skins, and glucose, each, 5 million dollars.

Seven groups of articles represent about one-half the entire value of our import trade, each of them exceeding 100 million dollars in the fiscal year 1916. Stated in order of magnitude, they are: sugar, estimated at 206 million in 1916, against 174 and 101 millions one and two years earlier; rubber and substitutes therefor, 159 million, against 87 and 76 million, respectively; hides and skins, 157 million, against 104 and 120; raw wool, 145, against 68 and 53; raw silk, 122, against 81 and 98; coffee, 117, against 107 and 111; and chemicals, drugs, etc., 108 million, against 84 and 95 million, respectively. Our leading imports are thus factory materials and foodstuffs.

Imports of manufactured fibers are estimated at 69 million dollars for 1916, against 62 and 82 million one and two years earlier; raw fibers, at 62 million, compared with 40 and 54 million; copper in ingots, bars, etc., 52 million, as against 20 and 41 million; wood manufactures, 51 million, as against 47 and 44 million; tin in bars, blocks, etc., 48 million, compared with 31 and 39 million; cotton manufactures, 47 million, compared with 46 and 71 million; and raw cotton, 42 million, compared with 23 and 19 million in 1915 and 1914, respectively.

Taking up the articles of lesser value and stating the 1916, 1915, and 1914 imports in millions of dollars, the figures run:

MINOR ARTICLES OF IMPORT

Classes	*1916	1915	1914	Classes	*1916	1915	1914
	Mil. Dol.	Mil. Dol.	Mil. Dol.		Mil. Dol.	Mil. Dol.	Mil. Dol.
Unmanufactured cocoa	34	23	21	Flaxseed....	20	13	11
Vegetable oils	34	36	47	Undressed furs.......	17	8	9
Diamonds...	31	12	25	Fish........	17	18	19
Silk mfrs.....	31	25	35	Cattle.......	15	18	19
Paper Mfrs..	26	26	28	Wool mfrs...	15	30	34
Meat and dairy products......	24	43	39	Spirits, wines, etc........	16	13	20
Breadstuffs..	24	20	37	Wood........	13	14	18
Iron and steel	23	23	32	Precious stonesother than diamonds......	13	3	8
Unmanufactured tobacco.....	23	27	35	Leather and tanned skins......	13	11	14
Copper ore..	22	11	14	Mineral oils..	13	10	14
Fruits........	22	27	34	Seeds other than flax..	12	10	9
Nuts........	21	17	20				
Art works....	21	18	35				
Tea.........	20	18	17				

* Estimated upon basis of 11 months.

The estimated import trade in the minor groups would include, vegetables, zinc ore, and hats and hat materials, each 11 million dollars; nickel, 10; spices, 9; antimony matte, sulphur ore, and fertilizers, each 7; earthen and chinaware, manganese, brass for remanufacture, bituminous coal, iron ore, tobacco manufactures, leather manufactures, each between 5 and 6 million; and lead, dyewoods, clocks and watches, asbestos, dressed furs, toys, plants, and platinum, each from 3 to 4 million dollars.

The estimate of 6½ billion dollars as the value of American foreign trade in the fiscal year which ended June 30, 1916, recently announced by the Bureau of Foreign and Domestic Commerce, Department of Commerce, is confined by complete returns which have just been tabulated by that office.

The year's exports aggregated 4,334 million dollars, exceeding by more than 1½ billion the huge total for 1915 and by more than 2 billion dollars the annual average from 1911 to 1914. June alone gave a total of 465 million dollars, being slightly less than the record total of 475 million for May, but practically 200 million more than in June last year.

The year's imports amounted in value to 2,198 million dollars, exceeding by 524 million the 1915 total and by 476 million the annual average from 1911 to 1914. June imports totaled 246 million, the largest figure ever shown by a single month. It was 17 million dollars larger than that for May and 88 million larger than that for June last year.

The year's export balance reached the unequaled total of 2,136 million dollars, being practically double that for 1915 and more than four times that of 1914, which were 1,094 million and 471 million dollars, respectively. The month of June contributed 219 million dollars to the favorable trade balance of the year, which compares with an export balance of 111 million in June, 1915, and less than a half million dollars' import balance in June, 1914.

Of the year's imports 68 per cent entered free of duty, compared with approximately 62 per cent in 1915. Of the June imports 62.6 per cent were free of duty, as against 62.9 per cent in June, 1915.

The net inward gold movement amounted to 114 million dollars for June and 404 million for the year ending with June. The preceding fiscal year showed a net gold import of 25 million, while 1914 showed a net gold export of 45 million dollars. The year's imports of gold amounted to 494 million dollars, compared with 172 million in 1915 and 67 million in 1914; the year's exports of gold, 90 million dollars, as against 146 million in 1915 and 112 million in 1914. Gold imports averaged 58 million dollars per month for the period from August to December, 1915, averaged less than 13 million per month for the period from January to May, 1916, but in June rose to 123 million dollars. June exports of gold amounted to 8⅓ million dollars, or about 3 million less than the monthly average since December, 1915.

The Sault Ste. Marie Canal carries nearly all the tonnage of the Great Lakes, and the Erie and other New York canals carry more than two million tons of freight annually.

A partial report of the traffic movement on navigable streams of the country made by the Inland Waterways Commission, places the commerce by this means of transportation at 70,933,142 short tons.

Commerce (see also Foreign Import Duties):

Active cooperation of consular service in promoting foreign commerce, 6459.

Agreements with foreign powers regarding, discussed, 5615, 5747.
Proclaimed, 5576, 5583, 5587, 5684, 5688, 5693, 5698, 5714, 5716, 5718, 5800.

Belgian restrictions upon importation from the United States, 6325.

Berlin and Milan decrees affecting, discussed and referred to by President—

Jefferson, 409, 415, 430, 432, 434, 441, 446.

Madison, 467, 474, 476, 503, 513, 522.
Proclamations regarding, 457, 466.

Burden imposed upon, by Spain, 1456.

Collection of commercial regulations of foreign powers referred to, 632, 775.

Conditions of, discussed, 2808.

Conventions regarding. (See treaties under the several powers.)

Decline of, discussed and recommendations for advancement of, by President—
Arthur, 4650, 4727, 4831, 4837.
Grant, 4007, 4060, 4201.
Harrison, Benj., 5491.

Depredations on (see also claims under the several powers; Vessels, United States, seized)—
Referred to, 237, 329.

Discriminations against, by Maximilian's Government, 3584.

Discussed by President—
Adams, John, 226, 241, 247, 255.
Adams, J. Q., 978, 979.
Arthur, 4650, 4720, 4731, 4831, 4837.
Cleveland, 4921.
Grant, 4007, 4013, 4060, 4201.
Harrison, Benj., 5491, 5743, 5747, 5757.
Hayes, 4423, 4564.
Jackson, 1519.
Jefferson, 318, 361, 383.
Lincoln, 3259.
McKinly, 6241, 6359, 6381, 6436.
Madison, 559.
Monroe, 621, 667, 775.
Pierce, 2762, 2808.
Polk, 2274.
Roosevelt, 6645, 6788, 7052.
Taft, 7374, 7435, 7502, 7757.
Van Buren, 1719.
Washington, 58, 95, 175.
Wilson, 8017.

Extension of, with foreign powers, referred to, 559, 3259, 4837, 6266.

Fines imposed upon American shipping by Spain discussed, 4626, 4714, 4763.

First treaty of, referred to, 820.

Foreign vessels purchased by American citizens in aid of, 4823.

Hawaiian trade discussed, 6340.

Laws for regulating, must engage attention of Congress, 454, 525, 538, 672, 7032.

Laws of, having tendency to prolong war (1812) should be revised, 525.

Letter from Emperor of France regarding free trade and, referred to, 3112.

Merchandise transported from one port in United States, over Canadian territory, to another port therein, discussed, 5770.

Merchant marine discussed by President—
McKinley, 6359.
Roosevelt, 6653.

Not to be affected by imperial decree of France, 409.

Policy of United States in commercial intercourse discussed, 866.

Proof of increasing dangers to, referred to, 427.

Referred to, 2895, 4973, 5663.

Reciprocal Trade relations with foreign countries, 6266.

Resources locked up, 8016.

Spoliations committed on, referred to, 237, 329. (See also claims under the several powers; Vessels, United States, seized.)

Suspension of, caused by injustice of belligerent powers, 443, 467, 477.

Tariff laws modified. (See Foreign Import Duties.)

Treaties regarding. (See treaties under the several powers.)

With foreign powers (see also Foreign Import Duties)—
Austria, 1114, 2004.
Belgium, 2193.
Brazil, 3049, 4078, 4629, 5570, 5663.
British colonies, 652.
Canada, 2582, 2654, 3989, 3999, 5748. (See Welland Canal.)
  Conference on subject of, discussed, 5675, 5678, 5748.
  Treaty regarding, 4220.
China, 1114, 1790, 2066, 2743, 2977, 3446, 4060, 6367.
  Interruption of, by Great Britain referred to, 1839.
Colombia, 1124.
Confederate States. (See Confederate States.)
Consular reports, 6338, 6356, 6381, 6436, 6460.
Costa Rica, 3885.
Cuba, 1260, 1347, 2945, 4826, 4921, 5089, 5470, 5547, 6069, 6292.
  Report on, 6292.
  Treaty regarding, 4842, 4847, 4848.
Denmark, 1094, 1244, 2812, 2944.
Ecuador, 6435.
France, 170, 346, 409, 460, 467, 645, 669, 917, 961, 1069, 1911, 2976, 6330.
  Restraints on, removed and discussed, 278, 292, 294, 457, 466, 476, 917, 6262.
  Suspension of, 458.
Germany, 5617, 6061, 6330.

Great Britain—
Convention regarding, 548, 554, 608, 628, 764, 946.
Proclamation regarding, 555.
Discussed by President—
  Adams, John, 251.
  Adams, J. Q., 919, 933, 941, 967, 974.
  Jackson, 1043, 1064, 1115.
  McKinley, 6435.
  Madison, 459, 467, 476.
  Monroe, 608, 628, 645, 669, 818.
  Polk, 2428.
  Taylor, 2548.
  Washington, 88, 114, 138, 175, 184, 190, 191.
Renewal of relations, 453, 457.
Suspension of relations, 458, 476, 941, 948.
Greece, 1647, 6332.
Japan, 2703, 2743, 2769, 4060, 4242, 4448, 6373.
Mexico, 816, 1070, 1157, 2115, 4327, 4462, 5678, 5959.
Netherlands, 599, 918, 1369.
Newfoundland, 2867.
Nicaragua, 6435.
Oldenburg, 820.
Peru, 1159, 2745.
Portugal, 811.
  Vessel sent to protect American interests, 1099.
Prussia, 820.
Puerto Rico, 1260, 1347, 4826, 4921, 5989, 5470, 6069.
  Treaty regarding, 4842, 4847, 4848.
Russia, 820, 1068, 1113, 1369, 1704.
Salvador, 5663.
Santo Domingo, 287, 773, 5663, 6435.
  Complaints of France against, 379.
  Restrictions on, removed, 280, 285.
Sardinia, 820.
South America, 4014, 4826, 5509.
South American Republics, 2869, 4460.
  Report on, 4024.
Spain, 110, 112, 113, 139, 164, 5089, 5663.
  Treaty regarding, discussed, 4919.
States in insurrection. (See Confederate States.)
Sweden, 820.
Texas, 1964.
  Treaty with, regarding, 2030.
Trusts discussed, 6240, 6360, 6645.
Turkey, 1078. (See also Black Sea.)

Commerce, Interstate. (See Interstate Commerce.)

Commerce Court.—The Mann-Elkins act of June 18, 1910, created a new judicial body known as the Commerce Court to

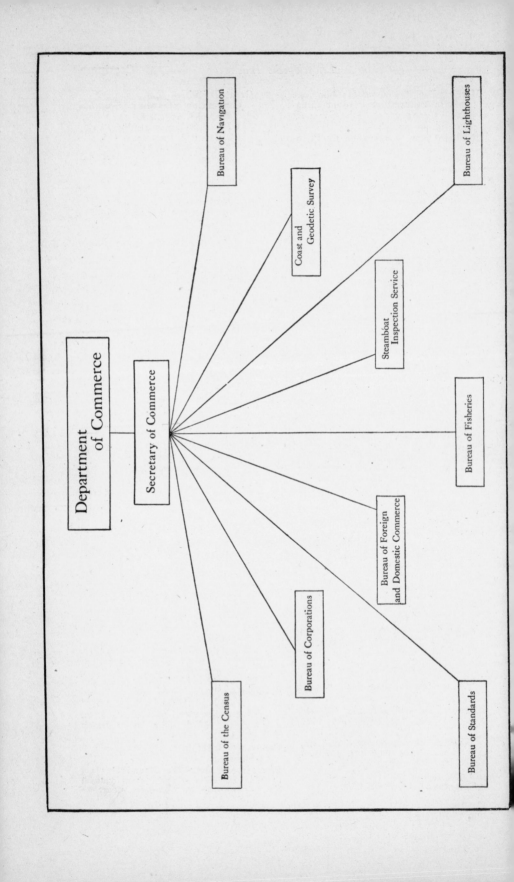

review the decisions of the Interstate Commerce Commission on appeal and to expedite rate cases formerly tried in the United States Circuit Courts.

It has the same jurisdiction as Circuit Courts in (1) all cases for the enforcement, otherwise than by adjudication and collection of a forfeiture or penalty or by infliction of criminal punishment, of any order of the Interstate Commerce Commission other than for the payment of money; (2) cases brought to enjoin, set aside, annul or suspend in whole or in part any order of the Interstate Commerce Commission; (3) such cases as by section three of the act entitled "An act to further regulate commerce with foreign nations and among the states," approved Feb. 19, 1903, are authorized to be maintained in a Circuit Court of the United States; (4) all such mandamus proceedings as under the provisions of section twenty or section twenty-three of the act entitled "An act to regulate commerce," approved Feb. 4, 1887, as amended, are authorized to be maintained in a Circuit Court of the United States.

The jurisdiction of the Commerce Court over cases of the foregoing classes shall be exclusive, but this act shall not affect the jurisdiction now possessed by any Circuit Court or District Court of the United States over cases or proceedings of a kind not within the above-enumerated classes.

The Commerce Court shall be a court of record, shall have a seal and be composed of five judges, to be from time to time designated and assigned thereto by the Chief Justice of the United States, from among the circuit judges of the United States, for the period of five years, except that in the first instance the court shall be composed of the five additional circuit judges to be appointed as hereinafter provided, who shall be designated by the President to serve for one, two, three, four and five years, respectively, in order that the period of designation of one of the said judges shall expire in each year thereafter. In case of the death, resignation or termination of assignment of any judge so designated, the Chief Justice shall designate a circuit judge to fill the vacancy so caused and to serve during the unexpired period for which the original designation was made. After the year 1914 no circuit judge shall be designated to serve in the Commerce Court until the expiration of at least one year after the expiration of the period of his last previous designation. The judge first designated for the five-year period shall be the presiding judge of said court, and thereafter the judge senior in designation shall be the presiding judge.

Each of the judges during the period of his service in the Commerce Court shall, on account of the regular sessions of the court being held in the city of Washington, receive in addition to his salary as circuit judge an expense allowance at the rate of one thousand five hundred dollars per annum. The President shall, by and with the advice and consent of the Senate, appoint five additional circuit judges, no two of whom shall be from the same judicial circuit, who shall hold office during good behavior and who shall be from time to time designated and assigned by the Chief Justice of the United States for service in the Circuit Court for any district, or the Circuit Court of Appeals for any circuit, or in the Commerce Court.

President Taft made the following appointments: Judge Martin A. Knapp, presiding, commissioned Dec. 31, 1910, for a term of five years; Judges Robert W. Archbald, William H. Hunt, John E. Carland and Julian W. Mack, each commissioned

Jan. 31, 1911 for terms of four, three and two years, and one year, respectively. The associate judges shall have precedence and shall succeed to the place and powers of the presiding judge whenever he may be absent or incapable of acting in the order of the date of their designations. Four of said judges shall constitute a quorum, and at least a majority of the court shall concur in all decisions.

The act further provides for the appointment of a clerk and marshal. Its regular sessions shall be held in Washington, but it may hold sessions in different parts of the United States as may be found desirable. In all cases within its jurisdiction it may exercise any and all the powers of a Circuit Court of the United States. Its jurisdiction may be invoked by the filing of written petitions setting forth the petitioner's cause of action and specifying the relief sought. Appeals may be taken to the Supreme Court of the United States. Upon expiration of the term for which they are appointed, they do not cease to be judges, but are assigned for duty within some judicial circuit, and other Circuit Judges are designated by the Chief Justice of the Supreme Court for service in this court.

The court was abolished Oct. 22, 1913, its jurisdiction transferred to the district courts and its judges were retained as circuit judges.

Commerce Court. (See Courts.)

Defended, 7755.

Decisions sustained by Supreme Court, 7757.

Establishment of, recommended, 7442.

Jurisdiction of, 7757.

Prompt decision of cases in, 7756.

Reasons for establishment of, 7756.

Record of, 7756.

Commerce, Department of.—In order to relieve some of the executive departments of the Government of the burden of greatly increased duties, and in response to the petitions of the industrial and commercial classes of the country for the establishment of a separate department of the Government to care for their interests, the Bureau of Labor was established June 27, 1804, and June 13, 1888, it was succeeded by the Department of Labor which was succeeded in turn by the Department of Commerce and Labor, created Feb. 14, 1903. The Sixty-second Congress, on the last day of its session (March 4, 1913), separated the Department of Commerce and Labor into the Department of Commerce and the Department of Labor.

Like the Department of the Interior the Department of Commerce is composed of unrelated bureaus and branches of the public service. The fundamental purpose of the department is to promote the foreign and domestic commerce, the mining, manufacturing, shipping, and fishing industries, and the transportation facilities of the United States. The new offices created by the act of 1903 were the Bureau of Corporations and the Bureau of Manufactures. The Light House Board, the Light House Establishment, the Steamboat Inspection Service, the Bureau of Navigation, the United States Shipping Commissioner, the National Bureau of Standards, the Coast and Geodetic Survey (q. v.), the Commissioner-General of Immigration, the Commissioners of Immigration, the Bureau of Immigration, the Immigration Service at Large, the Bureau of Statistics (q. v.), and the Alaska Fur Seal Service were taken over from the Department of the

Treasury. The Census Office was transferred to the Department of Commerce and Labor from the Department of the Interior. The Bureau of Foreign Commerce was taken from the Department of State and made a part of the Bureau of Statistics; the Fish Commission (q. v.) the Office of Commissioner of Fish and Fisheries, which 'had heretofore existed as independent branches of the public service, are now attached to the Department of Commerce. The division of Cotton and Tobacco Statistics was organized in 1916.

Important new lines of investigation planned by the department for 1917 are transportation by water and city cartage in relation to the cost of living, also the subjects of religious bodies, marriage and divorce.

Corporations.—The Bureau of Corporations, the head of which is a Commissioner, is one of the most important divisions of the department. It has authority to make investigations into the organization, conduct, and management of business of any corporation, joint stock company, or corporate combination (except common carriers) engaged in commerce among the several states and with foreign nations, and has the same power in respect to these as is conferred upon the Interstate Commerce Commission (see Interstate Commerce).

Manufactures.—It is the function of the Bureau of Manufactures to aid the manufacturing industries of the United States, and to assist them in gaining markets at home and abroad by supplying all available information concerning the various industries and their markets. To aid in this all consular offices, under the direction of the Secretary of State, are placed at the service of the Secretary of Commerce.

Following are the Secretaries of Commerce and Labor and the Presidents under whom they served:

PRESIDENT	Secretary of Commerce and Labor	Appointed
Roosevelt...	George B. Cortelyou, New York.	1903
" ...	Victor H. Metcalf, California...	1904
" ...	Oscar S. Straus, New York.....	1907
Taft........	Charles Nagel, Missouri........	1909
	Secretary of Commerce	
Wilson.....	William C. Redfield, New York.	1913

For more detailed information as to the scope of the activities of the Department of Commerce consult the index references to the Presidents' Messages and Encyclopedic articles under the following headings:

Bureau of Foreign and Domestic Commerce.
Bureau of Navigation.
Bureau of Standards.
Census.

Coast and Geodetic Survey.
Corporations.
Fisheries.
Light House Service.
Manufactures.
Steamboat Inspection Service.

Commerce and Labor, Department of:
Establishment recommended, 6649, 6716.
Established, 6784.

Commerce of Foreign Powers:
Consular reports on trade and industries referred to, 4986, 5122, 5201, 6338, 6356, 6381, 6436, 6460, 6673.
Consular regulations, 6797, 6913, 7421, 7504.

Disturbed by War between the States, 3327.
Referred to, 4851.
Report of Hamilton Fish on, 4024.

Commerce of the World, printing of special edition of, recommended, 6096, 6183, 6734, 6867.

Commerce with Near East, 7667.

Commercial Relations, printing of special edition of, recommended, 6096, 6183, 6338, 6356, 6381, 6436, 6460.

Commercial reports, publication and circulation of, referred to, 4539, 6338, 6356, 6381, 6436, 6460.

Commercial Rights of United States, decrees of belligerent powers of Europe affecting, referred to, 446.

Commercial Tariff. (See Foreign Import Duties; Import Duties.)

Commercial Treaties. (See treaties under the several powers.)

Commissariat.—The part of the army detailed to supply equipment, food and transportation.

Commissary General. (See War Department and Army.)

Commission.—The certificate clothing a person with authority in a position, as the commission of an ambassador.

Commission Form of Government.—The government of a city by a commission, instead of by a mayor and other city officials, was first instituted in Galveston, Texas, in 1901. Its usual form provides for the election of a certain number of commissioners from the city at large, who, in turn, elect one of their number to act as mayor and divide with each other the administration of the city departments. One commissioner may take charge of the police department, a second of the fire department, a third of a health department, and so on. A limited number of members of the commission, usually only five, has been the customary practice, in order to concentrate responsibility of government. Another object in limiting the number of commissioners is to secure a "short ballot." The commission movement has had added to it, in the case of some cities, the initiative, the referendum and the recall. In some cases, no recognition is given to political primaries or political parties; candidates for the office of commissioner being nominated by certificate.

History of the Commission Form of Government.—Washington, D. C., which came under the commission plan on June 11, 1878, by act of Congress, was the first city in the United States to adopt permanently this form of government. The application of the commission plan to the capital of the United States grew out of the relation of the National Government to the Federal city, and the capital was not at that time considered an example to other municipalities. The real beginning of the movement toward commission government in American cities was made in Galveston, Tex., in 1901. A destructive storm having overwhelmed the city in 1900, leaving it prostrate financially, the government was placed in the hands of a commission in the following year. The experience of Galveston under the commission plan was such that in 1905 it was adopted by Houston, Tex. Three more cities adopted the commission form in the calendar year 1907, 2 in 1908, 8 in 1909, 7 in 1910, 14 in 1911, 14 in 1912, 20 in 1913, 7 in 1914, and 3 in the early part of 1915. In all, 81 cities have adopted the commission form. According to the latest information available six more such cities have recently adopted the plan by popular vote, and in four of them it has already gone into effect. Thus there are 85 cities of over 30,000 inhabitants which are governed by commissions at the present time. These cities vary in population from 32,800 inhabitants in Boise, Idaho, to 465,000 in Buffalo, N. Y., and are scattered throughout 27 States, in addition to the District of Columbia, ranging from Massachusetts to Washington and from South Carolina to California. Five of them are in New England, 30 in other Northern States east of the Mississippi, 16 in Northern States between the Mississippi River and the Pacific Coast States, 9 in the Pacific Coast States, and 25 in the South.

The total population of the 85 commission cities on February 1, 1916, is estimated at 7,677,000, or 44 per cent of the aggregate population of the 195 cities of 30,000 to 500,000 inhabitants which were covered by the bureau's latest inquiry. Confining the figures to cities of 30,000 to 300,000 inhabitants, there are now operating under the commission form 82 such cities, with a total population of 6,480,000, or 45 per cent of the aggregate population of the 184 cities within these size limits. During the past 10 years the commission plan has also been adopted by many cities of fewer than 30,000 inhabitants.

Commission of Labor. (See Labor, Commission of.)

Commissioner.—A person appointed to attend to duties in connection with the government, as the Commissioner of Pensions, a civil service commissioner, etc.

Commissioner of Internal Revenue. (See Internal Revenue.)

Commissioner of Labor Statistics, Labor Department.—The Bureau of Labor Statistics, which was created in 1883, was really the seed from which sprang the present Department of Labor. The Bureau collects, collates, and reports facts regarding the welfare of wage-earners. It publishes serial bulletins concerning its findings, which cover a wide range,—for instance, Wholesale Prices; Retail Prices and the Cost of Living; Wages and Hours of Labor; Women in Industry; Workmen's Insurance and Workmen's Compensation; Conciliation and Arbitration in Labor Disputes. Under act of May 30, 1908, the Bureau also administers compensation to certain classes of employees of the United States for injuries sustained in the service of the government. The Commissioner of Labor Statistics is appointed by the President, by and with the consent of the President, and his yearly salary is $5,000. (See Labor Department.)

Commissioner of Naturalization.—(S e e Naturalization.) By act of June 29, 1906, the Bureau of Immigration in the Department of Commerce and Labor (q. v.) was changed to the Bureau of Immigration and Naturalization. When the Department of Labor (q. v.) was organized as a separate department of the Government in 1913, the Bureau was separated into the Bureau of Immigration (q. v.) and the Bureau of Naturalization. The Commissioner of Naturalization is appointed from the competitive classified civil service (q. v.) and his yearly salary is $3,500. He not only has charge of the naturalization activities of the government, but also records the registry, date of entrance, and other data concerning each immigrant, granting a certificate containing such data to the immigrant himself.

Commissioner-General of Immigration. —(See Immigration.) The office of Superintendent of Immigration was created in 1891, and was placed under the Treasury Department. The title of Commissioner-general of immigration was bestowed in 1895, and in 1903 the officer was transferred to the newly-created Department of Labor and Commerce, from which he was transferred to the Department of Labor when the latter was organized in 1913. The Commissioner-general of immigration is appointed by the President, by and with the consent of the Senate, at a yearly salary of $5,000; and he is assisted by a deputy commissioner of immigration at a salary of $3,500. The Bureau of Immigration applies the laws concerning the admission and rejection of immigrants to the United States, and also the deportation of aliens. The Commissioner-general is charged also with the protection of and assistance to immigrants reaching this country; and pays particular attention to the problem of distributing them as advantageously as possible throughout the United States. He co-operates with the other departments of the government concerning the education and employment of immigrants and other matters pertaining to their welfare. All the immigrant stations of the country are under his supervision, as is the prevention of the surreptitious entry and smuggling of immigrants.

Commissioners. (See the several commissioners.)

Commissioners, United States, jurisdiction to try misdemeanors recommended, 4939, 5879, 5968.

Commissions (see also Cherokee Commission; Mission Commission; Sioux Commission):

To treat with Indians for cession of lands discussed, 6271.

Commissions, Foreign, Visits of. (See Visits of Foreign Commissions.)

Committee.—One or more persons, elected or appointed, to whom any matter of business is referred, either by a legislative body or by a court or by any collective body of men acting together. It is the custom in all American legislative bodies to appoint committees for the transaction of their business. It is the duty of these committees to report to the central body their conclusions on all matters referred to them, thus presenting for discussion well-shaped or completed legislation, saving much valuable time and securing more concentrated effort. The committee system of conducting business was developed by the British House of Commons during Queen's Elizabeth's reign and was in full operation during the Commonwealth. It has, however, been partially superseded in England by the system of cabinet government. During early colonial days Virginia, Maryland, New York, Pennsylvania, and North Carolina copied the system from England, and the familiarity of the members of the Continental Congress with its workings naturally led to its use in that body. After the adoption of the Constitution Congress made sparing use of the committee system, but by 1820, under Speaker Clay, the system of standing committees had reached full development. The Senate followed slowly. The Senate appoints its own committees.

This was formerly the custom of the House, but soon their appointment was given to the Speaker, which adds greatly to his power.

Committee of the Whole.—It is the regular custom of legislative bodies both in this country and in Europe, to intrust or commit all proposed legislation to committees appointed for the purpose of considering special subjects. These make reports and recommendations to the whole body. For the purpose of deliberating upon matters of general interest not comprehended in the scope of the regular committees, the entire legislative body sometimes resolves itself into a committee of the whole, under the chairmanship of some member other than the regular presiding officer. In the United States Congress the rules and practice of the House recognize two Committees of the Whole—namely, the Committee of the Whole House on the State of the Union, to which are referred public business and bills appropriating public money or property, and the Committee of the Whole House, to which are referred private bills and private business. The rules of proceeding in the House are observed in the Committee of the Whole so far as they are applicable. No legislation can be enacted by the Committee of the Whole.

Committee on Public Information. (See Public Information Committee.)

Commodore.—Formerly a courtesy title given in the United States Navy to the senior officer of a squadron. By an act passed in 1857 the senior captain of a fleet was known as the flag officer. The grade of commodore was created in 1862, along with that of rear-admiral, and established as the grade next above that of captain. This grade had the relative rank of a brigadier-general in the Army. Until that year a captain was the highest naval officer recognized by law. A captain or flag officer who commanded more than one vessel at a time was by common consent called commodore, and the title, once applied, generally clung to him. The title of commodore was abolished by the navy personnel act approved March 3, 1899, and the number of rear-admirals was increased by the same act to eighteen.

Common Carriers.—The legal definition of common carrier applies to all who carry goods for hire indifferently for all persons. The term includes carriers by land and water. On the one hand they comprise railway companies, truckmen, teamsters and express companies, whether such persons undertake to convey goods from one part of a city to another or through the whole extent of the country, or between different states and countries; on the other hand they include owners and masters of every sort of vessel who undertake to carry freight for all who choose to employ them, whether between ports, along the coasts, or along navigable rivers, or across the seas. Common carriers are liable for all damages or loss during transportation from any cause except the act of God or the public enemy. Common carriers, when they undertake the general business of transportation, are obliged to carry all which offer and if they refuse without just excuse they are liable to action. They may qualify their common law responsibility by special contract. The bill of lading is the written evidence of the contract. The responsibility of the carrier begins on receipt of the goods from the owner. Common carriers of passengers are not held responsible as insurers of the safety of those they transport as common carriers are.

The regulation of common carriers by federal laws seemed unnecessary in the early history of legislation. The attention of Congress was finally engaged by a report submitted by the Cullom committee Jan. 18, 1886, which declared that "Unjust discrimination is the chief cause of complaint against the management of railroads in the conduct of business, and gives rise to much of the pressure upon Congress for regulating legislation." This report was based on 1,450 printed pages of testimony, and formed the basis of the Inter-State Commerce act of 1887.

The statute recognizes the fact that it is no business of a common carrier to foster particular enterprises or to build up new industries; but, deriving its franchise from the legislature and depending upon the will of the people for its very existence, it is bound to deal squarely with the public, to extend reasonable facilities for the transportation of persons and property, and to put all its patrons upon an absolute equality. The law of 1887 was amended by the Elkins act of 1903. This provided for a fine of from $1,000 to $20,000 on the company instead of imprisonment of the agent for wilful violation of the law, and provided for expediting cases before the federal courts. While the law virtually prevented the giving of direct rebates, yet it was found possible for the companies to grant indirect discriminations to favored shippers, especially those furnishing sidings, cars, or other facilities for transportation. The consolidation of competing roads was decided to be illegal in the Northern Securities case, decided March 14, 1904.

June 29, 1906, Congress passed the Hepburn law. This gave the Interstate Commerce Commission power to prescribe rates for common carriers, and broadened the definition to include all railroads, pipe lines, express and sleeping car companies; forbade the issue of free passes to any but employees and their families and a few prescribed others; forbade railroad companies to transport any commodities other than lumber produced or owned by the carrier; required schedules of all tariffs to be filed with the commission; imposed severe penalties for rebating; empowered the commission to prescribe a uniform method of bookkeeping.

During 1907 the Federal Government secured indictments against the following common carriers for discriminating between shippers and for giving rebates: The Great Northern Railroad, for giving rebates to the American Sugar Refining Company; the Chicago, Rock Island and Pacific, on twelve counts; the Chicago, Milwaukee and St. Paul, on thirteen counts; the lake steamer line of the New York Central Railroad (Western Transit Company), on twelve counts; the Central Vermont, for giving rebates to one of the constituent companies of the American Sugar Refining Company; the Atchison, Topeka and Santa Fé, for giving illegal rates; the New York, Chicago and St. Louis, the Lehigh Valley and the owners of a refrigerator car line, for giving and taking rebates; the Pennsylvania Railroad, the New York Central, the Standard Oil Company and one of its subsidiary companies, for illegal rates from Olean, N. Y., to points in Vermont; the Standard Oil Company, for accepting illegal rates on oil from Whiting, Ind., to East St. Louis, Ill.

Common Carriers, government control of, recommended, 7143.

Common Law.—Common Law is defined to be those rules of action which have grown up from old usage and the decisions of judges. In the United States the term "common law" means that of England, including unwritten maxims and customs immemorial in that Kingdom, and the statutes passed by the English Parliament before the independence of the Colonies. July 4, 1776, is the date fixed by many states, but the rule is not uniform. With the exception of Louisiana, this forms the basis of the jurisprudence of all states. In many of them it has been expressly adopted by statute or constitutional provision. Under the first Constitution of the Colonies the people were declared entitled to the benefits of the common law of England, but it was left for the colonial courts to decide what common law was. The courts placed various constructions upon existing statutes and colonial legislatures modified the text in various ways. After the Constitution was adopted the strict constructionists maintained that there was no common law in respect to the jurisprudence of the Federal government, the nationalists taking the opposite view. Federal courts sitting in a Territory adopt common law rules of decision in the absence of statutes; in a state they adopt the common law of that state. The United States as a district sovereignty has no common law, and therefore there can be no common law offenses against it, but the Federal courts adopt the common law definition of common law crimes not defined by statute.

"Common Sense."—A pamphlet by Thos. Paine, published in 1776. It was a stirring appeal for American independence. Washington ordered it read to his troops. (See Paine, Thomas, Biographic Index.)

Communism.—Common ownership and control of property as distinguished from individual ownership and control. (See Socialism.)

Compact.—Used generally as synonymous with *treaty* in diplomatic relations between countries.

Company.—In military parlance a body of troops fewer in number than a regiment or battalion. In time of war a company is supposed to consist of about one hundred men.

Compatriot.—A fellow-countryman.

Compensated Emancipation. (See Emancipation.)

Competitor, The, persons claiming American citizenship captured on, by Spanish authorities, 6180, 6183, 6262.

Compromise, Missouri. (See Missouri Compromise.)

Compromise of 1833.—The high tariff of 1828 caused much dissatisfaction throughout the south. By the act of July 14, 1832, amending the tariff law of 1828, many of the revenue taxes were reduced and the first tax was laid on woolen yarn. The oppressive features of these laws were more bitterly opposed in South Carolina than elsewhere, and resulted in the nullification of the law by that state. This was done by a convention held at Columbia, Nov. 19, 1832, which by ordinance declared the tariff acts of 1828 and 1832 null and void. Thus the question of nullification in its fullest development was brought into national prominence. March 1, 1833, Congress enacted a new tariff law

in the nature of a compromise. It was practically the same bill as that introduced in the Senate by Henry Clay. It provided for the gradual scaling down of the high duties then existing until after ten years a free-trade basis should be reached. This compromise took the place of a low-tariff measure then under consideration in the House. The latter provided for a gradual scaling down of all duties so that 20 per cent should be the standard duty in 1842. (See also Nullification.)

Compromise of 1833, diminution of duties under, referred to, 1955.

Compromise of 1850.—On Jan. 29, 1850, Henry Clay introduced six resolutions in the Senate relating to (1) the admission of California as a free state; (2) Territorial governments for Utah and New Mexico without conditions as to slavery; (3) boundaries of Texas; (4) payment of Texas debt; (5) suppression of the slave trade in the District of Columbia; (6) fugitive slave laws. A special committee of thirteen, with Clay as chairman, combined these resolutions into one omnibus bill, which failed of passage. After the defeat of this (Clay's omnibus) bill several separate bills, having practically the same purpose of compromising on the slavery question, were introduced and passed. Under the compromise Texas was allowed $10,000,000 for New Mexico, and the area of that territory was reduced. Sept. 9, 1850, California was admitted to the Union with her free constitution. On the same day bills were passed for establishing territorial governments in New Mexico and Utah. These laws contain Senator Soulé's slavery-option clause. Sept. 12 amendments to the fugitive-slave law of Feb. 12, 1793, were passed, denying arrested negroes trial by jury and prohibiting redress to free colored seamen imprisoned in southern ports.

Compromise of 1850 (see also Slavery): Adherence to, 2628, 2674.
Discussed, 2755.

Compromises of the Constitution.—Three important compromises were made by the Constitutional Convention in 1787. The most important question that agitated the members was whether each state's influence should be equal to that of any other state, or whether representation should be based upon population. The plan proposed by Edmund Randolph, of Virginia, and called the "Virginia plan," favored representation in both Houses according to population; that of William Paterson, of New Jersey, an equal vote for all states and only one House. As a compromise, proposed by William Samuel Johnson, of Connecticut, and originally suggested by George Mason, of Virginia, the Convention agreed to have two Houses with equal representation in the Senate and proportionate representation in the House. Secondly, it was proposed to tax both exports and imports at the discretion of Congress. Charles Cotesworth Pinckney, of South Carolina, declared that his state could not come into the Union under such a provision, as her wealth consisted mainly in one article of export—rice. It was therefore decided that no tax upon exports should be laid. Thirdly, North Carolina, South Carolina, and Georgia refused to enter into the Union if the slave trade was to be prohibited; so the third compromise agreed to was that Congress should not prohibit traffic in slaves before 1808 and that a fugitive-slave law should be enacted.

Comptroller of the Currency. (See Treasury Department.)

Comptroller of the Treasury.—The office of Comptroller of the Treasury was established by act of Congress in 1789. As defined by the law of 1894, the office is in charge of all appeals from the findings of the auditors (q. v.), and advises and aids the Treasury Department in determining the validity of all appropriations and payments passing through the Treasury Department. The Comptroller of the Treasury therefore passes legal judgment over all expenditures coming through the treasury of the United States; and, except for review by the courts, his decision is final. His yearly salary is $6,000, and he is assisted by an assistant comptroller, who receives a yearly salary of $4,500. (See Treasury Department.)

Comptroller of the Treasury, 785.

Compulsory Military Service.—A number of prominent Americans, notably ex-President Theodore Roosevelt and Major-General Leonard Wood, had been favoring compulsory military training for citizens of the United States even before the outbreak of the Great European War; but their efforts in this direction received little support from the mass of the American people. After August 1, 1914, however, a definite movement for military preparedness (see Preparedness) took shape in the United States, and the sentiment for universal military training became powerful. There arose also a strong antagonism to the proposal, and the discussion became bitter over the entire country.

Both the advantages and the disadvantages of the compulsory training are evident, and the question of its adoption hinges solely upon their relative values. Among the advantages may be cited the following: Compulsory military training is democratic, insofar as it places the burden of military service upon the shoulders of all alike, without distinction of wealth or of social station; whereas service in a small or even a considerable professional army is apt to be declined by the middle and upper classes. A trained standing army, with an even larger number of trained reserves, is always available for an emergency, whereas it requires months of training, to say nothing of legislation, to raise an army from the untrained citizenry. In times of war, the expense and the uncertainty of voluntary recruiting are abolished, along with the hectic campaign of hatred and vituperation towards the country's enemies which characterized England's campaign for recruits in the European War, for instance. Universal training also should have a beneficial effect upon the physical development of the individual, in addition to providing a definite census of the physical situation of the country's inhabitants, with provision for any defects which may need to be remedied. Universal training has been adopted by practically every European country, with the exception of England, and by Japan; so that, despite the large population of the United States, she could not put into the field in case of conflict with any of these countries an army which would bear comparison in size with their armies. And the example of France and of Switzerland is mentioned to prove that a country may adopt military training for all its inhabitants without becoming militaristic or without being fired by lust for conquest or by chauvinism.

Opponents of universal military training point out, on the other hand, that Germany, the country which today stands before the world as the greatest exponent of militarism (q. v.), is the country in which universal training received its impetus and highest development. France, they declare, adopted universal service too recently for the military spirit to overwhelm the French people, while countries like Switzerland are too small and have a population too scattered to nourish the seeds of militarism. These opponents claim further that war at its best.is a brutalizing influence, and that training for war is apt to have a brutalizing effect upon the individual. Military service means blind obedience to orders, and the consequent stunting of the individual initiative; and a democracy must perish when its people get out of the habit of thinking for themselves. The opposition of military training to the finer instincts of democracy is shown by the fact that many persons who found a place in our history as most serviceable Americans fled to this country to avoid serving in European armies. The physical improvement in the individual can be obtained with physical training methods aside from the military drill; and the United States, unlike the European countries, separated by a vast expanse of water from any possible enemies, need not fear an invasion upon a few days' notice. And although the possession of a large military strength need not imply a desire for the utilization of it, yet it may inculcate a psychological aggressiveness which will fan any latent war spirit in times of disturbance.

Germany was the first of the great European powers to inaugurate the system of universal military training, and her successes in 1866 and 1870 were so startling that her example was followed by most of the other European countries, with the exception of England, who relies upon her fleet for war strength. Under the German system, all men are called to the colors for two years' service when they reach the age of 20. Owing to the fact that there is a constitutional check of 1% of the population upon the size of Germany's standing army, there are many and liberal exemptions to the liability for military service. The men from the maritime cities and provinces recruit the navy. All the officers of the German army are professional military men, and those citizens who are trained for the upper classes in the military service receive only one year of training. From 22 to 27 the German man is under the first reserve, and from 27 to 45 in the second reserve. The normal professional army of Germany in peace times was about 870,000.

France, although with a smaller population, by a system of three years' military service and of fewer exemptions has been able to maintain a peace army of about 720,000, including her colonial troops—only 150,000 less than the German army. (See Swiss System of Military Training, Australian System of Military Training; also Armies of the World, Military Training in Schools, European War, Preparedness.)

Concessioner.—One who obtains a special privilege from the Government, like the privilege to cut timber or to use water-ways.

Concessions, The.—The privileges enjoyed by New Jersey as a Province in 1664; these privileges having been granted by Berkeley and Carteret, who held authority from Charles II. These privileges served as a constitution for the Province of New Jersey until the Revolution.

Concord (Mass.), Battle of.—One of the opening skirmishes of the Revolutionary War. A detachment of 800 British soldiers under Lieut.-Col. Smith and Maj. Pitcairn had been sent from Boston to destroy or capture some military stores collected at Concord by the Americans. After a brief engagement at Lexington they reached Concord April 19, 1775, where they were opposed by 300 minutemen under Col. Barrett and Maj. Buttrick. After a short conflict, in which several were lost on each side, the British fled to Boston under a harassing fire of the Americans. (See also Lexington (Mass.), Battle of.)

Concord, The, mentioned, 6298, 6414, 6766, 6769, 6771.

Concurrent Resolution.—A r e s o l u t i o n passed by the House of Representatives and the Senate not of sufficient importance to require the President's signature.

Confectionery.—As early as 1816 there were twenty confectioners in Philadelphia, and perhaps as many in New York. Each dealer, as a rule, manufactured his own stock by hand and sold it at retail. In 1845 machinery was introduced into the business, and the trade has so increased that today the manufacture of special machinery for confectioners' use has become a separate and important industry.

Among the pioneers in the business were Sebastian Henrion, succeeded in 1844 by Henrion & Chauveau and later by Sebastian Chauveau, who was the first to manufacture gum-drops, ju-jube paste and marshmallows in this country; Paul Lajas, who became a sugar refiner; George Miller, William N. Herring, S. S. Rennels and J. J. Richardson, of Philadelphia. In New York, Ridley & Co. was established in 1806; R. L. Stuart in 1828, followed by Thompson, Stryker and the Delmonico Brothers. In Boston, the Chases, Copenhagen, Nichols and Fenno were leaders, while in Baltimore the pioneers were Bouvey, Price and Bridges.

In 1850 there were in the United States 383 factories, employing 1,733 persons and producing $3,040,671 worth of goods, with an investment of $1,035,551. By 1900 the number of establishments had grown to 4,297, with a capital of $35,155,361, employing 33,583 persons, paying in wages $10,867,687, and turning out $81,290,543 worth of goods. Ten years later the value of the output was $134,795,000.

In 1884 the National Confectioners' Association of the United States was formed by leading candy manufacturers. One of its stated purposes is "to advance the standard of confectionery in all practicable ways, and absolutely to prevent harmful adulterations." In most states the sale of candy containing harmful ingredients is forbidden by law.

Confederacy, United Daughters of the.
—This organization was organized at Nashville, Tennessee, on September 10, 1894, with a membership of 90,000 in its 3,000 chapters. It is composed of the widows, wives, or female descendants of military or civil workers under the Confederacy. Its objects are the unification of the womanhood of the South, and the preservation of objects and data of historical interest.

Confederate Flags:

Captured, to be presented to Congress, 3309.

Return of Union and, to respective States recommended, 5163.

Proposition withdrawn, 5164.

Confederate Soldiers, proposed national care of graves, 7006.

President Wilson's speech at dedication of monument to, at Arlington, 7948.

Confederate States.—A government organized in February, 1861, by the states of South Carolina, Mississippi, Florida, Alabama, Georgia, Louisiana and Texas. Later Arkansas, North Carolina, Virginia, and Tennessee seceded from the Union and joined the Confederacy. The provisional Congress met at Montgomery, Ala., Feb. 4, 1861, and adopted a provisional constitution February 8. Jefferson Davis was elected provisional president and Alexander H. Stephens provisional vice-president. Later a permanent government was organized. A permanent constitution was adopted March 11, 1861. Mr. Davis and Mr. Stephens were elected president and vice-president, respectively, and they were inaugurated Feb. 22, 1862, at Richmond, Va., which was made the permanent seat of government.

The history of the Confederate States is almost entirely confined to a history of the Civil War. The United States Government denied the right of any state to secede from the Union, refused to recognize the Confederate States as anything more than rebellious members of the Union, and immediately took measures to bring them into subjection. The Confederate States were granted belligerent rights by most of the maritime nations, but their independence was recognized by none (pages 3327, 3565). Money was obtained by the issue of treasury notes and by loans on cotton. After a war of four years the government of the Confederate States practically came to an end with the surrender of Gen. Lee at Appomattox, April 9, 1865.

Confederate Cabinet.—The Confederate States had a cabinet composed of the heads of executive departments, similar to the United States Government and created for like purposes. The heads of the departments exercised similar powers and were clothed with duties and responsibilities corresponding to those of Cabinet officers in the United States. The President was empowered to remove members of his cabinet. Congress was authorized to provide for the admission of cabinet officers to a seat in either house, with the privilege of participating in debates pertaining to their department. This provision remained inoperative, as the congress failed to provide the appropriate legislation. The secretaries of state were Robert Toombs, of Georgia, Robert M. T. Hunter, of Virginia, and Judah P. Benjamin, of Louisiana; of the treasury, Charles G. Memminger and George A. Trenholm, of South Carolina; of war, L. Pope Walker, of Alabama, Judah P. Benjamin, of Louisiana, George W. Randolph, of Virginia, James A. Seddon, of Virginia, and John C. Breckinridge, of Kentucky; of the navy, Stephen R. Mallory, of Florida; postmaster-general, John H. Reagan, of Texas; attorneys-general, Judah P. Benjamin, of Louisiana, Thomas Bragg, of North Carolina, Thomas H. Watts, of Alabama, and George Davis, of North Carolina. The last member of this cabinet, John H. Reagan, died at Palestine, Texas, on March 6, 1905.

Confederate Congress.—The provisional congress of the seceding southern states met at Montgomery, Ala., Feb. 4, 1861. Two sessions were held here. The government removed to Richmond, Va., May 24, 1861. The last two sessions were held in the latter city, final adjournment taking place Feb. 17, 1862. The first Confederate Congress held four sessions between Feb. 18, 1862, and Feb. 18, 1864, to organize the Confederacy, frame a constitution, and devise means for carrying on the war. It consisted of twenty-four senators and about one hundred representatives. The second Confederate Congress had two sessions between May 2, 1864, and March 18, 1865.

Confederate Constitution.—The constitution adopted by the Confederate States of America at Montgomery, Ala. A provisional congress, composed of delegates from the seceding states, met in that city Feb. 4, 1861, and on the 8th adopted a provisional or temporary constitution. March 11 they agreed upon a permanent constitution, which was afterward ratified by all the seceding states. It was based upon that of the United States, with the following chief exceptions: It recognized the principle of state sovereignty and the protection of slavery in all new territories; it prohibited internal improvements at federal expense and contained a prohibition against laying any duties on imports "to promote or foster any branch of industry"; new states were to be admitted by a vote of the states; state legislatures could impeach Confederate officers acting within their jurisdiction; the president was to be elected for a term of six years and was ineligible for re-election; the appropriating power of congress was limited, and the right of debate in congress was extended to heads of departments.

Commissioners to Europe.—There were sent abroad to secure assistance and co-operation in Europe William L. Yancey and James M. Mason to the Court of St. James, John Slidell to Paris, Pierre A. Rost to Madrid, A. Dudley Mann to Brussels, and L. Q. C. Lamar to St. Petersburg, although each made visits to other capitals. The arrest of Mason and Slidell aboard a British steamer and their subsequent release upon demand of Great Britain points to the probability of intervention by that power in behalf of the Confederate States.

Confederate States (see also Confederate Constitution; Reconstruction; Restoration; Secession; Slavery; Southern States; Civil War):

Acts for admission of certain Southern States vetoed, 3846, 3848.

Acts to provide for more efficient government of rebel states vetoed. (See Reconstruction.)

Agents of, abroad, suits instituted in English courts against, 3661.

Aid furnished to, by Great Britain. (See Alabama claims.)

Belligerent rights accorded, by foreign powers discussed, 3259, 3327, 3565.

Recognition and aid from foreign powers invoked by, 3221, 3246.

Blockade of ports of. (See Blockades.)

Circuit courts to be re-established in, recommendations regarding, 3556.

Correspondence regarding, referred to, 3576.

Claims against citizens of, and means of collecting discussed, 3251.

Commercial intercourse with, prohibited, 3238, 3366, 3483.

Restrictions on, removed from certain ports, 3290, 3310, 3372, 3375, 3417, 3431, 3482, 3507, 3515, 3524, 3529, 3531, 3537.

Constitution of. (See Confederate Constitution.)

Courts of justice for, recommended by President Lincoln, 3251.

Direct tax, collection of, referred to, 3589.

Envoys of, sent to France and Great Britain. (See Mason and Slidell.)

Executive departments of, historical statement of Gen. Sherman concerning public policy of, referred to, 4850.

Flags of—

Captured, to be presented to Congress, 3381.

Return of, to respective States, recommended, 5163.

Proposition withdrawn, 5164.

Government employees assisting in rendition of public honors to rebel living or dead, referred to, 3591.

Government of, first located at Montgomery, Ala., 3225.

Transfer of, to Richmond, Va., 3225.

Governments to be re-established in—

Act to guarantee republican form of government to states whose governments have been overthrown, 3424.

Discussed, 3390.

Proclamations regarding, 3414, 3423.

In which insurrection exists proclaimed, 3238, 3293, 3358, 3366.

Proclamations declaring insurrection at an end, 3627, 3632.

Joint resolution declaring certain States not entitled to representation in electoral college discussed, 3461.

Joint resolution excluding electoral votes of states lately in rebellion, vetoed, 3849.

Policy of President of United States toward, referred to, 3667.

President of. (See Davis, Jefferson.)

Products of, authority given to purchase, 3441.

Rebel debt, referred to, 3583, 3588.

Reconstruction of. (See Reconstruction.)

Restoration of. (See Restoration.)

Secretary of War of. (See Seddon, James A.)

Union and Confederate flags, return of, to respective States recommended, 5163.

Proposition withdrawn, 5164.

Confederate Veterans. (See United Confederate Veterans.)

Confederate Veterans, United. (See United Confederate Veterans.)

Confederate Veterans, United Sons of. —This organization was formed in Richmond in 1896 for charitable, historical and social purposes. It is composed of male descendants of men who served the Confederacy actively during the Civil War.

Confederation, Articles of.—The Second Continental Congress appointed on June 11, 1776, a committee to draw up Articles of Confederation and Perpetual Union. This committee presented a draft to Congress July 12, 1776. Nov. 15, 1777, they were adopted with amendments as "Articles of Confederation and Perpetual Union between the States." July 9, 1778, the Articles were signed by delegates from eight states. March 1, 1781, the delegates from Maryland also signed, and on the same date the final ratification was ordered by Congress. The original is indorsed: "Act of Confederation of the United States of America." These Articles provided for a single House of Congress with power to raise money by requisition on the states. Ratification of the articles by all the states was necessary, and they could not be amended save by the consent of every state. They did not operate on individuals and could not command respect abroad or enforce order at home. After numerous futile attempts to amend them a convention, following the suggestion of the Virginia and Maryland boundary commissioners, was called at Annapolis, Md., in 1786, which in turn called a convention at Philadelphia in 1787. The last-named body rejected the Articles of Confederation and framed instead the present Constitution, which, after its ratification by nine states, became the supreme law of the land (page 5).

Confederation, Articles of, 5.

Signers of, 13.

Congo Conference, at Berlin, referred to, 4823, 4855, 4865, 4915.

Congo Free State.—A dependency of Belgium in the heart of Africa. It extends from 5° 30′ north of the equator to about 12° south, and from the central lake region north and west to the Congo River. The northwest boundary follows that river to its mouth, which provides an outlet to the Atlantic Ocean. The exact boundaries were defined by the neutrality declarations of August, 1885, and December, 1894, after treaties with Great Britain, Germany, France and Portugal. The country has access to the Nile at the Lado *enclave*, of which that river forms the eastern boundary. The area of the country is estimated at more than 900,000 square miles, and the inhabitants at 20,000,000. The European population, Jan. 1, 1908, numbered 2,943, including forty-seven Americans. The state had its origin in the companies formed for trade and exploration in that region.

The African International Association, founded in 1877, sent Henry M. Stanley on an expedition up the Congo River to establish trading posts and report on the possibilities of travel and transportation. After Stanley's return the Comité d'Etudes du Haut Congo was formed under the auspices of Leopold II, King of Belgium, and in 1879 this became the International Association of the Congo. This organization again sent Stanley up the great river. He and his men built roads, founded trading stations and made more than 400 treaties with native chiefs, conveying the sovereignty of these chiefs to the International Association of the Congo. The association then appealed to the Powers of the world for permission to combine these numerous sovereignties into one independent state. The United States was the first country to recognize the International Association of the Congo as a sovereign independent power, under the name of the Congo Free State. This was done in accordance with the report of the Committee on Foreign Relations of the Forty-eighth Congress, which reported that the acts of the native chiefs were clearly within their rights and that the association could lawfully accept them (pages 4823, 4914). Within a year Austria, France, Germany, Great Britain, Italy, the Netherlands, Portugal, Russia, Spain, and Sweden followed the example of the United States.

A general act of the International Congo Conference, held at Berlin in 1885, established freedom of trade in the basin of the Congo, declared absolutely free the navigation of the Congo, its tributaries and the lakes and canals connected with it, laid down rules for the protection of the natives and the suppression of the slave trade, and imposed upon the powers which signed the act the obligation to accept the mediation of one or more friendly governments should any serious trouble arise in the Congo basin. The United States declined to ratify this act, on the ground that such action i..posed upon it international obligations at variance with its traditional policy. The Conference placed the state under the sovereignty of King Leopold II of Belgium, on the basis of personal union with Belgium, though perpetually neutral and free to the trade of all nations, and guaranteed equality of treatment to all settlers of whatever nationality. By a will dated Aug. 2, 1889, Leopold bequeathed to Belgium all his sovereign rights in the Congo Free State.

July 21, 1890, the territory of the state was declared inalienable, but a convention of July 3, 1890, reserved to Belgium the right to annex the Congo after a period of ten years. A treaty for annexation was signed Nov. 28, 1907, approved by the Belgian legislature in August, 1908, and by the King Oct. 18, 1908. By February, 1909, Germany had recognized the annexation. The exports of the country consist of rubber, ivory, palm nuts, palm oil, white copal, cocoa, coffee, gold and copper ore. Cottons, provisions, clothing, wines and spirits, machinery, building material, arms, ammunition are sold to the country. The bulk of the trade is with Belgium.

In 1914 the Congo completed its sixth year as a Belgian colony. The Belgian Parliament provided for its administration and appointed Baron Wahis governor. Many complaints have been made of cruel treatment of natives by traders. Great Britain withheld her recognition of the annexation until there was evidence of satisfactory conditions in the Congo. Nov. 21, 1911, British consuls in the country reported that conditions in general had improved but that abuses continued in those districts where rubber is demanded in lieu of taxation. (See also Belgium.)

Congo Free State:

Act for reform of revenue tariff of, referred to, 5621.

Arms and ammunition, act prohibiting sale of, to natives of, recommended, 5868.

Discussed, 4914.

International Association of the Congo recognized by United States, 4823, 4914.

Referred to, 4988.

Slave trade in—
Conference at Brussels for suppression of, 5543.
Recommendations regarding, 5868.
Valley of Congo opened to commerce, discussed, 4762.

Congo, Treaties with.—The International Association of the Congo declared in 1884 that by treaties with the legitimate sovereigns of the basin of the Congo and adjacent territory on the Atlantic it had established supervision over the commerce of the several countries and adopted a common standard for said free states consisting of a blue flag with a golden star in the center. Recognition of this flag was accorded by the United States by declaration of Secretary Frelinghuysen April 22, 1884.

Congress.—A formal meeting or association of persons having a representative character for the enactment of laws, or the consideration of some special subject, or the promotion of some common interest. In the United States all legislative powers are granted by the Constitution to Congress. This body consists of the Senate (*q. v.*) and the House of Representatives (*q. v.*). The powers of Congress are enumerated in the Constitution, Article I, section 8, and all the powers not delegated to the United States by the Constitution nor prohibited by it to the states are reserved to the states respectively or to the people. The power of Congress is absolute within the scope of its authority except as it may be restrained by the veto of the President. The Senate is composed of two members from each state regardless of size or population. The members of the House are apportioned on the basis of Federal population. The Constitution provides (Article V) that "no state, without its consent, shall be deprived of its equal suffrage in the Senate." The Senate is presided over by the Vice-President of the United States, who is also President of the Senate, and the House of Representatives by a Speaker chosen by its members. The Vice-President has no power except in cases where the Senate is equally divided. Congress is required to "assemble at least once in every year, and such meeting shall be on the first Monday in December unless they shall by law appoint a different day." Measures that have passed both Houses are sent to the President, who may either approve or veto them, or do neither, in which latter case the measure becomes a law after ten days from the time it is presented to him, unless in the meantime Congress shall have adjourned. If he approve the bill and sign it, it becomes a law, but if he disapprove it he must return it with his objections to the House in which it shall have originated for reconsideration by them. In such a case, after reconsideration, it requires the affirmative vote of two-thirds of the members in each of the two bodies to pass the measure. Legislation which exceeds the constitutional power of Congress may be declared unconstitutional and void by the Supreme Court of the United States when that body is properly appealed to by either party in any controversy arising in an attempt to enforce such legislation. Each House is by the Constitution "the judge of elections, returns, and qualifications of its own members" (page 17). (See also Senate and House of Representatives; United States, Government of, and Apportionment.)

Congress:

Act appointing day for annual meeting of, vetoed, 1450.

Act of—
Approved, but not signed, whether in force, discussed, 856.
Duly certified and approved, which had not passed, discussed, 1353.
Effect on, of adjournment of Congress before expiration of 10 days after presentation to President, discussed, 3797.

Acts of, to be published in certain newspapers, 4116.

Address from committee of public safety of France transmitted to, 181.

Adjournment of—
Postponement of recess requested, 6092.
Postponement of, recommended, 3021, 3286, 4034.
Resolution authorizing, not approved, 257.

Appropriations, power to designate officer to expend, discussed, 3128.

Appropriations should not be made by, unless necessary, 1248.

Bills, time allowed for consideration of, discussed, 2993, 3060.

Capital, longitude of, west of Greenwich, report, 688.

Capitol prepared for. (See Capitol.)

Carpenter's painting of Lincoln and Cabinet at reading of Emancipation Proclamation presented to, 4435.

Constitution, copies of, printed for members of, 634, 678.

Constitutional amendments recommended to. (See Constitution.)

Contingent expenses of, discussed, 3179.

Declaration of Independence, first copperplate of, bequeathed to, by Lafayette, letter of son presenting, 1342.

Diligence and good temper of, admired, 7913.

Desk on which Declaration of Independence was written presented to United States by heirs of Joseph Coolidge, Jr., 4540.
Letter of Robert C. Winthrop regarding, 4541.

Discretionary authority which can be regulated by, should not be exercised by Executive, 1387.

District of Columbia should be represented in, 1091, 1120, 3652.

Extraordinary sessions of, convened by proclamation of President—
Adams, John, 222.
Cleveland, 5828.
Harrison, W. H., 1876.

Hayes, 4399, 4472.
Jefferson, 345, 412.
Lincoln, 3214.
McKinley, 6470.
Madison, 476, 509.
Pierce, 2927.
Taft, 7586.
Van Buren, 1538.
Information regarding foreign affairs requested by, refused, 186, 2232, 2281, 2416, 2452, 2690, 2691, 2695, 6101.
Joint resolution of—
Declaring freedom of Cuba and authorizing intervention, etc., 6297.
Discussed, 6311.
Regarded by Spain as ''equivalent to an evident declaration of war,'' 6312.
Loyal Senators and Representatives denied admission to seats in, discussed, 3644.
Mail, rates of transportation of, should be regulated by. (See Postal Service.)
Meeting of—
Act appointing day for annual, vetoed, 1450.
Constitutional amendment regarding, recommended, 240.
Members of. (See Representatives; Senators.)
Notification to, of discontinuance of addresses, by President Jefferson, 313.
Permanent seat of Government occupied by. (See Seat of Government.)
Protests of Presidents against action of. (See Protests.)
Public and private acts of, list of, transmitted, 3963.
Requested by President Cleveland not to take recess until enactment of financial legislation, 6092.
Resolutions of, thanking Samuel T. Washington for sword of Washington and staff of Franklin, 2120.
Right of states to representation in, discussed, 3644.
''Shall make no law respecting religious establishment,'' application of, 475.
Testimonials of Gen. Grant offered to, by Mrs. Grant, 4857.
Schedule of, 4859.
Thanks of, tendered. (See Thanks of Congress.)
Two Houses of, independent of each other, 516.
War with—
Algiers should be declared by, 539.
Great Britain—
Declared by, 497.

Special session called on account of threatening aspect of, 413.
Spain declared by, 6348.
House of Representatives (see also Representatives)—
Address of, in reply to President Washington's inaugural, 48.
Reply of President, 49.
Address of, to President Adams on death of Washington, 290.
Calls on President, 290.
Contested elections in, act regulating taking of testimony in, reasons for applying pocket veto to, 2108.
Expresses regret upon being notified of President Washington's intention to retire, 200.
Information regarding foreign intercourse refused, 186, 2281, 2416, 2452.
Referred to, 2529.
Letter of John Randolph, Jr., demanding punishment of certain officers of Army and Navy for insulting conduct, referred to, 291.
Members of. (See Representatives.)
Privileges of, letter relating to, transmitted, 293.
Protests of Presidents against action of. (See Protests.)
Treaties—
Assent of, to, not required, 188.
Transmission of, to, declined, 2601.
Senate (see also Senators)—
Address of, in reply to President Washington's inaugural, 46.
Reply of President, 47.
Address of, to President Adams on death of Washington, 288.
Breach of duty by public officer in publishing executive business of, discussed, 2691.
Calls on President, 288.
Can hold only correspondence with the President in executive session, 2174.
Correspondence respecting relations with Spain refused, 6101.
Executive and, independent of each other in cases of appointment to office, 516.
Expresses regret upon being notified of President Washington's intention to retire, 198.
Extraordinary sessions of, convened by proclamation of President—
Adams, John, 306, 1220.
Adams, J. Q., 997.
Arthur, 4621, 4873.
Buchanan, 3026, 3081, 3156, 3203.
Cleveland, 5428, 6230.
Fillmore, 2646, 2726.
Referred to, 2726.

Grant, 3966, 4087, 4171, 4278, 4390.
Harrison, Benj., 5817.
Hayes, 4591.
 Referred to, 4588.
Jackson, 1508.
Jefferson, 449.
Johnson, 3719.
Lincoln, 3362, 3474.
McKinley, 6470.
Madison, 571.
Monroe, 856.
Pierce, 2959.
Polk, 2539.
Tyler, 2220.
Van Buren, 1857.
Washington, 130, 204, 571.
 (See also Congress, *ante*.)
Free confidential communication with Executive should be preserved, 893.
In confidential correspondence with President, 144, 495, 652.
In executive session can only hold correspondence with President, 2174.
Information regarding—
 Annexation of Texas refused, 2232.
 Negotiations with Great Britain, Costa Rica, and Nicaragua, refused, 2690.
 Nominations to. (See Executive Nominations.)
 President Washington meets and advises with, respecting treaty with Indians, 53.
 Proposition to annex Hawaiian Islands, refused, 2691, 2695.
Protests of Presidents against action of. (See Protests.)
Requested by President Adams to postpone adjournment of, 257.
Treaties, power to make, vested in President with consent of, 187.
Congress, Confederate. (See Confederate Congress.)
Congress, Continental. (See Continental Congress.)
Congress, Members of. (See Appendix.)
Congress, Number of.—Each congress is numbered and holds two annual sessions, respectively termed the long and the short session, each assembling on the first Monday in December and may be called in special session by the President or by joint resolution of both houses. The life of a congress lasts from 12 o'clock noon on March 4 of the odd-numbered year following the election of representatives until 12 o'clock noon on March 4 of the next odd-numbered year. To determine the years covered by a given congress multiply the number of the congress by two and add the product to 1789. The result will be the year in which the congress closed. Example: Sixty-second Congress. Twice 62 is 124; adding 124 to 1789 gives 1913, the year during which (on March

4) the Sixty-second Congress must expire. To find the number of a congress sitting in any given year subtract 1789 from that year; if the result be an even number, half that number will give the congress of which the year in question saw the close; if the result be an odd number, add one, and half the sum will give the congress of which the year in question was the first year.
Congress of Nations. (See Panama, Isthmus of.)
Congressional Elections:
 Federal supervision of, recommended, 5490, 5562, 5766.
 Gerrymander discussed, 5643.
Congressional Globe.—That part of the proceedings of Congress which was published between 1833 and 1873. The Globe was first issued as a newspaper. Later it succeeded the Register of Debates. It was succeeded by the Congressional Record. The Congressional Globe was started as a private enterprise Dec. 7, 1833. Volume I, No. 1, began with the proceedings of the Twenty-third Congress. It was published weekly and each volume was devoted to one session of Congress. The second session of the Fortieth Congress, 1869, was comprised in one volume of five parts, aggregating more than 5,000 pages. (See also Annals of Congress; Congressional Record; Register of Debates.)
Congressional Library. (See Library of Congress.)
Congressional Record.—A complete record of the debates and proceedings of Congress from December, 1873, to the present time. It is the successor to the Congressional Globe, and is printed and circulated by the Government. The Congressional Record is issued daily during the sessions of Congress. Each member of Congress is gratuitously supplied with a specified number for his constituents. It may also be obtained by subscription, the price being $8 for the long and $4 for the short session. The Congressional Record began with the special session of the Forty-third Congress, convened with the inauguration of President Grant for the second term, March 4, 1873. One volume is devoted to the proceedings of each session, but the volumes are generally bound in several parts. Vol. XLV, covering the proceedings of the second session of the Sixtieth Congress, Dec. 6, 1809-June 25, 1910, consists of eight parts, aggregating more than 10,000 pages. (See also Annals of Congress; Congressional Globe, Register of Debates.)
Congressman.—A member of the United States Congress or Legislature,—either in the Senate or the House of Representatives; more commonly used to designate a member of the House of Representatives.
Congressman-at-Large.—A member of United States House of Representatives elected by the voters of an entire state, and not, as is customary, by those of a Congressional district. The election of a Congressman-at-large is a device adopted by a state to secure proper representation in Congress under a Federal apportionment act pending the passage of a state law redistricting the state in accordance with the Federal allowance of Representatives. The apportionment act of Jan. 16, 1901, provides that after March 3, 1903, the House of Representatives shall be composed of 86 members apportioned as fol-

lows: Alabama, 9; Arkansas, 7; California, 8; Colorado, 3; Connecticut, 5; Delaware, 1; Florida, 3; Georgia, 11; Idaho, 1; Illinois, 25; Indiana, 13; Iowa, 11; Kansas, 8; Kentucky, 11; Louisiana, 7; Maine, 4; Maryland, 6; Massachusetts, 14; Michigan, 12; Minnesota, 9; Mississippi, 8; Missouri, 14; Montana, 1; Nebraska, 6; Nevada, 1; New Hampshire, 2; New Jersey, 10; New York, 37; North Carolina, 10; North Dakota, 2; Ohio, 21; Oregon, 2; Pennsylvania, 32; Rhode Island, 2; South Carolina, 7; South Dakota, 2; Tennessee, 10; Texas, 16; Utah, 1; Vermont, 2; Virginia, 10; Washington, 3; West Virginia, 5; Wisconsin, 11; Wyoming, 1. It also provided that Congressmen shall be elected from districts composed of contiguous territory and containing as nearly as possible an equal number of inhabitants, the number of such districts equaling the number of Representatives to which the state is entitled; but "in case of an increase in the number of Representatives which may be given to any state under this apportionment such additional Representative or Representatives shall be elected by the state at large and the other Representatives by the districts now prescribed by law until the legislature of such state, in the manner herein prescribed, shall redistrict such state." The present membership of the House is thus, 435. (See Apportionment and House of Representatives.)

Connecticut.—One of the thirteen original states of the American Union; nickname, "The Nutmeg State"; motto, "Qui transtulit sustinet" (He who transplanted still sustains). It lies between lat. 41° and 42° 3' north and long. 71° 55' and 73° 50' west, an area of 4,965 square miles. It is bounded on the north by Massachusetts, on the east by Rhode Island, on the south by Long Island Sound, and on the west by New York. Connecticut is largely a manufacturing State, due to its position which gives easy access to the large distributing centers; its chief products are hardware, firearms, silks, cotton and woolen goods, and clocks. Connecticut was settled by English Colonists from Plymouth, Mass., about 1635, although the Dutch had been there somewhat earlier. Charles II granted a charter to the Connecticut and New Haven Colonies in 1662, and soon thereafter they united. The present constitution was adopted in 1818.

Statistics of agriculture collected for the last Federal census place the number of farms in the State at 26,815, comprising 2,185,788 acres, valued, with stock and improvements, at $159,399,771. The value of domestic animals, poultry, etc., was $14,163,902, including 195,318 cattle, valued at $6,730,287; 46,341 horses, $5,739,400; 52,372 swine, $472,741; 22,418 sheep, $112,349; poultry, $988,653. The yield and value of the field crops of 1911 was: corn, 59,000 acres, 2,862,000 bushels, $2,375,000; oats, 11,000 acres, 386,000 bushels, $216,000; rye, 8,000 acres, 148,000 bushels, $138,000; potatoes, 23,000 acres, 1,955,000 bushels, $2,053,000; hay, 490,000 acres, 539,000 tons, $12,666,000; tobacco, 17,000 acres, 27,625,000 pounds, $5,663,125. The mineral products of the State are unimportant. The capital employed in manufactures in the State, reported in 1908, was $373,383,580; number of wage earners, 181,605, to whom was paid $87,942,091. There were 3,447 establishments. The cost of the raw material was $191,303,881, and the value of the output was $369,082,091. Population in 1910, 1,114,756.

The number of manufacturing establishments in Connecticut having an annual out-

put valued at $500 or more at the beginning of 1915 was 4,106. The amount of capital invested was $620,194,000, giving employment to 254,498 persons, using material valued at $288,454,000, and turning out finished goods worth $545,249,000. Salaries and wages paid aggregated $160,730,000.

Connecticut:

Ratification of amendment to Federal Constitution by, referred to, 249.

Refusal of governor of, to furnish militia for defense of frontier, 501.

Connecticut River, practicability of connecting Lake Memphremagog with, 873.

Conquest.—The capture of territory by military force.

Conscientious Objectors.—The term applied in England to those persons with inner objections to participating in war so strong that they refused to allow themselves to be subjected to military service. The term was used to describe both those whose conscientious scruples against war were limited to direct military service, and who hence accepted non-combatant service as an alternative; and to those who refused to perform any service under military orders, whether combatant or non-combatant, or even to assist in any way their government while it was at war. It is estimated that of these latter class there were in England almost 5,000 in jail on June 1, 1917. The conscientious objectors are not to be confused with the "slackers" (q. v.).

Conscription.—An enforced enlistment for army or navy service. (See Drafts.)

Conservation Commission.—The National Conservation Commission was created by President Roosevelt June 8, 1908, as the result of a conference, held at the White House, May 13, 1908, of the governors of the states and territories. The President had invited these officials and other eminent men to confer on the subject of national resources. Among the notable addresses were those of Andrew Carnegie, on iron and coal in relation to their exhaustion; Elihu Root, urging the states to exercise their sovereignties in preserving their natural resources; James J. Hill, on the wasteful use of the soil; William J. Bryan, John Mitchell, Governor Glenn, of North Carolina; Gifford Pinchot, and James R. Garfield.

The object of the conference was to arouse the public conscience to the unnecessary waste and destruction of the forests, streams and mineral deposits, and the depletion of the soil, and to encourage by public sentiment and laws the conservation and development of the bountiful provisions of nature for the happiness and welfare of man.

Within a month after the creation of the national commission the governors of five states had appointed state conservation commissioners and an equal number of organizations of national scope had named conservation committees. By January, 1909, thirty-six states and territories had formed conservation commissions, and the indications were that all the remaining states would soon take similar action. Besides these, forty-one national organizations had appointed conservation committees. Under the direction of the national commission the first inventory of the natural resources of the United States ever made was accomplished.

The aim and scope of the Conservation Commission is summarized in the following brief extracts from the report made to the President Dec. 7, 1908:

"The duty of man to man is no greater than the duty of each generation to the next, and the obligation of the nation to the actual citizen is no more sacred than its obligation to the citizens to be. In this country, blessed with natural resources in unsurpassed profusion, the sense of responsibility to the future has been slow to awaken. Forests have been cleared away as obstacles to the use of land. Neglect of the waterways and approaching exhaustion of the forests directed attention to the rapid depletion of the coal and iron deposits and the misuse of the land.

"In the present stage of our national development wise and beneficial uses are essential and the checking of waste is absolutely demanded. The most reprehensible waste is that of destruction, as in forest fires, uncontrolled flow of gas and oil, soil wash, and abandonment of coal in mines. Nearly as bad is the waste arising from misuse, as the consumption of fuel in furnaces and engines of low efficiency, use of ill-adapted structural materials, growing of ill-chosen crops, and the perpetuation of inferior plants and animals, all of which may be remedied.

"Even as we have neglected our natural resources so have we been thoughtless of life and health. Natural resources are useless without men and women to develop them; we cannot, therefore, too soon enter upon the duty of conserving our chief source of strength by the prevention of disease and the prolongation of life.

"At the present rate of coal production the supply will approach exhaustion by the middle of the next century. The supply of high-grade iron ore, at the present rate of consumption, cannot be expected to last beyond the middle of the present century. Petroleum, though increasing in supply, is also enormously misused and wasted, and cannot be expected to last beyond the middle of the present century. The daily waste of natural gas is enough to supply every city in the United States of over 100,000 population.

"Of the total area of our lands, but little more than two-fifths is in farms, and less than one-half of the farm area is improved and made a source of crop production. The area of cultivated land may possibly be doubled. In addition to the land awaiting the plow 75,000,000 acres of swamp land can be reclaimed, 40,000,000 acres of desert land irrigated and millions of acres of brush and wooded land cleared. We must greatly increase our yield per acre. The average yield of wheat in the United States is less than fourteen bushels per acre; in England it is thirty-two bushels and in Germany twenty-eight. We get thirty bushels of oats per acre; England nearly forty-five and Germany more than forty-seven. Proper management will double the yield and produce more than three times our present population can consume."

As an outgrowth of the joint conservation conference in December, 1908, President Roosevelt invited President Diaz of Mexico and the Governor-General and Premier of Canada to a North American conservation conference. These governments sent representatives to a meeting held at the White House Feb. 18, 1909. The principles of the original commission were endorsed and an invitation was extended to forty-five other nations to send delegates to a world's conference to be held at The Hague on a date to be later decided upon.

As a result of the agitation against destruction of the natural resources of America, other national societies have been organized and are actively at work on the task of educating the people and securing the passage of laws for protecting mineral deposits, forests, water power, fauna and flora.

The National Conservation Association, with headquarters in the Colorado Building, Washington, D. C., is now the organized head of the conservation movement in the United States. The association came into existence because of an urgent need for an organization open to every man and woman who stood for conservation which would give them immediate opportunity for united and active work. Its objects are thus stated:

"The National Conservation Association is fighting for the prompt and orderly development of our natural resources, for the welfare of ourselves and our children, and for the rights of the plain people. The association is bound neither by political considerations nor official connections. It is free to speak the whole truth.

"That conservation means the use of our natural resources for the benefit of us all and not merely for the profit of a few is already household knowledge. The task which the National Conservation Association has set itself is to get this principle put into practical effect."

The association is maintained by dues from membership, which are divided into the following classes: Members, $1.00 a year; Active Members, $3.00 a year; Contributing Members $20.00 a year; Patrons $100 a year; Life Membership, $1,000 a year.

The organization of the National Conservation Association is as follows: Gifford Pinchot, President, Washington, D. C.; Charles W. Eliot, Honorary President, Cambridge, Mass.; Overton W. Price, Vice-President and Treasurer, Washington, D. C.; Harry A. Slattery, Secretary, Washington, D. C.

The National Conservation Congress first met at Seattle, Wash., in August, 1909, under the auspices of the Washington Conservation Association.

The objects of the Congress are: To provide for discussion of the resources of the United States as the foundation for the prosperity of the people. To furnish definite information concerning the resources and their development, use and preservation. To afford an agency through which the people of the country may frame policies and principles affecting the conservation and utilization of their resources to be put into effect by their respective representatives in state and federal governments.

There is no official connection between the National Conservation Congress and the National Conservation Association, although the two are working closely together along the same lines. The Congress confines its work to an annual gathering of citizens appointed by state and municipal officials and delegates. The Association maintains a permanent working organization throughout the year. The officers are: President, J. B. White, Kansas City, Mo.; Executive Secretary, Thomas R. Shipp, Washington, D. C.; Treasurer, D. Austin Latchaw, Kansas City, Mo.

Conservation Commission:

Appropriation for, urged, 7268.

Commission report submitted, 7258.

Conservatives.—A faction of the Democratic party who from 1837 to 1840 voted with the Whigs against the sub-treasury bill. On other questions the Conservatives acted with their party. The term is generally applied to those members of a political party who oppose radical measures of any kind.

Conspiracies, Unlawful. (See Illegal Combinations.)

Conspiracy.—The combined action of two or more persons for illegal purposes, especially plots against the Government.

Constantinople, Turkey:

Expulsion of Greeks from, 2774.

International conference to be held at, upon subject of cholera, referred to, 3576.

Robert College at, referred to, 3900.

Constellation, The.—The flagship of Commodore Thomas Truxtun of the squadron sent to protect American shipping in the West Indies during troubles with France in 1799. The *Constellation* was built at Baltimore, and commissioned in 1798. Feb. 9, 1799, she defeated and captured the French frigate *L'Insurgente*, of 40 guns. Feb. 1, 1800, she defeated *La Vengeance*, of 54 guns, which, after a fierce engagement, escaped, owing to a storm. Congress presented Truxtun with a gold medal and a vote of thanks for his bravery during this engagement.

Constituency.—The voters in a given political division.

Constitution.—Fundamental law in a limited or free government. As applied to the United States of America, or to any state of the American Union, the constitution is a written statement of the powers of government. The people who hold the elective franchise are by prescribed forms called upon to establish their constitution which they may subsequently amend in accordance with its provisions. When established the constitution is paramount to the government organized under it. If any department of the government exceeds its authorized powers, the act is irregular and void. Thus, if an act of Congress or of a state legislature does not conform in its terms to the constitution, which declares itself to be the supreme law of the land or of the state, as the case may be, the Federal or State Supreme Court, as the case may be, may decide the act in question to be unconstitutional and therefore of no effect. In Great Britain the constitution consists of customs, traditions, royal charters, statutes of Parliament, the common law, the Magna Charta, the Declaration of Rights, the Act of Settlement, the Reform Bill, etc. The British constitution has never had the direct sanction of the people ; the Constitution of the United States and of each state of the Union has received such sanction. The Constitution of the United States was framed in a convention of the states, except Rhode Island, at Philadelphia, in 1787, and went into effect March 4, 1789, having been ratified by eleven of the thirteen states. North Carolina and Rhode Island ratified it Nov. 21, 1789, and May 29, 1790, respectively. (See also Amendments.)

Constitution:

Amendments to—

Fourteenth, recommendation that disabilities imposed under, be removed, 4107, 4209.

Proclamation directing discontinuance of prosecutions, 4130.

Joint resolution proposing, 3841.

Joint resolution proposing fourteenth, opposed, 3589.

Proposed by Taft, 7390, 7392.

Question of Congress proposing, until after admission of loyal Senators and Representatives of unrepresented states referred to, 3589.

Ratification of. (See Ratification of, *post.*)

Referred to, 595, 786, 3722.

Relative to—

Abolishing slavery—

Defeated, 3453.

Recommended, 3556.

Ratification of referred to, 3570, 3644.

Approval of separate items of bill and veto of others recommended, 4196, 4725, 4774, 4840.

Distribution of surplus revenue among states suggested, 1015.

Expenditures for education, suggested, 397, 444, 587.

Gradual emancipation of slaves recommended, 3337.

Income tax recommended, 7390, 7392.

Internal improvements suggested, 398, 553, 587, 760.

Legislation in extra session of Congress suggested, 4196.

Maintenance of free schools by States, 4288.

Mode of election of President and Vice-President suggested, 1010, 1081, 1120, 1168, 1253, 1336, 1395, 1478, 3837, 3889, 4196.

Mode of election of United States Senators, 3849, 3889.

Postponement of meeting of Congress suggested, 240.

Selection of Presidential electors recommended, 5644.

Slavery recommended, 3169.

Suability of States ratified, 250.

Successor to President in event of vacancy in Presidency and Vice-President recommended, 3837, 3889, 4950.

Tenure of office by judiciary of United States recommended, 3841, 3889.

Centennial anniversary of framing, proposition to celebrate, discussed, 5118.

Journal of acts and proceedings of convention which formed, published, 634, 678.

Legislation to supplement guaranties afforded by fourteenth amendment recommended, 4775.

Ratification of—
Fifteenth amendment referred to, 3998, 4001, 4007, 4801.
Discussed, 4009.
Fourteenth amendment referred to, 3664, 3665, 3667, 3722, 3795, 3836, 3837, 3843.
Proclamation regarding enforcement of, 4088.
Proclaimed, 3854, 3855, 3856, 3857, 3858.
Withdrawal of, by Ohio and New Jersey, 3836.
Ratification of, by states. (See the several states.)
Recommendation of legislation to supplement guaranties afforded by fourteenth amendment, 4775.
Referred to, 95, 101.
Right to make and alter, basis of our political system, 200.
Secret journal of Congress of Confederation published, 678.
Signers of, 26.
Text of, 15.

Constitution, Confederate. (See Confederate Constitution.)

Constitution, The.—A famous American frigate, known also as *"Old Ironsides."* She was built at Boston in 1797, and carried 44 guns. July 17, 1812, she encountered a fleet of five British frigates, but through the masterly seamanship of Capt. Hull eluded capture. Aug. 19 she was attacked by the British frigate *Guerrière*, carrying 38 guns. Within half an hour the latter was a wreck and 85 of her men killed and wounded. Dec. 29, 1812, the British man-of-war, *Java*, carrying 38 guns, surrendered to the *Constitution* (507). The British loss was only 34. Feb. 20, 1815, the *Constitution* captured the *Cyane*, 20 guns, and the *Levant*, 18 guns. British los 77 and American loss 15. (See illustration opposite 505.)

Constitution, The:
British frigate *Guerrière* captured and destroyed by, 502.
British frigate *Java* captured and destroyed by, 507.
Capt. Bainbridge in command of, 507.
Capt. Hull in command of, 502.

Constitution, The (slave ship), proceedings of court regarding, 895.

Constitutional.—In accord with the constitution, as in the case of a law which the courts hold to be constitutional.

Constitutional Rights discussed. (See powers of Federal and State Governments.)

Constitutional Treasury System:
Recommended by President Polk, 2256.
Successful operation of, discussed, 2406, 2498.

Constitutional Union Party.—The issues of 1860 and the years immediately preceding disrupted the Whig party. May 9 of that year representatives of the party held a convention at Baltimore and nominated John Bell, of Tennessee, for President, and Edward Everett, of Massachusetts, for Vice-President. Delegates were present from about twenty states. They took the name of the Constitutional Union party. They denounced the platforms of the other parties as tending "to widen political divisions," and declared their principles to be "the Constitution of the country, the Union of the States, and the enforcement of the laws." In the election of 1860 the party carried three states—Kentucky, Tennessee, and Virginia, polling 589,581 votes and gaining 39 electoral votes.

Constitutionalist.—Any one who consistently abides by the Constitution, or who desires to see governmental activities determined only by the Constitution is now called a Constitutionalist.

Constitutionalists.—A political party in Pennsylvania which under the Constitution of 1776-1790 favored the maintenance of that instrument as opposed to those who demanded a stronger government than could be had under it. They were the local forerunners of the Democrats and Anti-Federalists of later times. Between 1804 and 1808 a party arose which desired to amend the Constitution. They were called Conventionalists and the party opposed to them Constitutionalists.

Constitutions, State.—At the time of the Declaration of Independence only a few of the Colonies had local governments of their own. These were only temporary organizations. Constitutions were first adopted by the thirteen original states as follows: Maryland, New Hampshire, New Jersey, North Carolina, Pennsylvania and Virginia in 1776; Georgia and New York in 1777; South Carolina in 1778; Massachusetts in 1780; Delaware in 1792; Connecticut in 1818; Rhode Island in 1842.

Construction and Repair, Bureau of, Navy Department. (See Bureau of Construction and Repair.)

Consul.—A representative of a government delegated to reside in a city of a foreign government for the purpose of maintaining friendly and commercial relations, and of gathering and distributing information on industrial enterprises.

Consul-General, title of, should be abandoned, 4923.

Consular Appointments, State Department.—(See Civil Service.) The first consul sent from the United States to a foreign government was William Palfrey, of Massachusetts, who was despatched as consul to France in 1780. The present system of consular appointments is the result of thorough re-organization by President Roosevelt, in 1906. His re-organization provided for five inspectors of consulates; demanded notarial services from consuls in office; forbade any consul to engage in business or law, or to receive any compensation other than his consular salary; and applied the Civil Service principle to the service as a whole. At present a board of examiners passes upon all candidates, who must be American citizens between the ages of 21 and 50, and who must show moral, mental and physical fitness for consular work. All candidates must receive a grade of at least 80% in an extensive examination covering English and at least one foreign language, the present trade and commercial situation of the United States and the possibilities of its expansion, both international and common law, modern history, and other subjects. Successful candidates are appointed to the eighth and ninth grades in the consular service, from which, with few exceptions, promotions are made. (See Consuls; State Department; Consular Service; Trade Information and Publicity.)

Consular Bureau, Department of State.
—The chief of the consular bureau has supervision over the administration of the consular service (q. v.), attends to arrangements for commercial and other consular agreements, and is in charge of other details in the activities of the consular service. (See Consuls; State Department.)

Consular and Diplomatic Service (see also Consular Reform):

Act making appropriations for—
Approved and reasons therefor, 4331.
Returned, 4807.

Classified service needed, 7022.

Commercial attachés proposed, 6939, 6940.

Consular system referred to, 1246, 3382, 3393, 3471, 3592, 3794, 3837.

Cost of, 6797, 6798.

Costumes of persons in, referred to, 3115, 3834.

Discussed, 5468, 5547.

Elevation of missions, 6335, 6673.
Recommended, 5468.

Inspector of consular offices discussed, 6155.

Larger salaries needed in, 7022.

Organization of class of supernumerary secretaries of legation abroad recommended, 4654.

Promotions, removals and appointments in, 4672.

Referred to, 3067, 3393, 3471, 3592, 4069, 4123, 4795, 4801, 4849.

Reorganization of, recommended by President—
Arthur, 4718, 4829, 4838.
Cleveland, 4922, 5091, 5370, 5874.
Roosevelt, 6673, 6674, 6913, 7022, 7023.

Consular Conventions.—The first practical step toward close diplomatic relations between nations is the establishment of the consular office within its dominions. This is brought about by treaties and agreements which are called consular conventions. The terms and conditions upon which consuls are established in foreign countries by the United States have been, generally speaking, the same. Consequently treaties of this nature bear such close resemblance to one another that they are here grouped for purposes of comparison, and only specific differences are noted. Such treaties provide that consuls-general, consuls, and vice-consuls shall be reciprocally received and recognized on presentation of their commissions, in the way and manner customary in the several nations, and according to the court etiquette of the particular nation. An exequatur (q. v.) shall be issued to the representative by the government of the country to which he is sent. These representatives are to be treated with respect, dignity, and honor, due to the country whence they come. They are exempt from military service, public duty, and all personal and direct taxation, whether Federal, state, or municipal. If, however, the consular representative of a foreign na-

tion is a resident of the country in which he acts, he is amenable to all of the laws, and pays taxes and performs public duties which his citizenship demands of him. Consuls have the right to hoist the flag of their nation over their official residence, or upon an official vessel. They are relieved of public witness duty, and when their evidence is necessary in connection with the administration of justice, their depositions may be taken in writing or at their dwellings.

Consular offices and dwellings are inviolable; local authorities may not invade them for any purpose; papers and documents deposited there may not be seized or examined; and the houses cannot be used as an asylum for the refuge or protection of criminals or fugitives from justice. Consuls-general and consuls have the power to appoint as consular agents any citizen of their own country, of the nation to which they are representatives, or of any other country, who shall be acceptable to the respective governments, and that consular agent shall have full authority to act when so certificated.

All consular officials of whatever rank have power and authority to take evidence, or depositions of captains, seamen, crews, passengers, or citizens of their own country, at the official residence, and may there execute any papers or documents. Consular representatives have the right of acquiring property and of disposing of it in any way; may conduct business, trade, or profession, exactly as do in these respects the citizens of the country in which they reside; and they may not be discriminated against in any way by reason of their being aliens. The discipline and internal order of the vessels of their country are entirely under the control of the consuls of the ports at which such vessels may be; and these officers may use the local judicial machinery freely for the arrest, detention, and punishment of deserters or mutineers, or for the preservation of the public peace. Expenses of such police judicial action must be borne by the consuls. A definite time for the detention of deserters or criminals so arrested without trial is set by treaties and varies from two to three months. (See also Treaties.)

Argentine Republic.—The consular convention with this country is contained in the treaty of friendship, commerce, and navigation, of 1853. (See Argentine Republic, Treaties with.)

Austria-Hungary.—The consular convention was concluded in 1870 and ratified June 29, 1871.

Belgium.—The consular conventions of 1868, which expired in 1880, and that of 1880, still in force, govern the conduct and appointment of consuls.

Bolivia.—Agreement regarding consuls is contained in the treaty of peace, friendship, commerce, and navigation, of 1858. (See Bolivia, Treaties with.)

Brazil.—The consular convention with this nation is contained in the treaty of amity, commerce, and navigation, of 1828.

China.—Consular regulations with China are contained in the several commercial treaties with that nation. (See China, Treaties with.)

Colombia.—Consular regulations are contained in the treaty of peace, amity, navigation, and commerce, of 1846, with New Granada, and in the consular convention with Colombia of 1850. (See Colombia, Treaties with.)

Costa Rica.—Consular regulations were covered by the treaties of friendship, commerce, and navigation, of 1851. (See Costa Rica, Treaties with.)

Denmark.—The convention of friendship, commerce, and navigation, of 1826, and the consular convention of 1861, regulate the conduct and appointment of consuls.

France.—The consular convention with France was concluded Feb. 23, 1853.

German Empire.—The consular convention was concluded Dec. 11, 1871.

Greece.—The consular convention was concluded Nov. 19, 1902.

Haiti.—Consular regulations are contained in the treaty of amity, commerce, navigation, and extradition, of 1864. (See Haiti, Treaty with.)

Honduras.—Diplomatic and consular regulations are provided in the treaty of friendship, commerce, and navigation, of 1864.

Italy.—The consular convention was concluded May 8, 1878, and a supplement was added on Feb. 24, 1881, covering the settlement of shipping disputes.

Japan.—The treaty of commerce and navigation of 1894 regulates consular and diplomatic relations.

Liberia.—The treaty of commerce and navigation of 1862 provides for the consular office.

Mecklenburg-Schwerin.—Consular office and functions are provided for in the treaty of commerce and navigation of 1847.

Morocco.—Consular provisions are contained in the treaty of peace and friendship of 1836, and in the convention as to protection of 1880.

Muscat.—Consular provisions are contained in the treaty of amity and commerce, of 1833.

Netherlands.—The consular convention was concluded May 23, 1878.

Ottoman Empire.—The treaty of commerce and navigation of 1830 provides for consular intercourse.

Paraguay.—Diplomatic and consular privileges are secured by the treaty of friendship, commerce, and navigation, of 1859.

Persia.—Diplomatic privileges are secured by the treaty of friendship and commerce of 1856.

Roumania.—The consular convention of 1881 secures diplomatic and consular privileges.

Russia.—The treaty of commerce and navigation of 1832 secures diplomatic and consular privileges.

Servia.—The consular convention of 1881 secures consular privileges.

Siam.—The treaty of amity and commerce of 1856 provides for the appointment of a consul to reside at Bangkok.

Spain.—The treaty of peace of 1898, known as the treaty of Paris, provides for the consular office.

Sweden and Norway.—The treaty of commerce and navigation of 1827 provides for the consular office and privileges.

Switzerland.—The convention of friendship, commerce, and navigation, of 1850, provides for consular office and privileges.

Tonga.—The consular office and jurisdiction is regulated by the treaty of amity, commerce, and navigation, of 1886.

Tripoli.—The treaty of peace and amity of 1805 provides for consular residence at Tripoli.

Tunis.—The consular office is secured by the treaty of amity, commerce and navigation of 1797.

Zanzibar.—The treaty as to duties on liquors, and consular powers, of 1886, governs the consular office.

Consular Conventions with—

Austria, 4023.

Belgium, 3888, 3893, 3997, 4539.
Referred to, 4561.

Chile, 2957.

France, 49, 2726.
Referred to, 75.

Germany, 4114, 4142.

Italy, 3800, 4436, 4448, 4588, 4626.
Expirations of discussed, 4418.

Netherlands, 4437, 4520.

Roumania, 4622, 4627.
Referred to, 4757.

Salvador, 4070, 4212, 4247.

Servia, 4627, 4658.
Referred to, 4757.

Consular Courts. (See Courts Consular.)

Consular Laws discussed, 243, 1117, 2713.

Consular Officers, salaries of, 7938.

Consular Offices, inspection of, discussed, 6155.

Consular Pupils, referred to, 3347.

Consular Reform (see also Consular and Diplomatic Service.)
Discussed, 6071, 6154.
Order regarding examination for consular offices, 6056.

Consular Regulations, amendment of, 6704.

Consular Reports:

On production of and trade in coffee among Central and South American States, referred to, 5201.

On taxation, referred to, 5201.

On trade and industries of foreign powers, referred to, 4986, 5122, 5201, 6460, 6673.

Publication of, discussed, 6338.
Recommended, 4564, 4631, 5091.

Value and importance of, discussed, 5091.

Consular Service.—Consular officers include consuls-general, consuls and commercial agents. Their chief duties and powers are connected with our commercial interests, to protect ships, seamen and other Americans, to send home destitute seamen, and to give certificates for various purposes. They are sent to the principal ports or markets of a country. Some diplomatic powers also attach to their office, and in non-Christian countries they have sometimes the right, by treaty, to act in a judicial capacity between citizens of the United States. A consul-general has jurisdiction over several consuls. Commercial agents are accredited to smaller places. The consular officers are appointed by the President and confirmed by the Senate after passing an examination as to fitness and ability in accordance with an executive order of President Roosevelt. Officers of the service are under the control and direction of the State Department.

Consular officers are expected to endeavor to maintain and promote all the rightful interests of American citizens, and to protect them in all privileges provided for by treaty or conceded by usage; to visa and, when so authorized, to issue passports; when permitted by treaty, law or usage, to take charge of and settle the personal estates of Americans who may die abroad without legal or other representatives. (See Consular Appointments.)

Consuls.—In international law an agent appointed and commissioned by a sovereign state to reside in a foreign city or town to defend the personal rights and to protect the business interests of such citizens of his country as may reside therein, and to collect and forward to the home government information on industrial and economic matters. He is not a diplomatic agent. He must be formally recognized by the power within whose jurisdiction he serves before he can legally discharge the functions of his office.

From the early days of the Government the United States has maintained a consular service. The title of consul-general was first introduced in 1855. In 1866 the consular service was reorganized upon a basis requiring the examination, by a board which has remained substantially unchanged to the present day. In 1895 President Cleveland issued an order requiring the examination, by a board composed of three members to be named by the Secretary of State, of applicants for appointment to places the salaries of which are more than $1,000 and less than $2,500 per year. By an order of Nov. 10, 1905, President Roosevelt extended the operations of this order so that it now applies to applicants for all consular places, irrespective of the salaries attached to them.

Duties.—Consular officers are expected to endeavor to maintain and promote all the rightful interests of American citizens, and to protect them in all privileges provided for by treaty or conceded by usage; to visé and when so authorized, to issue passports; when permitted by treaty, law or usage, to take charge of and settle the personal estates of Americans who may die abroad without legal or other representatives, and remit the proceeds to the treasury in case they are not called for by a legal representative within one year; to ship, discharge, and, under certain conditions, maintain and send American seamen to the United States; to settle disputes between masters and seamen of American vessels; to investigate charges of mutiny or insubordination on the high seas and send mutineers to the United States for trial; to render assistance in the case of wrecked or stranded American vessels, and, in the absence of the master or other qualified person, take charge of the wrecks and cargoes if permitted to do so by the laws of the country; to receive the papers of American vessels arriving at foreign ports and deliver them after the discharge of the obligations of the vessels toward the members of their crews, and upon the production of clearances from the proper foreign port officials; to certify to the correctness of the valuation of merchandise exported to the United States where the shipment amounts to more than $100; to act as official witnesses to marriages of American citizens abroad; to aid in the enforcement of the immigration laws, and to certify to the correctness of the certificates issued by Chinese and other officials to Chinese persons coming to the United States; to protect the health of our seaports by reporting weekly the sanitary and health conditions of the ports at which they reside, and by issuing to vessels clearing for the United States bills of health describing the condition of the ports, the vessels, crews, passengers, and cargoes; and to take depositions and perform other acts which notaries public in the United States are authorized or required to perform.

Promotion of Commerce.—A duty of prime importance is the promotion of American commerce by reporting available opportunities for the introduction of our products, aiding in the establishment of relations between American and foreign commercial houses, and lending assistance wherever practicable to the marketing of American merchandise abroad.

In addition to the foregoing duties, consular officers in China, Turkey, Siam, Maskat, Morocco, and a few other so-called un-Christian countries, are invested with judicial powers over American citizens in those countries. These powers are usually defined by treaty, but generally include the trial of civil cases to which Americans are parties, and in some instances extend to the trial of criminal cases.

Consuls of United States (see also the several powers):

Active cooperation in commerce, 6460, 6673.

Advances made by, should be reimbursed, 243.

Engaged in business in violation of law, referred to, 3068.

Examination, by, of American atrocities in Turkey discussed, 5989, 6069.

Expenditures to, refused by Turkey, 6092, 6148.

Expenses of, appropriation for, recommended, 4109, 4159.

Fees collected by—
From American vessels, 4667.
In connection with authentication of invoices. 4670.

Fees of, referred to, 4000, 4067, 4109, 4110, 4159, 4210, 4258, 4736.

Imprisonment of, in Cuba, 329.

Jurisdiction of. (See Courts, Consular.)

Laws in regard to, should be revised, 243, 1117, 2713.

List and returns of, transmitted, 2133, 4109.

May not act in a fiduciary capacity while in office abroad, 6704.

Number of, who speak or write language of country where they are located, 4115.

Order regarding examinations for consular offices, 6056.
Discussed, 6071.

Presents from foreign states to, disposition of, discussed, 1256.
Referred to, 1258, 1200.

Referred to, 75, 78, 111, 169, 363, 2539.

Reports of. (See Consular Reports.)

Reports of consular agents referred to, 4069, 6248, 6299, 6338, 6356, 6460, 6673.

Requested by Swiss Government to protect its citizens in countries where it is not represented, 4627.

Rights of, in Cuba discussed, 6069.

Salary of—
Appropriations for expenses of, discussed, 4159.
Discussed, 238, 243, 1031, 1910, 1953.
Fees of consular agents referred to, 3718, 4109.

Fees of consular officers referred to, 4000, 4067, 4110, 4159, 4210, 4258.

Recommendations regarding, 4109.

Consuls to United States:
Exequaturs revoked—
Consul of—
Belgium, 3420.
Chile, 3625.
France, 260.
Frankfort, 3709.
Great Britain, 2924, 2925.
Hanover, 3709.
Hesse, 3709.
Nassau, 3709.
Oldenburg, 3710.
Spain, 2588.
Sweden and Norway, 3626.
Revocation annulled, 3630.
Vice-consul of—
Portugal, 4038.
Sweden and Norway, 3627.
Revocation annulled, 3630.

Fees demanded by Spanish, discussed, 4714.

Legislation for protection or punishment of, recommended, 2654, 2713.

Tax upon incomes of, discussed, 3383.

Consulting Board, Naval. (See Naval Consulting Board.)

Contagious Diseases (see also Cholera; International Sanitary Conference; Plague; Quarantine Regulations; Yellow Fever):
Among animals, discussed, 4578, 4580, 4771, 5112, 4383, 5764, 5887, 6597, 6604, 7078.
Conference on subject of, to be held at—
Rome, 4898.
Washington, 4564.
Legislation to prevent introduction of, into United States. (See Quarantine Regulations.)

Contested Elections in Congress, act regulating taking of testimony in, reasons for applying pocket veto to, 2108.

Contested Presidential Elections. (See Presidential Elections and Electoral Commission.)

Continental Congress.—On receipt of the news of the passage of the Boston Port Act the Virginia assemby in 1774 advised a congress of all the Colonies. Upon this recommendation the First Continental Congress assembled in Philadelphia Sept. 5, 1774, all the Colonies being represented except Georgia. Resolutions were passed commending the people of Massachusetts for their temperate resistance to the execution of the objectionable measures of Parliament and declaring that all America ought to support such opposition. This Congress also recommended an agreement not to import British goods after Dec. 1, 1774, and not to export goods to England after Sept. 10, 1775, unless such grievances as were set forth in a declaration of rights and wrongs were redressed by the parent Government. The First Continental Congress sat until Oct. 26, 1774.

The Second Continental Congress convened at Philadelphia, May 10, 1775. This Congress was composed of delegates from each state, generally elected by the legislature. Each state was allowed one vote. It declared the independence of the United States and carried on the war with Great Britain. This body remained in session until Dec. 12, 1776, and then adjourned to meet at Baltimore, where it reassembled Dec. 20; remaining in session until Feb. 27, 1777, on which date adjournment was had until March 12, when it reassembled at Philadelphia, remaining in session there until the 18th of the following September, when it adjourned to meet at Lancaster, Pa., Sept. 27, remaining there but one day. Oct. 1 it resumed its session at York, Pa. June 27, 1778, it adjourned to meet at Philadelphia, where it reassembled July 7, remaining there until June 21, 1783. Its next meeting was at Princeton N. J., June 30, remaining in session at that place until Nov. 4, when it adjourned to meet at Annapolis, Md., Nov. 26, where its sessions were held until June 8, 1784. Adjourning, it next met at Trenton, N. J., Nov. 1. Dec. 24 it adjourned to meet at New York, where it remained in session until its final adjournment, Oct. 21, 1788. The sessions here were as follows: Jan. 11 to Nov. 4, 1785; Nov. 7, 1785, to Nov. 3, 1786 (new officers being chosen at the commencement of this session); Nov. 6, 1786, to Oct. 30, 1787 (new officers again elected at beginning of session); Nov. 5, 1787, to final adjournment. It is a fact worthy of record that as the old Congress died, so the new was born, in the City of New York.

Continental Money.—On the authority of the Second Continental Congress an issue of paper money was begun in 1775 and continued till 1779. This "money" was in the nature of bills of credit and its value necessarily fluctuated with the fortunes of the Government which promised redemption. About $242,000,000 were put forth. At first the bills circulated on a par with gold, but later greatly depreciated. In 2 years they had become depressed to half the value of gold. In 1779 they were reduced to one-twentieth of their face value and afterward to one-fortieth. Congress then ordered the notes brought up at their market value, replacing them by a new issue at the rate of 20 to 1, to bear interest at 5 per cent. The old notes sank as low as 1,000 to 1 and finally disappeared.

Continentalist.—In the early history of the United States the continentalist faction comprised those who advocated a strong union of the states.

Contingent Expenses. (See Expenditures, Public.)

Contraband of War.—A term said to have been first employed in the treaty of Southampton between England and Spain in 1625. The treaty of the Pyrenees between France and Spain, signed Nov. 7, 1659, modified the previously entertained notions of articles contraband of war, and a still more liberal construction was put upon the word by the Declaration of Paris, April 26, 1856. All arms, ammunition, and supplies which may be of use in carrying on war or aiding in defense are by the laws of war contraband, and are liable to seizure by either belligerent should a neutral attempt to convey them to the other belligerent. In most of our treaties with foreign countries all articles contraband of war are specified. Gen. B. F. Butler in 1861 pronounced slaves of persons in rebellion against the United States Government contraband.

Contraband of War:

On British vessels for insurgents, 3352.

Trade in, and protection for neutral vessels, order regarding, 3377.

Contracts, Government, recommendations regarding, 3171.

Contreras (Mexico), Battle of.—Aug. 7, 1847, Gen. Twiggs's division began its march upon the City of Mexico. By the 18th the entire army was at San Augustine, 9 miles from the city. On the 19th a preliminary assault was made upon Contreras Hill, a fortified position about 4 miles from the city, held by Gen. Valencia with 6,000 men. Early the next morning Contreras Hill was taken by sudden assault, Valencia's army being completely routed, with a loss of 2,500 men. Among the prisoners were 4 generals. By this brilliant dash the Americans had gained one of the several strong positions by which the roads to the City of Mexico were guarded. The American loss was 50 men killed and wounded. The Mexicans lost heavily in cannon, muskets and ammunition. (See illustration opposite 2153.)

Contreras (Mexico), Battle of, referred to, 2386.

Controller Bay (Alaska):

Opening to settlement of lands in, discussed, 7599.

Convention.—1. In its political sense a body of delegates, selected by the members of a political party, meeting together and nominating candidates and adopting platforms for the party. 2. The same as *treaty* when applied to international relations.

Convention, Nominating.—An assembly of delegates or representatives for consultation on important political concerns and the nomination of candidates for office. Early American candidates for office either made a public announcement of their candidacy or were placed in nomination by a caucus more or less select. Out of this custom grew the Congresssional caucus of party leaders and, at a later period, the legislative caucus. This was defective in that parties having no legislative delegates had no caucus delegates. This was remedied by sending caucus delegates from those districts not represented by legislative delegates. This immediate step was succeeded by the nominating caucus or convention as at present conducted, both in the several states and in the nation, consisting of delegates from all parts of a state or of the nation chosen for the express purpose of making nominations. The first state convention of which we have any record was held at Harrisburg, Pa., in 1788. The first national nominating convention was that held at Baltimore in September, 1831, by the Anti-Masons. In December of the same year the National Republicans, who were the progenitors of the Whigs, held a national convention at Baltimore. In May, 1832, a Democratic national convention nominated Jackson for president and Van Buren for vice-president. About 1840 both parties adopted this practice, since which time it has become universal.

Convention, Revolutionary.—Previous to and at the beginning of the Revolution the royal governors of the Colonies dissolved the legislative assemblies because of their opposition to the oppressive measures of the Crown and Parliament. These assemblies immediately met in what were called revolutionary conventions. In a short time these bodies acquired all authority over the people, to the exclusion of the parent Government.

Conventions. (See International Conventions; Treaties.)

Convicts, Foreign, involuntary deportation of paupers, idiots, insane persons, and, to United States, 4852.

Conway Cabal.—A plot hatched by Gen. Thomas Conway, who was a "foreign officer of great pretensions," Generals Gates and Mifflin, and Samuel Adams, "with two or three others of the New England delegation in Congress, and one of the Virginia deputies," to remove Washington from chief command of the Continental forces.

Thomas, count de Conway, was born in Ireland, but taken to France while young. In 1777, through the influence of Silas Deane, he came to the United States, was commissioned brigadier-general May 13, 1777, and fought at Brandywine and Germantown, 1777. Washington's defeats caused widespread discontent in 1777, especially when the British occupied Philadelphia. Burgoyne's surrender gave Gates the prestige of a great success. Such men as John Adams, Samuel Adams, Richard Henry Lee, Thomas Mifflin, etc., began to doubt Washington's fitness for the chief command. Conway did not originate the cabal for Washington's removal, but was so active in it that it bears his name. Gates willingly lent his influence, in the hope of obtaining the command himself. There was correspondence derogatory to Washington between Gates, Mifflin, and Conway during the summer and autumn of 1777. In the new board of war, organized November, 1777, the faction was represented by Gates as president, and Mifflin and others as members. Conway, against Washington's remonstrance, was promoted major-general, and made inspector-general of the army. A vain attempt was made to win Lafayette by offering him an army to invade Canada; but these intrigues, when known to the army, were heartily reprobated, nor did the state legislatures approve them. In spite of disasters to the army, Washington retained the confidence and affection of soldiers and people; and most of the conspirators shrunk from avowing their share in the plot. Conway, ordered to the northern department, complained to Congress, and offered his resignation. It was accepted, and he tried in vain to obtain a reinstatement. He was wounded soon after in a duel with Gen. Cadwallader, and, believing his end near, wrote an apology to Washington for his course. He recovered however, and returned to France.

Cooly Trade referred to, 2907, 3127, 3261, 3837, 3991, 4034, 4190.

Copper, act regulating duties on, vetoed, 3903.

Copper Coins, weight of, reduced to one pennyweight, sixteen grains, 183.

Copper Mines referred to, 764, 803.

Copperhead.—A term of opprobrium applied to citizens of the north who sympathized with the Southern Confederacy during the Civil War. The name was first used in a political sense in 1863 in reference to persons who favored peace on any terms. The epithet had its origin in the charge that those to whom it was applied were secret and insidious foes to the Union. The term has recently (1899) been applied to those who are not in sympathy with the prevalent ideas concerning the annexation of territory gained by the recent war with Spain, especially to those who are quietly endeavoring to foment discord among the people at home and the soldiers in the Philippines.

Copyright.—As defined by Drone, copyright is the exclusive right to multiply and dispose of copies of an intellectual production. Before the organization of the Federal Government the states issued copyrights. The Constitution authorized Congress to grant copyrights to authors and patents to inventors. Accordingly Congress passed a law in 1790 giving authors the exclusive right to their works for fourteen years, with the privilege of renewal for fourteen years, by themselves, or their heirs, executors or assigns. In 1831 the period was extended to twenty-eight years, with the right of renewal of fourteen years, the right being extended to the widow or children of a deceased author. In 1856 the protection of copyright was extended to dramatic works and in 1865 to works of art and photographs. Clerks of the district courts of the United States at first issued copyrights, but the act of 1870 provided that the right to issue should be vested in the Librarian of Congress, and in 1897 an office of Register of Copyrights, acting under the direction of the Librarian of Congress, was created.

Foreign Copyright.—In 1891 the international copyright law passed, extending the privilege of American copyright to authors in such foreign countries as granted the same privilege to American authors. This reciprocal privilege, which is determined and effected by proclamation of the president, according to the terms of the law, has been availed of by several European and American nations, as follows: Austria, Belgium, Chile, Costa Rica, Cuba, Denmark, France, Germany, Great Britain and her possessions, Italy, Luxemburg, Mexico, Netherlands and possessions, Norway, Portugal, Spain, Sweden, Switzerland, Tunis.

Copyright treaties have also been entered into with China, Japan and Hungary (the latter in effect on October 16, 1912). The Copyright Convention of Mexico of 1902 has been ratified by the United States and is effective from July 1, 1908, as between the United States and Costa Rica, Guatemala, Honduras, Nicaragua and Salvador.

The copyright law approved March 4, 1909, which took effect on July 1, 1909, provides that the application for registration of any work "shall specify to which of the following classes the work in which copyright is claimed belongs:" (a) Books, including composite and cyclopaedic works, directories, gazetteers, and other compilations; (b) periodicals including, newspapers; (c) lectures, sermons, addresses, prepared for oral delivery; (d) dramatic or dramatico-musical compositions; (e) musical compositions; (f) maps; (g) works of art; models or designs for works of art; (h) reproductions of a work of art; (i) drawings or plastic works of a scientific or technical character; (j) photographs; (k) prints and pictorial illustrations. An amendment of August 24, 1912, adds: (l) motion picture photo plays; (m) motion pictures other than plays. The applica-

tion for registration of any article should distinctly specify to which one of these classes the work belongs. An article is not entitled to registration unless it is reasonably possible to class it under one or the other of the designations named in the statute.

The steps necessary to secure copyright registration are: For works reproduced in copies for sale: 1. Publish the work with the copyright notice. The notice may be in the form "Copyright, 19..(year date of publication) by..........(name of copyright proprietor)." 2. Promptly after publication, send to the Copyright Office, Library of Congress, Washington, D. C., two copies of the best edition of the work, with an application for registration and a money order payable to the Register of Copyrights for the statutory registration fee of $1.

For works not reproduced in copies for sale: Copyright may also be had of certain classes of works (see a, b, c, below) of which copies are not reproduced for sale, by filing in the Copyright Office an application for registration, with the statutory fee of $1, sending therewith: (a) In the case of lectures or other oral addresses or of dramatic or musical compositions, one complete manuscript or typewritten copy of the work. This privilege of registration, however, does not exempt the copyright proprietor from the deposit of printed copies of a dramatic or musical composition or lecture where the work is later reproduced in copies for sale. (b) In the case of photographs not intended for general circulation, one photographic print. (c) In the case of works of art (paintings, drawings, sculpture); or of drawings or plastic works of a scientific or technical character, one photograph or other identifying reproduction of the work. In all these cases, if the work is later reproduced in copies for sale, two copies must then be deposited.

Duration of Copyright.—The original term of copyright runs for twenty-eight years. Within one year prior to the expiration of the original term, the author, if living, or the widow or widower of the author, or the children of the author if he be not living; or if none of these be living then the author's executors, or in the absence of a will, the author's next of kin may secure a renewal for a further term of twenty-eight years, making fifty-six years in all. In case of composite works, if the proprietor secured the original copyright, he may also secure the renewal. Copyrights are assignable by any instrument in writing.

Copyright:

Correspondence with—

Switzerland and France regarding international, referred to, 5115.

Switzerland and Italy regarding international, referred to, 4989.

Foreign holders of, to be privileged in United States discussed, 4828, 5478, 5561.

International law of—

Convention regarding with—

Germany, 5626.

Great Britain, 2725, 2763.

Correspondence with Great Britain regarding, referred to, 2003.

Recommended, 5478, 5561.

Law of, needs revision, 7011, 7012.

Proclamation granting privilege to—
Belgium, France, Great Britain and
Switzerland, 5582.
Chile, 6125.
Germany, 5713.
Italy, 5736.
Mexico, 6122.
Norway, 6954.
Spain, 6024.

Copyright Convention, International:
At Berne, discussed, 4919, 5090.
Negotiations for, referred to, 4625.

Copyright Laws. (See Copyright.)

Corea. (See Korea.)

Corisco Islands. (See Spain.)

Corn. (See Agricultural Products.)

Corporal's Guard.—A few soldiers under a
corporal's command; in John Tyler's administration his few followers in Congress were
facetiously referred to as a corporal's guard:
thus the leaders of one political party ridi-
cule the following of the opposition leaders
by insinuating that they amount to only a
corporal's guard.

Corporate Securities, protection for investors in, 7079.

Corporation Income Tax same as excise tax, 7391.

Corporation Tax.—Taxes on corporations
are levied by most of the states in proportion to the number of shares into which
they are divided. The laws of the states
are so diversified in this respect that many
corporations find it profitable to become
incorporated in states distant from the
scenes of their operation. President Roosevelt and Taft both recommended federal
taxes on the earnings of corporations and
in response to Mr. Taft's request Congress
in 1909 passed a federal corporation tax
requiring every corporation, joint stock company or association organized for profit,
and every insurance company to pay annually an excise tax of one per cent upon its
entire net incomes in excess of $5,000. This
was justified by the existing deficit in the
treasury. The law also provided for a form
of publicity which gave the government supervision over all corporations.

The income tax law of 1913, passed
after the adoption of the sixteenth amendment, supersedes the Taft law. This measure provides for the payment of one per cent
upon the net income from all property owned and of every business, trade or profession, joint stock company or corporation.

The Revenue bill approved on Sept. 8,
1916, provided for a system of taxation
upon corporations as follows:

All corporations, not including partnerships, must pay a tax of 2% on their net
incomes. Similar provisions are enacted
providing for taxation to the same extent
of foreign corporations doing business in
the United States, the taxable basis of such
foreign corporations being that amount of
their incomes which is derived in this country.

The following corporations, however, are
exempt from paying the corporation tax:
Labor, agricultural and horticultural organizations; mutual savings banks not having capital stock represented by shares;
fraternal societies or orders entirely of a
beneficial and non-profit-making nature;
domestic building and loan associations and
co-operative banks, without capital stock,
and operated for mutual purposes without
considerations of profit; cemetery companies

of a similar nature; corporations or associations organized and conducted for religious, civic, social welfare, scientific or
educational purposes, and none of the income of which accrues to any individual
representing them; clubs of a non-profit-
making nature; various farmers or other
relief associations of a purely local character, and the asessments of which are paid
merely to meet operating expenses; farmers', fruit-growers' or similar associations
which operate without profit as selling
agents only; holding corporations of any
of the above.

In addition, federal land banks and national farm-loan associations are exempt
from the operations of the tax as are joint
stock banks as to income derived from
bonds or debentures of other joint stock
banks or any Federal land bank belonging
to such joint stock land banks.

All corporations manufacturing any kind
of explosives or military supplies are taxed
12½% on their net profits. This tax is
to be effective for one year after the close
of the European War. This tax is to take
effect only from Jan. 1, 1916, and excludes
income derived from contracts made before that date. To determine net profits,
provision is made that from the gross receipts shall be deducted the cost of raw
materials, running expenses, interest paid
on debts or loans, taxes, losses and depreciation of the plant.

There is an additional tax of $0.50 on
each thousand dollars of capital, surplus or
undivided profits of all corporations capitalized above $99,000. In addition, there
is a special tax of 1% on the net profits of
smelters, when the amount thereof is between $25,000 and $1,000,000; and of 2%
when it is above this latter figure.

There are special taxes on brokers,
amusement resorts, liquors, tobacco.

An act of Congress approved March 3,
1917, places a tax of 8% on the amount
by which the net income of a corporation
or partnership exceeds $5,000 and 8% of
the actual capital invested. However, from
the income to be taxed is excluded income
from life, health and accident insurance
combined in one policy on the weekly premium payment plan. A similar tax, corresponding in its details to the tax upon
corporations of the United States is placed
upon the income derived by foreign corporations by activities in this country.

The term actual capital in the above "excess profits" tax means the actual cash paid
in, the actual cash value of assets other
than actual cash paid in, and paid in or
earned surplus and undivided profits, excepting money or property borrowed.

Income is exempt when derived from a
public utility or the exercise of governmental function by any state or subdivision of
a state.

Net income is to be ascertained by deducting from the gross income all ordinary
and necessary expenses, including all usual
and necessary rentals; all losses for which
there is no compensation by insurance or
otherwise, including a "reasonable" amount
for depreciation of plant and property; the
amount of interest paid in indebtedness,
not in excess (a) of the entire amount
of the capital stock outstanding, or if no
capital stock, the entire amount of the
capital employed in the business for the
year for which the tax is to be paid, and
(b) one-half of the corporation's interest-
bearing indebtedness; and taxes, etc.

The fiscal year for which the tax is to be
paid ends on Dec. 31. By March 1 of the
following year, returns must be made to
the collector of internal revenue for the

district in which the corporation is located. The assessments on the returns must be handed in by June 1, and must be paid by June 15.

There is a provision in the law that any collector, inspector, or other governmental agent making known in any manner except that prescribed by law any information concerning the conduct of a business which may have come to him through his investigations shall be punished by dismissal from the government service and shall be fined not more than $1,000 or imprisoned for not more than 1 year.

Any individual failing to comply with the provisions of this law shall be fined not less than $20 nor more than $1,000; and if the official of a corporation, shall be fined not more than $2,000 or imprisoned for not more than 1 year or subjected to both penalties.

For the fiscal year of 1916, there were collected from corporations $56,993,658. Returns were received from 336,443 corporations within the meaning of the law. Of these, 190,911 reported a net income of $5,184,442,000; and 175,532 reported either no profits or profits less than those on

which a tax might be levied. Of the 15 districts for collecting the corporation tax, the district in which New York City is located reported collections of more than $10,000,000, and the district containing Chicago more than $4,500,000.

The report of the Federal Trade Commission (Bureau of Corporations) for 1915 indicates that the various states collect about $300,000,000 of their revenue from corporations, not including taxes of local subdivisions of the states. Railroad, banking and insurance corporations contribute about 40% of the total revenue of the states.

War Corporation Tax.—By provision of the bill signed by the President on October 5, 1917, there is levied upon the income of all corporations, in addition to the tax described in the earlier bills, a tax of 4%.

War Profits Tax.—In addition to taxes already existing, there is levied a tax of 20% of the net income on "excess profits," not in excess of 15% of the invested capital; 25% of the amount of the net income in excess of 15% and not in excess of 20% of the net capital; 35% of the net income in excess of 20% and not in excess of

The returns of the corporation tax by states in 1916 and 1917 were as follows:

States and Territories.	Returns received in 1916	Returns showing tax due in 1916	Total tax assessed in 1916	Per cent increase over 1915	Total tax assessed in 1917
Alabama	4,244	1,790	$ 206,198	20.6	$ 887,906
Alaska	208	88	28,532	354.6	49,132
Arizona	1,286	467	165,232	137.7	637,993
Arkansas	2,353	1,518	110,958	27.6	306,310
California	20,849	8,709	2,031,463	21.8	6,147,289
Colorado	8,177	3,165	632,208	76.9	1,789,597
Connecticut	6,288	2,887	1,261,621	95.6	3,872,638
Delaware	981	533	1,100,340	832.6	2,791,067
District of Columbia	1,165	605	156,357	24.2	579,311
Florida	3,023	1,419	108,672	1.1	327,655
Georgia	4,246	3,146	434,603	35.9	1,218,831
Hawaii	551	378	341,049	71.6	909,818
Idaho	2,429	847	122,080	27.4	217,479
Illinois	22,009	12,010	5,049,485	37.8	14,359,537
Indiana	8,560	5,612	832,493	29.3	2,261,049
Iowa	9,401	6,233	516,654	17.4	1,252,992
Kansas	4,355	3,151	658,479	180.6	2,349,847
Kentucky	5,379	3,054	417,655	10.4	1,252,485
Louisiana	3,996	2,149	438,503	20.8	1,269,121
Maine	3,436	1,854	322,342	14.2	815,750
Maryland	3,883	2,034	549,987	41.2	1,401,954
Massachusetts	16,382	7,500	2,858,713	61.1	9,320,716
Michigan	9,733	5,941	2,152,922	63.4	6,565,769
Minnesota	9,321	5,227	1,900,349	54.0	4,618,464
Mississippi	1,945	1,181	95,837	49.4	246,829
Missouri	13,844	7,867	1,629,797	49.2	4,596,170
Montana	4,448	1,699	265,127	89.2	776,719
Nebraska	5,078	3,289	331,015	46.6	779,615
Nevada	1,052	319	54,990	9.0	75,423
New Hampshire	1,141	729	105,907	36.2	283,837
New Jersey	12,424	5,561	1,685,207	19.6	5,250,581
New Mexico	1,058	444	134,766	112.8	300,134
New York	48,644	24,169	15,352,575	52.3	46,566,951
North Carolina	4,934	3,122	315,522	3.0	1,232,609
North Dakota	2,674	2,189	101,675	45.6	218,771
Ohio	17,002	11,082	3,667,020	63.1	12,873,403
Oklahoma	7,788	3,068	422,209	61.7	2,231,436
Oregon	5,461	2,103	194,661	10.1	406,931
Pennsylvania	21,571	11,643	6,971,613	46.2	24,238,266
Rhode Island	2,634	1,144	466,511	67.0	1,339,290
South Carolina	5,827	2,656	176,284	100.0	498,116
South Dakota	2,385	1,717	76,043	28.2	182,248
Tennessee	4,784	2,543	324,824	32.6	942,090
Texas	10,606	6,412	949,986	49.7	2,611,153
Utah	5,066	1,447	430,857	82.2	1,148,676
Vermont	1,123	695	82,456	45.5	184,547
Virginia	6,170	3,054	651,354	49.0	1,837,125
Washington	9,726	3,445	425,628	34.3	1,187,702
West Virginia	4,229	2,195	357,702	12.2	1,460,908
Wisconsin	11,267	6,115	804,693	31.2	2,716,523
Wyoming	1,367	706	75,904	43.7	184,694
Total	366,443	190,911	$58,547,081	66.5+	$179,372,887

25% of the net capital; 45% of the net income in excess of 25% of the net capital and not in excess of 33% of the net capital; 60% of the income in excess of 33% of such capital. For a definition of excess profits, the reader must be referred to the lengthy and complicated provisions of the act itself, as for a definition of the net income, net capital and businesses coming under this section. The years 1911, 1912, and 1913 are chosen as the years by which to gauge the normal income.

Corporation tax a tax on privilege and not on property, 7391.

Corporations (see Commerce and Labor, Department of):

Bond issuance by, power of Territorial legislatures to authorize, 1757.

Business stability would be assured by corporations being under Federal control, 6976.

Created by law, should be controlled by law, 6648.

Evils of trusts and monopolies discussed and recommendations regarding, 5358, 5478, 6176, 6711, 6899, 6974, 6976, 7137, 7191, 7199.

Exclusion of American insurance companies from Germany, 6061, 6099, 6183.

Federal supervision of incident to tax on, 6648.

Federal control urged for, 6711, 6974, 7143, 7191, 7199, 7391.

Honest, need not fear supervision, 6785.

Inspection and returns of, 7960.

International commerce promoted by, 6646.

International importance of, 6646.

National Control exemplified in national banking act, pure food law, meat inspection law, 7080.

Overcapitalization of discussed, 6976, 7039, 7132, 7137, 7191, 7199.

Political contributions from, 7023.

Publicity for, 6648, 7199.

Stock in other corporations, right to hold, 7079.

Tariff does not affect, 6712.

Taxes upon franchises of, recommended, 7042.

Treatment of American insurance companies in Russia discussed, 5961.

Work of Bureau discussed, 6859, 6785, 6901.

Corporations, Bureau of. (See Bureau of Corporations.)

Corporations, Bureau of, policy and work of, discussed, 6785, 6901.

Corps of Engineers. (See Engineer Corps.)

Corrupt Leaders, types of, discussed, 7034.

Corruption of Blood, prohibited except during life of person attainted of treason, 24.

Cost of Living.—The historian of the future, in evaluating the different forces which affected the status of society during the first decades of the twentieth century, will be compelled to give much attention to the phenomenon described as the high cost of living during that period. Excepting only the war in Europe, no other factor seems to have played so large a part in the daily lives of the entire population of the United States. Although the rise in the cost of commodities was steady from 1896, the years following the outbreak of war in 1914 saw a tremendous acceleration.

In 1916, food prices increased 125% from the prices in 1896. From October, 1915, to December, 1916 alone, the increase was 50%. (The increase in food prices from 1900 to 1910 was only about 20%, although during this period the price of butter increased 30%, of eggs 60%, and of bacon and pork, 135%.) The rapid increase in the war years may be seen by comparing these figures with the increase of only 60% in the 23 years between 1890 and 1913. In September, 1917, it was calculated that the increase in the cost of living over only 1 year had been 40% and over 3 years, 70%, with an increase of 100% in the ten year period from 1907.

Considering some particular foodstuffs, from 1900 to 1916, the rate of increase was as follows: Wheat, 140%; Corn, 190%; Flour, 130%; Beef, 80%; Milk, 90%; Eggs, 118%; Bread, 20%; Pork, 200%; Butter, 40%; Codfish, 95%; Sugar, 50%; Potatoes, 365%.

In the ten years preceding 1910, the general wholesale price level increased 14½%, with wages increasing about 15%. In 1914, wholesale prices had increased about 55% from 1896. Of particular commodities between 1900 and 1916, the increase was as follows: Hides and leather, 93%; cotton, 125%; ginghams, 60%; steel billets, 45%; copper, 75%; lead, 55%; anthracite coal, 30%; bituminous coal, 100%.

The significance of these figures can be understood only by comparing them with increase in wages during the same periods. Speaking generally, it must be said that wages did not increase proportionately to the cost of living, and to that fact may be ascribed much of the unrest in the ranks of labor, as typified by the increase in the strength of such organizations as the I. W. W. and the Socialist Party. From 1890 to 1913, it is estimated that the cost of living increased 60%, with the increase in wages only about 30%. From 1907 to 1915, wages increased 12%, but their purchasing power decreased 10%. From 1915 to 1916, wages increased about 28%, but prices increased 38%. The increase in income, however, came to only a slight extent to those working on salaries rather than on wages; and the middle class was probably harder hit, comparatively, by the high cost of living than those receiving wages.

In studying the above figures, it must be remembered that the increase in food prices was greater than the increase in other commodities. Thus figures of $844.94 as the minimum on which a family of five could subsist decently in New York increased in 1917 to $980.41, or only 16%. It is extremely difficult to get the exact figures for wages in recent years.

Cost of Living:
International Commission on, 7724.
Not caused by high tariff, 7403.

Costa Rica.—Costa Rica occupies part of the southern and narrowing isthmus of Central America, between Nicaragua and Panama, with a regular coast line on the Atlantic of about 200 miles, and a broken and varied coast on the Pacific, with two bold promontories—that of Nicoya in the north and Dulce in the south, each enclosing a gulf of the same name.

Physical Features and Climate.—The country is mainly an elevated tableland, intersected by lofty volcanic ridges, running from northwest to southeast. Although close to the Equator (between 8° 17'-11° 10' N. latitude), and lying entirely within the tropical zone, the climate of Costa Rica is not unhealthy. Malaria and rheumatism are common in the coastal regions, but the climate of the plateau (at an elevation of 3,000-5,000 feet) is equable, with a mean temperature of 68° and a variation of only 5° between the extremes.

History.—For nearly three centuries (1530-1821) Costa Rica formed part of the Spanish American dominions, the seat of administration being Cartago. In 1821 the country threw in its lot with the other Central American provinces and became independent of Spain. From 1824-1839 Costa Rica was one of the "United States of Central America."

AREA AND POPULATION

Provinces and Capitals	Area in English Sq. Miles	Population 1912
Alajuela (Alajuela)	——	95,382
Cartago (Cartago)	——	61,439
Guanacaste (Liberia)	——	34,952
Heredia (Heredia)	——	43,304
Limon (Limon)	——	19,647
Puntarenas (Puntarenas)	——	20,591
San José (San José)	——	124,109
Total	23,000	399,424

Ethnography.—The inhabitants are mainly of Spanish blood, descendants of the colonists of the sixteenth and nineteenth centuries, with an admixture of mestizos or Spanish Indians. The aboriginal Indians were almost exterminated under three centuries of Spanish rule, and number about 4,000, while there are about 25,000 negroes, mostly Jamaicans and mainly employed on banana farms. The foreign white population amounts to 5,000 or 6,000, mainly Spaniards and Italians, with some German, British, and United States settlers.

Government.—The present constitution rests upon the fundamental law of Dec. 22, 1871, as modified in 1882, 1903, and 1913, and is that of a centralized Republic, with a President elected by direct vote for four years (and ineligible for an immediate term) and a single chamber legislature. President of the Republic (May 8, 1910-1914).—Ricardo Jimenez, born Feb. 6, 1859.

Congress consists of forty-three Deputies, elected for four years by the direct vote of all adult self-supporting citizens, one-half of the deputies retiring biennially.

There are magistrates' courts in all centers and superior courts in each province, with a supreme court, two appeal courts and a court of cassation at the capital.

Service in the Army is compulsory in time of war on all able-bodied citizens between the ages of eighteen and fifty. A small permanent army of about 1,000 of all arms is maintained, and there is an organized militia with a reserve and a national guard. In time of war a partly trained force of 50,000 could be raised.

Primary Education is compulsory and free, the schools are well attended, and the proportion of illiterates is being rapidly reduced. There are secondary schools at San José, Cartago, Alajuela and Heredia, and colleges of law and medicine at San José.

Debt.—An agreement, made between the Costa Rican Government and Mr. Minor C. Keith, providing for the issue of £2,-000,000 Gold Refunding, to be applied to the Conversion of the External Debt, with all arrears of interest, and the Limon Sanitation Bonds (for which together £1,617,-200, the balance, £382,800, being reserved for the Government's requirements), was finally accepted by the Foreign Bondholders in July, 1911.

These Bonds are payable in 1958, through the operation of a cumulative sinking fund of not less than 1 per cent. annually, commencing in 1921, and bear interest at the rate of 4 per cent. per annum for the first ten years, and at the rate of 5 per cent. thereafter, and are secured by a first charge on the Customs Revenue. The July, 1911, coupons and subsequent coupons were duly paid, and the conversion has been duly made.

In November, 1911, the Government of Costa Rica issued in Paris a new 5 per cent. Loan for 35,000,000 francs, for the purpose of paying off the Bonds of the Pacific Railway and the Internal Debt. This Loan is secured by a first charge on the Government Liquor Monopoly, and has been given a quotation on the Paris Bourse. The proceeds of this issue have been applied to the payment of the Internal Debt and Pacific Railway Bonds in the early part of 1912, the Government, under the agreement with the French Bankers, having received 80 per cent. of the nominal value of the Loan coupons paid.

The Internal Debt amounted, on Dec. 31, 1912, to 2,465,272 colones. The gold colon is equal to 46½ cents of United States money.

Production and Industry.—More than two-thirds of the population are engaged in agriculture, the most important crops being coffee and bananas, the latter in annually increasing quantities. Coffee, rice, maize, sugar-cane, potatoes and beans are grown in the interior and bananas, cocoa, and rubber are produced in the coast lands. The soil is extraordinarily fertile, and for this reason the republic fully deserves the name of "Rich Coast," bestowed upon it (possibly on account of its reputed auriferous wealth) in the sixteenth century. There are vast forest-covered tracts on the Atlantic and Pacific slopes where cedar, mahogany, rosewood, ebony and dye-woods are obtained. Gold, silver, copper, iron, lead and zinc are believed to exist in many districts, but the gold fields alone are worked.

Chief Exports (1912).—Bananas 10,647,-702 bunches, value £1,018,918; coffee 196,-211 bags, value £729,527; gold and silver bullion, £155,514; raw sugar, cacao, rubber, cedar and hides.

Percentage of Imports (1912).—United States, 50.58; Germany, 17.11; United Kingdom, 16.59; France, 4.82; other countries, 11.40.

Railways.—About 420 miles of railway were open for traffic in 1911, the Pacific and Atlantic being connected via the capital. The Costa Rica Railway runs from Limon to the capital, San José (104 miles), in six hours, and is continued 13 miles to Alajuela. The Northern Railway runs from Limon as terminus, and comprises 142 miles of main line and branches, running through the banana districts on the Atlantic coast. The Government own and operate the Pacific Railway, from San José to Orotina (46 miles), and the coast section of the same, Esparta to Puntarenas (13 miles) ; a new section from Orotina to join the Puntarenas section was opened in 1910. The journey from the capital to Puntarenas (76 miles) takes 5½ hours.

Shipping.—In 1912, 552 foreign vessels (1,256,093 tons) entered at Costa Rican ports, the mercantile marine of the country consisting only of a few small sailing and motor-driven vessels. The chief port is Limon, on the Atlantic coast, through which the whole of the important banana trade with the United States is done, as well as by far the larger part of the other exports and imports. Puntarenas is the most important harbor on the Pacific coast.

Towns.—Capital, San José. Estimated population (1912) 32,449. Other towns are Heredia, Limon, Alajuela, Cartago, Puntarenas, and Liberia.

Trade with the United States.—The value of merchandise imported into Costa Rica from the United States for the year 1913 was $3,514,908, and goods to the value of $3,098,735 were sent thither—a balance of $416,173 in favor of the United States.

Costa Rica:

Boundary question with Colombia discussed, 4627, 5868.

Boundary question with Nicaragua—

Arbitration referred to President of United States, and award of, 5369, 6427.

Settlement of, indspensable to commencement of ship canal, 2702.

Survey of port and river of San Juan, 3444.

British protection over, correspondence regarding, transmitted, 2583.

Claims of United States against, 3048, 3100.

Commission to adjust, discussed, 2664.

Convention for adjustment of, 3175, 3185.

Commercial relations with, 3885.

Consul of United States in, referred to, 3832.

Correspondence regarding, transmitted, 2722, 2894.

Dispute with Panama settled by arbitration, 7657.

Fugitive criminals surrendered to United States by, 5868.

Negotiations with, transmission of information regarding, refused, 2690.

Transmitted, 2695.

Outrages committed on American citizens in, 3048.

Postal convention with, 3284.

Relations with, 2690, 2691, 2695.

Rupture with Nicaragua amicably settled, 6325.

Territorial controversies between States on San Juan River, 2736.

Treaty with, transmitted and discussed, 2675, 3175, 3185.

Exchange of ratification of recommendations regarding, 3201.

Costa Rica, Treaties with.—July 10, 1851, a treaty of friendship, commerce and navigation was concluded, containing the most-favored-nation clause, granting equal treatment and equal trade privileges to the citizens of each country in the territory of the other ; exempting from military duty the citizens of either country in the territory of the other, and providing for the exchange of consular and diplomatic officers. It was provided that at any time after seven years either of the contracting parties might give notice of termination.

Claims.—July 2, 1860, a claims convention was concluded providing for a commission to act upon all claims for damages to persons and property sustained by citizens of the United States in Costa Rica. The commission met in Washington Feb. 8, 1862, and adjourned the following November, and awarded $25,704.14 against Costa Rica.

President McKinley by proclamation of Oct. 19, 1899, extended copyright privileges to Costa Rica, and in 1900 a protocol was concluded for the construction of an inter-oceanic canal.

Arbitration.—Differences which may arise of a legal nature or relating to the interpretation of existing treaties which it may not have been possible to settle by diplomacy shall be referred to the Permanent Court of Arbitration at The Hague, according to a convention signed at Washington Jan. 13, 1909.

Costa Rica also became a party to the convention between the United States and the several republics of South and Central America for the arbitration of pecuniary claims and the protection of inventions, etc., which was signed in Buenos Aires in 1910 and proclaimed in Washington July 29, 1914. (See South and Central America, Treaties with.)

Cotton Cases, suits pending in Court of Claims known as, 4003.

Cotton Crop.—The cotton plant is indigenous to tropical India and America. Cotton cloth is mentioned by Herodotus, was known in Arabia in the time of Mahomet, and was introduced into Europe by his followers. It was used by the Chinese in the thirteenth century, and was grown and woven in Spain in the tenth century. Cotton fabrics were worn by the American Indians when first visited by Columbus. The first cotton factory in America was set up at East Bridgewater, Mass., in 1787.

The first effort to cultivate cotton in the United States was made in Virginia in 1621. Later, experiments in cotton culture were made in Maryland, Delaware. Pennsylvania and New Jersey, but conditions of climate in those states were found unsuitable. It was introduced into South Carolina in 1733 and into Georgia in 1734. It was being grown in Louisiana in 1741. Cotton was not grown as a staple crop, however, until 1770, at which time shipments of American cotton to Liverpool were recorded as: "Ten bales from Charleston, three bales from New York, four bags from Virginia, and three barrels from North Carolina." After the Revolutionary War the cultivation of cotton spread more rapidly. The crop of 1790 produced 3,138 equivalent bales of 500 pounds each. 379 of which were exported. Sea island cotton was first grown in 1786.

Cotton is grown in many localities within a globe-encircling belt about five thousand miles wide, but the total area devoted to its cultivation constitutes only a small part of the entire land surface within this belt. A number of conditions are requisite for the successful production of cotton, the most important factor being a suitable climate. The cotton plant requires a long warm season in which to come to full maturity, as well as adequate moisture. In some localities where the rainfall is insufficient, recourse is had to irrigation.

Altogether the greatest cotton-growing section in the world, both in extent and in production, is located in the southern and southeastern parts of the United States. It includes small portions of Virginia, Kentucky, Missouri, Kansas, and New Mexico, and the states lying to the south. This cotton-producing area is about 1,500 miles long, from east to west, and about 500 miles in width. Within the past few years the cultivation of cotton has been undertaken in Arizona and California, on irrigated land, with considerable success, especially in the latter state. The growing of other valuable crops, however, will likely prevent any appreciable increase in the production in these states.

Some idea of the importance of cotton production in the United States from an economic standpoint may be had when it is considered that, next to corn, cotton is the most valuable crop grown in the country, and that cotton is the largest single item of export. The value of the cotton crop of 1909 represented 15 per cent of the total value of all the crops of the country. The value of cotton exported during the fiscal year 1913 amounted to $547,357,195, or 22.5 per cent of the total value of all articles of domestic merchandise exported during the year. These large exports, combined with the more than 5,000,000 bales consumed in domestic manufacture, strikingly indicate the importance of cotton in the economic affairs of the Nation. Of the total production of commercial cotton in 1913 the United States contributed 60.9 per cent.

Cotton now leads all other fibers as a textile material. The position attained by this staple and its manufactures in the industrial and commercial world renders reliable information regarding it of great importance. The international trade in no other single article equals that in cotton and the products made from it. In its various stages—from the seed to the completed fabric—it furnishes employment to a considerable portion of the entire human race. It affects not only those who are engaged directly in producing, handling, and consuming the fiber and its products, but also large numbers who touch it, so to speak, as merchants, bankers, manufacturers of fertilizers and ginning machinery, and, in fact, some of those engaged in almost any line of endeavor.

Cotton crop in specified years, 1903 to 1915, acreage harvested, production, and farm value:

Year	Area	Fibre	Seed	Total value
	Acres	Bales [1]	Short tons	Dollars
1903....	28,016,893	9,851,129	4,716,000	660,550,000
1904....	30,053,739	13,438,012	6,427,500	652,030,000
1905....	26,117,153	10,575,017	5,060,000	632,300,000
1906....	31,374,000	13,273,809	5,913,000	721,650,000
1907....	31,311,000	11,107,179	5,952,000	700,960,000
1908....	32,444,000	13,241,799	4,904,000	681,230,000
1909....	32,044,000	10,004,949	5,462,000	812,090,000
1910....	32,403,000	11,608,616	4,175,000	943,520,000
1911....	36,045,000	15,692,701	6,997,000	869,690,000
1912....	34,283,000	13,703,421	6,104,000	904,130,000
1913....	37,089,000	14,156,486	6,305,000	1,026,700,000
1914....	36,832,000	16,134,930	7,186,000	720,080,000
1915....	31,535,000	11,191,820		

[1] The figures represent equivalent 500-pound bales, gross weight.

The following table shows the cotton production by States in 1915, including linters, and the total annual production for four preceding years:

State	Gross Equivalent of 500-lb. Bales		Per cent of total ginned [1]	Rank in production [1]
	Cotton	Linters		
Alabama..............	1,020,839	71,854	9.1	4
Arkansas..............	816,002	54,060	7.3	6
Florida..............	47,831	(²)	0.4	12
Georgia..............	1,908,673	171,239	17.1	2
Louisiana..............	341,063	32,158	3.1	9
Mississippi..............	953,965	83,345	8.5	5
Missouri..............	47,999	4,724	0.4	11
North Carolina........	699,494	52,531	6.3	7
Oklahoma..........	639,626	48,446	5.7	8
South Carolina........	1,133,919	67,337	10.1	3
Tennessee..............	303,420	53,430	2.7	10
Texas..............	3,227,480	227,150	28.8	1
Virginia..............	15,809	....	0.2	13
All Others [3]..........	35,700	14,506	0.3	....
Total for 1915..........	11,191,820	880,780	100.0	....
Total for 1914..........	16,134,930	856,900	100.0	....
Total for 1913..........	14,156,486	638,881	100.0	....
Total for 1912..........	13,703,421	609,594	100.0	....
Total for 1911..........	15,692,701	557,575	100.0	....

[1] Based on equivalent 500-pound bales, excluding linters.
[2] Included in "All other states," to avoid disclosure of individual operations.
[3] Includes Arizona, California, Kansas, Kentucky, and New Mexico, and the linter production of Illinois.

The needs of the world markets are shown in the following table of cotton consumption of the world:

500-lb. Bales	Great Britain	Continent	United States	Total World
1904–1905...	3,620,000	5,148,000	4,310,000	15,612,000
1905–1906...	3,774,000	5,252,000	4,726,000	16,435,000
1906–1907...	3,892,000	5,460,000	4,950,000	16,999,000
1907–1908...	3,690,000	5,720,000	4,227,000	16,281,000
1908–1909...	3,720,000	5,720,000	4,912,000	17,164,000
1909–1910...	3,175,000	5,460,000	4,533,000	16,189,000
1910–1911...	3,776,000	5,460,000	4,485,000	16,750,000
1911–1912...	4,160,000	5,720,000	5,210,000	18,566,000
1912–1913...	4,400,000	6,000,000	5,531,000	19,642,000
1913–1914...	4,300,000	6,000,000	5,680,000	19,858,000
1914–1915...	3,000,000	3,250,000	5,806,000	15,917,000

The world's production of commercial cotton for two recent years is given in the annexed table for purposes of comparison:

COTTON PRODUCTION (BALES OF 500 POUNDS NET)

Country	1913	1912
United States............	14,156,000	13,113,000
India *.................	3,801,000	3,328,000
Egypt..................	1,470,000	1,492,000
China..................	1,200,000	1,074,000
Russia..................	1,004,000	917,000
Brazil..................	420,000	315,000
Mexico..................	150,000	140,000
Peru..................	110,000	110,000
Persia..................	140,000	137,000
Turkey..................	130,000	115,000
All other countries........	285,000	235,000
Total........	22,866,000	20,976,000

* The amounts for India do not include cotton used in home manufacture, although such cotton is included in the reports of cotton produced compiled by the Indian Government.

[The statistics for the United States were collected by the Census Bureau. Those for other countries have been compiled from a number of sources, among them being *The Cotton Gazette*, Liverpool, England; Mitsui & Co., Osaka, Japan; Reinhart & Co., Alexandria, Egypt; Commercial Intelligence Department of the Indian Government; Russian Department of Agriculture; E. T. Craig, Mexico City; Pan-American Union; and the United States Consular Reports.]

See illustrations opposite 980, 1837, 3007.

Cotton Goods Made in the United States.
—A Census Bureau report issued June 17, 1911, showed that the number of establishments engaged in the manufacture of cotton goods in the United States in 1909 was 1,206, an increase of 24 per cent since 1899, and that the value of the products was $616,297,000, an increase of 85 per cent since 1899. The following is a tabular statement of the kinds of products of cotton goods by kind, quantity and value in 1914:

Number of establishments..................... 1,325

PRINCIPAL MATERIALS	Pounds	Cost
Cotton, raw..............	2,523,500,837	$330,315,223
Domestic...............	2,431,405,884	312,586,001
Foreign................	92,094,953	17,729,222
Dyed, bleached, and other prepared cotton.......	1,052,836	111,423
Cotton waste.............	54,116,105	3,542,631
All other fibers............	4,276,476	3,203,262
Cotton yarns.............	139,482,027	39,793,131
All other yarns...........	3,309,277	4,793,221
Total value........................		² $701,152,268

PRODUCTS	Square Yards	Value
Woven goods..............	6,815,645,683	$488,728,054
Ducks.................	248,539,379	47,921,989
Ginghams..............	489,661,133	36,706,542
Fancy weaves, total.....	1,422,787,368	131,813,609
Drills..................	289,969,885	21,256,698
Twills, sateens, etc.......	392,108,735	32,891,854
All other fancy weaves...	740,708,748	77,665,057
Napped fabrics..........	263,862,227	24,352,020
Velvets, corduroys, plushes, etc...........	29,128,703	8,540,143
Toweling and terry weaves	75,732,241	9,805,232
Mosquito netting and similar fabrics.........	97,981,783	2,820,524
Bags and bagging.......	129,357,002	9,705,616
Tapestries..............	10,137,710	5,411,592
All other woven goods....	4,048,458,137	211,650,787
Yarns manufactured for sale	497,986,999	127,363,952
Thread..................	26,507,023	22,917,099
Twine..................	13,284,875	2,792,125
Cordage and rope.........	5,515,658	891,223
Cotton waste not used.....	317,360,019	14,421,929
All other products, value................		44,037,886

¹ A minus sign (—) denotes decrease.
² In addition, cotton goods to the value of $6,538,130 were produced in 1914 by establishments engaged primarily in other lines of industry.

Cottonseed Products.—Prior to the introduction of oil mills cotton seed was practically valueless, except for planting purposes. Although it was used to some extent for fertilizing and for planting, a very large proportion of the total amount produced was considered a waste product and treated accordingly. The manufacture of oil from cotton seed first reached importance in England. That country, with a crush of about 200,000 tons of cotton seed annually, was the leading cottonseed-oil producing country in the world as late as 1870. A few mills were constructed in the United States prior to the Civil War, but the growth of the industry was very slow, and at the census of 1880 only 45 such establishments were reported in the United States. Since that time the industry has shown marvelous growth in this country, there being 870 establishments engaged in the crushing of cotton seed during the season of 1913-14, with a crush of more than 4,750,000 tons.

Many changes have been brought about in this industry, that of delinting the seed preparatory to crushing being of particular interest in a report on the cotton crop. The first mills erected were not equipped with machinery for this purpose, as the seed treated were usually of the sea-island or Egyptian varieties, which are smooth and comparatively free from lint. Practically all of the seed treated in the United

States are of the upland varieties of cotton, and these seed, unless specially reginned, are covered with short fibers, which prevent a complete separation of the meats from the hulls, as small particles of the former become enmeshed in the fibers and are carried away with the hulls. When seed were first delinted, not more than 25 or 30 pounds of linters were obtained per ton of seed treated. With the increase in the value of oil and meal, efforts were made to increase the yield of these products, and machinery was devised for the closer delinting of seed. Accordingly improved machinery of this character has very generally been installed, and now many establishments obtain more than 100 pounds of linters per ton of seed treated, some obtaining as much as 150 or 160 pounds per ton.

Cotton Exposition.—From Sept. 18 to Dec. 31, 1895, was held at Atlanta, Ga., the Cotton States Industrial Exposition, having for its chief purpose the display of the agricultural, manufacturing and mineral resources of the southern states. The site covered an area of 189 acres in Piedmont Park, on which some thirty exhibition buildings were erected. The Federal government and many foreign countries and various states of the Union, as well as South and Central America Republics made exhibits. Numerous congresses of educational and industrial interests were held in the auditorium, and to nearly every day was assigned some special feature of interest. The total attendance was 1,179,889. The receipts from admissions were $500,-000; from concessions, $125,230; from rent of floor space, $79,000, a total of $704,230, as against a cost of $960,930.

Cotton Expositions. (See Atlanta, Ga.; New Orleans, La.)

Cotton Loan referred to, 3583.

Cotton State.— Alternative nickname for Alabama. (See Land of Flowers.)

Council Bluffs, Iowa, act authorizing purchase of ground for Government offices in, vetoed, 5258.

Council of National Defense.—Provision for a Council of National Defense was made in the Army Appropriation Bill approved on August 29, 1916, in order to provide for the "coordination of industries and resources for the national security and welfare." The Board consists of the Secretary of War (Chairman), and the secretaries of Navy, Interior, Agriculture, Commerce and Labor. The development of the work of the Council is best described by President Wilson himself as the "coordination of all forms of transportation and the development of the means of transportation to meet the military, industrial and commercial needs of the nation" and "the collection of complete information as to our present manufacturing and productive facilities adaptable to the many-sided uses of modern war." Provision was made also for the appointment by the President of an advisory committee of seven, on the nomination of the Council, to assist in the administration of the program of the Council. The members of the advisory committee serve without pay, but are allowed expenses incurred in the performance of their duties. The following men were appointed as the advisory committee: Daniel Willard, President of the Baltimore and Ohio Railroad; Samuel Gompers, President of the American Federation of Labor; Dr. Franklin H. Martin, a distinguished surgeon recommended by the associated medical societies of the country; Mr. Howard E. Coffin, an automobile engineer, formerly chairman of the committee on industrial preparedness of the Naval Consulting Board (q. v.); Mr. Bernard Baruch, a New York financier; President Hollis Godfrey, of the Drexel Institute, Philadelphia; and Julius Rosenwald, president of the largest mail-order establishment in the United States. The director of the advisory committee is Mr. W. S. Gifford. The work of the Council has been subdivided into seven sub-committees, over each of which presides a member of the advisory committee, as follows: Committees on Medicine and Sanitary Conditions, Labor, Transportation, Science and Research, Raw Materials, Munition Manufacturing, and Supplies.

Council of Soldiers' and Workmen's Delegates. (See Russia, Russian Revolution.)

Council of War.—Meeting of army officers to determine the course of military action.

Counselor, Department of State.—Appropriation of $7,500 as yearly salary for a counselor to the Department of State was first made in the appropriation act of June 17, 1910. This officer is appointed by the President, by and with the consent of the Senate, and in the Department of State he ranks next to the Secretary of State. As his title indicates, he advises the department on matters of law and policy which are of especial importance. In addition, he is in charge of Far Eastern affairs (q. v.) and of relations with belligerents affecting trade. In addition, he is charged with the conduct of the Information Bureau of the department (q. v.). (See State Department.)

Counterfeit.—An imitation of money, bonds or other things of value.

Counterfeiting:

Of foreign and domestic coins, 1136, 1268.

Pardons granted counterfeiters, etc., referred to, 3818.

Country Life Commission.—In August, 1908, President Roosevelt, desirous of improving social, sanitary and economic conditions on American farms, invited Prof. L. H. Bailey, of the New York College of Agriculture, at Ithaca; Henry Wallace, of *Wallace's Farmer*, Des Moines, Ia.; Kenyon L. Butterfield, president of the Massachusetts Agricultural College, at Amherst; Gifford Pinchot, of the United States Forest Service, and Walter H. Page, editor of *The World's Work*, New York, to assist him by acting as a committee of investigation, or "Commission on Country Life." The immediate purpose of the president in appointing the Commission was to gain from them information and advice which would enable him to make recommendations to Congress.

The Commission carried on its inquiries and investigations by correspondence and by personally holding meetings in rural sections at which the farmers themselves discussed their needs. The letters and speeches of the farmers formed, when classified and arranged, a condensed and comprehensive consensus of the opinions of farmers as to what are the chief rural problems and what are the remedies for evils and deficiencies. Prof. L. H. Bailey, N. Y. State College of Agriculture, Ithaca, N. Y., is chairman of the Commission.

Country Life Commission:

Report submitted, 7253.

County.—Originally the territory of a count or earl. County government was early established in this country. In 1639 Virginia had eight counties, originally called shires. By 1680 the number was increased to twenty. In South Carolina the original subdivision of the Colony was parish. Southern counties generally had officers and courts similar to those of England. Massachusetts first incorporated counties in 1643. In most Colonies, however, county government was established with English rule. Each state of the Union, except Louisiana, which adheres to the parish system, is now divided into counties, each of which contains a county seat, in which is usually located a court-house and a jail or prison.

Coupon.—The interest check attached to a bond, to be cut off, or "clipped," and presented for payment.

Coupon Bond.—A bond with the interest check attached.

Courier, The, officers and men of, rescued by Spanish ship *Sabina*, 2005. Compensation for, requested, 2005.

Court Martial. (See Courts Martial.)

Court of Arbitration (International). (See Hague Peace Conference.)

Court of Claims.—This court was established by act of Congress, Feb. 24, 1855. It has general jurisdiction of all "claims founded upon the Constitution of the United States or any law of Congress except for pensions, or upon any regulation of an Executive Department, or upon any contract, expressed or implied, with the Government of the United States, or for damages, liquidated or unliquidated, in cases not sounding in tort, in respect of which claims the party would be entitled to redress against the United States, either in a court of law, equity, or admiralty, if the United States were suable, except claims growing out of the late Civil War and commonly known as war claims," and certain rejected claims. It has jurisdiction also of claims of like character which may be referred to it by any Executive Department, involving disputed facts of controverted questions of law, where the amount in controversy exceeds $3,000, or where the decision will affect a class of cases or furnish a precedent for the future action of any Executive Department in the adjustment of a class of cases, or where any authority, right, privilege or exemption is claimed or denied under the Constitution. In all the above-mentioned cases, the court, when it finds for the claimant, may enter judgment against the United States payable out of the public treasury. An appeal, only upon questions of law, lies to the Supreme Court on the part of the defendants in all cases, and on the part of the claimants when the amount in controversy exceeds $3,000. The findings of fact by this court are final and not subject to review. The statute of limitations prevents parties bringing action on their own motion more than six years after the cause of action accrued. Any of the departments, however, may refer claims at any time if they were pending therein within a period of six years.

Under an act of March 2, 1887, the Secretary of the Navy referred to this court all cases growing out of claims for bounty for war vessels captured or destroyed by the United States Navy during the late war with Spain, involving the consideration of every naval conflict that took place during that war and the rights of all the officers and men engaged. This court was also vested with jurisdiction over certain Indian depredation claims by an act of March 3, 1891. By the act of April 29, 1902, Congress conferred upon this court jurisdiction over all claims against the United States arising out of the payment of custom duties to the military authorities in the Island of Puerto Rico upon articles imported from the several states.

The act of June 25, 1910, "An act to provide additional protection for owners of patents of the United States, and for other purposes," conferred a new jurisdiction. There are five judges, who sit together in the hearing of cases, the concurrence of three of whom is necessary for the decision of any case. The court sits at Washington, D. C., on the first Monday in December each year and continues into the following summer and until all cases ready for trial are disposed of. Cases may be commenced and entered at any time, whether the court be in session or not.

Chief Justice—Edward K. Campbell, Ala. Associate Judges—Charles B. Howry, Miss.; Fenton W. Booth, Ill.; Geo. W. Atkinson, W. Va.; Samuel S. Barney, Wis. Salaries, Chief Justice, $6,500; Justices, $6,000.

Court of Claims (see also Southern Claims Commission; War Claims):

Act in relation to new trials in, vetoed, 4168.

Claims pending in, referred to, 4205, 5755.

Joint resolution to refer certain claims to, discussed, 4741.

Judgments of, should be made final, 3252.

Method of verifying claims against Government, recommendations regarding, 4303.

Suits pending in, known as cotton cases, 4003.

Court of Customs Appeals.—On account of widespread criticism of the rulings of customs officials and the consequent appeals to the federal courts by importers, Congress on Aug. 5, 1909, passed an act creating a Court of Customs Appeals to hear and determine such cases. The law was amended Feb. 25, 1910, and provides that there shall be a United States Court of Customs Appeals, which shall consist of a Presiding Judge and four Associate Judges, each of whom shall be appointed by the President, and shall receive a salary of seven thousand dollars a year. The Presiding Judge shall be so designated in the order of appointment and in the commission issued to him by the President; and the Associate Judges shall have precedence according to the date of their commissions. Any three members of said court shall constitute a quorum, and the concurrence of three members shall be necessary to any decision thereof.

If the importer, owner, consignee, or agent of any imported merchandise, or the Collector or Secretary of the Treasury, shall be dissatisfied with the decision of the Board of General Appraisers as to the construction of the law and the facts respecting the classification of such merchandise and the rate of duty imposed thereon under such classification, or with any other appealable decision of said board, they, or either of them, may, within sixty days next after the entry of such decree or judgment, and not afterward, apply to the Court of Customs Appeals for a review of the questions of law and fact involved in such decision.

The judges of the court appointed by President Taft were: Presiding Judge, Robert M. Montgomery; Associate Judges, James F. Smith, Orion M. Barber, Marion De Vries, George E. Martin, Attorney-General, George W. Wickersham, Assistant Attorney-General, William L. Wemple.

Court of Private Land Claims:

Difficulty in administering law establishing, discussed, 5638, 5760.

Organization of, discussed, 5632.

Court, Supreme. (See illustration, frontispiece, Vol. XVI.)

Allotment of justices of, to circuits, 3324, 3376.

Appeals to, from courts of District of Columbia and Territories, recommendations regarding, 4939, 5103.

Bill for relief of, discussed, 5560.

Building for, recommended, 6343.

Decisions in joint traffic association and trans-Missouri cases of no practical effect, 7076.

Delay of justice in, discussed and intermediate court recommended, 4453, 4526, 4574, 4640, 5362, 5477.

Circuit courts of appeals discussed, 5968.

Act regarding, vetoed, 5679.

Distribution of decisions of, referred to, 2130, 2212.

Justices of—

Salaries of, increase in, recommended, 3996.

Should be exempted from other duties, 830.

Limitation upon right in felony cases to review by, recommended, 5632, 5880.

Reports, of. (See Supreme Court Reports.)

Vacancies in, and reasons for not filling discussed by President Lincoln, 3250.

Courts.—Public tribunals for the administration of justice and the interpretation of law were authorized by the Constitution, and the First Congress established the United States Supreme Court. John Jay, of New York, was made chief justice, and the first session was held in 1790.

The salary of the Chief Justice of the United States is $15,000; of Associate Justices, $14,500.

The Supreme Court at present consists of the following justices:

Year of Birth.	JUSTICES	Appointed
	Chief Justice	
1845	Edward D. White, Louisiana	1910
	Associate Justices	
1843	Joseph McKenna, California	1898
1841	Oliver W. Holmes, Mass.	1902
1849	William R. Day, Ohio	1903
1857	John H. Clarke, Ohio	1916
1859	W. Van Devanter, Wyo	1910
1858	Mahlon Pitney, N. J.	1912
1862	James C. McReynolds, Tenn.	1914
1856	Louis D. Brandeis, Mass.	1916

The Supreme Court is the highest tribunal of the United States. It consists of a Chief Justice and eight associate justices and holds its sessions annually in the Capitol at Washington, commencing the second Monday in October. All its members are appointed by the President, with the advice and consent of the Senate, and hold office during good behavior, receiving a compensation which may not be diminished during their term of office. They have the privilege of retiring at the age of seventy if they have served ten years and of drawing their salaries for the remainder of life.

The jurisdiction of the Supreme Court extends to all cases in law and equity arising under the Constitution, the laws of the United States, and treaties which are made under their authority ; to all cases affecting ambassadors or other public min-

TABLE SHOWING DISTRICTS COMPRISING EACH JUDICIAL CIRCUIT, THE DISTRICT AND CIRCUIT JUDGES THEREIN, AND THE JUSTICES OF THE SUPREME COURT ASSIGNED THERETO.

Circuits and Districts	District Judges	Circuit Judges	Justices
FIRST CIRCUIT:			
Maine...................	Clarence Hale........	William L. Putnam.	
Massachusetts...........	James M. Morton, Jr.	Frederic Dodge.....	Oliver W. Holmes.
New Hampshire...........	Edgar Aldrich........	G. H. Bingham.....	
Rhode Island.............	Arthur L. Brown.....		
SECOND CIRCUIT:			
Connecticut..............	Edwin S. Thomas.....		
New York, northern........	George W. Ray.......		
	Martin T. Manton...	Charles M. Hough..	
New York, southern........	Learned Hand........	Alfred C. Coxe.....	
	Julius M. Mayer......	Henry G. Ward.....	Louis D. Brandeis.
	Augustus N. Hand..	Martin A. Knapp*..	
New York, eastern........	Thomas Ives Chatfield	Henry Wade Rogers	
	Van Vechten Veeder..		
New York, western........	John R. Hazel.......		
Vermont..................	Harland B. Howe....		
THIRD CIRCUIT:			
Delaware.................	Edward G. Bradford..		
New Jersey...............	John Rellstab........		
	Thomas G. Haight....	Joseph Buffington...	
Pennsylvania, eastern......	J. Whitaker Thompson	John B. McPherson.	Mahlon Pitney.
	Oliver B. Dickinson...	Victor B. Woolley...	
Pennsylvania, middle.......	Chas. B. Witmer......		
Pennsylvania, Western.....	Chas. P. Orr........		
	W. H. Thomson......		
FOURTH CIRCUIT:			
Maryland.................	John C. Rose.........		
North Carolina, eastern....	Henry G. Connor....		
North Carolina, western....	Jas. Edmund Boyd...		
South Carolina, eastern....	Henry A. M. Smith..	Jeter C. Pritchard. .	
South Carolina, western....	Joseph T. Johnson...	Charles A. Woods..	Edward D. White.
Virginia, eastern..........	Edmund Waddill, Jr..		
Virginia, western..........	Henry C. McDowell...		
West Virginia, northern.....	Alston G. Dayton....		
West Virginia, southern.....	Benjamin F. Keller...		
FIFTH CIRCUIT:			
Alabama, northern........	William I. Grubb.....		
Alabama, middle and northern...................	Henry D. Clayton....		
Alabama, southern.........	Robert T. Ervin.....		
Florida, northern..........	Wm. B. Sheppard.....		
Florida, southern..........	Rhydon N. Call......		
Georgia, northern..........	William T. Newman...		
Georgia, southern..........	Emory Speer.........	Don A. Pardee.....	
Louisiana, eastern.........	Rufus E. Foster......	Robert L. Batts....	James C. McReynolds
Louisiana, western.........	Aleck Boarman.......	Richard W. Walker.	
Mississippi, northern and southern.................	Henry C. Niles......		
Texas, northern...........	Edward R. Meek.....		
Texas, southern...........	Waller T. Burns......		
Texas, eastern............	Gordon Russell.......		
Texas, western............	DuVal West.........		
Canal Zone...............	William H. Jackson...		
SIXTH CIRCUIT:			
Kentucky, eastern.........	A. M. J. Cochran.....		
Kentucky, western.........	Walter Evans........		
Michigan, eastern.........	Arthur J. Tuttle.....		
Michigan, western.........	Clarence W. Sessions..		
Ohio, northern............	John M. Killits.....	John W. Warrington	
	D. C. Westenhaver...	Loyal E. Knappen..	William R. Day.
Ohio, southern............	John E. Sater.......	Arthur C. Denison..	
	Howard C. Hollister...		
Tennessee, eastern and middle.................	Edward T. Sanford...		
Tennessee, western........	John E. McCall.....		

* No successor to be appointed (act Oct. 22, 1913; Public, No. 32).

TABLE SHOWING DISTRICTS COMPRISING EACH JUDICIAL CIRCUIT.—*Continued*

Circuits and Districts	District Judges	Circuit Judges	Justices
SEVENTH CIRCUIT:			
Illinois, northern............	Kenesaw M. Landis... / George A. Carpenter..	Francis E. Baker.... Samuel Alschuler....	
Illinois, eastern............	Francis M. Wright....	Christian C. Kohl-	
Illinois, southern...........	J. Otis Humphrey.....	saat..............	John H. Clarke.
Indiana...................	Albert B. Anderson...	Julian W. Mack.....	
Wisconsin, eastern........	Ferdinand A. Geiger..	Evan H. Evans....	
Wisconsin, western........	Arthur L. Sanborn....		
EIGHTH CIRCUIT:			
Arkansas, eastern..........	Jacob Trieber.......		
Arkansas, western..........	Frank A. Youmans....		
Colorado.................	Robert E. Lewis......		
Iowa, northern............	Henry Thomas Reed..		
Iowa, southern............	Martin J. Wade......		
Kansas...................	John C. Pollock......		
Minnesota................	Page Morris.......... / Wilbur F. Booth......	Walter H. Sanborn	
Missouri, eastern..........	David P. Dyer.......	William C. Hook...	
Missouri, western.........	Arba S. Van Valken-	Kimbrough Stone...	Willis Van Devanter.
	burgh.............	John Emmett Car-	
Nebraska.................	Joseph W. Woodrough / Thomas C. Munger...	land............. Walter I. Smith....	
New Mexico..............	Colin Neblett........		
North Dakota.............	Charles F. Amidon....		
Oklahoma, eastern.........	Ralph E. Campbell...		
Oklahoma, western.........	John H. Cotteral.....		
South Dakota.............	James D. Elliott......		
Utah....................	Tillman D. Johnson...		
Wyoming.................	John A. Riner........		
NINTH CIRCUIT:			
Arizona..................	William H. Sawtelle...		
California, northern.......	William C. Van Fleet.. / Maurice T. Dooling...		
California, southern........	Oscar A. Trippett.... / Benjamin F. Bledsoe..		
Idaho...................	Frank S. Dietrich.....		
Montana.................	George M. Bourquin..		
Nevada..................	Edward S. Farrington.		
Oregon..................	Charles E. Wolverton. / Robert S. Bean.......		
Washington, eastern.......	Frank H. Rudkin.....		
Washington, western.......	Edward E. Cushman.. / Jeremiah Neterer.....		
ALASKA..................	Robert W. Jennings, Div. No. 1......... John Randolph Tucker, Div. No. 2......... Frederick M. Brown, Div. No. 3......... Charles E. Bunnell... Div. No. 4.........		
HAWAII.................	Alexander G. M. Rob- ertson, chief justice. Ralph P. Quarles, asso- ciate justice....... James L. Coke, asos- ciate justice........ Clarence W. Ashford.. Samuel B. Kemp, judge first circuit......... Wm. J. Robinson, judge first circuit......... Wm. S. Edings, judge second circuit...... James W. Thompson, judge third circuit.. Clement K. Quinn, judge fourth circuit. Lyle A. Dickey, judge fifth circuit......... Horace W. Vaughan, U. S. district judge Joseph B. Poindexter, U. S. district judge	William B. Gilbert.. Erskine M. Ross.... William W. Morrow. William H. Hunt...	Joseph McKenna.

isters and consuls; to all admiralty and maritime cases; to controversies to which the United States is a party; to contro-versies between two or more states, between citizens of different states, between citizens of the same state, claiming lands under grants of different states, between a state and foreign states and between citizens of a state and foreign states. citizens or sub-jects. In all cases affecting ambassadors or other public ministers and consuls and those in which a state shall be a party the Supreme Court has original jurisdiction. In all the other cases aforementioned it has appellate jurisdiction both as to law and fact. The Supreme Court also has appellate jurisdiction over cases from the United States circuit courts where more than $2,500 is involved. (See Judiciary.)

In accordance with the provision of the Constitution establishing a Supreme Court and conferring upon Congress power to create inferior tribunals, a regular system of courts has been formed. The system at first adopted has not been changed in any essential manner. The latest change of importance was the creation of the Circuit Court of Appeals.

Circuit Courts.—The judiciary act of 1789 provides for United States circuit courts and district courts inferior to the Supreme Court. No provision having been made for circuit judges, the circuit courts up to 1869 were held by justices of the Supreme Court and district judges. In 1801 Congress passed a law providing for sixteen circuit judges, but it was repealed the following year. In 1869 special judges were provided for the circuit courts, and the New York circuit has since been given an additional one. Circuit courts were abolished at the close of December 31, 1911.

The following table shows the judges of the nine circuits and the dates of their appointment:

Circuit	Judges	Appointed
First......	Geo. H. Bingham, R. I........	1913
	William L. Putnam, Me.......	1892
	Frederic Dodge, Mass.........	1912
Second....	E. Henry Lacombe, N. Y......	1887
	Alfred C. Coxe, N. Y.........	1902
	Henry G. Ward, N. Y.........	1907
	Henry W. Rogers, Ct.........	1913
	Charles M. Hough, N. Y......	1916
Third......	Victor B. Woolley, Del.......	1914
	Joseph Buffington, Pa.........	1906
	John B. McPherson, Pa.......	1912
Fourth.....	Chas. A. Woods, S. C........	1913
	Peter C. Pritchard, N. C......	1904
Fifth......	Don A. Pardee, Ga...........	1881
	Robert L. Batts, Tex.........	1917
	Richard W. Walker, Huntsville..	1914
Sixth	Arthur C. Denison, Mich......	1911
	John W. Warrington, Ohio.....	1909
	Loyall E. Knappen, Mich......	1910
Seventh....	Evan A. Evans, Wis..........	1916
	Samuel Alschuler, Ill.........	1915
	Frank E. Baker, Ind.........	1902
	Christian C. Kohlsaat, Ill.....	1905
	Julian W. Mack, D. C........	1911
Eighth.....	Walter H. Sanborn, Minn.....	1892
	William C. Hook, Kan.......	1903
	John Emmett Carland, D. C....	1911
	Walter I. Smith, Ia..........	1911
	Kimbrough Stone, Mo........	1916
Ninth......	William B. Gilbert, Ore.......	1892
	Erskine M. Ross, Cal........	1895
	William W. Morrow, Cal......	1897
	Wm. H. Hunt, D. C..........	1911

Salaries $7,000 each. The Judges of each circuit and the Justice of the Supreme Court for the circuit constitute a Circuit Court of Appeals.

Circuit Court of Appeals.—Supreme Court cases having accumulated beyond the capacity of the court to consider them promptly, Congress March 3, 1891, provided for an additional circuit judge in each circuit and established circuit courts of appeals, to consist of the circuit judges of each circuit, the district judges therein, and the justice of the Supreme Court assigned thereto. Three judges make up the court, two constituting a quorum; but one or more of the district judges of the circuit may be called on by the court to make up a quorum.

These circuit courts of appeals have final jurisdiction over appeals from the district and circuit courts except in questions of the jurisdiction of those courts and in constitutional, prize and capital cases.

The act to codify, revise and amend the laws relating to the judiciary, approved March 3, 1911, abolished the circuit courts of the United States as courts of original jurisdiction, transferred the functions of these courts to the Federal district courts and limited the duties of the circuit judges to service on the circuit courts of appeals. The act took effect Jan. 1, 1912. The circuit courts of appeals exercise appellate jurisdiction to review by appeal or writ of error final decisions in the district courts, including the territorial courts of Alaska and the United States Court for China in all cases other than those in which appeals and writs of error may be taken to the Supreme Court, and, except as to the right of the Supreme Court to interfere through certiorari, the judgments and decrees of the

DISTRICT COURTS OF THE UNITED STATES

Districts	Judges and Addresses	Appointed
Ala.: N. & M..	Henry D. Clayton, Montgomery.	1914
" S. D....	Robert T. Ervin, Mobile....	1917
Alaska......	R. W. Jennings, Juneau......	1913
"	John R. Tucker, Nome......	1913
"	F. M. Brown, Valdez........	1913
"	Charles E. Bunnell, Fairbanks	1915
Ariz.......	Wm. H. Sawtelle, Tucson.....	1913
Ark.: E. D...	Jacob Trieber, Little Rock....	1901
" W. D....	F. A. Youmans, Fort Smith...	1911
Cal.: N. D...	M. T. Dooling, San Francisco.	1913
" N. D...	Wm. C. Van Fleet, San Francisco................	1907
" S. D.....	Oscar A. Trippett, Los Angeles	1915
" S. D.....	Benjamin F. Bledsoe, Los Angeles.................	1914
Canal Zone...	W. H. Jackson, Ancon......	1914
Colorado....	Robert E. Lewis, Denver.....	1906
Connecticut..	Edwin S. Thomas, New Haven	1913
Delaware....	Ed. G. Bradford, Wilmington.	1897
Fla.: N. D...	W. B. Sheppard, Pensacola..	1908
" S. D.....	Rhydon M. Call, Jacksonville.	1913
Ga.: N. D...	Wm. T. Newman, Atlanta....	1886
" S. D.....	Emory Speer, Macon........	1885
Hawaii......	Horace W. Vaughan, Honolulu	1916
"	Joseph B. Poindexter, Honolulu	1917
Idaho.......	Frank S. Dietrich, Boisé....	1907
Ill.: N. D...	Kenesaw M. Landis, Chicago..	1905
" N. D...	G. A. Carpenter, Chicago....	1910
" S. D.....	J. O. Humphrey, Springfield..	1901
" E.....	F. M. Wright, Urbana.......	1905
Indiana......	A. B. Anderson, Indianapolis.	1902
Iowa.: N. D..	Henry T. Reed, Cresco.......	1904
" S. D.....	Martin J. Wade, Davenport..	1915
Kansas......	John C. Pollock, Kansas City.	1903
Ky.: W. D...	Walter Evans, Louisville....	1899
" E. D....	A. M. J. Cochran, Maysville.	1901
La.: E. D....	Rufus E. Foster, New Orleans.	1909
" W. D....	George W. Jack, Shreveport..	1917
Maine.......	Clarence Hale, Portland......	1902
Maryland....	John C. Rose, Baltimore.....	1910
Mass.......	Jas. M. Morton, Jr., Fall River	1912
Mich.: E. D..	Arthur J. Tuttle, Detroit....	1912
" W. D...	C. W. Sessions, Grand Rapids.	1911
Minnesota...	Wilbur F. Booth, Minneapolis	1914
"	Page Morris, Duluth........	1903
Miss.: N. & S.	Henry C. Niles, Kosciusko...	1892
Montana....	G. M. Bourquin, Butte......	1912
Mo.: E. D...	David P. Dyer, St. Louis....	1907
" W. D....	A. S. Van Valkenburgh, Kansas City...............	1910
Nebraska....	Joseph W. Woodrough, Omaha	1916
"	Thos. C. Munger, Lincoln...	1907
Nevada......	E. S. Farrington, Carson City.	1907
N. Hamp....	Edgar Aldrich, Littleton....	1891
New Jersey...	John Rellstab, Trenton......	1909

DISTRICT COURTS OF THE UNITED STATES—*Cont'd*

District	Judges and Addresses	Appointed
New Jersey...	Thomas G. Haight, Jersey City	1914
"	J. Warren Davis, Trenton...	1916
New Mexico..	Colin Neblett, Santa Fe.....	1917
N. Y.: N. D...	George W. Ray, Norwich.....	1902
" W. D...	John R. Hazel, Buffalo......	1900
" S. D...	Julius M. Mayer, N. Y. City..	1912
" S. D...	August N. Hand, N. Y. City.	1914
" S. D...	Martin T. Manton, N. Y. City	1916
" S. D...	Learned Hand, N. Y.City....	1909
" E. D...	T. I. Chatfield, Brooklyn....	1907
" E. D...	Van V. Veeder, Brooklyn.....	1911
N. C.: E. D...	H. G. Conner, Wilson.......	1909
" W. D...	James E. Boyd, Greensboro..	1901
N. Dakota...	Chas. F. Amidon, Fargo.....	1897
Ohio.: N. D...	John M. Killits, Toledo......	1910
" N. D...	D. C. Westenhaver, Cleveland...............	1917
" S. D...	H. C. Hollister, Cincinnati...	1910
" S. D...	John E. Sater, Columbus....	1909
Okla.: E. D...	R. E. Campbell, Muskogee..	1908
" W. D...	John H. Cotteral, Guthrie...	1908
Oregon.......	C. E. Wolverton, Portland...	1906
"	Robert S. Bean, Portland...	1909
Pa.: E. D...	J. W. Thompson, Philadelphia	1912
" E. D...	O. B. Dickinson, Philadelphia	1914
" M. D...	Charles. B. Witmer, Sunbury	1911
" W. D...	M. H. S. Thomson, Pittsburgh.	1914
" W. D...	Chas. P. Orr, Pittsburgh....	1909
Porto Rico...	P. J. Hamilton, San Juan....	1913
R. Island....	A. L. Brown, Providence....	1896
S. Carolina...	H. A. M. Smith, Charleston..	1911
S. Dakota....	Jas. D. Elliott, Sioux Falls...	1911
Tenn.: E. & M	Ed. T. Sanford, Knoxville...	1908
" W. D...	John E. McCall, Memphis...	1905
Tex.: E. D...	Gordon Russell, Sherman....	1910
" W. D...	DuVal West, San Antonio ...	1916
" N. D...	Edw. R. Meek, Dallas.......	1899
" S. D...	W. T. Burns, Houston......	1902
Utah.......	Tillman D. Johnson, Ogden..	1915
Vermont.....	Harland B. Howe, St. Johnsbury....................	1915
Va.: E. D....	E. Waddill, Jr., Richmond...	1898
" W. D....	H. C. McDowell, Lynchburg.	1901
Wash.: W. D..	Ed. E. Cushman, Tacoma....	1912
" W. D..	Jeremiah Neterer, Seattle....	1913
" E. D..	F. H. Rudkin, Spokane.....	1911
W. Va.: N. D..	A. G. Dayton, Philippi.....	1905
" S. D...	B. F. Keller, Charleston....	1901
Wis.: E. D....	F. A. Geiger, Milwaukee.....	1912
" W. D...	A. L. Sanborn, Madison.....	1905
Wyoming....	John A. Riner, Cheyenne.....	1890

Circuit Courts of Appeals are final in all cases in which the jurisdiction is dependent entirely upon the opposite parties to the suit being aliens and citizens of the United States or citizens of different states; in all cases arising under the patent laws, the copyright laws, the revenue laws, the criminal laws, and in admiralty cases.

The First Circuit consists of Maine, Massachusetts, New Hampshire, Rhode Island.

Second—Connecticut, New York, Vermont.

Third—Delaware, New Jersey, Pennsylvania.

Fourth—Maryland, North Carolina, South Carolina, Virginia, West Virginia.

Fifth—Alabama, Florida, Georgia, Louisiana, Mississippi, Texas.

Sixth—Kentucky, Michigan, Ohio, Tennessee.

Seventh—Illinois, Indiana, Wisconsin.

Eighth—Arkansas, Colorado, Oklahoma, Iowa, Kansas, Minnesota, Missouri, Nebraska, New Mexico, North Dakota, South Dakota, Utah, Wyoming.

Ninth—Alaska, Arizona, California, Idaho, Montana, Nevada, Oregon, Washington, Hawaii.

District Courts.—District Courts are limited in jurisdiction to one state. Every state is a district and has at least one United States Court, while some have two or more. These are the admiralty and bankruptcy courts. They have jurisdiction in cases where an alien sues, and where the United States or an officer thereof or a foreign consul is a party. The district courts also have jurisdiction of such crimes as are not capital as the United States takes cognizance of. They have concurrent jurisdiction with the circuit courts or with the state courts where an alien sues for a tort in violation of a treaty. The classes of questions of which these courts take cognizance are determined by Congress. Originally each state constituted a district, but later some of the states were divided. There are now ninety-nine of these lowest grades of Federal courts.

The salary of a district judge is $6,000 and appointments are permanent, except for removal under charges. Following are the judges in the various districts with addresses, date of appointment. Districts are designated as North, South, East, West and Middle.

Courts, Consular:

Jurisdiction referred to, 4654.

Of acting consuls and vice-consuls of United States in China, 2951.

Regulations for, 3111, 5388, 6590.

In China, 4675, 7069.

Japan, 4072, 4630.

Korea, 5675, 6939.

Recommended, 5368, 5471.

Reorganization of, recommended, 4923.

Courts, District. (See Courts, Federal.)

Courts, Federal:

Act regarding establishment of circuit courts of appeals and regulating jurisdiction of, vetoed, 5679.

Carelessness in preparing statutes, discussed, 7216.

Change in procedure of, recommended, 7026.

Delays in, 6918.

Extension of jurisdiction of, recommended, 131.

Fee system as applicable to officials of, abolition of, discussed, 6161.

Recommended, 4939, 5879, 5968.

Modifications in system of, recommended, 4640, 4939.

Offenses against court officers should be made cognizable in, 5477, 5633.

Offenses against treaty rights of foreigners in United States should be made cognizable in, 5618.

Power of, over Executive Departments discussed, 1720.

Process of, should be uniform, 75.

Removal of cases from State courts to, restrictions on, recommended, 4939.

Removal of cases involving international obligations from State courts to, 1928, 1956.

Circuit—

Allotment of justices of Supreme Court to, 3324, 3376

Appeals from, recommendations regarding, 4939.

Extension of system of, recommended, 1024, 1121, 1168, 3250.

Resumption of authority of, in States where rebellion had existed recommended, 3556.

Correspondence regarding, transmitted, 3576.

Transfer of original jurisdiction of, to district courts recommended, 4939.

Circuit courts of appeals—
Act regarding, vetoed, 5679.
Discussed, 5968.

Commissioners, jurisdiction to try misdemeanors recommended, 4939, 5879, 5968.

District—
Act providing for trials in, vetoed, 496.

Transfer of original jurisdiction of circuit courts to, recommended, 4939.

Courts-Martial.—Military tribunals in the United States army are classified as courts-martial, courts of inquiry, and military commissions. Courts-martial are of four kinds —general, garrison, regimental and summary. A general court-martial may consist of any number of officers from five to thirteen and a judge-advocate. The President, any general officer, a colonel commanding a separate department, or the Superintendent of the Military Academy may order a court-martial. Garrison and regimental courts-martial are composed of three members and a judge-advocate. The summary court-martial is composed of one officer designated by the commanding officer of the post, camp or fort. This court cannot try officers, cadets or candidates for promotion. Courts-martial derive their existence from Congress and their jurisdiction is limited to maintaining military discipline.

Courts of inquiry may be demanded by an officer or soldier whose conduct is to be investigated. A court of inquiry consists of not to exceed three officers and a recorder. Military Commissions are for the trial of offenders against the laws of war.

Courts-Martial:
In Army discussed, 4933.
Navy referred to, 892.
Regulations for government of, 5602, 6034.

Courts, Military, order in relation to trials by, 3638.

Courts of Appeals, Circuit. (See Courts, Federal.)

Courts, Provisional, in Louisiana, order regarding, 3323.

Courts, State:
Removal of cases from, to Federal courts, restriction on, recommended, 4939.

Removal of cases involving international obligations from, to Federal courts, 1928, 1956.

Covenant.—As used in diplomatic agreements the term refers to the promise of one contracting party to the other.

Covoda (N. Mex.), Battle of.—After Gen. Phil. Kearny had established the authority of the United States securely, as he thought, in New Mexico, he proceeded toward the Pacific, leaving small forces in the garrisons behind. Jan. 15, 1847, Governor Bent, Sheriff Elliott, and twenty others were murdered by insurgent Mexicans at San Fernando de Taos and seven others at Turley's, eight miles distant, in the valley of the Moro. Col. Sterling Price, who was in command at Santa Fé, learning of the uprising, Jan. 23 started for the scene with a force of about 400. He encountered a force of 1,500 at the village of Covoda, which he dispersed after a severe engagement.

Covode Investigation.—A committee of the House of the Thirty-sixth Congress was appointed, with John Covode, of Pennsylvania, as chairman, to investigate charges made by two Anti-Lecompton Democrats, who alleged that President Buchanan had used corrupt influences to induce them to vote for the Lecompton bill. The investigating committee consisted of five members. The three Republicans voted to sustain the charges and the two Democrats to exonerate the president. No action was taken.

Covode Investigation, 3145, 3150.

Cowans Ford (N. C.), Battle of.—Feb. 1, 1781, Cornwallis, who had a second time invaded North Carolina, attempted to prevent the junction of Morgan's division of the American army with the main body under Gen. Greene. The Americans, pursued by the British, crossed the Catawba River at Cowans Ford. Gen. Davidson with 300 militia was left to oppose the crossing of Cornwallis. Davidson was killed and the militia scattered.

Cowpens (S. C.), Battle of.—One of the events following Gen. Greene's taking command of the Southern army in the Revolution, which decided the fate of the war in that quarter. Cornwallis, in command of the British army and in possession of South Carolina, meditated an invasion of North Carolina. Tarleton, with the advance guard of Cornwallis's army, consisting of about 1,100 men, pressed Morgan across the Pacolet, a branch of the Broad River, and back to the Cowpens, an extensive pasture ground on the Broad River about 2 miles south of the boundary line between the Carolinas. Morgan's force consisted of about 900 men. Jan. 17, 1781, Tarleton began the attack. The battle was well fought and displayed remarkable generalship on the part of Morgan. With his 900 men he surrounded and nearly annihilated Tarleton's 1,100, Tarleton and 270 men only escaping. The Americans lost but 12 killed and 61 wounded. Two standards, 100 horses, 35 wagons, 800 muskets, and 2 cannon were captured.

Coyote State.—A nickname for South Dakota, (q. v.). (See also States); sometimes also nicknamed Blizzard State.

Cracker State.—Alternative nickname for Georgia. (See Empire State of the South.)

Cradle of Liberty.—A name applied to Faneuil Hall, Boston, an old building used as a market house and place of public meeting from the early days of the settlement. It has been the scene of some of the most stirring appeals to patriotism by American citizens, particularly during and previous to the Revolutionary War. Upon being refused the use of Faneuil Hall for a meeting in March, 1850, Daniel Webster wrote: "I shall defer my visit to Faneuil Hall, the cradle of American liberty, until its doors shall fly open on golden hinges to lovers of Union as well as liberty." The appellation has since clung to the building.

Craney Island, Va.:

British attack on, repulsed, 524.

Evacuation of batteries on, referred to, 3313.

Crater Lake National Park. (See Parks, National.)

Credentials.—Papers accrediting an officer or other public servant, showing authority for action.

Credit, extension of, necessary to facilitate business, 7880.

Crédit Mobilier.—A joint stock company originally chartered by the Pennsylvania legislature under the name of the Pennsylvania Fiscal Agency, with a capital of $2,-500,000. The charter was purchased by a company having contracts for the construction of the Union Pacific Railroad. The value of the stock, which depended upon the liberality of the contracts made by Congress, rose to an enormous price and paid large dividends earned in the construction of the Union Pacific road. In the presidential election of 1872 the Democrats charged the speaker of the House of Representatives, the secretary of the treasury, the vice-president and the vice-president-elect with accepting Crédit Mobilier stock as an indirect bribe for political influence. An investigation followed, in which it was developed that several members of Congress were holders of this company's stock. One senator was recommended for expulsion, but as his term was about to expire no action was taken. Representatives Oakes Ames, of Massachusetts, and James Brooks, of New York, were censured by the House.

Credit, Public:

Act to strengthen, referred to, 4415.

Bank of United States attempts to impair, 1232.

Discussed. (See Finances discussed.)

Faith of nation must be preserved, 334, 2079.

Indebtedness of States works injury to, 2061.

Progress of, witnessed by rise of American stock abroad, 73, 124.

Progressive state of, 76, 77, 95, 122, 317, 463, 549.

Provision for preservation of, recommended, 3073.

"Strength and security of Government rest upon," 212.

Support of, provision for, recommended, 58, 60, 61, 228, 2060, 2079, 2118, 3073.

System of, should not be left unfinished, 159.

Credit System discussed by President Van Buren, 1541.

Creditors, Government, payment of, in depreciated currency referred to, 1777, 1806, 1807, 1808, 1810.

Creek Indian War.—Tecumseh, the ambitious Shawnee chief, and his brother, the Prophet, in their efforts to work up a conspiracy of all the North American Indians against the United States, joined with the British in the War of 1812. Tecumseh was defeated by Harrison at Tippecanoe and was killed in the battle of the Thames, Oct. 5, 1813, but his schemes agitated and divided the Creek Nation. Weathersford, or Red Eagle, became so troublesome as the leader of the war faction that bodies of militia were sent against him from Tennessee and Georgia. The first serious outbreak of the Creeks was the massacre of the garrison and refugees at Fort Mines, Aug. 30, 1813. As a result, Alabama was almost abandoned by whites. Self-protection and a desire for revenge took possession of the people of Georgia and Tennessee. Gen. Jackson entered the field at the head of the Tennessee militia. Gen. Floyd led the Georgians to avenge the massacre, and Gen. Claibourne was acting at the head of troops from Louisiana and Mississippi. The war received its death blow at the hands of Jackson at Horse Shoe Bend, March 27, 1814. It lasted only 7 months. Taken alone it was of minor importance, but considered in connection with the War of 1812 it had an important bearing. With the subjugation of the Creeks perished all hope of Indian aid in the Southwest for the proposed occupation of the Mississippi Valley.

Creek Indians. (See Indian Tribes.)

Creole Case.—During the passage of the brig *Creole* from Hampton Roads to New Orleans with a cargo of slaves, in November, 1841, some of the negroes rose against the officers of the vessel, killed one of the owners, and ran the vessel into Nassau, New Providence. All were here set at liberty by the English authorities except those charged with murder. Great Britain refused to surrender them on demand of the United States (1944), but the matter was finally settled by a treaty in 1842. During the negotiations for this treaty resolutions embodying the principles of the Anti-Slavery party were offered in Congress by Joshua R. Giddings, of Ohio. He was censured by the House and thereupon resigned. Returning to Ohio he was reelected by a large majority, with instructions to present the resolutions again.

Creole State.—Alternative nickname for Louisiana. (See Pelican State.)

Creole, The, liberation of cargo of slaves on, at Nassau, New Providence, 1944, 1954.

Crescent City, The, not allowed to land passengers and mail at Havana, Cuba, 2770.

Crete:

Resolution of Congress declaring sympathy for suffering people of, referred to, 3891.

Revolution in, referred to, 3660.

Crime, international convention for suppression of, 4115.

Crimes and Misdemeanors:

Abduction of foreigners claiming protection of United States should be made a crime, 2550.

Convictions, executions, and pardons for capital offenses referred to, 991.

Degrees in crime of murder should be recognized, 5755, 5880, 5968.

Limitation upon right in felony cases to review by Supreme Court recommended, 5632, 5880.

Trial of misdemeanors by United States commissioners recommended, 4939, 5879, 5968.

Criminal Code, revision of, recommended, 561, 2550, 2672.

Criminal Law, abuse of administration of, referred to, 4940, 5879, 7003.

Criminals. (See Fugitive Criminals.)

Criminals, Foreign, introduction of, into United States referred to, 2368, 4588.

Cristóbol Colón, The, mentioned, 6317.

Crittenden Compromise.—This was one of the numerous schemes to compromise the slavery question on a peaceful basis. John J. Crittenden was a Senator from Kentucky and tried to harmonize North and South on the slavery question. He hoped to evade the impending war by proposing in 1860 a constitutional amendment which should divide the United States into slaveholding and nonslaveholding portions. He proposed dividing the two sections by the parallel of 36° 30′, the United States to pay the owner for every fugitive slave captured. The proposition, which included other compromise measures, was never submitted to the states.

Crook, U. S. Transport, collision of, 6935.

Crop Estimates, Bureau of. — This bureau of the Department of Agriculture is the successor of the old Bureau of Statistics. The latter had for many years been the chief statistical office of the Federal Government, but gradually its special duties were transferred to other departments or bureaus where they more appropriately belonged, leaving it little more than the agricultural forecasts. Then the name was changed to Bureau of Crop Estimates. As successor of the Bureau of Statistics it collects and digests reports of agricultural production; the area annually sown to each of the leading crops, their condition on the first day of each month, the quantitative results at the close of each crop year, and the estimated farm value December 1. Besides this regular work the bureau collects periodical information on minor crops of importance, meadows and pastures and the principal foreign crops. The stock of corn, wheat and oats on United States farms at certain regular fixed dates is estimated, with the proportion shipped out of the country where grown; the number and value by species of animals on United States farms at the beginning of each year, and the annual losses from diseases and exposure; also the annual clip of wool and average weight of fleeces by States and territories. It also computes the world's production of the chief crops by countries, and the prices of principal agricultural products in various United States markets.

Especially qualified field forecast agents and crop specialists are employed who spend their entire time investigating actual crop conditions within their territories. By cooperation with the Weather Bureau and the Post-Office Department the information gathered is placed promptly in the hands of newspapers, farmers and shipping men.

Crop Values. (See Agricultural Products.)

Cross Keys (Va.), Battle of.—During Stonewall Jackson's movement up the Shenandoah Valley in the summer of 1862 Generals Frémont and Shields were both on the alert to capture him. Frémont reached Strasburg June 1, just after Jackson had passed through. At Port Republic the Shenandoah River divides, and on the larger of the two branches, at a village known as Cross Keys, Frémont brought Ewell's division of Jackson's army to bay June 8. A slight skirmish ensued and Ewell retired during the night. Jackson soon after effected a junction with Gen. Lee, and together they fought the battles around Richmond.

Crow Creek Indians. (See Indian Tribes.)

Crow Creek Reservation. (See Sioux Reservation.)

Crow Indians. (See Indian Tribes.)

Crow Reservation, Mont., opened to settlement by proclamation, 5727.

Crown Point (N. Y.), Capture of.—Immediately after the capture of Ticonderoga, May 12, 1775, Col. Seth Warner, with a small detachment of men, proceeded to Crown Point, on Lake Champlain, about 90 miles north of Albany. The place was strongly fortified and mounted 114 cannon, but was garrisoned by only 12 men. These were captured and the fort manned by Warner's men.

Cruise of the Battleship Fleet.—The most notable achievement of the Navy in time of peace was the voyage of the battleship fleet. This proved an epoch-making cruise, the longest ever undertaken by such a number of battleships, and enlisted the interested attention of the naval world.

Late in the spring of 1907 it was decided to send the Atlantic Fleet on a practice cruise to the Pacific, and in August of that year the final arrangements were determined upon.

The fleet sailed from Hampton Roads Dec. 16, 1907, after a review by the President, and made the passage to various ports for coaling and incidental stops at points in South America; engaged in target practice upon arrival at Magdalena Bay, Mexico, arranged by permission of the Mexican government; and reached San Francisco, May 1, 1908, without a single mishap to mar the voyage.

The fleet consisted of sixteen battleships, six torpedo boats, four auxiliaries. The number of men in the crews aggregated 15,000. The length of the cruise was 13,772 miles, and the duration of the voyage was 135 days.

After visits to Honolulu and Manila the fleet set sail for home, leaving Manila Dec. 1, and arrived at Suez Jan. 1, 1909. The itinerary included passage through Suez Canal, and coaling at Port Said.

The following was the itinerary after passing into the Mediterranean: *Connecticut* and *Vermont*, arrive Villefranche, Jan. 14, leave Jan. 27; *Minnesota* and *Kansas*, arrive Marseilles Jan. 14, leave Jan. 27; *Georgia*, *Nebraska* and *Kentucky*, arrive Genoa Jan. 15, leave Jan. 27; *Rhode Island* and *New Jersey*, arrive Leghorn Jan. 15, leave Jan. 27; *Louisiana* and *Virginia* arrive Malta Jan. 15, leave Jan. 19; *Louisiana* and *Virginia* arrive Algiers Jan. 22, leave Jan. 30; *Ohio* and *Missouri* arrive Athens Jan. 13, leave Jan. 25; *Wisconsin*, *Illinois* and *Kearsarge*, arrive Naples Jan. 17, leave Jan. 27. After leaving the above ports—First Division arrive Negro Bay Jan. 31.

leave Feb. 3 ; First Division, arrive Gibraltar Feb. 3, leave Feb. 6 ; Second, Third and Fourth Divisions, arrive Negro Bay Feb. 1, leave Feb. 1 ; fleet reassemble off Gibraltar and proceed to United States, arrive Feb. 22, 1909, at Hampton Roads, Virginia.

When the purpose of giving this assemblage of battleships the privileges and advantages of a practice cruise, under such severe conditions, was announced, criticism from high technical quarters was heard. It was suggested that the undertaking was too monumental ; that a battleship is too vast and complicated a piece of mechanism to send around the globe on an ordinary occasion ; that dangers more than multiplied with numbers in such a case ; that disaster lurked on every submerged ledge and was borne on every unknown tidal current ; that the skeletons of some of the ships would doubtless be left in the Straits of Magellan ; that, if the fleet should succeed in rounding South America, it was reasonably certain that the individual ships would, one by one, arrive with machineries loose and almost unserviceable, with crews reflecting the demoralized condition of the matériel, and that a woeful spectacle of failure would thus be presented.

As to the matériel, the cold facts are that the ships practically took care of their own repairs on the cruise. The repair lists turned in at the United States naval station at Cavite, P. I., were significant, since they substantially showed what was needed after the voyage to the eastern borders of the Pacific by way of Australia and Japan, and they were negligible. The performance of the *Oregon* in 1898 was substantially repeated.

With respect to its effect upon the discipline of the men, this was highly beneficial. Too much cannot be said of the magnificent conduct of the enlisted personnel throughout the history of the voyage and in the presence of an unprecedented succession of entertainments and shore hospitalities. The occasion brought to the front that element of greatest strength in our navy—the personal characteristics of the enlisted force. The tact, ability and mastership of their profession shown by the officers, from the lowest to the highest, is likewise worthy of earnest commendation.

The result was to give us an opportunity to get better acquainted with the republics to the south of us ; with our own island possessions ; with the new and vigorous branch of the British Empire in Australia ; and, particularly, with Japan ; and it has afforded the people living in those countries a better opportunity to get acquainted with us. It has been everywhere, in the South American countries and most notably in Australia and Japan, understood and accepted, as it was intended, as the reaching out of a strong hand in friendly greeting on the part of America ; and the cordial and enthusiastic hospitality extended to our fleet will no doubt be long remembered and has, unquestionably, exerted a powerful reflex influence on feeling in this country. Between the United States and every country visited there is a feeling of deeper interest and friendship than existed before the fleet sailed. Our own Pacific coast and island possessions have been placed in sight and touch with the strength of the nation.

Whatever may be said in technical criticism of the navy, the American people, to whom the ships belong and who paid for them, know, as the result of this extended cruise, at least, that the vessels will float ; that their officers and men can handle them ; and, so far as actual tests in time of peace can show, that the ships and the men are fit in every particular for any duty.

See illustration opposite 7060.

Cuartel Lot, survey and disposal of land known as, discussed, 5504.

Cuba.—Cuba is the largest island of the "West Indies," and extends in the shape of an irregular crescent at the entrance of the Gulf of Mexico, which the western horn divides into the Florida Channel on the north and the Yucatan Channel on the south. The western extremity (Cape San Antonio) is in 84° 57′ W. longitude, and the easternmost point (Cape Maisi) in 74° 7′ W. longitude. The most northerly point, close to Havana, is 93 miles distant from Key West on the Florida coast in 23° 13′ N. latitude, while Cape Santa Cruz, the inner extremity of the eastern horn and the most southerly point of the island, extends to 19° 48′ N. latitude, and is about 80 miles north of the Jamaican coast. Cape Maisi, at the outer extremity of the eastern horn, is 50 miles distant from the west coast of Haiti, and about 55 miles southwest of the nearest island of the Bahama group. The total length of the island is about 750 miles, its average width being about 50 miles, with a maximum of 160 and a minimum of 23 miles. There are many dependent islands, of which the Isle of Pines in the Archipelago de los Canarreos (inside the western horn of the main island) is by far the largest, with an estimated area of nearly 1,200 square miles.

Physical Features and Climate.—The island is distinctly mountainous, with a cross range in the southeast and central groups from end to end of the island. Some of the finest harbors in the world are situated both north and south of the island. The rivers of Cuba are generally short and tempestuous. The only river of any length is the Cauto, about 250 miles from its source in the Sierra Maestra to its outflow into the Caribbean Sea. The Sagua la Grande is also navigable for about 20 miles.

Cuba lies entirely within the tropical zone, and possesses a dry season from November to April and a wet season for the remaining half year. The climate is equable with a high mean temperature, the range being between the winter and summer means of 70°-80° F. In the months of October and November the island is liable to severe and destructive hurricanes. Yellow fever has ceased to be a scourge since the preventive action of the United States army of occupation after the Spanish-American War. Smallpox has been similarly stamped out by sanitary education, but consumption is still prevalent. The hygienic conditions of the whole island have been almost miraculously improved since the intervention of the United States.

History.—The island of Cuba was visited by Christopher Columbus, during his first voyage, on Oct. 27, 1492, and was then believed to be part of the western mainland of India. Early in the sixteenth century the island was conquered by the Spaniards, to be used later as a base of operations for the conquest of Mexico and Central America, and for almost four centuries Cuba remained under a Spanish Captain-General. The slave trade was abolished early in the nineteenth century and the slaves were emancipated from 1880-1886. The government of Spain was marked by a generally corrupt administration, complicated by internal unrest fomented by external influences, and the various attempts at independence met with severe military repression. The separatist and autonomous agitation culminated in the closing years of the nineteenth century in a fierce and bloodthirsty war, and although a conciliatory movement was evinced by the Madrid authorities in 1897, the struggle was continued by the party of separation in the island. (See opposite 5565 and 5613.) In 1898 the government of the United States put into execution of threat of interference by the dispatch of the battleship *Maine* to Havana harbor, and in February of that year the vessel was sunk by an explosion the cause of which appears likely to remain an unsolved mystery. On April 20, 1898, the United States Government demanded the evacuation of Cuba by the Spanish forces, and a short Spanish-American war led to the abandonment of the island, which was occupied by United States troops. From Jan. 1, 1899, to May 20, 1902, Cuba was under United States military rule, and reforms of the widest and most far-reaching character were instituted. On May 20, 1902, an autonomous government was inaugurated with an elected President, and a legislature of two houses. The island was, however, again the prey of revolution from July to September, 1906, when the United States Government resumed control. On Jan. 28, 1909, a republican government was again inaugurated.

AREA AND POPULATION

Provinces and Capitals	Area in English Sq. Miles	Population 1910
Camaguey (Puerto Principe)	10,068	128,669
Havana (Havana)	3,173	555,178
Matanzas (Matanzas)	3,244	255,308
Oriente (Santiago)	14,218	461,394
Pinar del Rio (Pinar del Rio)	5,211	252,421
Santa Clara (Santa Clara)	8,264	497,142
Total	44,178	2,150,112

Nearly 60 per cent. of the inhabitants are of Spanish descent, the colored races numbering about 30 per cent. (including mixed blood), foreign-born wh es 10 per cent. and Chinese barely 0.5 per cent. Slavery was abolished in 1886, and the colored races are increasing equally with the whites. There is little racial antagonism.

Government.—The government is that of a centralized republic, with a President, Vice-President, and nominated Cabinet, and a legislature of two houses. The President is elected by indirect vote for four years, and is ineligible for more than two consecutive terms. President of the Republic of Cuba (May 20, 1913-May 19, 1917), Mario G. Menocal.

Congress consists of a Senate and a House of Representatives. The Senate contains twenty-four members (four from each province) elected by indirect vote for eight years and retiring by halves every four years. The House of Representatives consists of eighty-three members (one for each 25,000 inhabitants) elected for four years by direct vote of all male citizens aged twenty-one years and half renewed every two years. Five years' residence qualified for naturalization and the franchise.

The six provinces contain ε i elective governor and assembly, with wide powers of self-government, but financial autonomy is restricted by the economic clauses of the treaty with the United States, which aim at development within the financial resources of the island. The smaller administrative unit is the municipality with elective councils and mayors (alcaldes), their jurisdiction frequently extending over a wide rural territory.

Justice is administered by courts of first instance in the municipal areas, and their contiguous rural territories, with superior courts in each province and a supreme court at Havana.

The external relations of Cuba are regulated by the protection of the United States in the case of any attempt to interfere with the independence of the island. The armed forces are therefore directed to the preservation of internal order. There is a mounted gendarmerie of 5,000 men known as the guardia rural.

Education.—A great impetus was given to education by the United States occupation of 1899-1902 and elementary schools were established in every municipality. Primary education is compulsory and free and about 82 per cent. of attendance is secured.

Finance.—The revenue and expenditure of Cuba for the six years 1907-1908—1911-1912 are stated as follows:

Year	Revenue	Expenditure
1907-08	$24,447,657	$22,377,168
1908-09	29,615,263	24,285,292
1909-10	33,824,746	31,070,409
1910-11	} 41,614,700	40,593,400
1911-12		
1912-13		

More than half the revenue is derived from customs. The principal items of expenditure, in addition to the cost of civil government, are debt service ($6,400,000), education ($4,320,000), public works ($3,600,000), and sanitation ($4,140,000).

Debt.—By treaty with the United States Cuba has undertaken "not to borrow more than she can pay," and the total debt, including the obligations of the revolutionary junta, amounts to less than two years' income. The debt was of the following descriptions on Aug. 1, 1911:

External Debt:
6% bonds 1896	$732,000
5% loan 1904	33,980,000
	$34,712,000

Internal Debt:
5% bonds	10,871,000
4½% loan	16,500,000
	$27,371,000

Total Debt	$62,083,000

Production and Industry.—Of the total area (about 28,000,000 acres) less than 1,000,000 acres are cultivated, but much of the remaining surface is dense forest, marsh or pastoral savannah. More than half the cultivated area is under sugar cane and about 30 per cent. under tobacco, sweet potatoes and bananas in equal proportions. Rice, coffee, cocoa and Indian corn are grown and many tropical fruits (oranges, coco-nuts, pineapples, etc.) are cultivated. The sugar crop is increasing and amounted in 1911 to nearly 2,000,000 tons. Agricultural conditions are still very primitive. Forestry is much neglected, although mahogany is exported and cedar used in the boxing of tobacco.

Iron, copper and manganese are plentiful and are easily worked. The principal mining districts are in Oriente province, where the Sierra Maestra was for centuries the largest copper-producing center in the world. Of non-metallic minerals petroleum and asphalt are found, and the former is exploited to some extent. Almost the whole mineral output is sent to the United States.

The only manufactures of any importance are connected with the tobacco and sugar-cane industries, cigars and cigarettes being made in great quantities in the capital, and sugar, rum and whisky in the neighborhood of the plantations.

Trade.—The imports and exports of merchandise for the five years 1908-1912 are stated as follows in dollars:

Year	Imports	Exports	Total
1908	$86,368,767	$98,849,091	$185,217,858
1909	83,856,835	115,637,321	199,494,156
1910	98,239,539	144,036,697	242,266,236
1911	102,692,888	128,114,937	230,807,825
1912	125,902,241	172,978,328	298,880,569

The principal exports are sugar, 80 per cent., and tobacco; the imports are mainly machinery, foodstuffs and textiles. The exchange was with the principal countries as under, in 1912:

Country	Imports from	Exports to
United States	$65,426,475	$145,185,933
United Kingdom	15,397,649	11,446,336
France	7,706,064	2,574,735
Germany	8,431,201	6,199,172
Spain	9,774,790	658,323

Railways.—In 1910 there were 2,516 miles of government and private line open for traffic. A line runs from Pinar del Rio to Santiago, thus traversing the island from west to east, and there are many lines from both coasts connecting with this principal system, particularly in the tobacco districts of the west and the mining region of the east.

Shipping.—In 1911 the mercantile marine consisted of fifty-four steamers (58,410 tons) and six sailing vessels (1,035 tons). The principal harbors are Havana, Matanzas, Cardenas, Bahia Honda, Neuvitas and Nipe on the north coast, and on the south Santiago, Cienfuegos and Guantanamo.

Cities.—Capital, Havana, on the northern coast almost due south of Key West, Fla., from which it is distant ninety-three miles, is the largest city and principal commercial center of the West Indies. Its Spanish name is San Cristobal de la Habaña. The city contained in 1907 a census population of 297,159, and the municipio of Havana a population of 302,526. Havana contains many fine buildings, including a seventeenth century cathedral and many churches. Its principal buildings are of limestone, which is plentiful in the neighborhood. The harbor is one of the finest in the world.

Other cities are:

Santiago	45,500	Guantanamo	14,600
Matanzas	36,000	Manzanillo	14,500
Cienfuegos	30,000	Guanabacoa	14,000
Puerto Principe		Santa Clara	14,000
(or Camaguey)	30,000	Sagua la Grande	13,000
Candeñas	25,000	Sancti Spiritus	12,750
		Trinidad	11,000

The Metric System of Weights and Measures is in general use. There is no Cuban currency, but the coinage of Spain (twenty-five peseta gold pieces, "centenes," five peseta silver pieces and silver pesetas), American dollars and French louis d'or are current. Public accounts are kept in dollars, of United States money.

Trade with the United States.—The value of merchandise imported into Cuba from the United States for the year 1913 was $70,581,154, and goods to the value of $126,088,173 were sent thither—a balance of $55,507,019 in favor of Cuba.

Cuba:

Acquisition of, by U. S.—Opposed by President Fillmore, 2701.

Proposition regarding, referred to, 3066.

Recommended by President Buchanan, 3041, 3066, 3092, 3173.

Affairs of—

Communications regarding, transmitted, 6098.

Discussed, 2649, 2700, 6660, 6741, 6743, 6780, 6871, 7056, 7234.

Mediation or intervention by United States in, referred to, 6101.

African slave trade in, discussed, 2777, 3041, 3124, 3126.

Agitations in, and abuse of American neutrality laws, 4826.

Aid furnished inhabitants of, by American citizens and Red Cross, 6284, 6308, 6320.

American citizens in—

Assaulted and murdered, 4002, 4004, 4022, 4023, 4196, 6182.

Condemned to death, 4690.

Death of, 6178, 6184.

Destitute, appropriation for, 6248, 6263.

Estates of deceased, referred to, 2893, 2894.

Property of, confiscated, 4019, 4022, 4023.

Treatment of, discussed, 6256.

Appropriation for starving inhabitants of, recommended, 6292.

Army, U. S., in 6693, 6694.

Autonomous government for, discussed, 6152, 6261, 6284, 6308, 6658.

Blockade of ports of, proclaimed, 6472, 6481.

Discussed, 6290, 6312.

Removal of, referred to, 6321.

Census ordered, 6594.

Chinese laborers introduced into, referred to, 4116.

Civil and political conditions in, referred to, 3998, 3999.

Commercial convention with, in 1902, 6741, 6743, 6780.

Commercial relations with, 1260, 1347, 2945, 4826, 4921, 5089, 5470, 5547, 6069, 6292.

Report on, 6292.

Treaty regarding, 4842, 4847, 4848.

Competitor, capture of alleged American citizens on the, 6180, 6183, 6262.

Conditions in, report on, transmitted, 6292.

Constitutional convention assembled, 6448.

Consul of United States in, imprisonment of, 329.

Consular officers of United States in, rights of, discussed, 6069.

Copyright reciprocity with, 6871.

Correspondence regarding, 4631, 4942.

Creation of offices in, 6589, 6591, 6607.

Diplomatic intercourse with Captain-General of, not allowed, 2742.

Renewal of, to be requested, 2742.

Evacuation of Havana, order regarding, 6583.

Exiles from, arrival of, in United States, 456.

Expeditions against—
Discussed, 2549, 2585, 2643, 2649, 2779.
Proclamations against, 2545, 2647, 2805.
Referred to, 2741.

Government for, discussed, 6322, 6377.

Grants of public or corporate rights in, order regarding, 6583.

Graves of American soldiers in, to be marked, order regarding, 6578.

Hurricane in, in 1844, referred to, 2869.

Importations into, modifications of laws regarding, 2869.

Indemnity for, discussed, 2869.

Imprisonment of—
American citizens in, 329, 2538, 2676, 2677, 2765, 3115, 4023, 5516, 6068, 6100, 6181, 6182, 6184.
Released, 6284.
Persons claiming to be American citizens, 6180, 6183.

Independence of, recognition of, by United States opposed and precedents cited, 6286.

Insurrection in (see also Spanish-American War).
Armistice proposed by United States discussed, 6285.
Autonomous government for, discussed, 6152, 6261, 6284, 6308.
Claims of United States against Spain growing out of, 4051, 4099, 4448, 5871, 6180.
Concentration policy of Gen. Weyler discussed, 6256, 6283, 6284, 6308.
Revoked, 6285.
Forcible intervention in, by United States discussed, 6261.
Recommended, 6289.
Friendly offices of United States tendered, refusal of, referred to, 6255, 6282.

Illustrations of, opposite 5565, 5613.

Neutrality proclamations of President Cleveland, 6023, 6126.

Policy of United States regarding, discussed, by President—
Cleveland, 6068, 6148.
Referred to by President McKinley, 6291.
Grant, 3985, 4018, 4051, 4101, 4143, 4245, 4290.
Referred to by President McKinley, 6259, 6284, 6291.
Hayes, 4438, 4448.
McKinley, 6248, 6280, 6307.

Provisional government proclaimed, 7056.

Questions with Spain growing out of, 4115, 4195, 4196, 4245, 4520.

Recognition of—
Belligerency by United States deemed unwise by President—
Cleveland, 6071, 6151.
Grant, 3985, 4018, 4292.
McKinley, 6258.
Independence by United States opposed and precedents cited, 6286.
Referred to, 4004, 4024.

Resignation of President of, 7436.

Spain directs Gen. Blanco to suspend hostilities, 6292.

Surrender of insurgents referred to, 4437.

Termination of, announced, 4448.

Joint resolution of Congress declaring freedom of, authorizing intervention, etc., 6297.
Discussed, 6311.
Regarded by Spain as "equivalent to an evident declaration of war," 6312.

Lopez expedition, pardon and release of members of, by Spain, 2678.

Mail and passengers not allowed by Captain-General to land in, 2701, 2770.

Maine, destruction of the, in harbor of Havana, 6277, 6290, 6308.
Findings of court of inquiry discussed, 6277, 6290.
Number of lives lost by, report on, 6294.
Proposition of Spain to investigate causes of, referred to, 6290.

Maritime jurisdiction of Spain in waters surrounding, 3380.

Military commission to superintend Spanish evacuation of, 6322.

Military occupation of, by United States, instructions regarding, 6575.

Piracies in, repressed, 782.

Policy of United States regarding, referred to, 2693.

Ports of entry constituted in, 6580.

Possession of, agreement to disclaim intention to obtain, declined by United States, 2701.

Postal communication of United States with Santiago, order regarding, 6577.

Privateering in ports of, referred to, 2345.

Proclamation of Captain-General of, authorizing search of vessels, referred to, 3986.

Reciprocity with United States, 6682, 6690, 6717, 6741.

Relations with, 4758, 6658, 6663, 6682, 6690, 6717, 6741.

Revolutionary movements in, 2585.

Right of search, questions with, regarding, 3986.
Sanitary problems connected with, referred to, 6341.
Shipping agreement with United States, 6690.
Slavery in, discussed, 4100, 4143, 4194, 4196.
Release of persons held in, 4194.
Tariff laws of, evidence of modifications of, proclaimed, 5583.
Referred to, 5615, 5747.
Treaty between Spain, France, and Great Britain respecting, referred to, 2676.
Tripartite convention on subject of, discussed, 2701, 2719.
Vessels of Spain from, discriminating duties on, suspended by proclamation, 4810, 5075, 5155.
Discussed, 5089.
Revoked, 5074.
Vessels of United States—
Discriminating duties and fines on, in, 1242, 4626, 4714, 4763, 4786, 4788, 5961, 6069, 6378.
Abolished, 4810, 5155.
Retaliatory measure discussed, 4763.
Fired upon by Spanish vessel, 6068.
Not allowed to enter ports of, 2770.
Seized by Spanish authorities in, 2767, 2778, 2869, 4023.
Warned against insurrectionary habit, 7437.

Cuba, Treaties with.—By a commercial convention concluded with Cuba Dec. 11, 1902, all Cuban merchandise imported into the United States shall be admitted at a reduction of 20 per cent in the rate of duty on said articles and reciprocally all produce of the soil or industry of the United States shall be admitted into the Republic of Cuba at a reduction of 20 per cent of the rate of duty prescribed for such products by the Republic of Cuba. It is further provided that certain articles of merchandise of the United States shall be admitted to Cuba at further reductions as follows:

To be admitted at a reduction of 25 per cent: Machinery and apparatus of copper or its alloys or machines and apparatus in which copper or its alloys enter as the component of chief value; cast iron, wrought iron and steel, and manufactures thereof; of crystal and glass, except window glass; ships and water borne vessels of all kinds, of iron or steel; whiskies and brandies, fish, salted, pickled, smoked or marinated; fish or shellfish, preserved in oil or otherwise in tins; certain articles of pottery or earthenware.

To be admitted at a reduction of 30 per cent: Butter; flour of wheat; corn; flour of corn or corn meal; chemical and pharmaceutical products and simple drugs; malt liquors in bottles; non-alcoholic beverages; cider; mineral waters, colors and dyes; window glass; complete or partly made up articles of hemp, flax, pita, jute, henequen, ramie, and other specified vegetable fibers; musical instruments; writing and printing paper, except for newspapers; cotton and manufactures thereof, except knitted goods; all articles of cutlery; boots, shoes and slippers; gold and silver plated ware; drawings, photographs, engravings, lithographs, cromolithographs, oleographs, etc., printed from stone, zinc, aluminium, or other material, used as labels, flaps, bands and wrappers for tobacco or other purposes, and all the other papers (except paper for cigarettes, and excepting maps and charts), pasteboard and manufactures thereof, common or ordinary soaps, vegetables, pickled or preserved in any manner; and nearly all wines.

To be admitted at a reduction of 40 per cent: Manufactures of cotton, knitted, and all manufactures of cotton not included in the preceding schedules; cheese; fruits, preserved; paper pulp; perfumery and essences; certain articles of pottery and earthenware; porcelain; soaps, other than common; umbrellas and parasols; dextrine and glucose; watches; wool and manufactures thereof; silk and manufactures thereof; rice; cattle.

It is agreed that the tobacco, in any form, of the United States or of any of its insular possessions, shall not enjoy the benefit of any concession or rebate of duty when imported into the Republic of Cuba.

Coaling and Naval Stations.—By an agreement entered into in 1903 the United States leases from the island of Cuba for $2,000 per annum land and water for coaling and naval stations at Guantanamo and Bahia Honda.

Political Relations.—In fulfillment of the declaration contained in the joint resolution of April 20, 1898, "for the recognition of the independence of the people of Cuba, demanding that the Government of Spain relinquish its authority and government in the island of Cuba, and to withdraw its land and naval forces from Cuba and Cuban waters, and directing the President of the United States to use the land and naval forces of the United States to carry these resolutions into effect," the President is hereby authorized to "leave the government and control of the island of Cuba to its people" so soon as a government shall have been established in said island under a constitution which, either as a part thereof or in an ordinance appended thereto, shall define the future relations of the United States with Cuba, the several conditions were enacted into a permanent treaty substantially as follows:

That the government of Cuba shall never enter into any treaty or other compact with any foreign power or powers which will impair or tend to impair the independence of Cuba, nor in any manner authorize or permit any foreign power or powers to obtain by colonization or for military or naval purposes or otherwise, lodgment in or control over any portion of said island.

That said government shall not assume or contract any public debt, to pay the interest upon which, and to make reasonable sinking fund provision for the ultimate discharge of which, the ordinary revenues of the island, after defraying the current expenses of government shall be inadequate.

That the government of Cuba consents that the United States may exercise the right to intervene for the preservation of Cuban independence, the maintenance of a government adequate for the protection of life, property, and individual liberty, and for discharging the obligations with respect to Cuba imposed by the treaty of Paris on the United States, now to be assumed and undertaken by the government of Cuba.

That all Acts of the United States in Cuba during its military occupancy thereof are ratified and validated, and all lawful rights acquired thereunder shall be maintained and protected.

That the government of Cuba will execute, and as far as necessary extend, the plans already devised or other plans to be mutually agreed upon, for the sanitation of the cities of the island, to the end that a recurrence of epidemic and infectious diseases may be prevented, thereby assuring protection to the people and commerce of Cuba, as well as to the commerce of the southern ports of the United States and the people residing therein.

That the Isle of Pines shall be omitted from the proposed constitutional boundaries of Cuba, the title thereto being left to future adjustment by treaty.

That to enable the United States to maintain the independence of Cuba, and to protect the people thereof, as well as for its own defense, the government of Cuba will sell or lease to the United States lands necessary for coaling or naval stations at certain specified points to be agreed upon with the President of the United States.

That by way of further assurance the government of Cuba will embody the foregoing provisions in a permanent treaty with the United States. This treaty was concluded May 22, 1903, and proclaimed by the President July 2, 1904.

Cuba also became a party to the convention between the United States and the several republics of South and Central America for the arbitration of pecuniary claims and the protection of inventions, etc., which was signed in Buenos Aires in 1910 and proclaimed in Washington July 29, 1914. (See South and Central America, Treaties with.)

Cuban Claims discussed, 3040, 3091, 3172. (See also Spain, claims against.)

Cuban Insurrection. (See Cuba, insurrection in.)

Culebra Island, reservation of lands on, 6703.

Cumberland, The, engagement with the *Merrimac* referred to, 3345.

Cumberland Road.—A national highway authorized by Congress and constructed at the expense of the General Government. Appropriations for the purpose of building and maintaining this road were opposed by various presidents and members of Congress on the ground that Federal aid to local internal improvements was unconstitutional. March 29, 1806, the president was authorized to appoint three commissioners to lay out a road from Cumberland, on the Potomac, to the Ohio River, and $30,000 was appropriated for that purpose (406). The road was extended from time to time, reaching Illinois in 1838, when it was superseded by railways. The total amount appropriated was $6,821,246. President Monroe vetoed a bill for the repair of the road May 4, 1822 (711). This highway was also called the National road. (See also Internal Improvements.)

Cumberland Road:

Act for repair of, vetoed, 711.

Amendment providing for internal repairs recommended, 759.

Appropriations for, referred to, 785, 955.

Commissioners for—
Appointed, 406.
Duties of, 683.
Report of, 428, 445.

Constitutional amendment providing for internal improvements recommended. (See Internal Improvements.)

Expenditures for, referred to, 933.

Provision for repair of, recommended, 962.

Referred to, 786, 1406.

Route of, approved, 428.

Superintendent of, 816.

Report of, 1491.

Survey of, referred to, 1036.

Currency Laws.—Strictly speaking, any medium of exchange that is current, or everywhere received as money, is currency, whether it be coin or paper. The term has, however, come to be applied in the United States exclusively to paper money. The paper money of this country is of four kinds: first, legal tender notes; second, national bank notes; third, gold certificates; fourth, silver certificates.

Legal Tender Notes.—The legal tender notes of the United States are bills issued merely on the credit of the government and originally constituted a sort of a forced loan based on the promise to pay the face value upon demand, but the legal tender quality given them by Congress made payment in similar notes possible and legal. (See Fiat Money.) The acts of 1875 and 1882, however, direct the Treasurer of the United States to hold $100,000,000 as a reserve for their redemption. There were outstanding on September 1, 1865, $432,553,000 of legal tender notes. This was reduced to $346,681,016 by January 1, 1879, at which amount it has since legally remained. There are now actually outstanding $337,923.706. These notes are issued in denominations of one, two, five, ten, twenty, fifty, one hundred, five hundred, one thousand, five thousand and ten thousand dollars. Previous to 1879 (when specie payments were resumed) bills for fractions of a dollar, fractional currency as it was called, were issued. The legal tender notes were issued by the government during the war as a means of raising revenue, and the issue was generally regarded merely as a war measure, but the Supreme Court has declared their issue constitutional and legal, though issued in time of peace.

National Bank Notes.—The national bank notes are issued by the national banks and guaranteed by the government, the banks depositing United States bonds as security. (See Banks, National.) There is now outstanding $716,261,921 of this sort of currency.

Coin Certificates.—Gold and silver certificates are issued by the government against deposits of gold and silver coin, and are exchangeable for the coin on demand. The treasury holds the coin so deposited as a trust fund. The certificates represent the coin and are used in preference to it merely because of greater convenience in handling. There is now in circulation an aggregate of $1,008.532,749 in gold certificates and $470,189,192 in silver certificates.

"Lawful money" includes gold coin, silver dollars, United States notes and Treasury notes. United States notes are by regulation receivable for customs so long as they continue redeemable in coin. There are still in use small amounts of $1 and $2 national bank notes; also $500 and $1,000 silver certificates. Treasury notes were issued for purchases of silver bullion, which was coined into dollars wherewith the notes are being redeemed as rapidly as practicable. The issue of national bank notes is practically dependent upon the market price of United States bonds. When the premium is high it is not profitable to issue notes.

Denominations of notes and coins and their legal tender quality are shown below:

question of the panic of 1873 in the very first paragraph of his fifth annual message and discusses its relations to the currency supply on pages 4198, 4199 and 4200. By the time the next session of Congress met Grant was able to present specific remedial legislation which he does at the outset of his sixth annual address. (Pages

	Gold Certificates	Silver Certificates	United States Notes	Treasury Notes of 1890	National Bank Notes
Limit of issue...	Unlimited for gold coin unless gold reserve falls below $100,000,000.	Amount of silver dollars coined, $562,173,530.	$346,681,016.	No further issues; volume steadily diminishing by redemption in silver dollars.	Not to exceed capital of banks.
Denominations..	$10,000, $5,000, $1,000, $500, $100, $50, $20, $10.	$100, $50, $20, $10, $5, $2, $1.	$1,000, $500, $100, $50, $20, $10, $5, $2, $1.	$1,000, $500, $100, $50, $20, $10, $5, $2, $1.	$1,000, $500, $100 $50, $20, $10, $5.
Legal tender....	Not a tender.	Not a tender.	For all debts, public and private, except customs and interest on public debt.	Unlimited, unless otherwise contracted.	Not a tender.
Receivable......	For all public dues.	For all public dues.	For all public dues.	For all public dues.	For all public dues except customs.
Exchangeable...	For subsidiary and minor coin.	For silver and minor coin.	For subsidiary and minor coin.	For silver and minor coin.	For subsidiary silver and minor coin.
Redeemable....	In gold coin at the Treasury.	In silver dollars at the Treasury.	In gold at the Treasury.	In gold at the Treasury.	In "lawful money" at the Treasury, or at bank of issue.

Coin.—The amount of gold coin in circulation in 1913 was $608,979,598; and of silver, $226,782,060.

From the above figures it will be seen that the total amount of money in circulation is about $3,370,000,000 or less than $35 per capita. It becomes necessary, therefore, for many persons and business organizations to do considerable business on credit.

Financial Panics.—When payments fall due and loans are called, demands are made on the principal money centres for currency with which to cancel obligations, interest rates are advanced by those holding currency and a panic ensues among those compelled to borrow money at high rates of interest (if able to borrow at all) or lose securities pledged for loans. Securities are offered for sale at far below their value to secure needed currency, and business halts for want of sufficient circulating medium. These panics have been of frequent occurrence in the United States, and have usually been terminated by the removal of the most apparent underlying cause, but not until many honest business persons have been financially ruined. (See Panics.)

Government Relief.—Congress should devise some means for preventing panics has long been the opinion of many able statesmen and bankers. President Monroe discussed the panic of 1816-1819 learnedly in his third annual message (page 630).

The money stringency of 1837 forms the subject of a special message by President Van Buren, in which the causes and the whole history of that memorable panic are discussed. (Pages 1541 to 1563.) President Tyler's discussion to the relation of the circulating medium to the national treasury are set forth in his second annual address, pages 2027 to 2060. In 1857 the widespread poverty of the circulating medium was rehearsed by President Buchanan, and its causes were plainly laid before Congress with suggestions for relief. (Pages 2967 to 2972.) These were confined mainly to appeals to the patriotism and honesty of the business world, particularly the bankers. In his second annual message he renews the appeals and recommends an effective federal bankruptcy act. (Pages 3051, 3052.) President Grant takes up the

4238, 4239, 4240 and 4241.) President Hayes announced his belief that the national currency should rest solely upon a coin basis. (Page 4397.)

The business depression of 1893, following the Silver Purchase Act, caused President Cleveland to call an extra session of Congress to repeal the act and take such measures as would restore confidence in established values. (Pages 5833 to 5837.) President Roosevelt calls attention to inflated credits and high rates of interest in his sixth annual message, pages 7429, 7430.

President Taft recommended to Congress and the country a careful study of the currency question and the report of the Monetary Commission (page 7893), and the subject of a National Reserve Association formed by banks and representatives of the government in Part II of his annual message of 1912.

Emergency Currency.—In 1908 Congress passed the Aldrich-Vreeland Currency Law to render the currency of the country more elastic by providing for the issue by the Treasury of emergency money to the national banks to the extent of 50 per cent. of their capital, secured by state, county, municipal or other approved bonds or securities, whenever the necessities of the country demanded an increase in money. This to be retired by a tax whenever its apparent need had passed. (See Aldrich-Vreeland Currency Law.)

Federal Reserve Banks.—When the Democratic Administration came into full power with President Wilson in 1913, he made an urgent appeal to Congress to enact adequate currency laws (page 8259), and the result was the Glass-Owen Federal Reserve Banking Law, which is here briefly summarized. At the breaking out of the European war in 1914, the organization of the system had not been perfected, and the drop in prices of securities consequent upon European liquidation of their American holdings necessitated its postponement and the continued use of the emergency currency under the Aldrich-Vreeland law in 1914.

The chief provisions of the Glass-Owen law are as follows:

The Secretary of the Treasury, the Secretary of Agriculture and the Controller of the Currency, acting as the Reserve Bank Organization Committee, shall designate not less than eight nor more than twelve cities to be known as federal reserve cities, and shall divide the continental United States, excluding Alaska, into districts, each district to contain only one such federal reserve city.

Every National banking association within such districts shall be required, within thirty days after notice from the Organization Committee, to subscribe to the capital stock of such federal reserve bank in a sum equal to six per cent. of the paid up capital stock and surplus of such bank.

No individual, copartnership or corporation other than a member bank of its district shall be permitted to hold at any time more than $25,000 par value of stock in any federal reserve bank. No federal reserve bank shall commence business with a subscribed capital less than $4,000,000.

Each federal reserve bank shall establish branch banks within the federal reserve district in which it is located. Such branches shall be operated by a board of seven directors, four of whom shall be selected by the reserve bank and three by the Federal Reserve Board.

Upon deposit with the Treasurer of the United States of any bonds of the United States in the manner provided by existing law relating to national banks, each bank shall receive from the Controller of the Currency circulating notes, registered and countersigned as provided by law, equal in amount to the par value of the bonds so deposited, such notes to be issued under the same conditions and provisions of law which relate to the issue of circulating notes of national banks secured by bonds of the United States bearing the circulating privilege, except that the issue of such notes shall not be limited to the capital stock of such federal reserve bank.

The capital stock of each federal reserve bank shall be divided into shares of $100 each.

If any member bank shall be declared insolvent and a receiver appointed therefor, the stock held by it in said federal reserve bank shall be cancelled, without impairment of its liability, and all cash paid subscriptions on said stock, with one-half of one per cent. per month from the period of last dividend, not to exceed the book value thereof, shall be first applied to all debts of the insolvent member bank to the federal reserve bank, and the balance, if any, shall be paid to the receiver of the insolvent bank.

After all necessary expenses of a federal reserve bank have been paid or provided for, the stockholders shall be entitled to receive an annual dividend of six per cent. on the paid in capital stock, which dividend shall be cumulative.

A Federal Reserve Board is created which shall consist of seven members, including the Secretary of the Treasury and the Controller of the Currency, who shall be members ex-officio, and five members appointed by the President, who shall devote their entire time to the work of the Board, and shall receive a salary of $12,000 per year.

The Federal Reserve Board is authorized to examine the accounts, books and affairs of each federal reserve bank and to require such statements and reports as it may deem necessary.

There is created a Federal Advisory Council, which shall consist of as many members as there are federal reserve districts.

The Federal Advisory Council shall have power to confer directly with the Federal Reserve Board on general business conditions and the general affairs of the reserve banking system.

Any federal reserve bank may receive from any of its member banks and from the United States deposits of current funds in lawful money, national bank notes, federal reserve notes or checks and drafts upon solvent member banks, payable upon presentation; or, solely for exchange purposes, may receive from other federal reserve banks deposits of current funds in lawful money, national bank notes or checks and drafts upon solvent member or other federal reserve banks, payable upon presentation.

Every federal reserve bank shall have power: to deal in gold coin and bullion at home or abroad, to make loans thereon, exchange federal reserve notes for gold, gold coin, or gold certificates, and to contract for loans of gold coin or bullion; to buy and sell, at home or abroad, bonds and notes of the United States, and bills, notes, revenue bonds and warrants with a maturity from date of purchase of not exceeding six months, issued in anticipation of the collection of taxes or in anticipation of the receipt of assured revenues by any state, county, district, political subdivision, or municipality in the continental United States, including irrigation, drainage and reclamation districts; to purchase from member banks and to sell bills of exchange arising out of commercial transactions, to establish from time to time rates of discount to be charged by the federal reserve bank for each class of paper, which shall be fixed with a view of accommodating commerce and business; to open and maintain banking accounts in foreign countries, appoint correspondents and establish agencies in such countries.

The moneys held in the general fund of the treasury, except the five per centum fund for the redemption of outstanding national bank notes and the funds provided in this act for the redemption of federal reserve notes, may, upon the direction of the Secretary of the Treasury, be deposited in federal reserve banks.

No public funds of the Philippine Islands or of the postal savings or any government funds shall be deposited in the continental United States in any bank not belonging to the system established by this act.

Federal reserve notes, to be issued at the discretion of the Federal Reserve Board for the purpose of making advances to federal reserve banks through the federal reserve agents, are hereby authorized. The said notes shall be receivable by all national and member banks and federal reserve banks and for all taxes, customs and other public dues. They shall be redeemable in gold.

Any federal reserve bank may make application to the local federal reserve agent for such amount of the federal reserve notes as it may require.

Every federal reserve bank shall maintain reserves in gold or lawful money of not less than thirty-five per centum against its deposits and reserves in gold of not less than forty per centum against its federal reserve notes in actual circulation. Whenever federal reserve notes issued through one federal reserve bank shall be received by another federal reserve bank, they shall be promptly returned for credit or redemption to the federal reserve bank through which they were originally issued.

No federal reserve bank shall pay out notes issued through another under penalty of a tax of ten per centum upon the face value of notes so paid out.

In order to furnish suitable notes for circulation as federal reserve notes, the Controller of the Currency shall, under the direction of the Secretary of the Treasury, have printed such notes of the denominations of $5, $10, $20, $50, $100.

Every federal reserve bank shall receive on deposit at par from member banks or from federal reserve banks, checks and drafts drawn upon any of its depositors, and when remitted by a federal reserve bank checks and drafts drawn by any depositor in any other federal reserve bank or member bank upon funds to the credit of said depositor in said reserve bank or member bank.

After two years from the passage of this act, and at any time during a period of twenty years thereafter, any member bank desiring to retire the whole or any part of its circulating notes may file with the Treasurer of the United States an application to sell for its account, at par and accrued interest, United States bonds securing circulation to be retired.

Demand liabilities within the meaning of this act shall comprise all deposits payable within thirty days, and time deposits shall comprise all deposits payable after thirty days, and all savings accounts and certificates of deposit which are subject to not less than thirty days' notice before payment.

By amendments approved June 21, 1917, the federal reserve banking system is altered as follows:

The Board may permit or require Federal reserve banks to establish branch banks within their districts and the number of the directors of such banks shall, at the option of the Board, be not more than seven nor more than three.

Subject to the provisions of the Federal reserve act and to the regulations of the board made pursuant thereto, any State bank or trust company which becomes a member of the Federal Reserve System shall retain its full charter and statutory rights and may continue to exercise all corporate powers granted to it by the State in which it was created and shall be entitled to all the privileges of member banks; *Provided, however,* That no Federal reserve bank may discount for such a member bank any note, draft, or bill of exchange of any one borrower who is liable to the member bank for more than 10 per cent of its capital and surplus.

State banks and trust companies which are member banks are made subject to examinations made by direction of the Federal Reserve Board or of the Federal reserve bank by examiners selected or approved by the Federal Reserve Board. Examinations by State authorities when approved by the directors of the Federal reserve bank may be accepted in lieu of examinations by examiners approved by the Federal Reserve Board. Reports of condition and of payments of dividends must be made to the Federal reserve bank instead of the Comptroller of the Currency as in the past. State banks and trust companies which have become member banks are authorized to withdraw from the Federal Reserve System after six months' written notice.

Federal reserve banks are authorized, solely for purposes of exchange or of collection, to receive deposits of currency, checks, drafts, and maturing notes or bills from any nonmember bank or trust company which maintains with the Federal reserve bank a balance sufficient to offset the items in transit held for its account by the Federal reserve bank.

Any member bank is authorized to make reasonable charges to be determined and regulated by the Federal Reserve Board, but in no case to exceed 10 cents per hundred dollars or fraction thereof for the collection or payment of checks and drafts and remission therefor by exchange or otherwise. Federal reserve banks, however, are not subject to these charges.

The Board is authorized to permit member banks to accept drafts and bills or exchange drawn against shipments of goods or against warehouse receipts covering readily marketable staples up to 100 per cent of the capital and surplus of the accepting bank; and to give its consent to or require reserve banks to open and maintain accounts in foreign countries, etc., and also to provide for participation accounts.

Provision is made for the issue of Federal reserve notes upon the security of gold or gold certificates and so as to provide that gold or gold certificates held by the Federal reserve agent as collateral security shall be counted as part of the gold reserve which the Federal reserve bank is required to maintain against its notes in actual circulation.

Provision is made for the issue of Federal reserve notes on the security of the 15-day notes of member banks secured by eligible commercial paper or by bonds or notes of the United States.

The Treasurer or any assistant treasurer of the United States is authorized to receive deposits of gold or gold certificates when tendered by any Federal reserve bank or Federal reserve agent for credit to its or his account with the Federal Reserve Board.

A national bank is no longer required to maintain a minimum deposit of bonds with the Treasurer of the United States.

Provision is made for an immediate transfer of all reserves to Federal reserve banks. Under this section, as amended, the total amount of reserves to be maintained by a member bank must be carried with the Federal reserve bank of its district. The amount of these reserves is as follows:

	Demand Deposits	Time Deposits
	Per cent	Per cent
Country banks	7	3
Reserve city banks	10	3
Central reserve city banks	13	3

Member banks are no longer required to maintain any reserves in their own vaults.

Currency (see also Reserve Banking System, Gold Certificates, Silver Certificates):

Defects in law pointed out and remedial legislation urged, 7049, 7050, 7080, 7081, 7879.

Discussed. (See Finances discussed.)

Elasticity in—

Secured, 8151.

Urged, 6715, 6914, 6989, 7080, 7082, 7879.

Emergency, recommended, 7080.

Integrity of, 6787.

Law, special address urging enactment of, 7879.

Of the Constitution, precious metals, discussed, 1465.

Plan of legislation for, indorsed by President Cleveland, 5985.

Discussed, 5993, 5999, 6073, 6091, 6175.

Precious metals, currency of the Constitution, 1465.

Reduction in, 630.

Reform of, discussed, 7373, 7513, 7879, 7908.

Should be responsive to commercial demands, 6654.

Uniformity of, necessity for, 58, 60, 549, 550, 563, 1896.

Cushing, American vessel, attacked by aeroplane, 8062.

Custer Massacre.—Maj.-Gen. George A. Custer led with his regiment Gen. Terry's column in an expedition against the Sioux Indians in 1876. June 25, coming upon an encampment of Indians on the Little Big Horn River, in Montana, he divided his regiment (the Seventh Cavalry) into several detachments, one of which, under Maj. Reno, was ordered to attack in the rear, while Custer led 5 companies to the front. Reno was driven back and the Indians fell upon Custer and massacred his entire command of about 276 men (4327). See illustrations opposite 4534 and 5231.

Custom-Houses:

In New York—

Authority for instituting investigation demanded, 1952.

Expenses of, referred to, 2010.

Investigated, 1952, 2007, 4423.

Report of commissioners referred to, 2005, 2014, 4402.

Reply of President, 1952.

Officers of, claims of, for additional pay discussed, 2722.

Partisan control over, order regarding, 4402.

Customs Administration Board discussed, 5549.

Customs Appeals, Court of. (See Courts.)

Customs, Collector of, compensation of, recommendations regarding, 4102.

Customs Districts, consolidation of, recommended, 4767.

Executive order designating, 7989.

Customs Duties. (See Import Duties.)

Customs Revenue, Commissioner of, creation of office of, recommended, 3985.

Customs Service:

Collection districts designated, 7989.

Order relating to and providing for fines for dishonest manifests in Canal Zone, 7963.

Reorganization of, 7863.

Treasury Department given authority over officers of an inforcement of neutrality laws, 7964.

Cyane, The, sent to Greytown, Nicaragua, to demand reparation for injuries sustained by United States, 2816.

Bombardment by, discussed, 2816. (See also Greytown, Nicaragua.)

Czecho-Slovaks and Jugoslavs, National Aspirations of.—The Czechs, or Bohemians, belong to the great Slavic family of mankind and, together with the

Poles, form the Western Slavic division of the Slavs. They inhabit a large part of Bohemia, an even larger part of Moravia, certain portions of both Prussian and Austrian Silesia, and large districts in northern Hungary, all of this territory being contiguous; and, in addition, certain other sections of Lower Austria, especially Vienna, and many districts in the Russia of the Tsar, especially Volhynia. They have a language and a literature of their own, although in the nineteenth century the Czechs outside of Bohemia developed a written language which in some respects differs from that of Bohemia. The Czechs are thus bounded on three sides by German peoples and influences and only in the east come into contact with their fellow-Slavs.

At the time of the outbreak of the European War, the number of Czechs was usually placed at 8,000,000 (about 28% of the total population of Austria), but their losses under the Austrian flag in the war were very great.

Bohemia.—The early history of Bohemia is vague and unverifiable. The Bohemians certainly formed one of the powerful groups of the barbarian invaders of the Roman Empire several hundred years after the beginning of the Christian era, and lived for some centuries in a primeval condition based upon tribal allegiances and relations. In the Dark Ages the Bohemians formed part of the Moravian kingdom of Svatopluk, which was destroyed in the tenth century by the Magyars, the present dominating, although by no means the most numerous, group in modern Austria-Hungary. At the time, however, the Bohemians fell under German rather than under Magyar suzerainty, their numerous kings and overlords paying at least a nominal allegiance to Teutonic powers.

By the thirteenth century, the Bohemians had succeeded in establishing a political autonomy of their own, and for some years were one of the important countries of Europe, even if they were too far to the north to represent as high a type of culture and civilization as other nationalities even in those days of darkness and superstition. Before 1400, however, Bohemia had once more fallen under German domination.

Bohemia was the centre in the fourteenth century of one of the significant movements of all times, the movement for religious reform led by John Hus, which notably helped to blaze the way for the later Reformation under Luther. The Reformation, accordingly, found Bohemia no virgin soil in which to cast its seeds, and the bitter Thirty Years' War raged throughout the length and breadth of Bohemia with fury and devastation. From the unprecedented slaughter of that struggle even the Czech race of today can hardly be said to have fully lost the traces. In 1620 Bohemia lost its independence, its crown became hereditary in the Hapsburg family, and the Czechs passed under Austrian rule.

Recrudescence of Nationalistic Feeling.—The Czechs fell strongly under the impulse of the rebirth of the souls of minor and suppressed nationalities which became the social movement of probably the farthest-reaching significance at the beginning of the nineteenth century. The disregard for nationalistic divisions displayed in the settlement of the Napoleonic Wars and the policy of suppressive reaction led by the Austrian Metternich fed the flames of the new feeling for Bohemian independence, and the Austrian government was not slow to see the danger therein contained for the Dual Monarchy. A strong policy of repression of the Czechs, literary, political, social, economic, was carried into effect, and the antagonism between the Czechs and the

Magyar and German elements in control of Austria-Hungary became pronounced.

Even in Austria, however, as the years rolled on, the movement for constitutional government could not be altogether disregarded, and in 1860 a pretense of representative government was established. The Czechs were given a representation far below that to which their numbers entitled them, and their elected representatives showed their anger by remaining away from the Imperial Parliament until 1879. Some years previously the Czech nationalistic aspirations had divided along conservative and radical lines, or into the parties of the Old Czechs and the Young Czechs. The establishment of a national university at Prague was an event of prime importance for the cultural and literary side of the Czech movement. At the outbreak of the European War, Bohemia had its own Diet of 242 members and was represented by 130 of the 516 members in the Lower House of the Austrian Reichsrat. Voting, however, is only through stringent property and other qualifications. So strong had the antagonism to the powers in control of the Dual Monarchy become by 1913 that in that year Franz Josef's government suspended the autonomous government of Bohemia.

The Slovaks are a race kindred to the Czechs, with whom they are connected by close ties. They are about 2,000,000 in number (about 10% of the total population of Hungary), and they inhabit northern Hungary adjacently to the Czechs. Their language is a Czech dialect and their history and their aspirations are practically identical with those of the Czechs.

With the outbreak of the European War, the Czecho-Slovak problem became intensified. The Germans in Austria had oppressed the Czecho-Slovaks no less than the Magyars, and there was among this suppressed nationality a deep hatred of everything German. Moreover, they were not to be aroused by the Russian menace, as they were a branch of the Slavic family of which the Great Russians were the most numerous. They were opposed to the political aspirations of the Central Powers, and realizing that an Entente victory would probably mean the breakup of the Dual Monarchy, their sympathies were more with their country's enemies than with their country. But they were powerless under compulsion, and were forced into the battle-line, the Austrian officials taking pains to see that the posts of greatest danger were given to them. Nevertheless, great numbers deserted to the Russian forces, especially after the Russian Revolution; and after peace with Russia was officially proclaimed, thousands of Czecho-Slovaks either remained in Russia and refused to return to their homes or else endeavored to join the Allied forces, especially after President Wilson had made it clearer and clearer that the Allies' war aims were concerned to a great extent with the freedom of the minor and subject nationalities of Europe. Many enlisted in the United States to fight the Central Powers.

Jugoslavs (South Slavs).—In many respects, the Jugoslav nationalistic movement is akin to that of the Czecho-Slovaks, although the details of their problem are different from those of their northern kinsmen. The Jugoslavs form the southern branch of the great Slavic family of nations, and live not only in Austria, but also in Serbia, Bosnia, Herzegovina, Bulgaria, Macedonia, Montenegro. They comprise about 1,400,000 Slovenes, living in the Austrian provinces of Carinthia, Carniola, and Styria; and about 8,000.00 Serbo-Croatians living in the southern Hungarian provinces

ng.—One of
he history
tates is
, in

neighborhood. It has been found, however, that the labor and expense of daily hauling the entire milk product of patrons' farms to the creamery, often several miles distant, is too great a tax upon the industry. A movement toward relief of the patrons and economy in creamery management has been the establishment of neighborhood "skimming stations," equipped only with a parator and power to operate it, as anches of the central plant. From these stations the cream is transported to the parent butter-making factory.

It is interesting to note that while the extension of the creamery system has been such as to raise the product of these establishments in ten years from 15 per cent to 28 per cent of the total butter product of the United States, with a net increase of 131.7 per cent, the quantity of butter made on farms has, nevertheless, increased nearly fifty million pounds. As a rule the states producing the greatest quantities of butter in factories are also those in which the quantities made on farms are greatest. Ohio is a notable exception. It produced 79,551,299 pounds of butter on farms, which is more than any other state, while its creamery product was comparatively small, being only 8,117,321 pounds.

Other new elements which are influencing a modification of the creamery system are the invention of the Babcock fat test for milk, and the adoption of the farm separator in sizes for either hand or power. The Babcock test is a chemico-mechanical contrivance, not difficult to operate, by which the percentage of butter fat in either milk or cream may be measured with mathematical accuracy, and the value of the butter-making elements thus fixed so far as quantity is concerned. Milk delivered at creameries and cheese factories is now generally tested in this way and paid for on the basis of the fat it contains. Farm and creamery methods are so much simplified by these improvements that many dairy farmers are procuring private separators. The State Dairy Commissioner of Iowa reports more than five thousand of these farm separators owned by patrons of creameries. This new form of cream gathering is rapidly extending, and cream again forms a large share of the raw material received at the factories for butter making.

Butter.—The quantity of butter packed solid or in prints and rolls varies with the market requirements. In New England the numerous cities and large towns easy of furnish markets where butter can be rectly to retail dealers or consumers. re, Vermont excepted, the cream- this section pack twice as much n the form of bricks, prints, or they do in solid tubs or firkins. Island and Connecticut, with re- s at their doors, the factories mes as much of their product tubs. Philadelphia and the arkets in general have long xcellent print butter. From Minnesota and South Da- t be sent long distances to rally goes mainly in bulk. e for butter throughout cents a pound; that s averages 19 cents, and small packages By careful computa- 22½ pounds of milk ne pound of butter. in connection with tter forms a basis estimate the profit

pon as a by-product

of the creameries, and is figured as worth about ten or eleven cents per hundred pounds. It is usually returned to the farmers at this price and fed to young stock. Some of it is used for making casein which sells for three to five cents a pound.

Cheese.—Cheese factories are run on about the same general principles as creameries. The bulk of the product, although different in form, size, color, and quantity, is nearly all made upon the same general plan, closely resembling the English cheddar. Hence a uniform type was established, which became known as "Standard American" or "Full Cream Factory" cheese, often called cheddar.

Successful efforts have been made in the older cheese-making states to imitate noted foreign brands. Neufchâtel, Limburger, Swiss, Camembert, Brie and other varieties are made as part of the regular output and find ready sale in competition with the imported varieties.

Condensed Milk.—The condensed milk industry was started about the same time as the factory system for making butter and cheese. Some method had long been sought for preserving milk, but none was successful until the invention of Gail Borden. After ten years of experimenting he decided that a semi-liquid state was the best form of preservation and in 1856 settled upon the process which has since popularized the product in every quarter of the globe. The present extensive industry, in Europe as well as America, with its many different establishments and various commercial names and brands, is based upon Mr. Borden's methods. This applies to the unsweetened article as well as to that preserved with sugar, for "plain condensed milk" was first introduced and put upon the market in 1861. It was then mainly in open vessels and intended for early use. Between 1860 and 1870 milk in both forms had become well known, and four or five factories were in operation, each producing about 5,000 one-pound cans per day.

Number and value of milch cows in the United States, 1890 to 1916. (Source—Reports of the Department of Agriculture.) :

Year Jan. 1	Number.	Value.
1890	15,952,883	353,152,133
1891	16,019,591	346,397,900
1892	16,416,351	351,378,132
1893	16,424,087	357,299,785
1894	16,487,400	358,998,661
1895	16,504,629	362,601,729
1896	16,137,586	363,955,545
1897	15,941,727	369,239,993
1898	15,840,886	434,813,826
1899	15,990,115	474,233,925
1900	16,292,360	514,812,106
1901	16,833,657	505,093,077
1902	16,696,802	488,130,324
1903	17,105,227	516,711,914
1904	17,419,817	508,841,489
1905	17,572,464	482,272,203
1906	19,793,866	582,788,592
1907	20,968,265	645,496,980
1908	21,194,000	650,057,000
1909	21,720,000	702,945,000
1910	21,801,000	780,308,000
1911	20,823,000	832,209,000
1912	20,699,000	815,414,000
1913	20,497,000	922,783,000
1914	20,737,000	1,118,487,000
1915	21,262,000	1,176,338,000
1916	21,988,000	1,185,119,000

The entire dairy and cattle raising business of the United States for the last census year may be summed up as follows :

Cows and heifers kept for milk born before Jan. 1, 1909	20,625,432
Cows and heifers not kept for milk born before Jan. 1, 1909	12,023,682
Heifers born in 1910	7,295,880
Steers and bulls born before Jan. 1, 1909	7,598,258
Steers and bulls born in 1909	5,450,289
Calves born after Jan. 1, 1910	7,806,539
Milk produced (pounds)	9,888,727,303
Cream produced (pounds)	1,406,143,908
Value of milk, cream and skimmed milk	$213,811,589
Pounds of butter produced, 1909	* 1,619,415,263
Pounds of cheese produced, 1909	† 320,532,181

* In addition, 2,381,212 pounds of butter produced in establishments engaged primarily in the manufacture of products other than butter, cheese or condensed milk.

† In addition, 49,413 pounds of cheese produced in establishments engaged primarily in the manufacture of products other than butter, cheese or condensed milk.

Computation of the per capita consumption of dairy products annually in this country is a simple matter so far as butter and cheese are concerned. To the aggregates made on farms and in factories, the imports must be added and the foreign and domestic exports deducted. Dividing this sum by the population figures gives each individual about 20 pounds as his share of butter for a year and 3½ pounds of cheese.

Export Trade.—Cheese, butter, and butter fats are again becoming important factors in our export trade after a long period of comparative inactivity. Fifteen or twenty years ago the United States was selling abroad between 20,000,000 and 30,000,000 pounds of butter, from 50,000,000 to 80,000,000 pounds of cheese, and from 5,000,000 to 10,000,000 pounds of imitation butter annually. In later years, however, exports of this class decreased in a marked degree and in the fiscal year 1914 had fallen far below the quantities named. In the year just ended there was a distinct revival in all these lines, with totals closely approximating the high levels touched in the decade from 1890 to 1900.

The large gains made by domestic dairy products and butter substitutes are well illustrated by figures published by the Bureau of Foreign and Domestic Commerce. Department of Commerce, in the June "Summary of Foreign Commerce." Butter, usually averaging about 3,500,000 pounds annually in our export trade, in 1915 went to nearly 10,000,000 pounds. During this period imports of butter were reduced by more than one-half, falling from a little less than 8,000,000 pounds in 1914 to less than 4,000,000 pounds last year.

American cheese, running at about 2,500,-000 pounds a year, went to 54,000,000 pounds in the fiscal year 1915. Here also, as in the case of butter, the trade balance was transferred to the export side, for the year's imports of cheese last year only totaled 50,000,000 pounds, a decrease of 13,-750,000 pounds from the total for 1914.

Exports of condensed milk, usually exported in sums valued at between $1,000,000 and $2,000,000 annually, in 1915 rose to $3,000,000 in value, the quantity (37,000,000 pounds) being double that of 1914.

Imitation butter contains, in addition to oleomargarine oil, some butter fat. The exports of this article also doubled, rising from 2,500,000 pounds in 1914 to 5,250,000 pounds last year.

England has become our largest foreign market for butter, cheese, and condensed milk, having taken 3,333,000 pounds of butter, out of a total export of 10,000,000 pounds; 48,500,000 pounds of cheese, out of a total export of 54,000,000 pounds; and 4,000,000 pounds of condensed milk, out of a total export of 37,000,000 pounds. Canada, Cuba, Panama, Australia, and Venezuela also take considerable quantities of American butter; Panama and the West Indies are important markets for our cheese; while Cuba, Belgium, the Netherlands, China, Japan, Hongkong, Russia, Chosen, Panama, and Brazil take large amounts of American condensed milk.

These exports, while important, represent a very small proportion of the annual products of the 60,000,000 cattle on American farms, valued at more than $2,333,000,000. As long ago as 1909, the latest period covered by the national census, we produced 1,619,000,000 pounds of butter, 321,000,000 pounds of cheese, and 5,814,000,000 gallons of milk, while the quantity of oleomargarine on which internal revenue tax was paid in 1914 aggregated 142,000,000 pounds.

Official reports give the number of milch cows in the United States in 1915 as 21,-262,000, valued at $1,176,338,000.

Purity of Products—Public interest has recently been aroused in the dairy business by the demands of the people through various state and city boards of health for pure milk and butter, and by the members of many organizations of farmers and dairymen who are interested in the profitable production of butter, milk and cheese.

Public Exhibits.—The sixth annual exhibition of the National Dairy Show, held in Chicago in the autumn of 1911, set a milestone in the progress of the industry. More than one thousand of the leading dairy breeds of cattle were shown; and the exhibits of dairy machinery and appliances excelled those of previous years. National, state and city governments made many excellent exhibits in connection with the inspection of milk and milk products. A feature of this meeting was the attendance of President Taft, who, in a brief address, commended the scope of the enterprise and emphasized the importance of the dairy industry. In 1900 dairy cows constituted about one-fourth of the total number of cattle in the United States, but the number increased until with the census report of 1910 cows made up one-third of the total number of cattle. The causes of this change were the increase in the consumption of milk, the cutting up of large ranges, and the increased cost of feed, which added materially to the cost of raising beef, so that the balance of profit was swung in favor of the milch cow. (See also Agricultural Products; Butter, Cheese and Condensed Milk Industry.)

Dakota, erecting North and South Dakota into a separate Internal Revenue district, 6608. (See also North Dakota and South Dakota.)

Dakota Central Railway Co., agreement for right of way to, through Sioux Reservation, Dak., transmitted, 4775.

Dakota Indians. (See Indian Tribes.)

Dakota Territory (see also North Dakota; South Dakota):

Creation and organization of, referred to, 3254.

Dakotah Indians. (See Indian Tribes.)

Dallas, Tex., bill to authorize construction of addition to public building in, vetoed, 5519.

Dames of the Revolution.—The Society of Dames of the Revolution was organized in 1896. The regulation as to membership is that the society shall be composed entirely of women above the age of eighteen years, of good moral character, who are descended in their own right from an ancestor who, either as a military, naval or marine officer or official in the service of any one of the thirteen original colonies or states, or of the National Government representing or composed of those colonies or states, assisted in establishing American independence during the War of the Revolution, April 19, 1775, when hostilities commenced, and April 19, 1783, when they were ordered to cease. Local chapters may be organized when authorized by the Board of Managers of the Society.

Danbury Hatters' Case. (See Loewe vs. Lawlor et al.)

Danish West Indies. (See Virgin Islands.)

Dardanelles, restrictions on passage of Straits of Bosphorus and, by ships of other nations, 4078.

Darien, Isthmus of, canal across. (See Panama Canal.)

Darien Naval Radio Station, established, 7961.

Dartmoor Massacre.—In 1815, Dartmoor prison, in Devonshire, England, contained 10,000 French and 6,000 American prisoners of war, as well as impressed American seamen who had refused to fight against their country. The prisoners of war had been taken in the War of 1812 and the seamen had been impressed for several years prior to the war and were impatient for their liberty, the war having ended. On the 6th of April a number of sailors, in attempting to escape, came into collision with the guards and 33 Americans were wounded and 7 killed. After an investigation ample satisfaction was made by the British Government.

Dartmouth College vs. Woodward.—A celebrated case decided by the Supreme Court of the United States, in 1819. June 27, 1816, the New Hampshire legislature amended the charter of Dartmouth College, increased the number of trustees to twenty-one, and changed the name from Dartmouth College to Dartmouth University, creating a new corporation, to which the property of the old corporation was transferred. Woodward was the secretary and treasurer of the corporation under the new charter. The old trustees began suit against him for the recovery of the property. The State court decided against them. The case was taken on writ of error to the United States Supreme Court. The latter tribunal reversed the decision of the State court, declaring that the "charter of Dartmouth College is a contract within the meaning of that clause of the Constitution which prohibits States from passing any law impairing the obligation of contracts." The New Hampshire law was therefore declared unconstitutional and void. Daniel Webster conducted the case for the plaintiffs. This decision is one of the most important ever rendered by the Supreme Court. It settled the law holding that a charter granted to a private corporation is a contract, which cannot be altered in a material point without the consent of those who hold it unless the power of revision is reserved to the legislature by a clause in the charter or a general law of the State.

Daughters of the American Revolution. —The Society was organized in the city of Washington, D. C., Oct. 11, 1890. The headquarters are in Washington. Its present membership is reported by the Secretary-General to be 47,111. Seven hundred and fifty state chapters exist in forty-five states and territories and the District of Columbia, presided over by regents. Chapter regents have been appointed for England, Cuba and the Philippines.

Any woman may be eligible for membership who is of the age of eighteen years, and who is descended from an ancestor who, "with unfailing loyalty, rendered material aid to the cause of independence as a recognized patriot, as a soldier or patriot, or as a civil officer in one of the several colonies or states, or of the United Colonies or States," provided that the applicant shall be acceptable to the society. Every application for membership must be indorsed by at least one member of the National Society, and is then submitted to the Registrars-General, who report on the question of eligibility to the Board of Management, and upon its approval the applicant is enrolled as a member.

Daughters of the Confederacy, United. (See Confederacy, United Daughters of the.)

Daughters of the Revolution.—The General Society was organized in the City of New York, Aug. 20, 1891. Eligibility to membership is restricted to "women who are lineal descendants of an ancestor who was a military or naval or marine officer, soldier, sailor or marine in actual service under the authority of any of the thirteen colonies or states, or of the Continental Congress, and remained always loyal to such authority, or descendants of one who signed the Declaration of Independence, or of one who as a member of the Continental Congress or of the Congress of any of the colonies or states, or as an official appointed by or under the authority of any such representative bodies, actually assisted in the establishment of American independence by service rendered during the War of the Revolution, becoming thereby liable to conviction of treason against the Government of Great Britain, but remaining always loyal to the authority of the colonies or states." State societies exist in a large number of states. The office of the General Society is 156 Fifth Avenue, New York.

Dauphine Island, Gulf of Mexico, fortification at, of importance to defense of New Orleans and Union, 688.

Referred to, 695.

Davids Island, New York Harbor, new building for recruiting service at, referred to, 4664.

Dawes Commission discussed, 6272, 6346, 6389.

Dead Letters. (See Division of Dead Letters.)

Death Penalty.—Capital punishment prevails in all the states and territories of the Union, except Michigan, Minnesota,

Wisconsin, Rhode Island, Kansas and Maine. It was abolished in Iowa in 1872 and restored in 1878. It was also abolished in Colorado, but was restored in 1891. In New York, Virginia and Ohio execution is by electricity. (See Capital Punishment.)

Death Rate.—The death rate for 1915 (13.5 per 1,000 population), is the lowest ever recorded, the most favorable year prior to 1915 having been 1914, for which the rate was 13.6. It is markedly lower than the average rate for the five-year period

[Data given by color for states with a colored population of at least 10 per cent of total and for cities with a colored population of 10,000 or over in 1910.]

Area.	Population estimated as of July 1, 1915	Death rate per 1,000 Population 1915
Total, registration area..........	67,336,992	13.5
REGISTRATION STATES [1]....	62,092,925	13.3
California......................	2,848,275	13.7
Colorado......................	935,799	11.3
Connecticut....................	1,223,583	14.9
Indiana.......................	2,798,142	12.7
Kansas........................	[2] 1,807,221	10.1
Kentucky (total)..............	2,365,185	12.3
White......................	2,115,315	11.1
Colored....................	249,870	22.0
Maine.........................	767,638	15.6
Maryland (total)..............	1,351,941	15.8
White......................	1,120,770	14.1
Colored....................	231,171	24.1
Massachusetts.................	3,662,339	14.5
Michigan......................	3,015,442	13.4
Minnesota.....................	2,246,761	10.1
Missouri......................	3,391,789	12.0
Montana.......................	446,054	11.4
New Hampshire.................	440,584	16.1
New Jersey....................	2,881,840	13.8
New York......................	10,086,568	14.6
North Carolina [3] (total).....	487,359	17.3
White......................	322,668	13.5
Colored....................	164,691	24.9
Ohio..........................	5,088,627	13.0
Pennsylvania..................	8,383,992	13.8
Rhode Island..................	602,765	14.8
Utah..........................	424,300	9.9
Vermont.......................	362,452	14.7
Virginia (total)..............	2,171,014	14.2
White......................	1,493,687	11.6
Colored....................	677,327	19.8
Washington....................	[2] 1,471,043	[2] 8.1
Wisconsin.....................	2,473,533	10.8
CITIES OF 100,000 POPULATION OR OVER IN 1910.		
Birmingham Ala. (total)........	174,108	15.6
White......................	108,679	11.3
Colored....................	65,429	22.7
Los Angeles, Cal. (total)......	475,367	12.3
White......................	454,791	12.0
Colored....................	20,576	19.4
Oakland, Cal..................	190,803	11.4
San Francisco, Cal. (total)....	456,009	15.9
White......................	439,379	15.6
Colored....................	16,630	24.9
Denver, Colo..................	253,161	13.3
Bridgeport, Conn..............	118,434	15.4
New Haven, Conn...............	147,095	15.7
Washington, D. C. (total)......	358,679	18.1
White......................	259,650	15.1
Colored....................	99,029	26.2
Atlanta, Ga. (total)..........	184,972	15.1
White......................	126,990	11.4
Colored....................	57,982	23.3
Chicago Ill. (total)..........	2,447,845	14.3
White......................	2,393,678	14.0
Colored....................	54,167	23.9
Indianapolis, Ind. (total).....	265,578	14.7
White......................	240,692	13.9
Colored....................	24,886	22.5

Area.	Population estimated as of July 1, 1915	Death rate per 1,000 Population 1915
Louisville, Ky. (total)	237,012	15.0
White	195,216	13.0
Colored	41,796	24.2
New Orleans, La. (total)	366,484	21.2
White	270,741	16.4
Colored	95,743	34
Baltimore, Md. (total)	584,605	17.1
White	496,682	15.2
Colored	87,923	28.1
Boston, Mass. (total)	745,139	16.1
White	729,061	16.0
Colored	16,078	23.0
Cambridge, Mass	111,669	13.1
Fall River, Mass	126,904	15.9
Lowell, Mass	112,124	16.2
Worcester, Mass	160,523	15.4
Detroit, Mich	554,717	15.7
Grand Rapids, Mich	125,759	12.5
Minneapolis, Minn	353,460	11.5
St. Paul, Minn	241,999	10.7
Kansas City, Mo. (total)	289,879	14.7
White	263,113	13.5
Colored	26,766	26.7
St. Louis, Mo. (total)	745,988	13.8
White	696,866	13.0
Colored	49,122	24.5
Omaha, Nebr	163,200	12.2
Jersey City, N. J	300,133	14.5
Newark, N. J	399,000	13.1
Paterson, N. J	136,374	13.2
Albany, N. Y	103,580	20.0
Buffalo, N. Y	461,335	14.9
New York, N. Y. (total)	5,468,190	13.9
White	5,354,428	13.7
Colored	113,762	23.7
Rochester, N. Y	250,747	13.9
Syracuse, N. Y	152,534	13.2
Cincinnati, Ohio (total)	406,706	15.6
White	384,701	14.8
Colored	22,005	29.9
Cleveland, Ohio	657,311	13.4
Columbus, Ohio (total)	209,722	14.0
White	194,466	13.6
Colored	15,256	19.7
Dayton, Ohio	125,509	13.6
Toledo, Ohio	187,840	15.4
Portland, Oreg	[2] 272,833	[2] 8.4
Philadelphia, Pa. (total)	1,683,664	15.6
Pittsburgh, Pa. (total)	571,984	15.3
Scranton, Pa	144,081	14.7
Providence, R. I	250,025	14.6
Memphis, Tenn. (total)	146,113	19.8
White	92,252	13.9
Colored	53,861	29.9
Nashville, Tenn. (total)	115,978	17.2
White	79,857	14.0
Colored	36,121	24.4
Richmond, Va. (total)	154,674	18.9
White	99,156	15.9
Colored	55,518	24.3
Seattle, Wash	[2] 330,834	[2] 7.4
Spokane, Wash	[2] 142,990	[2] 8.1
Milwaukee, Wis	428,062	11.4

[1] Includes District of Columbia.

[2] These rates are based on estimates of population computed on the assumption that the annual numerical increase since 1910 has been the same as the average numerical increase between 1900 and 1910. This method probably results, in the cases of the states and cities for the years indicated, in an exaggeration of the estimated population and a consequent reduction of the apparent death rate below the true figure.

[2] Includes only municipalities having a population of 1,000 or over in 1910.

1901 to 1905, which was 16.2. The decrease thus amounts to 16.7 per cent, or almost exactly one-sixth, during a little more than a decade.

The adjoining table shows the population and death rates in the registration area, 1915.

Debenture. (See Drawback.)

Debt, Public.—The debt of the United States, as reported to the first Congress at its second session, 1790-1791, by Alexander Hamilton, Secretary of the Treasury, consisted of the foreign debt, domestic debt and state debts. The Secretary recommended that these latter be assumed by the general government, and after considerable discussion this was agreed to. The debt then stood:

Domestic debt $42,414,085
Foreign debt 11,710,378
State debts (as finally assumed) 18,271,786

Total $72,396,249

The foreign debt consisted of money due in France, Holland and Spain, for loans made to us during the Revolution.

The debt was funded and in 1796 the total was $83,800,000. It then began to decrease, and, though swelled $15,000,000 by the Louisiana Purchase, it was brought down to $45,200,000 in 1812. The War of 1812 increased the amount till in 1816 the debt reached $127,000,000. By 1835, however, it was virtually extinguished. It then began to grow.

In 1836 the treasury had on hand a surplus of over $40,000,000, all but $5,000,-000 of which was ordered by Congress to be distributed among the states, on certain conditions and in four installments. Three of these were paid, but the turn taken by financial affairs rendered the payment of the fourth inexpedient. The increase between 1847 and 1849 was due to the Mexican War. Between 1852 and 1857 over $53,000,000 of the debt was purchased in the market by the government, about $8,-000,000 being paid as premium. After the panic of 1857 the debt began to increase; the sudden enormous increase in 1862 was caused by the Civil War. The total amount of loans issued by the government up to the outbreak of the Civil War was $505,-353,591.95; between that time and July 1, 1880, there was issued $10,144,589,408.69; and since then 3½ per cent. bonds to the amount of $460,461,050, matured 5 and 6 per cent. bonds extended being at that rate, and 3 per cent. bonds to the amount of $304,204,350, for the purpose of extending the above-mentioned 3½ per cent. bonds. (See Refunding.) The prosperity of the country, enormous revenues from customs, and the successive fundings of the debt at lower rates of interest reduced it by 1876 to $2,180,395,067. By 1886 it had further contracted $1,783,438,607, but the Spanish War caused it to grow again till in 1899 it amounted to $2,092,686,024.

Of this debt, $830,000,000, bearing interest at seven and three-tenths per cent., matured in 1867 and 1868, and about $300,-000,000 other debt matured in the same period. To meet this there were issued in 1865 $332,998,950, fifteen years, six per cent. bonds; in 1867 $379,616,050, fifteen years, six per cent. bonds; in 1868 $42,-539,350, fifteen years, six per cent. bonds; in 1867 and 1868 $85,150,000 demands, three per cent. certificates. The refunding act of 1870 authorized the issue of not more than $200,000,000, ten years, five per cent. bonds; of not more than $300,000,000, fifteen years, four and a half per cent. bonds; of not more than $1,000,000,000, thirty years, four per cent. bonds. In 1871 this was amended, increasing the amount of five per cent. bonds to $500,000,000, the total issue, however, not to be increased thereby. Under this act there were issued a total of $412,806,450 of five per cent.

bonds, and after 1876 $250,000,000 four and a half per cent. bonds. In 1879 a bill was passed authorizing the issue of $10 certificates, bearing four per cent. interest and exchangeable into the four per cent. bonds of the acts of 1870 and 1871. These certificates were issued as a part of the refunding scheme, and were intended to supply a safe means of investment for people of small means, an object that was defeated by the premium at which the four per cent. bonds were selling, which acted as an inducement to buy up these certificates and to exchange them for the bonds. In 1879 over $741,000,000 four per cent. bonds were issued under the acts of 1870 and 1871. The net result of all these changes was that the national debt, considerably more than one-half of which was in 1865 oustanding at six per cent. and over, was in 1879 costing but four and four and a half per cent. for more than one-half of its then principal. In 1881 over $670,000,000 of the public debt running at five and six per cent. matured. Congress failed to provide the means for meeting it, and there was at the disposal of the Secretary for this purpose only the surplus revenue and somewhat over $100,000,000 of four per cent. bonds under the acts of 1870 and 1871. Under these circumstances Secretary Windom, forced to act on his own responsibility, made a general offer to the holders of these bonds to extend the bonds of such as might desire it at three and a half per cent., redeemable at the pleasure of the government. This measure was a complete success, over $460,-000,000 bonds being extended at three and a half per cent. The next Congress (in 1882) authorized three per cent. bonds, redeemable at the pleasure of the government, to be issued instead of the bonds extended at three and a half per cent., and more than $300,000,000 were so issued. Meanwhile the reduction of the debt proceeded so rapidly that the last of the three and a half per cents. were called for payment November 1, 1883, and the last of the three per cents. July 1, 1887, leaving outstanding only the four and a half and four per cent. bonds.

The present debt of the United States may be divided into three parts: (1) the interest-bearing debt, consisting of bonds of various denominations; (2) the debt on which interest has ceased since maturity, which is a total of overdue bonds outstanding that have never been presented for payment; (3) debt bearing no interest, which includes old demand notes, the legal-tender notes, certificates of deposit, and gold and silver certificates.

An official statement of the public debt of the United States and the participation of each individual therein will be found in the table of the financial growth of the country in the article on Finances.

Public debts, as represented in government bonds are regarded by some financiers as real increases in national wealth. To add to present wealth by taking from the future a part of what it is sure to produce is looked upon today as a fair means of stabilizing financial transactions. The increase in commercial intercouse and the rising standards of national and civic life require great development of public improvements. To meet the most of all these at one time by taxation would amount almost to confiscation of taxable property. The expenses of a state are incapable of sudden contraction, while its revenues necessarily fluctuate. The existence of a large volume of demand obligations is an embarrassment to the treasury and impairs the credit of a state.

Following is a statement of outstanding principal of the public debt of the United States annually, from 1793 to 1914, on the dates mentioned.

Year Ending	Total Debt	Year Ending	Total Debt
January 1		July 1	
1793......	$80,352,634.04	1857....	$28,699,831.85
1794......	78,427,404.77	1858....	44,911,881.03
1795......	80,747,578.39	1859....	58,496,837.88
1796......	83,762,172.07	1860....	64,842,287.88
1797......	82,064,479.33	1861....	90,580,873.72
1798......	79,228,529.12	1862....	524,176,412.13
1799......	78,408,669.77	1863....	1,119,772,138.63
1800......	82,976,294.35	1864....	1,815,784,370.57
		1865....	2,680,647,869.74
1801......	83,038,050.80	1866....	2,773,236,173.69
1802......	86,712,632.25	1867....	2,678,126,103.87
1803......	77,054,686.30	1868....	2,611,687,851.19
1804......	86,427,120.88	1869....	2,588,452,213.94
1805......	82,312,150.50		
1806......	75,723,270.66	1870....	2,480,672,427.81
1807......	69,218,398.64	1871....	2,353,211,332.32
1808......	65,196,317.97	1872....	2,253,251,328.78
1809......	57,023,192.09	1873....	2,234,482,993.20
1810......	53,173,217.52	1874....	2,251,690,468.43
		1875....	2,232,284,531.95
1811......	48,005,587.76	1876....	2,180,395,067.15
1812......	45,209,737.90	1877....	2,205,301,392.10
1813......	55,962,827.57	1878....	2,256,205,892.53
1814......	81,487,846.24	1879....	2,340,567,232.03
1815......	99,833,660.15		
1816......	127,334,933.74	1880....	2,128,791,054.63
1817......	123,491,965.16	1881....	2,077,389,253.58
1818......	103,466,633.83	1882....	1,926,688,678.03
1819......	95,529,648.28	1883....	1,892,547,412.07
1820......	91,015,566.15	1884....	1,838,904,607.57
		1885....	1,872,340,557.14
1821......	89,987,427.66	1886....	1,783,433,697.78
1822......	93,546,676.98	December 1	
1823......	90,875,877.28	1887....	$1,664,461,536.38
1824......	90,269,777.77	1888....	1,680,917,706.23
1825......	83,788,432.71	1889....	1,617,372,419.53
1826......	81,054,059.99	1890....	1,549,206,126.48
1827......	73,987,357.20	1891....	1,546,961,695.61
1828......	67,475,043.87	1892....	1,563,612,455.63
1829......	58,421,413.67	November 1	
1830......	48,565,406.50	1893....	$1,549,556,353.63
		1894....	1,626,154,037.68
1831......	39,123,191.68	1895....	1,717,481,779.90
1832......	24,322,235.18	1896....	1,785,412,640.00
1833......	7,001,698.83	1897....	1,808,777,643.40
1834......	4,760,082.08	1898....	1,964,837,130.90
1835......	37,513.05	1899....	2,092,686,024.42
1836......	336,957.83	1900....	2,132,373,031.17
1837......	3,308,124.07	1901....	2,151,585,743.89
1838......	10,434,221.14	1902....	2,175,246,168.89
1839......	3,573,343.82	1903....	2,218,883,772.89
1840......	5,250,875.54	1904....	2,304,697,418.64
		1905....	2,293,846,382.34
1841......	13,594,480.73	December 1	
1842......	26,601,226.38	1906....	$2,429,370,043.54
July 1		November 1	
1843......	$32,742,922.00	1907....	$2,492,231,518.54
1844......	23,461,652.50	1908....	2,637,973,747.04
1845......	15,925,303.01	1909....	2,661,426,301.04
1846......	15,550,202.97		
1847......	38,826,534.77	December 1	
1848......	47,044,862.23	1910....	$2,704,142,281.69
1849......	63,061,858.69	November 1	
1850......	63,452,773.55	1911....	$2,831,330,305.66
		1912....	2,906,750,548.66
1851......	68,304,796.02	1913....	2,926,434,343.69
1852......	66,199,341.71	1914....	2,809,262,118.66
1853......	59,803,117.70	October 1	
1854......	42,242,222.42	1915....	3,225,734,627.16
1855......	35,586,858.56	October 31	
1856......	31,972,537.90	1916....	1,080,562,441.76

(For detailed statement of the public debt see Financial.)

Debt, Public (see also Bonds; Loans): Act directing payment of surplus in Treasury on, reasons for applying pocket veto to, 5073.

Act to facilitate refunding of, vetoed, 4589.

Discussed. (See Finances discussed.)

Extinction of, 1379, 1382.

Near approach of, 1014, 1160, 1247. Referred to, 2252.

Increase in, 675, 2402, 2441, 3055.

In consequence of Mexican War, 2441.

Interest on, reduction of, recommended, 3874, 4415.

Payment of—

From surplus revenue before due, recommended, 2660, 2713.

In coin, discussed, 3991.

Payments on. (See Finances discussed.)

Progress of refunding, discussed, 4423.

Provision for, 98, 823, 1379.

Vacant lands sold for reimbursing, 100, 317, 584.

Debtors, Insolvent (see also Bankruptcy):

Modifications in law regarding, recommended, 958, 1017, 1119, 1727.

Public officers availing themselves of benefits of act must be discussed, 1107.

Debts, British.—The treaty with Great Britain in 1783 provided for the payment of all debts owed by Americans to British subjects. Many obstacles were thrown in the way of prompt payment, however, some of the state governments going so far as to provide, even after the ratification of the treaty, that such debts might be paid to the state treasury, and the state would then refuse to entertain suits on the part of creditors. The Supreme Court decided in 1796 that such debts must be paid and that no state law could repudiate them. (See also Ware *vs.* Hylton.)

Decimal System of Coinage, Weights, and Measures.—In 1782 Gouverneur Morris reported a decimal currency system designated to simplify the money of the United States. He ascertained that the 1440th part of a Spanish dollar was a common divisor for the various currencies. With this as a unit he proposed a coinage of ten units to be equal to one penny; ten pence to one bill; ten bills to one dollar (equal to about seventy-five cents of the present money); ten dollars to one crown. In 1784 Mr. Jefferson, as chairman of a committee of Congress, proposed to strike four coins upon the basis of the Spanish dollar, viz., a gold piece worth ten dollars, a dollar of silver, tenth of a dollar in silver, and a one hundredth of a dollar in copper. Congress adopted this proposition, making the dollar the unit, July 6, 1785, and the coins became known as the cent, dime, dollar and eagle. Jan. 1, 1858, Canada adopted the decimal system of currency in use in the United States. By an act of Congress of May 16, 1866, the 5-cent nickel piece was made to conform to the decimal or metric system as to size and weight. The use of the metric system of weights and measures was authorized by Congress by a permissive act, not mandatory, and a table of equivalents was approved by Congress July 28, 1866.

Declaration.—In customs parlance, a statement as to goods imported, used by customs officers as the basis for fixing duties—usually after investigation.

Declaration of Independence. — The unanimous expression of the delegates in Congress of the thirteen original states, setting forth the rights of men in general and of the colonists in particular, citing their grievances against the British Government, and declaring "that these united colonies are and of right ought to be free and independent states." North Carolina took the first step toward independence by a resolution, April 12, 1776, "to concur with those in the other colonies in declaring independence," the same state having previously (May 31, 1775), in her famous Mecklenburg resolutions (*q. v.*), which were forwarded to the Continental Congress, declared the people of the colonies "a free and independent people, under the control of no other power than that of our God and the general government of the Congress." The title of the document was suggested by Virginia in her resolution of May 17, 1776, directing her representatives to propose in Congress a "declaration of independence." Such a resolution was introduced by Richard Henry Lee on June 8th, but was not adopted until July 2d. The document was prepared by a committee composed of Thomas Jefferson, John Adams, Benjamin Franklin, Roger Sherman and Robert R. Livingston. The draft was made by Jefferson. Congress made in the Declaration as presented by the committee eighteen suppressions, six additions and ten alterations, many of them, however, not being important. The Declaration was adopted July 4, 1776, by the unanimous vote of twelve states, New York alone not voting. It was afterward ratified by a convention of that state. It was engrossed and signed on Aug. 2d, by all the members present, six signatures being afterwards added. The signers of the Declaration were:

John Hancock, President of the Congress.

New Hampshire—Josiah Bartlett, William Whipple, Matthew Thornton.

Massachusetts Bay—Samuel Adams, John Adams, Robert Treat Paine, Elbridge Gerry.

Rhode Island—Stephens Hopkins, William Ellery.

Connecticut—Roger Sherman, Samuel Huntington, William Williams, Oliver Wolcott.

New York—William Floyd, Philip Livingstone, Francis Lewis, Lewis Morris.

New Jersey—Richard Stockton, John Witherspoon, Francis Hopkinson, John Hart, Abraham Clark.

Pennsylvania—Robert Morris, Benjamin Rush, Benjamin Franklin, John Morton, George Clymer, James Smith, George Taylor, James Wilson, George Ross.

Delaware—Cæsar Rodney, George Read, Thomas M'Kean.

Maryland—Samuel Chase, William Paca, Thomas Stone, Charles Carroll, of Carrollton.

Virginia—George Wythe, Richard Henry Lee, Thomas Jefferson, Benjamin Harrison, Thomas Nelson, Jr., Francis Lightfoot Lee, Carter Braxton.

North Carolina—William Hooper, Joseph Hewes, John Penn.

South Carolina—Edward R u t l e d g e, Thomas Heyward, Jr., Thomas Lynch, Jr., Arthur Middleton.

Georgia—Button Gwinnet, Lyman Hall, Charles Walton.

(See Frontispiece, Vol. 1.)

Declaration of Independence:

Analysis by President Wilson, 7952.

Desk on which it was written presented to United States by heirs of Joseph Coolidge, Jr., 4540.

Letter of Robert C. Winthrop regarding, 4541.

Facsimile of, see illustration opposite 4.

First copperplate of, bequeathed to Congress by Lafayette, letter of son presenting, 1342.

Signers of, 4.

Signing of, see illustration opposite 1.

Text of, 1.

Declaration of Rights.—The earliest general declaration of rights of which we have any official record was that of the Stamp Act Congress in 1765, which published what it called a "Declaration of Rights and Grievances of the Colonists of America." In this document they vigorously protested against the Stamp Act and all other plans to tax them by a parliament in which they had no representation. They demanded all the rights of British subjects. In 1774 the Continental Congress made a similar declaration against later aggressions of Parliament. Declarations of the same character were incorporated in the Declaration of Independence. (See also Bill of Rights.)

Declaration of War.— An announcement or resolution authorized by a country, making known the fact that the country officially declares war upon some other country. In the United States, the power of declaring war is vested in Congress by the Federal Constitution.

Decoration Day.—The custom of strewing flowers on the graves of their dead soldiers early in the spring of each year originated among the women of the South before the close of the Civil War. In some parts of the North a similar custom grew up, but its observance was not universal. May 5, 1868, while Gen. John A. Logan was commander-in-chief of the Grand Army of the Republic, he issued an order fixing the 30th day of May of that year as a day for the general observance of the custom by members of the Grand Army and their friends. Since that time May 30 had been regularly observed as Decoration Day throughout the country. It is known as Confederate Memorial Day in the South. The particular days observed there are April 26th in Alabama, Florida, Georgia and Mississippi, and May 10th in North Carolina and South Carolina, while Virginia observes May 30th and Louisiana May 3d (Jefferson Davis' birthday) under this title. In all states except Florida, Georgia, Idaho, Louisiana, Mississippi, North Carolina and South Carolina, Tennessee and Texas it is a legal holiday. Congress has by law declared Decoration Day a holiday in the District of Columbia and the territories.

Decoration Day. (See National Cemeteries.)

De Facto and De Jure.—These terms are generally used in connection with the holding of office. One who has actual possession of an office and exercises its functions is said to be an officer *de facto*, or in fact ; one who is entitled to an office, but does not actually fill it, is said to be an officer *de jure*, or by right. A *de facto* officer may hold his office without wrongful intent, though without legal sanction, as when there have been technical irregularities in the appointment, or

when the law under which he was appointed is afterward declared unconstitutional by the courts. The acts of a *de facto* incumbent are valid as respects third persons and the public generally if the officer holds his position by color of right (that is, with supposed authority based on reasonable grounds), if he holds it with some degree of notoriety, if he is actually in exercise of continuous official acts, or if he is in actual possession of a public office.

Defalcation of Public Officers:

Application of public money for private uses should be made a felony, 1709.

Freedom from, discussed, 5542, 5746.

Inquired into, 2918, 5800.

Defenses, Public (see also Forts and Fortifications):

Board to examine and report upon, appointed, 4899.

Correspondence regarding, referred to, 3261.

Council of, recommended, 7697.

Provision for, recommended by President—

Adams, John, 226, 243, 255, 270, 281, 297, 301.

Adams, J. Q., 955.

Arthur, 4638, 4724, 4767, 4798, 4833.

Cleveland, 5099, 5878, 5966, 6159.

Grant, 4202, 4271.

Harrison, Benj., 5476, 5550, 5631, 5755.

Hayes, 4571.

Jackson, 1411, 1433.

Jefferson, 373, 407, 416, 421, 447.

Lincoln, 3246.

McKinley, 6449.

Madison, 455, 471, 551.

Monroe, 763, 793.

Roosevelt, 7000, 7113, 7284.

Tyler, 1942, 1943, 1955, 2055.

(See also Navy, vessels for.)

Referred to, 245, 247, 266, 269, 283, 286, 301, 800, 1807.

Defensive Sea Areas.—In accordance with authority granted by acts of Congress, approved March 4, 1909, and March 4, 1917, President Wilson issued an executive order on April 5, 1917, establishing certain defensive sea areas, as follows : Mouth of the Kennebec River, Portland, Portsmouth, Boston, New Bedford, Newport, Long Island East, New York East, New York Main Entrance, Delaware River, Chesapeake Entrance, Baltimore, Potomac, Hampton Roads, Wilmington-Cape Fear, Charlestown, Savannah, Key West, Tampa, Pensacola, Mobile, Mississippi, Galveston, San Diego, San Francisco, Columbia River, Port Orchard, Honolulu, Manila, York River. Outer and inner limits for these areas were drawn and announced. The regulations pertaining to these areas were as follows :

A vessel desiring to cross a Defensive Area must proceed to the vicinity of the entrance to the proper channel, flying her national colors, and there await communication with the Harbor Entrance Board. When permission to enter is received, a vessel must proceed in accordance with the instructions received at the same time. Permission to enter a Defensive Area will be withheld from vessels other than public vessels of the United States between sunset and sunrise, and during weather conditions which make navigation difficult or dangerous. A vessel arriving off a Defensive Area after sunset shall anchor or lie-to at least a mile outside the limits of the area until the following sunrise; otherwise, it renders itself liable to be fired upon. No vessel shall proceed within the limits of a Defensive Sea Area at a speed greater than five knots.

Deficiency Bill. (See General Deficiency Bill.)

De Fuca Explorations. (See San Juan de Fuca Explorations.)

De Jure. (See De Facto and De Jure.)

Delagoa Bay.—The southernmost part of Portuguese East Africa. It is about 70 miles long and 20 miles across. Being partly enclosed by Inyack peninsula it affords the finest harbor on the east coast of Africa. In 1887 Colonel Macmurdo, an American, chartered a company and built a railroad from Lorenzo Marquez, on its shore, to the Transvaal frontier, which was extensively used for transporting gold from the interior. Upon the death of the concessioner the Portuguese government seized the road, and in 1890 the matter was referred to international arbitration. After ten years of litigation the Portuguese were ordered to pay an indemnity of $3,000,000. A British blockade of the port during the Boer war led to international complications.

Delagoa Bay Railway, seizure of, by Portuguese Government, 5470.

Claims regarding, submitted to arbitration, 5546, 6433.

Delaware.—One of the thirteen original states, and next to Rhode Island the smallest in the Union, its total area being 2,370 square miles, of which 405 square miles is water. Nickname, "The Diamond State"; motto, "Liberty and independence." It is bounded on the north by Pennsylvania, on the east by New Jersey and the Atlantic Ocean (Delaware River and Bay separating it from New Jersey), and on the south and west by Maryland. Delaware is essentially an agricultural State, 85 per cent of its land area being devoted to farming. The crops are corn, wheat and fruit. About 16,000 acres are devoted to raising tomatoes, the canning and shipping of which is a flourishing industry.

Delaware was originally settled by Swedes under Peter Minuit in 1638, passing under the rule of the Dutch in 1655, and of the English in 1664. In 1682 it was united with Pennsylvania. In 1703 it received a separate assembly, but had a governor in common with Pennsylvania until the Revolution. It was the first state to ratify the Federal Constitution, Dec. 7, 1787. Though a slave state, it remained in the Union throughout the Civil War. It is sometimes called the "Blue Hen State" and its citizens the "Blue Hen's Chickens." Its population in 1910 was 202,322.

Statistics of agriculture collected for the last Federal census place the number of farms in the State at 10,836, comprising 1,038,806 acres, valued with stock and improvements at $63,179,201. The value of domestic animals, poultry, etc., was $6,817,123, including 3,451,791 cattle, 764,133 mules, 337,910 swine, 36,898 sheep, and 876,081 fowls. The yield and value of field crops in 1911 was: corn, 195,000 acres, 6,630,000 bushels, $4,044,000; wheat, 113,-

000 acres, 1,887,000 bushels, $1,698,000; oats, 4,000 acres, 120,000 bushels, $56,-000; rye, 1,000 acres, 15,000 bushels, $14,-000; potatoes, 11,000 acres, 660,000 bushels, $634,000; hay, 72,000 acres, 63,000 tons, $1,418,000. The manufacturing statistics reported to the Federal Census Bureau in 1910 placed the number of establishments in the State at 726, capitalized at $60,906,000, and employing 23,984 persons. The largest number of men employed in any one industry are engaged in tanning leather. These numbered 3,045; machinery and iron casting gave employment to 2,210 wage-earners; paper and wood pulp-making to 1,525; canning and fruit preserving, 1,369; ship-building and the production of timber and lumber, 1,413.

Delaware:

Circuit court in, time of holding, 249.

Constitution of United States, evidence of ratification of amendment to, 65, 170.

Resolutions of general assembly of, transmitted, 65.

Delaware Bay, erection of piers near, recommended, 786.

Delaware Indians. (See Indian Tribes.)

Delaware River, canal from Chesapeake Bay to. (See Chesapeake and Delaware Canal Co.)

Delegate.—In politics, a person selected by voters of a political district to represent them in convention; or a person selected or appointed as a representative of a territory in the United States Legislature.

Delivery, City. (See City Delivery, Division of.)

Delivery, Rural. (See Division of Rural Delivery.)

Demagogue.—In usual parlance, an orator whose representations and promises are without integrity.

Democratic Party.—One of the fragments of the disrupted Democratic-Republican party. Andrew Jackson was the leader of the party and the first President elected.

The party favored internal improvements; State banks; removal of deposits from favored banks; a sub-treasury; State rights; free trade; tariff for revenue only; annexation of Texas; the Mexican war; the compromise of 1850; the Monroe Doctrine; the Dred Scott decision; fugitive slave law; acquisition of Cuba; frugal public expenditure. Opposed agitation of the slavery question in any form or place; coercion of the seceded states; Chinese immigration.

From the time of Jackson up to 1860 the Democrats by skillful party management won all the Presidential elections but two—those of 1840 and 1848. They adopted in general the tenets of the Democratic-Republican party (*q. v.*). They carried the country through the war with Mexico, annexed Texas and the Californias, and abolished the United States Bank. With the introduction of the slavery question into politics the party began to lose strength in the North. The Democratic party was always strongest in the South, however. In 1860 the party split into two factions and the Republicans won the election. Then came the Civil War, and though many Democrats supported Lincoln and the Union the party lost power and prestige in the North generally, and the Republicans remained in control until 1884, when war issues had been superseded in the minds of many by economic questions.

The party candidates in 1864 were George B. McClellan, of New Jersey, and George H. Pendleton, of Ohio ; in 1868, Horatio Seymour, of New York, and Francis P. Blair, of Missouri ; in 1872 the party in convention at Baltimore, July 1, ratified the nominations of the Liberal Republican party (*q. v.*) that had separated from the Republican party and named Horace Greeley, of New York, and B. Gratz Brown, of Missouri, as Presidential candidates. The minority held a convention at Louisville, Kentucky, and nominated Charles O'Conor, who declined. Greeley was unsuccessful. In 1874 the Democrats regained control of the House of Representatives, which they kept until 1880. In 1876 the candidates were Samuel J. Tilden, of New York, and Thomas A. Hendricks, of Indiana. The election was contested (see Electoral Commission), but finally settled in favor of the Republicans. In 1880 the nominees were Winfield S. Hancock, of Pennsylvania, and William S. English, of Indiana. In 1882 the Democrats regained control of the House, and in 1884 elected as their candidates, Grover Cleveland, of New York, and Thomas A. Hendricks, of Indiana, in a campaign made largely upon the personal character and "records" of the opposing candidates. The party was not in full control of the Government, however, as the Republicans held the majority in the Senate. In 1887, by his message to Congress, President Cleveland brought the tariff question to the front, and in 1888, the Democratic candidates, Grover Cleveland, of New York, and Allen G. Thurman, of Ohio, were defeated upon that issue. In that year the party lost control of the House as well. They regained control of the House in 1890, however, and in 1892 the party candidates, Grover Cleveland, of New York, and Adlai E. Stevenson, of Illinois, were elected. The party also gained control of the House and Senate. During this administration the Democrats repealed the Sherman silver purchase act (see Sherman Act), and passed the Gorman-Wilson tariff bill, with an income tax provision which was later declared unconstitutional. A political reaction began in 1893, helped by the commercial depression of that time, and the Democrats lost control of the House in 1894.

The strength of the radical free silver wing of the party now grew steadily, and in 1896 controlled the Chicago convention and nominated William J. Bryan, of Nebraska, and Arthur Sewall, of Maine, on a platform declaring for the free coinage of silver at the ratio of 16 to 1. This resulted in the formation of the National Democratic (Gold Democrats) party, opposed to free silver, which held a convention at Indianapolis and nominated John M. Palmer, of Illinois, and Simon B. Buckner, of Kentucky. This party received no electoral vote but had an important influence on the election by drawing votes from Bryan and Sewall. The nomination of the Democratic candidate was endorsed by the National Silver party, which was made up chiefly of silver Republicans, and Bryan was also nominated by the People's party (*q. v.*). The Democratic party was defeated, its popular vote being 6,509,052 and the electoral vote 176. The Democratic party supported the war measures of the Republican administration in the war with Spain, but disagreed with it as to the settlement of problems growing out of the war, particularly the question of the acquisition of the Philippines. In 1900 the Democrats declared "imperialism" to be the "paramount issue" and favored "an immediate declaration of the nation's purpose

to give the Filipinos : (1) a stable form of government; (2) independence; and (3) protection from outside interference." The question of the free coinage of silver also entered into this campaign inasmuch as the party ratified the Chicago platform of 1896, and nominated William J. Bryan for President, and Adlai E. Stevenson for Vice-President. The popular vote was 6,358,729 and the electoral vote 155.

In 1904 free silver was in abeyance and the Democratic candidate declared himself in favor of the gold standard. The party platform also declared in favor of a promise of future independence for the Filipinos, the reduction of the tariff, and restrictive measures in dealing with trusts. The party candidates were Alton B. Parker, of New York, and Henry G. Davis, of West Virginia, who were unsuccessful, the popular vote being 5,112,565, and the electoral vote 140. In 1908 the National Democratic convention was held in Denver, Colo., July 7 to 10, and nominated William Jennings Bryan, of Nebraska, for President, and John W. Kern, of Indiana, for Vice-President. The platform declared for publicity of campaign contributions, reduction of the tariff on the necessities of life and the admission, duty free, of articles competing with products controlled by trusts, internal improvements and conservation of natural resources, and the exclusion of such Asiatic immigrants as cannot become amalgamated with our population. The Democratic candidate for President received 6,393,182 votes against 7,637,676 for the Republican candidate. The electoral vote was 162 for the Democratic candidate to 321 for the Republican.

At the national convention in Baltimore, Md., June 25, 1912, they nominated Woodrow Wilson, governor of New Jersey, for President, and Governor Thomas R. Marshall, of Indiana, for Vice-President. A platform was adopted declaring in favor of a tariff for revenue only ; vigorous prosecutions of trusts ; popular election of senators ; presidential primaries ; an adequate navy ; revised banking laws ; inspection of food and the safeguarding of miners ; the full and free exercise by the State of their reserved sovereign rights ; income tax ; publicity of campaign expenses ; supervision and regulation of rates of railroad, express and telephone companies ; rural credits and improved waterways ; encouragement of merchant marine without bounties ; exemption from Panama Canal tolls of American ships engaged in coastwise trade, and forbidding the use of the canal to railroad owned ships in competitive trade ; and establishment of parcel post. (See Wilson.)

President Woodrow Wilson and Vice-President Thomas Riley Marshall were renominated, June 16, 1916, by the Democratic National Convention in session at St. Louis, Mo. President Wilson, by a vote of 1092 to 1. Delegate-at-Large, Robert Emmet Burk, of Chicago, casting the dissenting vote ; and Vice-President Marshall by acclamation.

The convention adopted the party platform exactly as approved by President Wilson and approved by the resolutions committee, including the plank on Americanism and that favoring woman suffrage.

The platform endorsed the Wilson Administration and called attention to the following achievements : Enactment of the Federal Reserve Act, creation of the Federal Trade Commission, adjustment of the tariff, protection of labor, increase in efficiency of the parcel post, enlargement of postal savings system, the placing of Post Office system on a self-supporting basis, with actual surplus in 1913, 1914 and 1916, and the enactment of legislation instituting economic reforms. The following planks were incorporated in the platform: The Underwood Tariff law was unreservedly endorsed, the doctrine of a tariff for the purpose of providing sufficient revenue for the operation of the government economically administered was reaffirmed and the proposed non-partisan tariff commission was cordially endorsed.

Americanism was declared to be the supreme issue of the day.

Democratic-Republican Party.—Individual liberty rather than strict government is a paramount sentiment in many American hearts. Those who originally looked with apprehension on the possibility of the central Government's encroachment upon the personal liberties of the people or the rights of States formed the nucleus of the National Democratic-Republican party.

The chief tenets of the party were succinctly set forth by Mr. Jefferson in his first inaugural address. These tenets he characterized as essential principles of our Government. His definition of the principles of the party is thus expressed: "Equal and exact justice to all men, of whatever state or persuasion, religious or political; peace, commerce, and honest friendship with all nations, entangling alliances with none; the support of the State governments in all their rights, as the most competent administrations for our domestic concerns and the surest bulwarks against anti-republican tendencies; the preservation of the General Government in its whole constitutional vigor, as the sheet anchor of our peace at home and safety abroad; a jealous care of the right of election by the people—a mild and safe corrective of abuses which are lopped by the sword of revolution where peaceable remedies are unprovided; absolute acquiescence in the decisions of the majority, the vital principles of republics, from which is no appeal but to force, the vital principle and immediate parent of despotism; a well-disciplined militia, our best reliance in peace, and for the first moments of war, till regulars may relieve them; the supremacy of the civil over the military authority; economy in the public expense, that labor may be lightly burthened; the honest payment of our debts and sacred preservation of the public faith; encouragement of agriculture, and of commerce as its handmaid; the diffusion of information and arraignment of all abuses at the bar of public reason; freedom of religion; freedom of the press, and freedom of person under the protection of the *habeas corpus*, and trial by juries impartially selected" (page 311).

Sympathy with the French revolutionists in 1789 and a desire that the Government should aid France in her war with England drew a number of disciples to the party entertaining these sentiments. Under the leadership of Thomas Jefferson the party took the name of Democratic-Republican and opposed the Federalists. After Monroe's time it was commonly known as the Democratic party, though previously it had been known as the Republican party. From its inception in 1792 to 1801 it was the party of opposition. When the party got control of the Government it lost sight of some of its tenets, and many of its members at certain times supported measures tending toward nationalization. After the War of 1812 the Democrats had a clear field of operations until the second election of Monroe in 1820. Subsequently dissensions began to appear. Adams and Clay and their followers advocated protection, national aid to internal improvements, and a broader construction of the Constitution. The party split in the

campaign of 1824, and never after appeared in a national campaign.

Demonetization.—The act of depriving money of its official standard value, whether by direct order of the governing power or by such legislation as would logically bring about the same result; for example, the gold standard advocates believed that the success of the Sixteen to One propaganda in 1896 would amount to the demonetization of gold.

Demun and Chouteau, depredations committed on property of, by Mexicans, 1448.

Denationalize.—To take away the national character or meaning; as in the case of confining a practice to states or localities.

Denatured Alcohol:
Use of, recommended, 7224.

Denmark.—The Kingdom of Denmark consists of a portion of the European mainland and of a neighboring archipelago, with the detached island of Bornholm in the Baltic, and the Faeroes (or Sheep Islands) in the North Atlantic. Its dependencies are Iceland in the Arctic Ocean, Greenland, and the West Indian Islands of St. Thomas, St. John and St. Croix. The continental portion, or Jutland, occupying the northern extremity of the Cimbrian Peninsula, forms two-thirds of the total area. The northern extremity is The Skaw (Skagen) in 57° 45' N. latitude, the southern boundary adjoining the German territory of Schleswig-Holstein. The coast is washed on the west by the North Sea, on the north by the Skaggerack and on the east by the Kattegat.

The archipelago lies to the east of Jutland, and consists of three main groups (a) Fünen, with Langeland, Ærö and Taasinge; (b) Zealand (or Sjaelland) with Moën, Falster, Laaland, Samsö, Amager and Saltholm; and (c) Bornholm. Detached from the main groups are Laesö and Anholt, off the eastern coast of northern Jutland. The mainland and the archipelago lie between 54° 33'-57° 45' N. latitude and 8° 4' 54"-12° 47' 25" E. longitude, to which must be added Bornholm, which lies across 15° E. and between 55°-55° 18' N. and the Faeroes, a group of 21 islands in the North Sea between Iceland and the Shetlands clustering round the intersection of 7° E. and 62° N.

Physical Features.—The mainland and all the islands of the archipelago are low lying, the highest point being Bavnehoi (565 feet) in Randers and the Himmelbjerg (560 feet) in the Aarhus province of eastern Jutland. In 1825 the North Sea burst through the western coast between the amter of Thisted and Ringkjobing, and the northern provinces of Thisted and Hjorring are thus insular, detached from the remainder of Jutland by a succession of fjords from the North Sea to the Kattegat.

AREA AND POPULATION

Territories	Area in English Sq. Miles	Population 1911
Kingdom of Denmark.....	15,042	2,757,076
Faeroes or Sheep Islands.	539	18,000
Iceland..	40,448	85,089
Greenland................	50,000	12,968
West Indies..............	138	27,086
	106,167	2,901,219

History.—The ancient Kingdom of Denmark was at the head of the tripartite League of Kolmar (Denmark, Norway and Sweden) from 1397-1448, in which year the death of King Christopher III. led to the election of Count Christian of Oldenburg as King Christian I. of Denmark and Norway, while Sweden seceded from the league. In 1814 Norway became an independent kingdom in union with Sweden. From 1448-1863 the crown was in fact hereditary in the male line of the House of Oldenburg, the hereditary principle becoming recognized by the legislature in 1660. At the death of Frederik VII. without male heirs, in 1863, the Crown fell to Prince Christian of Schleswig-Holstein-Sonderburg-Glücksburg under the terms of a previous convention with the Powers, ratified by Denmark on Jan. 28, 1852. The exclusion by the Salic Law of Duke Christian of Sonderburg Augustenburg from the duchies of Schleswig and Holstein, which formed part of the kingdom of Denmark, led to the intervention of Austria and Prussia, and to a gallant but hopeless struggle against the overwhelming power of Prussia. The Prusso-Danish war of 1864 deprived Denmark of the two duchies, which now form part of the Kingdom of Prussia.

Government.—The government is that of a constitutional monarchy under a statute which received the royal sanction on July 28, 1866. King of Denmark (of the Wends and of the Goths) Christian X. (Christian Charles Frederick Albert Alexander William), born at Charlottenlund, Sept. 26, 1870.

The executive is vested in the Sovereign, aided by a Council of State (Statsraad), which includes all the Ministers.

The Rigsdag consists of two houses, the Landsting and the Folketing, and meets in annual session. The Landsting consists of sixty-six members, of whom twelve are nominated for life by the Sovereign, and fifty-four elected by indirect vote for eight years and renewed as to one-half every four years (seven are elected by the Capital, forty-five by electoral districts, one by the island of Bornholm and one by the Faeroes). The Folketing consists of 114 members (one per 21,000 inhabitants), elected by direct vote for three years.

The Kingdom is divided into eighteen counties (Amter), each Amt being under an Amtmann or Civil Administrator, with elective County Councils (Amstraad) and Parish Councils for local affairs. Municipalities have Burgomasters appointed by the Sovereign (except in the capital where the Burgomaster is elective) with elective Municipal Councils.

Justice is administered in hundred-courts for each hundred (herred), or group of hundreds, under a Justice. There is a Supreme Court at Copenhagen, where also there is a Court of Commerce and Navigation. Prospective litigants are first heard by "Committees of Conciliation" which endeavor to compose matters in dispute without recourse to the Courts of Law, and more than half of the cases are thus settled.

Army.—Service in the National Militia is compulsory and universal for all able-bodied Danes between the years twenty and thirty-six. Peace Effective 13,000 of all ranks, but at certain times of the year 75,000 men are under arms. (See Armies of the World. For Navy see Navies of the World.)

Education.—The educational system is thorough and effective. Primary Education is compulsory and free from seven to fourteen years and the schools (maintained by local taxation) are extremely well attended. Copenhagen University, founded in 1479, and rebuilt in 1836, is attended by over 2,000 students and possesses a library of 200,000 volumes, an observatory and botanical garden.

Production and Industry.—Two-fifths of the population are employed in agriculture and pastoral industries. Of the total area (9,470,000 acres) there were (in 1907) 7,000,000 acres under crops and grass, and 800,000 acres of woods and plantations.

The industrial population is closely organized and trade unions had a membership in 1910 of close on 150,000, while industrial disputes are frequent. The principal industries are those of marine engineering and shipbuilding; woolens, cottons and linen; sugar refineries; paper mills; and brewing and distilling. The State and private porcelain factories from the deposits of porcelain clay are important.

Railways.—There were (1911) 2,135 miles of railway open, of which 1,212 were state owned and 923 private lines.

Shipping.—The mercantile marine consisted in 1911 of 553 steamers of 671,828 gross tons and 310 sailing vessels of 64,734 net tons. In 1911 Danish vessels carrying 2,101,407 tons of merchandise, and foreign vessels carrying 1,661,639 tons entered at Danish ports.

Cities.—Capital, Copenhagen (in the Island of Zealand). Population (1911) 462,161 (including suburbs, 560,000). The urban population is less than 35 per cent. of total of the Kingdom. There were in 1911 six cities with populations exceeding 20,000, and nine others exceeding 10,000.

The Metric System of Weights and Measures is compulsory. The Unit of Currency is the Krone of 100 Ore. The gold coins are 20 and 10 kroner pieces; silver, 2 kroner, 1 krone and 25 and 10 öre; copper, 5, 2 and 1 öre. The krone is equivalent to 26 4/5 cents United States money.

THE FAEROES or Sheep Islands are an integral part of the Kingdom of Denmark. The group consists of twenty-one islands in the North Sea between Iceland and the Shetland Islands, clustering round the intersection of 7° E. longitude, and 62° N. latitude. The islands have belonged to Denmark since 1386 and form a county (Amt) of the kingdom, sending a representative to each house of the Rigsdag at Copenhagen.

ICELAND is a large volcanic and treeless island in the North Atlantic, partly within the Arctic Circle. The island consists of two elevated table-lands, connected by a narrow isthmus, and contains over 100 volcanoes, some of which are still active, the largest being Askja, with a crater thirty-four sq. miles in extent, the most famous Hekla, in the Laki chain, and the highest Oeraefajökull, 6,424 feet above sea level. Iceland was a republic from 930 to 1262 and was afterwards under Norwegian rule for many years, until the establishment of the League of Kalmar (see Denmark, History) brought the island under the Danish crown, in the year 1397. The government now rests upon the constitution granted in 1874.

GREENLAND is a vast island-continent, largely within the Arctic Circle, with smaller islands to the north, with a total length of nearly 1,700 miles and an extreme breadth of about 800 miles. The total area is believed to exceed 830,000 square miles, of which the ice-free portion of about 50,000 square miles belongs to Denmark, the trade being a monopoly of the Danish crown. The inhabitants numbered 12,968 in 1911, of whom about 300 were Europeans, the remainder being Eskimos. The principal settlement is Godthaab, on the west coast, and there are about sixty others on the west and south-east coast. The principal exports are seal oil, skins and furs, and fishery products, the imports are breadstuffs and clothing, the import of spirits being prohibited.

Trade with the United States.—The value of merchandise imported into Denmark from the United States for the year 1913 was $18,687,794, and goods to the value of $2,974,670 were sent thither—a balance of $15,713,124 in favor of the United States.

Denmark:

Cession of St. Thomas and St. John Islands to United States, treaty regarding, 3777, 3779, 3796, 3886.

Claims of, against United States, 344, 365, 634.

Claims of United States against, 469, 867, 909, 976, 1008, 1044, 1068, 1109, 1157, 1243, 2173, 4462, 5369.

Agreement to submit, to arbitration, 5388.

Award of arbitrator, 5545.

Payment of, 976, 1008, 1068, 1112, 1157, 1243.

Commercial relations with, 1094, 1244, 2812, 2944.

Consuls of United States in, 90, 109.

Convention with, 3996.

Convicts in, banished to United States, 3835.

Copyright privilege extended, by proclamation, 5827.

Referred to, 5874.

Fugitive criminals, failure to negotiate convention with, for surrender of, 4561.

Importation of American products into, degrees placing restrictions upon, 6100.

Minister of, to United States, grade of, raised, 4718.

Naturalization treaty with, 4160, 4193.

Payment of claims of the United States against, 976, 1008, 1068, 1112, 1157, 1243.

Sound dues, treaty regarding, 2867, 2994, 3001.

Treaty with, transmitted and discussed by President—
Adams, J. Q., 911, 919.
Buchanan, 2994, 3001.
Grant, 3996.
Jackson, 1044, 1093, 1137.
Johnson, 3779, 3891.
Ratification of, by Denmark, 3819.

Vessels of, captured by American ships and claims based thereon, 3271.

Vessels of United States—
Seized or interfered with by, 5388.
Tolls levied on, discussed, 2812, 2867, 2944.

Denmark, Treaties with.—The convention of friendship, commerce, and navigation of 1826, containing the most favored-nation clause and permitting freedom of trade and equality as to shipping was abrogated by notice April 15, 1856, and renewed April 11, 1857, except as to sound and belt dues, which were expressly discontinued as to United States vessels from the date of the latter treaty. A claims convention was concluded in 1830 and a Consular convention in 1861. A naturalization treaty was proclaimed in 1873, and trade-mark and copyright privileges were exchanged in 1892 and 1893 respectively. The extradition treaty of 1902 was supplemented by a treaty signed in 1905, extending its provisions to the island possessions of the contracting parties and including the crime of bribery. An agreement was effected by an exchange of notes of June 22 and June 26, 1906, with respect to the protection of industrial designs or models; and the protection of trade-marks in China was effected in the same manner in 1907. International arbitration was agreed to May 18, 1908.

Department of Agriculture. (See Agriculture, Department of.)

Department of Commerce. (See Commerce, Department of.)

Department of the Interior. (See Interior, Department of.)

Department of Justice. (See Justice, Department of.)

Department of Labor. (See Labor, Department of.)

Department of Navy. (See Navy, Department of.)

Department of Post-Office. (See Post-Office, Department of.)

Department of State. (See State, Department of.)

Department of Treasury. (See Treasury, Department of.)

Department of War. (See War, Department of.)

Departmental Solicitors. (See Solicitors, Departmental.)

Dependencies (Insular):
Porto Rico and Philippines discussed, 6720, 6799, 6928, 7017, 7051, 7232, 7299, 7301, 7374, 8110.

Dependent-Pension Law discussed, 5552, 5762, 5883, 5977.

Deportation.—The act of sending a foreigner out of the country because of his undesirability or unfitness.

Deposits, Public, Removal of.—In 1833 and prior thereto, the public funds of the Government were deposited in the Bank of the United States. President Jackson determined to discontinue this practice and to deposit the funds collected in state banks, while those in the Bank of the United States should be withdrawn as needed. William J. Duane, the Secretary of the Treasury, was opposed to the removal of the funds, particularly before the meeting of Congress. After fruitless effort to have him change his opinion on the subject, the President requested his resignation. It was given, and on the same day, Sept. 23, 1833, Roger B. Taney, the Attorney-General, was appointed Secretary of the Treasury. He promptly made the necessary orders. The Senate passed a resolution of censure of the President and also rejected the nomination of Mr. Taney as Secretary of the Treasury. In a paper which he read to his Cabinet the President gave his reasons for removing the Government funds from the Bank of the United States, 1224.

Deposits, Public, Removal of:
President Jackson's paper to Cabinet on, 1224.
Refuses to transmit to Senate, 1255.
Recommended, 1163, 1236.
Referred to, 1386.
Views of President Tyler on, 1897.

Depredations on Commerce. (See the several powers, claims against.)

Derne Expedition.—Gen. William Eaton, United States consul at Tunis, in 1805, espoused the cause of Hamet, Pasha of Tripoli, against the latter's usurping brother. With the co-operation of the United States naval forces in the Mediterranean, they defeated the usurper at Derne April 27, 1805. After this success a treaty highly favorable to the United States was negotiated with the Pasha.

Desert Lands. (See Lands, Desert.)

Desert State.—Alternative nickname for Utah. (See Mormon State.)

Desertion.—The act of leaving service, especially in the Army or Navy, without honorable discharge.

Desertion, from Army and Navy, 6684.

Des Moines Rapids, act for continuing improvement of, vetoed, 2921.

Des Moines River, acts to quiet title of settlers on lands on, vetoed, 4996, 5412.

Detention Camp.—In military usage, an enclosed or guarded space for the detention by one government of subjects of, or sympathizers with, another government in time of war.

Detroit, The, mentioned, 6365.

Detroit, Mich.:
Civil authority over, recommended, 190.
Lands—
Ceded for post of, 421, 426.
Lying near, referred to, 355.
Memorials for district of, 430.
Town and fort of, surrendered to the British, 500.
Recovery of, referred to, 524.

Detroit (Mich.), Surrender of.—In August, 1812, Col. Proctor, in command of the British troops in Canada, was joined by Gen. Brock with a body of militia and some Indians under Tecumseh. The forces at Sandwich amounted to 1,330 men, 600 of whom were Indians. Gen. Hull, in command at Fort Detroit, on the opposite side of the river, had 1,000 men available for duty. Aug. 16 the British sent a party of Indians and regulars across the river to assault the works. Hull surrendered the fort and the whole territory of Michigan, of which he was governor, without the discharge of a gun. About 2,000 men in all became prisoners of war. During tue firing by the British 7 Americans were killed and several wounded. Gen. Hull was afterwards convicted of cowardice by a court-martial and condemned to death, but was pardoned by President Madison in consideration of his age and his services in the Revolutionary War. Subsequent investigations greatly modified the blame attached to Gen. Hull.

Deutschland.—The first German submarine to cross the Atlantic Ocean. In July, 1916, it arrived at Baltimore after a trip of sixteen days from Bremen. The *Deutschland* officers claimed to have traveled only ninety miles of the trip under water, although one whole night was spent motionless on the bottom of the ocean because of rough weather. The vessel was strictly a merchant ship, carrying a load of dye-stuffs to the United States, and was not armed in any fashion. It was 315 feet long, with a beam of thirty feet. Its engines were oil-burning, and it had enough oil unused after docking in Baltimore to carry it back to Germany. Of a tonnage of 791, its speed on the surface was 14 knots and under the surface 7 knots. It was submergible to a depth of 300 feet and could remain under the water for four days. A supposed sister-submarine, the *Bremen*, never completed its predicted voyage to America, although the *Deutschland* returned for a second trip, docking at New London, Connecticut. (See Submarines, and illustration opposite 8112.)

Devils Lake Reservation, N. Dak., right of way for railroad through bill for, 4952, 5177.

Diamond State.—Nickname for Delaware (q. v.), (See also States); sometimes also nicknamed the Blue Hen State.

Dime.—The smallest piece of silver now coined by the United States. In value it is the tenth part of a dollar. The word is taken from the French dixième, one-tenth, and was spelled "disme" on some of the first coins. Authorized in 1792 with a weight of 41.6 grains, it was afterwards (in 1853) reduced to 38.4 grains. The first dimes were issued in 1796.

Dingley Tariff Act.—The tariff act passed in 1897. (See Tariff.)

Dingley Tariff Act, revision of, recommended, 7379, 7393, 7395.

Diplomatic Agents. (See Consuls; Ministers.)

Diplomatic and Consular Service.—The officers of the foreign service of the United States are divided into two branches, diplomatic and consular. Ambassadors—The former, called in general ambassadors, diplomatic agents, includes envoys extraordinary, ministers plenipotentiary, ministers resident and secretaries of legation. The first may be appointed for special purposes, but the title is usually added to that of ministers plenipotentiary. These ambassadors have the right to negotiate treaties and generally to represent our government in the state to which they are sent. They are sent only to great nations. Ministers resident are accredited to less important nations, but their powers are about the same as those of ministers plenipotentiary. Secretaries of legation are appointed to assist principal ambassadors.

Ambassadors extraordinary and plenipotentiary are now sent to Argentina, Austria-Hungary, Brazil, Chile, France, Germany, Great Britain, Italy, Japan, Mexico, Russia, Spain and Turkey with salaries of $17,500.

Envoys extraordinary and ministers plenipotentiary are sent to Belgium, Bolivia, Bulgaria, China, Colombia, Costa Rica, Cuba, Denmark, Dominican Republic, Ecuador, Greece, Guatemala, Hayti, Honduras, Luxemburg, Montenegro, Morocco, Netherlands, Nicaragua, Norway, Panama, Paraguay, Persia, Peru, Portugal, Rumania, Salvador, Servia, Siam, Sweden, Switzerland, Uruguay, and Venezuela, with salaries ranging from $10,000 to $12,000.

There are five consuls-general at large, with salaries of $5,000 each.

Consuls.—Consular officers include consuls-general, consuls and commercial agents. Their chief duties and powers are connected with our commercial interests, to protect ships, seamen and other Americans, to send home destitute seamen, and to give certificates for various purposes. They are sent to the principal ports or markets of a country. Some diplomatic powers also attach to their office, and in non-Christian countries they have sometimes the right, by treaty, to act in a judicial capacity between citizens of the United States.

A consul-general has jurisdiction over several consuls. Commercial agents are accredited to smaller places. The various diplomatic and consular officers are appointed by the President and confirmed by the Senate. The highest salary is $17,500, paid to ambassadors to great powers and the lowest is $2,000, paid to consuls at unimportant ports. Officers of the foreign service are under the control and direction of the State Department.

Diplomatic Appointments, State Department.

—The Bureau of Appointments in the Department of State has charge over applications, examinations, and appointments to the diplomatic service. It issues and files extradition warrants, and also has custody of the Great Seal of United States. It is controlled by both the assistant and the third assistant secretary of state. (See State Department; Seal of United States; Diplomatic Service.)

Diplomatic Bureau, State Department.

—This bureau was organized by the President on August 29, 1833, on the recommendation of Secretary of State McLane. It has administration over the diplomatic service at large—its staffs, the ceremonies attending the making of treaties, the preparation of diplomatic correspondence with foreign governments, and other miscellaneous matters of diplomatic importance. Together with the Consular Bureau (q. v.), it is the oldest bureau in the Department of State, and it is under the supervision of the second assistant secretary of state (q. v.). (See State Department.)

Diplomatic Negotiations, Breaking of.

—In the history of the United States, severance of diplomatic relations has always been followed by war, although not always directly. In the summer of 1796, France suspended the functions of her minister to the United States, although he remained in the country to observe conditions. Pinckney succeeded Munroe as minister to France in December, 1796, but the French Government refused to receive him, and he obeyed a hint to return to his country in February, 1797. The first actual conflict between the two countries occurred in February, 1799. In 1809, the English minister to the United States was told that no further communication would be received from him by the United States Government. His successor was appointed later, and did not return to England until after war had formally been declared. In the meantime, the American minister to England, Pinckney, had left England in 1811. In the war with Mexico, the Mexican minister demanded his passports on March 6, 1845, and the American minister to Mexico was informed that diplomatic negotiations were at an end on March 28, 1845. War was declared on May 12, 1846. In the war with Spain, the Spanish and American ministers did not leave their respective posts until after war had formally been declared on April 19, 1898. On Feb. 2, 1917, Ambassador von Bernstorff from Germany was handed his passports, and the American ambassador, Gerard, was ordered at the same time to apply for his passports from Germany, although it was not until April 6, 1917, that war was formally announced. With respect to the difficulties with Mexico beginning in the early days of Wilson's first administration, diplomatic negotiations were never severed, although they did not remain dignified by the presence of ambassadors themselves in Washington and Mexico City.

Diplomatic Service. (See Consular and Diplomatic Service.)

Direct Election of U. S. Senators.

—A joint resolution providing for the direct election of senators was introduced in the second session of the Sixty-first Congress. It passed the House, but on Feb. 28, 1911, was defeated in the Senate by four votes. The joint resolution was reintroduced in the first session of the Sixty-second Congress, and on April 14, 1911, it passed the House of Representatives by a vote of 296 to 16. On June 12th the Senate passed the resolution with an amendment placing the control of federal elections under state government. The bill was then sent to a conference committee whence it had not emerged when Congress adjourned, so that it failed to become law. In several states, notably California, Kansas, Minnesota, Montana, New Jersey, Ohio and Wisconsin, the legislatures enacted laws providing for the Oregon plan of pledging candidates to the legislature to vote for the people's choice for United States Senators, as indicated in the general primary election to be held previously.

This method of expressing a choice for United States Senators was unsatisfactory, as it was not general and also because members of state legislatures were not bound by such expression of preference, and looked upon the vote merely as a recommendation, which they were at liberty to follow or disregard at pleasure.

The Sixty-second Congress, at its second session, adopted a joint resolution proposing an amendment to the constitution, making the election of United States Senators by direct vote of the people compulsory. This was ratified by a sufficient number of states (36) and declared in force May 31, 1913, being the seventeenth amendment to the Constitution.

Direct Nominations of Presidential Candidates. (See Presidential Primaries.)

Direct Taxes. (See Taxation; Taxes.)

Director of Bureau of Engraving and Printing. (See Engraving and Printing, Bureau of.)

Director of the Consular Service, Department of State.

—This office was created in 1910, and carries a yearly salary of $4,500. The director of the consular service is ranked after the counselor and assistant secretary of state, along with the second and third assistant secretaries of state and the solicitor to the department. He has charge of the Consular Bureau (q. v.), Consular Appointments (q. v.), the Emergency Fund, and Trade Information and Publicity (q. v.). (See Consular Service; State Department.)

Director of the Mint. (See Mint.)

Disability-Pension Act discussed, 5552, 5762, 5883, 5977.

Disarmament. (See Arbitration (International) and Disarmament.)

Discretionary Powers of President. (See Executive Nominations; President; Removing from Office.)

Discriminating Duties. (See Vessels, Foreign tonnage on.)

Diseases, Contagious. (See Cholera; Contagious Diseases; International Sanitary Conference; Plague; Quarantine Regulations; Yellow Fever.)

Diseases of Animals. (See Animals and Animal Products.)

Dispatch-Boat.—A vessel used for transporting communications.

Distilled Spirits (see also Liquors):
Sale of, in Siam by Americans, 4170.
Sale of, to Indians, recommendations regarding, 322, 6167.
Sale of, in Manila, information concerning transmitted, 6413.
Tax on—Discussed by President—
Arthur, 4723, 4765, 4831.
Harrison, Benj., 5474.
Washington, 91, 97, 104, 119, 122, 123, 125, 126, 142.
Division of United States into districts for collection of, 91, 97, 104, 126.
Laws for raising. (See Revenue, Public.)
Removal of, on spirits used in arts and manufactures discussed, 5474.

District.—A name applied in the United States to those portions of territory which are without elective or representative institutions—for instance, the District of Columbia. South Carolina counties were formerly called districts. From 1804 to 1812 that portion of the Louisiana purchase lying north of the northern boundary of the present state was called the District of Louisiana. Before their admission as states Kentucky and Maine were called districts, respectively of Virginia and Massachusetts. The name "district" is also applied to those divisions of a state grouping certain counties or wards into separate Congressional districts for the election of Representatives in Congress.

District Attorneys. (See Attorneys, District.)

District Courts. (See Courts, Federal.)

District of Columbia.—Congress is authorized by the Constitution to "exercise exclusive legislation in all cases whatsoever over such district (not exceeding ten miles square) as may, by cession of particular states and the acceptance of Congress, become the seat of the Government of the United States." July 16, 1790, after a long and bitter discussion, a district ten miles square lying on both sides of the Potomac River was selected. Maryland ceded sixty-four square miles on the north bank of the river and Virginia thirty-six square miles on the south bank. The District was first called the Territory of Columbia. The seat of Government was removed thither by 1800. July 9, 1846, the portion south of the Potomac was ceded back to Virginia. For a time the superintendence of the

District of Columbia was in the hands of three commissioners, but in 1802 Washington was incorporated and its government was placed in the hands of the people, with a president and a council, the former appointed by the President. In 1820 a mayor, to be elected by the people, was substituted for the president. From 1871 to 1874 the District had a Territorial government, the upper house and the governor being appointed by the President and the lower house selected by the people. This was found to be unsatisfactory, and in 1874, Congress provided for a board of three commissioners to take charge of all matters pertaining to the District government.

June 11, 1878, Congress provided for a permanent government, consisting of three commissioners, two to be appointed from civil life by the President, the third to be detailed from the officers of the Engineer Corps of the Army. The area is sixty-four square miles, practically all included in the City of Washington; population (1910), 331,069, of whom about 97,000 were negroes. The value of the property in the district was estimated in 1911 at $1,250,-000,000, of which about one-fourth was personal property, and three-fourths real estate.

Commissioners—Oliver P. Newman and Frederick L. Siddons (Democrats), whose terms expire July 19, 1916, and Lieut.-Col. Chester Harding (non-partisan), Corps of Engineers, United States Army, detailed during the pleasure of the President of the United States; Secretary, William Tindall. Offices of Commissioners, District Building, Washington, D. C.

Judiciary—Court of Appeals: Chief Justice, Seth Shepard; Associate Justices, Charles H. Robb, J. A. Van Orsdel. Supreme Court: Chief Justice, Harry M. Clabaugh; Associate Justices, Job Barnard, Thomas H. Anderson, Ashley M. Gould, Daniel T. Wright, Wendell P. Stafford.

District of Columbia (see also Washington City):
Act—
Fixing rate of interest on arrearages of taxes due in, returned, 5502.
For promotion of anatomical science and to prevent desecration of graves vetoed, 4998.
Prescribing times for sales and for notice of sales of property in, for taxes returned, 5212.
Prohibiting bookmaking and pool selling in, vetoed, 5528.
Referred to, 5551.
Providing for recording deeds, etc., in, vetoed, 4335.
Respecting circulation of bank notes in, vetoed, 3288.
To abolish board of commissioners of police, in, etc., vetoed, 4384.
To authorize reassessment of water-main taxes or assessments in, returned, 6102.
To pay moneys collected under direct tax of 1861 to States, Territories, and, vetoed, 5422.
To punish unlawful appropriation of property of another in, returned, 5672.

To regulate elective franchise in, vetoed, 3670.

To regulate practice of medicine and surgery in, etc., returned, 6102.

Appropriation for, recommended, 4108.

Armory of—
Damages to be incurred by repealing act providing for construction of, referred to, 2901.
Location of, referred to, 2911.
Site for, selected, 2899.

Benevolent institutions in, deserve attention of Congress, 3388, 3452, 4459, 4579, 5385.

Board of public works in, report of, referred to, 4119.
Work accomplished by, 4208.

Bonded indebtedness of, discussed and recommendations regarding, 4221.
Report on, 4256.

Boundaries of, referred to and proclaimed, 86, 92, 94.

Bridge over Rock Creek, construction of, referred to, 1844.

Bridges over Potomac River in, construction and repair of, discussed, 1171, 1257, 2710, 4638, 4679, 5114.
Injuries sustained by, referred to, 1448.

Buildings for offices of, recommended, 4578, 4840, 4950, 5114.

Buildings, public, in, construction of, referred to, 182.

Ceded to Congress for permanent seat of Government, 92.

Congress assembled in, 261, 295, 298.

Contagious diseases, provisions against, recommended, 854.

Courts of—
Appeals from, to Supreme Court, recommendations regarding, 4939, 5103.
Minister of Netherlands refuses to testify in, 2952.
Supreme Court, selection and service of jurors in, bill regarding, returned, 5396.

Crimes against chastity in, inadequacy of laws relating to, 5633.

Debt of, discussed, 4429.

Delegate in Congress to represent, recommended, 1091, 1120, 3652.

Depression in pecuniary concerns of, 1396.

Deputy marshals, bailiffs, etc., in, compensation to, referred to, 3664.

Distribution of arms, ordnance, stores, etc., to Territories and, regulations regarding, 5159, 5462.

Electric wires in, report of board to consider location, etc., of, transmitted, 5647.

Government of, discussed, 295, 298, 300, 1091, 1120, 1612, 4257.
Referred to, 4372.
Territorial government in, discussed, 4108, 4158.

Improvements to streets in, recommendations regarding, 4950.

Insane asylum in—
Appropriation for, 2708.
Construction of, discussed, 2750.
Erection of, recommended, 1621, 2204.
Estimate for deficiency appropriation for, 4677.

Institution of learning for, recommended, 4208.

Interests of, discussed by President—
Arthur, 4734, 4773, 4840.
Buchanan, 2994, 3060, 3107, 3184.
Cleveland, 4950, 5113, 5384.
Fillmore, 2628, 2673, 2710.
Grant, 4208, 4257.
Harrison, Benj., 5487.
Hayes, 4429, 4459, 4532, 4579.
Lincoln, 3254, 3452.
Pierce, 2825, 2873, 2943.
Polk, 2265.
Taylor, 2561.
Tyler, 1903, 1942, 2124, 2204.
Van Buren, 1612, 1720.

Laws of—
Commissioners appointed to revise and codify, 2873.
Proclamation fixing time and place of election for voting on adoption of code, 3021.
Referred to, 3014.
Revision of civil and criminal code recommended, 4840.
Revision of, necessary, 1396, 1478, 1492, 1611, 5114, 5384, 5633, 6943.
Statute of limitations for crimes should not be limited to 2 years, 1168.
Want of uniformity in, 1091.

Laws of adjoining States applicable to, insufficient, 326.

Legislation in, power of, should be taken from Congress and vested in people, 616.

Liberal spirit of Congress in relation to, 2750.

Liquors, amendment of laws regulating sale of, etc., in, recommended, 4950, 5114, 5385, 5487, 5766.

Military governor of. (See Wadsworth, James S.)

National celebration of the centennial anniversary, 6347, 6404, 6456.

Penitentiary in—
Compensation to inspectors of; referred to, 1036, 1091, 1495.
Completion of, referred to, 1091.
To be erected, 930.

Plan of, referred to, 105.

Police regulations of, recommendations that Commissioners be clothed with power to make, 5114.

Police system for, recommended, 1942.

Political rights to citizens of, extension of, recommended, 1396.

Prisoners in, provision for, recommended, 326.

Public schools in, aid for, recommended, 4430, 4532, 4578.

Discriminations against District in donation of lands for support of, 4459.

Referred to, 98, 182.

Reform school for girls in, construction of, recommended, 5632.

Reform school in, supply of blankets for, discussed, 4371.

Relinquishment of portion of, to Virginia discussed and recommendation that it be regained, 3252.

Commissioners appointed on affairs of, 4256.

Reservations in, appropriations for, recommended, 4430.

Seat of government—

Boundaries of, referred to and proclaimed, 86, 92, 94.

Removed from Philadelphia to Washington, 281, 295, 298, 299, 300.

Sewerage system of, committee to report upon, appointed, 5487.

Report of, transmitted, 5514.

Slavery in, abolished, 3274.

Steam railway lines—

Concentrating upon Washington, construction of, urged, 3351.

Controversies regarding occupation of streets by, 4950, 5114, 5385.

Recommendations regarding location of depots and tracks, 4459, 4579, 4651, 4734.

Street railroad companies in, report of board on amount chargeable to, referred to, 4273.

Survey of, commissioners directed to make, 86, 94.

Report of, referred to, 128.

Taxes in, remitted by Congress should be charged to National Treasury, 4806.

Disunionist.—A person who favored secession during the Civil War.

Division of Accounts and Disbursements. (See Accounts and Disbursements, Division of.)

Division of Dead Letters, Post-Office Department.—"Dead letters" is a generic term used to cover all pieces of mail matter which cannot be directly delivered because of faulty directions. Provision for handling such mail matter was begun in 1825. In 1916, 10,839,890 pieces were turned into this division, of which 3,667,194 were delivered, 111,485 were filed, 7,091,436 were destroyed, and 41,775 reserved for later

treatment. Checks, drafts, money orders and other valuable paper found inside "dead letters" and returned to their owners in 1916 amounted to $2,303,119.56. Under certain conditions, undeliverable merchandise is sold, and undeliverable currency is removed from letters turned into this division. Letters which have been advertised are obtainable only at an additional premium of one cent each, from which and other sources there was obtained in 1916 $64,665.69, making the division of dead letters almost self-supporting. An act of July 28, 1916 reduces the time during which letters with valuable enclosures must be held from the previous requirement of 4 years to 1 year. (See Post-Office Department; Postal Service.)

Division of Finance, Post-Office Department.—This division is under the supervision of the third assistant postmaster-general (q. v.). For the fiscal year ending June 30, 1916, the receipts of the Post-Office Department were $312,057,688.83, and the expenditures were $306,204,033.14. The chief sources of revenue in 1916 were as follows:

Stamped paper	$277,608,304.86
Money orders	8,130,545.47
Postal savings	695,000.00
Second class matter	11,385,929.78
Third and fourth class matter	8,791,443.91

The principal expenditures were as follows:

Assistant postmasters and clerks	$ 55,011,110.23
Railway mail transportation	57,498,186.61
Rural delivery	51,948,805.91
City delivery	43,193,431.48
Postmasters' compensations	31,135,234.45
Star routes	8,656,586.96

(See Post-Office Department; Mail Matter; Postal Service; Division of Stamps.)

Division Miscellaneous Transportation, Post-Office Department.—This division is under the direct supervision of the second assistant postmaster-general (q. v.). Mail transportation by electric and cable cars comprises 571 routes, covering 8,106 miles and an annual travel of 12,869,216 miles. Appropriations for this branch of the service in 1917 were $660,000. Wagon service comprises routes to the extent of 1,380 miles and an annual travel of 5,494,556 miles. Appropriations for this method of carrying the mail in 1917 were $2,905,000. On July 1, 1916, the first assistant postmaster general assumed the supervision of wagon service, as it comes under the head of urban delivery. The first assistant postmaster-general also assumed charge on the same date of pneumatic tube service, for which the appropriations in 1916 were $966,800; and of the mail messenger service, for which $2,160,000 was appropriated in 1916 to cover the 8,027 routes, 5,571 miles in length, and of an annual travel of 12,410,098 miles. The steamboat service comprises 260 routes, covering 32,481 miles, with an annual travel of 5,470,272 miles. For steamboat service the 1917 appropriations were $1,060,000. The Alaska star service comprises 21 routes, covering 4,544 miles, with an annual travel of 249,321 miles, and carrying an appropriation for 1916 of $305,100. (See Post-Office Department; Assistant Postmasters-General; Postal Service.)

Division of Money Orders, Post-Office Department.—Money orders were first utilized in 1864, by Postmaster-General Blair.

in order to accommodate Union soldiers who wished to send small sums of money to their homes. The supervision of money orders is now in the hands of the third assistant postmaster-general (q. v.). There were in operation, in 1916, 56,026 domestic money order offices and 11,518 international money order offices. Domestic orders issued in 1916 amounted in number to 121,663,818, and in amount to $719,364,950.46, an average of $5.91 per money order. The fees collected on these orders amounted to $6,718,550.45. Of international money orders there were issued 3,011,097, totalling $46,351,386.34, an average of $15.40. Although money orders are invalid one year from the last day of the month in which they are issued, yet they may be collected after the expiration of the time limit by special procedure. The fees are graded, as follows: On orders up to $2.50, 3 cents; between $2.50 and $5.00, 5 cents; between $5.00 and $10.00, 8 cents; between $10.00 and $20.00, 10 cents; between $20.00 and $30.00, 12 cents, up to orders between $75.00 and $100.00, 30 cents. (See Post-Office Department; Postal System.)

Division of Naval Militia Affairs. (See Naval Militia.)

Division of Postal Savings, Post-Office Department. (See Postal Savings Banks.)

Division of Postmasters' Appointments. (See Appointments Division of Postmasters'.)

Division of Post-Office Service.—In 1825, the Government delivered letters at a cost of two cents each to the person who received them. In 1836, newspapers and pamphlets were delivered in the same fashion at a cost of one-half cent each. Free delivery service in cities of more than 50,000 population was established under Lincoln's administration in 1863. In 1917, there were 34,114 letter-carriers, with an average salary of $1,115.46 yearly; there were 40,127 clerks in the city delivery service, earning an average yearly salary of $1,093.44. The division of post-office service falls under the supervision of the first assistant postmaster-general, and includes city parcel post delivery. (See Post-Office Department; First Assistant Postmaster-General; Postal Service.)

Division Railway Adjustment, Post-Office Department. — This bureau has charge of the adjustment of rates paid to the railways for the transportation of the United States mails, and is directed by the second assistant postmaster-general (q. v.). An act of Congress in 1916 makes provision for a readjustment of the rates on a basis of space, new rates to be determined by the Interstate Commerce Commission (q. v.). (See Post-Office Department; Postal Service; Railway Mail Service.)

Division of Publications. (See Publications, Division of.)

Division of Registered Mails, Post-Office Department.—This division of the postal service is directed by the third assistant postmaster-general (q. v.), and includes insurance on mail matter and collections on delivery. Registered letters were first provided for in 1855. In the fiscal year ending June 30, 1916, there were 39,236,569 registrations of mail matter, on which the fees amounted to $3,427,083.10; 24,936,082 pieces of mail matter were insured, bringing in fees of $1,067,192.29; and of collections on delivery, a feature confined to the parcel post system, there were 6,300,546, carrying fees of $630,054.60. The division of registered mails also attends to indemnity claims, which in most cases are settled within ten days of the receipt of the claim. In 1916, there were 33,032 claims approved, and $231,047.73 was appropriated to meet them, an average of $7.00 per piece of mail. The registry fee is 10 cents. (See Post-Office Department; Postal Service.)

Division of Rural Mails, Post-Office Department.—Rural free delivery was begun in 1897, and was definitely established on a large scale in 1902. It falls under the supervision of the fourth assistant postmaster-general (q. v.). After the delivery of second-class matter, the rural free delivery is the most costly branch of the government postal service, but all postmasters-general speak of it as possibly the most serviceable part of the postal system. The establishment of new routes is determined by the postmaster-general, usually after a petition signed by at least 150 persons, who must represent 75 per cent of the families along the proposed route. In 1916, the rural free delivery served 5,719,062 families, containing 26,307,686 persons, at a cost of $51,-715,616; but it is estimated that in that year there were still 2,000,000 families without any postal facilities. The rural free delivery routes in 1916 comprised 42,-927 routes, covering 1,091,852 miles, the average route being 25.435 miles. In that year there were 42,766 carriers, whose average salary was $1,162.50. Within this division fall also the "Star Routes" (q. v.). (See Post-Office Department; Postal Service.)

Division of Stamps, Post-Office Department.—This division is under the third assistant postmaster-general (q. v.). In 1916, revenue from stamped paper was $277,728,-025.20, and the report of the postmaster-general for 1916 estimates that the revenue for 1917 will amount to $300,000,000. In 1857 the per capita consumption of stamped paper was $.19; in 1916 it was $2.68. During this period, the population increased at a rate of 257 per cent, and the consumption of stamped paper at a rate of 4,968 per cent. In 1916 there were issued to the various postmasters throughout the country postage stamps, post cards, stamped envelopes, newspaper wrappings, international reply coupons, postal savings cards and stamps to the number of 14,650,243,326. (See Postage Stamps; Post-Office Department.)

Divorce.—The fact that an American couple may be regarded as man and wife in one state while divorced in another, or as never married at all in a third state has long been noted. Laws providing for the dissolution of the marriage tie exist in all the states, except South Carolina. In that state divorce is not granted on any grounds whatsoever, either by courts of justice or by acts of the legislature. In all other states infidelity and violation of the marriage vows are recognized as valid grounds for divorce. In New York adultery alone is a valid ground for absolute divorce. Impotence or physical inability in almost all states either justifies divorce or renders the marriage voidable.

There are thirty-five different causes for absolute divorce recognized in the different states. The principal grounds generally recognized are: infidelity, violation of marriage vows, willful desertion; habitual drunkenness; conviction of felony; intolerable, extreme, or repeated cruelty; desertion. Condonation, collusion, or connivance, with the purpose of procuring a divorce, is in all states regarded as a bar to the dissolution of marriage.

In the case of Haddock vs. Haddock, it was decided by the United States Supreme Court in 1906, four justices dissenting, that a divorce granted in a state where the defendant is not domiciled, without personal service of process or a voluntary appearance by the defendant, though valid in the state where decreed, need not be recognized by any other state.

On account of this ruling and the diversity of state laws on the subject, a conference was held in Washington in 1906, which was attended by representatives of forty states, the Territory of New Mexico, and the District of Columbia. In November of that year at a second session of the conference a model divorce law was agreed upon and submitted to the various state legislatures. This law specifies as the ground for the annulment of marriage, impotency, consanguinity and affinity, existing marriage, fraud, force, or coercion, insanity unknown to the other party, marriage where wife was under sixteen, or husband under eighteen unless confirmed after arriving at such age. The causes for absolute divorce recommended are adultery, bigamy, conviction of certain crimes, extreme cruelty, willful desertion for two years, and habitual drunkenness. The causes for legal separation recommended are adultery, extreme cruelty, willful desertion for two years, hopeless insanity of husband, and habitual drunkenness. The conference recommended that no additional causes be recognized. The proposed law provides that, except in cases of bigamy or adultery, jurisdiction shall depend upon two years' residence. If a party has moved into a state after the cause for divorce arose, no jurisdiction shall be taken unless this cause was recognized in the state in which such party resided at the time the cause arose. It also provides that every state adopting this law shall give full faith and credit to the decrees issued by any other state adopting it. This law was adopted by Delaware and New Jersey in 1907.

In 1889, the Commissioner of Labor made a report of the statistics of divorce covering the period of twenty years, 1867-1886. He showed that whereas in 1867 there were only 9,937 divorces recorded, there were during the last year considered, 25,535, an increase of 157 per cent, while the population increased only about 60 per cent. The total number of divorces recorded during the twenty years was 328,716. The ratio of divorces to marriages was in 1900 one divorce to each 15.4 marriages, and was at another period as high as one to every 8.5 marriages for the entire country and as high as one to every 5.7 for a single state.

In 1908 another report on marriage and divorce was made by the Census Bureau. This covered the twenty years 1887-1906. The total number of divorces reported for this period was 945,625, as compared with the 328,716 for the previous twenty years. These figures indicate about one divorce in every twelve marriages, and that the divorce rate is higher in the United States than in any other country supplying statistics. Two-thirds of the divorces during forty years were granted the wife. Only 3.9 per cent of the entire number for the last twenty years were granted solely on account of intemperance. The annual average rate of divorces in the United States was seventy-three to each 100,000 of population, Japan 215 divorces to each 100,000 of population, and Austria only one.

Next to the United States comes Switzerland with thirty-two, followed by Saxony with an annual average of twenty-nine to each 100,000 of population. (See also Marriage, Divorce and Polygamy.)

Divorce, uniform laws on, advocated, 6942, 7048.

Dixie.—A term applied originally to New York City when slavery existed there. According to the myth or legend, a person named Dixie owned a large tract of land on Manhattan Island and a large number of slaves. As Dixie's slaves increased beyond the requirements of the plantation many were sent to distant parts. Naturally the deported negroes looked upon their early home as a place of real and abiding happiness, as did those from the "Ole Virginny" of later days. Horace Dixie became the synonym for a locality where the negroes lived happy and contented lives. In the south Dixie is taken to mean the southern states. There the word is supposed to have been derived from Mason and Dixon's line, formerly dividing the free and slave states. It is said to have first come into use there when Texas joined the Union, and the negroes sang of it as Dixie. It has been the subject of several popular songs, notably that of Albert Pike, "Southrons, hear your country's call"; that of T. M. Cooley, "Away Down South where grows the cotton," and that of Dan Emmett, the refrain usually containing the word "Dixie," or the words "Dixie's Land." During the Civil War the tune of Dixie was to the southern people what Yankee Doodle had always been to the people of the whole Union and what it continued in war times to be to the northern people, the comic national air.

Dixie Highway.—One of the national road movements developed during the year 1915. It was officially launched at the conference of Governors of the States interested called to meet at Chattanooga, Tenn., April 3, 1915, by Governor Samuel Ralston, of Indiana. The system of highways, as designated by two commissioners, each appointed by the Governors of the States of Michigan, Illinois, Indiana, Ohio, Kentucky, Tennessee, Georgia and Florida, consists of two divisions and one loop each in the States of Michigan and Florida, with connecting links. The western division starts at Chicago, and is routed through the cities of Danville, Ill.; Indianapolis, Ind.; Louisville, Ky.; Nashville and Chattanooga, Tenn.; Rome, Atlanta and Macon, Ga.; Tallahassee, Kissimee, Bartow and Jupiter, Fla., where it connects with the eastern division. Indianapolis, Ind., is connected with a loop around the State of Michigan at South Bend, Ind. Joining the eastern end of the Michigan loop, which follows Lake Huron to Detroit, the eastern division of the highway is routed through the cities of Monroe, Mich.; Toledo, Dayton and Cincinnati, Ohio; Lexington, Ky.; Cumberland Gap and Knoxville, Tenn., to Chattanooga; thence to Atlanta, Ga., via Dalton; thence to Macon, via McDonough; thence to Jacksonville, Fla., via Fitzgerald and Waycross, Ga., and along the east coast of Florida to Miami. A connecting link from Indianapolis on the western division to Dayton, Ohio, on the eastern division, and from Tallahassee, Fla., on the western division, to Jacksonville, Fla., on the eastern division has also been designated.

The Dixie Highway has a total mileage of 4,206. In the eight States it traverses 163 counties. It will serve a territory with a population of almost forty million. There are over eight hundred thousand automobile owners in this territory, from which the

Dixie Highway can reasonably expect to attract tourists.

Dixie, The, mentioned, 6318, 6765, 6766, 6835.

Dock Yards for construction of large vessels, recommended, 600.

Appropriations for building, should be separated from those of naval service, 2625, 2670.

Construction of—

Appropriation for, recommended, 769, 1335.

Discussed, 333, 335, 2669.

Referred to, 769, 985, 2414.

Site for, 934.

Report of commission to select, transmitted, 5566, 5650.

Spanish war vessels repaired at American, 4005.

Dollar.—Derived from daler or thaler. The American silver dollar is modeled after the Spanish milled dollar. It was authorized by an act of Congress passed in 1792, which declared 371¼ grains of pure silver to be equal to 24¾ grains of pure gold and each equivalent to a dollar of account. It was made the unit of value. The silver dollar was first coined in 1794 and weighed 416 grains, 371¼ grains being of silver and the remainder alloy. In 1837 the weight was reduced to 412½ grains by decreasing the weight of alloy. In 1873 provision was made for a dollar of 420 grains for use in trade with China and Japan known as the "trade dollar." The gold dollar was issued under the act of March 3, 1849. Its coinage was discontinued in 1890. The coinage act of Feb. 12, 1873, tacitly suspended the coinage of silver dollars (except the trade dollar) and made the gold dollar the standard of value. The act of Feb. 28, 1878, authorized the Secretary of the Treasury to purchase each month, at market value, not less than $2,000,000 and not more than $4,000,000 worth of bullion, to be coined into silver dollars of 412½ grains each. This act was repealed by the act of June 14, 1890. By act of 1900, the gold dollar again became the standard of value in this country. (See Coinage Laws; Coins and Coinage.)

Dolphin, The (British cruiser), seizure of the *Catherine* by, discussed, 2070.

Dolphin, The (United States brig), seizure of the *Echo* by, discussed, 3058.

Dolphin, The (United States dispatch boat), contract regarding construction of, discussed, 4935.

Dominican Republic. (See Santo Domingo.)

Dominion State.—Formerly a nickname for New Jersey. (See Red Mud State.)

Doorkeeper.—By an act of March 3, 1805, the designation of Doorkeeper of the Senate was changed to Sergeant-at-Arms. He executes all orders relating to decorum and is officially charged with all matters relating to the keeping of the doors of the Senate. He orders persons into custody and makes arrests by direction of the Senate. The duties of the Doorkeeper of the House of Representatives are varied and complicated. Under the rules of the House he is required to enforce the rules relating to the privileges of the floor, and is responsible for the conduct of his employees—messengers, pages, laborers, etc. He also has charge of all the property of the House. He reports to Congress annually the amount of United States property in his possession, also the number of public documents in his possession subject to order of members of Congress. He has more patronage than any other officer of the House. The appointments made by him number between 160 and 200.

Dorr's Rebellion.—A forcible effort to overthrow the State government of Rhode Island in 1840-1842. After the Declaration of Independence Rhode Island retained her original colonial charter, which provided for only limited suffrage. Many of the citizens were dissatisfied with the State government. In October, 1841, a convention of delegates prepared a constitution. This was submitted to popular vote and, it was claimed, received a majority of the votes cast. The established government considered these efforts to be little short of criminal. A legislature elected under the new constitution assembled at Newport May 3, 1842, with Thomas W. Dorr as governor. Governor King proclaimed martial law. The Dorr party offered armed resistance, but their forces were dispersed and Dorr fled the State. Returning, he again offered resistance to the State authorities, but was captured, tried, and convicted of treason. He was pardoned in 1852. In September, 1842, a State convention adopted a constitution which embodied nearly every provision that had been advocated by Dorr and his followers.

Dorr's Rebellion:

Correspondence regarding, 2139.

Discussed, 2136.

Doughface.—A term first applied by John Randolph, of Virginia, to northern Congressmen who supported the Missouri Compromise of 1820. It was intended to apply to those who were easily molded by personal or unworthy motives to forsake their principles. It was generally applied to northern people who favored slavery, but was also sometimes used to stigmatize those southern citizens who opposed the prevailing sentiment of their section on the slavery question.

Douglas, The, indemnification for, to be made by Great Britain, 2111.

Down East State.—Alternative nickname for Maine. (See Pine Tree State.)

Draft:

Civil War—

Citizens liable to, not allowed to go abroad, 3322.

Deficiency in quota of states, referred to, 3412.

Orders regarding, 3321, 3433.

Evasions, warning against, 8269.

Exemption of government employees from, explained, 8320.

In war against Germany, announced and explained, 8256.

Registration for, in—

Alaska, 8303.

Continental United States, 8256.

Hawaii, 8304.

Porto Rico, 8302.

Rules and regulations for, 8306.

Drafting. (See Drafts.)

Drafts.—Conscription for obtaining men for the military forces of the government depend on the general principle that it is the duty of a citizen who enjoys the protection of a government to defend it. The state constitutions make citizens liable to military duty, and the Constitution of the United States (Article 1, section 8, clause 12) gives Congress power to raise armies, which the courts have held includes the right of conscription. There was some application of the draft principle in the early Colonial armies and in the Revolutionary Army. During the War of 1812 the necessity for troops led to the introduction of a bill in Congress, known as the "Draft of 1814," providing for a draft from the militia, but it failed to pass. During the Civil War the need of soldiers occasioned the passage of the Conscription Bill, which became law on March 3, 1863 (afterwards amended in February and July, 1864). This bill provided for the enrollment of all able-bodied citizens between eighteen and forty-five years of age. In default of volunteers to fill the quota from a congressional district, the deficiency was to be supplied by drafts from the enrolled citizens. Provisions were made for the acceptance of substitutes or a commutation of $300 in place of the drafted individuals. Persons refusing obedience were to be considered as deserters. A call for 300,000 troops was made by the President in May, and the application of the draft created serious riots. It was alleged that a disproportionate number of men had been demanded from Democratic districts; these discrepancies were corrected by the War Department. In October, 1863, the President issued another call for 300,000 men, and a draft was ordered for the following January to supply any deficiencies. Other drafts were subsequently made. The provision for exemption by the payment of $300 was repealed in 1864, but the provision for substitutes remained. The operation of the drafts was not satisfactory in the number of men directly obtained, and desertions were frequent among such as were drafted, but voluntary enlistments were quickened. It is estimated that only about 20,000 men were obtained by the draft principle for the Union armies in the Civil War. The Confederate States had very stringent conscription laws, which were rigidly enforced.

Draft Riots.—The attempt to enforce the draft in 1863 led to serious troubles in some sections of the country. Pennsylvania was disturbed in this way, but New York City was the scene of the greatest outrages. On July 13 a mob gained control of the city, and was not dispersed till four days had elapsed. The police force was too small to cope with the rioters, but a small force of United States regulars could be commanded, and the militia were absent at the seat of war. The enmity of the mob was directed especially against the negroes, several of them being hanged or otherwise killed, and the Colored Orphan Asylum being burned. Finally the regulars, the police and some militia that had returned after the battle of Gettysburg succeeded in quelling the riot. It is estimated that about 1,000 persons lost their lives, and the city was obliged to pay indemnities for loss of property amounting to over $1,500,000.

Drafts During the European War.— Among countries not recognizing the principle of universal military service, England did not resort to conscription until almost 22 months after war was declared, and Australia voted down a proposal for conscription for foreign service by referendum on October 28, 1916.

In the United States, President Wilson and Congress put aside the volunteer system as unwise from the very beginning of the war, and on May 18, 1917, 42 days after the announcement of the existence of a state of war with Germany, the Selective Draft Bill was signed. (See Army, Selective Draft Bill of 1917.) The first draft army was to consist of 547,197 officers and men, the age limits being 21 and 30, inclusive. All residents of the United States between those ages were required to register on June 5, and it was announced that training for those selected, whose names were to be obtained according to the jury-wheel system, would begin on or about September 1 of the same year. The Census Bureau estimated that there were in the country 10,-078,900 men of the draft age, so that in round numbers about 1 in every 20 men of draft age would be called to the colors.

Those exempted from the operation of the draft were officers and officials of the several states and of the Federal government; those in industry whom the President might deem it wise to withhold from military service, ministers and theological students, those belonging before the announcement of the draft to a well-established religious body whose tenets forbid participation in war, and those found upon examination to be physically or morally unfit for service. To fill up gaps in the National Guard ,the number to be drafted was finally placed at 687,000.

Registration for the draft occurred in June, 1917; and the numbers were drawn by lot in July. By December 31, the members of the new "National Army" were at cantonments receiving instruction. Gross quotas and net quotas demanded of the different states are shown in an adjoining table.

For the purposes of the draft, there was appointed by the President a draft board for each voting subdivision in the United States. These draft boards examined all candidates brought before it by the lot, rejecting those who seemed to be unfit and recommending the fit for service. Appeal might be taken from the decisions of the draft boards to a central district draft board, but appeals on industrial grounds could be taken even higher to the President. Married men generally were only exempted from service when it was proved that their families would necessarily become dependent in their absence. The ratio of exemptions was as a whole less than one for every two men called.

In November, 1917, President Wilson issued a proclamation (which will be found in its chronological position in the Index under his name) announcing a change of system in the selective draft. Under the new method, all registrants were to be divided into five classes, which would be summoned to service in order, so that demands would not be made upon members of one class until all members of the preceding class had been called to the colors. The five classes were defined as follows:

CLASS I

Div.

A—Single man without dependent relatives.

B—Married man, with or without children, or father of motherless children, who has habitually failed to support his family.

C—Married man dependent on wife for support.

D—Married man, with or without children, or father of motherless children ; man not usefully engaged, family supported by income independent of his labor.

E—Unskilled farm laborer.

F—Unskilled industrial laborer.

Registrant by or in respect of whom no deferred classification is claimed or made.

Registrant who fails to submit questionnaire and in respect of whom no deferred classification is claimed or made.

All registrants not included in any other division in this schedule.

CLASS II

A—Married man with children or father of motherless children, where such wife or children or such motherless children are not mainly dependent upon his labor for support, for the reason that there are other reasonably certain sources of adequate support (excluding earnings or possible earnings from the labor of the wife), available, and that the removal of the registrant will not deprive such dependents of support.

B—Married man, without children, whose wife, although the registrant is engaged in a useful occupation, is not mainly dependent upon his labor for support, for the reason that the wife is skilled in some special class of work which she is physically able to perform and in which she is employed, or in which there is an immediate opening for her under conditions that will enable her to support herself decently and without suffering or hardship.

C—Necessary skilled farm laborer in necessary agricultural enterprise.

D—Necessary skilled industrial laborer in necessary industrial enterprise.

CLASS III

A—Man with dependent children (not his own), but toward whom he stands in relation of parent.

B—Man with dependent aged or infirm parents.

C—Man with dependent helpless brothers or sisters.

D—County or municipal officer.

E—Highly trained fireman or policeman, at least three years in service of municipality.

F—Necessary custom house clerk.

G—Necessary employe of United States in transmission of the mails.

H—Necessary artificer or workman in United States army or arsenal.

I—Necessary employe in service of United States.

J—Necessary assistant, associate or hired manager of necessary agricultural enterprise.

K—Necessary highly specialized technical or mechanical expert of necessary industrial enterprise.

L—Necessary assistant or associate manager of necessary industrial enterprise.

CLASS IV

A—Man whose wife or children are mainly dependent on his labor for support.

B—Mariner actually employed in sea service of citizen or merchant in the United States.

C—Necessary sole managing, controlling or directing head of necessary agricultural enterprise.

D—Necessary sole managing, controlling or directing head of necessary industrial enterprise.

	Gross quota	Credits for enlistments	Net quota for the draft
Alabama	21,300	7,651	13,612
Arizona	4,478	998	3,472
Arkansas	17,452	7,155	10,267
California	34,907	11,786	23,060
Colorado	9,797	5,027	4,753
Connecticut ..	18,817	7,807	10,977
Delaware	2,569	1,363	1,202
Dist. of Col...	3,796	2,860	929
Florida	10,129	3,786	6,325
Georgia	27,209	8,825	18,337
Idaho	4,833	2,538	2,287
Illinois	79,094	27,304	51,653
Indiana	29,971	12,409	17,510
Iowa	25,465	12,672	12,749
Kansas	17,795	11,325	6,439
Kentucky	22,152	7,878	14,236
Louisiana	18,481	4,867	13,582
Maine	7,076	5,243	1,821
Maryland	14,139	7,018	7,096
Massachusetts .	43,109	22,448	20,586
Michigan	43,936	13,569	30,291
Minnesota	26,021	8,122	17,854
Mississippi ...	16,429	5,600	10,801
Missouri	35,461	16,740	18,660
Montana	10,423	2,553	7,872
Nebraska	13,900	5,691	8,185
Nevada	1,435	382	1,051
New Hampshire	4,419	3,027	1,204
New Jersey ..	35,623	14,896	20,665
New Mexico ..	3,856	1,557	2,292
New York	122,424	52,971	69,241
North Carolina	23,486	7,471	15,974
North Dakota .	7,737	2,118	5,606
Ohio	66,474	27,586	38,773
Oklahoma	19,943	4,344	15,564
Oregon	7,387	6,657	717
Pennsylvania .	98,277	37,248	60,859
Rhode Island .	6,277	4,465	1,801
South Carolina	15,147	5,040	10,081
South Dakota.	6,854	4,125	2,717
Tennessee	22,158	7,592	14,528
Texas	48,116	17,488	30,545
Utah	4,945	2,566	2,370
Vermont	3,243	2,188	1,049
Virginia	21,354	7,522	13,795
Washington ..	12,768	5,450	7,296
West Virginia.	14,848	5,721	9,101
Wisconsin	28,199	15,274	12,876
Wyoming	2,683	1,868	810
Alaska	710	13	696
Hawaii	2,403	4,397	0
Porto Rico ...	13,480	624	12,833
Total	1,152,985	465,985	687,000

CLASS V

A—Officers—legislative, executive or judicial —of the United States or of state, territory or District of Columbia.

B—Regular cr duly ordained minister of religion.

C—Student who on May 18, 1917, was preparing for ministry in recognized school.

D—Persons in military or naval service of United States.

E—Alien enemy.

F—Resident alien (not an enemy) who claims exemption.

G—Person totally and permanently physically or mentally unfit for military service.

H—Person morally unfit to be a soldier of the United States.

I—Licensed pilot actually employed in the pursuit of his vocation.

Member of well recognized religious sect or organization, organized and existing on May 18, 1917, whose then existing creed or principles forbid its members to participate in war in any form and whose religious convictions are against war or participation therein.

It was estimated that the first class would contain 2,000,000 names; and that the addition of those who had attained their majority since the last registration would add 500,000 names by Jan. 1, 1918.

Drafts, Government, sale or exchange of, for bank notes, and payment of Government creditors in depreciated currency, 1777, 1806, 1807, 1808.

Drago Doctrine.—When in the winter of 1902-1903 Germany, Britain and Italy blockaded the ports of Venezuela in an attempt to compel the latter country to settle its foreign indebtedness Dr. L. F. Drago, a noted jurist, of Argentina, maintained that force cannot be used by one power to collect money owing to its citizens by another power. Prominence was given to the contention by the fact that it was officially upheld by Argentina and favored by other South American republics. The principle embodied has become generally known as the "Drago Doctrine."

It was at this second Hague Peace Conference, which was attended by delegates from leading South American countries, that the "Drago Doctrine" came up for discussion and the power of a Pan-American alliance was disclosed to the world. Dr. Calvo, Argentine representative in European capitals, maintained that if European states do not make war upon each other for the sake of bondholders, they ought not to make war to collect debts, good or bad, in the case of South American nations. This doctrine was taken up by Dr. Drago, Argentine minister of foreign affairs, and has since been known as the Drago Doctrine, and has been called the "Monroe Doctrine of the Money Market."

The forcible collection by a foreign power of debts due its subjects by other governments was opposed by General Porter, of the United States. He proposed that the Peace Conference permit the employment of force for the collection of debts only after the debtor state had refused to conform to the decision of arbitrators. He declared that speculators and adventurers often dragged their governments into costly expeditions for the collection of paltry sums, and instanced a case where the actual debt turned out to be only three-fourths of one per cent of the amount claimed and the United States had used nineteen warships and spent nearly $4,000,000 to collect a debt of less than $100,000. The powers agreed "to take no military or naval action to compel the payment of such debts until an offer of arbitration has been made by the creditor and refused or left unanswered by the debtor, or until arbitration has taken place and the debtor state has failed to conform to the decision given."

Drago Doctrine, statement of, 7061.

Drawback.—A term used in commerce to signify the remission or refunding of tariff duties when the commodity upon which they have been paid is exported. By means of the drawback an article upon which taxes are paid when imported may be exported and sold ia foreign markets on the same terms as though it had not been taxed at all. The drawback enables merchants to export imported articles taxed at home and sell them in foreign markets on the same terms as those offered from countries where no tax is imposed.

Dred Scott Case.—A celebrated Supreme Court case, decided in 1857, important from its bearing on the Missouri Compromise of 1820. Scott was a Missouri slave, and upon being taken into territory covered by the Missouri Compromise sued for his freedom. Being then sold to a citizen of another State, he transferred his suit from the State to the Federal courts under the power given to the latter to try suits between citizens of different States. The case came on appeal to the Supreme Court of the United States. Chief Justice Taney, for the court, delivered an exhaustive opinion, holding that the Missouri Compromise was unconstitutional and void; that one of the constitutional functions of Congress was the protection of property; that slaves were recognized as property by the Constitution, and that Congress was therefore bound to protect slavery in the Territories. Scott was put out of court on the ground that he was still a slave and being such could not be a citizen of the United States or have any standing in Federal courts. Associate Justices Curtis and McLean filed dissenting opinions. The decision aroused great excitement throughout the country, particularly in the North.

Dred Scott Case, Supreme Court decision regarding, discussed, 2985, 3029, 3085, 3160.

Drifting mines and submarines:

Agreement on use of, suggested by President Wilson, 8057.

Defence of use of, by Germany, 8058.

Driver, The, ordered from and forbidden to reenter waters of United States, 391.

Dry Docks. (See Docks.)

Dry Tortugas, survey of, for naval station, 1038.

Duck Valley, Nev., payment of settlers for improvements on lands in, referred to, 4664, 4776.

Dudley, The, seizure of, and claims arising out of, 4114, 5198, 5547, 5673, 5873, 5962.
Award in case of, 6070.

Due Process of Law necessary before any person may be deprived of life, liberty or property, 29, 31.

Duel Between Burr and Hamilton. (See Illustration facing page 430.)

Duluth, Minn., act for erection of public buildings at, vetoed, 5054.

Dunkirk, N. Y., proclamation granting privileges of other ports to, 2859.

Durango, The, convention with Texas for adjustment of claims in case of, 1686.

Dutch East Indies, discriminating duties on vessels of, suspended, 5154.

Dutch West Indies. (See Netherlands.)

Duties. (See Foreign Import Duties; Import Duties; Vessels, Foreign, tonnage on.)

Dwamish Indians. (See Indian Tribes.)

Dyrenforth, Rain-Getter. (See Rain-Maker.)

E Pluribus Unum.—A Latin phrase meaning "Out of many, one," or "One of many." It alludes to the formation of one Federal Government out of several independent states. It is the motto of the United States, having been selected by a committee composed of John Adams, Benjamin Franklin, and Thomas Jefferson. They made their report on a design for a motto and great seal Aug. 10, 1776. The phrase is probably derived from "Moretum," a Latin poem by Virgil. It was also the motto of the "Gentleman's Magazine," which was quite popular in the Colonies at the time the selection was made. It first appeared on coin issued by New Jersey in 1786.

Eagan's Court Martial.—At the close of the Spanish-American War, complaint was made of the treatment of troops who had been removed to Camp Wikoff at Montauk Point, Long Island. General Miles brought charges against Commissary-General Eagan, who was tried by Court-Martial, found guilty and dismissed from the Army. The sentence was afterwards commuted to suspension from the Army for a period of six years.

Eagle.—1. American Eagle, the white-headed eagle (sometimes known as the bald-eagle) and which is a symbol of America. 2. The name is applied to a ten-dollar gold piece, and the twenty-dollar gold piece is called the double eagle. 3. A standard, bearing the image of an eagle, used in connection with the military forces. 4. An emblem of the Republican party used both in cartoon and at the head of the ballot.

Earthquakes in Peru, Ecuador, and Bolivia, 3885.

East Florida. (See Florida.)

East Florida Claims:
Discussed and payment of, recommended, 1727, 1906, 4520, 4536, 4560.
Reports on, referred to, 4541.

East River, N. Y., appropriation for removal of Flood Rock in, recommended, 4788.

East Tennessee University, act for relief of, vetoed, 4169.

Eastport, Me., proclamation granting privileges of other ports to, 2859.

Eastry, The, collisions of, 6774, 6933.

Echo, The, captured with more then 300 African negroes on board by U. S. brig *Dolphin,* near Key Verde, on the coast of Cuba, and taken as a prize to Charleston, S. C., 3058.
Recommendations regarding removal of, 3059.

Economics.—The science concerned with the laws governing the production, distribution, exchange, and consumption of economic goods—that is to say, of products which have value in that they are not free to all. Economics differs from sociology (q. v.) in that it is not concerned with individuals as such, but only with individuals as they form a social organism. Hence the alternative name often used of "political economy," as applying to the laws governing those elements of production which are not limitless, as are air and water, and in whose

use therefore economy must be practised by civilization; and governing these economic goods in the organized, or political aspects of modern life. Thus, economics deals with the laws governing wages, interest, and rent; with methods of producing goods; with credit and credit machinery; with the distribution of wealth; with the tariff (q. v.), the single tax (q. v.), Socialism (q. v.) and with all other theories affecting the methods by which men are enabled to live upon this planet—namely, by deriving the subsistence necessary for existence. Economic speculations were present from the days of ancient history, but modern scientific economics dates from the publication in 1776 of Adam Smith's "Wealth of Nations."

Economy and Efficiency:
Discussed by President—
Taft, 7370, 7423, 7505, 7736.
Wilson, 8019.

Ecuador.—The Republic is bounded on the west by the Pacific Ocean, on the north and northeast by Colombia, and on the south by Peru. The extreme limits, according to Ecuadorial geographers, are between 1° 38′ N.-6° 26′ S. latitude and 70°-81° W. longitude, but its northern, southern, and eastern boundaries are in dispute.
Physical Features and Climate.—The Cordillera Occidental contains the dome-shaped summit of Chimborazo (20,498 feet), and Iliniza (17,405 feet), Carahuairazo (16,515 feet), Cotocachi (16,301 feet), and Pichincha (16,000 feet); in the Cordillera Oriental are Cotopaxi (19,613 feet), Antisana (19,335 feet), Cayambe (19,186 feet), Altar, or Capac Urcu (17,730 feet), Sangay (17,464 feet), Tunguragua (16,690 feet), and Sincholagua (16,365 feet). Both ranges contain other summits above 14,000 feet; Cotopaxi, Sangay, and Pichincha are active volcanoes. The elevated Ecuadorian plateau between the two ranges consists of the Quito, Ambato, and Cuenca plains, of which the Quito plain is fertile and covered with vegetation. La Region Orientale is a forest-clad plain inhabited by aucas, or uncivilized Indians. Its boundaries and extent are indeterminate, and it is only partially explored. The Galápagos Islands, 600 miles west of the mainland, lying at the intersection of the Equator and 90° W. longitude, were annexed by the Republic of Ecuador in 1832. The Archipelago consists of six large and nine small islands with a total area of about 2,500 English square miles. The larger islands were formerly the resort of buccaneers and they possess alternative English and Spanish names, viz.:—Albemarle (or Isabela), Narborough (or Fernandina), Indefatigable (or Santa Cruz), Chatham (or San Cristobal), James (or San Salvador), and Charles (or Santa Maria). The name is derived from the giant tortoise (galápago) found on the islands. In the Gulf of Guayaquil, separated from the mainland by the narrow Morro Straits, is Puna Island, about 200 square miles in area, low-lying and densely wooded. Santa Clara in the same gulf, and La Plata and Salango off the coast of Manabi province, are the largest of the remaining islands of Ecuador. The river systems are divided by the Andes and consist of western rivers flowing into the Pacific, and of tributaries of the Upper Amazon.
History.—The aboriginal Indian tribes were conquered in the third century by southern invaders, who established the Kingdom of Quito in the territory now known as Ecuador, and this kingdom fell

before the superior military organization of successive Incas of Peru in the latter half of the fifteenth century. Early in the sixteenth century Pizarro's conquests led to the inclusion of the Kingdom of Quito as a province of the Spanish vice-royalty of Peru, to which it remained joined until a final revolutionary war, culminating in the battle of Mount Pichincha (May 22, 1822), secured the independence of the country. With the aid of Bolivar the Spanish rulers were expelled (1822-1823), and the country was united to the Colombia Confederation. In 1830 it seceded and adopted its present name. The present Constitution was promulgated Dec. 23, 1906.

AREA AND POPULATION

Provinces and Capitals	Area in English Sq. Miles	Estimated Population
Azuay (Cuenca)............	3,850	140,000
Bolivar (Guaranda)........	1,260	45,000
Cañar (Azogues)..........	1,520	70,000
Carchi (Tulcan)..........	1,500	40,000
Chimborazo (Riobamba)...	3,000	130,000
Esmeraldas (Esmeraldas)...	5,500	20,000
Galápagos Islands (San Cristoval).................	2,500	500
Guayas (Guayaquil).......	8,300	100,000
Imbabura (Ibarra)........	2,300	70,000
Léon (Latacunga)........	2,500	110,000
Loja (Loja)...............	3,700	60,000
Manabi (Puerto Viejo)....	8,000	65,000
Oriente (Archidona).......	60,000 (?)	80,000
Oro (Machala)............	2,250	35,000
Pichincha (Quito)........	6,250	200,000
Rios (Babahoyo)..........	2,300	35,000
Tunguragua (Ambato).....	1,700	100,000
Total................	116,530	1,300,500

The particulars in the above total include the area and estimated population of the Oriente Province as claimed by Ecuador, but the boundaries are in dispute with Colombia and Peru. Ecuador claims a wide extension northward into Colombia, while Peru claims a considerable portion of Ecuadorian Oriente, of the Ecuadorian claim from Colombia, and of an extension beyond that claim into Colombian territory.

Ethnography.—The Quitu and Cara Indians are estimated at 800,000, of whom about 200,000 are totally uncivilized, or aucas. The white population, descendants of the Spanish colonists, are believed to number 100,000, the mestizos, or mixed Spanish-Indians, 300,000, and the descendants of imported negroes about 40,000, of whom only 8,000 are of pure blood, the remainder being of mixed Indian and Spanish blood. The foreign population is stated at 6,000, mainly from neighboring republics, with some 700 from Europe and the United States, and about 300 Chinese.

Government.—The Government is that of a centralized republic, and rests upon the written constitution of 1830, with a President and Vice-President, elected by direct vote for four years (and ineligible for successive terms in the same office). President of the Republic (April 1, 1916-1920), Alfredo Bazuerizo Moreno.

Congress consists of a Senate and a Chamber of Deputies. The Senate contains thirty-two members (two for each province) elected for four years, half renewable every two years; the Chamber of Deputies is composed of forty-eight members (one per 30,000 inhabitants) elected for two years. The electors in each case are all male citizens above eighteen years who can read and write. Congress meets annually for sixty days from August 10.

Each of the sixteen provinces is administered by a Governor, appointed by the

Executive, and is divided into departments under political chiefs. The Galápagos Islands are administered as a territory.

There are civil courts of first instance under justices of the peace and police courts in all the smaller centers, with alcaldes in the municipalities; six superior courts at Quito, Guayaquil, Cuenca, Riobamba, Loja, and Porta Viejo, and a supreme court at the capital.

Army.—There is a Militia, with a permanent strength of about 5,000 of all ranks and a National Guard of three classes. (See Armies of the World.)

Navy.—The Navy consists of the cruiser Cotopaxi, the destroyer Bolivar and torpedo-boat Tarqui, with a force of about 200 of all ranks.

Education.—Primary education is compulsory and free, there being about 1,200 schools, with a total attendance of about 80,000. The University of Quito, founded in the seventeenth century, has about 300 students and thirty-two professors.

Finance.—The revenue and expenditure for the five years, 1907-1911, are stated as follows in condors. The condor is equal to $0.487 United States money.

Year	Revenue	Expenditure
1907.................	1,319,500	1,300,000
1908.................	1,272,450	1,540,180
1909.................	1,587,750	1,560,500
1910.................	1,520,700	1,550,950
1911.................	2,398,480	2,204,725

Debt.—Upon seceding in 1830 from the Confederacy, Ecuador was charged with 21½ per cent. of the debt of Colombia. In 1912 the External Debt amounted to $16,000,000, and the Internal Debt to $5,000,000, a total of $21,000,000. The Colombian debt, with arrears of interest, amounted to about 12,000,000 sucres. In 1895 a sinking fund was formed for the purposes of amortization by the payment into a special account of a 10 per cent. surtax on the import duties. This sinking fund amounted in 1910 to about 600,000 sucres ($300,000).

Production and Industry.—Wheat, maize, oats, barley, potatoes, and vegetables are grown in the northern uplands, but the staple product of the soil is cacao, grown principally in the valleys of the province of Guayas and in the Machala district of the province of Oro, which produce about one-third of the world's supply. Coffee of excellent quality is grown on the lower slopes of the Andes, and cotton, sugar, tobacco, and rice in the western plains, while rubber, cinchona bark, vegetable ivory (tagua nuts), and cabinet woods are obtained from the extensive, forest-clad plains of Oriente. There are immense tracts of grazing land on the lower slopes west of the Cordilleras, and also on the northern part of the plateau between the two ranges.

Gold, quicksilver, lead, iron, and copper are found, and there is a valuable petroleum field at Santa Elena, near the coast of the province of Guayas. Emeralds and rubies are occasionally discovered, and sulphur is abundant in many districts and in the Galápagos Islands.

The principal industry is straw-plaiting, and the manufacture of "Panama" hats for the foreign market. The fiber industry is widespread, and chocolate factories have been established in the cacao districts.

The principal exports are cocoa, vegetable ivory, rubber, cinchona bark, straw hats, coffee, and cattle and horses; the principal imports being textiles and clothing, iron manufactures and foodstuffs.

Railways.—In 1910 there were 356 miles of railway open, of which 300 miles constituted the line from Quito to Guayaquil, between the two ranges of the Andes.

Trade with the United States.—The value of merchandise imported into Ecuador from the United States for the year 1913 was $2,553,785, and goods to the value of $3,037,689 were sent thither—a balance of $483.904 in favor of the United States.

Ecuador?

Civil war in, 1319.

Claims of United States against, convention for adjustment of, 3348, 3402.

Failure of, to pay first installment of award under, 3584.

Commercial convention with, 1751.

Convention with, respecting case of Emilio Santos, 5957.

Diplomatic relations with, discussed, 4630, 5468.

Dispute with Peru, arbitration of, 7499.

Earthquakes in, 3885.

Fugitive criminals, convention with, for surrender of, 4160, 4247.

Imprisonment of American citizens in, 4856.

Released, 4915, 4990.

Treaty to settle claim regarding, 5369.

Naturalization treaty with, 4119, 4193.

Report of George E. Church upon, transmitted, 4744.

Treaty with, transmitted and discussed, 1784, 2051, 3348, 4160, 4247.

Expresses desire to negotiate, 1694.

Probably rendered abortive, 1933.

Ecuador, Treaties with.—June 13, 1839, a treaty of peace, friendship, navigation and commerce was concluded with Ecuador. This was terminated August 25, 1892, by notice from the Ecuadorean government.

In 1909, Ecuador signed the Hague arbitration convention with the United States to endure for a period of five years, and thereafter until the expiration of a year's notice.

Editors, Opinions of, 8033.

Education in the United States.—The history of education in the United States may be roughly divided into four different stages. In the first, extending from the settlement of the country until approximately 1750, the colonists patterned the instruction they gave their children after English models. Especially prominent was the apprentice system in New England and the middle Atlantic states. New England soon took up seriously the problem of schooling, and by various enactments showed its feeling for the responsibility of the state in education, whereas the South, after some experiments, left the problem of education largely to the individual household and to private schools. In New England provision was made for the instruction of girls along with boys in the elementary classes, but the academies, or secondary schools, which were established for the colleges which soon had arisen thickly in New England were for boys and young men.

The second stage of development would extend from about 1750 to 1825. In this period, the independent personality and national psychology of the United States made themselves evident, and the instruction given in the schools reacted to the new emphasis upon conceptions of liberty and political democracy, although there was little change in the educational systems, except in general enlargement and advanced work.

The third period would extend until close to the end of the nineteenth century. It represents on the administrative side of the school systems a strong tendency toward consolidation. The remarkable industrial expansion and urban development of the country greatly influenced the schools, as did the coming of large numbers of immigrants. Pedagogically, visitors to Europe were responsible for a knowledge of the theories of European educational reformers such as Pestalozzi and Froebel, and American education strive more and more toward freeing the individuality of the pupil. The establishment of the Bureau of Education (q. v.) had an integrating effect upon the country's school systems. This is also the period in which opportunities for higher education were opened to women.

The fourth period is too close to us for a definite characterization. It is undeniably a period of educational uncertainty and experimentation, and represents a reaction away from the previous individualism into a stronger emphasis upon social values. Especially noticeable is the reaction of the schools to the newly awakened social conscience, and more and more the schools have tended to become social as well as educational agencies in their communities. The European War also made inevitable the broadening of the school system to a consideration of all national, industrial and cultural problems, and to some extent nationalized the various school systems of the land.

Nevertheless, the school system of the United States is still a system of local rather than national control. Local schools are still administered generally according to district, township or county units, with supervision more or less close from a state educational system; and our schools are characterized more by the variety of their methods and programs than by their uniformity.

In 1916, there was an enrollment in the common schools of the United States of 20,-351,687, representing 76% of the school population. The average daily attendance was 15,358,927, and the average length of the school year was 160 days. The whole number of teachers was 623,371, of which 20% were men. The average monthly salary paid the teachers was $70.21, and the amount expended for schools, per capita of average attendance, was $41.72. $6,28 was expended per capita of population.

The Western states had the highest percentage of the school population enrolled, expended more per capita population, paid more per capita average attendance, and gave the highest salaries. The North Atlantic states had the highest average of attendance to enrollment and the South Central states had the greatest proportion of men teachers. Some figures follow:

	Monthly Salaries	Expenditure Per Capita Population
No. Atlantic	$80.15	$7.12
No. Central	68.14	7.72
So. Atlantic	50.65	3.18
So. Central	61.18	3.30
Western	95.05	9.53

The following table gives the figures of common schools by states:

	School Population Enrolled	Average Monthly Salaries	Cost per Capita Popu-lation	Cost per Capita Attend-ance
North Atlantic States:				
Maine	84.35%	$53.38	$5.18	$34.31
New Hamp..	68.70	56.74	4.86	39.44
Vermont ...	77.22	48.31	6.33	43.91
Mass'setts ..	72.76	88.03	7.35	53.75
Rhode I'd ..	63.23	74.27	5.87	50.32
Conn'cut ...	82.18	68.16	7.78	53.09
New York ..	69.59	101.70	6.69	52.15
New Jersey .	76.39	95.34	8.86	61.89
Pennsylv'a .	70.86	54.42	7.24	50.88
North Central States:				
Ohio	74.34	60.31	7.89	52.88
Indiana	80.19	74.88	8.53	51.77
Illinois	71.64	91.57	7.15	45.16
Michigan ...	82.62	70.40	7.88	47.66
Wisconsin ..	66.75	62.72	6.67	44.90
Minnesota ..	78.01	62.16	9.17	57.22
Iowa	90.11	60.90	9.35	52.15
Missouri ...	81.08	69.19	5.21	33.65
No. Dakota..	72.90	60.12	10.25	69.62
So. Dakota..	69.35	51.03	8.23	61.26
Nebraska ...	84.84	53.60	8.51	50.06
Kansas	83.28	69.91	8.41	49.40
South Atlantic States:				
Delaware ...	85.90	44.79	3.08	24.06
Maryland ..	68.00	63.04	3.84	30.93
Dist. Col....	82.18	112.34	10.10	74.09
Virginia ...	73.02	48.50	3.33	21.53
West Va....	78.25	51.69	4.66	28.85
No. Ca'lina..	84.07	42.57	2.29	12.31
So. Ca'lina..	76.63	54.14	2.20	12.80
Georgia	73.19	44.49	2.22	13.77
Florida	77.33	55.86	4.27	26.44
South Central States:				
Kentucky ..	76.78	52.33	3.51	23.56
Tennessee ..	88.81	53.72	2.96	15.76
Alabama ...	69.48	50.96	2.15	15.49
Mississippi .	77.57	37.99	1.48	9.30
Louisiana ..	55.91	63.10	3.01	23.36
Texas	73.26	84.82	4.76	30.50
Arkansas ...	81.99	49.62	2.56	14.63
Oklahoma ..	76.30	64.27	4.20	28.47
Western States:				
Montana ...	....	79.46	14.14	86.36
Wyoming ...	88.04	65.41	8.01	57.65
Colorado ...	81.94	75.79	7.83	55.90
N. Mexico ..	64.79	76.58	4.86	38.79
Arizona	81.58	96.30	10.44	77.85
Utah	85.96	88.95	10.31	50.84
Nevada	76.27	94.32	7.18	76.26
Idaho	84.68	95.85	9.65	63.56
Washington .	73.01	99.26	8.53	68.33
Oregon	77.61	86.15	8.04	52.50
California ..	94.47	113.46	10.93	78.16

The enrollment in the schools of the United States in 1916 was as follows:

	Public.	Private.	Total.
Elementary	18,895,626	1,665,075	20,560,701
Secondary .	1,485,119	215,718	1,700,837
Univs. and Colleges .	107,237	152,274	259,511
Professional Schools ..	12,336	57,540	69,876
Normal Schools ..	104,714	6,958	111,672
Special Schools ..	805,569	348,724	1,154,293
Totals ..	21,410,601	2,446,289	23,856,890

Colleges and Universities.—The first American institutions of higher learning were naturally patterned after the English model—indeed, were founded largely by graduates of English universities. Originally, they were training schools for the ministry, and admission was open to those who had completed what would now be considered a grammar school education with the addition of Latin and some mathematics.

Of the university and college students, in the first group there were 70,946 men and 36,291 women; and in the second group, 93,129 men and 59,145 women.

In 1916, the teachers of the country were distributed as follows:

Schools.	Men.	Women.	Total.
Public Elementary.	93,907	460,187	554,094
Public High.......	29,131	39,146	68,277
Private	26,656	36,131	62,787
Universities and Colleges	21,539	5,663	27,203
Professional	.....	.....	12,920
Normal	2,405	4,237	6,642
Others	21,180	17,090	38,270
Total	192,795	562,455	755,250

The enrollment in the elementary schools of the United States in 1916, by the different percentages in the different grades, was as follows:

	Grade 1st	Grade 2d	Grade 3d	Grade 4th
Unit'd States.	23½%	14¾%	14%	13¼%
No. Atlantic.	17¾	14½	13½	13
No. Central.	20½	13½	13½	13
So. Atlantic.	29	17½	15	13½
So. Central..	30	15¼	14½	14
Western	24	13¾	13	12¼

	Grade 5th	Grade 6th	Grade 7th	Grade 8th
Unit'd States.	11¼%	9¼%	7½%	6½%
No. Atlantic.	12	11	10	8½
No. Central..	11½	10½	8¾	8½
So. Atlantic.	10	7	5	2
So. Central..	11	7	5	3¼
Western	11	10	8½	8

The following table shows the distribution of the students in the secondary schools of the country and of the different sections in the year 1916:

	Year 1st	Year 2d	Year 3d	Year 4th
United States....	40½%	27%	18½%	14%
No. Atlantic	41½	27	18	13¼
No. Central	39	26½	19	15½
So. Atlantic	41¾	28	19	11
So. Central	41½	27½	18¼	12
Western	42	25½	17¾	14½

Harvard was established in 1636; William and Mary in 1693; Yale in 1701. In the eighteenth century, 21 colleges were established, 12 after the Revolution. In the nineteenth century, 153 were founded before the Civil War and 244 afterwards. In 1912, there reported to the United States Commissioner of Education 596 degree-granting institutions.

The development of strictly university, that is, post graduate and higher professional and research work, in the United States dates with the founding in 1876 of The Johns Hopkins University, patterned after German models, since when practically all of our great colleges have become universities as well as colleges. The course of study has become gradually lengthened and the requirements for admission heightened, so that whereas in the eighteenth century nineteen was the average age for graduation, it is to-day the average age for admission. The courses offered have also broadened to a remarkable extent, and the curriculum has become largely elective instead of compulsory. Few colleges or universities of the first rank are now under direct denominational auspices and control, although many retain a purely nominal sectarian character in their management.

A notable feature of American university progress has been the establishment of the great state universities, supported not by private funds, but by the state, and with low tuition charges and coeducation. An-

Institution	Founded	Faculty	Students
Amherst	1821	49	500
Barnard[1]	1889	115	736
Bryn Mawr[1]	1885	61	448
Carnegie Institute	1900	225	3,432
Catholic University	1889	83	1,655
Clark[2]	1889	23	90
College City New York	1847	281[4]	9,186[4]
Columbia	1754	1,042[3]	18,176[3]
Cornell[5]	1865	820	7,656
Dartmouth	1769	116	1,494
Georgetown	1789	220	1,500
George Washington[6]	1821	264	2,194
Goucher[1]	1885	55	709
Harvard	1636	892	6,306
Haverford	1833	29	170
Indiana[5][6]	1820	208	2,860
Johns Hopkins	1876	340	2,666
Lehigh	1866	81	653
Leland Stanford, Jr.[5]	1891	225	1,500
Massachusetts Inst. Technology[5]	1861	270	1,800
Mt. Holyoke[1]	1888	97	851
New York[5]	1831	507	8,075
Northwestern[5]	1851	495	5,274
Ohio State[5][6]	1872	516	5,761
Pennsylvania State[5][6]	1855	272	3,953
Princeton	1746	215	1,535
Purdue[5][6]	1869	265	2,415
Radcliffe[1]	1879	147	665
Smith[1]	1871	205	1,877
Syracuse[5]	1870	315	4,020
Teachers'[5]	1888	230	4,871
Univ. California[5][6]	1860	503	11,960
Univ. Chicago[5]	1891	322	10,448
Univ. Illinois[5]	1867	868	6,850
Univ. Michigan[5][6]	1837	414	7,517
Univ. Minnesota[5][6]	1868	608	13,279
Univ. Missouri[5][6]	1839	309	4,349
Univ. Nebraska[5][6]	1869	190	4,826
Univ. Notre Dame	1842	90	1,285
Univ. Pennsylvania[5]	1740	630	9,000
Univ. Wisconsin[5][6]	1848	490	5,318
U. S. Military Academy	1802	136	763
U. S. Naval Academy	1845	157	1,230
Vanderbilt[5]	1872	145	897
Vassar[1]	1861	138	1,100
Washington[5]	1853	226	1,304
Wellesley[1]	1875	138	1,609
Western Reserve[5]	1826	340	3,168
Yale	1701	478	3,254

[1] For women only; [2] graduate work only; [3] including extension, summer, professional schools and Barnard College; [4] including preparatory department; [5] coeducational; [6] state universities.

other feature to be mentioned is university extension work, whereby college instructors travel throughout the state or nation to present their services and information to those who cannot be reached within the college walls. Many colleges combine their academic and professional courses into a combination six-year course, whereas certain medical schools and law schools, etc., require the completion of the full four-year academic course before admission. Colleges for women are a phenomenon of the last seventy-five years, and are found mostly in the East, where the older colleges and universities still do not admit women to undergraduate work. Of recent years, the tendency of college courses has been to get away from the older classical and theoretical training and to provide training seen to be necessary by an examination of the features of modern American life.

A list of the more famous universities and colleges adjoins. In the case of the enrollment, it must be remembered that it contains many who do not pursue full courses, but do part-time work in summer schools, professional courses, etc.

Education (see also Indian Schools; Military Academy, National University; Naval Academy):

Act donating lands for benefit of agricultural colleges vetoed, 3074.

Appropriation of proceeds of sales of public lands for, recommended, 4106, 4157, 4558, 4578, 4645.

Constitutional amendment regarding, suggested, 397, 444, 587.

Constitutional amendment regarding maintenance of free schools by states, etc., recommended, 4288.

Government aid to, recommended by President—

Arthur, 4645, 4730, 4771, 4840.

Harrison, Benj., 5489.

Roosevelt, 7045.

In Alaska, appropriation for, recommended, 4667, 5483.

In Army discussed, 4570, 5879.

In Indian Territory, recommendations regarding, 6346.

Industrial, discussed, 7045, 8187.

Report on, transmitted, 5782.

In new national problems, requested of school officials, 8331.

Lands granted to states in aid of, 1029, 1045, 3587, 4206, 5974.

Recommended, 398, 470, 4065, 4208.

Of freedom discussed and referred to, 3995, 5489.

Recommendation that States be required to afford good common schools, 4310.

Recommendations regarding education in states, 4431, 4458, 4554, 4578.

Sectarian tenets not to be taught in public schools, 4310.

Technical, discussed, 7045.

Vocational, advocated, 8187.

Education, Bureau of. (See Bureau of Education.)

Education, Bureau of:

Discussed by President—

Grant, 4066, 4207.

Hayes, 4531, 4578.

Establishment of, referred to, 4036.

National, purposes of, 7227.

Education, Industrial, report on, transmitted, 5782.

Educational Land Grants, 1029, 1045, 3587, 4206, 5974.

Recommended, 398, 470, 4065, 4208.

Educational Requirements for Voters, recommended by President Grant, 4310, 4365.

Edwards, W. H., report of, transmitted, 5769.

Eel River Indians. (See Indian Tribes.)

Egypt.—Egypt occupies the northeastern corner of the African continent, between 22°-31° 35′ N. latitude and 16°-37° E. longitude. The northern boundary is the Mediterranean, and in the south Egypt is conterminous with the Anglo-Egyptian Sudan. The western boundary runs from the coast, near the Gulf of Sollûm (longitude 25° E.), inland in a southwesterly direction, and in the extreme southwest meets that of the French Sahara in 16° E. longitude; in the northeast a line drawn from the north of the Gulf of Akaba to Rafa on the Mediterranean (34° 15′ E. longitude) separates the Sinai Peninsula from Palestine, and the remainder of .the eastern boundary is washed by the Red Sea.

Physical Features.—The highlands of Abyssinia extend northward through Egypt along the Red Sea littoral and Gulf of Suez to the Sinai Peninsula, a triangular plateau in its northeast corner, with Mount Sinai (8,540 feet), near the apex in the south.

The principal feature of Egypt is the Nile Valley, where the river runs through cliffs, which, with the exception of granite round Aswân, are of sandstone from Wadi Halfa to near Esna, while from Qena to Cairo limestone predominates. These cliffs sometimes rise to nearly 2,000 feet above the level of the sea. The c.iff-enclosed valley increases in width to several miles, and on either side of the river, particularly to the west, lie the fertile lands upon which the prosperity of the country depends; after the Delta Barrage (14 miles north of Cairo) the country spreads out into an irregular, fan-shaped formation comprising the six Provinces of Lower Egypt, which contain the richest soil in the country. The Nile has a total length of about 3,700 miles from the Victoria Nyanza to its mouths, and for close on 900 miles of its course lies between the southern and northern boundaries of Egypt. The river has an almost constant rise and fall, the rise attaining its maximum in September, its fall being rapid for about fourteen weeks from that time, and then gradual to the end of May.

Between the western cliffs of the Nile Valley and the Tripolitan Valley is a vast plateau, known as the Libyan Desert, with a total area of about 270,000 square miles. On the eastern edge of the Libyan Desert, southwest of Cairo, stand the Great Pyramids of Giza.

The country between the Nile Valley and the Red Sea is known as the Arabian Desert.

History.—From B.C. 30 to A.D. 639 Egypt was a province of the Roman Empire, but in A.D. 640 the Christian inhabitants were subjugated by Moslem invaders, and Egypt became a province of the Eastern Caliphate. In 1517 the country was incorporated in the Ottoman Empire, and was governed by pashas sent from Constantinople until the beginning of the eighteenth century, when for about 100 years the ruler was chosen from among the mamelukes, or bodyguard. From 1802-1804 French troops occupied the country, with the ostensible object of suppressing the mamelukes and restoring the authority of the Sultan; and after their evacuation of the country Mohammed Ali, who was appointed governor in 1805, exterminated the mamelukes in 1811, and was eventually made hereditary governor of Egypt and the Sudan by a firman from the Sultan of Feb. 13, 1841. Mohammed Ali was succeeded before his death by his son Ibrahîm (1848 . whose nephew Abbâs I. ruled from 1848-1854. During the reign

of Saïd (1854-1863), a son of Mohammed Ali, the concession for the Suez Canal was obtained, and his successor Ismail (1863-1879), a son of Ibrahim, was granted (by firman of May 14, 1867) the title of Khedive, the previous rulers having held the title of Vali, or Governor. In the early years of Ismail's reign the Egyptian dominions were very largely extended, until in 1875 its territories comprised an area of nearly 1,500,000 square miles, with a population of about 16,000,000. The wild extravagance of Ismail drove him to raise enormous loans in Europe, which plunged the country into such financial embarrassment that the Governments of France and Great Britain intervened and forced Ismail to abdicate, appointing his son Tewfik (1879-1892) to succeed him.

By a Khedival decree oɪ Nov. 10, 1879, two Comptrollers-General were appointed for the reorganization of the administration and re-establishment of financial equilibrium, Major Evelyn Baring being the British and M. de Blignières the French representative. The Dual Control governed Egypt for two years, and a series of reforms was initiated, but further progress was interrupted by a military revolt, headed by an officer of the Egyptian Army (Ahmed Arâbi Pasha). The revolt assumed alarming proportions, but the French Government declined to intervene, and a British expedition was dispatched to re-establish the authority of the Khedive. Egypt is nominally subject to Turkey and pays an annual tribute of $3,300,-000, but in all internal and international affairs the Khedive is completely independent. In practice, however, the actual control is in the hands of Great Britain.

AREA AND POPULATION

Districts and Capitals	Area in English Sq. Miles	Population 1907
Lower Egypt—		
Alexandria	70	332,246
Cairo	19	654,476
Ismailia and Port Saïd	3	61,332
Suez	3	18,347
Beheira (Damanhûr)	1,725	830,015
Daqahlia (Mansûra)	1,018	912,428
Gharbia (Tanta)	2,436	1,484,814
Menuffa (Shebîn el Kôm)	609	971,016
Qaliûbia (Benha)	358	434,575
Sharqia (Zagazig)	1,323	886,346
Upper Egypt—		
Assiât (Assiât)	772	907,435
Aswân (Aswân)	169	234,602
Beni Suêf (Beni Suêf)	413	372,412
Fayûm (Medînet el Fayûm)	671	441,583
Girga (Sohâg)	579	797,940
Giza (Giza)	397	460,080
Minia (Minia)	759	663,144
Qena (Qena)	656	780,849
El 'Arîsh	} 11,200	{ 18,637
Sinai Peninsula		25,082
Libyan and Arabian Deserts	340,000	100,000
Total	363,181	11,287,359

The Dual Control was abolished by a decree of the Khedive (Jan. 18, 1883), and a British financial adviser was appointed in place of the Comptroller-General. In January, 1884, Sir Evelyn Baring (who had previously served as Comptroller-General) was appointed Consul-General for the United Kingdom, and the British expeditionary force, sent to quell the rebellion of 1882, remained in the country as an army of occupation. Meanwhile a revolt had broken out in the southern provinces, headed by Sheikh Mohammed Ahmed, of Dongola, who had proclaimed himself a Mahdi of Islam. This revolt led to the temporary abandonment of the territory now known as the Sudan Provinces (*q. v.*). In 1892 Tewfik was succeeded by his elder son Abbas II., the present Khedive.

Ethnography.—There are three distinct elements in the native population of Egypt. The largest, or "Egyptian" element, is a Hamito-Semitic race, known in the rural districts as Fellahin (fellâh = ploughman, or tiller of the soil). The fellahin have been mainly Muhammadans since the conquest of the country in the seventh century, but about 800,000 Coptic Christians are enumerated in the towns and villages. These Egyptian townsmen and peasantry exceed 10,000,000 in the total of the Census of 1907. A second element is the Bedouin, or nomadic Arabs of the Libyan and Arabian deserts, numbering in all about 750,000, of whom about one-seventh are real nomads, and the remainder semi-sedentary tent-dwellers on the outskirts of the cultivated land of the Nile Valley and the Fayûm. The third element is the Nubian of the Nile Valley, between Aswân and Wadi Halfa, of mixed Arab and negro blood. The Bedouins and Nubians are Muhammadans. At the Census of 1907 the foreign residents exceeded 220,000, including Turks, Greeks, Italians, ⌐ritish, French and Tunisians, Austro-Hungarians, Russians, Germans, other Europeans, and Persians.

Government.—Viscount Kitchener of Khartoum was appointed British Agent and Governor-General in 1911. The army is limited to 18,000, and the commander in chief is appointed by the Khedive with the consent of the British Government. The position of Egypt is thus somewhat complicated as a semi-independent tributary State of the Ottoman Empire, at present occupied by British troops. Ruler, Abbâs II. (Abbâs Hilmi), Khedive of Egypt; born July 16, 1874; succeeded his father (Mohammed Tewfik) Jan. 7, 1892.

Irrigation.—ᴋing Mena (B.C. 4000, approximately) is said to have been the founder of the first scientific system of using the Nile water for irrigation purposes; he employed what is known as the basin system, which is still used for the irrigation of all the land lying to the south of Deirût in Upper Egypt. By this system the land is divided into rectangular areas varying in size from 5,000 to 50,000 acres and surrounded by banks; water is admitted to these basins during the flood season (August) to an average depth of three feet, and is left on the land for about forty days; it is then run off and the seed is sown broadcast on the uncovered land. Since the British occupation the basin systems have been improved and provided with numbers of important masonry works. About 1820 Mohammed 'Ali Pasha introduced the system of perennial irrigation by digging deep canals in which the water could flow all the year round, by which means it was possible to grow two (or more) crops in one year, and to introduce the cultivation of cotton on a large scale. By these works, and by the construction of a vast network of canals perennial irrigation has been extended throughout middle and lower Egypt. The increase in the value of the land has been enormous, and some two million acres have been added to the cultivable area of Egypt. Harvests of wheat, barley, beans, clover, vetches and lentils are gathered in due course. In Lower Egypt, cotton, maize, wheat, rice, beans, barley, sugar cane and clover are the chief crops.

Railways.—There is a network of railways in the Delta, the principal lines radiating from Cairo to Alexandria (and on to Rosetta), Damietta, and Ismailia (continuing northward to Port Said and southward to Suez). From Cairo the line runs southward for a distance of 554 miles to Shellal, the First Cataract. At this point a steamer connection runs to Wadi Halfa, connecting the Egyptian State system with the Sudan Government Railways.

Caravan Routes.—The principal caravan routes lead to the Oases of the Libyan Desert. There are many well-known routes across the Arabian Desert to the Red Sea.

Cities.—Cairo, the capital, stands on the east bank of the Nile, about fourteen miles from the head of the Delta. Its oldest part is the fortress of Babylon in Old Cairo, with its Roman bastions and Coptic churches. The earliest Arab building is the mosque of 'Amr, dating from A.D. 643, and the most conspicuous is the Citadel, built by Saladin toward the end of the twelfth century. On the eᴅge of the desert west of Cairo are the Pyramids of Giza and the Sphinx, which can now be reached by tram in about forty minutes. Alexandria, founded B.C. 332 by Alexander the Great, was for over 1,000 years the capital of Egypt. Its great Pharos, or lighthouse, was one of the "seven wonders of the world."

Egypt:

American citizens in, proclamation regarding rights of, 4231, 4344. Discussed, 4244, 4357.

American representative in, death of, referred to, 3446.

Ancient obelisk presented to New York City by Government of, 4520, 4564.

Change of personal head of, 4520.

Commercial convention with, agreement regarding, 4849.

Consular courts in, discussed, 4759.

Consuls in, relieved of judicial powers discussed, 4192.

Diplomatic relations with, 4824. Resumed, 3446.

Disturbances in, and protection for American citizens discussed, 4715.

Expulsion of Greeks from, referred to, 2828.

Judicial code of reform tribunal of, to be revised, 4564.

Egypt, International Tribunals of.—In 1876, as the result of negotiations between the Ottoman and Egyptian Governments and the various Christian powers having representatives at Cairo, courts were created in Egypt for the trial of civil and commercial causes arising between natives and foreigners of different nationality, as well as all questions of real estate between any person and suits of foreigners against the Egyptian Government and members of the Khedival family. These mixed tribunals, in civil matters within their exclusive jurisdiction, superseded the consular courts. A mixed tribunal consists of five judges, three of whom are foreigners and two natives. The foreign judges are appointed by the Khedive on the recommendation of the great powers, each of which is represented by from one to three judges. There are three tribunals of original jurisdiction (first instance), one each at Cairo, Alexandria and Mansura, and a Court of Appeals at Alexandria. The United States

is represented in these courts by the following judges:
Court of Appeals.—Somerville P. Tuck, of New York (appointed 1908).
Court of First Instance.—William G. Van Horne, of Utah (appointed 1902); Pierre Crabités, of Louisiana (appointed 1911).

Egypt, Treaties with. — In November, 1884, a convention relative to commerce and customs was concluded with Egypt. It is identical with one concluded between Egypt and Greece during the same year. It contains the most favored-nation clause, and provides for the importation into Egypt of the productions of the soil and industry of the United States under a fixed duty based upon eight per cent *ad valorem* in the port of discharge. The importation of firearms into Egypt is forbidden, as well as tobacco in all its forms, and tombac, together with salt, natron, hashish, and saltpeter. The productions of the soil of Egypt, when sent to the United States, shall pay an export duty of 1 per cent *ad valorem* computed on the value of the goods at the port of exportation.

Eight-Hour Law.—Congress, as long ago as 1868, passed a law making eight hours a legal day's work for all laborers, workmen and mechanics employed by or on behalf of the government, and President Grant by proclamation decreed that no reduction in wages should be made in consequence of the shortening of the day. (Page 3969.) Failure of certain department heads to comply with the law brought forth an emphatic repetition of the proclamation for strict observance. (Page 4129.)
President Van Buren had, back in 1840, ordered a uniform day of ten hours in the executive departments.
The eight-hour law was evaded by contractors in navy yards and public buildings and work undertaken by contractors for many years. Finally in 1912 an act was passed to take effect Jan. 1, 1913, requiring all contracts for government work to contain a clause forbidding laborers or mechanics to work more than eight hours a day.

Eight-Hour Law should be extended, 7088, 7208.

El Caney (Cuba), Battle of. (See Santiago (Cuba), Battle of.)

El Caney, Cuba, captured by American troops, 6317, and illustration opposite 5994.

El Dorado.—Alternative nickname for California. (See Golden State.)

El Dorado of the North.—A nickname for Alaska (q. v.).

El Dorado, The, arrest and search of, by Spanish authorities, 2869, 2976.

Election Commission charged with inquiring into subject of election laws recommended, 5646, 5766.

Election.—The choosing of officials by vote.

Election Law, Federal, recommended, 5490, 5562, 5766.

Elections:
Act prohibiting military interference at, vetoed, 4484.
Army and Navy prohibited from interfering in, 3866.

Complications growing out of, in Southern States, and other disturbances, discussed, 4071, 4072, 4104, 4117, 4161, 4166, 4218, 4219, 4250, 4259, 4273, 4367, 4372.
Federal interference in, discussed, 4259.
Habeas corpus suspended in certain sections, 4090, 4093.
Revoked as to certain county, 4092.
Proclamation regarding, 4086, 4088, 4089, 4090, 4092, 4093, 4177, 4226, 4230, 4276, 4350.
Congressional and claims of members to seats discussed, 4466.
Constitutional conventional in Cuba, ordered, 6448.
Discussed, 4445, 4512, 4553.
Educational requirements for voters recommended, 4310, 4365.
Federal supervision of Congressional, recommended, 5490, 5562, 5766.
Gerrymander discussed, 5643.
In Arkansas, disturbances regarding, and claims of persons to governorship discussed, 4218, 4219, 4252, 4273.
Proclamation regarding, 4226.
In California, correspondence regarding national military forces to be used at, referred to, 4076.
In Louisiana, complications growing out of, discussed, 4161, 4166, 4250, 4259.
Federal interference in, discussed, 4259.
Proclamations regarding, 4177, 4230.
In Mississippi, proclamation regarding complications growing out of, 4276.
In the South and results of amendments to Federal Constitution discussed, 4445, 4553.
In Virginia, troops at polling places during, referred to, 4367, 4372.
Not to be held in Hawaii, 6590.
Partisan interference in, by public officers—
Discussed by President Tyler, 1905, 1942.
Order regarding, of President—
Cleveland, 5079.
Hayes, 4402.
President discussed. (See President of United States.)
Stimulus of personal interests in, should be restrained, 1942.
Troops stationed at polling places in Southern States discussed, 4367, 4372.

Elective Franchise to Freedmen:
Discussed by President—
Garfield, 4598.

Hayes, 4445, 4553.

Johnson, 3557.

Free exercise of right of suffrage discussed and recommendations regarding, 5490, 5562, 5643.

Elector.—A citizen having the franchise, or the right to vote; a member of the Electoral College (q. v.). (See Presidential Electors.)

Electoral Colleges.—Under the Constitution of the United States (Article II, Section 1), the President and Vice-President are chosen every four years by electors appointed by each state "in such manner as the legislature thereof may direct." Each state is entitled to as many electors as it has Senators and Representatives. No Senator or Representative or person holding an office of trust or honor under the United States may be an elector. The twelfth amendment to the Constitution prescribes how the electors shall meet and cast their ballots, and how Congress shall count the votes. The article provides that "the electors shall meet in their respective states and vote by ballot for president and vice-president, one of whom at least shall not be an inhabitant of the same state with themselves. They shall name in their ballots the person voted for as president, and in separate ballots the person voted for as vice-president, and they shall make distinct lists of all persons voted for as president and of all persons voted for as vice-president, and of the number of votes for each, which list they shall sign and certify and transmit, sealed, to the seat of the government of the United States, directed to the President of the Senate."

The term Electoral College has been informally used since 1821, and was probably suggested by the "College of Cardinals." The words "College of Electors" first appear in an act passed in 1845. The Colleges of Electors are state bodies, and their integrity as such is scrupulously guarded. Their method of appointment is left absolutely to the state legislatures. Till about 1820-1824 they were appointed direct by the legislature in most states; in 1824 popular election had superseded legislative appointment in all but six states. The last state to adopt popular choice of presidential electors was South Carolina, in 1868. The congress district system, which divides a state's electoral vote, has sometimes been tried as a party compromise, but at present all parties prefer the system of having all the electors on a general ticket. The state appoints the place of meeting and Congress has fixed the time—the second Monday in January, every fourth year. There is no organization of the college, but it is customary to select a chairman. On the second Wednesday in February following the meeting of the electors, both houses of Congress meet in the hall of the House of Representatives and the President of the Senate opens and counts the state returns. The state, by act of Feb. 3, 1887, is made absolute judge of all disputes over returns; its certificate is final between two sets of returns and Congress can only intervene if the state itself is unable to decide. (See Electoral Commission.)

In the presidential campaign of 1912 during the contest between President Taft for renomination and Mr. Roosevelt for the nomination for President before the Republican convention, some of the states chose presidential electors before the nominations were made. President Taft was nominated by the convention, and Mr. Roosevelt decided to run for President as the nominee of the (new) Progressive Republican party. Mr. Roosevelt claimed that the electors who had been chosen and instructed to vote for him before the nomination of Mr. Taft were still, notwithstanding the latter's nomination, in duty bound to carry out their obligations to the people, and vote for Mr. Roosevelt, and some of the electors expressed such intentions. The courts were appealed to in several states and ruled that electors regularly placed on the Republican ticket could not be removed because of the failure or success of any candidate before national convention, and that their obligations to the people were the same as if no convention had been held.

Electoral Colleges:

Increase of political power of Southern States in, due to constitutional amendments, discussed, 4445.

Joint resolution declaring certain States not entitled to representation in, discussed, 3461.

One branch of Congress formed into, productive of mischief, 1395.

Referred to, 2188.

Electoral Commission.—In the Presidential election of 1876 Rutherford B. Hayes and Samuel J. Tilden were the respective Republican and Democratic candidates. Charges of fraud were made concerning the electoral votes of Florida, Louisiana, Oregon and South Carolina. On Jan. 20, 1877, Congress appointed a commission, called the Electoral Commission, to investigate the charges and determine the validity of the returns. This is the only time a commission of this sort has been appointed and much doubt has been expressed as to its constitutionality. The commission consisted of fifteen members—three Republican Senators, two Democratic Senators, three Democratic Representatives, two Republican Representatives, and five Associate Justices of the Supreme Court. Its members were Justice Nathan Clifford (president of the commission), Samuel F. Miller, Stephen J. Field, William Strong, and Joseph P. Bradley; Senators George F. Edmunds, Oliver P. Morton, Frederick T. Frelinghuysen, Thomas F. Bayard, and Allen G. Thurman (replaced later by Francis Kernan), and Representatives Henry B. Payne, Eppa Hunton, Josiah G. Abbott, George F. Hoar, and James A. Garfield. The commission by a vote of eight to seven, on Feb. 9, 1877, decided to sustain the validity of the Hayes electoral ticket in Florida, and later gave similar decisions regarding the returns from the other states. After the work of the commission the vote of the electoral colleges stood 185 for Hayes and 184 for Tilden.

Electoral-Commission Bill approved and reasons therefor, 4376.

Electoral Messengers, compensation to, recommendations regarding, 4850.

Electors, Presidential:

Constitutional amendment regarding selection of, recommended, 5644.

Method of appointment of, and effect of gerrymander discussed, 5643.

Electrical Machinery, Apparatus and Supplies.—(From a bulletin of July 31, 1916, issued by the Bureau of the Census.)

This industry includes the manufacture of the machines and appliances used in the generation, transmission and utilization of electric energy, together with most of the parts, accessories and supplies for them. It does not include, however, the production of poles, whether of wood, iron or steel; nor does it include the manufacture of glass and porcelain ware made expressly for electrical purposes, that of bare iron and copper wire, or any of the group of electrochemical and electrometallurgical products.

The statistics for 1914 cover a period of depression due to the outbreak of the European war, from which the industry has since fully recovered.

Reports were received from 1,121 establishments engaged in this industry in 1914; with products valued at $359,412,676. Of these establishments, the principal business of 1,030 was the manufacture of electrical machinery, apparatus, and supplies, and 91, which were engaged primarily in other lines of manufacture, produced electrical machinery and apparatus to the value of $24,261,961.

It is to be noted that these statistics do not cover porcelain electrical supplies, manufactured by the clay-working industries—valued at $4,130,270 in 1914, as reported by the Geological Survey—nor globes and battery jars for electrical use, manufactured in glass works.

The output of dynamos, including parts and supplies, in 1914 was valued at $23,233,437. Under this head are included dynamotors, motor-generators, boosters, rotary converters, double-current generators, etc., 8,393 in number, with an aggregate capacity of 780,009 kilowatts and valued at $5,367,895.

STATEMENT OF THE MANUFACTURE OF ELECTRICAL MACHINERY, APPARATUS, AND SUPPLIES

	Census 1914	Per cent of increase for 5 years
Number of establishments......	1,030	2.1
Persons engaged in manufacture	144,712	37.0
Proprietors and firm members	368	*16.2
Salaried employees..........	26,266	46.7
Wage earners (average number)	118,078	35.3
Primary horsepower..........	227,731	43.4
Capital.......................	$355,725,000	32.8
Services.....................	109,097,000	56.8
Salaries....................	35,291,000	74.8
Wages.....................	73,806,000	49.5
Materials..................	154,728,000	42.5
Value of products............	335,170,000	51.4
Value added by manufacture (value of products less cost of materials)..................	180,442,000	60.0

* Decrease.

In addition, in 1914, 91 establishments, primarily engaged in other lines of manufacture, produced electrical machinery, apparatus, and supplies to the value of $24,261,961, and in 1909, 142 establishments of this character manufactured $18,728,916 worth of electrical machinery, apparatus and supplies as a subsidiary product.

Under the head of direct-current dynamos there were reported 208,548 small dynamos and automobile starter-generator sets, valued at $5,933,273, but this is not to be taken as the total output of such devices, since it is apparent that they were reported by the manufacturers in some cases with "motors for automobiles."

The transformers manufactured in 1914 aggregated 115,843 in number, with 2,644,794 kilowatts' capacity, and were valued at $13,120,065.

The 1914 output of motors, including parts and supplies, was valued at $44,176,235. Motors made in 1914 for industrial power and for railway use numbered 417,992, had an aggregate capacity of 2,882,795 horsepower, and were valued at $32,286,149. Of motors for automobiles, 11,880, having an aggregate horsepower of 36,858 and valued at $1,351,442, were produced in 1914. This output, however, probably includes a considerable number of starting motors for gasoline automobiles, not separately reported as such. Motors for fans to the value of $4,835,850 were reported for 1914, and motors for miscellaneous uses to the value of $1,190,564.

Other products reported for 1914 were: Light and power switchboards, panel boards, and cut-out cabinets, valued at $8,989,111; batteries, storage and primary, and parts and supplies, $23,402,455; incandescent lamps. $17,350,385; arc lamps, searchlights, projectors, and focusing lamps, $2,823,687; telephones, telephone switchboards, and parts and supplies, $22,815,640; telegraph apparatus, including wireless, switchboards, and parts and supplies, $2,248,375; electric heating apparatus, including air heaters, cooking devices, flatirons, and welding apparatus, $4,034,436; electric measuring instruments, $8,786,506; electrical therapeutic apparatus, $2,653,098; insulated wires and cables, $69,505,573; electric conduits, underground and interior, $4,874,709; magneto-ignition apparatus, spark plugs, coils, etc., $22,260,847; electric switches, signals, and attachments, $6,393,551, an increase of 18.9 per cent; carbons for furnace, lighting, brushes, battery, etc., $3,602,741, an increase of 86.2 per cent; annunciators, $263,806, an increase of 12 per cent; electric clocks and time mechanisms, $410,774, an increase of 16.5 per cent; and various other kinds of electric equipment, including sockets, receptacles and bases, some electric lighting fixtures, lightning arresters, fuses, circuit fittings, and unclassified electric machinery, apparatus, and supplies, $44,907,658, an increase of 56.3 per cent. The last item includes electric locomotives, mine and railway, of which there were reported 900, valued at $3,720,914.

Location of Establishments.—Of the 1,121 establishments reported for 1914, 234 were located in New York, 151 in Illinois, 129 in Ohio, 114 in Pennsylvania, 100 in Massachusetts, 83 in New Jersey, 46 in Connecticut, 46 in Indiana, 30 in California, 19 in Missouri, 18 in Minnesota, 17 in Rhode Island, 8 in Colorado, 7 in Maryland, 6 in New Hampshire, 5 in Iowa, 4 each in Delaware, North Carolina, Tennessee, Washington, and West Virginia, 3 in Kentucky, 2 each in District of Columbia, Louisiana, Nebraska, and Vermont, and 1 each in Alabama, Kansas, Oregon, South Carolina, Texas, and Virginia.

Electric Telegraph. (See Telegraph Lines.)

Electricians, International Congress of, at Paris, discussed and recommendations regarding, 4581, 4625, 4714.

Electricians, National Conference of, at Philadelphia, 4956.

Eleemosynary Institutions, Washington, D. C.—The Department of the Interior is charged with the Government administration and supervision over the following institutions in Washington: Government Hospital for the Insane (q. v.), Freedmen's Hospital (q. v.), Howard University (q. v.) and the Columbian Institution for the Deaf (q. v.), including Gallaudet College.

Elephant.—A symbol of the Republican party.

Elimination of local offices from politics, 7698.

Elk Refuge, land set apart for, 7988.

Emancipation of Slaves:
Compensation to states abolishing slavery recommended, 3269, 3292, 3334.
Draft of bill for, 3285, 3337.
Recommendation again to be made, 3297.
Constitutional amendment regarding, recommended, 3453, 3556.
Ratification of, 3570, 3643.
Discussed by President Hayes, 4394.

Emancipation Proclamation.—Early in the Civil War many persons began to agitate for a proclamation from the President declaring the slaves free. It was the intention of President Lincoln, as he declared, to preserve the Union without freeing the slaves, if possible. Sept. 22, 1862, he issued a preliminary proclamation (page 3297) as a war measure, calling upon all the people in rebellion against the United States to return to their allegiance, promising measures of relief in case of compliance, and threatening to free the slaves in those states and parts of states which should still be in rebellion on the 1st day of January next succeeding the proclamation. This had no effect. Accordingly, on Jan. 1, 1863, President Lincoln issued a supplementary proclamation (page 3358) declaring the freedom of the slaves in all the states which had seceded except forty-eight counties in West Virginia, seven counties in Virginia, including the cities of Norfolk and Portsmouth, and thirteen parishes of Louisiana, including the city of New Orleans. The thirteenth amendment to the Constitution, in force Dec. 18, 1865, completed the work of emancipation, by which 3,895,172 slaves were made free. (See illustrations opposite 3261.)

Emancipation Proclamation, 3358.
Carpenter's painting of Lincoln and Cabinet at first reading of, presented to Congress, 4435.
Notice given that slaves would be emancipated on Jan. 1, 1863, 3297.

Embalmed Beef.—A term used to characterize the canned meats supplied to the United States Army during the Spanish-American War—implying that the meats were so badly decomposed that they had to be treated with preservative chemicals. (See Eagan's Court-Martial.)

Embargo.—A prohibition imposed by a country to prevent its vessels or those of neutral or hostile powers leaving its ports. The United States Government laid embargoes at various times between 1794 and 1815. Upon the breaking out of war between France and Great Britain in 1793 each country ordered the seizure of neutral vessels bound for the ports of the other. In consequence of the depredations of England and France upon the commerce of the United States, an act was passed April 18, 1806, prohibiting trade with Great Britain and her colonies. Dec. 22, 1807, Congress, at the suggestion of Jefferson, passed an embargo act prohibiting the sailing of any merchant vessel, save coasters, from any American port.
II

Jan. 9, 1808, another and more stringent act was passed. These measures failed to bring either France or England to terms, and, though somewhat modified by the act of March 12, 1808, they wrought much injury to shipping and export trade of the United States. They were extensively evaded, and March 1, 1809, were repealed and replaced by the nonintercourse law, which forbade French and English vessels entering American ports. Another embargo act was passed Dec. 10, 1813, during the second war with Great Britain.

Embargo:
During war with Germany—
On coin, bullion and currency, 8355.
On various commodities, 8333.
Imposed by Washington, 144, 145.
On American vessels referred to, 427.
On foreign vessels—
For 60 days recommended, 484.
Governors requested to call forth militia if necessary to enforce, 144.
Imposed, 458.
Removed, 457, 466.

Embassy.—The official name of the building in which an ambassador officially resides.

Embezzlement. (See Defalcation.)

Emblem.—A design used to symbolize an organization, a sentiment, or an idea, as evenly balanced scales symbolize justice.

Emergency Fleet Corporation, powers of, 8316.

Emergency Peace Federation. (See Peace Societies.)

Emigrants to United States. (See Immigration.)

Emigration of Negroes. (See Negroes.)

Emigration to the West. (See illustrations opposite 900, 1057, 2246, 2929.)

Eminent Domain.—The original or superior ownership retained by the people or state by which land or other private property may be taken for public use or benefit. This is the most definite principle of the fundamental power of the government with regard to property and the most exact idea of property remaining in the government or in the aggregate body of the people in their sovereign capacity, giving the right to resume original possession in the manner directed by law whenever its use is essential to the mutual advantage and welfare of society. If, for instance, the proper authorities deem it necessary for the general good to open a street, lay out a park, dig a canal, abate a nuisance, charter a railroad, etc., and the owners of the land on the route or space desired refuse to sell or demand an exorbitant price for their property, the state, by eminent domain, has the power of control, and the courts may compel the surrender of the property upon due compensation being determined by a board of appraisers. The Constitution of the United States limits the exercise of the right of eminent domain to cases where public good demands it and requires compensation to those from whom property is taken.

Empire State.—A nickname for New York (q. v.). (See also States.)

Empire State of the South.—A nickname for Georgia (q. v.), (See also States); sometimes also nicknamed the Cracker State.

Employees. (See Government Employees; Officers, Public.)

Employers' Liability and Workmen's Compensation Legislation.—The term "employers' liability" may be used in either a general or a legal and legislative sense. In the former, it would cover the responsibility of the employer for conditions in his establishment, and consequently for any injury sustained by the employee as a result of those conditions.

In the common law, however, the term became involved with contractual and master-and-servant relations, so that its legal bearing until the last several decades was at variance with the common-sense meaning described above. According to this interpretation, the employee made himself responsible for all the ordinary risk of employment when he voluntarily entered it. Especially was he responsible for any injury inflicted as a result of action by a "fellow-servant;" and the latter term included any one working for the same employer, even a manager or superintendent.

In the second half of the nineteenth century, public opinion became aware of the unfairness of this current legal conception of employers' liability, and in 1880 an enactment of the English Parliament paved the way for reform. That example was followed by other countries, the United States legislation, by constitutional requirements, being state legislation.

But in most cases involving employers' liability, the employee was still at a distinct disadvantage. He could seldom obtain the damages due him without lengthy and expensive law suits, which would cost a large share of the sum he finally received and cause much delay; and as a result he was usually forced to compromise on appreciably less than was due him. There arose accordingly a series of enactments providing for automatic award of damages, according to definite principles, although these laws of "workmen's compensation" vary in the different states. The employers met the new demand upon their funds by insuring themselves against the necessity for such payments, either through state or through private agencies; and there arose hence the principle of Employers' Liability or Workmen's Compensation Insurance.

Germany provided for compulsory workmen's compensation in 1884 and England in 1897; but the movement in the United States did not realize definite achievements until 1910. In some of the states, the amount of the compensation is fixed by the enactment in accordance with the injury received; in others, there are commissions to determine the compensation. Some of the legislation is compulsory; but much is still elective, although it provides special inducement for coming under the provisions of the law.

On September 7, 1916, the Federal government passed legislation providing for automatic compensation for all civilian employees of the Government and of the Panama Railroad. In 1917, provision was made also for automatic pensions for injuries received by those in the Army and Navy as a result of the war against Germany. (See Soldiers' and Sailors' Insurance.)

In the United States, the Supreme Court has verified the constitutionality of the employers' liability and workmen's compensation laws.

According to the latest figures, there were thirty-seven states and three territories which enjoyed workmen's compensation privileges. The states in which no such legislation had been passed were as follows: Alabama, Arkansas, District of Columbia (Federal employees covered by the Federal Law), Florida, Georgia, Mississippi, Missouri, North Carolina, North Dakota, South Carolina, Tennessee, Virginia. It will be seen that practically all of these states are Southern states.

Every state law passed provides for some exemptions from the operation of the workmen's compensation enactments. Accordingly, although the states with such enactments contain between 75% and 80% of the country's workers, in reality less than 35% of the workers are protected. In only 8 states is the automatic compensation compulsory.

In only New Jersey and Hawaii are 90% of the workers covered by the provisions of the law, and in only 7 states are 80% of the workers so protected. In most of the states, agricultural, domestic and casual laborers are excluded from the operations from the law. Indeed, agricultural labor is specifically included in only one law and is specifically excluded in 23 of the states.

Another group of laws extends compensation only to those industries of particular danger to the employees; and still another group excludes workers in small shops, one law even excluding workers in shops employing less than twelve persons.

Some idea of the varying natures of the state laws may be gained from the fact that in one state, Oregon, the widow and children of a man killed in industry receive $13,480; in another state, Vermont, they receive only $1,830; and in a third, Oklahoma, they receive nothing.

However, the workmen's compensation legislation is constantly being improved and amended; and hardly a state legislature holds a session without altering the then law to some extent.

By 1917, the principle of workmen's compensation had been enacted into law by 51 foreign countries, including every European country except Turkey.

Employers' Liability and Workmen's Compensation Commission, 7692. Report of, 7729.

Employers' Liability Law proposed for District of Columbia, 6728, 6896, 6980, 6982.

Acts making service on station agents sufficient in suits under, 7449.

Discussed by President Roosevelt, 6728, 6896, 6980, 6982, 7036, 7087, 7088, 7126, 7206, 7216.

Government employees injured in service, compensation for, recommended, 7127.

Needed for railways, 7912.

Employment Bureau, Federal, advocated, 8029.

Emucfau (Ala.), Battle of.—In January, 1814, Jackson, with 930 volunteers, and 200 friendly Indians, again took the field against the hostiles. Jan. 21, with Gen. Coffee, he camped near Emucfau, on a bend in the Tallapoosa, in southern Alabama. Indications pointed to the presence of Indians, and the whites kept vigil all the night. At dawn of the 22d the savages made the attack. Gen. Coffee repulsed the Indians, driving them back 2 miles. The Indians then rallied, attacking a second time, but were again repulsed. Gen. Coffee was wounded. His aid-de-camp and 2 or 3 others were killed. Several privates were wounded. Jackson abandoned his excursion after the battle and retired toward Fort Strother.

Enacting Clause.—The preamble or preliminary clause in a legislative bill, starting with the words: "Be it enacted," etc.

Encomium, The, seizure of slaves on board, referred to, 1499.
Compensation by Great Britain in case of, referred to, 1732, 1784.

Encroachment of spheres of government harmful, 211.

Encyclopedic Index to Messages and Papers of the Presidents, services of, outlined by James D. Richardson, in Prefatory Note, vol. I.

Endicott Board, report of, 7284.

Enfranchisement.—The clothing of persons, or classes of persons, with the right to vote; as the enfranchisement of women.

Engines and machine tools, reduction of tariff on, vetoed, 7751.

Engineer Corps:
Entitled to consideration, 471.
Increase in, recommended, 873, 954, 1387, 1474, 1607, 4638.
Officers of, referred to, 1685.
Recommending increase in, 873, 954, 1387, 1474, 1607, 4638.

England. (See Great Britain.)

Engraving and Printing, Bureau of. —In 1862 the government took over the work of printing its own notes and securities and in 1874 the Bureau of Engraving and Printing was established, in accordance with an act passed by Congress in 1872.
In 1878 a separate building was erected for the exclusive use of the bureau at a cost of $300,000. This was soon found to be inadequate to the needs of the work and a new building was erected in 1902 in the grounds adjoining, and the old building was renovated and arranged for the offices of the auditors.
The bureau designs, engraves, prints and finishes all the securities and other similar work of the government printed from steel plates, embracing United States notes, bonds and certificates, national bank notes, internal revenue, postage and customs stamps, treasury drafts and checks, disbursing officers' checks, licenses, commissions, patent and pension certificates, and portraits authorized by law of deceased members of Congress and other public officers." From its presses come the million dollars of new paper money demanded by the commerce of the United States every day; the billions of stamps that are affixed to the nation's mail, and the millions of internal revenue stamps with which the nation collects its domestic taxes. The engraving is guarded with the utmost secrecy, and the original plate is never printed from.
When the superintendent of the plate-printing division wants plates to fill an order for printing which he receives from the Chief of Division, he makes a requisition upon the custodian, stating the plate required, its class, etc.; the same is then charged to him upon the book of delivery and a replica is forwarded by a messenger, with a receipt for the same, which is signed on its delivery. After the proper complement is printed, the replica is returned to the custodian and checked from the superintendent's account. It is then repaired or waxed, as the case may be, and placed away in the vault. In conducting the operations of the bureau the discipline and order observed are remarkable, and if not perfect it is still difficult to know where to begin or what to improve. While there is no ostentatious display of authority, that authority is felt. and the pressure tends, as that on the key of the arch, to hold the fabric together. There is no noise except that of the machinery. The directions are conveyed quietly from one to another by printed and written tickets, so that every transaction has its check and countercheck. The silk-fibre paper used in the notes is a closely guarded trade secret, and every sheet is accounted for from the time it leaves the mills in Massachusetts, till it is stamped in the Treasury. (See illustration opposite 1105.)

Engraving and Printing, Bureau of, economies effected in, 7509.

Ensign.—A minor officer in the Navy.

Entangling Alliances:
Discussed by President Wilson, 7943.
Should be avoided, 205, 8204.
United States no longer to remain isolated, 8288.

Entente Allies.—The term applied during the European War (q. v.) to the opponents of the Central Powers (q. v.). The term *Entente* is a French term signifying "understanding," and included during the war the following countries: England, France, Italy, Servia, Rumania, Montenegro, Portugal, Japan, Russia, Belgium, Cuba, and the United States. (See Triple Entente.)

Entente Allies (See European War):
Interference with mails by, 8165.
Replies of—
To Central Powers' offer to open peace negotiations, 8193.
To protest of United States against interference with mails, 8165.
To Wilson's proposal for peace conference, 8195.
War aims of, 8293.

Enterprise, The.—An American brig of fourteen guns which, while cruising off the coast of Maine, Sept. 5, 1813, under command of Capt. Burrows, met and captured the British brig *Boxer*, also of 14 guns. The fighting was desperate and lasted 40 minutes, during which both captains were killed. The captured brig was towed into Portland, Me.

Enterprise, The (brig), seizure of slaves on board, referred to, 1499.
Compensation by Great Britain in case of, referred to, 1732, 1784.

Enterprise, The (schooner), engagement with Tripolitan cruiser, 315.

Entomology, Bureau of, Agriculture Department.—This is a bureau of the Department of Agriculture which has supervision of quarantine to prevent the spread of gypsy and browntail moths and other insect pests.

It makes studies of bugs and worms affecting agriculture and forestry, including means for repression of insects injurious to crops, animals and man. It also studies beneficial insects—both those which are the source of industries, like the honey bee, the silk worm, and the fig-fertilizing insect, and those indirectly beneficial by preying upon injurious ones. It maintains large collections of insects and insecticidal machinery and chemicals.

The largest problem, from the point of view of financial expenditure, which comes under the work of this bureau is the effort to restrict the spread of the gypsy moth and the browntail moth, which have long been doing an enormous amount of damage to the trees of New England. These insects have been most successfully fought by the importation of their natural enemies, which feed upon them, thus gradually taking their places in the infested area, which was estimated in 1910 to be nearly 11,000 square miles in extent.

The orange groves of California have been saved from annihilation by insects through the efforts of this bureau. The Bureau of Entomology, through its study of insects and their relation to man, is the housekeeper's best aid in her warfare against flies, mosquitoes, ants, moths, and other insects which carry filth, transmit disease, or destroy clothing and furniture. (See Agriculture, Department of.)

Ephemeral and Nautical Almanac. (See Nautical Almanac.)

Epidemics. (See Contagious Diseases; International Sanitary Conference; Quarantine Regulations.)

Equality of All Men, declared in the Declaration of Independence, 1.

Equality of Nations and Rights necessary for enduring peace, 8201.

Era of Good Feeling.—A period of American political history between 1817 and 1823. All political issues seemed to have been settled by the War of 1812. The Federalist party had dwindled to an insignificant few, and the grounds of their contentions seemed to have disappeared. The Democrats held undisputed sway in Government and the best of feeling prevailed everywhere. The inaugural address of Monroe in 1817 (573) was calculated to promote harmony and soothe the feelings of the minority. The President made a tour through New England and was enthusiastically received. In 1820 he was almost unanimously reelected, only one electoral vote being cast against him. The later issues of the tariff and internal improvements at public expense had not yet developed, but with the election of John Quincy Adams in 1824 opposition to his policy began to grow, with Jackson as a center. Jackson had been the popular candidate for the Presidency in 1824. Failing of a majority in the electoral college, he was defeated in the House by a coalition of the friends of Clay and Adams, who later formed the Whig party, and the Era of Good Feeling ended.

Erie, The, claims of Sweden for alleged misconduct of commander of, 1172.

Erie and Oswego Canal, memorial in favor of enlarging docks of, 3282.

Erie Canal.—The construction of the Erie Canal was due to the never-ceasing agitation of Governor Clinton, of New York, under whose administration the first excavation was made on Independence Day, 1817. The canal was formally opened in 1825 by Governor Clinton, who, as shown in the picture opposite 932, poured a keg of water taken from Lake Erie into the Atlantic Ocean, with which water communication with the Great Lakes was established by the opening of the canal. The original cost of the canal was $7,602,000, but up to 1912 the maintenance of the canal had cost the State of New York more than $50,000,000. Recently provision has been made for enlarging the canal to a depth of twelve feet, and to improve it in other ways so that it will accommodate barges of 2,500 tons.

Erie, Lake. (See Lake Erie.)

Erie (Pa.) Marine Hospital tendered United States for use of soldiers' and sailors' home, 4786.

Erwin, Miss., riot at, 6731.

Espionage Law.—In the last session of the Sixty-fourth Congress, a bill, commonly called the Espionage Bill, or Spy Bill, was introduced to extend and to clarify the regulations concerning espionage and treason, but the bill, although it passed the Senate, was not reported out of the committee in the House. A similar bill was passed by the Sixty-Fifth Congress and was approved by the President on June 15, 1917. Its main provisions were as follows :—

Title I—Whoever obtains information respecting any place connected with the national defense with intent or reason to believe that such information is to be used to the injury of the United States, including the taking of photographs or blue prints, etc. ; or who receives or agrees to receive or stimulates the acquisition of such information for such intent or reason ; or who permits the transmission of such information to any one not entitled to receive it, through intent or through gross negligence, shall be punished by a fine of not more than $10,000 or by imprisonment for not more than two years, or by both.

Whoever, with such intent or reason, transmits or assists in the transmission of such information relating to the national defense to a foreign government or to any agent thereof shall be punished by imprisonment of not more than 20 years ; *provided* that whoever so acts in time of war shall be punished by death or by imprisonment of not more than 30 years, and that whoever, with intent that it shall be furnished the enemy, collects or attempts to collect such information, in time of war, is punishable by death or by imprisonment for not more than 30 years.

Whoever in time of war wilfully makes false statements to interfere with the operation of the forces of the United States or attempts to cause insubordination in the forces of the United States or to obstruct the recruiting or enlistment service of the United States, to the injury of the service or of the United States, is punishable by a fine of not more than $10,000 or by imprisonment for not more than 20 years or by both.

Any person who conspires to violate the above provisions shall be punishable as any person who performs them. Any person concealing or harboring a person who he suspects has violated these provisions is punishable by a fine of not more than $10,000 or by imprisonment for not more than two years or by both.

Title II gives the Secretary of the Treasury power over all vessels in the territorial waters of the United States whenever the President proclaims that a national emergency for this purpose exists. Punishment is provided for those who resist the exercise of such power or who cause or permit the destruction or injury of such vessels or permit them to harbor persons who have committed offenses against the United States.

Title III provides punishment for any person who injures or tampers with or places bombs on any vessel in the territorial waters of the United States or any vessel of American registry anywhere.

Title IV provides punishment for any person who attempts to interfere with the exportation abroad of articles or to injure such articles.

Title V gives the President the right to refuse clearance and to detain vessels during a war in which the United States is a neutral. It also provides that any person breaking internment is subject to arrest and confinement and for the punishment of any person under the jurisdiction of the United States who shall aid or persuade any such person to break internment.

Title VI provides for the regulation of the seizure of arms or munitions of war unlawfully attempted to be exported from the United States.

Title VII gives the President power to proclaim certain exports unlawful, but only during the war against the Central Powers.

Title VIII provides for the punishment of any person who wilfully makes an untrue statement under oath, with knowledge of a possibility that such statement may influence the conduct of any foreign government or of the United States, to the injury of the latter; and of any person who falsely pretends to be an official of a foreign government, and obtains any thing of value because of such misrepresentation; and of any person within the jurisdiction of the United States who carries out a conspiracy, wherever made, to injure property, etc.

Title IX changes passport regulations.

Title X provides for the punishment of any person who attempts to counterfeit a government seal or uses a government seal unlawfully.

Title XI provides extensive regulations concerning search warrants and their applicability.

Title XII refers to the use of the mails. Any writing or publication of any kind violating any of the above provisions is declared to be non-mailable. No person, however, except an employee of the Dead Letter Office authorized thereto or another person working upon an authorized search warrant, is permitted to open a letter not addressed to himself.

Any writing or publication containing any matter advocating treason or resistance to the laws of the United States is declared non-mailable. Whoever attempts to use the mails or the Postal Service to mail matter thus declared to be unmailable shall be fined not more than $5,000 or imprisoned not more than five years or both.

Title XIII contains general provisions and definitions regarding the language and jurisdiction of the preceding articles.

By regulations of Postmaster-general Burleson, made at the direction of President Wilson, seditious publication in accord with the provisions of the Espionage Act is defined as follows:

Any matter advocating or urging treason, insurrection, or forcible resistance to the laws of the United States.

Any matter conveying false reports or false statements intended to interfere with the operation or success of the military or naval forces of the United States, or to promote the success of its enemies.

Any matter intended to cause insubordination, disloyalty, mutiny, or refusal of duty in the military or naval forces of the United States.

Any matter intended to obstruct the recruiting or enlistment service of the United States, to the injury of the service of the United States.

Any matter the circulation or the publication of which involves the violation of any of the criminal provisions of the Espionage Act.

By act of Congress approved May 16, 1918, the penalty of twenty years' imprisonment or fine of $10,000 or both was extended to cover cases of any one who utters, writes or publishes any "disloyal, profane, scurrilous or abusive language" regarding the United States government, Constitution, flag, military or naval forces, and uniform or any language intended to bring them into contempt or disrepute; and of any one who shall urge the curtailment of the production of any goods of value to the country in the prosecution of the war, with intent to hinder such prosecution; and of any one who advocates or defends such acts, or supports or favors the cause of a country with which the United States is at war or by word or act opposes the cause of the United States in that war.

Moreover, during the war the Postmaster General "upon evidence satisfactory to him" that any person is using the mails in violation of the provisions of the law may declare that all mail addressed to such person is undeliverable.

Espionage Law, rules and regulations under, supplemented, 8433.

Essex, The.—A United States frigate of 32 guns. Aug. 13, 1812, she was attacked by the *Alert*, a British sloop of war carrying 26 guns. One broadside from the *Essex* nearly sunk the *Alert* and caused her surrender. Among the midshipmen of the *Essex* at this time was David Glasgow Farragut, then 11 years old. Later the *Essex* started for the Pacific on an independent cruise. At this time she carried 46 guns. Under command of Capt. David Porter she seized nearly all the British whaling vessels off the coast of South America, capturing or destroying $2,500,000 worth of the enemy's property, 360 seamen, and over 100 cannon. In February, 1814, she was surprised in the harbor of Valparaiso, Chile, by 2 British men-of-war—the *Phoebe*, carrying 52 guns, and the *Cherub*, 28 guns. March 28 the *Essex*, already crippled by a squall in the attempt to get to sea, tried to escape, but was surrendered a helpless wreck to the enemy after a bloody battle, in which one-half of her men and all but one officer were wounded or slain. (See illustration opposite 521.)

Estate Tax. (See Inheritance Tax.)

Estelle, The, order to United States marshal in Rhode Island to take possession of, 4443.

Esthonia. (See Baltic Provinces.)

Ethiopia. (See Abyssinia.)

Ethiopia, Treaties with.—Dec. 27, 1903, a treaty to regulate commercial relations was signed with Menelik II., King of Ethiopia, granting freedom to citizens of the United States to travel and transact business in that country and guaranteeing security of persons and property.

Europe.—The area of Europe is about 3,800,000 square miles, and it forms about one-fourteenth of the land surface of the globe. Its length from the North Cape,

71° 12′ N., to Cape Matapan, in the south of Greece, 36° 23′ N., is about 2,400 miles, and its breadth from Cape St. Vincent to the Urals is about 3,300 miles. The political boundary between Europe and Asia extends some distance beyond the Urals, to include the mining regions; in the southeast it follows the valley of the Manych, north of the Caucasus.

The nations of Europe, with the form of government and capital of each follow:

*Albania (Principality), Scutari.
Austria-Hungary (Monarchy), Vienna.
  Austria (Empire), Vienna.
  Hungary (Kingdom), Budapest.
Belgium (Kingdom), Brussels.
*Bulgaria (Kingdom), Sofia.
Denmark (Kingdom), Copenhagen.
France (Republic), Paris.
German Empire (Empire), Berlin.
*Greece (Kingdom), Athens.
Italy (Kingdom), Rome.
Luxemburg (Grand Duchy), Luxemburg.
*Montenegro (Kingdom), Cettinje.
Netherlands (Kingdom), The Hague.
Norway (Kingdom), Christiania.
Portugal (Republic), Lisbon.
Rumania (Kingdom), Bucharest.
Russia-in-Europe (Republic), Petrograd.
*Servia (Kingdom), Belgrade.
Spain (Kingdom), Madrid.
Sweden (Kingdom), Stockholm.
Switzerland (Republic), Berne.
*Turkey (Empire), Constantinople.
United Kingdom (Kingdom), London.

The Balkan States are Albania, Bulgaria, Greece Montenegro, Servia and Turkey-in-Europe.

Physical Features.—The coast-line is irregular owing to the large number of islands and of deep gulfs and inlets separated by peninsulas. The Baltic, with its inner branches, the Gulf of Bosnia and the Gulf of Finland, reaches toward the White Sea on the north, and partly isolates Scandinavia. On the west coast are the peninsulas of Denmark, Cotentin, Brittany, and the Iberian Peninsula. The Mediterranean is divided into gulfs, peninsulas, and islands, of which Italy, the Adriatic, the Balkan Peninsula, the Ægean, the Sea of Marmora, the Black Sea and the Crimea, and Corsica, Sardinia, Sicily, Crete and Cyprus are the largest.

Structurally Europe may be divided into plateaus and fold mountains. The main plateaus are the old plateau of northwestern Europe, the Central Plateau of France, the Meseta of the Iberian Peninsula, the Schwarzwald (or Black Forest), Taunus, Hunsruck, Erzgebirge, and the Russian Platform. The main fold mountains are the Pyrenees, the Alps, the Carpathians, the Balkans and their branching spurs. The folded mountains contain the highest summits, Mont Blanc (15,775 feet) being the culminating point of Europe, if the Caucasus be included in Asia. In Scandinavia the rivers are short and torrential on the West Coast. Though useless for navigation, they provide in their waterfalls valuable power, which is now being extensively utilized. To the southeast is the Russian or Eastern Lowland, the rivers of which drain into the Arctic, the Baltic, and the Black and Caspian Seas. The Dwina and Petchora flow into the Arctic, the Düna and Niemen into the Baltic, the Volga and Ural into the Caspian, and the Don, Dnieper, Bug and Dniester into the Black Sea.

Through the Central Lowlands flows the Vistula, which rises in the Tatra, and the Oder, which has its source in the Sudetes. The Elbe and its tributaries rise in the mountains which bound the Bohemian plateau, the Erzgebirge, Bohemian Forest, Moravian Plateau and Sudetes, and the Weser rises in the Thuringian Forest. Both these rivers flow into the North Sea. The Rhine rises in the St. Gothard group in the Alps and flows through the Lake of Constance to Basel, where it turns north. Numerous lakes, Zurich, Lucerne, Thun, Neuchâtel, are traversed by the tributaries of the Aare, which joins the Upper Rhine. The principal Atlantic rivers of France are the Seine, which rises in the Cote d'Or, the Loire from the Cevennes, and the Garonne from the Pyrenees. The Mediterranean Drainage of Europe includes the Ebro in Spain, the only large river on the eastern side, and the Rhone, which rises near the sources of the Rhine and flows through the Lake of Geneva. With the Saône, its northern tributary, it forms the longest north to south valley in Europe. The west coast of Italy has several comparatively long rivers, the Arno and the Tiber, the Apennine watershed lying nearest to the Adriatic Coast. In North Italy is the Po and its tributaries. The Danube rises in the Black Forest and receives many tributaries from the Bavarian Plateau. (Details of the history, government, etc., of the several countries will be found in the regular alphabetical order.)

Europe, policy of neutrality should be followed towards nations of and quarrels in, 213.

Railway Systems of, 3270.

Europe and the Near East, political conditions in, 8047.

European and West Virginia Land and Mining Co., agreement with agents of Mexico referred to, 3723.

European War.—The unbiased, neutral and detached history of the greatest armed conflict in the history of all civilization must wait for calmer days than these. Belligerent nations are naturally prejudiced in their interpretation of events, and when most of the world is at war, even neutral nations have their sympathies. Moreover, many of the facts necessary to a complete understanding of the developments of the holocaust will not be disclosed until many months after peace will have been signed; and a contemporary chronicler can merely record events as they occurred.

Whatever be the final verdict of history upon the causes which produced the holocaust, however, one fact stands indisputably clear. The war was in no sense an isolated phenomenon, but had its roots in the previous relations between the various European states. Indeed, as one surveys the diplomatic history of the latter half of the nineteenth century, one must ask oneself if the partition of Europe into two hostile camps delicately balanced on a vague and complicated theory of the balance of power could have resulted otherwise than in war.

The outstanding feature of European history of the last seventy-five years is the remarkable growth and increase of power of the German empire. At the beginning of the nineteenth century, Germany was but an unintegrated conglomeration of petty kingdoms and principalities, most of which were still in medieval conditions. The rise of Prussia under the Fredericks, together with their remarkable ability both to wage war and to form national federations, was the medium which conceived and finally gave birth to modern Germany.

The strength of this newest and most virile of the European countries was indicated when it proceeded to annihilate Denmark in 1864; and was plainly shown when it completely defeated Austria in 1866, and paved the way for that domination of the Hapsburg kingdom which has continued until the present day. But even the best informed statesmen of Europe rubbed their eyes in astonishment at the rapidity and the ease with which Prussia brought France to her knees in 1870. After that time, there was no nation which would have denied that Germany was dominating all Europe.

Bismarck foresaw that France would never forget or forgive his annexation of Alsace and Lorraine; and the foundation of his diplomacy lay in the absolute isolation of France. (It was a bitter disappointment to him that France was able to pay promptly the enormous indemnity which he had laid upon her.) By a series of negotiations which have probably never been equalled for astuteness, he succeeded in arranging alliances with every country which might possibly unite with France against him.

Despite the humiliation of Austria by Germany in 1866, Bismarck played upon her fear of Russia sufficiently to consummate an offensive and defensive alliance with Austria. He then played upon Russia's conflicting interests with Austria in the Balkans and probably upon her possible rivalry with England in the East to conclude a similar alliance with Russia. Italy and Austria were at loggerheads about the "Irredenta," and the rising threat of the Catholic party in France filled Italy with uneasiness; so that Germany was able to conclude an alliance with Italy in return for protection against France and Austria. England had no interests upon the Continent; and as Germany had not yet challenged her commercial supremacy and had not even thought of colonial expansion, England presented no problem.

The leadership of Germany was well shown at the Congress of Berlin, in 1878, called to adjust the results of Russo-Turkish war. The various nations there represented took the law practically as Bismarck laid it down to them.

When William II, the present German emperor, came to the throne in 1888, however, he soon evinced impatience with the aged Chancellor, and in 1890, "dropped the pilot" altogether. Soon afterwards, the system of protection which Bismarck had devised for Germany began to fall apart.

Russia's interests in the Balkans and her desire for Constantinople could hardly be reconciled with Austria's interests; and Germany no longer had been able to keep both of them on her string. William chose to retain Austria; and as Russia was sadly in need of the funds which frugal and therefore prosperous France could lend her for her internal improvements, an offensive and defensive alliance between France and Russia resulted. Moreover, Italian bitterness against Austria could no longer be restrained, and as France soon disestablished Church and state, and thereby removed the danger of the Catholic animus against Italy, there is every reason to believe that Italy let it be known secretly to Germany that she could not be counted upon in the plans of that latter country, although publicly the "Triple Alliance" between Germany, Austria and Italy seemed to be firm.

Moreover, with the beginning of the twentieth century, German efficiency had begun to undermine England's industrial supremacy, and the commercial competition between the two countries became bitter. Probably to develop new fields for her marvelous factories, Germany also began to lay plans for colonial expansion, and England awoke with a start to the danger presented by her isolation. The contemplated German railroad to Bagdad menaced the road to India, and England came eagerly into an "entente" with France and Russia.

Nevertheless, Germany was still all-powerful in European diplomacy. In 1904, she demanded the retirement of the French foreign minister, the able and anti-German Delcassé, and despite the utter humiliation involved, France did not see her way clear to resist the demand, although she defeated Germany in the diplomatic conference following the Moroccan troubles in 1905. Moreover, Russia's prestige was sadly diminished as a result of her defeat by Japan. In 1908, Germany again dominated when she supported Austria in the latter country's absorption of Bosnia and Herzegovina, when the Entente again felt itself too weak to resist.

It was in 1911, as a result of the Agadir dispute concerning Morocco, that Germany's challenge was met by France, supported by England and Russia. Germany's demands were refused, and for a period war hung almost by a hair. But Germany did not risk it, and for the first time in more than forty years she could not dominate.

In the spring of 1918, Prince Lichnowsky, German ambassador to Great Britain at the outbreak of the war, made public memoranda confessing that Great Britain had steadily tried to bring about a "rapprochement" with Germany and to bind the two nations in a more friendly relationship. In his statement denying many of Prince Lichnowsky's statements, the Foreign Minister under whom he served, von Jagow, admitted the implication of the diplomatic history sketched above—namely, that Germany recognized that she could no longer dominate Europe in peaceful diplomatic negotiations, and that she could regain or even strengthen her former position of domination only by war, or by threat of war.

These political and diplomatic developments, however, had their roots in almost every phase of European activity. Particularly, they were made possible by the growth of the nationalistic impulse throughout the nineteenth century. At the close of the Napoleonic Wars, the partition of Europe was arranged with scant heed to the cultural demands of various suppressed nationalities. Within Austria-Hungary were many national elements with little in common; the Balkan peninsula was a hotbed of racial groups, with now one in the saddle, now another, but with the powerful always repressing the weaker; neither France nor the inhabitants of Alsace-Lorraine could rest contented while those provinces were a part of German culture; Russia might be Slavic, but some of her elements, for instance the Ukrainians and the Lithuanians, had no desire to wrap up their destinies with those of the Great Russians; more than one hundred years of partition and dependence had failed to shake the longing of the Poles for a country and a literature of their own; and the geographical boundaries of Italy were not broad enough to include those lands and peoples which inherently were a part of Italian national life. Dominating all this smouldering volcano was the so-called Pangerman movement—a movement of a new and young nation which had developed its own national life in so brilliant a fashion as virtually to assume the leadership of the world, but in which success had inculcated so heedless and so unscrupulous a national pride that Germany held itself justified in forcing its civilization and culture upon all other peoples, no matter what the civilization and culture of the latter and no matter how distasteful to them might be the German idea.

Forming the frame for this ferment of unrestrainable forces were the industrial needs of the last twenty-five years. The extent to which economic competitions and aggressions were responsible for a situation which could make possible the outbreak of a world war is a matter of individual opinions, varying in accordance with the amount of influence assigned economic motives in one's philosophy of life. But it is undeniable that the tremendously accelerated production due to new mechanical inventions had made national markets no longer adequate for the great enterprises of the great nations, and the wealth and influence of those nations were dependent upon the extent of the new markets which they could control. Preferential tariffs; colonies and colonial expansions; access to the natural wealth of the great undeveloped lands of the earth, especially Africa and Siberia; the control of the important harbors of maritime traffic, with their coaling facilities, and of international waterways and canals; the manipulation of international finance and banking—all these aspirations were the pawns pitted against each other by the Great Powers of Europe on their chessboard of the world.

Succeeding events in European diplomacy are hazy, especially those concerned with the Balkan wars. But through them all ran the fact that the Entente was becoming stronger and Germany weaker in their jockeying for position. And only in the light of this development may the following events be understood.

June 28, 1914, the Austrian Archduke Francis Ferdinand, heir to the throne of Austria, and his wife, the Duchess of Hohenberg, were assassinated in Sarajevo, Bosnia, by a Servian student. An inquiry was begun, at which evidence was introduced to show that the assassin's work was part of a plot for the revolt of the southern Slav provinces of Austria, instigated by Servians with the connivance of the Servian government. Austria demanded a voice in the investigation and punishment of the crime, and sent an ultimatum to Servia. The latter country agreed to all the demands except that to allow Austrian officials to participate in the inquiry.

July 27, the Austrian foreign office issued a statement claiming that the Servian answer was hypocritical and that Servia had no intention of ending intrigues in its territory against Austria.

Russia notified Austria that it could not allow Servian territory to be invaded. Semi-officially, Germany let it be known that no one must interfere with the Austro-Servian entanglement—an intimation that Germany would back Austria.

Sir Edward Grey, the British Foreign Secretary, made the definite proposal that mediation between Servia and Austria be undertaken by a conference of the Ambassadors in London. France and Italy accepted the proposal. Germany and Austria declined. Next day came an announcement from Austria-Hungary that it considered itself at war with Servia.

The following day the Czar of Russia issued an imperial ukase calling all reservists to the colors.

Germany then asked Russia to cease mobilization and asked for a reply within twenty-four hours. England notified Germany that if a general conflict should occur it could not stand aloof and see the balance of power in Europe destroyed.

July 31st, Premier Asquith announced in the British House of Commons that he understood that Germany was about to mobilize if Russia did not heed a German ultimatum to the effect that the Tsar must countermand his mobilization orders.

Russia paid no attention to the German ultimatum, but M. Gorymykin, president of the Council of the Empire, issued a manifesto announcing that Russia was determined to protect Servia from the power of Austria.

August 1, 1914, the German Ambassador handed the declaration of war to the Russian Foreign Minister. On the same day, the French Government issued a general mobilization order.

August 2d, Germany began the invasion of France through the Duchy of Luxemburg. This territory had been neutralized by the powers, including Germany, in 1867, but no resistance was made by the Ducal army of less than 450 men, though the Grand Duchess made formal protest.

August 3d, Germany sent to Belgium demanding passage for her troops and offering compensation therefor. Germany said that it already had information that France was to use Belgium as a military base. Despite many attempts on the part of Germany to prove that Belgium was unneutral in both intent and need, the verdict of most unbiased observers has been that the Germans did not substantiate their charges against King Albert's land. Belgium refused entrance to German troops and demanded that Germany respect her neutrality, but on the morning of the 4th German troops entered Belgium. Sir Edward Grey, British Foreign Minister, in the House of Commons, read a telegram addressed to King George by King Albert of Belgium, asking "the diplomatic intervention of Your Majesty's Government to safeguard the integrity of Belgium."

Italy proclaimed her neutrality, although a member of the Triple Alliance. This alliance, her statesmen explained, was intended to protect the parties to it against an attack. Italy interpreted Germany's and Austria's acts as amounting to an aggressive war.

August 4th, the German Emperor gave the Russian Ambassador his passports and England sent an ultimatum to Germany, demanding a satisfactory reply by midnight on the question of the neutrality of Belgium. No reply having been received the British foreign office announced that a state of war existed with Germany, dating from 11 P.M. August 4, 1914. Meanwhile Germany had given his passports to the British Ambassador in Berlin.

August 5th, President Wilson tendered the good offices of the United States in an attempt to bring about a settlement of the European difficulties.

Declarations of war were made as follows:

Austria v. Belgium, August 28, 1914.
Austria v. Japan, August 27, 1914.
Austria v. Montenegro, August 9, 1914.
Austria v. Russia, August 6, 1914.
Austria v. Serbia, July 28, 1914.
Brazil v. Germany, October 26, 1917.
Bulgaria v. Serbia, October 14, 1915.
China v. Austria, August 14, 1917.
China v. Germany, August 14, 1917.
Costa Rica v. Germany, May 23, 1918.
Cuba v. Austria, December 16, 1917.
Cuba v. Germany, April 7, 1917.
France v. Austria, August 13, 1914.
France v. Bulgaria, October 16, 1915.

France v. Germany, August 3, 1914.
France v. Turkey, November 5, 1914.
Germany v. Belgium, August 4, 1914.
Germany v. France, August 3, 1914.
Germany v. Portugal, March 9, 1916.
Germany v. Rumania, September 14, 1916.
Germany v. Russia, August 1, 1914.
Great Britain v. Austria, August 13, 1914.
Great Britain v. Bulgaria, October 15, 1915.
Great Britain v. Germany, August 4, 1914.
Great Britain v. Turkey, November 5, 1914.
Greece (provisional government) v. Bulgaria, November 28, 1916.
Greece (provisional government) v. Germany, November 28, 1916.
Greece (Government of Alexander) v. Bulgaria, July 2, 1917.
Greece (Government of Alexander) v. Germany, July 2, 1917.
Guatemala v. Austria, April 22, 1918.
Guatemala v. Germany, April 22, 1918.
Haiti v. Germany, July 12, 1918.
Honduras v. Germany, July 19, 1918.
Italy v. Austria, May 24, 1915.
Italy v. Bulgaria, October 19, 1914.
Italy v. Germany, August 28, 1916.
Italy v. Turkey, August 21, 1915.
Japan v. Germany, August 23, 1914.
Liberia v. Germany, August 4, 1917.
Montenegro v. Austria, August 8, 1914.
Monenegro v. Germany, August 9, 1914.
Nicaragua v. Germany and her allies, may 7, 1918.
Panama v. Austria, December 10, 1917.
Panama v. Germany, April 7, 1917.
Portugal v. Germany, November 23, 1914. (Resolution passed authorizing military intervention as ally of Great Britain.)
Portugal v. Germany, May 19, 1915. (Military aid granted.)
Roumania v. Austria, August 27, 1916. (Allies of Austria also consider it a declaration.)
Russia v. Bulgaria, October 19, 1915.
Russia v. Turkey. November 3, 1914.
San Marino v. Austria, May 24, 1915.
Serbia v. Bulgaria, October 16, 1915.
Serbia v. Germany, August 6, 1914.
Serbia v. Turkey, December 2, 1914.
Siam v. Austria, July 21, 1917.
Siam v. Germany, July 21, 1917.
Turkey v. Allies, November 23, 1914.
Turkey v. Roumania, August 29, 1916.
United States v. Austria-Hungary, December 7, 1917.
United States v. Germany, April 6, 1917.

Severance of diplomatic relations has been as follows :
Austria against Japan, August 26, 1914.
Austria against Portugal, March 16, 1916.
Austria against Serbia, July 26, 1914.
Austria against United States, April 8, 1917.
Bolivia against Germany, April 14, 1917.
Brazil against Germany, April 11, 1917.
China against Germany, March 14, 1917.
Costa Rica against Germany, September 21, 1917.
Ecuador against Germany, December 7, 1917.
Egypt against Germany, August 13, 1914.
France against Austria, August 10, 1914.
Greece against Turkey, July 2, 1917 (government of Alexander).
Greece against Austria, July 2, 1917 (government of Alexander).
Guatemala against Germany, April 27, 1917.
Haiti against Germany, June 17, 1917.
Honduras against Germany, May 17, 1917.
Liberia v. Germany, May 8, 1917.
Nicaragua against Germany, May 18, 1917.

Peru against Germany, October 6, 1917.
Turkey against United States, April 20, 1917.
United States against Germany, February 3, 1917.
Uruguay against Germany, October 7, 1917.
At war with Germany or her allies on June 1, 1918 :
Serbia, France, Great Britain, Montenegro, Japan, Belgium, Italy, San Marino, Portugal, Greece, Cuba, Panama, Siam, Liberia, China, Brazil, Guatemala, Nicaragua, Costa Rica, and the United States.
The various belligerents, soon after their respective entrances into the war, published their own official versions of the circumstances which led to their participation. These versions were in the forms of booklets, and were named by the color of the covers, as follows :
Blue Books, England and Servia ; Gray Book, Belgium ; Green Book, Italy ; Orange, Russia and Holland ; Red, Austria-Hungary ; Red, White and Blue, United States ; White, Germany and Portugal ; Yellow, France.

After a heavy bombardment of two days German forces entered the strongly fortified city of Liège, Belgium, August 7, and proceeded westward, taking successively Louvain, Brussels, Namur and Antwerp About the middle of August Japan sent an ultimatum to Germany demanding the immediate surrender of Kiau Chau, China, which was leased by Germany in 1898, and later made a protectorate. This was surrendered to the Japanese in November.
Meantime, although Germany had made some progress along the shores of the Baltic Sea, the Russian forces had invaded Galicia in Austria and East Prussia.
In France the German line extended diagonally across the northeastern frontier, with the left resting on Mülhausen. Turning on the left base the armies pressed rapidly by way of Nancy, Verdun, Montmedy, Reims, Amiens, westward and south to within twenty-five miles of Paris and along the Marne River. Here, with the aid of British forces, the Germans were checked. The French government moved from Paris to Bordeaux. The allied forces attempted an enveloping manœuvre, and the German line was extended northward, falling back to the eastward at the same time.

Battle of the Marne.—During the retreat of the French and allied armies from Brussels toward Paris they had received constant accessions, while the Germans were compelled to transfer part of their forces to the eastern theatre of the war to oppose the invasion of Prussia by the Russians. Sept. 6, General Joffre called a halt in the Franco-British line, then extending from Paris to Verdun, with its center south of the River Marne. Along this line of 140 miles were more than 1,500,000 of the allies, while the Germans numbered but 900,000. From left to right the order of the French line was: the Sixth French army, the British army, the Fifth, Ninth, Fourth and Third French ; the Germans from right to left were those of Von Kluck, Von Bülow, Von Hausen, Grand Duke Albrecht of Württemberg ; and the Crown Prince of Prussia. The German left was secure but their right was exposed to attack. To protect their communications two corps facing west were stationed behind the River Ourc, which flows from the north into the Marne, about thirty-five miles east of Paris. Early on the morning of Sept. 6, General Joffre advanced the Sixth French army from Paris north of the Marne toward the Oure, and then began the famous retreat of Von Kluck, which exposed the flank of Von Bülow, whose retreat in turn exposed the flank of Von Hausen, and the whole German line swung rapidly back to the eastward, at the same time extending northward to avoid enveloping movements by the enemy. On the 12th and 13th the pursuit was brought to an unexpected halt by the German army at bay on the hills north of the River Aisne.

Fall of Antwerp.—During September, 1914, while the German armies held their positions in northern France, the Belgian army had been reorganized and began an aggressive campaign against the German communications. The German general staff then determined to capture Antwerp and complete the conquest of Belgium.

The entire Belgian defense centered in Antwerp, which was considered one of the strongest fortresses in Europe. The city had a population of more than 300,000. It was defended by two rings of forts—an inner one of eight forts, about two miles from an old enceinte which encircled the city, and an outer ring of fifteen forts, at distances varying from six to nine miles from the enceinte. Four special features contributed to the strength of Antwerp: (1) the close proximity of the neutral Dutch frontier on the north and northwest, which reduced the front to be defended; (2) the existence of a large inundated area on the west and northwest, which served the same purpose; (3) the position of the River Scheldt, which protected the city on the west and offered a secure passage through Holland for supplies from the sea; (4) the position of the River Nethe, which runs close to the rear of the outer ring of forts and furnishes an inundated area for the protection of the city on the southeast.

Sept. 28 the German guns opened upon two of the forts of the outer ring south of the city. On the 29th one of these was blown up and the other was destroyed the following day. The next two forts to the right were silenced Oct. 1, and the Belgian infantry were compelled to withdraw across the Nethe, where they were supported by the British. On the 5th the Belgian army withdrew and the Germans crossed the Nethe and occupied Antwerp, coming into complete possession by the 9th. A war tax of $7,000,000 a month was levied upon the city and a civil governor placed in charge. Many stories were told of attacks by civilians upon the soldiers after surrender and of retaliatory measures by the Germans which were calculated to excite the sympathies of neutrals. Indeed, it is not too much to say that her procedure in Belgium was the strongest of the many factors which condemned the Kaiser's government at the bar of international public opinion.

Battle of the Aisne.—The Aisne River is a sluggish canalized river about 170 miles long flowing generally westward into the Oise through a valley from half a mile to two miles wide between plateaus 400 feet high on each side. While on the drive to Paris the Germans had prepared a strong position on the northern plateau upon which to make a stand in case of possible retreat. Concrete platforms had been built for heavy guns, and commodious trenches with overhead protection against shrapnel had been constructed for the infantry. The right of the position rested on the Noyon Hills west of the Oise, north of its junction with the Aisne. From this point the line ran east along the Aisne about forty miles and then south by east by Reims to Verdun. Four

railways ran back from this position into Belgium and a fifth ran east and west at a convenient distance in the rear of the lines. The German retreat abruptly halted Sept. 12 at Soissons, where the river is about sixty yards wide. Here the armies were deadlocked from the Noyon Hills to the Swiss frontier. The allies sent out forces to turn the German right and strike the railways in their rear, but each expedition resulted only in a pitched battle and the extension of the German lines northward. By Oct. 7, the 25th day of the fighting along the Aisne, the lines had been prolonged to La Bassee, ten miles from the Belgian frontier, and the net result of the fighting after ten months was the extension of the lines from the confluence of the Aisne and Oise rivers into Flanders and as close to the English Channel coast as operations of the British navy would permit. This line was roughly marked by the towns of Vermelles, Armentieres, Ypres, Bixshoote and Dixmude, which became the scenes of fierce struggles. French reserve troops, detachments from the French active army, the British expeditionary force, British Indians, Senegalese, and Turcos went to make up the prolongation of the allies' front.

On the southeast end of the German line the Crown Prince in September sent out several army corps to cut the line south of Verdun, but only succeeded in reaching St. Mihiel, which during the first half of 1915 continued to be a starting point for aggressive movements.

Fighting in Flanders.—Having taken Antwerp the Germans began sending large armies toward Dunkirk and Calais. The Belgian army held the Germans back of the Yser River at Nieuport, and, assisted by British warships in the Channel, forced them from the coast. Between Nieuport and Ypres the German advance was checked by cutting the dykes and flooding the country.

Battle of Ypres.—About the middle of October, 1914, the Germans began massing their troops in the vicinity of Ypres, and the attacks grew fiercer each day. Their evident intention was to force their way to Calais. By Nov. 5 the attacks ceased. The allies, on the defensive, lost 100,000 men, killed, wounded and missing, and it is supposed the German offensive cost twice as many, so that the losses about Ypres must have reached close to 300,000 men.

From the time of the establishment of the lines of trenches in October, 1914, to the end of 1915, little progress was made by either side in the fighting in the western theatre of the war. The opposing forces were arrayed in parallel lines from the North Sea to the Swiss frontier, a distance of 350 miles, the number of combatants on each side per mile of front probably varying from 3,000 to 10,000. Artillery duels took place nearly every day and occasional charges by the men at arms resulted in Anglo-French gains here and German gains there, but the main lines remained generally parallel.

A section of France north of Arras, known as the "Labyrinth," was selected by the Anglo-French allies in May, 1915, as the objective point of a determined effort to break the German line. Ample preparations were made, and the fighting began May 30 and was carried on continuously to June 17. The gains made were insignificant, and were partially recovered by the Germans later.

A second drive along the entire front in France and Belgium was begun in September, 1915, and fighting continued almost uninterruptedly, the heaviest actions being carried on in the Champagne district between Arras and Ypres and east of Loos.

The Eastern Theatre of War.—Operations against Germany and Austria on the east covered two separate fields : (1) that along the Vistula River in Poland and East Prussia and (2) the Austrian province of Galicia, which lies north of the Carpathian Mountains. At the beginning of the war the Russians invaded East Prussia, defeated the Germans at Gumbinnen (Aug. 17-23), captured Allenstein and invested Königsberg.

In the south the Russian invasion of Galicia resulted in the capture of Lemberg, Sept. 2, Jaroslav, Sept. 23, and the strong fortress of Przemysl, on the San River, March 22, 1915, after a long siege.

The invasion was proceeding favorably for the Russians until General Von Hindenberg transported a large German force from Belgium, and during the last three days of August completely annihilated two Russian army corps in the vicinity of Allenstein, Ortlesburg and Tannenberg, and on Sept. 1 reported to Berlin the capture of 70,000 prisoners, including two generals, 500 officers, and the equipment of the two corps.

Before the middle of November, 1914, seven Russian armies were advancing upon the Austrians and Germans between the Baltic Sea and the Carpathian Mountains, and pushing them to the west and south. The Russians held a line 100 miles long in East Prussia parallel to the frontier, extending from Stalluponen on the right via Goldap and Lyck to the vicinity of Soldau. Here occurred a gap in the line, which began again in Russian territory near the Vistula and ran generally parallel to the frontier, and at no great distance from it, to the vicinity of Cracow, Austria. The Russians held the German town of Pleschen, about 65 miles northeast of Breslau. Although there were gaps in this line, it was almost continuous for 350 miles. In Galicia, Russian armies, moving west, were about 75 miles from Cracow, and another army, approaching from the northeast, was reported to be within 25 miles of that city. The full strength of the Russian Empire was engaged in one grand concerted movement, with its single purpose the overthrow of the Teutonic power of central Europe.

Early in December the Germans occupied Lodz, in East Prussia, and began an impetuous advance toward Warsaw, Poland, while the Russians made Cracow, in Galicia, their objective. Russian bombardment of Cracow was halted Dec. 23 by the arrival of Austro-German reinforcements.

The spectacular advance of the Germans along the 100-mile front, extending from the Baltic Sea near Libau in a southeasterly direction to the northern tributaries of the River Niemen, continued unchecked. Libau, in the province of Courland, was captured May 8, and the invaders pushed onward toward Riga.

In north Poland German forces successively occupied Przasynsz and Novo Georgievsk in July, 1915, and continued their drive on to Warsaw, which was taken Aug. 1.

Further south, in Galicia, the strongly fortified towns of Przemysl and Lemberg were retaken by the Germans in June.

Invasion of Servia.—From July 29 to Aug. 12, 1914, the Austrians bombarded Belgrade, capital of Servia, whence the administrative offices were moved, first to Kragujevac and later to Nish. Aug. 16, 50,000 Austrians crossed the Danube into Servia and were met and defeated on the 18th and 20th by four Servian corps. The Servians, elated with their victories, invaded Austria early in September and besieged Sarajevo, capital of Bosnia. They were driven back, however, and an Austrian force of some 250,000 men moved against the northwest corner of Servia, meeting the Servians at Valievo Sept. 15 and defeating them Nov. 15. The Austro-Hungarian siege of Belgrade, which had begun July 29, ended Dec. 2, when the Servians were driven out by assault. The outlook for Servia was indeed gloomy when, to the surprise of the world, a desperate attack on the center divided the Austrian army, crushed the right wing and drove the invading armies from the Servian soil. Dec. 14, 1914, King Peter reentered Belgrade with his victorious army and reported the land wholly free from the invading Teutons.

Coincident with the Bulgarian invasion of Servia in October, 1915, Austro-German forces crossed the Danube at Belgrade and drove the Servians before them down the Morava Valley and formed a junction with the Bulgars on the 26th at a point on the Salonika-Nish railway and captured Nish, the temporary capital, and Kragujevac, the principal arsenal, in November. By the 1st of December, 1915, Austro-Hungarian, German and Bulgarian armies had swept over the entire country of Servia, the army was scattered and the King in flight.

Turkey's Entrance into the War.—The German cruisers *Goeben* and *Breslau*, pursued by hostile war ships at the beginning of the war, sought escape by passage through the Dardanelles and safety in the Turkish harbors beyond. Instead of being compelled to put to sea or intern within a reasonable time, the cruisers were alleged to have been bought by Turkey. The powers protested, but Turkey not only retained the vessels but announced the abrogation of her capitulations wherein she had in times past restricted her sovereignty or conferred special privileges upon foreign nations. The first act of hostility was the bombardment of the Russian Black Sea port of Theodosia, Oct. 29, 1914, by the *Goeben*, changed in name to the *Midullu*. Other hostile acts followed, and Nov. 5, Great Britain and France declared war on Turkey. The former also annexed the island of Cyprus and declared Egypt an independent state.

Kut-el-Amara, Siege of.—The outbreak of the war found British troops to the number of 8,000 or 10,000 in Mesopotamia, under command of Gen. Townshend. After a defeat by the Turks at Ctesiphon, Townshend retreated to Kut-el-Amara, a city built on a peninsula on the left bank of the Tigris river. The Ottoman troops settled down in front of the place, while heavy flanking parties swept by on both banks of the river and speedily cut off the British line of communication. The Turks then assumed the simple task of maintaining the siege until necessity should compel the British surrender. Ineffectual attempts were made at rescue, and unusual floods prevented aggressive operations. After a siege of 143 days the British flag was hauled down, and the army surrendered its arms to the Turks, April 29, 1916.

Helgoland Naval Battle.—Aug. 28, 1914 Admiral David Beatty, with a British battle squadron, consisting of the *Fearless*, the *Arethusa* and about twenty destroyers, engaged a German squadron off the naval base of Helgoland in the North Sea. Three German cruisers were sighted—the *Mainz*, the *Coln* and the *Ariadne*. During the ensuing fight the British battle cruisers *Lion*, *Queen Mary*, *Invincible* and *New Zealand* came upon the scene. The three German cruisers and two destroyers were sunk, and 2,500 sailors were reported lost.

Activities of German Cruisers.—In spite of British supremacy at sea Germany was able to inflict severe damage upon her commerce through the activities of the cruisers *Karlsruhe*, *Emden*, *Königsberg*, *Scharnhorst*, *Gneisenau*, *Dresden*, *Leipsic*, *Nürnberg* and *Geier*, most of which had been interned in neutral ports or destroyed by the first of 1915.

The German cruiser *Karlsruhe* was in the West Indies when hostilities broke out in Europe. Though said to have been chased by British warships, the *Karlsruhe* had by Aug. 23 sunk 15 English merchantmen in the Atlantic. On the 26th she took the *Vandyck*, valued, with her cargo, at $2,000,000. The *Emden* appeared in the Bay of Bengal Sept. 10, and by the 20th had captured six British ships, sinking five and sending the other to Calcutta, with the crews. Then she bombarded Madras and set two oil tanks on fire. Entering the harbor of Penang, Straits Settlements, she torpedoed and sunk the Russian cruiser *Zhemtchug* and a French destroyer. Next the *Emden* turned her attention to the wireless telegraph plant on Cocos Island. Nov. 9 she landed a small party to destroy the station, but the operator had called the Australian cruiser *Sydney* to his assistance, and the *Emden* put to sea, leaving the landing party ashore. The *Sydney*, being a superior vessel, defeated and burned the *Emden*. The German loss was 200 killed and 30 wounded, while the loss on the *Sydney* was trifling. The Cocos Island landing party, after a series of miraculous escapes, heroic adventures and physical sufferings, reached Hodeida, on the east coast of the Red Sea, in friendly territory.

The *Königsberg*, on Sept. 20, 1914, attacked and destroyed the British cruiser *Pegasus*, which was undergoing repairs in Zanzibar harbor. After a thorough search of East African waters the German raider was discovered by the British cruiser *Chatham* in shoal water six miles up the Rufigi River, in German East Africa. There she was bottled up by sinking colliers in the channel.

Off Coronel, Chile.—A British squadron consisting of the three armored cruisers, *Good Hope*, *Monmouth* and *Glasgow*, commanded by Admiral Cradock, encountered the German cruisers *Scharnhorst*, *Gneisenau*, *Dresden*, *Nürnberg* and *Leipsic*, under Admiral Von Spee, off the coast of Coronel, Chile, on Nov. 3, 1914. The fight took place near sunset and lasted about three-quarters of an hour. A broadside from the Germans sank the *Monmouth* and the *Good Hope*, while the *Glasgow* escaped. Rear-Admiral Cradock, in command of the fleet, and 1,500 British sailors were lost. The German losses were insignificant.

Off the Falklands.—Dec. 5, 1914, the augmented British squadron encountered the German cruisers *Leipsic*, *Scharnhorst*, *Gneisenau*, *Nürnberg* and *Dresden* off the Falkland Islands. All were sunk except the *Dresden*, which escaped. The British loss was reported as seven killed and four wounded.

Oct. 17, 1914.—The British cruiser *Undaunted*, supported by four destroyers, engaged and sunk four German destroyers off the Dutch coast; 193 German officers and sailors were reported lost.

Jan. 24, 1915, a large German fleet, while attempting a raid on the English coast, was engaged by a British fleet. The German battle cruiser *Bluecher* (15,550 tons) and the smaller cruiser *Kolberg* were reported lost, and the British cruisers *Lion* and *Tiger* badly damaged.

Capture of German Colonies.—By the end of 1916, practically all of Germany's colonial possessions were in the hands of the Entente Allies. Soon after the outbreak of the war, the German islands in the Pacific surrendered to English marine and territorial forces, including German Samoa, which surrendered on August 29, 1914. In Africa, Togoland also soon was under the English flag, as was most of the large and important colony, Kamerun. In July, 1915, General Botha, of Boer War fame, completed the occupation of German Southwest Africa, although a small portion of the Kamerun succeeded in resisting capture until 1916 and German East Africa to late in 1917. Altogether, the German colonies acquired by the Allies comprised a territory of 2,000,000 square miles.

War Zone Operations.—Early in the year 1915 a British order in council declared that all foodstuffs destined to Germany, though intended for the civilian population, subject to seizure and confiscation. This was based on Germany's national regulation of the food supply, which was construed to mean confiscation for army uses. Germany in reply to this order declared a war zone to be in existence around the British isles after Feb. 15, 1915, and warned neutral vessels of the dangers of navigation. Submarines were sent into the designated waters, and reports came daily of the sinking of English, French and neutral vessels.

Munitions Shipments.—Soon after the outbreak of the war, the Entente Allies proceeded to purchase in the United States both munitions of war and the raw materials for manufacturing them. Because of the Entente mastery of the seas, the Central Powers were not able to use the resources of the United States in a similar fashion.

The refusal of the United States to interfere in this trade in munitions caused much bad feeling against her in the Central Powers, coupled with charges that by permitting such trade the United States had in fact, if not in theory, joined hands with the Entente. Indeed, on June 29, 1915, Austria-Hungary lodged with the United States an official protest against the trade in munitions between this country and the Entente. The reply of the United States pointed out that this trade was sanctioned by international law, that Germany had itself similarly indulged in such trade with belligerents in wars in which she had been neutral, and that inability of a belligerent to purchase supplies in neutral countries would to a marked degree increase the amount of war preparation indulged in by all countries in peace times.

Agents of the Central Powers in the United States attempted to thwart the trade in munitions between the United States and the Entente by dynamiting factories and encouraging strikes. As a result, recall of the Austrian ambassador, Dumba, was requested by the United States in September, 1915, it having been proved that he had engineered such actions, and similar action was taken with respect to von Papen and Boy-ed, connected with the staff of the German ambassador to the United States, in December of the same year. Other German agents in the United States were imprisoned for offenses against the peace of the country and for other crimes.

Lusitania Case.—The German embassy in America called attention to the war zone and repeated the warning to neutral and enemy vessels. Despite the warning, which had been personally brought to the attention of the passengers, the *Lusitania* sailed from New York May 1st, and May 7th, when off Kinsale, Ireland, was struck by a mine or torpedo and sank within fifteen minutes with great loss of life, including more than one hundred Americans. (See Wilson, Woodrow.)

The *Lusitania* was built in 1907, and was one of the largest and fastest of British ships and was valued at about $10,000,000. Besides passengers and crew to the number of 2,159 persons aboard, she carried about 1,500 tons of cargo, valued at $735,579. The principal items of the cargo were for war consumption, and included sheet brass, valued at $50,000; copper and copper wire, $32,000; beef, $31,000; furs, $119,000; copper manufactures, $21,000; military goods, $66,000; ammunition, $200,000. The latest official figures showed that 1,396 lives were lost. The total number of survivors was 763, including 462 passengers and 301 of crew; the number injured was 30 passengers and 17 of crew; of the survivors 45 died from exposure or injuries; the number of Americans who died was 107. There were 81 American survivors, 23 American identified dead and 84 Americans missing and undoubtedly dead.

Forcing the Dardanelles.—The Strait of the Dardanelles, the ancient Hellespont of Xerxes and Alexander the Great, is a narrow channel separating southeastern Europe from Asia, and connecting the Sea of Marmora with the Aegean Sea. It is about forty-two miles long and varies in width from one to four miles. The approach to Constantinople from the west by water can only be made by way of this narrow strait, which is strongly fortified on both sides with modern works and heavy guns. A treaty between Turkey and the great powers of Europe in 1841 provided that no war ship of any nation save Turkey should pass the Dardanelles without express consent of Turkey. This agreement was confirmed at London in 1871 and at Berlin in 1878, but an agreement of 1891 gave the Russian volunteer fleet the right of passage.

Early in February, 1915, a fleet of the Anglo-French allies undertook the difficult task of forcing the Dardanelles as a part of the operations against Turkey, as well as to secure possession of large quantities of Russian wheat which were said to be stored in Odessa. The allied fleet under command of the British Vice-Admiral Carden included the super-dreadnought *Queen Elizabeth,* said to be the most powerful fighting machine afloat, the *Agamemnon, Irresistible, Vengeance, Cornwallis, Triumph, Albion* and *Majestic,* and the French battleships *Gaulois, Suffren,* and *Charlemagne,* as well as minor vessels, bringing the total up to more than fifty, including the greatest and newest British dreadnoughts. Heavy losses sustained by the allied fleet soon made it apparent that an attack by sea alone could not succeed, and Sir Ian Hamilton, with the British and French forces which had been assembled in Egypt, was landed on the Gallipoli peninsula for land operations.

The *Queen Elizabeth,* from a position beyond the range of the guns of the forts, reduced the outer works, Seddul-Bahr and Kum Kaleh, on Feb. 26. The fleet then began an advance up the strait, sweeping the mines and reducing the forts on the European side of the entrance. March 18, the French warship *Bouvet,* the English *Irresistible* and *Ocean* were sunk, and the *Gaulois* and *Inflexible* were disabled.

The task of this joint expedition, numbering eventually upward of 300,000 effectives, was to occupy the lower end of the Gallipoli Peninsula, reducing the forts on the Dardanelles shores where these come to their narrowest span. After six months, during which time three violent assaults had been repulsed, the question of abandoning the enterprise was seriously considered.

During the first week of January, 1916, the entire expedition was withdrawn. The attempted landing at Suvla Bay failed. The Turks claimed possession of $10,000,000 booty after the departure of the British.

Bulgaria, which had maintained a strict neutrality up to that time, mobilized her army Sept. 21, 1915, and during the following month crossed the Danube into Servia and advanced to the Belgrade-Nish-Salonika railroad. In the meantime Austro-German forces had crossed the Save and Danube and pressed southward, driving the Serbs before them. Efforts of the Anglo-French allies to induce Greece and Rumania to interfere in behalf of Servia were futile. The Bulgars advanced steadily westward to Monastir, in the extreme southwest corner of Servia, where they established themselves and strengthened their lines to the borders of Greece.

Montenegro in the War.—Montenegro declared war on Austria Aug. 7, and the Montenegrin forces proceeded to invade Bosnia, in conjunction with a Servian army, and to assist the British and French to besiege Cattaro. They later occupied Mostar, capital of Herzegovina. After the occupation of Servia by the central powers, Austrian armies turned their attention to Montenegro, recovered the Bosnian provinces and placed Montenegro under military control of the Austrians.

Siege of Tsing-tau.—On the outbreak of hostilities in Europe, Japan sent an ultimatum to Germany, demanding that she withdraw her warships from Oriental waters and evacuate the entire leased territory of Kiao-chau, with a view to its eventual restoration to China. Kiao-chau, of which Tsing-tau is the capital, lies on the east coast of the Chinese province of Shan-tung. It has a population of about 33,000, of whom some 1,500 are white. It was seized by Germany in November, 1897, and later occupation was confirmed under a 99-year lease. It is surrounded by a neutral zone thirty miles wide. Germans spent $100,000,000 in improving the port. The siege lasted till Nov. 7, 1914, when the German garrison of 4,600, which included many business men, was forced to surrender. The Japanese besiegers, reported at 45,000, lost 1,500 men. The Japanese cruiser *Takachiho,* with a crew of 344 men, was sunk by a German submarine, and the Austrian cruiser *Kaiserin Elizabeth,* which took part in the defense, was sunk by her crew to escape capture.

In the Caucasus.—For more than eighteen months the Czar's armies had made little headway in the Caucasus. Preparations were begun by Grand Duke Nicholas in the fall of 1915, and an army estimated at 300,000 men, operating from a base at Batum on the Black Sea and on Tiflis and Baku, began a drive on Armenia in February, 1916. Erzerum, which lies 60 miles from the Russian frontier and 625 miles from Constantinople, stands on a plateau 6,000 feet high, and was defended by eighteen forts. The city is flanked by two high mountain ranges. After an assault lasting five days the Russians took the place by storm, Feb. 26, 1916. More than 300 pieces of ordnance and 13,000 prisoners were taken.

After the capture of Erzerum the Russians pushed on in three main divisions. The first, along the Black Sea coast, supported by warships, moved toward Trebibond, taking Ishpir and Rizeh on the way, and on March 7, Trebizond. The second column, from the Lake Van region, captured Mush and Bitlis. The third, fighting in Persia, took Kermanshah, Feb. 25, and advanced to Kirind, 130 miles from Bagdad.

Aerial Warfare.—Soon after the breaking out of the war it became evident that air craft of various designs were to play an important part, both in scouting and offensive operations. The Germans had developed the Zeppelin airship to a high state of perfection, and in the early advance through Belgium and into France Zeppelins flew high in advance of the uhlans, communicating their observations to headquarters. On Aug. 24, bombs were dropped on Antwerp. A month later other Belgian towns, as well as Paris and Warsaw, were bombarded from the air. Contradictory stories of the effects of these attacks reached the outside world from the headquarters of the belligerents. In October German aviators dropped bombs in Paris, killing three persons and wounding 20; Dec. 30 Dunkirk was shelled from the air and 15 persons were killed. In January, 1915, a fleet of Zeppelins raided the English coast, bombarding six towns and killing five persons. Other air raids followed, but without accomplishing any military purpose. By February, 1915, the Anglo-French allies had built a fleet of 30 to 40 air and seaplanes and made retaliatory raids on Dunkirk, Ostend, Zeebrugge and other towns within the German lines.

On the western battle front, at least four types of aeroplanes are in constant use. (1) Scouting machines. They are swift, and capable of long flights. They carry a large store of gasoline, photographic apparatus, machine guns and even wireless stations. Their biplanes have a spread of 45 feet and the motors often attain 150 horse power.

(2) Bombing planes. They are heavy and slow, and carry great weights of bombs, all of which must be discharged before return, as the shock of descent would explode any bombs remaining upon the machine. They must usually be protected by lighter machines, and accordingly make night attacks the rule.

(3) Artillery planes, used for observing the explosions of shells among the enemy. They are light and stable.

(4) Battle planes, which are very light and swift, and are especially adapted to climb quickly.

In addition, there are the huge heavier-than-air Zeppelins, used by the Germans, which are dirigible balloons; and the captive balloons used by all belligerents for observation purposes.

During 1917, especially after the summer months, the Germans increased their night aerial raids upon England, and especially upon London, often killing many children, women and other non-combatants. These machines used the captured sections of Belgium as their base; and it was difficult for the English to make reprisals, for this territory was inhabited chiefly by Belgian non-combatants, and the territory of Germany itself was too far distant to offer much prospect of success for air raids. The Germans defended their bomb-throwing upon unified cities by the Allied food blockade and consequent attempt to starve German women, children and other non-combatants. From a tactical point of view, the raids were of service to Germany in keeping a large number of airplanes in England to meet the German airplanes, and hence diminished the number of machines utilized by the English on the battle-front. Even neutral opinion, however, unqualifiedly condemned such raids on unfortified places as not only in direct violation of the Hague regulations of war, but also as manifestations of a savage and brutal philosophy.

Verdun, Siege of.—German offensive operations against the French fortress of Verdun began in February, 1916. For three weeks, in half a dozen places on a front of more than 450 miles, from the North Sea to the Swiss frontier, the Germans had been feinting with an intensity that gave each separate thrust a look of latent enterprise, and then abruptly, to the north of Verdun, on a continuous battle line of twenty-five miles, they developed operations of the first magnitude.

Verdun is the first and strongest of a line of fortified French places (Verdun-Toul-Epinal-Belfort) facing the German frontier. It had withstood the German attack at the outbreak of the war, and now, greatly strengthened, it was attacked, Feb. 19, by the army of the Crown Prince, 300,000 strong, under the eye of the Kaiser. After six days' fighting Fort Douaumont, the most northerly outpost of the fortified area, was taken. Hardaumont, to the east, and Champneuville, to the west, were taken Feb. 26. The British line in Flanders was lengthened so that reinforcements might be sent to Verdun. The attack on the west side of the Meuse was made on a narrow front of not more than a mile and a half, between Vauquois and Malancourt and toward the town of Avocourt. Repeated assaults resulted in the formation of the French defense on the line of a double salient, with one apex at Avocourt and the other at Le Mort Homme. Malancourt was captured by the Germans March 31, who then shifted their attack to the town of Vaux, on the east bank of the Meuse. Penetrating the French lines on hills 265 and 295, the Germans during April and May almost daily attacked Le Mort Homme and Hill 304. Early in June the attacks centered on Fort Vaux, which fell to the Germans on the 7th, and Thiaumont on the 23d. June 25 the Anglo-British allies began a strong offensive movement (see Somme, Battle of) extending along the line from La Bassee in the north to Verdun in the south. The effect of these counter-attacks was to quell the German offensive, and by the end of the month the vast German siege was admittedly a failure. The French counter-attacks regained practically all of the ground which the Germans had gained.

Somme, Battle of.—During the early spring of 1916, the German attacks in France were mainly directed against Verdun. From the first of February till late in June the most terrific warfare recorded in history took place in this fortified area (See Verdun, Battle of.) The British lines in the north were extended so as to send reinforcements to the French defenders. Finally, June 25th, a general advance by the Franco-British allies began. Fighting in July centered along the advance between the Ancre and the Somme rivers, by way of La Boiselle, Cortalmaison, Montaubon, Pozierès, the Faureaux and Delville woods. Guilement-Ginchy and Combles were taken from the Germans in August and by the end of September the Allies claimed to have captured 117 square miles of territory, including forty-four villages, from the invaders since the beginning of the combined offensive. The end of October, 1916, found the Anglo-French allies still fighting furiously to maintain positions on the roads connecting Peronne and Bapaume.

Rumania in the War.—Rumanian participation in the war was a finality foreseen by all close observers of the great struggle, but it was questionable at all times prior to the actual declaration as to which of the belligerents would gain the support of the inland kingdom, surrounded by warring neighbors. The Austrian Red Book says the late King Charles was informed in July, 1914, of Austria's proposed ultimatum to Servia, and promised to keep hands off. King Charles worked hard to maintain Rumanian neutrality, despite the Allies' constantly increasing pressure. Crown Prince Ferdinand, later King, insisted, however, the nation wanted war with Austria. Oct. 9, 1914 King Charles, utterly discouraged, said to the Austrian envoy, "I have only to die and see the end of this." The King died Oct. 10, 1914.

June 25, 1916, the Austro-Hungarian minister predicted that a critical time had arrived. "The minister reported that the Entente was threatening Rumania, and that it would consider no Rumanian wishes in the peace conference if Rumania did not enter the war now. July 27 the minister reported that King Ferdinand declared: 'I have the same intentions as my late uncle, but not the same authority.'" August 8 Premier Bratiano asked the cession of a part of Bukowina, alleging that this might strengthen the partisans of neutrality. The minister, following instructions, declined, since the cession would not prevent Rumania from attacking Austria-Hungary whenever she thought the moment propitious. August 12 the Austro-Hungarian Foreign Minister instructed the minister at Bucharest to point out in a friendly tone that Rumania left the Russian frontier unprotected while it made strong war preparations against Austria-Hungary. The King's answer to these representations on August 26, the minister reports, was evasive, as usual. The night of the 26th Premier Bratiano declared in a conversation with the minister that Rumania would enter the war only if attacked. On the 27th Rumania declared war on the side of the Entente.

Invasion of Rumania.—During the late summer of 1916, the Germans had launched sporadic attacks against Rumania, but on October 18, 1916, the campaign for the complete subjugation of the country was undertaken in earnest. The Germans invaded from two points, with one division under the command of Mackensen and the other under Falkenheyn. Both the division proceeding through Transylvania and the division proceeding through the Dobruja swept all before it, despite the fact that the Rumanian armies were reinforced by Russian troops; and the two German armies effecting a union before Bucharest, the capital fell early in December, and Rumanians, like Serbians, became a people without a country.

Battle of Jutland.—During the spring and summer of 1916, both the German and the British fleets had been making long sweeps, in divisions, through the North Sea; and it hence was inevitable that they should meet. At 2 P. M. on May 31, 1916, a British division under Sir David Beatty encountered, off the northwest coast of Jutland, a German division under Admiral Hipper. The British division consisted of 2 squadrons of battle cruisers, 3 squadrons of light cruisers, and 4 torpedo boat destroyers, supported by 4 super-dreadnaughts. The German division, consisting merely of 5 squadrons of battle cruisers, supported by light craft, was outnumbered, and attempted to fall back on the main German fleet steaming up from Helgoland. Beatty, however,

pursued the Germans, with the two hostile divisions stretched out in almost parallel lines, although the pursuit carried him closer to the main German fleet and farther away from the main British fleet under Jellicoe, which also was steaming up to join in the conflict. At 3.48 P. M. action commenced at a distance of about 20,000 yards. Each side soon got busy with torpedoes, and the English "Indefatigable" was the first vessel to sink, although the Germans soon lost two destroyers when their attack was met by an attack from the British destroyers. The latter, however, lost heavily when they pursued their advantage to attempt an attack upon the German light cruisers. The "Queen Mary" also soon went to the bottom; and by 4.30 the conflict was raging fiercely.

At 4.45 P. M., Beatty sighted the advance of the main German battle fleet, and fell back to the main British fleet, which was now also approaching, and which soon engaged the enemy. A heavy haze, however, gave rise to a condition of "low visibility," and it was difficult to strike a decisive blow; and action practically ceased by 9 P. M. Jellicoe attempted during the fight and later during the night to cut off the German fleet from its base, but found in the morning that he had not succeeded; and the English could not follow, because of the danger of mines. Although the battle of Jutland remains probably the greatest naval battle fought in the history of the world, yet the results were indecisive. The British seem to have suffered the heavier losses, but the Germans indisputably fled. The British loss comprised 3 battle cruisers, 3 cruisers, and 8 destroyers, a total loss in tonnage of 114,100 tons. The Germans confessed to a loss of 1 battleship, 2 battle cruisers, 5 cruisers and 5 destroyers—a total loss in tonnage of 60,720 tons. The British claimed, however, that the Germans lost in addition tonnage to the extent of 47,800 tons; and the German denials of this claim must be discredited because of the fact that Berlin admitted that she had for some time refused to verify the claim of the British concerning two of the vessels listed above as lost, "for military purposes." It must be remembered also that, since the British fleet is more than twice as powerful as the German fleet, any German loss of more than 50% of the British loss is in its effects a defeat for Germany.

Protest to Great Britain.—The protest of the United States against the enforcement of the British Order in Council declaring a blockade of neutral European ports was rejected by Great Britain in three notes made public by the State Department. The main British contention was that no principle of international law was violated by the British blockade. It was held that there is only one immutable principle underlying the right of blockade, namely, that of "cutting off by effective means the seaborne commerce of the enemy." Instances were cited of Federal interference with neutral traffic during the civil war in America when goods were destined ultimately for States in rebellion.

Peace Proposals.—Chancellor von Bethmann-Hollweg, December 12, 1916, handed to the envoys of the United States, Spain and Switzerland—the three neutrals that represent German interests in hostile capitals—a note proposing peace negotiations. The text of the note and the replies thereto will be found on pages 8187 to 8194.

One week after the German proposal President Wilson, through Secretary of State Lansing, sent a note to each of the belligerent powers, suggesting that they take the initiatory steps to bring about peace.

The note to the entente groups was delivered to Great Britain, France, Italy, Japan, Russia, Belgium, Montenegro, Portugal, Rumania and Serbia; that to the central allies, to Germany, Austria-Hungary, Turkey and Bulgaria, and also to all neutral governments for their information. For the text of the note and replies, see 8190, et seq.

The Entente Allies' message in reply to President Wilson's peace note outlined terms which would have indicated defeat for Germany in the war, but which had the saving grace of being definite.

Entente Peace Terms.—The proposals of the Entente Allies for a peace settlement, after repeating the statement in their reply to the peace proposals of Germany which insisted that all danger to the world of future aggression on the part of Germany must be removed, included the following features: "The restoration of Belgium, Servia and Montenegro, and the indemnities which are due them; the evacuation of the invaded territories of France, of Russia and of Roumania, with just reparation; the restitution of provinces or territories wrested in the past from the Allies by force or against the will of their populations (this reference being to Alsace and Lorraine); the liberation of Italians, of Slavs, of Roumanians, and of Tcheco-Slovaques from foreign domination (reference including those Austrian portions of the Italian peninsula and Adriatic shores desired by Italy); the enfranchisement of populations subject to the bloody tyranny of the Turks; the expulsion from Europe of the Ottoman Empire (including Constantinople);" and the fulfilment of the intentions of Russia to grant freedom to all of Poland.

Germany, in reply to the President's note, refused to mention any definite terms on which she would be willing to consider the establishment of peace; but asserted her willingness to discuss peace terms with representatives of the countries with which she was at war.

Entrance of the United States into the War.—On Jan. 31, 1917, Ambassador von Bernstorff laid before the State Department a communication from the Imperial German Government which retracted the assurances previously given by that power regarding limitations upon its submarine campaigns. The defense offered by Germany for this retraction was a statement that her enemies had resorted to illegal warfare until Germany was compelled to do likewise. The communication announced that beginning with February 1, 1917, all ships entering a blockade zone established around the British Isles and France, and also a blockade zone in the Mediterranean Sea around France and Italy, would be sunk on sight, with no provision for the safety of their crews and irrespective of their purposes and cargoes. Due time would be given for ships sailing before this warning was made public to reach their destinations in safety, the German note continued; but thereafter no ship, belligerent or neutral, would be safe from unannounced attack in the blockade zones. American ships would be allowed only this privilege—they might sail to and from, the port of Falmouth, according to a course laid down by Germany, provided that only one ship a week took advantage of this offer, and provided that such ship did not carry contraband in the German interpretation of that word.

The response of the United States to Germany's announcement was prompt and decisive. On February 3, President Wilson

announced to Congress that Ambassador von Bernstorff had been given his passports, and expressed a fervent wish that this action would convince the Imperial German Government of the determination of the United States to defend its own honor, and would induce Germany not to commit an overt act which would lead to war. The American Ambassador to Germany, James W. Gerard, was instructed at the same time to ask for his passports.

For some weeks, the outcome of the situation was awaited over the entire civilized world with breathless interest, but there was no indication that Germany was considering receding from the position she had taken. On February 27, one week before the adjournment of the Sixty-fourth Congress, President Wilson asked it for power to arm American merchant vessels, in accordance with a policy of armed neutrality; but a small group of Senators, whom the President characterized as a group of "wilful men representing no opinion but their own," was enabled to take advantage of the Senate's rules of debate to prevent a vote upon the bill embodying President Wilson's request. The result of their action was the immediate amendment of the rules of the Senate to provide for shutting off debate by certain regulations (closure); and the policy of armed neutrality was put into effect. It soon became evident, however, that, in the President's words, "the policy proved to be impracticable." American ships were still being mercilessly sunk, and the Sixty-fifth Congress was summoned into special session on April 2, 1917. On the evening of the same day, the President addressed the Congress assembled in joint session, and asked it to declare that the actions of Germany had compelled this country to proclaim that a state of war existed between the United States and the Imperial German Government. With only 6 Senators and 50 Representatives voting in the negative, the Congress followed the President's request, and official announcement of the entrance of the United States into the conflict was made by the President on April 6. But a few days later, Cuba followed the example of the country which had made her free.

German Intrigues in the Western World.—The decision of the United States to recognize that a state of war existed with Germany was hastened by announcement made on February 28, 1917, that an incriminating note from the German foreign secretary, Zimmermann, had been intercepted by the United States Secret Service. The note was dated from Berlin, on January 19, 1917, and was addressed to the German minister in Mexico. The text of the note is as follows:

"Berlin, Jan. 19, 1917.

On the 1st of February we intend to begin submarine warfare unrestricted. In spite of this, it is our intention to endeavor to keep neutral the United States of America.

If this attempt is not successful, we propose an alliance on the following basis with Mexico: That we shall make war together and together make peace. We shall give general financial support, and it is understood that Mexico is to reconquer the lost territory in New Mexico, Texas, and Arizona. The details are left to you for settlement.

You are instructed to inform the President of Mexico of the above in the greatest confidence as soon as it is certain that there will be an outbreak of war with the United States, and suggest that the President of Mexico, on his own initiative, should communicate with Japan suggesting adherence at once to this plan. At the same time, offer to mediate between Germany and Japan.

Please call to the attention of the President of Mexico that the employment of ruthless submarine warfare now promises to compel England to make peace in a few months.

ZIMMERMANN."

There is no evidence that either Japan or Mexico, if they received the note, considered acting in accordance with its suggestions. On April 8, the Government of Austria-Hungary severed diplomatic negotiations with the United States, although war was not declared, and this example was soon followed by Turkey. Later in April, Brazil severed relations with Germany, because of the sinking of Brazilian ships, but war was not declared. Many of the countries of Central and South America followed the example of Brazil.

Throughout 1917, the State Department of the United States made public a number of documents which proved beyond question that Germany had made wide-spread unneutral propaganda in neutral countries. The German minister to Argentina had made use of diplomatic facilities extended him through the courtesy of Sweden to transmit to his government information regarding the sailing of Argentine ships, with directions that they be sunk without trace, "spurlos versenkt." Count Bernstorff, the German ambassador to the United States, for months had been expending vast sums of money in causing strikes and destruction of property in American manufacturing establishments and in endeavoring to influence American public opinion.

For *Relief of the destitute in Belgium and northern France,* see Belgian Relief.

For the *Russian Revolution,* see Russia; Russian Revolution.

For *Socialists and the War,* see Socialism.

Preparations of the United States for Participation.—Immediately upon the announcement by the President and Congress of the existence of a state of war, the country went into extensive preparations to prosecute its share in the conflict with the utmost of its energy and resources. Plans made for the enlargement of the Army (q. v.) and the Navy (q. v.) and for the industrial and social integration of the country for the conflict were put into immediate effect; and new plans were made by newly-created boards and commissions. (See Council of National Defense; Naval Consulting Board; National Food Board; United States Shipping Board.) A conscription act was passed, providing for a first war army of 500,000 men, in addition to the recruiting of the Army and Navy up to their full war strength. Ex-President Roosevelt pleaded for permission to lead a division of volunteers into France, and went ahead with plans for the organization of such a force while Congress and the President were considering the advisability of granting his request. The Secret Service force was most efficient in rounding up and arresting German spies and plotters in this country, and practically none of the anticipated schemes for blocking the progress of the country's war plans was carried into effect. Commissions from England, Italy and France, to consult and to give advice about our participation in the war, were received with open arms, and a commission from the United States to her new ally, the democratic Government of Russia, was dispatched. Without a dissenting vote, Congress passed a first war budget of $7,000,000,000; and $2,-000,000,000 offered in bonds as the Liberty Loan (q. v.) was offered generally to the country, to be largely oversubscribed. Extensive war credits were granted to our new allies. State and municipal governments co-operated extensively in governmental plans, specially in the elimination of waste, in the production of food, and in the encouragement of thrift and economy. Registration of all men between the ages of 21 and 31 was set for June 5. On May 19, President Wilson announced that a division of the regular army (about 28,000 men) would be dispatched immediately to France under the command of General Pershing. Aviation and hospital units from the United States also were dispatched about the same time. President Wilson announced also on May 19 that he did not contemplate at that time the acceptance of Ex-President Roosevelt's offer to lead an expeditionary force into France.

From June throughout 1917, American troops were dispatched to France, where they received intensive training before being sent to the firing lines.

On July 20, 1917, the numbers were drawn for the draft army, which had been increased to 687,000, and by December all those drawn in the lottery were in cantonments receiving training.

The Sixty-fifth Congress, by its adjournment early in October, had passed appropriations totalling $21,000,000,000. Seven billions of this amount, however, was for loans to the other Entente Allies; and much additional was for future expenditure. The President sought and obtained legislation enabling him to mobilize and direct the entire economic resources of the country. For the war taxes levied, see Internal Revenue. Mr. Herbert Hoover, formerly head of the Belgian Relief Commission, was made food administrator, although his powers fell far short of those of a food dictator. The Red Cross was re-organized; the problem of providing ships for transportation of men and supplies to Europe was attacked vigorously; and the entire business structure of the land was re-organized for food purposes.

The First Liberty Loan of $2,000,000,000 was offered to the people in June, 1917, and was largely oversubscribed, as was the Second Liberty Loan, offered in October, in which more than $4,000,000,000 was collected.

A feature of the war administration of President Wilson was the suppression of papers criticising our entrance into and prosecution of the war to the point where the post-office authorities declared that such criticism was hindering the country's endeavors.

Domestic activities concerned with the prosecution of the War, such as the *United States Shipping Board, War Trade Board, Alien Property Custodian, Shipbuilding, Income and Corporation Taxes, Espionage Law, Fuel Administration, Food Administration, Railroad Federalization, Conscription,* are described under their respective heads.

For detailed account of the war activities of the bureaus within the War and Navy Department, look under those heads. Separate activities like those concerned with Shipping, Aircraft Production, Liberty Loans, Conscription, Council of National Defence, Fuel Administration, War Trade Board, Red Cross, Alien Property Custodian, etc., are described under those heads.

Prosecution of the War, 1917.—During the winter of 1916-1917, the forces struggling on land maintained their *status quo.* In the Western theatre of war, desultory trench fighting and minor maneuvers continued. In England, the Asquith coalition cabinet had resigned in December, 1916, to be succeeded by a war council of five members entrusted with the prosecution of the conflict, under the direction of the new premier, Lloyd-George. In March, the Briand Ministry in France resigned, and the new Cabinet was headed by Ribot as premier. General Nivelle, who had succeeded Marshall Joffre as commander-in-chief of the Allied armies in the West was in turn succeeded in April by General Petain, with practically dictatorial war powers. Field Marshal von Hindenburg was given supreme command of the German armies and General Falkenhayn was made chief of staff. The disruption in Russia due to the revolution in March would probably have been made by Germany the occasion for a new onslaught in the East, had not the Allies launched a new and terrible offensive.

In July, growing unrest in Germany forced the government to promise widespread franchise reforms, to take effect in the Reichstag elections for the coming year. Dissatisfaction with Chancellor von Bethman-Hollweg forced his retirement, and the succession to the premiership of Michaelis, who was succeeded on October 29, 1917, by the Prussian Prime Minister, Count George F. von Hertling.

In England, King George renounced the title of the head of the House of Hanover, because of its German derivation, and the family name of the ruling family of England will hereafter be the House of Windsor. In France, the Ribot ministry was forced to resign in September because of the opposition of the Socialists, and it was succeeded by the ministry under the premiership of Paul Painlévé, in turn yielding to the ministry of Clemenceau. For the Russian military collapse, and the Vatican's peace proffer, see below. In August, China also declared war on Germany.

Throughout the summer and fall of 1917, the situation on the Western front changed but little. The costly trench fighting made the gains slight, but most of them seemed to fall to the lot of the Allies. The chief source of military interest lay in the activities of the German submarines, for which see below; and the feeling among the Allies that the undersea warfare had failed to counterbalance the addition of the United States to their ranks caused them to believe that their final victory was only a matter of time.

On November 16, Georges Clemenceau became premier of France, and succeeded as had none of his predecessors during the war in rallying the various political forces of France behind his ministry.

Developments in Greece.—By treaty obligations, Greece was bound to defend Servia in case of attack; but Greece nevertheless refused to act when Roumania attacked Servia in 1915. It seemed that the mass of the Greek people were pro-Entente in their sympathies, but the sympathies of the King and the Court were pro-Teuton. The powerful and able premier, Venizelos, demanded that Greece be faithful to her treaty with Servia, but the King refused, and finally suspended constitutional government. Dissention reigned in the land. Finally, in 1917, the Allies announced that they could no longer shut their eyes to what they declared were the German intrigues of the King, and compelled him to resign on June 12, 1917. He was succeeded by his second son, Alexander; Venizelos returned to power; and Greece soon afterwards cast in her lot with the Entente Allies.

Stockholm Conference.—In April, 1917, neutral Socialists called an international conference at Stockholm, Sweden, for the purpose of resurrecting the Internationale (the international Socialist organization). German and Russian Socialists were ready to attend, but the conference came to naught through the refusal of the British, French and United States governments to grant passports to the delegates selected from their countries, on the ground that the conference was a German peace machination. The action of the British government led to the resignation from the British Cabinet of Arthur Henderson, the leader of the powerful British Labor Party.

Vatican Peace Proffer, 1917.—On August 14, 1917, the Pope dispatched a proffer of peace to all the belligerents. The Pope proposed as the basis for negotiations the establishment of arbitration; the freedom of the seas; disarmament; the absence of indemnities of a punitive nature; the evacuation of Belgium with guarantees for independence; the return of northern France and also of the German colonies; and the settlement of the territorial problems represented by Alsace and Lorraine, Italia Irredenta, the Balkan problem, etc., by negotiations after the war.

The President replied to the Pope on August 29, in a communication which spoke also for the allies of the United States. The President, after expressing appreciation of the Pope's motives in offering mediation, drew up an indictment of Germany as a faithless menace to the organization of the world, and declared that while the German government remained autocratic, there could be no guarantee that a peace with it would be lasting, secure or just. Denying that the United States would take part in an economic league against Germany after the war, President Wilson declared that until Germany was ruled democratically by its people instead of autocratically by a caste, there could be no peace negotiations with her. The President did not state what definite changes would meet the requirements of the Allies, nor did he comment upon the other definite proposals of the Pope.

The German and Austrian replies to the Vatican, published soon after the President's reply, after asserting that Germany and Austria had always been peace-loving, assented to the Pope's proposal of reciprocal limitation of armaments, and the establishment of international arbitration.

The text of the Pope's offer and of the replies to it will be found in their chronological position in the text of the Messages and Papers of the Presidents, under the administration of President Wilson.

Battle of Arras.—Early in February began the first of the great German retreats since the Battle of the Marne. The Battle of the Somme had allowed the British to drive a wedge into the German lines, and persistent attacks had gradually widened that wedge until the German lines were no longer tenable. The Germans prepared their new line of resistance (the Hindenburg line) very carefully and retreated to it in masterly fashion, taking up a position facing the towns of Arras and Soissons. The Germans pursued their policy of frightfulness by deliberately wasting the country they were forced to abandon, in such wanton fashion as to impoverish it for years to come.

Against the new German line, the English launched a general attack at dawn of Easter Monday, April 9, 1917. The offensive was along a 45-mile front, with Lens as the objective at one end and St. Quentin at the other end. Despite the fact that the attack was launched in bitter weather, it was irresistible, and day after day the Germans retreated, the English taking above 10,000 prisoners daily. Not since the beginning of the war was the attack by air so comprehensive, and the artillery bombardment rivalled that around Verdun in the previous year. From the day of the inauguration of the offensive, when the Canadians captured the Vimy ridge, to the end of ten days, the Allies gained more ground than they had previously gained in the 6 months since the Battle of the Somme. After the first 5 days, the French also delivered smashing blows; and the retreat of the Germans along their whole line covered a considerable number of miles. By May 1, the end of the offensive was in sight, and by May 15, Germany was able to deliver several successful counter-attacks.

Russian Military Collapse, 1917.—For several months after the Russian Revolution (q. v.), Germany seems to have refrained from any attacks upon that country because of the hope of concluding a separate peace with her. A strong Russian offensive in July, however, was final proof that Russia was determined to stick by her allies, and Germany accordingly launched a heavy attack later in the month. The inevitable re-action from the enthusiasm of the Revolution at this time was convulsing Russia, and she was unable to to present any considerable resistance to the German advance. Many of the radicals and the pacifists were not in favor of continuing the war, and the consequent disorganization in the army made Germany's task easy. On September 3, Riga was occupied, and in October, German warships penetrated into the Gulf of Riga.

In July, the Socialist Kerensky had replaced Lvoff as premier, and the government became more radical in its personnel. Kerensky displayed remarkable powers of organization, and made great strides toward resurrecting Russia's military strength. The Bolsheviki, or uncompromising Socialists, nevertheless at latest reports were increasing in power; and the date on which Russian armies could again be of great assistance to their allies was problematical.

On September 9, 1917, General Korniloff, who had succeeded Brusiloff, the successor of Alexieff as commander-in-chief, raised the standard of revolt in behalf of the constitutional democrats, or moderates, against the Socialist government, but was unsuccessful, and saw his revolt put down by Kerensky with little trouble. Shortly afterwards, the Cabinet proclaimed Russia a republic. Before the end of 1917, Kerensky had been replaced by a government of the Bolsheviki (q. v.), under Lenine and Trotsky. In December, an armistice between Russia and Roumania and Germany was announced.

Through January, 1918, the representatives of the Bolshevist government and of Rumania discussed terms of peace with the spokesmen of the Central Powers at Brest-Litovsk. Lenine asked the Allied governments to join the negotiations, but was told that the Allies would not discuss peace with a victorious and uncontrolled German government. On February 15, 1918, the German government finally rejected all peace propositions of the Bolsheviki, and three days later resumed hostilities against Russia, which was not in a condition to oppose even a weak resistance to the German advance. The Germans soon crossed the Dvina River at Dvinsk and, Petrograd being menaced, the seat of the Russian government

was removed to Moscow, and the Bolsheviki were forced to accept terms of peace as dictated by Germany.

In addition to being bound by certain economic and political concessions, Russia lost Russian Poland, Courland, Livonia, Esthonia and the Ukraine (q. q. v.). In Asia Minor Russia was compelled to leave Armenia entirely to the Turks and to cede to Turkey in addition Batum, Kars and Erivan. Bessarabia (q. v.) was also surrendered; and the Russian army was to be demobilized and the Russian warships dismantled.

Moreover, Germany recognized Ukrainia's right to independence, and even after the terms of peace had been signed, marched her armies through Russia under the pretext of aiding Ukrainia to rid itself of Bolshevist influence. By May, the Germans had penetrated far into a country with which they were supposed to be at peace, and had established their influence in the freed and occupied territory. In the Baltic provinces, German influence openly took the ascendancy, and although Lithuania was recognized as independent in May, German influence there also dominated the country.

The commercial treaty forced upon Russia by Germany contained favored nation clauses to be effective until 1925; and in addition, the Bolsheviki were compelled to put an end to all propaganda and agitation in their territories against the German form of government.

In addition to losing the territory mentioned above, the Cossacks of the Caucasus region seceded from Russia and set up a government of their own; and even before the end of 1917 Finland had become a nation distinct from Russia, although its hopes for national self-expression were jeopardized by German intrigues and activities.

Rumanian-Central Powers Peace. — At the same time as the peace negotiations between the Central Powers and the Socialist Government of Russia at Brest-Litovsk, and largely under the same conditions, Rumania entered upon peace negotiations with the Central Powers. Final terms of peace were signed on May 7, 1918, and as made public included the following chief features:

The Rumanian army is demobilized, except for two divisions to protect the borders of Bessarabia and eight in Moldavia, the total not to exceed 20,000 infantry and 3,200 cavalry.

Rumania cedes all of Dobruja. Bulgaria obtains that portion which she had ceded to Rumania in the treaty of Bucharest in 1913, and the Central Powers that portion of Dobruja north of the new Bulgarian frontier line to the mouth of the Danube.

There is general rectification of the frontier in favor of Austria, the latter acquiring most of the important passes and many valuable mine lands. The population in the ceded territory is given the right of emigration.

Punitive indemnities are waived, but arrangements are made for the payment of damages caused by the war.

The Danube is to be under free navigation, Rumania abandoning all right to collect tolls on the river. The Central Powers obtain the right to maintain warships anywhere on the river. Rumania is guaranteed a trade route to the Black Sea by way of Tchernavoda and Constanza (Kustenje).

The economic relations of Rumania with the Central Powers are regulated by separate agreements going into effect simultaneously with the treaty, and functioning to the advantage of the Central Powers.

The Central Powers agree to the annexation of Bessarabia to Rumania.

Shipping Built in United States During War.—Between April 6, 1917, and November 11, 1918, 2,985 ships were built in United States shipbuilding plants. The total tonnage represented was 3,091,695 gross, an average of 1,035 gross tons each. Of the total built, 506 were ocean-going steel vessels, aggregating 2,056,814 tons, an average of slightly more than 4,000 gross tons each. Ocean-going wooden vessels aggregated 403, with a gross tonnage of 753,156. For further details of our shipbuilding program during the War, see the article in volume XX under "Shipbuilding."

Month by month the number of ships built in the United States was as follows:

Months.	Seagoing.						Nonseagoing.		Grand total.	
	Steel.		Wood.		Total					
	Number.	Gross Tons.	Number.	Gross Tons.	Number.	Gross Tons.	Number.	Gross Tons.	Number.	Gross Tons.
1917.										
April	7	34,364	9	17,233	16	51,597	123	9,201	139	60,798
May	11	36,086	19	33,004	30	69,090	162	22,137	192	91,227
June	22	97,908	9	31,216	31	129,124	196	22,877	227	152,001
July	14	54,891	7	14,113	21	69,004	184	20,148	205	89,152
August	9	46,716	14	12,155	23	58,871	152	27,171	175	86,042
September	9	35,073	12	12,513	21	47,586	80	28,999	101	76,585
October	13	44,420	22	35,879	35	80,299	87	10,386	122	90,685
November	19	50,660	11	10,872	30	61,532	87	15,736	117	77,268
December	17	85,917	16	20,611	33	106,528	52	16,053	85	122,581
1918.										
January	12	53,748	6	6,468	18	60,216	39	4,579	57	64,795
February	17	94,242	14	17,874	31	112,116	53	5,485	84	117,601
March	29	115,040	12	20,776	41	135,816	97	11,329	138	147,145
April	31	130,637	15	21,017	46	151,654	119	11,396	165	163,050
May *	*40	157,598	13	16,453	53	174,051	132	20,413	185	194,464
June	42	163,034	16	26,985	58	190,019	130	11,406	188	201,425
July †	37	146,981	38	72,727	75	219,708	118	†10,223	193	229,931
August	49	191,102	39	91,997	88	283,099	89	12,750	177	295,849
September	46	177,765	54	123,668	100	301,433	70	7,037	170	308,470
October	57	228,203	53	117,165	110	345,368	91	12,164	201	357,532
Nov. 1 to Nov. 11.	25	112,429	24	50,430	49	162,859	15	2,235	64	165,094
Grand total	506	2,056,814	403	753,156	909	2,809,970	2,076	281,725	2,985	3,091,695

* Includes 1 cement vessel of 3,427 gross tons.   † Includes 1 cement vessel of 325 gross tons.

Invasion of Italy.—From the very moment of the declaration of war against Austria, Italy had confined her exertions in the conflict to the occupation of Italia Irredenta (q. v.) and to surrounding territory lying along the border between the two countries. That border is composed of mountain ranges almost inaccessible, and the Italian progress, although sure, was slow. By November, 1917, a broad belt of Austrian territory more than 30 miles in width had been conquered and occupied by the Italian armies under General Cadorna; and the Italian flag was getting closer and closer to Trieste.

On November 1, 1917, however, the German General Staff launched two attacks as terrible as they were unexpected against the Italian line, which had become considerably extended. The attacking forces were largely of seasoned German troops under von Mackensen. One force advanced through Plezzo and Tolmino while the other was making a flanking movement to the northeast. The first attack drove the Italians southwest to the plains around Udine and Cividale, and bent the Italian line so sharply that Gorizia and the surrounding land to the south had also to be abandoned. The German flanking force to the northeast meanwhile was not to be denied, and Cadorna was confronted by the threat of being altogether surrounded. The only escape lay in a general retreat into Italy; and despite the rapidity with which he was able to reach the Tagliamento River in Italy with the loss of 180,000 prisoners and 1,500 cannon. The Teutons were thus enabled to occupy the northern boundary of Italy to the extent of more than thirty-five miles.

At the Tagliamento River a stand was made, but the Germans continued their flanking movements, and a general retreat still farther into Italy was ordered. There seemed to be hope that Venice could be saved from the invaders, and that a successful winter stand could be made farther north than the Adige or the Po rivers.

The Italian disaster called forth great re-inforcements from the Allies, especially in supplies; and the consciousness among the Allied leaders that the disaster had been made possible largely by the lack of unified management of the war among the Entente Allies led to the formation of a central Allied war council, with power to direct all military operations.

Until the summer of 1918, the Austro-Italian battleline then remained comparatively quiescent. On June 15, 1918, however, a pretentious Austrian attack was launched on a front stretching more than 100 miles from the Adriatic inland. Austrian gains, however, were slight, and even in the region of their greatest advance, the land between the Piave and Venice along the Adriatic, they did not penetrate beyond a depth of five miles. Within ten days, the Italians launched counterattacks, and the Austrians abandoned most of the territory they had acquired at heavy loss.

Battle of Cambrai.—On the morning of Monday, November 19, 1917, the British launched a carefully-prepared and carefully-concealed attack upon the German trenches in front of the village of Cambrai. The attack was led by many "tanks," or tractors, which had been massed before the

Man Power Under Arms on Jan. 1, 1918.—
According to the most reliable figures available, there were at the beginning of 1918
some 38,000,000 persons in the Armies and
Navies of the nations engaged in the great
struggle, distributed as follows:

ENTENTE ALLIES

Russia	9,000,000
France	6,000,000
Great Britain	5,000,000
Italy	3,000,000
Japan	1,400,000
United States	more than 1,000,000
China	540,000
Rumania	320,000
Serbia	300,000
Belgium	300,000
Greece	300,000
Portugal	200,000
Montenegro	40,000
Total	**27,400,000**

CENTRAL POWERS

Germany	7,000,000
Austria-Hungary	3,000,000
Bulgaria	300,000
Turkey	300,000
Total	**10,600,000**

point of attack without the knowledge of
the enemy, and which succeeded in batter-
ing down the German trenches in their advance so that the British troops could pour
through. There was tremendous artillery
activity on a front of almost 32 miles, from
Quéant almost to St. Quentin, but the advance proper was on a front of about 12
miles.

The attack lasted four days before it
spent itself, and by that time the British
had advanced six miles at certain points,
averaging a five-mile advance along a seven
mile front, and gaining altogether more
than fifty square miles of territory and some
10,000 prisoners. This gain of ground represents the greatest Allied advance since
the Battle of the Marne, and more than was
gained in four months' fighting at the
Somme. Cambrai itself, an important railroad and highway center, was not occupied,
however.

Once recovered from their surprise, however, the Germans launched terrific counter-
attacks against the advanced positions of
the British, winning many of them back.
These counter-attacks continued well into
December, and succeeded in retrieving practically all of the ground which the British
had captured.

Capture of Jerusalem.—Soon after the
entrance of Turkey into the war, a Turkish
attack against Egypt and the Suez Canal
was launched across the Sinai peninsula.
In November, 1914, the Turks arrived within striking distance of the Canal at several
points, but after several months were driven
back a considerable distance.

In June, 1916, however, the Turks advanced again, and got to within fifteen miles
of the coveted water passage, only to be defeated again.

In December, 1916, the British finally
succeeded in driving the Turks altogether
out of Egypt, and inaugurated an advance
of their own into Palestine. By March,
1917, they had advanced to the site of ancient Hebron, fifteen miles south of Jerusalem. The heated summer weather compelled a lull in operations and a retirement
until the following Fall; but by November,
Beersheba and Gaza were in British hands,
and by December Hebron had again been
taken, and Jaffa, the port of Jerusalem,
also was under the British flag. The city

was thus surrounded, but the invading
forces proceeded with caution, so as not to
injure the holy places of the city; and
Jerusalem was not finally surrendered until December 9, 1917.

Later Peace Negotiations.—After an armistice between Germany and the New Russia, as represented by the Bolshevist government under Lenine and Trotzky, had been
declared late in 1917, peace negotiations between the two countries were entered upon.
The Russian terms were comprised within
the formula, "No punitive indemnities, no
forcible annexation of territory, and the
right to self-development of all nationalities, large and small." While seeming to
agree to this formula, the German representatives interpreted it in such fashion as
to place Russia's Baltic provinces and parts
of Poland under German control, and the
negotiations were broken off. One effect of
these negotiations, however, was to call
forth new statements of war aims from the
British premier, Lloyd-George, on January
6, 1918, and from President Wilson two
days later. The latter's pronouncement,
placed in the form of an address to Congress, will be found in its chronological
position in his messages and papers.

The President expressed deep sympathy
with the Russian people in their plight, but
expressed regret that these and similar negotiations were hampered by the fact that
t ere was no knowing if and when the German representatives expressed the will of
the people of Germany of the Reichstag, or
merely of the ruling military group within
the German empire. Coming out unqualifiedly for open and public diplomacy in all
future international relations, President
Wilson formulated fourteen articles as comprising the war aims and basis of peace
terms of the Entente Allies. (See pages
8423-8425.)

The statement of Lloyd-George had been
similar to President Wilson's, although he
was not so specific upon so large a number
of international problems. The British
statesman, moreover, had not spoken with
so much friendliness of the Russians, and
had mentioned Alsace-Lorraine simply as a
problem needing attention, rather than as
representing a wrong to be righted.

On April 2, 1918, Count Czernin, the
Austrian premier, announced that "shortly
before the beginning of the offensive in the
West" Premier Clemenceau of France had
asked him upon what basis he was ready to
negotiate for peace, and that the conversations were broken off by France after
Count Czernin had answered that only
France's demand for Alsace-Lorraine stood
in the way of peace negotiations. Premier
Clemenceau immediately denied that the negotiations had been started by France, asserting that Austria had taken the initiative
in asking France's peace terms; and that
France had replied that no negotiations
were possible until Austria recognized the
justice of France's claims for Alsace-Lorraine. On April 11, 1918, Paris further issued an official note, asserting that on
March 31, 1917, Prince Sixtus de Bourbon,
the brother-in-law of Emperor Charles of
Austria, had communicated to the French
President and Premier a letter to him signed
by Emperor Charles, saying in part:

". . . . It is a special pleasure to me to
note that, although for the moment adversaries, no real divergence of views or
aspirations separates my Empire from
France, and that I am justified in hoping
that my keen sympathy for France, joined
to that which prevails in the whole
(Austro-Hungarian) monarchy, will forever
avoid a return of the state of war, for
which no responsibility can fall on me.

The Results of Submarine Warfare.—The following table shows the merchant tonnage of the world on July 1, 1914, the tonnage lost through acts of war (chiefly submarine attacks), the tonnage built during the war, and the tonnage of the world on January 1, 1919. The figures are in gross tons.

	July 1, 1914	Lost in War	Built in War	January 1, 1919
United Kingdom	20,100,000	7,757,000	4,557,000	16,900,000
United States	1,875,000	395,000	4,239,000	5,719,000
Other Allies	7,675,000	2,592,000	1,757,000	6,840,000
Central Powers	6,325,000	3,000,000	750,000	*4,360,000
Neutral Nations	6,640,000	1,998,000	1,144,000	5,786,000
Total	42,615,000	15,742,000	12,447,000	39,605,000

* 2,400,000 tons of Central Powers' shipping were seized at the outbreak of the War and during the War.

The net loss of merchant shipping due to the war, that is, the difference between the tonnage lost and the tonnage constructed, may be placed at 4,250,000. But under normal conditions it is estimated that there would have been constructed from August, 1914 to November, 1918 some 12,000,000 tons of shipping, so that the total shortage in world shipping as a result of the war may be placed at 16,250,000.

It is estimated that Germany lost 200 submarines during the War.

"With this in mind, and to show in a definite manner the reality of these feelings, I beg you to convey privately and unofficially to President Poincaré that I will support by every means, and by exerting all my personal influence with my allies, France's just claim regarding Alsace-Lorraine.

"Belgium should be entirely re-established in her sovereignty, retaining entirely her African possessions without prejudice to the compensations she should receive for the losses she had undergone. Serbia should be re-established in her sovereignty and, as a pledge of our good-will, we are ready to assure her equitable natural access to the Adriatic, and also wide economic concessions in Austria-Hungary. On her side, we will demand, as primordial and essential conditions, that Serbia cease in the future all relation with, and suppress, every association or group whose political object aim. at the disintegration of the monarchy, particularly the Serbian political society, Narodni Ochrana; that Serbia loyally and by every means in her power prevent any kind of political agitation, either in Serbia or beyond her frontiers, in the foregoing direction, and give assurances thereof under the guarantee of the Entente Powers. The events in Russia compel me to reserve my ideas with regard to that country until a legal definite government has been set up there.

"Having thus laid my ideas clearly before you, I would ask you in turn, after consulting with these two powers, to lay before me the opinion first of France and England, with a view thus to preparing the ground for an understanding on the basis of which official preliminary negotiations could be taken up and reach a result satisfactory to all. . . . .   CHARLES."

German Offensive, 1918.—Throughout the latter months of 1917 and the early months of 1918 there were persistent reports that Germany was preparing the most gigantic blow she had yet delivered, to annihilate the Entente forces before sufficient United States troops could be transported to France to alter conditions on the firing line. The first stage of the German offensive *(Battle of Picardy)*, which developed immediately into the most terrific and comprehensive battle in the history of all civilization, was begun on the morning of March 21, 1918, after a brief but severe artillery preparation, on a fifty mile front opposite the British forces between Arras and La Fère. Before the battle had ceased, the British Premier described the battle in the House of Commons in a remarkably frank manner, and from his statement the following description of the struggle could be gleaned:

Notwithstanding the heavy casualties of 1917, the British Army was considerably stronger on January 1, 1918, than on January 1, 1917. Before the collapse of Russia in November, 1917, the German combatant strength was as two to the Allies' three. The German offensive in March was reinforced with the German troops removed from the Eastern front, with a certain amount of support from Austria, especially in guns and ammunition. Nevertheless, when the battle began, the Germans were still slightly inferior to the Allies in infantry and in artillery and markedly inferior in aircraft.

Accordingly, the Germans reorganized their troops in smaller divisions, so as to get a greater number of divisions. They had fewer men in a battalion and fewer battalions in a division. The particular advantage enjoyed by the Kaiser's troops was that of the offensive and the knowledge where the attack would be delivered, whereas the Allies had to strengthen their line along practically its entire length. The Germans concentrated in front of both the British and the French troops, bringing up their latter forces to the support of the former by night. The Germans enjoyed also remarkably advantageous weather conditions. But the chief advantage which the Germans enjoyed was that of a unified command, as opposed to the divided authority of all the Entente forces.

One result of the Allied withdrawal was the appointment of the French military leader, General Ferdinand Foch, as generalissimo of all the Allied forces, the first time that the Allied armies had been placed under one leader.

The attack was made by about ninety-seven divisions, on the widest front which up to that time had been engaged. The German object was the severance of the British and French forces and the capture of the Channel ports and Amiens, a railroad and supply centre of well-nigh incalculable importance. In this aim, the Germans almost succeeded. They broke through the British Third and Fifth Armies, and there was a serious gap opening up the road to Paris which was finally closed only by the heroic efforts of troops under General Carey.

After the retirement of the Fifth Army, the French reserves came up with comparatively great rapidity and by April 10th the impetus of the German attack was halted. The total German gain represented more than all the ground in this region won by the Allies since the first German

Casualties of the War.—It is difficult to present accurate figures as to the total casualties of the war. Many soldiers originally reported as missing are later found to have been killed or captured, many were wounded more than once, and many killed were previously included in the wounded column. The following figures, however, are compiled from official reports of some of the belligerents, with the figures for the other belligerents acquired by using the ratio of total casualties to deaths obtaining among these official reports:

ENTENTE ALLIES

	Dead	Wounded	Total Casualties
Russia	1,700,000	3,500,000	7,500,000
France	1,366,200	3,000,000	5,000,000
British Empire	900,000	2,800,000	4,200,000
Italy	462,000	950,000	2,700,000
Servia, Montenegro	125,000	290,000	575,000
Belgium	102,000	235,000	450,000
Roumania	100,000	230,000	440,000
United States	49,000	230,000	286,000
Greece	7,000	16,000	30,000
Portugal	2,000	4,000	7,000
Total	4,813,000	11,255,000	21,188,000

CENTRAL POWERS

	Dead	Wounded	Total Casualties
Germany	1,620,000	3,700,000	6,000,000
Austria-Hungary	800,000	2,000,000	4,100,000
Turkey	250,000	575,000	800,000
Bulgaria	100,000	400,000	700,000
Total	2,770,000	6,675,000	11,600,000
Grand Total	7,583,000	17,930,000	32,788,000

Estimates of the losses in wars of the nineteenth and twentieth centuries are as follows, although the data are extremely meagre and unreliable, except in the case of the Union forces in the Civil War, where the figures may be regarded as official:

Civil War—Union Army:			*Casualties*
Forces Engaged	2,320,272	War of 1812	50,000
Total Deaths	359,528	Mexican War	50,000
Wounded	275,175	Napoleonic Wars	6,000,000
Confederate Army:		Crimean War	285,000
Forces Engaged	600,000	Russo-Turkish War	225,000
Total Deaths	155,000	Russo-Japanese War	550,000
Wounded	70,000	British-Boer War	175,000

retreat from the Marne in November, 1914. The entire first stage of the drive lasted for about fifteen days. The territory gained was about 1,000 square miles, the depth of the German penetration at the widest point being more than 40 miles.

The ground gained was roughly in the form of a right angle triangle, of which the hypotenuse rested on the old line of battle. The apex was just south of Lens, and the altitude was just east of Arras and Amiens; for the Germans were unable to capture either of these centres, although their line was so close to them that their artillery rendered them untenable. By this attack, the Germans were within 70 miles of Paris. Each side gave due credit to the courage of the other, the Germans laying their success to the poor handling of the Allied forces.

Another result of the battle was the brigading of the United States forces with the French and British troops, at least until the danger of the German drive was spent. After the Germans had consolidated their gains, they disclosed a gun of a range sufficient to reach Paris from their lines, a distance of at least seventy miles, and began the bombardment of the French capital.

Second Phase (Battle of Flanders).—The second phase of the German offensive occurred to the north of the first, and represented a more direct drive for the Channel ports. It opened on April 9, the defending troops being chiefly British and Portuguese. Before the momentum of the drive was finally halted at the end of the month, the Germans had gained about 500 square miles, again representing more territory than they had evacuated in this region since their entrenchment after the first Battle of the Marne. Again the German gains were roughly in the shape of a right angle triangle, stretching from a point just east of Dixmude on the north to La Bassée, some ten miles above the northernmost point of the first stage of their offensive. On April 26, Mount Kemmel, the highest point of the Messines ridge, was captured, but beyond that point the Germans were not able to advance, nor did they succeed in capturing Ypres.

On April 12, the Field Marshal of the British Forces, General Sir Douglas Haig, addressed his army in a special order of the day, in part as follows:

"Many among us now are tired. To those I would say that victory will belong to the side which holds out the longest. The French Army is moving rapidly and in great force to our support. There is no other course open to us but to fight it out. Every position must be held to the last man. There must be no retirement. With our backs to the wall, and believing in the justice of our cause, each of us must fight to the end. The safety of our homes and the freedom of mankind depend alike upon the conduct of each one of us at this critical moment."

Third Phase (Battle of the Champagne or Second Battle of the Marne).—The third phase of the German attack was inaugurated on May 26th, on a fifty-five mile front extending from Noyon to Betheny, the latter point just north of Rheims. Like the other phases of the offensive, the attack was preceded by only several hours of severe artillery preparation, and the same methods were used in the onslaught as have been described above. This time, however, the Germans were able to advance without narrowing their front so generally as in the previous phases of the offensive, and as a result the ground gained was more in the shape of a square than that of a triangle. The attack was more precipitous than even its predecessors, as may be judged from the fact that although it was stopped earlier than the previous ones, it gained more ground than they had gained. By the time the French and American reserves had checked Ludendorff's forces on June 4, about 1300 square miles had been lost.

The territory gained adjoined immediately upon that gained by the first phase of the Germany offensive, not separated from it by a considerable expanse of battle line as in the case of the second and first phases of the offensive. By June 5th, slight gains were made against the attacking Germans, notably by the United States marines. But from Craonne to Bouresches, the deepest line of gain, the Germans had covered more than 40 miles, and had brought themselves within 43 miles of Paris. Rheims itself was not captured, and remained a French outpost in the eastern flank of the German drive.

Several weeks later, the French withdrew from the salient projecting between the area of the first and third phases of the German attack, thus throwing into one solid mass stretching from Arras to Rheims the territory gained by the Kaiser's armies in their first and third great attacks in the summer of 1918.

Allies' Successes, Summer, 1918.—After the great German gains in the third phase of their attacks in the summer of 1918, the German army rested for almost a month while making preparations for a fourth, and possibly a final drive from Chateau Thierry, at the apex of their new salient. As Chateau Thierry was a bare forty miles from Paris, another considerable German success in this region would have well-nigh compelled the evacuation of Paris, with all the grave consequences to the Allies' cause. The French realization of this fact made the approaching onslaught a final test of the power of the German war machine. The awaited German attack was launched on July 15. It covered the entire front gained in the third phase of the German attack about one month previously and the adjacent wings, being especially severe against Rheims, which formed the apex of the French salient into the German lines. Accordingly, the line of attack was along the unprecedented front of eighty miles.

But from the very beginning of their attack, the Germans struck a snag. They made no impression against the defences of Rheims, and even around Chateau Thierry, they gained but two miles or thereabouts on the first day of attack. And on the second day, their combined American and French opponents stopped them completely. Then began the Allied counterattack, and the immediate German rout.

Gaining six miles on the first day, Foch's forces so irresistibly swept aside the German defense that Hindenburg and Ludendorff decided that to oppose the whole fronting army of the Crown Prince was to court its complete annihilation or surrender, and a general German retreat from the salient was ordered. The German General Staff evidently hoped that rear guard actions would give the Crown Prince's army time to retire in good order, but so precipitate was the American and French advance that the Germans had to retreat in great disorder, and enormous stores of war materials and great numbers of prisoners fell into the Allies' hands. The Allied attack beginning at the apex of the salient, by July 20 it spread around the sides. By July 23, every German had been driven across the Marne, and by July 27, the German army abandoned all pretense of strong resistance until it could reach the Vesle, where the Germans established themselves and entrenched by August 5th. Their line was thus much shorter, and their evident need for a shortening of the front gave every indication that the German forces were no longer strong enough to maintain against the Allies' forces a battle line much lengthened over the Hindenburg line of 1917. The Germans accordingly gave up the entire salient which had cost them so dear.

The turning of the tide of battle against the Germans had a significance which can hardly be overestimated. In the first place, it proved that the climax of the German power still saw France undefeated. Secondly, it proved that the Germans were by no means invincible, even when not outnumbered. Thirdly, it proved the benefits of unified command among the Allies and the abilities of Foch. Fourthly, it had a most depressing effect upon the German morale both in the army and at home, and a corresponding stimulating effect upon the morale in the Allied countries. Fifthly, it weakened German influence, not only among neutrals and especially in Russia, but even among its co-belligerents, Austria, Turkey and Bulgaria. And finally, although by no means last in importance, this engagement being the first of considerable importance in which the United States forces had been present, it proved that they were magnificent fighters, magnificently trained, and magnificently led; and that there could no longer be doubt that the inability of Germany to stop the transporting of all the armed might of America to France meant her final overthrow, and that sooner than had seemed probable before the battle on the banks of the Marne in the closing weeks of July, 1918.

The Beginning of the End.—When the Crown Prince's Army entrenched itself on the Vesle on August 5, 1918, it seemed probable that another period of trench warfare, possibly continuing up to the following spring, was in order; for it looked as though the Allies needed several months to consolidate the salient which they had regained, and to prepare strong forces to attack the German position.

But Foch's resources were greater than probably any one except himself knew. Within two days, that is, on August 7, he ordered an advance of the British forces against the army of Prince Rupprecht, one hundred miles to the north, on the Lys salient. The next day, August 8, another attack was launched halfway between the Crown Prince's line and Rupprecht's army—on the Somme and directed against the lines of communication feeding the new position of the Crown Prince on the Vesle. The strength of the new attack may be gauged from the fact that on the first day the English army under Rawlinson gained no less than nine miles. By August 12, Lassigny had been taken and 40,000 prisoners were in the Allies' hands. Before August 18, when the Germans attempted to make a new stand, they had given up much ground and had surrendered at least one-fifth of the Lys and Picardy salients.

Simultaneously, attacks on the Crown Prince's line had made it impossible for him to consolidate his resources, and by August 18, his army had been driven back about ten miles from the Vesle. By this time, the whole line from the coast to Switzerland was active, and contemporaneous history becomes impossible. One can only take up different sections in order.

On the Lys salient, the Germans were compelled before September to withdraw forces to prevent a rout farther south, where Foch was hammering in Picardy ; and the British constantly took advantage of these withdrawals to launch attacks which cut deeply into the German line. By August 25, Merville was in Allied hands and by August 30, Bailleul. On the next day Mount Kemmel itself was re-occupied by the British and by September 10, Wytschaete was evacuated.

In the Picardy salient, the centre of the entire Allied thrust was taking place, and was dominating the whole line, gains in Picardy necessitating both withdrawals and transferrals of German troops from other sectors to bolster the Picardy lines. On August 25, the Allied forces had reached the Hindenburg Line on the north, and there the Germans once more endeavored to make a stand.

The Hindenburg line represented the line held by the Germans through the winter of 1917-8 and hence the line from which their advances in the spring of 1918 had been launched. It was the strongest natural line of defense for the Germans and also the shortest, while if it were once seriously broken, the entire German line in Belgium and northern France would have been threatened. The entire world therefore looked to see that line held by the Germans up to the last man and the last ounce of resources.

Foch, however, had no intention of allowing the Germans sufficient breathing space to make a stand. The Allies advanced as quickly as the Germans retreated. It was therefore significant when Haig was able within several days to cut the Hindenburg line to the north near Arras, and to carve out the first salient into the Hindenburg line since the beginning of the war, a salient toward Cambrai, developing considerable proportions by August 27th. By the end of the month, Mont St. Simeon fell and Mont St. Quentin, dominating the road up the Oise and Peronne. By the middle of the month of September, the Hindenburg line was being attacked along its whole length, and had been pierced in several important sections toward Cambrai.

On the Vesle front, there was little attacking between the middle of August and the first of September. The German withdrawals to the north, however, were threatening the Crown Prince with the danger of being flanked, and on September 5 he ordered a wide retreat to a point some twenty miles back of the Vesle. His retreat broke whatever had been left of the German military morale, and by October 1, the Hindenburg line had been cleared of Germans and the battlefront was rolling far to the north and east. Meanwhile the surrender of Bulgaria exposed Germany and Austria on the east and Turkey on the west.

The German Rout.—From the middle of September, the history of the war on the western front is an uninterrupted story of Allied gains and German retreats. By September 16, there could no longer be question of final defeat of Germany. Her losses had been tremendous all through the year, but by the end of the summer she could show nothing as recompense for them. Her condition in the military sense was dynamic, not static ; on no front except that of Lorraine was she able to

catch her breath. There was no longer possibility of making a stand—she had risked all, and was losing all, and there was no middle ground she could hold. She had decided to abandon the slow trench warfare, had won tremendous victories in the open, but now that the Allies had utilized the open fighting for victories of their own, Germany no longer could resort to trenches. The only problem now on the western front was the number of men and guns Germany could save before she reached the Rhine there was strong probability that the rate of her retreat had been so accelerated that even at the Rhine no stand could be made. After the middle of September, moreover, the American army west of the Vesle was ready with its thrust.

American Troops Capture St. Mihiel Salient.—For more than four years, from September, 1914, to September, 1918, the German forces had occupied the so-called St. Mihiel salient—stretching over the plain of the Woevre River. Its apex toward France was the town of St. Mihiel, on the Meuse, and it protected as its base the great iron fields of Briey, the most productive in the world, while still farther in the rear it served as a bulwark for the strongest of all German fortresses, Metz, with its many surrounding forts.

On September 12, 1918, the first American army ever mobilized in France launched a tremendous attack against the entire salient. Pershing himself led the attack, and under him was the flower of the troops sent across the seas, trained, supplied and reserved to break for all time the threat of German world domination. It was no mere chance which gave the Americans probably the most difficult position to attack along the whole line—fortified as it had been for all of four long years over almost every square foot of its two hundred miles.

The operation itself was along the so-called pincers plan. One claw of the pincers rested on the Moselle near Pont-a-Mousson —about ten miles thick. The other was to the east of the river, near Haudimont— about seven miles thick.

The artillery preparation began about midnight, and lasted several hours. The chief opposition was encountered on the west front, at the northern tip of the salient, slightly southwest of Fresnes ; but before the end of the day the advance here had almost equalled the advance on the southern end of the salient. The attack was led by a great army of tanks, reported by correspondents to be between 500 and 1,000.

On the first day, the northern attacking force had advanced from five to seven miles, while on the second it had got about twelve miles into the salient, reaching the Moselle at Jaulny. On the first day alone, some 10,000 prisoners were taken, the Germans being unable to offer much resistance to the force of the attack.

Early in the second day, the forces attacking from the south, which had had the easier task, met the northern forces at Haudicourt, and the junction of the two forces gave them all the ground back of them, in all, about 100 square miles. The combined forces then advanced along the entire line. By September 16, the guns of Metz itself got into action, and for the first time the Germans were able to offer stiff resistance, and some of the American advances were checked. Nevertheless by the seventeenth, the Americans had advanced to Ronvaux and Haumont. By the eighteenth, the attack slackened to consolidate the positions won, especially near the regions from which the pincers had first begun to close in upon the German lines.

In five days, accordingly, probably the most strongly-fortified German salient had been captured, with more than 20,000 prisoners and 200 guns; Verdun had for all time been freed from danger of further attack; more than 200 square miles of territory had been gained; the Moselle had been reached; and Metz was finally under fire, while the Briey iron fields were at least menaced.

Every military observer then realized that the war was practically over and the only uncertainty lay in the length of time before the German forces degenerated into a rabble and Germany would admit defeat, ask peace on the Allies' terms, and lay prostrate before the mercies of the Allies.

Germany herself answered the question. On September 15, 1918, Austria asked peace. The peace negotiations are described elsewhere, and it will suffice here to say that from that moment until the armistice was signed on November 11, the defeat of Germany and her inability for further resistance were confessed by herself and on the battlefronts only rearguard machine actions obstructed the steady advance of the Allies toward German territory.

Capitulation of Bulgaria.—The check to the German advance in the summer of 1918, and the forward progress of the Allies beyond even the line which the Germans had held through the winter of 1917, lowered morale among Germany's allies as well as in Germany itself throughout August and September, 1918. Coupled with these military events was the ever-increasing faith, not only among the Entente Allies, and not only among the neutrals, but even among the common people of the Central Powers, in the potency and promise of President Wilson's program of international political idealism.

The first sign of the defection of Germany's Allies was the peace overture from Austria-Hungary, described elsewhere. The second, and even more significant, was the agreement by Bulgaria to an armistice on the terms of the Allies.

On September 14, 1918, a carefully prepared but carefully concealed campaign was opened against Bulgaria. The British and Greek forces, which had long been held at Saloniki and other places in Greece as protection against a possible invasion of Greece by German, Austrian or Turkish forces, were no longer needed in this capacity because of the inability of Germany to detach any of her forces from her hard-pressed western front. Accordingly, the British-Greek forces struck the Bulgarian line with great vehemence between the Vardar River and Lake Doiran. Serbian forces soon afterwards made for Charevo and the Serbian-French forces made east of Monastir for Uskub, while there was a general enflanking movement of the Italians eastward through Albania. Within ten days, progress to the extent of one hundred miles had been made, and in a few days more the capture of Strumitza severed the two wings of the Bulgar-German army.

On September 27, 1918, Bulgaria asked for an armistice, and being refused any armistice except one on the Allies' terms, agreed to the latter proposal; and on September 29, 1918, it was announced that Bulgaria had withdrawn from the war. The terms she received were purely military, containing no provisions of a political nature, the armistice being in force until a final general peace was declared.

Bulgaria agreed to evacuate all the territory she occupied in Greece and Serbia; to demobilize her army at once; to surrender all means of transportation to the Allies, including her boats; to grant control of navigation on the Danube; to give the Allies free passage for military operations through her territory; to permit the Allies to occupy all strategic military points, and to store her arms and ammunition under the control of the Allies.

Thus in addition to losing an ally, with the consequent loss of prestige and weakening of morale, Germany's direct route to the East was broken, the Berlin-to-Bagdad Railroad was blocked, the solid belt of German territory through Central Europe (Mitteleuropa) was dissipated and Turkey was practically isolated.

Palestine Lost to Turks.—On September 18, 1918, General Allenby struck with all the might of the British army in Asia Minor against the Turkish armies in central and northern Palestine; and the Turks were soon in full retreat. In connection with Arabs under King Hussein, the British forces advanced rapidly from the Mediterranean at Haifa on a line extending across all of Palestine to the Arabian desert. On October 1, Damascus, the capital of Syria, was taken and occupied. By October 8, the Allied forces had captured the towns of Zaleh and Rayek, thirty miles from Damascus. On the same day, a French naval division entered Beirut, 150 miles north of Damascus, and made for Aleppo, the seat of the Turkish military power in Asia Minor; and it soon fell into their hands.

Simultaneously, the British forces along the Euphrates and Tigris, in Mesopotamia, advanced toward Allenby's army.

Before the surrender of the Turkish army, Allenby had captured some 125,000 prisoners, including some Austrian and German troops and officers.

So complete was Allenby's victory that the road to the Aegean sea and the Dardanelles was opened and Turkey was in no position to resist further. By the middle of October, all Palestine was free of Turkish forces, and with Allenby threatening an advance to the north and east, Turkey sued for peace. A note addressed to the United States on October 11 asked for peace terms and indicated willingness to yield whatever points were demanded, but before the Allies, busy with negotiations with Austria and Germany, could reply, Allenby's threat had become so great that Turkey surrendered to him early in November and granted the terms of armistice demanded by him, of a nature to make Turkey impotent, to await her final fate from the world war at the hands of the Allied representatives at the final peace negotiations.

It was announced by the Allied Governments that Palestine would be administered pending final settlement of its status by a government representing the Allies. In 1918 both Great Britain and France announced that Palestine would be an autonomous state, and that Jews would be protected in their organization of the long-cherished Zionist hope, a separate and independent Jewish state. In a semi-official letter to Rabbi Wise, of New York (see page 8575), President Wilson also endorsed the Zionist program with respect to Palestine.

Intervention in Russia.—All through the summer of 1918, there was doubt as to the policy which the Allies should pursue in Russia. On the one hand were those who demanded intervention on the ground that Russia was helpless under

The Cost of the War.—The following figures show the cost of the War to the spring of 1919, almost six months after the termination of hostilities. They represent most of the direct outlay for military purposes, but naturally the cost of the War, in items such as pensions, etc., will continue for many years after the signing of the peace.

ENTENTE ALLIES

British Empire	$ 38,000,000,000
France	26,000,000,000
United States	22,000,000,000
Russia	18,000,000,000
Italy	13,000,000,000
Other Entente Allies	6,000,000,000
Total	**$123,000,000,000**

CENTRAL POWERS

Germany	$ 39,000,000,000
Austria-Hungary	21,000,000,000
Turkey and Bulgaria	3,000,000,000
Total	**$ 63,000,000,000**
Grand Total	**$186,000,000,000**

War Debts.—The following table shows the pre-war and post-war debts of the belligerent nations:

	Pre-War	Post-War
Germany	$ 1,200,000,000	$ 39,000,000,000
U. Kingdom	3,500,000,000	34,000,000,000
France	6,600,000,000	27,000,000,000
United States	1,300,000,000	24,000,000,000
Aust.-Hungary	4,000,000,000	23,000,000,000
Italy	2,900,000,000	11,000,000,000
Russia	5,100,000,000	25,000,000,000
Total	**$24,600,000,000**	**$183,000,000,000**

German domination; that Germany was unhindered in obtaining war and food supplies from that hapless land; that the Bolshevist regime, under Lenin and Trotsky, if not actually under the influence of Germany, was at least conducting the affairs of Russia in such manner as to assist Germany at the expense of the Allies; and that Russia's precipitate withdrawal from the war had released a large number of German troops from the eastern front and had thus made possible the great German successes of the spring and summer of 1918.

On the other hand were those who claimed that ethically the Allies had no right to intervene in a country which desired to remain neutral; that, if left alone, Russia would soon tire of German domination and return to the ranks of the Allies; that the Bolshevist regime was falling and that Allied intervention would re-strengthen it by consolidating all Russians back of it in repelling Allied intervention.

On August 3, 1918, it was finally announced that the Allies had decided upon military intervention in Russia. Actually, intervention had already occurred several weeks previously. The immediate cause assigned was the extrication of some 50,000 Czecho-Slovaks who had been Austrian prisoners of war in Germany, but who were now anxious to join the Allied ranks in France and whose progress was being impeded both by former German prisoners in Russia and by Bolshevist troops. There was also involved the question of preventing military stores and supplies at Vladivostok and other places from falling into German hands.

Intervention came from two directions, combined forces of Japanese and Americans,

each about ten thousand strong, under the general direction of a Japanese leader, from Vladivostok and other Pacific ports westward; and a joint Allied force from Archangel and other points on the Murman coast southward. Soon afterward, the United States Committee on Public Information published a series of documents tending to prove that Lenin and Trotsky and other Bolshevist leaders were in German pay and both de jure and de facto German agents. The authenticity of these documents was strongly questioned, both in Europe and the United States, and from sources most strongly supporting the Allied governments in their prosecution of the war, but the Committee on Public Information took steps to prove them in the main authentic.

It can hardly be said that from a positive point of view Allied intervention in Russia was a complete success, although from a negative point of view it may have prevented much further German exploitation of Russian resources and of the Russian people. To a man, the Russian people resisted the Allied troops, and although the Allied forces both from the north and the east were able to advance, their advance was only at the expense of many pitched battles against the Bolshevist troops. The Czecho-Slovaks were unable to proceed much farther than southeastern Siberia and there is no evidence that they participated in the battles on the western or Bulgarian fronts which caused Germany's final downfall.

Within Russia itself, the Allied intervention gave the leaders the excuse they needed for more stringent methods to enforce their rule, and by November, Russia was under the iron heel of a dictatorship of the proletariat. Stern measures were adopted for the suppression of all anti-Bolshevist agitation; the rights of private property were even further narrowed; civil liberties almost disappeared; and a Constituent Assembly still was unconvened. It is impossible to characterize these measures objectively. Those sympathetic towards the Bolsheviki described them as regular proceedings of martial law, necessary to preserve at least a slight degree of law and order and to prevent Russia from lapsing into even more complete anarchy and famine. Those hostile to the Bolsheviki described them as altogether autocratic, brutal, and fanatical—calculated to thwart the real desires and longings of the majority and to keep in the saddle a reckless and selfish band of adventurers bent on verifying a dogma rather than on establishing true peace and happiness. Whatever one's personal reaction towards Russia, however, there could be no denial of the facts that the Soviet form of government represented a most ingenious and workable system of representation according to industries; that Lenin was revealing remarkable powers of administration and organization; and that the sources from which information was spread about Russia were on the whole anti-Bolshevist.

In October, 1918, President Wilson felt called upon to address a public memorandum to the nations of the world, calling attention to the chaos and violence which reigned in Russia and to the wide-spread prevalence of robbery, violence, imprisonment and even murder; and asking concerted action wherever possible to end the conditions which were so appalling to him.

Within the Allied countries, intervention in Russia had been opposed by the Labor and Socialist elements in France, Italy and Great Britain, and helped to widen the breach between those elements and their governments. It was announced that simultaneously with the military intervention great economic and industrial aid would be furnished Russia by a visiting commission clothed with plenary powers, but the results of the military intervention were such that no such economic aid was rendered.

Austria's Internal Troubles and Defeat in Italy.—During the spring and summer of 1918 evidences of racial discontent within the Austrian Empire and opposition to the government, aggravated by the desperate food situation, grew more and more pronounced. A Conference of Oppressed Austrian nationalities met at Rome on April 10 and declared the necessity of the disintegration of the Empire and the establishment of a unified, independent Jugo-Slav nation. On May 5 Emperor Charles dissolved the Reichsrat, in which the Germans were in the minority. Demonstrations against Germany became more and more frequent. Risings in Bohemia led to the establishment of martial law at Prague and the suppression of Czech newspapers. The disintegrating forces were fostered by organized Italian propaganda in the Austrian army and by a statement issued by the Allied War Council at Versailles in favor of an independent Polish state and freedom for the Czecho-Slovaks and Jugo-Slavs. Numerous mutinies occurred among the Slavic troops and Bohemian troops began to join the Italian army.

On July 16, Baron Burian, Austro-Hungarian Foreign Minister, addressed the Austrian and Hungarian Premiers on the eve of the meeting of the new Reichsrat in answer to President Wilson's Mount Vernon address, protesting against the Allied attitude toward so-called "peace offensives" and attempted interference with the internal affairs of Austria-Hungary. Shortly after, the Austrian cabinet, headed by Von Seidler, resigned and his successor, Baron Hussarek, declared that Austria was ready to conclude an honorable peace but stood in firm union with Germany.

On September 15, however, very shortly after the recognition of the Czecho-Slovaks as a de facto independent nation by Great Britain and the United States, the Austrian government addressed a note to belligerent and neutral powers suggesting a meeting for a preliminary and non-binding discussion of war aims. The President of the United States summarily rejected the proposal within an hour of its receipt, and it was later rejected by the Allied Governments. Germany announced her readiness to participate in the exchange of ideas suggested.

On October 5 Austria-Hungary appealed directly to President Wilson to conclude an armistice immediately and to start negotiations for peace on the basis of the fourteen principles announced by him. President Wilson replied on October 19 stating that the recognition of the Czecho-Slovak nation had altered the attitude of the United States upon the tenth of the fourteen principles, regarding the autonomous development of the peoples of Austro-Hungary. Meanwhile, on October 17, a proclamation had been read at a meeting of the Hungarian parliament declaring Hungary to be an independent state. The following day Emperor Charles announced steps for the organization of Austria-Hungary on a federalized basis and Baron Burian resigned. The Provisional Government of the new Czecho-Slovak nation proclaimed its independence of Austria-Hungary, and the Czechs seized Prague where a general strike had broken out.

On October 25, General Diaz led his Italian army in a powerful frontal attack against the Austrian positions, and within three days there was little left which could be called an Austrian army. On the 29th, the Austro-Hungarian government declared its willingness to adhere to all the conditions laid down by the American government and asked for an immediate armistice on all fronts without waiting for the outcome of other negotiations. By this time, the defeat of the Austrians in Italy had become a complete débacle, and Austria was menaced too vitally by the Italian army to be able to await the result of further peace negotiations. Accordingly, she turned directly to General Diaz, and on November 4, 1918, an armistice was concluded on terms which amounted to unconditional surrender.

Final Peace Negotiations.—When the Austrian note asking for negotiations looking toward peace was handed to President Wilson on September 16, 1918, there was little doubt of Germany's knowledge and approval of the move. Accordingly, there was no surprise when Germany herself took up the burden of the peace move, after the President had peremptorily told Austria that the United States had previously stated her peace conditions and that therefore he must refuse to re-state them or to enter into conversations on the subject.

The direct peace overture came from Germany on October 6, signed by Prince Max, who had supplanted von Hertling as the power of the military oligarchy of Germany waned at home under the pressure of the retreat of the German armies under Foch's blows in the field. The course of the negotiations and the final terms of the armistice may be seen by consulting pages 8603 to 8617.

President Wilson, before replying to the German overture, asked on October 8 three questions of the German government, concerned with—(1) the acceptance by Germany of his terms of peace laid down on January 8th (the 14 points) and on other occasions; (2) the willingness of the Central Powers to abandon all invaded territory as a requisite to an armistice; (3) the extent to which the German government was still uncontrolled by the German people and the Reichstag.

On October 12, the German government returned answers to these queries indicating their willingness to accept the President's terms of peace and to relinquish invaded territory and asserting that recent changes in the German political structure had given the German people control over their Government.

On October 14, President Wilson replied, calling the German government's attention to the fact that an armistice would have to be left to the military leaders of the Allies and would be of a nature calculated to maintain the contemporaneous Allied military supremacy and to render Germany impotent in the field; that no peace could be considered by the Allied governments while Germany persisted in her inhuman practises on sea and on land; and that one feature of the only peace to which the Allies would consent would be the final overthrow of the autocratic and unchecked military group in control of the German people.

By this time, the German forces in France were no longer able to maintain even a pretense of strong resistance to the oncoming Allied troops, and Germany was compelled to assent to the conditions, or rather the observations, of the note of President Wilson of October 14. In a reply of October 18, Germany indicated her willingness to grant even the last points insisted upon by the President, accompanying her acceptance with a memorandum, not made public, indicating the recent changes toward complete democratization which had taken place in Germany since September.

Accordingly, on October 23, the President replied, saying that he would lay the German request before the Allies, but still insisting that the terms of the armistice would necessarily be severe, because of the untrustworthy nature of the German government. The Interallied War Council was immediately convened at Versailles, Colonel House being the chief of the American delegates, and arranged terms of an armistice. On November 5, 1918, President Wilson informed the German government that the Allies had decided upon the terms on which an armistice would be granted Germany, and that Germany could obtain them by application to Marshal Foch. At midnight on November 10, 1918, the armistice was signed, and actual hostilities ceased six hours later (eleven A. M., November 11, French time). As will be seen by consulting the terms of the armistice in President Wilson's address to Congress on November 11, 1918, they are of such a nature as to constitute complete surrender, and to mark the end of the war.

The most stupendous of all wars lasted from August 1, 1914, to November 11, 1918, killed more than 8,000,000 men, permanently wounded and disabled almost as many more, cost well-nigh $175,000,000,000, and involved 28 nations. Fundamentally, it ended for all time the hope of the German militarists to dominate the world, unseated the Czar and demolished the last vestige of royalty in Russia, broke up the Austro-Hungarian government into its racial groups, ended the isolation of America and brought her as an active member into the family of the world's nations, and at the very end not only overthrew the Hohenzollern and all other royal dynasties within the German empire and restored the German people to independence, but also dissipated for all time that creed of might and force which the world to its cost had come to know as German Kultur. More important than any other achievement, it brought the great nations of the world into agreement, and gave hope that the international world order of the future would be one permeated no longer by lack of organization and competitive negotiations supported by force, but one of organization of the nations of the world into a league whose foundations lie in justice and goodwill and friendship.

Battle-line at Close of Hostilities.— When the guns of battle ceased their roar from both the Allied and the German lines in northern France and Belgium at exactly one minute before o'clock (six o'clock, French time), the line of battle was approximately as follows:

From Belgium at the boundary with Holland near Selzaete (all the Belgian seacoast had been cleared of Germans) south through Ghent, southeast through Grammont, along the west bank of the Dandre River to Ath; 4 miles east of Mons, crossing the Sammbre at the boundary with France, several miles southwest of Thuin. Then for some distance almost exactly along the French-Belgian frontier to Rocroi, thence on to French soil proceeding just north of Messieres and Sedan, along the Meuse until the river begins to turn directly south; then away from the Meuse some ten miles north and east of Verdun, through Fresnes, being retired close to the French-German frontier

near Conflans and Mars la Tour, some twelve miles north and east of Nancy, then again well onto French territory straight across to the frontier again in the Vosges mountains directly east of Saint Die, where it passed into Lorraine, extending almost due southwest of Mulhausen until it ended near the point where Germany, Switzerland and France touch.

Position of American Forces at End of Hostilities.—On November 11, 1918, scattered forces of American troops were scattered along the entire battle-front from the North Sea to Switzerland; but the main military strength of the United States, as represented by its First and Second American Armies, lay as follows:

First American Army.—Running south to north, from north of the Chateau D'Hannonville (about ten miles east by southeast of Verdun) slightly northwest, passing east of Blanzee and Grimaucort, then steadily northwest, passing east of Bezonvaux, north of Chaumont, north of Remoiville, striking the Meuse east and north of Stenay, then north and east of the Meuse, passing north and east of Sedan, ending the sector north of Nouzon, along the Meuse. This sector was only about seven miles from the Belgian frontier at its northernmost point, and fifteen miles at its southern end from the German frontier along Lorraine, although about thirty miles from the German and Luxembourg frontier along the middle of the sector.

Second American Army.—Running south to north, from Nomeny (due east of St. Mihiel and Pont á Mousson, and just west of the German frontier in Lorraine), west by north through Eply, to the Moselle River less than a mile south of Pagny, then west slightly south of Preny; then west through Remberecourt to the north edge of Lake Lauchausee, through St. Hilaire, Marcheville and Riaville to a point slightly south of Ville-en-Woevre. The American front covered 52 miles.

American Forces in Battle.—The number of American soldiers to reach France was 2,084,000. Of these, some 1,390,000 saw active service in the front battle-lines. The number of divisions dispatched overseas was 42, and in addition some 200,000 troops were sent in auxiliary services. Of the 42 divisions sent to France, only 29 took active part in hostilities as such, the remainder being utilized as replacement troops or arriving in France just before the termination of hostilities. Of these 29 divisions, whose record comprises the greater part of the battle record of the United States, 7 were of the Regular Army, 11 were of the National Guard and 11 were of the National Army.

During the 200 days of battle in which American troops were engaged, they performed 13 major operations, of which 11 were performed in conjunction with French, British and Italian troops and 2 were distinctively American undertakings.

The period of greatest activity of the American Army was in the second week of October, when all the 29 divisions were in line, holding 101 miles, or 23 per cent., of the western battle-front. A resumé of the American record is as follows:

Total Battle Advances, miles	485
Prisoners Captured	63,000
Artillery Captured, Pieces	1,378
Trench Mortars Captured	708
Machine Guns Captured	9,650

The thirteen major operations in which American troops were engaged were as follows, together with the number of American troops involved:

West Front—Campaign of 1917:
Cambrai, Nov. 20 to Dec. 4..... 2,200
West Front—Campaign of 1918:
German offensive, Mar. 21 to July 18—
Somme, Mar. 21 to Apr. 6..... 2,200
Lys, Apr. 9 to 27............ 500
Aisne, May 27 to June 5....... 27,500
Noyon-Montdidier, June 9 to 15 27,000
Champagne-Marne, July 15 to 18 85,000
Allied offensives, July 18 to Nov. 11—
Aisne-Marne, July 18 to Aug. 6. 270,000
Somme, Aug. 8 to Nov. 11.... 54,000
Oise-Aisne, Aug. 18 to Nov. 11.. 85,000
Ypres-Lys, Aug. 19 to Nov. 11.. 108,000
St. Mihiel, Sept. 12 to 16...... 550,000
Meuse-Argonne, Sept. 20 to
Nov. 11....................1,200,000
Italian Front—Campaign of 1918:
Vittorio-Veneto, Oct. 24 to Nov. 4 1,200

The Strength of the American Army.—The following table shows the strength of the army of the United States in Europe and as a whole during the participation of the United States in the Great War.

1917—	In Europe	As a Whole
April		200,000
May		290,000
June		390,000
July	20,000	500,000
August	35,000	551,000
September	45,000	691,000
October	65,000	948,000
November	102,000	1,100,000
December	139,000	1,189,000
1918—		
January	176,000	1,315,000
February	225,000	1,425,000
March	153,000	1,639,000
April	320,000	1,796,000
May	424,000	1,953,000
June	722,000	2,112,000
July	996,000	2,380,000
August	1,293,000	2,658,000
September	1,576,000	3,001,000
October	1,843,000	3,433,000
November	1,971,000	3,634,000

Casualties.—Battle casualties in the American Expeditionary Forces were as follows:

Dead	48,909
Killed in Action...... 34,180	
Died of Wounds...... 14,729	
Wounded	230,074
Severely 80,130	
Slightly 110,544	
Degree Undetermined. 39,400	
Missing in Action............	913
Prisoners	434
Total	286,339

The comparative mortality in battle and from disease in recent wars of the United States has been as follows:

War	Battle Rate	Disease Rate
Mexican, 1846-48	12%	88%
Civil (Union forces), 1861-5	34%	66%
Spanish, 1898	16%	84%
European (Sept., 1917-June, 1918)	50%	50%

Fourth Liberty Loan.—The campaign for the Fourth Liberty Loan opened on September 28, 1918, and closed on October 19, 1918. The amount was set at $6,000,000,-000; the rate of interest was 4¼%; and the bonds will mature on October 15, 1938, although they may be redeemed at the pleasure of the United States at par and accrued interest any time after October 15, 1933.

In spite of undeniable evidence that the Central Powers were in the last stages of

their resistance to the Allies and that the end of the war would probably be in sight before the end of the year, and despite a violent epidemic of influenza which swept the country from one end to another, disarranging all activities of the American people and bringing sorrow and desolation to tens of thousands of American households, the loan was an unqualified success. When the books had closed, it was found that the loan had been oversubscribed more than 14%, the total subscriptions being above $6,850,000,000, making this the largest popular loan ever floated in the history of the world. The number of subscribers was above 21,000,-000, as compared with 4,500,000; 9,500,000; and 18,300,000 in the First, Second, and Third Liberty Loans respectively.

The quotas and the subscriptions of the several Federal Reserve Districts were as follows:

District	Quota	Subscription	P. C.
Boston .....$	500,000,000	$ 632,221,850	126.44
Richmond ..	280,000,000	352,688,200	125.95
Philadelphia	500,000,000	598,763,650	119.75
Cleveland ..	600,000,000	702,059,800	117
Dallas	126,000,000	145,944,450	115.82
Minneapolis.	210,000,000	241,028,300	115.06
SanFrancisco	402,000,000	459,000,000	114.17
St. Louis...	260,000,000	296,388,550	113.99
New York...	1,800,000,000	2,044,778,000	113.59
Atlanta ...	192,000,000	217,885,200	113.48
Kansas City	260,000,000	294,646,450	113.32
Chicago	870,000,000	969,209,000	111.40
U.S.Treas...	....	33,329,850	....
Total .....$	6,000,000,000	$6,987,943,300	116.45

A fifth Liberty Loan, probably of short maturity, was announced for the spring of 1919.

The amount of the war obligations of the United States, at the time of the signing of the armistice on November 11, 1918, was as follows:

	Amount	Redeemable
First Liberty Loan.....$	2,000,000,000	1932-1947
Second Liberty Loan...	3,808,000,000	1927-1942
Third Liberty Loan....	4,176,000,000	1928
Fourth Liberty Loan...	6,988,000,000	1933-1938
War Savings Stamps...	879,000,000	1923
Total $17,851,000,000		

Expenditures.—For the 25 months from April 1, 1917 to May 1, 1919, the Treasury disbursements of the United States were $23,363,000. Charging $2,069,000,000 as normal peace expenses, the direct cost of the War to the United States for 25 months may be placed at $21,294,000,000. In addition, there was loaned to our Allies the sum of $8,850,000,000. Of the total war expenditure, there was expended on the Army $14,244,061,000. The *daily cost of the War* to the United States at different periods was as follows:

May 15, 1917 ....$	2,000,000
February 1, 1918	22,500,000
January 1, 1919	44,700,000

The expenditures in the Army from April 1, 1917 to May 1, 1919 were divided as follows:

Quartermaster Corps* ..$6,242,745,000	
Ordnance Department.	4,087,347,000
Pay of the Army	1,831,273,000
Air Service	859,291,000
Engineer Corps	638,974,000
Medical Department	314,544,000
Signal Corps	128,920,000
Chemical Warfare Service	83,299,000
Provost Marshal General	*24,301,000
Secretary of War and Miscellaneous	†33,367,000

* Exclusive of pay of the Army.
† December 31, 1918.

The total cost of the War to the United tates averaged well above $1,000,000 *an* our for more than two years.

United States Navy Activities.—Owing to 1e fact that the German naval campaign fter the United States entered the War as confined to its submarine operations, 1e United States navy played a purely de- nsive and protective part in the conflict. ithout its protection, however, combined 1th the protection of the navies of the llies, not only could few American troops 1ve been dispatched to Europe, but also 1ere would have been a lack of the supplies 1herewith to support them there. The nited States Navy assisted materially in 1e transportation of more than 2,000,000 nited States troops to Europe without the 1ss of a single American troopship sailing 1st and with the loss of only a few hun- ed soldiers altogether on the high seas. At the close of the War, the United cates naval forces in European waters 1mprised 338 vessels with a personnel of 1me 75,000—representing a force larger 1an the entire navy before the entrance the United States into the War.

Four naval vessels were lost in the War 1 a result of submarine attacks—the des- oyer *Jacob Jones;* the converted yacht *lcedo;* the Coast Guard cutter *Tampa;* and 1e cruiser *San Diego* (sunk by mine). The 1llier *Cyclops* was also lost in a fashion 1hich made its disappearance a complete 1ystery.

One definite achievement of the United cates Navy was the laying of a mine 1rrage against submarines in the North 1a. For this purpose 100,000 mines 1ere manufactured and more than 85,000 1ipped abroad.

On July 1, 1918, the enlisted and com- 1ssioned personnel of the naval aviation rces of the United States included 823 1ained naval aviators, 2,052 student offi- rs, 400 ground officers, 7,300 trained me- 1anics, and 5,400 mechanics in training. 1e total naval aircraft personnel was in 1e neighborhood of 30,000.

When war was declared between the 1ited States and Germany the navy com- ised 66,000 men. At the signing of the 1mistice, this number had increased to 1°7,000. When the war was declared, the 1vy had 197 ships in commission; at the 1 gning of the armistice, this number had creased to more than 2,000. During the 1me period the Naval Reserve increased om 85,000 to 290,000.

The Peace Conference.—As has been seen, 1rmany surrendered, and her surrender 1s accepted by the Allies, largely upon 1e basis of the principles and programs 1unciated by President Wilson in the 1urse of the United States' participation the War. President Wilson therefore 1t called upon to go in person to the de- 1erations of the peace conferences in 1ris which sealed the greatest of all wars. 1e other members of the American dele- tion were Secretary of State Robert 1nsing, Mr. Edward M. House, General 1sker H. Bliss and Mr. Henry White. The 1ench delegation was headed by Premier 1emenceau, the British by Premier Lloyd- 1orge, the Italian by Premier Orlando and 1e Japanese by Baron Makino. But the rms of the peace were arranged almost 1tirely by the three premiers and the 1erican President, although Japan was 1o one of the great Powers, thus making 1e in all, in whose hands lay all the 1cisions of the Conference.

A full summary of the peace treaty with 1rmany will be found on pages 87:37 to

8756. The kernel of the treaty was the Covenant of the League of Nations, al- though it was much circumscribed in power from the outlines of such a league as those outlines had been drawn by Presi- dent Wilson before the Conference. It was evident that the President had been de- feated in most of the deliberations by a combination of the French, Japanese and Italian votes, although he was usually sup- ported by the British point of view. The dominating figure of the Conference was Clemenceau, and in order to gain a league of nations, the American and British delega- tions were forced to submit to a number of settlements which were admitted to be unjust, in the hope that they would later be altered by the action of the League of Nations.

By the terms of the treaty, Germany lost Alsace-Lorraine, her colonies, much terri- tory on her eastern frontier inhabited by Poles, two small pieces of land on her western frontier inhabited chiefly by Flem- ish, and control over the Sarre basin for a period of fifteen years at least. Her army was reduced to 100,000, she was forbidden to resort to conscription, and a wide sweep of territory east of the Rhine had to re- main unfortified and without the presence of troops and garrisons. She was com- pelled to pay an indemnity estimated in the neighborhood of $25,000,000,000, and for practical purposes her trade and her com- merce were placed in the hands of the Allies. Her fleet was practically dismantled and, temporarily, at least, she was excluded from the League of Nations.

As a result of the war, the old empire of Austria-Hungary disappeared. The Czechs and Slovaks formed the new nation of Czecho-Slovakia, and the South Slavs formed the new nation of Jugo-Slavia, with the old Servia and Montenegro as a basis. The portions of the old Austro-Hungarian empire inhabited chiefly by Roumania were given to the latter country, and the por- tions inhabited chiefly by the Ukrainians (Ruthenians) were given to the new Ukrai- nia. Italy was given not only Italia Irre- denta, but also portions of the Austrian Tyrol and Dalmatia in which the Austrian and the Slav nationalities, respectively, were in the ascendancy. Austria was for- bidden to join Germany, although the rul- ing race in Austria was German. The new nations of Austria and Hungary were penalized, by the terms of the treaties with them, in much the same fashion as Germany had been by the German treaty.

Another nation arising from the ashes of the war was Poland, re-assuming the national existence which had been termi- nated by partition at the end of eighteenth century.

Although the treaties with Turkey and Bulgaria were far from completion by the beginning of the winter of 1919-1920, it was evident that they, too, woud be pena- lized sharply. Obviously, Bulgaria would have to surrender territory to Roumania and Greece and it was considered axiomatic that Turkey would be driven altogether from Europe, with the possible exception of the territory immediately surrounding Con- stantinople, which, with the Dardanelles, the Sea of Marmora and the Bosphorus, would possibly be internationalized.

Most of the colonies taken from Germany were to be administered by the great Powers as mandatories for the League of Nations. Japan was given temporary occupation of the German rights upon the Shantung pen- insula of China. However, certain portions of the old German colonial possessions were acquired outright by Great Britain, who, along with France, acquired also valuable concessions in Syria, Mesopotamia, Persia, etc.

The Peace Conference opened in Paris on January 18, 1919 and the treaty with Germany was signed at Versailles, France, on the following June 28.

European War (For activities in United States during and for index in greater detail, consult the Index under Wilson, Woodrow)—

Aircraft, attack on United States vessel by, 8062.

Alsace-Lorraine, wrong of, must be righted by, 8424.

America—
  Aims of, in, 8232, 8250, 8270, 8277, 8450.
  Citizens of, stranded abroad, relief for, 7962.
  Flag of, misused in, 8055.
  Foreign policy of, affected by, 8282, 8288.
  Isolation of, ended by, 8222, 8288.
  Trade of, affected by, 8015.
  Troops of, record of, praised, 8638, 8653, 8694, 8720, 8728.
  Losses of, at sea, 8637.
  United by, 8382, 8399, 8501.
  Veterans of, civil service concessions to, 8551, 8700, 8701.
  Re-employment for, 8642, 8715.

Ancona, protest on sinking of, 8117, 8120.

Armed neutrality, policy of, discussed, 8209, 8217, 8222, 8227, 8296.

Armistice—
  Congratulatory messages between United States and allies on, 8622-8626.
  Negotiations, 8603-8613.
  With Germany, terms of, 8613-8617.

Asia, German domination in, must be ended by, 8401.

Austria-Hungary—
  Anxious for peace, 8388.
  German domination over, discussed, 8278, 8388, 8401, 8403.
  Notes of, on—
    American protest on sinking of *Ancona*, 8118.
    Mediation, 8189.
    Pope's offer of mediation, 8345.
    Serbian murder of Archduke of Austria, mere step in Pan-Germanism, 8278.
  Notes to, on sinking of *Ancona*, 8117, 8120.
  Peoples of, must be granted autonomy, 8401, 8421. (See also Jugo-Slavs and Czecho-Slovaks.)
  Prime minister of, reply of, to President Wilson's Address of January 8, 1918, discussed, 8448.
  Statement of, on German peace disposal, 8189.

War with, declaration of—
  Asked, 8404.
  Made, 8406.

Balkan States—
  German domination over, must end, 8401, 8483.
  Internal autonomy to be granted to, 8425.

Belgium—
  Freedom and restoration of, essential, 8401, 8424, 8451.
  Reply of, to United States peace proposal, 8196.
  Sympathy of America for, 8287.

Berlin-to-Bagdad Railroad, purpose of, discussed, 8388.

Blockade of European waters, protest to British and French governments against, 8059.

Brest-Litovsk peace parleys discussed, 8421, 8595.

Bucharest, treaty of (1918), discussed, 8595.

Central Powers. See Germany and Austria-Hungary.

Château-Thierry, American victory at, 8638, 8729.

Contraband, food-stuffs should not be classed as, 8057.

Co-operation of all forces necessary to win, 8250, 8255, 8256, 8260.

Cost of living as affected by, 8764.

Czecho-Slovak troops in Russia, need of assistance for, 8591.

Dardanelles must be internationalized at settlement of, 8425.

Declarations of London—
  Invalid during European War, 8284.
  Praised and explained, 8284.

Destruction wrought by, 8015.

Diplomacy, secret and, discussed, 8422, 8423.

Disarmament to the point of domestic safety must result from, 8424.

Economic barriers between nations must be removed by, 8424.

Entente Allies (See also Great Britain and France)—
  Notes of, on—
    American proposal for peace, 8194.
    American protest against interference with mails, 8163.
    Central Powers' peace proffer, 8193.
  Notes to. See Great Britain, Notes to.
  Secret treaties among, discussed, 8703.
  Unity among, 8422.
  War aims of, 8293.

First years of, effect on America, 8221.

Foch, Marshal, armistice terms presented to Germany by, 8612, 8613.

Foodstuffs—
Germany's position on importation of, 8058.
Interference with shipments of, 8057.
Force to the utmost to decide, 8484.
France (See also Entente Allies)—
Alsace-Lorraine, wrong of, must be righted, 8424.
Evacuation and restoration of, essential, 8401, 8424.
Protest to, against blockade of European waters, 8059.
Treaty with—
Discussed, 8735, 8762.
Text of, 8764.
Freedom of the Seas—
Discussed, 8202, 8283, 8424.
Reservation concerning, in armistice terms, 8612.
Violated by Germany, 8289, 8290.
Fry, sinking of, discussed, 8210.
Germany—
Achievements of, praised, 8387, 8401, 8425.
Arbitration treaty with, absence of, deplored, 8289.
Armistice with. See Armistice.
Autonomy of, not to be attacked, 8402, 8425.
Belgium must be restored by, 8401, 8424, 8451.
Challenge of, to force, accepted, 8484.
Chancellor of, reply of, to President Wilson's Address of January 8, 1918, discussed, 8448.
Conquests of, 8388.
Diplomatic relations with, severed, 8206.
Domination of, over other countries must cease, 8388, 8401, 8403.
Fleet of, surrender of, 8616, 8621.
Freedom of the seas violated by, 8289, 8290.
Government of—
Ambitious to rule world, 8389, 8290, 8296, 8297, 8298, 8405.
And people, distinction between, 8278.
Autocratic character of, 8230, 8606, 8609.
Crimes of, 8226, 8271, 8290, 8296, 8298, 8785.
Destroyed, 8618.
Instigator of the war, and why, 8389.
International intercourse may be denied, 7400, 8402.
International law violated by, 8289.
Kultur aims of, denounced, 8288.
Notes from, on—
American protests against submarine warfare, 8057, 8127.
Attempt to embroil Mexico into war with United States, 8216.

Entente Allies' charges, 8197.
Peace offer, 8187, 8188, 8193.
Peace Proposals by—
Pope, 8344.
President Wilson, 8197.
Peace without Victory Address, 8204.
Submarine warfare resumption, 8205.
Notes to, on—
Lusitania sinking, 8062.
Mail interference by Entente, 8056.
Submarine warfare, 8055.
Sussex sinking, 8125.
Overt act by—
Necessary to bring America into the war, 8209.
Temporarily avoided, 8210.
Pan-Germanism, denounced, 8278.
Peace proposals of, 8187.
Analysed, 8292, 8293.
Replies to, 8193.
Peace treaty with. See Peace Treaty.
People of—
And government, distinction between, 8232, 8278.
Faith of America in, 8291.
Not free, 8403.
Responsible for acts of Government, 8785.
Susceptible to spirit of freedom, 8388.
Poland and, boundary between, 8791.
Reichstag peace resolutions discussed, 8450.
Russia betrayed by, 8483, 8595.
Spy system of, denounced, 8231.
Strict accountability of, for destruction of American ships, 8056.
Submarine warfare of. See Notes to.
Subsidy system of, denounced, 8387.
Victory of, evil results which would flow from, 8280.
War Aims of, 8293, 8483, 8595.
War practises of, cessation of, demanded, 8606.
War with, recognition and announcement of, 8226, 8242.
Great Britain—
Controversy with, soon after outbreak of war, discussed, 8287.
Notes from, on—
American protest against blacklist, 8178.
Central Powers' peace proffer, 8193.
Notes to, on—
Blacklisting of American firms, 8143.
Neutral rights violation, 8059.
Use of neutral flags, 8056.
Premier of, address of, discussed, 8422.
Housatonic, sinking of, discussed, 8210.

"How the War Came to America,''
(See Red, White and Blue Book).
International law—
American support of, 8057.
Violated by Germany, 8290.
Italy—
Boundaries should be extended according to nationality, 8424, 8704.
Claims to Fiume discussed, 8703, 8789.
Jugo-Slavs, territory disputed by Italy and, 8703, 8789. (See also Austria-Hungary.)
League of Nations—
Covenant of, 8673-8683.
Discussed, 8669-8686, 8787.
Need of, discussed, 8191, 8200, 8288, 8402, 8425, 8596, 8652, 8657, 8663, 8665, 8722, 8733.
Lusitania, sinking discussed, 8062, 8290.
Lyman M. Law, sinking of, discussed, 8210.
Mails, interference with by Entente Allies, 8165.
Militia called into national service, 8306.
Mines, drifting, discussion on use of 8057, 8058.
Monroe Doctrine—
Assaulted by Germany, 8290.
World-wide application of, necessary 8203.
Montenegro, evacuation and restoration of, 8424.
Munitions, sale of, to belligerents while neutral, discussed, 8289.
Nationalities, self-determination of, principle of, to be applied after, 8202, 8424, 8450.
Neutral flags—
Protest against use of by belligerents, 8056.
Use of, mentioned, 8055.
Neutrality in—
Appeal to citizens to observe, 7978.
Followed, 8286.
Discussed, 7978, 8102.
Proclamations of, 7969, 7974, 7975, 7976, 7977, 8014, 8065, 8141, 8142.
Terminated, 8297.
Neutral rights, violation of. See Germany and Great Britain.
Objects of belligerents, as officially stated, the same, 8191.
Order in Council, protest against carrying out of, 8059.
Pact of London discussed, 8703.
Pan-Germanism, denounced, 8278, 8295.
Peace—
Covenants must be open, 8423.
Formula, "No annexations, no contributions, no punitive indemnities," discussed, 8400.

German terms of, imperialistic, 8421.
League for, conditions under which United States would join, 8200
Negotiations. See Armistice.
Note from President Wilson, and replies thereto, 8190.
Analyzed, 8293.
Overtures from—
Austria, 8189.
Germany, 8187.
Insincere, 8448.
The Pope, 8340.
Replies thereto, 8341, 8344, 8345.
United States, 8190.
Pacifists cannot obtain, 8389.
Perpetual, bases of, analyzed, 8200 et seq., 8451.
Proposals of Germany, 8193.
Analyzed, 8292.
Terms of—
Defined, 8399, 8400, 8406, 8421, 8423.
Should be stated, 8192.
Principles of, reaffirmed, 8402, 8406.
Without Victory—
Address of President Wilson, 8199.
Analyzed, 8295.
Response to, from Germany, 8204.
Analyzed, 8295.
Necessity of, 8192.
Peace Conference at Paris—
President Wilson in attendance on, 8646 et seq.
Work of, discussed, 8691 et seq., 8728.
Peace Treaty with Germany—
Discussed, 8727, 8785.
Signing of, announced, 8726.
Summary of, 8737-8756.
Poland—
Freedom essential to, 8202, 8403, 8425, 8451.
Germany and, boundary dispute between, discussed, 8791.
Pope of Rome—
Mediation offer from, 8340.
Replies to, 8341, 8344, 8345.
Prayer for peace, day of, proclaimed, 8007.
Prayer for victory in, day of, set apart, 8377, 8495.
Red Cross, American—
Children urged to enroll in, 8358.
Services of, discussed, 8501.
Support urged for, 8264, 8494, 8648.
Red Cross, International, listing of alien enemies for, 8274.
Red. White and Blue Book, text of, 8282.
Rumania, evacuation and restoration of, 8424.

Russia—
    America will support, 8423, 8501.
    Betrayal of, by Germany, denounced, 8483.
    Free development of, must not be hindered, 8424.
    German betrayal of, denounced, 8483, 8595.
    Intervention by Entente Allies and United States in, discussed, 8590.
    Message to, 8270, 8469.
    Peace proposals of, discussed, 8421.
    People of—
        Misled, 8403.
        Praised, 8422.
    Revolution in, praised and discussed, 8230, 8299.
    Terrorism in, denounced, 8589.
St. Mihiel, American victory at, 8638.
Secret treaties. See Pact of London.
Serbia—
    Access to the sea must be granted, 8425.
    Evacuation and restoration of, essential, 8403, 8424.
Status quo ante, the cause of the conflict and must be altered, 8271.
Submarine warfare. See Germany.
Trade conditions must be equal for nations after, 8424.
Turkey—
    Dardanelles must be internationalized, 8425.
    German domination over, must end, 8401.
    Internal autonomy of, not to be hindered, 8401, 8425.
    Nationalities under, to be free, 8425.
United States and. See America.
Woman suffrage movement and, 8601, 8639.
World court, establishment of, long desired by America, 8285.

Eutaw Springs (S. C.), Battle of.—Lieut.-Col. Stewart had succeeded Lord Rawdon in command of the southern division of the British army and established headquarters at Orangeburg, S. C. Gen. Greene, who had been resting the American army on the hills of the Santee River, had been reenforced by 700 North Carolina continentals. His army thus increased to more than 2,500 men, Greene determined to attack Stewart, whose force did not exceed 2,000. Stewart fell back about forty miles to Eutaw Springs, near the Santee River, in South Carolina. Here Sept. 8, 1781, a fierce but indecisive battle was fought. Stewart kept the field, but at night retired toward Charleston, and Greene took possession of the battle ground and sent detachments in pursuit of the British. The total American casualties as given by Gen. Greene were 408. The British loss was 693.

Excise Laws.—As early as 1790 a national excise law was passed. Alexander Hamilton, then Secretary of the Treasury, insisted that such a tax was necessary, but the law was not passed without a fierce debate. The tax imposed at first varied from 25 to 40 cents a gallon on imported spirits, from 9 to 25 cents on domestic distilled liquors, and from 11 to 30 cents when the material was molasses or other imported product. This tax was reduced in 1792. Opposition to it was strong throughout the country, culminating in the Whisky Insurrection in western Pennsylvania in 1794. Under Jefferson the excise tax was abolished. It was revived again in 1813, during the war with Great Britain. In 1817 it was again repealed and no excise tax was collected by the General Government until 1862, during the Civil War. In 1864 the excise rates were raised, the rates on liquor rising from 60 cents to $2 per gallon, while in 1865 the rates were still further increased. After that time the excise rates gradually declined, till in 1875 the liquor tax stood at 90 cents per gallon. Excise rates remained thus until 1894 when the tax on liquor was raised to $1.10. During the Spanish War, however, excise rates were again raised, those on fermented liquors being doubled. By an act of March, 1902, however, the last of the war taxes were removed and the rate of excise was left as it was before the war.

Excise Tax, power to levy rests in national government, 7391. (See Taxation.)

Executive.—That branch of a government to which the execution of laws is entrusted. The executive may be a king, an emperor, or a president, or a council or other body. From 1775 to 1789 the United States Government had no other executive than Congress, which, however, created a Board of War, Board of Treasury, etc. The Constitution invested the President with executive power, sharing only the powers of appointment and treaty making with the Senate.

Executive Departments were established by the First Congress under the Constitution. Governors appointed by the Crown exercised the executive functions of the Colonies, except in Rhode Island, Connecticut, and for a short time in Massachusetts, where governors were elected by the people. At the outbreak of the Revolution, when the royal governors had been deprived of their powers, and before the State constitutions had been adopted, executive power was vested in a committee of safety. In some Colonies an executive council, with a president or chairman, was chosen by the provincial congresses. Most of the state constitutions provided for governors.

In the United States the Executive is one of the three great branches of government, the other two being the legislative and the judicial. Historically the legislative branch is first, because it was placed first in order in both the work of the Convention and in the final draft of the Constitution. Practically the executive branch is clearly prior in consideration so far as foreign powers are concerned. Under some Administrations executive power has been greatest in influence; under others perhaps smallest of the three. The weight of the Executive has steadily increased since the inauguration of the Government, not only on account of the appointing power, which is shared with the Senate and which grows with the expansion of the Republic, but for other reasons. The President's functions are constantly exercised when Congress and the judiciary are taking recess. Besides, he is the one person who represents to the average citizen the concrete majesty of law—the embodiment of authority in a democratic representative government.

Executive Cabinet.—Official conduct of, complimented, 2203, 2714.

Executive Departments.—The executive branch of the United States Government comprises the following ten subordinate Departments, each of which is presided over and directed by a head who is known as the Secretary of the Department. The Secretaries of the various Departments constitute what is termed the "Cabinet" (q. v.). They are chosen by the President, but must be confirmed by the Senate. Each acts under the authority of the President. The annual salary is $12,000. (1) State, which administers foreign affairs; (2) Treasury, which has charge of the finances; (3) Justice, which is the legal counsel of the Government; (4) War, which administers military affairs; (5) Post-office, which has charge of the postal service; (6) Navy, which has charge of naval affairs; (7) Interior, which has charge of matters pertaining to home affairs, including public lands, Indians, patents, pensions, education, railroads, and census; (8) Agriculture, which collects and disseminates information on agricultural subjects; (9) Commerce, which cares for the commercial, manufacturing, census, corporations, fisheries and navigation interests of the country.; (10) Labor, which has charge of the immigration bureau and statistics of labor. The Department of Labor, which was created June 13, 1888, and absorbed into the Department of Commerce and Labor on its establishment, Feb. 14, 1903, was an independent Executive Department, although its head was known as a Commissioner, instead of Secretary, and was not a member of the Cabinet. The Department of Commerce and Labor was again divided in 1913.

Executive Departments (see also the several Departments):

Acts regarding advertising of, vetoed, 4388.

Advertising in newspapers by, inquired into, 2911.

Aliens employed in, report on number of, transmitted, 6102.

Applications to, should be in writing, 3456.

Appointment of laborers, 6707.

Appointments and promotions in, order regarding preference to be given veterans in, 3637, 6703.

Appointments in, having relation to civil service, 4990. (See also Executive Nominations.)

Buildings occupied by, referred to, 3897.

Canvassing for outside support for promotion forbidden, 6703.

Circulars asking for political contributions circulated in, 4784.

Closed for Thanksgiving, 3245.

Communications to be transmitted to head of proper Department, order regarding, 3859, 3981.

Employees in—
Official conduct of, complimented, 2714.

Order permitting—
To participate in decoration of graves of soldiers, 3862, 4118, 4137, 4184, 4237, 4282, 4352, 4402, 4443, 4508, 4552, 4603, 4712, 4753, 4818, 4899, 5078, 5350, 5463, 5540, 5609, 5832, 5949, 6046.

To participate in public exercises, 4879, 6590, 6595, 6611.

To witness inauguration of President Cleveland, 4881.

Ordered to organize into companies for defense of Washington, 3323.

Partisan interference in elections by. (See Elections.)

Referred to, 3585.

Rendering honors to rebel living or dead, inquired into, 3591.

Wages of, not to be affected by reduction in hours of labor, 3969, 4129.

Examination of operations of, invited, 6058.

Extension of power to make temporary appointments of heads of, recommended, 3348, 5568.

Personal interviews with heads of, order regarding, 3546.

Postage accounts of, referred to, 2360.

Power of judiciary over, discussed, 1720.

Record of efficiency of persons in, 5642.

Recommended, 5615.

Redistribution of bureaus among, recommended, 6989, 7105, 7229.

Superannuated employees, 7706.

Transfer of duties among, recommended, 2264, 4060.

Vacancy occasioned by death of head of, recommendations regarding filling, 3348, 5568.

Executive Mansion. (See White House.)

Executive Mansion:

Completion of, 595.

Furniture should be provided for, by Congress, 595.

Improvement of, 808.

Restoration of, 6729, 6739.

Executive Nominations (see also Removals from Office):

Act—
Prescribing oath of office to be taken by persons who participated in rebellion discussed, 4076.

Regulating tenure of certain civil offices vetoed. (See Tenure-of-Office Act.)

Appointing power discussed by President—
Buchanan, 3190.
Fillmore, 2616.

Jackson, 1261, 1272, 1351.
Johnson, 3690, 3767, 3820.
Tyler, 1903, 1958.
Appointments—
Applicants refused by President Tyler, 1958.
For limited period, 638.
Referred to, 3662.
Relation of members of Congress to, discussed, 4557.
Discussed, 3062.
Errors in, arrangements for corrections of, recommended, 802.
Interviews with President, 5831.
Persons appointed or permitted to continue in office without consent of Senate inquired into, 3663.
President Madison declines to confer with Senate regarding, 515.
Rejections of, President Jackson's message asserting that Senate is not required to give reasons for, 1261.
Renewal of, 2646.
Request of—
House for names of applicants for office refused by President Tyler, 1958.
Senate for correspondence regarding, right to make, denied by President Jackson, 1272.
Senate for reasons for making, refused by President Jackson, 1261, 1351.
Resolution of Senate regarding, and reply of President Hayes, 4433.
Rules regulating interviews with President regarding, discussed, 5831.
Withdrawal of, by President—
Harrison, W. H., not acted on by Senate, 1876.
Jackson, not acted on by Senate, 1002.
Executive Orders. (See the several subjects.)
Executive Salaries. (See Salaries, Executive.)
Executive Session.—The Constitution of the United States provides that the president "shall have power, by and with the advice and consent of the senate, to make treaties, provided two-thirds of the senators present concur; and he shall nominate and, by and with the advice and consent of the senate, shall appoint ambassadors, other public ministers, and consuls, judges of the Supreme Court, and all other officers of the United States whose appointments are not herein otherwise provided for, and which shall be established by law." A rule of the senate providing for the manner of advising and consenting to executive recommendations requires that "when acting upon confidential or executive business, unless the same shall be considered in open executive session, the senate chamber shall be cleared of all persons except the secretary, the chief clerk, the principal legislative clerk, the executive clerk, the

12

minute and journal clerk, the sergeant-at-arms, the assistant doorkeeper, and such other officers as the presiding officer shall think necessary, and all such officers shall be sworn to secrecy." The senate is then said to be in executive session. The house holds no executive sessions. It may go into secret session, however, whenever confidential communications are received from the president, or whenever the speaker or any member shall inform the 'house that he has a communication which ought to be kept secret for a time.

Exequatur.—A Latin word meaning "Let him execute." In diplomatic usage the word is used to signify a document authorizing an official to act in the capacity of agent or representative. Usually a written recognition of a person in the character of consul or commercial agent issued by the government to which he is accredited and authorizing him to exercise his powers. The government from which an exequatur is asked has the right to refuse it either on political or personal grounds. The government may also withdraw it. When deprived of his exequatur a consul may withdraw with his records or delegate his powers to another, according to instructions.

Exequaturs:
Refusal of Turkey to grant exequaturs to consuls of United States referred to, 6092, 6148.
Revoked—
Consul of—
Belgium, 3420.
Chile, 3625.
France, 260.
Frankfort, 3709.
Great Britain, 2924, 2925.
Hanover, 3709.
Hesse, 3709.
Nassau, 3709.
Oldenburg, 3710.
Spain, 2588.
Sweden and Norway, 3626.
Revocation annulled, 3630.
Vice-Consul of—
Portugal, 4038.
Sweden and Norway, 3627.
Revocation annulled, 3630.

Exhibits, Office of, Agriculture Department.—The Bureau of Forestry in the Department of Agriculture, in the prosecution of its educational work, makes exhibits consisting of models, specimens, maps, drawings, transparencies and bromide enlargements of its work at county and state fairs and national expositions. More than 1,700 lantern slides were loaned to 386 persons engaged in educational work. Traveling exhibits of photographs, maps, drawings and wood samples were loaned to 172 schools and libraries.

The Office of Public Roads and Rural Engineering in the prosecution of its educational work, delivers lectures and makes exhibits consisting of models and enlarged photographs illustrating the best methods of road, bridge and culvert construction, road drainage, maintenance, repair, roadside treatment, road building, equipment, machinery, etc., at expositions, congresses, conventions, and fairs. A "good roads" train, with motion picture equipment, makes tours of the country.

Other bureaus maintain similar equipment

and educational exhibits and transport the same from place to place upon request of a sufficient number of interested persons. Requests for this service and reports thereon for convenience are made through the Office of Exhibits.

Exhibitions (see also Adelaide; Antwerp; Arcachon; Atlanta; Barcelona; Bergen; Berlin; Boston; Brussels; Caracas; Chicago; Cincinnati; Hamburg; London; Louisville; Madrid; Melbourne; Munich; New Orleans; Oporto; Paris; Philadelphia; Sydney; Vienna):

Discretionary authority to send delegates to, recommendations regarding, 4714, 4763, 4827, 5546, 6325.

Expansion.—The term has been particularly applied to the territorial growth of the United States, as when Louisiana Territory and Alaska were purchased. The term was used especially in the campaign of 1900 when the Democrats assailed the Republican policy of expansion on the question of the acquirement of the Philippines and Porto Rico, and of control over Cuba.

Expansion, Territorial:

Annexation discussed. (See Alaska; California; Cuba; Florida; Gadsden Purchase; Hawaiian Islands; Louisiana Purchase; New Mexico; Philippine Islands; Puerto Rico; St. John Island; St. Thomas Island; Santo Domingo; Texas; Yucatan.)

Foreign policy discussed by President—

Adams, John, 228.

Adams, J. Q., 862, 868, 884, 895, 903, 922, 950.

Buchanan, 2966, 2998, 3037, 3041, 3066, 3089, 3092, 3173, 3177.

Cleveland, 4912, 5867, 5871, 5873, 5892, 5955, 5963, 6064, 6068, 6087, 6148.

Fillmore, 2614, 2656, 2701, 2715.

Grant, 3985, 4006, 4015, 4018, 4050, 4053, 4082, 4101, 4143, 4176, 4192, 4245, 4290, 4365.

Harrison, Benj., 5445, 5618, 5750, 5783.

Harrison, W. H., 1873.

Hayes, 4418, 4420.

Jackson, 1159, 1222, 1324, 1370, 1378, 1456, 1484, 1500.

Jefferson, 311, 346, 349.

Johnson, 3564, 3581, 3777, 3886, 3888.

Lincoln, 3248, 3255, 3327, 3444.

McKinley, 6248, 6281, 6295, 6307.

Madison, 452, 473.

Monroe, 573, 582, 624, 627, 639, 672, 685, 762, 787, 791, 817, 829.

Pierce, 2731, 2745, 2807, 2864, 2904.

Polk, 2229, 2236, 2248, 2276, 2322, 2337, 2361, 2386, 2431, 2437, 2444, 2480.

Taylor, 2548, 2555.

Tyler, 1890, 2049, 2064, 2160, 2169, 2171, 2176, 2190, 2193, 2206.

Van Buren, 1590, 1702, 1748, 1819.

Washington, 120, 213.

Expatriation.—The voluntary renunciation of the rights and liabilities of citizenship in one country to become the citizen or subject of another. The right of expatriation has been sanctioned by custom and usage in the United States. The government has even in a number of instances refused protection to native-born and naturalized citizens on the ground that they had expatriated themselves. An act of Congress of July 27, 1868, declared it the natural and inherent right of all people, and any denial or restriction thereof contrary to the fundamental principles of government. An act of Congress, approved March 2, 1907, defined the conditions under which an American citizen may expatriate himself. It provides that any American citizen shall be deemed to have expatriated himself when he has been naturalized in any foreign state in conformity with its laws, or when he has taken an oath of allegiance to any foreign state. When any naturalized citizen shall have resided for two years in the foreign state from which he came, or for five years in any other foreign state, it shall be presumed that he has ceased to be an American citizen, and the place of his general abode shall be deemed his place of residence during said years: Provided, however, that such presumption may be overcome on the presentation of satisfactory evidence to a diplomatic or consular officer of the United States, under such rules and regulations as the Department of State may prescribe: And provided also, that no American citizen shall be allowed to expatriate himself when this country is at war.

Any American woman who marries a foreigner shall take the nationality of her husband. At the termination of the marital relation she may resume her American citizenship, if abroad, by registering as an American citizen within one year with a consul of the United States, or by returning to reside in the United States, or, if residing in the United States at the termination of the martial relation, by continuing to reside therein. Any foreign woman who acquires American citizenship by marriage to an American shall be assumed to retain the same after the termination of the marital relation if she continues to reside in the United States, unless she makes formal renunciation thereof before a court having jurisdiction to naturalize aliens, or if she resides abroad she may retain her citizenship by registering as such before a United States consul within one year after the termination of such marital relation. A child born without the United States of alien parents shall be deemed a citizen of the United States by virtue of the naturalization of or resumption of American citizenship by the parent: Provided, that such naturalization or resumption takes place during the minority of such child: And provided further, that the citizenship of such minor child shall begin at the time such minor child begins to reside permanently in the United States. All children born outside the limits of the United States who are citizens thereof and who continue to reside outside the United States shall, in order to receive the protection of this government, be required upon reaching the age of eighteen years to record at an American consulate their intention to become residents and remain citizens of the United States, and shall be further required to take the oath of allegiance to the United States upon attaining their majority. Expatriation has been frequently pleaded before the Supreme Court, but the plea has always been overruled. Though the right be admitted, except in the case of persons subject to military service, holding public trusts, or charged with crime the difficulty remains to give evidence of the mode of expatriation. British subjects cease to be such upon being naturalized in other countries, and such persons, in order to be again considered British subjects, must be renaturalized on their return to Great Britain. In France and Germany the somewhat indefinite claim of domicile in a foreign land is accepted as evidence of expatriation.

Expatriation. (See Naturalization Laws.)

Expedition.—A journey by an organized body for the accomplishment of some definite end, as the expedition of a force of the United States army in pursuit of the Mexican bandit, Villa.

Expeditions Against Foreign Powers (see also Neutrality):
Discussed by President—
Arthur, 4640.
Buchanan, 2978, 2997, 3180.
Fillmore, 2643, 2649, 2697.
Jefferson, 394, 395, 400, 417.
Johnson, 3640, 3655, 3658.
Monroe, 582, 583, 590, 592, 601, 609, 769.
Pierce, 2741, 2779.
Polk, 2455.
Taylor, 2549, 2585.
Van Buren, 1616.
Washington, 146.
Proclamations against, by President—
Buchanan, 3027.
Cleveland, 6023, 6126.
Fillmore, 2647, 2648.
Grant, 4039, 4045.
Jefferson, 392.
Johnson, 3631.
Madison, 546.
Pierce, 2804, 2805, 2921.
Taylor, 2555.
Tyler, 1925.
Washington, 149.

Expeditions, Exploring. (See Exploring Expeditions.)

Expeditions, Unlawful. (See Expeditions Against Foreign Powers.)

Expenditures, Public.—In 1794 the annual expenditures of the Federal Government amounted to only $6,300,000. In 1814 they ran up, on account of the war with Great Britain, to $34,700,000. They fell in 1834 to $18,600,000. In 1854 they were $55,000,000. During the last year of the Civil War (1865) they amounted to $1,-295,000,000; but in 1878 they had declined to $237,000,000. For the following ten years the expenditures averaged $260,000,-000 per annum. For the fiscal year ending June 30, 1893, they were $459,400,000, made up largely of interest and pensions. In 1896 they were $434,678,654, and for the year ending June 30, 1899, they had increased to $605,072,180. Since the Spanish War the expenditure has naturally been re-

duced; for the year ending June 30, 1905, it was $567,411,611, or some $23,987,752 in excess of the revenue. In 1907 the expenditures were $578,360,592, and the revenues amounted to $665,306,134, which is $86,-945,543 more than the expenditures. The grand total of expenditures of the government for the years 1911-1912, appropriated by the Sixty-first Congress at its third session, was $1,025,489,661.54. The receipts for the fiscal year ending, from customs, amounted to $701,372,375. Expenditures for the year ended June 30, 1913, were $1,-010,812,449, including postal.

Expenditures, Public (see also Foreign Intercourse):
Act making appropriations for—
Approved and reasons therefor, 3128, 4327.
Vetoed, 4488.
Act making appropriations to supply deficiencies vetoed, 6115.
Congress warned about, 6238.
Contingent fund, account of, rendered, 80, 127, 325, 343, 354, 366, 382, 405, 421, 447, 482.
Discussed. (See Finances discussed.)
Economy in, recommended, 5890, 6177.
Estimates, etc., of, referred to, 281, 297, 4213, 4523.
Failure of Congress to provide for, discussed, and recommendations regarding, 3073, 3102, 4322, 4404, 4472.
Provisions for, recommended by President—
Buchanan, 3073.
Hayes, 4472.
Van Buren, 1541.

Experiment Stations, Office of.—These are public institutions for ascertaining facts useful to the agriculturist. Scientific conduct of experiments in the growth and improvement in plants and animals requires close attention, long time and the outlay of considerable money. Thus only the fortunate individual possessing these essentials can seriously devote himself to experiments which often result in discouraging failure and which, when successful, often inure to the benefit of few and at the expense of many. Consequently the state and Federal governments have established public stations where experiments may be methodically carried on and the successful results freely given to the public.

The first agricultural experiment station in America was begun at Wesleyan University, at Middletown, Conn., in 1875, though similar work had previously been done at some of the agricultural colleges. By 1887 there were seventeen stations in fourteen different states. That year Congress passed what is generally referred to as the Hatch Act, giving to each state and territory $15,000 a year from the national treasury to maintain an experiment station as a department of the agricultural college established under the land-grant act of 1862. It was presumed that the states would provide the land, buildings and equipment, and spend the money carrying on the experiments and reporting the results. There are now sixty-five of these stations.

The work of the stations is thus outlined in the act: "It shall be the object and duty of said experiment stations to conduct original researches or verify experiments on the physiology of plants and animals, the diseases to which they are severally subject, with the remedies for the same ; the chemical composition of useful plants at their different stages of growth ; the comparative advantages of rotative cropping as pursued under a varying series of crops ; the capacity of new plants or trees for acclimation ; the analysis of soils and water ; the chemical composition of manures. natural and artificial, with experiments designed to test their comparative effects on crops of different kinds ; the adaptation and value of grasses and forage plants ; the composition and digestibility of the different kinds of food for domestic animals ; the scientific and economic questions involved in the production of butter and cheese ; and such other researches or experiments bearing directly on the agricultural industry of the United States as may in each case be deemed advisable, having due regard to the varying conditions and needs of the respective states and territories."

Under this act agricultural experiment stations are in operation in all the states and Alaska, Hawaii. Porto Rico and Guam. A number of substations are also maintained. The states have in recent years greatly increased their appropriations to these stations to supplement the Federal funds. The total annual appropriation to the several stations is now between $4,000,-000 and $5,000,000.

Experiment Stations, discussed, 5384, 5888, 5980, 6347. (See also Agriculture, Department of.)

Experiment Stations, Agricultural, report of, 6733, 6861.

Exploration.—An investigation of unknown parts, as the Lewis and Clark exploration. (See Lewis and Clark Expedition.)

Explorer.—A person venturing into sections previously unknown.

Exploring Expeditions (see also Arctic Expeditions; *Jeannette* Polar Expedition: Lady Franklin Bay Expedition; Pacific Ocean Exploring Expedition; South Sea Exploring Expedition; Wilkes Exploring Expedition).

Across continent recommended, 341, 886.

Naval expeditions referred to, 4449.

Explosives, order to prevent shipment of, 4815.

Export Duties, levied by foreign powers referred to, 4744.

Exports.—The value of American export trade has generally kept pace with the development of domestic business. In 1892 it passed the billion dollar mark, and until the outbreak of the European War in 1914. it promised to pass two and a half billion in that year. The figures for the period 1900-1913 follow in an adjoining table :

Exports for the 12 months ending with September, 1916, were, in round terms, $5,000,000,000. The precise figures announced by the Bureau of Foreign and Domestic Commerce of the Department of Commerce were $4,971,945,883. as against $3,177,764,184 in the preceding 12 months and an annual average of $2,453,000,000 in the five years preceding 1915-16. Our exports of domestic products in the month of

September were larger than those for the entire fiscal year 1875, the closing year of our first centenary.

For the year ending with September, 1916, imports totaled $2,307,766,567, compared with $1,681,298,913 for 1915 and an annual average of $1,725,000,000 for 1911-1915.

Year Ending June 30	Exports		Total Exports
	Domestic	Foreign	
1901...	$1,460,462,806	$27,302,185	$1,487,764,991
1902...	1,355,481,861	26,237,540	1,381,719,401
1903...	1,392,231,302	27,910,377	1,420,141,679
1904...	1,435,179,017	25,648,254	1,460,827,271
1905...	1,491,744,641	26,817,025	1,518,561,666
1906...	1,717,953,382	25,911,118	1,743,864,500
1907...	1,853,718,034	27,133,044	1,880,851,078
1908...	1,834,786,357	25,986,989	1,860,773,346
1909...	1,638,355,593	24,655,511	1,663,011,104
1910...	1,710,083,998	34,900,722	1,744,984,720
1911...	2,013,549,025	35,771,174	2,049,320,199
1912...	2,170,319,828	34,002,581	2,204,322,409
1913...	2,428,506,358	37,377,791	2,465,884,149
1914...	2,329,684,025	34,895,123	2,364,579,148
1915...	2,716,178,465	52,410,875	2,768,643,532
1916...	4,272,397,774	61,261,091	4,333,658,865

The effect of the war in Europe upon the business of the United States is shown by a comparison of the exports for the month of August, 1913, and those of 1914 :

	1913	1914
Belgium	$9,322,252	$432,527
France	10,750,624	7,420,800
Germany	21,301,274	68,737
Russia	1,500,854	112,372
United Kingdom	38,355,184	32,951,250
Argentine	5,139,819	971,129
Australia	3,875,282	1,823,453
Italy	5,274,678	1,169,326

Exports:

Aggregate of, to France referred to, 768.

Embargo on—
Modification of laws regarding, recommended, 527.
Recommended, 526.

Laws in regard to, 528, 866.

Prohibition on—
Recommended, 517.
Removal of, recommended, 527.

Value of, for year ending June—
1845, 2252; 1846, 2346; 1847, 2401; 1848, 2496; 1851, 2658; 1852, 2705; 1877, 4422; 1881, 4633; 1884, 4830; 1885, 4925; 1886, 5093; 1890, 5555; 1891, 5627; 1892, 5743; 1893, 5875, 5887; 1894, 5964, 5978; 1896, 6156, 6171; 1899, 6357; 1900, 6439.

Value of, from commencement of Government, 1045.

Expositions. (See Exhibitions.)

Express, The, American vessel attacked by, 2675, 2680.

Expunging Resolutions.—March 28, 1834, the Senate passed a resolution censuring President Jackson and declaring that in removing the Federal deposits from the Bank of the United States he had assumed authority not conferred by the Constitution and the laws. Through the effort of Senator Benton an "expunging resolution" was passed Jan. 16. 1837. A black line was drawn around the resolution of censure in the Journal and across it was written the words "Expunged by order of the Senate this 16th day of January, 1837." The expunging resolution was strenuously opposed by Webster, Clay, and Calhoun.

Extension Banks.—Under the provisions of the Reserve Banking law of 1914 any national banking association possessing a capital and surplus of $1,000,000 or more may file application with the Federal Reserve Board for the purpose of securing authority to establish branches in foreign countries or dependencies of the United States for the furtherance of the foreign commerce of the United States, and to act, if required to do so, as fiscal agent of the United States.

Extradition, International.—Extradition treaties have been concluded by the Government of the United States with the principal governments of the world and many of the smaller ones. The first was that with Great Britain negotiated by John Jay in 1794. Congress, however, made no law for carrying out its provisions. Again, in 1842 a second treaty was negotiated. This was found to be inadequate in many ways. For instance, a criminal whose offense was not covered by the treaty was extradited on another charge and then tried for his real offense. This called forth a protest from Great Britain. By 1886 the treaty of 1842 was found to be entirely inadequate to existing conditions. The Phelps-Rosebery convention of that year offered a more satisfactory system, but was rejected by the Senate. That body, however, ratified the Blaine-Pauncefote convention of 1889, which accomplished the desired result. The United States has now extradition treaties with forty nations, but has no such treaties with the following countries: Bulgaria, China, Costa Rica, Dominican Republic, Egypt, Greece, Honduras, Korea, Morocco, Paraguay, Persia, Roumania, and Siam. The latest extradition treaties made were those with Cuba and Uruguay in 1905. Crimes which are recognized as extradital with all nations are: murder, and attempts to murder, arson, robbery, embezzlement, forgery and counterfeiting. Crimes at sea are extradital with all but France. Burglary, criminal assault, abduction, perjury and destruction of railroads are extradital under the majority of the treaties. (See Treaties.)

Extradition Treaties.—(See also Fugitive Criminals.) The United States has concluded extradition treaties with all of the principal countries of the world and many of the smaller. These vary greatly in the extraditable crimes. But the general conditions and means of extradition of all are the same. The essential principle of all of these treaties is that a fugitive from justice cannot be extradited from a country for one crime and tried upon another, without having ample opportunity and time to depart from it. The requisition for extradition is made through the diplomatic agents, or when such are wanting through the consular office. Sufficient proof of guilt within the law of the country from which extradition is sought must accompany the requisition; or if the fugitive has been sentenced or convicted prior to his escape, a legalized copy of the sentence of the judge, or of the warrant for arrest, must accompany the requisition. In urgent cases the provisional arrest of the fugitive may be secured by telegraphic or mail request, in which cases proceedings must be begun against the prisoner within a period of, usually, two months.

Political offenses or crimes are not extraditable, and an extradited person cannot be tried subsequently for a political offense, or connection with one prior to extradition. Where the person whose extradition is sought has committed an offense against the laws of the country of the asylum he must be tried, and, if guilty, fulfill his punishment before being handed over to the other nation. Expenses of the extradition are to be borne by the country seeking requisition. No extradition is possible if the offense with which the fugitive is charged is unpunishable by reason of the statute of limitation of the country of asylum. All articles and property in possession of the fugitive at the time of arrest are so far as is practicable to be returned with him, whether or not the proceeds of crime.

Where requests for the extradition of the same person come to a nation from more than one other country, unless directed otherwise by treaty provisions, he is to be handed over to the officers of the country first making requisition. The countries with which the United States has extradition treaties in force and the extraditable offenses are as follows::

Argentine Republic—(1896). — Homicide, assassination, parricide, poisoning, infanticide, manslaughter, or the attempt to commit any of these crimes; arson, burglary, house-breaking, shopbreaking, robbery with violence, larceny of the value of $200; forgery, counterfeiting, embezzlement of public monies or of private funds exceeding $200; fraud or breach of trust of $200; perjury or subornation of perjury; rape, abduction, kidnapping or child-stealing; train-wrecking, accomplished or attempted; piracy, mutiny, destroying or attempting to destroy a ship; assaults on shipboard; and trading in slaves where such is prohibited by the laws of both countries.

Austria-Hungary—(1856).—Murder, assault with intent to kill, piracy, arson, robbery, forgery, making or circulating counterfeit money, or embezzlement of public monies.

Baden—(1857).—Murder, attempt to commit murder, piracy, arson, robbery, forgery, making or circulation of counterfeit money, or embezzlement of public money.

Bavaria—(1853).—Murder, assault with intent to commit murder, piracy, arson, robbery, forgery, making or circulating counterfeit money, or embezzlement of public money.

Belgium—(1901).—Murder, parricide, assassination, poisoning, infanticide, attempt to commit murder, rape, attempt to commit rape, bigamy, abortion, arson, piracy, mutiny on shipboard, larceny, burglary, house-breaking, forgery, making or circulating counterfeit money, embezzlement of public money, or of private funds, exceeding $200 or 1,000 francs; train-wrecking, obtaining money or goods under false pretences, kidnapping of minors, and reception of stolen articles.

Bolivia—(1900).—Murder, assassination, parricide, infanticide, poisoning, attempt to commit murder, manslaughter, arson, robbery, burglary, forgery, counterfeiting, embezzlement exceeding $200; fraud or breach of trust when $200 or more is involved: perjury, subornation of perjury, rape, abduction, kidnapping, train-wrecking, piracy, mutiny, destroying a vessel, assaults at sea, slave-trading in violation of the laws of both countries.

Brazil—(1898).—Same as Bolivia.

Chile—(1900).—Same as Bolivia.

China.—No extradition.

Colombia—(1888).—Same as Bolivia.

Cuba.—1. Murder, comprehending the offenses expressed in the Penal Code of Cuba as assassination, parricide, infanticide and poisoning; manslaughter, when voluntary; the attempt to commit any of these crimes. 2. Arson. 3. Robbery, defined to be the act of feloniously and forcibly taking from the person of another money, goods, documents, or other property, by violence or putting him in fear; burglary; house-breaking and shop-breaking. 4. Forgery, or the utterance of forged papers, or falsification of the official acts or documents of the Government or public authority, including courts of justice, or the utterance or fraudulent use of any of the same. 5. The fabrication of counterfeit money, whether coin or paper, counterfeit titles or coupons of public debt, bank-notes, or other instruments of public credit; of counterfeit seals, stamps, dies and marks of state or public administration, and the utterance, circulation or fraudulent use of any of the above-mentioned objects. 6. Embezzlement by public officers or depositaries; embezzlement by persons hired or salaried to the detriment of their employers; obtaining money, valuable securities or other personal property by false devices, when such act is made criminal by the laws of both countries and the amount of money or value of the property so obtained is not less than two hundred dollars in gold. 7. Fraud or breach of trust (or the corresponding crime expressed in the Penal Code of Cuba as defraudation) by a bailee, banker, agent, factor. trustee, or other person acting in a fiduciary capacity, or director or member or officer of any company, when such act is made criminal by the laws of both countries and the amount of money or the value of the property misappropriated is not less than two hundred dollars in gold. 8. Perjury; subornation of perjury. 9. Bribery; defined to be the giving, offering or receiving of a reward to influence one in the discharge of a legal duty. 10. Rape, bigamy. 11. Wilful and unlawful destruction or obstruction of railroads, trains, bridges, vehicles, vessels or other means of transportation or public or private buildings, when the act committed endangers human life. 12. Crimes committed at sea, to wit: (a) Piracy, by statute or by the law of nations. (b) Revolt, or conspiracy to revolt, by two or more persons on board a ship on the high seas against the authority of the master. (c) Wrongfully sinking or destroying a vessel at sea, or attempting to do so. (d) Assaults on board a ship on the high seas with intent to do grievous bodily harm. 13. Crimes and offenses against the laws of both countries for the suppression of slavery and slave-trading. 14. Kidnapping of minors or adults, defined to be the abduction or detention of a person or persons in order to exact money from them or their families, or for any other unlawful end. 15. Larceny, defined to be the theft of money, effects, documents, horses, cattle, livestock or any other movable property of the value of more than fifty dollars. 16. Obtaining by threats of doing injury, money, valuables or other personal property. 17. Mayhem and other wilful mutilation causing disability or death. Extradition is to take place for participation in any of the crimes and offenses mentioned in this treaty not only as principal or accomplices, but as accessories in any of the crimes or offenses mentioned in the present article, provided such participation may be punished, in the United States as a felony and in the Republic of Cuba by imprisonment, hard labor or capital punishment.

Denmark.—Same as Belgium; supplemented by a treaty signed in 1905 extending its provisions to the island possessions of the contracting parties, and including the crime of bribery.

Ecuador—(1872).—1. Murder, including assassination, parricide, infanticide and poisoning. 2. The crime of rape, arson, piracy, and mutiny on shipboard when the crew or a part thereof, by fraud or violence against the commanding officer, have taken possession of the vessel. 3. The crime of burglary, this being understood as the act of breaking or forcing an entrance into another's house with intent to commit any crime, and the crime of robbery, this being defined as the act of taking from the person of another, goods or money with criminal intent, using violence or intimidation. 4. The crime of forgery, which is understood to be the wilful use or circulation of forged papers or public documents. 5. The fabrication or circulation of counterfeit money, either coin or paper, of public bonds, bank bills and securities, and in general of any kind of titles to or instruments of credit, the counterfeiting of stamps, dies, seals, and marks of the state, and of the administrative authorities, and the sale or circulation thereof. 6. Embezzlement of public property, committed within the jurisdiction of either party by public officers or depositaries.

France—(1843).—Murder, assassination, parricide, infanticide, poisoning, attempted to commit murder, rape, forgery, arson, and embezzlement. By the treaty of 1845: Robbery, burglary, and house-breaking. By the treaty of 1858: Making or circulating counterfeit money and embezzlement by hired or salaried persons. By the treaty of 1909: 1. Murder, assassination, parricide, infanticide and poisoning; manslaughter, when voluntary; assault with intent to commit murder. 2. Rape, abortion, bigamy. 3. Arson. 4. Robbery, burglary, housebreaking or shop-breaking. 5. Forgery; the utterance of forged papers, the forgery or falsification of official acts of Government, of public authority, or of courts of justice, or the utterance of the thing forged or falsified. 6. The counterfeiting, falsifying or altering of money, whether coin or paper, or of instruments of debt created by national, state, provincial, municipal or other governments, or of coupons thereof, or of bank-notes, or the utterance or circulation of the same; or the counterfeiting, falsifying, or altering of seals of state. 7. Fraud or breach of trust by a bailee, banker, agent, factor, executor, administrator, guardian, trustee or other person acting in a fiduciary capacity, or director or member or officer of any company, when such act is made criminal by the laws of both countries, and the amount of money or the value of the property misappropriated is not less than $200 or 1,000 francs. Embezzlement by public officers or depositaries; embezzlement by persons hired or salaried, to the detriment of their employers. 8. Larceny; obtaining money, valuable securities or other property by false pretenses, when such act is made criminal by the laws of both countries, and the amount of money of the value of the property fraudulently obtained is not less than two hundred dollars or one thousand francs. 9. Perjury, subornation of perjury. 10. Child-stealing, or abduction of a minor under the age of fourteen for a boy and of sixteen for a girl. 11. Kidnapping of minors or adults. 12. Wilful and unlawful destruction or obstruction of railroads, which endangers human life. 13. (a) Piracy, by the law of nations. (b) The act by any person, being or not being one of the crew of a vessel, of taking possession of such vessel by fraud or violence. (c) Wrongfully sinking or destroying a vessel at sea. (d) Revolt or conspiracy to revolt, by two or more persons on board a ship on the high seas, against the authority of the captain or master. (e) Assaults on board a ship on the high seas, with intent to do grievous bodily harm. 14. Crimes and offences against the laws of both countries for the suppression of slavery and slave-trading. 15. Receiving money, valuable securities or other property knowing the same to have been unlawfully obtained, when such act is made criminal by the laws of both countries and the amount of money or the value of the property so received is not less than $200 or 1,000 francs.

Great Britain—(1889).—Voluntary manslaughter, counterfeiting, embezzlement, larceny, receiving stolen goods, fraud, perjury, subornation of perjury, rape, abduction, child-stealing, kidnapping, burglary, house-breaking, piracy, mutiny, destroying a vessel, assault at sea, slavery and slave-trading. By a supplement of 1900 there were added: Obtaining money under false pretenses, train-wrecking, and procuring abortion.

Greece.—No extradition.

Guatemala—(1903).—Same as Bolivia, with the addition of: Mayhem, bigamy, bank robbery, embezzlement of bank funds, obtaining money or property by threat and receiving same.

Haiti—(1864). — Murder, assassination, parricide, infanticide, poisoning, attempt to commit murder, piracy, rape, forgery, counterfeiting, arson, robbery, and embezzlement.

Honduras.—Until 1909 we had no extradition treaty with Honduras. During that year Secretary Root negotiated a convention covering a longer list of extraditable offenses than the existing treaty with Mexico, which had theretofore been considered fairly complete and a model form for application to contiguous territory. They are: 1. Murder, comprehending the crimes designated by the terms of parricide, assassination, manslaughter, when voluntary; poisoning or infanticide. 2. The attempt to commit murder. 3. Rape, abortion, carnal knowledge of children under the age of twelve years. 4. Bigamy. 5. Arson. 6. Willful and unlawful destruction or obstruction of railroads, which endangers human life. 7. Crimes committed at sea: (a) Piracy, as commonly known and defined by the law of nations, or by statute. (b) Wrongfully sinking or destroying a vessel at sea or attempting to do so. (c) Mutiny or conspiracy by two or more members of the crew or other persons on board of a vessel on the high seas, for the purpose of rebelling against the authority of the captain or commander of such vessel, or by fraud or violence taking possession of such vessel. (d) Assault on board ships upon the high seas with intent to do bodily harm. 8. Burglary, defined to be the act of breaking into and entering the house of another in the night time with intent to commit a felony therein. 9. The breaking into and entering into the offices of the Government and public authorities, or the offices of banks, banking houses, saving banks, trust companies, insurance companies, or other buildings not dwelling with intent to commit a felony therein. 10. Robbery, defined to be the act of feloniously and forcibly taking from the person of another, goods or money by violence or by putting him in fear. 11. Forgery or the utterance of forged papers. 12. The forgery or falsification of the official acts of the Government or public authority, including courts of justice, or the uttering or

fraudulent use of the same. 13. The fabrication of counterfeit money, whether coin or paper, counterfeit titles or coupons of public debt, created by national, state, provincial, territorial, local, or municipal governments, bank-notes or other instruments of public credit, counterfeit seals, stamps, dies, and marks of state or public administrations, and the utterance, circulation, or fraudulent use of the above mentioned objects. 14. Embezzlement or criminal malversation committed within the jurisdiction of one or the other party by public officers or depositaries, where the amount embezzled exceeds $200 (or Honduran equivalent). 15. Embezzlement by any person or persons hired, salaried, or employed, to the detriment of their employers or principals, when the crime or offense is punishable by imprisonment or other corporal punishment by the laws of both countries, and where the amount embezzled exceeds $200 (or Honduran equivalent). 16. Kidnapping of minors or adults, and to be the abduction or detention of a person or persons, in order to exact money from them or their families, or for any other unlawful end. 17. Larceny, defined to be the theft of effects, personal property, or money, of the value of twenty-five dollars or more. 18. Obtaining money, valuable securities or other property by false pretenses or receiving any money, valuable securities or other property knowing the same to have been unlawfully obtained, where the amount of money or the value of the property so obtained or received exceeds two hundred dollars (or Honduran equivalent). 19. Perjury or subornation of perjury. 20. Fraud or breach of trust by a bailee, banker, agent, factor, trustee, executor, administrator, guardian, director, or officer of any company or corporation, or by any one in any fiduciary position, where the amount of money or the value of the property misappropriated exceeds two hundred dollars (or Honduran equivalent). 21. The extradition is also to take place for participation in any of the aforesaid crimes as an accessory before or after the fact, provided such participation be punishable by imprisonment by the laws of both contracting parties.

Italy—(1868, 1869, 1884).—Murder, assassination, parricide, poisoning, infanticide, attempt to commit murder, rape, arson, piracy, mutiny, burglary, robbery, forgery, counterfeiting, and embezzlement. By the addition of 1884: Kidnapping.

Japan—(1886).—Same as Haiti.

Luxemburg—(1883).—Same as Great Britain.

Mexico—(1889 and 1902).—The extent of extraditable offenses is greater in the case of Mexico than in any other treaty of the United States, probably on account of the contiguity of territory. The list of extraditable offenses includes: Murder, assassination, parricide, poisoning, infanticide, rape, bigamy, arson, piracy, destroying a vessel, murder, burglary, housebreaking, bank robbery, robbery, forgery, fraudulent use of the courts, counterfeiting, introduction of counterfeiter's tools, embezzlement of public or private funds, embezzlement of bank or trust funds, embezzlement by hired or salaried persons, kidnapping, mayhem, endangering human life by destruction of railroads, bridges, and the like; obtaining money or property by violence, threats, or false pretenses; receiving or buying goods known to have been wrongfully obtained; larceny to the extent of twenty-five dollars or more, or receiving goods to that value, knowing them to have been stolen. By the addition of 1902, bribery was added.

Morocco—No extradition.

Netherlands—(1887).—Same as Great Britain, with the addition of bigamy, abortion, larceny, and embezzlement. Extended in 1904 to the insular possessions of both countries.

Nicaragua—(1905).—Practically the same as with Honduras.

Norway—(1893).—Same as Netherlands.

Ottoman Empire—(1874).—Same as Haiti.

Panama—(1904).—1. Murder; 2. Arson; 3. Robbery; 4. Forgery; 5. Counterfeiting; 6. Embezzlement where the embezzlement exceeds the sum of $200; larceny. 7. Fraud, breach of trust by a bailee, banker, agent, factor, trustee, or other person acting in a fiduciary capacity, or director or member or officer of any company, when such act is made criminal by the laws of both countries and the amount of money or the value of the property misappropriated is not less than $200. 8. Perjury; subornaton of perjury. 9. Rape; abduction; kidnapping. 10. Willful and unlawful destruction or obstruction of railroads which endangers human life. 11. Crimes committed at sea: (*a*) Piracy, by statute or by the laws of nations; (*b*) Revolt, or conspiracy to revolt, by two or more persons on board a ship on the high seas against the authority of the master; (*c*) Wrongfully sinking or destroying a vessel at sea, or attempting to do so: (*d*) Assaults on board a ship on the high seas with intent to do grievous bodily harm. 12. Crimes and offenses against the laws of both countries for the suppression of slavery and slave trading. 13. Bribery. Extradition is also to take place for participation in any of the crimes and offenses mentioned in this Treaty, provided such participation may be punished, in the United States as a felony, and in the Republic of Panama by imprisonment at hard labor.

Paraguay.—No extradition.

Persia.—No extradition.

Peru—(1899).—Same as Bolivia.

Portugal—(1908).—Same as Honduras, with the understanding that no death penalty shall be enforced upon surrendered criminals.

Prussia—(1852).—This treaty was concluded by the king of Prussia for Prussia and other states. It was acceded to by Bremen, Mecklenburg-Schwerin, Mecklenburg-Strelitz, Oldenburg, Schaumburg-Lippe, and Württemberg. It includes as extraditable crimes: Murder or assault with intent to commit murder, piracy, arson, robbery, forgery, or the utterance of forged papers, counterfeiting, and embezzlement of public moneys.

Roumania.—No extradition.

Russia—(1887).—Same as Great Britain.

Salvador—(1911).—Same as Honduras with few minor exceptions.

Servia—(1901).—Same as Netherlands.

Siam.—No extradition.

Spain.—Extradition treaties of 1877 and 1882 abrogated by the treaty of friendship of 1902, and reestablished in 1904 by the signature of a treaty similar to that with Honduras.

Sweden—(1893).—Same as Netherlands.

Switzerland—(1900).—Same as Belgium.

Venezuela.—No extradition.

Extraordinary Session Messages. (See Special Session Messages.)

Extraordinary Sessions of Congress, proclamations convening, by President—

Adams, John, 222.

Cleveland, 5828.

Harrison, W. H., 1876.

Hayes, 4399, 4472.

Jefferson, 345, 412.

Lincoln, 3214.

McKinley, 6470.

Madison, 476, 529.

Pierce, 2927.

Roosevelt, 6780.

Taft, 7586.

Van Buren, 1538.

Extraordinary Sessions of Senate, proclamations convening by President—

Adams, John, 306, 1220.

Adams, J. Q., 997.

Arthur, 4621, 4873.

Buchanan, 3026, 3081, 3156, 3203.

Cleveland, 5428, 6230.

Fillmore, 2646, 2727.

Referred to, 2726.

Grant, 3966, 4087, 4171, 4278, 4390.

Harrison, Benj., 5817.

Hayes, 4591.

Referred to, 4588.

Jackson, 1508.

Jefferson, 449.

Johnson, 3719.

Lincoln, 3362, 3474.

Madison, 571.

Monroe, 856.

Pierce, 2959.

Polk, 2539.

Roosevelt, 6779, 6951, 6967.

Tyler, 2220.

Van Buren, 1857.

Washington, 130, 204, 571.

Ezra's Church (Ga.), Battle of.—July 27, 1864, Maj.-Gen. O. O. Howard was appointed to the command of the Army of the Tennessee and Gen. Hooker resigned the command of the Twentieth Corps, being succeeded by Gen. H. W. Slocum. The Army of the Tennessee was moved from the extreme left to the extreme right of the position before Atlanta. Gen. Hood, taking advantage of this movement, July 28 made an attack on the Fifteenth Corps, under Logan, at Ezra's Church. Logan was well supported by Blair's and Dodge's corps. The Federal accounts represent that the fighting continued from noon till 4 o'clock P. M., when the Confederates retired with a loss of 2,000. The Federal loss was 600. Gen. Sherman says that the Confederates sustained an overwhelming defeat. Gen. Hood states that no material advantage was gained by either opponent, and that the loss was small in proportion to the numbers engaged.

Fabian Socialist.—In the strict sense of the term, a member of the Fabian Society. This English organization had its beginnings in 1888, and is composed of Socialists who pursue a method of cooperation with existing governmental and social agencies, in order thus to sow the seeds of Socialism among them; whereas most Socialists refuse to cooperate or to join with other reform movements. The Society is composed of intellectuals, rather than of workingmen, and among its most famous members are Bernard Shaw and Sidney and Beatrice Webb. In a loose sense, a Fabian Socialist has come to mean any Socialist who desires to achieve the Socialistic ends by opportunist methods. (See Socialism.)

Faction.—A portion of an organization setting itself up in opposition; sometimes seceding from the organization proper.

Fair Oaks (Va.), Battle of. (See Seven Pines (Va.), Battle of.)

Falkland Islands.—Two large islands surrounded by a group of smaller ones in the South Atlantic between the parallels of 51° and 52° 45′ S., some 300 miles east of the main land of Patagonia, opposite the Strait of Magellan. The combined area of the group is about 7,510 square miles. The islands were visited by John Davis in 1592. In 1761 Commodore Byron took possession of them in the name of Great Britain, and they now constitute a crown colony. The principal occupation of the inhabitants is sheep raising, 2,325,000 acres being devoted to the pasturage of 724,736 sheep in 1910, besides 5,382 cattle and 3,314 horses. The principal exports are wool, hides and tallow. The population is about 2,500.

Falkland Islands:

Claims of Argentina respecting acts of American minister at, 4910.

Outrages committed on American citizens and vessels at, 1116, 1246.

Fanfare.—A flourish of trumpets, especially in military ceremonies.

Far Eastern Affairs, Department of State.—This department was created in 1909, by Secretary of State P. C. Knox. The chief of the Bureau is appointed by the Secretary of State, and the act making appropriations for his office made his salary either $4,500 or $3,000 yearly, at the discretion of the Secretary. The division of Far Eastern Affairs has supervision over matters other than administrative in Japan, China, Siberia, Hongkong, French Indo-China, Siam, Straits Settlements, Borneo, East Indies, India and other Far Eastern countries. (See Department of State; Counselor, Department of State.)

"Farewell Address."—The last address of President Washington, delivered September 17, 1796, at the conclusion of his eight years' of service in the Presidency, is regarded as one of the ablest of American State Papers. Reading of it, in whole or in part, is required before the Army and Navy on Washington's Birthday (see 3306); and by proclamation, as well as by custom, it is read generally to the people on Washington's Birthday. (See 3289.)

Farewell Address of President—
Jackson, 1511.
Washington, 205.
Army orders regarding reading of, 3306.

Proclamation recommending reading of, on Feb. 22, 3289.

Farm and Arm.—Catch-phrase used by ex-President Roosevelt in a Chicago speech immediately after President Wilson's message asking Congress to declare war against Germany, forcefully suggesting the need of systematic methods for food production, as well as of systematic fighting.

Farmers' Welfare:
Credits for, needed, 7908.
Discussed by President—
Roosevelt, 7046.
Wilson, 7908.

Farm Loan Act.—This is an act to provide capital for agricultural development, to create standard forms of investment based upon farm mortgage, to equalize rates of interest upon farm loans, to furnish a market for United States bonds, to create Government depositaries and financial agents for the United States, and for other purposes. The short title of this act is "The Federal Farm Loan Act." Its administration is under the direction and control of the Federal Farm Loan Board. Its chief provisions are:

Federal Farm Loan Board.—There shall be established at the seat of government in the Department of the Treasury a bureau charged with the execution of this act and of all acts amendatory thereof, to be known as the Federal Farm Loan Bureau, under the general supervision of a Federal Farm Loan Board.

Said Federal Farm Loan Board shall consist of five members, including the Secretary of the Treasury, who shall be a member and chairman ex officio, and four members to be appointed by the President of the United States, by and with the advice and consent of the Senate. Of the four members to be appointed by the President, not more than two shall be appointed from one political party, and all four of said members shall be citizens of the United States and shall devote their entire time to the business of the Federal Farm Loan Board; they shall receive an annual salary of $10,-000 payable monthly, together with actual necessary traveling expenses.

One of the members to be appointed by the President shall be designated by him to serve for two years, one for four years, one for six years, and one for eight years, and thereafter each member so appointed shall serve for a term of eight years, unless sooner removed for cause by the President. One of the members shall be designated by the President as the Farm Loan Commissioner, who shall be the active executive officer of said board. The following board was appointed by President Wilson:

William G. McAdoo, Chairman (ex officio).
George W. Norris, Farm Loan Commissioner.
Charles E. Lobdell.
W. S. A. Smith.
Herbert Quick.   W. W. Flannagan, Secretary.

Federal Land Banks.—The Federal Farm Loan Board shall divide the continental United States, excluding Alaska, into twelve districts, which shall be known as Federal land bank districts, and may be designated by number. Said districts shall be apportioned with due regard to the farm loan needs of the country, but no such district shall contain a fractional part of any State.

The Federal Farm Loan Board shall establish in each Federal land bank district a Federal loan bank, with its principal office located in such city within the district as said board shall designate. Each Federal land bank shall include in its title the name of the city in which it is located.

Each Federal land bank shall be temporarily managed by five directors appointed by the Federal Farm Loan Board. Said directors shall be citizens of the United States and residents of the district. They shall each give a surety bond, the premium on which shall be paid from the funds of the bank. They shall receive such compensation as the Federal Farm Loan Board shall fix.

After the subscriptions to stock in any Federal land bank by national farm loan associations, hereinafter authorized, shall have reached the sum of $100,000, the officers and directors of said land bank shall be chosen and upon becoming duly qualified, take over the management of said land bank from the temporary officers.

The board of directors of every Federal land bank shall consist of nine members, each holding office for three years. Six of said directors shall be known as local directors, and shall be chosen by and be representative of national farm loan associations; and the remaining three directors shall be known as district directors, and shall be appointed by the Federal Farm Loan Board and represent the public interest.

Directors of Federal land banks shall have been for at least two years residents of the district for which they are appointed or elected, and at least one district director shall be experienced in practical farming and actually engaged at the time of his appointment in farming operations within the district.

Capital Stock.—Every Federal land bank shall have, before beginning business, a subscribed capital of not less than $750,000. The capital stock of each Federal land bank shall be divided into shares of $5 each, and may be subscribed for and held by any individual, firm, or corporation, or by the Government of any State or of the United States. Stock held by national farm loan associations shall not be transferred or hypothecated, and the certificates therefor shall so state. Stock owned by the Government of the United States in Federal land banks shall receive no dividends, but all other stock shall share in dividend distributions without preference. Stock owned by the United States shall be voted by the Farm Loan Commissioner, as directed by the Federal Farm Loan Board.

It shall be the duty of the Federal Farm Loan Board to open books of subscription for the capital stock of a Federal land bank in each Federal land bank district. If within thirty days after the opening of said books any part of the minimum capitalization of $750,000 herein prescribed for Federal land banks shall remain unsubscribed, it shall be the duty of the Secretary of the Treasury to subscribe the balance thereof on behalf of the United States, said subscription to be subject to call in whole or in part by the board of directors of said land bank upon thirty days' notice with the approval of the Federal Farm Loan Board; and the Secretary of the Treasury is hereby authorized and directed to take out shares corresponding to the unsubscribed balance as called, and to pay for the same out of any moneys in the Treasury not otherwise appropriated.

After the subscriptions to capital stock by national farm loan associations shall amount to $750,000 in any Federal land bank, said bank shall apply semiannually to the payment and retirement of the shares of stock which were issued to represent the subscriptions to the original capital twenty-five per cent of all sums thereafter subscribed to capital stock until all such original capital stock is retired at par.

At least twenty-five per cent of that part of the capital of any Federal land bank for which stock is outstanding in the name of national farm loan associations shall be held in quick assets, and may consist of cash in the vaults of said land bank, or in deposits in member banks of the Federal reserve system, or in readily marketable securities which are approved under rules and regulations of the Federal Farm Loan Board; *Provided,* That not less than five per cent of such capital shall be invested in United States Government bonds.

Government Depositaries.—All Federal land banks and joint stock land banks organized under this act, when designated for that purpose by the Secretary of the Treasury, shall be depositaries of public money, except receipts from customs, under such regulations as may be prescribed by said Secretary; and they may also be employed as financial agents of the Government; and they shall perform all such reasonable duties, as depositaries of public money and financial agents of the Government, as may be required of them.

National Farm Loan Associations.—A national farm loan association may be organized in any community where 10 citizens owning land desire to borrow an aggregate of not less than $20,000. The land must be unincumbered or the proceeds of the loan must be used, in part, to remove any lien. Loans may be as small as $100, or as large as $10,000.

They must first make application, in writing, for a charter to the Federal land bank of the district in which the association desires to do business. This application must be signed by all those desiring to form the association, stating specifically the name under which they desire to do business, the amount each one desires to borrow, the estimated value of the security each one offers, the territory in which the association desires to do business, how the proceeds of the loan are to be used, and other details set forth in the blank forms which are furnished.

The application having been signed, together with another blank form furnished, called an "organization certificate," the applicants become a tentative organization and elect an agent to represent them, called a "secretary-treasurer"; they also select a committee of three, called a "loan committee." This agent will then receive, from each of the applicants, a subscription to the stock of the association they are forming equal to 5 per cent of the loan they severally desire, which is not required to be paid unless the loan is granted. That is, each borrower must subscribe for such stock to the amount of 5 per cent of his own loan and no more.

The application for the charter having been signed, the signatures must be acknowledged before a notary public or other officer qualified to administer oaths, and then it must be forwarded by the secretary-treasurer to the Federal land bank of the district.

Upon its receipt the bank will send its agent to examine into the representations made in the application and, if found satisfactory, a charter will be granted.

Upon the granting of the charter, the individuals signing the application become a body corporate, which gives it the right to do the business authorized by the farm loan act, to extend its benefits to others by taking in new members from time to time, and to have succession indefinitely. New members must be borrowers whose loans may be as small as $100 or as large as $10,000.

Let it be plainly understood that farmers can organize at once, but they can not borrow money until the land banks are established.

After the charter is granted the applicants no longer act in their individual capacity, but become merged as shareholders into a corporation, which has a separate existence created by law, under the same name which has been chosen and set forth in the original application and organization certificate. This corporation will have directors and officers selected by the shareholders to do its business in accordance with the by-laws which the shareholders make for their guidance. The active executive officer of the association will be the secretary-treasurer, and his duties are set forth in section 7 of the farm loan act.

These associations are organized for the primary purpose of giving to each borrower the benefit of the combined credit of all its members to the extent of the capital contributed and the limited liability they each incur, and hence the associations are required to indorse every loan made to members. It is also through these associations that the borrowers will ultimately become the owners of the Federal land banks. The association decides whether any loan shall be made or not by refusing the application for every loan which is considered unsafe or even doubtful. No loan can be made unless it is approved by the loan committee after examination of the land offered as security.

The national farm loan associations are not limited as to the number of their members. After one is organized it may serve an entire neighborhood by receiving new members. Each association may obtain in loans for its members twenty times the amount of its stock in the Federal land bank, no matter how large its holdings of stock may become by the growth of the association.

1. No loan may be made except upon the security of first mortgages.

2. The amount of the mortgage can not exceed one-half the appraised value of the land and 20 per cent of the permanent improvements thereon, which must be insured.

3. The proceeds of the loan must be used for the extinguishment of pre-existing indebtedness or for productive purposes, which includes the purchase of live stock, fertilizers, equipment and improvements.

4. Every mortgage must contain an agreement to pay off the debt (principal and interest) in fixed annual or semiannual installments.

5. The amount of each installment may be fixed by the borrower, but can not be less than sufficient to pay off the debt in 40 years, nor greater than to pay it off in 5 years.

6. The rate of interest charged any borrower can not exceed 6 per cent per annum.

7. The borrower can not be called upon to pay the debt except by the installments he originally fixes, unless he defaults, but after five years he may pay off the whole or any portion at his option at any installment period. (See Rural Credits.)

Farm Loan Bureau. (See Farm Loan Act.)

Farm Management, Office of, Agriculture Department.—One of the special functions developed by the Bureau of Plant Industry of the Department of Agriculture. Investigations by the bureau developed the fact that there was an utter lack of system in the management of farm enterprises. Too little attention has been given to standardizing systems of farm work. An astonishing variation in the number and kind of operations on the corn crop alone were found on different farms and in different localities. No reasons for the variation could be given, except custom. It was found that a wide difference existed between the profits shown by an average farm in Wisconsin and an average farm in Massachusetts.

It was shown that neighboring farmers, with similar types of farming, devote very different amounts of time to the various classes of enterprises on their farms because of the lack of standard systems of management of these enterprises, and it is not always the man who devotes the most time to an enterprise who makes the largest profits from it. Lack of system means lost motion and useless work.

In order that the farm may be profitable the crops and live stock maintained upon it must be adapted not only to local conditions of soil, and climate but also to existing economic conditions.

The income per animal unit is a very important factor in profit. Yield per acre is also important, but less so than the income per animal unit. Moderate yields may be more profitable than very high yields.

It is for the purpose of developing these points and bringing them to the attention of the farmer that the Office of Farm Management was established.

Farm Products. (See Agricultural Products.)

Farmville (Va.), Battle of.—After the evacuation of Richmond, Lee's army was moving westward toward Farmville, where he hoped to cross the Appomattox, burn the bridges and check the pursuit of the Federals. Meantime Ord, with his command of the Army of the James, was also advancing toward Farmville to burn the bridges and intercept Lee at that point. His advance consisted of 2 regiments of infantry and a squadron of cavalry under Gen. Theodore Read. At Farmville the Confederates made a short halt. Read appearing, he was attacked by Lee. In the conflict Read was killed, his column brushed aside and the retreating army crossed the river. After the death of Read, Ord's command arrived, and the Confederates began to intrench themselves. On the same afternoon, April 7, 1865, Sheridan struck the enemy farther back, capturing 16 pieces of artillery and 400 wagons, and held them in check until the arrival of the Second Corps, when a general attack was ordered, resulting in the capture of 6,000 or 7,000 prisoners.

Fashion, The, 2997, 3001, 3017. (See Walker, William.)

Fasting and Prayer (see also Thanksgiving Proclamations):

Special day of, set apart by proclamation of President—

Lincoln, 3237, 3365, 3422.

Referred to, 3437.

Fatherland.—Native country. Often applied to Germany.

Federal Courts. (See Courts.)

Federal Courts, procedure in, 6918.

Enforcement of criminal laws discussed, 7003.

Right of appeal by Government in criminal cases on questions of law recommended, 7023.

Federal Election Law recommended, 5490, 5562, 5766.

Federal Farm Loan Act. (See Farm Loan Act.)

Federal Inspection and control of interstate commerce advocated, 7074, 7087, 7130. (See also Corporations.)

Federal Jurisdiction inadequate to enforce treaty obligations within states, 7055.

Federal Reserve Banking Law. (See Reserve Banking System.)

Federal Reserve Banks. (See Currency Laws and Reserve Banking System.)

Federal Reserve Board. (See Reserve Banking System.)

Federal Supervision of Corporations incident to tax on incomes of, 7391.

Federal Trade Commission. (See Trade Commission.)

Federal White Slave Act. (See White Slave Law.)

Federalist Party.—The first political party organized in the United States after the achievement of independence. Its leaders were Washington, Adams, Hamilton, Jay, Marshall, and others of high rank and ability. During the French Revolution the Federalists sympathized with England rather than with the Red Republicans of France. At this time Jefferson, Burr, and others organized the Republican party, whose distinctive features were to intensify the feeling of hostility toward England. They accused the Federalists of being enemies of the masses of the people and of favoring aristocratic government.

The looseness of the Union under the Articles of Confederation had unsettled business, and all citizens that were injured by this state of affairs were in favor of a stronger government. Moreover, the feeling that thus only could we become a nation among nations had much weight in inclining the more thoughtful to favor the Constitution. Washington, Jefferson, Madison and Randolph were all Federalists in the earlier and wider meaning of the term. The adoption of the Constitution left the anti-Federalists without a cause, and the Federal party went into power with Washington at its head practically unopposed. During the first session of Congress the departments of the government were organized. At the second session Alexander Hamilton introduced his financial measures. The foreign debt was to be paid in full, the continental debt was to be paid at par, and the debts of the several States were to be assumed. To the second of these propositions Madison dissented, but it was nevertheless carried. The third aroused enormous opposition, and it was hotly debated both in and out of Congress. After one defeat it was reintroduced and carried by means of a bargain. At the third session a bill taxing distilled spirits was passed and the Bank of the United States was incorporated. These measures Jefferson and Randolph opposed. The party had thus gradually strengthened the broad construction view of the Constitution and had attained real principles and party life.

The Federalists elected Washington and John Adams. Hamilton's financial measures had been acceptable to those who desired strong government—the commercial classes—and those who wished to see the Union drawn still more closely together in the direction of centralization and national consolidation. In 1797 the majority of the party favored war with France. The following year they passed the Alien and Sedition Laws (q. v.), and in 1800 their candidates, Adams and Pinckney, were defeated by Jefferson and Burr for President and Vice-President, respectively. The unpatriotic course of the party in the War of 1812 and the odium excited by the Hartford Convention (q. v.) destroyed it entirely.

Federalist, The.—A series of essays, eighty-five in number, in favor of the new Constitution of the United States, originally published in the *Independent Journal*, of New York, between Oct. 27, 1787, and April 2, 1788. The authors were Alexander Hamilton (who wrote fifty-one of the essays), James Madison (who wrote twenty-nine), and John Jay (who wrote five), who addressed the public over the common signature of "Publius." The purpose of the letters was to create in the minds of the people a sentiment favorable to the new Federal Constitution proposed by the Convention of Sept. 17, 1787. These essays were gathered into two volumes in 1788, and have been reprinted in many editions.

Fee System, abolition of, as applicable to certain Federal officers, discussed, 6161.

Recommended, 4939, 5879, 5968.

Felonies, limitations upon right in felony cases to review by Supreme Court recommended, 5632, 5880.

Fellow-Countryman.—A person belonging to the same country as the user of the term.

Fenians.—An organization of Irish-Americans and Irish revolutionists, whose object was the forcible separation of Ireland from Great Britain and the establishment of an Irish Republic. The Fenian Brotherhood was founded in New York in 1857 by Michael Doheny, William R. Roberts, John O'Mahony, and Michael Corcoran, the last named being afterwards a brigadier-general in the United States Army. About the same time a similar organization, existing in Ireland under the name of the Phœnix Society, was developed by James Stephens, who came to the United States in 1858 and reported an enrollment of 35,000 disciplined followers in Ireland. O'Mahony was the first president of the American organization. Nov. 3, 1863, the first national congress of Fenians met in Chicago, representing an enrolled membership of 15,000, one-half of whom were in the Union Army. This convention declared Ireland to be an independent nation with James Stephens at its head. When the second Fenian congress assembled at Cincinnati in January, 1865, the circles had increased fivefold. The fourth Fenian congress met in New York Jan. 2, 1866, when an invasion of Canada was decided upon. Military operations were conducted by Gen. Thomas W. Sweeney, a former officer of the Union Army. In May, 1866, the United States authorities seized 750 stand of arms at Eastport, Me., about 1,200 stand at Rouses Point, N. Y., and 1,000 stand at St. Albans, Vt., all intended for the Fenian invasion of Canada. May 31, 1866, about 1,200 Fenians, under Col. O'Neill, crossed the Niagara River at Buffalo and occupied Fort Erie, whence they were driven two days later. On returning they were intercepted by United States forces and paroled under promise to go to their homes. Similar arrests were made on the Vermont line. United States troops under Gen. Meade kept close watch on the Canadian frontier. President Johnson issued a proclamation warning citizens of the United States against participation in the unlawful proceedings (3631). The Fenian leaders were arrested, but afterwards released. Several outbreaks were suppressed in Ireland, and dissensions soon arose among the leaders of the movement. A second invasion of Canada was projected, but the vigilance of the United States authorities prevented its accomplishment. In April, 1867, the brig *Erin's Hope* sailed from New York with arms, ammunition, and officers for a brigade, but was unable to land and returned. During 1867 a number of Fenian riots occurred in Ireland, but all were quelled and many of the leaders were imprisoned or 'hanged. Many of the wrongs for which the Fenians sought redress have been corrected by legislation.

Fenians:

Release of, 4114.

Resolution urging, referred to, 3595.

Trial of, in Canada referred to, 3718.

Unlawful expeditions of, discussed, 3640, 3655.

Proclamation against, 3631.

Fenix, The, provision for captives of, recommended, 1097.

Fernandina, Fla., blockade of port of, removed by proclamation, 3431. Referred to, 3446.

Ferrocarriles de Porto Rico, Compaina de los, concessions to, 6933, 6934.

Ferrolana, The, American vessel attacked by, 2869, 2976.

Fever. (See Contagious Diseases; Yellow Fever.)

Fiat Money.—A term given to irredeemable paper currency during the greenback agitation following the Civil War in the United States. The greenback party claimed that the fiat of the government could itself give value to a circulating medium of no intrinsic value and not even containing a promise to pay, but issued by the state with the bare assertion of its identity with true money. The Latin word "fiat" means "Let it be done." (See Currency.)

Field Products. (See Agricultural Products, also Crop Values.)

"Fifty-four Forty or Fight."—A campaign cry of the Democrats in 1844. This was during the northwestern boundary discussion. The treaty with Spain in 1819 fixed the parallel of 42° as the northern limit of that country's possession in America. Between that parallel and 54° 40' lay the territory of Oregon, claimed by both America and England. To avoid clashes a joint occupation of the whole territory west of the Rocky Mountains was agreed upon in 1818, to last for ten years. A new convention in the year 1827 decided to continue joint occupation indefinitely. This arrangement created much dissatisfaction : Americans had made surveys as far north as 49° and settlements were springing up. English fur traders had passed south of that line, and for a time war seemed inevitable ; but a treaty was arranged in 1846 fixing the boundary at lat. 49° north. It was during the presidential campaign that the cry "Fifty-four Forty or Fight" orig-

inated. The supporters of Mr. Polk in that campaign vigorously proclaimed that the northwestern boundary line should be established as far north as 54° 40' or the United States should fight. It was during his administration that the line was fixed at 49°. When criticised by his political opponents for the failure to locate the line at 54° 40' he excused and justified his administration by stating that "all conflicting title to the Oregon Territory south of the forty-ninth degree of north latitude, being all that was insisted upon by any of my predecessors, 'has been adjusted" (2484). (See also Northwestern Boundary.)

Fiji Islands, report of agent to, for investigation of claim of B. H. Henry and others, 6098.

Filibuster.—From the Spanish word filibustero, meaning "freebooter" or "buccaneer." In 1849-1851 the term was applied by the Cubans to Narciso Lopez and his followers, and from that time became a common name for military adventurers who fitted out expeditions against the Spanish-American countries. The object of most of these filibusters has been to free the Spanish-American countries from their European rulers. After Lopez the most famous filibuster was Gen. William Walker, who invaded Sonora, Mexico, in 1853. In 1855 he took possession of Nicaragua and was elected president. He did not long enjoy this distinction, for 'he was soon compelled to surrender to the forces of the United States, but escaped punishment. In 1857 he organized a second expedition to Nicaragua, but was again compelled to surrender to the United States Government. Escaping punishment a second time, in 1860 he organized an expedition against the Government of Honduras, but was captured and, by order of the president of Honduras, shot. In the United States the term filibuster, when used in a legislative or political sense, means that method pursued by the members of the minority of a legislative body who seek to delay or defeat the adoption of measures obnoxious to them by obstructive and dilatory tactics, such as repeated motions to adjourn, for a recess, calls for the yeas and nays, etc. (See illustration opposite 2769.)

Fillmore, Millard.—July 10, 1850-March 4, 1853.

Sixteenth Administration (continued)— Whig.

President pro tem. of the Senate—
William R. King.

Secretary of State—
Daniel Webster.
Edward Everett.

Secretary of the Treasury—
Thomas Corwin.

Secretary of War—
Charles M. Conrad.

Secretary of the Navy—
William A. Graham.
John P. Kennedy.

Secretary of the Interior—
James A. Pearce.
Alex. H. H. Stuart

Postmaster-General—
N. K. Hall.
Samuel D. Hubbard.

Attorney-General—
John J. Crittenden.

Fillmore succeeded to the presidency on the death of Zachary Taylor, July 9, 1850.

Opposition.—Nominated to the Vice-Presidency by the Whig National Convention. he was opposed by William O. Butler, of Kentucky.

EXTENT OF THE UNITED STATES DURING THE ADMINISTRATION OF PRESIDENT FILLMORE, 1850-1853.

(NOT INCLUDING TERRITORIES)

MAINE
1820

VT.
1791

N. H.
1788

MASS.
1788

CONN.
1788

R. I.
1790

NEW YORK
1788

N. J.
1787

PENNSYLVANIA
1787

DEL.
1787

MD.
1788

VIRGINIA
1788

NORTH CAROLINA
1789

SOUTH CAROLINA
1788

FLORIDA
1845

MICHIGAN
1837

OHIO
1803

INDIANA
1816

KENTUCKY
1792

TENNESSEE
1796

GEORGIA
1788

ALABAMA
1819

WISCONSIN
1848

ILLINOIS
1818

MISSISSIPPI
1817

IOWA
1846

MISSOURI
1821

ARKANSAS
1836

LOUISIANA
1812

TEXAS
1845

CALIFORNIA
1850

FLAG OF 1853

COPYRIGHT BY BUREAU OF NATIONAL LITERATURE (INC.)

Vote.—The electoral vote stood : Fillmore, 163 ; Butler, 127. Fillmore was the seventh Vice-President which the State of New York supplied and the second to succeed to the Presidency through the death of the President. His succession occurred at a most critical time in the history of the United States.

Party Affiliation.—Fillmore's political career is contemporaneous with the birth and death of the Whig party. In the State legislature of New York he drafted the bill abolishing imprisonment for debt, passed in 1831. In Congress he was the author of the tariff bill of 1842 ; as comptroller of the State of New York (1847) he advocated a national bank with currency issue secured by United States stocks—a principle which is the basis of the present national bank system. As Vice-President with Taylor on the Whig ticket, he presided in the Senate during a seven months' controversy covering such questions as California's admission, slavery in the new territories, surrender of fugitive slaves, and Clay's "omnibus bill."

Tariff.—In his First Annual Message (page 2620) President Fillmore discusses the tariff and advocates a uniform, permanent, specific tariff. He says : "The power to lay these duties is unquestionable, and its chief object is, of course, to replenish the Treasury. But if in doing this an incidental advantage may be gained by encouraging the industry of our own citizens, it is our duty to avail ourselves of that advantage. . . . A high tariff can never be permanent. It will cause dissatisfaction and will be changed. It excludes competition. . . . What a manufacturer wants is uniformity and permanency, that he may feel confident that he is not to be ruined by sudden changes. . . . *Ad valorem* duties fluctuate with the price and offer strong temptations to fraud and perjury. Specific duties, on the contrary, are equal and uniform in all ports and at all times, and offer a strong inducement to the importer to bring the best article, as he pays no more duty upon that than upon one of inferior quality." There was, however, no tariff revision by Congress until the act of 1857. In his Third Annual Message (page 2706) the President again calls the attention of Congress to the need of a revision of the tariff and adds another reason for its consideration. ". . . that the present tariff in some cases imposes a higher duty upon the raw material imported than upon the articles manufactured from it, the consequence of which is that the duty operated to the encouragement of the foreigner and the discouragement of our own citizens."

Foreign Policy.—The policy of his administration is laid down (page 2614) in his First Annual Message : "To maintain a strict neutrality, in foreign wars, to cultivate friendly relations, to reciprocate every noble and generous act, and to perform punctually and scrupulously every treaty obligation—these are duties which we owe to other States." . . . In his Second Annual Message (page 2652), speaking of the invasion of Cuba, the President says : "In proclaiming and adhering to the doctrine of neutrality and nonintervention, the United States have not followed the lead of other civilized nations ; they have taken the lead themselves and have been followed by others." In his Third Annual Message (page 2700) he deprecates the addition of Cuba to the Union in these words : "Were this island comparatively destitute of inhabitants or occupied by a kindred race, I should regard it, if voluntarily ceded by Spain, as a most desirable acquisition. But under existing circumstances, I should look upon its incorporation into our Union as a very hazardous measure. It would bring into the Confederacy a population of a different national stock, speaking a different language, and not likely to harmonize with the other members."

Internal Improvements.—President Fillmore had no doubt of the power of Congress to make appropriations for the making of internal improvements. In his First Annual Message (page 2626) he argues the question of the constitutionality of such acts. "This authority I suppose to be derived chiefly from the power of regulating commerce with foreign nations and among the States and the power of laying and collecting imposts." Lighthouses, wharves, beacons, buoys, breakwaters, and dredging then become necessities to such regulation. He sees no more reason for refusing appropriations for navigable rivers than for sea-coast improvements. He cites an important geographical fact in these words : "I may add, as somewhat remarkable, that among all the thirty-one States there is none that is not to a greater or less extent bounded on the ocean, or the Gulf of Mexico, or one of the great lakes, or some navigable river."

Slavery—By signing the fugitive slave act and the other compromise measures of 1850, President Fillmore lost the friendship and the support of a large number of his party in the North. He was influenced by the written opinion of the Attorney-General on the constitutionality of the Fugitive slave act, and also by the concurrence of his able Cabinet. In his First Annual Message (page 2629) the President discusses these compromises and says : "The series of measures to which I have alluded are regarded by me as a settlement in principle and substance—a final settlement of the dangerous and exciting subjects which they embraced. . . . By that adjustment we have been rescued from the wide and boundless agitation that surrounded us, and have a firm, distinct, and legal ground to rest upon." In a special message (page 2637) he discusses the disturbances attending the enforcement of these laws and announces his intention to see the laws enforced. By proclamation of Feb. 18, 1851 (page 2646) support of the laws by the citizens of the country is called for. In his Second Annual Message (page 2674) the President says : "Looking at the interests of the whole country, I felt it to be my duty to seize upon this compromise as the best that could be obtained amid conflicting interests and to insist upon it as a final settlement, to be adhered to by all who value the peace and welfare of the country."

Fillmore, Millard:

Annual messages of, 2613, 2649, 2699.

Appointing power of President discussed by, 2616.

Biographical sketch of, 2599.

Cuba—

Acquisition of, discussed by, 2701.

Affairs of, discussed by, 2649, 2700.

Incorporation of, into Union not desired, 2701.

Death of, announced, and honors to be paid memory of, 4236.

Death of President Taylor announced to, and reply of, 2589.

Communication of, to Senate, 2590.

Discussed by, 2593, 2600, 2613.

Finances discussed by, 2619, 2658, 2704.

Foreign Policy discussed by, 2614, 2656, 2701, 2715.

Information regarding negotiations with Great Britain, Costa Rica, and Nicaragua refused by, 2690.

Information regarding proposition to annex Hawaiian Islands refused by, 2691, 2695.

Internal improvements discussed by, 2626.

Oath of office, time and place of taking, mentioned, 2590.

Portrait of, 2598.

Powers of Federal and State Governments discussed by, 2626.

Proclamations of—

Discriminating duties on vessels of Chile suspended, 2612.

Extraordinary session of Senate, 2646, 2727.

Military expedition to—

Cuba, 2647.

Mexico, 2648.

Texas boundary line, 2643.

Unlawful combinations in Boston, 2645.

State of the Union discussed by, 2613.

System of government discussed by, 2614.

Tariff discussed by, 2619, 2659, 2661, 2705.

Finances.—The first financial measure of the Continental Congress was a loan of £6,000, in 1775. Franklin urged the Congress to continue to raise money by loans, but the majority favored the issue of paper money. One delegate said: "Do you think, gentlemen, that I will consent to load my constituents with taxes when we can send to our printer and get a wagon load of money, one quire of which will pay for the whole?" Previous to 1776 $6,000,000 in paper had been issued, redeemable in four years, beginning with 1783. Subsequent issues during the Revolutionary war increased this sum to more than $200,000,000 and it rapidly depreciated until in 1781 it ceased to pass as money. By 1783 the loans of the United States amounted to $42,000,000, of which $7,885,085 were obtained abroad. Home creditors received no interest and some of them sold their claims for as low as 10 per cent of their face value. After the adoption of the federal constitution these claims were paid in full by Alexander Hamilton, while Secretary of the Treasury. Before this, however, Robert Morris had been made Superintendent of Finance. He systematized the finances, improved the foreign credit and established a bank. When unable to borrow money on the credit of the government he used his own money and his own credit on behalf of the nation.

During Hamilton's five years as head of the Treasury Department he established the public credit on a firm basis. Albert Gallatin was appointed Secretary of the Treasury by Jefferson, and during his service of twelve years he reduced the public debt from $83,000,000 in 1801 to about $50,000,000 in 1813, besides providing funds for the purchase of Louisiana and the expenses of the War of 1812.

In 1835 and 1836 the country was practically out of debt, and nearly $40,000,000

was realized from the sale of public lands. Congress voted to distribute all the surplus in excess of $5,000,000 among the states, but before this had been accomplished a panic overspread the country and the government was on the verge of bankruptcy.

At the beginning of the civil war Salmon P. Chase was Secretary of the Treasury. Congress authorized a loan of $250,-000,000 in 3-year 7-30 treasury notes and 20-year bonds with interest not to exceed 7 per cent, and in lieu of a portion of said loan the Secretary was authorized to pay salaries or other debts or to exchange for coin non-interest-bearing treasury notes payable on demand and receivable for all public dues, to the extent of $50,000,000. Secretary Chase obtained an advance of $50,000,-000 from the banks of New York, Boston and Philadelphia. Subscription books were then opened in all the loyal cities and the public took about $45,000,000 of the 3-year notes. This was turned over to the banks and they advanced another $50,000,000, but the third attempt failed, and Congress authorized the issue of $150,000,000 of legal tender notes. (See Currency.) Three of such issues were made aggregating $450,-000,000. Within the year 1863 gold fluctuated between $125 and $160. In 1863 the National Banking Act was passed establishing a uniform currency, and the issue of bonds became a settled policy of the Treasury. The four leading points in Secretary Chase's policy were moderate interest, general distribution, future controllability and incidental utility.

The most important financial measures of recent times have been the enactment of the Aldrich-Vreeland law and the Regional Reserve bank law, both of which aim to stabilize the money market by the issue of emergency currency based on collateral securities.

Finances:

Act—

Directing coinage of silver bullion in Treasury vetoed, 5915.

Directing payment of surplus in Treasury on public debt, reasons for applying pocket veto to, 5073.

To authorize coinage of standard silver dollars, etc., vetoed, 4438.

To facilitate refunding of national debt vetoed, 4589.

To fix amount of United States notes and circulation of national banks vetoed, 4222.

Authority to Secretary of Treasury to accumulate gold for final redemption recommended, 4303.

Bank deposits, discussed. (See Deposits Public, State Banks.)

Bland-Allison Act—

Discussed by President—

Arthur, 4633, 4720, 4830.

Cleveland, 4927, 5097, 5373.

Harrison, Benj., 5475.

Hayes, 4511, 4568.

Vetoed by President Hayes, 4438.

Clearing houses recommended, 4199.

Condition of the Treasury, 7681.

Conference provided for in act to authorize coinage of silver dollars, etc., appropriation for, recommended, 4438.

FINANCIAL GROWTH OF THE COUNTRY AND THE PEOPLE SINCE 1800, AS REPORTED BY THE
DEPARTMENT OF COMMERCE

Year	Area Sq. miles[1]	Population June 1 [2]	Population per square mile[3]	Wealth[4]		Public debt, less cash in Treasury July 1	
				Total	Per capita	Totals[5]	Per capita
1800	892,135	5,308,483	6.12			$82,976,294.35	$15.63
1810	1,720,122	7,239,881	4.29			53,173,217.52	7.34
1820	1,792,223	9,638,453	5.50			91,015,566.15	9.44
1830	1,792,223	12,866,020	7.34			48,565,406.50	3.77
1840	1,792,223	17,069,453	9.73			3,573,343.82	.21
1850	2,997,119	23,191,876	7.88	$7,135,780,000	$307.69	63,452,773.55	2.74
1852	2,997,119	24,802,000	8.42			66,199,341.71	2.67
1853	3,026,789	25,615,000	8.61			59,803,117.70	2.33
1854	3,026,789	26,433,000	8.89			42,242,222.42	1.60
1855	3,026,789	27,256,000	9.16			35,586,956.56	1.31
1856	3,026,789	28,083,000	9.44			10,965,953.01	1.14
1857	3,026,789	28,916,000	9.72			9,998,621.76	.99
1858	3,026,789	29,758,000	10.01			37,900,191.72	1.51
1859	3,026,789	30,596,000	10.29			53,405,234.19	1.91
1860	3,026,789	31,443,321	10.57	16,159,616,000	513.93	59,964,402.01	1.91
1861	3,026,789	32,064,000	10.78			87,718,660.80	2.74
1862	3,026,789	32,704,000	11.00			505,312,752.17	15.45
1863	3,026,789	33,365,000	11.22			1,111,350,737.41	33.31
1864	3,026,789	34,046,000	11.45			1,709,452,277.04	50.21
1865	3,026,789	34,748,000	11.68			2,674,815,856.76	76.98
1866	3,026,789	35,469,000	11.93			2,636,036,163.84	74.32
1867	3,026,789	36,211,000	12.18			2,508,151,211.69	69.26
1868	3,026,789	36,973,000	12.43			2,480,853,413.23	67.10
1869	3,026,789	37,756,000	12.69			2,432,771,873.09	64.43
1870	3,026,789	38,558,371	12.96	30,068,518,000	779.83	2,331,169,956.21	60.46
1871	3,026,789	39,555,000	13.30			2,246,994,068.67	56.81
1872	3,026,789	40,596,000	13.65			2,149,780,530.35	52.96
1873	3,026,789	41,677,000	14.01			2,105,462,060.75	50.52
1874	3,026,789	42,796,000	14.39			2,104,149,153.69	49.17
1875	3,026,789	43,951,000	14.78			2,090,041,170.13	47.53
1876	3,026,789	45,137,000	15.18			2,060,925,340.45	45.66
1877	3,026,789	46,353,000	15.59			2,019,275,431.37	43.56
1878	3,026,789	47,598,000	16.00			1,999,382,280.45	42.01
1879	3,026,789	48,866,000	16.43			1,996,414,905.03	40.85
1880	3,026,789	50,155,783	16.86	43,642,000,000	870.20	1,919,326,747.75	38.27
1881	3,026,789	51,316,000	17.25			1,819,650,154.23	35.46
1882	3,026,789	52,495,000	17.65			1,675,023,474.25	31.91
1883	3,026,789	53,693,000	18.05			1,538,781,825.15	28.66
1884	3,026,789	54,911,000	18.46			1,438,542,995.39	26.20
1885	3,026,789	56,148,000	18.88			1,375,352,443.91	24.50
1886	3,026,789	57,404,000	19.30			1,282,145,840.44	22.34
1887	3,026,789	58,680,000	19.73			1,175,168,675.42	20.03
1888	3,026,789	59,974,000	20.17			1,063,004,894.73	17.72
1889	3,026,789	61,289,000	20.61			975,939,750.22	15.92
1890	3,026,789	62,947,714	21.16	65,037,091,000	1,035.57	890,784,370.53	14.15
1891	3,026,789	63,844,000	21.47			851,912,751.78	13.34
1892	3,026,789	65,086,000	21.88			841,526,463.60	12.93
1893	3,026,789	66,349,000	22.31			838,969,475.75	12.64
1894	3,026,789	67,632,000	22.74			899,313,380.55	13.30
1895	3,026,789	68,934,000	23.18	77,000,000,000	1,117.01	901,672,966.74	13.08
1896	3,026,789	70,254,000	23.62			955,297,253.70	13.60
1897	3,026,789	71,592,000	24.07			986,656,086.14	13.78
1898	3,026,789	72,947,000	24.53			1,027,085,492.14	14.08
1899	3,026,789	74,318,000	24.99			1,155,320,235.19	15.55
1900	3,026,789	75,994,575	25.55	88,517,307,000	1,164.79	1,107,711,257.89	14.58
1901	3,026,789	77,612,569	26.10			1,044,739,119.97	13.46
1902	3,027,789	79,230,563	26.64			969,457,241.04	12.24
1903	3,026,789	80,848,557	27.18			925,011,637.31	11.44
1904	3,026,789	82,466,551	27.73	107,104,212,000	1,318.11	967,231,773.75	11.73
1905	3,026,789	84,084,545	28.27			989,866,772.00	11.77
1906	3,026,789	85,702,533	28.82			964,435,686.79	11.25
1907	3,026,789	87,320,539	29.36			878,596,755.03	10.06
1908	3,026,789	88,938,527	29.90			938,132,409.38	10.55
1909	3,026,789	90,556,521	30.45			1,023,861,530.79	11.31
1910	3,026,789	92,174,515	30.99			1,046,449,185.25	11.35
1911	3,026,789	93,792,509	31.54			1,015,784,338.46	10.83
1912	3,026,789	95,410,503	32.08	187,739,071,000		1,027,574,697.28	10.77
1913	3,026,789	97,028,497	32.63			1,028,564,055.14	10.60
1914	3,026,789	98,646,491	32.59			1,027,257,009.56	10.41
1915	3,026,789	100,264,485	32.79			1,090,148,006.00	10.87
1916	3,026,789	102,431,000	33.81			989,219,621.85	9.66

[1] The figures relate to continental United States. [2] For other than census years prior to 1890, the figures are for July 1
[3] The figures are based upon the land area of continental United States and upon population as given in the preceding column. [4] True valuation of real and personal property; the figures are those of the Bureau of the Census, Department of Commerce, relate to continental United States, and cover census years. [5] 1800 to 1855, outstanding principal of the public debt Jan. 1.

RECEIPTS AND DISBURSEMENTS, YEARS ENDED JUNE 30, 1909, TO 1916, ETC.

RECEIPTS AND THEIR SOURCES

Source	1910	1911	1912	1913	1914	1915	1916
Customs revenue....	333,683,445	314,497,071	311,321,672	318,891,396	292,320,015	209,786,672	213,185,846
Internal revenue.....	289,933,519	322,529,201	321,612,200	344,416,966	380,041,007	415,669,460	512,702,031
Miscellaneous (net)..	51,894,751	64,346,103	58,844,593	60,802,868	62,312,145	72,454,696	53,776,678
Ordinary receipts..	675,511,715	701,372,375	691,778,465	724,111,230	734,673,167	697,910,828	779,664,555
Public-debt receipts .	31,674,292	58,334,725	53,726,749	23,400,850	23,021,222	22,486,955	....
Total receipts, exclusive of postal.	707,186,007	759,707,100	745,505,214	747,512,080	757,694,389	720,397,783	....
Postal Revenues.....	224,128,658	237,879,824	246,744,016	266,619,526	287,934,566	287,248,165	312,057,689
Total receipts, including postal...	931,314,665	997,586,924	992,249,230	1,014,131,606	1,045,628,955	1,007,645,948	1,128,411,639[1]

[1] Included Panama Canal receipts, proceeds of bonds and excess of deposits to retire national bank notes over redemptions.

DISBURSEMENTS AND THEIR OBJECTS

Object	1910	1911	1912	1913	1914	1915	1916
Legislative.........	13,616,496	13,344,838	12,729,950	13,291,813	13,468,828	13,577,399	13,848,007
Executive:							
Executive, proper..	520,208	734,603	923,979	592,015	564,134	3,065,880	395,940
State.............	4,909,558	4,902,175	4,511,475	4,978,380	5,253,912	4,908,607	6,444,594
Treasury.........	87,425,755	87,718,816	88,558,324	85,013,058	83,003,813	94,010,189	73,737,018
War.............	158,172,957	162,357,100	151,048,896	162,607,913	175,759,874	175,188,627	166,853,552
Navy............	123,974,208	120,728,786	136,389,660	134,092,417	140,543,059	142,721,524	155,915,296
Interior..........	201,189,691	201,968,761	197,761,594	217,775,366	216,311,438	215,587,935	201,678,833
Post Office.......	10,117,907	1,812,594	3,461,232	3,196,710	2,236,202	8,531,466	7,270,710
Agriculture........	16,976,022	17,666,228	19,471,567	20,469,028	22,208,141	29,131,112	28,031,540
Commerce	19,221,704	18,503,443	14,466,998	11,263,457	10,958,882	11,499,099	11,403,722
Labor	1,010,454	1,373,589	1,388,562	3,347,380	3,768,904	11,499,099	11,403,722
Justice..........				1,523,068	1,588,573	3,783,612	3,531,144
						1,538,126	1,509,582
Independent bureaus and offices.	2,323,799	2,555,974	2,553,747	2,878,326	3,232,180	5,738,774	7,221,803
District of Columbia	11,650,497	12,335,940	12,959,542	12,841,211	12,756,971	13,220,663	13,633,853
Total Executive.	637,492,760	632,658,009	633,495,576	660,578,329	678,186,083	708,925,614	715,340,118
Judicial..........	8,596,135	8,135,151	8,328,437	8,900,564	8,599,579	8,896,746	9,152,881
Ordinary disbursements.........	659,705,391	654,137,998	654,553,963	682,770,706	700,254,490	731,399,759	724,492,999
Panama Canal disbursements......	33,911,673	37,063,515	35,327,371	41,741,258	34,826,941	29,187,042	17,503,728
Public-debt disbursements,........	33,049,696	35,223,337	28,648,328	24,191,610	8,599,579	8,896,746	24,668,914
Total exclusive of postal paid from postal revenues..	726,666,760	726,424,850	718,529,662	748,703,574	762,042,758	777,840,292	766,665,640
Postal disbursements.	224,128,658	237,660,705	246,744,016	262,108,875	283,558,103	287,248,165	306,228,453
Total disbursements including postal.	950,795,418	964,085,555	965,273,678	1,010,812,449	1,045,600,861	1,065,088,457	1,072,894,093

FINANCIAL STATEMENT OF THE UNITED STATES GOVERNMENT
(Formerly issued as "Statement of the Public Debt")
PUBLIC DEBT—MARCH 31, 1918

Debt Bearing no Interest (Payable on presentation)	Debt on which Interest has Ceased since Maturity (Payable on presentation)
Obligations required to be reissued when redeemed:	Funded Loan of 1891, continued at 2%, called for redemption May 18, 1900....$ 4,000.00
United States Notes................$346,681,016.00	Funded Loan of 1891, matured September 2, 1891.................. 20,850.00
Less gold reserve.................. 152,979,025.63	Loan of 1904, matured February 2, 1904. 13,050.00
Excess of notes over reserve...... 193,701,990.37	Funded Loan of 1907, matured July 2, 1907 .... 494,250.00
Obligations that will be retired on presentation:	Refunding Certificates, matured July 1, 1907 .... 11,330.00
Old demand notes................. 53,012.50	Old Debt matured prior to January 1, 1861, and other items of debt matured subsequently 900,620.26
National-bank notes and Federal reserve bank notes for which money has been deposited for their retirement 36,134,454.50	Certificates of Indebtedness, at 3, 3¼, 3½, and 4 per cent, matured............ 77,000.00
Fractional currency.................. 6,845,598.23	
Total 236,735,055.60	Total 1,521,100.26

MARCH 31, 1918

Balance held by the Treasurer of the United States as per daily Treasury Statement for March 31, 1918......$1,012,094,761.10		Settlement warrants, matured interest obligations, and checks outstanding:	
		Treasury warrants..................$ 17,168,072.17	
Deduct—		Matured interest obligations[1]....... 5,278,004.66	
Net excess of payments over receipts in March reports subsequently received 39,537,751.68		Disbursing officers' checks......... 133,016,110.97	
		Balance 817,094,821.62	
			972,557,009.42
Revised balance..................... 972,557,009.42			

[1] The unpaid interest due December 15, 1917, on First Liberty Loan, is estimated on the basis of receipts of the Treasurer of the United States for principal of bonds. It includes interest on interim certificates not exchanged for bonds and a calculation on account of bonds and interim certificates converted.

RECAPITULATION

Gross Debt	Net Debt
Debt bearing no interest.............$ 236,735,055.60	Gross debt (opposite)..............$10,402,497,619.77
Debt on which interest has ceased... 1,521,100.26	Deduct—
Interest-bearing debt............... 10,164,241,463.91	Balance available to pay maturing obligations 817,094,821.62
Gross debt..................... 10,402,497,619.77	* Net debt................... 9,585,402,798.15

* The amount of $4,668,829,750 has been expended to above date in this and the preceding fiscal year from the proceeds of sales of bonds authorized by law for purchase of the obligations of Foreign Governments. When payments are received from Foreign Governments on account of the principal of their obligations, they must be applied to the reduction of the interest-bearing debt of the United States.

Constitutional treasury recommended by President Polk, 2256.
Successful operation of, discussed, 2406, 2498.
Credit of the United States, 7682.
Currency legislation, plan of, indorsed by President Cleveland, 5985.
Discussed, 5993, 5999, 6072, 6091, 6175.
Discussed by President—
Adams, John, 228, 243, 252, 265, 281, 297.
Adams, J. Q., 869, 923, 952, 977.
Arthur, 4632, 4719, 4763, 4829.
Buchanan, 2967, 2988, 3019, 3052, 3073, 3104, 3179.
Cleveland, 4924, 5092, 5097, 5165, 5371, 5833, 5875, 5964, 5985, 5993, 5999, 6072, 6091, 6155, 6175.
Fillmore, 2619, 2658, 2704.
Garfield, 4600.
Grant, 3983, 3991, 4061, 4101, 4146, 4197, 4238, 4247, 4268, 4301, 4354, 4379.
Harrison, Benj., 5472, 5548, 5628, 5753.
Hayes, 4397, 4413, 4422, 4449, 4509, 4523, 4566.
Jackson, 1014, 1088, 1118, 1159, 1224, 1246, 1326, 1379, 1458.
Jefferson, 315, 332, 343, 348, 354, 361, 366, 375, 382, 396, 417, 443.
Johnson, 3562, 3648, 3769, 3872.
Lincoln, 3248, 3330, 3350, 3384, 3447.
McKinley, 6236, 6242, 6244, 6339, 6437, 6465.
Madison, 455, 461, 472, 480, 504, 513, 523, 535, 549, 563.

Monroe, 584, 613, 629, 646, 675, 756, 761, 780, 785, 822.
Pierce, 2746, 2817, 2870, 2940.
Polk, 2252, 2346, 2401, 2406, 2441, 2496.
Roosevelt, 6645, 6654, 6715, 6787, 7082, 7198.
Taylor, 2555.
Taft, 7681.
Tyler, 1895, 1916, 1934, 1955, 1959, 2052, 2057, 2079, 2117, 2119, 2199.
Van Buren, 1541, 1596, 1686, 1706, 1751, 1757, 1789, 1822.
Washington, 75, 98, 121, 133, 159, 177.
Elasticity of currency needed, 6914, 6989.
Exchequer, plan of, recommended, 2057, 2119.
Gold accumulation for final redemption authorized, 4303.
Gold certificates, recommendations regarding issue of, 4633.
Gold reserve discussed and recommendations regarding, 5935, 5985, 5993, 5999, 6075, 6090.
Gold standard, effects of, 6654.
Greenbacks discussed, 6073.
Retirement of, recommended, 6078, 6175.
Legal-tender act, repeal of portion of, recommended, 4302.
Legal-tender notes, redemption of, recommended, 4303, 4379, 4511, 4567.
Monetary Commission, 7683.
Monetary Reform, 7683.
Paper currency discussed. (See Currency.)
Power of Federal Government over collection and disbursement of, discussed, 1459.

INTEREST-BEARING DEBT. (Payable on or after specified future dates.)

Title of Loan	Authorizing Act	Rate	When Issued	When Redeemable or Payable	Amount Issued	Outstanding March 31, 1918
Consols of 1930	March 14, 1900	2 per cent	1900	Pay. after April 1, 1930	$646,250,150.00	$599,724,050.00
Loan of 1908-1918	June 13, 1898	3 per cent	1898	Red. after Aug. 1, 1908; Pay. Aug. 1, 1918	198,792,660.00	63,945,460.00
Loan of 1925	January 14, 1875	4 per cent	1895-96	Pay. after Feb. 1, 1925	162,315,400.00	118,489,900.00
Panama Canal Loan: Series 1906	June 28, 1902, and Dec. 21, 1905	2 per cent	1906	Red. after Aug. 1, 1916; Pay. Aug. 1, 1936	54,631,980.00	48,954,180.00
Series 1908	June 28, 1902, and Dec. 21, 1905	2 per cent	1908	Red. after Nov. 1, 1918; Pay. Nov. 1, 1938	30,000,000.00	25,947,400.00
Series 1911	Aug. 5, 1909, Feb. 4, 1910, and Mar. 2, 1911	3 per cent	1911	Pay. June 1, 1961	50,000,000.00	50,000,000.00
Conversion Bonds	December 23, 1913	3 per cent	1916-17	Pay. 30 yrs. from date of issue	28,894,500.00	28,894,500.00
One-Yr. Treasury Notes	December 23, 1913	3 per cent	1917-18	Pay. 1 year from date of issue	50,902,000.00	27,362,000.00
Cert's of Indebtedness[1]	September 24, 1917	4 per cent	1917-18	Pay. on or before Apr. 22, May 9 and June 25, 1918	4,420,180,500.00	2,208,708,000.00
Cert's of Indebtedness	September 24, 1917	4½ per cent	1918	Red. on or before May 28 and June 18, 1918	1,042,792,500.00	1,042,792,500.00
First Liberty Loan of 1917[2]	April 24, 1917	3½ per cent	1917	Red. on or after June 15, 1932; Pay. June 15, 1947	1,986,625,405.57	1,986,625,405.57
Second Liberty Loan of 1917[3]	September 24, 1917	4 per cent	1917	Red. on or after Nov. 15, 1927; Pay. Nov. 15, 1942	3,807,736,497.19	3,807,736,497.19
Postal Savings Bonds (1st to 13th series)	June 25, 1910	2½ per cent	1911-17	Red. after 1 yr. from date of issue; Pay. 20 yrs. from date of issue	10,758,560.00	10,758,560.00
Postal Savings Bonds (14th series)	June 25, 1910	2½ per cent	1918	Red. after Jan. 1, 1919; Pay. Jan. 1, 1938	302,140.00	302,140.00
War Savings and Thrift Stamps[4]	September 24, 1917	4 per cent	1917-18	Pay. Jan. 1, 1923	5 144,725,891.80	144,000,871.15
Aggregate of Interest - bearing Debt					5 12,634,908,184.56	10,164,241,463.91

1 The interest rate and maturity are given in respect of the certificates outstanding March 31.
2 These amounts represent receipts of the Treasurer of the United States on account of principal of the First Liberty Loan Bonds to March 31, and include the principal of bonds which have been converted under the authority of section 11 of the act of September 24, 1917, into 4% bonds.
3 These amounts represent receipts of the Treasurer of the United States on account of principal of the Second Liberty Loan Bonds to March 31.
4 The average issue price of War Savings Stamps for the year 1918 with interest, at 4 per cent per annum compounded quarterly for the average period to maturity will amount to $5 on January 1, 1923. Thrift Stamps do not bear interest.
5 This amount represents receipts of the Treasurer of the United States on account of proceeds of sales of War Savings Certificate Stamps and U. S. Thrift Stamps.

Relations with **Mexico, China,** and other gold standard countries, 6825.

Revenue laws, need for readjustment, 6988.

Seigniorage discussed, 5875.

Sherman Act—
Discussed, 5548, 5628.
Repeal of purchasing clause of, discussed, 5875, 6073, 6074.
Recommended, 5833.

Silver certificates—
Discussed, 5474.
Repeal of act for issuance of, recommended, 4633, 4720.
Suspension of issuance of, recommended, 4830.

Silver-purchase clause of act of 1890, repeal of, discussed, 5875, 6073, 6074.
Recommended, 5833.

Sinking-fund law, repeal of, recommended, 5754.

Specie payments discussed. (See Specie Payments.)

Subtreasury system discussed. (See Subtreasury System.)

Trade dollars discussed, 4767, 4831.

Treasury notes. (See Treasury Notes.)

Finances, Collection of.—The expense of collecting the customs and internal revenues of the United States includes all sums paid for salaries of clerks, inspectors, revenue agents, surveyors of distilleries, gaugers, storekeepers, paper for printing internal revenue stamps, and detecting and punishing violations of revenue laws. To this must also be added traveling expenses of special agents, weighing, measuring and appraising imported goods, as well as rents for buildings not owned by the government. Maintenance of custom houses and other buildings owned by the government is paid out of specific appropriations for those purposes.

The expense of collecting the internal revenue has not exceeded 2 per cent since 1898, while in 1871 collection expenses were more than 5 per cent. The customs revenue costs something more than 3 per cent to collect, and varies, of course, with the tariff. With the lowering tariff rates and the increased imports the cost of collection advances. In 1915 it cost 4.42 per cent to collect the customs.

Finances, Superintendent of.—On Feb. 7, 1781, the Continental Congress passed an act establishing the office of Superintendent of Finance. Robert Morris was appointed to the position. Previous to this the Committee of Claims and the Treasury Office of Accounts were combined in what was called the Treasury Board, consisting of five members of Congress. This board expired with the appointment of Morris. He was authorized to examine into the state of the country's finances, report plans for improvement, direct the execution of orders respecting revenue and expenditure, and control the public accounts. Morris resigned in 1784 and the finances of the Government were placed under a board of three commissioners, where they continued until 1789, at which time, the first Congress established the present Treasury Department (q. v.).

The following table shows the amount of customs and internal revenue receipts for recent years, and the expenses of collecting the same:

INTERNAL REVENUE.

Year ended June 30—	Revenue.	Expenses of Collecting.	Per Cent.
	Dollars.	*Dollars.*	
1892....	153,971,072.57	3,879,082.31	2.52
1893....	161,027,623.93	4,144,927.02	2.57
1894....	147,111,232.81	3,749,029.22	2.55
1895....	143,421,672.02	3,754,935.45	2.62
1896....	146,762,864.74	3,846,887.55	2.62
1897....	146,688,574.29	3,606,798.85	2.46
1898....	170,900,641.49	3,705,256.95	2.17
1899....	273,437,161.51	4,350,543.05	1.59
1900....	295,327,926.76	4,446,318.98	1.51
1901....	307,180,663.77	4,404,986.68	1.43
1902....	271,880,122.10	4,360,144.97	1.60
1903....	230,810,124.17	4,496,479.28	1.95
1904....	232,904,119.45	4,507,867.83	1.94
1905....	234,095,740.85	4,338,184.70	1.85
1906....	249,150,212.91	4,391,660.65	1.76
1907....	269,666,772.85	4,641,169.95	1.72
1908....	251,711,126.70	4,650,049.89	1.85
1909....	246,212,643.59	4,547,715.05	1.85
1910....	289,933,519.45	5,008,191.77	1.73
1911....	322,529,200.79	5,027,871.39	1.55
1912....	321,612,199.66	5,059,286.49	1.57
1913....	344,416,965.65	5,166,301.36	1.50
1914....	380,041,007.30	5,542,353.55	1.46
1915....	415,669,646.00	6,236,046.55	1.50
1916....	512,723,287.77	6,259,047.67	1.22

CUSTOMS REVENUE.

1892....	177,452,964.15	6,646,276.05	3.74
1893....	203,355,016.73	6,756,790.98	3.32
1894....	131,818,530.62	6,791,872.86	5.15
1895....	152,158,617.45	6,736,690.92	4.43
1896....	160,021,751.67	7,237,796.40	4.52
1897....	176,554,126.65	7,075,372.05	4.01
1898....	149,575,062.35	7,152,276.58	4.78
1899....	206,128,481.75	7,361,562.83	3.57
1900....	233,164,871.16	7,467,692.48	3.20
1901....	238,585,455.99	7,713,418.82	3.23
1902....	254,444,708.19	7,967,472.39	3.13
1903....	284,479,581.81	8,468,710.19	2.98
1904....	261,274,564.81	8,665,636.37	3.32
1905....	261,798,856.91	9,115,499.44	3.48
1906....	300,251,877.77	8,997,669.41	3.00
1907....	332,233,362.70	9,436,752.68	2.55
1908....	286,113,130.29	9,580,626.25	3.35
1909....	300,711,933.95	10,261,073.33	3.41
1910....	333,683,445.03	10,665,770.12	3.20
1911....	314,497,071.24	11,015,254.24	3.50
1912....	311,321,672.22	10,804,979.15	3.47
1913....	318,891,395.86	10,285,613.95	3.23
1914....	292,320,014.51	9,804,771.72	3.35
1915....	209,786,672.21	9,268,403.58	4.42
1916....	213,185,845.63	9,074,471.95	4.26

Fine Arts Commission.— The Fine Arts Commission was established in 1910 by act of Congress in order to give advice and to assist in the selection and location of monuments erected under the supervision of the Government; and also to help in the choice of artists and of models in that connection. The Commission, which consists of seven members appointed by the President for a term of four years, must approve all plans for public buildings erected in Washington, and in a general way also gives advice to the Government on all matters of art in the country.

Fine Arts, International Exhibition of, to be held at Munich, Bavaria, 5193.

Fines:
Imposed upon Gen. Jackson, remission of, recommended, 2062.
Remitted by Executive, inquired into, 637.

Fingal, The, engagement with the *Weehawken* referred to, 3392.

Finland. (See Russia.)

Fire Engines referred to, 649.

First Assistant Postmaster-General. (See Assistant Postmasters-General.)

"First Liberty Congress." (See Imperialism.)

First United States Volunteer Regiment of Cavalry, mentioned, 6637.

Fiscal Bank of United States.—After the repeal of the subtreasury act in 1841, the Whig majority in Congress passed an act chartering the Fiscal Bank of the United States. This was vetoed by President Tyler. A bill was then passed chartering the Fiscal Corporation of the United States, which it was thought would meet his approval, but this also was vetoed.

Fiscal Bank of United States, act to incorporate subscribers to, vetoed, 1916.

Fiscal Corporation of United States, bill to incorporate, vetoed, 1921.

Fiscal Policy. (See Finances.)

Fiscal Year, change in termination of, 2117.
Recommended, 1611.

Fish Commission. (See Commerce and Labor, Department of.)

Fish Lake Forest Reserve (Utah), proclaimed, 6964.

Fisheries.—The right to catch fish on the high seas is open to all; but by international law, as the sea for a marine league is under the jurisdiction of the sovereign of the adjoining land, no one can fish in such waters without express permission given by law or treaty. After the Revolution the people of Canada disputed the right of citizens of the United States to fish off the banks of Labrador, Newfoundland, and the Gulf of St. Lawrence. By the treaty with Great Britain in 1783 citizens of the United States were given the right to take, cure, and dry fish on the coasts, bays, and creeks of any unsettled British possessions. Permission was also given them to take fish without curing or drying them, on the coasts of Newfoundland. On the coasts, bays, and creeks of Nova Scotia, Magdalen Islands, and Labrador, after they should become settled, the right to take and cure fish was given only with the consent of the inhabitants or proprietors of the ground. American fishermen were not slow to take advantage of the opportunities provided by this treaty, and Canadian resentment became more pronounced. The War of 1812 dissolved this treaty, and in the treaty of Ghent (q. v.) in 1814, the question of fishery rights was not mentioned, thus virtually allowing the old rights to stand.

In 1818 a convention of the United States and England decided that the citizens of the former should have the perpetual right to fish on the western and northern coasts of Newfoundland within certain limits, on the shores of the Magdalen Islands, and on those of Labrador from Mount Joly eastward and northward. The right of drying and curing fish on the western and southwestern coasts of Newfoundland and the coast of Labrador was granted so long as they remained unsettled, but afterwards only with the consent of the proprietors. This agreement, however, did not improve the situation on account of the various interpretations given to the "Three-mile limit." Between 1854 and 1866 a reciprocity treaty, virtually between Canada and the United States, permitted the citizens of the latter to fish in all the British possessions except Newfoundland, where the right was denied. From 1866 to 1871 the conditions of the treaty of 1818 prevailed.

By the treaty of Washington in 1871 Canadian fishermen were permitted to take any fish except shell-fish, shad, and salmon in the waters of the United States as far south as lat. 39°. United States fishermen to have the same privilege in Canadian waters. The Canadians, however, insisted that the concessions to United States fishermen were far more valuable than those awarded themselves. (See Fortune Bay Outrages.) As a result of this contention a joint commission was appointed to determine the excess of advantages enjoyed by the United States and the amount to be paid therefor. (See Halifax Commission.)

June 30, 1885, the provisions of the treaty of Washington relating to fisheries ceased to be operative, after due notice by the United States. This abrogation revived the provisions of the convention of London, which were not satisfactory to either party. In May, 1886, the *David J. Adams*, a United States fishing schooner, was seized on the charge of having purchased bait on forbidden coasts. Several other seizures were made, causing great excitement in the United States and Canada. March 3, 1887, Congress pased a retaliation act, providing that whenever the president shall be satisfied that our fishing vessels are illegally, unjustly, or vexatiously restricted or harassed in the exercise of their business or denied the privileges accorded to the vessels of the most favored nation in respect to touching or trading by the authorities of the British North American dominions he may by proclamation close our ports and waters against the vessels and products of all or any part of said British dominions. President Cleveland, instead of exercising this power, moved for a commission to amicably adjust the points of dispute under the convention of London. Thomas F. Bayard, William L. Putman, and James B. Angell were selected to represent the United States, and Joseph Chamberlain, Sir Lionel Sackville-West, and Sir Charles Tupper represented Great Britain. Feb. 15, 1888, a treaty was signed and immediately laid before the two Governments for ratification. Great Britain abandoned her claim that the three-mile limit extended from headland to headland, and agreed that, except in cases specially mentioned of bays more than ten miles wide, the marine league should be measured outward from a line drawn across them, and also agreed that the United States fishing vessels should have the same rights in Canadian ports as Canadian vessels, except that the purchase of bait was forbidden. The treaty also contained a reciprocity clause. It was rejected by the Senate Aug. 21, 1888. Since that period good relations have been maintained by virtue of a *modus vivendi* terminable at will. In 1890

Canada raised this *modus vivendi* to the status of a law of the Dominion.

At a meeting of conferees of the two powers held at Washington in May, 1898, it was agreed to submit the question of the fisheries, among others, to a joint high commission.

This commission assembled at Quebec in August, 1898, and adjourned to Washington in the winter following, but arrived at no agreement thereon.

The differences between the United States and Great Britain regarding the interpretation of the Treaty of 1818 were submitted to The Hague Tribunal in September, 1910. The issues may be presented in the form of the following seven questions:

First: Must any reasonable regulations made by Great Britain, Canada, and Newfoundland, in the form of municipal laws, ordinances, or rules governing the time or implements for fishing be subject to the consent of the United States? Second: Have inhabitants of the United States a right to employ in crews fishing on treaty coasts, persons not inhabitants of the United States? Third: Can Americans, exercising their right to take, dry, and cure fish on treaty coasts, be subjected to requirements of custom-house entry or report, or payment of dues, or any similar conditions, without the consent of the United States? Fourth: Can the treaty rights to enter certain bays or harbors for shelter, repairs, wood, and water be made conditional upon the payment to customs officials of light, harbor, or other dues, or similar conditions? Fifth: From where must be measured the three marine miles within which Americans may not fish? Sixth: Does the treaty give Americans rights to fish in the bays, harbors, and creeks of Newfoundland as in Labrador? Seventh: Are American fishermen operating on treaty coasts to have the commercial privileges accorded generally to American trading vessels?

The Hague Tribunal decided the first and fifth questions in favor of Great Britain and the remainder in favor of the United States. The following judges heard the case: Lammasch, of Vienna (president); Judge Gray, of Delaware; Chief Justice Fitzpatrick, of Canada; Dr. Drago of Argentina; and Dr. Savarin-Lohman, of Holland.

With regard to the first question it was decided that Great Britain's right to regulate her fisheries without the consent of the United States is inherent in her sovereignty, but that she must not violate the treaty of 1818 or give local fishermen an advantage over Americans. The award further provided that existing regulations should be examined as to their justice and propriety by a committee composed of two experts, one from each country, together with Dr. Paulus Hock, fisheries adviser to Holland; that if they report unanimously, The Hague Tribunal shall incorporate such findings in its award; and that if they fail of unanimity the local regulations will be examined by the Tribunal itself. The award decreed that future Anglo-American disputes regarding fisheries shall be considered by the committee headed by Dr. Hoek.

The successful claim of Great Britain regarding the fifth point was that the three marine miles within which the United States had agreed not to take fish should be measured from an imaginary line drawn across the mouth of a bay, no matter how wide, from headland to headland; the United States, on the other hand, contended that the line should follow the sinuosities of the coast, thus permitting Americans to fish in bays, providing they maintain three marine miles of water between themselves and the nearest coast.

The decision on other points made it unnecessary for American fishermen to report to customs-houses or to pay light, harbor, or other dues; permits the employment of Newfoundlanders on American fishing vessels, and gives American fishing vessels the right to purchase supplies and to enjoy other commercial privileges.

The decision has been received with mixed satisfaction by the herring fishery interests of both countries. One of the remarkable incidents of the case was that the Canadian Chief Justice, Fitzpatrick, voted against Great Britain on the five points ceded to the United States, and Judge Gray, of Delaware, voted against the United States on the two points ceded to England. Senator Elihu Root argued the cause of the United States. Only one judge, Dr. Drago, upheld the American contention that the three-mile barrier should follow the sinuosities of the coast.

A report of the Census Bureau for 1908 gives the following figures for the fisheries industry in the United States:

Sections	Vessels	Employees	Value Products
South Atlantic..	534	17,961	$ 4,034,000
Gulf States	915	15,387	4,824,000
Middle Atlantic..	3,165	54,163	16,302,000
New England...	1,623	22,157	15,139,630
Great Lakes....	319	8,533	3,767,000
Rivers, etc.....	39	11,825	3,125,000
Pacific Coast*...	1,038	28,936	9,300,672
Alaska*	541	23,994	26,156,559
Totals	8,174	233,555	$82,648,861

* Figures for 1915.

The estimated value of the fisheries products of some of the world's greatest fish producing nations is as follows:

United States (1908)	$82,648,861
Japan (1911)	63,147,550
Russia (1911)	50,034,825
England (1916)	36,686,011
Canada (1915)	35,860,708
China, Korea, etc.	34,000,000
France (1913)	33,034,497

The total value of the fisheries product of the world was estimated in 1912 at slightly under $500,000,000.

Fisheries (see also Bering Sea Fisheries; Fortune Bay Outrages; Geneva Tribunal; Halifax Commission; Halifax, Nova Scotia):

Capture and detention of American fishermen, 853, 855, 4068.

Commission on subject of, recommended, 4757, 4917, 5114.

Commission to be organized, 2867, 4075.

Correspondence regarding, with—
France, 3233.
Great Britain, 3233, 5121, 5193.

Discussed by President—
Adams, John, 241.
Jefferson, 334.
Washington, 77.

Dispute between Great Britain and United States, Hague award in, 7409, 7492.

Federal control of interstate recommended, 7229.

International, 7229.

Interstate, 7230.

Joint commission between United States and Great Britain relating to preservation of, 6183.

Joint high commission between United States and Great Britain on subject of, to sit at Washington, 4075.

Outrages committed on American fishermen, 4542, 4558.

Papers for protection of vessels engaged in, referred to, 1774.

Preservation of, Anglo-American joint agreement for, 7495.

Questions growing out of, with Great Britain (see also Bering Sea Fisheries; Fortune Bay Outrages; Geneva Tribunal; Halifax Commission; Halifax, Nova Scotia)—

Discussed by President—
Cleveland, 4916, 5084, 5114, 5188, 5205, 5213, 5364, 5384.
Fillmore, 2675, 2694, 2699, 2724, 2726.
Grant, 4012, 4056, 4068, 4075, 4097, 4141.
Harrison, Benj., 5469.
Johnson, 3581, 3888.
Pierce, 2741, 2761, 2867.
Tyler, 2112.

Regulations of Great Britain, France, and Germany respecting, referred to, 1127.

Salmon, decrease in, 7230.

Treaty with Great Britain regarding, 2775, 2780, 2810, 2944, 4164, 4867, 5188. (See also Geneva Tribunal.)
Acts passed to give effect to, passage of, proclaimed, 4179.
Meetings of commissioners referred to, 5196.
Rejection of, discussed, 5205, 5364.
Termination of, discussed, 4757, 4916.
Proclaimed, 4867.

Unfriendly treatment of American fishermen by Canadians, 4012, 4056, 5114.

Vessels sent to protect American fishermen, 2694.

Fisheries, Bureau of.—(Department of Commerce.) The work of the Bureau of Fisheries comprises (1) the propagation of useful food fishes, including lobsters, oysters and other shellfish, and their distribution to suitable waters; (2) the inquiry into the causes of decrease of food fishes in the lakes, rivers and coast waters of the United States, the study of the waters of the coast and interior in the interest of fish-culture, and the investigation of the fishing grounds of the Atlantic, Gulf and Pacific coasts, with the view of determining their food resources and the development of the commercial fisheries; (3) the collection and compilation of the statistics of the fisheries and the study of their methods and relations. The bureau also has jurisdiction over the fur-seal herds and the salmon fisheries of Alaska.

An idea of the extent of the fishing industry of the country may be gained from the table at the bottom of this page compiled by the Department of Commerce from reports of 1908.

For the fiscal year ending June 30, 1916, the Bureau distributed 425,700,794 eggs; 4,329,300,337 fry; and 92,261,435 fingerlings, yearlings and adults—a total of almost 5,000,000,000.

Fisheries, Bureau of, should include Alaska fur seal service, 7230.

Fisheries Exhibition, International, at London, discussed, 4688.

Fishermen, American:
Capture and detention of, 853, 855, 4068.
Outrages committed on, 4542, 4558.
Unfriendly treatment of, by Canadians, 4012, 4056, 5114.
Vessels sent to protect, 2694.

Fishers Hill (Va.), Battle of.—Early's retreat from the Opequan after the battle of Sept. 19, 1864, did not stop at Winchester, but continued to Fishers Hill, south of Winchester and about 12 miles from the scene of the battle of Opequan Creek. Here Early rallied his forces. To drive him from this position, Sheridan dispatched Torbert with 2 divisions of cavalry by a circuitous route to the Confederate rear, and on the evening of Sept. 22 the Sixth and Nineteenth Corps engaged Early in front, while Torbert's forces fell upon the rear. The Confederates retreated and Sheridan followed them through Harrisonburg, Staunton, and the gaps in the Blue Ridge Mountains. Sheridan then devastated the valley so as to render it untenable for Confederate troops. At Fishers Hill he captured 1,100 prisoners and 16 guns.

Sections	Vessels Employed		Persons Employed	Capital Invested	Value of Products
	No.	Tons			
South Atlantic States....................	534	5,029	17,961	$2,324,000	$4,034,000
Gulf States.............................	915	13,665	15,387	3,901,000	4,824,000
Middle Atlantic States..................	3,165	45,208	54,163	11,105,000	16,302,000
New England States.....................	1,623	44,219	22,157	11,970,000	15,139,630
Great Lakes............................	319	4,499	8,533	4,814,000	3,767,000
Mississippi River and Tributaries........	39	273	11,825	1,440,000	3,125,000
Pacific Coast States.....................	294	15,618	13,855	6,468,000	6,839,000
Alaska Territory (1912).................	504	98,978	24,263	38,263,457	18,877,480
Total........................	7,393	227,489	168,144	$80,285,457	$72,908,110

Pacific Fisherman's (January, 1913, issue) estimate of Pacific coast (including Alaska) canned salmon pack in 1912: Chinooks and king, 346,901 cases; sockeye and Alaska red, 2,099,673 cases; cohoes, silversides, 456,508 cases; pinks and chums, 2,060,280 cases; steelheads, 7,198 cases. Total, 4,960,377 cases of 48 pounds.

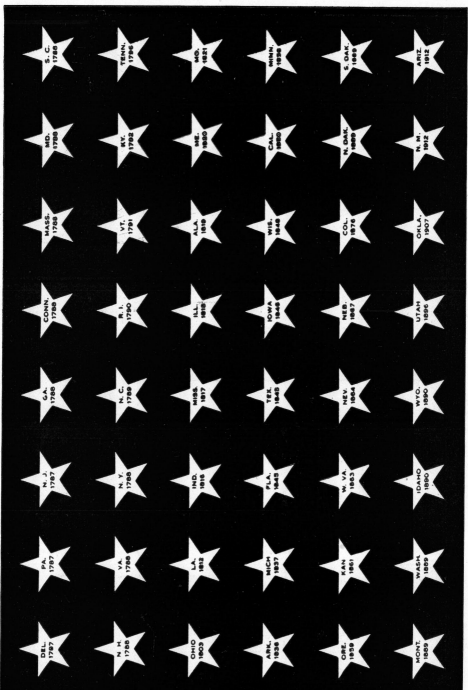

FIELD OF THE FLAG

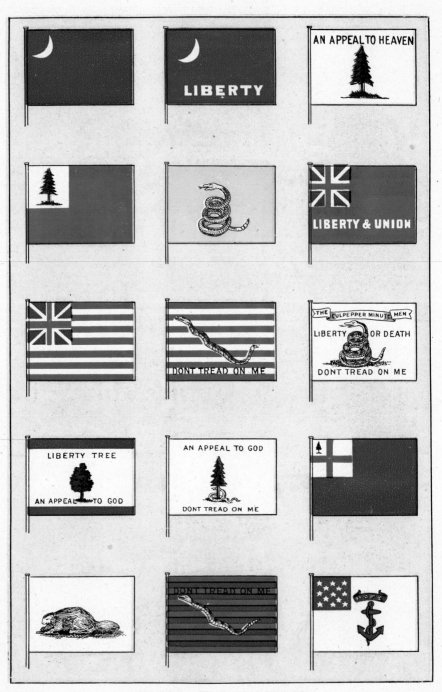

EARLY AMERICAN FLAGS

Fishery Commissions. (See Fisheries and Bering Sea Fisheries.)

Fish Packers licensed, 8497.

Five-cent Piece.—In 1792 Congress authorized the coinage of a silver half dime of 20.8 grains in weight. This was the first coin struck by the United States Mint. In 1853 the weight was reduced to 19.2 grains. There were no issues of this coin in 1798, 1799, 1804, and from 1806 to 1828. In 1866 the nickel 5-cent piece was authorized and the legal-tender value reduced from $5 to 30 cents. Coinage of the silver half dime was discontinued in 1873.

Five Civilized Tribes. (See Indian Tribes.)

Five Forks (Va.), Battle of.—March 27, 1865, Gen. Sheridan, with 10,000 cavalry, returned with his raid through the Shenandoah Valley and rejoined the Army of the Potomac before Richmond. On the 29th Grant began a movement to turn the Confederate right or destroy their line of retreat south. Sheridan, with the Fifth Corps, under Gen. Warren, and about 9,000 cavalry, crossed Hatchers Run and proceeded by way of the Boydton plank road toward Dinwiddie Court-House. Warren found the Confederates in force on the White Oak road. Sheridan, passing Dinwiddie, turned north. Lee had sent a stronger force, chiefly the divisions of Johnson and Pickett, to meet the threatened attempt on the roads to his rear. March 31 this column met and defeated Warren and then attacked Sheridan at Five Forks and drove him back toward Dinwiddie. The next morning, April 1, Sheridan advanced with his cavalry and the Fifth Corps, about 12,000 strong. By 2 P. M. the Confederates had retired into their main works. Ayres, on the left of the Fifth Corps, made a charge, carrying all before him, and taking 1,000 prisoners; Griffin captured the works in his front, taking 1,500 prisoners; Crawford seized the Ford road in the Confederate rear; Merritt's cavalry made a charge, and the day was won, but not without a desperate resistance. Lee's army was virtually overwhelmed. For 6 miles it fell back along the White Oak road. More than 5,000 prisoners were taken, with 6 guns and 13 colors. Sheridan's loss was about 1,000, of whom 634 were of Warren's Corps.

Five-Forties.—Bonds redeemable by the Government after five years, but payable in full at the end of forty years.

Five-Twenties.—Bonds redeemable by the Government after five years, but payable in full at the end of twenty years.

Flag.—A banner or ensign, sometimes called colors. There are records of ensigns in the earliest traces of ancient civilization—for instance, among the Greeks, Persians, Romans. The Roman eagle, especially in time of war, was particularly able to command attention and devotion. Through the medieval ages, again, ensigns were much in evidence, but were largely the personal insignia of individual leaders. The flag in its modern significance of typifying the ambitions and ideals of an entire nation becomes evident only with the emergence of the modern nation, around the thirteenth century.

Among the early American colonies, the British ensign was naturally much in evidence. In many cases, however, the insignia or mottoes of the several colonies were added. There is even a tradition that an early colonial leader cut out with his sword the St. George's cross from the flag because the cross was a symbol of Romanism. Around the end of the seventeenth century, there was in general use a flag for all of New England which consisted of a white field with the St. George's cross and the letters J. R. (Jacobus Rex).

When the colonies began their war of independence from Great Britain, each colony naturally came into the field with its own devices, the number of which was almost legion. Connecticut had on its flag the arms of the colony, with the motto, "Qui transtulit sustinet" (He who brought us across will sustain us). The colony of New Amsterdam, soon to be known as New York, used the arms which constitute, practically untouched, the present arms of New York City, the beaver denoting both industry and the wealth of the fur trade. This flag was used in the early years of the Revolution by ships plying from New York harbor. Soon after the battle of Bunker Hill, Putnam displayed a flag with a red ground—on one side the Connecticut motto described above and on the other the words, "An Appeal to Heaven." The latter phrase was a favorite Massachusetts motto. Most of the early vessels sailing under the control of General Washington used a pine tree, another favorite device among the colonists, but many private men-of-war used also the device of a mailed hand grasping a bundle of thirteen arrows. A flag in use among the Southern colonists was blue with a white crescent. Another favorite device among the colonists was a rattlesnake, usually with thirteen rattles, and often with the words, "Don't Tread on Me."

On January 2, 1776, Washington displayed a flag which had been designed by a committee, which consisted of thirteen stripes of red and white, with the British Union Jack where the stars now are, thus showing that the colonists at that time still had not lost all feeling of allegiance toward Great Britain.

An interesting, but hardly verifiable legend is connected with the design of the first American flag. The story runs that in June, 1776, a committee of Congress, consisting of George Washington, Robert Morris, and Colonel George Ross, waited upon the widow of Colonel Ross's nephew in her upholstery shop in Philadelphia, and asked for assistance concerning the design of the new flag to be adopted by the Congress. The committee had already planned a flag consisting of thirteen stars and thirteen stripes, but the stars were six-pointed. When Betsy Ross advised, however, five-pointed stars, and showed how they could be cut with but one clip of her scissors, the committee adopted her suggestion. It is said that it was Washington who suggested that the stars be arranged in a circle, in order to show that all the states were equal, and that no one of them was entitled to take precedence over any other. The house in which this story is centered is located at 239 Arch Street, Philadelphia, and is called the Betsy Ross House.

June 14, 1777, the flag of the United States had its statutory beginning in the following resolution: "Resolved, that the flag of the United States be thirteen stripes, alternate red and white; that the union be thirteen stars, white in a blue field, representing a new constellation." The banner of the United States is commonly supposed to have been based upon the Washington coat-of-arms. Paul Jones claimed to have been the first to use the new flag at sea, and on land it was first used over Fort Stanwix on August 6, 1777, and in battle first in the battle of Brandywine, September 11, 1777.

The first victory of any American flag,

however, had been in 1776, when Commander Manley, of the *Hancock*, defeated a British armed vessel off Boston harbor. On a contemporary picture of the battle, Manley's flag is shown as the pine-tree.

The first occasion when an American flag floated over foreign soil was on March 3, 1776, when Commander Hopkins, of the Congress fleet, landed several hundred men on the Bahamas. The flags then used were described as the thirteen stripes with the British Union and also the rattlesnake flag with its motto.

Vermont was admitted to the Union in 1791 and Kentucky in 1792, but the flag was not altered until 1794, when by Congressional resolution two more stars and two more stripes were added. In spite of the admission of new states from time to time, the flag remained as indicated above until April 4, 1818, when by act of Congress it was reestablished with thirteen stripes, representing the thirteen original states, and twenty stars, one star for each new state admitted, to be added to the flag on the 4th of July succeeding such admission.

From what evidence can be obtained, it seems that the stars in the field of the flag were placed in rows for the first time in 1818, previous flags having the stars arranged in a circle or in the shape of a large star.

There are several stories concerning the christening of the flag "Old Glory." One is to the effect that the christener was a famous Salem skipper, Captain Stephen Driver, who doffed his hat and hailed as "Old Glory" a flag (which had been presented him by friends) as it was raised aloft on his ship when he was about to depart on a long cruise. Another story is to the effect that the captain (whose Christian name was William) at the outbreak of the Civil War was living in lonely retirement in Nashville. Fearing that his beloved flag would be taken from him, he sewed it dexterously into his bed quilt; and when the city was taken by the Union forces in 1862, he carried his saved treasure to the Capitol Building, and as it was spread out to the breeze, for the first time christened it "Old Glory."

It seems that after the establishment of the Union the flag was not officially carried into battle until the Mexican War. At that time, it had 29 stars. In the Civil War, the flag had 35 stars; in the war against Spain, it had 45 stars; and in the war against Germany, it had 48.

When the Southern states seceded from the Union, they had the same confusion about flags as the early American colonists had had. Finally, late in 1861, a flag was adopted with a broad white horizontal bar between two broad red horizontal bars, with a blue union in which there were seven stars in a circle, the number being later changed to thirteen. But the Confederate flag usually used in battle was a blue St. Andrew's cross with a white border and thirteen white stars. In 1863, the battle flag was placed on a white field, but this flag was so often mistaken for a flag of truce that in 1865 a red bar was placed across the white field.

Military, but not necessarily civil regulations, demand the observance of the following ceremonies concerning the flag:

It should not be hoisted before sunrise nor allowed to remain up after sunset.

At "retreat," sunset, civilian spectators should stand at "attention" and uncover during the playing of the "Star Spangled Banner." Military spectators are required by regulation to stand at "attention" and give the military salute.

When the National colors are passing on parade, or in review, the spectator should, if walking, halt, and if sitting, arise and stand at attention and uncover.

When the flag is flown at half staff as a sign of mourning it should be hoisted to full staff at the conclusion of the funeral.

In placing the flag at half staff, it should first be hoisted to the top of the staff and then lowered to position, and preliminary to lowering from half staff, it should be first raised to the top.

On Memorial Day, May 30, the flag should fly at half staff from sunrise to noon and full staff from noon to sunset.

Government ships entering foreign ports are expected to display the flags of these countries, together with a salute of guns.

When the flag is hung reversed, or with the union down, distress is indicated. A salute of the flag usually consists of three "dips," a dip consisting of lowering the flag slightly from the top of the mast and then raising it again.

The flags in most common use in the United States are reproduced on the adjoining plate.

The President's flag is broken at the main of any vessel of the United States which the President is visiting, at the moment that he reaches the deck. The flag is kept flying as long as he is on board. The President usually directs that his flag be displayed from the staff in the bow of his barge. When the President passes in a boat flying his flag, vessels of the United States Navy parade the full guard, four ruffles are beaten on the drum, four flourishes are blown on the bugle, the National Anthem is played by the band and the officers and men salute. All saluting ships, when passing a ship flying the President's flag, fire a national salute, as do all naval batteries when the President's flag goes past.

The Union Jack is flown from the jackstaff (the staff at the bow) of vessels at anchor, from morning to evening colors. When hoisted at the fore mast, it is a signal for a pilot. When hoisted at the mizzen mast or at a yard arm, it indicates that a general court martial or a court of inquiry is in session. The jack is carried on a staff of the bow of a boat of the navy bearing on an official visit a diplomatic officer of the United States of or above the rank of chargé d'affaires or the naval governor of Guam, Tutuila or the Virgin Islands, within the limit of his government. Yachts may fly the Union Jack from 8 a. m. to sunset, while at anchor and when no wash clothes are triced up.

The United States Army flags used to designate its several branches are of two kinds—colors and standards. The colors are used by unmounted troops and the standards by mounted forces. The chief points of difference between them are the smaller size of the standards and the absence of cords and tassels on the standards.

In garrison, the standards or colors are kept in the offices or quarters of the colonel. They are escorted thereto and therefrom by the color guard. In camp, the colors or standards are displayed before the colonel's tent, when not in use, with the national color or ensign on the right.

The names and dates of battles in which regiments or battalions have participated are engraved on silver bands, which are then placed on the pikes of the colors or the lance of the standard. The War Department decides upon the battles which are important enough to be thus utilized.

The flag of the Secretary of the Interior has a brown bison upon a green field, with a yellow star in each corner.

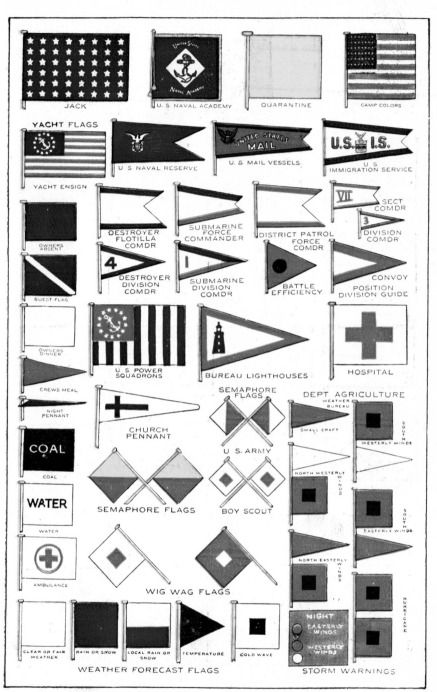

FLAGS IN COMMON USE IN THE UNITED STATES

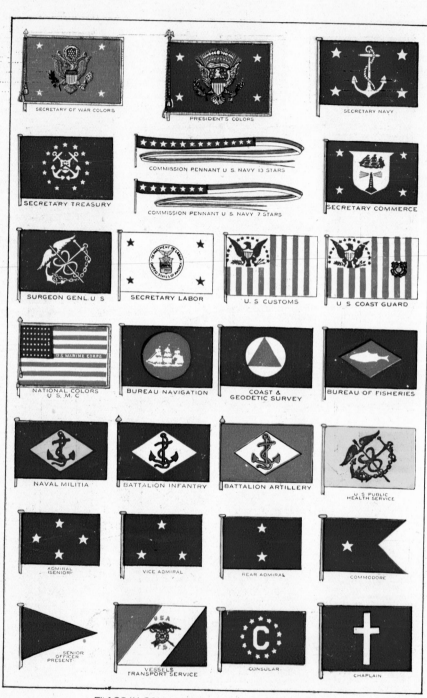

FLAGS IN COMMON USE IN THE UNITED STATES

The Assistant Secretary of War's flag is similar in design to that of the Secretary of War, but is on a white field instead of on a red and the four corner stars are red instead of white.

The flag of the assistant secretary of the navy is the same as that of the secretary, with the colors reversed.

The flags of the assistant secretaries of commerce and treasury are the same as those of their chiefs, with the color scheme reversed.

When generals, lieutenant generals, major generals or brigadier generals are in automobiles or upon boats, a red flag is flown with four, three, two or one white stars, as the case may be. (See table of insignia under Army.)

The Chief of Staff's colors have a field of a red and a white triangle, the red having its base on the staff. In the centre is the spread eagle of the national coat-of-arms imposed upon a white star. There is a white star at the right angle of the red triangle and a red star in the corresponding position in the white.

As shown in the adjoining plate, the flags of the admiral, vice admiral and rear admiral have a blue field, but when these are officers of a junior grade, they fly flags with the white stars upon a red field in the presence of senior officers of their grades. A commodore of naval militia flies a flag of the same shape as that of the commodore of the navy, but the upper half only is of blue, the lower being yellow and the white star being placed upon the blue field.

The corps and regimental colors of the Marine Corps have the Marine Corps device upon a blue field, with red scrolls above and below.

The Coast Artillery Corps colors are similar in design and color to those of the Secretary of War, except that there are no large stars in the corner and that under the eagle are the crossed cannon device and a yellow scroll containing in red the words "U. S. Coast Artillery Corps."

The device of the Engineers' Corps is a castellated fort. On the Engineers' colors, this device is placed over a white lettered scroll, the field of the flag being red. Above the fort and the scroll is the spread eagle device to be found on the flag of the Secretary of War.

The field of the colors of the United States Cadet Corps is gray. Instead of the national coat of arms there is an escutcheon bearing the national colors on which there is a cap of Mars and which is surmounted by an eagle.

The field artillery standard is of similar design, except that the field is of red and the scroll is of yellow.

The mounted engineers' standard is similar to that of the field artillery, except that the scroll is of white and that there is a white castellated fort above it.

The standard of the Signal Corps also has the spread eagle device upon a red field, the scroll being white and placed under the crossed semaphore flag device.

The cavalry standard has a field of yellow, upon which is placed the same device as on the flag of the Secretary of War. Under this device is a red scroll containing the words "U. S. Cavalry."

Each troop of cavalry carries a guidon with the upper half red and the lower, white. The white numeral upon the upper half indicates the regiment and the red letter upon the lower half, the troop. The guidon of the field artillery has a solid red field, with the letter and numeral also in yellow and a crossed cannon device also in yellow. The guidon of the mounted engineers has a white castellated fort upon a red field, with the letter and numeral also in white. The guidon of the Signal Corps has a red field with the device of the crossed semaphore flags. The aero squadron guidon is similar, with the addition of the flying eagle device.

The motor truck company guidon is triangular, with a red, white and blue field. Upon the white section of the field is the device of the eagle over the starred wheel and the crossed sword and key.

The field hospital guidon has the caduceus of Hermes in white upon a purple field. The guidon of the ambulance company is similar, except that the former has the white letters "F. H." and the latter, "A. C." The field hospital flag is the red cross on a white field, as is the ambulance flag.

Ammunition trains display a red triangular pennant, with a large white numeral. This pennant is given the right of way in time of battle.

A blue anchor on a white field is the device of the flag flown at the jackstaff by vessels of the Coast Guard patrolling large harbors of the United States.

Flag:

Day, 8173, 8276.

Address of President Wilson, 8276.

Significance of, 8277.

Sizes and Proportions of, fixed, 8172.

Flags:

Confederate, captured, to be presented to Congress, 3309.

Neutral, protest against use of, by belligerents, 8056.

Union and Confederate, return of, to respective States recommended, 5163.

Proposition withdrawn, 5164.

Flathead Indians. (See Indian Tribes.)

Treaty with, 2913.

Fleet.—Several ships, particularly warships, under the same commanding officer.

Fleet Naval Reserve. (See Naval Reserve.)

Flogging.—A chastisement by beating or whipping. It was a punishment inflicted in the United States Navy until 1850, when it was abolished. In 1861 it was prohibited in the Army.

Florida.—One of the southern group of states; nickname, "The Everglade State"; motto, "In God We Trust." It lies between lat. 31° and 24° 30' north and long. 79° 48' and 87° 38' west, an area of 58,666 square miles. It is bounded on the north by Georgia and Alabama, on the east by the Atlantic Ocean, on the south by Florida Strait and the Gulf of Mexico, and on the west by the Gulf of Mexico and Alabama (separated from the latter by the Perdido River). The east coast of the State contains many favorite winter resorts for tourists.

Florida was discovered by Juan Ponce de Leon on Easter Sunday in 1513. It was named, some say, from the profusion of flowers in bloom at the time of its discovery; others, from the day of its discovery, which in Spanish is called Pascua florida, or Flowery Easter. Expeditions fitted out at Cuba and Puerto Rico by Spaniards made futile attempts at settlement between 1516 and 1540. The French Admiral De Coligny sent three colonies of Huguenots from France to settle the country, but they were massacred by the Spaniards, and in 1565 St.

Augustine was permanently established by the Spanish under Menendez. The territory was ceded to Great Britain in 1763 and returned to Spain in 1783. In February, 1819, East and West Florida were ceded to the United States, Spain receiving therefor $5,000,000. The territory was the scene of the Seminole war. It was admitted to the Union in 1845, seceded Jan. 10, 1861, and was readmitted by act of Congress June 25, 1868. The present constitution was adopted in the latter year. In 1910, the population was 752,619. The estimated population on Jan. 1, 1917, was 904,839.

Statistics of agriculture collected for the last Federal census place the number of farms in the State at 50,016, comprising 5,253,538 acres, valued, with stock and improvements, at $143,138,183. The average value of all land per acre was $17.84, against $7.06 in 1900. The value of domestic animals, live stock, poultry, etc., was $20,591,187, including 845,188 cattle, valued at $9,262,262; 45,640 horses, $4,854,-699; 23,333 mules, $3,545,821; 810,069 swine, $1,848,731; 113,701 sheep, $256,166, and poultry, $673,814. The yield and value of the field crops in 1911 was: Corn, 636,-000 acres, 9,286,000 bushels, $7,429,000; oats, 43,000 acres, 580,000 bushels, $435,-000; rice, 700 acres, 18,000 bushels, $14,-000; potatoes, 10,000 acres, 900,000 bushels, $1,305,000; hay, 18,000 acres, 23,-000 tons, $426,000; tobacco, 2,600 acres, 2,444,000 pounds, $684,320, and cotton, 73,-000 bales. The chief mineral product is phosphate, which was produced to the extent of $9,563,084 in 1913. The production has fallen off considerably of recent years, that of 1915 being only 1,358,611 long tons, valued at $3,762,239. Even so, this amount constituted three-fourths of the amount produced in the United States. The tobacco manufactories of Key West and Tampa compete with Havana, Cuba, in the manufacture of fine cigars. Besides lumber and timber, the forests produced, in 1905, 12,-872,869 gallons of turpentine and 1,445,902 barrels of rosin. Florida is the premier state in the production of Fuller's earth, a variety of clay used for filtering and clarifying animal, mineral, and vegetable oils. The harbor of Pensacola is now thirty feet deep at low tide. The government has deepened and improved the harbors and channels of Jacksonville and Key West. In 1912 there were 4,808 miles of steam railway and 150 miles of electric railway. The Florida and East Coast Railway extension to Key West was opened Jan. 22, 1912. The population in 1910 was 751,139.

In 1916, the chief agricultural product was corn, of which 12,600,000 bushels were produced, to the value of $11,340,000. 43,000 bales of cotton were produced, of the value of $6,412,000. 1,110,000 bushels of potatoes, worth $2,220,000 and 70,000 tons of hay, worth $1,120,000, also were produced.

In 1914, there were 2,518 manufacturing establishments in the state, employing some 55,000 wage-earners, representing an investment of $88,319,000 and paying out annually in wages $24,822,000.

Florida (see also Confederate States):
   Acquisition of, by United States—
      Discussed, 624, 672, 929, 956, 1029.
      Effect of, discussed, 2878.
      Treaty regarding. (See Spain, treaty with, discussed by President Monroe.)
   Archives of, to be delivered to United States, 1156, 1243, 1317.

   Contravention of treaty regarding, discussed, 672.
   Portion of, delivered, 1369.
   Army in, called into action only on written requisition of officers of Territory, 696.
   Bonds of, referred to, 1807, 1808, 1844.
   Boundary line with. (See Spain.)
   Boundary line with Georgia discussed, 895, 961, 1124, 1260.
   Canal routes in, survey of, 1254.
   Cedar Keys, interference with collector of customs at, 5507.
   Change of possession of, from Spain to other power objected to, 473. (See also Monroe Doctrine.)
   Claims arising out of invasion of. (See East Florida Claims.)
   Constitution of, transmitted, 3832.
   Courts of United States in, obstructions to execution of process of, 5539.
   Depredations of Indians, 1645, 2007, 2052.
   Expeditions against, 582, 590, 592, 601, 609, 620. (See also Expeditions Against Foreign Powers.)
   Fisheries on coast of, 2725.
   Fourteenth Amendment to Constitution ratified by, referred to, 3854.
   Government should be established in, 674.
      Referred to, 696.
   Governor and other officers appointed for, 673.
   Inability of Spain to check Indian movements in, 600, 609.
   Indian depredations in, 1645, 2007, 2052.
   Indians in—
      Authority to use certain funds in purchase of lands for, bill for, 5197.
      Hostile acts of, 1433, 2007.
      Referred to, 2128.
      Removal of, discussed, 2583, 2707, 2720. (See also Indians, removal of.)
   Indian Wars in (see also Indian Wars)—
      Brevet nominations for army officers for services in, 2008.
      Correspondence regarding, referred to, 1796.
      Discussed, 2007, 2051.
      Disposition of Indians to treat for peace, 1647.
      Referred to, 600, 1754, 1833, 1933, 2007, 2052.
   Insurrection in, proclamation regarding, 3217.
   Interference with collector of customs in Cedar Keys, and action of Government discussed, 5507.

Lands granted to, in aid of railroads referred to, 3580.

Lands in—
Claims to, 772, 993.
Titles to, 803, 993.

Legislative council of—
Memorial from, regarding government, etc., for, 769.
Resolutions of, referred to, 2073.

Maj.-Gen. Jackson's entrance into, discussed, 611.

Courts-martial of Arbuthnot and Ambristie [Ambrister] referred to, 612.

Idea of hostility toward Spain not entertained, 612.

Not an encroachment upon rights of Spain, 611.

Orders to Gen. Matthews, Col. Mc-Kee, and Governor Mitchell, regarding possession of, 491.

Possession of, transferred from Spain to another power objected to, 473.

Power to use certain funds for the purchase of lands for Indians in, 5197.

Progress in, checked by malady at Pensacola, 759.

Property owners in, should be compensated for losses sustained, 1474.

Provisional governor for, appointed and restoration of, into Union discussed, 3527.

Railroads, lands for, 3580.

Smuggling practiced by citizens of. (See Smuggling.)

Spanish authority in, almost extinct, 600, 609.

System of buccaneering organized in, 609.

Territorial government established
Laws of, referred to, 766.
in, 756.

Territorial judges in, authority of, to act as Federal judges, referred to, 2268.

Transmission of Constitution of, 3832.

Unlawful combinations in, 609.

Florida, The.—A Confederate cruiser fitted out in England under the name of the *Oreto.* For two years she did much damage to the Union cause. After having been twice seized and having twice escaped from the Federal cruisers, her name was changed to *Florida.* Oct. 7, 1864, in the harbor of Bahia, Brazil, in violation of the rights of neutrals and under the guns of the Brazilian corvette, she was captured by the *Wachusett* (sister ship to the *Kearsarge*), commanded by Capt. Napoleon Collins. Subsequently she was taken to Hampton Roads and sunk in a collision.

Florists, Society of American, act in-corporating, vetoed, 6010.

Flour, duty on, referred to, 1115.

Flour-Mill and Grist-Mill Industry.—(From a report of the census bureau, April 7, 1913.) The report on this industry distinguishes three classes of mills: (1) Mer-

chant mills whose chief products are intended for human consumption; (2) merchant mills whose chief products are those commonly used as feed for live stock, and (3) mills engaged exclusively in custom grinding. Mills reporting the purchase of any part of the grain which they grind are classified as merchant mills, even though a large part of their business may consist in custom grinding. Custom mills, on the other hand, are those engaged exclusively in custom grinding, whether for toll or for a stipulated charge, including those where grain already ground is sometimes given in exchange for the grain to be ground. Practically all of the custom mills are very small, and so also are a considerable number of the merchant mills.

Of the 23,652 mills canvassed for 1909, more than half (11,961) were custom mills, but of the total value of products—$938,699,958—only $55,115,553, or 5.9 per cent., was contributed by this class of mills. More than three-fourths of the merchant mills were engaged chiefly in the manufacture of wheat flour and other products intended for human consumption, and the value of the products of these mills was $832,790,364, or 88.7 per cent. of the total for all mills combined.

In 1909, of the number of merchant mills reported for the flour-mill and grist-mill industry, 19.4 per cent. were under corporate ownership, as compared with 17.2 per cent. in 1904. While corporations thus controlled represented less than one-fifth of the number of establishments, the value of the products of these establishments represented 66.6 per cent. of the value of products for all merchant mills engaged in the industry.

In 1909, of the number of wage-earners reported for merchant mills, 9,053, or 22.9 per cent., were employed in establishments under individual ownership; 7,488, or 19 per cent., in those under firm ownership; and 22,912, or 58.1 per cent., in those owned by corporations.

Minnesota, the most important flour-producing state, showed a decrease of 68 in the number of wheat-flour mills, and a decrease was shown for each of the five classes of mills except those producing less than 1,000 barrels. Decreases in the number of mills which produced wheat flour took place also in New York, Ohio and Missouri, which ranked third, fifth and sixth, respectively, in the production of such flour in 1909, but the number increased slightly in Kansas and Illinois, which ranked second and fourth, respectively.

The flour-mill and grist-mill industry is one in which the cost of materials constitutes a very large proportion of the value of products, the process of manufacture itself being relatively simple and inexpensive. The cost of the materials used by all mills in 1909 was $813,891,347, which was equal to about seven-eighths (86.7 per cent.) of the value of products, while the value added by manufacture (that is, the value of products less the cost of materials) was only $124,808,611.

The flour-mills and grist-mills of all classes combined gave employment in 1909 to an average of 88,849 persons, of whom 46,467 were wage-earners, and paid out $35,167,693 in salaries and wages. The quantity of grain ground was 872,950,743 bushels, the greater part being wheat and corn.

Minnesota is by far the most important state in the flour-mill and grist-mill industry, ranking first at the censuses of both 1909 and 1904 in the average number of wage-earners employed in merchant mills, in value of products, and in value added by manufacture. During 1909, 104,042,999

| 1909 | FLOUR-MILLS AND GRIST-MILLS, MERCHANT AND CUSTOM | | | |
| | Merchant Mills | | Custom Mills | Total |
	Manufacturing Chiefly for Human Consumption	Manufacturing Chiefly Feed for Live Stock		
Number of establishments.......	9,162	2,529	11,961	23,652
Persons engaged in the industry..	59,188	6,866	22,795	88,849
Proprietors and firm members...	11,365	3,205	15,634	30,204
Salaried employees...........	11,378	653	147	12,178
Wage-earners (average number)	36,445	3,008	7,014	46,467
Primary horsepower...........	853,584	(1)	272,763	1,126,347
Capital.....................	$326,654,430	$22,497,349	$21,258,510	$370,410,289
Expenses....................	$781,274,162	$46,248,187	$48,110,565	$875,632,914
Services...................	$32,062,511	$1,918,642	$1,186,540	$35,167,693
Salaries...................	$12,021,161	$495,606	$47,828	$12,564,595
Wages.....................	$20,041,350	$1,423,036	$1,138,712	$22,603,098
Materials..................	$724,294,494	$43,281,985	$46,314,868	$813,891,347
Miscellaneous..............	$24,917,157	$1,047,560	$609,157	$26,573,874
Value of products..............	$832,790,364	$50,794,041	$55,115,553	$938,699,958
Value added by manufacture (value of products less cost of materials)................	$108,495,870	$7,512,056	$8,800,685	$124,808,611
Grain ground, bushels..........	736,013,881	70,234,080	66,702,782	872,950,743

(1) Included in total for merchant mills.

bushels of wheat and 12,340,167 bushels of other grains were used in the merchant mills of that state, and 22,737,404 barrels of wheat flour were produced or more than one-fifth of the total for the United States. The number of wage-earners employed in the merchant mills of that state increased 7.7 per cent. during the decade ending with 1909, and the value of products 67.7 per cent.

In New York, which ranked second among the states, the merchant mills used 30,073,-407 bushels of wheat and 40,271,986 bushels of other grain in 1909. More corn, buck-wheat and oats were ground in New York than in any other state. Larger percentages of increase from 1899 to 1909 are shown for New York than for Minnesota.

Kansas ranked third in value of products and in value added by manufacture in 1909. Of the nine states that led in respect to value of products, Kansas shows the most rapid development in the milling industry during the period from 1899 to 1909, the number of wage-earners increasing 68 per cent. and the value of products 221.1 per cent. Still higher percentages of increase, however, are shown for some of the states in which the industry has attained importance only during recent years, such as Oklahoma, Idaho, Louisiana, Wyoming and Nevada.

There was considerable variation in the relative importance of the establishments operated by individuals, firms and corporations, respectively, in the different states. Thus in Minnesota, the principal flour-producing state, establishments controlled by corporations constituted 38.2 per cent. of the number of establishments, gave employment to 85.3 per cent. of the wage-earners, and reported 87.2 per cent. of the total value of products. In Pennsylvania, on the other hand, corporations controlled only 4 per cent. of the establishments, and these establishments gave employment to only 20.2 per cent. of the wage-earners, and contributed only 27.4 per cent. of the value of products.

Of the 11,691 merchant mills reported for 1909, 138, or 1.2 per cent., manufactured products valued at $1,000,000 or over.

On the other hand, the small establishments—that is, those manufacturing products valued at less than $20,000—constituted more than one-half (51.2 per cent.) of the number of merchant mills. The great bulk of the output of the merchant mills was turned out by establishments hav-

ing products valued at $100,000 or over, such establishments reporting 72.6 per cent. of the value of products.

The quantity of grain during 1909, 872,-950,743 bushels, represented an increase of 37,807,118 bushels, or 4.5 per cent., over the amount reported for 1899. The merchant mills devoted primarily to the manufacture of products intended for human consumption used 84.3 per cent. of the quantity reported for 1909; those producing mainly feed for live stock 8 per cent., and the mills engaged exclusively in custom grinding 7.6 per cent.

The value of breakfast foods manufactured in 1909 and included with "food preparations" approximated $37,000,000.

Of the total quantity ground in merchant mills, wheat constituted 61.6 per cent., corn formed 26 per cent. and oats formed 6.2 per cent.

The quantity of wheat flour reported for 1909, 107,108,461 barrels, represents an increase of 3,584,367 barrels, or 3.5 per cent., over 1899. On the basis of the quantity of wheat and wheat flour reported, an average of 4.7 bushels of wheat was used to produce a barrel of flour.

Food Administration.—Nothing proved that the Great War was being fought on an international rather than on a national scale, and that the results would be determined largely by the matter of material production, better than the food problem created by and during the conflict. Even before the United States officially recognized a state of war with the Imperial German Government on April 6, 1917, it had been exporting foodstuffs in such quantity to Europe that the effects of a food shortage and of increased prices due to stimulated demand had been felt by most American citizens.

Whatever food control had existed before the war in this country had been concerned chiefly with the enforcement of pure food and drugs laws (see Food and Drugs Act) and with the encouragement and direction of farm production through the Department of Agriculture (q. v.). So that the active steps necessary to federal control over the food problem in this country were almost unprecedented in the history of the United States.

It was not until May 17, 1917, that President Wilson took the preliminary steps towards federal food control by asking Herbert C. Hoover to organize a food administration of the United States. Mr. Hoover, a sketch of whom appears in the Biographical Index, had achieved world-wide fame by his direction of the Belgian Relief work (q. v.). On August 10, 1917, Congress enacted a law "to provide further for the national security and defence by encouraging the production, conserving the supply, and controlling the distribution of fuel products and fuel." As authorized under this law, the activities of the Food Administration fell chiefly under the following three heads: (1) To guide food trade so as to eliminate speculation, extortion and waste and to stabilize prices in essentials: (2) To regulate exports so as to leave within the country sufficient food to meet just demand at home, and to co-operate with the Allies of the United States to prevent inflation of prices: (3) To stimulate food saving to enable necessary exportation to be made to foreign countries.

Accordingly, the Food Administration headed and guided by Mr. Hoover was but a temporary branch of the Government, deriving its powers through executive orders directly from the President. The administration itself was accordingly not divided into a number of bureaus with sharply divided duties like a permanent Government department; but the entire food question was treated as a series of problems and each problem was placed in the hands of an individual, Mr. Hoover having called to his assistance men from all parts of the country who were qualified to serve him.

Through the hotel and restaurant section of the Food Administration, all public eating places fell into a food conservation arrangement by which no meat was served on Tuesdays (later Saturday becoming a day on which no pork was served), and Wednesdays (and later Mondays) became days on which no wheat was served. There was to be one wheatless meal and one meatless meal per day. The pledge card division of the Administration achieved similar results in private households by getting pledges to this effect from more than two-thirds of the seventeen million households in the country.

Each state had a federal food administrator appointed by the President, to attend to the detailed program of the food conservation campaign within that state, and there was created a separate division of the United States Food Administration to correlate the work of the separate state food administrations. All in all, therefore, the work depended more on voluntary co-operation than on the food dictation practised in Europe.

Among the achievements of the Food Administration during the first year of its existence may be mentioned the following: The fixing of wheat prices had saved the American people about $60,000,000 monthly. From July 1, 1917, to March 31, 1918, 80,000,000 bushels of wheat had been shipped to our Allies. On May 15, 1917, when Mr. Hoover was appointed Food Administrator, the price of flour at Minneapolis was $16.75 per barrel, whereas one year later it had decreased to $9.80. On the former date, the difference between the price paid the farmer for his wheat and the wholesale price for flour was $5.68 a barrel, whereas on the latter date the difference had decreased to about $.65.

Sugar prices declined one cent during 1917, and the margin between the prices of raw and refined sugar decreased almost 50%. Pork exports for March, 1918, were more than 50% higher than in any month in the preceding seven years; of beef products, more than 20% higher; of rye and rye flour, 32% higher than in the preceding year; of barley, 55% higher; and of oats and oatmeal, 35% higher.

It was estimated that 10,000,000 signatures were obtained in the house-to-house campaign inaugurated in November, 1917, pledging co-operation with the Food Administration. Efforts in the home concentrated upon saving and using substitutes for wheat; pork, mutton and beef; milk: fats and eggs. The greater use of corn and oat products, fish, and vegetables was encouraged.

Food Administration:

Agriculture Department, relation of, to, 8262.

Bureaucracy will not result from, 8263.

Conservation of food asked, 8379, 8431.

Grain Corporation created, 8324.

Licensing of—

Bakers 8383, 8443.

Beverage manufacturers, 8498.

Coffee dealers, 8443.

Commodities, 8362.

Farm equipment industry, 8499.

Fish packers, 8497.

Fishermen, 8430.

Importation, manufacture, etc., of feeds and foods, 8429.

Poultry dealers, 8498.

Sugar importers and refiners, 8352.

Wheat and rye elevators and millers, 8322.

Profits, reasonable, determination and enforcement of, left to Food Administrator, 8398.

Prohibition legislation should not be included in bill for, 8305.

Requisition of foods and feeds, provision for, 8376.

Treasury Department assigned certain details of, 8351.

Food Adulteration, discussed, 5384.

Food and Drugs Act.—The Pure Food act, approved June 30, 1906, for preventing the manufacture, sale or transportation of adulterated or misbranded or poisonous or deleterious foods, drugs, medicines and liquors, and for regulating traffic therein, and for other purposes took effect Jan. 1, 1907.

The first section of the act makes it unlawful for any person to manufacture within the District of Columbia or any Territory, any article of food or drug which is adulterated or misbranded, under a penalty not to exceed $500, or one year's imprisonment, or both, at the discretion of the court for the first offence, and not to exceed $1,000 and one year's imprisonment, or both, for each subsequent offence.

The second section of the act makes it applicable to food or drugs introduced into any state from any other state, and from or to any foreign country.

The examinations of specimens of food and drugs are to be made in the Bureau of Chemistry of the Department of Agriculture, or under the direction and supervision of such bureau, for the purpose of determining from such examinations whether such articles are adulterated or misbranded within the meaning of this act; and if it shall appear from any such examination that any of such specimens is adulterated or misbranded within the meaning of this act, the Secretary of Agriculture shall cause notice thereof to be given to the party from whom such sample was obtained. After judgment of the court, notice shall be given by publication in such manner as may be prescribed by the rules and regulations aforesaid.

The term "drug," as used in this act, includes all medicines and preparations, recognized in the United States Pharmacopoeia or National Formulary for internal or external use, and any substance or mixture of substances intended to be used for the cure, mitigation or prevention of disease of either man or other animals. The term "food," as used herein, shall include all articles used for food, drink, confectionery or condiment by man or other animals, whether simple, mixed or compound.

For the purposes of this act an article shall be deemed to be adulterated:—

In case of drugs—If, when a drug is sold under or by a name recognized in the United States Pharmacopoeia or National Formulary, it differs from the standard of strength, quality or purity, as determined by the test laid down in the United States Pharmacopoeia or National Formulary official at the time of investigation: Provided, That no drug defined in the United States Pharmacopoeia or National Formulary shall be deemed to be adulterated under this provision if the standard of strength, quality or purity be plainly stated upon the bottle, box, or other container thereof, although the standard may differ from that determined by the test laid down in the United States Pharmacopoeia or National Formulary, and if this strength or purity fall below the professed standard or quality under which it is sold.

In the case of confectionery—If it contain terra alba, barytes, talc, chrome yellow, or other mineral substance or poisonous color or flavor, or other ingredient deleterious or detrimental to health, or any vinous, malt, or spirituous liquor or compound or narcotic drug.

In the case of food—If any substance has been mixed and packed with it so as to reduce, or lower, or injuriously affect its quality or strength. If any substance has been substituted wholly or in part for the article. If any valuable constituent of the article has been wholly or in part extracted. If it be mixed, colored, powdered, coated or stained in a manner whereby damage or inferiority is concealed. If it contain any added poisonous or other added deleterious ingredient which may render such article injurious to health: Provided, That when in the preparation of food products for shipment they are preserved by any external application applied in such manner that the preservative is necessarily removed mechanically, or by maceration in water, or otherwise, and directions for the removal of said preservatives shall be printed on the covering of the package, the provisions of this act shall be construed as applying only when said products are ready for consumption.

If it consist in whole or in part of a filthy, decomposed, or putrid animal or vegetable substance, or any portion of an animal unfit for food, whether manufactured or not, or if it is the product of a diseased animal, or one that has died otherwise than by slaughter.

The term "misbranded," used herein, shall apply to all drugs, or articles, or food, or articles which enter into the composition of food, the package or label of which shall bear any statement, design or device regarding such article, or the ingredients or substances contained therein which shall be false or misleading in any particular, and to any food or drug product which is falsely branded as to the state, territory or country in which it is manufactured or produced.

For the purposes of this act, an article shall also be deemed to be misbranded:—

In case of drugs—If it be an imitation of or offered for sale under the name of another article, or if the contents of the package as originally put up shall have been removed, in whole or in part, and other contents shall have been placed in such package, or if the package fail to bear a statement on the label of the quantity or proportion of any alcohol, morphine, opium, cocaine, heroin, alpha or beta eucaine, chloroform, cannabis indica, chloral hydrate or acetanilide, or any derivative or preparation of any such substances contained therein.

In case of food—If it be an imitation of or offered for sale under the distinctive name of another article.

If it be labelled or branded so as to deceive or mislead the purchaser, or purport to be a foreign product when not so, or if the contents of the package as originally put up shall have been removed in whole or in part and other contents shall have been placed in such package, or if it fail to bear a statement on the label of the quantity or proportion of any morphine, opium, cocaine, heroin, alpha or beta eucaine, chloroform, cannabis indica, chloral hydrate, or acetanilide, or any derivative or preparation of any such substance contained therein.

If in package form, and the contents are stated in terms of weight or measure, they are not plainly or correctly stated on the outside of the package.

If the package containing it or its label shall bear any statement, design or device regarding the ingredients or the substances contained therein, which statement, design or device shall be false or misleading, in any particular: Provided, That an article of food which does not contain any added poisonous or deleterious ingredients shall not be deemed to be adulterated or misbranded in the following cases:

In the case of mixtures or compounds which may be now or from time to time hereafter known as articles of food, under their own distinctive names, and not an imitation of or offered for sale under their own distinctive names, and not an imitation of or offered for sale under the distinctive name of another article, if the name be accompanied on the same label or brand with a statement of the place where said article has been manufactured or produced.

In the case of articles labelled, branded or tagged so as to plainly indicate that they are compounds, imitations or blends, and the word of "compound," "imitation" or "blend," as the case may be, is plainly stated on the package in which it is offered for sale: Provided, That the term blend as used herein shall be construed to mean a mixture of like substances not excluding harmless coloring or flavoring ingredients used for the purpose of coloring and flavoring only: And provided further, That nothing in this act shall be construed as requiring or compelling proprietors or manufacturers of proprietary foods which contain unwholesome added ingredients to disclose their trade formulas, except in so far as the provisions of this act may require to secure freedom from adulteration or misbranding.

No dealer shall be prosecuted under the provisions of this act, when he can establish a guaranty signed by the wholesaler, jobber, manufacturer or other party residing in the United States, from whom he purchases such articles, to the effect that the name is not adulterated or misbranded within the meaning of this act, designating it.

The remaining provisions of the act provide the methods of prosecuting offenders and destroying goods imported or offered for import which are adulterated or falsely labelled.

Food and Drugs Inspection, Board of.—

A Federal board under the jurisdiction of the Department of Agriculture which considers, in conjunction with state officials, all questions relating to the enforcement of the food and drugs act.

It had long been recognized that inconsistencies between the Federal food and drugs act and the food, drug, and dairy laws of the different states, as well as lack of uniformity in state legislation, have greatly hindered the prevention of fraud, adulteration and misbranding of food and drugs, and have made it difficult to induce manufacturers to improve their products.

To avoid the waste occasioned by duplication of the work of Federal and state officials the Secretary of Agriculture called a conference of state food and drug officials to meet in Washington Nov. 13 and 14. 1913, to determine ways and means of bringing about better coordination of functions and closer cooperation.

Agreements were reached at this conference to establish in the Department of Agriculture a board to prevent duplication of research and investigation and to make food and drug control more effective. The country was divided into several general inspection districts, each in charge of a competent official, and all laboratories and inspectors working in that territory put under the same immediate direction.

The amendment to the act of August 23, 1912, provides specifically that drugs are misbranded if their labels contain false and fraudulent statements concerning their curative and therapeutic effects.

In 1913, the Bureau of Chemistry (q. v.), in order better to enforce the Food and Drugs Act, was divided into three districts, with headquarters at Washington, Chicago and San Francisco. In 1916, there were 46 inspectors engaged in enforcing the act.

In the three years from 1913 to 1916, some 22,000 samples of food and drugs were collected and analysed. More than 9,000 hearings were granted to manufacturers and shippers and 2,250 cases were sent to the Department of Justice for prosecution. Of the 3,000 cases decided in this period, practically all were in favor of the government. About 50,000 importations were examined, with the result that some 3,000 were refused entry and some 15,000 had to be relabeled.

In the year 1917, 358 recommendations for seizure were made and 424 cases were referred for criminal prosecution. 847 cases terminated in the courts, of which number 751 were decided in favor of the government. 4,483 official samples and some 4,000 additional informal samples were collected.

Food Control Law.—

The main provisions of the Food Control Law, approved by the President on August 10, 1917, are as follows:

Section 3 provides that no person acting as an agent of the United States shall induce or attempt to induce any person to make a contract of any kind or to furnish goods of any kind to the United States if such agent has any pecuniary interest in such contract or furnishing or is connected with any person or association thus pecuniarily interested. Any such agent must, moreover, if such contract be consummated without his influence, make a statement of the extent to which he is materially interested in such contract; nor shall he participate in the awarding of such contract.

Section 4 forbids any person to destroy any necessaries for the purpose of enhancing their price or restricting the supply; knowingly to commit waste or to permit preventable deterioration; to hoard any necessities, as defined in section 6; to monopolize or to attempt to monopolize any necessities; to engage in any discriminatory, unfair, deceptive or wasteful practice or to make any unreasonable charge in connection with the handling of necessities; to conspire or combine to limit the facilities for handling necessaries, to restrict their supply or distribution, to limit their manufacture or production, or to exact excessive prices for any necessaries.

Section 5 provides that no person shall engage in the importation, manufacture, mining, storage or distribution of any necessaries without procuring a license therefor, after the President has made public announcement that such license must be procured. The President is authorized to prescribe regulations and details concerning this licensing system. The President is further authorized to stop any unfair practice by any licensee, and to find what is a just and fair storage charge, commission, profit and practice. Punishment by a fine of not more than $5,000, or imprisonment for not more than two years, or both is provided for those violating the provisions of this section. It is expressly stated, however, that this section does not apply to farmers nor to retailers doing a business of less than $100,000 annually nor to common carriers.

Section 6 provides punishment by fine of not more than $5,000 or imprisonment for not more than two years, or both for wilful hoarding, which is defined as holding or contracting for any necessaries beyond reasonable requirements for a reasonable time, whether for private consumption or for seasonable business needs or withheld from the market for the purpose of increasing prices. The activities of any exchange, however, as defined in section 13 and of farm-- etc., are not to be defined as hoarding.

Section 7 provides for the seizure and sale of such commodities found to have been hoarded.

Sections 8 and 9 provide for the punishment of persons found guilty of limiting output, destroying necessaries, etc.

Section 10 permits the President to requisition foods, feeds, fuels and other supplies necessary for the common defense, to provide storage facilities for the same and to provide ay just compensation therefor. If such compensation be not satisfactory in amount to the person to be compensated, he shall be paid 75% of it and may bring suit against the United States to recover the remainder of what he shall conceive to be due him. Requisition may not be taken, however, of any foods or seeds necessary for the consumption or use of any individual and his dependents.

Section 11 authorizes the President to buy and to sell at reasonable prices, for cash, wheat, flour, meal, beans and potatoes, such prices not to be lower than the minimum prices theretofore fixed for them, according to section 14.

Section 12 authorizes the President to take over, for Government use or operation, whenever he finds it necessary for the common defence, any factory, packing house, mine, oil pipe line, or other plants, or any parts thereof. The compensation provided for such action follows the procedure described in section 10.

Section 13 authorizes the President to prescribe regulations for the activities of any exchange, board of trade, etc., in order to prevent undue fluctuation of prices, speculation, etc. It also authorizes him to require the keeping of records, accounts, and the making of statements to disclose all the facts relating to transactions, not only of the above organizations, but also of clearing houses and similar organizations.

Section 14 authorizes the President, in case of necessity, to fix and announce a reasonable guaranteed price for wheat, according to the different grades, to assure producers of it a reasonable profit. The Government thereupon guarantees that each producer obeying the Government regulations will receive not less than the guaranteed price within eighteen months of the period prescribed in such notice. The guaranteed prices for the crop of 1918 shall be based upon No. 1 northern spring or its equivalent at not less than $2.00 a bushel, to be binding until May 1, 1919. Wheat imported into the United States shall be taxed, if necessary, sufficiently to prevent its lowering of the domestic price below the standard fixed. The President is authorized also to purchase and sell wheat whenever necessary to make the provisions of this section effective.

Section 15 forbids the utilization, after thirty days of the approval of the act, of any foods or food materials in the production of distilled spirits for beverage purposes, except that, within the discretion of the President, such materials may be used for the production of distilled spirits exclusively for other than beverage purposes, or for the fortification of sweet wines as defined in the revenue act approved Sept 8, 1916. Nor shall any distilled spirits be imported into the United States. Whenever the President finds it necessary, he may also limit or prohibit the use of food or of food materials in the production of malt or vinous liquors for beverage purposes or to limit the alcoholic content of such. Nothing in this section permits the licensing of the manufacture of any liquors where the manufacture of such is already prohibited by law. Section 16 authorizes the President to commandeer any distilled spirits, when necessary, for redistillation, the compensation for such action to be determined as above.

Section 20 provides that no person employed under this act shall thereby be excused from the operations of the draft law. Section 23 defines the word person as used in the act to include businesses, partnerships, etc. Section 24 provides that the provisions of the act are effective only during the existing war with Germany.

Section 25 authorizes the President, in case of necessity, to fix the price of coal and coke, wherever and whenever sold, and to regulate their production, transportation, distribution, etc. It also authorizes him, in case this plan be preferred in his discretion, to have all coal and coke sold to the United States, through an agency to be designated by the President, and thence to redistribute and sell them.

Section 27 authorizes the President to procure such stocks of nitrate of soda and to sell them at cost, for increasing agricultural production, as may be necessary.

The terms of the Act define necessaries as foods, fuels, feeds, fuel oil and natural gas, fertilizer and fertilizer ingredients, and tools, utensils, implements, machinery, and equipment required for the actual production of foods, feeds, and fuel.

Food Control, statement concerning, 8262.

Foodstuffs:

Contraband of war, should not be classed as, 8057.

Germany's position on importation of, 8058.

Interference with shipments of, 8057.

Force Bill.—Several bills introduced into Congress have been given this name. When the South Carolina nullifiers attempted to prevent the execution of the tariff act of 1828, it became necessary to enact special laws for carrying out its provisions to enforce collections under it. March 2, 1833, the "Force bill" or "Bloody bill" was enacted for this purpose. The trouble was adjusted later by a compromise. A bill to enforce the fourteenth and fifteenth amendments, which passed Congress May 31, 1870, was also known as the "Force bill," as was an act passed the following year on the same subject. (See Ku-Klux-Klan.) The name was applied later by many persons to the election bill which was introduced in the House by Mr. Lodge, of Massachusetts, during the Fifty-first Congress, "to amend and supplement the election laws of the United States and to provide for their more efficient enforcement." This bill was passed by the House, but was defeated in the Senate.

Force Bill. (See Federal Election Law.)

Ford Peace Expedition. (See European War.)

Forefathers' Day.—The anniversary of the landing of the Pilgrim Fathers at Plymouth, Mass., Dec. 21, 1620. They touched shore on Monday, Dec. 11th, old-style calendar. In December, 1769, the Old Colony Club was formed by seven citizens of Plymouth to celebrate the "landing of our worthy ancestors in this place." In order to accommodate the date to the new-style or Gregorian calendar, the Old Colony Club, thinking that Dec. 22d new style corresponded to Dec. 11th old style, established the anniversary on Dec. 22d instead of Dec. 21st. New England societies have been established in many states of the Union and the celebration of Forefathers' Day is becoming more general. The celebrations are held in December, the date of the preliminary landing, rather than in the January following, when the landing for settlement took place.

Foreign Affairs, Secretary of.—Jan. 10, 1781, the Continental Congress created the office of Secretary of Foreign Affairs at the solicitation of representatives in other countries. Robert R. Livingston, of New York, was the first incumbent of the office. His duties also comprehended the adjustment of affairs between states. The scope of the office was much enlarged by reorganization in 1782. John Jay occupied the position between 1784 and 1789. July 27, 1789, the two Departments of Home (q. v.) and Foreign Affairs were combined in the Department of State. (See also State, Department of.)

Foreign Ambassadors and Ministers to the United States. (See Ambassadors.)

Foreign and Domestic Commerce, Bureau of. (See Bureau of Foreign and Domestic Commerce.)

Foreign Bill.—A bill of exchange drawn on a person or firm in another country.

Foreign-built Ships, admission of, to American registry, 8006.

Foreign Coins:
Assay of, referred to, 935.
Ceased to be legal tender, 239.
Counterfeiting of, should be made a crime, 1136, 1268.
Overvaluation of gold in, 1845.
Referred to, 2407.
Spanish milled dollars legal tender, 239.
Spanish milled doubloons referred to, 304.
Value of Alfonsino and Louis fixed by order, 6616.

Foreign Commissions, Visits of. (See Visits of Foreign Commissions.)

Foreign Criminals, introduction of, into United States referred to, 2368, 4588.

Foreign Import Duties (see also Vessels, Foreign, tonnage on):
Imposed upon American products, 5117.
By Colombia, 5672.
Retaliatory measures proclaimed, 5700.
By Haiti, retaliatory measures proclaimed, 5702.
By Venezuela, 5672.
Retaliatory measures proclaimed, 5703.
Modifications of tariff laws—
Discussed, 5615, 5747, 5956, 6058, 6239, 6652, 6713, 7189, 7393.
Evidence of, proclaimed—
Austria-Hungary, 5718.
Brazil, 5576.
British Guiana, 5688.
British West Indies, 5688.
Cuba and Puerto Rico, 5583, 5890-5892.
Dominican Republic. (See Santo Domingo, *post.*)
Germany, 5693.
Great Britain. (See British Guiana; British West Indies, *ante.*)
Guatemala, 5716.
Honduras, 5714.
Nicaragua, 5698.
Salvador, 5684, 5800.
Santo Domingo, 5587.
Spain. (See Cuba and Puerto Rico, *ante.*)
Vessels refused clearance by Haiti discussed, 5869.

Foreign Intercourse:
Action recommended on the publication of confidential items, 2281.
Appropriations for, 190, 448.
Reduction in, discussed, 4356.
Unexpended, referred to, 3828.

Contingent expenses—
Funds on deposit with Baring Brothers & Co. for, referred to, 3828.
Public interests demand that confidential items be not published, 2281.
Funds on deposit with Baring Brothers & Co., 3828.
Provision for, recommended, 58, 190.
Requests of House and Senate for information regarding, refused, 186, 2281, 2416, 2452, 2690, 2691, 2695, 6101.
Referred to, 2529.

Foreign Mail Service, Department of.
—This department of the postal service is under the direction of the second assistant postmaster-general (q. v.). Its total cost in 1916 was $3,287,000.73; and the estimated appropriations for 1917 are $3,800,-800. In 1916, the mail transported in the foreign mail service weighed 26,241,304 pounds. The contract service for foreign mails applies to five routes, and its cost in 1916 was $1,090,918. Foreign mails carried over the other routes are carried on a weight basis of payment. There are reciprocal domestic rates on letters between the United States and Canada, Cuba, Mexico, Panama, the Bahamas; Barbadoes Islands; British Guiana; British Honduras, the Dutch West Indies; the Leeward Islands; Newfoundland and New Zealand. Further application of the reciprocal mail service to apply to all countries of the Western Hemisphere was prevented by the European War. The United States has parcel post conventions with 53 countries and colonies. (See Post-Office Department; Postal Service; Postal Conventions; Mail Matter.)

Foreign Mail Service, unsatisfactory condition of, 7109.
To South American countries, subsidy recommended, 7109.

Foreign Mails, transmission of, through United States referred to, 2175. (See also Postal Service.)

Foreign Ministers. (See Ministers.)

Foreign Paupers:
Introduction of, into United States, 1686, 2368.
Legislation respecting, recommended, 4757.
Request of President to withdraw articles regarding, from consideration of House, 1692.
Involuntary deportation of convicts, idiots, insane persons, and, to United States referred to, 4219, 4588.

Foreign Policy of United States (see Annexation for policy as applicable to various countries):
Discussed by President—
Adams, John, 228.
Adams, J. Q., 862, 868, 884, 895, 903, 922, 950.
Buchanan, 2966, 2998, 3037, 3041, 3066, 3089, 3092, 3173, 3177.

13

Cleveland, 4912, 5867, 5871, 5873, 5892, 5955, 5963, 6064, 6068, 6087, 6148.

Fillmore, 2614, 2656, 2701, 2715.

Grant, 3985, 4006, 4015, 4018 4050, 4053, 4082, 4101, 4143, 4176, 4192, 4245, 4290, 4365.

Harrison, Benj., 5445, 5618, 5750, 5783.

Harrison, W. H., 1873.

Hayes, 4418, 4420.

Jackson, 1159, 1222, 1324, 1370, 1378, 1456, 1484, 1500.

Jefferson, 311, 346, 349.

Johnson, 3564, 3581, 3777, 3886, 3888.

Lincoln, 3248, 3255, 3327, 3444.

McKinley, 6241, 6248, 6281, 6295, 6307.

Madison, 452, 473.

Monroe, 573, 582, 624, 627, 639, 672, 685, 762, 787, 791, 817, 829.

Pierce, 2731, 2745, 2807, 2864, 2904.

Polk, 2229, 2236, 2248, 2276, 2322, 2337, 2361, 2386, 2431, 2437, 2444, 2480.

Roosevelt, 6921-6926, 6990-6998, 7118.

Taft, 7492, 7656.

Taylor, 2548, 2555.

Tyler, 1890, 2049, 2064, 2160, 2169, 2171, 2176, 2190, 2193, 2206.

Van Buren, 1590, 1702, 1748, 1819.

Washington, 120, 213.

Wilson, 7877, 7884, 7907, 7929, 7933, 7934, 7969, 7970, 7978, 7982, 7984.

Foreign Postal Arrangements. (See Postal Service.)

Foreign Powers. (See Powers, Foreign.)

Foreign Relations:

American representative at coronation of King of Siam, 7667.

Arbitration, 7656.

Arbitration between Panama and Costa Rica, Colombia and Haiti, 7657.

Buenos Aires convention ratified, 7672.

Central America-Honduras and Nicaragua treaties proposed by President Taft, 7663.

Chambers of foreign commerce suggested, 7674.

Chamizal boundary question not satisfactory, 7658.

Chinese loans, 7664.

Claim of Alsop & Co. settled, 7657.

Commerce with the Near East, 7667.

Coronation of King George V., 7668.

Europe and the Near East, 7667.

Extension of American banking to foreign countries recommended, 7674.

Fur seal treaty (North Pacific) concluded with Great Britain, Japan and Russia, 7670.

Improvement in foreign service noted, 7675.

International opium commission, 7671.

International prize court, 7670.

Latin America.—Venezuela, 100th anniversary of independence celebrated, 7658.

Liberia; loan to ameliorate conditions in, 7669.

Need for American merchant marines, 7674.

Neutral advisor proposed for China in matter of foreign loans, 8046.

Panama, 7664.

Pan-American Union, 7664.

Presentation to Germany of replica of Von Steuben, 7669.

Protection of industrial property union, 7671.

Recognition of Portuguese republic, 7669.

Russia, concerning treaty of 1832, 7669.

Settlement of long standing differences with Great Britain, 7668.

Spitzbergen Islands, 7670.

Trade with other countries, 7672.

Treaty of commerce and navigation with Japan, 7666.

United States army and navy forces mobilized on border of Mexico to protect American interests, 7658.

Foreign Service, improvement in, noted, 7675.

Foreign Trade. (See Commerce of Foreign Powers.)

Foreign Vessels. (See Vessels, Foreign.)

Foreigners in United States. (See Aliens; Naturalized Citizens.)

Forest, Belle, The, destruction of, in Chinese waters, 4464.

Forest Fires. (See illustration opposite 5199.)

Forest Preservation discussed, 6656, 6657-6660, 6908-6911, 7005, 7218.

Forest Reserve.—July 1, 1905, the control of the national forest reserves together with everything pertaining to the use, care and development of the timber, water, grazing, etc., passed from the Department of the Interior to the Department of Agriculture. In 1908 about four-fifths of the total wooded area of the country was in the hands of private owners, and the remainder in charge of Forest Service. The consumption of timber in the United States in 1908 was three times the annual increment.

Dec. 31, 1908, there were 145 National Forests, embracing 168,681,039 acres in nineteen states and territories, including Alaska and Porto Rico. During 1908 severe droughts visited many parts of the country and forest fires were frequent and destructive, the estimated loss due to fire being $50,000,000. The most serious of these fires were in Minnesota, Michigan and Wisconsin, as well as New York, Pennsylvania and Montana. During this time the National Forests suffered little loss owing to the system of patrol, by which many smaller fires are extinguished before gaining destructive headway.

Previous to 1905 the Bureau of Forestry merely gave expert advice, on request, to the Department of the Interior concerning the application of forestry to the forest reserves. The change of name from "forest reserves" to "national forests" was made in 1906, in order to correct the impression that the forests were, as "reserves," withdrawn from use. Since the Forest Service took charge of them the fundamental aim has been to open them to the widest use consistent with their proper protection.

The reserves set aside were as follows: By President Harrison, 13,416,710 acres; by President Cleveland, 25,686,320 acres; by President McKinley, 7,050,000 acres; by President Roosevelt, 148,346,924 acres. During the administration of President Taft 3,891,800 acres have been eliminated from the national forests, making their area at the close of the fiscal year 1911, 190,608,243 acres. The eliminations threw out land which was found to be better suited for agricultural and other purposes than for forestry. An act of Congress, passed in 1907, prohibits any additions by the President to the national forest area in Washington, Oregon, Idaho, Montana, Wyoming and Colorado.

In pursuance of the policy that the forests are for the use of the people under proper restrictions, grazing privileges, timber cutting, haying and other smaller privileges are let under government supervision. From these sources there were received in 1908, for grazing, $962,829.40; timber sales, $849,027.24; special uses, $30,425.23; total from all sources, $1,842,281.87. Under the law 25 per cent. of the gross revenues goes to the state wherein the reservation is situated, to be applied for school and road purposes, and the balance to the federal treasury. The expenditures on the national forests for 1908 were $3,118,267.21, an excess of about $1,200,000 over the receipts. In addition to the privileges for which charges are made the free use of some timber and some pasturage is granted to settlers near the forests, no charge or permit being required for pasturing a limited number of stock. The entire cost of managing the National Forests is less than two cents per acre per year.

Location, date latest proclamation effective, and area of the National Forests on June 30, 1915: By States. [Source: Reports of the Forest Service, Department of Agriculture.]

State and forest	Latest proclamation effective.	Net area.
Arizona:		Acres.
Apache	Feb. 17, 1912	1,184,582
Chiricahua[1]	July 1, 1910	348,160
Coconino	Dec. 8, 1915	1,599,677
Coronado	June 19, 1912	959,961
Crook[1]	Feb. 17, 1912	867,102
Dixie[1]	May 10, 1916	17,680
Kaibab	May 19, 1913	1,072,170
Manzano[1]	Sept. 10, 1914	27,708
Prescott	Oct. 7, 1910	1,434,122
Sitgreaves	Feb. 17, 1912	667,408
Tonto	Sept. 26, 1910	1,996,280
Tusayan	July 1, 1910	1,605,823
Total		11,780,433
Arkansas:		
Arkansas	Feb. 23, 1916	622,003
Ozark	Feb. 17, 1916	294,916
Total		916,919

[1] National forest extending into two States.

State and forest.	Latest proclamation effective.	Net area.
California:		Acres.
Angeles	Aug. 23, 1916	829,216
California	Oct. 12, 1910	822,364
Cleveland	Apr. 24, 1916	591,750
Crater[1]	July 19, 1915	46,980
Eldorado[1]	July 28, 1910	549,350
Inyo[1]	Feb. 23, 1911	1,268,604
Klamath[1]	June 21, 1912	1,470,848
Lassen	Aug. 9, 1916	918,147
Modoc	Dec. 23, 1910	1,182,298
Mono[1]	June 30, 1911	801,485
Monterey	Aug. 5, 1916	288,112
Plumas	Nov. 17, 1914	1,146,645
Santa Barbara	June 9, 1915	1,695,175
Sequoia	July 1, 1915	2,196,199
Shasta	June 19, 1912	828,367
Sierra	Apr. 27, 1915	1,493,474
Siskiyou[1]	May 4, 1914	349,650
Stanislaus	Apr. 13, 1915	809,679
Tahoe[1]	Sept. 1, 1916	546,166
Trinity	June 7, 1912	1,428,168
Total		19,263,277
Colorado:		
Arapaho	Jan. 26, 1915	636,899
Battlement	Mar. 1, 1913	651,199
Cochetopa	Mar. 3, 1913	907,532
Colorado	Jan. 26, 1915	494,656
Durango	July 1, 1911	614,275
Gunnison	May 27, 1913	908,109
Hayden[1]	Aug. 8, 1910	66,718
Holy Cross	Dec. 16, 1910	576,945
La Sal[1]	Feb. 9, 1914	27,444
Leadville	Mar. 3, 1913	935,229
Montezuma	Aug. 15, 1910	700,571
Pike	Sept. 16, 1916	1,138,551
Rio Grande	Aug. 29, 1913	1,137,067
Routt	Nov. 21, 1916	833,659
San Isabel	May 27, 1910	598,912
San Juan	July 1, 1911	618,075
Sopris	Dec. 16, 1910	596,852
Uncompahgre	Apr. 1, 1912	790,589
White River	June 15, 1915	848,337
Total		13,081,647
Florida:		
Florida	July 1, 1911	309,546
Idaho:		
Boise	Dec. 24, 1910	1,054,302
Cache[1]	July 1, 1915	514,317
Caribou[1]	Apr. 18, 1914	686,349
Challis	May 21, 1914	1,260,600
Clearwater	July 1, 1911	785,179
Coeur D'Alene	July 1, 1911	650,336
Idaho	Mar. 23, 1912	1,193,513
Kaniksu[1]	May 6, 1910	199,190
Lemhi	May 19, 1913	1,067,741
Minidoka[1]	Jan. 24, 1916	510,003
Nezperce	July 1, 1911	1,703,168
Palisade[1]	July 1, 1910	297,020
Payette	July 26, 1916	832,033
Pend Oreille	May 6, 1910	678,054
St. Joe	June 4, 1912	577,135
Salmon	May 19, 1913	1,621,477
Sawtooth	May 19, 1913	1,203,554
Selway	July 1, 1911	1,694,171
Targhee[1]	Apr. 21, 1916	694,372
Weiser	July 1, 1911	562,743
Total		17,785,257
Michigan:		
Michigan	July 1, 1915	89,466
Minnesota:		
Minnesota	May 23, 1908	197,852
Superior	Sept. 21, 1912	857,330
Total		1,045,162

State and forest.	Latest proclamation effective.	Net area.
Montana:		
Absaroka	June 19, 1912	843,443
Beartooth	Apr. 15, 1912	662,855
Beaverhead	May 19, 1913	1,338,197
Bitterroot	Apr. 30, 1912	1,047,895
Blackfeet	June 19, 1912	873,414
Cabinet	Apr. 30, 1912	831,494
Custer	June 19, 1912	[430,142
Deerlodge	July 1, 1910	[834,709
Flathead	June 19, 1912	1,812,019
Gallatin	Sept. 4, 1912	565,575
Helena	Sept. 4, 1912	688,346
Jefferson	Sept. 28, 1914	1,042,912
Kootenai	June 19, 1912	1,337,991
Lewis and Clark	June 19, 1912	811,727
Lolo	Apr. 30, 1912	850,505
Madison	Sept. 24, 1912	960,120
Missoula	Sept. 24, 1912	1,028,127
Sioux[1]	May 2, 1913	98,805
Total		16,058,186
Nebraska:		
Nebraska	Dec. 1, 1915	206,074
Nevada:		
Dixie[1]	May 10, 1916	282,543
Eldorado[1]	July 28, 1910	400
Humboldt	June 19, 1912	691,758
Inyo[1]	Feb. 23, 1911	72,817
Mono[1]	June 30, 1911	465,012
Nevada	Oct. 28, 1912	1,237,943
Ruby	June 19, 1912	343,185
Santa Rosa	Nov. 3, 1911	270,072
Tahoe[1]	July 28, 1910	14,687
Toiabe	May 10, 1916	1,907,643
Total		5,286,060
New Mexico:		
Alamo	Apr. 3, 1916	610,529
Carson	Jan. 14, 1914	854,562
Chiricahua[1]	July 1, 1910	126,478
Datil	July 3, 1916	2,671,706
Gila	May 9, 1910	1,437,147
Lincoln	Apr. 1, 1912	551,760
Mazano[1]	Sept. 10, 1914	755,894
Santa Fe	July 1, 1915	1,355,034
Total		8,363,110
North Dakota:		
Dakota	Nov. 24, 1908	6,045
Oklahoma:		
Wichita	Oct. 13, 1910	61,480
Oregon:		
Cascade	July 1, 1911	1,016,569
Crater[1]	July 15, 1915	787,454
Deschutes	July 15, 1915	1,287,486
Fremont	July 15, 1915	888,887
Klamath[1]	June 21, 1912	3,998
Malheur	July 1, 1911	1,057,682
Mina	July 1, 1911	398,068
Ochoco	July 1, 1911	716,482
Oregon	Oct. 11, 1912	1,031,902
Santiam	July 1, 1911	606,776
Siskiyou[1]	May 4, 1914	997,139
Siuslaw	July 1, 1908	541,280
Umatilla	July 1, 1911	486,183
Umpqua	July 9, 1914	1,011,417
Wallowa	July 1, 1911	993,181
Wenaha[1]	Mar. 8, 1916	425,504
Whitman	July 1, 1911	877,564
Total		13,127,590
South Dakota:		
Black Hills	July 1, 1915	483,782
Harney	Apr. 29, 1912	556,220
Sioux[1]	May 2, 1913	75,844
Total		1,115,864

State and forest.	Latest proclamation effective.	Net area.
Utah:		
Ashley[1]	Oct. 7, 1910	982,493
Cache[1]	Apr. 21, 1915	267,066
Dixie[1]	May 10, 1916	432,784
Fillmore	May 6, 1914	700,626
Fishlake	June 27, 1913	661,699
La Sal[1]	Feb. 9, 1914	519,644
Manti	July 1, 1916	781,800
Minidoka[1]	Jan. 26, 1916	69,402
Powell	Sept. 26, 1910	689,685
Sevier	June 19, 1912	729,614
Uinta	June 30, 1916	1,005,252
Wasatch	June 30, 1916	607,732
Total		7,447,797
Washington:		
Chelan	Mar. 2, 1916	677,389
Columbia	July 1, 1908	776,480
Colville	May 9, 1910	756,395
Kaniksu[1]	May 6, 1910	258,776
Okanogan	July 1, 1911	1,487,136
Olympic	Mar. 2, 1907	1,534,680
Rainier	Mar. 28, 1914	1,316,057
Snoqualmie	Oct. 23, 1911	695,332
Washington,	July 1, 1908	1,454,356
Wenaha[1]	Mar. 8, 1916	313,434
Wenatchee	July 1, 1910	657,644
Total		9,927,679
Wyoming:		
Ashley	Oct. 7, 1910	5,987
Bighorn	July 2, 1908	1,123,430
Black Hills	July 1, 1915	144,759
Bridger	July 1, 1916	707,661
Caribou[1]	Apr. 18, 1914	6,707
Hayden[1]	Aug. 8, 1910	322,222
Medicine Bow	July 1, 1910	469,786
Palisade[1]	July 1, 1910	254,964
Shoshone	July 1, 1908	1,576,349
Targhee[1]	Apr. 21, 1916	84,970
Teton	Aug. 16, 1916	1,919,476
Washakie	July 1, 1916	858,482
Wyoming	July 1, 1908	899,980
Total		8,375,173
Alaska:		
Chugach	Aug. 9, 1916	5,429,858
Tongass	Feb. 16, 1909	15,454,110
Total		20,883,968
Porto Rico:		
Luquillo	Jan. 17, 1903	12,504
Grand total of 155 national forests		155,153,228

[1] National forest extending into two states.

Forest Reserves. (See also Lands, Public, set apart.)

Dividing administrative site in Oregon, 7989.

Lookout Station established on Twin Sisters Mountain, 7966.

Ranger Station established for, 7990.

Forest Reservations.—March 1, 1911, Congress gave consent to each of the several states of the Union to enter into any agreement or compact, not in conflict with any law of the United States, with any other state or states for the purpose of conserving the forests and the water supply of the states entering into such agreement or compact. The sum of $200,000 was appropriated and made available until expended, to enable the Secretary of Agriculture to co-operate with any state or group of states, when requested to do so, in the protection from fire of the forested watersheds of navigable streams; and the Secretary of Agriculture is authorized, and on such conditions as he deems wise, to stipulate and agree with any state or group of states to co-operate in the organization and maintenance of a system of fire protection on any private or state forest lands within such state or states and situated upon the watershed of a navigable river: Provided, That no such stipulation or agreement shall be made with any state which has not provided by law for a system of forest fire protection: Provided further, That in no case shall the amount expended in any state exceed in any fiscal year the amount appropriated by that state for the same purpose during the same fiscal year.

There was appropriated for the fiscal year ending June 30, 1910, the sum of $1,000,000, and for each fiscal year thereafter a sum not to exceed $2,000,000, for use in the examination, survey and acquirement of lands located on the headwaters of navigable streams or those which are being or which may be developed for navigable purposes: Provided, That the provisions of this section shall expire by limitation on the 30th day of June, 1915.

It also provided that a commission, to be known as the National Forest Reservation Commission, consisting of the Secretary of War, the Secretary of the Interior, the Secretary of Agriculture and two members of the Senate, to be selected by the President of the Senate, and two members of the House of Representatives, to be selected by the Speaker, be created and authorized to consider and pass upon such lands as may be recommended for purchase and to fix the prices at which such lands may be purchased, and no purchases shall be made of any lands until such lands have been duly approved for purchase by said commission.

The Secretary of Agriculture is authorized and directed to examine, locate and recommend for purchase such lands as in his judgment may be necessary to the regulation of the flow of navigable streams, and to report to the National Forest Reservation Commission the results of such examinations: Provided, That before any lands are purchased by the National Forest Reservation said lands shall be examined by the Geological Survey and a report made to the Secretary of Agriculture, showing that the control of such lands will promote or protect the navigation of streams on whose watersheds they lie. The Secretary of Agriculture is authorized to purchase, in the name of the United States, such lands as have been approved for purchase by the National Forest Reservation Commission at the prices fixed by said commission. Such acquisition may in any case be conditioned upon the exception and reservation to the owner from whom title passes to the United States of the minerals and of the merchantable timber, or either or any part of them, within or upon such lands at the date of the conveyance, but in every case such exception and reservation and the time within which such timber shall be removed and the rules and regulations under which the cutting and removal of such timber and the mining and removal of such minerals shall be done shall be expressed in the written instrument of conveyance, and thereafter the mining, cutting and removal of the minerals and timber so excepted and reserved shall be done

only under and in obedience to the rules and regulations so expressed. (See National Forests.)

Forest lands acquired under the Weeks Law: Areas, June 30, 1915. [Source: Reports of the Forest Service, Department of Agriculture.]

State and area.	Areas under protection.		
	Acquired	Additional approved for purchase.	Total.
Georgia:	Acres.	Acres.	Acres.
Georgia...........	31,450	28,097	59,547
Savannah (south part)...........	11,346	25,492	36,838
Total........	42,796	53,589	96,385
Maine:			
White Mountain (part)...........	....	24,825	24,825
New Hampshire:			
White Mountain...	195,216	85,223	280,439
North Carolina:			
Boone.............	....	38,930	38,930
Mount Mitchell....	34,818	27,332	62,150
Nantahala........	31,711	2,422	34,133
Pisgah...........	49,704	30,695	80,399
Savannah (north, part)...........	16,879	17,275	34,154
Total........	133,112	116,654	249,766
South Carolina:			
Savannah (south, part)...........	....	17,270	17,270
Tennessee:			
Cherokee.........	72,468	59,032	131,500
Unaka............	....	44,569	44,569
White Top (part)..	27,809	19,326	47,135
Total........	100,277	122,927	223,204
Virginia:			
Massanutten......	23,212	33,320	56,532
Natural Bridge.....	32,265	48,722	80,987
Potomac (part)....	20,722	16,456	37,178
Shenandoah (part)..	84,378	20,391	104,769
White Top (part)...	11,358	795	12,153
Total........	171,935	119,684	291,619
West Virginia:			
Monogahela.......	22,810	28,263	51,073
Potomac (part)....	27,511	9,200	36,711
Shenandoah (part)..	13,318	1,118	14,436
Total........	63,639	38,581	102,220
Grand Total...	706,975	578,753	1,285,728
Approved acreage....	....	....	1,329,487
Surveyed acreage.....	....	....	1,285,728
Difference	....	....	43,759

Forest Service.—One of the bureaus of the Department of Agriculture. It has charge of the administration and protection of the national forests and also promotes the practice of forestry through investigations and the diffusion of information.

The work of the Government in forestry was initiated by the appointment of Dr. Franklin B. Hough in 1876 as special agent in the Department of Agriculture. In 1881 a division of forestry was created in that department. In 1901 this division became the Bureau of Forestry, and in 1905, when the care of the national forests was given to this bureau, its name became the Forest Service.

Previously the care of the national forests had been in the hands of the Department of the Interior.

A law authorizing the president to set apart forest reserves was passed in 1891, but no provision for their administration and use was made until 1897. (See Forest Reserve.)

Our forests now cover 550,000,000 acres, or about one-fourth of the United States. Forests publicly owned contain one-fifth of all timber standing. Forests privately owned contain at least four-fifths of the standing timber. The timber privately owned is not only four times that publicly owned, but it is generally more valuable.

The original forests of the United States contained timber in quantity and variety far beyond that upon any other area of similar size in the world. They covered 85,000,000 acres, with a stand of not less than 5,200,000,000,000 board feet of merchantable timber, according to present standards of use. There were five great forest regions—the northern, the southern, the central, the Rocky Mountain and the Pacific.

The present rate of cutting is three times the annual growth of the forests of the United States. The great pineries of the lake states are nearing exhaustion and heavy inroads have been made upon the supply of valuable timber throughout all parts of the country.

The heavy demands for timber have been rapidly pushing the great centres of lumber industry toward the south and west. In consequence, the State of Washington has led for several years in lumber production, now followed in order by Louisiana, Mississippi, North Carolina and Oregon. In 1912 the production of yellow pine lumber amounted to fourteen and one-half billion feet; the Douglas fir of the northwest held second place, with nearly five and one-quarter billion feet; while white pine ranked third, though less was produced than in the preceding year; oak came first among the hardwoods with four and one-third billion feet, and was followed in order by maple, red gum, tulip, poplar, chestnut, beech and birch.

We take from our forests yearly, including waste in logging and in manufacture, 30,000,000,000 cubic feet of wood, valued at about $1,875,000,000.

We use in a single year 90,000,000 cords of firewood, 40,000,000,000 board feet of lumber, 135,000,000 hewed ties, 1,686,000,-000 staves, over 444,500,000 board feet for veneer, over 136,000,000 sets of heading, over 353,000,000 barrel hoops, 3,300,000 cords of native pulp wood, 165,000,000 cubic feet of round mine timbers, nearly 1,500,000 cords of wood for distillation, over 140,000 cords for excelsior, and nearly 3,500,000 telegraph and telephone poles.

In 1912 about 4,330,000 cords of wood were used in the manufacture of paper, of which about 940,000 cords were imported from Canada. The demand for wood pulp is making a severe drain on the spruce forests, which furnish the principal supply, though a number of other woods, such as poplar, hemlock, pine and balsam, are now being used in considerable quantities. The Forest Service of the United States Department of Agriculture is conducting investigations to determine what other woods, such as scrub pine, white fir, tupelo and the like, can be successfully used.

A larger drain upon our forest resources is made by the demand for railroad ties. White oak, hitherto the chief source of supply, is not plentiful enough to meet this demand indefinitely, and to many parts of the country the supply of chestnut, cedar and cypress is dwindling; however, methods of treating woods with preservative solutions are being used, and in this way cheaper and more plentiful woods, such as Southern pine, Douglas fir, tamarack and hemlock, are coming into demand. A great saving has been effected in the naval stores industry, also largely through the work of the Forest Service, by the introduction of the so-called "cup" systems of turpentining in place of the old destructive system of "boxing." The new systems insure a larger product of better quality and prolong the life of the long-leaf pine forests upon which the industry depends.

The total appropriation for the Forest Service in the fiscal year 1914 is $5,399,-679, as against $5,343,045 for 1913, with a further provision of $200,000 available for fighting and preventing forest fires in cases of extraordinary emergency.

The grazing receipts for 1913 were paid by the holders of 22,032 permits to graze 1,557,118 cattle, horses and hogs, and of 5,434 permits to graze 7,867,851 sheep and goats. The receipts from timber sales were paid by approximately 5,800 purchasers, who cut the equivalent of 495,668,000 board feet of timber. The receipts from special uses were paid by the holders of approximately 5,000 permits. In other words, these receipts represent profitable use of the forests by at least 38,000 individuals or concerns. To the use for which payment was made must be added the heavy free use of the forests by the public.

In issuing permits for reservoirs, conduits, power-houses and transmission lines for commercial power development the Forest Service has steadfastly insisted on conditions designed to prevent speculative or perpetual holdings and to secure the full development of available power and the payment of reasonable charges for the use of land. The total stand of timber on the national forests is estimated at nearly six hundred billions board feet.

The following table shows the local cut of timber in board feet from the national forests in the fiscal year 1913:

State	Cut Under Sale	Cut Under Free Use	Total Cut
	Board Feet	*Board Feet*	*Board Feet*
Montana.....	82,757,000	18,513,000	101,270,000
Idaho........	78,199,000	21,405,000	99,604,000
Arizona......	58,532,000	4,459,000	62,991,000
California....	52,419,000	9,153,000	61,572,000
Oregon.......	52,362,000	12,049,000	64,411,000
Colorado.....	42,446,000	11,002,000	53,448,000
Alaska........	33,535,000	96,000	33,631,000
Washington...	29,149,000	2,611,000	31,760,000
Arkansas.....	20,104,000	187,000	20,291,000
New Mexico..	14,815,000	14,611,000	29,426,000
Utah.........	10,988,000	12,026,000	23,014,000
South Dakota.	9,085,000	5,080,000	14,165,000
Wyoming.....	7,915,000	7,750,000	15,665,000
Nevada.......	3,122,000	2,638,000	5,760,000
Michigan.....	130,000	54,000	184,000
Minnesota....	57,000	65,000	122,000
Florida.......	40,000	12,000	52,000
Oklahoma.....	13,000	232,000	245,000
North Dakota.	......	42,000	42,000
Totals......	495,668,000	121,985,000	617,653,000

The value of the public property administered by the Forest Service is estimated at over two billion dollars.

Forest Service. (See Agriculture, Department of.)

Forestry, report of Commissioner of Agriculture on, transmitted, 4432, 4462, 4535.

Forestry, Bureau of, work of, 6656.

Forestry System:
Inauguration of, discussed, 6346, 6390.
Plans for, to be formulated by commission, 6167.

Forests. (See Lands, Timber.)

Formosa Island, ship's company of American bark *Rover* murdered by inhabitants of, 3829.

Fort.—An enclosed place armed and manned for the protection of a city, a harbor, etc.

Fort Berthold Reservation, N. Dak.:
Agreement for cession of portion of, to United States, 5118.
Allotment of lands in severalty to Indians on, referred to, 4783.
Portion of, opened to settlement, proclaimed, 5579.

Fort Bliss, Tex.:
Title of United States to, referred to, 4665, 4736.
Troops ordered to, referred to, 4991.

Fort Bridger, Idaho, treaty of, 6687.

Fort Brown (Tex.), Attack on.—In consequence of the annexation of Texas the War Department, apprehending trouble with Mexico, sent all the available troops in the South and West to the frontier. The territory between the Nueces and Rio Grande Rivers was claimed by both Texas and Mexico. Gen. Zachary Taylor collected an army of 4,000 men at Corpus Christi, near the mouth of the Nueces, in November, 1845. Jan. 13, 1846, he was ordered to advance to a position on the Rio Grande, and on March 25 he occupied Point Isabel, on the coast of the Gulf of Mexico, just north of the mouth of the river. During April Gen. Taylor had advanced his army up the Rio Grande to a point opposite Matamoras, which was occupied by the Mexican army under Gen. Arista. Here the Americans built a fort under the direction of Major Brown and named it in his honor. Learning that bodies of Mexicans had crossed the river both above and below him with the intention of cutting him off from his supplies at Point Isabel, Taylor fell back toward the latter place May 1. Learning of his departure, the Mexicans on May 3 began a heavy bombardment of Fort Brown, which was continued at intervals until the 10th. It was gallantly defended by Maj. Brown and Captains Hawkins and Mansfield. The former was killed during the engagement. The only other fatality was that of Sergt. Weigert. Thirteen privates were wounded.

Fort Cameron Reservation, Utah, disposal of, recommended, 4740.

Fort Delaware, Del., title to island on which it stands referred to, 1099, 1125.

Fort Dodge Military Reservation, Iowa. Disposal of, referred to, 4690.

Fort Donelson (Tenn.), Capture of.—After the taking of Fort Henry the next logical move against the Confederate line of defence in the West was the reduction of Fort Donelson. This was a large field-work of 100 acres, on a bluff 100 feet high, near the town of Dover, Tenn., on the Cumberland River, about 63 miles from Nashville. It mounted 65 guns and was garrisoned by 21,000 men under Gen. Floyd. Feb. 12, 1862, Brig.-Gen. Grant with 15,000 men moved upon the works by way of the roads leading from Fort Henry. While Grant was placing his forces in position Commodore Foote arrived in the river opposite the fort with a fleet of 6 gunboats, 4 of them ironclad. On the 14th he opened fire. In a desperate attack 2 of the vessels were disabled and the others withdrew after a loss of 54 men. The guns on the bluff were too high to be silenced from the water level. On the day of the unsuccessful attack by the gunboats Gen. Wallace arrived with reenforcements, swelling Grant's command to 27,000. On the 15th Floyd made an attempt to force his way through the surrounding Federal lines. Fighting continued all day during most intensely cold weather. When night fell upon Donelson the Confederates retired to their works. During the night Floyd surrendered the command to Pillow and he to Buckner. The two former escaped by way of the river during the night, and next morning Buckner surrendered the fort unconditionally to Grant. Sixty-five guns, 17,600 small arms, and 14,623 prisoners fell into the hands of the victors. Grant's losses were 2,832 in killed, wounded, and missing. The Confederates lost 2,500 in killed and wounded.

Fort Erie (Canada), Battle at.—June 1, 1814, Maj.-Gen. Brown established headquarters at Buffalo with the intention of retaking the lower peninsula of Canada. His army consisted of 2 brigades of infantry, commanded by Generals Scott and Ripley, respectively, and to each were added a train of artillery and a squad of cavalry. There was also a brigade of 1,100 New York and Pennsylvania volunteers and 500 Indians. July 3 the American Army crossed the Niagara and demanded the surrender of Fort Erie, the first British post on the Canada side. Maj. Buck, with the garrison of 170 men, yielded without a struggle. Aug. 5 Gen. Gaines arrived at Fort Erie to take command of the American army of 2,500, which had retired to the southward after the battle of Lundys Lane. Here he was besieged by Lieut.-Col. Drummond with 5,000 men. The latter subjected the fort to a heavy bombardment all day Aug. 14, and on the 15th, between midnight and dawn, made a series of desperate assaults, showing no quarter to Americans who fell into their power. The British were driven off, with a loss of 221 killed, 174 wounded and 106 prisoners. The American loss was 17 killed, 56 wounded, and 11 missing. After this repulse the British kept up a constant bombardment of the fort for several weeks. Gen. Gaines was seriously injured, and Gen. Brown resumed command, though in ill health and suffering from wounds received at Lundys Lane. Sept. 17 a sortie was made by about 1,000 regulars and the same number of militia upon the British outposts, and all their batteries were captured or destroyed. This saved Buffalo and perhaps all of western New York and seriously crippled the enemy. The loss to the British during the sortie was 500 killed, wounded, and missing, and 385 prisoners. The American loss was 79 killed and 216 wounded. After this disaster Drummond retired precipitately and the Americans abandoned and destroyed Fort Erie.

Fort Erie, Canada, reduction of, by American arms, 524.

Fort Fisher (N. C.), Capture of.—In November, 1864, an expedition was planned against Fort Fisher, N. C. This fort occupies a peninsula on the south coast of North Carolina, between the mouth of the Cape Fear River and the Atlantic Ocean, about 18 miles from Wilmington. It formed the principal defence of that city, which was the most important seaport through which the Southern Confederacy received foreign supplies, and from which departed blockade runners laden with cotton and other products of the South. It was also deemed a point of considerable strategic importance. Fort Fisher and its connected works mounted 75 guns. The armament of the works guarding the approaches to Wilmington was about 150 guns, including some 150-pounder Armstrong guns. The garrison of the fort and outworks consisted of 2,300 men. Dec. 13, 1864, the expedition started. It was composed of a fleet of 73 vessels, carrying 655 guns, some of them of the largest caliber, and a land force of 6,500 men under Gen. Butler. The expedition was accompanied by a boat loaded with 215 tons of gunpowder, which it was designed to explode in the vicinity of the fort, with the object of igniting and exploding the magazines. This proved a failure. Dec. 24 the fort was bombarded by the fleet for an hour and a half. The next day, after a reconnaissance by the land troops, Butler ordered their reembarkation and return. Butler was relieved of the command and superseded by Gen. Terry, with the addition of 1,500 men and a small siege train. Jan. 13, 1865, the fort was again attacked. The troops were landed under the protection of Porter's guns. On the 14th a small advance work was taken by the Federals. The ships reopened fire on the 15th. At 3 P. M. a general assault was made, and for five hours a desperate hand-to-hand encounter was maintained. Not until 10 P. M. was resistance ended and the garrison forced to surrender. Two thousand and eighty-three prisoners were taken, including Gen. Whiting and Col. Lamp. The Federal loss was 110 killed and 530 wounded. The Confederate loss in killed and wounded was about 500. The next morning by the accidental explosion of a magazine 200 men were killed and 100 wounded.

Fort Gaines (Ala.), Reduction of. (See Mobile Bay (Ala.), Battle of.)

Fort Gaines, Ala., reduction of, and orders regarding celebration of, 3439.

Fort George (Canada), Capture of.—After the occupation of Toronto, April 27, 1813, the Americans turned their attention to the British forts along the Niagara River. On the west side of the river and near its mouth stood Fort George, which was held by about 1,800 regulars, 350 militia, and 50 Indians, under Brig.-Gen. Vincent and Colonels Harvey and Meyers. Nearly opposite Fort George was the American Fort Niagara, in and about which had been collected some 4,000 troops under command of Gen. Dearborn. Acting under him were Maj.-Gen. Morgan Lewis, Generals Boyd, Winder, and Chandler, and Col. Winfield Scott. May 27, 1813, an attack was made on Fort George. The army was transported to the Canadian soil by the fleet under Commodore Chauncey and Capt. Perry. After a severe battle of 20 minutes the British fled in confusion toward Beaver Dams, 18 miles distant, to rendezvous. At the end of 3 hours Fort George and its dependencies, with the vil-

lage of Newark, were in the hands of the Americans. Their loss was about 40 killed and 100 wounded. The loss of the British regulars was 51 killed and 305 wounded, missing, and prisoners. The number of Canadian militia made prisoners was 507, making the total British loss 863, as well as large quantities of ammunition and stores. July 8, 1813, a party of 40 Americans under Lieut. Eldridge, in attempting to drive off a small detachment of British and Indians who had approached to within a couple of miles of Fort George, were ambushed by Indians under Blackbird, and only 10 of the party escaped. The wounded and prisoners were massacred.

Fort George, Canada, reduction of, by American arms, 524.

Fort Griswold (Conn.), Capture of.—Sept. 6, 1781, after Arnold and the Tories had secured New London, they carried by assault Fort Griswold, on the opposite side of the river. The Americans offered a stubborn resistance. Out of the garrison of 150 men 73 were killed, including Col. Ledyard, the commander, and 30 were wounded, many after having surrendered.

Fort Hall Reservation, Idaho, agreement with Indians for disposal of lands on, for use of railroad, 4655, 4779, 5187.

Opened to settlement, 6687, 6863, 6865.

Fort Harrison (Ind.), Attack on.—Capt. (afterwards General and President) Zachary Taylor, Sept. 4, 1812, held, until reenforcements reached him, a blockhouse on the Wabash River, Ind., with a garrison of 50 men, ill or convalescing from fever, against a fierce assault of Indians. The savages set fire to the blockhouse. Taylor's loss was 3 killed and 3 wounded.

Fort Henry (Tenn.), Capture of.—The main line of Confederate defense in the West in January, 1862, extended from Columbus, Ky., on the Mississippi River, to the Cumberland Mountains, in eastern Tennessee. On this line of defense were Forts Henry and Donelson, in the northern part of Tennessee, the former on the eastern bank of the Tennessee River and the latter on the western bank of the Cumberland, about 12 miles apart. Gen. Halleck, commander of the Department of Missouri, determined to make an attack on Fort Henry, which was near the center of the line. Jan. 30 an expedition was sent out from Cairo, consisting of 7 gunboats, 4 of them ironclad, under command of Commodore Foote, and a land force of 15,000 men commanded by Brig.-Gen. Grant. On the night of Feb. 5 the infantry were landed 4 miles from the fort. The gunboats anchored abreast until 10 o'clock the next morning, when they began to advance. Fort Henry mounted 17 guns and was garrisoned by 2,724 men, under command of Brig.-Gen. Tilghman. The attack was to have been made by the gunboats, seconded by the land forces. Foote began the bombardment before the arrival of Gen. Grant, whose march was delayed by muddy roads and swollen streams. Tilghman answered the fire of the gunboats for 1 hour and 20 minutes and then surrendered unconditionally, the greater part of his garrison having already escaped to Fort Donelson. Grant arrived half an hour after the battle, and the fort was turned over to him. The part of the garrison that surrendered consisted of about 56 able-bodied men and 60 invalids. Tilghman's loss was 21 killed, and wounded. The Federal loss was 48.

Fort Henry, Tenn., thanks of President to forces capturing, 3305.

Fort Jackson, Ala., treaty with Indians concluded at, 886.

Fort Leavenworth, Kans.:
Estimates for barracks at, referred to, 4666, 4674.

Military prison at, use of, as Government penitentiary, discussed, 6161.

Recommended, 5969.

Fort Lewis, Colo., estimates for post at, 4677.

Fort McAllister (Ga.), Capture of, and Fall of Savannah.—After the destruction at Atlanta and its railroad connections Gen. Sherman took up his march toward Savannah. His army was composed of the Fourteenth, Fifteenth, Seventeenth, and Twentieth Corps. Gen. Howard commanded the right wing and Gen. Slocum the left. The cavalry was under the direction of Gen. Kilpatrick. Sherman passed down the peninsula between the Ogeechee and Savannah rivers and about the middle of December appeared before Savannah, held by the Confederate General Hardee with 15,000 men. To the south of Savannah, on the Ogeechee River, stands Fort McAllister, which had resisted many attacks from the sea and effectually prevented the ascent of the river by the Federal gunboats. The defenses of the fort were weak to the landward and a garrison of less than 300 men held the works. Fort McAllister mounted 23 guns in barbette and 1 mortar. Dec. 13, 1864, Gen. Hazen's division of the Fifteenth Corps crossed the river and assaulted the fort from the rear. The garrison was overpowered and in 15 minutes after the bugle sounded "Forward" the fort was taken. Communication was now open to Dahlgren's fleet, lying in the harbor. Siege guns were brought from Hilton Head, and when the investment of Savannah was completed Sherman demanded its surrender. Hardee refused, but on the night of Dec. 20, when all the arrangements for the assault had been completed, he evacuated the city. It was occupied next day by Sherman's army. Two hundred guns and 35,000 bales of cotton fell into Federal hands. Thus ended Sherman's march from Atlanta to the sea, a distance of more than 300 miles. Out of the entire army of 66,000 men 63 were killed, 245 wounded, and 260 were captured on the march, which consumed 27 days.

Fort McHenry (Md.), Bombardment of.—In September, 1814, the British planned to take Baltimore by a combined land and sea attack. The night after the battle of North Point the British remained on the field. The following morning, Sept. 13, 1814, the British fleet, consisting of 16 heavy vessels, 5 of them bomb ships, began the attack on Fort McHenry, 3 miles southeast of the city. The fort was defended by Maj. Armistead with about 800 men. The bombardment continued 25 hours. The American loss was 4 killed and 24 wounded. It was during this bombardment that Francis Scott Key wrote "The Star-Spangled Banner." The British withdrew after losing 2 vessels and a large number of men.

Fort McKinney (Wyo.), estimates for completion of post at, 4680.

Fort Mackinaw (Mich.), Capture of.—The War of 1812 was proclaimed June 18 (497). The British in Canada learned of it sooner than their adversaries across the lakes. July 17 a force of 600 British and Indians under Capt. Roberts surprised and captured the garrison of 61 officers and men under Lieut. Hancks at Fort Michilimackinac, or Mackinaw. An attempt to recapture it in 1814 was unsuccessful.

Fort Mackinaw, Mich., attempted reduction of, referred to, 534.

Fort Madison (Iowa), Defense of.—Sept. 5, 1812, about 200 Winnebago Indians attacked Fort Madison, on the Mississippi River above St. Louis, and were repulsed after 3 days' fighting. The garrison consisted of a small detachment under Lieutenants Hamilton and Vasques. The Americans lost one man.

Fort Maginnis, Mont., estimates for post at, 4687.

Fort Malden, Canada, reduction of, by American arms, 524.

Fort Marcy, Military Reservation (New Mex.), disposed of, 6872.

Fort Meigs (Ohio), Bombardment of.—In April, 1813, Col. Proctor, with a force of 1,000 British regulars and Canada militia and 1,500 Indians, set out on an expedition against Fort Meigs, on the Maumee River, about 12 miles from its mouth. Gen. Harrison was there with about 1,100 effective men. May 1 the British, having erected batteries at Maumee City, opposite the fort, opened fire, which they kept up for 5 days with slight injury to fort or garrison. Meantime Harrison was reenforced by Gen. Clay and 1,100 Kentuckians. Eight hundred of these, under Col. Dudley, were detached with orders to attack the British rear. They were successful at first, but instead of obeying the order to return they pursued the flying foe into the woods and fell into an Indian ambush. Of the 800 in Dudley's command only 170 escaped. After the fruitless bombardment, the Indians deserting Proctor, he abandoned the expedition.

Fort Meigs, Ohio, British attack on, repulsed, 524.

Fort Mercer (N. J.), Attack on.—Though the British forces under Gen. Howe had occupied Philadelphia in September, 1777, Washington's army in the immediate vicinity controlled the navigation of the Delaware and Schuylkill rivers. Just below the mouth of the latter stream, and on the opposite side of the Delaware, at Red Bank, N. J., was Fort Mercer, in command of Col. Greene, with a force of about 400 men. Admiral Lord Howe having arrived at Newcastle with his fleet early in October, the necessity of opening the river to British navigation became urgent. Oct. 22, an attack was made on Fort Mercer by the British ships and some 1,200 Hessian troops. The assailants were repulsed with a loss of 400. One of the ships grounded and 2 others were burned. The American casualties were 35.

Fort Mifflin (Pa.), Attack on.—One of the principal defenses of the Delaware River after the occupation of Philadelphia in September, 1777, was Fort Mifflin, just below the mouth of the Schuylkill. On the arrival of Admiral Howe with his fleet off Newcastle, Del., early in October, it became necessary to open the river to British navigation. Fort Mifflin was in command of Lieut.-Col. Smith, of Baltimore, with a garrison of about 400 men. Failing disastrously at Fort Mercer, the British turned to Fort Mifflin. A combined attack by the land and water batteries, begun on the 10th, resulted in the retreat of the American garrison to Fort Mercer on the night of Nov. 15, 1777, with the loss of 250 men. The next day the Royal Guards occupied the works. The British loss was 37.

Fort Mims (Ala.) Massacre.—In the summer of 1813 the inhabitants of Alabama, frightened by the hostile actions of the Creek Indians, took refuge at Fort Mims, near Montgomery, Ala., 10 miles above the junction of the Tombigbee and Alabama rivers. The place was garrisoned by 16 regulars and about 240 volunteers. At noon, Aug. 30, 1813, about 1,000 Indians under Weathersford and the prophet Francis surprised the fort. Of the 550 persons (more than 300 of whom were women and children) who at the time were at Fort Mims, 400 were massacred, including all the women and children. The whites resisted desperately. The negroes were made slaves to the Indians. Twelve men of the garrison escaped into the swamp.

Fort Morgan (Ala.), Reduction of. (See Mobile Bay (Ala.), Battle of.) Orders regarding celebration of, 3439.

Fort Moultrie, Charleston (S. C.), Defense of.—In 1776 Clinton was charged with holding the Southern Colonies and Cornwallis was sent to his aid with troops under convoy of Sir Peter Parker's fleet. Charles Lee commanded the Americans in the vicinity of Charleston. William Moultrie was in charge of a little fort of palmetto logs on Sullivans Island, S. C. June 4 the hostile fleet appeared and on the 28th bombarded Fort Moultrie. Clinton's troops had already landed on Long Island. The Americans fired with precision and effect, and one ship was abandoned. Clinton's forces failed to attack, and in a few days the British withdrew. The American loss was 12 killed and 24 wounded. The British loss was 205, and only one of their vessels remained seaworthy. An incident of this battle was the replacing by Sergt. Jasper of a flag which had been shot from the bastion. This fort was abandoned by the Federals under Maj. Robert Anderson Dec. 26, 1860, and was seized by the Confederates, who served a battery from it during the bombardment of Fort Sumter, April 12-14, 1861.

Fort Myer, Va., meteorological observatory at, establishment of, recommended, 4792.

Fort Niagara (N. Y.), Bombardment of.—Nov. 21, 1812, Fort Niagara sustained a severe bombardment at the hands of the British artillery at Forts George and Newark, on the Canadian side of the Niagara River. The Americans returned the fire and silenced the batteries of the enemy. The loss to the Americans was 9; British loss was not known.

Fort Omaha Military Reservation, Nebr., act to provide for lease of, to Nebraska, vetoed, 6119.

Fort Pillow (Tenn.), Capture of.—This fort was located on the Chickasaw Bluff, in the Mississippi River, 40 miles above Memphis. It was built by the Confederates during the Civil War. It was occupied by the Federal troops June 5. 1862. its evacuation having been compelled by the destruction of the Confederate flotilla on the previous day. The Federal forces not long afterwards abandoned it in consequence of operations on the Tennessee River. April 12, 1864, the fort was garrisoned by 19 officers and 538 men of the Union Army, about one-half of whom were negro troops. On that day Gen. Forrest with Confederate cavalry assaulted and captured it.

Fort Polk, Tex., removal of, referred to, 2603.

Fort Powell (Ala.), Reduction of. (See Mobile Bay (Ala.), Battle of.) Orders regarding celebration of, 3439.

Fort Preble Military Reservation, Me., additional land for, recommended, 4777.

Fort Riley, Kans., bridge over Republican River at, reconstruction of, recommended, 4777.

Fort Ripley Military Reservation, Minn., Indian school at, establishment of, referred to, 4683.

Fort St. Philip (La.), Bombardment of.—Jan. 9, 1815, while the British were burying their dead before New Orleans, a portion of the fleet attacked without success Fort St. Philip, at a bend in the Mississippi. 65 miles below the city. It contained a garrison of 366 men under Maj. Overton. The bombardment was continued for five days. Two Americans were killed and 7 wounded.

Fort Selden, N. Mex., estimates for post at, referred to, 4670.

Fort Sherman Military Reservation (Idaho), disposition of, 6937, 6953.

Fort Sill Indian Sub-Agency, referred to, 6695.

Fort Smith, Paris and Dardanelle Railway, act granting right of way to, etc., vetoed, 5278.

Fort Stedman (Va.), Assault on.—When in March, 1865, it became apparent to Lee that he must evacuate Richmond, he planned an assault on Fort Stedman, on Grant's right. During the assault Longstreet and Hill were to retire to the south, followed by the assaulting column, and join Johnston. The assault took place March 25. The batteries were carried and 500 prisoners captured. The Confederates were gathered in the works they had taken. March 27 the surrounding artillery of the Union army was brought to bear on the position, and 1,900 of the Confederates surrendered. The Federal loss was 919.

Fort Stephenson (Ohio), Attack on.—In July, 1813, Maj. Croghan was sent with 160 men to garrison Fort Stephenson, or Lower Sandusky, now Fremont, Ohio, about 20 miles from Sandusky Bay. Here he was attacked Aug. 1, 1813, by Gen. Proctor, with 400 British regulars and several hundred Indians, while Tecumseh, with 2,000 Indians, held the roads leading to the fort, so as to cut off reenforcements. The firing was maintained all night from Proctor's gunboats and from howitzers landed by the British. Aug. 2 a general assault was made, which the garrison repulsed with the loss of 1 man killed and 7 slightly wounded. The British loss was 120. The Indians kept out of harm's way.

Fort Sullivan, Me., legislation to authorize sale of post at, recommended, 4783.

Fort Sumter (S. C.) Fired on.—At 3:30 o'clock on the morning of April 12, 1861, Gen. Beauregard, in command of the Confederate troops in and around Charleston, S. C., demanded the surrender of Fort Sumter, in Charleston Harbor, about 3½ miles from the city. The fort was garrisoned by Maj. Anderson with 70 men. Beauregard had a force of 7,000 men. Anderson having refused to surrender, at 4:30 A. M. the bombardment was begun. The firing was kept up until dark and renewed on the morning of the 13th. Buildings in the fort were several times set on fire. Anderson was only able to return a feeble fire, and it was impossible to furnish him with the number of reenforcements necessary to hold the fort. Accordingly, on April 14 he evacuated the works lowering the flag with a salute, and with the garrison sailed north. This was the first conflict of the Civil War. There were no casualties on either side.

Fort Sumter, S. C., assault upon, and reduction of, discussed, 3222, 3278.

Flag floating over, at time of, to be raised on ruins of, by Gen. Anderson, 3484.

Fort Thornburg, Utah, estimates for construction of post at, referred to, 4670.

Fort Wagner (S. C.), Battle of.—In order to test the efficacy of monitors and ironclads as against land fortifications, Admiral Dupont attempted to force the defenses of Charleston Harbor with a fleet of such vessels. April 7, 1863, he started to attack Fort Sumter. His fleet consisted of 7 Ericsson monitors, the frigate *Ironsides,* partially ironclad, and the *Keokuk,* a frailer ironclad. The opposing forts mounted 300 guns. The expedition signally failed. June 12 Gen. Gillmore was placed in command of an expedition against the same fort with 11,500 men, 66 guns, and 30 mortars. Admiral Dahlgren was to cooperate with him with the frigate *Ironsides* and 6 monitors. Gillmore's intention was to capture Fort Wagner, on Morris Island, and then proceed against Fort Sumter. July 10, 1863, a combined attack by sea and land was made on that fortification. He advanced within musket range of Fort Wagner, but delayed the assault till the next day, when it was repulsed. In these operations Gillmore lost about 150 men, the Confederates 300. July 18 another attempt was made to reduce the place, but it was completely repulsed, with a loss of 1,200. Gillmore now determined to approach the fort by a series of parallel trenches. The first was opened July 24 and the third Aug. 9. Beauregard was in command of Fort Sumter. Aug 17 Gillmore opened on that fort. By the 23d Sumter was battered to ruins. Additional parallels were opened toward Fort Wagner. Final operations began Sept. 5, with 17 siege and cohorn mortars, 13 Parrott rifles, and the 11-inch shells of the *Ironsides.* An assault was to have been made Sept. 7, but during the previous night the garrison evacuated the place. Though 122,300 pounds of metal were thrown against the work, the bombproofs were found intact.

Fort Wagner, S. C., Indian agency at, removal of, 967.

Fort Wallace Military Reservation (Kans.), act to provide for disposal of, vetoed, 5308.

Fort Washington (N. Y.), Capture of.—One of the most serious disasters to the Americans of the early days of the Revolution. Howe sent an expedition to dislodge the Americans from Forts Lee and Washington, the principal defenses of the Hudson, which Congress had decided, against the advice of Washington, should be held. The garrison withdrew from Fort Lee in safety. Fort Washington was carried by storm Nov. 16, 1776, after a severe struggle, 2,600 men and all the munitions of war falling into the hands of the British. The American loss in killed and wounded did not exceed 130, while the loss of the combined British and Hessian troops amounted to about 450.

Fort Yuma Military Reservation (Ariz.) disposed of, 6704, 6705.

Fortification.—Any kind of construction artificially made or adopted to prevent capture or defeat by enemy.

Fortress.—A fortified place.

Forts Clinton and Montgomery (N. Y.), Loss of.—Forts Clinton and Montgomery were situated on the west side of the Hudson River, about 6 miles below West Point. Fort Montgomery was a large, unfinished work north of Poplopen Creek, its garrison consisting of one company of artillery, a few regulars, and some half-armed militia under Col. Lamb. Fort Clinton was south of the mouth of the creek, thoroughly built, and garrisoned by a few regulars and militia under Brig.-Gen. James Clinton. Oct. 6, 1777, these forts were stormed and carried by the British under Gen. Henry Clinton. The Americans lost about 300 in killed, wounded, and missing, besides 100 cannon and large quantities of ammunition. The British loss was about 200 killed and wounded.

Fortress Monroe, Va.:

Artillery schools of practice at, 940.

Estimates for barracks and quarters at, referred to, 4666.

Forts.—Strictly speaking a fort is a permanent, strongly built detached enclosure with mounted guns, capable of independent defense, and manned by an organized military force. A fortress is a fort of especial size and strength. The only application of the latter term in America was to Fort Monroe, Va. Both are used for the defense of cities or the entrance to harbors. A fortification is a series of defensive works, temporary or permanent, consisting of a parapet and ditch, and may be of earth or masonry. A post is a permanent military camp, with or without defensive fortifications. The military posts of the western part of the United States were originally fortified against attacks by Indians. There are 160 forts and garrisoned posts in the United States.
Adams—Three miles from Newport, R. I.
Andrews—Nine miles from Boston, Mass.
Apache—Ninety miles from Holbrook, Ariz.
Armistead—Eight miles from Baltimore, Md.
Armstrong—Honolulu, H. T.
Army and Navy General Hospital—Hot Springs, Ark.
Augusta Arsenal—Three miles from Augusta, Ga.
Baker—Four miles from San Francisco, Cal.
Banks—Two miles from Boston, Mass.
Barrancas—Eight miles from Pensacola, Fla.
Barry—Seven miles from Fort Baker, Cal.
Bayard—Two miles from Bayard, N. Mex.
Benicia Arsenal—Army Point, Cal.
Benjamin Harrison—Ten miles from Indianapolis, Ind.
Bliss—Fort Bliss, Tex.

Boisé Barracks—Two miles from Boisé, Idaho.
Brady—One mile from Sault Ste. Marie, Mich.
Canal Zone—Canal Zone.
Canby—Ten miles from Fort Stevens, Ore.
Carroll—Eight miles from Baltimore, Md.
Casey—Fifty-three miles from Port Townsend, Wash.
Caswell—Two miles from Southport, N. C.
Cayey—See Henry Barracks.
Clark—Ten miles from Spofford Junction, Tex.
Columbia—Four miles from Fort Stevens, Ore.
Columbus Barracks—One mile from Columbus, Ohio.
Constitution—Three miles from Portsmouth, N. H.
Crockett—Galveston, Tex.
Crook—Nebraska.
Dade—Thirty-five miles from Tampa, Fla.
D. A. Russell—Wyoming.
Davis—Nome, Alaska.
De Russy—Four miles from Honolulu, H. T.
Des Moines—Five miles from Des Moines, Iowa.
De Soto—Thirty-four miles from Tampa, Fla.
Douglas—Douglas, Ariz.
Douglas—Four miles from Salt Lake City, Utah.
Du Pont—Two miles from Delaware City, Del.
Eagle Pass—Eagle Pass, Tex.
Ethan Allen—Vermont.
Flager—Five miles from Port Townsend. Washington.
Foster—Six miles from Portsmouth, N. H.
Frankford Arsenal—One-half mile from Bridesburg, Pa.
Fremont—Twelve miles from Beaufort, S. C.
Gaines—Thirty miles from Mobile, Ala.
Galveston—Galveston, Tex.
George Wright—Four miles from Spokane, Wash.
Getty—Five miles from Newport, R. I.
Gibbon—Tanana, Alaska.
Governors Island—See Fort Jay, N. Y.
Greble—Five miles from Newport, R. I.
Hamilton—Seven miles from Brooklyn, N. Y.
Hancock—Six miles from Highlands, N. J.
Heath—Three-quarters of a mile from Highlands, Mass.
Henry Barracks—Cayey, P. R.
H. G. Wright—Eight miles from New London, Conn.
Howard—Seventeen miles from Baltimore, Md.
Huachuca—Seven miles from Huachuca Siding, Ariz.
Hunt—Fifteen miles from Washington, D. C.
Jackson Barracks—Six miles from New Orleans, La.
Jay—Governors Island, New York City.
Jefferson Barracks—Jefferson Barracks, Mo.
Kamehameha—Honolulu, H. T.
Key West Barracks—Key West, Fla.
Lawton—Two miles from Interbay, Wash.
Leavenworth—Leavenworth, Kan.
Leavenworth—Fort Leavenworth, Kan.
Levett—Four miles from Portland, Me.
Lincoln—Four miles from Bismarck, N. Dak.
Liscum—Three miles from Port Valdez, Alaska.
Logan—Colorado.
Logan H. Roots—Four miles from Little Rock, Ark.
Lyon—Four miles from Portland, Me.
McDowell—Seven miles from San Francisco, Cal.
McIntosh—One mile from Laredo, Tex.
Mackenzie—Three miles from Sheridan, Wyo.
McKinley—Five miles from Portland, Me.

McPherson—Four miles from Atlanta, Ga.
McRee—Ten miles from Pensacola, Fla.
Madison Barracks—Sacketts Harbor, N. Y.
Mansfield—Seven miles from Westerly, R. I.
Meade—Two miles from Sturgis, S. Dak.
Michie—Eleven miles from New London, Conn.
Miley—Six miles from San Francisco, Cal.
Missoula—Four miles from Missoula, Mont.
Monroe—Fort Monroe, Va.
Morgan—Thirty miles from Mobile, Ala.
Mott—Six miles from Salem, N. J.
Moultrie—Six miles from Charleston, S. C.
Myer—Four miles from Washington, D. C.
Niagara—Seven miles from Lewiston, N. Y.
Oglethorpe—Eleven miles from Chattanooga, Tenn.
Omaha—Five miles from Omaha, Neb.
Ontario—Oswego, N. Y.
Philip Kearny—One mile from Saunderstown, R. I.
Philippine Islands—Manila, P. I.
Pickens—Nine miles from Pensacola, Fla.
Plattsburg Barracks—Plattsburg, N. Y.
Porter—Three miles from Buffalo, N. Y.
Preble—Three miles from Portland, Me.
Presidio of Monterey—Two miles from Monterey, Cal.
Presidio of San Francisco—Five miles from San Francisco, Cal.
Presidio of San Francisco—Letterman Gen. Hosp. Cal.
Revere—One-quarter mile from Stony Beach, Mass.
Riley—Fort Riley, Kan.
Robinson—Fort Robinson, Neb.
Rock Island Arsenal—One mile from Rock Island, Ill.
Rodman—Four miles from New Bedford, Mass.
Rosecrans—Six miles from San Diego, Cal.
Ruger—Six miles from Honolulu, H. T.
St. Michael—Fort St. Michael, Alaska.
St. Philip—Six miles from Buras, La.
Sam Houston—Two miles from San Antonio, Tex.
Sandy Hook Proving Ground—Six miles from Highlands, N. J.
San Jacinto—Galveston, Tex.
San Juan—San Juan, P. R.
Schofield Barracks—Twelve miles from Honolulu, H. T.
Schuyler—Three miles from Westchester Station, N. Y.
Screven—Fort Screven, Ga.
Shafter—Three miles from Honolulu, H. T.
Sheridan—Fort Sheridan, Ill.
Sill—Fort Sill, Okla.
Slocum—Two miles from New Rochelle, N. Y.
Smallwood—Eleven miles from Baltimore, Md.
Snelling—Seven miles from St. Paul, Minn.
Springfield Armory—Springfield, Mass.
Standish—Seven miles from Boston, Mass.
Stark—Three miles from Portsmouth, N. H.
Stevens—Fort Stevens, Ore.
Strong—Five miles from Boston, Mass.
Sumter—Six miles from Charleston, S. C.
Terry—Thirteen miles from New London, Conn.
Texas City—Texas City, Tex.
Thomas—Newport, Ky.
Totten—Two miles from Whitestone, N. Y.
Travis—Galveston, Tex.
U. S. Military Prison—Fort Leavenworth, Kan.
U. S. Military Prison—Four miles from San Francisco, Cal.
Vancouver Barracks—Vancouver, Wash.
Wadsworth—Rosebank, N. Y.
Walter Reed General Hospital—Five miles from Washington, D. C.
Ward—Eleven miles from Seattle, Wash.
Warren—Seven miles from Boston, Mass.
Washington Barracks—Washington, D. C.

Washington—Thirteen miles from Washington, D. C.
Watertown Arsenal—Six miles from Boston, Mass.
Watervliet Arsenal—One mile from Troy, N. Y.
Wayne—Four miles from Detroit, Mich.
West Point—West Point, N. Y.
Wetherill—Two miles from Newport, R. I.
Whipple Barracks—One mile from Prescott, Ariz.
Whitman—Twelve miles from Mount Vernon, Wash.
Wm. H. Seward—Haines, Alaska.
Williams—Four miles from Portland, Me.
Winfield Scott—Winfield Scott, Cal.
Wood—Three miles from New York, N. Y.
Worden—Fifty-one miles from Seattle, Wash.
Yellowstone—Five miles from Gardiner, Mont.
Yosemite—Fifteen miles from El Portal, Cal.

Forts and Fortifications (see also Army, Defenses, Public):

Appropriations for—
Bill for, defeated, 1388.
Recommended, 395, 471, 614, 688, 927, 955, 1388, 2711, 2895, 3993, 4798, 4833.
Armaments for, 770.
Appropriation for, recommended, 2895, 4798.
Recommended, 4271.
Board of Ordnance and Fortifications discussed, 5373.
Ceded to United States, 102, 146, 384.
Constructed with view to permanence, 630.
Construction of, progress made in. 635, 647, 677, 688, 800, 983, 1251.
Defense of, necessary, 435.
Expenditures for, 635, 907, 983.
In Lawrence, Kans., referred to, 3894.
Referred to, 99, 161, 178, 230, 297, 318, 614, 780, 894, 1785, 1807, 2266.
Requisite on seacoasts, 586, 688, 1901.
Sale of, on Staten Island to United States proposed, 934.
Sites for, referred to, 435.

Fortune Bay Outrages.—The treaty of Washington (q. v.) ratified in 1871, granted to American fishermen the right to take and cure fish on the Canadian coasts, and the Halifax Commission (q. v.) determined upon the compensation to be made for such privileges. The Newfoundlanders, however, continued to regard American fishermen as intruders, and in January, 1878, inhabitants of Fortune Bay, Newfoundland, attacked some Gloucester fishermen who were taking on cargoes of frozen herring, cut their nets and drove away the crews. The Newfoundland people asserted that the local laws were being violated. The British Government, however, decided that these could not stand in conflict with the treaty. The injured fishermen claimed damages amounting to $105,305, of which the British Government paid about $73,000. During President Cleveland's first administration (1884-1888) there was a renewal of the fishery disputes at Fortune Bay and other places along the Canadian coast. For a time feeling ran high in the United States, and retaliatory laws were enacted in 1888, and a *modus vivendi* was agreed upon. (See also Fisheries.)

Fortune Bay Outrages, discussed, 4518, 4542, 4558.
Claims arising out of, paid, 4625.

"Forty-Niners."—Name by which the California gold seekers were known. (See opposite 2488.)

Foundry, National, for cannon to be common to both Army and Navy of the United States, in order to regulate quality and secure uniformity, erection of, recommended, 1607, 1714.

Four Years' Law.—In May, 1820, Congress passed a law making the term of certain postmasters and revenue collectors four years. Though it was claimed that the only object of the bill was to have public accounts submitted for inspection every four years, its effect was to greatly increase the power of the president in making appointments.

Fourth Assistant Postmaster-General. (See Assistant Postmasters-General.)

Fourth of July. (See Independence Day.)

Fourth of July, oration by President Wilson, 7952.

Fourth of July Accidents.—In recent years much progress has been made toward securing a sane and rational celebration of the Fourth of July. A few cities like Trenton, N. J.; Cleveland, Ohio; Washington, D. C., and Baltimore, Md., have adopted ordinances prohibiting the sale and use of fireworks, and in New York, Chicago, Toledo, Ohio, and a few other cities the use of fireworks has been restricted. Injuries and fatalities due to the discharge of explosives on the Fourth of July are, however, still far too numerous.
From records kept by the *Journal of the American Medical Association* it is shown that the average number of casualties between 1904 and 1910 were 170 persons killed and 4,600 injured. The year preceding the taking of this average the number of persons killed was 466, and in 1911, after repeated caution and the passage of judicious city ordinances, only 57 persons were reported killed and some 1,500 injured.

Fourth of July Claims.—This name is given to a class of claims arising during the Civil War. The claims were for quartermaster and commissary stores and supplies taken from loyal citizens in certain territory named for the use of and actually used by the Union armies. The first act of Congress providing for the payment of these claims was passed July 4, 1864, from which fact the name arose.

Fourth of July Claims (see also War Claims):
Payment of, referred to, 4148.
Transfer of, to Southern Claims Commission recommended, 4361, 4425.

Fox Reservation. (See Sac and Fox Reservation.)

Fox River, Wis., act regarding improvement of, vetoed, 4336.

Fractional Currency.—Paper money issued during the Civil War in denominations of less than a dollar.

France.—France is the most westerly state of Central Europe, extending from 42° 20' to 51° 5' N. latitude and from 7° 45' E. to 4° 45' W. longitude. It is bounded northwest by the North Sea, Straits of Dover and the English Channel; west by the Atlantic Ocean; southwest and south by Spain; southeast by the Mediterranean; east by Italy, Switzerland and Germany; and northeast by Belgium. The greatest length from north to south is 600 miles; the greatest breadth from east to west 530 miles. Its 3,300 miles of boundary are nearly two-thirds water, 400 miles being Mediterranean, 700 North Sea, etc., and 900 Atlantic.

Physical Features.—The Pyrenees, which divide France from Spain, extend from the Atlantic to the Gulf of Lyons, the highest point in French territory being the Vignemale (10,800 feet) in the center of the range. The Alps form the eastern frontier of France, their highest point (the highest summit of Europe) being Mont Blanc (15,800 feet) near the junction of the Franco-Swiss-Italian frontier. The narrow Rhone valley separates the Alps from the mountainous region of south-central France. The Rhone rises in Mont St. Gothard (Switzerland), and at Lyons is joined by the Saône from the Faucilles and Vosges. The Garonne rises in the Spanish Pyrenees, flows into the Atlantic as the Gironde. The Charente rises in Haute Vienne, and flows into the Atlantic near Rochefort. The Loire rises in the Vivarais Mountains and flows into the Atlantic at St. Nazaire. The Seine rises in the Langres plateau, and flows into the English Channel at Havre. The Rhine and the Meuse both rise in French territory (in the northeast), but their main course is in Germany and Belgium.

Area and Population.—Continental France has an area of 207,076 square miles, and is divided politically into eighty-seven departments, containing a total population of 39,602,258 according to the census of 1911.

History.—The monarchical system was overthrown by the French Revolution (1789-1793), which established a Republic during the closing years of the eighteenth century. In 1804 Napoleon founded the "First Empire," which gave place to a restoration of the Bourbon Dynasty in 1814-1815 until the "Second Empire" under Napoleon III. 1848 (-1852)-1870. Since 1870 France has enjoyed prosperity under the third Republic.

In August, 1914, when Germany declared war against Russia, an ally of France, preparations were made to repulse the German invasion which followed by way of Liège, Belgium. The Germans had advanced to within a day's march of Paris by Sept. 1, when with the aid of English troops they were checked.

Government.—Since 1870 France has enjoyed an increasing security under the Third Republic. The head of the Republic is the President, elected for seven years by the two Houses of Legislature (Senate and Deputies) in joint session as the National Assembly. All French citizens are eligible for the office of President, except members of any royal family which has ever reigned in France. President (Feb. 18, 1913-1920), M. Raymond Poincaré, born at Bar-le-Duc (Meuse), Aug. 20, 1860, elected Jan. 17, 1913.

The Executive is vested in the President and is exercised by a Cabinet of Responsible Ministers, the chief of whom is selected by the President of the Republic from one of the principal political parties of the legislature.

The President is aided in determining constitutional and administrative questions by a Conseil d'Etat, which consists of twenty-one Councillors, thirty-seven Maîtres des Requêtes and forty Auditors.

The lowest Courts are those of the Juges de Paix in each of the 3,005 cantons, where minor civil and criminal cases are determined. More serious charges are dealt with by the tribunaux de première instance in each of the 377 arrondissements, the 227 tribunaux de commerce dealing with mercantile cases. Appeals from the tribunals are heard in twenty-six courts of appeal, throughout the Republic. Assizes are also held periodically in each department, with juries, whose verdict depends on a mere majority. The highest tribunal is the Cour de Cassation at Paris. In criminal cases a preliminary inquiry is held in secret by a judge d'instruction, who may dismiss the accused or remand the case for prosecution by a procureur before a criminal tribunal. All judges are appointed by the President of the Republic. Transportation to a penal colony (New Caledonia or Guiana) is in force for convicts condemned to hard labor.

For the French army and navy, see Armies of the World and Navies of the World.

Education.—The educational system of France is highly developed. The Central Administration comprises (a) Ministry of Public Instruction; (b) Superior Educational Council, charged with the actual administration; (c) Consultative Committee (advisory); (d) Educational Bureaux and Inspecting Staffs, whose heads report direct to the Minister. By the Law of July, 1904, all congregational institutions are to be suppressed within ten years, and many were at once closed. Primary Education is secular, compulsory and free. Age 6-13. Special Schools are numerous, many public institutions being dependent on ministries other than that of Public Instruction; the Ecole des Beaux Arts, the Conservatoire de Musique et Déclamation at Paris, and the School of Forestry at Nancy being justly famous. In addition to Paris University, there are Universities at Aix, Algiers, Angers, Bordeaux, Caen, Clermont, Dijon, Grenoble, Lille, Lyon, Marseilles, Montauban, Montpelier, Nancy, Nantes, Poitiers, Rennes, and Toulouse.

Production and Industry.—Of the total area (132,389,000 acres) there were in 1910 90,392,677 acres under crops and grass.

The coasts support a large fishing population, over 159,899 persons being directly employed. The principal forests, Ardennes, Compiègne, Fontainebleau and Orléans, consisting chiefly of oak, birch, pine, beech, elm, chestnut, and the cork-tree in the south. Fruit trees abound and are productive, the principal being the olive, chestnut, walnut, almond, apple, pear, citron, fig, plum, etc.

The mineral resources of France are mainly coal and iron, but copper, lead, silver, antimony, and salt are also produced.

The most important industries are metals, watches, jewelry, cabinet work, carving, pottery, glass, chemicals, dyeing, paper making, woolens, carpets, linen, silk, and lace, and leather work, the clothing and textile industries generally employing close on 2,000,000 hands.

Finance.—The revenue, inclusive of loans, in 1913 amounted to 4,738,882,438 francs and the expenditures nearly as much. The national debt is the heaviest incurred by any nation and was stated in 1911 as more than thirty-three billion francs, carried at an interest cost stated in 1912 as 1,465,289,000 francs.

Cities.—Paris, the capital, has a population of 2,846,986, and there are some forty cities with population in excess of 50,000.

Trade with the United States.—The value of merchandise imported into France from the United States for the year 1913 was $146,100,201, and goods to the value of $136,877,990 were sent thither—a balance of $9,222,211 in favor of the United States.

FRENCH COLONIES.—The Colonial possessions of the French Republic have a total area of 10,586,778 square kilometres (4,084,463 square miles), including Algeria (which is an integral part of France) and Morocco, in which country French influence is predominant. The following Table exhibits the area and population of French territory outside of Europe:

Continent	Area Square Miles	Estimated Population 1911
Asia—		
French India	200	282,472
French Indo-China	310,000	16,990,229
Total Asia	310,200	17,272,701
Africa—		
Algeria	221,947	5,563,828
Morocco	193,000	5,000,000
Tunis	46,300	1,956,762
French Sahara	923,692	450,000
French West Africa	1,509,733	11,344,076
French Equatorial Africa	560,913	9,000,000
French East Africa	46,296	208,061
Madagascar, etc.	225,515	3,247,895
Mayotte and Comora Islands	836	....
Réunion	926	177,677
Total Africa	3,729,158	36,948,299
Islands of Kerguelen, St. Paul and Amsterdam	1,355	———
America—		
St. Pierre and Miquelon	93	4,209
Guadaloupe, etc.	687	190,273
Martinique	380	185,385
French Guiana	34,159	49,009
Total America	35,319	428,876
Oceania—		
New Caledonia, etc.	7,196	50,500
Society Island, etc.	1,182	30,563
Total Oceania	8,378	81,063
Grand Total	4,084,410	54,730,039

AMERICAN POSSESSIONS.—France possesses two small groups of islands off the southeast coast of Newfoundland, of which St. Pierre and Miquelon are the largest respectively; their combined area is about 95 square miles, with a total population in 1907 of 4,768, and they form an excellent basis for the French cod fishery.

In the West Indies two of the most fertile of the Lesser Antilles belong to France, viz., Martinique (capital Port de France), area about 380 square miles; population in 1910 of 184,004; and Guadaloupe and Basse Terre (capital Pointe-à-Pitre), area 687 square miles, population 190,273 in 1906.

In South America, Cayenne or French Guiana has an area of 33,880 square miles, and an estimated population of about 39,117 in 1906.

Trade with the United States.—The value of merchandise imported into the French West Indies from the United States for the year 1913 was $1,723,124, and goods to the value of $79,736 were sent thither—a balance of $1,643,388 in favor of the United States.

The value of merchandise imported into French Guiana from the United States for the year 1913 was $337,714, and goods to the value of $86,386, were sent thither—a balance of $251,328 in favor of the United States.

France (see also Arcachon; Paris):

American citizens in—

Impressed into military service of. (See Naturalized Citizens.)

Outrages committed on, 490.

Passports used by, referred to, 3902.

Presented at court of, 3265.

Amity and friendship expressed in address to the people of the United States, 181.

Arbitration, resolution of French Chambers favoring treaty of, referred to, 6060.

Army of persons to serve in, must be citizens of, 3171.

Attempts to draw United States into its contest with Great Britain, 437.

Claim of W. H. Frear against, 5198.

Claims of—

Against United States, 406, 568, 591, 696, 2585, 2995, 3399, 6291.

Appropriation for, recommended, 4799.

Convention regarding, 4534, 4559, 4743.

Payment of, 4916.

Requested, 144, 6345.

Against Venezuela, 4761.

Growing out of war between the States paid, 4916.

To persons in United States for military service, 3715.

Claims of United States against, and relations with (see also Vessels, United States, seized)—

Act—

Making appropriations for French spoliation claims vetoed, 6115.

Providing for ascertainment and satisfaction of French spoliation claims vetoed, 2316.

Providing for ascertainment of French spoliation claims vetoed, 2840.

Admitted but not paid, 1320, 1371.

Amicable settlement of, 1446, 1592.

Appropriations for, discussed, 1322, 1371.

Awards of commissioners referred to, 4960.

Commission for adjudication of, 4743, 4757, 4807, 4852, 4864, 4865.

Convention regarding, 4534, 4559, 4743.

Correspondence regarding, 273, 834, 1348, 1354, 1397, 1412.

Referred to, 1407.

Discussed by President—

Adams, John, and replies of House and Senate, 224, 230, 232, 233, 234, 240, 245, 247, 252, 254, 255, 256, 260, 262,

266, 267, 268, 270, 271, 272, 274, 280, 283, 284, 287, 296, 304.
Adams, J. Q., 867, 913, 949, 974.
Jackson, 1007, 1069, 1111, 1195, 1239, 1319, 1371, 1407, 1446
Johnson, 3654.
Madison, 476.
Monroe, 778, 818.
Van Buren, 1592.
Washington, and replies of House and Senate, 137, 168, 195, 198, 199, 201, 202.
Errors in report of, referred to, 1443.
First installment of, not paid, 1240.
List of papers touching unpaid spoliation claims transmitted, 4972.
Mediation offered by Great Britain for adjustment of dispute regarding, 1432, 1434.
Accepted by United States, 1432.
Correspondence regarding, 1436.
Rendered unnecessary, 1435.
Minister of France recalled, 1375.
Minister of United States given passports, 1375, 1416.
Minister of United States instructed to quit France if not settled, 1354.
Payment of, 1446.
Pledges made by, for payment of, not redeemed, 1321, 1323.
Referred to, 271, 4807, 4851.
Reference to convention, regarding, 4743.
Report on spoliation claims referred to, 4916, 4965, 4972, 4982, 5199, 6290, 6291.
Settlement of, France expresses readiness to make, 1440.
Treaty for settlement of, 303, 305, 1111, 1239.
Treaty in regard to, must be executed by France, 1411.
Unless paid, reprisals should be authorized by Congress, 1325.
Colony to be established by, from coast of Africa, 3015.
Colors of, presented to United States through minister of, on the occasion of the presentation of an address by the Committee of Public Safety to the United States, 181.
Commerce and free trade, letter from Emperor of, regarding, referred to, 3112.
Commerce of United States, Berlin and Milan decrees affecting, discussed by President—
Jefferson, 409, 415, 430, 432, 434, 441, 446.
Madison, 467, 474, 476, 503, 513, 522, 6260, 6267, 6270, 6271, 6346.

Proclamations regarding, 457, 466.
Commercial relations with, 170, 346, 409, 460, 467, 645, 669, 917, 961, 1069, 1911, 2976, 6330.
Reciprocal modifications in tariff on certain commodities specified and announced by proclamation, 6479.
Restraints on, removed and discussed, 278, 292, 294, 457, 466, 476, 917.
Suspension of, 458.
Complaint of, against commerce between United States and San Domingo, 379.
Confederate envoys sent to. (See Mason and Slidell.)
Congratulations of the people of the United States to, on the establishment of a republican form of government, 2455.
Constitution of, accepted by King of, 109.
Consular convention with, 49, 2726.
Referred to, 75.
Consuls of, to United States—
Compulsory attendance of, in court, complaints regarding, discussed, 2811, 2835.
Difficulties between authorities in California and, 2835.
Satisfactorily settled, 2868.
Exequaturs to, revoked, 260.
Consuls of United States, in, 165, 170, 350.
Convention with, 755, 764, 818, 867, 1127, 3012.
Alleged violation of, by United States regarding the Pactole, 1172.
Copy of correspondence from the Minister of, to the United States referred to, 2436.
Ratification of, 772, 4698.
Copyright privilege extended, by proclamation, 5582.
Referred to, 5625.
Correspondence with, concerning injuries sustained by American citizens, 834.
Dauphin, death of the, referred to, 54.
Differences of Belgium and, with Venezuela discussed, 6070.
Differences of, with Hawaiian Islands, 2656.
Differences with, correspondence regarding. (See Claims against, ante.)
Diplomatic intercourse with, suspension of, 260, 1375, 1410.
Resumed, 1455, 2548.
Faure, President, death of, referred to by President McKinley, 6367.

Fisheries of, referred to, 1127.
Fugitive criminals, convention with, for surrender of, 2125, 2166, 2219, 3012.
Referred to, 5869.
Greytown bombardment and claims arising out of. (See Greytown, Nicaragua.)
Hostile disposition of, toward United States, 138, 262, 266, 267, 268, 476.
Imperial decree of, not to affect commerce of United States, 409.
Importation of American products into, restrictions upon, 4963, 4758, 4789, 5194, 5545.
Decrees regarding, referred to, 5517, 6100.
Imprisonment of American citizens by, 6060, 6098.
Indians should be restrained by, from committing hostilities against United States, 600.
Individuals bearing commissions granted by enemies of, to be treated as pirates, 271.
Instruction to Minister, 1354.
International expositions in. (See Arcachon; Paris.)
King of—
Constitution accepted by, 109.
Letter from, complimenting Jefferson, 81.
Referred to, 1064.
Salute fired by the *United States* in honor of birthday of, accident caused by, 1273.
Compensation to injured recommended, 1273.
Lands purchased by United States from, 956. (See also Louisiana, *post*.)
Letter of Emperor of, regarding commerce and free trade referred to, 3112.
Louisiana, cession of—
To, referred to, 331, 338.
To United States discussed and referred to, 346, 348, 350, 669, 853, 929, 3255, 6346.
Effect of, discussed, 2878.
Mexican ports blockaded by. (See Blockades.)
Minister of, to United States—
Appointment of, discussed, 138.
Claim of Capt. Beziers presented by, 1647.
Claim of Lafitte & Co., memorial relating to, presented by, 1648.
Correspondence with, referred to, 2436.
Letter of, covering address from Committee of Public Safety transmitted on the occasion of presentation of colors to, 181.
Passports requested by, 1420.

Recall of, 1375.
Requested, 142.
Received, 4718.
Title of ambassador conferred upon, 5874.
Minister of United States to, 50, 107, 147, 148, 224, 235, 272, 274, 296, 339, 429, 445.
Death of, referred to, 513.
Instructions to, to quit France if claims of the United States against France are not settled, 1354.
Intercourse suspended, 1375, 1410.
Passports given, 1375, 1416.
Protection of, for North Germans in France, revoked, 4050.
Recall of, requested, 147.
Refused, 224, 266.
Relations with. (See Claims against.)
Sent to press payment of claims, 1241.
Title of ambassador conferred upon, 5874.
To be commissioned when France appoints minister to United States, 1449.
Will not be sent unless respected, 256, 269.
Minister of United States to Spain denied passage through, discussed, 2811.
National Assembly of—
Decree of—
Making enemy's goods in friendly vessels lawful prize, 138.
Responding to resolution of Congress tendering congratulations to France, 2455.
Letter of President of, and decree of, respecting death of Benjamin Franklin, 87, 6237.
Neutral vessels—
Deemed lawful prize by, 432.
Laden with English merchandise declared lawful prize by, 253, 6345.
Neutrality of United States in war with—
Germany, 7969.
Austria-Hungary, 7977.
Ocean cables, convention with, for protection of. (See Ocean Cables.)
Orders and decrees of, violating commerce and neutral rights of United States, 474.
Owners of vessels, relief of, 645.
Peace convention with, regarding, 303, 305, 320.
Expenses of, 322.
Political affairs of, referred to, 2679.
Postal convention with, 4250.
President of—
Arbiter in case of the *General Armstrong*, 2655.

Award of Emperor, 2722.
Assassination of, 5910.
Resolutions of Senate and House on, transmitted to widow of, 5957.
Privateers of, must not interfere with vessels within waters of United States, 252, 490.
Proclamation suspending duties on vessels, 752, 2371, 3711, 3969, 3973, 4182.
Protectorate over districts in Africa proclaimed by, and action of United States discussed, 5751, 5862.
Relations of, with Venezuela discussed, 4629.
Relations with. (See Claims against, *ante*.)
Republican form of government established in, 2429.
Congratulations of American people on, responded to, 2455.
President Polk's message regarding, 2429.
Reestablishment of, discussed, 4050.
Referred to, 2436, 2480.
Revolution in, referred to, 2737.
Spoliations committed on commerce of United States by vessels of. (See Claims against, *ante*.)
Statue of Liberty Enlightening the World presented to United States by citizens of. (See Liberty Enlightening the World.)
Steamship line between Havre and New York referred to, 2011, 2173.
Trade-marks, treaty with, regarding, 3967.
Treaty of, with—
Allied powers, 185.
Nicaragua, 3121.
Treaty with, transmitted and discussed by President—
Adams, John, 241, 245, 247, 262, 266, 268, 272, 280, 284, 303, 305.
Buchanan, 3012.
Grant, 3967.
Jackson, 1111, 1121, 1125, 1127, 1320, 1345, 1442.
Jefferson, 320, 434.
Johnson, 3722.
Monroe, 645, 755, 764, 818.
Tyler, 2125, 2166, 2219.
Washington, 198, 199.
Decree of France contravening, 226.
Disregarded, 266, 268.
Execution of, refusal of, to make provision for, 1345.
Letter of John Forsyth regarding, 1345.
Ratification of, 772.
Referred to, 5869.
Troops of, in Mexico. (See Mexico.)

Vessels of—
Collision with United States steamer, 3343.
Discriminating duties on—
Modification in law regarding recommended, 2135.
Representation of chargé d'affaires regarding, 81.
Suspended by proclamation, 752, 2371, 3711, 3969, 3973, 4182.
Referred to, 755, 1568.
Suspension terminated by proclamation, 4132.
Embargo on, removed, 466.
Discussed, 468.
Entitled to same rights as most favored nations, 669.
Entry of, to ports of United States should be prohibited, 1411.
Interfered with by United States (See *La Manche*, The.)
Owners ignorant of duties on, relieved, 645.
Repayment of duties on, recommended, 1776.
Vessels, neutral:
Deemed lawful prize, 136.
Laden with English merchandise declared lawful prize by, 253.
Vessels of United States—
Seized or interfered with by vessels of, 138, 243, 252, 387, 490. (See also Claims against, *ante*.)
War of Great Britain and, with China, neutrality of United States in, 3037, 3089, 3174.
War with, preparation for, by United States recommended, 262, 268, 270, 1411.
War with—
China, 4823.
Germany—
Correspondence regarding, 4068, 4434.
Diplomatic relations resumed, referred to, 4098.
Neutrality of United States in, 4050.
Proclaimed, 4040, 4043, 4045.
Suspension of hostilities recommended by President Grant, 4055.
Great Britain, etc., neutrality of United States in, proclaimed, 148.
Santo Domingo and United States, commerce between, complaints about, 379.
War with Spain—
Privateers, commissions not granted to, 779.
Referred to, 821.
Wines, duty on, imported into the United States, modified by reciprocal trade relations, proclamation concerning, 6479.

Wines imported into United States, treaty regarding duty on, 1321.

France, Treaties with.—The basis of diplomatic relations of the United States with France was the treaty of amity and commerce of 1778, abrogated by Congress on July 7, 1798. In this abrogation was also included the treaty of alliance with France to carry on war with Great Britain. In 1782 an agreement was made to repay in twelve equal annual installments of 1,500,000 livres, the indebtedness of 18,000,000 livres to the king of France; and the loan of 10,000,000 livres to the king of Holland. In 1783, a new loan of 6,000,000 livres was negotiated from France, and its repayment provided for by treaty of that year. A consular convention of 1788 was abrogated by the act of 1798. The treaty of amity, peace and commerce, of 1800, expired by its own limitations in 1809.

The treaty of 1803 ceded Louisiana to the United States in what is known as the Louisiana Purchase, and is of historical importance as defining the extent of the cession. The convention of 1803 provided for the purchase money of Louisiana out of $11,250,000 six per cent stock in annual payments of not less than $3,000,000, to commence after fifteen years from the date of ratification of the treaty. A claims convention of 1803 provided for the payment of claims of United States citizens against France, not to exceed 60,000,000 francs.

The convention of navigation and commerce of 1822 provided that United States goods imported into France in American bottoms should pay twenty per cent more duty than when carried in French bottoms. Goods of French manufacture, produce, or growth, imported into the United States should pay an excess duty not to exceed $3.75 per ton of merchandise over that charged upon similar goods when carried in American bottoms. These excess duties shall not apply to goods of either country imported for the express purpose of re-exportation, however carried. To facilitate the estimation of a ton of merchandise not usually so computed, quantities of certain classes of goods are specified as making a ton. Other excess charges than those already specified shall never exceed, on United States vessels in France, five francs per ton, computed on its American register, and for French vessels in the United States, ninety-four cents per ton, computed on the vessel's French passport. Provision is made for the arrest, transport, and punishment of deserting or mutinous sailors when in the country of the other. The life of the treaty was specified as two years, and failing notice of intention to terminate by either party at the expiration of that date, to continue in force until such notice should be given. If no such notice be given within the period, it was agreed that the excess duties provided for in the first sections of the treaty should diminish by one-fourth of their whole amount year by year until extinguished. (For the extradition treaty of 1843, see Extradition Treaties. For the consular convention of 1853, see Consular Conventions. For the trade-mark convention of 1869, see Trade-Mark Conventions.)

A reciprocal agreement of 1898 specified that mutual concessions on the rates of duties on certain classes of goods be made by each country to be continued during the pleasure of the two contracting parties. By an amendment, made in 1902, it was agreed that the provisions of this agreement extend to Algeria and Porto Rico.

In 1904 the United States renounced the right of invoking in Tunis the stipulations of the treaties made between the United States and the Bey of Tunis in August, 1797, and February, 1824, in return for which the French government assured to the consuls and citizens of the United States in Tunis the same rights accorded them in France. Mutual protection of trade-marks in China was agreed to in 1905. The reciprocal trade agreement of 1908 was terminated under the tariff act of 1909.

An arbitration agreement in accordance with the provisions of The Hague convention of 1899 was signed Feb. 10, 1908, and renewed in 1909.

Franchises of street railway and similar corporations, tax upon, recommended, 7042.

Francis and Eliza, The, indemnification asked for by owners of, 1258.

Franco-Prussian War. (See Wars, Foreign.)

Frankford, Pa., arsenal at, referred to, 4661.

Frankfort, exequatur issued consul of, revoked, 3709.

Franking Privilege.—A right enjoyed by Government officials of sending letters and packages free by mail. It was first granted by Congress in January, 1776, to private soldiers actually in service, and was gradually extended to the President, Vice-President, Cabinet officers, members of Congress, bureau officials, postmasters, etc. The franking privilege covered letters, newspapers, executive papers, documents, and printed matter. Many abuses grew up under the system, and Postmaster-General Creswell, in his report, in 1872, estimated that the franked matter, if paid for, would yield a revenue of $3,500,000. Jan. 31, 1873, Congress passed an act entirely abolishing the privilege. Certain features have since been restored. By acts passed June 23, 1847, and March 3, 1875, those documents ordered printed for the use of Congress were admitted for free transmission through the mails and the privilege was restored to President, Vice-President and Cabinet officers with regard to their official correspondence. By special acts the privilege has been extended to widows of Presidents. The act of Jan. 12, 1895, gives to members of Congress the right to frank through the mails all correspondence not exceeding one ounce in weight on official and departmental business.

Franking Privilege:

Abolition of—

Proposed and discussed, 2560, 2943.

Recommended, 3994, 4063, 4152.

Abuses of, referred to, 1335, 2123.

Expenses for transportation of matter before abolition of, referred to, 4216.

Recommendations regarding, referred to, 2626, 4063.

Substitute for, recommended, 3056.

Franklin at French Court. (See illustration opposite 98.)

Franklin or Frankland.—The first constitution of North Carolina made provisions for a future state within her limits on the western side of the Alleghany Mountains. In May, 1794, North Carolina ceded to the United States her territory west of the Alleghanies, provided Congress would accept it within two years. The general opinion among the settlers and people of that territory was that it would not be accepted by Congress, and in this they were correct. For a period of two years, not being under the protection of the Government of the United States nor of the State of North Carolina, they could not receive support from abroad and could not command their own resources at home, for the state had subjected them to the payment of taxes to the United States Government. During this period of uncertainty the Indians were committing frequent depredations, which added to the discontent among the settlers. Under these circumstances a majority of the people within the territory concluded to adopt a constitution and organize a state of their own. This they proceeded to do, and called a convention, which met at Jonesboro Aug. 23, 1784. Delegates assembled from portions of the territory and appointed a committee to consider their condition. The convention adjourned after issuing an address to the people.

In the following November the delegates again assembled at Jonesboro. They did not adopt a constitution, but broke up in confusion because of the fact that in October of that year North Carolina repealed the act of cession. Dec. 14, 1784, another convention assembled at Jonesboro and adopted a constitution which was to be ratified or rejected by a convention called to meet at Greenville, Nov. 14, 1785. In the meantime a general assembly was elected, which met at Greenville early in 1785 and chose John Sevier for governor and other officers. The new state which they attempted thus to create was named in honor of Benjamin Franklin, and is therefore properly called Franklin and not Frankland. It is not perfectly clear that at first these people intended the new state to become part of the Union. One of the provisions in their proposed form of government was that "the inhabitants within the limits of the proposed state agree with each other to form themselves into a free, sovereign, and independent body politic or state by the name of the Commonwealth of Franklin." Later they concluded they would seek admission to the Union, and accordingly they made an effort to have Congress recognize the new state.

The boundary lines of the proposed state show that it included what are now fifteen counties of Virginia, six of West Virginia, one-third of Kentucky, one-half of Tennessee, two-thirds of Alabama, and at least one-fourth of Georgia. This territory is rich in mineral wealth. There is probably more iron and coal in it than can be found in the same area elsewhere in the United States. The convention met in Greenville in November, 1785, to adopt a constitution, but when the constitution proposed was submitted it was rejected and in lieu thereof the constitution of North Carolina was adopted.

This was the beginning of the trouble which ended in the overthrow of the state. The assembly or legislature of the state continued to meet for several years, during which time dual governments existed in the territory. Courts were held in the same counties, one under the Franklin and the other under the North Carolina government; the same militia was called out by officers appointed by each government; laws were passed by assemblies of both states; taxes were laid by authority of both states, but as the people said they did not know which government had the right

to receive their taxes, they adopted the easy solution of paying to neither. The people of the territory became divided, some adhering to Governor Sevier, while others yielded to the authority of North Carolina. Acts of violence were committed by one party against the other, the provocation on the one side being surpassed in the way of retaliation by a still greater provocation on the other. In October, 1788, Sevier was arrested and carried to North Carolina for trial, his property having been attached in January or February of that year. Soon after his arrest the government of Franklin collapsed and North Carolina passed an act of "pardon and oblivion," resuming her authority over these people. Later North Carolina passed a second act ceding the territory to the United States, and Aug. 7, 1790, President Washington appointed William Blount governor of the territory. The State of Tennessee was soon thereafter organized out of this territory.

Franklin (Tenn.), Battle of.—With the purpose of drawing Sherman's army out of Georgia, Gen. Hood evacuated Atlanta early in September, 1864, and marched north, threatening Sherman's communication with his base of supplies at Nashville. Oct. 29, Hood crossed the Tennessee River at Florence with about 35,000 infantry and 10,000 cavalry. (He stated his effective force at 40,000, Sept. 20.) His army was formed in 3 corps, under Cheatham, Stewart, and S. D. Lee; the cavalry under Forrest. Sherman had sent Gen. Thomas to Nashville and placed under his command Gen. Stanley with the Fourth Corps, Gen. Schofield with the Twenty-third, and most of Wilson's cavalry—a force aggregating, according to Federal accounts, 27,000 men. Schofield was in command of the field, and upon Hood's advance he fell back toward Nashville. By Nov. 30 Schofield's army had reached Franklin, on the south bank of the Harpeth River, about 18 miles south of Nashville. Hood here assailed him. His first blow fell upon two brigades of Wagner's division, which had been posted outside the hastily erected works. The Union troops lost 1,000 men in the attack. Schofield's line was broken and defeat seemed imminent, when Gen. Opdycke, commanding one of Wagner's brigades, made a brilliant charge and saved the day. The Confederates made several assaults, each of which was repulsed with terrible loss. Schofield succeeded in getting his troops over Harpeth River in retreat, and by daylight he was well on his way to Nashville. The Federal statement of losses in this battle is as follows: Union, 189 killed, 1,033 wounded, and 1,104 missing, a total of 2,326; Confederates, 1,750 killed, 3,800 wounded, and 702 prisoners, a total of 6,252.

Fraser, Trenholm Co., agents of Confederate Government, suits instituted in English courts against, 3661.

Fray.—A fight between belligerents,—not of sufficient importance to be called a battle.

Frayer's Farm (Va.), Battle of.—One of the Seven Days' Battles before Richmond. June 30, 1862, Longstreet and A. P. Hill crossed the Chickahominy in pursuit of McClellan's retreating army. Huger and Magruder marched around the White Oak Swamp to operate on his flank, and a brigade was brought over the James River from Fort Darling. At 4 o'clock in the afternoon Longstreet and Hill made the attack. Huger and Magruder failed to arrive.

The fighting was furious and the advantage with the Confederates. Nearly one-fourth of McCall's division, upon whom the attack was made, were killed. Of the Confederate loss Gen. Pryor, of the Fifth Brigade of Longstreet's corps, reported the Fourteenth Alabama Regiment nearly annihilated. Of the 1,400 men with whom he crossed the Chickahominy June 26, 860 had been lost up to this time.

Fredericksburg (Va.), Battle of.—After the battle of Antietam (or Sharpsburg) McClellan occupied Harpers Ferry Sept. 22, 1862. Nov. 7 he was relieved of his command by Gen. Burnside. Lee's army was at that time at Culpeper and westward of the Blue Ridge Mountains. Burnside divided the army, now numbering about 110,000 men, into three grand divisions of two corps each. By Nov. 17 he had moved this army down the left bank of the Rappahannock to Falmouth, opposite Fredericksburg. Here the advance was delayed, awaiting the pontoon train from Washington. In the meantime Lee had concentrated the Confederate army of about 80,000 in the hills behind Fredericksburg. Dec. 11, 1862, the pontoons were laid, and on the 12th Franklin's division crossed. The Union forces were formed with Franklin on the left, Hooker's division in the center, and Sumner's on the right. The battle was opened by Franklin on the morning of the 13th, and continued in a series of disconnected and unsuccessful attacks on the Confederate works until night. On the 14th and 15th a truce was obtained by the Federals for burying their dead. On the evening of the latter day they retired across the river and the Confederates again occupied Fredericksburg. The Federal losses were 1,284 killed, 9,600 wounded, and 1,769 missing—a total of 12,653. The Confederates lost 608 killed, 4,116 wounded, and 653 captured or missing—a total of 5,377. Later in the month the Federal army went into winter quarters at Falmouth, and Jan. 25, 1863, Burnside was relieved of the command at his own request. Gen. Burnside testified before the Committee on the Conduct of the War that he had 100,000 men in action at the battle of Fredericksburg. Col. Walter H. Taylor, late adjutant-general of the Army of Northern Virginia, stated that Gen. Lee had actively engaged in the battle less than 20,000 men.

Fredericksburg, Va., battle of, discussed, 3360.

Free and Unlimited Coinage. (See Silver.)

Free Banking System.—April 11, 1838, the New York legislature passed the free-bank act, under the provisions of which any person or persons might establish a bank by depositing stocks, bonds, and mortgages as security for its circulating notes. This law was afterwards amended, requiring at least half of the securities to be New York State stocks. Previous to the passage of the free banking law of New York charters were granted by special act of the legislatures of various states, and their circulating medium was often far in excess of their capital. This caused heavy losses to note holders. The action of the New York legislature was followed by that of many other states and was made the basis of the national banking act of 1863.

Free-Booter. (See Bandit, also Pirate.)

Free Coinage of Silver. (See Silver Coinage, under Coins and Coinage.)

Free-Delivery System (see Post-Office, Department, of):
Discussed and recommendations regarding, 4204, 4769, 4836, 4937, 5102, 5376, 5756, 5881, 5971.
Extension of, to towns of 5,000 population recommended, 5633.
Inadequate facilities extended rural districts, 5633, 6451.

Free Goods.—Merchandise admitted into the country by import without the burden of customs taxes.

Free List. (See Import Duties.)

Free Negroes.—The first census taken in the United States showed nearly 60,000 free colored population. Of this number about half were in the southern states. The fact that they were considered a dangerous element by many persons led to a movement for colonizing them in Liberia, and they were put under certain disabilities, especially in the southern states. In the Dred Scott decision it was held that they were not citizens of the United States.

Free Negroes. (See Negroes.)

Free Ships, Free Goods.—The Declaration of Paris (1856) holds that "neutral goods in enemies' ships and enemies' goods in neutral ships, except contraband of war, are not liable to capture." As the United States refused to surrender the privilege of privateering, it could not subscribe to this declaration of the leading nations as the conduct of war. The United States Government has always held to the doctrine that in time of war all goods, whether belonging to neutrals or to belligerents, are, if carried in neutral vessels, thereby exempted from capture unless they are by nature contraband of war. During the war between England and France in 1793-1815 the United States contended for the recognition of this principle. England, on the other hand, always maintained that the ownership of the property itself should determine the question of seizure. This was a contributory cause of the War of 1812. The treaty of Ghent did not settle the question. The motive for privateering which once existed has been obviated by the addition of numerous cruisers to the Navy.

Free Silver. (See Silver.)

Free-Soil Party.—The southern leaders of the Democratic party determined to prevent the nomination of Martin Van Buren for the presidency in the convention of 1844. This was accomplished by declaring the vote of two-thirds of the convention necessary to nominate. These tactics caused a split in the Democratic party, especially in New York State, where the Van Buren faction became known as the Barnburners and their opponents the Hunkers. At the national convention in 1848 Van Buren's followers joined the remnants of the Liberal party and formed the Free-Soil party, which nominated Van Buren and Charles Francis Adams.

The platform was a strong protest against the extension of Slavery, and contained the epigrammatic declarations: "A free soil for a free people," and "Congress has no more power to make a slave than to make a king."

The popular vote in 1848 was Van Buren and Adams, 291,342; Cass (Democrat), 1,219,962; Taylor (Whig), 1,360,752. Van Buren received no electoral votes. Again in 1852 the party nominated a presidential ticket led by John P. Hale and George W. Julian, but obtained no electoral votes and a less popular vote than in 1848. During its existence the party always had from fifteen to twenty representatives in Congress, among them Charles Sumner, Salmon P. Chase and David Wilmot. It opposed the Kansas-Nebraska bill. It finally became part of the Republican party.

Free-Soilers.—That one of the anti-slavery political parties which came into existence in 1848. It was composed of the Liberty party, the Barnburner Democrats of New York, and a number of northern Whigs, who favored the Wilmot Proviso to the appropriation bill to conclude the treaty of peace with Mexico. Wilmot's amendment provided that there should be no slavery in the territory acquired under the appropriation. It passed the House, but was defeated in the Senate. In the next session it failed to pass either House. Resolutions of the same import as the Wilmot Proviso were introduced in the Whig and Democratic conventions of 1846, but were rejected. Upon this many prominent men of New York, Massachusetts, and Ohio withdrew and formed the Free-Soil party. At Buffalo in 1848 they nominated Martin Van Buren and Charles Francis Adams for President and Vice-President. These candidates received no electoral votes and only 291,263 popular votes. At Pittsburg in 1852 they nominated John P. Hale and George W. Julian, but their vote only reached 156,149. In 1856 the Free-Soilers joined the Republican party.

Free Trade.—In politics this term is used to signify an exchange of merchandise between the people of different countries without the imposition of any tax by the government. A tariff tax imposed by the government for the protection of home manufactures is held by the advocates of free trade to be contrary to sound principles of political economy and unjust to the consumers of the articles so taxed.

Free Zone. (See *Zona Libre.*)

Freedman's Savings and Trust Co., affairs of, discussed and recommendations regarding, 5113.

Freedmen (see also Civil Rights):

Act to protect all persons in United States in their civil rights and furnish means of vindication vetoed, 3603.

Violations of act referred to, 3666.

Appropriations for settlement under treaties of, and descendants upon lands in Oklahoma recommended, 4785.

Colonization of. (See Negroes.)

Condition of, discussed, 5490.

Education of, recommendations regarding, 3995, 5489.

Elective franchise to, discussed by President—

Garfield, 4598.

Hayes, 4445, 4553.

Johnson, 3557.

Emigration of. (See Negroes.)

Free exercise of right of suffrage by, discussed and recommendations regarding, 5490, 5562, 5643.

Memorial from, in Alabama asking for rights of citizenship, 4258.

Protection of rights and privileges of, discussed, 4395, 4412, 5490.

Provisions in amended constitutions of Southern States regarding, referred to, 3586.

Freedmen's Aid Societies, letter to President from, referred to, 3395.

Freedmen's Bureau.—An office of the War Department, created during the Civil War, to protect the interests of negroes who had been freed; its further purpose was to look after the education of refugees.

Freedmen's Bureau:

Abandoned lands, etc., to be turned over to, order regarding, 3538, 3547.

Act—

For discontinuance of, vetoed, 3852.

To continue, and to amend act to establish, vetoed, 3620.

To establish, vetoed, 3596.

Continuation of, vetoed, 3620.

Commissioner of—

Ordered to settle questions arising from lands set apart for benefit of refugees and freedmen, 3549.

Report of, referred to, 3569, 3571.

Establishment of, 3538.

Lands abandoned, ordered to be turned over to, 3538, 3547.

Operations of, referred to, 3586.

Property in Alabama to be transferred to, order regarding, 3550.

Reports of assistant commissioners of, referred to, 3577.

Transfer of, War Department, 4147.

Transportation required by, order regarding provision for, 3547.

Freedmen's Hospital.—This institution was established in Washington as a continuation of Government provision for sick freedmen. Every year it administers treatment to some 3,500 patients, and it conducts a training school for nurses. Government supervision is exercised through the Interior Department.

Freeholders, number of taxable inhabitants who are not, referred to, 988, 990.

French-American.—An American of French birth or extraction.

French Cable Co., stipulations with, referred to, 4738, 4744.

French Exhibit and Representation at the World's Fair, Chicago, in 1893, a reason for the United States participating largely at Paris, 6276.

French Revolution, claims of United States against France growing out of (see also France, Claims against): Referred to, 2808.

French Spoliation Claims.—In July, 1796, the Directory of the Republic of France announced to the world that French cruisers and privateers had been ordered to treat

Encyclopedic Index

vessels of neutral and allied powers, either as to search, seizure, or confiscation, in the same manner as they (the neutral or allied powers) should suffer the English to treat them. It was claimed that the United States did not exercise close enough vigilance over the belligerent rights and treaty stipulations between themselves and the warring European powers. England claimed the right to seize goods contraband of war under any flag. Though the United States disputed this claim, the Government did not feel justified in going to the extreme lengths desired by the French Government to enforce their protests. American commerce thereupon became a prey to French cruisers. By a convention between the United States and France ratified in 1801 the differences were adjusted, and the United States urged the claims of their citizens for damages sustained, amounting to $20,000,000. France made a counter-claim many times as great for damages sustained by her citizens resulting from failure of the United States to keep their treaty obligations. The result of this convention was a mutual surrender of these claims. The United States Government, it is claimed, became responsible to its citizens for indemnification. The claims were repeatedly pressed upon Congress, and the subject has engaged the attention of some of our ablest lawyers and statesmen. Bills for their payment were vetoed by President Polk in 1846 (2316), and by President Pierce in 1855 (2840). Jan. 20, 1885, Congress passed an act authorizing the claimants to apply to the Court of Claims for adjudication of their claims. This act was approved by President Arthur. The court has reported to Congress favorably on a large number of these claims. The Fifty-first Congress passed an act appropriating something more than $1,000,000 to pay such of the claims as had been reported favorably by that court to Congress, which was approved by President Benj. Harrison. A similar bill, carrying over $1,000,000 for their payment was vetoed by President Cleveland June 6, 1896 (6115). March 3, 1899, President McKinley approved an act to pay over $1,000,000 of these claims.

French Spoliation Claims (see also France, Claims against):
Act making appropriations for, vetoed, 6115.
Act providing for—
Ascertainment and satisfaction of, vetoed, 2316.
Ascertainment of, vetoed, 2840.
Reports on, transmitted, 4916, 4956, 4972, 4982, 5199.

Frenchtown (Mich.), Battle of.—Gen. Harrison having succeeded Hull in command of the Army of the Northwest, resolved to regain what that unfortunate commander bad lost. He dispatched Gen. Winchester with 2,000 men to Detroit, with orders to cross the river if opportunity offered and take Fort Madden. From his camp (at Presque Ile) Winchester on Jan. 17, 1813, detailed Col. Lewis with 660 men to advance to Frenchtown (now Monroe, Mich.), on the River Raisin. Lewis arrived on the 18th, and the British garrison, consisting of 200 Canadian militia and 400 Indians, were driven into the woods. The Americans lost 12 killed and 55 wounded. The loss to the enemy was considerable and occurred chiefly in the forest.

Friars' Lands in Philippine Islands, disposition of, 1069.

Friendly Islands. (See Tonga Islands.)
Friends, Society of. (See Society of Friends.)
Frigates. (See Vessels.)
"Frolic."—The British Sloop of War captured by "The Wasp" in command of Captain Jones in the War of 1812. (See Wasp, The.)
Frolic, The, engagement with the *Wasp*, 506.
Frontiers (see also Indians; Militia):
Affairs on southeastern frontier, 2909.
Posts should be established for protection of, 614.
Protection of—
Necessity of, 76, 86, 87, 96, 101, 133, 166, 551, 1817, 2819, 3447.
Sufficient, 648.
Referred to, 165, 398, 824.

Fruit Growing and Preserving.—Horticulture as a distinct branch of farming is of recent growth in the United States. The early settlers found growing wild in America many of the common fruits familiar to them in Europe. Besides cultivating these, they imported other varieties and grafts from their former homes. The early efforts of the colonists were limited to raising enough fruit for the family, with little thought of commerce, though an orchard of 2,500 apple trees is said to have existed in Virginia in 1686. In New England, too, large apple orchards were not uncommon, but their products were mostly used for making cider. There are about 150 species of fruits grown in the United States, ranging from the plums and apples of the north to the figs, oranges, lemons and other tropical fruits of Florida and California. They are classified for convenience into tree fruits, vine fruits, small fruits and herbs. With the improvements in transportation and packing came the shipment of tropical fruits to northern markets.
Scientific breeding and cross-breeding of native species has developed some distinct varieties suited to the requirements of the markets. Pioneers in this line were Munson of Texas, Burbank of California, and Webber of the Department of Agriculture.
From 1800 to 1830 about the only fruit imported was an occasional bunch of bananas. In the latter year J. V. T. Pearsall of New York brought in a cargo of 1,500 bunches. In 1832 a cargo of oranges arrived from Sicily, and for the next thirty years Italian fruits held undisputed possession of the American markets, during which time much speculation was indulged in and the auction system of marketing was established. Some of the early dealers were Devlin & Rose ; Chamberlain, Phelps & Co., James Robinson & Co., Lawrence, Giles & Co., of New York ; Daniel Draper & Co., and Conant & Co., Boston ; Dix & Wilkins, Baltimore ; S. S. Scattergood & Co., and Isaac Jeanes & Co., Philadelphia.
The first green fruit shipped across the continent from California arrived in New York in 1867. This shipment proved a failure, but next year one car of Tokay grapes and three cars of pears from California consigned to N. R. Doe, New York, arrived in good order and brought $3.50 to $5 a box for the pears and $10 to $15 per 40-pound crate for the grapes. Thousands of carloads of fruit are now shipped every year, the refrigerator-car service v. the railroads facilitating the transporta

tion. The freight rate across the continent has been reduced, in some instances, as much as fifty per cent, in the last thirty-five years. The Italian fruit grower can land fruit in New York after paying a duty, and sell cheaper than the growers in California and Florida, yet the domestic products seem to hold their own. Florida and California ship about 8,000,000 boxes of oranges a year and Florida adds to this 10,000,000 pineapples and $250,000 worth of limes. Our fruit export trade consists largely of apples, which are sent to London, Glasgow, Liverpool and Berlin.

Canning and Preserving.—There are 2,789 establishments in the United States engaged in canning and preserving fruits and vegetables. They are collectively capitalized at $67,313,423, and employ 47,448 persons, including firm members, wage-earners and salaried attendants. The value of the output is figured at $91,439,161, of which $28,895,539 is added in the process of packing and preserving.

California is by far the most important state in the canning and preserving industry, largely on account of its fruits. The establishments in California are on the average much larger than those of most other states, but show relatively fewer wage-earners than the others. This doubtless is due to the growing use of improved machinery and appliances. The number of wage-earners decreased 5.4 per cent during the decade ending with 1909, but the value of the output increased 120.3 per cent. New York ranked second and Maryland third.

In the production of canned tomatoes, the most important of vegetables, Maryland has led all other states for the last thirty years, reporting 40.9 per cent of the total in 1909. Six states: Maryland, Delaware, New Jersey, Indiana, Virginia and California—each reported more than a million dollars' worth of canned tomatoes in 1909. California puts up eighty per cent of the canned peaches, pears and apricots as well as dried fruits.

Fruits, American, restrictions upon importation of, into Germany and Switzerland, 6331.

Fuel Administration.—The increased consumption of fuel due to the increased demand in industry as a result of the European War led to the inclusion of fuel among the products over which the President was given control in the so-called Food Control Bill. The general powers granted under that bill are described under the head of "Food Administration," but separate provisions regarding fuel in the bill authorize the President to requisition and take over mines for use or operation by the government; to fix the price of coal and coke, when sold by either producer or dealer; and to establish rules for their distribution and transportation. He is further empowered to prescribe regulations governing the work of employees in the mines, and to require, if necessary, all producers to sell only to the United States through an agency to be designated by the President. Various orders by the President in carrying out these powers may be found by consulting the headings Fuel and Coal in the Index under Wilson, Woodrow.

To give merely one example of the difficulties attending the fuel problem, it might be stated that whereas the railroads of the country used approximately 125,000,000 tons of coal in 1916, some 170,000,000 tons were used by them in 1917. If the same ratio was preserved in all the other forms

of American industrial activity, our net consumption of coal increased in 1917 to 635,000,000 tons from 475,000,000 tons in 1916. The scarcity of labor, due to increasing wages in other industries and the draft, combined with the severest winter known in the recent history of the Weather Bureau, made the coal problem among the most serious met by our Government in its prosecution of the war.

On August 21, 1917, the President officially fixed coal prices (see page 8327), altering them later on November 28, 1917 (see page 8398). On August 23, 1917, Harry A. Garfield, formerly president of Williams College, was appointed Fuel Administrator. The seriousness of the coal situation was probably the chief determining factor in the federalization of the railroads in the country (see pages 8409, 8412, 8418). But the severe and unprecedented cold waves and snow storms of January, 1918, hindered the solution of the coal problem, industries shut down because no coal could be obtained, private homes remained unheated, suffering became intense, especially among the poor; and accordingly Fuel Administrator Garfield announced on January 17, 1918, that all factories and manufacturing plants except those specifically mentioned as being engaged in the production of essential war material would remain closed from January 18 to January 22, inclusive; and that on all Mondays from January 21 to March 18, inclusive, all work except that absolutely indispensable to the public health and welfare would cease. The suddenness with which the order came caused a furor throughout the country, but it was loyally and faithfully obeyed: and the results, especially those concerned with the coaling of ships, were favorable.

Indeed, the order regarding "Workless Mondays" was rescinded for Southern states after February 4, 1918, and for the remainder of the country after February 11, 1918.

Another noteworthy feature of the campaign for fuel conservation during the war was the elimination of unnecessary lighting, such as that of an ornamental or advertising nature. In addition, there was organized a campaign for more economical firing, etc., in both domestic and industrial heating plants.

Among the agencies used by the Fuel Administration were a campaign to urge that rooms and houses be not heated above 68° Fahrenheit and the reduction of the supply of fuel whenever necessary to industries classed as non-essential.

Fuel Administration:

Licensing of—

Ammonia industry, 8428.

Coal and coke distributors, 8471.

Cotton dealers, 8498.

Fertilizer industry, 8460.

Fuel oil industry, 8444.

Regulations for, 8472.

Fuel Administrator, appointment of 8330.

Fuel Prices. (See Coal Prices.)

Fugitive Criminals. (See Extradition.)

Laws regarding, amendment of, recommended, 5090, 6334.

Opinion of Attorney-General regarding right of Executive to surrender, when crime is committed out of United States, 1808.

Reports of International American Conference on subject of, referred to, 5514.

Surrender of—
Ashburton treaty regarding, discussed, 2016.
By Costa Rica, 5868.
Convention regarding, with—
Austria, 2911.
Baden, 2898.
Bavaria, 2760.
Belgium, 2724, 4129, 4216, 4247, 4695, 4715.
Central America, 4055.
Chile, 2912.
Columbia, 4587, 5200.
Denmark, failure to negotiate, 4561.
Ecuador, 4160, 4247.
France, 2125, 2166, 2219, 3012.
Referred to, 5869.
Germany, 2689.
Discussed, 4824.
Great Britain, 2016, 4989, 5470.
Demands made under, 2131, 2213.
Discussed, 4917.
Questions arising under, 4419.
Referred to, 4802, 5545.
Refusal of, to comply with, discussed, 4321, 4324, 4368.
Guatemala, 4067, 5123, 5179, 5199.
Haiti, 3459.
Hanover, 2834.
Honduras, 4161, 4210.
Italy, 3828, 3888, 3896, 4806.
Referred to, 5546, 5959.
Japan, 4987, 5086.
Luxemberg, 4782.
Mexico, 2602, 3264, 4867.
Demands made under, 4791.
Extension of time of ratification of, recommended, 3274.
Questions arising under, 5090, 6333.
Report of Secretary of State regarding, 2690.
Netherlands, 2910, 2952, 2994, 4542, 4562, 5176, 5397.
Withdrawn from Senate, 2916.
Nicaragua, 4067, 4100.
Peru, 4068, 4247, 6434.
Termination of, referred to, 4919.
Prussia, 2267, 2689, 2719.
Ratification of, refused, 2450.
Russia, 5398, 5871.
Salvador, 4033, 4212, 4247.
Questions arising under, 5961.
Santo Domingo, 3669.
Sicily, 2870.
Spain, 4376, 4699, 4738.
Referred to, 4757.
Sweden and Norway, 3114, 5871.
Swiss Confederation, 2356.
Turkey, 4258, 4296.
Venezuela, 2917, 3185.
Discussed, 5962.
Conventions regarding, recommended, 5868.

Fugitive-Slave Laws.—Article IV., section 2, of the Constitution provides: "No person held to service or labor in one state, under the laws thereof, escaping into another, shall, in consequence of any law or regulation therein, be discharged from such service or labor, but shall be delivered up on claim of the party to whom such service or labor may be due." In pursuance of this provision Congress in 1793 passed the first fugitive-slave law, providing that on the owner's giving proof of ownership before a magistrate of the locality where the slave was found the magistrate should order the slave to be delivered to his owner without trial by jury. Hindering arrest or harboring a fugitive slave was punishable by a fine of $500. In 1850, as a part of the compromise measures of that year, a law was passed providing for United States commissioners to aid in the more strict enforcement of the law. Proof of identity and two witnesses to the fact of escape were all that were required in evidence. The negro could neither testify nor have jury trial. In all the Colonies laws had been passed providing for the return of fugitive slaves. The New England Confederation of 1643 had provided for mutual extradition of slaves. Extradition from British territory had been denied in the decision of the Sommersett case in 1771. In the case of Prigg vs. Pennsylvania (1842) the Supreme Court held that the execution of the law of 1793 devolved upon Federal authorities alone; that state authorities could not be forced to act. Several states thereupon forbade action by their officials. The act of 1850 aroused much bitter feeling in the north, and "personal liberty" laws were passed in many of the states, some of them conflicting with Federal laws and some even with the Constitution itself. The Civil War ended the whole matter, and the laws were repealed.

Fugitive Slaves:

Acts passed to defeat laws regarding, discussed, 3160.
Execution of laws for return of, forcibly resisted at Boston, 2637, 2673.
Proclamation regarding, 2645. (See opposite 2692.)
Legislation regarding restoration of, recommended, 2673.
Negotiations with Great Britain regarding surrender of, 988, 2131.
State laws regarding, discussed, 2874, 2933.
Surrender of, referred to, 988.

Fundamental Constitutions of Carolina.—In 1669 John Locke, the celebrated English philosopher, drew up an elaborate constitution for the Colony of Carolina, providing for several orders of nobility. At the present day it is of interest only as a sample of early constitutions and an attempt to establish an American aristocracy. The scheme comprehended a grand court of proprietors and a parliament of landgraves and caciques having entailed estates.

Funeral of Nineteen American Sailors and Marines, President Wilson's Address at, 7939.

Furlough.—Absence from military duty by consent of authority ; also in the navy signifying absence from duty on half-pay, either by one's own request, or as mild punishment for a petty offense.

Furniture Manufacture.—Colonial furniture, as the term is understood today, was unknown to the American colonists. In the early struggles for existence little attempt was made to evolve a distinctive style of furniture. The New Englanders copied the designs of the pieces brought over with them or reproduced from memory as nearly as they were able with the rude tools at hand and their productions were of heavy wood with severe lines and little carving. The southern planters imported richly carved pieces from England and France in the style of Elizabethan and Jacobean periods in England and the Renaissance in France, while the Dutch settlers of New York brought their styles from Holland and the Orient.

In 1776 the home of a well-to-do American was fitted up in about the same style as that of an Englishman of the same social and financial standing. Chippendale was the vogue, with pieces in the modified Greek style of Adam. From the French Empire came the massive mahogany with rope-carved pillars and lion-claw feet.

The early cabinet shops were like the secondhand repair shops to be found in all the large cities today. The cabinet-makers continued to reproduce the styles imported from Europe and these long continued on the simple Chippendale lines. Gradually the Empire fashions, which were making themselves felt all over Europe, spread to America, and the shapes became heavier and more pretentious, mahogany being used almost exclusively. Heads of animals were used, and claw feet became a general feature. Cabinet-makers soon changed their ideas and began making a debased rococo style, which did not have the elegance or character of the Louis XV, but was covered with a florid ornamentation in which the main idea seems to have been display. About 1830 efforts were made to produce furniture in the Gothic style, but the lack of artistic training of American cabinet-makers caused these to be abandoned, and the rococo furniture held sway for many years.

The application of steam to cabinet-makers' machinery in 1815 revolutionized furniture making, bringing labor-saving devices into more general use, and enabling the manufacturer to supply the rapidly increasing demand. In 1825 Mr. Richardson, of Philadelphia, introduced the circular saw, and Taylor, Rich & Co. erected the first mahogany mill in America, using a number of these saws. Ordinary furniture, which until now had been quite plain, began to take on endless scrollwork, moldings and ornaments, so easily produced by the new machines. The value of the furniture product in 1850 was estimated at about $15,-000,000, and the industry gave employment to 37,000 people, out of a population in excess of 23,000,000.

Up to this time the furniture industry had been confined to the Eastern States, principally in and around Boston, but a number of factories were now started in the West. These factories, equipped with new machinery and using the native forests of oak, ash, walnut, etc., with which they were surrounded, produced a useful grade of furniture, in which art seems to have been little considered, but which answered the purposes of the rapidly increasing population of the newly developing territory. Trade kept increasing with the general wealth, and by 1860 the production had reached $25,500,000, but the number of working men employed in the industry, owing to improvements in machinery, had declined to 28,000. The population had then reached almost 31,500,000. At this time all industry received a serious blow by the civil war.

After the war came a movement in favor of more perfect construction, and the use of straight lines exclusively became general, the stiff apparance being relieved by an abundant use of arches, spindles, turnings, etc. This style allowed the manufacturer to do the greater part of the work by machinery, for which it seemed specially adapted. The awakened public interest in furniture developed the trade in an unprecedented manner, the production for 1870 being $68,500,000, two and a half times that of 1860. The number of men employed at this time shows a similar increase, being 55,800, out of a population of 38,-500,000.

The amount of business done in 1890 was not equal to the increase in population. The value of the output for that year was $86,362,685, an increse of eleven per cent. over 1880, but the amount per capita of population dropped to $1.38 as compared with $1.55 in 1880, and $1.77 in 1870.

The woods used in furniture are subject to frequent changes. Early in the 19th century mahogany, maple, and black walnut were in favor; then cherry and ash became fashionable ; toward 1880, oak, so long forgotten, took a prominent place. At the end of the century we find black walnut almost out of use. Oak has kept its vogue for the hall, the library and the dining room. Mahogany, curly birch, and maple are still extensively used ; all of them for the bedroom and mahogany for the dining room and the drawing-room in the better grades of furniture.

The furniture industry of the United States has reached a magnitude unknown elsewhere, and the perfect equipment and organization of our mammoth factories capable of an enormous production, make it imperative that some outlet should be found for it outside the home demand. Intelligent efforts are being made in this direction by a number of manufacturers, and there is every prospect of our being able eventually to secure a large foreign trade.

Fur Seals:

Killing of, regulated by Tribunal of Paris, 7063.

Problem of, discussed by President Taft, 7779, 7823.

Threatened extinction of, 7063.

Fur Seals. (See Bering Sea.)

Fur Seal Treaty (North Pacific) concluded with Great Britain, Japan and Russia, 7670, 7877.

Fur Trade, persons killed while engaged in, referred to, 1128.

Gadsden Purchase.—This term is applied to a tract of land consisting of 45,-535 square miles in Arizona and New Mexico, extending from the Gila River to the Mexican boundary. It was acquired from Mexico by a treaty negotiated by James Gadsden, Dec. 30, 1853. The United States paid Mexico $10,000,000 for the land, but Mexico relinquished claims against the United States for damages for Indian depredations amounting to from $15,000,000 to $30,000,000. For this transaction Santa Anna, President of Mexico, was banished as a traitor.

Gadsden Purchase, treaty with Mexico respecting, 2762.

Gag-Law.—A parliamentary rule for the purpose of eliminating or shutting off debate. From 1840 to 1844 a rule in the House of Representatives existed amounting to a denial of the Constitutional right of liberal debate. John Quincy Adams effected the repeal of the rule.

Gag Rule.—May 26, 1836, Congress passed a resolution providing that thenceforth all petitions, memorials, resolutions, propositions, or papers relating in any way to the subject of slavery or the abolition of slavery should lie upon the table without being printed or referred. John Quincy Adams led a strong and bitter opposition to this infringement upon the right of petition. The cry of "gag rule" was raised in the north and served to increase the spirit of petition in that section. Dec. 3, 1844, the rule was abolished.

Gaines Mill (Va.), Battle of.—One of the series of engagements which took place June 25 to July 1, 1862, before Richmond, commonly known as the Seven Days' Battles. June 27, the day after the battle of Mechanicsville, Fitz-John Porter retired to Gaines Mill Heights, about 5 miles east of his former position. Here he was attacked shortly after noon by A. P. Hill's corps. Slocum's division was sent to reenforce Porter, increasing his army to 35,000. During the afternoon Jackson joined Hill and Longstreet, swelling the Confederate forces to about 60,000. Severe fighting was continued until dark. Porter succeeded in defending the bridges across the Chickahominy allowing the heavy guns and wagon train to pass in safety on their way to the James. During the night he himself crossed over, destroying the bridges. The loss of the Confederates was reported at 3,284. Porter lost 894 men killed, 3,107 wounded, and 2,836 missing, a total of 6,837. He also lost 22 cannon.

Gainesville, McAlester and St. Louis Railway Co., act regarding grant of right of way to, through Indian Territory returned, 6099.

Gallantry.—In military parlance, brave, undaunted action and bearing on the part of soldiers, either singly or en masse.

Gallantry, instances of, rewarded:
Bertholf, Ellsworth P., 6352.
Call, Dr. Samuel J., 6352.
Dewey, George, 6296.
Farragut, David G., 3440.
Grant, Ulysses S., 3305.
Hobson, Richmond P., 6306.
Jarvis, David H., 6352.
Merritt, Wesley, 6491.
Sampson, William T., 6573.

Gallaudet College. (See Columbian Institution for the Deaf.)

Galveston, Tex.:
Equipment of privateers at, must be suppressed, 583.
Illicit introduction of slaves through, must be suppressed, 583.
Referred to, 590, 592.

Game, Big, preservation of, 6764, 7186, 7393.

Garden City Forest Reserve, proclaimed, 7289.

Garden State.—A nickname for Kansas (q. v.). (See also States) ; sometimes also nicknamed the Sunflower State.

Garfield, James A.—March 4, 1881-Sept. 19, 1881.

Twenty-fourth Administration—Republican.
  Vice-President—Chester A. Arthur.
Secretary of State—
    James G. Blaine.
Secretary of the Treasury—
    William Windom.
Secretary of War—
    Robert T. Lincoln.
Secretary of the Interior—
    Samuel J. Kirkwood.
Secretary of the Navy—
    William H. Hunt.
Postmaster-General—
    Thomas L. James.
Attorney-General—
    Wayne MacVeagh.

Nomination.—Garfield's nomination at the Republican Convention, at Chicago, June 2-3, 1880, has been characterized as one of the greatest political struggles ever known in American history. He was accepted as the compromise candidate between the Grant and Blaine factions on the thirty-sixth ballot.

Platform.—The Republican platform of 1880 reviewed the work of the party during its twenty years of political ascendency, enumerating among its achievements, the suppression of the rebellion, the enfranchisement of 4,000,000 negroes, suppression of the Fugitive Slave law, the raising of the value of paper from 38 to par, and increased railways from thirty-one thousand miles in 1860, to more than eighty-two thousand miles in 1879 ; increased foreign trade, reduced the public debt, and brought prosperity to the country. It stood upon this record ; acknowledged the supremacy of the Constitution ; advocated national promotion of popular education ; reaffirmed non-sectarianism ; repeated its confirmation of revenue for tariff and for protection ; urged restriction of Chinese immigration ; endorsed the administration of President Hayes ; arraigned the Democratic party ; and affirmed the restoration of harmony to the Union.

Opposition.—The Democratic National Convention, at Cincinnati, June 22-24, 1880, nominated General Hancock. The National Greenback party, at Chicago, June 9-11, 1880, nominated James B. Weaver. The Prohibition party, at Cleveland, on June 17, 1880, nominated Neal Dow.

Vote.—The popular vote cast by thirty-eight States gave Garfield 4,454,416 ; Hancock, 4,444,952 ; Weaver, 308,578 ; with 10,-305 scattering. The electoral vote, counted on Feb. 9, 1881, gave Garfield 214, and Hancock, 155.

Party Affiliation.—Garfield seems never to have voted before 1856, when he cast his ballot for Frémont, the first candidate of the Republican party. The leading part that he played in Congress for twenty years as chairman of most important com-

EXTENT OF THE UNITED STATES DURING THE ADMINISTRATION OF PRESIDENT GARFIELD, 1881.

(NOT INCLUDING TERRITORIES)

mittees, saw the rendering of faithful and brilliant service to Republican interests. From March, 1866, he continued his aggressive policy of promoting the resumption of specie payment. He was the representative in Congress of the "Sound Money" principle. In reconstruction times, he opposed the policy of President Johnson. In the Forty-fifth Congress, as leader of the opposition in the House, he contributed greatly in compelling the Democratic majority to make the appropriations which they were withholding. His report of the tariff commission in April, 1880, confirmed him as a firm believer in the policy of protection.

One of the first acts of Garfield was the removal of Gen. Edwin A. Merritt from the position of Collector of the Port of New York and the appointment of Mr. Robertson without consulting the New York Senators. Postmaster-General James and Senators Conkling and Platt protested, but without avail. This resulted in the resignation of both Senators.

Political Complexion of Congress.—In the Forty-seventh Congress (1881-1883) the Senate, of 76 members, was composed of 37 Democrats, 37 Republicans, 1 American, and 1 Readjuster; and the House, of 293 members, was made up of 130 Democrats, 152 Republicans, 9 Nationals, and 2 Readjusters. In the Forty-eighth Congress (1883-1885) the Senate, of 76 members, was made up of 36 Democrats and 40 Republicans; and the House, of 225 members, was made up of 200 Democrats, 119 Republicans, 4 Independents, and 2 Nationals.

Civil Service.—In his Inaugural Address (page 4601) President Garfield said: "The civil service can never be placed upon a satisfactory basis until it is regulated by law. For the good of the service itself, for the protection of those who are entrusted with the appointing power against the waste of time and the obstruction to the public business caused by the inordinate pressure for place, and for the protection of incumbents against intrigue and wrong, I shall at the proper time ask Congress to fix the tenure of the minor offices of the several Executive Departments and prescribe the grounds upon which removals shall be made during the terms for which the incumbents have been appointed." It was in connection with the civil service and the making of appointments that the memorable struggle over the patronage of New York occurred, which resulted in the resignation of Senators Conkling and Platt.

Finance.—In his Inaugural Address (page 4600) President Garfield said: "By the experience of commercial nations in all ages it has been found that gold and silver afford the only safe foundation for a monetary system. Confusion has recently been created by variations in the relative value of the two metals, but I confidently believe that arrangements can be made between the leading commercial nations which will secure the general use of both metals."

President Garfield was shot July 2, 1881, in the Baltimore and Potomac railroad station in Washington and died Sept. 19 following at Elberon, N. J.

Garfield, James A.:

Biographical sketch of, 4593.

Civil service discussed by. (See also Civil Service.) 4601.

Death of—

Action of Congress on, 4615.

Action of Senators and Representatives in Washington on, 4608.

Announcement of, to Vice-President and reply to, 4604.

Announcements of, and honors to be paid memory of, 4603, 4604, 4605, 4606, 4607.

Condolence on, of—

Guatemala, 4627.

Russia, 4626.

Day of humiliation and mourning in memory of, appointed, 4621.

Discussed, 4620, 4624.

Official bulletin of autopsy on body, 4614.

Finances discussed by, 4600.

Funeral of—

Announcement of, and arrangements for, 4610.

Orders of heads of Executive Departments relating to, 4608.

Inaugural address of, 4596.

Portrait of, 4592.

Statue of, to be erected in Washington, appropriation for, recommended, 4795.

Unveiling ceremonies, order regarding, 5162.

Garland Case.—In 1860 Augustus H. Garland was admitted to practice in the United States Supreme Court. Not very long after the State of Arkansas had seceded from the Union in 1861 he was sent to the Confederate Congress, where he served until the surrender of Gen. Lee in 1865. He was included in the general amnesty extended to citizens of the southern states. July 2, 1862, Congress enacted a law requiring all candidates for office to take an oath that they had never engaged in hostilities against the United States, and on Jan. 24, 1865, this oath was required of persons admitted to the bar of any circuit or district court of the United States or Court of Claims. Garland refused to take the prescribed oath on the ground that it was unconstitutional and void as affecting his status in court, and that if it were constitutional his pardon released him from compliance with it. The court sustained him in his contention on the ground that the law was ex post facto. Justice Field, delivering the opinion, said: "It is not within the constitutional power of Congress thus to inflict punishment beyond the reach of Executive clemency." Chief Justice Chase and Justices Miller, Swayne, and Davis dissented.

Garrison.—The soldiers residing for defensive purposes in a fort or fortress.

Gas, Illuminating and Heating.—The history of the gas industry, not only of the United States but of the world, covers little more than a century. The possibility of making gas for lighting purposes was investigated simultaneously in France and England in the latter part of the eighteenth century—in England by William Murdock and in France by Philippe Le Bon—and it is an open question as to which of the two countries is entitled to the credit of discovery.

The story of the manufacture of coal gas in this country dates from 1806, when David Melville, of Newport, R. I., lighted his premises with gas, which he made thereon. This was nine years after Murdock's experiments. Melville patented his process in 1813, and shortly thereafter cotton mills were lighted by coal gas, and in 1817 it was used in a lighthouse. In 1816 a company was chartered in Baltimore, Md., followed by the establishment of plants in Boston in 1822, New York, in 1823, Brooklyn, N. Y., and Bristol, R. I., in 1825, and New Orleans in 1835.

The Lowe process of making water gas was established at Phoenixville, Pa., in 1873. By this process hydrogen and the oxides of carbon, produced by the action of steam upon carbon at a high temperature, are mixed and then combined with richly carburated gases, usually from petroleum, thus producing the power of illumination. At present the amount of water gas is about 75 per cent of the entire quantity manufactured.

Returns were received by the Department of Commerce from 1,284 establishments in 1914, the total products of which for the year were valued at $220,237,781. Of these 1,284 establishments, 427 produced carbureted water gas; 274, straight coal gas; 156, mixed coal and water gas or mixed coal, water, and oil gas; 150, oil gas; and 165, acetylene. The principal product of the remaining establishments, 112 in number, was gasoline gas. The 150 oil-gas plants included 61 which manufactured Pintsch gas and 4 which produced Blau gas; and the 165 acetylene plants included 36 which distributed the gas in containers.

Location of Establishments.—Of the 1,284 establishments reported for 1914, 131 were located in New York, 113 in Iowa, 99 in Pennsylvania, 75 in Illinois, 66 in California, 61 in Massachusetts, 60 in Indiana, 59 in Michigan, 48 in Nebraska, 47 each in Minnesota and Wisconsin, 43 in New Jersey, 35 in Missouri, 27 each in Connecticut and Texas, 25 in Ohio, 22 in Virginia, 20 in North Carolina, 19 in Georgia, 18 in Maryland, 17 each in Maine and South Dakota, 14 each in Alabama, Florida, and New Hampshire, 13 each in Kentucky and Washington, 12 each in Kansas, South Carolina and Tennessee, 9 each in Arizona, North Dakota, Oregon, and Vermont, 8 each in Colorado, Delaware, and Mississippi, 6 each in Montana and Rhode Island, 5 each in Oklahoma and West Virginia, 4 each in Idaho, Louisiana, and Utah, 3 each in the District of Columbia and Nevada, 2 in New Mexico, and 1 each in Arkansas and Wyoming.

Gaugers. (See Weighers and Gaugers.)

Gayhead, Mass., land designated at, for lighthouse, 1221.

"Gazette" Articles.—A series of articles written by John Adams, and published in 1765 in the Boston "Gazette" supporting the refusal of the Colonists to use stamps as required by the Stamp Act (q. v.). These articles set forth the arguments against taxation without representation in convincing style, and therefore were helpful in arousing the public sentiment which led to the Declaration of Independence.

Geary Law, sustained by Supreme Court, discussed, 5868.

Gem of the Mountains.—A nickname for Idaho (q. v.). (See also States.)

General.—Formerly highest rank in the United States Army, conferred in recognition of distinguished military services. It was first created by act of Congress March 2, 1799, and conferred upon George Washington; was abolished in 1802, but was revived July 25, 1866, for Ulysses S. Grant. William T. Sherman succeeded to the rank, March 4, 1869, Grant having become President, and held it until his retirement, Feb. 8, 1884. The grade was revived June 1, 1888, for Philip H. Sheridan, who held it until his death, Aug. 5 of that year, when it ceased to exist. The rank of General was also highest in the Confederate Army. (See Army.)

General Allotment Act, mentioned, 6674.

General Armstrong, The:
Claims of owners of, against Portugal, 2268, 2759.
Distribution of fund appropriated for relief of owners and crew of, referred to, 4987.
President of France selected as arbiter in case of, 2655.
Award of Emperor of France, 2722.

General Deficiency Bill.—A bill passed by Congress to provide appropriations omitted from special appropriation bills.

General Grant National Park. (See Parks, National.)

General Land Office. (See Interior, Department of.)

General Land Office:
Appropriations for—
Estimates of, submitted, 4677.
Recommended, 1433.
Business of, suspension of, recommended, 1433.
Creation of new offices in, recommended, 4658.
Discussed, 5638.
Estimates of appropriations required for, submitted, 4677.
Increase in clerical force of, recommended, 4663.
Improvements in, recommended, 1381.
Surveyor-general's district for Missouri, Illinois, and Arkansas should be divided, 1131.
Work of, 6656.

General Land Office, Commissioner of:
Bill to increase salary of, 4658.
Reports of, 986, 1098, 2130.

General Supply Committee.—The General Supply Committee was created in lieu of the board (Board of Awards) provided for in section 3709 of the Revised Statutes as amended, and is composed of officers, one from each of the executive departments, designated by the head thereof. Its duties are to make an annual schedule of required miscellaneous supplies for the use of each of said departments and other Government establishments in Washington, to standardize such supplies, eliminating all unnecessary grades and varieties, and to solicit bids based upon formulas and specifications drawn up by such experts in the service of the Government as the committee may see fit to call upon, who shall render whatever assistance they may require. Provided, that the articles intended to be purchased in this manner shall be those in common use by or suitable to the ordinary needs of two or more such departments or establishments. Every purchase or drawing of such supplies from the contractor is immediately reported to said committee. No disbursing officer may be a member of the committee.

General Urrea, The, capture off the coast of Texas of, by the *Natchez* and restoration of, referred to, 1617.

Geneva Convention.—An agreement entered into at Geneva, Switzerland, Aug. 22, 1864, by representatives of France, Belgium, Switzerland, Portugal, Holland, Italy, Spain, Denmark, Baden, and Prussia. It has since been agreed to by all the military powers of Europe and of America, except Brazil. Of Asiatic countries Persia has also consented to be governed by its provisions. The convention provides for the neutrality of ambulances, no distinction of nationality to be made in caring for the sick and wounded. Natives of an invaded country who bring aid to sick and wounded shall be free and respected. If they receive the wounded into their houses, they shall be exempt from military contributions and quartering of troops. Hospitals and their attachés, unless defended by a military force, shall be recognized as neutral. Nurses, surgeons, physicians, and those in charge of administration and transportation shall be marked by a distinctive flag or arm badge, consisting of a red cross on a white ground. The sick and wounded who fall into the hands of the enemy shall, when cured, be returned to their own country, if incapable of service; otherwise they shall be paroled.

In 1868 a second convention at Geneva extended the operations of the system to naval warfare so far as possible. Influenced by the agreement between nations, many Red Cross societies have been organized by humane civilians, whose work has done much to alleviate the horrors of war. The credit of originating the idea of neutralizing the sick and wounded is due to two Swiss gentlemen, Heinrich Dumont, a physician, and his friend, Gustave Moynier, chairman of the Society of Public Utility.

Geneva Convention, for relief of wounded in war referred to, 4631, 4653, 4670.

Geneva Tribunal.—The settlement of the Alabama Claims was referred by the Treaty of Washington to five arbitrators, to be appointed by the President of the United States, the Queen of Great Britain, the King of Italy, the President of the Swiss Confederation and the Emperor of Brazil. These rulers, in the above order, named as arbitrators Charles Francis Adams, Lord Chief Justice Sir Alexander Cockburn, Count Federigo Sclopis, Mr. Jaques Staempfli and Baron Itajuba. J. C. Bancroft Davis and Lord Tenterden, respectively, represented as agents the United States and Great Britain. The tribunal met at Geneva, Switzerland, on Dec. 15, 1871, and Count Sclopis was made president. Each government submitted its proofs and arguments, which were carefully considered by the arbitrators. The United States claimed damages both for direct and for indirect losses, and for injuries occasioned by thirteen vessels. The tribunal decided to allow only direct losses caused by the *Florida* and the *Alabama,* with their tenders, and by the *Shenandoah* during part of their cruise. Various rules of international law were laid down which supported most of the contentions of our government. It was decided that the expenses incurred in pursuing the cruisers and the prospective earnings of the destroyed merchant vessels should not be included in the award; that net, and not gross, freights should be allowed, and that reasonable interest should be included. Fi-

nally, on Sept. 14, 1872, the tribunal "awarded to the United States a sum of $15,500,000 in gold as the indemnity to be paid by Great Britain to the United States as the satisfaction of all the claims referred to the consideration of the tribunal." The English representatives cast the only dissenting vote, but Great Britain accepted the decision and paid the award within a year. (See also Alabama Claims.)

Geneva Tribunal (see also Halifax, Nova Scotia):

For settlement of questions pending between United States and Great Britain, discussed, 4097, 4138.

Award of, 4138.

Commissioners to report on distribution of, appointment of, recommended, 4139, 4190.

Payment of, 4190.

Case of United States and counter case referred to, 4115, 4118, 4119.

Differences of opinion regarding powers of, 4120, 4122.

Legislation in connection with, urged, 4164.

Referred to, 4161.

Geodetic Association, International, invitation to United States to become a party to, 5192.

Geographer of United States.—By an act passed May 20, 1785, Congress created a national geographer, whose duty it was to supervise and submit plats to the Treasury Department. The United States Coast and Geodetic Survey now has control of this work.

Geographic Board.—By an Executive Order of Aug. 10, 1906, the official title of the United States Board on Geographic Names was changed to United States Geographic Board, and its duties enlarged. The Board passes on all unsettled questions concerning geographic names which arise in the departments, as well as determining, changing, and fixing place names within the United States and its insular possessions, and all names hereafter suggested by any officer of the Government shall be referred to the Board before publication. The decisions of the Board are to be accepted by all departments of the Government as standard authority. Advisory powers were granted the Board concerning the preparation of maps compiled, or to be compiled, in the various offices and bureaus of the Government, with a special view to the avoidance of unnecessary duplication of work; and for the unification and improvement of the scales of maps, of the symbols and conventions used upon them, and of the methods of representing relief. Hereafter, all such projects as are of importance shall be submitted to this Board for advice before being undertaken.

Geographic Names, Board on, Executive order constituting, 5647, 6461.

Geographical Congress of Venice, 4626.

Geographical Survey, practicability of consolidating with Geological Survey discussed, 4218.

Geological Explorations, discussed, 4307.

Geological Survey.—Expeditions for the special purpose of making geological inquiry have been provided for by the General Government and by nearly all the states, beginning with North Carolina, whose legislature authorized a survey of the state in 1823. Such work carried on by the Federal Government is under the supervision of the Department of the Interior. The United States at first attached geologists to exploring parties, but in 1834 sent out a special geological survey under Featherstonhaugh. Similar expeditions set forth in 1839, 1845, 1847, and 1848. In 1867 F. V. Hayden was authorized to survey Nebraska, extending his work later into other territories. In 1871 J. W. Powell was commissioned to survey the country bordering upon the Colorado River, and G. M. Wheeler was put in charge of a topographical survey.

In March, 1879, the United States Geological Survey was established, and the Hayden, Powell, and Wheeler surveys consolidated with it. The five branches of the Survey are: (1) Administrative; (2) Geologic, including the making of the geologic map and the study of economic geology; (3) Topographic, including the making of the basic topographical map which has been extended over 31 per cent of the area of the United States; (4) Hydrographic, including the Reclamation Service which has Irrigation (q. v.) work in charge and which determines the flow and discharge of rivers; (5) Publication Branch. The Directors of the Geological Survey have been Clarence King, 1879-1881; Major J. W. Powell, 1881-1894; Charles D. Wolcott, 1894-1896; George Otis Smith. The first appropriation for the work (1879) was $106,000. (See Department of the Interior.)

Geological Survey. (See also under Interior Department.)

Practicability of consolidating with Geographic Survey discussed, 4218.

Report of Director of, discussed, 4577, 6656.

Georges Shoals, survey of, completed, 1610.

Georgetown, D. C.:

Act transferring duties of trustees of colored schools in Washington and, vetoed, 3903.

Water supply for, referred to, 2698, 2725, 2750.

Georgia.—One of the thirteen original states; nickname, "The Empire State of the South"; motto, "Wisdom, Justice, Moderation." It lies between lat. 30° 20′ and 35° north and long. 80° 40′ and 85° 38′ west, an area of 59,265 square miles. It is bounded on the north by Tennessee and North Carolina, on the east by South Carolina (separated by the Savannah River) and the Atlantic Ocean, on the south by Florida, and on the west by Alabama (separated in part by the Chattahoochee River). The surface is level in the south, rolling in the center, and mountainous in the north. Georgia was settled by English colonists under Oglethorpe in 1733. It is one of the leading States in the production of cotton. Lumber, rice, gold, iron, and coal are also produced. The manufacture of cotton and woolen goods and the production of iron are industries which have rapidly developed in recent years.

Statistics of agriculture collected for the last Federal Census, place the number of farms in the State at 29,027, comprising 26,953,413 acres, valued with stock and improvements at $580,546,381. The average value of land per acre was $13.74 against $5.25 in 1900. The value of domestic animals, poultry, etc., was $80,393,993. Georgia marble has a high reputation throughout the country.

The bonded debt amounted to $7,034,202 in 1909. The assessed valuation of property was $725,018,197. The principal port is Savannah, which has lately been deepened and improved by the government.

Georgia passed an ordinance of secession Jan. 19, 1861. It was restored to the Union by act of Congress June 25, 1868. Population (1910), 2,609,121.

The number of manufacturing establishments in Georgia having an annual output valued at $500 or more at the beginning of 1915 was 4,639. The amount of capital invested was $258,849,000, giving employment to 118,574 persons, using material valued at $160,199,000, and turning out finished goods worth $253,320,000. Salaries and wages paid amounted to $49,962,000.

Georgia (see also Atlanta; Augusta; Confederate States):

Act of legislature ratifying resolution of Congress, referred to, 168.

Africans landed on coast of, referred to, 3065, 3069, 3086.

Arsenal in. (See Augusta.)

Articles of agreement and cession with United States referred to, 992.

Boundary line between—

Florida and, 895, 961, 1124, 1260.

United States, and, 329.

Branch mint in, referred to, 1383, 1495.

Campaign in, discussed. (See Civil War.)

Citizens of, must not trespass upon Indian lands, 936.

Claims of, against Creek Indians, 652.

Colored members in legislature of, unseated, discussed, 3982.

Constitution of, referred to, 3832.

Deposits of provisions at posts in, contracts regarding, 598.

Fourteenth amendment to Constitution ratified by, proclamation announcing, 3858.

Indian depredations in, 1645.

Indian titles in, extinguishment of, referred to, treaty for, recommended, 637.

Indians attempt to establish government in, 1020.

Internal-revenue tax due from, suspension of collection of requested, 3588.

Lands donated to, for benefit of colleges and mechanic arts, accepted, 3587.

Lands in—

Compact with United States regarding, 803, 850, 936, 1085.

Conflicting claims regarding, of—

Indians and State, 936, 939, 941, 990, 991.

United States and State, 290.

Extinguishment of Indian title to, 769, 771.

Recommended, 637.

Treaty for, referred to, 684.

Sale of, act for, 167.

Military authorities in, not vested with authority to interfere with contracts between individuals, order regarding, 3548.

Payment of amount due citizens of, under treaty with Creeks referred to, 968.

Payment of amount due, from United States recommended, 568.

Political and civil condition of, referred to, 3998.

Property owners in, should be compensated for losses sustained, 1474.

Provisional governor for, appointed, and restoration of into Union, discussed, 3516.

Reconstruction of, referred to, 4002.

Georgia, The.—A Confederate cruiser built at Glasgow, Scotland, and sent out to prey upon the commerce of the United States during the Civil War. The *Georgia* sailed from Glasgow in April, 1863, under the name of the *Japan*, and destroyed a number of Federal merchant vessels off the coast of France. Aug. 15, 1863, she was seized by the U. S. S. *Niagara*, Capt. Craven, and taken to England.

Georgiana, The, seizure of, by Spanish or Cuban authorities, referred to, 2679.

Claims arising out of, referred to, 2721, 2900.

Convention with Peru regarding claims arising out of capture of, 3353.

German-Americans.—Americans of German birth or descent. Soon after the outbreak of the European War, the term became applied in the United States to those German-Americans who were faithful to their fatherland, even at the expense of the United States, who thus were dominated by the spirit of "Hyphenated-Americanism" (q. v.). Many of the persons falling within this latter restricted use of the term endeavored to cause strikes in munition factories, prevent by illegal methods the exportation of United States goods, and in other ways embarrass the United States in order to help Germany. This latter unpatriotic group, however, as President Wilson himself consistently declared, formed but a small percentage of the entire group of German-Americans. (More persons have immigrated to the United States from Germany than from any other country—see Immigration.) After the United States formally recognized the existence of a state of war with Germany, trouble was feared from the smaller group of German-Americans whose pro-German (q. v.) activities had brought discredit upon the larger group of German-Americans, but such fears were discovered to be groundless.

German Efficiency.—A term used in admiration to characterize the efficient scientific methods of the Germans, and in derision to characterize the complete efficiency of the Imperial German Government in accomplishing its ends regardless of means.

14

German Frightfulness.—A term of opprobrium used to characterize the inhuman conduct of the Imperial German Government in the European War,—especially the sinking of merchant ships and passenger vessels without warning by the submarine, and the use of poison gas in the trenches.

German Insurance Companies.—Because of the uncertainty of the status of insurance companies incorporated under the laws of the German Empire but doing business in the United States, during the war between the United States and Germany, President Wilson on April 6, 1917, issued a proclamation on the subject. The proclamation announced that the German insurance companies were allowed to continue their business in the different states as though a state of war did not exist, provided that funds belonging to or held by such companies should not be sent outside the United States or used as a basis for the establishment of any credit for an enemy of the United States or for any allies of such enemy.

Germanic Association of Customs and Commerce:

Establishment and growth of, referred to, 2113.

Treaty with, regarding duty on agricultural products, 2167.

Germantown (Pa.), Battle of.—After the American defeat at Brandywine Creek and the British occupation of Philadelphia, Washington determined to attack the main body of Howe's army, which was quartered in Germantown, a suburb of Philadelphia. The American army was encamped at Skippock Creek, 20 miles from Philadelphia, and consisted of about 10,000 men. About two-thirds of these, under Generals Sullivan and Wayne, started for Germantown on the evening of Oct. 3, 1777. Washington accompanied Sullivan's division. The battle opened about 7 A. M. on the 4th. The attack failed on account of fog and a misunderstanding among the officers. After 3 hours of severe fighting the Americans were obliged to retreat with a loss of 673 killed and wounded and some 400 prisoners. The British loss was reported at 535, including Gen. Agnew and Lieut.-Col. Bird, though 800 is claimed to be a more approximate figure. Washington retired to his former camp and Gen. Howe returned to Philadelphia.

Germany.—The German Empire is a Federation of Central European States, extending from the Alps on the south to the Baltic on the north. The Empire lies between 47° 16'-55° 54' North latitude and 5° 52'-22° 53' East longitude, and is bounded on the east by Russia, on the south by Austria, Liechtenstein, and Switzerland, on the west by France, Luxemburg, Belgium, and the Netherlands, and on the north by Denmark and the North and Baltic Seas.

Physical Features.—The Vosges or Wasgau Mountains (Alsace), the Hardt Mountains (Rhine Palatinate), the Schwarzwald or Black Forest (Baden and Württemberg), the Schwabischer Jura (Württemberg), the Franconian Jura and Fichtel, Elster and Erz Mountains (Bavaria), and the Bayerische and Böhmer Wald (East Bavaria) are the principal mountains of the southern plateau. In the northern division are the Hartz Mountains (Central Prussia), with the Brocken (3,750 feet) and the Taunus (Southern Prussia).

The principal rivers of Northern Germany are the Memel or Niemen, Pregel, Vistula and Oder, and the Elbe, Weser and Ems.

The great rivers of Southern Germany are the Rhine and the Danube. The Rhine (800 miles) from Lake Constance to Basel (120 miles) forms a boundary with Switzerland. It is navigable throughout its entire course in the empire. The Danube (1,750 miles) rises in the Schwarzwald (Baden). Only 350 miles of its course is in German territory, and it is navigable for 220 miles to Ulm (Württemberg).

Owing to the extent and diversity of the land surface there is a great variety in the climatic conditions. The Elbe is closed for navigation for a short time in severe winters, and the Vistula is generally ice-bound for some months every year.

AREA AND POPULATION

States and Capitals	Area in English Sq. Miles	Population Census 1910
Kingdoms—		
Bavaria (Munich)	29,292	6,887,291
Prussia (Berlin)	134,616	40,165,219
Saxony (Dresden)	5,789	4,806,661
Württemberg (Stuttgart)	7,534	2,437,574
Grand Duchies—		
Baden (Karlsruhe)	5,823	2,142,833
Hesse (Darmstadt)	2,966	1,282,051
Mecklenburg-Schwerin (Schwerin)	5,068	639,958
Mecklenburg-Strelitz (Neu-Strelitz)	1,131	106,442
Oldenburg (Oldenburg)	2,482	483,042
Saxe-Weimar (Weimar)	1,397	417,149
Duchies—		
Anhalt (Dessau)	888	331,128
Brunswick (Brunswick)	1,418	694,339
Saxe-Altenburg (Altenburg)	511	216,128
Saxe-Coburg-Gotha (Coburg and Gotha)	764	257,177
Saxe-Meiningen (Meiningen,)	953	278,762
Principalities—		
Lippe (Detmold)	469	150,937
Reuss—Elder Line (Greiz)	122	72,769
Reuss—Younger Line (Gera)	319	152,752
Schaumburg-Lippe (Bücke-burg)	131	46,652
Schwarzburg-Rudolstadt (Rudolstadt)	363	100,702
Schwarzburg-Sondershausen (Sondershausen)	333	89,917
Waldeck (Arolsen)	433	61,707
Hanse-Towns—		
Bremen	99	299,526
Hamburg	160	1,014,664
Lübeck	115	116,599
Reichsland—		
Alsace-Lorraine (Strassburg)	5,604	1,874,014
Total	208,780	64,925,993

KINGDOMS OF GERMANY.—Prussia comprises the larger portion of Germany, and consists of thirteen provinces. The government is that of a constitutional monarchy, the Crown being hereditary in the male line. The executive is vested in the King, aided by a Council of Ministers. King, William II., German Emperor. Capital, Berlin. The Parliament (Landtag) consists of the Herrenhaus of Princes, heads of noble families, elected peers, appointed life members, and representatives of universities and towns; and the Abgeordnetenhaus, or Chamber of Deputies, of 433 members elected indirectly for a maximum of five years.

Bavaria.—The second Kingdom in size and population of the Empire.

The Crown is hereditary in the male line; the executive power is in the Sovereign, who acts through a responsible ministry or Staatsrat. King, Ludwig III., b. Jan. 7, 1845, proclaimed King Nov. 5, 1913. Capital, Munich. There is a Parliament of two houses, the Chamber of Reichsräte—

Princes, and hereditary nobles and members appointed for life, or by virtue of their office, and the Chamber of Abgeordneten (Representatives), elected directly for six years.

Saxony.—Third in importance and population of the German kingdoms. The Crown is hereditary in the male (and eventually the female) line. The Executive is vested in the King, aided by a Ministry of State. King, Frederic Augustus III., b. May 25, 1865, succeeded Oct. 15, 1904. Capital, Dresden. The legislature (Ständeversammlung) consists of two co-ordinate houses, of which the first is made up of Princes, landed proprietors and official and appointed members; and the second of 91 members, elected directly by the people for six years.

Württemberg is a Kingdom of South Germany, mainly between Bavaria and Baden. The Crown is hereditary and the monarchy constitutional, the executive being vested in a Ministry of State. King William II., b. Feb. 25, 1848; succeeded Oct. 6, 1891. Capital, Stuttgart. There is a Landstände of two estates, the first chamber (Standesherren) being of princely, noble or territorial rank, with certain official and nominated members; the second (Abgeordnetenhaus) consists of 92 members, elected by direct and secret ballot for six years.

GRAND DUCHIES.—*Baden.*—A State of the German Empire, situate in the southwestern part. The Rhine forms its southern and western boundary, separating it from Switzerland and Alsace. There is a legislature of two houses. A great part of the surface is mountainous, and includes the Black Forest and Odenwald. Grand Duke, Frederick II., b. July 9, 1857; Grand Duke, Sept. 28, 1907. Capital, Karlsruhe.

Hesse.—A central State in the west of Germany, comprising two disconnected territories nearly equal in size. There is a bicameral legislature. Grand Duke, Ernest Louis, b. Nov. 25, 1868; succeeded March 13, 1892. Capital, Darmstadt.

Mecklenburg-Schwerin.—Comprises an area of 5,135 square miles on the Baltic, with a population of 639,958. The Legislative power is vested in representatives of the towns and of the Knights' estates. Grand Duke, Frederick Francis IV., b. April 9, 1882; succeeded April 10, 1897. Capital, Schwerin.

Mecklenburg-Strelitz.—Consists of two detached parts (Strelitz and Ratzeburg), separated by Mecklenburg-Schwerin. There is a diet of two estates, the Rittenschaft and Landschaft. Grand Duke, Adolphus Friedrich, b. July 22, 1848. Capital, Neu-Strelitz.

Saxe Weimar Eisenach. — The Grand Duchy consists of three detached districts and 24 scattered enclaves, the population being mainly Lutherans. There is a British and American church at the capital. There is an executive ministry and a single chamber diet of 38 members, elected for six years. Grand Duke, William Ernest, b. June 10, 1876; succeeded Jan. 5, 1901. Capital, Weimar.

Oldenburg is situate on the North Sea and the Weser, between the sea and Hanover, with the detached Principalities. More than 80 per cent. of the inhabitants are Protestants. There is an executive ministry and a single chamber (Landtag) of 45 members. Grand Duke, Frederic Augustus, b. Nov. 16, 1852; succeded June 13, 1900. Capital, Oldenburg. Population, 28,565.

DUCHIES.—*Anhalt.*—A Duchy of Central Germany, in two principal portions, surrounded by Prussian Saxony, containing 906 square miles and a population of 331,128. Single chamber diet of 46 members, elected for six years. Duke, Friedrich II., b. Aug. 19, 1856; succeeded Jan. 24, 1904. Capital, Dessau.

Brunswick.—A State of Northern Germany, consisting chiefly of three detached parts. Duke, Ernest Augustus, b. Nov. 17, 1887, married daughter of the German Emperor; proclaimed Nov. 3, 1913. Capital, Brunswick.

Saxe-Altenburg.—Duke, Ernest, b. Aug. 31, 1871; succeeded Feb. 7, 1908. Capital, Altenburg.

Saxe - Coburg - Gotha.—A State consisting of two principal and several smaller detached portions. Coburg has a diet of 11 and Gotha of 19 members. The diet meet in joint session for common affairs. Duke, Charles Edward (H. R. H. Duke of Albany), b. July 19, 1884.

Saxe-Meiningen.—The single chamber diet has 24 members, elected for six years. Duke, George II., b. April 2, 1826; succeeded Sept. 20, 1866. Capital, Meiningen.

The Principalities are:

Lippe.—Prince, Leopold.

Reuss (Elder Line).—Prince, Henry XXIV.

Schaumburg-Lippe.—Reigning Prince, Henry XXVII.

Schaumburg-Lippe.—Reigning Prince, Adolphus.

Schwartzburg-Rudolstadt.—Prince, Gunther.

Schwarzburg - Sondershausen. — Prince Gunther.

Waldeck.—Prince, Frederick, Prince of Waldeck-Pyrmont, Count of Rappolstein, Seigneur of Hohenack and Geroldseck, Wasziegen, etc.

HANSE TOWNS.—The Free Hanse Towns comprise the three cities of Lübeck, Bremen, and Hamburg, each with a small rural territory, retaining their sovereignty and local self-government, like the other States of the Empire; they are situated in the North of Germany, on the Trave, Weser, and Elbe, respectively. Lübeck is situate near the Baltic, and is connected with the Elbe by the Elbe-Trave Canal; its commerce is principally with Denmark, Norway, Sweden, and Russia. Bremen is much smaller, but very prosperous, and only second in commercial importance to Hamburg. It is connected by railway with the outport of Bremerhaven, thirty-five miles distant, and carries on a very extensive American trade. Hamburg is the great emporium of Germany, and is sixty-five miles from Cuxhaven, to which port it is connected by railway.

"REICHSLAND."—Alsace-Lorraine (Elsass-Lothringen), which was annexed by France from the old German Empire between 1648 and 1697, and restored to Germany in 1871, embraces the fertile plain between the Rhine and the Vosges, and stretches beyond these mountains as far as Luxemburg. Wine, tobacco, and hops, iron and coal are among its leading productions, and the cotton industry is most flourishing. There is a *Landtag* of two chambers, of which the first consists of representatives of the churches, university towns and professional classes, and the second of 60 members, elected by secret ballot.

Principal towns, Strassburg, Mühlhausen, Metz, and Kolmar.

Language and Religion.—While the vast majority of the Emperor's subjects are German-speaking people it is notable that a considerable number adhere to the vernacular of their original sovereignty. A recent language census gives the following figures: German, 51,883,131; Polish, 3,328,751; French, 223,551; Danish, 141,061; Czech, 107,398; Lithuanians, 106,305; Others, 224,063.

The generally accepted religion of the people is Lutheran, but there are many congregations of Catholics and others. The census of 1910 showed: Protestants, 39,991,421; Catholics, 23,821,453; Other Christians, 283,946; Jews, 615,021; Others (or of unknown religions), 214,152.

GERMAN COLONIES.—Area and population.

Colony	Area in English Sq. Miles	Estimated Population
Africa—		
East Africa	384,079	7,645,000
South-west Africa	322,348	120,000
Cameroon	295,000	3,500,000
Togoland	33,659	1,000,000
Total, Africa	1,035,086	12,265,000
Pacific—		
New Guinea	90,000	463,300
Solomon Islands	4,200	33,000
Marshall Islands	160	10,550
Eastern Carolines	} 800	78,600
Western Carolines		
Samoan Islands	1,050	34,500
Total, Pacific	96,210	619,950
Asiatic—		
Kiao Chao	193	190,000
Sphere of Interest	2,750	84,000
Total, Asiatic	2,943	274,000
Grand Total	1,134,239	13,158,950

History.—The Germans, or Teutons, are an Aryan race, first mentioned in history in the fourth century B. C. The German Roman Empire was founded by Charlemagne A. D. 800, and this dynasty was extinguished about 911 A.D. The reign of Otto, which followed shortly (936-977 A. D.), was the most successful of the Middle Ages. This was followed by the succession of the Hohenstaufen dynasty (1138-1268 A. D.). The imperial power was restricted by the electors between 1273 and 1806. Napoleon overthrew the empire and brought Germany under the confederation of the Rhine in 1806. This was dissolved in 1813, and an alliance made with Austria in 1815, and the North German confederation was formed in 1866. Prussia was the leading factor in the Franco-Prussian war of 1870-71, in which she was joined by Southern Germany. William I., King of Prussia, was elected German Emperor in the Reichstag on the initiative of all the reigning German princes in 1871.

Aug. 1, 1914, upon learning of the mobilization of troops in Russia to attack Austria, which was then at war with Servia, Germany declared war against Russia, and upon the beginning of hostilities between the two countries France began to prepare for the inevitable invasion of her territory without a declaration of war. German forces started for the French border by way of Liège, Belgium. Belgium protested against the violation of her territory and appealed to Great Britain for protection. England was pledged to both the protection of France and the neutrality of Belgium, and when on Aug. 4, 1914, Germany declared war on Belgium, Great Britain replied with a declaration of war upon Germany.

Government.—The Empire, according to the Constitution of April 16, 1871, is a Confederate League, bearing the name German Empire—Deutsches Reich—under the hereditary presidentship of the King of Prussia, who holds the title of German Emperor—Deutscher Kaiser—and whose eldest son is styled His Imperial and Royal Highness. The Emperor as such represents the Empire in all matters affecting international law; in the name of the Empire he declares war and makes peace, concludes alliances and treaties with foreign States, and accredits and receives Ambassadors. Except to repel an attack on the territory or the coasts of the League, the Emperor cannot declare war without the consent of the Federal Council, Bundesrat, which represents the sovereignty of the Federated States of the Empire. The Bundesrat, with the Emperor's consent, has the power to dissolve the Reichstag. Amongst the matters belonging to the competence of the Empire are all those that refer to the army and navy; the common, civil and penal law of the Empire; posts and telegraphs (excluding Bavaria); inland navigation; customs; weights and measures; coinage; banking; patents; copyright; foreign trade; the German mercantile marine; the Press; everything relating to the right of forming corporations; police; sanitation; colonization. A majority of the Federal Council and Reichstag is necessary, and also sufficient, for the validity of a law. The laws of the Empire take precedence of the laws of the Federated States within the scope of the Constitution of the Empire; they are compulsory on all Governments of the Empire.

Ruler, His Imperial Majesty William II., German Emperor, King of Prussia, born at Berlin Jan. 27, 1859.

The legislative power of the Empire is exercised within certain prescribed limits by the Bundesrat (or Federal Council) and the Reichstag. The Bundesrat is composed of 61 plenipotentiaries nominated by the governments of the States which form the Empire, viz.:—Prussia (17), Bavaria (6), Saxony and Württemberg (4), Baden and Hesse (3), Mecklenburg-Schwerin and Brunswick (2), the remaining States and the three Hanse Towns (1 each), and Alsace-Lorraine 3 delegates (with limited voting powers). The Reichstag is composed of 397 Deputies, elected by universal suffrage for a maximum of five years. The Federal Council and Reichstag must be summoned to meet every year.

The Supreme Court of the Empire is the Reichsgericht with a President and 100 Judges, appointed by the Emperor, with the advice of the Bundesrat. This is a Court of Appeal from the remaining courts, which are State appointed and maintained, the legal system being identical in each.

Army and Navy.—The Emperor is the Bundesfeldherr, or Federal Commander-in-Chief of the whole German Army. In time of war he holds supreme command; in time of peace the Kings of Bavaria, Saxony, and Württemberg retain their sovereign rights as heads of their respective armies. On the other hand, the German Navy is Imperial (kaiserlich), and the Emperor as such is the supreme Admiral-in-Command of the Imperial German Navy in peace as well as war. Service in the Army is universal and compulsory on all German subjects between the ages of 17 and 45, service commencing at the age of 20. (For the army establishment see Armies of the World and for the navy see Navies of the World.)

Education.—The German educational system is remarkable for the ease with which it meets the requirements of every social class. Its efficiency is best exemplified by the annual military recruiting statistics, which in 1907 disclosed a proportion of only .02 per cent. of illiterate recruits. It is, moreover, practically homogeneous in all branches throughout the Empire. The Prussian administration may be cited as typical, comprising a general control by the Minister of Public Instruction over all educational establishments, public or private, a provincial organization charged with management of public elementary schools, and Spe-

cial Provincial Boards charged with th management of Secondary and Norma Schools, their curricula, appointment o teachers, and leaving examinations. Pr mary is Compulsory and free, age 6-14 Average attendance, 95 per cent. Evenin continuation schools for children of workin classes (partly compulsory); city intermedi ate schools in two grades; gymnasia prepar ing for university and learned profession with a nine-years' course. Special School are numerous throughout the Empire, spe cial attention being devoted to agriculture commerce, mining, forestry and music. Uni versities, State-maintained and administered are: Berlin, Bonn, Breslau, Erlangen, Frei burg, Giessen, Göttingen, Greiswald, Halle Heidelberg, Jena, Kiel, Königsberg, Leipzig Marburg, München, Münster, Rostock Strassburg, Tübingen and Würtzburg.

Finance.—The Revenue of the Empire i derived mainly from Customs and Excise stamps, posts and telegraphs, railways, an contribution in lieu of Customs and Excis duties from certain states with matricula levies on the constituent States of the Em pire, and (since 1913) a direct Property Tax. The revenue for 1913 was 3,696,033, 200 marks, and the expenditure was the same amount. The debt at the beginning of the year 1913 was 4,922,242,000 marks For ordinary computations five marks are reckoned as equal to one dollar of United States money.

The Imperial War Treasure stored in the Julius Tower at Spandau amounted, March 31, 1911, to 120,000,000 marks ($24,000,-000). Under the law of 1913, this amount is to be doubled, and in addition a silver reserve created amounting to an additional 120,000,000 marks.

Pensions.—The German scheme of social legislation gives all subordinate bread-winners in the Empire a legal right to pecuniary subvention when unfitted for work through sickness, accident, premature infirmity, or old age. Insurance is compulsory. The National Insurance is based on mutual insurance and self-administration. The Infirmity Insurance Act came into force Jan. 1, 1900. The insured include all persons working for wages or salary as workpeople, in so far as the incomes do not exceed Mk. 2,000—including foreigners working in Germany under these categories. Pensions for premature infirmity are given to insured persons when unfit for work; old age pensions to all insured persons on attaining the age of 70, though still capable of work.

Production and Industry.—In 1907, 32.6 per cent. of the population were supported by agriculture, 37 per cent. by industries and mining, and 11.5 per cent. by trade and traffic. The approximate number of persons engaged in agricultural and pastoral pursuits (exclusive of their dependents) in 1907 was 9,750,000; in mining and industries, 11,230,000; in trade and commerce, 3,500,000; and in domestic and other service, 1,750,000.

Of the total area in 1907, 78,632,139 acres were cultivated (including 60,347,914 acres arable) and 34,272,141 acres were woods and forests.

Prussia contains the principal mining districts (in Silesia, Rhineland and Saxony), coal, lignite, and iron ore being largely produced; the Reichsland also contains valuable coal and iron ore, and the Hartz mountains yield copper and silver.

Germany is becoming more and more a manufacturing country, the industries centering round the coal and iron fields, particularly in Prussia, the Reichsland, Bavaria, and Saxony. In Prussia (iron, linens, glass, etc.) the principal industrial centres are

Berlin, Breslau, Cologne, Aix, Düsseldorf, Dortmund, Magdeburg, and Cassel, while Solingen and Essen are the centres of the steel industry. In Saxony the woolen industry of Chemnitz, the machinery of Zwickau, and the book trade of Leipzig vie with the "Dresden china" industry of Meissen. In Bavaria and the Reichsland, cottons and silk; and in almost all the kingdoms and States, brewing. Gotha contains the largest and most justly famous geographical institute in the world. The textile industries increase annually in importance and centre in Crefeld, Elberfeld-Barmen, Mühlhausen, Chemnitz, and the provinces of Westphalia and Silesia.

Sea fish to the value of nearly 75,000,-000 marks were consumed in 1912, the amount imported being valued at 46,000,000 marks. About 35,000 persons were employed in the fisheries.

Railways, etc.—In 1912 there were 56,-062 kilometres (35,380 miles of State railways and 3,701 kilometres (2,300 miles) of private lines, with 2,215 kilometres of narrow gauge line. The number of registered automobiles and motor cycles on 1st Jan., 1913, was 77,789.

In addition to some 6,000 miles of navigable rivers there are over 1,500 miles of canals and 1,600 miles of ship canals. Length of telegraph lines, 228,600 kilometres (length of wires, 1,907,200 kilometres); post offices, 40,987; telegraph offices, 46,444; wireless stations, 14; telephone call-stations, 37,970. The number of employés in the service of posts, telegraphs and telephones was 310,363.

Shipping.—On Jan. 1, 1913, the Mercantile Marine consisted of 2,098 sea-going steamers of 17.65 register tons and upwards (4,380,348 tons gross register), and of 2,420 sailing vessels (447,870 tons gross register); number of seamen, 77,746. Germany now ranks second in the list of maritime countries. There were completed in 1912 at German yards for German firms, 659 sea-going ships of 383,090 tons gross, and at German yards for foreign firms, 124 sea-going ships of 31,238 tons gross.

Towns.—Capital of the German Empire, Berlin. There were 48 towns at the Census of December, 1910, with a population exceeding 100,000.

The unit of value is the mark of 100 pfennige. One mark is equal to $0.238 United States money. One dollar United States money is equal to 4 marks 81 pfennige.

Trade with the United States.— The value of merchandise imported into Germany from the United States for the year 1913 was $331,684,212, and goods to the value of $188,963,071 were sent thither—a balance of $142,721,141 in favor of the United States.

Germany (see also Berlin; Hamburg):

Caroline Islands, dispute with Spain regarding, 4916, 6370.

Commercial relations with, 5617, 6061, 6369.

Compulsory insurance of workingmen in, referred to, 5782.

Consular convention with, 4114, 4142.

Copyright privilege extended, by proclamation, 5713.

Referred to, 5752.

Diplomatic relations with, discussed, 2549.

Emperor of—

Arbitrator in northwestern boundary dispute, 4097.

Award of, 4139.

Thanks of United States tendered, 4140.

Death of, 5367.

Expulsion of Julius Baumer from, referred to, 4460.

Fruits, American, restrictions upon importation of, into, discussed, 6331.

Fugitive criminals, convention with, for surrender of, 2689.

Discussed, 4824.

Government of United States of North Germany referred to, 3780.

Immigration treaty with, 4419.

Importation of American products into, restrictions upon, discussed, 4758, 4789, 4916, 5957, 6061, 6328, 6429.

Decree regarding, 6100.

Insurance companies, American, excluded from, 6061, 6099, 6183.

Minister of Hamburg, received in United States, 949.

Minister of, to United States, title of ambassador conferred upon, 5874.

Minister of United States to—

Recalled, 2549.

Salary of, increase in, recommended, 4074.

Title of ambassador conferred upon, 5874.

Naturalization treaty with, 3828, 3829, 3830, 3888.

Questions arising under, referred to, 4419, 4520, 4625, 4916, 5084, 5471, 5869.

Neutrality of United States in war with—

Russia, 7969.

France, 7969.

Great Britain, 7974.

Belgium, 7976.

Italy, 8142.

Japan, 7976.

Roumania, 8142.

Portugal, 8141.

Peace overtures, 8187.

To the Vatican, 8188.

Reply of Entente Allies to, 8193.

Germany's reply to, 8197.

Political questions in, 4017.

Postal convention with, 3775, 3783, 4203.

Samoan affairs discussed. (See Samoan Islands.)

Shipping interests of, report of consul-general on, referred to, 4973.

Tariff laws of, evidence of, modifications of, proclaimed, 5693.
Discussed, 5747.
Tariff laws of United States, protest against provisions of, imposing discriminating duty on sugar, 5957.
Tobacco imported into (see also Agricultural Products)—
Duties on, referred to, 2909.
Treaty regarding, 2167.
Trade-marks, treaty with, regarding, 4114, 4142.
Treaty of United States with—
Hamburg, 988, 991, 2686.
States composing the Zollverein, 2168, 2169, 2205.
Negotiations regarding, and rejection of, discussed, 2192.
Transmitted and discussed, 2689, 4824.
Union of States of, discussed, 4074.
Vessels of—
Claims of, to interest on dues illegally exacted, 5084, 5367.
Destroyed at Samoan Islands, 5479.
Duties on, suspended by proclamation, 5326.
Proclamation revoking, 6129.
Vessels of Hamburg, application for rights regarding, 621.
Discriminating duties on, suspended, 607.
War with France—
Correspondence regarding, 4068, 4434.
Diplomatic relations resumed, referred to, 4098.
Neutrality of United States in, 4050.
Proclaimed, 4040, 4043, 4045.
Suspension of hostilities recommended by President Grant, 4055.
German Empire, Treaties with.—When the German Empire was formed in 1871, certain treaties in force with the individual component States were abrogated; many, however, remained in force and are to be found under the headings of Baden, Bavaria, Prussia, Saxony, etc. A consular convention was concluded in 1871.
In 1900 a reciprocal commercial arrangement was made with Germany. It contains certain concessions of import duties upon specified classes of goods coming from Germany; and Germany makes compensating concessions upon classes of goods going into Germany. This agreement was made subject to three months' notice of intention to terminate and was denounced by Germany to take effect Feb. 28, 1906. Agreements were effected by the exchange of notes for the reciprocal protection of trade-marks in Morocco in 1901 and in China in 1905. A reciprocal trade agreement was entered into in 1906, and superseded by another in 1907, and this was terminated on notice given by the United States under direction of the tariff act of 1909. The patent convention of 1909 is still in force.
Samoan Islands—In 1889 a general act providing for the neutrality and autonomous government of the Samoan Islands was concluded between the United States,

Germany and Great Britain. This provided for the establishment of a supreme court for the islands, and confirmed titles to lands. Interference in political struggles in the islands in 1899 by commanders of British and American warships resulted in the appointment of a court of claims. King Oscar of Sweden was agreed upon as arbitrator. His decision held the United States and Great Britain responsible for all damages caused by unwarranted military operations in the islands. By a convention of Dec. 2, 1899, the general act and treaties relating to Samoa were annulled and a new article was signed by the three powers in which Germany and Great Britain renounce in favor of the United States all their claims to Tutuila and all other islands of the Samoan group, while the United States renounced to Germany all claims to the islands of Upolu, Savaii and other islands west of long. 171° west. (See also Samoan Islands; Tutuila.)
Gerrymander.—An arbitrary arrangement of the legislative or Congressional districts of a state regardless of geographical contiguity and compactness, whereby a minority of the voters of one party may be so grouped as to elect all or a majority of the representatives in Congress or a state legislature. The word was coined in 1811 from the name of Elbridge Gerry, who as governor of Massachusetts signed a bill passed by the Democratic majority of the legislature grouping the sections which gave the Federalists majorities into one district, with a fancied resemblance to a salamander.
Gerrymander, discussed, 5643.
Get-Rich-Quick.—A term opprobriously applied to the class of Americans who have made money on a very large scale, and quickly, occasionally where the fortune is presumed to have been accumulated by questionable means.
Gettysburg Address.— Immediately after the battle of Gettysburg, Congress set aside the battlefield as a national burial-ground for soldiers; and it was at the dedication of the new national cemetery on November 19, 1863, that Lincoln delivered the address which has forever afterwards been called by the name of the little town in Pennsylvania. There is some dispute as to the manner in which the address was prepared, one legend running that Lincoln wrote it in a few minutes on the back of an official Government envelope while on the special train which was conveying him to the dedication ceremonies. The consensus of valid opinion, however, indicates that the address was prepared with great care in Washington some days before it was delivered, although Lincoln may have slightly revised it on the evening before or the day of the dedication itself. Lincoln held a written copy of his remarks in his hand when he rose to speak after the two hours' address of Edward Everett, whose sonorous and polished phrases had mightily moved the audience before him. The fewness and the simplicity of Lincoln's immortal words, after Everett's lengthy peroration, could not but engrave them indelibly on the minds of those who were privileged to hear them.
The speech stands out as an acknowledged classic,—many scholars pronouncing it the greatest short speech ever delivered. Lincoln made several autograph copies, by request, for different individuals and patriotic institutions. Various slight alterations appear in the various reproductions, and it is not certain which of the manuscripts is precisely correct. Between 3371 and 3372, Volume VIII, appears a facsimile of one

manuscript. We quote below the full text of a facsimile of another manuscript; the latter being the one found in Nicolay and Hay's life of Lincoln, which does not purport to be the original, but is a copy made by Lincoln especially for the Soldiers and Sailors Fair at Baltimore in 1864:

"THE GETTYSBURG ADDRESS.

Fourscore and seven years ago our fathers brought forth on this continent a new nation, conceived in liberty, and dedicated to the proposition that all men are created equal.

Now we are engaged in a great civil war, testing whether that nation, or any nation so conceived and so dedicated, can long endure. We are met on a great battle-field of that war. We have come to dedicate a portion of that field, as a final resting-place for those who here gave their lives that that nation might live. It is altogether fitting and proper that we should do this.

But, in a larger sense, we cannot dedicate,—we cannot consecrate,—we cannot hallow this ground. The brave men, living and dead, who struggled here have consecrated it, far above our power to add or detract. The world will little note, nor long remember, what we say here, but it can never forget what they did here. It is for us, the living, rather to be dedicated here to the unfinished work which they who fought here have thus far so nobly advanced. It is rather for us to be here dedicated to the great task remaining before us,—that from these honored dead we take increased devotion to that cause for which they gave the last full measure of devotion—that we here highly resolve that these dead shall not have died in vain,—that this nation, under God, shall have a new birth of freedom—and that government of the people, by the people, for the people shall not perish from the earth.   ABRAHAM LINCOLN."

Gettysburg (Pa.), Battle of.—After the remarkable success of the Confederate arms at Chancellorsville, and in response to a general demand of the people of the Confederacy, Gen. Lee determined upon an invasion of the Northern States. In the early days of June, 1863, he started his army on the northward march into Pennsylvania. Passing up the Shenandoah Valley by way of Winchester (at which latter place he defeated Gen. Milroy, capturing 4,000 prisoners and 28 cannon), he crossed the Potomac at Williamsport and Shepardstown, arriving in Hagerstown, Md., with a force of 68,352 effectives, according to Confederate accounts, or 97,000 men and 280 guns, according to some Federal accounts. Hooker's army numbered almost 80,000. By June 27, Lee had reached Chambersburg, Pa., with Longstreet's and Hill's corps, Ewell having pushed on as far as Carlisle and York. While the Confederates moved up the west side of the Blue Ridge Mountains Hooker marched along the east side, keeping always between his adversary and Washington. The movement of the Confederates toward the east through Chambersburg threatened Harrisburg and Columbia, and eventually Baltimore. Hooker asked to be relieved of command, which request was immediately granted, and he was succeeded by Gen. George G. Meade, who assumed command June 28. Meade was now reenforced by 15,000 men from Washington and 2,100 from the Middle Department and granted the privilege of calling upon the 11,000 at Harpers Ferry, making the two armies thus advancing to battle on Northern soil numerically equal, according to Northern statements.

Lee, learning on June 28 that Meade was just across the South Mountain, and fearing the latter might attempt to cut off his communications with the Potomac by an advance through the mountain gaps in his rear, determined upon an eastern movement. Meade surmised that Lee would attempt a movement south on the east side of the South Mountain, and prepared to meet him and give battle at Pipe Creek, near Taneytown, Md., 15 miles southeast of Gettysburg. The left wing of the Federal army, consisting of the First, Eleventh, and Third corps, was sent forward to Gettysburg to mask the Pipe Creek movement.

On the morning of July 1, 1863, Buford's cavalry, which had moved west of Gettysburg on the Chambersburg road, encountered the Confederate advance under Hill and Heth and were driven back to Seminary Ridge, west of the town. The corps were scarcely placed in line of battle when Gen. Reynolds was mortally wounded and the command of the field devolved upon Howard. He was later in the day superseded by Gen. Hancock. During the afternoon Ewell's corps and two-thirds of Hill's reenforced the Confederates and drove Reynolds's and Howard's corps to Cemetery Hill, south of the town, inflicting upon them a loss of nearly 10,000 men and 16 guns. Gen. Lee ordered Ewell to press forward and take the hill. Ewell failed to push on. On the advice of Hancock, Meade moved his whole army during the night and occupied Cemetery Hill. Lee's army was posted along Seminary Ridge, west of the town. July 2 the fighting of both armies was directed toward securing good positions, the Confederates gaining in two or three advance movements and capturing some trophies and prisoners. The attack on Cemetery Hill, while nearly successful, was disjointed, the Confederates retiring with their prisoners. The Union loss the second day was 10,000, Sickles losing half of his men. The Confederate losses were also great. July 3, the day of the decisive action, opened with slight skirmishing. After noon a heavy cannonade was kept up between the two armies for 2 hours. About 3 o'clock in the afternoon the Confederates, under Pickett, made a grand assault. They went forward in the face of a terrible fire and met with almost complete destruction. Hay's division took 2,000 prisoners and 15 colors; Gibbon's division took 2,500 prisoners and 12 colors. The charge on the left was under Pettigrew, and was made with the same desperate valor. The entire Federal losses at Gettysburg were 3,155 killed, 14,529 wounded, and 5,365 missing—a total of 23,049. The Confederate losses footed up, according to official reports, a total of 20,451 of whom 2,592 were killed, 12,709 wounded, and 5,150 taken prisoners. This report does not include the artillery losses. Gettysburg was probably the crucial battle of the Civil War. (See illustration opposite 3405.)

Gettysburg Battlefield, work of locating and preserving lines of battle at, 5879.

Ghent, Treaty of, between United States and Great Britain, 537, 819.

Commissioners—

   Copy of journal of, transmitted, 1026.

Disagree in opinions on, 777, 819.

Expenses of, referred to, 650.

To conclude, communications from and instructions to, 536, 537.

To make international boundary in Passamaquoddy Bay according to description of, 6063.

Construction of, referred to Emperor of Russia for arbitration and interpretation of, 645, 672.

Decision of, 756.

Opinion of Attorney-General on, 966.

Ratification of, 767.

Convention for payment of claimants under, 959.

Copy of journals of the United States Commissioners to, transmitted, 1026.

Expresses incurred under, referred to, 6282.

Exportation of slaves by Great Britain in violation of, 629.

Proclaimed, 545.

Referred to, 581, 591, 597, 629, 672, 756, 775, 813, 868, 895, 945, 995, 1006.

Restitution of slaves referred to, 591, 617.

Settlement of boundaries under Article IV. of, referred to, 581, 597.

Gibbons vs. Ogden.—An important Supreme Court case denying the right of a State to grant the exclusive privilege of navigating the waters of the State extending to the coastwise traffic of another State. Aaron Ogden had obtained through assignment the exclusive right to navigate for thirty years, with boats propelled by fire or steam, the waters within the jurisdiction of the State of New York. In 1808 the New York court of chancery granted an injunction forbidding Thomas Gibbons from running steamboats between New York, Elizabethtown, and other places in New Jersey. Gibbons appealed and the New York court of errors having sustained the chancery court, the Supreme Court rendered judgment for the appellant Gibbons on the ground that the granting of exclusive navigation of waters within the State of New York by the State's legislature, extending to coastwise traffic with another State, was repugnant to the clause of the Constitution of the United States authorizing Congress to regulate commerce, and was void. Ogden's bill was dismissed, the decree of the two New York courts having been annulled. The case occupies 240 pages of a large volume of the Supreme Court Reports. Daniel Webster appeared for the appellant. Chief Justice Marshall delivered the opinion.

Gila Bend Reservation, Ariz., removal of Indians on, bill for, transmitted, 5499.

Gila Valley, Globe and Northern Railway, act granting right of way to, through San Carlos Reservation, Ariz., vetoed, 6003.

Gilsonite, disposition of lands in Utah containing, discussed, 6168.

Glacier National Park. (See Parks, National.)

Glass-Owen Act.—Act providing for Federal Reserve Banks. (See Currency Laws,—Federal Reserve Banks.)

Glen, The, appropriation for illegal capture of, recommended, 3396.

Globe, Congressional. (See Congressional Globe.)

Gloucester, The, mentioned, 6318.

God Reigns and the Government at Washington Still Lives.—These were the closing words of a brief address made by James A. Garfield, then a representative in Congress, to a large assemblage in Wall Street, New York, on April 15, 1865, the morning after the assassination of Lincoln. The crowd was about to move for an attack on the World newspaper office, which had violently opposed Lincoln. Suddenly Garfield's voice was heard to calm their passions. He spoke briefly as follows: "Fellow-citizens! Clouds and darkness are round about Him. His pavilion is dark waters and thick clouds of the skies. Justice and judgment are the establishment of His throne. Mercy and truth shall go before His face. Fellow-citizens! God reigns, and the government at Washington still lives!"

Gold and Silver Money, fixed ratio for Mexico and China, 6735, 6787, 6825, 6941.

Gold Standard, effect of, on public credit, 6654.

Gold.—The most valuable of the metals in general use among civilized or barbarous nations, both in ancient and modern times. Its earliest use was probably for personal adornment. It was extensively employed by the Oriental nations, such as the Hindus, Akkadians, Assyrians, Egyptians, and the Persians. Although it never was used to the same extent among the Greeks, they obtained it by their intercourse with the Phenicians and other navigators and merchants of the Mediterranean, and adorned their temples and made ornaments for their wealthier classes with it. Neither was gold in common use at an early day in Rome. Gold as money was not coined so early as silver. The Lydians made coins of the metal 860 B. C., but it had been in earlier use in the shape of rings, rods, etc., in the cities of the Chaldeans and in Assyria, and also among the Egyptians. The metal has been found most abundantly in South America, South Africa, and North America. Ancient gold mines of Russia were reopened in 1699 and those of the Ural Mountains have since been richly productive.

PRODUCTION OF GOLD IN UNITED STATES IN CALENDAR YEAR 1915.

States and Territories	Fine Ounces	Value
Alabama	247	$ 5,100
Alaska	808,346	16,710,000
Arizona	220,392	4,555,900
California	1,090,731	22,547 400
Colorado	1,089,928	22,530,800
Georgia	1,684	34,800
Idaho	56,628	1,170,600
Montana	240,825	4,978,300
Nevada	574,874	11,883,700
New Mexico	70,632	1,460,100
North Carolina	8,258	170,700
Oregon	90,321	1,867,100
Philippine Island	63,898	1,320,900
Porto Rico	34	700
South Carolina	174	3,600
South Dakota	358,145	7,403,500
Tennessee	329	6,800
Texas	87	1,800
Utah	189,045	3,907,900
Virginia	24	500
Washington	22,330	461,600
Wyoming	672	13,900
Total	4,887,604	$101,035,700

Gold is said to have been first discovered in Peru and Mexico in the sixteenth century by the Spaniards. It was found in Malacca in 1731, in Nueva Andalucia in 1785, in Ceylon in 1800, in New Zealand in 1842, in California in 1848, in Australia in 1851, in British Columbia in 1856, in Nova Scotia in 1861, in the Transvaal in 1868, in the Bendigo gold fields, Western Australia, in 1870, and in the Klondike region of the Yukon in 1896.

GOLD PRODUCTION FROM MINES IN THE UNITED STATES: 1792 TO 1915

(From Reports of the Director of the Mint, Treasury Department.)

Calendar Year	Fine ounces (troy)	Value
Apr. 2, 1792-July 31, 1834	677,250	$14,000,000
July 31, 1834-Dec. 31, 1856	22,278,670	460,537,000
1857	2,660,625	55,000,000
1858	2,418,750	50,000,000
1859	2,418,750	50,000,000
1860	2,225,250	46,000,000
1861	2,080,125	43,000,000
1862	1,896,300	39,200,000
1863	1,935,000	40,000,000
1864	2,230,087	46,100,000
1865	2,574,759	53,225,000
1866	2,588,062	53,500,000
1867	2,502,196	51,725,000
1868	2,322,000	48,000,000
1869	2,394,362	49,500,000
1870	2,418,750	50,000,000
1871	2,104,312	43,500,000
1872	1,741,500	36,000,000
1873	1,741,500	36,000,000
1874	1,620,122	33,490,000
1875	1,619,009	33,467,900
1876	1,931,575	39,929,200
1877	2,268,662	46,897,400
1878	2,477,109	51,206,400
1879	1,881,787	38,900,000
1880	1,741,500	36,000,000
1881	1,678,612	34,700,000
1882	1,572,187	32,500,000
1883	1,451,250	30,000,000
1884	1,489,950	30,800,000
1885	1,538,373	31,801,000
1886	1,686,788	34,869,000
1887	1,603,049	33,136,000
1888	1,604,478	33,167,500
1889	1,594,775	32,967,000
1890	1,588,877	32,845,000
1891	1,604,840	33,175,000
1892	1,597,098	33,015,000
1893	1,739,323	35,955,000
1894	1,910,813	39,500,000
1895	2,254,760	46,610,000
1896	2,568,132	53,088,000
1897	2,774,935	57,363,000
1898	3,118,398	64,463,000
1899	3,437,210	71,053,400
1900	3,829,897	79,171,000
1901	3,805,500	78,666,700
1902	3,870,000	80,000,000
1903	3,560,000	73,591,700
1904	3,892,480	80,464,700
1905	4,265,742	88,180,700
1906	4,565,333	94,373,800
1907	4,374,827	90,435,700
1908	4,574,340	94,560,000
1909	4,821,700	99,673,400
1910	4,657,017	96,269,100
1911	4,687,053	96,890,000
1912	4,520,719	93,451,500
1913	4,271,562	88,301,023
1914	4,572,976	94,531,800
1915	4,887,604	101,035,700

The production of gold has been steadily increasing in recent years by reason not only of new discoveries but of the improved scientific methods of mining and of extracting the pure metal from the ore. The estimated value of all the gold in the world in 1848 was $2,500,000,000. In 1875 the amount had probably doubled. There was a large increase in the world's production of gold in 1897, the output for that year being twice that of 1890. More than 90 per cent of the supply was furnished by seven countries, viz., the United States, the Transvaal, Australia, Russia (Siberia), British India, Canada, and Mexico.

The world's output is worth about a million and a quarter dollars a day. The Bank of England under a law passed in 1866 is bound to buy all the gold offered to it at the rate of $19.05 per ounce of standard fineness, pure gold being credited at $20.81 per ounce. The greatest hoard of gold in the world is stored in the vaults of the United States Treasury. The Director of the Mint reported more than 500 tons on hand in November, 1914. (See illustration opposite 4344.)

Gold and Silver:

Adoption of, as standard of value discussed, 1465.

Coinage of. (See Coins and Coinage.)

Depreciation in price of silver discussed, 5548, 5628.

Discovery of—
Gold discussed, 2486, 3451, 4355.
Silver discussed, 3451.

Export of, discussed, 5875, 5964, 6156.

Imports of, discussed, 5964.

International action for restoration of silver to full use as money referred to, 4587.

International agreement for free use of silver as a coin metal discussed, 5548.

International conference at Brussels, Belgium, in 1892 to consider enlarged use of silver, 5752.

Postponement of, discussed, 5876.

Report of, transmitted, 5784.

International conference for adopting ratio between, discussed, 4447, 4464, 4474, 4510.

Appropriation for, recommended, 4438.

International conference to consider free coinage of silver, information regarding, refused, 5673.

International ratio of, establishment of, referred to, 4929, 4955.

Price of silver, depreciation of, discussed, 5548, 5628.

Production of, discussed, 3771, 3879, 5876, 5965, 6156.

Production of gold in California discussed, 2660.

Silver-purchase clause of act of 1890, repeal of, discussed, 5875, 6073.

Recommended, 5833.

Use of, as medium of exchange. (See Medium of Exchange.)

Value of gold compared with national currency discussed, 4061, 4102.

Gold Certificates. (See Currency Laws.)

Gold Certificates, recommendations regarding issue of, 4633.

Gold Democrats. (See Sound Money Democrats.)

Gold Mines. (See Mines.)

Gold Reserve discussed, and recommendations regarding, 5835, 5985, 5993, 5999, 6075, 6091.

Golden Circle, Knights of. (See Knights of the Golden Circle.)

Golden State.—A nickname for California (q. v.). (See also States) ; sometimes also nicknamed El Dorado.

Good Return, The:
Protocol relative to claim on Chile in case of, transmitted, 4214.
Reparation made by Chile in case of, 4289.

Gopher State.—A nickname for Minnesota (q. v.), (See also States) ; sometimes also nicknamed North Star State.

Gordon, Ironsides and Fares Company, reimbursement of, 6857.

Gosport, Va., site for docks at, 934.

Government. (See United States.)

Government Bonds. (See Bonds; Debt, Public.)

Government Contracts, recommendations regarding, 3180.

Government Creditors, payment of, in depreciated currency referred to, 1777, 1806, 1807, 1808, 1810.

Government Drafts, sale or exchange of, for bank notes and payment of Government creditors in depreciated currency, 1777, 1806, 1807, 1808, 1810.

Government Employees. (See also Officers, Public):
Official conduct of, complimented, 2714.
Order permitting, to—
Participate in public exercises, and ceremonies, 4879, 6590, 6595, 6611.
Participate in dedication of Washington Monument, 4879.
Witness inauguration of President Cleveland, 4881.
Ordered to organize into companies for defense of Washington, 3323.
Partisan interference in elections by. (See Elections.)
Rendering honors to rebel living or dead inquired into, 3591.
Wages of, not to be affected by reduction in hours of labor, 3969, 4131.

Government Hospital for the Insane.—
This institution was established by act of Congress approved March 3, 1855. It is sometimes called St. Elizabeth's Hospital. Its usual population is above 3,000, for which it cares in the most approved methods for helping the insane, at an annual expenditure of about $800,000. The Hospital is under the supervision of the Interior Department. The District of Columbia is represented more largely than any other state or territory in the number of inmates, but there is liberal provision for the admittance of inmates from other states.

Government Hospital for Insane:
Appropriation for, 2708.
Construction of, discussed, 2750.
Erection of, recommended, 1621, 2204.
Estimate for deficiency appropriation for, 4677.

Government, local. (See Local Government.)

Government Notes, may become necessary to issue, as medium of exchange, 551.

Government Penitentiaries. (See Penitentiaries.)

Government Printing Office.—The Public Printer has charge of all business relating to the public printing and binding. He appoints the officers and employees of the Government Printing Office, and purchases all necessary machinery and material. The foreman of printing has charge of all matter which is to be printed. His department consists of the following divisions : the document, job, specification, press, folding, stereotype, and Congressional Record rooms, as well as the various branch offices. The Superintendent of Documents has general supervision of the distribution of all public documents, excepting those printed for the use of the two Houses of Congress and the Executive Departments. He is required to prepare a comprehensive index of public documents and consolidated index of Congressional documents, and is authorized to sell at cost any public document in his charge, the distribution of which is not specifically directed. The following are the official heads of the several departments : Public Printer, Cornelius Ford ; Secretary to the Public Printer, Joseph P. O'Lone ; Deputy Public Printer, Henry T. Brian ; Congressional Record Clerk, William A. Smith ; Superintendent of Work, D. V. Chisholm ; Superintendent of Documents, Josiah H. Brinker.

See illustration opposite 6567.

Government Printing Office:
Civil service extended over, 6046, 6055.
Order permitting employees of, to—
Participate in decoration of graves of soldiers, 4753, 4818, 4899, 5078, 5350, 5463, 5540, 5609, 5832, 5949, 6046.
Participate in dedication of Washington Monument, 4879.
Transfer to Department of Commerce and Labor recommended, 7229.
Witness inauguration of President Cleveland, 4881.
Overproduction of, 6728, 6914.

Government Service:
Abolition of local offices, 7703.

Accounting and reporting, 7711.
Auditing offices, consolidation of, recommended, 7741.
Budget (the) as an annual programme, 7714.
Business methods in, 7706.
Character of accounts required, 7712.
Citizens' interest in expenditures, 7715.
Classification of local officers, 7704.
Constructive results obtained by investigation, 7713.
Documents, distribution of, 7744.
Economy and efficiency in, 7698, 7736.
Efficiency of personnel, 7706.
Excessive cost of travel, 7710.
First complete investigation into, 7700.
General technical services, 7703.
Lack of specifications, 7709.
Lighthouse and lifesaving services, consolidation of, recommended, 7739.
Local postoffices, should be included in classified service, 7739.
Magnitude of inquiry into, 7699.
Merit system, legislation needed to establish, 7739.
Methods of purchasing, 7711.
Modifications recommended, 7713.
Need for labor saving devices, 7708.
Outlines of organization, 7701.
Pension agencies, should be included in classified service, 7738.
Plan of investigation of, 7700.
Plan for inquiry, 7702.
Prosecution of inquiry into, 7717.
Public welfare questions, 7715.
Reasons for inquiry into, 7699.
Reports on particular services, 7702.
Reports required by Congress, 7713.
Revenue Cutter Service, abolition of recommended, 7740.
Subsistence, storage, communication, etc., expenses, 7711.
Superannuation, 7706.
Uniformity in classification and methods, 7712.
Unnecessary cost of in copy work, 7708.
Handling and filing correspondence, 7707.
Insurance, 7709.
Waste in the distribution of public documents, 7708.
Wasteful use of properties and equipment, 7709.

Governor.—The executive head of each of the states of the Union. When the first settlements were made in America the term governor was used in England to designate the head of large trading corporations like the East India Company, Massachusetts Bay Company, etc. In the Colonies, therefore, which operated under charters similar to the trading companies the executive head became known as the governor. In the royal Colonies he was appointed by the Crown, in the proprietary Colonies by the proprietors, and in Rhode Island, Connecticut, and most of the time in Massachusetts he was chosen by the people. After the Revolution the constitutions of the states provided for a single head, to be called the governor. Terms of the governors of the states vary from one to four years, and the salaries from $1,000 to $10,000. To them is intrusted the execution of the laws, and they are usually invested with the veto and pardoning powers. In our early history the governors of many of the states were chosen by the legislatures thereof. At present the uniform practice is to elect the governor by popular vote.

Governors Island, N. Y., appropriation for sea wall on, recommended, 4744.

Governors, Provisional. (See Provisional Governors.)

Graduated Inheritance Tax, recommended, 7370, 7390.

Graft.—Illegal gains obtained by corrupt practice, particularly on the part of public officials or politicians.

Grain Statistics.—The Bureau of Statistics of the Department of Agriculture makes a careful estimate of the amount of grain sown each year and reports the condition of the crops monthly until harvest, and then publishes a bulletin of the yield and the average price received in leading markets. (See Agricultural Products.)

Granada, The, seizure of, by Canadian revenue cutter at Port Hood, Nova Scotia, 4070.

Granadian Confederation, convention with, referred to, 3268.

Granby Token.—An authorized coin issued by John Higley, of Granby, Conn., in 1737. It was made of copper and on the obverse bore a deer with the words, "Value me as you please," the Roman numerals III, and a crescent. The design on the reverse consisted of three hammers, on a triangular field, each bearing a crown. The legend was, "I am good copper."

Grand Army of the Republic.—A fraternal, charitable, and patriotic organization composed exclusively of ex-soldiers and ex-sailors of the Union Army, Navy, and Marine Corps who served during the Civil War and were honorably discharged. It was planned by Dr. B. F. Stephenson, ex-surgeon of the Fourteenth Illinois Infantry. The first post was organized at Decatur, Ill., April 6, 1866, and the first regular convention was held at Indianapolis, Ind., Nov. 20, 1866. Forty posts were represented, and Gen. S. A. Hurlbut, of Illinois, was chosen commander-in-chief. The organization now has branches in all parts of the Union. Its objects are to bring together in a spirit of friendship all former soldiers and sailors in the Civil War, to care for the widows and orphans of their deceased comrades, to cultivate a spirit of devotion to the Union, and to perpetuate the memory of their dead. There are forty-four departments, and the Commander-in-Chief is Washington Gardiner, Albion, Mich. Jan. 1, 1913, there were 5,663 posts, with a membership of 180,203. Losses by death the previous year were 11,338. Auxiliary to the Grand Army is the Women's Relief Corps, an organization of women having the same objects as the Grand Army and numbering 140,523 members.

Grand Army of the Republic:
Addresses to, 8073, 8075.
Appropriation for reception and entertainment of, in Washington recommended, 5672.
Decoration of graves by, 4137, 4184.
Parade of, in Washington discussed, 5763.
Order permitting members employed in public service to participate in, 5740.

Grand Canyon of the Colorado, proposed as National Park, 7393.

Grand Canyon Forest Reserve, boundaries of, 1104.

Grand Jury.—A jury whose duty it is to inquire into charges for offenses and to determine whether indictments shall be brought against alleged criminals in any court. Provisions of the Federal and state constitutions prohibit the criminal prosecution of any person except upon presentment or indictment by a grand jury for any except the less serious crimes or misdemeanors or military or naval offenses. The custom is very ancient and has been scrupulously guarded as a safeguard of civil liberty since the time of Ethelred, an Anglo-Saxon king of the ninth century. At common law (and usually by statute) the grand jury consists of not less than twelve nor more than twenty-three members, and the concurrence of twelve is necessary to the finding of an indictment. They sit in absolute secrecy, and may either pass upon bills presented by the prosecuting officer of the state or upon presentments made by one of their own number, or upon evidence laid before them of any violation of law. The proceedings are entirely ex parte. Witnesses for the prosecution only are examined. If the requisite number of jurors are satisfied, from the evidence presented, of the truth of the accusation, the foreman of the grand jury writes on the back of the indictment the words "A true bill," signs his name as foreman, and adds the date of the finding; but if the evidence is unsatisfactory the endorsement is "Not a true bill." After all the indictments have been considered the work of the grand jury is ended and the cases are turned over to the court and petit jury for trial.

Grande Ronde Reservations, Oreg., relief of Indians on, bill for, 4780.

Grange.—A farmers' organization instituted for the mutual benefit of its members.

Grangers.—A common name for the patrons of Husbandry, a secret association for the promotion of agricultural interests. The society had its origin in the depressed condition of agriculture immediately succeeding the Civil War. Its object was to redress the grievances of the farmers against the middlemen and railroad companies. The plan of organization embraces a secret ritual. It was organized in Washington, Dec. 4, 1867, by employees of the Department of Agriculture. In a manifesto issued in 1874 the objects of the Grangers are declared to be "to develop a better

and higher manhood and womanhood; to enhance the comforts of our homes; to buy less and produce more; to discountenance the credit system, the fashion system, and every other system that tends to prodigality and bankruptcy." Though nonpolitical, the order has exerted a strong influence in various state legislatures and in elections.

Granite State.—A nickname for New Hampshire (q. v.). (See also States.)

Grant, Ulysses S.—1869-1877.
(FIRST TERM, 1869-1873.)
Twenty-first Administration—Republican.
Vice-President—Schuyler Colfax.
Secretary of State—
Elihu B. Washburn.
Hamilton Fish.
Secretary of the Treasury—
George S. Boutwell.
Secretary of War—
John A. Rawlins.
William T. Sherman.
William W. Belknap.
Secretary of the Navy—
Adolph E. Borie
George M. Robeson.
Secretary of the Interior—
Jacob D. Cox.
Columbus Delano.
Postmaster-General—
John A. J. Creswell.
Attorney-General—
E. Rockwood Hoar.
Amos T. Ackerman.
George H. Williams.
Nomination.—Grant was elected by the Republican party, Nov. 3, 1868. He was nominated at the National Convention, at Chicago, May 20-21, 1868, by a unanimous vote of the 650 delegates.
Platform.—The platform of the Republican party endorsed the reconstruction policy of Congress; equal suffrage; denounced repudiation; recommended equalization of taxation; advised the extension of the time of payment of the public debt to a fair and reasonable period; advocated economical administration; deplored the death of Lincoln and denounced President Johnson's administration; placed naturalized citizens on a level of equality with the native-born; upheld the gallant conduct of soldiers and sailors in the Civil War; encouraged immigration; and commended the spirit of the Southern people in their assistance in reconstruction.
Opposition.—The Democratic National Convention, held in New York, July 4-11, 1868, nominated Horatio Seymour, after the twenty-second ballot, over Pendleton, Hendricks, and Hancock.
Vote.—The popular vote of thirty-four States, including that of Georgia, gave Grant 3,015,071; and Seymour, 2,709,613. The electoral vote, counted Feb. 10, 1869, gave Grant 214 and Seymour 80; 23 cast no vote.
Renomination.—In 1872, President Grant was renominated enthusiastically by acclamation at the Republican National Convention, at Philadelphia, June 5-6.

(SECOND TERM, 1873-1877.)
Twenty-second Administration—Republican.
Vice-President—Henry Wilson.
Secretary of State—
Hamilton Fish (continued).
Secretary of the Treasury—
William A. Richardson.
Benjamin H. Bristow.
Lot M. Morrill.
Secretary of the Interior—
Columbus Delano.
Zachariah Chandler.

Secretary of War—
  W. W. Belknap (continued).
  Alphonso Taft.
  James D. Cameron.
Secretary of the Navy—
  George M. Robeson (continued).
Postmaster-General—
  John A. J. Creswell (continued).
  James W. Marshall.
  Marshall Jewell.
  James N. Tyner.
Attorney-General—
  George H. Williams.
  Edwards Pierrepont.
  Alphonso Taft.

SECOND TERM—Opposition.—The opponents of the Grant administration, under the name of the Liberal Republican party, had met in Cincinnati, May 1, 1872, and nominated Horace Greeley. The Democratic (Straight Out) Convention, at Louisville, Ky., Sept. 3, 1872, nominated Charles O'Conor, of New York. The Labor Reform Convention, at Columbus, Ohio, Feb. 21-22, 1872, nominated David Davis. The Prohibition Convention, at Columbus, Ohio, Feb. 22, 1872, nominated James Black.

Vote.—The popular vote of thirty-seven State cast in November gave Grant 3,597,-070; Greeley, 2,834,079; O'Conor, 29,489; and Black, 5,608. The electoral vote, counted on Feb. 12, 1873, gave Grant 286; Hendricks, 42; Brown, 18; Jenkins, 2; Davis, 1; and not voting, 17. The death of Horace Greeley on Nov. 29, 1872, caused the Democratic and Liberal Republican electors to cast their votes for others.

Party Affiliation.—General Grant, though nominated unanimously by the Republican party, never cast a Republican vote until after his term of office expired. He had never taken an active part in politics, and voted but once for a President, James Buchanan, the Democratic candidate in 1856, though his earlier associations had been with the Whig party. Though approached at this election by Democratic politicians and urged to accept the Democratic nomination, he declined the offer, for at heart he was more of a Republican than anything else. He favored a national banking system, a protective tariff, internal improvements, and equity of laws.

Political Complexion of Congress.—In the Forty-first Congress (1869-1871) the Senate, of 74 members, was composed of 11 Democrats, 61 Republicans, with 2 vacancies; and the House, of 243 members, was made up of 73 Democrats and 170 Republicans. In the Forty-second Congress (1871-1873) the Senate of 74 members was composed of 17 Democrats and 57 Republicans; and the House, of 243 members, was made up of 104 Democrats and 139 Republicans. In the Forty-third Congress (1873-1875) the Senate, of 74 members, was composed of 19 Democrats, 54 Republicans, with 1 vacancy; and the House, of 292 members, was made up of 88 Democrats, 203 Republicans, with 1 vacancy. In the Forty-fourth Congress (1875-1877) the Senate, of 76 members, was composed of 29 Democrats, 46 Republicans, with 1 vacancy; and the House, of 293 members, was made up of 181 Democrats, 107 Republicans, 3 Independents, with 2 vacancies.

Tariff.—The tariff act of July 14, 1870, "to reduce internal taxes, and for other purposes," reduced the duties on several articles named and also increased the free list. By the act of May 1, 1872, the duty on tea and coffee was repealed. Taxes on imports were still further reduced by the act of June 6, 1872, and this latter act was amended by the tariff act

of March 3, 1873. Two amending acts were passed in 1875, that of March 3 increased the duties on imported molasses, sugar, and other articles. In his Second Annual Message (page 4061) the President said: "The tax collected from the people has been reduced more than $80,-000,000 per annum. By steadiness in our present course there is no reason why in a few short years the national tax-gatherer may not disappear from the door of the citizen almost entirely. With the revenue stamp dispensed by postmasters in every community, tax upon liquors of all sorts, and tobacco in all its forms, and by a wise adjustment of the tariff, which will put a duty only upon these articles which we could dispense with, known as luxuries, and on those which we use more of than we produce, revenue enough may be raised after a few years of peace and consequent reduction of indebtedness, to fulfill all our obligations. A further reduction of expenses, in addition to a further reduction of interest account, may be relied on to make this practicable. Revenue reform, if it means this, has my hearty support."

Fifteenth Amendment.—The Fifteenth Amendment to the Constitution was adopted Feb. 26, 1869, ratified by the requisite three-fourths of the States, and declared in force on March 30, 1870. President Grant had recommended this measure and when he proclaimed its adoption he sent a special message to Congress (page 4009) in which he said that this "is indeed a measure of grander importance than any other one act of the kind from the foundation of our free Government to the present day." Again he says that "the adoption of the Fifteenth Amendment to the Constitution completes the greatest civil change and constitutes the most important event that has occurred since the nation came into life."

Civil Service.—In his Second Annual Message (page 4062) President Grant advocates "reform in the civil service of the country. I would have it go beyond the mere fixing of the tenure of office of clerks and employees. . . . I would have it govern, not the tenure, but the manner of making all appointments. . . . The present system does not secure the best men. The elevation and purification of the civil service of the Government will be hailed with approval by the whole people of the United States." In his Third Annual Message (page 4109) the President reports the appointment by him of a board to revise rules and regulations to effect the needed reforms. In his Fifth Annual Message (page 4209) the President asks Congress to appoint a committee to confer with his Civil-Service-Board regarding proper recognition of the rules formulated by it.

Public Debt.—The public debt of the United States during the administration of President Grant stood as follows: July 1, 1869, $2,432,771,873.09; 1870, $2,331.-169,965.21; 1871, $2,246,994,068.67; 1872, $2,149,780,530.35; 1873, $2,105,462,060.75; 1874, $2,104,149,153.69; 1875, $2,090,041,-170.13; 1876, $2,060,925,340.45.

In his First Annual Message (page 3983) President Grant said: "The vast resources of the nation, both developed and undeveloped, ought to make our credit the best on earth. With a less burden of taxation than the citizen has endured for six years past, the entire public debt could be paid in ten years. But it is not desirable that the people should be taxed to pay it in that time. Year by year the ability to pay increases in a rapid ratio." The President advocates the payment of the interest and

EXTENT OF THE UNITED STATES DURING THE ADMINISTRATION OF PRESIDENT GRANT, 1869-1877.

(NOT INCLUDING TERRITORIES)

MAINE 1820

N. H. 1788

MASS. 1788

CONN. 1788

R. I. 1790

VT. 1791

NEW YORK 1788

N. J. 1787

PENNSYLVANIA 1787

MD. 1788

DEL. 1787

VIRGINIA 1788

WEST VIRGINIA 1863

NORTH CAROLINA 1789

SOUTH CAROLINA 1788

FLORIDA 1845

OHIO 1803

KENTUCKY 1792

GEORGIA 1788

MICHIGAN 1837

INDIANA 1816

TENNESSEE 1796

ALABAMA 1819

ILLINOIS 1818

WISCONSIN 1848

MISSISSIPPI 1817

MISSOURI 1821

ARKANSAS 1836

LOUISIANA 1812

IOWA 1846

MINNESOTA 1858

NEBRASKA 1867

KANSAS 1861

TEXAS 1845

COLORADO 1876

NEVADA 1864

OREGON 1859

CALIFORNIA 1850

FLAG OF 1877

the funding of the public debt. On page 3991, the President highly commends the action of Congress in passing the joint resolution providing that the debt be paid, both principal and interest in coin.

Finance.—In his First Annual Message (page 3983) the President said: "Among the evils growing out of the rebellion, and not yet referred to, is that of an irredeemable currency. It is an evil that I hope will receive your earnest attention. It is a duty and one of the highest duties of Government to secure to the citizen a medium of exchange of fixed, unvarying value. This implies a return to a specie basis and no substitute for it can be devised. I earnestly recommend to you then such legislation as will secure the gradual return to specie payments, and put an immediate stop to fluctuations in the value of currency." When, in 1874, Congress passed the "Inflation Bill" increasing the paper currency of the country $100,000,000, the President vetoed it (page 4223) and stated that the opinions formerly expressed by him had undergone no change. The bill was not passed over his veto and the whole country sustained his action. Writing on June 4, 1874, President Grant said: "I believe it a high and plain duty to return to a specie basis at the earliest practical day, not only in compliance with legislative and party pledges, but as a step indispensable to national lasting prosperity." Congress as a result of the President's earnestness and unanswerable argument passed the "Resumption Act" in 1875. The financial results of President Grant's administrations may be summed up thus: There had been a reduction of over $300,000,000 in the taxes, over $450,000,000 in the public debt, over $60,000,000 in the interest, and a change from $130,000,000 of balance of trade against the country to that amount in its favor.

Grant, Ulysses S.:

Advancement and progress made by United States discussed by, 4286.

Annexation of Santo Domingo discussed by. (See Santo Domingo.)

Annual messages of, 3981, 4050, 4096, 4138, 4189, 4238, 4286, 4353.

Biographical sketch of, 3957.

Brigadier-general, thanks of President tendered, 3305.

Captain-general of Army, appointment of, as, recommended, 4572.

Civil Service discussed by, 4063, 4108, 4159, 4177, 4208, 4217. (See also Civil Service.) 4254.

Congress requested by, to postpone adjournment, 4034.

Constitutional amendment regarding—

Approval of separate items of bill and veto of others recommended by, 4196.

Election of President and Vice-President referred to by, 4196.

Legislation during last 24 hours of Congress recommended by, 4196.

Legislation in extra session of Congress recommended by, 4196.

Cuban insurrection and policy of United States regarding, dis-

cussed by, 3985, 4018, 4051, 4101, 4143, 4245, 4290.

Referred to by President McKinley, 6259, 6286, 6291.

Death of, announced and honors to be paid memory of, 4893, 4900, 4901, 4902, and illustration opposite 4927.

Executive acts performed during absence of President from seat of Government discussed by, 3559.

Exequatur issued vice-consul of Portugal revoked by, 4038.

Finances discussed by, 3983, 3991, 4061, 4101, 4146, 4197, 4238, 4247, 4268, 4301, 4354, 4379.

First lieutenant by brevet, nomination of and reasons therefor, 2520.

Foreign policy discussed by, 3985, 4006, 4016, 4018, 4050, 4053, 4082, 4101, 4143, 4176, 4192, 4245, 4290, 4365.

General of United States Army—

Nomination of, 3595.

Nomination of, upon retired list, 4867.

Recommended, 4858.

Requested to proceed to Mexican frontier and communicate with American minister, 3641.

Relieved from duty, 3641.

Habeas corpus, writ of, suspended in South Carolina by, 4090, 4093.

Revoked as to Marion County, 4092.

Inaugural address of—

First, 3960; Second, 4175.

Legislation in last 24 hours of Congress, 4829.

Lieutenant, first, by brevet, nomination of, and reasons therefor, 2520.

Lieutenant-general—

Commander of armies of United States assigned to, 3435.

Negotiations for and correspondence regarding restoration of peace, 3461.

Nomination of, 3400.

Report of, referred to, 3471.

Major-general, thanks of Congress tendered, and gold medal presented to, 3432.

Monroe doctrine reasserted by, 4015, 4054, 4083.

Official and civil career of, discussed by, 4353.

Pension to, recommended, 4840.

Pocket veto of, 4274.

Portrait of, 3956.

Powers of Federal and State Governments discussed by, 3992, 4126, 4170, 4196, 4259.

Proclamation of—

Admission of Colorado, 4346.

Alabama Claims, extending time of Commission of, 4278.

American citizens in Ottoman dominions, rights of, 4231, 4344.

Centennial Exposition at Philadelphia, 4181. (See illustration opposite 4376.)

Consular jurisdiction over crews of foreign vessels in American waters, 4038, 4129.

Day for submitting constitution to voters of—
Mississippi, 3970.
Texas, 3971.
Virginia, 3967.

Directing discontinuance of proceedings to remove persons from office, 4130.

Discriminating duties suspended on vessels of—
France, 3969, 3973, 4182.
Revoked, 4132.
Japan, 4131.
Portugal, 4080.
Spain, 4128.

Enforcement of fourteenth amendment, 4088.

Exequatur of vice-consul of Portugal revoked, 4038.

Extraordinary session of Senate, 3966, 4087, 4171, 4278, 4390.

Facsimile of, opposite 3976.
Military expedition to Canada, 4039.
Neutrality in Franco-German War, 4040, 4043, 4045.

Recommending filing of historical sketches of counties and towns, 4345.

Reduction in hours of labor not to affect wages of Government employees, 3969, 4129.

Thanksgiving, 3972, 4046, 4092, 4132, 4182, 4231, 4279, 4346, 4351.

Treaty with—
Great Britain, acts to give effect to, 4179, 4227.
Hawaiian Islands, 4348.

Unlawful combinations in—
Arkansas, 4226.
Louisiana, 4177, 4230.
Mississippi, 4276.
South Carolina, 4086, 4089, 4350.
Habeas corpus suspended, 4090, 4093.
Revoked as to Marion County, 4092.

Reconstruction of Southern States discussed by, 3982, 4050.
Recommendations regarding, 3965.
Referred to, 4354.

Removals from office discussed by, 3992.

Report of, on condition of Southern States, 3571.

Restoration of Southern States recommended by, 3965.

Secretary of War, authorized to act as, *ad interim*, 3754, 3781.

Correspondence with President Johnson regarding vacation of office of, 3800.

State of the Union discussed by, 3981, 4050, 4107, 4138, 4238, 4259, 4286, 4353.

Swords and testimonials of, offered to government by Mrs. Grant, recommendation regarding, 4857.
Schedule of, 4859.

Tariff discussed by, 3984, 4061, 4102, 4201, 4247, 4303.

Termination of official career of, referred to, 4367.

Thanksgiving proclamations of, 3972, 4046, 4092, 4132, 4182, 4231, 4279, 4346, 4351.

Tomb of, see illustration opposite 4943.

Veto messages of—
Abolishing police board in District of Columbia, 4384.
Advertising of Executive Departments, 4388.
Amendment to act for improvement of Fox and Wisconsin rivers, 4336.
Congratulations from Argentine Republic and Pretoria, 4384.
Equalizing bounties of soldiers in war, reasons for applying pocket veto, 4274.
Fixing salary of President, 4334.
Homestead entries, 4383.
Indian trust funds, 4332.
New trials in Court of Claims, 4168.
Paving Pennsylvania avenue, 4341.
Pension to—
Blumer, Eliza Jane, 4338.
Crawford, Richard B., 4126.
Hinely, Lewis, 4274.
Montgomery, Mary Ann, 4126.
Ryan, Abigail, 4126.
Placing Daniel H. Kelly's name on muster roll, 4386.
Post-office statutes, 4336.
Recording conveyances in District of Columbia, 4335.
Relief of—
Best, J. Milton, 4126.
Brock, Michael, 4339.
Burtch, Alexander, 4273.
Children of John M. Baker, 4125.
Contractors for war vessels, 4079.
Cooper, Charles, and other signers of bond, 4078.
Denniston, William H., 4222.
East Tennessee University, 4169.
Hanks, John F., estate of, 4124.
Hile, James A., 4333.
Johnston, James T., 4125.
Jussen, Edmund, 4168.
Leland, Edward A., 4389.
McCullah, James A., 4170.
Owners of salt works, 4170.
Spencer and Mead, 4225.
Tiffany, Nelson, 4337.

Turner, Junius T., 4343.
  Objections to bill withdrawn, 4343.
Tyler and Luckett (assignees), 4334.
Wallace, Thomas B., 4127.
White, Rollin, 4034.
Willman, Henry, 4070.
Removal of charge of desertion from record of Alfred Rouland, 4387.
Restoration of Edward S. Meyer's name to army list, 4339.
Sale of Indian lands, 4341.
  President requests that bill be returned for approval, 4342.
  Request denied, 4342.
Union troops in Alabama and Florida, fixing status of, 4035.
United States notes and national bank circulation, 4222.
Grant's Tomb. (See illustration opposite 4943.)
Graphophone. (See Phonograph.)
Greaser.—A name given to Mexicans in the United States, particularly in the border states.
Great Britain. (See British Empire for History and Description.)
Great Britain (see also British Empire, Canada, Dominion of; London):
Action of United States in Boer War to preserve neutrality and to produce peace, 6371.
Aid to American interests in Spanish jurisdictions rendered by consuls of, 6331.
American citizens—
  Attacked by force from, discussed, 1618.
  Militia called forth to protect, 1620.
  Claims of, against, 6858.
  Illegally taken by, 485.
  Treatment of, referred to, 3718.
  Unlawfully put to death in, and retaliatory measures discussed, 522.
American interests in Spanish jurisdiction confided to consuls of, 6331.
Arbitration, negotiations with United States for. (See Arbitration.)
Attempted occupation of portion of Alaska by Canada and, referred to, 6097.
Attempts of Canada and, to establish post routes in Alaska referred to, 5501.
Attempts of, to draw recruits from States during war with Russia discussed, 2864.
Attempts to draw United States into its contest with France, 437.
Bering Sea questions discussed. (See Bering Sea Fisheries.)

Blockade declared by, without presence of adequate force, 486.
Boundary dispute of, with Liberia, 4716, 4762.
Boundary dispute of, with Venezuela regarding British Guiana, 5204, 5471, 5616, 5873, 5958, 6064, 6087, 6154, 6380.
  Arbitration of—
    Discussed, 6337.
    Recommended by President Cleveland, 6064.
  Treaty regarding, 6154.
  Monroe doctrine reasserted and attitude of United States respecting, discussed by President Cleveland, 6064, 6087.
Boundary line with (see also Alaska; Ghent, Treaty of; Northeastern Boundary; Northwestern Boundary)—
  Commission for determining, dissolved, 3989.
  Commission to settle, recommended, 4056, 4141.
  Commission selected referred to, 4191.
  Expenses of commission referred to, 3899.
  Referred to, 965, 3112, 3117, 4098, 4191.
  Settlement of, 4138, 4357.
  Treaty regarding, referred to, 3894, 3956.
Canal navigation in Canada discussed. (See Canada, Dominion of.)
Central America, relations between United States and, regarding. (See Central America.)
Cession of keys on Bahama Banks to United States, negotiations regarding, 913.
Claims of, against United States, 242, 621, 1125, 1258, 2995, 3247, 3580, 4191, 4243, 4975, 5662. (See also Lord Nelson, The.)
  Agreement to discharge, 329.
  Award of commission, 4191.
    Payment of, 4243.
  Commission for adjustment of, 2741.
  Convention regarding, 2726, 3894, 6097.
Claims of, growing out of War between the States, 4191.
Claims of United States against (see also Alabama Claims; Fisheries; Fortune Bay Outrages; Vessels, United States, seized)—
  Arising from injuries to United States during War between the States. (See Alabama Claims.)
  Commission for adjustment of, 2741, 2917.
  Recommended, 4056.
  Convention regarding, 932, 935, 2726, 3894, 3956.

Correspondence regarding, 3999.
Discussed and referred to by President—
Adams, John, 242, 253.
Adams, J. Q., 869, 895, 919, 932.
Grant, 3964, 3965, 3987, 4191.
Jackson, 1109, 1268.
Jefferson, 383, 411, 433.
Johnson, 3565, 3655, 3777, 3890.
Madison, 458.
Tyler, 2111, 2112, 2191, 2219.
Van Buren, 1732, 1784.
Washington, 88, 89, 145, 146, 192.
Indemnification to be allowed, 2111.
Letter from minister regarding it, 383.
Payment of, 242, 935, 945, 986, 4625.
Treaty regarding, rejected by Senate, 3987.
Colonial trade of United States with—
Prohibited by proclamation, 941, 947.
Proposition made to Great Britain in regard to, 1043, 1064, 1134, 1135.
Referred to, 920, 932, 1095, 1109, 4122, 4123.
Commerce of United States—
Decrees affecting. (See Berlin and Milan Decrees.)
Restrictions placed upon by, during South African War, 6429.
Spoliations committed on. (See Claims against, *ante*.)
Commercial reciprocal conventions concluded with, on behalf of colonies, 6381.
Commercial relations of United States with colonies of. (See British Colonies.)
Commercial relations with, and questions regarding—
Convention in regard to, 548, 554, 608, 628, 764, 946.
Proclamation regarding, transmitted, 555.
Discussed, by President—
Adams, John, 251.
Adams, J. Q., 919, 933, 941, 967, 974.
Jackson, 1043, 1064, 1115.
Madison, 459, 467, 476.
Monroe, 608, 628, 645, 669, 818.
Polk, 2428.
Taylor, 2548.
Washington, 88, 114, 138, 175, 184, 190, 191, 458, 476, 941, 948.
Renewal of, 453, 457.
Suspension of, 458, 476, 941, 948.
Commissioners' award in the claims of United States against, 6276.
Conduct of, toward United States before War of 1812, discussed, 484.
Confederate envoys sent to. (See Mason and Slidell.)

Confederate States, aid furnished to, by, and claims of United States arising out of. (See Alabama Claims.)
Consuls of, to United States, exequaturs to, revoked, 2924, 2925.
Convention with—
Proposition to refer differences regarding, to arbitration, 2895.
Referred to, 771, 935, 958, 969, 2763, 2776, 2908, 2917.
Conventional regulations of passage of Chinese laborers across American frontier proposed to, 5544.
Copyright privilege extended, by proclamation, 5582.
Referred to, 5625.
Distressed operatives of Blackburn, Referred to, 3358.
Duties—
Claims of, for return of, settled, 2296.
Remitted to citizens of United States by recommendations regarding, 568.
Edicts of, unjust, 487.
Export duties, return of, to American merchants demanded, 2112.
Claims regarding, settled, 2296.
Financial policy of, discussed, 2504.
Fisheries, controversy with United States regarding. (See Bering Sea Fisheries.)
Fisheries of, referred to, 1127.
Flag of, order directing salute to, by Army and Navy forces at Yorktown, 4624.
Referred to, 4625.
Fortifications of, on northern frontier of United States, 1803, 1815, 1817.
Gen. Macomb's letter regarding, 1815.
Gen. Scott's letter regarding, 1804.
Fugitive criminals, convention with, for surrender of, 2016, 4989, 5470.
Demands made under, 2131, 2213.
Discussed, 4917.
Questions arising under, 4419.
Referred to, 4802, 5545.
Refusal of, to comply with, 4321. 4324, 4368.
Fugitive slaves in. (See Fugitive Slaves.)
Greytown bombardment and claims arising out of. (See Greytown, Nicaragua.)
Hostile disposition of, toward United States, 476, 479, 483, 484.
Import duties collected in contravention of treaty between United States and, 596, 2274, 2296.
Importation of American products to, restrictions upon, discussed, 4519, 5764, 6178.
Importations of, suspension of act prohibiting, recommended, 399.

Imposition of commercial restrictions upon the products and manufactures of the United States sought to be introduced into, 4519, 5764, 6178.

Imprisonment of American citizens by authorities of, 963, 969, 990, 1123, 1575, 1622, 1687, 1909, 1928, 2521, 3718, 3827, 3897, 4005, 4602, 4674, 6101.
Correspondence regarding. (See Greely, Ebenezer S.)
Released, 1110.
Trial and conviction of, 3800, 3827, 3833, 3834, 4782.

Imprisonment of citizens of, by United States, 1840.
Referred to, 1894, 1927, 2286, 2303.

Improper publication regarding proposition to adjust claims discussed, 2691.

In state of war with United States while latter remains in state of peace, 489.

Interference with cargoes in neutral bottoms during Boer War by, 6429.

Invasion of northern frontier of United States by troops of, discussed, 1618, 1676, 1695, 1840, 1929.

Island of Tigre, forcible seizure and occupancy of, by, referred to, 2570, 2601.

Lease of station by Hawaii to, for submarine telegraph cable, recommendations regarding, 5991.

Licenses of, acceptance of, prohibited. (See Licenses.)

Light-house dues of, referred to, 4117.

Mediation offered by, in dispute between United States and France, 1432, 1434.
Accepted by United States, 1432.
Correspondence in regard to, 1436.
Rendered unnecessary, 1435.

Military operations of, against China terminated by treaty, 2066.

Military preparations of, referred to, 1803, 1815, 1817.

Minister of, to United States—
Intercourse with, terminated by President Pierce, 2908.
Resumed, 2972.
Interference of, in political affairs of United States and action of President Cleveland regarding, 5365, 5396.
Recalled, 459.
Received, 2972.
Title of ambassador conferred upon, 5874.

Minister of United States to—
Correspondence of, transmitted, 463.
Letter of, transmitted, 6254.
Nomination of, 146.

Pretoria protects British and other interests, 6371.

Recall of, referred to, 4070.

Title of ambassador conferred upon, 5874.

Monetary disturbances in, referred to, 5549, 5556.

Naturalization treaty with, 3894, 3956, 4014, 4056, 4077.

Naval force on Lakes, agreement with, regarding, 581, 602, 605, 1805, 1817, 5768.
Desire of Great Britain to annul, 1818.
Proclamation regarding, 605.

Navigation acts of, alterations in, referred to, 2548.

Navigation with, referred to, 331, 559, 960, 2548.

Negotiations with, 843, 913.
Transmission of information regarding, refused, 2690.

Neutral rights of United States disregarded by, 486.

Neutral trade between ports unfriendly to, interdicted by, 415.

Neutrality, alleged violation of, by, referred to, 1738.

Neutrality of United States in war with—
Austria-Hungary, 7975.
Germany, 7974.
Turkey, 8014.

Nicaragua, authority and aggressions of, in, discussed, 2571.

Northeastern boundary line with United States. (See Northeastern Boundary.)

Northwestern boundary line with United States. (See Northwestern Boundary.)

Officers of, misbehavior of, toward American vessels of war, 271.

Operations against China terminated by treaty, 2066.

Oregon Territory dispute with United States regarding boundary of. (See Northwestern Boundary.)

Payment of duties due, 568.

Postal arrangements to be made with, 2413.
Referred to, 2175, 2428.

Postal convention with, 2528, 2560, 2724, 3650, 3775, 3833, 3883.

Ramsden, Fred W., Consul at Santiago de Cuba, death of, referred to, 6331.

Refusal of, to abide by action of minister to United States, 458.

Relations with, discussed, 147, 251, 327, 328, 329, 434, 437, 778, 1617, 2690, 2691, 4024.

Restrictions upon products, 4519.

Renounces rights under Clayton-Bulwer treaty, 6849.

Ruatan Island, convention with Honduras regarding, 2955.
Salvador, differences with, 2643.
Samoan affairs discussed. (See Samoan Islands.)
San Juan Island, claim of United States and, to. (See San Juan Island.)
Satisfaction demanded from, for outrages committed by vessels of, 414.
Seamen of United States impressed by, referred to, 383, 430.
Account of J. B. Cutting for expenses in liberating, 108.
Search, right to, claimed by, but denied by the United States, 484, 1930, 2048, 2082.
Mutual right to, discussed, 1943.
Secret agent employed by, to foment disaffection in United States, 483, 488.
Sioux Indians, pursuit of hostile bands of, referred to, 3399.
Slave trade, convention with, for suppression of. (See African Slave Trade.)
Slaves exported by, in contravention of treaty of Ghent, 629, 6280.
Soldiers enlisted within United States by, discussed, 2864, 2895, 2908, 2943.
Spoliations committed on commerce of United States by. (See Claims against, *ante*.)
Tariff on productions of, referred to, 2571.
Tariff system of, discussed, 2350.
Territorial relations with, referred to, 1732, 1738.
Trade-marks, treaty with regarding, 4408, 4419.
Treaty and negotiations with, regarding—
Canals. (See Nicaragua Canal; Panama Canal.)
Tehuantepec route. (See Tehuantepec, Isthmus of.)
Treaty of peace with, Commissioners were Albert Gallatin, John Quincy Adams and James A. Bayard.
Appointed in May, 1813.
Proclamation regarding, 545.
Transmitted, 537.
Treaty of, with—
Honduras, referred to, 3170.
Nicaragua, 3168.
Treaty with, transmitted and discussed by President—
Adams, John, 251, 280, 282, 285, 296.
Adams, John Q., 932, 935.
Cleveland, 4917, 4989.
Fillmore, 2602, 2617.
Grant, 4055, 4086, 4097, 4161.
Harrison, Benj., 5470.
Jefferson, 327, 329, 409, 433.
Johnson, 3722.
Lincoln, 3272, 3281, 3395, 3401.
Madison, 537, 545, 548, 554.
Monroe, 605, 618, 619, 707, 764, 777, 810.
Pierce, 2775, 2780, 2810, 2951.
Polk, 2245, 2528.
Taylor, 2580.
Tyler, 2016, 2047, 2068, 2082, 2110.
Washington, 88, 143, 144, 170, 175, 184, 186, 190, 192, 197.
(See also Ashburton Treaty; Clayton-Bulwer Treaty; Geneva Tribunal; Ghent, Treaty of, and Hay-Pauncefote Treaty.)
Acts to give effect to, passage of, proclaimed, 4179, 4227.
Referred to, 4243.
Ashburton. (See Ashburton Treaty.)
Commissioners to conclude—
Communications from and instructions to, 536, 537.
Communications received in regard to, 536, 537, 2583.
Construction of, discussed. (See Clayton-Bulwer Treaty; Ghent, Treaty of.)
Emperor of Russia construes, 645, 672, 756.
Proclamation regarding, by President—
Arthur, 4867.
Madison, 545.
Pierce, 2858, 2922.
Ratification of, 767.
Referred to, 945, 946, 2760, 2943, 2944, 2952, 5196.
Regarding—
British North American fisheries. (See Fisheries.)
Dominion over Central America. (See Central America.)
Property and slaves taken in violation of treaty of Ghent, 932.
Trade with Canada, 4220.
Rejected by Senate, 3982.
Signed at Ghent. (See Ghent, Treaty of.)
Termination of, proclaimed, 4867.
Tribunal at Geneva to settle questions pending between United States and. (See Geneva Tribunal.)
Troops of—
About to encroach upon territory of United States, 147.
Landed in Nicaragua referred to, 5908.
Vessels of—
Committing depredations shall not reenter waters of United States, 390, 410, 419.
Contraband on, for use of American insurgents discussed, 3352.

Embargo on—
Imposed, 458.
Referred, 468, 476.
Removed, 457.
Intercourse with, forbidden, 419.
Interfered with by United States.
(See *Albion*, The; *Glen*, The;
Perthshire, The; *Sibyl*, The.)
Ports of United States opened to,
by proclamation, 753, 1060.
Referred to, 755.
Presented to United States. (See
Lady Franklin Bay Expedition.)
Restrictions on, removed, 603, 605.
Seized in Oregon, 2636.
To be restored to, 2953, 4856.
Violate American flag, 485.
Vessels of United States—
In Great Lakes granted facilities
for returning, 6331.
Mutual right to search, discussed,
1943.
Question amicably settled, 3038,
3171.
Restricted in South Africa, 6429.
Right to search, claimed by, denied
by United States, 484, 1930,
2048, 2082.
Referred to, 2286, 2297.
Seized or interfered with by, dis-
cussed by President—
Adams, John, 242, 264, 271.
Buchanan, 3062.
Cleveland, 4990, 5198.
Fillmore, 2603, 2675, 2680.
Grant, 4068, 4070, 4114.
Jefferson, 410, 414, 420, 433, 441.
Madison, 454, 478, 481.
Polk, 2286, 2297.
Tyler, 1909, 1920, 1929, 2016,
2076, 2111, 2215, 2219.
Van Buren, 1676, 1693, 1695,
1732, 1784, 1806, 1839, 1840,
1857.
Washington, 118.
(See also *Chesapeake*, The; **War
of 1812** discussed.)
War of France and, with China,
neutrality of United States in,
3037, 3089, 3174.
War with France, neutrality of
United States in, proclaimed, 148.
War with Russia—
Attempts of Great Britain to draw
recruits from United States,
2864.
Neutrality of United States in,
2864.
Wars with United States. (See Rev-
olutionary War; War of 1812.)
Welland Canal, navigation of, and
questions growing out of. (See
Welland Canal.)
Workingmen in, correspondence of
President Lincoln with, transmit-
ted, 3358.

Great Britain, Treaties with.—Many of
the treaties made between the United States
and Great Britain have been either abrogated by wars or have been superseded by
later treaties. All are, however, of great
historic importance on account of the part
they played in establishing the boundaries
and determining the relations of the two
countries.
Protocol Ending Revolution.—The provisional treaty of peace of 1782 was concluded
at Paris, Nov. 30, 1782. By it, Great
Britain acknowledged the independence of
the United States, relinquished all claims,
and specified the boundaries between the
United States and Canada. It was the
vagueness of the boundary description of
the east that led to the difficulties with
Canada, settled by the Webster-Ashburton
treaty. Fishery rights were conferred upon,
and confirmed to the United States in all
parts in which its people had been accus-
tomed to fish. The collection of debts
was facilitated; recommendations were made
for the restitution of confiscated estates;
confiscations and persecutions were to
cease; prisoners of war on both sides were
to be liberated; and Great Britain was to
withdraw all forces, and to restore all
State records, archives, deeds, and papers,
which had fallen into the hands of any
British officers. The navigation of the Mississippi was to be open to the citizens both
of the United States and Great Britain.
Armistice.—There was signed at Versailles on Jan. 20, 1783, an armistice declaring a cessation of hostilities, upon which
the several provisions of the preceding
treaty went into effect.
Peace.—The definitive treaty of peace
between Great Britain and the United States
was signed at Paris on Sept. 3, 1783. It
was in effect a reiteration of the terms and
conditions of the protocol.
*Amity Commerce and Navigation (Jay
Treaty).*—The treaty of amity, commerce,
and navigation of 1794 is known as the Jay
treaty. A part of it expired by limitation
in 1807, and the rest of it was annulled
by the War of 1812. It contained more
definite location of the St. Croix river—a
part of the eastern boundary; and provided
for the adjustment of claims on both sides.
Peace and Amity (Treaty of Ghent).—
The treaty of peace and amity of 1814,
known as the Treaty of Ghent, closed the
war of 1812. It was signed at Ghent on
Dec. 24, 1814. It declared peace between
the two countries, provided for the restoration of territory and of archives; proclaimed
a cessation of hostilities; and ordered the
release of prisoners on both sides. The
northeastern boundary was determined and
laid down, the northern boundary from the
St. Croix to the St. Lawrence, and the
northern boundary from the St. Lawrence to
Lake Superior, and thence from Lake Huron to the Lake of the Woods, were defined. It defined the powers of the boundary
commission. The United States obligated
itself to put an end to hostilities of the
Indians; and slave trade was abolished. To
this treaty were appended many annotations
and explanations of the boundaries between
the United States and Canada.
Commerce.—The convention of commerce
and navigation of 1794 is continued in force
by the treaties of 1815 and 1818, and indefinitely extended by the convention of
1827. It agreed to freedom of commerce
and navigation throughout the dominions of
both powers; provided for the equitable
levying of imports, taxes, and tolls. It
was stipulated that trade with the British
West Indies and with British America
should not in any degree be affected by
this treaty. Trade with these parts of the

British Empire was opened by the proclamation of President Jackson, on Oct. 5, 1830. (Page 1060.) The trade of the principal British ports of the East Indies was thrown open to the United States, but was limited to direct trade from a British to an American port. Coastwise trade was excluded from the provisions. Both countries were permitted to appoint consular representatives in the several ports to safeguard their commercial interests. A declaration was appended to the treaty to the effect that as the island of St. Helena was to be the abode of exile of Napoleon Bonaparte, American vessels were excluded therefrom.

Naval Forces on the Great Lakes.—In 1817 an arrangement was effected between the two countries which limited and prescribed the armed force that each country should maintain on the Great Lakes. (See Proclamation page 605).

Fisheries Boundary and the Restoration of Slaves.—The convention of 1818 respecting fisheries, boundaries, and the restoration of slaves, conferred upon the United States the privilege of taking fish on the southern, western, and northern coasts of Newfoundland, and upon the southern coast of Labrador. The United States relinquished the right to take or to cure fish within three miles of the coast in any other parts of the British dominions. Privilege was extended to the United States to enter ports, creeks, harbors, or bays, in any other part only for the purpose of procuring water, food, or for repairs, and protection from stress of weather. The boundary of the regions from Lake of the Woods to the Stony Mountains and thence west of the Stony Mountains, was defined. Commercial relations were extended for a period of ten years, in terms of the treaty of 1815. Compensation for the restitution of slaves was also provided for.

Indemnification for Slaves.—In 1822 a claims convention was agreed to for effecting the compensation for such slaves as had been carried away by British troops. Indemnity to the amount of $1,204,960 was awarded for this purpose by the convention of 1826.

Boundaries Suppression of Slave Trade and Extradition (Webster-Ashburton).—The convention of 1842 as to boundaries, suppression of slave trade, and extradition, defined the northeastern boundary, the northern boundary from Lake Huron to Lake of the Woods, and opened the river St. John, in New Brunswick, to both parties. Prior grants of land within the disputed territory were confirmed; the "Disputed Territory Fund" was provided to defray expenses and to pay claims arising from the dispute over territory. A commission was established to settle the northeastern boundary dispute. Channels in the St. Lawrence, Detroit, and St. Clair rivers were declared open to navigation by both parties. For the suppression of the slave trade on the coasts of Africa, it was agreed to support a naval force of sufficient strength. Remonstrances with other powers were decided upon to help suppress the trade in slaves. Provision was made for the extradition of fugitive criminals charged with the commission of the more serious crimes.

Northwest Boundary.—The boundary of the country west of the Rocky Mountains was established by the treaty of 1846. The navigation of the Columbia River was free and open to both parties and the Puget Sound Agricultural Company was confirmed in its possessions.

Isthmian Canal (Clayton-Bulwer).—The convention of 1850, known as the Clayton-Bulwer treaty, dealt with the ship canal connecting the Atlantic and the Pacific oceans. It was superseded by the convention of 1901.

Ceding Horse-Shoe Reef.—Horse-Shoe Reef in the Niagara River was ceded to the United States by protocol of Dec. 9, 1850.

Reciprocity as to Fisheries, Duties and Navigation.—A reciprocity treaty was concluded in 1854 to settle by commission the question of fisheries, duties and navigation in British North America. The work of the commission was nearly concluded when in 1866 the United States exercised its right to terminate the treaty.

Suppression of African Slave Trade.—A treaty for the suppression of the slave trade was concluded in 1862, by which war vessels were empowered to search for slaves on suspected ships other than those of the navies of the two contracting powers. This right shall be exercised in a manner prescribed by the treaty and only within a distance of two hundred miles from the coast of Africa. In cases of illegal search and wrongful detention, the government of the country whose vessel was at fault shall be responsible for the payment of proper indemnity. Courts were established at Sierra Leone, Cape of Good Hope, and New York, for the convenient trial and settlement of cases. Conditions, apparatus, and supplies, which may be regarded as evidence of guilt, are specified in the treaty, and their presence on board a ship shall justify its detention or capture, and no indemnity may be collected by the owners of such vessel. Vessels engaged in such traffic shall be destroyed and the parts sold, or the vessel may be purchased by either of the contracting powers. The officers and crew of such condemned vessel shall be punished in accordance with the laws of their native country or that to which the vessel belongs. Slaves taken from such vessels are to be set at liberty and their freedom guaranteed by the country making the capture. The treaty was further supplemented by an agreement of 1863, and another in 1870, when mixed courts were abolished and the machinery of the ordinary courts of countries submitted therefor.

Alabama Claims, Fishery Rights, Navigation and Boundary.—The treaty of 1871, known as the Treaty of Washington, was drawn up for the settlement of all causes of difference between the two countries. The articles which referred to the Alabama claims, the Civil War claims commission, and the fisheries, are no longer effective. The River St. Lawrence in that part wholly within the Dominion of Canada is open to free navigation; the Yukon, Porcupine, and Stikine rivers are also open to free navigation by both parties. Reciprocal use of the Welland, St. Lawrence, and other canals of Canada, and of the State canals in the United States, is urged upon both governments. Lumber cut in the State of Maine upon the head waters of the River St. John, may be floated down the river to its mouth, and there shipped free of duty. In 1872, the Emperor of Germany, to whom was referred the question of the northwestern boundary, made an award of the island of San Juan to the United States. By protocol of 1873, the matter of the northwestern boundary was more fully established.

Fur Seals in Bering Sea.—The convention of 1892, relating to fur-seals in Bering Sea, established a tribunal of arbitration consisting of seven members—two named by the United States, two by Great Britain, one each by the president of France, the king of Italy, and the king of Sweden and Norway. All details for the meeting and conduct of the tribunal were laid down, their duties, the points for their decision, and the matter of the adjustment of the expenses were all clearly set forth. The award of the tribunal was made on Aug. 15, 1893. While the decision of the tribunal was pending a *modus vivendi* declared that all citizens of the United States and all subjects of Great Britain were prohibited from killing fur-seals in the eastern part of Bering Sea. The tribunal recommended that both governments prohibit the killing of fur-seals within a limit of sixty geographic miles of Pribilov Islands, or, during the season from May 1st to July 31st in each year anywhere north of the 35th degree of north latitude, and east of the 180th meridian of longitude. Sailing vessels are allowed to take part in seal fishing and these must bear a certificate from their home government and carry a distinguishing flag of their nation. The result as to number and sex of the catch, and the locality fished in during each day, must be entered in the vessel's log. Nets, firearms, or explosives must not be used. Men engaged in seal fishing must give to their respective governments evidence of their skill in the use of weapons. The regulations do not apply to Indians dwelling on the coasts who fish for food and livelihood by the customary means. The regulations to remain in force until superseded by a satisfactory agreement between the two countries.

For the extradition treaty of 1889, see Extradition Treaties.

Deserting Seamen.—By a treaty of 1892, deserting seamen may be arrested in ports by the consul of the country from whose vessels they have deserted, except such deserting seamen be citizens or subjects of the country in which he deserts.

Alaskan Boundary.—By a convention of 1892, provision was made for the appointment of a commission to conduct the survey for the determination of the Alaskan boundary between Canada and the United States. Also for a commission to mark the boundary in Passamaquoddy Bay. By a convention of 1894 the term of the Alaskan commission was extended until 1895, by reason of the difficulty of the task. In accordance with the decision of the tribunal, losses sustained by the seizure of British vessels by the United States in connection with the seal fisheries were paid by a claims convention commission of 1896. The award was $473,151.26 against the United States.

Disposition of Property of Deceased Persons.—A treaty of 1889 provides for the disposition of the real and personal property of citizens of one country within the dominions of the other, both as to the holding, the sale, and the succession and inheritance, as well as the administration of the affairs of deceased owners. The consular officers may personally, or by delegation to others, act for heirs until they be represented. This treaty was opened to accession by colonists of Great Britain, except Canada, and nearly all acceded to its provisions.

Alaskan Boundary.—A *modus vivendi* fixed a temporary boundary between Alaska and Canada in 1899, without prejudice to any rights of owners.

Isthmian Canal (Hay-Pauncefote).—The treaty of 1901, known as the Hay-Pauncefote Treaty, was concluded to facilitate the construction of a ship canal. It superseded the old treaty of 1850, or Clayton-Bulwer Treaty. The construction of the canal is provided for under the auspices of the United States Government. The canal is to be free and open to vessels of commerce and war of all nations, on equitable conditions and charges for traffic. It shall never be blockaded, nor shall any act of war or hostility occur within it. A belligerent may not revictual or take on other than strictly necessary stores within the canal, nor shall the passage of such vessels through the canal be unnecessarily delayed. Prizes shall conform to rules just as do the vessels of the belligerent power. Troops may not be embarked or disembarked, nor shall munitions of war be loaded or unloaded within the canal, except in case of accident. The limits of the canal shall extend a distance of three marine miles beyond each end. Except in cases of distress, vessels of war of a belligerent power shall not remain within the canal longer than twenty-four hours, and a vessel of war of one belligerent shall not depart within twenty-four hours of the departure of a vessel of war of another. All the buildings, plant, and equipment of the canal, shall be regarded as a part thereof, and shall enjoy entire immunity, from injury and attack at all times. (See illustration opposite 7762.)

Import Duties, Light and Harbor Dues of Zanzibar.—A treaty of 1902 fixed the import duties at the port of Zanzibar at a sum not to exceed ten per cent of the value of the goods at the port of importation. All of the rights, privileges and immunities of commerce are extended to the United States in the conduct of trade with the protectorate. A treaty of 1903 fixed the light and harbor dues at Zanzibar at one anna per registered ton for light and one anna per registered ton for harbor dues on all vessels of the United States entering ports on the islands of Zanzibar and Pemba. The payment of these dues is conditional upon the provision of adequate lights and buoys. Extraterritorial rights in Zanzibar were relinquished by treaty of 1905.

Alaskan Boundary.—The convention as to the Alaskan boundary was concluded on Jan. 24, 1903. It provided for the establishment of a tribunal of three members appointed by the President of the United States and three by the king of England. The details of procedure, the list of questions to be decided, the time of meeting, and the rendering of the decision, were all provided for in the convention. The decision was rendered Oct. 20, 1903. It was signed by Baron Alverstone for England (the two Canadian members not fully concurring in all of the decisions and answers), and by Elihu Root, Henry Cabot Lodge, and George Turner, for the United States. The agreement was effected by exchange of notes March 25, 1905.

Canadian Boundary.—April 11, 1908, a treaty was concluded providing for the appointment of commissioners to define the entire boundary line between Canada and the United States from Passamaquoddy Bay to the Pacific Ocean.

Fisheries.—A *modus vivendi* between the United States and Great Britain was effected in September, 1907, in regard to inshore fisheries on the treaty coast of Newfoundland. Rights of coast fishermen formed the subject of treaties of 1908 and 1909.

Arbitration.—Differences of a legal nature or as to the interpretation of treaties impossible of settlement by diplomacy are to be referred to the Permanent Court of Arbitration at The Hague according to a convention signed at Washington, April 4, 1908, and in 1909 the whole matter of the North Atlantic coast fisheries was submitted to the Permanent Court of Arbitration, and an agreement was effected Sept. 8, 1909.

Further stipulations for the submission of differences to arbitration are contained in the following treaty, which is given almost entire for the reason that it follows the general terms and form of all arbitration treaties growing out of the Hague Conference:

Aug. 3, 1911, a general arbitration treaty, in the interest of peace, between the United States and Great Britain, was signed at Washington by Philander C. Knox, Secretary of State, on behalf of the United States, and James Bryce, the British Ambassador, on behalf of Great Britain.

On the same day a treaty of the same import between the United States and France was signed in Washington by Philander C. Knox, Secretary of State, on behalf of the United States, and in Paris by Jean Jules Jusserand, French Ambassador, on behalf of France.

The two treaties are alike except as to the necessary differences in phraseology pertaining to the respective names of the two countries and the persons who are parties to the agreements.

The following is the text of the British treaty:

The United States of America and his Majesty the King of the United Kingdom of Great Britain and Ireland and of the British Dominions Beyond the Seas, Emperor of India, being equally desirous of perpetuating the peace, which has happily existed between the two nations, as established in 1814 by the Treaty of Ghent, and has never since been interrupted by an appeal to arms, and which has been confirmed and strengthened in recent years by a number of treaties whereby pending controversies have been adjusted by agreement or settled by arbitration or otherwise provided for, so that now for the first time there are no important questions of difference outstanding between them, and being resolved that no future differences shall be a cause of hostilities between them or interrupt their good relations and friendship;

The high contracting parties have, therefore, determined, in furtherance of these ends, to conclude a treaty extending the scope and obligations of the policy of arbitration adopted in their present arbitration treaty of April 4, 1908, so as to exclude certain exceptions contained in that treaty and to provide means for the peaceful solution of all questions of difference which it shall be found impossible in future to settle by diplomacy.

All differences hereafter arising between the high contracting parties, which it has not been possible to adjust by diplomacy, relating to international matters in which the high contracting parties are concerned by virtue of a claim of right made by one against the other, under treaty or otherwise, and which are justifiable in their nature by reason of being susceptible of decision by the application of the principles of law or equity, shall be submitted to the Permanent Court of Arbitration established at The Hague by the convention of October 18, 1907, or to some other arbitral tribunal, as may be decided in each case by special agreement, which special agreement shall provide for the organization of such tribunal if necessary, define the scope of the powers of the arbitrators, the question or questions at issue, and settle the terms of reference and the procedure thereunder.

The provisions of Articles XXXVII to XC, inclusive, of the convention for the pacific settlement of international disputes concluded at the second peace conference at The Hague on Oct. 18, 1907, so far as applicable, shall govern the arbitration proceedings to be taken under this treaty.

The high contracting parties further agree to institute, as occasion arises, and

as hereinafter provided, a Joint High Commission of Inquiry, to which upon the request of either party, shall be referred for impartial and conscientious investigation any controversy between the parties within the scope of Article I, before such controversy has been submitted to arbitration, and also any other controversy hereafter arising between them, even if they are not agreed that it falls within the scope of Article I; provided, however, that such reference may be postponed until the expiration of one year after the date of the formal request therefor, in order to afford an opportunity for diplomatic discussion and adjustment of the questions in controversy, if either party desires such postponement.

Whenever a question or matter of difference is referred to the Joint High Commission of Inquiry, as herein provided, each of the high contracting parties shall designate three of its nationals to act as members of the Commission of Inquiry for the purpose of such reference; or the commission may be otherwise constituted in any particular case by the terms of reference, the membership of the commission and the terms of reference to be determined in each case by an exchange of notes.

The Joint High Commission of Inquiry is authorized to examine into and report upon the particular questions or matters referred to it, for the purpose of facilitating the solution of disputes by elucidating the facts, and to define the issues presented by such question, and also to include in its report such recommendations and conclusions as may be appropriate.

See illustration opposite 7618.

Fur Seals Preservation.—The final treaty for the preservation of fur seals was signed July 7, 1911, by representatives of United States, Great Britain, Russia and Japan.

Wrecking, Salvage and the Conveyance of Prisoners.—Reciprocal rights in the matters of conveyance of prisoners, and wrecking and salvage for the United States and Canada were provided for in a treaty concluded May 18, 1908.

Great Eastern. (See illustration opposite 3562.)

Great Falls Land Case, opinion of Judge Brewer in, referred to, 3072.

Great Lakes.—Five large bodies of fresh water on the northern line of the United States. They are Superior, Michigan, Huron, Erie, and Ontario. Lake Superior is the largest sheet of fresh water in the world; elevation above sea level, about 600 feet; length, about 370 miles; area, about 32,000 square miles. Lake Michigan is about 340 miles long and has a depth of 870 feet; elevation above sea level, 582 feet; area, over 22,000 square miles. Lake Huron has a length of 270 miles; depth, from 300 to 1,800 feet; elevation above sea level, 581 feet; area, about 23,800 square miles. Lake Erie is the southernmost and shallowest of the lakes, and is about 250 miles long; elevation above sea level, 573 feet; area, 9,600 square miles. Lake Ontario is the smallest and easternmost of the lakes, and is 190 miles long; elevation above sea level, 234 feet; area, about 7,500 square miles.

Great Lakes (see also the several lakes):

Canal from, to Atlantic Ocean, commission to consider construction of, 6179.

Fortifications of, referred to, 3261.

Jurisdictions of United States and Canada in, discussed, 6064.

Naval force on—

Agreements with Great Britain regarding, 581, 602, 1805, 1817, 5768.

Desire of Great Britain to annul, 1818.

Proclamation regarding, 605.

Arrangement limiting, referred to, 3459.

Necessity for increasing, discussed, 3447.

Regulations with regard to rescue and savings of life and property on, referred to, 4519, 5366.

Vessels of United States in, granted facilities for returning, 6331.

Great Miami River, lands purchased on, 105.

Great Osage Indians. (See Indian Tribes.)

Great Sioux Reservation. (See Sioux Reservation.)

Greater Republic of Central America, establishment of, discussed, 6264, 6325.

Greece.—Greece is a maritime kingdom of southeastern Europe, the mainland and Eubœa lying between 35° 50'-41° N. lat. and 19° 20'-26° 15' E. long., and occupying the southern portion of the Balkan Peninsula, with certain islands in the surrounding seas. In 1912-13 Greece took part in a successful war of the Balkan League (Greece, Bulgaria, Servia and Montenegro) against Turkey, gained a great extension of territory northward, and seized many of the Ægean islands. In July, 1913, war broke out between Greece and Servia on the one side and Bulgaria on the other, and against the last named Rumania threw in the weight of an unexhausted army. By the treaty of Bucharest the Greco-Bulgarian frontier was fixed to start from the new Serbo-Bulgarian frontier, on the east of the Belashitza Range, to terminate at the mouth of the river Mesta, on the Ægean, leaving Serres, Drama and Cavalla to Greece, who thus increased her acquisitions at the expense of Bulgaria. An irregular land frontier on the north separates the kingdom from Albania, Servia and Bulgaria, and on the west, south and east are the Adriatic and Ionian, the Mediterranean and the Ægean Seas. The mainland comprises the Peloponnesus (Morea), joined by the narrow Isthmus of Corinth to a larger northern territory, which extends over portions of Albania and Macedonia wrested from Turkey in the war of 1912-13. In the western sea are the Ionian Islands of Corfu, Leucas, Ithaca, Cephalonia and Zante; in the Mediterranean are Crete, Cerigo and Cerigoto; and in the Ægean the Northern Sporades, the Cyclades, and the islands of Samothrace, Lemnos, Strati, Mitylene, Psara, Chios, Nikaria, Themina, Samos, and other Ægean islands captured from the Turks in 1912-13.

Physical Features.—The kingdom is everywhere mountainous. The principal plains are those of Thessaly, Eubœa, Messenia, Argos, Elis, and Marathon, the last named (in Attica) being the site of battle of B. C. 490, in which the Athenians and Platæans defeated the armies of Persia. Macedonia extends three promontories southwards into

the Ægean, and the easternmost of these peninsulas is known as Mount Athos. Mount Athos is a semi-independent tributary state with a total area of about 200 square miles, belonging to twenty Christian monasteries, and is ruled by an elective committee of twenty members, who appoint an executive council. The population is close on 9,000, of whom 3,000 are monks and the remainder lay brothers.

AREA AND POPULATION

Departments (Nomoi) and Capitals	Area in English Sq. Miles	Population 1907
Acarnania and Aetiolia (Missolonghi)	2,007	141,405
Achæa (Patras)	1,169	150,918
Arcadia or Morea (Tripolitsa)	1,682	162,324
Argolis (Nauplia)	995	81,943
Arta (Arta)	531	41,280
Attica (Athens)	1,207	341,247
Bœotia (Livadia)	1,196	65,816
Cephalonia (Argostoli)	290	71,235
Corfu (Corfu)	270	99,571
Corinth (Corinth)	914	71,229
Cyclades (Hermopolis)	1,042	130,378
Elis (Pyrgos)	775	103,810
Eubœa (Chalcis)	1,505	116,903
Euritania (Karpenisi)	887	47,192
Karditsa (Karditsa)	1,022	92,941
Lacedemon (Sparta)	1,200	87,106
Laconia (Gythium)	493	61,522
Larissa (Larissa)	1,500	95,066
Leucas and Ithaca (Leucas)	177	41,186
Magnesia (Macrinitsa)	785	102,742
Messenia (Messini)	645	127,991
Phocis (Salona)	810	62,246
Phthiotis (Lamia)	1,775	112,328
Trikkala (Trikkala)	1,178	90,548
Triphylia (Kyparissia)	617	90,523
Zante (Zante)	160	42,502
	24,822	2,631,952
Acquired Territory, Mainland	14,200	1,400,000
Acquired Territory, Islands	4,500	600,000
Total in 1913	43,522	5,000,000

Ethnography.—The principal races are the Hellenes, the Albanians and the Vlachs, with a foreign element in which Turks preponderate. The Hellenes are the modern representatives of the ancient Greeks, the Albanians are descended from fourteenth century immigrants from the north; the Vlachs are believed to be descendants of the Roman colonists and owe their name to their rusticity (Βλήχας =a bleater). The Orthodox Church is the official religion of the kingdom.

History.—Greece formed part of the Ottoman Empire from the middle of the fifteenth century until the awakening of the national spirit led to a Greek War of Independence, 1821-1829, which culminated in the Treaty of Adrianople (Sept. 12, 1829), whereby an Independent Monarchy was constituted. The independence was confirmed by the Convention of London (May 7, 1832), and a Bavarian prince reigned from 1832-1862 as King Otto I. A constitution was granted in 1844.

In 1862 a revolution drove Otto from the throne, and by the Treaty of London (July 13, 1863) a new dynasty was inaugurated, the throne being accepted by Prince William George of Schleswig-Holstein-Sonderburg-Glücksburg (second son of King Christian IX. of Denmark), while the Ionian Islands Commonwealth was transferred to the new government. Successful wars in 1912-13 against Turkey and Bulgaria increased the Hellenic dominions both on the mainland and in the Ægean.

Government.—The constitution rests upon the fundamental law of Nov. 28, 1864, the crown being hereditary in the male (and eventually in the female) line of King George I., who reigned from 1863-1913. King of the Hellenes : His Majesty Constantine, born at Athens July 21 (Aug. 3), 1868 ; succeeded to the throne (on the assassination of his father, King George) March 18, 1913.

The Executive authority is vested in the sovereign, who governs through a Council of Ministers, appointed by himself, but responsible to the Chamber.

There is a single-chamber legislature of 177 deputies, elected for 4 years by the direct vote of all males over the age of 21. No law can be passed without a clear majority of the House, and no sitting is valid unless one-third of the total number are present.

Justice is administered by correctional tribunals and justices of the Peace in minor cases, with 26 courts of first instance, 5 Courts of Appeal and a Court of Cassation at Athens.

The land and sea forces are in process of reorganization. (For the details see Armies of the World and Navies of the World.)

Production and Industry.—Agriculture conducted by primitive methods is the principal industry of the kingdom, and employs about half the population. About 10,000 persons are employed in the various mines and quarries. The industrial population does not exceed 30,000 hands.

Finances.—The revenue is chiefly derived from customs and direct taxes and monopolies ; one quarter of the ordinary expenditure is for debt service.

January 1, 1913, the public Gold Debt of Greece amounted to $179,365,400, and the Currency Debt to $32,799,700. The total debt charges in 1913 were estimated at $7,957,860. In 1898 the administration of the debt was intrusted to an International Commission, sitting at Athens, consisting of representatives of the Governments of Great Britain, France, Germany, Russia, Austria-Hungary, and Italy. To them are assigned the revenues from all sources and proportional payments are made.

Shipping.—The mercantile marine of Greece in 1912 consisted of 298 steamers and 110 sailing vessels, all vessels of 100 tons and upwards with many smaller vessels. Much of the trade of the Ottoman Empire is carried in Greek vessels. A Ship Canal through the Isthmus of Corinth was opened for traffic in 1893, but its use is mainly confined to Greek vessels, owing to the higher rate of dues on foreign shipping. The principal harbors of Greece are the Piræus (the port of Athens), Syra, Patras, Volo and Corfu.

Cities.—Capital, Athens, in the southeast of Attica, a modern capital, occupying an extensive area around the site and remains of the classical city. There were, in 1913, 25 towns with a population exceeding 10,-000. The unit of value is the gold drachma equal to $0.19.3 United States money.

Trade with the United States.—The value of merchandise imported into Greece from the United States for the year 1913 was $1,216,195, and goods to the value of $3,-179,816 were sent thither—a balance of $1,963,816 in favor of Greece.

Greece:

Commercial relations with, 1647.

Condition of Greeks referred to, 790.

Currants from, duties imposed upon, discussed, 6410.

Differences with, amicably settled, 2868.

Diplomatic relations with, recommendations regarding, 3656, 4520, 4630, 4718.

Expulsion of Greeks from—

Constantinople, 2774.

Egypt, 2828.

Independence of, hope for, manifested by United States, 762, 786, 785, 950.

Russia furnished aid to, 950.

Sympathy of American people for, acknowledged by, in letters of thanks, 950.

Treaty with, 1647, 1706.

Vessels of, discriminating duties on, repealed by proclamation, 1539.

War with Turkey, hope for independence of Greece manifested by United States, 762, 786, 828, 875, 950.

Greece, Treaties with.—A treaty of commerce and navigation was concluded Dec. 22, 1837, which conferred freedom of commerce, with attendant rights, privileges, protection, and security in all rivers, ports, and places where foreign commerce is permitted within the two countries. The treaty provides for the customary equitable tonnage duties and port charges ; equal rights of imports into the two countries in vessels of either nation ; and of exports from the two countries, except so far as coastwise trade is concerned, and passage from one port in the nation to another port in the same nation which is not permitted. No prohibition of the import of the products of one country into the other shall ever be made. A vessel may enter a port of the other nation, and if it is not desirable to break cargo, may proceed on its voyage without incurring any charges other than those of pilotage, wharfage, and light, so long as all regulations are conformed to. If only a part of a cargo be unloaded at a port, the charges to be levied at that port shall be *pro rata* for that port only. Charges due upon a vessel at one port are to be paid at the first port of entry and not again at another port visited.

No quarantine shall be imposed on vessels coming directly to a port from a port within its own dominions and possessing a clean bill of health, so long as there is no malignant disease on the vessel, nor shall have been since leaving the home port. Should a port be blockaded within either of the countries, no merchant vessel shall be subject to capture for making a first attempt to enter a port, but may be so if, after one warning, the attempt be repeated. The treaty was made to run ten years from date, with a year's notice of intention to terminate. Jan. 30, 1890, a protocol was signed explaining and clarifying certain clauses of the treaty of 1837. (See also Consular Conventions.) There are no extradition treaties with Greece.

Green Bay, cession of lands at, for benefit of New York Indians, 1127.

Greenback Party.—Opposition to the resumption of specie payments caused a political party to be organized at Indianapolis, Ind., Nov. 25, 1874, called the Greenback party. The platform adopted advocated the withdrawal of all national and State bank currency and the substitution therefor of paper currency, or greenbacks, which should be exchangeable for inconvertible bonds bearing interest sufficiently high to keep them at par with gold, and that coin should only be used in payment of interest on the national debt.

In 1876 the Greenback party nominated Peter Cooper, of New York, for President. He received 81,740 votes, mostly from the Western States. In 1878 the Greenback party united with the Labor Reform party, the two forming the Greenback-Labor party. The new party, in their platform adopted at Toledo, Feb. 22, 1878, reiterated the demands of the original Greenback party, and in addition declared for an eight-hour law, prohibition of Chinese immigration, suffrage without regard to sex, and against grants of land to railroads and special grants to corporations. Fourteen members of Congress were elected on this platform. June 9, 1880, at their national convention held at Chicago, they nominated Gen. James B. Weaver, of Iowa, for President, and B. J. Chambers, of Texas, for Vice-President. Their popular vote reached 307,740. In 1884, with Gen. B. F. Butler as their candidate, they polled only 133,825 votes. The party has now become extinct.

Greenbacks.—The common name for the legal-tender Treasury notes, printed on one side in green ink, issued by the Government during the Civil War. The right of the Government to issue bills of credit was disputed by many statesmen and financiers, but the exigencies of the time seemed to render some such measure necessary and the Supreme Court finally established their validity. Issues of $150,000,000 each were authorized by the laws of Feb. 25 and July 11, 1862, and March 3, 1863. The result was that, as compared with greenbacks, gold was held at an average of 220 throughout 1864, and at one time actually rose to 285, and did not again touch par with greenbacks till Dec. 17, 1878, nearly seventeen years after the last previous sale of gold at par. By the specie resumption act of Jan. 14, 1875, it was ordered that on and after Jan. 1, 1879, all legal-tender notes presented to the assistant treasurer of the United States at his office in New York should be redeemed in coin. The term "greenback" has been applied to other forms of United States securities printed in green ink. (See Currency.)

Greenbacks:

Discussed, 6073.

Retirement of, recommended, 6078, 6175.

Green Mountain State.—A nickname for Vermont (q. v.). (See also States.)

Greenwich, Meridian of, starting point for computing longitude, 4827.

Greer County:

Boundary dispute regarding, 4902, 4904.

Proclamation against selling lands involved in, 5325.

Proclamation declaring lands in, in state of reservation, 6122.

Grenada, Island of, duties on vessels from, suspended by proclamation, 5930.

Grenade.—An explosive charge, not so large as a bomb, which may be hurled from a cannon, or by catapult, or by hand. Grenades are made of iron, in ball-shape,—

though in former times they were made of various other metals, and even of wood and glass.

Greytown, Nicaragua (see also Central America and Nicaragua and illustration opposite 2817.)

Bombardment of, and reasons therefor, 2814.

Claims arising out of, 2995, 3049.

Complaints of foreign powers regarding, 2817.

Vessels from, duties on, suspended by proclamation, 4872.

Grierson's Raid.—In the spring of 1863 Gen. Hurlburt, with the approval of Gen. Grant, ordered Col. B. H. Grierson to proceed from La Grange, Tenn., with the Sixth Illinois (his own regiment), the Seventh Illinois, and the Second Iowa, by way of Pontotoc, in the northern part of Mississippi, to Baton Rouge, La., cutting the southern railroads and destroying bridges on the way. April 17, 1863, the expedition started and on the 19th the Second Iowa was detached below Pontotoc and the two Illinois regiments proceeded to Baton Rouge, where they entered the Union lines May 2. The results of the expedition are thus summed up in Grierson's report: About 100 of the enemy killed and wounded; 500 prisoners (many of them officers) captured and paroled; between 50 and 60 miles of railroad and telegraph destroyed; more than 3,000 stand of arms and other stores captured and destroyed, and 1,000 horses and mules seized. Federal loss, 3 killed, 7 wounded, 5 left sick on the route, and 9 missing.

Griffon, The, seizure of, by Brazilian authorities, 2779.

Gros Ventre Indians. (See Indian Tribes.)

Groveton (Va.), Battle of, or Second Battle of Manassas.—After eluding Pope's army and destroying the military stores at Bristow Station and Manassas, Stonewall Jackson retired across the battlefield of Bull Run and awaited reenforcements. Longstreet arrived on Aug. 29, swelling the numbers of the Confederate army to 49,000. Pope's army numbered about 40,000. On the evening of the 28th Kearny had driven the Confederate rear guard out of Centreville, and Pope, feeling sure of crushing Longstreet and Jackson, ordered an attack to be made at daylight next morning. Sigel began the attack, which soon became general. McDowell's corps arrived upon the scene of battle late in the afternoon. Fitz-John Porter never came into action, though ordered up by Pope. For alleged disobedience of orders in this connection charges were preferred against Porter by Pope. At night both armies rested on the field. The next day, Aug. 30, the battle was renewed. The fiercest fighting took place about 5 o'clock in the afternoon, and on the ground where the battle of Bull Run had been fought July 21, 1861. The result was a victory for the Confederates under Lee and the defeat of Pope's army. The loss of the Federals was about 15,000, that of the Confederates about 8,400. This battle is also called the Second Battle of Manassas.

Guadalupe Hidalgo, Treaty of.—Named from the Mexican village where Nicholas P. Trist, on behalf of the United States, Feb. 2, 1848, signed the treaty with Mexico (2423), terminating the war and ceding territory now comprising Nevada, Utah, most of Arizona, a large part of New Mexico, parts of Colorado and Wyoming, and all of California, to the United States, and accepting the Rio Grande as the boundary between Mexico and Texas. The United States agreed to pay Mexico $15,000,000 (page 2437) and to assume the claims of its citizens against Mexico arising before the treaty. Mexicans in the ceded territory were allowed to remain at their option and were assured protection as citizens. (See also Mexico, Treaties with.)

Guadalupe Hidalgo, Treaty of:
Abrogation of eleventh article of, referred to, 2771.
Amendments to, discussed, 2529.
Claims arising out of, 2636, 2771.
Discussed, 2423, 2437, 2529.
Fraudulent claims arising under, 2683.
Proclamation regarding, 2477.
Ratifications of, exchanged at Queretaro, 2437.
Referred to, 2545, 2551, 2565, 2566, 2580, 2623, 2636, 2665, 2705, 2744, 2765, 2903, 2926.

Guadeloupe:
Extraordinary commission of, apply to Congress for aid, 143.
Tonnage on American vessels at, referred to, 1123.
Vessels of, duties on, suspended by proclamation, 5327.

Guam.—The island of Guam, the largest of the Mariana Archipelago, was ceded by Spain to the United States by Article II of the Treaty of Peace, concluded at Paris Dec. 10, 1898. It lies in a direct line from San Francisco to the southern part of the Philippines, and is 5,044 miles from San Francisco and 1,506 miles from Manila. It is about 30 miles long and 100 miles in circumference, and has a population of 12,517. The inhabitants are mostly immigrants or descendants of immigrants from the Philippines, the original race of the Mariana islands being nearly extinct. The prevailing language is English. Spanish and Chamorro are also spoken. Nine-tenths of the islanders can read and write. The island is thickly wooded, well watered, and fertile, and possesses an excellent harbor. The productions are tropical fruits, cacao, rice, corn, tobacco, and sugar cane. The island of Guam was discovered by Hernando de Magallanes on March 6, 1521.

The island was captured by the U. S. S. Charleston, Captain Henry Glass commanding, June 21, 1898, the American flag raised over Fort Santa Cruz, and a salute fired. Later the island was made a naval station, and Commander E. D. Taussig, of the U. S. S. *Bennington,* took possession Feb. 1, 1899. The Governor is a naval officer, and the island has a marine garrison as well as a station ship.

During the year ending June 30, 1911, the imports, general cargo, were as follows: From United States, $28,112.69; Hawaiian Islands, $17,406.16; Philippines, $815.71; Japan, $89,469.07; Saipan, $3,115.76; Great Britain, $1,088.86; Germany, $197.- 83; total imports, $140,326.08. Exports, and copra to Japan, $51,058.80.

Guam, Island of, cable communication with, recommended, 6354.
Release of prisoners on, 6735.

Guano:
Claim of American citizens to, on Alta Vela Island, 3827.
Deposits of, on Arcas Cays, 5679.
Discovery of, in Jarvis and Baker Islands, referred to, 3017.
Importation of, from Peru—
Desired, 2619, 2745, 2764.
Negotiations regarding, 2764.
Referred to, 3018, 3068.

Guantanamo (Cuba), Battle of.—As a preliminary step to the capture of Santiago, June 10, 1898, a force of 600 American marines, under the protecting fire of the *Oregon, Marblehead, Dolphin, Yankee, Yosemite, Porter,* and *Vixen,* was landed at Guantanamo Bay, on the south coast of Cuba, 35 miles east of Santiago, where it had been decided to establish a naval station. This important point was taken after a severe bombardment, and the position so won was held by the marines, assisted by 50 Cuban allies, despite desperate attempts to dislodge them. Seven Americans (including Surg. John B. Gibbs) were killed and 8 wounded, and 2 Cubans were killed and 4 wounded while holding Guantanamo prior to the arrival of Gen. Shafter's army. The enemy's loss was much greater, 40 of their dead being left on the field. Seventeen prisoners were taken. After several naval demonstrations on the north coasts of Cuba and Porto Rico it became evident that well-ordered land operations were indispensable to the reduction of the forts. Accordingly a land force of 15,738 men, under Gen. W. R. Shafter, sailed from Tampa, Fla., June 14, and by the 24th had landed at Daiquiri, near Guantanamo. The landing was assisted by Cubans under Gen. Garcia. Little resistance was encountered from the Spaniards.

Guantanamo Bay, Cuba, landing of American marines and subsequent fighting at, discussed, 6317.

Guatemala.—The Republic is the most northerly of the Central American States, and is situated between 13° 42'-17° 49' N. lat. and 88° 10'-92° 30' W. long. It is bounded on the west and north by Mexico, on the northeast by British Honduras, east by the Republic of Honduras, and southeast by the Republic of Salvador, with a coast line washed on the east by the Gulf of Honduras (Atlantic) and on the west and south by the Pacific Ocean.

Physical Features.—The Sierra Madre traverses the country from west to east, and forms a precipitous barrier between the narrow plains of the Pacific Coast and the rest of the country. The mountain barrier contains several volcanic peaks, and earthquakes are frequent. The highest summits are Tacana (14,000), Acatenango, Tajamulco, Fuego, Santa Maria, Agua, Atitlán, and Pacaya, all except the first named being dormant or active volcanoes. On the Atlantic side of the Sierra Madre are highlands between parallel ranges.

There are numerous rivers in Southern Guatemala, in addition to the torrents flowing from the Sierra Madre to the Pacific. The Rio Grande or Motagua has a total length of 250 miles from its source in the Atlantic to its outflow into the Gulf of Honduras.

A northern extension of the republic from the Sierra de Chama to 7° 49' N. lat., and between Mexico and British Honduras, consists of the great Plain of Peten, with a total area of nearly 16,000 square miles.

History.—Guatemala was conquered by the Spaniards under Pedro de Alvarado early in the sixteenth century, and formed part of the Spanish colonial dominions until 1821, when the Captaincy-General, in which it was included, revolted and established its independence. In 1823 the country formed part of a larger republic of Central America, from which it seceded in 1847, and since that year it has been an independent republic.

Ethnography.—Guatemala has an area of 47,424 English square miles, with an estimated population of 2,000,000. Of the people more than half are pure-blooded Indians, mainly of the Maya and Quiché stock, the remainder being largely mestizos, or half-caste Spanish Indians, with a proportion of Spaniards, descendants of the colonists of the sixteenth-nineteenth centuries. The foreign element, estimated at 12,000, includes Italians, Germans and other Europeans, and many Jewish immigrants from the United States. The language of the country is Spanish, and the majority of the inhabitants are Roman Catholics.

Government.—The government is that of a centralized republic, with a constitution fixed in the year 1879, and amended in 1887 and 1897. The President is elected by direct vote of the nation for six years. President of the Republic (March 15, 1911-1917), Manuel Estrada Cabrera, born Nov. 21, 1857, elected Oct. 2, 1898, reelected 1904 and 1910.

The President is assisted by a cabinet of six Secretaries of State.

Congress consists of a Council of State and of a National Assembly. The Council of State contains 13 members, partly elected by the Assembly and partly nominated by the President. The National Assembly consists of 69 members elected for 4 years by universal adult male suffrage.

The Republic is divided into twenty-three Departments, each under a *jefe politico*, and subdivided into districts and municipalities. There are municipal councils under the presidency of an alcalde (mayor), elected by direct vote of the inhabitants.

Service in the army is universal and compulsory on all subjects between the ages of 18-30, with a further term of 20 years in the reserve. The Peace Effective of the army is about 50,000; of the Reserve 30,000. The permanent force numbers about 7,000 in regular service.

Education.—Primary education is free and nominally compulsory, but more than 75 per cent of the inhabitants are absolutely illiterate. Large planters are compelled to provide elementary school accommodation for their employés' children free of cost to the public.

Production and Industry.—Coffee is the principal crop. Sugar, bananas, tobacco, cocoa, indigo, rubber, vanilla, grain, sweet potatoes and beans are also grown. The workers on the plantations are mainly Indians, and many of them are attached to the soil by the burden of undischarged debts, due to their improvident expenditure of wages paid in advance. The coffee produced (over 70,000,000 lbs. in 1912) is of the finest quality, and the industry is mostly in the hands of German settlers. The Forest produce includes cedar, mahogany, and other cabinet woods, rubber and dye woods.

Gold and silver are found, and have been worked for many centuries. There are indications of lead, tin, copper, mercury, antimony, coal, salt and sulphur, but the extent and value of the deposits are unknown. Two strong mining companies have commenced operations in the Departments of Huehuetenaugo and Chiquimula.

Railways.—In 1911 there were 430 miles of railway in operation, the lines crossing the country from Atlantic (Puerto Barrios) to Pacific (San José) via the capital, and extending along the Pacific coast between the ports of San José and Champerico. The exports for 1912 amounted to 13,156,538 pesos, more than four-fifths being coffee. Textiles, manufactured metals, and provisions were imported—50 per cent from the United States and 25 per cent from Germany.

Cities.—Capital, Guatemala (Guatemala) population (1912) about 90,000. Other towns are: Quezaltenango, Totonicapam, Coban and Sololá.

The unit of value is the peso of 100 centavos of the nominal value of about $0.97 United States money, but the currency is in paper pesos varying in value from 70c. to 90c. United States money.

Finance.—The revenue and expenditure for the five years 1908-9 to 1912-13 are stated in paper pesos (for the value of which see "Currency" at end of article) as follows:

Year	Revenue	Expenditure
1908– 9	37,336,000	44,930,000
1909–10	49,233,000	70,554,000
1910–11	51,571,000	45,959,000
1911–12	62,047,000	69,162,000
1912–13	71,014,726	44,970,483

The revenue is mainly derived from customs and excise; the service of the debt accounts for more than half of the expenditure.

The amount of outstanding indebtedness on Jan. 1, 1913, was stated to be:

4% External Debt	$7,414,000
4% Gold Debt (13,700,000 gold pesos)—	13,000,000
Arrears of interest	4,655,000
Internal Debt (84,786,000 paper pesos)—about	5,000,000

representing a total indebtedness of close on $30,000,000. By an arrangement concluded with the foreign bondholders in May, 1913, the government paid to them the current interest due on the loan for the fiscal year July 1, 1913—June 30, 1914, during the month of July. These payments are to be made annually.

Trade with the United States.—The value of merchandise imported into Guatemala from the United States for the year 1913 was $3,658.587, and goods to the value of $3,106,981 were sent thither—a balance of $551,606 in favor of the United States.

Guatemala:

Boundary dispute with Mexico, 4627, 4716, 4802.

Arbitration of, submitted to United States minister, 6066, 6265.

Diplomatic relations with, 4562.

Fugitive criminals, convention with, for surrender of, 4067, 5123, 5179, 5199.

Minister of United States to, action of, regarding seizure of Gen. Barrundia on the *Acapulco* and subsequent recall of, discussed, 5544.

Papers regarding, transmitted 5565.

Political affairs of, referred to, 5870.

Relations with, 4667.

Tariff laws of, evidence of modifications of, proclaimed, 5716.

Discussed, 5747.

Treaty with, transmitted and discussed, 2572, 4067, 5123, 5179, 5199.

Extension of time for ratification of, recommended, 2686.

War in Central America caused by, discussed, 4911.

War with Salvador, 5543.

Guatemala, Treaties with.—A treaty of peace, friendship, commerce, and navigation was signed March 3, 1849; two claims conventions were signed in 1900, and a trade-mark agreement in 1901. A convention of 1901 provides for the tenure and disposition of personal and real property. A period of three years, reasonably extended if necessary, is given to those who are by the laws of the country disqualified from holding inherited property within either country, to dispose of the property to advantage and to close up their affairs. Full power is given for the disposal by sale, testament, gift or otherwise by citizens of one country within the dominions of the other, on terms identical with those of native citizens. The consular office is empowered to act either directly or by delegation for distant heirs of a deceased owner until they may be properly represented. (See also Extradition Treaties, and Trade-Mark Conventions.)

Guatemala also became a party to the convention between the United States and the several republics of South and Central America for the arbitration of pecuniary claims and the protection of inventions, etc., which was signed in Buenos Aires in 1910 and proclaimed in Washington, July 29, 1914. (See South and Central America, Treaties with.)

Guerrière, The, capture and destruction of, by the *Constitution,* 502.

Guiana, British. (See British Guiana.)

Gulf of Mexico. (See Mexico, Gulf of.)

Gulf State.—Alternative nickname for Florida. (See Everglade State.)

Guilford Court-House (N. C.), Battle of.—The American army, when arranged for battle at Guilford Court-House, N. C., March 15, 1781, consisted of 4,404 men, including 1,400 regular infantry and 161 cavalrymen, under command of Gen. Greene. The remainder were raw militia. Cornwallis's army was not more than 2,200 strong. The conflict lasted two hours, and the Americans were repulsed after having killed or wounded nearly one-third of the British army. Cornwallis and Leslie were the only British general officers not wounded. The exact number of British killed and wounded was officially reported at 544. The total American casualties were reported as 1,311. Lord Cornwallis retreated after the battle to the coast. Pitt and other great leaders in Great Britain regarded this engagement as the precursor of ruin to British supremacy in the South.

Gun Factory for Army, establishment of, at Watervliet Arsenal, N. Y., discussed, 5374.

Gun-Foundry Board:

Appointed in 1890, report of, transmitted, 5565.

Discussed, 4797, 4833.

Referred to, 4798, 4849.

Gun Manufactory, erection of, recommended, 1608, 1714.

Gunboats. (See Vessels, United States.)

Habeas Corpus.—In law a writ issued by a judge or court requiring the body of a person restrained of liberty to be brought before the judge or into the court, that the lawfulness of the restraint may be investigated and determined. The writ of habeas corpus is one of the chief bulwarks of civil liberty, being perhaps the best security against the grosser forms of tyranny ever devised. Its foundation is in the Magna Charta of England. The power to suspend it is naturally a subject of the gravest importance. The Constitution of the United States, Article I., section 9, provides: "The privilege of the writ of habeas corpus shall not be suspended unless when, in cases of rebellion or invasion, the public safety may require it." The writ has been suspended many times in England. It was suspended in Rhode Island by state authority during Dorr's Rebellion. July 5, 1861, Attorney-General Bates gave an opinion in favor of the President's power to suspend the writ. March 3, 1863, Congress approved this opinion, and thereafter many arrests were made for disloyal practices. Sept. 15, 1863, the suspension of the writ was made general so far as it concerned persons arrested by military officers for disloyalty. In 1866, in the case of Milligan, arrested in Indiana in 1864, and sentenced to death by a military tribunal, the Supreme Court, having been appealed to, decided that the privilege of the writ could not be suspended in districts where the action of the civil courts was not interrupted, except that military commissioners might be given jurisdiction to try residents of rebellious states, prisoners of war, and persons in the military and naval services. Milligan, being a civilian, was exempt from the laws of war, and could only be tried by a jury. (See also Merryman case; Milligan Case.)

Habeas Corpus:

Authority given by President Lincoln to suspend writ of, 3217, 3218, 3219, 3220, 3240, 3300, 3313, 3322.

Referred to, 3225.

Suspension of writ, by President Lincoln, 3299, 3371, 3420.

Revoked as to certain States by President Johnson, 3529, 3531.

Suspension of writ, in South Carolina by President Grant, 4090, 4093.

Revoked as to Marion County, 4092.

Hague Peace Conference.—May 18, 1899, there assembled at The Hague an international conference of delegates from the principal countries of the civilized world. These representatives met in response to an invitation of the Czar of Russia, and their objects were to secure concerted action for the maintenance of a general peace between nations and the amelioration of the hardships of war, as well as the reduction of the naval and military armaments of the world. One hundred delegates were present representing the United States, Mexico, China, Japan, Persia, Siam and twenty-one European powers. No delegates from South or Central America attended. The sessions were presided over by Baron de Staal, of Russia, and continued from May 18 to July 29.

To facilitate the work of the conference three grand committees were formed dealing respectively with the three subjects of discussion, viz.: Armaments and engines of destruction; humane regulations in warfare; and mediation and arbitration. Each of the powers was represented on each committee and each had one vote on every proposal submitted to the conference. The conclusions of the conference were embodied in a final act signed July 29 by all the states represented. This act consists of three conventions, three declarations, and six resolutions. The conventions relate to the pacific adjustment of international disputes, and with the laws and usages of war on land, and provide for the adaptation of the rules of maritime warfare to the principles of the Geneva Convention of 1864 (q. v.) The three declarations prohibit the use of projectiles or explosives from balloons for a period of five years (adopted unanimously); the employment of projectiles which diffuse asphyxiating or other deleterious gases (not accepted by England and the United States); and the use of bullets which expand or flatten easily in the human body. In the six resolutions the conference expresses the opinion that the military burdens which now weigh so heavily on the world may be lightened, in the interest of the moral and material well being of humanity (unanimously agreed to); that the duties of neutrals, the inviolability of private property in maritime warfare, and the question of the bombardment of towns should be referred to a future conference, and that the questions of the types and calibers of marine artillery and small arms and the size of naval and military budgets should be studied with a view to establishing uniformity in the former and a reduction of the latter.

The first convention, which relates to the pacific adjustment of international disputes, proved the most important work of the conference. According to this convention the signatory powers agree to resort to mediation in cases of serious international disputes, and agree that mediatory advances by a third party shall not be considered by the disputants as an unfriendly act; where neither honor nor essential interests are concerned a commission of inquiry is provided for.

International Court of Arbitration.—With a view to the settlement of disputes between countries by arbitration a Permanent Court of Arbitration was created. This tribunal is composed of persons eminent in international law chosen by the parties to a dispute from a permanent list of arbitrators nominated by the signatory powers. Each power is allowed to nominate four members for a term of six years.

The following powers are members of the court: Argentine Republic, Austria-Hungary, Belgium, Bolivia, Brazil, Bulgaria, Chili, China, Colombia, Cuba, Denmark, Dominican Republic, Ecuador, France, German Empire, Great Britain, Greece, Guatemala, Haiti, Italy, Japan, Luxemburg, Mexico, Montenegro, Netherlands, Nicaragua, Norway, Panama, Persia, Peru, Portugal, Rumania, Russia, Salvador, Servia, Siam, Spain, Sweden, Switzerland, Turkey, United States, Uruguay and Venezuela.

Court of Arbitration.—Oct. 21, 1904, the United States proposed a second Peace Conference for the purpose of granting jurisdiction to The Hague Tribunal through treaties of arbitration, and for other purposes. This second conference convened in the Hall of Knights, The Hague, June 15, 1907. It was presided over by M. Nelidoff, and the sittings continued from June 15 to Oct. 18, 1907. The permanent Court of Arbitration was perfected by making it to consist of fifteen judges, eight of whom should be appointed by the six great European nations, Japan and the United States, the other seven to be appointed by the minor powers and to sit in rotation, according to the maritime importance of the countries they represent. Other questions discussed were the declaration of war and the time to elapse between that event and the beginning of hostilities. It was finally decided that no military action was to be taken until a formal declaration of war was made and neutrals notified. In relation to naval warfare it was decided that before bombardment from the sea due notice would be given neutrals and non-combatants.

The powers agreed "to take no military or naval action to compel the payment of debts until an offer of arbitration has been made by the creditor and refused or left unanswered by the debtor, or until arbitration has taken place and the debtor state has failed to conform to the decision given."

No decision was arrived at on the great question of the disarmament of nations.

The actual accomplishments of The Hague Conference are as follows: It established the inviolability of neutral territory and the right of asylum in that territory for prisoners of war; prohibited belligerents from establishing wireless telegraph stations in neutral territory; forbade belligerent ships of war to take on fuel or revictual in neutral ports; provided that hostilities shall not begin without a previous declaration of war; ordered that neutral powers be notified of a state of war; revived the declarations which had lapsed in 1904, viz.: prohibition to drop projectiles from balloons, to diffuse deadly gases, or to use bullets of an unusually cruel kind; required indemnification by any belligerent who violates any of the rules of war; provided a definite period of grace allowance to belligerent merchantmen in the enemy's harbors at the beginning of hostilities; prohibited the use of submarine anchored torpedoes for the purpose of restricting commercial navigation; and the use of floating mines, unless they be made so as to become harmless within an hour after having passed beyond human control, and also the use of anchored mines which do not become harmless after they have broken their moorings; prohibited the bombardment of undefended places; insisted on the inviolability of fishing boats and of the postal service; ratified the humanitarian recommendations of the Geneva Red Cross Convention of 1906; established the international prize court; agreed to the American adaptation of the Drago Doctrine, namely, that one nation shall not attempt to collect by force debts claimed by its citizens from the government of another nation unless the question of indebtedness be first submitted to arbitration.

Reservation by United States.—Both Hague conventions were signed by the plenipotentiaries of the United States under reservation of the following declaration: "Nothing contained in this convention shall be so construed as to require the United States of America to depart from its traditional policy of not intruding upon, interfering with, or entangling itself in the political questions of policy or internal administration of any foreign state; nor shall anything contained in the said convention be construed to imply a relinquishment by the United States of America of its traditional attitude toward purely American questions."

In ratifying and signifying American adherence to the second Hague convention, the Senate expressly excluded Article XXIII thereof concerning the rights and duties of neutral powers in naval war, which is in the following words: "Article XXIII.—A neutral power may allow prizes to enter its ports and roadsteads, whether under convoy or not, when they are brought there to be sequestrated pending the decision of a prize court. It may have the prize taken to another of its ports. If the prize is convoyed by a war ship, the prize crew may go on board the convoying ship. If the prize is not under convoy, the prize crew are left at liberty."

It was further resolved by the Senate that the "United States adheres to this convention with the understanding that the last clause of Article III implies the duty of a neutral power to make the demand therein mentioned for the return of a ship captured within the neutral jurisdiction and no longer within that jurisdiction." "Article III.—When a ship has been captured in the territorial waters of a neutral power, this power must employ, if the prize is still within its jurisdiction, the means at its disposal to release the prize with its officers and crew, and to intern the prize crew. If the prize is not in the jurisdiction of the neutral power, the captor government, on the demand of that power, must liberate the prize with its officers and crew."

See illustration opposite 6724.

Hague Conference, first peace conference, 6664.

  Advancement made, 7118.

  Collection by governments of debts due their citizens, from other countries, by force of arms, referred to, 7060.

  Instrumental in maintaining peace between nations, 7060.

  Proposal for convening a second conference, 6923, 6991.

Hague, The, International Statistical Congress at, referred to, 4082.

Hague Tribunal, Arbitration of Venezuelan cases before, 6941.

  Mexican disputes referred to, 6718.

Hail Columbia.—A popular national song written by Judge Joseph Hopkinson, of Philadelphia, in 1798, when war with France seemed imminent. The air to which Mr. Hopkinson's words were sung, and indeed for which they were expressly written, was first known as "General Washington's March" and latter as "The President's March." It was composed by Professor Feyles, leader of the orchestra of the John Street Theater, New York, in 1789, and played when Washington went to New York to be inaugurated President. The song was first sung by an actor named Fox in a Philadelphia theater, and immediately became a great favorite.

Haiti.—Haiti (or San Domingo, or Hispaniola) is the second largest of the Greater Antilles in the "West India" Islands, and lies between 17° 37'-20° 10' N. lat. and 68° 20'-74° 28' W. long. Two-thirds of the island form the Dominican Republic (q. v.), the western third, between 18°-20° 10 N. lat. and 70° 40'-74° 28' W. long., being the Republic of Haiti.

History.—The island was visited in Dec. 6, 1492, by Christopher Columbus, who named it Espagnola, the native name being Haïti (mountainous) or Quisquica (vast). The Spaniards explored the island and almost exterminated the 2,000,000 native Indians, whom they replaced with African negroes. By the Treaty of Ryswick (1697) the western portion of the island was ceded to France, and in 1803 the territory was abandoned by the French, and a republic was proclaimed under the aboriginal name of Haiti.

During its existence the so-called republic has had twenty-four rulers, the majority of whom have died at the hands of their enemies before the expiration of the terms for which they were elected. Aug. 8, 1912, President Cincinnatus Leconte was killed by an explosion which destroyed the national arsenal at Port au Prince, and Tancrede Auguste succeeded him. He was succeeded May 4, 1913, by Michel Oreste. In July, 1915, President Guilaume was murdered by a mob, and, amid the disorder following United States marines were landed by Admiral Caperton, July 29. Under American protection Gen. Dartiguenave was elected President Aug. 12, and the United States assumed a protectorate over the republic.

Haiti:
> Claims of United States against, 1857, 2067, 2760, 4665, 4716, 4918, 5120, 5369, 6099, 6100.
> Award referred to, 5123.
> Settlement of, 6332.
> Correspondence with, transmitted, 5907.
> Diplomatic intercourse with, provision for, recommended, 4716.
> Dispute with Colombia settled by arbitration, 7657.
> Duties imposed upon American products by, retaliatory measures proclaimed, 5702.
> Fugitive criminals, convention with, for surrender of, 3459.
> Imprisonment of American citizens by, 3829, 4665, 4918, 5020, 5123, 5369, 5869, 6099.
> Independence of, recognition of, by United States recommended, 3248.
> Instructions to naval officers in command on coast of, referred to, 4023.
> Insurrections in, discussed, 4824, 4918, 5368, 5471.
> Mission to, elevation of, recommended, 5468.
> Naval force at, referred to, 3832.
> Recognition of, by United States referred to, 5471.
> Relations with, discussed, 3885.
> Social condition of, discussed, 3885.
> Treaty with, transmitted and discussed, 3329, 3459.
> Vessels of United States seized or interfered with by, 2680, 5368, 5390.
> Vessels refused clearance by, discussed, 5869.

Haiti, Treaties with.—A treaty of amity, commerce, navigation, and extradition was concluded Nov. 3, 1864, and provides for most favored nation treatment, immunity of the citizens of the one country in the dominions of the other in time of war between the two countries and of their goods for a period of six months after declaration of war, together with exemption from seizure of money debts or shares.

The citizens of the one country shall be exempt from military service and forced loans or exactions and shall not pay any higher contributions than those demanded from the citizens of the other country. Perfect freedom in the conduct of trade is accorded to all in whatever direction they may legally elect. The books, papers, or accounts of citizens of either country residing within the jurisdiction of the other, may be examined only upon the order of a competent judicial authority. Liberty of conscience and protection of the dead is secured. Property may be disposed of by sale, testament, or gift, with full liberty and without embarrassment.

Importation and exportation of goods may be conducted with equal privileges, regardless of the nationality of the vessels so engaged. The coasting trade is not included in this agreement. The imposition of duties on products of both countries shall be the same for each as for the goods of other countries, and no prohibition of the import of the products of either country into the other shall be made. Provision is made for extension of humane treatment to the shipwrecked on the shores of both countries. Vessels of either nationality attempting to enter a blockaded port of the other shall not be captured on the first attempt, but may be if the attempt is repeated or persisted in. The principle that free ships make free goods is recognized by both parties, and that the property of neutrals on an enemy's vessel is not subject to confiscation unless contraband. Arms, munitions of war, and military equipment of all kinds form a class of contraband of war. Provision is made to facilitate the examination of ships' papers and the search during war as well as the disposition of captured vessels and goods. The customary provision is made for the establishment of consular offices on terms usually described in consular conventions. The terms of extradition recited in the treaty are to be found under Extradition Treaties. The term of the treaty was originally for eight years, with renewal, subject to one year's notice of intention to terminate. (See also Naturalization.)

Haiti also became a party to the convention between the United States and the several republics of South and Central America for the arbitration of pecuniary claims and the protection of inventions, etc., which was signed in Buenos Aires in 1910 and proclaimed in Washington, July 29, 1914. (See South and Central America, Treaties with.)

"Half-Breeds."—In political parlance, a name used in derision to describe the partizans who favored the withdrawal of troops from Southern States in support of the action of President Hayes; and who also urged Civil Service reform in the matter of appointments. The partizans opposing these views came to be known as "Stalwarts" (q. v.). (See also Civil Service.)

Half - Holiday for government employees in summer recommended, 7208.

Halifax Commission.—A commission consisting of representatives of the United States and Great Britain which met in 1877 at the city of Halifax, Nova Scotia, to decide what amount should be paid by the former country for the fishing privileges granted its citizens by the treaty of 1871. Great Britain and the United States each named one of the commissioners, and the third was named by Austria. The Canadians insisted that the concessions granted to the citizens of the United States by that instrument were much more valuable than those obtained by themselves in the reciprocal privileges given them by it. The commission decided that the United States Government should pay the sum of $5,500,-000, and Congress appropriated that amount with the proviso that the articles in the treaty relating to fisheries ought to be terminated at the earliest period consistent with other provisions of the same treaty. These articles were terminated on July 1, 1885, and three years later a new treaty was negotiated but was rejected by the United States Senate on Aug. 21, 1888. Since then the question has been in abeyance under a *modus vivendi*.

Halifax, Nova Scotia:

American prisoners of war in, 507.

Fishery Commission held at, under treaty of Washington referred to, 4419, 4435, 4437, 4438.

Award of commission and appropriation for, discussed, 4448. (See also Geneva Tribunal.)

Hall of Fame.—March 5, 1900, the Council of New York University accepted a gift of $100,000, afterward increased to $250,-000, from a donor, whose name was withheld, for the erection on University Heights, New York City, of a building to be called "The Hall of Fame for Great Americans." A structure was built in the form of a semi-circle, 170 feet, connecting the University Hall of Philosophy with the Hall of Languages. On the ground floor is a museum 200 feet long by 40 feet wide, consisting of a corridor and six halls to contain mementos of the names that are inscribed above. The colonnade over this is 400 feet long with provision for 150 panels, each about 2 feet by 6 feet each to bear the name of a famous American.

Only persons who shall have been dead ten or more years are eligible to be chosen. Fifteen classes of citizens were recommended for consideration to wit: Authors and editors, business men, educators, inventors, missionaries and explorers, philanthropists and reformers, preachers and theologians, scientists, engineers and architects, lawyers and judges, musicians, painters and sculptors, physicians and surgeons, rulers and statesmen, soldiers and sailors, distinguished men and women outside the above classes. Fifty names were to be inscribed on the tablets at the beginning, and five additional names every fifth year thereafter, until the year 2,000, when the 150 inscriptions will be completed. In case of failure to fill all the panels allotted, the vacancies are to be filled in a following year.

Every nomination seconded by a member of the university senate is submitted to an electorate of one hundred eminent citizens selected by the University council. The number of names submitted to the electorate for first ballot was 252. Of these each judge returned a vote for fifty. The rule required that no candidate receiving less than fifty-one votes could be accepted. The returns showed that but twenty-nine candidates received the required number and were chosen. These were as follows: George Washington, Abraham Lincoln, Daniel Webster, Benjamin Franklin, Ulysses S. Grant, John Marshall, Thomas Jefferson, Ralph Waldo Emerson, Henry W. Longfellow, Robert Fulton, Washington Irving, Jonathan Edwards, Samuel F. B. Morse, David G. Farragut, Henry Clay, Nathaniel Hawthorne, George Peabody, Robert E. Lee, Peter Cooper, Eli Whitney, John J. Audu-

bon, Horace Mann, Henry Ward Beecher, James Kent, Joseph Story, John Adams, William E. Channing, Gilbert Stuart, Asa Gray.

In October, 1905, under the rules named above, the senate received the ballots of 95 electors out of 101 appointed, of whom only 85 undertook to consider the names of women. A majority of 51 was demanded, but in the case of the names of women, a majority of only 47. The following persons were found to be duly chosen: John Quincy Adams, 59; James Russell Lowell, 58; William Tecumseh Sherman, 58; James Madison, 56; John Greenleaf Whittier, 53; Alexander Hamilton, 88; Louis Agassiz, 83; John Paul Jones, 54; Mary Lyon, 58; Emma Willard, 50; Maria Mitchell, 48.

The hall was dedicated May 30, 1901, when twenty-five or more national associations each unveiled one of the bronze tablets in the colonnade, and on May 30, 1907, the eleven new tablets were unveiled, orations being given by the governors of New York and Massachusetts.

Since the deed of gift was amended to admit memorials to famous foreign born Americans, the roll of electors has been amended in like manner. Mr. Andrew Carnegie, a native of Scotland, succeeding to the place of ex-President Grover Cleveland, deceased.

In October, 1910, the next ballot was taken, the number cast being 97 and the number required for a choice being 51. The following persons had the requisite number of votes: Harriet Beecher Stowe, 74; Oliver Wendell Holmes, 69; Edgar Allen Poe, 69; Roger Williams, 64; James Fenimore Cooper, 62; Phillips Brooks, 60; William Cullen Bryant, 59; Frances E. Willard, 56; Andrew Jackson, 53; George Bancroft, 53; John Lothrop Motley, 51. There were 211 nominees.

Hamburg (see also Germany):

International Agricultural Exhibition to be held in, referred to, 3348, 3398.

International Cattle Exhibition at, 4714.

International Polar Congress at, referred to, 4535.

Minister of, received in United States, 949.

Treaty with, 988, 991, 2686.

Vessels of—

Application for rights regarding, 621.

Discriminating duties on, suspended, 607.

Hamburg, S. C., slaughter of American citizens in, referred to, 4329.

Hampton Normal Agricultural Institute. Indians to be educated at, 4455.

Hampton Roads (Va.), Battle of.—One of the most celebrated maritime conflicts known to history. Aside from the dramatic interest that surrounds the battle of Hampton Roads, it is important from the fact that it marks the transition from the old to the new style of naval warfare, the passing of the ancient wooden frigate and the advent of the modern navy. When the navy-yard at Norfolk was seized by the Confederates in April, 1861, they found the steam frigate *Merrimac* (40 guns) scuttled and sunk. She was afterwards raised and her deck covered with a slanting roof made of 3 layers of iron, each 1¼ inches thick. This armor extended 2 feet below the water line and rose 10 feet above. The bow was provided with a ram. Her armament consisted of eight 11-inch guns, 4 on each side, and a 100-pounder rifled Armstrong gun at each end. She was then named the *Virginia.* About noon March 8, 1862, she came down the Elizabeth River under command of Commodore Franklin Buchanan, who had been an officer in the United States Navy. The sloop of war *Cumberland,* 24 guns and 376 men, stood athwart her course and opened fire. The projectiles of the *Cumberland* from thirteen 9 and 10-inch guns struck the oncoming monster and glanced from her armor. Advancing with all her speed in the face of 6 or 8 broadsides, the massive hulk of iron rammed her prow into the *Cumberland* just forward of the main chains and instantly opened fire from every gun that could be brought to bear. The *Cumberland* sank in 54 feet of water, her flag flying, and guns firing as she went down, taking with her over 100 dead, sick, and wounded of the crew. The *Merrimac (Virginia)* then turned her attention to the *Congress.* One shot killed 17 men at one of the latter's guns. When the flag of surrender was run up only 218 survived of a crew of 434 men. At 7 o'clock in the evening the iron-clad retired behind Sewells Point. Next morning (Sunday, March 9) she approached the *Minnesota,* which had grounded on a bar. Before getting near enough to administer a shot a strange-looking vessel, called the *Monitor,* commanded by Lieut. John L. Worden, stood across her path. The *Merrimac* proceeded and sent a shell toward the *Minnesota.* The answer was 2 shots from the 11-inch guns in the revolving "cheese-box," which the turret of the *Monitor* resembled. The effect of these was to attract the undivided attention of the *Merrimac.* Rising only 10 feet out of the water, the *Monitor* was not a tempting mark, and the shot that did strike glanced off harmlessly. For the most part the shot flew over the low deck. Five times the *Merrimac* tried to run down the *Monitor,* and at each attempt received the fire of her 11-inch guns at close quarters. After having been twice aground and receiving 2 broadsides from the *Minnesota,* the *Merrimac* withdrew from the conflict, badly disabled and almost unmanageable. On the *Merrimac* 2 men were killed and 19 wounded. Lieut. Worden was injured. (See also *Merrimac,* The ; *Monitor,* The.)

Hampton Roads, Va.:

Conference at, discussed and correspondence regarding restoration of peace, 3461.

Monitor-Merrimac naval engagement in, 3313.

Tercentenary of settlement at Jamestown, to be celebrated at, 6913, 6952, 7006.

Hand-Grenade.—A grenade suitable to be thrown by hand. (See Grenade.)

Hanging Rock (S. C.), Battle of.—On the evening of Aug. 6, 1780, Col. Sumter, with a force of 150 men, attacked the British post at Hanging Rock, a large bowlder jutting out from the high bank of the Catawba River, in South Carolina, 11 miles from Rocky Mount. A body of North Carolina refugees under Col. Bryan fled upon the approach of Sumter, but the Prince of Wales Regiment defended the post for 4 hours and was almost annihilated, the British loss aggregating 269. The American loss was 12 killed and 41 wounded.

Hanover:

Exequatur issued consul of, revoked, 3709.

Fugitive criminals, convention with, for surrender of, 2834.

State dues, treaty with, for abolition of, 3260, 3265.

Referred to, 3328.

Treaty with, transmitted and discussed, 1811, 2303, 2479, 2834, 3260, 3265.

Referred to, 1821, 3328.

Vessels of, discriminating duties on, suspended by proclamation, 970.

Hanover Court-House (Va.), Battle of.—May 24, 1862, while McClellan's army was advancing up the peninsula toward Richmond, Gen. Fitz-John Porter was sent with 12,000 men to Hanover Court-House, 17 miles north of Richmond, to meet and facilitate the advance of McDowell's corps, which was to join McClellan by way of Fredericksburg. Here, May 27, Porter met and defeated the Confederates under Gen. Branch. The Federal loss was 387 ; that of the Confederates between 200 and 300 killed and 730 taken prisoners. McDowell was recalled and Porter returned to his former camp at Gaines Mill.

Hans, The, appropriation to owners for detention of, recommended, 6298, 6336, 6457.

Hanseatic Republics, Treaties with.—These comprise Bremen, Hamburg, and Lübeck, and were incorporated into the North German Union on July 1, 1867. The treaty of 1827 on friendship, commerce, and navigation provides for equality of duties, import and export duties. Especial provision is made for conditions arising from the small population and area which these towns possess, and the three towns are considered an entity in the clearance of ships. Citizens may possess and dispose of property by sale, testament, or otherwise, and have full privileges of winding up estates and affairs in every respect as do citizens. (See also Germany, Treaties with.)

Harbor Island, referred to, 6701.

Harbors. (See Rivers and Harbors.)

Hard Cider Campaign. (See Log Cabin and Hard Cider Campaign.)

Harlem Heights (N. Y.), Battle of.—After Washington had successfully withdrawn the American troops from Long Island he proceeded to strengthen and fortify his lines at Kings Bridge, on Harlem Heights. Sept. 15, 1776, the British ships in the East River landed a small force at Kips Bay, and on the 16th Gen. Howe sent a regiment and two battalions of infantry to dislodge the Americans. The British were driven back with a loss of nearly 200 in killed and wounded.

Harlem River, N. Y., navigation of, report of coast survey on the possibility and expense of rendering navigable for commercial purposes, 3120.

Harpers Ferry (Va.), Capture of.—After Stonewall Jackson was detached from Lee's army in Maryland he recrossed the Potomac at Williamsport Sept. 12, 1862,

EXTENT OF THE UNITED STATES DURING THE ADMINISTRATION OF PRESIDENT B. HARRISON, 1889-1893.

(NOT INCLUDING TERRITORIES)

MAINE 1820

VT. 1791

N. H. 1788

MASS. 1788

CONN. 1788

R.I. 1790

NEW YORK 1788

N.J. 1787

DEL. 1787

MD. 1788

PENNSYLVANIA 1787

WEST VIRGINIA 1863

VIRGINIA 1788

NORTH CAROLINA 1789

SOUTH CAROLINA 1788

GEORGIA 1788

FLORIDA 1845

OHIO 1803

KENTUCKY 1792

TENNESSEE 1796

ALABAMA 1819

MISSISSIPPI 1817

MICHIGAN 1837

INDIANA 1816

ILLINOIS 1818

MISSOURI 1821

ARKANSAS 1836

LOUISIANA 1812

WISCONSIN 1848

IOWA 1846

MINNESOTA 1853

NORTH DAKOTA 1889

SOUTH DAKOTA 1889

NEBRASKA 1867

KANSAS 1861

TEXAS 1845

MONTANA 1889

WYOMING 1890

COLORADO 1876

IDAHO 1890

NEVADA 1864

WASHINGTON 1889

OREGON 1859

CALIFORNIA 1850

FLAG OF 1893

and proceeded down the Virginia side of the river to Harpers Ferry. Sept. 13 he occupied Loudon Heights, meeting with but little opposition. On the night of the 14th Col. Davis with 2,000 cavalry crossed the river between the Confederate forces and escaped. Jackson opened fire on the garrison on the evening of the 14th and continued on the morning of the 15th until Col. Dixon S. Miles, mortally wounded, surrendered 11,583 men, 73 guns, 13,000 small arms, 200 wagons, and large quantities of supplies. The killed and wounded on the Union side numbered 217, while the Confederates sustained no loss.

Harpers Ferry, Va., insurrection at, discussed, 3084.

Harrisburg Convention.—The high-tariff woolen bill of 1827 passed the House of Representatives, but was rejected in the Senate by the casting vote of the Vice-President. The protectionists thereupon called a convention to meet at Harrisburg, Pa., the following year. This body was made up mainly of delegates from the New England and Middle States. It presented the idea of protection to the people and decided to ask for an increased duty upon woolens and also upon other manufactured articles. The activity of the delegates to this convention and the sentiment aroused resulted in the passage of the high-tariff law of 1828, which its enemies nicknamed "The bill of abominations."

Harrison, Benjamin.—1889-1893.

Twenty-sixth Administration—Republican.

Vice-President—Levi P. Morton.
Secretary of State—
    James G. Blaine.
    John W. Foster.
Secretary of the Treasury—
    William Windom.
    Charles Foster.
Secretary of War—
    Redfield Proctor.
    Stephen B. Elkins.
Attorney-General—
    William H. H. Miller.
Postmaster-General—
    John Wanamaker.
Secretary of the Navy—
    Benjamin F. Tracy.
Secretary of the Interior—
    John W. Noble.
Secretary of Agriculture—
    Jeremiah M. Rusk.

Nomination.—Harrison was elected by the Republican party at the election of 1888. The convention met at Chicago on the 19th of June. For some time the work of the convention was delayed awaiting word from Blaine, who was in Europe, as to his possible candidacy. On the withdrawal of his name, the leading candidates were Sherman, Gresham, Alger, and Harrison. Sherman led for the first six ballots but on the seventh the nomination went to Harrison.

Platform.—The platform of 1888 paid tributes to the memories of the great leaders of the party of the past; reaffirmed support of the Constitution; committed the party uncompromisingly to the policy of protection; opposed foreign cheap labor and Chinese immigration; opposed trusts, combines, and monopolies; restricted public lands to settlers' use; confirmed constitutional government by the Territories; condemned Mormonism; supported bimetallism; favored postage reduction; endorsed free schools; urged the rehabilitation of the merchant-marine; favored increase of the navy; advocated a more courageous foreign policy; condemned the Democratic party and the Republican de-

serters of 1884; urged greater pension relief for soldiers; and arraigned President Cleveland for excessive veto in this direction.

Opposition.—The Democratic party in convention at St. Louis, on June 5, 1888, unanimously renominated President Cleveland. Two Labor parties met at Cincinnati on May 15, 1888. The Union Labor party nominated Andrew J. Streator; and the United Labor party put forward Robert H. Cowdrey.

Popular Vote.—The popular vote on Nov. 6, 1888, gave Cleveland 5,536,242; Harrison, 5,440,708; Streator, 146,836; and Clinton B. Fisk (Prohibitionist), 146,876. The electoral vote, counted on Feb. 13, 1889, gave Harrison 233 and Cleveland 168.

Party Affiliation.—Benjamin Harrison's political career began with the birth of the Republican party. In 1860 he became conspicuous in Indiana by a thorough canvass of the State when a candidate for the office of reporter of the Supreme Court. By oversight of the respective campaign committees he and Governor Hendricks were cast to speak at Rockville on the same day, and by agreement divided the time between them. Harrison acquitted himself in debate in an amazingly creditable way. From that time, Harrison was active in every campaign in the State, except for the interruption by his Civil War career. For his support in the campaign of 1880, President Garfield offered Harrison a Cabinet position. In the Senate he was a strong partisan against the administration of Cleveland. His acceptability to what were regarded as doubtful States decided his nomination for President in 1888.

Political Complexion of Congress.—In the Fifty-first Congress (1889-1891) the Senate, of 84 members, was composed of 37 Democrats and 47 Republicans; and the House, of 330 members, was made up of 156 Democrats, 173 Republicans, and 1 Independent. In the Fifty-second Congress (1891-1893) the Senate, of 88 members, was composed of 39 Democrats, 47 Republicans, and 2 Alliance; and the House, of 332 members, was made up of 235 Democrats, 88 Republicans, and 9 Alliance.

Public Debt.—The public debt of the United States during the administration of President Harrison stood as follows: July 1, 1889, $975,939,750.22; 1890, $890,-784,370.53; 1891, $851,912,751.78; 1892, $841,526,463.60.

In his Second Annual Message (page 5549) President Harrison attributes the great reduction of the public debt to "the efforts of the Secretary to increase the value of money in circulation by keeping down the Treasury surplus to the lowest possible limit. That this substantial and needed aid given to commerce resulted in an enormous reduction of the public debt and of the annual interest charge is a matter of increased satisfaction. There has been purchased and redeemed since March 4, 1889, 4 and 4½ per cent. bonds to the amount of $211,832,450 at a cost of $246,-620,741, resulting in the reduction of the annual interest charge of $8,967,609 and a total saving of interest of $51,576,706."

Foreign Policy.—In his Third Annual Message (page 5617) the President makes suggestions regarding the rights of aliens domiciled in the United States as a deduction from the lynching in New Orleans of several Italian subjects. In the affair with the government of Chile the President was earnest and insistent in his demands, which after a display of great patience, became peremptory and were satisfactorily complied with. The onus of the Bering Sea adjustment was thrown upon the President by the illness of Secretary Blaine, and it was not long until treaty adjustment was made. There is no doubt that the presentation of the "five points" upon which the arbitrators were asked to arbitrate was the work of President Harrison and are a good illustration of his legal acumen.

Civil Service.—In his First Annual Message (page 5488) the President acquaints the country with the fact that the book of eligibles in the hands of the Commission is now open for inspection and no longer secret. "This secrecy was the source of much suspicion and many charges of favoritism in the administration of the law."

Tariff.—President Harrison was an out-and-out protectionist. In his First Annual Message (page 5473) he said: "I recommend a revision of our tariff law both in its administrative features and in the schedules. . . . The inequalities in the law should be adjusted, but the protective principle should be maintained and fairly applied to the products of our farms as well as of our shops. . . . The free list can very safely be extended by placing thereon articles that do not offer injurious competition to such domestic products as our home labor can supply. . . . If safe provision against fraud can be devised, the removal of the tax upon spirits used in the arts and manufactures would also offer an unobjectionable method of reducing the surplus." In speaking of the McKinley tariff act of 1890, in his Second Annual Message (page 5556) the President said while the act had been in force at the time of speaking only sixty days, "it is curious to note that advance in prices of articles wholly unaffected by the tariff act was by many hastily ascribed to that act." "No bill was ever framed, I suppose, that in all of its rates and classifications had the full approval of even a party caucus. Such legislation is always the product of compromise as to details, and the present law is no exception." In his Third Annual Message (page 5627) the President said: "I think there are conclusive evidences that the new tariff has created several great industries, which will within a few years give employment to several hundred thousand American working men and women." In his Fourth Annual Message (page 5744) the President said: "I believe the protective system, which has now for something more than thirty years continuously prevailed in our legislation, has been a mighty instrument for the development of our national wealth and a most powerful agency in protecting the homes of our workingmen from the invasion of want. I have felt a most solicitous interest to preserve to our working people rates of wages that would not only give daily bread, but supply a comfortable margin for these home attractions and family comforts and enjoyments without which life is neither comfortable nor sweet." He expressed regret that the results of the recent elections indicate a change of tariff policy and the accompanying disruption of trade conditions which uncertainty in tariff legislation invariably brings.

Harrison, Benjamin:

Annual messages of, 5467, 5542, 5615, 5741.

Arbitrator in boundary dispute between Argentine Republic and Brazil. (See Cleveland, Grover, arbitrator.)

Biographical sketch of, 5438.

Bland-Allison Act discussed by, 5475.

Civil Service discussed by, 5487, 5555, 5642, 5766. (See also Civil Service.)

Centennial celebration of Washington's inauguration, 5371.

Commercial and industrial interests of United States discussed by, 5741.

Constitutional amendment regarding selection of Presidential electors recommended by, 5644.

Finances discussed by, 5472, 5548, 5628, 5753.

Foreign policy discussed by, 5445, 5618, 5750, 5783.

Inaugural address of, 5440.

Interoceanic canal construction begun by an Amercian company, 5470.

Member of Mississippi River Improvement Commission, resignation of, referred to, 4589.

Portrait of, 5437.

Powers of Federal and State Governments, discussed by, 5489, 5562, 5766.

Proclamations of—

Admission of—

Montana, 5459.

North Dakota, 5455.

South Dakota, 5457.

Washington, 5460.

Agreement with Great Britain for *modus vivendi* in relation to Bering Sea fisheries, 5581.

Anniversary of discovery of America, 5724.

Centennial celebration of inauguration of Washington, 5453.

Collisions at sea, 5537.

Contracts for grazing on Cherokee Outlet declared void, 5532.

Time for removing stock extended, 5534.

Copyright privilege to—

Belgium, France, Great Britain, and Switzerland, 5582.

Germany, 5713.

Italy, 5736.

Division of portion of Sioux Reservation, 5529.

Duties on vessels from Tobago suspended, 5598.

Duties upon imports from—

Colombia, 5700.

Haiti, 5702.

Venezuela, 5703.

Extraordinary session of Senate, 5817.

Indian titles to lands in Nebraska extinguished, 5535.

Insurrection in Idaho, 5723.

Lands—

Opened to settlement, 5450, 5579, 5591, 5707, 5710, 5727.

EXTENT OF THE UNITED STATES DURING THE ADMINISTRATION OF PRESIDENT WM. H. HARRISON, 1841.

(NOT INCLUDING TERRITORIES)

FLAG OF 1841

MISSOURI 1821
ARKANSAS 1836
LOUISIANA 1812
MISSISSIPPI 1817
ALABAMA 1819
GEORGIA 1788
SOUTH CAROLINA 1788
NORTH CAROLINA 1789
TENNESSEE 1796
KENTUCKY 1792
ILLINOIS 1818
INDIANA 1816
MICHIGAN 1837
OHIO 1803
VIRGINIA 1788
PENNSYLVANIA 1787
NEW YORK 1788
MD. 1788
DEL. 1787
N.J. 1787
CONN. 1788
MASS. 1788
R.I. 1790
N.H. 1788
VT. 1791
MAINE 1820

Set apart as public reservation, 5577, 5590, 5595, 5686, 5695, 5705, 5719, 5722, 5786, 5792, 5795, 5797, 5804, 5810, 5811, 5814, 5815.
Pardons to polygamists, 5803.
Prevent extermination of seals in Bering Sea, 5449, 5533, 5578, 5581, 5697.
Tariff laws of—
  Austria-Hungary, 5718.
  Brazil, 5576.
  British West Indies, 5688.
  Cuba and Puerto Rico, 5583.
  Dominican Republic, 5588.
  Germany, 5693.
  Guatemala, 5716.
  Honduras, 5714.
  Nicaragua, 5698.
Thanksgiving, 5454, 5536, 5597, 5736.
Tolls upon Canadian vessels, 5725.
  Revoked, 5812.
Unlawful combinations in—
  Idaho, 5723.
  Wyoming, 5725.
World's Columbian Exposition, 5575.
Samoan Islands, treaty with Germany concerning, 5469.
Sherman Act discussed by, 5548, 5628.
State of the Union discussed by, 5467, 5542, 5741.
Tariff discussed by, 5473, 5556, 5626, 5744.
Thanksgiving proclamations of, 5454, 5536, 5597, 5736.
Veto messages of—
  Authorizing Ogden, Utah, to assume increased indebtedness, 5518.
  Authorizing Oklahoma City to issue bonds to provide right of way for railroad, 5571.
  Bookmaking and poolselling in District of Columbia, 5528.
  Referred to, 5551.
  Changing boundaries of Uncompahgre Reservation, 5522.
  Declaring retirement of C. B. Stivers from Army legal, 5526.
  Establishing circuit courts of appeals and regulating jurisdiction of United States courts, 5679.
  Establishing Record and Pension Office of War Department, 5573.
  Extending time to purchasers of Indian lands in Nebraska, 5525.
  Issuance of railroad bonds by Maricopa County, Ariz., 5523.
  Number of district attorneys and marshals in Alabama, 5785.
  Public building at—
    Bar Harbor, Me., 5571.
    Dallas, Tex., 5519.
    Hudson, N. Y., 5521.
    Tuscaloosa, Ala., 5521.
  Relief of—
    Administratrix of estate of G. W. Lawrence, 5574.
    Charles P. Choteau, 5528, 6115.
    Portland (Me.) Company, 5527.
  Submitting claim of William McGarrahan to Court of Private Land Claims, 5680.
  Suits against United States, 5682.
Washington's inauguration, celebration of centennial of, 5371.

Harrison, William Henry.—March 4, 1841-April 4, 1841.

Fourteenth Administration—Whig.
Vice-President—John Tyler.
Secretary of State—
  Daniel Webster.
Secretary of the Treasury—
  Thomas Ewing.
Secretary of War—
  John Bell.
Secretary of the Navy—
  George E. Badger.
Postmaster-General—
  Francis Granger.
Attorney-General—
  John J. Crittenden.

Nomination.—William Henry Harrison was elected by the Whig party in the election of 1840. He was nominated at the National Whig Convention that met at Harrisburg, Pa., Dec. 4-7, 1839, to consider the claims of several rivals for the nomination, especially Harrison, Clay, and Scott. No platform was adopted by the Whigs.

Opposition.—The Democrats met in convention at Baltimore, May 5, 1840, and nominated Martin Van Buren for reelection, but chose no Vice-Presidential candidate.

Platform.—For the first time in election history, a national party platform was adopted. It set forth strict construction, opposed Federal assumption of State debts; opposed Federal fostering of one industry to the exclusion or neglect of another; and national banks; strongly asserted State rights; separation of government money from banking institutions; and endorsed the principles of Jefferson, as set forth in the Declaration of Independence. The Liberty party met in convention at Warsaw, N. Y., and, later, at Albany, N. Y., on April 1, 1840, and nominated James G. Birney on a platform of abolition of slavery. The party thus formed was the beginning of the modern Republican party. The campaign of 1840 was one of the most remarkable in the political history of the United States. It was the first in which all of the people manifested intense interest and excitement. The attempts to belittle Harrison on account of his humble origin were taken up as catch-words, and the "Hard Cider and Log-Cabin" campaign became the "political hurricane of 1840."

Popular Vote.—The popular vote cast at the election of Nov. 3 by twenty-six States stood: Harrison, 1,275,017; Van Buren, 1,128,702; and Birney, 7,059. The electoral vote, counted Feb. 10, 1841, gave Harrison 234 votes, and Van Buren, 60.

Party Affiliation.—The great services that made Harrison so popular were military rather than political. His first nomination for the Presidency was in 1835 by a Whig convention. The second nomination, in 1839, was by a convention composed of

Whigs, National Republicans, and Anti-Masons. His failure of election in 1835 was largely due to the fact that the opponents of Van Buren and Jackson did not concentrate upon Harrison as they did in 1840. President Harrison was not a strong party man. In his Inaugural Address (page 1847) he deprecates party influence. "If parties in a republic are necessary to secure a degree of vigilance sufficient to keep the public functionaries within the bounds of law and duty, at that point their usefulness ends." And again: "To me it seems perfectly clear that the interest of the country requires that the violence of the spirit by which these parties are at this time governed must be greatly mitigated, if not entirely extinguished, or consequences will ensue which are appalling to be thought of."

Political Complexion of Congress.—In the Twenty-seventh Congress (1841-1843) the Senate, of 52 members, was made up of 22 Democrats, 28 Whigs, and 2 Independents; and House, of 242 members, was composed of 103 Democrats, 132 Whigs, 6 Independents, and 1 vacancy. In the Twenty-eighth Congress (1843-1845) the Senate, of 52 members, was made up of 23 Democrats and 29 Whigs; and the House, of 223 members, was composed of 142 Democrats and 81 Whigs.

Foreign Policy.—In his Inaugural Address (page 1874) the President outlines his policy in these words: "Long the defender of my country's rights in the field, I trust that my fellow-citizens will not see in my earnest desire to preserve peace with foreign powers any indication that their rights will ever be sacrificed or the honor of the nation tarnished by any omission on the part of their Chief Magistrate unworthy of their former glory."

Harrison, William Henry:

Biographical sketch of, 1858.

Death of—

Announcements of, 1877.

Certificate of, 1885.

Day of fasting and prayer recommended in consequence of, 1887.

Honors to be paid memory of, 1879.

Report of physicians on, 1886.

Resolution of Congress on, 1908.

Foreign policy discussed by, 1873.

Governor of Indiana Territory, success of troops under command of, 481.

Inaugural address of, 1860.

Major-general, military talents of, commented on, 520.

Nominations of, unacted on, withdrawn by, 1876.

Portrait of, 1857.

Proclamation of, convening extraordinary session of Congress, 1876.

Provisions for family of, for expenses incurred in removing to Washington recommended, 1893.

Remains of, removal of, to North Bend, Ohio, for interment, 1907.

Correspondence regarding, 1906.

Hartford Convention.—Hartford, Conn., has been the scene of two historic conventions with almost opposite purposes. In the autumn of 1780 delegates from all the Northern States assembled there to devise means to strengthen the financial system of the Federal Government and to raise and equip troops for the prosecution of the War of Independence. A second convention was held there Dec. 15, 1814-Jan. 5, 1815, and had for its object the denunciation of the war with Great Britain. It consisted of delegates from Massachusetts, Connecticut, Rhode Island, New Hampshire and Vermont, and was held behind closed doors. The New England Federalists were much opposed to the War of 1812, as it wrought great damage to their commercial interests. They denounced the policy of the Government in drafting men for the Army and demanded reforms in the direction of state's rights. Having been accused of an attempt to disrupt the Union, the convention denied "any present intention to dissolve the Union," but admitted that "if a dissolution should become necessary by reason of the multiplied abuses of bad administration it should, if possible, be the work of peaceable times and deliberate consent." It laid down the general principle that "it is as much the duty of the state authorities to watch over the rights reserved as of the United States to exercise the powers that are delegated." The resolutions of the convention were endorsed by the legislatures of Connecticut and Massachusetts and passed upon by Congress. No attention was there paid to them. They are of interest as showing that secession was contemplated in New England at an early date in our history. The strength of the Federalist party in the states where it had been strongest began to wane after the holding of this convention.

Hatchers Run (Va.), Battle of.—Oct. 27, 1864, in an attempt to seize the South Side Railroad and get nearer Richmond, the Second Army Corps, under Hancock, and two divisions of the Fifth Corps forced a passage of Hatchers Run, the termination of the Confederate works on the right, and moved up on the south side of it to the point where the run is crossed by the Boydton plank road. In support of the movement Butler made a demonstration on the north side of the James River and attacked the Confederates on both the Williamsburg and York River railroads. The Confederates moved across Hatchers Run and made a fierce attack upon Hancock, but were driven back into their works. During the night Hancock retired to his old position, having lost 1,900 men, one-third of whom were missing. Feb. 5, 1865, Grant made another attempt to turn the Confederate lines at Hatchers Run. The only gain was an extension to the westward of the Federal lines. The losses in the attempt were 2,000 on the Federal and about 1,000 on the Confederate side.

Hatteras Expedition.—Aug. 26, 1861, an expedition against Forts Hatteras and Clark was sent out from Fortress Monroe under Commodore Stringham and Gen. Butler. The naval force consisted of the *Minnesota* and four other vessels and transports and the land force about 900 men. Fort Clark was occupied on the 27th without serious opposition. On the morning of the 28th bombardment of Fort Hatteras began, and on the 29th at eleven o'clock, the fort surrendered. Butler occupied the works with his land forces. Capt. Barron and 615 prisoners were sent north on the flagship *Minnesota*. Twenty-five pieces of artillery, 1,000 stands of arms, and a large quantity of ordnance stores, provisions, etc., fell into the hands of the victors.

Hatters' Case. (See Loewe v. Lawlor.)

Havana, Cuba (see also Cuba):

Destruction of the *Maine* in harbor of, 6277, 6290, 6305.

Findings of court of inquiry discussed, 6277, 6290.

Number of lives lost in, 6296.

Proposition of Spain to investigate causes of, referred to, 6290.

Hawaii.—A dependent territory of the United States consisting of a group of twelve islands (four of which are uninhabited), lying near the middle of the Pacific Ocean, between 18° 54′ and 22° 2′ north latitude and between 155° and 161° west longitude. From Honolulu, capital of Oahu, to San Francisco the distance is 2,100 miles; to Yokohama, 3,440 miles; to Hong Kong, 4,893 miles. The group was named by Capt. Cook, their discoverer, Sandwich Islands, in honor of the Earl of Sandwich, first lord of the British admiralty at the time of their discovery, but the natives called them the Hawaiian islands and that term is now officially recognized. The eight principal islands are Hawaii, Maui, Oahu, Kauai, Lanai, Kahulaui, Molokai, and Niihau. They are mountainous and volcanic. The total area of the group is 6,449 square miles, of which 4,000 is the island of Hawaii.

History.—During the greater part of the nineteenth century the islands formed an independent kingdom. Jan. 17, 1893, Queen Liliuokalani was deposed and a provisional government was formed, with Sanford B. Dole at the head; and annexation to the United States asked. A treaty of annexation was concluded with President Harrison, but before it could be ratified by the Senate President Cleveland was inaugurated; he at once withdrew it and sent James H. Blount as special commissioner to investigate the affairs of the islands. The restoration of the Queen was attempted, but failed, mainly because she refused to grant an amnesty. On July 4, 1894, a Republic was proclaimed with Mr. Dole as its president. During President McKinley's first term, another treaty of annexation was sent to the Senate, but, pending its consideration, a joint resolution passed Congress annexing the islands. The resolution was approved on July 7, 1898, and the formal annexation occurred on Aug. 12 of the same year. The islands were constituted the Territory of Hawaii in June, 1900, and by act of April 30 of the same year citizenship of the United States was bestowed on all citizens of the former Republic of Hawaii; territorial franchise has been given to those who had been resident in the territory for one year, provided they were able to read and write the English or Hawaiian language. The government rests in a legislature of two houses—a senate of fifteen members (elected for four years) and a house of representatives of thirty members (elected for two years). The governor and secretary are appointed for four years by the President of the United States. The territory is represented in the United States House of Representatives by a delegate elected biennially.

The first United States census of the islands was taken in 1900 with the following result: Hawaii Island, 46,843; Kauai Island, 20,562; Nihau Island, 172; Maui Island, 25,416; Molokai Island and Lanai Island, 2,504; Oahu Island, 58,504. Total of the Territory, 154,001. The population of the city of Honolulu was 39,306. The population of Hawaii according to the 1910 census, made by the United States Census Bureau, was 191,909, Honolulu City having a population of 52,183.

Trade with the United States.—The exports from Hawaii to the United States in the twelve months ending June 30, 1911, were valued at $41,180,195. The imports into Hawaii from the United States for the same period were valued at $21,677,213. The imports from foreign countries for the same period were $5,190,449, exports $730,642.

Sugar and rice are the staple products, but coffee, hides, sisal, bananas, pineapples and wool are exported. The sugar crop of 1908 amounted to 521,123 tons. For the year ended June, 1908, the imports from foreign countries amounted to $4,682,399, and the exports to foreign countries, $597,640. The shipments of domestic merchandise from the United States to Hawaii amounted to $15,303,325, and those from Hawaii to the United States to $41,640,815. Several lines of steamers run regularly between Hawaii and the United States. Canada, Australia, the Philippines, China, and Japan. There are seventeen steamers plying between island ports. There are 160 miles of railway and 600 miles of telephone line. The city of Honolulu has electric lights and electric street railways.

The total population was found by the census of 1910 to be 191,909. (See illustration opposite 5087.)

Hawaiian Islands:

American policy in, 6660, 6799, 6921, 7018, 7051, 7231.

Annexation of, to United States, 6332, 6399. (See also Control over, *post.*)

Action of American minister regarding, discussed by President Cleveland, 5873, 5892.

Discussed by President—

Harrison, Benj., 5783.

McKinley, 6332.

Dispatch of Henry A. Pierce regarding, 4085.

Information regarding, refused, 2691, 2695.

Pearl Harbor, improvement of, urged, 7232.

Shipping interests between Pacific mainland and, discussed, 7232.

Treaty for, transmitted by President Benj. Harrison, 5783.

Withdrawn by President Cleveland, 5825.

Discussed, 5873, 5892.

Cable communication with, recommended, 4565, 5086, 5368, 5751, 6354, 6449, 6661, 6719.

Surveys for, in progress, 5623, 5663, 5679.

Commission to report upon legislation concerning, 6333.

Control over—

Must not pass to foreign powers, 2064, 2555, 2650, 3887, 5783.

Not sought by United States, 2064.

Customs relations with foreign powers after annexation to the United States discussed, 6333.

Differences of, with France referred to, 2656.

Discussed by President—

Cleveland, 5085, 5873, 5892.

Fillmore, 2656, 2691, 2695.

Harrison, Benj., 5783.

Johnson, 3887.

McKinley, 6399, 6453.

Taylor, 2555.

Tyler, 2064.

Duties wrongfully levied, 5545.

Efforts of, to seek replenishment of population discussed, 4630.

Government of—

Change in, and interference of American minister in, discussed, 5873, 5892.

Proposed change referred to, 5181.

Troops landed under direction of American minister in, discussed, 5873, 5892.

Recognition of, by United States, 5958.

Independence of—

Desired by United States, 2064, 2555, 2656, 3887.

First recognized by United States, 2656.

Instructions to diplomatic and naval representatives of United States in, transmitted, 5904.

Insurrection in—

Report on, transmitted, 5998.

Treatment of American citizens and action of United States Government discussed, 6065.

Invitation to, to attend international conference at Washington, extension of recommended, 5468.

King of—

Coronation of, discussed, 4761.

Death of, in United States, 5623.

Visit of, to United States, 4630.

Lease of station to Great Britain by, for submarine telegraph cable, recommendation regarding, 5991.

Lighthouse establishment in, 6497.

Minister of, to United States, recall of, discussed, 6065.

Minister of United States to—

Instructions to, and correspondence with, referred to, 5905, 5906, 5907, 5908, 5909, 5910, 5911, 6000.

Letter of Sanford B. Dole to, referred to, 5906, 5907.

Provisional Government recognized by, discussed by President Cleveland, 5873, 5892.

Mission to, elevation of, recommended, 5468.

Queen of—

Referred to, 5623.

Restoration of, to throne discussed, 5783.

Surrender of sovereignty by, discussed, 5903.

Questions between Japan and, settled, 6333.

Relations with, referred to, 5784.

Special commissioner sent to, report of, discussed by President Cleveland, 5873, 5892.

Transfer of, to United States, 6264, 6332.

Treaty with, transmitted and discussed, 2563, 2619, 2870, 2884, 3399, 3664, 3721, 3891, 3996, 4272, 4289, 4296, 4358, 4842, 5783.

Extension of, recommended, 5058.

Proposition regarding, 4805, 4824.

Referred to, 5368.

Modification of, 4716, 4761.

Proclaimed, 4348.

Recommended, 3882.

Referred to, 5121, 5782.

Withdrawn, 5825.

Discussed, 5873, 5892.

Vessels of, discriminating duties on, suspended by proclamation, 3713.

Hawkeye State.—A nickname for Iowa (q. v.). (See also States.)

Hay.—The hay crop of the United States is important and profitable, its annual value amounting in 1915 to more than 900 million dollars. The yield is something less than two tons per acre, and the price advanced in ten years from $8 per ton to $15 per ton, but showed a decrease in 1915, and an advance again in 1916.

The estimated acreage, production, and value of the hay crop, 1908 to 1914, and in 1915 by states is shown in the table herewith: (Source: Reports of the Department of Agriculture.)

Year	Acreage	Total Farm Value Dec. 1
1908	46,486,000	$635,423,000
1909	45,744,000	689,345,000
1910	45,691,000	747,769,000
1911	43,017,000	694,570,000
1912	49,530,000	856,695,000
1913	48,954,000	797,077,000
1914	49,145,000	779,068,000
State		
Alabama	250,000	4,489,000
Arizona	147,000	4,512,000
Arkansas	350,000	5,768,000
California	2,511,000	50,624,000
Colorado	970,000	16,218,000
Connecticut	365,000	9,860,000
Delaware	70,000	1,428,000
Florida	51,000	976,000
Georgia	300,000	5,210,000
Idaho	677,000	14,076,000
Illinois	2,400,000	39,917,000
Indiana	2,020,000	33,330,000
Iowa	3,098,000	48,511,000
Kansas	1,766,000	22,747,000
Kentucky	875,000	15,312,000
Louisiana	250,000	4,511,000
Maine	1,215,000	20,815,000
Maryland	390,000	7,582,000
Massachusetts	470,000	15,510,000
Michigan	2,470,000	42,188,000
Minnesota	1,680,000	20,538,000
Mississippi	250,000	3,850,000
Missouri	3,050,000	39,406,000
Montana	775,000	11,625,000
Nebraska	1,650,000	24,882,000
Nevada	225,000	5,062,000
New Hampshire	504,000	8,770,000
New Jersey	361,000	9,937,000
New Mexico	201,000	3,890,000
New York	4,500,000	91,845,000
North Carolina	350,000	10,692,000
North Dakota	440,000	3,762,000
Ohio	2,812,000	51,422,000

State	Acreage	Year Farm Value Dec. 1
Oklahoma	460,000	5,925,000
Oregon	850,000	17,765,000
Pennsylvania	3,100,000	67,704,000
Rhode Island	57,000	1,598,000
South Carolina	220,000	4,462,000
South Dakota	610,000	6,466,000
Tennessee	950,000	19,404,000
Texas	450,000	6,044,000
Utah	394,000	7,880,000
Vermont	970,000	20,305,000
Virginia	700,000	14,836,000
Washington	812,000	20,174,000
West Virginia	730,000	16,425,000
Wisconsin	2,576,000	44,629,000
Wyoming	550,000	9,438,000
Total, 1915	50,872,000	$912,320,000

Hay-Herran Treaty, terms of, 6902, 6903. (See Colombia, Treaties with, under Ship Canal.)

Hay-Pauncefote Treaty, terms of, 6902. Invoked in opposition to control of Panama Canal, 7758.

(See Great Britain, Treaties with, under Isthmian Canal.)

Hayes, Rutherford B.—1877-1881.
Twenty-third Administration—Republican.
Vice-President—William A. Wheeler.
Secretary of State—
  William M. Evarts.
Secretary of the Treasury—
  John Sherman.
Secretary of War—
  George W. McCrary.
  Alexander Ramsey.
Secretary of the Navy—
  Richard W. Thompson.
  Nathan Goff, Jr.
Secretary of the Interior—
  Carl Schurz.
Postmaster-General—
  David McK. Key.
  Horace Maynard.
Attorney-General—
  Charles Devens.

Nomination.—Hayes was nominated by the Republican National Convention at Cincinnati, June 14-15, 1876, on the seventh ballot, after a most exciting contest with James G. Blaine.

Platform.—The Republican platform of 1876 pledged the party to the complete pacification of the South and the protection of its people; demanded specie payment; sought improvement in the civil service; recommended non-sectarian schools; advocated tariff for revenue and equalized protection; opposed grants of public lands to corporations and monopolies; advocated naturalization treaties with foreign powers; questioned the moral and material effect of Chinese immigration; sympathized with equal rights for women; denounced polygamy; renewed pledges to soldiers and sailors; deprecated sectional feeling; and severely criticised the Democratic party and its administrations.

Opposition.—The Democratic National Convention at St. Louis, June 27-29, 1876, nominated Samuel J. Tilden. The Greenback Convention at Indianapolis, May 17, 1876, nominated Peter Cooper, on a platform opposing specie payment. The Prohibition Convention at Cleveland, May 17, 1876, nominated Green Clay Smith. The American party nominated James B. Walker.

Popular Vote.—The popular vote of thirty-seven States on the election on Nov. 7, 1876, gave Tilden 4,284,757; Hayes, 4,033,-

950; Cooper, 81,740; and Green Clay Smith, 9,522. The popular vote in Florida and Louisiana was in dispute between the two parties; and Congress passed an act creating an Electoral Commission as a court of last resort to settle the dispute. By a vote of 8 to 7, the Commission decided in favor of Hayes and the electoral vote was declared on March 2, 1877, to stand 185 for Hayes and 184 for Tilden.

Party Affiliation.—In his early career, Hayes always voted with the Whig party, supporting Clay in 1844, Taylor in 1848, and Scott in 1852. From long-cherished anti-slavery feelings, he joined the Republican party on its organization and supported Frémont in 1856, and Lincoln in 1860. General Hayes was in the field when he was nominated for Congress in 1864 by a Republican convention at Cincinnati. To a friend who suggested that he take leave of absence to go home to canvass, General Hayes replied: "Your suggestion about getting a furlough to take the stump was certainly made without reflection. An officer fit for duty who at this crisis would abandon his post to electioneer for a seat in Congress ought to be scalped." In Congress he voted with his party on reconstruction, voted against repudiation, voted for the impeachment of President Johnson; advocated Civil Service reform. In his career as three times Governor of his State, he strongly advocated the honest money system. In his letter of acceptance, General Hayes laid especial stress upon civil service reform, the currency, and pacification of the South.

Political Complexion of Congress.—In the Forty-fifth Congress (1877-1879) the Senate, of 76 members, was composed of 36 Democrats, 39 Republicans, and 1 Independent, and the House, of 293 members, was made up of 156 Democrats and 137 Republicans. In the Forty-sixth Congress (1879-1881) the Senate, of 76 members, was composed of 43 Democrats and 33 Republicans; and the House, of 293 members, was made up of 150 Democrats, 128 Republicans, 14 Nationals, and 1 vacancy.

Civil Service.—In his letter of acceptance, General Hayes said "that public officers should owe their whole service to the Government and to the people," and that "the officer should be secure in his tenure so long as his personal character remained untarnished, and the performance of his duties satisfactory." In his Inaugural Address (page 4396) he asked for "a reform that shall be thorough, radical, and complete." He points out that reform was advocated by both great political parties prior to the election, a demonstration of its necessity. In his First Annual Address (page 4418) he says: "I have endeavored to reduce the number of changes in subordinate places usually made upon change of the general administration, and shall most heartily cooperate with Congress in the better systematizing of such methods and rules of admission to the public service and of promotion within it as may promise to be most successful in making thorough competency, efficiency, and character the decisive tests in these matters." The recommendations of the President were not acted upon by Congress and no appropriation was made for the Civil Service Commission. Republican senators and congressmen were dissatisfied with the efforts of the President in this direction and great opposition was experienced.

Finances.—The President favored the coinage of silver but only in moderate quantity. In his Third Annual Message (page 4511) he said: "I would, however, strongly urge upon Congress the importance of authorizing the Secretary of the

EXTENT OF THE UNITED STATES DURING THE ADMINISTRATION OF PRESIDENT HAYES, 1877-1881.

(NOT INCLUDING TERRITORIES)

FLAG OF 1881

CALIFORNIA 1850

OREGON 1859

NEVADA 1864

COLORADO 1876

TEXAS 1845

KANSAS 1861

NEBRASKA 1867

MINNESOTA 1858

IOWA 1846

WISCONSIN 1848

MISSOURI 1821

ILLINOIS 1818

LOUISIANA 1812

ARKANSAS 1836

MISSISSIPPI 1817

TENNESSEE 1796

KENTUCKY 1792

INDIANA 1816

MICHIGAN 1837

OHIO 1803

ALABAMA 1819

GEORGIA 1788

SOUTH CAROLINA 1788

NORTH CAROLINA 1789

WEST VIRGINIA 1863

VIRGINIA 1788

PENNSYLVANIA 1787

NEW YORK 1788

FLORIDA 1845

MD. 1788

DEL. 1787

N. J. 1787

CONN. 1788

MASS. 1788

R. I. 1790

VT. 1791

N. H. 1788

MAINE 1820

Treasury to suspend the coinage of silver dollars upon the present legal ratio. The market value of the silver dollar being uniformly and largely less than the market value of the gold dollar, it is obviously impracticable to maintain them at par with each other if both are coined without limit." In his Fourth Annual Message (page 4568) the President said: "It is obvious that the legislation of the last Congress in regard to silver, so far as it was based on an anticipated rise in the value of silver as a result of that legislation, has failed to produce the effect then predicted. The longer the law remains in force, requiring as it does the coinage of a nominal dollar which in reality is not a dollar, the greater becomes the danger that this country will be forced to accept a single metal as the sole legal standard of value in circulation, and this a standard of less value than it purports to be worth in the recognized money of the world." He urges that the coinage of silver dollars containing only 412½ grains of silver be stopped and that silver dollars be made the equivalent of gold.

Public Debt.—The public debt of the United States during the administration of President Hayes stood as follows: July 1, 1877, $2,019,275,431.37; 1878, $1,999,-382,280.45; 1879, $1,996,414,905.03; 1880, $1,919,326,747.75.

In his First Annual Message (page 4415) the President advocated the refunding of the public debt so as to reduce the interest by one-third and the repayment of the debt in gold. He said: "During the time of these issues the only dollar that could be or was received by the Government in exchange for these bonds was the gold dollar. To require the public creditors to take in repayment any dollar of less commercial value would be regarded by them as a repudiation of the full obligation assumed. It is far better to pay these bonds in that coin than to seem to take advantage of the unforeseen fall in silver bullion to pay in a new issue of silver coin thus made so much less valuable. It was the great merit," he said, "of the act of March, 1869, in strengthening the public credit, that it removed all doubt as to the purpose of the United States to pay their bonded debt in coin."

Hayes, Rutherford B.:

Annual messages of, 4410, 4444, 4509, 4553.

Arbitrator in boundary question between Argentine Republic and Paraguay, 4449.

Biographical sketch of, 4391.

Bland-Allison Act—
Discussed by, 4511, 4568.
Vetoed by, 4438.

Civil service discussed by, 4396, 4417, 4501, 4502, 4507, 4513, 4555. (See also Civil Service.)

Constitutional amendment regarding election of President recommended by, 4397.

Cuban insurrection and policy of United States regarding, discussed by, 4438, 4448.

Death of, announced and honors to be paid memory of, 5818.

Election of, discussed by, 4398.

Finances discussed by, 4397, 4413, 4422, 4450, 4509, 4523, 4566.

Foreign policy discussed by, 4418, 4420.

Inaugural address of, 4394.

Portrait of, 4390.

Powers of Federal and State Governments discussed by, 4445, 4466, 4475, 4484, 4488, 4493, 4497, 4512, 4543, 4544, 4553.

Proclamations of—
Discriminating duties on vessels of China suspended, 4552.
Extraordinary session of—
Congress, 4399, 4472.
Senate, 4591.
Thanksgiving, 4409, 4442, 4500, 4551.
Unauthorized occupancy of Indian Territory, 4499, 4550.
Unlawful combinations in—
Maryland, 4400. (See illustration opposite 4470.)
New Mexico, 4441.
Pennsylvania, 4401.
West Virginia, 4399.

Reconstruction of Southern States discussed by, 4394, 4410, 4445.

Special session messages of, 4404, 4472.

State of the Union discussed by, 4410, 4444, 4509, 4553.

Tariff discussed by, 4422, 4511.

Thanksgiving proclamations of, 4409, 4442, 4500, 4551.

Veto messages of—
Appropriations—
For judicial expenses, 4493.
For legislative, executive, and judicial expenses, 4488.
For support of Army, etc., 4475.
To pay fees of marshals, etc., 4497.
To supply deficiencies, etc., 4543.
Coinage of standard silver dollars, 4438.
Military interference at elections, 4484.
Mississippi courts, 4440.
Refunding national debt, 4589.
Regulations of pay and appointments of deputy marshals, 4544.
Relief of Joseph B. Collins, 4496.
Restricting Chinese immigration, 4466.

Haymarket Riot.—A riot which took place at Haymarket Square, Chicago, May 4, 1886, involving the police and a number of anarchists. An open-air meeting, in which certain labor troubles were under discussion, was in progress The police attempted to break up the meeting because of the inflammatory utterances of some of the speakers. In the fight which ensued a bomb was thrown and 7 policemen were killed and 60 wounded. Albert R. Parsons, August Spies, Adolph Fischer, George Engel, Michael Schwab, Louis Lingg, Samuel Fielden and Oscar W. Neebe, prominent anarchists, were arrested and tried for complicity in the outrage.

The case attracted universal attention and resulted in the hanging of the first four Nov. 11, 1887. Lingg escaped the gallows by committing suicide in prison. Fielden and Schwab were sentenced to imprisonment for life and Neebe for 15 years. They were pardoned by Governor Altgeld in 1893. (See illustration opposite 4596.)

Hayti. (See Haiti.)

Haytien Republic, The, seizure and delivery of, referred to, 5390.

Health, Board of. (See National Board of Health.)

Health, Bureau of:

Conflict of rival schools regarding, deprecated, 7543.

Formation of, recommended, 7438, 7543.

Legislation to strengthen, 7194.

Health Insurance.—Compulsory insurance of the workingman against illness is present in Austria (covering some 33% of the workers); in Hungary (30%); in Russia (40%); and in Germany, Great Britain, and Norway, where practically all the workers are thus protected.

The first system of insurance against the distress incident upon illness was put into effect by Germany in 1884, and it still remains the most efficient system and that after which most of the systems of other countries are patterned. In 1914, the system was broadened to include domestic workers, although this extension was postponed until after the war. The German system is not compulsory for workers earning more than $500 a year. The organization of the system is left to different kinds of local organizations. Two-thirds of the funds for this purpose are contributed by the workers and one-third by the employer.

The minimum insurance is for free medical service and medicines for 26 weeks of illness, with a pension of one-half the wage of ordinary unskilled labor in the locality in which the insurance is being paid. There is also a minimum pension to women for six weeks surrounding child-birth; and a minimum funeral benefit of twenty times the average daily wage.

The extent to which amounts greater than the minimum may be paid is left to the individual organizations. Some of these pay a year's benefit of three-fourths of the wage, others pay a stated sum to dependants, others give hospital treatment for a year, others give larger funeral benefits, and so forth. However, the amount contributed must not exceed 6% of the wages, the average being 3½%. Each local organization must have at least 100 members.

The executive committee managing the health insurance of the various organizations is composed of two representatives of the workingmen for one of the employer. In case of permanent illness or disability the workman passes under the supervision of the Invalidity Insurance Law.

In 1905, there were some 12,000,000 persons insured against illness in the German Empire. 256,000,000 marks was paid for pensions. The receipts during the same period were 340,000,000 marks, of which 16,000,000 marks was paid for administration expenses.

Systems modelled on the German were adopted by Austria in 1888, Hungary in 1891, Norway in 1909, Servia in 1910, Russia and Rumania in 1912.

The system adopted by Great Britain in 1911 is usually considered to be inferior to the German system. Recognition was given to volunteer friendly benefit organizations. Workmen contribute 4/9 of the benefit, the employer 3/9 and the state 2/9. Working-women contribute 3/8, the employer 3/8 and the state 2/8 of the fund.

There is also much provision for voluntary health insurance in France, Italy, Denmark, Netherlands, Sweden. In the United States the movement for insurance against ill health is gaining ground, but at present only about one-eighth of the workmen of the country receive illness benefits through their trades unions or through benefit associations.

In 1917, the following states had created commissions to study social insurance and health insurance: California, Connecticut, Illinois, Massachusetts, New Hampshire, Ohio, Pennsylvania, Wisconsin. California had provided for the submission to a referendum of the voters of the state of an amendment to the state constitution providing for a system of health insurance, either voluntary or compulsory.

Health of the nation not properly studied, 7870.

Health, Public, protection of, 7228. (See also Quarantine Regulations.)

Health Service.—The United States Public Health Service is a bureau of the Treasury Department. The head of the bureau is granted the title of Surgeon-General. The work of the Service is administered, under direction of the Surgeon-General, by seven bureau divisions—Personnel and Accounts, Scientific Research, Foreign and Insular Quarantine, Domestic Quarantine, Sanitary Reports and Statistics, Marine Hospitals and Relief and Miscellaneous.

Appointments in the corps are made to the grade of Assistant Surgeon, after successful examination. Qualifications for examination are graduation from a reputable medical college, one year's hospital experience or two years' professional work after graduation, and testimonials from responsible persons as to professional and moral character. Applicants for examination must be between the ages of 23 and 32 years.

The Public Health Service maintains twenty-two marine hospitals and 125 other relief stations throughout the country. Fifty-one quarantine stations in the United States and twenty-five stations in its insular possessions are also operated, and eighty-one stations for the medical inspection of immigrants. Eighteen officers are stationed at American consulates abroad to assist in the administration of quarantine and the inspection of immigrants.

At the Hygienic Laboratory, located in the city of Washington, research work in connection with investigations of disease, sanitation and water pollution is carried on, and tests are made of the purity and potency of viruses, serums and toxins, with the supervision of the manufacture and sale of which the Public Health Service is charged by law.

The Public Health Service co-operates with state and local Boards of Health in the eradication of epidemic diseases, such as plague, cholera, yellow fever, typhus fever, smallpox and leprosy. Details of officers are also made, on request from state and municipal health authorities, to assist in the suppression of typhoid fever, infantile paralysis, cerebro-spinal meningitis, and other diseases. The Public Health Service has supervision of measures for the prevention of the spread of infectious and contagious diseases in interstate traffic; the administration of matters in relation to the Interstate Quarantine Regulations regarding the prevention of the use of the common towel and common drinking cup on vehicles or vessels operating in interstate traffic and the certification of water and ice furnished by common carriers for passengers in interstate traffic. Among the signal achievements of the Service in recent years in the field of public health work have been the eradication of bubonic plague in California and Porto Rico, and the suppression of yellow fever in the South.

In addition to the commissioned medical corps, the services of 241 Acting Assistant Surgeons (physicians appointed locally and not subject to change of station) were required to conduct the operations of the Service during the fiscal year ending June 30, 1913. During this year 50,604 patients were treated—14,097 in hospitals and 36,507 at dispensaries. At quarantine stations 7,821 vessels, carrying 599,955 passengers and crews, were inspected and 1,737 vessels disinfected. Immigrants to the number of 1,574,371 were inspected and 38,558 certified for rejection on account of physical and mental defects. At the immigrant hospitals at Ellis Island, N. Y., conducted by Service officers under the supervision of Commissioner of Immigration, 10,165 patients were admitted to treatment.

In 1916, the medical staff consisted of 1 surgeon-general, 13 senior surgeons; 72 surgeons; 37 passed assistant surgeons; 63 assistant surgeons; and 250 acting assistant surgeons. In that year 12,120 vessels and 853,073 passengers and crew were inspected and 1,794 ships were fumigated. 478,527 immigrants were examined. 68,398 patients received treatment by the Service—17,464 in hospitals and 50,934 as dispensary and out-patients.

In 1917, there were 61 quarantine stations in the United States, 26 stations in its insular possessions, and 89 stations for the medical inspection of immigrants under the United States Health Service. In 1917, 12,431 vessels were inspected at quarantine stations, carrying 709,770 passengers and crew. 2,796 vessels were fumigated. 528,648 immigrants were examined, and 64,033 patients were treated in the 20 marine hospitals and the 119 other relief stations under the Marine Hospital and Relief Division.

The Health Service also has charge of the lepers in the United States, estimated at 500 in number. On February 3, 1917, a bill was signed by the President authorizing the construction of a national home for lepers.

Health Service:

Transferring Deadman's Island to, 7979.

Hebrew-American.—An American of Hebrew or Jewish descent.

Helderberg War.—Demonstrations made at various times between 1839 and 1845, by the Anti-Renters of Albany, Rensselaer, Columbia, Greene, Delaware, Schoharie, and Otsego counties, N. Y., and the efforts of the State government to suppress them. Large tracts of land in these counties had been granted by the Government of Holland to the early Dutch settlers or patroons. The patroons sublet the land in perpetuity to tenants who agreed to pay the rent in produce. On the death of Stephen Van Rensselaer in 1839 his tenants, who had long been dissatisfied, refused to pay his successor the rent. Men disguised as Indians terrorized the region. A sheriff and posse who attempted to collect the rents were outnumbered and their efforts proved futile. In 1844 there was again armed opposition to the payment of rent. In 1845 an officer named Steele was shot while trying to collect rent in Delaware County. Governor Wright proclaimed the county in a state of insurrection. Two persons were convicted and sentenced to death for this murder, but they were afterward pardoned. The court of appeals in 1852 rendered a decision which in the main sustained the tenants and practically ended the movement.

Helena (Ark.), Assault on.—To strengthen the army before Vicksburg, Grant had withdrawn troops from all the neighboring posts. Helena, Ark., was left in charge of 3,800 men under Gen. B. M. Prentiss. June 26 the Confederate Generals T. H. Holmes and Sterling Price left Little Rock with about 8,000 men to surprise and capture the place. July 4, 1863, the day Vicksburg surrendered, they made an assault on one of the batteries with 3,000 men. They were repulsed with a loss of 1,111 men. Four regiments then attacked a fort on Hindman Hill, but were defeated. A third assault was made by Marmaduke, with 1,750 men, upon a fort on the north side of the place, but was likewise repulsed with a loss of one-fifth of the assailants. The Confederate loss was officially reported as 173 killed, 687 wounded, and 776 missing—in all, 1,636. The Federal loss did not exceed 250 in all.

Hemp, Russian, import duties on, referred to, 3990.

"Henning's Statutes at Large."—A collection of Virginia laws before the Revolution, suggested by Jefferson, who did the larger part of the work.

Henrick, The, indemnification for loss of claimed, 344, 365, 634.

Henry Crosby, The, fired upon at Azua, Santo Domingo, 6095.

Henry Documents.—Sir James H. Craig, the Governor of British North America, in January, 1809, sent an adventurer, John Henry by name, into the New England States to report the feeling of that section of the country on the question of secession from the Union, and possibly to increase the discontent already caused among these people of commercial interests by the Embargo Act and the Non-Intercourse system of the government. Failing of the reward he sought from the British ministry, Henry sold to President Madison for $50,000 his correspondence with the English officials, and these papers became known as the Henry documents. Madison submitted the letters to Congress and claimed that they proved a design on the part of England to annex the New England States. The evidence of the documents was not conclusive.

Henry Street Settlement. (See Social Settlements.)

Hepburn Law, money needed to enforce, 7190.

Hepburn vs. Griswold.—One of the Supreme Court cases involving the constitutionality of the issue of United States legal-tender notes. June 20, 1860, Mrs. Hepburn proposed to pay Mr. Griswold $11,250 on Feb. 20, 1862. At the time gold and silver only were legal tender. Feb. 25, 1862, the United States issued $150,000,000 of its own notes, to be received as lawful money in payment of all debts, public and private, within the United States. This was five days after the note became due. Mrs. Hepburn in March, 1864, after suit had been brought, tendered these notes in payment, and they were refused. The notes were then tendered and paid into court in Louisville, Ky. The Louisville court of chancery declared the debt absolved. The Kentucky court of errors and appeals reversed the chancellor's judgment, and the United States Supreme Court at the December term, 1867, affirmed the judgment of the court of errors and appeals. This ruling was afterwards reversed. (See Juilliard *vs.* Greenman.) Chief Justice Chase, in delivering the opinion of the court, said: "We can not doubt that a law not made in pursuance of an express power, which necessarily and in its direct operation impairs the obligation of contracts, is inconsistent with the spirit of the Constitution." "We are obliged to conclude," he continued, "that an act making mere promises to pay dollars in legal tender in payment of debts previously contracted * * * is inconsistent with the spirit of the Constitution, and that it is prohibited by the Constitution." Justices Miller, Swayne, and Davis dissented.

Hermitage, The.—The name given by Andrew Jackson to his home, situated about 10 miles from Nashville, Tenn., near the Cumberland River. At this place President Jackson died and is buried. The premises and a portion of his farm have become the property of the State of Tennessee and have been converted into a state home for aged, indigent or disabled ex-Confederate soldiers.

Hermitage, The, tendered to United States, 2954.

Appropriations for keeping in repair, asked, 7104.

Hero, The, seizure of, and claims arising out of, 4114, 5198, 5547, 5673, 5873, 5962.

Award in case, 6070.

Hesse, convention with, 2169, 2210.

Hesse-Cassel:

Convention with, 2297.

Treaty of, with France, 185.

Hesse, Electorate of, exequatur issued consuls of, revoked, 3709.

Hiatt & Co., relief of, draft of bill for, transmitted, 5119.

Hickey Plot.—A conspiracy headed by Thomas Hickey, one of Washington's Life Guards, to assassinate the general at New York in 1776. The plot was discovered. Hickey was hanged in June, 1776, and David Matthews, mayor of New York, was imprisoned for his connection with the affair; Governor Tryon was also suspected of complicity.

High License.—A term generally used to specify a high tax on the retail sellers of intoxicating liquors. The objects of high license are to increase the price of liquor to some extent, so as to limit its consumption and place its sale on a more respectable basis, and to collect large sums of money for public purposes. Several states have passed high-license laws, and some communities have in addition placed local restrictions on the traffic in intoxicants.

Higher Law.—William H. Seward, while making an anti-slavery speech in the United States Senate March 11, 1850, in referring to the moral law, declared: "There is a higher law than the Constitution."

Highlander, The, watch to be presented to commander of, by British privy council for services rendered, 3400.

Highwayman. (See Bandit.)

Highways. (See Transcontinental Highways.)

Historians, value of opinions of, 7997.

Hobkirks Hill (S. C.), Battle of.—April 25, 1781, Lord Rawdon, with about 950 British, made a sudden attack on the Americans under Greene at Hobkirks Hill, two miles north of Camden, S. C. The American force consisted of 1,446 men. Greene was defeated, but both armies withdrew from the field. The British lost 258 in killed, wounded and missing. The total casualties on the American side were 271.

Hockaday & Leggit, act for relief of, vetoed, 3201.

Holding Companies, should be prohibited, 7917.

Holidays, Legal.—There is no national holiday, not even the Fourth of July. Congress has at various times appointed special holidays. In the second session of the Fifty-third Congress it passed an act making Labor Day a public holiday in the District of Columbia, and it has recognized the existence of certain days as holidays for commercial purposes, but, with the exception named, there is no general statute on the subject. The proclamation of the president designating a day of Thanksgiving only makes it a legal holiday in the District of Columbia and the territories.

Every Saturday after 12 o'clock noon is a legal holiday in California in public offices, Illinois (in cities of 200,000 or more inhabitants), Maryland, Michigan, New York, New Jersey, Ohio, Pennsylvania, Rhode Island, Virginia, the District of Columbia (for banking purposes), and in New Orleans, La., and Charleston, S. C.; in Louisiana in all cities exceeding 10,000 inhabitants; in Missouri in cities of 100,000 or more inhabitants; in Tennessee, for state and county officers, and in Colorado during June, July and August; in Indiana, first Saturday in June to last Saturday in October, inclusive, for all public offices in counties having a county-seat of 100,000 population or more; in New Hampshire in state offices.

There are no statutory holidays in Mississippi, but by common consent the Fourth of July, Thanksgiving and Christmas are observed. In New Mexico, Washington's Birthday, Decoration Day, Labor Day, Flag Day (June 14) and Arbor Day are holidays when so designated by the Governor. In South Carolina, Thursday of Fair Week is a legal holiday.

Arbor Day (*q. v.*) is a legal holiday in many states, although in some it is observed as designated by the Governor.

Jan. 1st, New Year's Day.—In all states (including District of Columbia, Porto Rico and Alaska), except Arkansas and Massachusetts. (In Maine a bank holiday only legally.)

Jan. 8th, Anniversary of the Battle of New Orleans.—In Louisiana.

Jan. 19th, Lee's Birthday.—In Florida, Georgia, North Carolina, South Carolina, Virginia, Alabama, Mississippi and Arkansas.

Mardi-Gras.—In the parish of Orleans, Louisiana.

Feb. 12th, Georgia Day.—In Georgia.

Feb. 12th, Lincoln's Birthday.—In California, Colorado, Connecticut, Delaware, Illinois, Iowa, Indiana, Kansas, Michigan, Minnesota, Montana, Nevada, New Jersey, New York, North Dakota, Oregon, Pennsylvania, South Dakota, Utah, Washington, West Virginia and Wyoming.

Feb. 22d, Washington's Birthday.—In all the states, District of Columbia, Porto Rico and Alaska.

Mardi-Gras Day, Shrove Tuesday.—In Alabama and Florida (in counties having a carnival).

March, First Wednesday prior to Spring election at which Circuit Judges are elected and in counties and cities where offices are filled at Spring election in Michigan.

March (Third Tuesday), Primary Election Day.—(Every Presidential year) in North Dakota.

March 2d, Anniversary of Texan Independence.—In Texas.

March 4th, Inauguration Day.—In District of Columbia in years when a President of the United States is inaugurated.

March 22d, Emancipation Day.—In Porto Rico.

April (First Monday in 1916 and every four years thereafter), Presidential Primary.—In Michigan.

Good Friday—In Alabama, Connecticut, Delaware, Florida, Louisiana, Maryland, Minnesota, New Jersey, Pennsylvania, Porto Rico, Tennessee.

April 12th, Halifax Independence Resolutions.—In North Carolina.

April 13th, Thomas Jefferson's Birthday. —In Alabama.

April 19th, Patriots' Day.—In Maine and Massachusetts.

April 21st, Anniversary of the Battle of San Jacinto.—In Texas.

April 26th, Confederate Memorial Day.— In Alabama, Florida, Georgia and Mississippi.

May 10th, Confederate Memorial Day.— In North Carolina and South Carolina.

May (Second Friday), Confederate Day.— In Tennessee.

May 20th, Anniversary of the Signing of the Mecklenburg Declaration of Independence.—In North Carolina.

May 30th, Decoration Day.—In all the states (and District of Columbia, Porto Rico and Alaska) except Arkansas, Florida, Georgia, Louisiana, Mississippi, North Carolina, South Carolina and Texas.

June 3d, Jefferson Davis's Birthday.—In Florida, Georgia, Alabama, Mississippi, Texas, Arkansas and South Carolina. In Louisiana, known as "Confederate Memorial Day." In Virginia, in public schools.

June 11th, Kamehameha Day.—In Hawaii.

June 15th, Pioneer Day.—In Idaho.

June (Last Wednesday), Primary Election Day.—In North Dakota.

July 4th, Independence Day.—In all the states, and District of Columbia, Porto Rico and Alaska.

July 10th, Admission Day.—In Wyoming.

July 24th, Pioneers' Day.—In Utah.

July 25th, Landing of American Troops. —Porto Rico.

July (Fourth Saturday), Primary Election Day.—In Texas.

August, Primary Election Day.—In Missouri. In Michigan (last Tuesday in August preceding every general November election).

Aug. 1st, Colorado Day.—In Colorado.

Aug. 16th, Bennington Battle Day.— In Vermont.

Sept. (First Monday), Labor Day.— in all the states (and District of Columbia and Alaska). In Louisiana, observed in Orleans Parish.

Sept., Primary Election Day.—In Wisconsin, First Tuesday. In Oregon, even years.

Sept. (Third Saturday), Regatta Day.— In Territory of Hawaii.

Sept. 9th, Admission Day.—In California.

Sept. 12th, "Old Defenders' Day."—In Baltimore, Md.

Sept. (Second Monday), Election Day.— In Arkansas, Maine.

Oct. 12th, Columbus Day.—In Alabama, Arkansas, California, Colorado, Connecticut, Delaware, Idaho, Illinois, Indiana, Kansas, Kentucky, Maine, Maryland, Massachusetts, Michigan, Missouri, Montana, Nebraska, Nevada, New Hampshire, New Jersey, New Mexico, New York, Ohio, Oklahoma, Pennsylvania, Rhode Island, Vermont, Washington.

Oct. 18th, Alaska Day.—In Alaska.

Oct. 31st, Admission Day.—In Nevada.

Nov. 1st, All Saints' Day.—In Louisiana.

Nov. (first Friday), Pioneer Day.—In Montana, observed in public schools.

Nov. Gen. Election (1st Tuesday). In Alabama, Alaska, Arizona, California, Colorado, Delaware, Florida, Idaho, Illinois, Indiana, Iowa, Louisiana, Maine, Maryland, Michigan, Minnesota, Missouri, Montana, Nevada, New Hampshire, New Jersey, New Mexico, New York, North Carolina, North Dakota, Ohio (from 5.30 A. M. to 9 A. M. only), Oklahoma, Oregon, Pennsylvania, Rhode Island (biennially in even years), South Carolina, South Dakota, Tennessee, Texas, Virginia, Washington, West Virginia, Wisconsin and Wyoming, in the years when elections are held therein. In 1914 in states holding such elections the date is November 3d.

Nov. 26, 1914, Thanksgiving Day (usually the last Thursday in November).—Is observed in all the states, and in the District of Columbia, Porto Rico and Alaska, though in some states it is not a statutory holiday.

Dec. 25th, Christmas Day.—In all the states and District of Columbia, Porto Rico and Alaska.

Holland. (See Netherlands.)

Holland Company, treaty of, with Seneca Indians, 335.

Holland Patent.—A grant of land made in 1686 by Governor Dongan, of New York, to 6 Dutch patentees. The land was situated in what is now Orange County, N. Y., and was to be held in free and common socage of King James II.

Holstein-Schleswig War referred to, 2548.

Holston, Treaty of, referred to, 118.

Home Department.—A name given for a time to the office of Foreign Affairs (see Foreign Affairs, Sec. of) which afterward developed into the State Department. The term Home Department was also given for a time to the Interior Department (q. v.).

Home Rule for Ireland.—The term "Home Rule" was composed and first applied to the struggle for Irish freedom in the year 1873, although Irish nationalists had been blazing the trail towards Irish independence for some years previous to that date. The legislative union of Ireland with Great Britain dates from July, 1800, and for some time afterwards the social condition of the masses in one country was probably as bad as that of the masses in the other. The great reform measures inaugurated in England in 1832 were reflected but slightly in

Ireland, however, as the economic situations of the two countries were becoming more and more dissimilar. The misery of the Irish people, and the inadequacy of the measures proposed for their relief from London finally gave rise to a feeling in Ireland that she alone was able and ethically justified to work out her own salvation, and that hence the legislative union with Great Britain should be abrogated. In the forties this feeling developed under the leadership of Daniel O'Connell, who obtained many followers but no success. An open rebellion broke out in 1848, but was soon quelled. For the next twenty years there was little open trouble, although the fires were smouldering under the surface, and considerable disturbance was created by the Fenians (q. v.), an organization of Irish nationalists organized in America.

In 1868 London began attempts to legislate understandingly concerning the Irish question, and Prime Minister Gladstone disestablished and disendowed the Anglican Church in Ireland in that year. In 1870, the disturbances throughout Ireland became particularly severe, and Gladstone carried through Parliament his so-called "three F" measures—providing for Fair Rent, Fixity of Tenure, and Free Sale. In 1878 Charles Stewart Parnell became the leader of the Irish nationalists; and London was showing greater interest in co-operating to remedy conditions in Ireland when the assassination of Lord Cavendish brought on severe repressive measures. Cavendish, chief secretary for Ireland, was stabbed to death, along with a deeply-hated subordinate, in Phoenix Park, Dublin, on May 6, 1882. For this crime, five men were hanged, three sentenced to life imprisonment, and others received jail terms of various length. The Irish nationalist who turned state's evidence at the trial was later murdered in South Africa, and his assassin in turn was brought to London and hanged for the crime. Nevertheless, the Irish Nationalist party became stronger and stronger, and in 1885 finally achieved the balance of power in the House of Commons. It was on April 6, 1886, that Gladstone made his momentous announcement that he had been converted to Home Rule, and introduced his Home Rule Bill, thereby disrupting the old Liberal Party, only to have the bill itself defeated on June 7, 1886. In 1898, Gladstone for a second time introduced a Home Rule measure into Parliament, and carried it successfully through the House of Commons, only to see it defeated in the House of Lords.

The third and successful Home Rule Bill was introduced into Parliament by Premier Asquith in April, 1912. The House of Lords defeated the Bill in January, 1913, but Asquith held an advantage which Gladstone did not enjoy. For in the years between 1898 and 1913, the veto power of the House of Lords had been curbed; and the Bill became law without the consent of the House of Lords on its third passage through the House of Commons on March 5, 1914, by a vote of 351 to 274. The Bill differs in about important features from Gladstone's proposals. It creates an Irish Parliament of 164 members, with a House of Lords to be nominated. However, the Lord Lieutenant of Ireland has the power to veto any legislation or to refer it for approval to the English Parliament. Forty-two Irish members are given seats in the English Parliament, with full power to vote upon all questions. Disputes concerning the measures and applications of the Bill are to be decided by a Joint Exchequer Board, consisting of two members from Ireland, two from Great Britain, and of a chairman to be appointed by the King. Broadly, the Irish Parliament

is given the power to legislate upon all questions except those which do not pertain to Ireland; except certain specific questions reserved for treatment exclusively by the Imperial government; and except treason and foreign treaty regulations. The Irish Parliament is also forbidden to establish, endow, or to make preferential regulations concerning any religion; nor may it veto any legislation on an Irish problem passed by the Imperial Parliament. The Irish Parliament is also without the power to legislate upon land purchase, tax collection, and public loans. Right to deal with old age pensions, labor exchanges and various schemes for government insurance was withheld until 1915; right to deal with the police laws until 1918; and the right to deal with savings banks and friendly societies until 1922. The Imperial Government is to collect all the Irish revenue, returning, however, the sum needed for administration under the Irish Parliament. The Irish Parliament, on the other hand, may levy taxes of its own, and is given the administration of the Irish customs; but the receipts on any increase of taxes of more than 10% must be turned over to the Imperial Government.

Delay in the application of the Bill has been due to the opposition of Ulster County. Unlike the remainder of Ireland, Ulster is almost entirely industrial and Protestant, and objects to being controlled by the agrarian and Catholic Irish majority. In September, 1912, under the leadership of Sir Edward Carson, a solemn pledge was signed in Ulster to refuse to abide by the authority of any act establishing Home Rule. Ulster raised a volunteer army which was reliably reported to number at least 100,000 men, and the army was recruited and drilled with the greatest care. A provisional government was planned, arms and ammunition were extensively imported, and other preparations for civil war were made, of so serious a nature that the Government delayed its application of Home Rule. On July 26, 1914, a serious struggle broke out in the streets of Dublin, concerning the smuggling of some arms into Ireland for revolutionary purposes, and the proximity of this date to August 1, 1914, the date on which the Great European War broke out, is often commented upon. On April 20-25, 1916, a revolt in Dublin disclosed extensive preparations to establish Irish independence by force, and its leader, Sir Roger Casement, was executed for treason on August 2 of the same year. Interest in Home Rule in the United States has not been confined to Americans of Irish birth or descent, and shortly after the entrance of the United States into the great European struggle on April 6, 1917, a petition signed by more than two hundred members of Congress was dispatched to our new ally, England, respectfully requesting her to establish Home Rule without further delay. (See section Ireland under British Empire.)

On May 17, 1917, Premier Lloyd-George announced that he had submitted to the Irish Nationalists proposals for the immediate application of Home Rule, with the exclusion of Ulster. This exclusion would be reconsidered by Parliament after a space of five years. In the meantime, control of all Ireland would be vested in a Council of Ireland, consisting of two delegations equal in number from the nationalist and the excluded areas. This proposal meeting with little favor, the Premier called a general Irish convention, representing all factions, to suggest solutions of the Irish problem.

The convention sat continuously for eight months, from July 25, 1917, under the presidency of Sir Horace Plunkett, making its report finally on April 12, 1918, three days after Premier Lloyd-George had announced that the Government proposed to extend conscription for the war against Germany to Ireland, and one day before the bill to that effect passed the House of Commons. The Sinn Fein (q. v.) element refused to be represented in the convention, which finally consisted of seventy-seven delegates, representing chiefly the Nationalists, Ulster Unionists, Southern Nationalists and Laborites. The report of the convention was adopted by a vote of 44 to 29, which Premier Lloyd-George declared to be too small a majority to justify his acceptance of the report. When the question of conscription was brought before the convention, it decided, by a vote of 54 to 17, that conscription in Ireland would be impracticable except with the consent of an Irish Parliament.

The letter of Sir Horace Plunkett transmitting the report of the convention revealed the following facts concerning it:

The majority of the Nationalists, all the Southern Unionists, and five of the seven Labor delegates endorsed the final proposals of the convention for Home Rule (see below). The scheme of the minority of the Nationalists differed from the scheme of the majority in only one important proposal. Therefore "the convention laid a foundation for an Irish agreement unprecedented in history." "The difficulties of the Irish Convention may be summed up in two words, 'Ulster' and 'Customs'."

The Ulsterites in a separate statement denied that the convention had laid the basis for a settlement of the Irish question and that unanimity had ever been in sight.

The chief features of the proposals favored by the majority of the convention were as follows, the figures in brackets indicating the votes by which they were favored:

(1) The Irish Parliament to consist of the King, Senate and House of Commons. The supreme power of the Imperial Parliament nevertheless to remain unaffected and undiminished over all persons, matters and things in Ireland and every part thereof. (51-18)

(2) The Irish Parliament to have general powers to make laws for peace, order and good government in Ireland. (51-19)

(3) The Irish Parliament to have no power to make laws on the following subjects: Crown and succession; peace and war; army and navy; treaties and foreign relations; dignities and titles of honor; control of harbors necessary for military and naval purposes; coinage, weights, measures, copyrights, patents. Subject to the imperial exigencies, the Imperial and the Irish Parliaments jointly to arrange for the unified control of the Irish police and postal services during the war with Germany, the administration of these two services to become subject to the Irish Parliament only, after the cessation of hostilities. (49-16)

(4) The following restrictions on the power of the Irish Parliament to be made: Prohibition of laws interfering with religious equality; Special provisions protecting the position of Freemasons; . . . . Money bills to be founded only on a vice-regal message; Privileges and qualifications of the members to be the same as those of the bill of 1914 (see above); Rights of existing Irish officers to be safeguarded. (46-15)

(6) Executive power in Ireland to remain in the King, to be exercised through the Lord Lieutenant, on the advice of an Irish executive committee. (45-15)

(9) The Senate to be constituted as follows: Lord Chancellor; 4 Roman Catholic Bishops; 2 Church of Ireland Bishops; Representative of the General Assembly; 3 Lord Mayors of Dublin, Belfast, Cork; 15 peers resident in Ireland, to be elected by peers resident in Ireland; 11 persons selected by the Lord Lieutenant; 15 representatives of commerce and industry; 4 representatives of labor, one from each province; 8 representatives of the county councils. Total, 64. (48-19)

(10) Ordinary personnel of the House of Commons to be 160. National University and Universities of Dublin and Belfast to have 2 members each, to be elected by the graduates. Principle of proportional representation to be followed wherever constituency returns two or three members; special representation for urban and industrial centres by applying to them a smaller electoral quota than to the remainder of the country. Forty per cent of the membership to be guaranteed to the Unionists—in pursuance of this plan, the Lord Lieutenant to nominate 20 members to represent interests not otherwise adequately represented in the provinces of Leinster, Munster and Connaught, and 20 additional members to be elected by Ulster to represent commercial, industrial and agricultural interests—but the nominated membership to disappear wholly or partly after 15 years. Extra Ulster representation not to cease except on the decision of a three-fourths majority of both houses sitting together. The House of Commons to continue for five years, unless previously dissolved. (45-20)

(11) Money bills to originate only in the House of Commons, not amendable by the Senate. (45-22)

(12) Disagreement between the Houses to be solved by joint sitting. (45-22)

(13) Representation in the British Parliament to continue unchanged. (44-22)

(14) Finance and exchequer as in act of 1914 (see above). (44-22)

(15) Control of excise and customs by the Irish Parliament to be postponed for further consideration within 7 years after the war. Until then the United Kingdom's Board of Excise and Customs to include persons nominated by the Irish Treasury. A joint exchequer board to be set up to determine the real income of Ireland, and the revenue due to Ireland, as found by this board, to be paid into the Irish Exchequer. All other branches of taxation to be under the Irish Parliament. (38-30)

(20) General civil service requirements to be applied to all holding public service positions. (42-18)

(22) This report to be submitted to the Imperial Government. (42-35)

Other provisions than those noted above generally re-affirm proposals in the act of 1914.

In May, 1918, the Lloyd-George Government of Great Britain announced that the Allied reverses in the European War compelled the Government to advocate a policy of conscription in Ireland, and despite opposition on the part of Nationalists and Sinn Fein, supported by many Liberals, Parliament passed a bill granting the Government's request. This action immediately brought to a head discontent in Ireland, and resistance was openly preached. A number of Sinn Fein leaders were arrested and confined in the Tower of London on the charge of having conspired with Germany; but although the Government published evidence in support of such charges (evidence which the Irish ridiculed as inconclusive), it announced that it would not proceed against the prisoners for treason.

So bitter was the opposition, not only in Great Britain and Ireland, but also in the United States, to Irish conscription that there was little doubt that such a policy would be carried into effect only by force of arms, and after civil war on a large scale. Accordingly, the Government announced that it would postpone conscription pending another recourse to voluntary enlistments; but this policy also proved ineffectual, and on June 23, 1918, Lloyd-George announced that the Government had decided not to go ahead with either conscription or Home Rule in Ireland.

Home Squadron, proposed extension of duties of, referred to, 2129.

Homestead-Exemption Laws. — Legislation enacted by most of the states to secure a home and shelter for a family or individual by exempting, under certain conditions, the residence occupied by the family or individual from liability to be sold for the debts of its owner and by restricting his right of free alienation. The purpose of the homestead-exemption laws are to protect the family, secure to it a home, and to provide against its members being deprived thereof by misfortune, improvidence, or incapacity of the head of the family. These laws exist in nearly all the states, varying in their terms and limitations. In 15 states homestead-exemption is part of the constitution.

Homestead Law.—A law enacted by Congress May 20, 1862. It provided that any citizen might, upon payment of the nominal fee of $5 or $10, enter upon and hold any unappropriated quarter section of the public lands valued at $1.25 per acre or any one-eighth section valued at $2.50 per acre, and after 5 years' residence become the sole owner. This measure proved of great value in settling the lands of the West.

Homestead Lands. (See Lands, Homestead.)

Homestead Laws (see also Lands, Public, opened to settlement):

Act—
    Granting Indians privileges of, recommended, 4428, 4528.
    In relation to proof required in homestead entries vetoed, 4383.
    To secure homesteads to settlers on public domain vetoed, 3139.
Amendment of, recommended, 5107.
Bill to allow Indian homestead entries referred to, 4783.
Confirmation of entries in Michigan referred to, 4665.
Discussed, 3560, 3651, 5484.
Working of, in the West, 6725.

Home-builders, public lands for, 6725, 6800.

Honduras.—Honduras is the middle state of Central America, between 13° 10′-16° N. lat. and 83° 10′-88° 40′ W. long., bounded on the south by Salvador, on the east by Nicaragua, and on the west by Guatemala.

Physical Features and Climate.—Close to the southern boundary an eastern arm of the Sierra Madre traverses the republic from west to east with heights of 10,000 feet, and along the Atlantic coast the Sierra de Pija rises to a considerable height. The rest of the country is generally mountainous, with intervening plains, of which the plains of Comayagua and Plancho are the most considerable. The largest rivers on the Atlantic side are the Ulua, the Chamel-

econ, the Roman, the Negro, and the Aguan. Into the Pacific flow the Goascoran, the Nacome and the Choluteca. The wet season lasts from May to November and the climate of the lowlands of the Atlantic coast is oppressive, but the elevated plateaus of the interior are salubrious and temperate.

History.—Christopher Columbus landed at Cape Honduras in 1502, and in 1524 the country was settled by the Spaniards. In 1525 Hernando Cortes founded the city of Puerto Cortes, and from 1539 to 1821 the country formed part of the Captaincy-General of Guatemala. The republic was part of the Confederation of Central America from 1821 to 1839, but since that date has been independent. Politically the country is divided into seventeen departments.

Government.—The Constitution rests upon a charter proclaimed in October, 1894, and re-invoked in September, 1907. The Government is that of a centralized republic, with a President elected for 4 years by the direct vote of all male subjects of 21 years (or married citizens of 18 who can read and write). The President is eligible for one successive term. President of the Republic (1913), Dr. Don Francisco Bertrand.

The President is aided by six Secretaries of State.

Congress consists of one house of 42 deputies, elected for 4 years by universal adult male suffrage.

The Supreme Court at the capital consists of five judges elected by the people, and there are four Courts of Appeal.

Army and Navy.—Service in the Army is universal and compulsory between the ages of 21 and 35, with a further liability of 5 years in the Reserve. The permanent force is limited to about 2,000 of all ranks, the effective war strength exceeding 50,000.

The Navy consists of the armed cutter General Barahona.

Area and Ethnography.—The area of the republic is given as 42,658 square miles, with a population of 553,500 as ascertained by the last census. Politically the country is divided into seventeen departments. The aboriginal Indians include Xicagues and Poyas in the eastern districts and Caribs in the coastal regions of the north and in the Bay Islands, where they were transported from the British Island of St. Vincent at the end of the eighteenth century. The most numerous element is the Spanish-speaking half-caste or mestizo, while in the Mosquitia district are the mixed Indian-negroes, known as Sambos.

Production and Industry.—The principal agricultural products are bananas, coconuts, coffee, indigo and tobacco, while cereals, rubber, sugar and cocoa are also grown. The forest products include mahogany and other cabinet woods, and dye woods. The republic contains great mineral wealth. Gold and silver are produced, and platinum, copper, lead, antimony, nickel, iron and coal, and nitrate deposits are believed to be fairly plentiful and await development. Almost all the common necessaries of life are imported, including provisions, textiles and metal, and hardware, the only local industries being the plaiting of straw hats, distilling, and brick making.

In 1914, cattle numbered 489,185, grazing being an important item in the country's enterprises. The banana crop in 1915 was 6,070,000 bunches. The only important manufactures are Panama hats and cigars.

Education.—Primary education is free, secular and compulsory, and there are schools in every centre. Ability to read and write is the qualification for the franchise. There are Government secondary schools and training colleges in each department, a school of jurisprudence at Comayagua, and a central institute and university at the capital.

In 1916, there were 865 primary schools, 1,083 teachers and 38,000 pupils.

Finance.—The expenditures keep nearly even pace with the revenues, which average about 4,500,000 pesos annually. There is a foreign public debt of 64,800,000 pesos ($1,620,000), upon which interest has not been paid since 1872. The peso is equal to about $0.40 United States money.

Most of the trade is with the United States, the imports generally exceeding the exports. The principal export is bananas, others being coconuts, coffee, hides, rubber and timber ; the imports are principally textiles, with metal and hardware, and provisions. The capital is Tegucigalpa and there are some half a dozen towns with a population in excess of 10,000.

In 1915, imports amounted to $5,874,780 and exports to $3,858,857. Imports from the United States amounted to $5,177,000 and exports to the United States to $2,987,-000.

Honduras:

American bankers fund debt of, and finance railways in, 7500.

Diplomatic relations with, discussed, 5468.

Fugitive criminals, convention with, for surrender of, 4161, 4210.

Imprisonment of American citizens by, 5825.

Postal convention with, 5377.

Refusal of, to receive American commercial agent, 2917.

Report of Thomas C. Reynolds on condition and commerce of, transmitted, 5116.

Ruatan Island, convention of, with Great Britain regarding, 2955.

Tariff laws of, evidence of modifications of, proclaimed, 5714.

Discussed, 5747.

Treaty of, with Great Britain referred to, 3170.

Treaty with, transmitted and discussed, 3116, 3458, 4161, 4210.

Regarding Honduras Interoceanic Railway, 3116.

Vessels of United States—

Fired upon by authorities of, and disavowal of act by, discussed, 5869.

Seized and used by insurgents in, questions regarding, 5869.

Honduras and Nicaragua Treaties proposed by President Taft, 7663.

Honduras, Treaties with.—A treaty of friendship, commerce, and navigation of 1864 provides for freedom of commerce, except in the coasting trade, with the customary immunity from higher, other, or discriminating duties, charges, or restrictions. The importation and exportation of goods is conducted upon equal terms by vessels of either nationality. Citizens are protected in all conditions, and under all circumstances have the same rights and privileges as those of the dominions of each of the parties at home. In case of death of a citizen of one country residing in the other the administration of his estate and the protection of his property may be conducted by consular authorities. Privileges in the use of the Honduras Interoceanic Railway are accorded to the United States by this treaty.

A naturalization treaty was signed in June, 1908, and an extradition convention in 1909. Honduras also became a party to the convention between the United States and the several republics of South and Central America for the arbitration of pecuniary claim and the protection of inventions, etc., which was signed in Buenos Aires in 1910 and proclaimed in Washington, July 29, 1914. (See South and Central America, Treaties with.)

"Honest Abe."—A nickname given to Abraham Lincoln.

Hongkong, consulate at, referred to, 4534.

Honolulu Harbor, dredging needed for, 6921.

Hoosier State.—A nickname for Indiana (q. v.). (See also States.)

Hoover, Herbert C., qualifications of, for position of food administrator, 8263.

Hops.—The hop plant can be grown generally throughout the United States, but up to the present its production in commercial quantities has been confined to California, Oregon, New York and Washington. American hops find ready sale in England, where the consumption is about 66,-000,000 pounds annually against a production of 36,000,000 pounds. A machine has been invented which is capable of picking 60,000 pounds of hops a day. For 1909, when the latest computation was made by the Department of Commerce and Labor, there were 44,693 acres in hops in the United States. The yield was 40,718,748 pounds, valued at $7,844,744, an increase of 92 per cent. in ten years.

In 1915, the acreage of hops was 44,700 ; the yield, 52,986,000 pounds ; the value, 11.7 cents per pound, for a total of $6,203,-000. In 1916, the corresponding figures were 43,900 acres, 50,537,000 pounds and 12 cents, $6,071,000. California produced 112,000 bales, Oregon, 90,000 bales and Washington, 28,000 bales, the crop in New York falling to 10,000 bales. (A bale contains 200 pounds.) In 1917, the figures were 29,900 acres, 27,788,000 pounds, 33.7 cents and $9,363,000.

Hornet, The.—An American sloop of war carrying 18 guns, commanded by Capt. Lawrence during the War of 1812. Feb. 24, 1813, near the mouth of the Demerara River, she attacked the British brig *Peacock*, of 18 guns. The *Peacock* was soon in a sinking condition, and struck her colors. Before the wounded could be removed she went down, carrying with her 9 British and 3 American seamen. March 23, 1815, off the Cape of Good Hope, the *Hornet* captured and sunk the British brig *Penguin*, also of 18 guns, the latter losing her commander in the engagement. Shortly after the battle the *Hornet* was chased by the British frigate

Cornwallis, 74 guns, and only escaped capture by throwing her guns and heavy stores overboard.

Hornet, The, British sloop of war destroyed by, 513.

Horse Shoe Bend (Ala.), Battle of.— When Gen. Jackson was informed of the arrival of Creeks in considerable numbers in Tallapoosa County he resolved to strike a decisive blow. He sent his stores down the Coosa River from Fort Strother in flatboats and marched his army against the gathering Indians. March 27, 1814, with 2,000 effective men, he halted within a few miles of the breastworks at the Horse Shoe Bend of the Tallapoosa River, where 1,200 Indians (one-fourth of whom were women and children) had entrenched themselves with an ample supply of food. The whites and their Indian allies soon surrounded the camp. The Indians fought desperately. They were attacked in front with bayonet and ball, and the torch was applied to their camp in the rear. The battle lasted all day, and in the evening 557 Creek warriors were dead in the little peninsula and some 200 more were killed while trying to escape. The loss to the whites was 32 killed and 99 wounded. The Cherokees lost 18 killed and 36 wounded. Some 300 women and children were taken prisoners. The spirit of the Indians was broken by this battle. Weathersford, the chief, appeared personally before Gen. Jackson and offered to surrender. He was permitted to go free and counsel peace among his dejected followers.

Horticultural Board.—A federal board under the jurisdiction of the Department of Agriculture which has charge of the administration of the laws for inspection and quarantine of diseased or infested plants. On August 20, 1912, Congress passed an act to regulate the importation of nursery stock and to maintain quarantine districts. The board is appointed from the bureaus of Entomology and Plant Industry and the Forest Service of the Department of Agriculture and representatives of the State, Treasury and Post-Office departments, and horticultural inspectors of the several states.

Four foreign quarantines have been promulgated by the board, viz: Against the white pine blister rust of Europe and Asia, the potato wart of portions of Canada and several European countries, the Mexican fruit fly, and the pink boll cotton worm of Egypt.

Four domestic quarantines have also been promulgated by the board, viz: against the Mediterranean fruit fly in Hawaii, the gypsy and brown-tail moths in New England, date palm scale insects in Arizona, California and Texas, and the pink boll cotton worm in Hawaii.

Hosiery and Knit Goods.—The art of knitting is said to have been invented in Scotland in the fifteenth century and to have found its way from there to France where it became a recognized industry. In 1589 William Lee, of Nottingham, England, invented a knitting frame, which entirely altered the knitting trade, and developed a business which has ever since been an important feeder to the commerce of Great Britain. An apparatus for ribbing was invented by Jedediah Strutt in 1758. The circular knitting machine was invented in 1816, but it did not meet with much success until 1847, since which time it has received many improvements, chief of which was the tumbler or latch needle invented by Townsend in 1858. Two Americans, W. C. Gist and Almet Reid, by their ge-

nius added to the practical value of the knitting machine. Nottingham and Leicester are the centers of the industry in England, while in America, Pennsylvania, New York and Massachusetts lead in production.

The growth of the business in the United States has been remarkable. In 1850 there were only eighty-five establishments, with a combined capital of $554,734, and an aggregate annual output worth $1,028,102.

There were in 1909, 1,374 establishments in which 136,130 persons were engaged, of whom 129,275 were wage-earners. The amount paid in salaries and wages was $52,431,680. The value of the products was $200,143,527; the cost of materials $110,241,053, equivalent to 55.1 per cent of the value of the products; and the value added by manufacture was $89,902,474. During the preceding ten years the business more than doubled, and prices materially advanced.

Returns were received by the Department of Commerce from 1,647 establishments engaged in the manufacture of hosiery and knit goods in 1914 the products of which were valued at $263,925,855.

As to the distribution of the industry, Pennsylvania led with 464 establishments, employing an average of 38,206 wage-earners, and making goods to the value of $49,657,506; New York, with 360 establishments and 35,950 employees, turned out finished goods to the value of $67,130,-296; Massachusetts made $14,736,025 worth of goods in 65 factories with the aid of less than 10,000 employees. No other state comes anywhere near these in the value of output. Of the total numbers given, 30 establishments in 1914, with products valued at $5,042,856, were engaged primarily in the manufacture of other products, such as cotton, silk, or woolen goods, men's clothing, etc., and made hosiery and knit goods only as subsidiary products.

In the underwear industry the United States excels the world. More machine made knitted goods are turned out annually here than in all other countries combined. Our people wear more underwear than other people. They are not only obliged to wear more for climatic reasons, but they can afford to wear more, and the general desire for personal comfort in wearing apparel results in an enormous distribution of the products of these mills. The beginnings of the industry are well within the lifetime of many manufacturers still living. The total value of underwear manufactured in 1914 was $93,153,515.

Until 1832 the knitting of socks and stockings remained mostly a household industry—the only form of textile work which the machine had not wrested from the housewife. In that year Egbert Egberts successfully applied the principal of knitting by power at Cohoes, N. Y. His machine was simply the square stocking frame of William Lee adapted to power. From that adaptation dates a revolution in underwear, which had previously consisted wholly of flannel, fashioned and sewed at home, according to the individual needs. The revolution gathered momentum gradually, as invention after invention—almost all of American origin—perfected the knitting machine: but once the new industry was fairly and firmly established it spread with amazing rapidity. In the decade between 1880 and 1890 the number of knit goods mills doubled, and the value of the annual product jumped from $29,167,227 to $67,241,013.

The production of hosiery in 1914 amounted to 75,227,704 dozen pairs, valued at $98,136,265. The output of sweaters increased from 2,221,410, valued at $22,430,-817, in 1909, to 2,249,142, valued at $26,195,002, in 1914. Of hoods, scarfs, etc., the production in 1914 amounted to 987,178 dozen, valued at $3,456,326.

The great variety of goods made facilitates the tendency, peculiar to this industry, toward the building of comparatively small mills, requiring but moderate capital; and it happens in consequence that these mills spring up all over the country, and can now be found in thirty-eight of the forty-eight states. Many of them employ only cotton as a raw material; others use chiefly wool; and still others manufacture what are known as merino knit or mixed goods—cotton mixed with wool in proportions varying from fifty to seventy-five and ninety per cent. of cotton, according to the particular market sought. The tendency to the larger use of cotton in these goods is perceptible not necessarily because of greater cheapness or a desire to adulterate, but because of the liability of wool to shrink, and its excessive warmth, lead many to prefer undergarments in which cotton is an equal or predominating material. In 1858 E. E. Kilbourne invented a machine for automatically knitting full fashioned underwear, and this machine has gradually wrought a second revolution in the industry. The amount of hand labor now done is reduced to the minimum—to the mere sewing on of buttons, so to speak.

In 1909 the total number of knitting machines reported by establishments in the industry was 115,019, as against 69,047 in 1899, an increase of 45,972, or 66.6 per cent. Over 96 per cent. of all the knitting machines in 1909 were power machines. There was an increase of 3,167, or 21.8 per cent. in the number of spring beard needle machines between 1899 and 1909. Latch needle machines constituted 84.6 per cent. of the total number of machines in 1909. Circular hosiery automatic machines formed 80.7 per cent. of the total number in 1909.

Location of Establishments.—Of the 1,647 establishments reported for 1914, 1,325, or over 80 per cent, were located in the 7 states of Pennsylvania, New York, Massachusetts, North Carolina, Wisconsin, New Jersey, and Illinois, in the order in which named. In 1909 these states reported 1,112 establishments—about the same proportion as in 1914. The remaining 322 establishments in 1914 were distributed among 27 states, the number in each ranging from 1 each in 6 states to 39 in Ohio. In 1914 Pennsylvania and New York together reported 989 establishments, as compared with 837 in 1909. Of the 152 new factories shown for the later year, 123 were located in New York.

Hospitals. (See Marine Hospitals.)

Hostage.—A person held by the enemy, with or without his consent, as a means of enforcing the fulfillment of a promise or compelling the performance of an involuntary act.

Hot Springs, exploration party ascends Washita River, 387.

Hot Springs Commission discussed, 4456.

Hot Springs Reservation, Ark. (see also Parks, National):
Appropriation for improvement of, recommended, 4661.

Bath houses and bath-house sites at, granting leases of, referred to, 4787.
Condition, occupancy, and area of, referred to, 3665.
Payment of damages to persons in recommended, 4668.

Hough, Judge, opinion cited in anti-trust decision, 7131.

Hours of Labor:
Referred to, 6348.
Uniform course regarding, recommended, 1819.
Wages of Government employees not to be affected by reduction in, proclaimed, 3969, 4129.

House of Representatives.—The lower house of the Congress of the United States. The Constitution provides (Article I., sections 1 and 2) that "all legislative powers herein granted shall be vested in a Congress of the United States, which shall consist of a Senate and House of Representatives. The House of Representatives shall be composed of members chosen every second year by the people of the several states. * * * No person shall be a representative who shall not have attained to the age of twenty-five years and been seven years a citizen of the United States, and who shall not, when elected, be an inhabitant of that state in which he shall be chosen." Members of the House of Representatives are apportioned among the several states according to population as shown at each decennial census, and are elected by a direct vote of the people in Congressional districts fixed by state law. The original proportion was 1 to 30,000; at present it is 1 to 212,407. Each organized territory is entitled to 1 delegate in the House of Representatives. Delegates may participate in debate, but may not vote. The sole power of impeachment is given to the House of Representatives, and in this House must originate all general appropriation bills and bills for raising revenue. Members of the House receive a salary of $7,500 a year, besides mileage. They are privileged from arrest during attendance at the sessions of the House and in going to and returning from the same, and may not be questioned in any other place for any speech or debate in the House. The membership at present (1916) consists of 435 representatives and two delegates and three resident commissioners. (See illustration, frontispiece, Vol. XIV.) (See also Apportionment; Congress; Gerrymander.)

House of Representatives. (See Congress.)

Houston, James, district judge, nomination of, 390.

Howard University.—This institution is located in Washington, and exists for the higher education of the colored race. It was incorporated by act of Congress dated March 2, 1867, for the "education of youth in the liberal arts and sciences." In 1915, its register contained 1,452 students from 36 states and 6 foreign countries, and 205 students were graduated at its annual commencement. The University is divided into the College of Arts and Sciences; Teachers' College; School of Manual Arts and Applied Sciences; Conservatory of Music; School of Theology (undenominational); School of

Medicine (ranked as Class A); School of Law; and the two divisions of the secondary department—the Academy and the Commercial College. It was first given Government support in 1893, and at the present time the Government furnishes about half of its annual budget, which is slightly above $200,000. Government supervision of the school is through the Interior Department.

Huamantla (Mexico), Battle of.—Gen. Lane set out from Vera Cruz about the 1st of October, 1847, with 2,000 men to re-enforce the garrisons between there and the City of Mexico. Santa Anna, learning of Lane's approach to Puebla, set out to intercept him with 4,000 men and six pieces of artillery. On the night of Oct. 8, 1847, the Mexicans were encamped in the city of Huamantla and Capt. Walker was sent forward with a company of cavalry to give them battle. Walker's cavalry fought desperately in the face of superior numbers until the arrival of the infantry put the Mexicans to flight, with a loss of 150. Capt. Walker was killed in the fight and of his company of 75 men only 17 were able to keep the saddle at the close of the engagement.

Hubbardton (Vt.), Battle of.—Upon Burgoyne's advance toward Albany, July 6, 1777, Gen. St. Clair, whom Schuyler had left in command at Ticonderoga, being hard pressed by the enemy under the Hessian General Riedesel, began a retreat toward Rutland. The left wing of the British army, under Gen. Fraser, pursued the Americans, and in the afternoon of the 7th came upon Colonels Warner, Francis, and Hale, with about 900 effective men, at Hubbardton, Vt. The British force was officially reported as 858. The Americans maintained their ground with resolution and bravery, but the arrival of Riedesel forced them to retire. Col. Francis was killed and Col. Warner fled toward Rutland. The American casualties were about 360. The British loss amounted to 183, including Maj. Grant.

Hudson, The:

Seizure of, by British authorities referred to, 4114.

Thanks of Congress to officers and men of, for rescuing the *Winslow* at Cardenas, Cuba, recommended, 6302.

Hudson, N. Y., bill for erection of public building at, vetoed, 5521.

Hudson River, act to authorize New York and New Jersey Bridge Companies to construct bridge across, at New York, vetoed, 5912.

Hudsons Bay Company.—A trading corporation chartered by Charles II. in 1670 to Prince Rupert and other noblemen, to discover a new passage to the South Sea and to trade in the products of British North America. The original charter secured to Prince Rupert and his associates the absolute proprietorship, subordinate sovereignty, and exclusive traffic of an undefined territory which, under the name of Rupert's Land, comprised all the regions discovered or to be discovered within the entrance of Hudson Strait. The company afterwards combined with the Northwest Company and became a formidable rival of the United States in claiming the northwestern portion of America. Notwithstanding the fact that the treaty of 1783 vested the right to certain territory in the United States, the Hudsons Bay Company persisted in making settlements therein and

discouraging American colonists. Their efforts to hold Oregon by force almost resulted in a war with England, but the boundary was finally settled in 1846.

Hudsons Bay Company:

Claim of, against United States, 3888.

Award of commission referred to and appropriation for, recommended, 3989.

Encroachments of agents of, upon trade and territory of Alaska, 3898.

Extinguishment of rights of, in Oregon Territory, referred to, 2453.

Fur trade of, referred to, 1097.

Lands in Oregon Territory granted to, by British Government, 2073.

Location of, 4056.

Rights of, in Oregon, 2633.

Rights of, to navigation of Columbia River, 2811.

Treaty with Great Britain regarding, 3395, 3401.

Commissioners appointed under, 3447.

Value of possessory rights of, referred to, 2866.

Hugh McCulloch, The:

Mentioned, 6297.

Recognition of services of commander of, in battle of Manila Bay, Philippine Islands, recommendations regarding, 6305.

Huguenot Society of America.—This Society was organized April 13, 1883, and has its office in New York at No. 105 East Twenty-second Street. Descent from Huguenot ancestors is the qualification necessary for membership.

Hull House. (See Social Settlements.)

Hundred.—An ancient English subdivision of a county. It was used to a limited extent in the American colonies, notably Delaware, Maryland and Virginia. The chief officer of the hundred was the constable. It corresponds roughly to the present township.

Hungary (see also Austria-Hungary):

Agent of United States sent to, during war with Austria, referred to, 2550, 2579, 2632.

Exiles from, report on, 2612.

Kossuth liberated. (See Kossuth, Louis.)

War of, with Austria, sympathy of American Government with Hungary, 2550, 2579.

Hunkers.—A name applied to a faction of the Democratic party of New York and later to the conservative element of that party in other states. The name came into use in 1844. The Hunkers in New York opposed the Locofocos, the Barnburners and the Radicals. (See Barnburners.)

Hunkpapa Indians. (See Indian Tribes.)

Huns.—Originally one of the barbarian tribes which overran the Roman Empire's Province of Gaul around 350 A. D., compelling its then barbarian occupants to migrate into Italy itself. The origin and the fate of the Huns are uncertain, but they seem to have been a Mongolian race. The Huns acquired in their conquest a name for utter ruthlessness and savagery; and it was this characteristic which led many Englishmen, in their hatred of the German people, to apply the name "Huns" to them in the European War.

Hustings.—A speaker's platform, especially where political questions are discussed. In American politics the word has come to mean the place, or places, where a political campaign is waged. Thus, a man undertaking any kind of electioneering is said to go on the hustings.

Hyde vs. Continental Trust Co. (See Income Tax Cases, also Pollock vs. Farmers' Loan and Trust Co.)

Hydrographic Commission of the Amazon, claims of members of, against Panama, 6099.

Hydographic Office.—This office is under the Bureau of Navigation (q. v.) of the Navy Department (q. v.), and provides the United States Navy (q. v.) and Merchant Marine (q. v.) with charts, maps, and sailing directions covering the seas of the entire world. Its work in making new surveys is continuous, as is its publication of general marine data, such as movements of ice bergs and ice fields. It issues daily memoranda for the use of navigators, and maintains an ice patrol in the North Atlantic Ocean.

Hydrographic Office, transfer of, to Navy Department recommended, 5973.

Hygienic Congress at Turin, 4626.

Hylton vs. United States.—This was a case first coming before the United States Supreme Court in the May term, 1795, involving the question of direct or indirect taxes. Hylton was indicted before the circuit court for the district of Virginia for refusing to pay duty upon certain carriages which he claimed were kept for his own private use. The decree was against the defendant. When the case came before the Supreme Court the argument turned upon the question of the tax being direct or indirect. The justices read their opinions *seriatim*. Judgment was affirmed for defendant. Justice Wilson briefly stated that he upheld the constitutionality of the law of 1794, under which the case arose. The other justices differed in their treatment of the law, whether to deny its constitutionality in express terms or not. (See Income Tax Cases.)

Hyphenate.—A person dominated by Hyphenated-Americanism (q. v.)

Hyphenated.—The term came into general use with the European War as an opprobrious characterization of a naturalized citizen suspected of greater allegiance to his native country than to America, as German-Americans, etc. (See Hyphenated-Americanism.)

Hyphenated-Americanism.—A term coined by President Wilson soon after the outbreak of the European War, to describe the spirit which seemed to animate those persons of foreign descent living in this country who were endeavoring to assist their native country in the war at the expense of the United States itself. The phrase arose from the fact that many such persons acted not as Americans, but, for instance, as German-Americans (q. v.); and the implications of President Wilson's phrase were that such persons not only were not unadulterated Americans, but also that of the two words which, when connected by a hyphen, formed the compound word by which they described themselves, they placed the emphasis upon the word which preceded the word "American."

Idaho.—One of the western group of states; nickname, "Gem of the Mountains;" motto, "Esto perpetua" ("May it last forever"). It lies between lat. 42° and 49° north, and long. 111° and 117° 10' west. The area is 83,888 square miles. It is bounded on the north by British Columbia and Montana, on the east by Montana and Wyoming, on the south by Utah and Nevada, and on the west by Washington and Oregon. The Bitter Root and Rocky Mountains form the eastern border. It also contains the Salmon River Mountains. It was a part of the Louisiana Purchase. Later it formed part of Oregon Territory and was also at one time part of Washington Territory. In 1863, together with the present Montana and part of Wyoming, it was organized as a separate Territory. It was admitted as a State in 1890.

The State has constructed 3,789 miles of irrigating ditches to reclaim the arid lands and the federal government has supplemented this work with 300 miles. In this way 3,346,386 acres have been rendered productive and the reclamation of 400,000 acres more is under way. Wheat is the most important crop, 232,000 acres being sown to this cereal in 1908, the yield amounting to 6,960,000 bushels, valued at $5,150,000. Other breadstuffs produced the same year were 5,588,000 bushels of oats, 2,132,000 bushels of barley, besides potatoes and hay. Some 25,000 tons of beet sugar are manufactured. Live stock is extensively raised. In 1908 the number of sheep reported was 3,575,000, from which 5,692,000 pounds of scoured wool was clipped, valued at $3,-757,000.

The State has about 20,000,000 acres of timber lands, which supply the raw material for 260 lumber mills, one of these, at Potlatch, having a capacity of 750,000 feet daily, the largest in the world.

Statistics of agriculture collected for the last Federal census, place the number of farms in the State at 30,807, as compared with 17,471 in 1900, comprising 5,183,604 acres, and valued, with stock and improvements, at $305,317,185. The value of domestic animals, poultry, etc., was $49,775,-309; including 453,807 cattle, valued at $11,330,639; 197,772 horses, $19,832,423; 4,036 mules, $481,301; 178,346 swine, $1,-398,727; 3,010,478 sheep, $15,897,192. In 1911, 15,860,000 bushels of wheat, valued at $10,468,000, was produced on 517,000 acres; 14,564,000 bushels of oats, $5,826,-000, on 331,000 acres, and 330,000 bushels of corn, $280,000, on 11,000 acres.

The mineral product of chief value in Idaho, according to the United States Geological Survey, is lead, which forms about 60 per cent of the state's total mineral production, having somewhat more than twice the value of Idaho's silver output, which ranks second among the state's mineral products. The total value of the mineral products of Idaho increased from $21,816,-390, in 1912, to $24,565,826, in 1913.

In 1913 the recoverable lead content of the ores mined in Idaho amounted to 158,-936 short tons, valued at $13,986,366, against 142,093 short tons, valued at $12,-788,355, in 1912. Idaho ranks second among the states in the production of lead ores, its output of this product being exceeded by that of Missouri. The recoverable silver content of the ores mined in Idaho in 1913 was valued at $6,033,473, against $5,101,268, in 1912. Copper, gold and zinc are also produced in significant quantities in Idaho, the output of each having a value of over $1,000,000, in 1913. The total value of the metals contained in the ores mined in Idaho in 1913 was $24,168,339, or

98 per cent of the total mineral production. The total value of the nonmetallic products—coal (lignite), gem materials, clays, lime, mica, phosphate rock, salt, sand and gravel, sandlime brick, and stone—was $397,487. Small quantities of iron and tungsten ores are also produced in the state. The nonmetallic resource of greatest promise is phosphate rock, extensive deposits of which lie in the southeastern part of the state and extend into northeastern Utah and southwestern Wyoming. As the agricultural industries of the western states are developed this necessary plant food, which is abundant in this region, should become one of the most important items in the mineral production of Idaho.

Idaho:

Admission of, into Union discussed, 5553.

Governor of, removal of, referred to, 3794.

Insurrection in, proclamation against, 5723.

Lands in—

Opened to settlement, 6026.

Set apart as public reservation, 6213, 6218, 6687.

Partial organization of, referred to, 3451.

Town sites reserved in, 6874.

Unlawful combinations in, proclamations against, 5723, 5932.

Identic Note.—A term used in diplomatic relations to designate a copy of a treaty or other agreement between two countries, which is sent to some other country for diplomatic reasons—often for the purpose of warning or admonishing the country receiving the copy.

Ikisima Island, Japan, Japanese subjects in, injured by target practice of American vessel, recommendations regarding, 5367, 5386.

Illegal Combinations (see also Amelia Island; Arizona; Arkansas; Boston; Burr, Aaron; California; Colorado; Dorr's Rebellion; Expeditions Against Foreign Powers; Harpers Ferry, Va.; Idaho; Illinois; Kansas; Ku-Klux-Klan; Louisiana; Maryland; Mississippi; Montana; New Mexico; New York, North Dakota; Pennsylvania; Rifle Clubs; Secret Lodges; South Carolina; Utah; Washington; West Virginia; White Leagues; Wyoming):

Discussed, 424, 4153.

Legislation for suppression of, recommended, 4640.

Proclamation against, 438.

Illinois.—One of the middle western group of states; nickname, "Prairie State," or "Sucker State"; motto, "National Union; State Sovereignty." It is bounded on the north by Wisconsin and Lake Michigan, on the east by Lake Michigan and Indiana, on the south by Kentucky (separated by the Ohio River), and on the west by Missouri and Iowa (separated by the Mississippi River). It has an area of 56,665 square miles. The surface is generally level. It is one of the leading states in the production of wheat, corn and oats. Though it is mainly an agricultural state, it has many flourishing manufactures, taking third rank among the manufacturing states. Its chief industries are slaughtering, meat packing, distilling, iron-founding, and the manufacture of general and agricultural machinery. It is the second State in the Union in the extent of its railways and the third in population.

Illinois was settled by the French in 1682; was ceded to Great Britain in 1763 and to the United States in 1783. It became part of the Northwest Territory in 1787 and part of Indiana Territory in 1800. It was made a separate Territory in 1809 and admitted into the Union in 1818.

Statistics of agriculture collected for the last Federal census place the number of farms in the State at 251,872, a decrease of 4.6 per cent, compared with 1900, and comprising 32,522,937 acres, valued, with stock and improvements, at $3,905,321,075, an increase of $1,901,004,178. The average value of land per acre was $95.02. The value of domestic animals, poultry, etc., was $308,804,431, including 2,440,577 cattle, valued at $73,454,745; 1,452,887 horses, $163,363,400; 147,833 mules, $18,-140,335; 4,686,362 swine, $36,210,179; 1,-059,846 sheep, $4,843,736. In 1911, 334,-950,000 bushels of corn was produced on 10,150,000 acres, and was valued at $184,-222,000; 121,536,000 bushels of oats, $51,-045,000, on 4,220,000 acres; 42,000,000 bushels of wheat, $37,380,000, on 2,625,-000 acres; 6,900,000 bushels of potatoes, $6,210,000, on 138.000 acres; 1,948,000 tons of hay, $33,116,000, on 2,376,000 acres.

The mineral products, consisting of coal and petroleum in 1910, were valued at $141,-809,121, a decrease from the previous year. The production of coal in the State in 1910 was 42,900,246 short tons, as valued at $52,405,897, as against 50,904,990 tons in 1903. The State was the scene of a strike of the mine workers which began April 1, 1910, and tied up the industry in most of the mining districts for nearly six months. As a result of the strike Illinois lost to West Virginia second place as a producer of coal. During the year 67,218 men out of a total of 72,264 mine operators were idle an average of 136 days.

For the biennial period ending Sept. 30, 1910, the state treasurer reported receipts of $21,611,919, and disbursements, $21,046,-572, balance in treasury, $4,424,610. The bonded debt of the State outstanding Oct. 1, 1910, was $17,500, consisting of bonds which have been called in by the governor and have ceased to draw interest, but have not been surrendered. The tax levy for 1909 was $83,269,865.

Chicago, next to New York, the largest city in the United States, and one of the greatest in the world, is a port on Lake Michigan, and has an immense trade through the great lakes.

The population, by the official United States census of 1910, was 5,638,591.

The number of manufacturing establishments in Illinois having an annual output valued at $500 or more at the beginning of 1915 was 18,388. The amount of capital invested was $1,943,836,000, giving employment to 95,130 persons, using material valued at $1,340,183,000, and turning out finished goods worth $2,247,323,000. Salaries and wages paid amounted to $469,388,000.

Illinois (see also Chicago):

Admission of, into Union, 615.

Bill relating to division of, into judicial districts, etc., returned, 5122.

Canal in, recommendations regarding, 3334.

Decisions of Supreme Court requested by legislature of, 2212.

Defalcation of officers in, 941.

Illinois and Michigan Canal tendered United States by, 4783.

Lands in, ceded to United States by Indians, 1257.

Mineral lands in, referred to, 2218.

Unlawful combinations in—

  Discussed, 4424.

  Proclamation against, 5931.

Volunteers from, thanks of President tendered, 3442.

Illinois and Michigan Canal tendered United States by Illinois, 4783.

Illinois Central Railroad, transportation of mails over, referred to, 2896.

Illinois Indians, treaty with, 127.

Immigration.—No official statistics of immigration were kept previous to 1820. By the act of Congress of March 2, 1819, collectors of customs were required to keep a record and make a return to the Treasury Department of all passengers arriving in their respective districts from foreign ports. As early as 1700 large numbers of Germans from the districts along the Rhine emigrated to America, most of them settling in Pennsylvania. Some 5,000 are said to have arrived in Pennsylvania from Germany in 1729.

The outbreak of the Revolution of course retarded immigration for a time. Then the breaking out of the European wars and their continuance until 1815 absorbed nearly all the surplus population for about forty years.

Various estimates have been made of the number of immigrants coming to the United States prior to 1820. These range from an average of 4,000 to 7,800 a year, some of the calculators, however, basing their estimates on returns for only a part of the time. Dr. Loring, of the United States Statistical Bureau, calculates that 250,000 immigrants came to the United States between 1775 and 1820. This is an average of 5,500 per year. In 1820, the first year of record, there were 8,385 arrivals. The following years showed a steady increase up to 1854, when the number reached 427,-833. Almost every year's figures show an increase over those of the preceding year. After 1854 there was a gradual falling off, until during the first year of the Civil War the number was reduced to 89,724—but little more than half the number of arrivals for the preceding year. The following year (1862) showed but 89,207, but this number was nearly doubled the next year, notwithstanding the result of the war was yet in doubt. After the war the tide of immigration again set toward our shores and in 1882 the arrivals reached 788,992.

The total immigration from Jan. 1. 1820. to the close of 1893 was more than 20,000,-000. This large influx of foreigners so disturbed the existing social conditions that remedial legislation was demanded. By an act of Congress in 1882 a head tax was laid upon every immigrant by sea, and commissioners were appointed to inspect vessels entering American ports, who should have the power to prevent the landing of any "convict, lunatic, idiot, or person likely to become a public charge." Such persons were to be returned to the port from which they came at the cost of the owners of the vessels bringing them to this country. A further law, passed in 1885, makes it unlawful to pay the transportation or to encourage in any way the immigration of aliens under contract or agreement to perform labor or service in the United States. The penalties attached to this act are $1,000 fine upon the person so encouraging such immigrant and $500 upon the captain of a vessel who knowingly transports the laborers.

The immigration laws were amended in 1887, 1888, 1891 and 1892 in the direction of protecting American workingmen from the ruinous competition with foreign pauper labor. These laws have served to reduce the number as well as to improve the class of arrivals. Between 1894 and 1901 the tide of immigration again ran low, falling below the half million mark. In 1905 more than a million arrivals were recorded and this number has been frequently exceeded since.

The problem of immigration is one of much concern to the public mind because of the accretion to our population of many undesirable elements in spite of existing restricting laws. In his fourth annual message (Dec. 6, 1904), President Roosevelt made a plea for the better regulation of the service. While there is no danger of having too many immigrants of the right kind, he said, in effect, "we should not admit masses of men whose standards of living and whose personal customs and habits are such that they tend to lower the level of the American wage-worker, and above all we should not admit any man of an unworthy type, any man concerning whom we can say that he will himself be a bad citizen, or that his children and grandchildren will detract from instead of add to the sum of the good citizenship of the country." (Page 6916.)

IMMIGRATION BY COUNTRIES IN 1915.

Austria-Hungary	18,511
Belgium	2,399
Denmark	3,312
France, including Corsica	4,811
German Empire	7,799
Greece	12,592
Italy, including Sicily and Sardinia	49,688
Netherlands	3,144
Norway	7,986
Portugal, including Cape Verde and Azore Islands	4,907
Roumania	481
Russian Empire and Finland	26,187
Spain, including Canary and Balearic Islands	2,762
Sweden	6,585
Switzerland	1,742
Turkey in Europe	2,411
England	21,562
Ireland	14,185
Scotland	4,668
Wales	1,007
Total Europe	**197,919**
China	2,660
India	161
Japan	8,613
Turkey in Asia	3,543
Other Asia	234
Total Asia	**15,211**
British North America	82,215
Mexico	12,340
Central America	1,252
West Indies and Bermuda	11,598
South America	3,801
Total America	**111,206**
Total Oceania	1,399
Total Africa	934
All other countries	31
Total immigrants	**326,700**

Immigrants arriving in the United States in 1910 numbered 1,041,570. Reports show Italy to have been the previous home of the majority, 182,882 arriving from that country and the adjacent islands of Sicily and Sardinia in 1911, and 215,537 in 1910. The Russian Empire and Finland contributed 158,721 in 1911. Austria and Hungary each averaged more than 100,000 a year for the two years. Arrivals of Jews are not reported as such, but are credited to the country whence they embark for America. Chinese to the number of 5,107 arrived in 1911, and 4,282 Japanese. During the fiscal year 119,753 persons left the United States for Canada, while 105,512 emigrated from Canada to the United States.

Of the whole number of immigrants in the fiscal year ending June 30, 1913, 892,-653 came through the customs district of New York, 32,833 through Baltimore, 54,-740 through Boston, 59,466 through Philadelphia, 5,554 through San Francisco and 47,822 through other ports; also 104,824 through Canadian ports.

The reported occupations of immigrants arriving during the fiscal year 1913 were as follows: laborers, 220,992; servants, 140,-218; farm laborers, 320,105; tailors, 22,-934; merchants and dealers, 13,919; carpenters and joiners, 15,035; shoemakers, 11,578; clerks and accountants, 14,025; mariners, 4,979; miners, 9,510. The number of professional immigrants (including 911 actors, 1,917 engineers, 1,254 musicians and 2,389 teachers) was 13,469; of skilled laborers, 160,108; other miscellaneous (including unskilled), 14,396; no occupation (including women and children), 297,188.

The following table shows the immigration into the United States from 1824 to 1915:

Year	Total Alien Passengers	Year	Total Alien Passengers
1789 to 1822 est.	266,038	1871	321,350
1824	7,912	1872	404,806
1825	10,199	1873	459,803
1826	10,837	1874	313,339
1827	18,875	1875	227,498
1828	27,382	1876	169,986
1829	22,520	1877	141,857
1830	23,322	1878	138,469
1831	22,633	1879	177,826
1832	60,482	1880	457,257
1833	58,640	1881	669,431
1834	65,365	1882	788,992
1835	45,374	1883	603,322
1836	76,242	1884	518,592
1837	79,340	1885	395,346
1838	38,914	1886	334,203
1839	68,069	1887	490,109
1840	84,066	1888	546,889
1841	80,289	1889	444,427
1842	104,565	1890	455,302
1843	52,496	1891	560,319
1844	78,615	1892	623,084
1845	114,371	1893	502,927
1846	154,416	1894	314,467
1847	234,968	1895	279,948
1848	226,527	1896	343,267
1849	297,024	1897	230,832
1850	369,986	1898	229,299
1851	379,466	1899	311,715
1852	371,603	1900	448,572
1853	368,645	1901	487,918
1854	427,833	1902	648,743
1855	200,877	1903	857,046
1856	195,857	1904	812,870
1857	246,945	1905	1,027,421
1858	119,501	1906	1,100,735
1859	118,616	1907	1,285,349
1860	150,237	1908	782,870
1861	89,724	1909	751,786
1862	89,207	1910	1,041,570
1863	174,524	1911	878,587
1864	193,195	1912	838,172
1865	247,453	1913	1,197,892
1866	163,594	1914	1,218,480
1867	298,967	1915	326,700
1868	282,189	1916	298,826
1869	352,569		
1870	387,203	**Total**	**32,652,950**

Aliens debarred and deported 1903-1915:

Year Ended June 30	Total Immigration	Debarred	Deported
1903	857,046	8,769	547
1904	812,870	7,994	779
1905	1,026,499	11,879	845
1906	1,100,735	12,432	676
1907	1,285,349	13,064	995
1908	782,870	10,902	2,069
1909	751,786	10,411	2,124
1910	1,041,570	24,270	2,695
1911	878,587	22,349	2,770
1912	838,172	16,057	2,456
1913	1,197,892	19,938	3,461
1914	1,218,480	33,041	4,610
1915	326,700	24,111	2,564
1916	298,765	18,867	2,781

According to races, the following shows the amount of money brought by immigrants, and the number debarred in the fiscal year 1914:

Race	Amount of Money	Debarred
Chinese	$98,676	410
English	4,332,732	1,808
French	1,265,444	884
German	4,621,022	1,375
Hebrew	3,032,445	2,506
Irish	1,673,875	832
Italian	7,887,778	6,748
Japanese	345,308	273
Polish	2,910,837	1,896
Russian	....	1,596
Scandinavian	2,043,329	414
Scotch	1,529,827	668

Chinese seeking admission to the United States for the year ended June 30, 1914:

Classes	Admitted	Deported
United States citizens	2,201	139
Wives of United States citizens	122	2
Returning laborers	1,000	7
Returning merchants	881	20
Other merchants	180	7
Members of merchants' families	807	130
Students	338	5
Travellers	29	3
Teachers	17	..
Officials	110	..
Miscellaneous	88	97
Totals	5,773	410

December 15, 1913, by a vote of more than two to one, the House Immigration Committee favorably reported the Burnett Immigration bill, with its stringent provisions barring from entry into the United States all Asiatics, militant suffragettes, advocates of sabotage and anarchists. The literacy test, requiring aliens to read or write one language, was also included. The bill was passed by both the House and the Senate, but was vetoed by President Taft, and the attempt to pass the bill over his veto failed by a narrow margin to obtain the necessary two-thirds vote. A similar bill was passed in President Wilson's first administration, but could not be passed over his veto. In his second administration, however, the bill was passed over his veto on February 6, 1917.

The bill provides, in addition to previous regulations, that on and after May 5, 1917, no alien over 16 years of age, physically able to read, shall be admitted to the United States if he cannot read English, or some other language or dialect, including Hebrew and Yiddish. Exception to this rule is made in favor of the father or grandfather over 55 years of age, the wife, the mother, the grandmother, or the unmarried or widowed daughter, if otherwise admissible, of any citizen of the United States, or of any alien previously or afterwards admitted. Exception is made also in favor of all persons fleeing from religious persecution, either by governmental laws or by overt acts. The literacy test which must be passed consists of reading between thirty and forty words, in ordinary use, of the language or dialect which the applicant for admission chooses, printed in legible type on slips of uniform size.

EMIGRATION FROM UNITED STATES

Year ended June 30	Emigrant Aliens	Non-Emigrant Aliens	Total
1908	395,073	319,755	714,828
1909	225,802	174,590	400,392
1910	202,436	177,982	380,418
1911	295,666	222,549	518,215
1912	333,262	282,030	615,292
1913	308,190	303,734	611,924
1914	303,338	330,467	633,805
1915	167,954	63,462	231,416
1916	129,765	111,042	240,807

Immigration:

Act to amend laws, vetoed, 6189.

Amendments recommended, 7006.

Chinese—

Act to execute certain treaty stipulations, 5215.

Acts regarding, vetoed, 4466, 4699.

Conventional regulation of passage of laborers across borders proposed to Mexico and Great Britain, 5544.

Discussed by President—
Arthur, 4716.
Cleveland, 4914, 4968, 4975, 5083, 5194, 5215, 5868.
Grant, 4242, 4309.
Harrison, Benj., 5469, 5476, 5632.
Hayes, 4521, 4540.
McKinley, 6240.
Roosevelt, 6644, 6651, 6916, 7006.
Taft, 7372, 7543.
Wilson, 8043.

Execution of acts regarding, 5495.

Head tax collected from Chinamen entering Canada, 5476, 5632.

Registration of Chinese laborers required—
Extension of time for, 5838, 5868.

Law regarding, sustained by Supreme Court, 5868.

Reports on, referred to, 4973, 4975.

Through Canada and Mexico discussed, 5476, 5632.

Treaty regarding, 4561, 4581, 5195, 5908, 5956.
Discussed, 4629, 4823, 5194, 5386.
Referred to, 4691, 5212, 5215.
Rejected by China, discussed, 5367, 5386, 5387, 5469.

Violation of laws restricting, discussed and recommendations regarding, 4762, 5632.

Convention for protection of emigrant passengers proposed, 3990.

Discussed by President—
Cleveland, 5370, 5877, 6157.
Lincoln, 3383, 3447.
Roosevelt, 6755, 6862, 7045, 7345.

Inland passage tickets for emigrants referred to, 3001.

Involuntary deportation of convicts, idiots, and paupers to United States discussed, 4219, 4588.

Laws, amendment of, recommended, 6649, 6862, 7045, 7046, 7386, 7387.

Legislation for protection of immigrants recommended, 4108, 4120, 4650.

Measures for health and safety of immigrants, 2772, 2775, 4120.

Of citizens of United States into Turkey referred to, 3661.

Dissatisfied citizens of United States into Mexico, 3571.

Laborers and *padroni* system discussed, 6055.

Mormons, laws to prevent, 4947.

Pardons granted foreigners on condition of emigration to United States discussed, 3653.

Paupers introduced into United States discussed, 1686, 2368.

Legislation respecting, recommended, 4757.

Request of President to withdraw articles regarding, from consideration of House, 1692.

Questions with Switzerland regarding, 4520, 4627.

To Southern States encouraged, 7007.

Treaties regarding, information respecting conflict of Senate bill with, transmitted, 5768.

Treaty regarding, with—

Bavaria, 3834.

China. (See Chinese, *ante.*)

Germany and claims arising under, discussed, 4419.

Prussia, 3827.

Veto of bill to regulate, 8043.

Immigration, Superintendent of, report of, discussed, 5877.

Immurement.—The act of enclosing and imprisoning—having especial reference to large bodies of persons when held by the enemy in time of war. (See Reconcentrados.)

Impeachment.—The exhibition of charges of maladministration against a civil officer before a competent tribunal. In the United States the House of Representatives has the sole power of impeachment of the president, vice-president and all civil officers of the United States. The Senate has the sole power to try all impeachments. The Chief Justice presides at the trial of a president. A two-thirds vote is necessary to convict. Most states have similar regulations regarding impeachment. This mode of trial of public officials comes to us from England, where impeachments are made by the House of Commons and tried by the House of Lords.

The Constitution of the United States, Article II., Section IV., provides that civil officers of the United States may be removed from office on impeachment and conviction of treason, bribery or other high crimes and misdemeanors; that the House of Representatives has the sole power of impeachment, and the Senate the sole power to try impeachments; that the Vice-President shall preside at impeachments except when the president is tried, when the Chief Justice of the Supreme Court shall preside; and that two-thirds of the members present must vote for conviction before a person impeached shall be deemed guilty. Only nine persons have been impeached and tried before the Senate, and only three of them have been convicted. The record is as follows:

William Blount, Senator from Tennessee; impeached July 7, 1797, for conspiring to wage war with Spain in favor of Great Britain, to excite the Cherokee Indians against Spain, and to create disaffection among the Indians toward the United States; trial December 17, 1798, to January 14, 1799; vote, 11 guilty, 14 not guilty; verdict, acquittal.

John Pickering, Judge of the District Court of the United States for the District of New Hampshire; impeached 1803 for drunkenness and disregard of the terms of the statutes; trial, March 3 to March 12, 1803; vote, 19 guilty, 7 not guilty; verdict, guilty; punishment, removal from office.

Samuel Chase, Associate-Justice of the Supreme Court of the United States; impeached 1804 for misconduct at trials of persons charged with breach of the Sedition Law; trial, November 30, 1804, to March 1, 1805; vote, 9 guilty, 30 not guilty, and 15 guilty, 19 not guilty, on different counts; verdict, acquittal.

James Peck, Judge of the District Court of the United States for the District of Missouri; impeached for tyrannous treatment of counsel, 1830; trial, May 11 to May 30, 1830, and from December 13, 1830, to January 31, 1831; vote, 21 guilty, 22 not guilty; verdict, acquittal.

West H. Humphreys, Judge of the District Court of the United States for the District of Tennessee; impeached 1862 for supporting the secession movement and unlawfully acting as Judge of the Confederate District Court; trial May 22 to June 26, 1862; vote, 32 guilty, 4 not guilty, and 38 guilty; verdict, guilty; punishment, removal from office.

Andrew Johnson, President of the United States; impeached for usurpation of the law, corrupt use of the veto power, interference at elections and high crimes and misdemeanors; trial, March 30 to May 26, 1868; vote, 35 guilty, 19 not guilty; verdict, acquittal. (Page 3907.) (See illustration opposite 3914.)

William W. Belknap, Secretary of War of the United States; impeached for accepting bribes; trial, April 5 to August 1, 1876; vote, 5 guilty, 25 not guilty; verdict, acquittal.

Charles Swayne, Judge of the District Court of the United States for the District of Florida; impeached 1905 for misconduct in office; trial, Feb. 6 to Feb. 7, 1905; vote, 55 guilty, 37 not guilty; verdict, acquittal.

Robert W. Archbald, Associate Judge of United States Commerce Court, was impeached July 11, 1912, on thirteen articles charging him with corrupt collusion with coal mine owners and railroad officials while in office. The Senate began his trial December 3, 1912, and ended January 13, 1913. Verdict guilty; removed from office.

Following are the Governors of states who have faced impeachment proceedings in the past, with the results that followed:

Seth Sothell, Colony of North Carolina, 1689, removed.

Charles Robinson, Kansas, 1862, acquitted.

Harrison Reed, Florida, 1868, charges dropped.

William W. Holden, North Carolina, 1870, removed.

Powell Clayton, Arkansas, 1871, charges dropped.

David Butler, Nebraska, 1871, removed.
Henry C. Varmoth, Louisiana, 1872, term expired and proceedings dropped.
Adelbert Ames, Mississippi, 1876, resigned.
William Sulzer, New York, 1913, removed.

Impeachment of President Johnson:
Articles of, exhibited by House of Representatives, 3907.
Answer of President, 3926.
Replication of House of Representatives, 3951.
Committee on, photograph of, opposite 3914.
Letter of Chief Justice Chase respecting proper mode of procedure, 3916.
Proceedings of Senate sitting for trial of, 3918.
Verdict of acquittal, 3955.

Imperial Mexican Express Co., organization of, referred to, 3575.

Imperialism.—A policy of territorial expansion. The charge of imperialism has been made against various administrations from Washington down to McKinley, especially in the epochs of United States history when territory has been acquired. "Imperialism" was hurled at the Republican party in 1900 as a party cry, especially urged by William Jennings Bryan. Bryan made many speeches, and finally compiled them into a book entitled "Republic or Empire?" in which he assailed the action of the administration in taking over the Philippines and Porto Rico. A National Anti-Imperialistic League was formed, and held what was termed the "First Liberty Congress" at Indianapolis in 1900. This league was made up largely of Sound Money Democrats, who were opposed to the so-called imperialism. After two days' debate a resolution was adopted condemning McKinley and favoring Bryan. A rump convention resulted from this meeting, and was subsequently held in New York, and the National Party resulted therefrom. (See National Party.)

Imperialism. (See Expansion, Territorial.)

Import Duties (see also Tariff; Revenue, Public):
Act—
In relation to immediate transportation of dutiable goods returned, 5502.
Regulating duties on copper, vetoed, 3903.
To extend for limited period present laws for laying and collecting, vetoed, 2033.
To provide revenue from imports etc., vetoed, 2036.
Protest of President Tyler against action of House in adopting report assailing his conduct regarding, 2043.
Ad valorem duties—
Offer strong temptations to fraud, 2620, 2662, 2706.
Recommended, 629, 667, 757, 870, 923, 952, 977.
Amount of, and statement in regard to, 1159, 1246, 1895, 4633.

Change of rate of, cause halt in business, 7369.
Collected by Great Britain and United States in contravention of treaty discussed, 596, 2274, 2296.
Commercial tariff should be regulated, 470.
Commission to revise, recommended, 4636, 4722.
Complaints of Spain and Portugal against operations of revenue act, 1956.
Compromise act, diminution of duties under, referred to, 1955.
Constitutionality of tariff questioned, 1086.
Correspondence with foreign governments regarding laws of, 2086.
Discussed by President—
Adams, J. Q., 979.
Arthur, 4636, 4721, 4839.
Buchanan, 2964, 3052, 3181.
Cleveland, 4926, 5093, 5169, 5359, 5890, 5984, 6173.
Fillmore, 2619, 2659, 2661, 2705.
Grant, 3984, 4061, 4102, 4201, 4247, 4303.
Harrison, Benj., 5473, 5556, 5626, 5744.
Hayes, 4422, 4511.
Jackson, 1012, 1086, 1119, 1160, 1247, 1380, 1470.
Jefferson, 397.
Johnson, 3773.
McKinley, 6238, 6246, 6439, 6465.
Madison, 470, 552.
Monroe, 675, 760, 784.
Pierce, 2747, 2871, 2941.
Polk, 2253, 2301, 2348, 2366, 2403, 2497, 2506.
Taylor, 2556.
Tyler, 1934, 1955, 1961, 2033, 2036, 2053, 2119.
Van Buren, 1752.
Effect of, on treaties with foreign powers, 2086.
Frauds in importation of foreign merchandise, discussed, 989, 4797.
Free List—
Increase in, recommended, 4102, 4247, 4723, 5474.
Sugar placed on, discussed, 5626.
Imposition of, as war measure, proposed, 2352, 2366.
Increase in, recommended, 760, 1961.
Laws levying, repealed. (See Vessels, Foreign, tonnage on.)
Moderate schedule of, recommended, 2054, 2620, 2662.
On—
American vessels. (See Vessels, United States.)

British vessels returned. (See Great Britain.)

Cotton from British North American colonies, 996.

Distilled spirits. (See Distilled Spirits.)

Flour, 1115.

Foreign mail matter, recommended, 4527.

French vessels. (See France.)

Hawaiian commodities wrongfully levied, discussed, 5545.

Luxuries discussed, 397.

Rice discussed, 1243, 1931, 2112, 2181, 2274.

Russian Hemp, and treaty obligations regarding, 3990.

Salt discussed, 397, 1470.

Tea and coffee—
Recommended by President—
Grant, 4303.
Hayes, 4422, 4511.
Polk, 2366, 2405.
Repeal of, recommended, 4062.

Tonnage repealed. (See Vessels, Foreign.)

Wines, 1131, 1321, 2127, 2250.

Wools discussed, 1247, 4247.

Works of foreign artists discussed, 4794, 4824, 4924, 5091.

Payment of amount due Great Britain, recommended, 568.

Protest of Germany against discriminating duty on sugar, recommendations regarding, 5957.

Reduction in, 1707, 1752, 2349, 2497, 4765.

Recommended by President—
Cleveland, 4926, 5093, 5165, 5359, 5374, 5890, 5984.
Grant, 4102, 4247.
Harrison, Benj., 5473.
Jackson, 1013, 1119.
Johnson, 3773.
Pierce, 2747, 2871, 2941.
Polk, 2253, 2301.
Taft, 7369, 7393, 7395, 7399, 7400, 7488, 7501, 7618.

Revision of Dingley act recommended, 7369.

Salt, rice and luxuries on, considered and discussed, 397.

Specific duties recommended, 2556, 2620, 2661, 2706, 3052, 3181, 4422.

Tariff discussed—
Of 1816, 760.
1842, 2254, 2301, 2349, 2402, 2497.
1846, 2402, 2497, 3051.
1890, 5556, 5626.
1894, 5984, 5998.
1909, 7393, 7403, 7625, 7631.

Tariff unsatisfactory, 980, 1013, 1961, 2253, 2301.

Warehousing system discussed, 1015, 2053, 2119, 2405.

Import Duties, Foreign. (See Foreign Import Duties.)

Imported Goods, misbranding of, 7228.

Imports:
Duties on. (See Import Duties; Vessels, Foreign, tonnage on.)
From France referred to, 768.
Increase in, 1155.
Into Cuba, modification of laws regarding, 2869.
Indemnity for, discussed, 2869.
Prohibition on—
Proclamation removing, 6025.
Recommendations regarding, 399, 527.
Reduction in, 1707.
Restrictions upon. (See Animals and Animal Products.)
Value of, for year ending June—

1845, 2252.	1885, 4925.
1846, 2346.	1886, 5092.
1847, 2401.	1891, 5626.
1848, 2496.	1892, 5743.
1851, 2658.	1893, 5875.
1852, 2705.	1894, 5964.
1877, 4422.	1896, 6155.
1881, 4633.	1899, 6357.
1884, 4830.	1900, 6439.

Imposts.—Taxes upon imported goods.

Impressment.—The act of compelling persons to enter the public service, usually applied to the seizure of sailors for service on naval vessels. Great Britain has always claimed the right to levy land and naval forces in time of war by compulsory process. This method has been limited in the case of land forces to times of actual invasion; but that country still claims the right to impress British seamen into service wherever they may be found. The exercise of this claim was among the causes that led to the War of 1812. Great Britain refused to allow the right of her seamen to change their allegiance by naturalization and claimed the right to search neutral vessels and decide by her visiting officers who among the crew of such neutral vessels were British subjects. Many American sailors were in this way wrongfully impressed into the British navy. Although by the treaty of Ghent Great Britain did not relinquish this claim, it has been abandoned so far as United States vessels are concerned. She has acceded to the doctrine of Webster that in every regularly documented American vessel the crew who navigate it will find protection in the flag which is over them. (See also Ghent, Treaty of.)

Impressment. (See Naturalized Citizens; Seamen, American.)

Imprisonment:
Citizens of United States and claims arising out of, in—
Algiers, 80, 90, 115, 140, 169, 192, 197, 199, 539.
Argentine Republic, 632.
Austria, 2742, 2889.
Brazil, 970, 2779.
Colombia, 4798.

Cuba, 329, 2538, 2676, 2677, 2765, 3115, 4023, 5516, 6068, 6100, 6181, 6182, 6184, 6345. (See also Spain.)

Persons claiming to be American citizens, 6180, 6183.

Released, 6367.

Ecuador, 4856.

Released, 4915, 4990.

Treaty to settle claim regarding, 5369.

France, 6060.

Great Britain, 963, 969, 990, 1123, 1575, 1622, 1687, 1909, 1928, 2521, 3590, 3718, 3827, 3897, 4005, 4602, 4674, 4678, 4679, 4693, 4699, 6101.

Colonies of. (See the separate British Colonies.)

Correspondence regarding. (See Greely, Ebenezer S.)

Released, 1110.

Trial and conviction of, referred to, 3800, 3827, 3833, 3834, 4782.

Haiti, 3829, 4665, 4918, 5120, 5123, 5369, 5869, 6099.

Honduras, 5825.

Ireland, 2521, 3590, 4678, 4679, 4693, 4699.

Released, 3902, 4713.

Trial and conviction of, referred to, 3800, 3827, 3833.

Mexico, 2720, 2834, 2837, 4376, 4672, 4678, 4692, 4696, 4852, 4991, 5086.

New Brunswick, 963, 969, 990, 1575, 1622, 1687.

Paraguay, 3884, 3898.

Peru, 5988, 6092, 6335.

Portugal, 3884.

Prussia, 1136.

Russia, 4162, 4789, 4793.

Santo Domingo, 4004, 4013.

Spain, 594, 2643, 4116, 5905. (See also Cuba.)

Pardon of, discussed, 2689, 2692.

Release, 6367.

Tripoli, liberated, 373.

Venezuela, 4789, 4803, 5198.

For debt. (See Imprisonment for Debt.)

Jails, use of, granted to United States, 103.

Of loyal citizens by forces in rebellion, 3235.

Prisoners—

Duties of sheriffs regarding, 67.

Provision for, recommended, 183.

Imprisonment for Debt:

Abolition of, except in case of fraud, recommended, 1017, 1119.

Referred to, 251.

Improvements, Internal. (See Internal Improvements.)

Inaugural Addresses of President—

Adams, John, 218.

Adams, J. Q., 860.

Arthur, 4620.

Buchanan, 2961.

Cleveland, 4884, 5821.

Garfield, 4596.

Grant, 3960, 4175.

Harrison, Benj., 5440.

Harrison, W. H., 1860.

Hayes, 4396.

Jackson, 999, 1222.

Jefferson, 309, 366.

Johnson, 3503.

Lincoln, 3206, 3477.

McKinley, 6236, 6465.

Madison, 451, 509.

Monroe, 573, 655.

Pierce, 2730.

Polk, 2223.

Roosevelt, 6930.

Taft, 7368.

Taylor, 2542.

Tyler, 1889.

Van Buren, 1530.

Washington, 43, 130.

Wilson, 7868, 8221.

Inauguration Day.—After the ratification of the Constitution by the several states the Congress of the old Confederation fixed upon the first Wednesday in January, 1789, for the choice of electors, the first Wednesday in February for the voting of the electors, and the first Wednesday in March for the inauguration of the president. The latter day fell on the 4th in that year, and the twelfth amendment to the Constitution settled upon this as the legal date. Bills have been frequently introduced in both Houses of Congress to change Inauguration Day from March 4th to various dates, some as late as April 30th. There has also been some agitation to make the date of inauguration considerably earlier, the advocates of this proposition claiming that the interval between election and inauguration is dangerously long.

Inauguration of Washington, Ceremonies initiatory to, 34-43.

Incendiary Speeches and mob violence discussed by President Roosevelt, 7032.

Income Tax.—A form of direct tax upon annual incomes in excess of a specified sum. According to the doctrine of Adam Smith, "the subjects of every state ought to contribute to the support of the government as nearly as possible in proportion to their respective abilities—that is, in proportion to the revenues which they respectively enjoy under the protection of the state." In pursuance of this principle all incomes should be taxed, but it is generally conceded among the advocates of such a tax that incomes below a certain amount should be exempt.

Aug. 5, 1861, Congress, to secure funds to suppress the rebellion, authorized a tax of 3 per cent. on all incomes over $800 per annum. July 1, 1862, an act was passed taxing all incomes under $5,000 5 per cent., with an exemption of $600 and house rent actually paid. Incomes of more than $5,000 and less than $10,000 were taxed 2½ per cent. additional, and on incomes of more than $10,000 5 per cent. additional with no exemptions. A tax of

5 per cent. on incomes of Americans living abroad and of 1½ per cent. on incomes from United States securities was levied, expiring in 1865. In 1864 a special tax of 5 per cent. was imposed on all incomes between $600 and $5,000 and 10 per cent. on incomes of more than $5,000. This law was repealed in 1872. The amount collected under it was $346,911,760.48. In August, 1894, the Wilson tariff law imposed a tax of 2 per cent. on all incomes in excess of $4,000. The Supreme Court in 1895 declared this law unconstitutional. (See Income-Tax Cases.)

Income taxes have been collected in England since 1799, when Mr. Pitt carried a proposition through Parliament for a graduated tax on all incomes in excess of £60 per annum. In 1803 the rate was fixed at 5 per cent. on all incomes above £150. Sir

The following table, from a report of the Commissioner of Internal Revenue, Treasury Department, shows the personal net income returns of persons reporting net income in excess of $3,000 for the year ended Dec. 31, 1916, by states.

State or Territory	$3,000 to $4,000	$4,000 to $5,000	$5,000 to $10,000	$10,000 to $15,000	$15,000 to $20,000	$20,000 to $25,000	$25,000 to $30,000	$30,000 to $40,000	$40,000 to $50,000	$50,000 to $75,000	$75,000 to $100,000	$100,000 to $150,000	$150,000 to $200,000	$200,000 to $250,000	$250,000 to $300,000	$300,000 to $400,000	$400,000 to $500,000	$500,000 and over	Total returns
Alabama	437	319	679	183	81	36	21	14	6	11	3		1	1					1,791
Alaska	33	21	31	6	5	1			1				1						100
Arizona	184	163	257	85	40	16	10	8	8	4	2	2	1						780
Arkansas	412	296	599	120	45	22	8	8	3	4		1							1,518
California	4,465	3,269	6,309	1,756	819	410	244	272	145	166	64	44	15	9	5	5	4	3	18,004
Colorado	839	576	1,052	301	125	65	42	38	35	26	12	9	4		1	1	2	1	3,129
Connecticut	1,317	1,184	2,610	730	390	249	158	180	106	126	37	25	13	14	3	3		8	7,153
Delaware	202	171	416	127	62	48	22	36	11	30	10	13	8	5	5	7	2	10	1,185
Dis. of Columbia	1,417	1,073	1,641	358	151	104	67	51	37	38	17	22	7	5	1	5		1	4,994
Florida	450	293	557	157	64	31	26	14	8	9	5	2				1		1	1,618
Georgia	683	544	1,135	301	137	63	35	33	14	20	3	8	2	1		2		1	2,982
Hawaii	172	135	234	72	45	24	22	20	13	12	8	1	1		1		1		781
Idaho	145	107	239	52	25	8	7	8	5	2	1	4	1			1			605
Illinois	5,660	5,323	10,463	2,762	1,332	792	519	538	329	391	184	138	54	26	15	18	12	20	28,576
Indiana	1,358	1,090	2,052	532	215	106	71	61	41	39	11	19	6	4	1		1		5,607
Iowa	1,789	1,320	2,477	582	211	113	57	81	32	30	8	12			1				6,713
Kansas	865	617	1,155	257	80	38	33	21	7	11	9	5	2	2					3,102
Kentucky	718	583	1,056	297	104	70	21	43	24	25	11	5	2	1					2,960
Louisiana	950	675	1,293	350	166	85	48	70	29	37	12	7	4	3		1			3,730
Maine	432	360	765	206	85	54	31	44	23	26	18	5	3	2			1	1	2,056
Maryland	1,487	1,337	2,526	633	346	154	117	118	60	81	24	27	7	3	2	3	1	3	6,929
Massachusetts	3,176	3,151	7,154	2,138	1,085	748	487	603	336	446	188	191	63	26	14	23	10	15	19,854
Michigan	1,719	1,503	3,043	967	451	267	158	190	96	121	68	53	22	9	1	4	4	9	8,685
Minnesota	151	761	1,798	508	271	193	103	137	81	81	28	34	4	8	2	5	1	2	4,168
Mississippi	263	194	390	106	48	26	12	12	9	5	2		1						1,068
Missouri	2,593	1,924	3,633	997	520	300	173	169	125	104	45	31	16	7	2	3	1	4	10,647
Montana	263	251	548	156	66	26	14	17	11	10		1	2	2	2				1,369
Nebraska	1,013	648	1,233	280	120	75	33	41	10	13	7	2	1		1	1			3,478
Nevada	85	53	101	23	9	1	1	1	1										275
New Hampshire	261	219	503	130	44	40	22	27	18	19	4	4	4						1,295
New Jersey	3,473	2,898	5,844	1,538	735	422	261	322	161	181	91	78	35	11	8	15	5	9	16,087
New Mexico	161	103	248	51	25	8	8	13	2	7	1								628
New York	11,840	11,571	25,663	8,116	4,213	2,744	1,830	2,173	1,310	1,638	745	656	291	160	105	106	57	191	73,409
North Carolina	404	384	700	170	80	30	21	15	5	10	5		1						1,829
North Dakota	61	160	452	96	40	15	13	12	3	5	1								858
Ohio	3,578	2,879	5,983	1,650	785	479	298	314	202	197	85	75	34	17	6	12	2	11	16,607
Oklahoma	338	300	540	148	56	31	29	26	23	33	13	12	4	3		1	1	4	1,562
Oregon	736	491	785	188	88	44	20	31	11	12	7	3	3		2				2,421
Pennsylvania	6,049	5,513	12,143	3,717	1,877	995	692	723	487	537	201	196	77	47	26	28	10	22	33,350
Rhode Island	512	431	1,020	325	140	100	69	77	48	45	28	22	13	7	5	4	3	5	2,854
South Carolina	316	229	413	92	34	20	8	9	3	5	2	2	1			1			1,135
South Dakota	64	140	283	77	25	14	9	6	3										621
Tennessee	886	636	1,162	324	145	68	38	42	15	22	9	5	2	1	1	1			3,356
Texas	2,034	1,472	2,905	762	353	184	105	122	67	72	23	16	5	3	1	1	1	1	8,127
Utah	188	173	371	96	47	34	13	27	6	16	3	4	2						980
Vermont	194	147	322	68	28	21	13	21	5	10	6	4		1			1	2	843
Virginia	861	644	1,226	338	163	78	46	46	27	19	9	6		1	1	1			3,463
Washington	1,315	854	1,280	318	138	68	43	47	29	27	5	9		4	1	1			4,139
West Virginia	447	375	711	195	87	41	31	34	11	14	9	6	2	1		2			1,966
Wisconsin	1,900	1,281	2,213	609	261	138	80	79	46	51	18	25	10	3	2		1	2	6,719
Wyoming	149	108	189	55	13	8	7	10	3	2	1						1		546
Total	69,045	58,949	120,402	34,102	16,475	9,707	6,196	7,005	4,100	4,791	2,056	1,793	724	386	216	254	122	329	336,652

Of the total number of those returning taxes, 266,153 were married and 47,583 were single men and 22,916 were single women. 4,819 were married women making separate returns.

Robert Peel's bill, passed in 1842, imposed a tax of 7d. per pound on annual incomes of £150 and upward, for three years. This law has since been extended at each period of its expiration, and the rate and exemptions frequently changed, but the law remains essentially the same in principle to-day as passed in the early forties. The rate has varied from 4d the pound (in 1865-67-70) to 1s. the pound (in 1904); yielded a revenue increasing irregularly from £571,055 in 1842, to £38,800,000 in 1903, and falling back to £31,860,000 in 1908. The immediate effect of Sir Robert Peel's measure was to cause the repeal of about £12,000,000 of direct taxes.

By virtue of the power granted under the sixteenth amendment to the Constitution the Sixty-third Congress passed an income tax measure as part of the tariff law of 1913. This provided for a normal tax of one per cent. on all incomes in excess of $3,000 for unmarried men and women, and in excess of $4,000 up to $20,-000 for married persons living together as man and wife, but only $4,000 of the aggregate income of man and wife living together is exempted. An additional one per cent. is assessed upon the amount by which the total net income exceeds $20,000 up to $50,000; two per cent. upon the amount in excess of $50,000 up to $75,000; three per cent. upon the amount in excess of $75,000 up to $100,000; four per cent. upon the amount in excess of $100,000 up to $250,000; five per cent. on the amount in excess of $250,000 up to $500,000, and six per cent. upon the amount in excess of $500,000. Early in 1917 the normal tax was raised to 2 per cent and the sur-taxes on large incomes were heavily increased, so that on June 1, 1917, the rates stood as follows:

On incomes under $20,000 (see previous paragraph for exemption limits), a tax of 2%; on incomes between $20,000 and $40,-000, an additional 1%, with an additional 1% for each $20,000, until an income between $80,000 and $100,000 is reached, when the tax is an additional 4%. After this point, there is an additional tax of 1% for each $50,000. until incomes between $250,000 and $300,000 are reached, upon which there is an additional tax of 8%. Incomes between $300,000 and $500,-000 pay an additional tax of 9% and incomes between $500,000 and $1,000,000 pay an additional tax of 10%, or 12% in total. There is then an additional tax of 1% for each $500,000, until incomes in excess of $2,000,000 yearly pay an additional tax of 13%, or a total income tax of 15%.

For 1916, the total income tax was $67,943,594, a gain of $26,800,000 from the figures of 1915. This amount was paid by 336,652 persons. Of this number, 266,153 were married and 47,583 were single men and 22,916 single women. Persons residing in or around New York City paid almost one-half of the total tax.

War Income Tax.—The rates on incomes were increased by provision of the so-called "War Tax Bill," signed by President Wilson on October 5, 1917, as follows:

(The tax is to be levied only for the duration of the war. Two thousand dollars is the exemption amount for married persons. $1,000 for unmarried persons. There is allowed an additional exemption of $200 for each dependent child.)

The former normal tax on the excess over the former exemption allowed ($4,000 for married persons and $3,000 for unmarried persons) is 2%, and is retained. The new normal tax on the excess over the new exemptions is an additional 2%. Thus a married man with an income of $5,000 pays 2% on $1,000 and 2% on $3,000, or a total normal tax of $80.

The former surtaxes (see above) are retained, with additional surtaxes as follows:

1% on amount above $5,000 and below $7,500.

2% on amount above $7,500 and below $10,000.

3% on amount above $10,000 and below $12,500.

4% on amount above $12,500 and below $15,000.

5% on amount above $15,000 and below $20,000.

7% on amount above $20,000 and below $40,000.

10% on amount above $40,000 and below $60,000.

14% on amount above $60,000 and below $80,000.

18% on amount above $80,000 and below $100,000.

22% on amount above $100,000 and below $150,000.

25% on amount above $150,000 and below $200,000.

30% on amount above $200,000 and below $250,000.

34% on amount above $250,000 and below $300,000.

37% on amount above $300,000 and below $500,000.

40% on the amount above $500,000 and below $750,000.

45% on the amount above $750,000 and below $1,000,000.

50% on the amount above $1,000,000.

In addition, there is a flat tax of 8% on incomes above $6,000.

Accordingly, on a married man with a net income of $10,000, there would be the following income taxes: $120 old normal tax; $160 new normal tax; old law surtax, none; new law surtax, (1% on $5,000-$7,500 and 2% on $7,500-$10,000), $75; additional 8% tax, $320—or a total income tax of $675.

A married man with an income of $5,000 is assessed a total tax of $80; with an income of $20,000, a total tax of $3,000; of $40,000, a tax of $6,300; of $100,000, a tax of $23,700; of $250,000, a tax of $89,200; of $500,000, a tax of $232,200; of $1,000,-000, a total tax of $554,700; of $3,000,-000, a total tax of $2,039,700.

The above figures are on the basis of a married man having no children. As explained above, the exemption rate is $1,000 lower for unmarried persons and $200 higher for each dependent child.

(For the "War Corporation Income Tax," see Corporation Tax.)

The provisions of the bill do not apply to Porto Rico or the Philippine Islands, the legislatures of which are given the right to assess income taxes to cover their own territory.

Contributions or gifts actually made within the year to corporations or associations organized and operated exclusively for religious, charitable, scientific, or educational purposes, or to societies for the prevention of cruelty to children or animals, no part of the net income of which inures to the benefit of any private stockholder or individual, to an amount not in excess of fifteen per centum of the tax-payer's taxable net income as computed without the benefit of this paragraph may be deducted from the income to be taxed.

Income is defined as all profits or gains from salaries, wages, compensation for personal service or from professions, trade, commerce or sales or dealings in real estate or personal property, interest, rent, except-

By states, the collection of income tax for the fiscal year ending June 30, 1917, was as follows:

State.	Individual Income Tax.	Corporation Income Tax.
Alabama ..$	200,385.29	$ 887,906.92
Alaska	20,772.03	49,132,34
Arizona ..	200,330.73	637,993.92
Arkansas ..	179,413.47	306,310.84
California .	3,870,314.24	6,147,289.14
Colorado ..	1,060,075.91	1,789,597.94
Connecticut	3,050,912.00	3,872,638.48
Delaware .	3,666,351.92	2,791,067.72
Dis. of Col.	1,816,133.33	579,311.46
Florida ..	305,879.91	327,655.04
Georgia ..	611,777.89	1,218,831.39
Hawaii ...	363,880.70	909,818.58
Idaho	176,711.97	217,479.58
Illinois ...	11,739,952.41	14,359,537.16
Indiana	1,233,845.52	2,261,049.58
Iowa	555,247.24	1,252,297.30
Kansas ...	568,181.91	2,349,847.01
Kentucky ..	393,271.63	1,252,485.55
Louisiana .	813,542.12	1,269,121.11
Maine ...	377,375.05	815,750.20
Maryland ..	1,947,336.47	1,401,954.27
Mass.	10,959,847.50	9,320,716.63
Michigan ..	3,627,884.25	6,565,769.68
Minnesota .	1,814,431.33	4,618,464.76
Mississippi.	197,456.70	246,829.38
Missouri ..	2,516,416.54	4,596,170.35
Montana ..	298,627.47	776,719.99
Nebraska ..	368,710.97	779,615.94
Nevada ...	15,425.53	75,423.06
New Hamp.	236,565.28	283,937.07
New Jersey	5,621,910.08	5,250,581.86
New Mexico	82,760.87	300,134.14
New York .	81,495,783.31	46.566,951.90
North Car..	551,189.51	1,232,609.13
North Dak.	74,159.64	218,771.77
Ohio	8,066,088.77	12,873,403.13
Oklahoma .	4,428,842.32	2,231,436.18
Oregon ...	413,684.24	406,931.70
Pennsylvania	17,860,341.18	24,238,266.36
Rhode Island	1,860,676.67	1,339,290.50
South Car..	81,874.28	498,116.17
South Dak..	49,164.33	182,248.15
Tennessee .	438,684.27	942,090.87
Texas	2,781,779.69	2,611,153.93
Utah	181,344.05	1,148,676.94
Vermont ..	369,879.07	184,547.33
Virginia ...	621,507.06	1,837,125.64
Washington.	855,286.77	1,187,702.79
West Va..	460,138.63	1,460,908.97
Wisconsin .	1,179,826.21	2,716,523.54
Wyoming ..	66,361.72	184,694.47

Total ...$180,108,340.10 $179,572,887.86

Calender year 1916 (act of Sept. 8, 1916)
Income tax, normal ......$ 55,742,230.89
Surtax :

Net incomes exceeding $20,000 and not more than

$40,000	6,969,051.71
$40,001 to $60,000......	6,493,954.37
$60,001 to $80,000......	6,071,465.16
$80,001 to $100,000....	5,730,101.63
$100,001 to $150,000....	11,099,321.57
$150,001 to $200,000....	8,189,595.69
$200,001 to $250,000....	6,241.807.10
$250,001 to $300,000....	5,196,876.83
$300,001 to $500,000....	12,969,686.27
$500,001 to $1,000,000..	14,501,213.51
$1,000,001 to $1,500,000..	7,531,893.76
$1,500,001 to $2,000,000..	4,888,040.10
Net incomes exceeding	
$2,000,000	16,145,856.30
Offers in compromise, etc..	15,994.50

Total $167,787,089.39

ing annuity or endowment payments from life insurance companies. Besides the $3,-000 and $4,000 above mentioned, there is exempt from taxation the necessary expenses of carrying on business; all interest paid on indebtedness, all taxes, bad debts, losses by fire or storm not covered by insurance, and an allowance for depreciation in value. Interest upon obligations of a state or political subdivision thereof and upon obligations of the United States or its possessions is also exempt from taxation.

In the case of corporations the same normal tax is payable upon the net income, to be computed up to the end of any calendar month the corporation may designate, the return to be made within sixty days after the close of its fiscal year. The net income is ascertained by deducting from the receipts of corporations all the necessary expenses of operation, including rentals; all losses by fire and storm not covered by insurance; depreciation (in the case of mines not to exceed five per cent. of the value of gross output) ; the amount of interest accrued and paid within the year upon bonds or other indebtedness; in the case of banks, interest paid during the year to depositors, or on moneys received for investment and secured by interest-bearing certificates.

Exemption from the corporation tax is extended to partnerships, mutual insurance companies, agricultural, labor and beneficiary societies, educational, religious and scientific associations not conducted for profit.

Persons, firms, companies, etc., having the payment of fixed annual or periodic income to other persons subject to tax shall in behalf of such persons deduct an amount equal to the normal income tax and make return of same with the name and address of such person.

Returns of taxable income are to be made by March 1, and payment is to be made by June 30th each year subject to a penalty of five per cent. and one per cent. a month on delinquents.

Income Tax:

Amendment, text of, see Amendments.

Constitutional amendment proposed, 7390, 7391.

Doubtful constitutionality of, 7390.

Increase in, suggested, 8113.

Power to levy sought by constitutional amendment, 7390, 7391.

Recommended by—
Grant, 3984.
Roosevelt, 7044, 7083.
Taft, 7390.

Upon certain corporate investments discussed, 5892.

Upon consuls to United States discussed, 3383.

Upon corporations, 7082.

Income-Tax Cases.—Famous cases involving the income-tax provision of the tariff laws of Aug. 28, 1894, and Oct. 5, 1913. The first to come before the Supreme Court was that of Pollock *vs.* Farmers' Loan and Trust Co., on appeal from the circuit court of the United States for the southern district of New York. April 8, 1895, it was decided that so much of the act cited as provided for levying taxes upon rents or incomes derived from real estate or from interest on municipal bonds was repugnant to the Constitution and therefore invalid. (See Hylton *vs.* United States.)

Incorporation Act, National, recommended by President Roosevelt, 7074.

Incorporation, Federal:

Arguments against, refuted, 7456.

Constitutionality of, discussed, 7457. Discussed and recommended, 7522.

Independence Day.—Fourth of July, so-called because of the date of the Declaration of Independence, July 4, 1776. (See Declaration of Independence.)

Independence Day, order regarding celebration of, 5079.

Independence Day addresses of President Wilson—

At Gettysburg, 7881.

At Philadelphia, 7952.

Independence, Declaration of. (See Declaration of Independence.)

Independence Party.—This party was created largely by William R. Hearst in 1908, and held its convention in Chicago July 27. Hearst declined the nomination for Presidency, and the choice fell on Thomas L. Hisgen. For Vice President, John Temple Graves was nominated. The basic clause in the platform read: "Our action is based on a determination to wrest the conduct of party affairs from the hands of selfish interests, political tricksters and corrupt bosses, and make the Government as the founders intended, an agency for the common good." The platform generally favored the interests of labor.

Independent National Party.—A party which came into existence in 1876, to oppose resumption of specie payments. In 1880 it merged into the Greenback Party (q. v.). (See also Populist or People's Party.)

Independent Voter, power of, 8031.

India.—The Indian Empire extends over a territory larger than the Continent of Europe without Russia. It is officially known as British India.

The Indian Empire adjoins Persia from the Gulf of Oman to near Zulfikar on the Harrirud; then the Russian Empire along the frontier laid down by agreement in 1885 as far as the Oxus at Khamiab; thence along the Oxus up to the Victoria Lake, and from the east end of that lake by the line demarcated in 1895 up to Povalo Schveikovski, where three empires —the British, Russian, and Chinese—meet. From this point the frontier—in many parts not yet clearly defined—touches the Chinese Empire, mainly along the crests of the Muztagh range and the Himalayas, till the limits of French Indo-China are reached on the Upper Mekong. The Indian frontier, on leaving the Mekong, adjoins Siam till it reaches the sea at Victoria Point, halfway down the Malay peninsula. Beyond the sea the Indian Empire includes the Andaman and Nicobar Islands, the Laccadive Islands, Aden and Perim, besides protectorates over Socotra, Bahrein, and various chiefships along the coast from Aden to the Persian Gulf. Continental India, including Baluchistan, reaches from 8° to 37° N. latitude, and from 61° to 101° E. longitude.

The reported deaths from plague up to the end of 1912 were about 8,034,000 in India as a whole. About 23,000 people are annually killed by snakes. According to the census of 1911 there were 110,000 lepers.

Ethnography.—Besides English the following languages are spoken: Bengali, Western Hindi, Bihari, Eastern Hindi, Telegu, Marathi, Punjabi, Tamil, Rajasthani, Kanarese, Gujarathi, Oriya, Burmese, and Malayalam. The religions professed, in the order of their numerical importance, are Hindus, Muhammadans, Buddhists, Animists, Christians, Sikhs, Jains, Parsis, Jews.

AREA AND POPULATION

Political Divisions	Area in English Sq. Miles	Population 1911 Census
Madras Presidency	141,726	41,405,404
Bombay Presidency	123,059	19,672,642
Bengal Presidency	78,699	45,483,077
Agra and Oudh	107,164	47,182,044
Ajmer Merwara	2,711	501,395
Andamans and Nicobars	3,143	26,459
Assam	53,015	6,713,635
Baluchistan	54,228	414,412
Bihar and Orissa	83,181	34,490,084
Burma	230,839	12,115,217
Central Province and Berar	99,823	13,916,308
Coorg	1,582	174,976
Delhi	557	391,828
N. W. Frontier Province	13,418	2,196,933
Punjab	99,222	19,974,956
Total British Territory	1,093,074	244,267,542
Native States and Agencies	709,118	70,864,995
Total Indian Empire	1,802,192	315,132,537

Government.—Under the King-Emperor. His Imperial Majesty's Secretary of State for India is the head of the Indian Administration in England. In all matters the Secretary of State can impose his orders on the Government of India. No expenditure from the revenue of India is legal unless sanctioned by him and a majority of his Council. The King-Emperor is George V., who succeeded to the Throne of England in 1910, proclaimed Emperor of India at Delhi in 1911. The supreme authority in India is vested in the Governor-General in Council, subject to the control of the Secretary of State in England. The Governor-General's Council consists of seven members, and, since March, 1909, one of these has been a native of India.

British India is partitioned into provinces, enjoying various degrees of independence. The Presidencies of Madras, Bombay and Bengal are each administered by a governor appointed direct from England.

The districts (of which there are over 250 in British Territory) are the administrative units of India.

The Presidencies of Madras, Bombay and Bengal, and also the Northwestern Provinces, have each a high court, supreme both in civil and criminal business, with an ultimate appeal to the judicial committee of the privy council in England.

Education.—A Department of Education has been created, and increased attention is being given to primary, commercial, and technical education. There are five Universities, viz., those of Calcutta, Madras, Bombay, Allahabad, and the Punjab.

Army.—The Army in India consists, first, of British troops, about 76,000; and, secondly, of native troops (largely Muhammadans), about 160,000. In addition, the native Army Reserves number 34,600 men, and the Imperial Service troops furnished by native states contribute 22,350, including cavalry, transport corps, and sappers. Further, there are 39,000 European and Eurasian volunteers (efficients).

Production and Industry.—About two-thirds of the population depend on agriculture. The cotton industry supports over 7,500,000 persons, more than two-thirds of whom depend on hand-weaving. There are 5,500,000 persons in Government service, civil or military. The State is the paramount landlord in India, and the land revenue is the State's share in the rent of the soil. In British territory in 1911-1912, 249 million acres were cropped, of which about 10 per cent were under wheat, 31 per cent under rice, and 37 per cent under other food-grains and pulses, 7 per cent under oilseeds, and 7 per cent under cotton, jute, and other fibers. Owing to the increasing world demand for raw cotton, great efforts are being made to cultivate a superior long-stapled cotton in India.

Poppy may be grown only in parts of Bengal and the United Provinces and in the Central Indian native States. Except in these States the manufacture is a Government monopoly. In 1911-1912 26,860 chests of Bengal opium were sold for export. The monthly auction sales at Calcutta realized £4,990,982, and the expenses of production, etc., were £729,432. Most of the opium produced is exported to China and the Straits Settlements. The cultivation of opium in India is being restricted as the exportation to China has been closed.

The output of coal in 1911 was 12,715,-000 tons, nine-tenths of the total coming from Bengal. The production of crude petroleum in India (chiefly Burma) has increased from 19,000,000 gallons in 1898 to 226,000,000 in 1911. The output of manganese ore in recent years has been much increased, and the quantity in 1911 was 536,000 tons. About 15,000 tons of saltpeter are produced annually and exported. The yield of gold (nearly all from Mysore) was about 583,000 ounces in 1911.

The ancient village handicrafts still survive, though they suffer more and more from the competition of machine-made goods. Cotton-weaving is by far the most important hand industry. Power mills have grown up under European auspices, but are now largely owned by natives. The 258 cotton mills at work in India in 1911-1912, mostly in Bombay and Ahmedabad, contained 6,427,000 spindles and 87,600 looms.

Railways.—Nearly all the railways in India are owned by the State and administered by a Railway Board, though many are leased to and worked by companies. The mileage open for traffic on December 31, 1912, was 33,484.

Shipping.—In 1912-1913 the number of vessels which entered from and cleared to foreign countries rose to 8,737, with a tonnage of 17,451,985 tons. Of this tonnage, approximately 51 per cent. was from or to the United Kingdom and British possessions; and 77 per cent. of the total trade of India was under the British flag. The chief ports are Calcutta and Bombay, which together do about 70 per cent. of the foreign trade.

Cities. — Capital, Delhi. Population (1911), 232,895. At the Census of 1911 there were 29 towns with populations exceeding 100,000, and 17 cities exceeding 350,000.

Madras was not only the oldest, but the most important, of the three original Presidencies of India before Clive's conquest of Bengal.

Bombay.—The island of Bombay was part of the dowry of the Infanta of Portugal (1662), and was made over by Charles II. to the East India Company in 1668. The greater part of the present territory was obtained by annexations from the Mahrattas, and by the lapse of the Satara State.

Bengal was placed under a Lieutenant-Governor in 1854, and was created a Presidency, under a Governor, in 1911. The old Bengal Presidency included practically all Northern and Central India, but the present administration comprises only a part of its former limits.

Agra and Oudh, called "Northwestern Provinces and Oudh" until 1902, form the upper part of the great Ganges plain to the west of Bengal, lying between the Himalayas and the hilly border of the central plateau.

Punjab Province occupies the northwestern angle of the great northern plain of India, and derives its name from the "Five Rivers" which, descending from the Himalayas, traverse the plain and unite in the Indus.

Burma is the largest province of the Indian Empire. Many immigrants come from Bengal, Madras, and China. It is thinly peopled; but, owing to remarkable prosperity, the population has increased nearly 15 per cent, in ten years.

Native or Feudatory States, whose chiefs are in subordinate alliance with, or under the suzerainty of, the King-Emperor, comprise about two-fifths of the area, but only two-ninths of the population of India. Their administration, with a few unimportant exceptions, is not under the direct control of British officials, but it is subject, in varying degrees, to the Supreme Government.

Indian Affairs, Office of. (See Interior, Department of.)

Indian Affairs, Bureau of:
Discussed by President—
Arthur, 4641.
Cleveland, 5103, 5977.
Harrison, Benj., 5761.
Employment of physicians by, 6893.
System of, recommendations regarding, 3333, 3388, 4641, 4942.

Indian Affairs, Commissioner of:
Appointment of, 6912.
Commission to perform duties of Assistant Commissioner and, recommended, 6168.

Indian Appropriation Bill, necessity of passing, discussed, 4033, 6272.

Indian Commission to perform duties of Assistant Commissioner and Commissioner of Indian Affairs, recommended, 6168. (See Indians.)

Indian Commissioners, appointment of 6 recommended, 4942, 5105.

Indian Commissioners, Board of:
Appropriation for defraying expenses of, recommended, 4656.
Report of, referred to, 4076, 4314, 4666, 4743, 4972.

Indian Commissioner. (See Commissions.)

Indian Corn, introduction of products of, into Europe, discussed, 5764.

Indian Lands. (See Lands, Indian.)

Indian Massacre. (See illustration opposite 1263.)

Indian Reservations:
Allotment of lands in severalty to Indians—
Discussed, 5381, 5480, 5552, 5637, 5761, 5976.
Recommended, 561, 4528, 4576, 4643, 4730, 4779, 4783, 4955, 5106.
Remonstrations against, 4669.
Survey necessary for, 4943.

Chehalis, allotment of lands in severalty to Indians on, referred to, 4779.

Cheyenne and Arapaho—
Opened to settlement by proclamation, 5710.
  Appropriation for, recommended, 5638.
  Unauthorized occupancy of, proclamation against, 4892.

Chippewa, disposition of timber on, referred to, 5566.

Choctaw, right of way for railroads through, 4653, 4655.

Colville, agreement for cession of lands on, 5648.

Crimes committed on statute for punishment of, recommended, 4837.

Crow, opened to settlement by proclamation, 5727.

Crow Creek. (See Sioux.)

Devils Lake, right of way for railroads through, bill for, 4952, 5177.

Disposition of damaged timber on, referred to, 4663.

Establishment of, opposed, 5483.

Fort Berthold—
  Agreements for cession of portion of, 5018.
  Allotment of lands in severalty to Indians on, referred to, 4783.
  Portion of, opened to settlement by proclamation, 5579.

Fort Hall, agreement for disposal of lands on, 4655, 5187.
  Compensation not paid by railroad, 4953.

Gila Bend, removal of Indians on, bill for, 5499.

Grande Ronde, bill for relief of Indians on, 4780.

Iowa, bill providing for sale of 4959.

Improvement of condition of Indians on, referred to, 4656.

Jicarilla Apache, payment for improvements at, recommended, 4696.

Lake Traverse—
  Agreement with Sioux for purchase of lands on, discussed, 5498.
  Opened to settlement by proclamation, 5707.
  Right of way for railroad through, referred to, 4788, 4954, 5178.

Lemhi, agreement for sale of lands on, 4779.

Malheur, referred to, 4669.

Menominee, sale of timber on, referred to, 4659.

Mescalero, payment to settlers for improvements on, recommended, 4982.

Old Winnebago, restoration of, to public domain, order regarding, declaring void, 4890.
  Discussed, 4943.

Otoe and Missouria—
  Right of way for railroad through, referred to, 4681.
  Sale of, bill for, referred to, 4656.

Pawnee, enlargement of, bill for, 4695.

Proceeds of, bill providing for use of, for Indians, 4973.

Pyramid Lake, agreement for cession of portion of, 5649.

Reduction of—
  Bill providing for, discussed, 5180.
  Discussed, 5552, 5637.
  Negotiations regarding, 5180.

Restoration of, to public domain, order regarding, declared void, 4890.
  Discussed, 4943.

Right of way for railroads through—
  Acts regarding, vetoed, 5057, 5278, 6003, 6008, 6012, 6014.
  Compensation to be paid for, referred to, 5178.
  Referred to, 5362.
  Timber depredations on, referred to, 4665, 4775.
  Unauthorized occupancy of, proclamation against, 4892.

Round Valley—
  Allotments of lands in severalty to Indians on, bill for, 4955.
  Payment for improvements on, recommended, 4692.
  Reduction of, bill for, discussed, 5178, 5494.

Sac and Fox—
  Bill providing for sale of, 4959.
  Cession of portion of, to United States proclaimed, 5591.
  Referred to, 4972.

San Carlos, coal lands on, referred to, 4683.

Shoshone, agreement for cession of portion of, 5649.

Sioux—
  Division of portion of, into separate reservations, etc., proclaimed, 5529.
  Compensation to for losses sustained in, 5568.
  Purchase of lands from, recommended, 4837.
  Restoration of, to public domain, declared void, 4890.
  Discussed, 4943.
  Right of way through, 4775.

Standing Rock, opened to settlement, 8047.

Uncompahgre, act to change boundaries of, vetoed, 5522.

Walker River, right of way for railroad through, 4736, 4776, 4953, 5178.

Yakima, lands, on, to be used by Northern Pacific Railway, 4864, 4954, 5178.

Indian Scouts employed in pursuing, hostile Indians, 5501.

Indian Territory (see also Oklahoma.)

Acts of United States marshals, etc., in, referred to, 4122.

Affray at court-house in Going Snake district, referred to, 4119.

Boundary line with Texas, commission to mark, 4902, 4904.

Proclamation against selling lands in dispute, 5325.

Constitution adopted by tribes in, and government of, discussed, 4073.

Departmental abuses in, 6938.

Education in, recommendations regarding, 6346.

Extension of laws of Arkansas over, recommended, 4643.

Federal court for, recommended, 5969.

Government of, discussed and recommendations regarding, 5482, 6346.

Homestead laws for, recommended, 4254.

Indian hostilities in, discussed, 4933, 4943.

Judicial district within, recommended, 4119.

Lands in—

Acquired by treaty of 1866, referred to, 4474, 4853.

Issuance of patents for, referred to, 4779.

Negotiations regarding cession of Indian, 5506.

Opened to settlement—

Action of Creeks regarding, 4855.

Discussed, 4659, 5392, 5482.

Proclaimed, 5450.

Questions regarding, 4853.

Survey of, referred to, 4435.

Population of, 5482.

·Proposed admission to Statehood, 7020.

Right of way for railroads through, referred to, 4653, 4986.

Bill granting, referred to, 4655.

Territorial government for, recommended, 4073, 4106, 4154, 4206, 4254.

Unauthorized occupancy or invasion of, referred to, 4214, 4473, 4529, 4832, 4933.

Penalty for, recommended, 4742.

Proclamations against, 4499, 4550, 4811, 4888.

Indian Treaties. (See Indians, treaties with.)

Indian Tribes:

Abnaki or Tarrateen—A confederacy of tribes of the Algonquian stock of Indians, who originally inhabited the northeastern part of the United States, including the present State of Maine and parts of adjoining states, and a portion of Canada. The Abnaki included the Penobscot, the Passamaquoddy, and the Amalicite tribes. They assisted the French in their wars with the English and were expatriated by the latter.

The name is interpreted as meaning "the whitening sky at daybreak," i. e., Eastern people.

Absentee Shawnee, agreement between Cherokee Commission and, 5514.

Proclaimed, 5591.

Alabama, encouraged to reduce themselves to fixed habitation, 446.

Algonquin—A tribe of the Algonquian stock of Indians. At the time of the advent of white settlers into America the Algonquian linguistic division occupied by far the largest area of any of the Indian nations. The name means "those on the other side of the river"—that is, the river St. Lawrence. They were spread over the territory from Labrador to the Rocky Mountains and from Hudson Bay to Pamlico Sound. Though this territory was not exclusively peopled by Algonquian Indians, some of their tribes had wandered to the west and south through hostile nations and established their family beyond the limits of the present stock. The Cheyennes and Arapahoes had strayed westward to the Black Hills and finally into Colorado, and the Shawnees had penetrated into South Carolina and Tennessee. There were hundreds of divisions of these Indians into tribes and confederacies, the principal of which were the Algonquin tribes. The latter tribe, from which the stock takes its name, occupied the basin of the St. Lawrence and its northern tributaries in Canada. They allied themselves with the French in the early wars.

Apache—A confederation of the Athapascan stock of North American Indians, consisting of a dozen or more tribes. In 1598 they inhabited northwestern New Mexico, and later spread over the valley of the Gila River. By 1800 their range extended from the Colorado River eastward to central Texas, and later they made incursions into Mexico as far south as Durango. They were the terror of the early Spanish settlers, and since the annexation of their territory to the United States they had given the Government much trouble under the leadership of such famous braves as Cochise, Mangus, Colorado, and Geronimo. White settlers opposed the plan of the Government to remove the Apaches to a reservation in New Mexico, and on April 30, 1871, over one hundred of the Indians were massacred at Fort Grant, Ariz.

Apache—

Agreement between Cherokee Commission and, 5768.

Appropriation for support of, etc., recommended, 4692.

Imprisonment of, by Government discussed and recommendations regarding, 5374, 5485, 5501, 5968.

Suppression of hostilities among, discussed, 4524, 4637, 4943, 5099, 5374.

Treaty with, 2727, 2762, 3394, 3573, 3796.

War with. (See Indian Wars.)

Apalachicola, treaty with, 1256.

Arapaho—A tribe of the Algonquian stock of Indians living on the headwaters of the Platte and Arkansas rivers, also ranging from the Yellowstone to the Rio Grande. The name is said to signify "tattooed people." They are at present divided between two reservations, one (the Arapaho) in Indian Territory, and the other (the Shoshone) in Wyoming.

Arapaho—
Agreement between Cherokee Commission and, 5565.
Lands acquired under, opened to settlement, 5710.
Appropriation to, recommended, 5761.
Disarming of, discussed, 4849.
Lands set apart for, referred to, 4680, 4778.
Treaty with, 3234, 3573, 3796, 3835.
Arickaree, allotment of lands in severalty to, referred to, 4783.

Aztecas or *Aztecs*—A branch of the Nahuatl stock of Indians, supposed to be the original inhabitants of Mexico. They appeared in the valley of Mexico about the middle of the thirteenth century, and are said to have been journeying southward for 600 years. The conquest of Mexico by Cortez in 1519 put an end to the power of the confederacy between the Aztecas, Tezucans, and the Tecpanecans. From analogy of language it is probable that they crossed the Pacific Ocean by the way of the Aleutian Islands from Asia. There are, however, various theories as to their origin. They founded Tenochtitlan on the present site of the City of Mexico in 1325, and ruled an empire of 30,000,000 people. They were well advanced in the arts and sciences, as is evidenced by the remains of their temples, roads and waterways. Only about 2,000,000 pure-blooded Aztecas are left in the mountains of Mexico. In stature they are small and somewhat resemble the Egyptians.

Bannock—
Agreement with, for disposal of lands for use of railroads, 4655, 4779.
Treaty with, 3898.
War with. (See Indian Wars.)
Belantse-Etoa. (See Minnetaree.)

Blackfeet—A savage and warlike tribe of the Siksika Confederation of the Algonquian stock of Indians. When not fighting among themselves they are generally at war with their neighbors. They formerly belonged to the Kena tribe, but separated from them and wandered up the Missouri River. The Sihasapa, an independent tribe, under the leadership of John Grass, was also known as the Blackfoot or Blackfeet Indians.

Blackfeet, treaty with, 2895, 3898.
Caddo—
Memorial from, regarding claims to lands in Oklahoma, 5671.
Treaty with, 1407.
Cahokia, treaty with, 616.
Calapona, treaty with, 2836.

Carib—A powerful and warlike tribe of Indians who occupied the northern part of South America and the Windward or Caribee Islands. Columbus encountered them at Guadelope and had a battle with them at Santa Cruz in 1493. After many disastrous wars with the Europeans and becoming mixed with fugitive negro slaves, they were transported to the vicinity of Honduras, where their descendants, the Black Caribs, now live.

Carmanchee, treaty with, 1407.

Cayuga—A small tribe of the Iroquois Confederacy of Indians (also called the Six Nations). They originally inhabited the district in the vicinity of Cayuga Lake, N. Y. During the Revolution they joined the British in making war on the colonists. They annoyed Gen. Clinton on his march to join Sullivan in 1779 and their villages were destroyed. After the war they ceded most of their lands to the State of New York and the tribe became scattered and almost totally disappeared. There are remnants of them in Oklahoma, Wisconsin, and Ontario, Canada. Their number is now insignificant.

Cayuse, treaty with, 2914.
Chasta, treaty with, 2836.
Chayenne. (See Cheyenne.)

Cherokee—An important tribe of the Iroquian stock of Indians. The name means "upland field." When first known to Europeans they occupied the mountains of southern Virginia, North and South Carolina, Georgia, Alabama, and Tennessee. In 1755 they ceded lands to Governor Glen and permitted the erection of forts within their territory. As the country about them filled up with whites they made repeated cessions of their territory until by the treaty of 1835 they sold all the remainder of their lands and removed west of the Mississippi River. The Cherokees rendered important service to Jackson's army in the War of 1812. They are now the most important and highly civilized tribe in Oklahoma.

Cherokee—
Act directing payment of certificates of, reasons for applying pocket veto to, 2182.
Agreement with, for cession of lands, 5671.
Bill for payment of money claimed by Eastern, 4971.
Bill securing to, proportion of proceeds of public lands, 4971.
Boundary line with United States, 1037.
Canal through country of, referred to, 987.
Citizenship solicited by, 442.
Commission to negotiate with, regarding claims to lands. (See Cherokee Commission.)
Commissioners' negotiations with, in the Indian Territory, 6271.
Conflict between Federal and Cherokee courts, 2909.
Convention with, referred to, 556, 834.
Difficulties among, 2262, 2279, 2308, 4743, 4744.
Enforcement of payment of taxes on products of, referred to, 4005.
Investigation of alleged frauds in affairs of, discussed, 2073.
Lands—
Containing iron ore relinquished to United States, 431.
Granted to, 1716.
Relinquished to United States, 108, 375, 384, 436, 808, 887, 1274, 1716.
Legal services rendered, payment of, recommended, 4694.
Neutral lands, treaty regarding, 3717.

New government to be formed by, 965.

Payment of—
Interest due, referred to, 2832.
Money to, 1716, 1823.
For lands ceded to United States, requested by, 4670, 4739.

Referred to, 1039, 4743, 4781.

Removal of, referred to, 1692, 1714, 4671.

Town of, destroyed, proclamation regarding, 129.

Treaty with, 71, 98, 103, 118, 167, 250, 271, 320, 378, 385, 389, 556, 566, 567, 589, 616, 811, 834, 968, 992, 1256, 1274, 1444, 1445, 1449, 1475, 1823, 2307, 3592, 3717.

Appropriation for, referred to, 2434.

Claims arising under, 2073, 2410.

Communication and agreement with Comanche, 5768.

Modification of, referred to, 1694.

Proclamation regarding, 72.

Trespasses upon lands of, by citizens of Georgia, 1039.

Troubles apprehended from, prevented, 1473.

War with. (See Indian Wars.)

Cheyenne—A tribe of the Algonquian stock of Indians. The word means "enemies." About 1800 they inhabited a region in and about the Black Hills and along the Platte River in Nebraska and the Cheyenne River in Dakota. In 1825 Gen. Atkinson made a treaty of peace with them. After this the tribe separated, and while the northern band located on the Tongue River Reservation, in eastern Montana, and remained peaceable, numerous encounters occurred between the settlers and the soldiers and the southern section of the tribe. Failure to fulfill their treaty obligations led to war in 1861. While negotiations for peace were being conducted in 1864, Col. Cheventon attacked the Sandy Creek village and massacred 100 Cheyennes. A bloody campaign followed. In 1865 the Indians agreed to go on a reservation, but the Dog Soldiers, whose village was burned by Gen. Hancock in 1867, kept up the warfare until defeated by Gen. Custer at Washita.

Cheyenne—
Agreement between Cherokee Commission and, 5565.

Lands acquired under, opened to settlement, 5710.

Appropriation to, recommended, 5761.

Authority to use certain funds for subsistence of, recommended, 4989.

Condition of, referred to, 4951, 5503.

Disarming of, discussed, 4849.

Disorderly conduct of, discussed, 4943.

Lands set apart for, referred to, 4680.

Title to, referred to, 4778.

Treaty with, 887, 912, 3234, 3573, 3796, 3835.

War with. (See Indian Wars.)

Chickamauga, depredations committed by, 118.

Chickasaw—A tribe of the Muskhogean stock of Indians, originally inhabiting the southern portion of the United States, mostly in the present States of Mississippi and Tennessee. In the eighteenth century their villages were about Pontotoc County, Miss., and their principal landing place Memphis. The treaty of 1786 fixed their northern boundary at the Ohio River, and as early as 1800 a part of the tribe migrated to Arkansas. In the early colonial wars they took the part of the English against the French, and in 1739 entered into friendly relations with Gen. Oglethorpe. In 1765 they met the Choctaws and whites at Mobile and entered into friendly trade relations. During the Indian wars generally they continued peaceful, aiding the whites against the Creeks in 1793. By treaties of 1805, 1816, and 1818 they ceded all their lands east of the Mississippi. In 1832 and 1834 they ceded the remainder of their lands and went to live with the Choctaws, with whom they dwelt harmoniously until 1855, when they were separated. During the early days of the Civil War they sided with the South.

Chickasaw—
Agreement with Choctaws referred to, 2835.

Appropriation to pay claim of, for lands ceded, recommendations regarding, 5637, 5664, 5761.

Boundary line with Choctaws, 2838.

Claims of, referred to, 2286, 2287.

Commissioners to treat with, for cession of lands, discussed, 6271.

Deed for release by, of lands, discussed, 5637, 5664, 5761.

Funds of, to be invested, 1406, 2719, 2726, 2736, 2808, 2828, 2893.

Lands ceded to, 108.

Lands ceded to United States by, 375.

Lands of, sold, 1810.

Removal of, 1715.

Stock of, to be transferred to Choctaws, referred to, 1837, 2271.

Subsistence to be granted, 1725.

Treaty with, 320, 378, 385, 566, 567, 614, 616, 1170, 1172, 1271, 1499, 2692, 2885, 3583.

Proclamation regarding, 72.

Chippewa—A tribe of the Algonquian stock of Indians, also known as the Ojibwa. They lived on the shores of Lakes Huron and Superior and extended westward to North Dakota. They allied themselves with the British during the Revolution, but made peace in 1785 and 1789. The confederacy formed by the Ojibwas, the Ottawas, and Pottawottomis was called the Three Fires. Having joined in the Miami uprising and been subjugated by Gen. Wayne, they again made peace in 1795. They renewed hostilities in 1812, but again came to terms in 1816, relinquishing all their lands in Ohio. Other treaties ceding lands were made, and by 1851 most of the tribe had moved beyond the Mississippi River.

Chippewa—
Agreement with, for cession of lands, 5781.
Agreements with, referred to, 5123.
Allotment of lands in severalty to, bill for, 4776.
Commission to negotiate with, 5500.
Disposition of bonds and funds of, referred to, 4660.
Negotiations with, for improvement of condition of, 4956.
Outbreak among, 6346.
Relinquishment of agreement with Ottawas, referred to, 3900.
Removal of, 1715.
Treaty with, 378, 422, 554, 566, 567, 590, 616, 635, 650, 913, 931, 940, 961, 963, 989, 996, 1027, 1029, 1257, 1345, 1444, 1447, 1498, 1612, 1622, 1646, 1733, 2063, 2304, 2414, 2829, 2835, 2838, 2884, 2954, 3110, 3363, 3397, 3400, 3403, 3411, 3460, 3581, 3718, 3835, 3900, 6286.
Instructions to commissioners negotiating, 6271.
Transmitted for exercise of powers for fulfilling, 6271.
Chippeway. (See Chippewa.)
Cho-bah-áh-bish, treaty with, 2912.

Choctaw—A tribe of the Muskhogean stock of Indians, originally occupying lands along the Gulf of Mexico. They were generally considered a friendly tribe, having acknowledged the sovereignty of the United States as early as 1786. They served in the war against England and in the Creek War. In 1820 they ceded part of their lands to the Government for territory west of Arkansas. In 1830 they ceded the remainder of their lands and moved west. Georgia assumed control of their lands in the East, granting them rights as citizens. New treaties were made in 1866. Their descendants now live in Oklahoma.

Choctaw—
Agreement with Chickasaws referred to, 2835.
Appropriation to pay claim of, for lands ceded, recommendations regarding, 5637, 5664, 5761.
Balance remaining from sales of orphan reservations of, 2910.
Boundary line with—
Chickasaws, 2838.
United States, 331, 338.
Claim of, to Greer County, 6122.
Claims of, referred to, 1348, 1353, 1613, 2286, 4463.
Opinion of Attorney-General regarding, referred to, 2433.
Commissioners to treat with, for cession of lands, discussed, 6271.
Deed for release by, of lands, discussed, 5637, 5664, 5761.
Lands of, proposition regarding cession of, 422.
Memorial from, regarding alleged violation of treaty by United States, 2003.
Proceedings of commission referred to, 2129.
Proceeds of sales of lands to be invested for, 1406.
Referred to, 1125.
Removal of, 1715.
Stock of Chickasaws to be transferred to, referred to, 1837, 2271.
Treaty with, 326, 351, 426, 448, 566, 567, 650, 770, 852, 856, 936, 989, 1092, 1095, 1105, 1499, 2885, 3583.
Advice of Senate regarding treaty for cession of lands east of Mississippi, requested, 1041.
President declines to appoint commission to conclude, 989.
Proclamation regarding, 72.
Referred to, 1093.
Transmitted for exercise of powers for fulfilling, 6271.
Christian—
Claims of, against United States, 1031.
Treaty with, 2953, 3110, 3400, 3835.

Cœur d'Alene—A small tribe of the Siliscean stock of Indians now living in Idaho and Washington. They call themselves Skitswish. Part of the tribe broke out into hostilities in 1858, but was subjugated and became peaceful. In 1867 a reservation was set apart for those in Idaho, and in 1872 a band in Paradise Valley was removed to a reservation between the Okinagan and Columbia Rivers. They numbered only about 427 in 1892.

Cœur d'Alêne, commission to negotiate with, for purchase of lands, 5493.
Cohnawaga, treaty with, referred to, 189.

Comanche—A savage tribe of the Shoshnoean stock of Indians, who were early engaged in disastrous wars with the Spanish settlers. In 1724 they were on the Upper Kansas River and later were south of the Red River, in Texas. Their recent territory was the extensive plains from the Rocky Mountains eastward into the Indian Territory and Texas, and they raided the country from Kansas southward as far as Durango, Mexico. They were expelled from Texas and became bitter enemies of that State. After harassing the settlers of the Southwest for some time they were finally located in the western part of Oklahoma. In 1868 they numbered about 2,500.

Comanche—
Agreement between Cherokee Commission and, 5768.
Claim of, discussed, 5762.
Treaty with, 2304, 2762, 3394, 3573, 3796.

Creek—A powerful confederacy of the Muskhogean stock of Indians, which in the early days of American history inhabited Alabama, Georgia, and part of Florida. At the instigation of Spaniards the Yamasi tribe made several attacks upon the settlers during the eighteenth century. They aided the British in the War of the Revolution, attacking Gen. Wayne in 1782. In 1790 they signed a treaty of friendship, but broke it two years later. In 1802 and 1805 they ceded lands to the whites. They joined the British in the War of 1812, and Aug. 30, 1813, they attacked Fort Mims and massacred 400 people. March 27, 1814, they were completely subjugated by Gen. Jackson, and ceded the greater part of their land to the whites. The Seminoles (q. v.) a renegade body of Creeks, made war upon the United States from 1835 to 1843. Part of the Creeks moved to Louisiana and part to Texas. Later Gen. Scott subjugated them, and they were removed to a reservation between the Canadian and Arkansas Rivers. In 1866 they ceded a large tract of land to the Government. The Creeks now occupy lands in Oklahoma, are well organized, and have a population, including mixed bloods, of 18,700.

Creek—
>   Charges against United States agent for, referred to, 965.
>   Commerce with, 69.
>   Commissioners to treat with, for cession of lands, discussed, 6271.
>   Conflicting claims of Georgia and, to lands. (See Georgia.)
>   Convention with, 378.
>   Court of inquiry relative to campaign against, 1508.
>   >   Opinion of, disapproved, 1508.
>   >   Proceedings of, transmitted for action thereon, 1510.
>   Difficulties of, with Seminoles, 2828, 2897.
>   Difficulties with, 143.
>   Frauds practiced upon, in land sales, 1622, 1697.
>   Hostilities of, ended, 1472, 1473.
>   >   Referred to, 1499.
>   Lands—
>   >   Ceded to United States by, 331, 362, 375, 960, 5450.
>   >   >   Amount of cession, 5481.
>   >   >   Proposition regarding, 4659, 5392.
>   >   Opened to settlement by proclamation, 5450.
>   >   Purchased for Seminoles from, 4786.
>   >   >   Additional proposition regarding, 5505.
>   >   Purchased from, title to, discussed, 4853.
>   Murdered by outlaws, 143.
>   Proposition of, to cede lands in Indian Territory, 4659, 5392.
>   >   Cession of, 5450.
>   Protection for lands of, invoked, 936.
>   Removal of, referred to, 1274, 1332, 1715.
>   Sales of reservations of deceased, 1733.
>   Treaty with, transmitted and discussed, 62, 68, 70, 71, 103, 159, 167, 191, 202, 385, 539, 654, 856, 872, 890, 909, 911, 936, 960, 964, 965, 968, 1072, 1132, 1256, 1733, 2214, 2775, 2916, 3394, 3591, 3900, 5392.

>   Correspondence regarding, 886.
>   Proclamation regarding, 72.
>   Ratified by proclamation, 6696.
>   Rights of, under, 936.
>   War with. (See Indian Wars.)

Crow—
>   Agreement with—
>   >   For sale of railroads, 4657.
>   >   Regarding individual allotments, 4957.
>   Appropriation for supplies for, recommended, 4781.
>   Treaty with, 913, 3835.

Crow Creek. (See Umpqua.)

Dakota. (See Sioux.)

Delaware—A confederacy of the Algonquian stock of Indians. They called themselves the Lenni-Lenape ("original men" or "preeminent men") and the French called them Loups (wolves). William Penn found them dwelling peaceably in the valley of the Delaware. He cultivated friendly relations with them and purchased much of their land. Their chief council fires blazed on the site of the present city of Philadelphia. In 1726 they refused to join the Iroquois in a war against the English and were stigmatized as "women." Later they became quite warlike, but were driven beyond the Alleghanies. Near the close of the Revolution a large number of Christian Delawares were massacred by Americans. The remnants of the tribe dwelt temporarily in Ohio, and in 1818 migrated to Missouri, in 1829, to Kansas, and in 1868 to the Indian Territory (now Oklahoma), where they live among the Cherokees and are well civilized.

Delaware—
>   Lands ceded to United States by, 360, 362, 1693.
>   Lands to be conveyed to Wyandottes, 2129.
>   Payment of amount of trust fund to, recommended, 5117.
>   Treaty with, 351, 361, 365, 378, 385, 463, 464, 539, 554, 590, 616, 1027, 1028, 1029, 1173, 2773, 3127, 3233, 3413, 3592.
>   >   Agreement with, for abrogation of article of, 3199.
>   Dwámish, treaty with, 2912.

Eel River—
>   Payment to, in lieu of annuities, 5115.
>   Treaty with, 351, 378, 385, 463, 464.

Five civilized tribes—
>   Discussed, 6270, 6346.
>   Relation of, to United States discussed, 5637, 6167.
>   Representation in Congress recommended, 5637.

Flathead—
>   Agreement with, for sale of lands, 4740, 4779.
>   Treaty with, 2913.

Fox—A tribe of the Algonquian stock of Indians. They followed the example of many other red men in joining with the British forces during the Revolutionary War. In 1804 they made a treaty ceding valuable lands of the Government. They renewed their alliance with the British in 1812. In 1824 and 1830 they ceded large tracts of land, and after taking part in the Black Hawk War (q. v.) were compelled to cede more of their territory by a treaty made with Gen. Scott. They have been successively driven from one place to another until the remainder of the tribe now occupies a small part of Oklahoma. They were incorporated at an early date with the Sac tribe.

Fox—
Agreement between Cherokee Commission and, 5510.
Proclaimed, 5591.
Hostile aggression of, 1251.
Treaty with, 363, 365, 554, 752, 888, 913, 1105, 1170, 1484, 1498, 1612, 2063, 2773, 3109, 3274, 3284, 3395, 3668, 3900.
Withdrawn, 4001.
War with. (See Indian Wars.)
F'peekskin, treaty with, 2836.
Great Osage. (See Osage.)
Gros Ventre—Two separate tribes of wandering Indians. The Gros Ventres of the prairie claim to have separated from the Arapahoes. After their separation they joined first one tribe and then another, and because of their infidelity suffered many hostile attacks from their neighbors. In 1824 they settled with the Blackfeet, near the Milk River. Their greatest chief was Sitting Squaw. Treaties were made with them in 1851, 1853, 1855, 1865, and 1868. In 1870 they were joined by their kindred, the Arapahoes, and are now occupying a portion of the Blackfeet Reservation in Montana.

Gros Ventre—
Allotment of lands in severalty to, referred to, 4783.
Treaty with, 3898.
Hunkpapa, treaty with, referred to, 912.
Illinois, treaty with, 127.
Iowa—
Agreement between Cherokee Commission and, 5511.
Proclaimed, 5591.
Treaty with, 913, 1484, 1612, 1729, 1733, 2773, 3274, 3900.
Withdrawn, 4001.
Iroquois—One of the great families of American Indians (formerly sometimes called the Long House, the Five Nations and later the Six Nations), composed of many tribes speaking languages of a common root. Most of the Iroquois tribes dwelt in early colonial days in the region of the Great Lakes, in what are now the Canadian Provinces of Ontario and Quebec and the States of New York and Pennsylvania. A small group of them (the Tuscaroras, etc.) occupied the region about the head waters of the Roanoke, Neuse, and branches of the Cape Fear Rivers, in North Carolina and Virginia. Intellectually and physically they were the foremost of American Indians. They were almost constantly at war with their neighbors or the whites. In the struggle for American independence nearly all of the Iroquois sided with Great Britain. They now have reservations in the Dominion of Canada. The Oneidas and Tuscaroras are now settled on reservations in New York, Pennsylvania, and Wisconsin.

Kansas—
Lands of, accounts for advertising sale of, 4664.
Treaty with, 883, 889, 912, 1040, 2273, 3109, 3277, 3413, 3717, 3965.
Withdrawn, 4001.
Kaskaskia—
Lands ceded to, 535.
Lands ceded to United States by, 347, 351.
Treaty with, 347, 351, 353, 616, 2775, 3270, 3716.
Ka-ta-ka, treaty with, 1612.
Kaw. (See Kansas.)
Kickapoo—A tribe of the Algonquian stock of Indians, who early inhabited the valleys of the Ohio and Illinois Rivers. The name was used by the Indians to describe smooth running rivers without rapids. In 1779 they allied themselves with the Americans against the British, but later turned and fought the new government until they were subjugated by Wayne in 1795, when they ceded part of their lands to the whites. In 1802, 1803, and 1804 the Kickapoos ceded more territory. They joined Tecumseh and fought against the whites at Tippecanoe in 1811. They united with the British in the War of 1812, but were badly defeated. By treaties made in 1815, 1816, and 1819 they ceded still more of their territory. Portions of them became roving bands. Some of them were removed to Kansas, and afterwards a portion of the tribe migrated to Mexico, whence about 400 were in 1873 returned by the Government and placed upon a reservation in the Indian Territory. In 1894 their number in the United States and Mexico was estimated at 762.

Kickapoo—
Agreement between Cherokee Commission and, 5638, 5649.
Settlement of estates of deceased, referred to, 4657, 4776, 4953.
Treaty with, 351, 464, 554, 566, 567, 635, 650, 654, 1173, 2773, 3284, 3716.
Kik-i-állus, treaty with, 2912.
Kiowa—
Agreement between Cherokee Commission and, 5768.
Claim of, discussed, 5762.
Treaty with, 1612, 2762, 3394, 3796.
Klamath—A tribe of Indians numbering some 600, distributed among eleven settlements in the Klamath Reservation, in Oregon. They formerly occupied a part of California, but the influx of whites led to trouble in 1851. Peace was soon restored. In 1864 they ceded large tracts of land to the Government and settled on a reservation.

Klamath, treaty with, 3470.
Kootenay—
Agreement with, for sale of lands, 4740, 4779.
Treaty with, 2913.
Little Osage. (See Osage.)
Lower Brulé, selling and trading of annuity goods by, 4671.
Maha, treaty with, 650, 888, 913.

Mahican—A tribe of the Algonquian family of Indians. The name is interpreted both as "wolf" and "seaside people." When first known to the whites they occupied both banks of the Hudson River, extending from near Albany to Lake Champlain. They were a distinct tribe from the Mohegans of the Connecticut River. The two tribes are generally confounded under the name of River Indians. The Mahicans were friendly to the English during the French and British struggles for supremacy in America. They assisted the colonists during the Revolution. Afterwards some of them became citizens.

Makah, treaty with, 2913.

Mandan—A tribe of the Siouan family of Indians. They were almost exterminated by smallpox in 1837. The survivors consolidated, and now occupy villages in common with the Hidatsa and Arikara, on the Fort Berthold Reservation, in North Dakota. They are of a light complexion.

Mandan—
Allotment of land in severalty to, referred to, 4783.
Treaty with, 888, 913.

Massachuset—A tribe of the Algonquian stock of Indians formerly inhabiting the eastern portion of the present State of Massachusetts and the basins of the Neponset and Charles Rivers. In 1617 they were much reduced by pestilence. The Massachuset Indians in 1650 were gathered into the villages of the Praying Indians and lost their tribal identity. They were always friendly to the whites.

Menominee—A tribe of the Algonquian family of Indians, which since it first became known to the whites has occupied lands in Wisconsin and upper Michigan, chiefly along the Menominee River and the west side of Green Bay, and extending south to the Fox River and west to the Mississippi. The name means "wild rice men," from their principal article of food. The French translated the name into "Folles Avoines," by which the Menominees are sometimes known. In the early Indian wars they sided with the British.

Menominee—
Lands ceded to United States by, 2501.
Referred to, 2838.
Sale of timber on reservation of, referred to, 4659.
Treaty with, 589, 913, 963, 996, 1104, 1198, 1491, 2501, 2521, 2773, 2896.

Me-sée-qua-guilch, treaty with, 2912.

Miami—
Distribution of money to western band of, 4660.
Funds of—
Bill authorizing application of, to relieve necessities of, 4958.
Consolidation of, 4661.
Payment to, in lieu of annuities recommended, 5115.
Treaty with, 351, 378, 385, 463, 464, 539, 554, 616, 931, 940, 964, 970, 1588, 1724, 1841, 2775, 3716.
Correspondence regarding, 1841.

Michigamia, treaty with, 616.

Minnetaree, treaty with, 913.

Mission—
Bill for relief of, 4786, 4954.
Commission to treat with, 5661.

Missouria—
Right of way of railroad through lands of, referred to, 4681.
Treaty with, 913, 1256, 1484, 1695, 2763, 2830, 3274, 3901.
Withdrawn, 4001.

Modoc—A tribe of the Lutunian family of Indians, which, with the Klamaths, formerly occupied the region of the Klamath Lakes and Sprague River, Ore., and extended southward into California. They began attacks on the whites as early as 1847. Hostilities continued until 1864, when they ceded their lands and agreed to go on a reservation. The Modocs became notorious through their conflict with the Government in 1872-73. They refused in 1872, to go to the Klamath Reservation, but instead took up strongly fortified positions in the lava beds near Fort Klamath, where in April, 1873, they murdered Gen. Canby and Commissioner Thomas, who had been sent to induce them to go to the reservation. War followed, and soon the Government troops compelled the Indians to surrender. Captain Jack, their leader, and two associates were executed and about eighty of his followers were removed to Indian Territory. The remainder reside on the Lower Colorado River, in Arizona.

Modoc—
Correspondence during war with, referred to, 4215.
Treaty with, 3470.

Mohave—A tribe of the Yuman Indians. They live along the Lower Colorado River in Arizona. About a third of them are on reservation ground.

Mohawk—A tribe of the Iroquois family of Indians. The name is said to be derived from the Algonquian word "maqua" meaning bears. Early settlers found them occupying the territory now included in New York State, extending from the St. Lawrence River to the Delaware River watershed and from the Catskills to Lake Erie. Their villages were along the Mohawk River. They were known as one of the Five Nations, and were the first tribe of the region to obtain firearms. The Mohawks were allies of the English in their wars with the French and Americans. In 1784, under Brant, they retired to Upper Canada.

Mohawk, treaty with, 255.

Mohegan—A tribe of the Algonquian family of Indians. They once lived chiefly on the Thames River, in Connecticut. The Mohegans claimed territory extending eastward into Massachusetts and Rhode Island. After the destruction of the Pequots, in 1637, they claimed the latter's lands. The death of King Philip, in 1676, left them the only important body of Indians in Southern New England. They finally became scattered, some joining the Brotherton Indians in New York. The Mohegans are often confounded with the Mahicans and called River Indians.

Mo-lal-la-las, treaty with, 2914.

Mo-lel. (See Mo-lal-la-las.)

Mosquito, correspondence regarding territory claimed by, referred to, 2722, 2894.

Munsee, treaty with, 378, 385, 1496, 1646, 1683, 1773, 2896, 3716, 3835, 3900.

Muscogee. (See Creek.)

Narraganset—A tribe of the Algonquian family of Indians which originally occupied a part of Rhode Island. They were friendly toward the early colonists, their wars being waged mostly against other tribes. Canonicus, their principal chief, gave Roger Williams a large tract of land and otherwise befriended him. Canonicus died in 1647, and King Philip, of the Pequots, induced the Narragansets to join him in a raid on the white settlements in violation of their treaty. King Philip and his allies, having ravaged the valley of the Connecticut in 1675 and 1676, returned to the land of the Narragansets, where the women and children of the tribes had been quartered and where supplies for the winter had been collected. They were surrounded by the whites and their villages were burned. Many of the Indians perished in the flames. Canonchet, the last chief of the Narragansets, was captured and killed. The few surviving Narragansets intermarried with the colonists and became civilized.

Navajo—An important tribe of the southern division of the Athapascan stock of Indians. From the time of their earliest discovery by the whites they have occupied the country along and south of the San Juan River, in northern New Mexico and Arizona, and extending into Colorado and Utah. They were surrounded by the Apache tribes except on the north, where the Shoshones show their neighbors. The Navajos are at present confined to the Navajo Reservations in Utah, New Mexico, and Arizona.

Navajo—
Practicability of restraining, within present reservation, etc., reports on, 5782.
Treaty with, 2571, 3834.

Nesqually, treaty with, 2836.

New York—
Cession of lands for benefit of, 1127.
Removal of, discussed, 1778.
Treaty with, 1496, 1684, 1729, 1778, 3394, 3896, 3897.
Withdrawn, 3667.

Nez Percé—The leading tribe of the Shahaptian stock of Indians. They are also known as the Chopunnish, Nomapu, Shahaptan, and Sahaptin. They were found by Lewis and Clark in 1804 inhabiting the country now comprised in western Idaho, northeastern Oregon, and southeastern Washington, and along the Columbia and Snake Rivers. They were good horsemen, but knew nothing of agriculture. The Nez Percés were always warlike. They derive their name from their custom of piercing the flesh of the nose for the reception of rings and ornaments. In 1877 the Nez Percés went to war with the whites in a vain attempt to defend their possessions. During this war Chief Joseph and White Bird gave orders to their people not to molest noncombatants, including women and children. October 1, Joseph and 500 of his followers were captured by United States soldiers. They now occupy the Nez Percé Reservation, in Idaho.

Nez Percé—
Campaign against, referred to, 4424.

Relief of, bill for, 4737, 4780.
Treaty with, 2914, 3403, 3893.
War with. (See Indian Wars.)

Nipmuc—A general name for the Indians of several tribes inhabiting in early colonial days south central Massachusetts and extending into Connecticut and Rhode Island. The majority of the Nipmucs did not at first join Philip in his war against the colonists, but were active against the English during the struggle in Connecticut in 1675. In January, 1676, the remnants of Philip's tribe, with the Narraganset, the Quaboag, and River Indians, joined the Nipmucs, and on the defeat of Philip fled north and west. Elliot's translation of the Bible is in the Natic dialect of the Nipmuc language. The word Nipmuc means "freshwater fishing place."

Noo-whá-há, treaty with, 2912.

Nook-we-cháh-mish, treaty with, 2912.

Northern Cheyenne. (See Cheyenne.)

N'Quentl-má-mish, treaty with, 2912.

Ogallala, treaty with, 912.

Ojibwa or *Chippewa*—A large tribe of the Algonquian stock of Indians. In the early history of the country their hunting grounds were along the shores of Lake Huron and Superior and across the State of Minnesota into the mountains of Dakota. Their name means "A puckering up" and is variously contended to refer to a puckering of the lips in a speaking or drinking, a peculiar seam in the moccasin, and the appearance of the flesh of roasted victims. They were known by the early French explorers as Saulteurs ("People of the falls"), having been first met with at Sault Ste. Marie. They were connected in a loose confederacy with the Ottawas and Pottawatomies and known as the Three Fires. After learning the use of firearms they greatly extended their territory by successful wars upon the Sioux, Foxes, and Iroquois. They joined Pontiac and were allies of England in the Revolution. They also participated in the Miami uprising. The Ojibwas ceded lands on Lake Erie in 1805. They again broke out into hostilities in 1812 and by the peace of 1816 relinquished all their lands in Ohio and retreated westward. By 1851 the remainder of the tribe in the United States was west of the Mississippi River. They now number about 30,000 in Canada and the United States, about one-half in each.

Old Settler. (See Cherokee.)

Omaha—A tribe of the Dhegiha division or confederacy of the Siouan stock of Indians. The name means "Those who went against the current." In 1815 and 1820, they ceded lands at Council Bluffs to the whites. In 1825 and 1830 they made similar treaties. In 1854 they gave up more of their lands and removed to a reservation in northeastern Nebraska. They number about 1,200.

Omaha—
Act to extend time of payment to purchases of land of, vetoed, 5525.
Claims of, against Winnebagoes, 4851.
Relief of, bill for, 4972.
Treaty with, 1484, 1695, 1729, 2768, 3574.

Oneida—A tribe of the Iroquois stock of Indians. They formerly occupied lands east of Oneida Lake, N. Y., and the head waters of the Susquehanna River to the south. The name means "Standing stone," or "People of stone." They usually acted independently of the other Iroquois and were not prominent in the confederacy. The early French settlers, with whom they were generally friendly, called them Oneiout. They took part with the Colonies in the Revolution. For this the British destroyed their villages. By a treaty in 1794 the Government made compensation for their losses. In 1785 and 1788 they ceded lands to New York State. In 1833 most of them removed to Green Bay, Wis., where they still remain, and others went to Canada. They number about 3,000.

Oneida—
> Lands of, proposition to sell, 256, 326.
> Treaty with, 335, 1684.

Onondaga—The leading tribe of the Iroquois stock of Indians. Their original hunting grounds were along the shores of the creek and lake in New York which bear their name. They claimed all the country between Lake Ontario and the Susquehanna River. The name is translated to mean "On the top of the mountain." In the councils of the Iroquois Confederacy they were called by a name meaning "They who keep the council fire." They fought on the side of the British in the Revolution and in the French wars. In 1788 they ceded all their land to the State of New York except a small portion, which they still hold.

Oregon, treaty with, 2393, 3593.

Osage—A tribe of the Dhegiha confederacy of the Siouan stock of Indians. They are divided into the Great or Highland Osage and Little or Lowland Osage, respectively referring in the native tongue to those who camped at the top of the hill, and those who camped at the foot of the hill, "waɔace" in the Siouan language denoting a camp on a hill. This has been corrupted into Osage. Through wars with the whites and Indian tribes of their own stock they were driven southward into Arkansas. In 1808 they ceded lands to the Government and made further cessions in 1815, 1818, 1822, 1825, and 1839. At the beginning of the Civil War about 1,000 of them went to the Indian Territory, and in 1865 and 1868 treaties were made looking to the removal of the remainder of the tribe. The last of their lands was ceded in 1870 to the Government and they went to their reservation in Oklahoma.

Osage—
> Decline to accede to terms reducing price of lands, 4673.
> Lands relinquished to United States by, 1693.
> Payment of interest due, referred to, 4691.
> Treaty with, 464, 474, 554, 614, 616, 767, 883, 889, 912, 1040, 3393, 3578, 3833, 3843.
> Referred to, 3578.
> Withdrawn, 4001.

Osette, rewards to, for rescuing crew of the *Umatilla* recommended, 4803.

Otoe—
> Right of way of railroad through lands of, referred to, 4681.

Treaty with, 589, 888, 913, 1256, 1484, 1695, 1729, 2768, 2830, 3901.
Withdrawn, 4001.

Ottawa—A tribe of the Algonquian stock of Indians. The Ottawas were first found along the Upper Ottawa River, in Canada. They were steadfast allies of the French. In 1646 they suffered defeat at the hands of the Iroquois and were driven westward along the southern shore of Lake Superior. In the early part of the eighteenth century the Ottawas established themselves about the site of the present city of Chicago, whence they spread in all directions. In 1763 they combined with other tribes in the South and West in an unsuccessful move against the English. During the Revolution they aided the British. They signed treaties in 1785 and 1789, but joined in the Miami uprising soon afterwards. They again made peace in 1795. Numerous treaties ceding territory to the United States followed, and a part of the tribe went south of the Missouri and soon lost their identity. Some of those living in Ohio migrated to the Osage country in 1836. In the same year the Michigan Ottawas ceded all their lands except reservations. In 1870 those in the Southwest were collected in the Indian Territory.

Ottawa—
> Disposition of bonds and funds of, referred to, 4660.
> Relinquishment of agreement with Chippewas referred to, 3900.
> Removal of, 1715.
> Treaty with, 378, 385, 422, 427, 448, 554, 566, 567, 590, 616, 888, 989, 991, 1027, 1029, 1124, 1199, 1257, 1345, 1444, 2304, 2884, 3283, 3716, 6271.
> Instructions to commissioners negotiating, 6271.
> Transmitted for exercise of powers for fulfilling, 6271.

Passamaquoddy—
> Fought for liberty of American people, 1026.
> Memorial of, presented to Congress in behalf of, 1026.

Pawnee—A confederacy of tribes of the Caddoan stock of Indians. They formerly inhabited the plains of Kansas and Nebraska and the banks of the Platte and Republican Rivers. This confederation has always been friendly to the Americans. By a treaty in 1833 they sold their lands south of the Nebraska. They were afterward attacked by the Sioux and the remainder of their hunting grounds was devastated. In 1857 the Pawnees sold more of their lands, and, the depredations of the Sioux continuing, the remnants of the Pawnee confederation were removed to a reservation in Oklahoma. They are now divided into four tribes—the Tcawi or Grand Pawnee, the Pitahauerat or Tapage, the Republican Pawnee, and the Skidi or Pawnee Loup.

Pawnee—
> Agreement between Cherokee Commission and, 5768.
> Aid for, recommended, 4314.
> Treaty with, 616, 888, 913, 1256, 2521, 2995.

Peoria, treaty with, 616, 1173, 2775, 3270, 3716.

Pequot or *Pequod*—A former tribe of the Algonquian stock of Indians. The name is translated "destroyers" or "ravagers." They were the most dreaded of all the southern New England Indians. When first known to the whites the Pequots formed one tribe with the Mohegans under Sassacus, but they seceded under Uncas and occupied a narrow strip of coast in southern Connecticut from the Niantic River to the Rhode Island boundary. They never exceeded 3,000. In 1634 they entered into a treaty with the colonists at Boston, but failed to keep the peace. Expeditions were sent against them and they in turn attacked Wethersfield and massacred many settlers. In 1637 they were surprised at a fort near the present site of Groton, Conn., and in the battle which ensued and the subsequent one at Fairfield Swamp the tribe was nearly annihilated. Many of them were sold as slaves and the others were scattered.

Piankeshaw—
Lands ceded to United States by, 362, 375.
Treaty with, 351, 362, 365, 389, 544, 1173, 2775, 3270, 3716.

Piegan, engagement of Col. Baker with, referred to, 4004.

Pi-Ute, agreement with, for right of way for railroad, 4736, 4776.

Ponca—
Commission appointed to investigate condition, etc., of, and report of, discussed, 4582.
Treaty with, 887, 912, 3015, 3263.

Poncarar, treaty with, 589.

Pottawatomie—A tribe of the Algonquian stock of Indians. When first known (about 1670), they lived on the Noquet Islands, in Green Bay, Wis. At the close of the seventeenth century they were established on the Milwaukee River, at Chicago, and on the St. Joseph River. At the beginning of the nineteenth century they possessed the country around the head of Lake Michigan from the Milwaukee River, Wis., to the Grand River, Mich., extending south into Illinois and in Indiana to the Wabash River. They took a prominent part in Pontiac's War and in the War of the Revolution, when they fought on the British side, as they also did during the War of 1812. The name Pottawatomie signifies "firemakers," and has reference to their secession from the Ojibwas and making fires for themselves. A large tract was assigned to them on the Missouri. In 1867, 1,400 of them became citizens, but the Prairie Band continued under the Indian Department.

Pottawatomie—
Agreement between Cherokee Commission and, 5514.
Proclaimed, 5591.
Location of lands ceded to Indiana by, 1098.
Removal of, 1715.
Treaty with, 351, 378, 385, 422, 427, 448, 463, 554, 566, 567, 590, 616, 888, 913, 931, 940, 961, 988, 989, 991, 996, 1027, 1029, 1170, 1257, 1345, 1354, 1446, 1491, 1498, 2304, 3262, 3356, 3580, 3717.

Complaints regarding, 3263.
Instructions to commissioners negotiating, 6271.
Transmitted for exercise of powers for fulfilling, 6271.

Pueblo—A common name for several distinct tribes and nations of Indians occupying western New Mexico, Arizona, Chihuahua, Texas and the valleys of the Rio Grande and Colorado Rivers. The Zuñis inhabit the largest pueblos or villages. They are distinct nations. When discovered by the Spaniards they occupied seven villages, known as the Seven Cities of Cibola, on the site of one of which stands the present pueblo of Zuñi. The Tañoan are also a distinct a distinct stock of Indians and comprise several tribes of closely allied dialects. The Tusayan is a confederacy of tribes inhabiting northeastern Arizona. The Pueblo Indians have always been friendly. The Supreme Court declared them citizens in 1857. The name was also applied by Spaniards to the early colonies established in California by authority of Philip II. Pueblo lands were vested either by proprietary right in the individual or in companies, reserving to them certain rights as citizens and colonists. The first settlers were also allowed money and supplies and permitted to elect their own magistrates, of whom the chief was the alcalde. They were allowed common use of the pasture lands reserved to the Crown outside the pueblo grants.

Puyallup—
Commission to treat with, 5663.
Treaty with, 2836.

Quapaw, treaty with, 616, 848, 855, 2829, 3716.

Qui-nai-elt, treaty with, 2913.

Quil-leh-ate, treaty with, 2913.

Ricara, treaty with, 888, 913.

River Crow, treaty with, 3898.

Rogue River, treaty with, 2762, 2836.

Sac—A tribe of the Algonquian stock of Indians who formerly lived near the mouth of the Ottawa River and along the Detroit River. They were driven thence by the Iroquois and settled about Green Bay, Wis. They allied themselves with the Fox tribe. About 1765 the Sacs took possession of land on both sides of the Mississippi, which they had conquered from the Illinois. From this time their history is the same as that of the Foxes. By 1810 they had overrun a large territory in Wisconsin, Illinois, Iowa, and Missouri. They aided Pontiac, and during the Revolution supported the English. They fought against the United States in 1812. In 1832 a part of the tribe, led by Black Hawk, rebelled and was defeated and removed to the Indian Territory, where most of the remainder of the two tribes, still live. The name Sac is a corruption of the Indian word "osagi," meaning "People at the mouth of the river," and refers to their early habitat.

Sac—
Agreement between Cherokee Commission and, 5510.
Proclaimed, 5591.
Annuities proposed to, 363.
Hostile aggression of, 1251.
Treaty with, 363, 365, 554, 566, 567, 767, 913, 1105, 1170, 1484, 1498, 1612, 2063, 2773, 3109, 3274, 3284, 3395, 3669, 3900.

Withdrawn, 4001.

War with. (See Indian Wars.)

Saginaw, treaty with, 1489.

So-heh-wamish, treaty with, 2836.

Sah-ku-méhu, treaty with, 2912.

St. Regis, treaty with, 1684.

Sam-áhmish, treaty with, 2912.

Scotan, treaty with, 2836.

Seminole—A tribe of the Muskhogean stock of Indians. The tribal name is translated to mean "renegade" or "separatist," and refers to their having separated from the Creek confederacy during the latter part of the eighteenth and the early part of the nineteenth century and settled in Florida. During the War of 1812 the British were materially aided by the Seminoles, and in 1817-18 they made many depredations on the settlements of Georgia and Alabama. By a treaty ratified in 1834 they ceded all their lands in the eastern part of the United States to the General Government and agreed to move to the Indian Territory. Their refusal to comply with the terms of this treaty led to a long and bloody war. (See Seminole Wars; Creeks.) The number of Seminoles finally removed in 1843 was officially reported as 3,824. They became one of the five civilized nations of the Indian Territory.

Seminole—

Authority to use certain funds in purchase of lands for, recommended, 5197.

Court of inquiry relative to campaign against, 1511.

Difficulties with Creeks, 2828, 2897.

Hostilities of, 1447, 1448, 1472, 1833, 2583.

Lands—

Purchased for, 4786, 5450.

Additional proposition regarding, 5505.

Purchased from—

Opened to settlement by proclamation, 5450.

Title to, discussed, 4853.

To be relinquished by, proposition regarding, 5392, 5396.

Cession of, 5450, 5482.

Removal of, arrangements made for, 1332, 2583, 2707, 2720.

Separation of from Creeks referred to, 1727.

Setting apart of land for, suggested, 1727.

Treaty with, 789, 1256, 2214, 2916, 3591.

War with. (See Seminole War.)

Seneca—A tribe of the Iroquois confederacy of Indians. The name is foreign to the language of the tribe, and is probably a corruption of a word meaning "red paint." They called themselves by a name meaning "people of the mountain." When first known they occupied lands in western New York between Seneca Lake and Genesee River. They allied themselves with Pontiac, destroyed Venango, attacked Fort Niagara, and cut out an army train near Devils Hole in 1763. They were conspicuous in the wars west of Lake Erie. On the defeat of the Erie and Neuter tribes they took possession of the territory westward to Lake Erie and southward along the Allegheny River into Pennsylvania, receiving by adoption many of the conquered tribes, which act made them the largest tribe of the Iroquois confederacy. They sided with the British in the Revolutionary War and their territory was devastated by the Americans. Peace was made with them in 1784. In the War of 1812 the tribe divided, those in New York taking part with the Americans and those in Ohio joining the hostile Western tribes. These were removed to the Indian Territory in 1831, the friendly tribes remaining in New York.

Seneca—

Conveyance made by, 940.

Memorial from, referred to, 2278.

Money held in trust for, 1019.

Portion of, opposed to treaty of Buffalo, 1784.

Remonstrance of, against allotment of lands in severalty to, 4668.

Treaty with 203, 249, 335, 539, 554, 590, 616, 1105, 1124, 1198, 2010, 2829, 3716.

Seven Nations. (See Cohnawaga.)

Shawanese, treaty with United States, 3717.

Shawnee—A tribe of the Algonquian stock of Indians. From their wanderings and the difficulties of identification their real habitat is uncertain. They seem to have wandered farther south than any other of the Algonquian tribes and to have been driven westward by the Iroquois. The name is translated to mean "Southerners." They were early known in the Cumberland Valley, in Tennessee, and along the Upper Savannah River, in South Carolina. About the middle of the eighteenth century they united in the Ohio Valley and were almost constantly at war with the whites. At first they aided the French, but were won over by the English. The Shawnees joined Pontiac, and from time to time continued hostilities until the peace of 1786. They took part in the Miami uprising, but were reduced by Gen. Wayne and submitted under the treaty of 1795. In 1812, under the leadership of Tecumseh, this tribe joined the English in their war against the Americans. They became scattered, and the Missouri band ceded their lands in 1825, the Ohio band in 1831. The main band ended their tribal relations in Kansas in 1854.

Shawnee—

Distribution of moneys to band of, referred to, 4659.

Lands of, treaty with, for purchase of, 1797.

Treaty with, 351, 378, 448, 539, 590, 616, 883, 1124, 1125, 1197, 1797, 2775, 2829, 3402, 3579, 3716, 3717.

Sheepeater—

Agreement with, for sale of lands, 4779.

Treaty with, 3898.

S'Homanish, treaty with, 2836.

Shoshone—The most northerly confederation of the Shoshonean stock of Indians. They are sometimes known as Snake Indians. There are some twenty known tribes of Shoshones. The division formerly occupied western Wyoming, part of central and southern Idaho, part of eastern Oregon, western and central Nevada, and a strip of

Utah west of the Great Salt Lake. The Snake River region of Idaho was their principal hunting ground. In 1803 they were on the head waters of the Missouri in western Montana, but they had earlier ranged farther east on the plains, whence they had been driven into the Rocky Mountains. Some of the bands near Great Salt Lake began hostilities in 1849. In 1862 California volunteers nearly exterminated one tribe. Treaties were made with various tribes later. They are at Fort Hall Agency and Lemhi Agency, Idaho.

Shoshone—
    Agreement with, for disposal of lands, 4655, 4779.
    Treaty with, 3397, 3898.
Sioune, treaty with, 912.

Sioux or *Dakota*—The principal division of the Siouan stock of Indians. The name is translated to mean "The snakelike ones." The early habitat of the Siouan family included parts of British America and the following States: Montana, Wyoming, the Dakotas, Minnesota, Iowa, Wisconsin, Nebraska, Kansas, Missouri, Oklahoma, Mississippi, Kentucky, the Carolinas, and Virginia. The Dakotas, generally known as the Sioux, have always been the most warlike of the stock. They have been hostile not only to whites and to the Indians of other stocks, but also to tribes of their own stock. The principal divisions of the family are the Dakota, Dhegiha, Tciwere, Winnebago, Mandan, Hidatsa, Tutelo, Biloxi, and Kataba.

The Sioux proper, or Dakotas, are divided into seven council fires, and they are sometimes known by an Indian name signifying that fact. They aided the English in 1812. In 1837 they ceded all their lands east of the Mississippi to the Government and in 1851 made further grants. In 1854 they engaged in war against the whites, but were subjugated in 1855. In 1862 a general Sioux uprising occurred, in which many whites and Indians were killed. They were defeated and scattered by Government troops, and a treaty was made with them by Gen. Sherman in 1868. Nevertheless, Sitting Bull and some of the other chieftains were unreconciled. June 25, 1876, Gen. Custer and 276 men were surprised by a force of 9,000 Sioux on the Little Big Horn River, Montana, and massacred. (See also Custer Massacre.) Sitting Bull, their chief, was killed near Fort Yates, N. Dak., in 1890, while resisting arrest.

Sioux—
    Agreement with, for purchase of lands, discussed, 5498.
        Proclaimed, 5707.
    Commission to treat with, for—
        Cession of lands, 5480, 5496.
        Modifications of treaties, 5742.
    Concessions obtained from, referred to, 4368.
    Hostile demonstrations of, referred to, 4327.
    Lands of—
        Opening of, to settlement refused by, 5381.
        Relinquished to United States, 5480.
    Outbreak among, discussed, 5636.
    Pursuit of hostile bands of, into Hudsons Bay territories, referred to, 3399.

    Removal of, to—
        Indian Territory, 4367.
        Nebraska, 3587.
    Report on condition of, referred to, 3897.
    Right of way for railroad through reservation of, 4775, 4780.
    Sioux expedition, referred to, 2912.
    Treaty with, 887, 888, 913, 1484, 1499, 1612, 1912, 2005, 2564, 2707, 3016, 3064, 3573, 3898, 3901.
    Reasons for concluding, 1912.
    War with. (See Indian Wars.)
Sisseton, treaty with, 3668.

Six Nations—A confederation of the Indian tribes of the Huron-Iroquois family. They were also known as Long House. They originally occupied the territory now included in New York State and southern Canada. The five original nations were the Mohawks, Senecas, Cayugas, Oneidas, and Onondagas. In 1712 the Tuscaroras, a branch of the Iroquois living in North Carolina, returned northward after their defeat by the white colonists, and joined their kindred. The confederation then became known as the Six Nations.

Six Nations—
    Conference with, 103, 166, 651.
    Depredations of, 57, 60, 61, 74, 76, 78.
    Negotiations with, 326.
    Opinion of Senate concerning treaty with, requested, 54.
    Referred to, 147.
    Treaty with, 54, 98, 159.
Skágit, treaty with, 2912.
Skai-wha-mish, treaty with, 2912.
S'Kallams, treaty with, 2913.
Skope-áhmish, treaty with, 2912.
Sk-táh-le-jum, treaty with, 2912.
Sk-táhl-mish, treaty with, 2912.
Smalhamish, treaty with, 2912.
Snake, treaty with, 3579.
Sno-ho-mish, treaty with, 2912.
Snoquálmoo, treaty with, 2912.
Soc, treaty with, 888.
Southern—
    Commissioners to, recall, 263.
    Negotiations with, 63.
    Treaty with, President meets Senate for discussion of, 53.
Squawksin, treaty with, 2836.
Squi-aitl, treaty with, 2836.
Squin-áh-mish, treaty with, 2912.
Ste'h-chass, treaty with, 2836.
Steilacoom, treaty with, 2836.
St-káh-mish, treaty with, 2912.
Stockbridge—
    Proceedings for relief of, referred to, 2167.
    Treaty with, 1496, 1646, 1683, 1773, 2529, 2896, 3716.
Stoluck-whá-mish, treaty with, 2912.
Suquámish, 2912.

Susquehanna or *Conestoga*—A tribe of the Iroquoian stock of Indians now extinct. They formerly lived in Pennsylvania and Maryland along the Susquehanna River and at the head of the Chesapeake Bay. They were close allies of the Dutch and Swedes, but treacherous in their dealings with the English. The Susquehannas were overthrown by the Iroquois in 1675, after a desperate struggle. A remnant of the tribe was massacred by whites at Lancaster, Pa., in 1763.

Swin-á-mish, treaty with, 2912.

Tamarois, treaty with, 616.

Ta-wa-ka-ro, treaty with, 1612.

Teton, treaty with, 912.

Tonawanda, treaty with, 3014.

Tonkawa, agreement between Cherokee Commission and, 5638, 5649.

Turtle Mountain—
Agreement with, for cession of lands, 5781.
Referred to, 5382.

Tuscarora—A tribe of the Iroquois stock of Indians. Their name means "Unwilling to be with others." They early separated from the parent stock and emigrated to the South. They were first known to Europeans on the Neuse River, in North Carolina. In 1711 they attacked the whites and were almost annihilated. The survivors returned to the Iroquois in New York and became one of the Six Nations.

Tuscarora, treaty with, 344.

Umatilla, treaty with, 2914.

Umpqua, treaty with, 2762, 2836.

Upper Pend d'Oreille—
Agreement with, for sale of lands, 4740, 4779.
Treaty with, 2913.

Utah (*Uta, Ute,* or *Youta*)—A division of the Shoshonean family of Indians. They formerly occupied the central and western portions of Colorado and the northeastern portions of Utah. The Utahs are divided into about fifteen tribes and have been generally friendly to the whites. Some disturbances occurred between them and the Mormons, and also the miners of Pike's Peak. In 1865 they ceded large tracts of land to the Government.

Utah, treaty with, 2571, 3393, 3577, 3663.
Agreement with, referred to, 4538, 4552, 4576.
Appropriation for Ute Commission recommended, 4672.
Negotiations with, referred to, 4464, 4465.
Payments to, referred to, 4434, 4533.
Removal of, 4637.
Suppression of hostilities among, 4524, 4528.
Treaty with, 3827.

Wabash—
Expeditions against, 104, 107, 118, 126, 159.
Treaty with, 127.
Instructions to commissioner in concluding with Indians, 6271.
Troops must be called forth to suppress, 53, 74.

Wahpeton, treaty with, 3668.

Walla Walla, treaty with, 2513, 2514.

Wampanoag—A tribe of the Algonquian stock of Indians. Their early habitation was the country to the west of Narragansett Bay. They also ruled the country from the bay to the Atlantic, including the island of Martha's Vineyard. The name means "Eastern lands." The Wampanoags were sometimes styled Pokanokets. after their principal village. They were at first very kindly disposed toward the whites. In 1621 they entered into a friendly compact with the Plymouth settlers, and Massasoit, the chief of the tribe, was on good terms with Roger Williams. They resisted all attempts to convert them to Christianity. Philip, the son of Massasoit, began a war against the whites in 1675, which, after great loss to the whites, resulted in the extermination of the tribe.

Wascoe, treaty with, 2513.

Wea—
Convention with, 463, 464.
Treaty with, 566, 567, 616, 650, 2775, 3270, 3416.
Trust lands of, referred to, 3400.

Wichita—
Agreement between Cherokee Commission and, 5638, 5648, 5671.
Lands of, title to, referred to, 4778.

Winnebago—A tribe of the Siouan stock of Indians. The name is a corruption of a word meaning "dirty water." They called themselves Hotcangara, meaning "parent speech." Early in the history of the Northwest Territory the Winnebagoes migrated eastward, but were forced back to the vicinity of Green Bay, Wis. They were nearly exterminated through wars with neighboring tribes in the seventeenth century. They aided the French in the wars between France and England and were allies of the British during both the Revolution and the War of 1812. The Winnebagoes were active in the Indian war of 1793-94 and were subdued by Gen. Wayne. A treaty of peace was made with them in 1816. In 1826 and 1827 treaties were made fixing the boundaries of their hunting grounds. In 1829 they ceded large tracts of land to the General Government, and after several removals they were in 1866 settled upon reservations in Nebraska and Wisconsin.

Winnebago—
Agent for, recommended, 4959.
Claim of Omahas against, 4851.
Treaty with, 913, 961, 963, 989, 991, 996, 1027, 1029, 1170, 1612, 2771, 2775, 2839, 3109, 3574.

Wyandot—A tribe of the Iroquoian family of Indians. When first known to the whites they occupied a narrow strip of land in Ontario, but between 1615 and 1650 they were almost exterminated in war with neighboring tribes. They joined with another tribe and soon spread along the south and west shores of Lake Erie and acquired considerable influence. The Wyandots sided with the French till the close of Pontiac's War and aided the British in the War of 1812. The word "Wyandot" means "calf of the leg," and refers to the manner in which they cut their meat. They were called "Hurons" by the French on account of the arrangement of their hair, which resembled the bristles of a wild boar.

Wyandot—
Lands to be conveyed to, by Delawares, 2129.
Treaty with, 351, 378, 385, 422, 427, 448, 539, 554, 590, 616, 1132, 1445, 2010, 2662, 2834, 6271.
Opinion of Senate concerning, requested, 54.
Referred to, 2837.
Transmitted for exercise of powers for fulfilling, 6271.
Yakama, treaty with, 2914.
Yancton, treaty with, 912.
Yanctonie, treaty with, 912.

Indian Wars.—From the earliest years of our history difficulties have been constantly occurring with the Indians within our borders. Only one of these has had any special political significance, and but a brief reference to some of the principal Indian wars will be attempted.

Apache Outbreak.—In the autumn of 1879 the Apaches of New Mexico began attacks on white settlers in their vicinity. They were driven into Mexico by United States soldiers and their chief Victoria was killed and most of the band were captured or killed.

A band of Apaches under Chiefs Geronimo and Natchez left their reservation in Arizona in the spring of 1882 and kept up an irregular warfare for three years. Sept. 1, 1885, Gen. Crook captured the band, but they escaped in a few days. Crook was superseded by Gen. Miles. In the pursuit of the Indians Capt. Crawford was killed by Mexicans through an alleged mistake, and the Indians continued their depredations until September, 1886, when they surrendered under pledges which prevented trial for murder. They were soon after removed to Florida, where their leaders were kept.

Again, in 1890, the Sioux began their war dances in South Dakota, and were soon joined by other tribes. Gen. Miles was in command in Dakota, and was joined by Gen. Brook and Col. W. F. Cody (Buffalo Bill). Dec. 15, 1890, the Indian camp was seized, and in the struggle Sitting Bull, his son Crow Foot, and others were killed. After this Chief Red Cloud counseled surrender, but Chief Big Foot and a band of about 160 warriors from the Cheyenne River repaired to the Bad Lands of Dakota. They were met at Wounded Knee Creek, Dec. 29, by Lieut. Hawthorne and the Seventh Cavalry and Maj. Whiteside's artillery. In the confused hand to hand fight the Indians were almost exterminated, including some 200 women and children. Capt. Wallace, Lieutenants Casey and Mann and several non-commissioned officers and privates were killed.

Black Hawk War.—In 1831 and 1832 the Sacs, Foxes and Winnebagoes, led by Black Hawk, refused to leave lands which they had ceded to the government, but the Black Hawk War, as the resulting disturbance is called, was soon ended and the leader captured.

In 1836 and 1837 there were minor disturbances in the South with the Creeks and Chicopees, connected with their removal west of the Mississippi.

Creek Indian Wars.—In 1813 and 1814 General Andrew Jackson conducted operations against the Creeks in the south, who were brought to terms by victories at Tallushatchie, Talladega and the Horse Shoe Bend of the Tallapoosa River.

Harrison's Expedition.—The Indians of the West formed a conspiracy some years later under Tecumseh and Elkswatama the Prophet, renewed hostilities, and were defeated in 1811 at Tippecanoe by General Harrison. During the war of 1812 the northern Indians joined their forces with the British and gave us much trouble; they, together with the British, were defeated at the River Thames in 1813 by Harrison, and Tecumseh was killed.

Miami Confederacy.—From 1790 to 1795 a war was waged with the Miami Confederacy in Ohio and neighboring territory. The confederacy was composed of the Miamias, Wyandots, Delawares, Potawatomies, Shawnees, Chippewas, and Ottowas. Generals Harmar and St. Clair met with reverses, but General Wayne crushed the outbreak in 1793.

Modoc War.—In 1872 the Modoc Indians in Oregon refused to go upon a designated reservation. They retreated before the troops to a volcanic region known as the lava-beds and could not be conquered. A peace conference held with them in April, 1873, was broken up by their treacherous murder of General Canby and Dr. Thomas. About the first of June, however, General Davis forced them to surrender; Captain Jack, their leader, and others were executed.

Nez Percé Outbreak.—In 1877 trouble with the Nez Percé Indians of Idaho, led by their chief Joseph, came to a head. General Howard was sent against them, they were soon hemmed in, and in October were completely defeated by Colonel Miles.

Pine Ridge Uprising.—On the last three days of December, 1890, and the first part of January, 1891, Major Forsyth was attacked in the Pine Ridge agency by dissatisfied Brûlés. They were repulsed and surrounded by Gen. Brook and the Second Infantry; about 4,000 Indians surrendered to Gen. Miles, who took some of their leaders to Washington to confer with President Harrison and Secretary Noble.

Seminoles.—In 1817 the Seminoles in Georgia and Alabama showed signs of hostility. General Jackson subdued them in the spring of the next year. In carrying out his campaign, thinking the Spaniards had encouraged the Indians, Jackson entered Florida, then a Spanish possession, and captured St. Marks. He seized two Englishmen, Arbuthnot and Ambrister, who were tried by court-martial on a charge of inciting the Indians, found guilty and executed. He then took possession of Pensacola and captured Fort Barrancas on the shore of the bay after a slight resistance. The execution of two British subjects raised such a storm of indignation in England that another war was threatened, but the English ministry admitted the justice of the act. Jackson's enemies endeavored to have Congress pass a vote of censure, but that body and the president supported him. Spain also complained of his proceeding, but without effect.

From 1835 to 1843 the Seminoles in Florida, led by Osceola, were in arms, refusing to remove to Western reservations. In December, 1835, Major Dade with a force of over a hundred men fell into an ambush and all but four of the command perished. Various battles were fought, but the Indians prolonged the war among the swamps of Florida for seven years. Colonel Zachary Taylor was among the leaders of our troops. Finally, after the expenditure of men and much money the persistent Indians were removed to the West.

Sioux Uprising.—In 1876 the Sioux Indians gave trouble in the Black Hills region on the borders of Montana and Wyoming. A large force of regulars was sent against them under Generals Terry, Crook, Custer and Reno. On June 25, 1876, the two latter attacked at different points a large Indian village situated on the Little Big Horn River. General Custer was killed with 261 men of the Seventh Cavalry and fifty-two were wounded. Reno held his ground till saved by re-enforcements. Additional troops were sent to the spot and the Indians were defeated in several engagements, and in the beginning of 1877 the Indian chief, Sitting Bull, escaped to Canada.

Ute Troubles.—In 1879 an outbreak of the Ute Indians cost the lives of the government agent, Major Thornburgh, and a number of soldiers before it was quelled.

Indian Wars:

Apache, discussed, 4524, 5099.
Bannock, discussed, 4454.
Cherokee, discussed, 1453, 1472.
Cheyennes, threatening attitude of, 4943.
Chippewa outbreak discussed, 6346.
Creek—
  Discussed, 1453, 1472.
  Probability of, 148.
Discussed by President—
  Adams, J. Q., 953.
  Arthur, 4625, 4723, 4767.
  Cleveland, 4933, 4943, 5099.
  Fillmore, 2623, 2668.
  Grant, 4360.
  Harrison, Benj., 5636.
  Hayes, 4424, 4454, 4524, 4528.
  Jackson, 1166, 1251, 1453, 1472, 1508, 1511.
  Johnson, 3774.
  Lincoln, 3333, 3345.
  Madison, 481, 524, 548.
  Monroe, 600, 610, 611, 617, 781.
  Polk, 2410, 2494.
  Tyler, 1933, 1944, 2007, 2051.
  Van Buren, 1833.
  Washington, 53, 74, 96, 107, 126, 132, 148, 159, 177.
Fox—
  Discussed, 1166.
  Termination of, 1251.
Gen. Gaines' requisition for volunteers in, not approved by President, 1453.
Instructions to Gen. St. Clair authorized him in 1789 to employ militia against the Wabash and Illinois.
Referred to, 1433, 1499, 1647, 2911, 3355, 4004, 4215, 4433, 4435, 4436.
Requisition for volunteers in, by Gen. Gaines not approved, 1453.
Statement of number of soldiers, Indians, etc., killed in, transmitted, 4580.
Surrender of Geronimo discussed, 5099.
Surrender of Sitting Bull discussed, 4625.
Treachery of Indians referred to, 1834.

Troops in, should be compensated, 1454.
Modoc, correspondence regulating, referred to, 4215.
Nez Percé—
  Discussed, 4424.
  Referred to, 4433.
Northern Cheyenne, discussed, 4454.
Piegan, engagement of Col. Baker with, referred to, 4404.
Ricaree, discussed, 781.
Sac—
  Discussed, 1166.
  Termination of, 1251.
Seminole—
  American forces in, and officers commanding, discussed, 611, 1472, 1833.
  Appropriation for suppression of, recommended, 1473.
  Brevet rank for officers of Army participating in, 2008.
  Discussed, 600, 611, 617, 1453, 1472, 1508, 1833, 1933, 2007, 2051.
  Massacre of Maj. Dade's command, 1834.
  Origin of, referred to, 1944.
  Spain furnishes aid to enemy in, 611.
  Termination of, 2051.
  Troops in, rations furnished, referred to, 594.
  Troops under Gen. Jackson referred to, 611.
Sioux, discussed, 3333, 4360, 5636.
Ute, discussed, 4524, 4528.
Wabash, troops must be called for to suppress, 53, 74.

Indiana.—One of the middle western group of states; nickname, "The Hoosier State." It is bounded on the north by Michigan and Lake Michigan, on the east by Ohio, on the south by Kentucky (separated by the Ohio River), and on the west by Illinois. The capital is Indianapolis.

Indiana was settled by the French (at Vincennes) in 1702 and was ceded to Great Britain in 1763 and to the United States in 1783. It became a part of the Northwest Territory in 1787 and was made a separate Territory in 1800, and was admitted to the Union Dec. 11, 1816. Area, 36,354 square miles. About 94 per cent. of the total area of the State is devoted to farming.

Statistics of agriculture collected for the last Federal census place the number of farms in the State at 215,485 (a decrease of 6,412 since 1900), comprising 21,-299,823 acres, valued, with stock and improvements, at $1,809,135,238. The average value of land per acre was $62.36. The value of domestic animals, poultry, etc., was $173,860,101, including 1,363,016 cattle, valued at $39,110,492; 813,644 horses, $87,118,468; 82,168 mules, $9,678,-014; 3,613,906 swine, $23,736,586; 1,336,-967 sheep, $5,908,496. In 1911, 174,600,000 bushels of corn was produced on 4,850,000 acres, and was valued at $94.284,000: 34,-354,000 bushels of wheat, $30,575,000, on 2,337,000 acres; 47,068,000 bushels of oats, $20,239,000, on 1,640,000 acres; 1,000,000 bushels of rye, $800,000, on 73,000 acres;

5,162,000 bushels of potatoes, $4,491,000, on 89,000 acres; 1,737,000 tons of hay, $29,182,000, on 1,848,000 acres, and 20,-020,000 pounds of tobacco, $1,561,000, on 22,000 acres.

The mineral products, consisting of coal, lime, cement, stone, clay products, and petroleum, produced in 1910 were valued at $59,039,303, of which $20,813,650 was coal. Only about 60 per cent. of the miners were affected by the coal strike of 1910, and these were idle only thirty-four days. Nearly half the coal was mined by machines. The average production per man (841 tons) was the greatest of any of the coal producing states.

The population, according to the census of 1910, was 2,700,876.

The number of manufacturing establishments in Indiana having an annual output valued at $500 or more at the beginning of 1915 was 8,022. The amount of capital invested was $668,863,000, giving employment to 233,270 persons, using material valued at $423,857,000, and turning out finished goods worth $730,795,000. Salaries and wages paid amounted to $155,854,000.

Indiana:

Boundaries of, referred to, 959.

Lands granted to, in aid of Wabash and Erie Canal discussed, 1725.

Lands in, referred to, 332.

Laws of, transmitted, 344.

Lead mines in, 359.

Location of lands ceded to, by Pottawattamies, 1098.

Sale of lands in, suspension of, requested, 1434.

Volunteers from, national thanks tendered, 3442.

Indians.—When Europeans first came to this hemisphere they called the natives Indians on the supposition that the land was India. This was soon found to be an error, but the name Indians has continued to be applied to the people of both North and South America. As the Indians were mostly barbarous, and as those who were partially civilized possessed no written records or reliable tradition, their origin and history became a problem for the ethnologist.

Morton makes two grand divisions of the South American Indians—the Toltecan nations, who were civilized, and the barbarous tribes, the former embracing the ancient Mexicans and Peruvians and the latter all the uncivilized tribes. The Mayas of Yucatan built pyramids and had a literature. Some ethnologists claim that the American Indian is a distinct type of the human race, as indigenous to this continent as its fauna and flora, and as having subsisted as such from the earliest ages of the world. Others regard them as a branch of the Mongolian race which, at a remote period of their history, wandered from Asia to the American continent, and there remained for thousands of years separated from the rest of mankind and passing through various stages of progress or retrogression. Dr. Robert Brown says in his "Races of Mankind": "Not only are the western Indians in appearance very like their nearest neighbors, the northeastern Asiatics, but in language and tradition it is confidently affirmed there is a blending of the people. The Eskimo on the American and the Tchuketchis on the Asiatic side understand each other perfectly." Anthropologists also admit that between the various tribes from the Arctic Sea to Cape Horn there is greater uniformity of physical structure and personal characteristics than is seen in any other quarter of the globe. Though the red men of Canada differ in many respects from the wandering Guranis of Paraguay and both from the Azteca of Mexico, all exhibit strong evidence of belonging to the same great branch of the human family, notwithstanding the wide diversity of language. Generally the physical characteristics are a low broad forehead; full face; back of head flattened; powerful jaws; full lips; prominent cheek bones; dark, deeply set eyes; hair long and wavy; no beard; copper-colored skin; erect and slender figure; about the average in height.

In Mexico and Peru the aboriginal inhabitants were a rich, powerful, and highly civilized people dwelling in walled cities. They had fixed laws and were acquainted with some of the higher arts and the sciences. Taking similarity of language as a basis of grouping, the Indians of North America were divided into some sixty linguistic stocks. These stocks were composed of many tribes of varying dialects, and tribes sometimes united temporarily for purposes of offense or defense into confederations. The most important of these stocks were the Eskimaun, Athapascan, Algonquian, Siouan, Iroquoian, Sallishan, Shoshonean, Muskhogean, Caddoan, Yuman, Piman, Sahaptian, Kiowan, and Timuquanan. The different tribes with which the United States have had dealings are mentioned under separate headings.

The total number of Indians in the United States, exclusive of Alaska, on June 30, 1910, was 304,950, of whom more than 100,-000 are members of the five civilized tribes of Cherokees, Chickasaws, Choctaws, Creeks and Seminoles, living on their own lands in Oklahoma and are practically self-supporting. About one-third the number wear citizen's dress and one-fourth the number read, write and converse in English.

The activity of the Bureau of Indian Affairs has always been directed toward two main ends—the improvement of the Indian's health and his education in self-supporting activity. In twenty-two western reservations demonstration farms have been established for the benefit of the Indians, and in some places the state authorities have co-operated with the Federal bureau in teaching. In the Yakima Reservation fifty-six Indians raised 23,000 bushels of wheat, while others raised alfalfa. Among the Nebraska Winnebagoes the value of the crops for 1911 was estimated at $90,000. For the education of children the Federal bureau maintains 223 day schools, seventy-nine boarding schools on reservations, and thirty-five non-reservation boarding schools. The enrollment for 1910 was 24,500. Carlisle (Pa.) and Hampton (Va.) Indian schools are the largest.

These groupings proved to be neither accurate nor permanent, as tribes frequently split into several parts and either allied themselves with existing tribes or formed new ones and the simple language of any one was easily acquired by the recruits from another branch or family. Each tribe called itself by a name in its own language, which often was metaphorical, and varied from time to time. Then, too, its several neighbors called it in their languages by other names, which, according to their existing relations, might be terms of obloquy, friendship or of simple topographical description. The attempts of English, French, Dutch and Spanish to imitate the native tongue added to the confusion, and when attempts were made to write the names further discrepancies appeared. While it is customary to refer to the Indian as fast becoming extinct, figures compiled by the Bureau of Indian Affairs show an increase from the 60,000 to 80,000 estimated in colonial times to more than 330,000 in 1913. This is due to intermarriage, adoption of whites and blacks and to the fostering care of the federal government which provides rations, clothing, schools and other supplies at a cost of some $20,000,000 a year and supports the titles to nearly 40,000,000 acres of land, rapidly increasing in value.

Early groupings and location of tribes and the numbers at the present time are shown in the tables on the next page:

The names and location of the principal tribes of the eight great families in the present area of the United States east of the Mississippi at the time of the first settlements were as follows:

I. *Algonquin tribes:*

Micmacs—East of the state of Maine.
Etchemins or Canoemen—Maine.
Abenakis—New Hampshire and Maine.
Narragansetts and Pokanokets or Wampanoags—Eastern Massachusetts and Rhode Island.
Pequots—Central Massachusetts and Rhode Island.
Mohegans—Western Massachusetts and Connecticut.
Delawares or Lenni Lenape—New Jersey, the valley, of the Delaware and Schuylkill.
Nanticokes—Eastern shores of Chesapeake Bay.
Powhatan Confederacy—Eastern Virginia and Maryland.
Corees—Eastern North Carolina.
Shawnees—South of the Ohio, western Kentucky, and Tennessee.
Miamis—Southern Michigan, N. Indiana, and northwestern Ohio.
Illinois—Southern Illinois and Indiana.
Kickapoos—Northern and central Illinois.
Pottawatomies—Northern Illinois.
Ottawas—Michigan.
Sacs and Foxes—Northern Wisconsin.
Menomonees and Chippewas or Ojibways —Southern shore of Lake Superior.

II. *Wyandot or Huron-Iroquois tribes:*

Eries (Huron or Wyandot-Iroquois)— Southern shore of Lake Erie.
Andastes (Huron or Wyandot-Iroquois)— Head-waters of the Ohio.
Wyandots (Huron or Wyandot-Iroquois) —Territory north of Lakes Erie and Ontario.
Senecas (Iroquois proper)—Western New York, Long House.
Cayugas and Onondagas (Iroquois proper) —Central New York.
Oneidas and Mohawks (Iroquois proper)— Eastern New York.
Tuscaroras (Iroquois proper)—Southwestern Virginia and North Carolina. Join the Iroquois of New York, 1713.
Chowans, Meherrins and Nottaways (Huron or Wyandot-Iroquois)—Southern Virginia.

III. *Catawabas:*
Western North and South Carolina.

IV. *Cherokees:*
Mountainous regions of Tennessee, Georgia, North and South Carolina.

V. *Uchees:*
About Augusta, Ga.

VI. *Natchez:*
Northwestern Mississippi.

VII. *Mobilian or Muskhogees:*
Chickasaws—Western Tennessee and northern Mississippi.
Choctaws—Eastern Mississippi and western Alabama.
Creeks or Muskhogees—Alabama and Georgia.
Seminoles—Florida.

VIII. *Winnebagoes:*
About Green Bay, Wisconsin.
The principal tribes west of the Mississippi between 1800 and 1830 were:
Dakotas (Sioux)—Wisconsin, west to Rocky Mountains.
Arapahoes—Wyoming, head-waters of Platte.
Cheyennes—Wyoming and Nebraska.
Kansas—Kansas, west.
Poncas—Dakota.
Omahas—Nebraska.
Mandans—Montana.
Assiniboins—Montana and Dakota.
Minnetaries (Gros Ventres)—Montana.
Missouris—Lower Missouri.
Iowas—Iowa.
Osages—Kansas, west.
Crows—Dakota.
Kaws—Kansas.
Pawnees—Kansas and Nebraska.
Caddos—Red River and Arkansas.
Shoshones or Snakes—Kansas to Oregon.
Kiowas—Kansas, west.
Utes—Utah and Colorado.
Comanches—Texas and New Mexico.
Apaches—New Mexico and Arizona.
Navajos and Mosquis—Arizona.
Yumas—Arizona and California.
Pueblos—Nevada and New Mexico.
Pimas—Arizona.
Bannocks—Idaho and Oregon.
Modocs and Nez Percés—Nevada and Oregon.
Flatheads—California, Oregon, and Nevada.
Klamaths—Oregon and northern California.

Indian Population of the United States, Exclusive of Alaska, June 30, 1916.

(Figures compiled from reports of Indian School superintendents, supplemented by information from 1910 census for localities in which no Indian Office representative is located.)

Grand Total	335,753
Five Civilized Tribes, including freedmen and intermarried whites	101,519
By blood 75,532	
By intermarriage 2,582	
Freedmen 23,405	
Exclusive of Five Civilized Tribes	234,234

INDIAN POPULATION BY STATES AND TERRITORIES

State	Pop.	State	Pop.
Alabama ...	909	Montana ...	11,450
Arizona ...	44,436	Nebraska ...	3,941
Arkansas ..	460	Nevada	7,915
California .	15,335	New Hamp..	34
Colorado ...	898	New Jersey.	168
Connecticut..	152	New Mexico	20,819
Delaware ..	5	New York ..	6,245
Dist. of Col.	68	North Car. .	8,096
Florida	578	North Dak...	8,887
Georgia ...	95	Ohio	127
Idaho	4,162	Oklahoma .*118,996	
Illinois	188	Oregon ...	6,544
Indiana ...	279	Rhode Island	284
Iowa	363	South Car..	331
Kansas	1,415	South Dak..	21,237
Kentucky ..	234	Tennessee ..	216
Louisiana ..	780	Texas	702
Maine	892	Utah	3,215
Maryland ..	55	Vermont ...	26
Massachusetts	688	Virginia ...	539
Michigan ..	7,514	Washington.	11,438
Minnesota .	11,758	West Va...	36
Mississippi .	1,253	Wisconsin .	9,997
Missouri ...	313	Wyoming ..	1,684

*Includes 23,405 freedmen and 2,582 intermarried whites.

Uncle Sam's Work Among the Indians.— A tremendous amount of time, money and attention is spent by Uncle Sam upon his Indians. The official care of more than 300,000 Indians is something more than mere child's play, especially when it is remembered that hundreds of millions of dollars' worth of property are owned by the redmen. In the month of September, 1916, over $7,000,000 in per capita payments is being distributed to the Choctaw, Chickasaw and Seminole tribes alone.

During the past three years under the administration of Secretary Lane more than $687,000 has been collected as tribal royalties on coal and asphalt lands belonging to the Choctaw and Chickasaw tribes; for the years 1913, 1914 and 1915 restrictions on alienation of 191,644 acres of land were removed, of which 159,000 acres were sold for the benefit of allottees, the amount derived from the sale being $1,568,000.

For the past three years there was collected as royalties of individual Indians from oil produced on restricted allotted lands the total sum of $5,563,000, the highest returns being for the year 1914, which was $2,113,000.

Of the original area allotted to members of the Five Civilized Tribes, amounting to over 15,000,000 acres, restrictions on alienation have been removed by operation of law, by the Secretary of the Interior, on over 12,000,000 acres, leaving 3,318,000 acres retained by only 32,540 restricted Indians of a total number of 101,521 enrolled members of the Five Civilized Tribes.

Aggressive work has been carried on during the same three years in all other departments of the Indian Office. In that time 13,000 allotments of land have been made, embracing more than 2,284,000 acres; the Fort Peck Reservation in Montana has been opened to settlement; the opening of the Colville Reservation in the State of Washington, making available for homestead entry 350,000 acres; the designation of 706 banks as depositaries of Indian moneys as against 450 banks in 1913, with amounts aggregating more than $20,000,000.

There has also been the withdrawal of lands in Arizona for the Papago Indians; the granting of new oil and gas leases in the Osage Reservation, Oklahoma, on the expiration of the Foster lease, procuring as a bonus value for the tribe $3,232,600, an increase in royalty from 12½ per centum to 16⅔ per centum and 20 per centum on oil, and an estimated increase in royalty on gas from 600 to 700 per centum over the amount paid on the old form of lease, which expired March 16, 1916.

Competency commissions have been appointed to pass on qualifications of Indians to individually handle their affairs and these commissions are at work in the Southwest, their recommendations so far having resulted in the fee patenting of over 132,000 acres, thereby placing within the taxing power of the States of Idaho, Montana, Oregon, Nebraska, North Dakota and South Dakota, considerably over two and one-half millions of dollars' worth of property.

Within the past three years there have been fee patented to Indians in States west of the Mississippi over 500,000 acres, thereby adding over $10,000,000 worth of property subject to State taxation. The total number of acres granted in fee to individual Indians and white purchasers during the past three years was 784,000 acres and a fair, conservative valuation thereof, subject to taxation by Western States, is $14,500,000.

Following are the Commissioners of Indian Affairs appointed since 1880:

	Appointed		Appointed
R. E. Trowbridge	1880	D. M. Browning	1893
Hiram Price	1881	Wm. A. Jones	1897
J. D. C. Atkins	1885	Fr. E. Leupp	1904
John H. Oberly	1888	R. G. Valentine	1909
T. J. Morgan	1889	Cato Sells	1913

Indians:

Act—

Making laws of States and Territories applicable to reservations recommended, 4643.

To establish peace with, referred to, 3796.

To transfer custody of trust funds of, vetoed, 4332.

Action recommended to enable Iroquois, Delaware and Abenaki, in Canada, to attend Exposition held at Omaha, Neb., 6304.

Act to refer claims for depredations by, to Court of Claims, vetoed, 6462.

Additional troops for Indian country recommended, 4330.

Agencies appointed. (See Indian Agents.)

Agents among. (See Indian Agents.)

Agricultural and manufacturing among, should be encouraged, 340, 347, 1391.

Allotment of lands in severalty to, recommended. (See Lands, Indian.)

Annual allowances given, 114, 347, 363, 378, 1031, 1391.

Annuities given, who fought with Great Britain against United States referred to, 1131.

Arms and ammunition furnished, orders and proclamation prohibiting, 3480, 4352, 4403.

Attempts to alienate affections of, discussed, 241, 245, 247.

Citizens, number of Indian, 6672.

Citizenship of, discussed, 7394.

Civilization of—

Appropriation for, 1334, 1391.

Discussed and referred to, 114, 177, 347, 415, 460, 648, 682, 683, 684, 825, 830, 1020, 1717, 2052, 2991, 4940.

Claims of, against United States (see also the several tribes)—

Appropriation for, recommended, 1031.

Settlement of, referred to, 2410.

Colonization of, recommended, 2991.

Commerce with, 96, 121, 133, 178, 251, 322, 347.

More capital should be employed in, 361.

Commission for settlement of differences with, recommended, 51.

Condition of—

Bill providing for improvement of, referred to, 4656.

Discussed by President—

Adams, J. Q., 981.

Arthur, 4641, 4730.

Cleveland, 4940, 5103, 5375, 5380, 5885, 5976, 6167.

Grant, 3992, 4106, 4206.
Harrison, Benj., 5480.
Hayes, 4427, 4454, 4528, 4575.
Jackson, 1020, 1082, 1117.
Monroe, 648.
Van Buren, 1715.
In Florida referred to, 894.
Report on, transmitted, 2609.
Control of Government over, must be complete, 615.
Conventions with. (See Treaties with, *post*.)
Corps of Indian auxiliaries recommended, 4454.
Crimes of—
Trial and punishment for, referred to, 4955.
Trial in United States courts recommended, 2279.
Debts due by, payment of, should be limited, 1446.
Depredations of, referred to, 74, 87, 96, 118, 122, 163, 1645, 2410.
Abuses in prosecution of claim, 5885.
Difficulties with, reports on, referred to, 4012.
Disarming of, law for, and compensation to, for weapons taken recommended, 4849.
Education of (see also Indian Schools), 6674, 7014.
Employed by Great Britain in war against United States, 500, 520.
Tribes receiving annuities after war referred to, 1131.
Enlistment and organization of, into companies discussed, 5631.
Enslaved in New Mexico, 3540.
Exhibition at Omaha, 6304.
Expeditions among, 2898.
Expenditures for. (See Indian Affairs, Bureau of.)
Farm lands for, recommendations regarding, 4528.
Frontiers must be protected from. (See Frontiers.)
General allotment Act, 6674.
Gospel propaganda among, 981.
Government established by, within States would not be recognized, 1020.
Government for, council at Ocmulgee for, 4073.
History and condition of, investigated, 2609.
Homestead entries for. (See Homestead Laws.)
Hostile attitude of Creeks, 1472, 1473.
Hunkpapa treaty with, 912.
Hostile disposition of, 128, 143, 3774.
Hostilities against United States, should be restrained by France from committing, 600.
Hostilities of. (See Indian Wars.)

Hostility of, to United States due to influence of British Government, 489, 500.
Hunting, should be encouraged to abandon, 340.
Husbandry, practice of, introduced among, 314.
Intermeddling of foreign powers with, referred to, 1728, 1806.
Lands—
Ceded to United States by. (See Lands, Indian; the several tribes.)
Donated to Jackson and Hawkins by, as mark of gratitude, 555.
Granted to, by United States. (See Indian Reservations; Lands, Indian; the several tribes.)
Lands to be reserved for, 3881, 4576.
Lands, tribal, 6674, 6875.
Laws regarding, modifications in, recommended, 2279.
Legal services for, rendered, payment of, recommended, 4694.
Liquors, prohibition of sale of—
To allottees, recommended, 6167.
To, requested by, 322.
Management of, committed to Society of Friends, 3992, 4063, 4106, 4154, 4206, 4254, 4306.
Military execution, death by, preferred to hanging, 322.
Military post among—
Increase in, recommended, 1475, 1940.
To be established, 436.
Militia sent to suppress. (See Indian Wars.)
Money invested for, 249.
Moral improvement of, 981.
Arrangements made for, 1391.
Neutral lands, treaty regarding, 3717.
Number of, in United States, 2991, 4940, 5885, 6167.
Pacific relations with, desired, 1332.
Paper from Society of Friends on affairs of, referred to, 4075.
Peace among, attempts made to preserve, 2117.
Peace policy, appropriation to carry out, recommended, 4106.
Persons charged with murder convicted by, 442.
Police force of, organized, 4575.
Population of, 2940, 2991, 5885, 6167.
Increased by enlargement of boundaries, 2623, 2664.
Presents to, from Great Britain, referred to, 2129.
Proceeds of reservations, bill providing for use of, for relief of, 4973.
Progress of, slow, 6911, 6912.
Public lands must be protected from. (See Frontiers.)

Referred to, 96, 100, 103, 107, 114, 117, 122, 123, 127, 133, 136, 159, 163, 178, 179, 191, 199, 346, 360, 374, 386, 395, 600, 651, 825, 1082, 1099, 2956.

Removal of, to lands lying westward—

Army engaged in, 1833.

Progress made in, discussed, 1128, 1167, 1332, 1390, 1472, 1475, 1608, 1714, 1833, 2261, 2355, 2410, 3388, 3587.

Recommended by President—

Fillmore, 2710, 2720.

Jackson, 1021, 1039, 1082, 1104, 1117, 1132, 1167, 1251, 1274, 1390.

Monroe, 759, 849.

Polk, 2279, 2303.

Tyler, 2007, 2201.

Van Buren, 1608, 1692, 1714, 1724, 1778.

Referred to, 4367.

Treaty regarding, 1251, 1475.

Rights of, citizens infringing, must be punished, 129, 177, 183, 937, 1099.

Schools provided for. (See Indian Schools.)

Supplies for, increase of items for transportation of, recommended, 4680.

Teachers sent among, 5375. (See also Indian Schools.)

Territorial government for, recommended, 4073, 4106, 4154, 4206, 4254.

Trade with, 773, 1099.

Act to regulate, discussed, 1099.

Trading establishments among, 766, 767, 849.

Recommended, 340, 342, 347, 436.

Treaties with (see also the several tribes), 1094, 2410, 2501, 2681, 2687, 2694, 2884, 2956, 3573, 3652, 3881, 4006.

Appropriation for fulfillment of, recommended, 2907, 2912.

Obligation of Congress to make, referred to, 4005.

Appropriation made for concluding, 872.

Compensation paid persons for negotiating, referred to, 1745, 1808.

Discussion of, in executive session referred to, 4006.

Exclusion of reservations from, discussed, 1724.

Instructions to commissioners negotiating within Indian Territory, 6271.

Irregularities in, discussed, 1901.

Laws regarding, modifications in, recommended, 2832.

Must be ratified by Government, 58.

Peace Commission of 1867 referred to, 4005.

Appropriation to carry out policy of, recommended, 4106.

Persons violating, shall be punished, 93, 129, 177, 183, 242.

Printed copies of, referred to, 1135.

Rejected by Senate, referred to, 2707.

Transmitted for exercise of powers for fulfilling, 285.

War between the States, attitude of tribes in. (See Civil War.)

Wars with. (See Indian Wars.)

Indigent Insane, act making grant of lands to States for benefit of, vetoed, 2780.

Industrial Congress Party.—In 1848 this ephemeral political party nominated Gerritt Smith for President and William S. Waitt for Vice President at Convention in Philadelphia.

Industrial Conditions, 6645, 6647.

Industrial Education, report on, transmitted, 5782.

Discussed by President Roosevelt, 7044.

Industrial Exhibitions. (See Exhibitions.)

Industrial Peace Committee.—The committee of the Norwegian Storthing entrusted with the distribution of the Nobel prize money in 1906 awarded to President Roosevelt that portion allotted to the person who should do the most to promote peace and fraternity among nations. The value of the prize was about $40,000. The President expressed a wish that this award be made the nucleus of a fund for the promotion of industrial peace at home, and Congress passed an act which he approved March 2, 1907, creating the Foundation for the Promotion of Industrial Peace. This law provided that the Chief Justice of the United States, the Secretary of Agriculture, and the Secretary of Commerce and Labor, and their successors in office, together with a representative of labor and a representative of capital and two persons to represent the general public, to be appointed by the President of the United States, be created trustees of the Foundation for the Promotion of Industrial Peace. The plan failed and the money was returned to Mr. Roosevelt.

Industrial Property, international convention at Paris for protection of, 4560, 4794, 4857, 5118.

Industrial Relations Commission.—The frequent interruption of peaceful relations between employers and wage-workers, especially on transportation lines and in the supply of commodities in general use, with the consequent loss and annoyance to the public, has been the subject of presidential concern in recent years, and the attention of Congress has been called to the necessity of federal action by Presidents McKinley, Roosevelt and Taft. The latter, in his message of February 2, 1912 (page 7725), recommended that a Commission be appointed to inquire into the question with the view of ascertaining the underlying cause of such disturbances. Congress accordingly passed a law in August, 1912, creating such a commission, charged with the following duties:

That the commission shall inquire into the general condition of labor in the principal industries of the United States, including agriculture, and especially in those which are carried on in corporate forms; into existing relations between employers and employees; into the effect of industrial conditions on public welfare and into the rights and powers of the community to deal therewith; into the conditions of sanitation and safety of employees and the provisions for protecting the life, limb and health of the employees; into the growth of associations of employers and of wage-earners and the effect of such associations upon the relations between employers and employees; into the extent and results of methods of collective bargaining; into any methods which have been tried in any state or in foreign countries for maintaining mutually satisfactory relations between employees and employers; into methods for avoiding or adjusting labor disputes through peaceful and conciliatory mediation and negotiations; into the scope, methods and resources of existing bureaus of labor and into possible ways of increasing their usefulness; into the question of smuggling or other illegal entry of Asiatics into the United States or its insular possessions, and of the methods by which such Asiatics have gained and are gaining such admission, and shall report to Congress as speedily as possible with such recommendation as said commission may think proper to prevent such smuggling and illegal entry. The commission shall seek to discover the underlying causes of dissatisfaction in the industrial situation and report its conclusions thereon.

The Commission appointed consisted of Frank P. Walsh, Chairman, Kansas City, Mo.; Prof. John R. Commons of Madison, Wis.; Mrs. J. Borden Harriman, New York City; Harris Weinstock, Sacramento, Cal.; S. Thurston Ballard, Louisville, Ky.; John B. Lennon, Bloomington, Ill.; James O'Connell, Washington, D. C., and Austin B. Garretson, Cedar Rapids, Iowa.

Industrial Relations, Commissions on, 7725.

Industries, importance of, during war with Germany, 8250.

Industrial Workers of the World. (See Socialism.)

Industrial System, limitations of, 7869.

Industry, Captains of, personal equation of, factor of success, 6646.

Infant Mortality. (See Children's Bureau.)

Infantile Paralysis. (See Poliomyelitis.)

Inflation Bill.—This bill was passed by Congress in 1874, and was calculated to make possible a great increase in paper currency. The bill was vetoed by President Grant as repugnant to the business interests of the country because of its delayal of specie payments.

Information Bureau, State Department. —The Division of Information in the Department of State was formed in 1909 by Secretary of State P. C. Knox. It falls under the supervision of the Counselor to the State Department (q. v.); and has charge of the "preparation and distribution to the foreign service of diplomatic, commercial and other correspondence and documents important to their information upon foreign relations." The Information Bureau also edits the department's publication called *Foreign Relations.* (See State Department.)

Information, International Bureau of, establishment of, at Washington recommended by International American Conference, 5506.

"In God We Trust."—"In God We Trust" first appeared on the copper two-cent issue of 1864, and was the first use of the word "God" in any Government act. The sentence was introduced by James Pollock, Director of the Mint, with the approval of the Secretary of the Treasury, Salmon P. Chase. It appeared on the 1866 issue of the double eagle, eagle, half-eagle, silver dollar, half-dollar, and nickel five-cent piece, in lieu of the long existing motto of "E Pluribus Unum." In the Trade Dollar issue (1873) both mottoes were retained, "In God We Trust" appearing on the obverse.

Some of the coinage of 1907 appearing without the customary legend, much criticism was aroused and Congress on May 18, 1908, passed the following act, restoring the motto to the coins: Be it enacted by the Senate and House of Representatives of the United States of America in Congress assembled, That the motto, "In God We Trust," heretofore inscribed on certain denominations of the gold and silver coins of the United States of America, shall hereafter be inscribed upon all such gold and silver coins of said denominations as heretofore.

Inheritance Tax.—A tax upon the estate of a deceased person has always been considered a proper and legitimate form of public revenue. The deceased, having enjoyed the protection of the state during life, and dying with the assurance that the state will carry out his last wishes, is under some obligation to the community, while the beneficiary will not feel the slight decrease in his legacy taken by the power that guarantees its legal transfer.

Federal Inheritance Tax.—The national government has imposed inheritance taxes temporarily on three different occasions. The first was in 1797, when war with France threatened; again in 1862, during the Civil war, and the third time during the Spanish-American war of 1898. President Roosevelt suggested it to Congress as a permanent source of revenue in his sixth annual message (page 7043), and repeats his recommendation in his seventh annual message and cites in support of his argument the fact that England, France and Germany collect such taxes. (Page 7083.) President Taft also recommended a graduated inheritance tax as a means of meeting a deficiency in the revenues. (Pages 7370 and 7390.)

By the revenue bills approved March 3, 1917, and September 8, 1916, upon the estates of all persons dying in the United States, whether residents or non-residents, there is placed a tax of 1½% of the net estate of any decedent which amounts to less than $50,000; 3% of the amount by which the estate exceeds $50,000 but not $150,000; 4½% on estates between $150,000 and $250,000; 6% on estates between $25,000 and $450,000; 7½% on estates between $450,000 and $1,000,000; and proceeding at a rate of increase of 1½% for each additional $1,000,000 until a tax of 15% is levied on all estates above $5,000,000.

The tax applies also to partnerships, corporations and associations.

The value of the estate of a decedent includes all the value at the time of his death of all his property, tangible or intangible, real or personal, wherever located. Any transfer of any of the decedent's property, except that made for proved business transactions, within two years of his death, is included in the amount of the estate which is to be taxed.

Deductions from the amount of the estate to be taxed include the funeral expenses of the deceased, the administration expenses of settling the estate, claims against the estate, unpaid mortgages upon it, losses incurred during the settlement of the estate (such as those by fire or shipwreck) and other charges recognized by law, and an exemption of $50,000. That is to say, estates of less gross value than $50,000 are not taxed.

The payment of the tax is due one year after the death of the owner of the estate, and there are provisions for discounts and penalties if the payment is rendered before or after it is due. For making false statements concerning the estate, there is a penalty of a fine of not more than $5,000 or not more than one year in jail or both.

War Inheritance Tax.—By provisions of the Revenue Bill approved October 5, 1917, the following are the net taxes levied upon estates: Estates under $25,000, exempt; $25,000-$50,000, 1%; $50,000-$100,000, 1½%; $100,000-$200,000, 3%; $200,000-$300,000, 4½%; $300,000-$500,000, 6%; $500,000-$1,050,000, 7½%; $1,050,000-$2,050,000, 9%; $2,050,000-$3,050,000, 10½%; $3,050,000-$4,050,000, 12%; $4,050,000-$5,050,000, 13½%; $5,050,000-$8,050,000, 15%; $8,050,000-$10,050,000, 17%; $20,050,00 and above, 20%.

State Inheritance Tax.—Most of the states tax inheritances and at the same time provide for the payment of preferred obligations of the deceased and the prompt and efficient settlement of the estate.

The following is a synopsis of several of the laws of the various states affecting the administration of the estate of a deceased person:

1. Who to Administer.—(a) If the deceased leaves a will, the duty of administration falls upon the executor. If no executor is named, or in the event of the death or refusal of the executor to act, the Court will grant administration under the will to some suitable person, generally selected from those most largely interested under the provisions of the will, such as the residuary legatees, if any. (b) If the deceased died intestate, letters of administration are granted to the following persons in practically all the states:

First—To the surviving husband or widow.

Second—To one or more of the next of kin entitled to share in the estate.

Third—If none of the above consent to act, to one of the creditors of the estate, except in localities where there is provided by law a Public Administrator, who is preferred to creditors. In practically all the states an administrator is required to give bond for the faithful performance of his duties in double the value of the estate to be administered.

In most of the states, if so provided by the will, no bond is required of an executor, except that in some states an executor is required to give a bond to cover the probable amount of the debts of the estate, and in practically all the states, in the discretion of the Court, for cause shown, an executor may be required to give a bond.

2. Claims of Creditors.—The procedure in the several states in presenting creditors' claims against the estate varies considerably. In the majority of the states the executor or administrator is required promptly to give public notice to creditors to present their claims to him, and the creditors are required so to present their claims supported by an affidavit that the same are justly due and owing from the estate, above any offsets or counter claims, within a period limited generally to six months or a year. The law of each state should be consulted for more specific details. Most of the states direct a final closing of the estate by the executor or administrator within a year or eighteen months after his appointment, though the time limit may be extended by the Probate Court if conditions require it.

3. Analysis of the laws of the several states, covering the inheritance or succession tax upon property received either by intestate laws, last will, or by gift or transfer, designed to take effect at death, excepting legacies for religious, charitable or educational purposes, which are tax exempt in most of the states. In the great majority of the states no distinction as to tax is made between real estate and personal property:

Alabama.—No inheritance tax.

Arizona.—To grandfather, grandmother, parents, husband, wife, child, brother, sister, son-in-law, or daughter-in-law, or adopted child, 1 per cent. $5,000 exempt to each beneficiary above named. Estates less than $10,000 exempt. To uncle, aunt, nephew, niece or descendant thereof, 2 per cent; $2,000 exempt to each beneficiary named. Estate less than $5,000 exempt. To others, 3 per cent up to $10,000; 4 per cent from $10,000 to $20,000; 5 per cent from $20,000 to $50,000; 6 per cent above $50,000. $500 exempt.

Arkansas.—On amounts not exceeding $5,000 the rate is 1 per cent to parents, husband or wife, child or adopted child, brother, sister, son-in-law or daughter-in-law. To all others the rate on the same amount is 3 per cent. $3,000 passing to widow or minor child and $1,000 passing to the other immediate relatives mentioned is exempt. The exemption to others more remote is $500. On amounts in excess of $5,000 the primary rates (1 per cent and 3 per cent respectively) are increased as follows: From $5,000 to $10,000, twice the primary rates; from $10,000 to $30,000, three times the primary rates; from $30,000 to $50,000, four times; $50,000 to $100,000, five times; $100,000 to $500,000, six times; $500,000 to $1,000,000, seven times; above $1,000,000, eight times.

California.—(a) To husband, wife, descendant, ancestor, adopted children or their issue, the tax is 1% up to $25,000; 2% between $25,000 and $50,000; 4% between $50,000 and $100,000; 7% between $100,000 and $200,000; 10% between $200,000 and $500,000; 12% between $500,000 and $1,000,000; and 15% on inheritances above $1,000,000. To widow or minor child, $24,000 is exempt from the tax; to others, $10,000. (b) To brother, sister or their descendants, or son-in-law or daughter-in-law, 3% up to $25,000; upon the increasing amounts in the preceding paragraph the rates are 6%, 9%, 12%, 15%, 20%, and 25%. $2,000 exempt from tax. (c) To uncles, aunts, or their descendants, 4% up to $25,000; upon the same increasing amounts the rates are 8%, 10%, 15%, 20%, 25%, and 30%. $1,000 exemption. (d) To others more remote in blood, 5% up to $25,000; the rates increase as above up to $500,000 as follows: 10%, 15%, 20%, and 25%, above $500,000 the rate is 30%. $500 exemption.

Colorado.—To parents, husband or wife, child, brother or sister, wife or widow of son, husband of daughter, lineal descendant, or adopted child the rate is 2 per cent, with $10,000 exempt. To uncle, aunt, nephew or niece or their descendants, 3 per cent. To all others above $500: On $500 to $10,000, tax is 3 per cent; $10,000 to $20,000, 4 per cent; $20,000 to $50,000, 5 per cent; $50,000 to $500,000, 6 per cent; above $500,000, 10 per cent.

Connecticut.—To parents, husband, wife, grandparents, adopted parent, descendant, adopted child or descendant thereof, 1% between $10,000 and $50,000; 2% between $50,000 and $250,000; 3% between $250,000 and $1,000,000; 4% above $1,000,000. To brother or sister, or their descendants, stepchild, son-in-law or daughter-in-law, 3% between $3,000 and $25,000; 5% between $25,000 and $50,000; 6% between $50,000 and $250,000; 7% between $250,000 and $1,000,000; 8% above $1,000,000. To others, 5% between $500 and $50,000; 6% between $50,000 and $250,000; 7% between $250,000 and $1,000,000; and 8% above $1,000,000.

Delaware.—Exempt to parents, grandparents, husband, wife, descendants, adopted child. To others exempt to $500 and taxable on excess as follows: To brothers, sisters or their descendants, 1 per cent; to uncles, aunts or their descendants, 2 per cent; to great-uncles, great-aunts or their descendants, 3 per cent; to those more remote in blood, 5 per cent.

District of Columbia.—No inheritance tax.

Florida.—No inheritance tax.

Georgia.—To parents, husband, wife, child, adopted child, lineal descendant, brother, sister or daughter-in-law, 1%. $5,000 is exempt. To all others, 5%.

Idaho.—Tax on estates less than $25,000 at following rates: (a) To husband or wife, lineal issue or ancestor, 1 per cent; exempt to widow or minor child, $10,000; to others of Class A, exempt, $4,000. (b) To brother or sister, or their descendants, or wife or widow of son, or husband of daughter, 1½ per cent; exempt, $2,000. (c) To uncles, aunts or descendants, 3 per cent; exempt, $1,500. (d) To great-uncles, great-aunts or descendants, 4 per cent; exempt, $1,000. (e) To more distant relatives or strangers in blood, 5 per cent; exempt, $500. On larger estates than $25,000 the above rates are multiplied as follows: $25,000 to $50,000, 1½ times above; $50,000 to $100,000, 2 times above; $100,000 to $500,000, 2½ times above; $500,000 and upward, 3 times above.

Illinois.—To parents, husband, wife, descendant, adopted child, brother, sister, wife of son, husband of daughter, on amounts from $20,000 to $100,000 the rate is 1 per cent; above $100,000, 2 per cent; exempt below $20,000. To uncle, aunt, niece, nephew or their descendants the rate is 2 per cent on amounts less than $20,000; 4 per cent on amounts in excess of $20,000; exempt below $2,000. To all others the rates vary with amounts as follows: Up to $10,000, 3 per cent; $10,000 to $20,000, 4 per cent; $20,000 to $50,000, 5 per cent; $50,000 to $100,000, 6 per cent; above $100,000, 10 per cent; exempt to $500.

Indiana.—On amounts not exceeding $25,000, the primary rates are: (1) To husband, wife, ancestor, descendant, adopted child, 1 per cent. Exempt $10,000 to widow and $2,000 to other parties just named. (2) To brother, sister or their descendants, or to son-in-law or daughter-in-law, 1½ per cent; exempt $500. (3) To uncle, aunt or their descendants, 3 per cent; exempt $250. (4) To great uncle, great aunt or their descendants, 4 per cent; exempt $100. (5) To others more remote, 5 per cent. On larger amounts the primary rates are multiplied as follows: (1) from $25,000 to $50,000, 1½ times; (2) from $50,000 to $100,000 twice; (3) from $100,000 to $500,000, 2½ times; (4) above $500,000, 3 times.

Iowa.—Property passing to parents, husband or wife, lineal descendants, adopted child or issue thereof is exempt. To others 5 per cent tax above $1,000. To alien nonresidents of the state tax is 20 per cent, unless alien is brother or sister, when tax is 10 per cent.

Kansas.—Property passing to husband, wife, ancestors, descendants, son-in-law, daughter-in-law, adopted children of their descendants is exempt from tax. To brothers or sisters, $5,000 is exempt, and rates are 3%, $5,000 to $25,000; 5%, $25,000 to $50,000; 7½%, $50,000 to $100,000; 10%, $100,000 to $500,000; 12½% above $500,000. To others more remote the rate is 5% up to $25,000, and on the increasing amounts stated above the rates are 7½%, 10%, 12½%, and 15%.

Kentucky.—On amounts not exceeding $25,000, the primary rates are: (a) To husband, wife, ancestor, descendant, adopted child, 1%, $10,000 exempt to widow and each minor child, to others in this class $5,000 exempt. (b) To brother, sister, or their descendants, or to son-in-law, or daughter-in-law, 1½%; exempt $2,000. (c) To uncle, aunt, or their descendants, 3%; exempt $1,500. (d) To great-uncle, great-aunt, or their descendants, 4%; exempt $1,000. (e) To others more remote, 5%; exempt, $500. On larger amounts the primary rates are multiplied at the same amounts and rates as provided by the Indiana statute (above).

Louisiana.—Exempt to $10,000 to parents or lineal ancestors, children or descendants; excess taxable at 2 per cent; to others 5 per cent.

Maine.—To ancestors, parents, husband, wife, descendants, adopted child, wife of son, husband of daughter, the rates are as follows: Up to $50,000, 1 per cent; $50,000 to $100,000, 1½ per cent; above $100,000, 2 per cent; $10,000 exempt to parents, husband, wife, child or adopted child. To brother, sister, uncle, aunt, nephew, niece or cousin, the rates on the above amounts are 4 per cent, 4½ per cent and 5 per cent; $500 exempt. To others, rates on the same amounts are 5 per cent, 6 per cent and 7 per cent; same exemption.

Maryland.—Exempt to parents, husband or wife, children, or lineal descendants; to others, 5 per cent above $500.

Massachusetts.—To husband, wife, ancestor, descendant, adopted child or its descendants, adopted parent or its ancestors, son-in-law, daughter-in-law, 1 per cent up to $50,000; 2 per cent $50,000 to $250,000; 3 per cent $250,000 to $1,000,000; 4 per cent above $1,000,000. To brother, sister, nephew or niece, 2 per cent up to $10,000; 3 per cent $10,000 to $25,000; 5 per cent $25,000 to $50,000; 6 per cent $50,000 to $250,000; 7 per cent $250,000 to $1,000,000; 8 per cent above $1,000,000. To others, 5 per cent up to $50,000; 6 per cent $50,000 to $250,000; 7 per cent $250,000 to $1,000,000; 8 per cent above $1,000,000. $10,000 passing to parent, husband or wife, child, adopted child or adopted parent is exempt. To others the exemption is $1,000.

Michigan.—Tax is 1 per cent to grandparents, parents, husband or wife, child, brother or sister, wife or widow of son, husband of daughter, lineal descendants, adopted child, or one to whom deceased stood in relation of parent, exempt to $2,000. To others, 5 per cent over $100. Exemption to widow is $5,000.

Minnesota.—Five classes of beneficiaries are recognized: (a) wife, or lineal descendant; (b) husband, parents, ancestors, adopted children or issue thereof; (c) brother or sister or their descendants, son-in-law or daughter-in-law; (d) uncles, aunts or their descendants; (e) others more remote. The rates for amounts not exceeding $15,000 (called the primary rates) for the classes given above are respectively 1 per cent, 1½ per cent, 3 per cent, 4 per cent and 5 per cent. On amounts from $15,000 to $30,000 the primary rates are multiplied 1½ times; from $30,000 to $50,000 twice; from $50,000 to $100,000, 2½ times; and above $100,000, 3 times. Exemptions are to classes (a) and (b), except ancestors, $3,000; to class (c) $1,000; to class (d) $250 and to class (e) $100.

Mississippi.—No inheritance tax.

Missouri.—All inheritances taxable at 5 per cent except to parents, husband or wife, adopted child or lineal descendants, which are exempt.

Montana.—Tax of 1 per cent to parents, husband, wife, child, brother, sister, descendant, adopted child, son-in-law, daughter-in-law, $7,500 exempt. To all others, 5 per cent over $500.

Nebraska.—Taxable at 1 per cent to parents, husband or wife, child, brother or sister, wife or widow of son, husband of daughter, adopted child and lineal descendants in lawful wedlock, exempt to $10,000. To uncle, aunt, nephew or niece, or descendants, 2 per cent; exempt to $2,000. To others, above $500 as follows: $500 to $5,000, 2 per cent; $5,000 to $10,000, 3 per cent; $10,000 to $20,000, 4 per cent; $20,000 to $50,000, 5 per cent; above $50,000, 6 per cent.

Nevada.—On amounts not exceeding $25,000 the primary rates are: (1) To husband or wife, ancestors, decendants or adopted child, 1 per cent. $20,000 exempt to widow or minor child: to others just named, $10,000 exempt. (2) To brother, sister, nephew, niece or their descendants, 2 per cent; $10,000 exempt. (3) To uncles, aunts or their descendants, 3 per cent, $5,000 exempt. (4) To great uncles, great aunts or their descendants, 4 per cent. (5) To all others, 5 per cent. On larger amounts the primary rates are multiplied as follows: $25,000 to $50,000, twice primary rates; $50,000 to $100,000, 3 times; $100,000 to $500,000, 4 times; above $500,000, 5 times.

New Hampshire.—Exempt to parents, husband or wife, lineal descendants, brother, sister, adopted child, or issue thereof, wife or widow of son, husband of daughter. To all others, 5 per cent.

New Jersey.—To parents, brother, sister, son-in-law, and daughter-in-law, the rates are 2%, from $5,000 to $50,000; 2½%, $50,000 to $150,000; 3% $150,000 to $250,000; 4% above $250,000. $5,000 is exempt. To husband or wife, child, adopted child, or lineal descendant the rates are 1% from $5,000 to $50,000; 1½% $50,000 to $150,000; 2% $150,000 to $250,000; 3% above $250,000. $5,000 is exempt. All others, 5%.

New Mexico.—No inheritance tax.

New York.—To parents, husband or wife, child, adopted child ($5,000 exempt), and to descendants ($500 exempt), 1% up to $25,000; 2% on the next $75,000; 3% on the next $100,000; 4% upon all additional sums. To brother, sister, son-in-law, or daughter-in-law, $500 exempt; 2% up to $25,000; 3% on the next $75,000; 4% on the next $100,000; 5% thereafter. To others more remote, $500 exempt; 5% up to $25,000; 6% on the next $75,000; 7% on the next $100,000; 8% thereafter.

North Carolina.—Exempt to husband or wife. (1) To lineal ancestors, or descendants, brothers or sisters, or where mutual relation of parents and child existed, ¾ per cent. (2) Descendants of brother or sister, 1½ per cent. (3) Uncles or aunts, or descendants, 3 per cent. (4) Great-uncles, great-aunts or descendants, 4 per cent. (5) To all others, $2,000 to $5,000, 5 per cent; $5,000 to $10,000, 7½ per cent; $10,000 to $25,000, 1 per cent; $25,000 to $50,000, 12½ per cent; above $50,000, 15 per cent; exempt $2,000 in all cases.

North Dakota.—To husband or wife ($20,000 exempt), father, mother, descendants, adopted child or its descendants, 1 per cent up to $100,000; 2 per cent from $100,000 to $250,000; 2½ per cent, $250,000 to $500,000; 3 per cent above $500,000. To brother or sister, son-in-law or daughter-in-law ($500 exempt), 1½ per cent up to $25,000; 2¼ per cent from $25,000 to $50,000; 3 per cent from $50,000 to $100,000; 3¾ per cent from $100,000 to $500,000; 4½ per cent above $500,000. To uncle, aunt or their descendants, 3 per cent up to $25,000; 4½ per cent from $25,000 to $50,000; 6 per cent from $50,000 to $100,000; 7½ per cent from $100,000 to $500,000; 9 per cent above $500,000. To others 5 per cent up to $25,000; 6 per cent from $25,000 to $50,000; 9 per cent from $50,000 to $100,000; 12 per cent from $100,000 to $500,000; 15 per cent above $500,000.

Ohio.—Exempt to parents, husband or wife, lineal descendants or adopted child. To others 5 per cent above $500 exempt.

Oklahoma.—To parents, husband or wife, child, brother, sister, son-in-law, daughter-in-law, adopted child, or lineal descendant, 1% up to $25,000; 2%, 25,000 to $50,-

000; 3%, $50,000 to $100,000; 4% above $100,000. $25,000 to widow, $10,000 to each child, and $5,000 to each other person named above is exempt. To others more remote, $2,500 exempt; tax above exemption, 5% up to $25,000; 6%, $25,000 to $50,000; 8%, $50,000 to $100,000; 10% above $100,000.

Oregon.—(a) Tax of 1 per cent to parents, husband or wife, child, brother or sister, wife or widow of son, husband of daughter, adopted child, lineal descendants or ancestors, $5,000 exempt to each person. Estate must exceed $10,000. (b) Tax of 2 per cent to uncle, aunt, niece, nephew or descendants, $2,000 exempt to each person. Estate must exceed $5,000. In all other cases above $500: $500 to $10,000, 3 per cent; $10,000 to $20,000, 4 per cent; $20,000 to $50,000, 5 per cent; above $50,000, 6 per cent.

Pennsylvania.—Estates less than $250 exempt. Exempt to parents, husband or wife, children or lineal descendants, stepchildren, adopted children, wife or widow of son. To all others, 5 per cent.

Rhode Island.—Estates under $5,000 tax exempt. To grandparents, parents, husband or wife, child, or descendant, adopted child, brother, sister, nephew, niece, son-in-law, or daughter-in-law, $25,000 is exempt. Rates on excess are: ½% below $50,000; 1%, $50,000 to $250,000; 1½%, $250,000 to $500,000; 2%, $500,000 to $750,000; 2½%, $750,000 to $1,000,000; 3% above $1,000,000. To others more remote $1,000 is exempt, and rates on excess are: 5% up to $50,000; 6%, $50,000 to $250,000; 7%, $250,000 to $1,000,000; 8%, above $1,000,000.

South Carolina.—No Inheritance tax.

South Dakota.—On amounts not exceeding $15,000 the primary rates of tax are: (1) To wife or lineal issue, 1 per cent. (2) To husband, ancestor or adopted child, 1½ per cent. (3) To brother, sister or their descendants, to son-in-law or daughter-in-law, 3 per cent. (4) To uncles, aunts or their descendants, 4 per cent; (5) to others, 5 per cent. On increased amounts the primary rate is multiplied from $15,000 to $50,000, twice; from $50,000 to $100,000, 2¼ times; above $100,000, 3 times. $10,000 is exempt to husband, wife, issue or adopted child; $3,000 is exempt to ancestor; $1,000 exempt to class (3), $250 to class (4) and $100 to class (5).

Tennessee.—To parents, husband, wife, child or descendants, $5,000 exempt. Upon excess 1 per cent up to $20,000; 1½ per cent above $20,000. To others, 5 per cent above $250.

Texas.—Exempt to parents, husband or wife or descendants. The rate of taxation on other legacies varies (above such sum as is exempt) with the amount of the legacy. Six divisions as to amount are recognized: (1) up to $10,000: (2) $10,000 to $25,000: (3) $25,000 to $50,000: (4) $50,000 to $100,000: (5) $100,000 to $500,000: (6) above $500,000. To ancestors, brothers, sisters or their descendants, the rates on the above amounts are 2 per cent, 2¼ per cent, 3 per cent, 3½ per cent, 4 per cent and 5 per cent: $2,000 being exempt. To uncles, aunts or their descendants the rates are 3 per cent, 4 per cent, 5 per cent, 6 per cent, 7 per cent and 8 per cent, $1,000 being exempt. To others more remote the rates are 4 per cent, 5½ per cent, 7 per

cent, 8½ per cent, 10 per cent and 12 per cent, $500 being exempt.

Utah.—Tax of 5% on all estates over $25,000 except that estates valued at no more than $10,000 are exempt and estates between $10,000 and $25,000 are taxed 3%.

Vermont.—Exempt to parents, husband or wife, lineal descendants, stepchild, adopted child, or lineal descendant thereof, wife or widow of son, husband of daughter. To all others, 5 per cent.

Virginia.—On amounts not exceeding $50,000 the primary rates are: (a) To grandparent, parent, husband or wife, child, descendant, brother or sister, 1%. $15,000 exempt. (b) To others more remote, 5%. On larger amounts the primary rates are multiplied as follows: (1) from $50,000 to $250,000, twice; (2) $250,000 to $1,000,000, 3 times; (3) above $1,000,000, 4 times.

Washington.—(a) Tax of 1 per cent above $10,000 to parents, husband or wife, lineal descendants, adopted child, or lineal descendant thereof. (b) To collaterals, including the third degree of relationship, 3 per cent up to $50,000, 4½ per cent from $50,000 to $100,000, and 6 per cent from $100,000 upward. (c) To those further removed, 6 per cent up to $50,000, 9 per cent up to $100,000, 12 per cent above $100,000.

West Virginia.—To lineal ancestor, husband, wife, descendant, the rate is 1 per cent on amounts up to $25,000; $25,000 to $50,000, 1½ per cent; $50,000 to $100,000, 2 per cent; $100,000 to $500,000, 2½ per cent; above $500,000, 3 per cent. Exempt up to $10,000, except in case of widow, where $15,000 is exempt. To brother or sister the rate is 3 per cent up to $25,000, and for the varying amounts stated above the rates are 4½ per cent, 6 per cent, 7½ per cent and 9 per cent. To others more remote the rates are 5 per cent, 7½ per cent, 10 per cent, 12½ per cent and 15 per cent.

Wisconsin.—(1) Tax of 1 per cent to husband, wife, lineal descendants, lineal ancestors, adopted child, and lineal issue thereof. (2) To brothers, sisters and descendants, wife or widow of son, or husband of daughter, 1½ per cent. (3) To uncles, aunts or their descendants, 3 per cent. (4) To great-uncles, great-aunts and their descendants, 4 per cent. (5) To all others, 5 per cent. When the estate is above $25,000 the above rates are multiplied as follows: $25,000 to $50,000, 1½ times on excess; $50,000 to $100,000, 2 times on excess; $100,000 to $500,000, 2½ times on excess; above $500,000, 3 times on excess. Exempt $10,000 to widow and lesser amounts to other relatives, down to $100 exemptions to strangers in blood.

Wyoming.—Tax of 2 per cent on amount above $10,000 to parents, husband or wife, child, brother, sister, lineal descendants, wife or widow of son, husband of daughter, adopted or acknowledged child for ten years. Except that to husband, wife or child resident of the state $25,000 to each is exempt. To others than above, tax of 5 per cent; $500 exempt.

Preferred Obligations.—In most states the preferred obligations are funeral expenses, administration, taxes, judgments in the order named.

17

The table on this page, reproduced from "Equity," shows the status of these measures in the different states of the Union.

Where Adopted	When	Statutory Initiative	Constitutional Initiative	Referendum	Recall †
South Dakota	1898	5%; *indirect		5%	
Oregon	1902	8%; direct	8%; direct	5%	
Nevada	1905 and 1912	10%, 1912; indirect		5%	25%
Montana	1906	8%; direct	10%, 1912; indirect	10%, 1905	25%, 1912
Oklahoma	1907	8%; direct	15%; direct	5%	
Maine	1908	12,000 voters		10,000 voters	
Missouri	1908	5%; direct	5%; direct	5%	
Michigan	1908 and 1913	8%, 1913; indirect	20% 1908, 10% 1913, direct		25%, 1913
Arkansas	1910	8%; direct	8%; direct	5%	Carried but killed by S. Ct.
Colorado	1910	8%; direct	8%; direct	5%	25%
Arizona	1911	10%; direct	15%; direct	5%	25%
New Mexico	1911			10%	
California	1911	5%; indirect. 8%; direct	8%; direct	5%	12% state; 20% local
Ohio	1912	3%; indirect. 6%; direct	10%; direct	6%	
Nebraska	1912	10%; direct	15%; direct	10%	
Washington	1912	10%; direct and indirect		6%	25% state; 35% local
North Dakota	1914	10%; direct	25%; indirect	10%	
Mississippi	1914	7,500 voters	7,500 voters	6,000 voters	
Kansas	1914				10%
Louisiana	1914				25%
Maryland	1915			10,000 voters	
Utah	1917	5%; indirect. 10%; direct		10%	

UTAH AND IDAHO: Initiative and Referendum amendments were adopted by the voters of Utah in 1900 and of Idaho in 1912; but in both cases without a self-enacting clause. In both of these states the amendments have remained a dead letter for lack of action by the legislature; hence omitted from above table under these dates.

† KANSAS AND LOUISIANA: Amendments for the Recall were adopted in 1914 by the voters of Kansas (10 per cent. petition for state, 15 per cent. for a county, and 25 per cent. for a municipality) and by the voters of Louisiana (25 per cent. petition).

* "Indirect," as applied to the Initiative and Referendum, means that opportunity must be given for action by the legislature on initiated measures before their submission at the polls. If not passed by the legislature, the measure must then go to the polls.

MUNICIPAL: The Initiative and Referendum and the Recall are now in operation, more or less completely, in over 300 municipalities, some under general state laws and others by special charter acts. Many such municipalities are in states not having the state-wide Initiative and Referendum or Recall. In 1917 only four states had no municipal or state-wide referendum, recall or initiative.

Inheritance Tax, recommended by President—

    Roosevelt, 7043, 7083.

    Taft, 7370, 7390.

Initiative, Referendum and Recall.—
Under these terms are comprised several propositions for bringing the entire body of voters into closer and more active participation in making and enforcing laws. In the opinion of many persons of various political faiths these ideas comprehend a simpler and more advanced form of democracy than at present obtains in most representative governments.

The initiative gives the people the power to originate laws. If a certain percentage of the voters sign a petition for a law and file it with the proper official it must come before the legislative body.

Reference of proposed laws to the people for their final acceptance or rejection is known as the referendum. The initiative is always coupled with the referendum.

The recall is a provision for the recall of an elective officer before the expiration of his term of office by petition of a certain proportion of those who voted for him and demanding another election.

The principle of the referendum has been employed in the United States as far back as 1778, when the legislature of Massachusetts submitted a constitution to the people, requiring a two-thirds majority for its ratification. This failed of passage at the hands of the voters, and in 1779 a popular vote was taken on whether to hold a constitutional convention. This proposal carried and a convention was called which framed a new constitution which was later submitted to the people and ratified. Constitutions have been referred to the people for ratification by nearly all the states.

The broader idea of the referendum as popularly advocated in the United States is copied from the Swiss republic, whence it dates back to the fourteenth century. About 1890 interest in this form of lawmaking was aroused. Its introduction was one of the demands of the Farmers' Alliance, and later of the People's party. It was thought that in this way legislation could be taken from the control of party politicians.

In 1898 South Dakota so amended its constitution as to require the submission to popular vote of any measure proposed by petition of five per cent of the qualified voters. Upon petition of the same percentage of voters any measure enacted by the legislature was required to be submitted to the people, provided such measure was not necessary to the immediate preservation of the public health, peace or safety for the support of the government or its existing institutions. South Dakota's adoption of the initiative and referendum was followed by Utah in 1900 and by Oregon in 1902.

The Oregon Plan.—The Oregon plan seems to have been the model after which other states formed their initiative and referendum laws. It requires that an initiative petition must be signed by eight per cent of the legal voters as shown by the vote for supreme judge at the last preceding general election, and filed with the Secretary of State four months before election. A referendum petition need only be signed by five per cent of the voters and filed with the Secretary of State ninety days after the final adjournment of the legislature passing the bill on which the referendum is demanded. The legislature may also refer to the people any act passed by it. The veto power of the governor does not extend to referendum measures passed on by popular vote. It is also provided that the Secretary of State shall, at the expense of the state, mail to registered voters a printed pamphlet containing a true copy of the title and text of each measure to be voted on, and the proponents and opponents are permitted to insert in the pamphlet, at the actual cost to themselves of paper and printing only, such arguments on the subject as they desire to present. The Republican legislature of Oregon was directed by the referendum to elect Governor Chamberlain, a Democrat, to the United States Senate.

The Ohio Constitutional Convention proposed an amendment to the Constitution of the State providing for Initiative and Referendum, requiring signatures of ten per cent of the electors to propose an amendment to the Constitution, and three per cent of the electors for a Referendum proposing a law. The amendment submitted to the people for approval, same to take effect October 1, 1912, was approved by vote of people at election held September 3, 1912. The Legislature of Ohio in 1913 passed following safety guards for the Initiative and Referendum petitions: Accepting money for signing, prohibited; applicable to each plan of organization in municipalities; giving money or value for signing, prohibited; printing and distribution of publicity pamphlets relative to measures submitted to people through Initiative and Referendum; provisions for Initiative and Referendum in municipal corporations; statement showing payments for circulating petitions.

Oklahoma was the first state to embody the initiative and referendum in its original constitution. Thirteen states have adopted the initiative and referendum—Arkansas, California (including the recall of judges), Colorado, Idaho, Illinois, Maine, Missouri, Montana, Nebraska, Nevada (referendum only), Oklahoma, Oregon, South Dakota and Utah. The legislature of Massachusetts has rejected the referendum. The question has also been submitted to the people of Florida, Iowa, Minnesota, North Dakota, Texas, Washington and Wisconsin. In Wyoming and Mississippi the required number of ballots was not cast, but of those voted the majority favored the proposition. In these states laws have been enacted for regulating the circulation of petitions.

The initiative and referendum is being largely used in cities, towns and counties to decide questions of public improvements, franchises, liquor traffic, etc. Los Angeles, Cal., adopted a form of initiative and referendum in 1902, and many other California cities have followed its example.

The California law of 1913, provides that the sheet or pamphlet containing Constitutional amendments, as well as any question, proposition or amendment to the Constitution to be submitted to the people by either Initiative or Referendum petition, shall also contain the corresponding Constitutional provisions as then in force, so as to facilitate comparison.

An amendment to the Constitution of Colorado became effective on Jan. 22, 1913, providing that every elective public officer may be recalled from office at any time; the initiation of the proceeding being a petition signed by electors equal in number to twenty-five per cent of the entire vote cast at the last preceding election for all candidates for the position which the incumbent sought to be recalled occupied. An amendment to the Constitution became effective on Jan. 22, 1913, providing for the recall of judicial decisions.

Returns on the Initiative and Referendum measures submitted to Montana's voters at the election in November, 1912, indicated that several of them were carried by heavy majorities. They provide for party nomination for state offices by direct vote, limiting the campaign expenditures of candidates to 15 per cent of the office salary for one year, and providing for the direct election of United States Senators and for a Presidential primary.

The Supreme Court of the United States on February 19, 1912, handed down a decision upon the claim of the Pacific States Telephone and Telegraph Company, that a tax upon it imposed by the Initiative and Referendum method in Oregon, was unconstitutional. The Court decided that only Congress and not the Supreme Court of the United States may object to the Initiative and Referendum.

Injunctions.—Judicial writs forbidding specified persons doing certain things, the commission or continuance of which would, in the opinion of a judge, work irreparable injury before the complaint could be settled in a court of equity were borrowed by the early English chancellors from Roman law to supplement the common law where inadequate to meet the ends of justice. The scope and application of these writs, now known as injunctions, have been broadened until to-day the injunction is one of the most widely used processes of the courts of equity.

Injunctions, which are summary proceedings, are only rightfully issued in cases where the remedy at law will be inadequate to give a party who is wronged the complete relief to which he is entitled. Popular interest has been aroused in the subject of injunctions by their employment in labor disputes, where labor union members and their friends and sympathizers have been enjoined from inducing or coercing other working people to quit work, thus inflicting damage or injury to their employers, and thereby forcing the employers to grant concessions demanded by the labor union members.

Injunctions have also been granted restraining labor unions from advising members of their own or allied organizations to withdraw their profitable patronage or services from employers against whom they have a grievance. (See Boycott.)

Trade unions have openly expressed hostility to the injunction as applied to their members, and have had a law passed providing that no writ shall be issued restraining any person from terminating employment, or from recommending others to do so; or from peaceful picketing; or from ceasing to patronize or to employ any party to a labor dispute; or from peacefully assembling; or from doing any act which might lawfully be done in the absence of a labor dispute.

Dec. 18, 1907, Judge Gould, of the Supreme Court of the District of Columbia, granted a temporary injunction against the officers of the American Federation of Labor, restraining them from publishing the name of the Buck's Stove and Range Company in their paper, *The American Federationist*, under the heading, "We Don't Patronize," or "Unfair List." This injunction was made permanent March 23, 1908, the judge declaring that, although individuals may refuse to patronize a firm, the inciting of others to do so constitutes a conspiracy in restraint of trade. It restrained Samuel Gompers, John Mitchell and Frank Morrison from "publishing or otherwise circulating, whether in writing or orally, any statement or notice of any kind or character whatever calling the attention of the complainant's customers, or of dealers or tradesmen, or the public, to any boycott

against the complainant, its business or its product and from advising any one not to purchase or handle the complainant's goods or by any other form of representation or statement interfering with his business." This injunction was violated and the defendants were sentenced by Judge Daniel Wright to imprisonment for one year, nine months and six months, respectively. The case was then taken to the Supreme Court of the United States. Meanwhile the Federation and the Bucks Company had come to an agreement. The court, therefore, in May, 1911, dismissed the original injunction suit brought by the company; and, while declaring the sentences in the contempt case to be excessive, ruled that the dismissal of the injunction suit did not prejudice the right of the original court to punish any contempt committed. After investigation by a committee appointed to inquire whether contempt had been committed, Justice Wright, in June, 1912, reimposed the sentences of twelve, nine and six months. The case was then taken again to the Court of Appeals of the District of Columbia. On May 5, that court, in a divided opinion, sustained the lower court in finding Messrs. Gompers, Mitchell and Morrison guilty of contempt, but modified the sentences to thirty days in jail for Gompers and $500 fine for each of the others.

In the latter part of May, 1913, counsel for the three defendants filed a petition in the Supreme Court of the United States for a writ of certiorari to obtain a review of the case. About the same time the Supreme Court of the District of Columbia filed a petition asking the same court to reverse that portion of the decision of the Court of Appeals which reduced the penalties imposed. June 19, the petition for a review of the case was granted, and May 11, 1914, the United States Supreme Court dismissed the case.

In 1893 the engineers on the Toledo, Ann Arbor and Michigan Railroad went out on strike. The engineers on connecting lines of road refused to handle cars of that road. An injunction was granted by Judge Taft (later President), forbidding the employees of other roads to refuse to handle the cars of the Toledo, Ann Arbor and Michigan road. This was the first judicial decision outlining the rights and duties of organized labor in interstate commerce. This opinion, while conceding the right of the engineers and employees of the Toledo Company to quit work, denied the right of the employees of other companies to refuse to handle the cars of the Toledo Company when offered them, such refusal being deemed part of a conspiracy in restraint of interstate commerce.

In 1894 the American Railway Union struck against the Pullman Car Company. Members of affiliated unions on all railways refused to handle the Pullman cars. The Cincinnati Southern Railway insisted on its employees hauling the cars, and an officer of the union was sentenced to jail for endeavoring to induce the men not to handle Pullman cars after an injunction had been granted by Judge Taft forbidding such refusal, on the ground of interference with interstate traffic.

In September, 1908, Judge Van Devanter, of the United States Circuit Court, at St. Louis, Mo., granted the St. Louis, Iron Mountain and Southern Railroad, and other roads operating in Arkansas, an injunction restraining the Arkansas State Railroad Commission from enforcing the two-cent-a-mile rate of fare law, on the ground that such rate was confiscatory and therefore unconstitutional.

In 1908 the Chicago Typographical Union

was enjoined by the Illinois Supreme Court not to practice "picketing." The union appealed the case and continued the practice complained of. The violators were fined by the court, who held that an appeal does not justify the violation of an injunction.

In 1908 a New York City Court judge issued an injunction restraining the police from interfering with certain theatrical performances on Sunday. This injunction was dismissed by the Appellate Division of the State Supreme Court, on the ground that an officer cannot be restrained from enforcing a valid law.

The Delaware, Lackawanna and Western Railroad Company sought, in 1908, to enjoin its switchmen from leaving its employ in violation of an alleged agreement to work under certain conditions for a specified time. The injunction was refused on the grounds that no violation of property rights was shown, and that members of labor organizations may peacefully withdraw from employment, even though such withdrawal involves a breach of contract.

Many interesting points of law have been raised on the subject of injunctions, and they have been officially discussed by President Roosevelt and President Taft.

Injunctions:
Abuse of, in labor disputes, mentioned, 7026, 7086, 7128, 7190, 7213.
Defended by President Taft, 7378.
Discussing powers of courts in, 7378.

Inland Bill.—A bill of exchange drawn in a country on a person or firm in the same country.

Inland Waterways, improvements recommended, 7222.

Innocuous Desuetude.—This phrase occurs in a message of President Cleveland, March 1, 1886 (4966), when he was discussing laws on the subject of suspensions from office. The Senate had asked him for his reasons for suspending certain officials.

Insane Asylum. (See Government Hospital for Insane.)

Insane Persons, act making grant of lands to States for benefit of, vetoed, 2780.

Insecticide and Fungicide Board.—A Federal board under the jurisdiction of the Department of Agriculture which has charge of the administration of the laws for the inspection of insecticides and fungicides. The Insecticide Act of 1910 was designed to regulate the interstate shipment, and to prevent the importation into the United States, of adulterated and misbranded insecticides and fungicides, and also to control the manufacture and sale of such products in the District of Columbia and the territories. By its provisions the Secretary of the Treasury, the Secretary of Agriculture, and the Secretary of Commerce and Labor are authorized to make uniform rules for its enforcement. The bureaus of Animal and Plant Industry, Chemistry and Entomology are represented on the board.

Laboratory and field experiments have been continued with various insecticides, especially lime and sulphur preparations, several arsenicals, and other toxic substances as possible substitutes for these nicotine sprays, distillate emulsions, etc. Some experiments have been undertaken to determine as exactly as possible the quantity of arsenate of lead which should be employed satisfactorily to control the codling moth and plum curculio on apples and peaches.

Insignia.—In military dress insignia are badges in the form of medallions, ribbons, or the like, signalizing rank or distinction.

Insolvent Debtors. (See Bankruptcy; Debtors, Insolvent.)

Inspection, Office of, Agriculture Department.—The Federal meat inspection service is coming to be recognized as the most effective existing agency for collecting, on a broad scale, data absolutely necessary to the success of any extensive program for the eradication from the food herds of the country of such diseases as tuberculosis and certain serious parasitic affections, the presence of which is not suspected in the living animal until the damage they do is beyond prevention. The eradication, or material reduction, of these diseases will enormously lessen losses on the farm, and in a corresponding measure remove the cause of the losses from condemnations under inspection.

The rules of condemnation on account of disease have been prepared by scientific and practical experts, and essentially conform to the views expressed by a commission of seven men outside of the department convened in 1907 by the Secretary of Agriculture to study the subject and give opinions as to the disposal of carcasses affected with disease and abnormalities. That the regulations are intelligently applied is indicated by the fact that all condemnations on the post-mortem inspection under the Federal system are determined by graduated veterinarians and then only after they have received instruction in the practical application of the rules after admission to the service. These inspectors, stationed in many states, make actual post-mortem examinations of upward of 60 per cent of the cattle, sheep, hogs, and goats slaughtered for food in the United States. This information, used in conjunction with live stock shipping records is sufficient, in most cases, to fix the territory of origin, and in many cases lead to the farm and herds whence the diseased animals have come.

In 1907 a Board of Food and Drug Inspection was organized to assist the Secretary of Agriculture in the enforcement of the Food and Drugs Act. Some of the important decisions of this board prohibited the coating of rice; restricted the use of coloring matter in food products; forbade the use of chemical preservatives known to be harmful; prohibited the bleaching of flour with nitrogen peroxide, the use of shellac for coating chocolates and other confections, the use of saccharin and copper sulphate in foods, importation and interstate traffic in absinthe, the shipment of immature, artificially colored citrus fruits; and restricted the sale of canned goods containing salts of tin. These boards were later, for purposes of economy, combined into the Office of Inspection.

Inspection, Sanitary. (See Animal Industry discussed.)

Inspector-General. (See War Department and Army.)

Inspector-General of Army, bill relative to department of, returned, 4855.

Inspector of Customs.—One who examines imported goods and baggage to forestall the effect of false declarations, and to prevent smuggling.

Inspector, Revenue. (See Revenue Inspector.)

Institutions of Learning. (See Education; Military Academy; National University; Naval Academy; Seminaries of Learning.)

Insular Affairs, Bureau of, War Department.—By act of July 1, 1902, the Bureau of Insular Affairs is charged with the administration of "all matters of civil government in the island possessions of the United States under the jurisdiction of the War Department." Under this head are included the Philippines (q. v.), Porto Rico (q. v.), and the other island possessions of the United States. (See War Department.)

Insular Possessions.—According to a report published by the National Geographic Society in June, 1914, the United States owns exactly 8,000 islands, supporting a population of 10,000,000. The report further shows that the commerce of these islands exceeds $300,000,000, or more than that of the United States in any year prior to 1850. American capital invested in the islands aggregates approximately $400,000,000, and from them there is shipped to the United States $100,000,000 worth of products every year and they take in exchange products of about equal value.

The feature of the report is the development of Porto Rico, Hawaii and the Philippine Islands. It shows that when Porto Rico came under American rule fifteen years ago there was but one school building on the island, while to-day there are 1,200. There were 25,000 pupils enrolled in the first year of American administration, now there are 175,000. Then there was but one good road of forty miles; now there are about 1,000 miles. Production of sugar has grown from 65,000 tons a year to 365,000. Foreign commerce was about $20,000,000 a year; now it is nearly $100,000,000.

Hawaii has been extremely prosperous since it came permanently under the American flag in 1900. The assessed value of the sugar crop more than doubled, deposits in banks trebled and in savings banks quadrupled. Hawaii's irrigation system is the marvel of the engineering world, and the quantity of sugar produced per acre far exceeds that of any other spot on the globe.

The Alaskan islands and mainland cost us $7,500,000, an expenditure that many believed to be unjustifiable; yet for many years the annual value of seal skins alone approximated the cost of the entire area. At present the value of the canned salmon sent us from Alaska in a single year is twice as much as the entire possession cost. (See Alaska, Guam, Hawaii, Puerto Rico, Philippines, Tutuila, Wake and other islands.)

Insular Possessions, U. S., mentioned, 7019, 7286, 7681.

Industrial development of, 7019.

Insurance Companies, American:

Exclusion of, from Germany, referred to, 6061, 6099, 6183.

Discussed by President Roosevelt, 6987, 7290.

Federal control of, advocated, 6987.

Treatment of, in Russia, 5961.

Insurrection.—Rebellion against legal authority, especially a small uprising within a country or state. (See Whiskey Insurrection.)

Insurrections. (See Illegal Combinations.)

Intercession.—A voluntary offer to mediate, especially on the part of one country towards another. It sometimes takes the form of force, as in the case of the intercession on the part of the United States in the difficulties between Cuba and Spain, which led to the Spanish-American War. (See Spanish-American War, and Intervention.)

Intercontinental Railroad:

Connection of Mexican railway system with, discussed, 5547.

Survey for, discussed, 5622.

To connect systems of North America with those of southern continent recommended, 5504.

Intercourse, Foreign:

Action recommended on the publication of confidential items, 2281.

Appropriations for, 190, 448.

Reduction in, discussed, 4356.

Unexpended, 3828.

Contingent expenses—

Funds on deposit with Baring Brothers & Co. for, 3828.

Public interests demand that confidential items be not published, 2281.

Expenditures for, to be paid from funds on deposit, 3828.

Provision for, recommended, 58, 190.

Requests of House and Senate for information regarding, refused, 186, 2281, 2416, 2452, 2690, 2691, 2695, 6101.

Referred to, 2529.

Interest Laws. (See Statutes of Limitations.)

Interior, Department of the.—An executive department of the government composed of a number of bureaus and offices whose duties have no connection with each other, but relate generally to internal affairs. It was created by an act of Congress approved March 3, 1849; in the original law it was called the Home Department (q. v.), the name being very soon changed. By the act of 1849, it was given jurisdiction over patents, formerly held by the State Department; Indian Affairs, formerly held by the War Department; pensions, formerly held by the War and Navy; and the census, formerly under the Treasury; while the General Land Office was transferred to it from the Treasury, together with the care of certain public buildings and the revision of court accounts. The Census Bureau was transferred in 1903 to the Department of Commerce and Labor (q. v.), while the reviewing of the accounts of courts and marshals is in the hands of the Department of Justice (q. v.). Numerous additions have since been made to its jurisdiction, including education, public surveys, the subsidized railroads, the distribution of certain public documents; labor matters now controlled by the Department of Labor (q. v.), territories, national parks, and the oversight of certain charitable institutions in the District of Columbia. The office of Assistant Secretary was created at its organization; an additional assistant secretary, with the title of First Assistant, was created in 1865.

Patent Office attends to the granting and issuing of patents on inventions. The first patent law was approved April 10, 1790. Only three patents were granted the first year, thirty-three the second, and

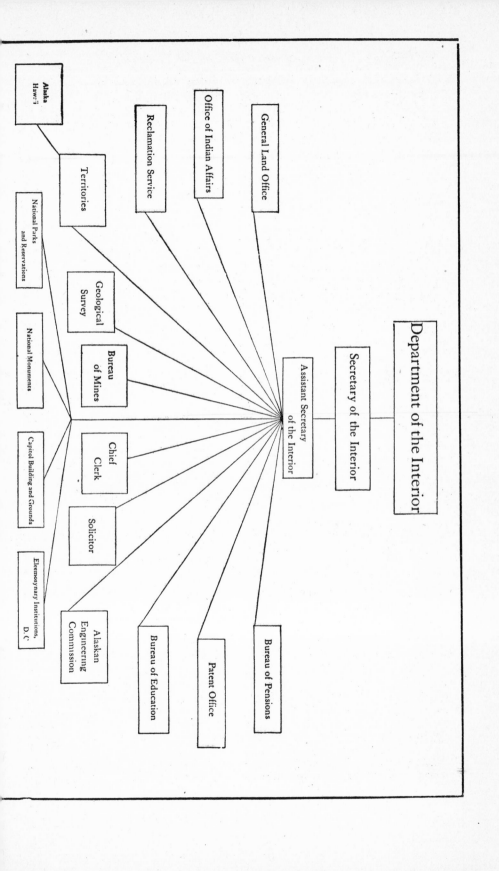

Department of the Interior

Secretary of the Interior

Assistant Secretary
of the Interior

General Land Office

Office of Indian Affairs

Reclamation Service

Territories

Alaska
Hawai'i

National Parks
and Reservations

National Monuments

Capitol Building and Grounds

Eleemosynary Institutions,
D. C.

Geological
Survey

Bureau
of Mines

Chief
Clerk

Solicitor

Alaskan
Engineering
Commission

Bureau of Education

Patent Office

Bureau of Pensions

eleven the third. In 1836 the Patent Office was burned, with all the records, and Congress then established the present system, substantially repealing the earlier laws. The office was created as a Bureau of the Department of State, the chief officer being the Commissioner of Patents. When the Department of the Interior was created, in 1849, the Patent Office was made a bureau thereof. The Commissioner of Patents supervises the issuing of patents and the registration of trade-marks. His decision is final in the Patent Office and he has appellate jurisdiction in the trial of interference cases and questions relating to the patentability of inventions. The Office publishes each month an Official Gazette, giving a description of each patent issued. (See Patents.)

Commissioner of pensions has charge of matters relating to pensions and bounty lands. Under him are two deputy commissioners and a chief clerk, each in charge of certain divisions of the Bureau. Up to 1833, the distribution of pensions had been supervised by the War and Navy Departments, each for its own pensioners. In that year Congress established the Pension Bureau, and placed J. S. Edwards in charge. He immediately assumed the business heretofore conducted by the War Department, and in 1849 naval pensions also. In the same year the Bureau was made a part of the new Interior Department. (See also Pensions.)

General Land Office has charge of the survey and sale of public lands. Until 1812 the Secretary of the Treasury acted as agent for the sale of public lands. After the office of Commissioner of the General Land Office was created, the Land Office remained a Bureau of the Treasury Department until it was made a part of the Interior Department at its organization.

The Bureau of Indian Affairs has jurisdiction over the Indians of the United States, except those in Alaska, and makes annual reports upon the condition of each tribe. Previous to 1832 all matters relating to the Indians had been transacted by the clerks of the War Department. By this time, however, the business relations between the Government and the Indians had grown to such proportions that it became necessary to establish a Bureau of Indian Affairs. Accordingly Congress authorized the President to appoint a Commissioner who should have general superintendence, under the Secretary of War, of all Indian Affairs. The first Commissioner was appointed July 9, 1832. It remained a part of the War Department until 1849, when it was transferred to the Department of the Interior. (See Indians.)

The Bureau of Education was originally established under the name of the Department of Education in 1867; the succeeding year it was made a Bureau of the Interior Department. Its head is the Commissioner of Education. His duties are to collect such statistics and facts as show the progress of education throughout the country, and to diffuse this and such other information as shall aid in educational progress. He also has charge of the education of the Indians in Alaska, and administers the endowment fund for the support of agricultural and mechanical colleges.

The Geological Survey was made a Bureau of the Interior Department in 1879, although geological and topographical expeditions had been sent out before that time. Its head, the Director of the Geological Survey, is charged with the classification of public lands, their examination as to geologic structure, mineral resources and products and the preparation of topographic and geologic maps; he makes investigations as to the water supply and the capacity of streams; and has charge of the reclamation of arid lands (popularly known as irrigation work) including the *disbursement of the reclamation fund*, created by the act of June 17, 1902, from the sale of arid lands. (See Irrigation; see Geological Survey.)

Following is a list of the secretaries of the interior and the presidents under whom they served:

President	Secretary of the Interior	Appointed
Taylor	Thomas Ewing, Ohio	1849
Fillmore	James A. Pearce, Maryland	1850
"	T.M.T.McKennan,Pennsylvania	1850
"	Alex. H. H. Stuart, Virginia	1850
Pierce	Robert McClelland, Michigan	1853
Buchanan	Jacob Thompson, Mississippi	1857
Lincoln	Caleb B. Smith, Indiana	1861
"	John P. Usher, Indiana	1863
Johnson	"	1865
"	James Harlan, Iowa	1865
"	Orville H. Browning, Illinois	1866
Grant	Jacob D. Cox, Ohio	1869
"	Columbus Delano, Ohio	1870
"	Zachariah Chandler, Michigan	1875
Hayes	Carl Schurz, Missouri	1877
Garfield	Samuel J. Kirkwood, Iowa	1881
Arthur	Henry M. Teller, Colorado	1882
Cleveland	Lucius Q. C. Lamar, Mississippi	1885
"	William F. Vilas, Wisconsin	1888
B. Harrison	John W. Noble, Missouri	1889
Cleveland	Hoke Smith, Georgia	1893
"	David R. Francis, Missouri	1896
McKinley	Cornelius N. Bliss, New York	1897
"	Ethan A. Hitchcock, Missouri	1899
Roosevelt	"	1901
"	James R. Garfield, Ohio	1907
Taft	Richard A. Ballinger, Washington	1909
"	Walter L. Fisher, Illinois	1911
Wilson	Franklin K. Lane, California	1913

For more detailed information as to the scope of the activities of the Department of the Interior consult the index references to the Presidents' Messages and Encyclopedic articles under the following headings:

Bureau of Education
Eleemosynary Institutions
General Land Office
Geological Survey.
Indians.
Land Grants.
Lands, Bounty.
Lands, Desert.
Lands, Homestead.
Lands, Indian.
Lands, Mineral.
Lands, Public.
Lands, Swamp.
Lands, Timber and Stone.
Mines, Bureau of
National Monuments
Patents.
Pensions.
Reclamation Service
Territories

Interior, Department of the:

Additional room for clerical force in, recommended, 4661.

Affairs of, discussed, 5760.

Appointments and removals in, referred to, 3669.

Establishment of, referred to, 2704.

Fire in, discussed and recommendations regarding, 4405, 4407.

Fireproof roof for, recommended, 4690.

Increased number of law clerks in, recommended, 4679.

Libraries in, consolidation of, referred to, 4738.

Separation of Patent Office from, recommended, 4155, 4206.

Transfer of—
Pension Bureau from, to War Department, recommended, 4060.
Territorial affairs from State Department to, recommended, 4060, 4145.

Internal Improvements.—There being no provision in the Constitution for internal improvements, the matter has always been a subject of dispute. Since Aug. 7, 1789, Congress has regularly appropriated money for such improvements as lie strictly within the Federal jurisdiction—harbors, beacons, buoys, lighthouses, piers, etc. March 29, 1806, Congress authorized the president to appoint three commissioners to lay out a national road from Cumberland, on the Potomac, to the Ohio River, and appropriated $30,000 for the expenses (406). The road was to pass through several states. A national road was also projected through Georgia, with New Orleans as its proposed western terminus. March 3, 1817, President Madison vetoed a bill to set apart the bonus and Government dividends of the national bank as a fund "for constructing roads and canals and improving the navigation of water courses," on the ground that Congress had no constitutional power to extend public revenue for such purposes (569). May 4, 1822, President Monroe vetoed an appropriation for preserving and repairing the Cumberland road, on the same general ground (711). President Jackson also vetoed several bills providing for internal improvements (1046, 1056, 1201, 1337). March 14, 1818, the House of Representatives passed a resolution declaring that Congress had the power to appropriate money for the construction of roads and canals and for the improvement of water courses. March 3, 1823, the first appropriation for the improvement of rivers and harbors passed Congress. In April, 1824, $30,000 was appropriated for the survey of such roads and canals as the president should deem of national importance, and the act of March 3, 1825, authorized the subscription of $300,000 to the stock of the Chesapeake and Delaware Canal. Since 1861 the question of internal improvements has ceased to be a party one, both parties recognizing the right of Congress to appropriate money for public improvements. (See River and Harbor Bills, Pacific Railroads and Irrigation, and illustrations opposite 2185, 2929.)

Internal Improvements (see also Rivers and Harbors):

Acts on subject of, vetoed by President—
Arthur, 4707.
Discussed, 4724.
Cleveland, 6109.
Grant, 4336.
Jackson, 1046, 1056, 1071, 1201, 1337.
Madison, 569.
Monroe, 711.
Pierce, 2789, 2790, 2919, 2920, 2921.
Polk, 2310, 2460.
Tyler, 2183.
Aid for, should be by separate bills, 4725.

Appropriations for, 1046.
Applied, 872.
On the Lakes referred to, 2957.
Recommended, 955, 2627, 4646.
Approval of bill for, explained, 1046.
(See also Rivers and Harbors.)
Board of Engineers for, examination made by, 853, 873.
Constitutional amendment relative to, suggested, 398, 553, 587, 759.
Referred to, 786.
Discussed by President—
Adams, J. Q., 954, 982.
Arthur, 4646, 4707, 4724.
Buchanan, 3130.
Cleveland, 6109.
Fillmore, 2626.
Grant, 4336.
Jackson, 1014, 1046, 1071, 1164, 1201, 1337.
Madison, 569.
Monroe, 587, 711, 713.
Pierce, 2751, 2789, 2790, 2919, 2920, 2921.
Polk, 2310, 2460, 2506.
Roosevelt, 7602.
Taft, 7665.
Tyler, 2183.
Expenditures for public works in States and Territories referred to, 3591.
Information regarding construction of roads transmitted, 594.
Lands granted in aid of, 1029, 3651, 4065, 4206, 5380.
Referred to, 872, 877, 879, 909, 987, 993, 1096, 1776, 2957.
Surveys for, transmitted, 1027.

Internal Revenue.—That part of the revenue of a country which is derived from duties or taxes on articles manufactured or grown at home, on licenses, stamps, incomes, etc.—in fact, all revenue not collected on exports or imports. The internal revenue of the United States is derived chiefly from taxes on liquors and tobacco and in cases of emergency upon commercial paper, bank circulation, and upon incomes. The receipts from these various sources have varied from $1,000,000, which figure was first reached in 1801, to $309,000,000, which was reached during the operation of the war tax in 1866. Later the taxes settled down to a normal basis of something like $150,000,000 a year.
The sources of internal revenue and the rate of taxation are as follows:
Special Taxes and Rates.—Rectifiers of less than 500 barrels a year, $100; rectifiers of 500 barrels or more a year, $200.
Wholesale liquor dealers, $100; retail liquor dealers, $25.
Wholesale dealers in malt liquors, $50; retail dealers in malt liquors, $20.
Manufacturers of stills, $50; and for stills or worms, manufactured, each, $20.
Brewers: Annual manufacture less than 500 barrels, $50; annual manufacture 500 barrels or more, $100.
Manufacturers of filled cheese, $400; wholesale dealers in filled cheese, $250; retail dealers in filled cheese, $12.
Manufacturers of oleomargarine, $600;

wholesale dealers in oleomargarine artificially colored in imitation of butter, $480; wholesale dealers in oleomargarine free from artificial coloration, $200; retail dealers in oleomargarine artificially colored in imitation of butter, $48; retail dealers in oleomargarine free from artificial coloration, $6.

Manufacturers of adulterated butter, $600; wholesale dealers in adulterated butter, $480; retail dealers in adulterated butter, $48; manufacturers of process or renovated butter, $50; manufacturers, packers or repackers of mixed flour, $12.

Distilled Spirits, etc.—Distilled spirits, per gallon, $1.10; stamps for distilled spirits intended for export, each, 10 cents; except when affixed to packages containing two or more 5-gallon cans for export, 5 cents.

Case stamps for spirits bottled in bond, 10 cents.

Wines, liquors or compounds known or denominated as wine, and made in imitation of sparkling wine or champagne, but not made from grapes grown in the United States, and liquors not made from grapes, currants, rhubarb or berries grown in the United States, but produced by being rectified or mixed with distilled spirits or by the infusion of any matter in spirits, to be sold as wine, or as a substitute for wine, in bottles containing not more than 1 pint per bottle or package, 10 cents; same, in bottles, containing more than 1 pint, and not more than 1 quart, per bottle or package, 20 cents (and at the same rate for any larger quantity of such merchandise, however put up or whatever may be the package). Grape brandy used in the fortification of pure, sweet wine under an act approved June 7, 1906 (to be assessed), per gallon, 3 cents.

Fermented Liquors.—Fermented liquors per barrel, containing not more than 31 gallons, $1 (and at a proportionate rate for halves, thirds, quarters, sixths and eighths of barrels); more than one barrel of 31 gallons, and not more than 63 gallons, in one package, $2.

Tobacco, Snuff, Cigars and Cigarettes.—Tobacco, however prepared, manufactured and sold, or removed for consumption or sale, per pound, 8 cents; snuff, however prepared, manufactured and sold, or removed for consumption or sale, per pound, 8 cents.

Cigars of all descriptions made of tobacco, or any substitute therefor, and weighing more than 3 pounds per thousand, $3; cigars of all descriptions made of tobacco, or any substitute therefor, and weighing not more than 3 pounds per thousand, 75 cents; cigarettes weighing more than 3 pounds per thousand, $3.60; cigarettes weighing not more than 3 pounds per thousand, 75 cents.

Oleomargarine, Adulterated Butter and Process or Renovated Butter.—Oleomargarine, domestic, artificially colored to look like butter, of any shade of yellow, per pound, 10 cents; oleomargarine, free from coloration that causes it to look like butter, of any shade of yellow, per pound, $\frac{1}{4}$ of one cent; oleomargarine, imported from foreign countries, per pound, 15 cents.

Adulterated butter, per pound, 10 cents; process or renovated butter, per pound, $\frac{1}{4}$ of one cent.

Filled Cheese.—Filled cheese, per pound, 1 cent; same, imported, per pound, 8 cents.

Opium.—Prepared smoking opium, per pound, $10.

Mixed Flour.—Mixed flour, per barrel of 196 pounds, or more than 98 pounds, 4 cents; half barrel of 98 pounds, or more than 49 pounds, 2 cents; quarter barrel of 49 pounds, or more than 24½ pounds, 1 cent; eighth barrel of 24½ pounds, or less,

$\frac{1}{2}$ of one cent. (Mixed flour imported from foreign countries, in addition to import duties, must pay internal revenue tax as above.)

Circulation of and Notes Paid Out by Banks and Bankers.—Circulation issued by any bank, etc., or person (except a national bank taxed under Section 5214, Revised Statutes, and Section 13, act March 14, 1900), per month, 1-12 of 1 per cent.

Circulation (except national banks) exceeding 90 per cent of capital, in addition, per month, 1-6 of 1 per cent.

Banks, etc., on amount of notes of any person, state bank, or state banking association, used for circulation and paid out, 10 per cent.

Banks, etc., bankers, or associations, on amount of notes of any town, city, or municipal corporation paid out by them, 10 per cent.

Every person, firm, association, other than national bank associations, and every corporation, state bank, or state banking association, on the amount of *their own notes* used for circulation and paid out by them, 10 per cent.

Every such person, firm, association, corporation, state bank, or state banking association, and also every national banking association, on the amount of notes of any person, firm, association, other than a national banking association, or of any corporation, state bank or state banking association, or of any town, city, or municipal corporation, used for circulation, and paid out by them, 10 per cent.

Playing Cards.—Playing cards, per pack, containing not more than 54 cards, 2 cents.

Following is a summary of internal revenue receipts from 1886 to 1917, inclusive:

Fiscal Years	Spirits	Tobacco	Fermented Liquors	Miscellaneous
1888...	$69,306,166	$30,662,432	$23,324,218	$ 154,970
1889...	74,312,206	31,866,861	23,723,835	83,893
1890...	81,687,375	33,958,991	26,008,535	135,555
1891...	83,335,964	32,796,271	28,565,130	256,214
1892...	91,309,984	31,000,493	30,037,453	239,532
1893...	94,720,261	31,889,712	32,548,983	166,915
1894...	85,259,252	28,617,899	31,414,788	1,876,509
1895...	79,862,627	29,704,908	31,640,618	1,960,794
1896...	80,670,071	30,711,629	33,784,235	1,664,545
1897...	82,008,543	30,710,297	32,472,162	1,426,506
1898...	92,547,000	36,230,522	39,515,421	2,572,696
1899...	99,283,534	52,493,208	68,644,558	9,225,453
1900...	109,868,817	59,355,084	73,550,754	11,575,626
1901...	116,027,980	62,481,907	75,669,908	13,448,921
1902...	121,138,013	51,937,925	71,988,902	13,360,130
1903...	131,953,472	43,514,810	47,547,856	7,723,345
1904...	135,810,015	44,655,809	49,083,459	3,354,722
1905...	135,958,513	45,659,910	50,360,553	2,209,000
1906...	143,394,055	48,422,997	55,641,859	1,644,027
1907...	156,336,902	51,811,070	59,567,818	1,948,232
1908...	140,158,807	49,862,754	59,807,617	1,836,772
1909...	134,868,034	51,887,178	57,456,411	2,001,095
1910...	148,029,311	58,118,457	60,572,288	23,236,988
1911...	155,279,858	67,005,950	64,367,777	34,719,897
1912...	156,391,487	70,590,151	63,268,770	30,067,365
1913...	163,879,342	a76,789,424	66,266,989	*36,073,054
1914...	159,098,177	79,986,639	67,081,512	†71,381,274
1915...	144,619,699	79,357,373	79,328,946	80,190,694
1916...	158,682,440	88,063,948	88,771,104	124,937,252
1917...	192,111,319	103,201,592	91,897,194	421,983,535

Of the receipts in 1913 classed as "Miscellaneous" $35,006,299 was from excise tax on corporations, $655,283 from playing cards and $401,910 from penalties. (a) Including $319,100 from sale of internal revenue stamps affixed to Philippine products, as provided for in the act of August 5, 1909. *Not including $1,259,987 from oleomargarine, $3,223 from mixed flour, $54,189 from adulterated butter, $98,241 from process or renovated butter. †Income tax.

Receipts of tax on Porto Rican products—spirits, cigars and cigarettes—year ended June 30, 1913, $591,356; on cigars and cigarettes from Philippines, $319,100.

Taxes Not Payable by Stamps.—Tax on deficiencies in production of spirits—On excess of materials used in production of spirits; on circulation of banks and bankers; on notes paid out by banks and others; on brandy used in the fortification of wine. Penalties of 50 and 100 per cent.

Corporation Taxes.—Excise tax on corporations, joint stock companies, associations and insurance companies (including 50 per cent additional), unassessed penalties, United States share of penalties recovered by suits, offers in compromise, interest, costs, fines, etc. (including duplicate payments, payments in excess, and payments after abatement). Rate of tax equivalent to 1 per cent of net income above $5,000.

Income Taxes.—The income tax for the year 1914 yielded $60,710,197.

Internal Revenue. (See Revenue, Public; Taxation.)

Internal-Revenue Collection Districts, reduction in, 4767.

Internal Revenue, Commissioner of, office of, discussed and recommendations regarding, 3985.

Internal-Revenue Stamps referred to, 3903.

Internal Taxation. (See Taxation.)

International African Association. (See Congo Free State.)

International American Bank:
Charter for, recommended by President Benj. Harrison, 5560.
Establishment of, recommended by International American Conference, 5505.
Discussed by, 5560.

International American Conference.— Oct. 2, 1889, on the invitation of the United States, an international conference of representatives from the United States and seventeen states of Central and South America, also including Mexico and Haiti, assembled at Washington. This conference is known as the Pan-American Congress. The object was to adopt some plan of arbitration for the settlement of disputes and the improvement of business relations and means of communication between the countries. Santo Domingo was the only state to refuse the invitation. Before assembling as a congress, the delegates were taken on a tour of the country to give them an idea of the extent and resources of the United States. After traveling 6,000 miles they returned to Washington. The proceedings of the congress resulted in extending a knowledge of the commercial status of the various countries and the publication of an extensive series of proceedings, debates and recommendations. The body adjourned April 19, 1890. The Bureau of American Republics (q. v.) was established at the suggestion of this congress.

International American Conference:
At Washington—
Centennial celebration of discovery of America, resolution of, regarding, 5512.
Discussed, 5369, 5467, 5542.
Extradition, reports on subject of, adopted by, 5514.
Importations and exportations, recommendations of, 5506.

Intercontinental railroad, survey of route for, recommended by, 5504.
International American bank, establishment of, recommended by, 5505.
Discussed, 5560.
International American monetary union, establishment of, recommended by, 5513.
International arbitration, reports on, adopted by, 5518.
Referred to, 5623, 5874.
International bureau of information at Washington, establishment of, recommended by, 5506.
International law, adoption of uniform code of, recommended by, 5513.
Latin-American library, establishment of, recommended by, 5506.
Memorial tablet in State Department to commemorate meeting of, erection of, recommended by, 5514.
Patents, trade-marks, and copyrights, report of, concerning protection of, 5512.
Post dues and consular fees, recommendations of, regarding uniform system of, 5514.
Postal and cable communication, establishment of improved facilities for, recommended by, 5511.
Public health, recommendations of, for protection of, 5513.
Reciprocal commercial treaties recommended by, 5509.
Statement of action in Panama Canal matter, 6827.
Steamship service, establishment of rapid, recommended by, 5491. (See also 5511.)
Weights and measures, report of, on, 5513.
At Rio Janeiro—
Collection by government of debts due their citizens, from other countries, by force of arms, referred to Hague Conference, by Conference of South American Republics, 7060.
Effective work of bureau of American Republics in, 7125.

International American Monetary Union, establishment of, recommended by International American Conference, 5513.

International Arbitration:
Attitude of Great Britain and United States respecting, discussed, 5874, 6154, 6178.
Failure of treaty for, referred to, 5623.

Reports adopted by International American Conference regarding, transmitted, 5518.
Referred to, 5623, 5874.
Resolution of French Chambers favoring treaty of, referred to, 6060.
Treaty with Great Britain regarding, discussed, 6178.
International Association of the Congo. (See Congo Free State.)
International Bureau of Exchanges, establishment of, recommended, 4681. (See also Exchanges for Official Documents.)
International Bureau of Information, establishment of, at Washington, recommended by International American Conference, 5506.
International Cattle Exhibition at Hamburg, discussed, 4714.
International Conference on Ratio between Gold and Silver. (See Gold and Silver.)
International Congress at Brussels for abolition of African slave trade, 5471.
International Congress of Electricians at Paris, discussed, 4581, 4625, 4714. (See also National Conference of Electricians.)
International Conventions:
Discretionary authority of President—
To invite nations to attend, on subject of coinage recommendations regarding, 5877.
To send delegates to, recommendations regarding, 4617, 4763, 4827, 5546.
For establishing standards of measure of color, perception, and acuteness of vision, recommendations regarding, 4780.
For protection of industrial property, 4794.
For suppression of crime, 4115.
International Copyright Convention:
At Berne, discussed, 4919, 5090.
Negotiations for, referred to, 4625.
International Court of Arbitration. (See Hague Peace Conference.)
International Exchange, Commission on, work of, 6941.
International Exhibition of Fine Arts, to be held at Munich, discussed, 5193.
International Exhibitions. (See Exhibitions.)
International Exposition of Labor at Barcelona, discussed, 5177, 5399.
International Fisheries Exhibition at London, discussed, 4688.
International Geodetic Association, invitation to United States to become a party to, 5192.
International Inventions Exhibition at London, discussed, 4827.

International Joint Commission. (See Mexico.)
International Law:
Claim of Great Britain to forcibly visit American vessels on the seas, not sustained by, 3038.
Propositions regarding, submitted by United States, discussed, 2945.
Uniform code of adoption of, recommended by International American Conference, 5513.
International Marine Conference at Washington, discussed, 5180, 5370, 5468, 5493, 5498, 5543.
International Meridian Conference:
At Washington discussed, 4718, 4800, 4827, 4841, 5180.
Invitation of Italian Government to United States to attend, 5546.
International Military Encampment to be held at Chicago:
During World's Fair discussed, 5609.
In 1887, foreign guests attending, not to pay duties on baggage, 5164.
International Monetary Conference (see also Coins and Coinage; Gold and Silver):
At Brussels in 1892, 5752.
Postponement of, discussed, 5876.
Reports of, transmitted, 5784.
At Paris in—
1867, 3776, 3792.
Report of S. B. Ruggles on, 4013.
1878, 4447, 4464, 4474, 4510.
Appropriation for, recommended, 4438.
1881, 4625.
1882, 4697.
International Money Orders discussed, 5881, 5971.
International Obligations of United States, removal of cases involving observance and execution of, from State to Federal judiciary recommended, 1928, 1956.
International Ocean Telegraph Co., charges made by, for messages referred to, 4069.
International Patent Congress at Vienna, report of John M. Thacher on, referred to, 4215.
International Peace Congress at Washington discussed, 4684, 4717.
Invitation extended countries of North and South America to attend, 4685.
Postponement of, referred to, 4717.
International Penitentiary Congress at London, referred to, 4162.
International Polar Congress at Hamburg referred to, 4535.
International Postal Conference at—
Berne, 4250.
Lisbon, 4938.

Paris, 3387.
New convention adopted by, 4453.
International Postal Union, convention for establishment of, 4250. (See also Universal Postal Union.)
International Prison Congress (see also National Prison Congress):
To be held at—
St. Petersburg, 5117.
Stockholm, 4406.
Proceedings of, referred to, 4464.
International Sanitary Conference at—
Rome, 4898, 4918.
Washington, 4564, 4622, 4631.
International Statistical Congress:
At St. Petersburg, 4142, 4221.
The Hague, 4082.
Invitation to hold meeting in United States recommended, 4142.
Internment.—The imprisonment by the authorities of a country of foreign citizens within its borders. The imprisonment is not intended as individual punishment, and occurs without reference to the conduct of the individual foreigner; it is a precaution taken against possible seditious conduct, and the imprisonment may amount to holding the foreigners as hostages in case reprisals become necessary. Internment differs from immurement (q. v.) in that immurement imprisons all nationalities who happen to be within the enclosure used for that purpose.
Interoceanic Canal Co., discussed, 5470.
Interparliamentary Union invited to St. Louis, 6796, 6923.
Interstate Commerce.—Commercial transactions and intercourse between residents in different states or carried on by lines of transport extending into more than one state. Power to regulate commerce between the states is invested in Congress by the Constitution (18). It is held that the power to regulate commerce of necessity includes the power to regulate the means by which it is carried on, so that the scope of authority given to Congress by this clause enlarges with the development of the industries of the country and the means of communication. The intent of the framers of the Constitution was to prohibit legislation by any state against the business interests of another state by taxation, discrimination or otherwise. It was intended also as a check upon the arbitrary power of state legislatures rather than upon private corporations or railroad companies. With the development of the great railway lines, traversing many states and bringing remote interior producers into close communication with the seaboard markets, came the necessity for regulating the rates of transportation by a more general law than it was within the power of any state to enact.
It was charged against the railroads that certain firms, or firms in certain cities made contracts by which their goods were carried over long distances at lower rates than were demanded for carrying the same goods short distances. The railroads claimed that competition between trunk lines forced them to take the long-distance freight at nearly the same rates as they received for local freight, where there was no competition. It was asserted that the railroads did not regulate freight rates by cost of carrying, but by what the business would bear.

The first attempts to regulate interstate commerce began in 1873, previous to which time the Grangers had had state laws for regulation of railroad charges enacted in some of the Western States. In 1878 John H. Reagan, of Texas, introduced a series of bills in the House, which culminated Feb. 4, 1887, after yearly debates on these and similar bills, in the act to regulate commerce. This law established an Interstate Commerce Commission of five to investigate complaints. It furthermore gives shippers the option of complaining to this commission or of instituting suits in the Federal courts; prohibits unjust discrimination between persons and places, the giving of special rates, etc., though the commissioners may suspend this rule in special cases; requires railroads to publish rates and adhere to them, and forbids pooling of freights of different and competing railroads; enforces the Safety Appliance Act of 1893, and requires from all common carriers doing an interstate business a monthly report of all accidents both to passengers and employees. The chairman of the Commission is directed to assist the Commissioner of Labor to endeavor to settle all disputes between railway companies and their employees. (See Assistant to the Attorney-General.)

Interstate Commerce Act. (See Assistant to the Attorney-General.):
Discussed by President—
Arthur, 4732, 4772.
Johnson, 3560.
Roosevelt, 6650, 6654, 6655, 6902, 7025, 7039, 7070, 7130, 7143.
Taft, 7368, 7432, 7441, 7452.
Interstate commerce rates reduced, after passage of law regulating, 7419.
New York Central and Hudson River R. R. convicted under, opinion and sentence of Judge Holt quoted, 7405.
Physical examination of railways recommended, 7130.

Interstate Commerce Commission.—Under "An act to regulate commerce," approved Feb. 4, 1887, as amended March 2, 1889, Feb. 10, 1891, Feb. 8, 1895, the "Elkins Act" of Feb. 19, 1903, and the amending act approved June 29, 1906, the Interstate Commerce Commission is composed of seven members. The regulating statutes apply to all common carriers engaged in the transportation of oil or other commodity, except water and except natural or artificial gas, by means of pipe lines, or partly by pipe line and partly by rail, or partly by pipe line and partly by water, and to common carriers engaged in the transportation of passengers or property wholly by railroad (or partly by railroad and partly by water when both are used under a common control, management, or arrangement for a continuous carriage or shipment). The statutes apply generally to interstate traffic, including import and domestic traffic, and also that which is carried wholly within any Territory of the United States. Only traffic transported wholly within a single state is excepted.
The commission has jurisdiction on complaint and after full hearing to determine and prescribe reasonable rates, regulations, and practices, and order reparation to injured shippers; to require any carriers to cease and desist from unjust discrimination

or undue or unreasonable preference, and to institute and carry on proceedings for enforcement of the law. The commission may also inquire into the management of the business of all common carriers subject to the provisions of the regulating statutes, and it may prescribe the accounts, records, and memoranda which shall be kept by the carriers, and from time to time inspect the same. The carriers must file annual reports with the commission, and such other reports as may from time to time be required. Carriers failing to file and publish all rates and charges, as required by law, are prohibited from engaging in interstate transportation and penalties are provided in the statute for failure on the part of carriers or of shippers to observe the rates specified in the published tariffs.

The following were the Commissioners in 1912: Judson C. Clements, of Georgia, Chairman; Charles A. Prouty, of Vermont; Charles C. McChord, of Kentucky; Franklin K. Lane, of California; Balthasar H. Meyer, of Wisconsin; Edgar E. Clark, of Iowa; James S. Harlan, of Illinois.

By amendment of June 18, 1910 ("Mann-Elkins law"), a Court of Commerce was created (q. v.) with jurisdiction to restrain or enforce orders of the commission. This court is composed of five judges selected from the circuit court judges of the United States, and the amendment contains specific provision as to jurisdiction and procedure. Telegraph, telephone, and cable companies are made subject to the commission. The jurisdiction of the commission is increased as to through routes and joint rates, freight classification, switch connections, long and short hauls, filing or rejection of rate schedules, investigations on own motion, making reasonable rates, suspension of proposed rates, and other matters. An important section authorizes the President to appoint a special commission to investigate issuance of railroad stocks and bonds.

The act of Feb. 11, 1903, provides that suits in equity brought under the act to regulate commerce, wherein the United States is complainant, may be expedited and given precedence over other suits, and that appeals from the circuit court lie only to the Supreme Court. The act of Feb. 19, 1903, commonly called the Elkins law, prohibits rebating, allows proceedings in the courts by injunctions to restrain departures from published rates, and provides that cases prosecuted under the direction of the Attorney-General in the name of the commission shall be included within the expediting act of Feb. 11, 1903.

Under the act of Aug. 7, 1888, all Government-aided railroad and telegraph companies are required to file certain reports and contracts with the commission, and it is the commission's duty to decide questions relating to the interchange of business between such Government-aided telegraph company and any connecting telegraph company. The act provides penalties for failure to comply with the act or the orders of the commission.

The act of March 2, 1893, known as the "Safety Appliance Act," provides that railroad cars used in interstate commerce must be equipped with automatic couplers, and draw-bars of a standard height for freight cars, and have grab irons or handholds in the ends and sides of each car; and that locomotive engines used in moving interstate traffic shall be fitted with a power driving-wheel brake and appliances for operating the train-brake system. The act directs the commission to lodge with the proper district attorneys information of such violations as may come to

its knowledge. The act of March 2, 1903, amended this act so as to make its provisions apply to territories and the District of Columbia, to all cases when couplers of whatever design are brought together, and to all locomotives, cars, and other equipment of any railroad engaged in interstate traffic, except logging cars and cars used upon street railways; and provides for a minimum number of air-braked cars in trains.

By act of April 14, 1910, the safety-appliance acts were supplemented so as to require railroads to equip their cars with sill steps, hand brakes, ladders, running boards, and grab irons, and the commission was authorized to designate the number, dimensions, location, and manner of application of appliances.

The act of June 1, 1898, known as the arbitration act, directs the chairman of the Interstate Commerce Commission and the Commissioner of Labor to use their best efforts, by mediation and conciliation, to settle controversies between railway companies engaged in interstate commerce and their employees. By amendment of this act March 4, 1911, any member of the commission, or of the Court of Commerce, may exercise the powers conferred upon the chairman of the commission.

By act of May 6, 1910, the prior accident-reports law was repealed and a new statute passed giving more power to the commission as to investigating accidents, and is more comprehensive than the former law.

The act of March 4, 1907, makes it the duty of the Interstate Commerce Commission to enforce the provisions of the act wherein it is made unlawful to require or permit employees engaged in or connected with the movement of trains to be on duty more than a specified number of hours in any twenty-four.

The act of May 23, 1908, by section 16 thereof, gives the Interstate Commerce Commission limited control over the street railroads in the District of Columbia.

The act of May 30, 1908, directs the Interstate Commerce Commission to make regulations for the safe transportation of explosives by common carriers engaged in interstate commerce. A penalty is provided for violations of such regulations.

The act of May 30, 1908, makes it the duty of the Interstate Commerce Commission to enforce the provisions of the act wherein it is provided that after a certain date no locomotive shall be used in moving interstate or foreign traffic, etc., not equipped with an ash pan which can be emptied without requiring a man to go under such locomotive. A penalty is provided for violations of this act.

Public resolution No. 46, approved June 30, 1906, and the sundry civil appropriation act of May 27, 1908, direct the commission to investigate and report on the use and need of appliances intended to promote the safety of railway operation.

The act of March 3, 1909, authorizes the commission to prescribe the form of bookkeeping for District of Columbia gas and electric companies.

The act of Feb. 17, 1911, confers jurisdiction upon the commission to enforce certain provisions compelling railroad companies to equip their locomotives with safe and suitable boilers and appurtenances thereto.

Interstate Commerce Commission. (See Assistant to the Attorney-General.)

Interstate Commerce Commission:
    Civil service extended to, 6143.

Legislation for protection of yard-
men and brakemen against accidents recommended, 5486, 5561,
5642, 5766.
Railroad transportation discussed,
6172.
Railroads, proposal to place under
jurisdiction of, 6878, 6879. 7358,
Work of, 6902.

Interstate National Guard Association.
—This association is composed of representatives of the organized militia of the
states of the Union, and its purpose is to
conserve the interests of that body of
troops.

Intervention.—A firm interference in the
actions of another country. It may take the
form of protest against the other country's
oppressor, or against a faction within the
other country in case of internal trouble.
Intervention usually presupposes armed
force, if necessary, to mitigate the evils
against which protest is made. Intervention
is, therefore, a stronger term than intercession. (See Intercession.)

Intrigue.—A secret plot against authority,
—usually on the part of comparatively few
persons.

Invasion.—A hostile entry into a country
by the armed forces of another country.

Inventions. (See Patent Office; Patents.)

Inventions, American.—The industrial
progress of the world is marked by inventions and discoveries which dot the path
from barbarism to the highest state of
civilization. While the first great inventions of gunpowder, printing, the mariner's
compass, the barometer, thermometer,
steam engine, spinning jenny, etc., were
brought to these shores by the earlier settlers, the world owes a great deal to America for original discoveries and inventions
as well as the development and practical
application of ideas from abroad. From
the day of the setting up of the printing
press and the drawing of electricity from
the clouds, the American inventive faculty
has been active, and, encouraged by the
patent laws and the resultant fame and
financial rewards, genius has run riot in
America.

Jeremiah Wilkinson's mule spinner, invented in 1774, was the basis of the cot-
ton-goods industry in New England, and
in the steamboat of John Fitch and the
steam road wagon of Oliver Evans, in 1786
and 1787, we find the nucleus of our present day steam-navigation service and the
automobile industry. The threshing machine was scarcely introduced from England than Eli Whitney gave us the cotton
gin. It was an American, John Stevens,
who first applied the idea of twin-screw
propellers to steam navigation and made
possible the ocean greyhound of to-day.
The breech-loading shotgun was patented
by an American before the breaking out of
the War of 1812. The eccentric lathe for
turning irregular wood forms was invented
by Thomas Blanchard, an American, in
1819, and John Walker patented friction
matches in 1827. Prof. S. F. B. Morse
conceived the electric telegraph in 1832,
and in the same year Saxton devised the
electro-magnetic machine, and M. W. Baldwin built "Old Ironsides," the first great
locomotive in the United States, and two
years later Obed Hussey and Cyrus Mc-

Cormick gave us the reaper and mowing
machine. Samuel Colt patented the revolving chambered firearm in 1836, and
three years later Charles Goodyear discovered how rubber can be vulcanized.
Charles Thurber had a practical typewriting
machine in operation in 1843. In 1844
Dr. Horace Wells discovered the use of
nitrous-oxide gas as an anæsthetic, and
two years later Dr. Morton used ether for
the same purpose. Robert Hoe's double-
cylinder printing press was immediately
followed by Elias Howe's sewing machine.
The laying of the first Atlantic telegraph
cable, which was conceived and executed
by Cyrus W. Field, gave an impetus to inventive genius along the line of rapid communication and transportation, and was
followed by many improvements in electrical apparatus, car couplers, air brakes,
printing, photography, farm machinery,
etc. Graham Bell had the telephone in
practical operation in 1876, and the following year Edison completed the phonograph,
which he followed immediately with the
incandescent electric light. An idea of the
many inventions in the line of electrical
appliances may be obtained from the fact
that Mr. Edison alone, according to the
records of the Patent Office, received 742
patents for electric devices between 1872
and 1900. As an indication that Edison
was not the only busy inventor, it may be
stated that during the same period some
forty others received from one hundred to
more than six hundred patents each. The
linotype machine, patented by Othmar Mer-
genthaler in 1884. wrought many changes
and improvements in the printing trade,
and the rear-drive chain safety bicycle,
which before the advent of the improved
automobile held sway as a rapid and economical mode of individual transportation,
was the invention of George W. Marble.
The extraction of aluminum and the manufacture of cement are also important
American inventions. For America's contributions to the science of navigating the
air, see the article entitled Aeronautics in
this volume. It is not the purpose of this
article to enumerate all the great inventions for which the world is indebted to
Americans, but merely to show that the
encouragement by the government has stimulated genius to a point even beyond the
fondest hopes of the early promoters of
the patent office. (See also Patent Office.)

Inventions Exhibition, International,
at London discussed, 4827.

Iowa.—One of the middle western group
of states; nickname, "The Hawkeye State";
motto, "Our liberties we prize and our
rights we will maintain." It was formed
from a part of the Louisiana territory purchased from France. The name signifies
"Here is the place to dwell in peace."
Iowa is bounded on the north by Minnesota,
on the east by Wisconsin and Illinois
(separated by the Mississippi River), on
the south by Missouri, and on the west by
Nebraska and South Dakota, and has an
area of 56,147 square miles.

The first white settlement was made, at
Dubuque by Julian Du Buque in 1788. In
1834 the territory was made a part of Michigan. In 1836 it was added to Wisconsin
Territory, and in 1838 the Territory of
Iowa was established. It was admitted to
statehood Dec. 28. 1846. Iowa is almost
exclusively an agricultural state.

Statistics of agriculture collected for the
last Federal census place the number
of farms in the State at 217,044 (a decrease of 11,578, or 5.1 per cent. as com-

pared with 1900), comprising 33,930,688 acres, valued, with stock and improvements, at $3,745,860,544, an average of $82.58 per acre, as compared with $36.25 in 1900. The value of domestic animals, poultry, etc., was $393,003,196, including 4,448,006 cattle, valued at $118,864,139; 1,492,226 horses, $177,999,124; 55,524 mules, $7,-551,818; 7,545,853 swine, $69,693,218; 1,-145,549 sheep, $5,748,836. In 1911 9,850,-000 acres produced 305,350,000 bushels of corn, valued at $161,836,000; 647,000 acres, 10,622,000 bushels of wheat, $9,348,000; 4,-950,000 acres, 126,225,000 bushels of oats, $51,752,000; 30,000 acres rye, $416,000; 174,000 acres, 12,876,000 bushels of pota- toes, $9,399,000, and 3,240,000 acres, 2,-592,000 tons of hay, $32,400,000.

The mineral products for 1910, consist- ing of coal, lime, clay products, and mineral water, amounted to $22,730,658. The coal production increased by 170,358 tons as a result of the coal strike in Illinois and In- diana. The general strike lasted only six weeks in Iowa, while it lasted six months in other states. There were 16,666 miners employed in the State, who worked an average of 218 days during the year 1910. The State has no bonded indebtedness. The assessed value of all property in 1911 was $757,336,279, which is one-fourth of the actual value. There was in the general State revenue fund June 30, 1911, $1,282,-539, with outstanding warrants of $173,745, leaving a net balance of $1,108,793.

There are 9,911 miles of steam railway in the State and 600 miles of electric line. The population ascertained by the United States census of 1900 was 2,231,853, and the State census of 1905 showed a decrease to 2,216,068. The Federal census of 1910, however, showed a slight advance during the next five years to 2,224,771.

The number of manufacturing establish- ments in Iowa having an annual output valued at $500 or more at the beginning of 1915 was 5,615. The amount of capital in- vested was $233,373,000, giving employment to 84,949 persons, using material valued at $205,538,000, and turning out finished goods worth $310,954,000. Salaries and wages paid amounted to $56,232,000.

Iowa (see also Cedar Rapids):

Acts to quiet title of settlers on Des Moines River lands in, vetoed, 4996, 5412.

Admission of, into Union, memorial from legislature requesting, 2130.

Boundary line with Missouri, dispute respecting, 1775, 1777, 1788.

Appropriation to defray expenses growing out of, requested, 1953.

Claims of, commissioners to be ap- pointed to examine, referred to, 3662.

Constitution of, appropriation to de- fray expenses of convention for formation of, requested, 1953.

Survey of northern boundary of, 2708.

Volunteers from, thanks of President tendered, 3442.

Iowa Indians. (See Indian Tribes.)

Iowa Reservation:

Cession of portion of, to United States proclaiming, 5591.

Sale of, bill for, 4959.

Ioway Indians. (See Iowa Indians.)

Ireland. (See British Empire, and Home Rule for Ireland.)

Imprisonment of American citizens in, 2521, 3590, 4678, 4679, 4693, 4699.

Released, 3902, 4713.

Trial and conviction of, 3800, 3827, 3833.

Military expedition to aid insurgent party in. (See Fenians.)

Iron:

Report relating to cost of production of, etc., transmitted, 5569.

Iron and Steel Industry.—Implements of iron having been found with those of stone and bronze amid prehistoric ruins afford conclusive proof of the antiquity of the use of this metal among the ancients. A piece of iron on exhibition in the British Museum taken from the Pyramid of Gizeh is believed to date from 4,000 years before Christ. Assyrians, Egyptians, Greeks and Indians used the metal freely for tools, weapons and ornaments 800 to 400 years B. C. During the prosperous days of the Roman Empire the use of iron became general throughout what was then the civilized world. When Julius Caesar in- vaded Britain, B. C. 55, he found the na- tives in familiar possession of spears, swords, hooks and scythes of iron.

Although one of the most abundant and useful of metals iron is seldom found in the native state, but combined with oxygen and other elements it is widely distributed as a constituent of rocks, and forms ex- tensive deposits in many parts of the world. Minerals from which iron ore is extracted for commercial purposes are: Magnetite, in which the iron occurs as mag- netic oxide, and contains, when pure, 72.40 per cent of iron; Hematite, including red, blue, and specular hematites and micaceous and fossil ores, containing about 70 per cent of iron; Limonite, or brown hematite, including bog ores, pipe ores, and other hy- drated oxides, containing less than 60 per cent of metal; Siderite, or spathic ore, including clay ironstone, blackband, and other ores, with about 48 per cent of iron.

In the United States mining is confined to the hematite, limonite and magnetite deposits, which carry from 50 to 60 per cent of iron. Hematite contributes four- fifths of the total production. A large part of this ore comes from the Lake Superior region, where immense deposits have been found in metamorphosed pre- Cambrian rocks. Five productive belts or ranges are worked. The Marquette, sit- uated in Michigan, east of the Keweenaw Peninsula, opened in 1856; the Menominee, on the border of Wisconsin and the upper peninsula of Michigan, developed in 1877; the Gogebec, wholly in Wisconsin, opened in 1884; the Vermilion and Mesabi, sit- uated northwest of Lake Superior, in Min- nesota, first worked in 1884. The deposits are found near the surface and are simply gathered up by steam shovels and dumped on cars. The total production for the United States in 1913 amounted to 61,-980,437 long tons, taken from 411 mines. One mine alone on the Mesabi Range in Minnesota produced 3,457,608 tons of hematite. The general average price of iron ore is $2.19 per ton. The nearest approach to the United States made by any other country in the production of iron is Germany, including the Duchy of Luxem- burg with about 30,000,000 tons. Next comes France with some 17,000,000 tons. The iron ore mined in the United States in 1915 reached 55,526,490 gross tons, the greatest output made in any year except 1910 and 1913. The shipments in 1915, namely, 55,493,100 gross tons, valued at $101,288,984, were a little less than the quantity mined. The quantity mined in 1915 was an increase of 14,000,000 tons over the output in 1914. The increases in quantity and in value of iron ore shipped amounted to about 40 and 41 per cent, respectively. The average value per ton in 1915 was $1.83, compared with $1.81 in 1914. The Lake Superior district alone in 1916 will possibly be 60,000,000 tons, and there will probably be an increase in price of 70 to 75 cents a ton for this ore.

Iron ore was mined in 23 States in 1915. As has been usual during recent years, the five States ranking highest in production in 1915 were Minnesota, Michigan, Alabama, Wisconsin, and New York.

The Lake Superior district mined nearly 85 per cent of the total ore in 1915, the Birmingham district about 8.5 per cent, or a little more than one-tenth as much.

To extract the pure metal from the various ores of iron requires some simple and cheap preliminary treatment, such as sorting and sizing the pieces of rock, washing away what earthy matter can be removed by water, crushing and concentrating by passing the broken rock through magnetized drums or screens to draw the ore from the non-ferrous gangue with which it is accompanied, and weathering to allow the disintegration of shale and sulphur. The direct or primitive method of extracting the iron from the ore was simply to apply heat to the mass and collect the drops of molten metal. The American bloomery was but a slight modification of the earliest form of forge. The resultant product was wrought iron or steel, according to the details of the process.

The distribution of the industry in the United States is shown by the following table for 1913:

State	Quantity in Long Tons	Per Cent of Total
Minnesota	38,658,793	62.37
Michigan	12,841,093	20.72
Alabama	5,215,740	8.42
New York	1,459,628	2.36
Wisconsin	1,018,272	1.64
Wyoming	537,111	.87
Pennsylvania	489,056	.79
Virginia	483,843	.78
Tennessee	370,002	.60
New Jersey	325,305	.53
New Mexico	164,085	.26
Georgia	155,236	.25
North Carolina	69,235	.11
Missouri	39,354	.06
Utah	14,690	.02
Other States	138,994	.19
Total	61,980,437	100.00

In order to prevent the great waste of iron caused by the combination of the gangue with some of the metal it was found necessary to use some substance with which the silica of the gangue will readily unite to form slag. Limestone is the most generally used for this purpose. All such articles added are called fluxes, and their use constitutes one of the most important discoveries ever introduced in the manufacture of iron. Charcoal early became generally used as fuel for heating the mass. The high temperature necessary to fuse lime slag requires a chimney-shaped furnace with appliances for forcing a draught of air through the molten rock. The contrivance used for this purpose is known as the blast furnace. It was first used in the Rhine provinces of Germany about the middle of the fourteenth century. Many important changes have been made in the blast furnace, until today the output of such furnaces frequently averages 600 tons of pig iron in twenty-four hours.

The production of pig iron, including ferroalloys, according to figures published February 26, 1916, by the American Iron and Steel Institute, was 29,916,213 gross tons in 1915, compared with 23,332,244 gross tons in 1914. The pig iron, exclusive of ferroalloys, sold or used in 1915, according to reports of producers to the United States Geological Survey, was 30,384,486 gross tons, valued at $401,409,604, a gain of 36 per cent in quantity and 34 per cent in value. The average price per ton at furnaces in 1915 as reported to the Survey was $13.21, compared with $13.42 in 1914. The ratio of pig iron produced to iron ore consumed was 53.15 per cent, compared with 57.45 per cent in 1914.

In 1855 and 1856 Henry Bessemer of London obtained patents for a process of converting pig iron into steel by forcing small jets of cold air through the molten iron, but his invention was not successful until modified by Robert F. Mushet, who added to the molten steel, after the blast had been stopped, a sufficient quantity of spiegeleisen (an alloy of iron and manganese) to neutralize the oxide of iron caused by blowing and to give the steel the proper degree of hardness and fluidity. Neither Bessemer nor his American rival, William Kelly of Pittsburgh, who obtained a patent for the same purpose, accomplished anything in America until 1866, when they combined their methods with those of Mushet, and the first plant to produce steel in commercial quantities was put into successful operation by the Pennsylvania Steel Company at Steelton, near Harrisburg, Pa., in June, 1867.

The "basic" open-hearth process of steelmaking was introduced into the United States in 1888 by Carnegie, Phipps & Co., at Homestead, Pa. This process consists of an ordinary open-hearth furnace lined with basic material, such as dolomite limestone or magnesite. When pig iron containing so much phosphorus as to render it unfit for conversion into steel by any other method is melted in such a furnace the basic lining, together with a basic flux which is added, removes the objectionable phosphorus and makes steel equal to that produced in the old open-hearth furnace. By this process immense deposits of iron ore so full of phosphorus as to be useless in steel making were made available for the highest kind of constructive work. High-grade structural material such as boiler and ship plates, bridge and building beams, high-grade castings, etc., is generally open-hearth steel, for the reason that it is considered more uniform in quality than the softer steel made by the Bessemer process.

The first steel rails rolled in the way of regular business were made by the Cambria Iron Company of Johnstown, Pa., in August, 1867, from ingots made by the Pennsylvania Steel Company. The production of Bessemer steel in 1867 was only 3,000 tons, while in 1913 it had grown to 9,545,706 tons. The rapid and enormous development of the Bessemer steel industry in the United States is attributable chiefly to the great extension of our railroads. Bessemer steel is also used for steel bars, merchant steel, and for tin plates. The basic Bessemer, or Thomas, process, though used in Germany to produce 4,888,054 tons in 1902, has not come into general use in this country.

Reports were received by the Department of Commerce from 436 establishments operating steel plants and hot-rolling mills, either or both, in 1914, the total products of which for the year were valued at $919,527,244. The rolled, forged, and other classified iron and steel products aggregated 25,586,715 tons, valued at $802,976,516, comprising 18,526,342 tons of finished rolled products and forgings, valued at $624,754,-421. 6,408,030 tons of partly finished rolled products—blooms, billets, slabs, sheet bars, tin-plate bars, muck bar, and scrap bar—valued at $130,674,909, and 652,343 tons of unrolled steel in the form of ingots and castings, valued at $47,547,136.

The statistics for 1914 covered a period of marked depression, the production of rolled iron and steel in that year, as reported by the American Iron and Steel Institute, being 25.9 per cent less than the output in 1913. This was followed by a recovery in 1915, as evidenced by the production of pig iron, which, after dropping from 12,500,000 tons for the first half of the year 1914 to less than 10,800,000 tons for the second half, increased to 12,233,791 tons for the first half of 1915 and to 17,682,422 tons for the second half.

The production of structural shapes in 1914 was 2,085,586 tons, valued at $57,561,-206, representing a decrease, as compared with 1909, of 38,044 tons, or 1.8 per cent, in quantity and of $8,003,387, or 12.2 per cent, in value.

The steel-works and rolling-mill industry is concentrated largely in the middle Atlantic and east north central states, and in the Panhandle of West Virginia.

The steel-works and rolling-mill industry comprises three classes of establishments: (1) Those equipped both with furnaces for making steel and with hot rolls for rolling it; (2) those equipped with steel furnaces but not with hot rolls; and (3) those equipped with hot rolls but not with steel furnaces. Most of the largest establishments belong to the first group. All steel plants operated in conjunction with blast furnaces are equipped also with rolling departments. On the other hand, no establishments of the second group have blast furnaces, but all buy pig iron and scrap for steel making. Establishments of the third group include those purchasing their material in the form of ingots, blooms, slabs or other shapes, pig iron for puddling furnaces, and also the few independent bloomeries.

Pennsylvania in 1909 contributed over half (50.7 per cent) of the total value of products: Ohio, about one-fifth (20.1 per cent); Illinois, 8.8 per cent; New York, 4 per cent, and Indiana, 3.9 per cent. Of the leading producing states, Indiana, owing to the recent great development at Gary, shows the highest percentages of increase—69.9 per cent in number of wage-earners, 128.4 per cent in value of products, and 108.7 per cent in value added by manufacture.

The average number of persons engaged in the industry in 1909 was 260,762, of whom 240,076, or 92.1 per cent, were wage-earners; 4,286, or 1.6 per cent, proprietors and officials, and 16,400, or 6.3 per cent, clerks. Individual proprietors and firm members were few in number, the industry being mainly controlled by corporations.

Of the number of wage-earners in 1909, 34.2 per cent were in establishments where the prevailing hours were sixty per week or ten hours a day for six days in the week, while 34.4 per cent were in establishments where the prevailing hours were over sixty per week, and 21.8 per cent where they were seventy-two per week and

over. The eight-hour day is not found to any large extent, only 9.3 per cent of the wage-earners being employed in establishments where the prevailing hours were less than fifty-four per week. The proportion in establishments in which the prevailing hours of labor were seventy-two or more per week was especially high in Illinois, Wisconsin and Indiana.

Location of Establishments.—Of the establishments reported for 1914, 178 were located in Pennsylvania, 67 in Ohio, 25 in Illinois, 23 in New York, 19 in Indiana, 15 in New Jersey, 15 in West Virginia, 12 in Massachusetts, 12 in Wisconsin, 9 in Michigan, 7 in California, 6 in Alabama, 6 in Kentucky, 5 in Delaware, 4 in Connecticut, 3 in Maryland, 3 in Missouri, 3 in Rhode Island, 2 in Virginia, and 1 each in Colorado, District of Columbia, Georgia, Maine, Minnesota, Oregon, Tennessee, Texas and Washington.

The tendency toward concentration in large establishments is very marked in the steel industry. There is no other industry in which so many plants of great size are found. In 1909, 41.7 per cent of the establishments reported products valued at $1,000,000 or more each. This group of establishments in 1909 included twenty-three, with products in excess of $10,000,-000 in value. The value of the output of the establishments with products valued at $1,000,000 or over formed 91 per cent of the total for all establishments in 1909, and that of the establishments with products valued at $10,000,000 or over constituted 43.2 per cent of the total.

In the distribution of the 19,276,237 tons of finished rolled products and forgings made by steel work and rolling mills in 1909, among the principal producing states Pennsylvania produced 51.4 per cent of the output of these products in 1909. Ohio increased its proportion of the output to 16.1 per cent in the latter year. Indiana and Illinois showed higher percentages of output in 1909 than in 1904; but the proportion reported by New York and West Virginia remained about the same.

There has been during each decade a marked increase both in the absolute and relative amount of open-hearth steel produced. Basic open-hearth steel constituted 1.3 per cent of the steel production in 1889, as against 56.2 per cent in 1909. Bessemer steel, on the other hand, although the output increased 153.8 per cent during this period, constituted only 39 per cent of the production in 1909, as compared with 86.6 per cent in 1889.

Iron and Steel, manufacturers of, tariff on (Schedule C) vetoed, 7749.

Tariff rates compared, 7750.

Irredenta. (See Italia Irredenta.)

Irrepressible Conflict. — An expression first used by William H. Seward in 1858 to denote the seemingly unending controversy between freedom and slavery.

Irrigation.—The ancient practice of increasing the productiveness of the soil by means of an artificial supply of water has been successfully applied to the arid plains of the western part of the United States. The subject became so extensive and important that in 1900 the leading political parties pledged themselves to enact laws looking to the reclamation of arid lands. Up to this time most of the public irrigation work was carried on under the Carey act of 1894, which granted to each of the arid states 1,000,000 acres of desert land on condition of its reclamation.

Under this law public lands are withdrawn from entry on application of the state. The state may then enter into contract with private companies to build irrigation canals, ditches, reservoirs, etc., the state agreeing to sell the land to settlers who have contracted with the canal builders for a supply of water at prices fixed in the contract with the state.

The number of projects and the amount expended on them to Jan. 1, 1915, are shown in the following table:

State And Project	Service Supply on completion Acres	Supply June 30, 1916 Acres
Arizona: Salt River..	191,648	191,648
Arizona-California:		
Yuma	128,000	72,440
California: Orland ..	20,193	20,193
Colorado:		
Grand Valley	53,000	900
Uncompahgre Valley	140,000	85,000
Idaho: Boise	255,000	230,000
Minidoka	120,300	120,300
Kansas: Garden City	10,677	....
Montana: Huntley....	32,905	32,905
Milk River	220,000	1,800
Sun River	174,022	16,322
Montana-North Dakota:		
Lower Yellowstone..	60,116	42,300
Nebraska-Wyoming:		
North Platte	129,891	129,891
North Platte, Fort		
Laramie Unit....	100,000	....
Nevada: Truckee-Carson	206,000	69,100
New Mexico: Carlsbad	24,796	24,796
Hondo	10,000	1,650
New Mexico-Texas:		
Rio Grande	155,000	85,000
North Dakota:		
North Dakota Pumping	26,273	12,239
Oklahoma: Lawton ..	2,500	....
Oregon: Umatilla	36,301	19,000
Oregon-California:		
Klamath	142,796	47,600
South Dakota:		
Bellefourche ......'.	97,916	78,591
Utah:		
Strawberry Valley ..	50,000	50,000
Washintgon:		
Okanogan	10,099	10,099
Yakima	146,664	126,746
Wyoming:		
Shoshone	147,365	42,665
Indian Projects (under Indian Office):		
Montana: Blackfeet ..	122,500	46,640
Flathead	152.00	63,000
Fort Peck	152,000	12,620
Grand Total	**3,117,862**	**1,690,244**

June 17, 1902, Congress passed the reclamation law, which provided for the construction of irrigation works by the United States Government. The law set aside the receipts from the sale of public lands in Arizona, California, Colorado, Idaho, Kansas, Montana, Nebraska, Nevada, New Mexico, North Dakota, Oklahoma, Oregon, South Dakota, Utah, Washington, and Wyoming, for the construction of irrigation works, under the direction of the Secretary of the Interior. The cost of the works is to be repaid by the settlers, who use the water, in ten annual installments, and when the payments have been made for a majority of the lands included in any project the management and operation of such project are to be turned over to the owners, to be maintained at their expense. The receipts from the sale of land and the use of water are to form a perpetual reclamation fund. Public lands included in reclamation projects may be acquired only under the terms of the homestead law, and

the commutation clause of that law does not apply to such lands.

Up to 1909 the Government had selected for reclamation more than two million acres at an estimated cost of nearly $90,-000,000. Under the Carey act the states have selected for reclamation and had assigned to them up to July 1, 1908, 3,239,-285 acres. Idaho and Wyoming, each having disposed of the 1,000,000 acres allowed them under the law, were granted an additional 1,000,000 acres for the same purpose.

The reclamation service having, however, embarked on various costly enterprises beyond the means of the reclamation fund, Congress was required to pass a new law in 1910 authorizing the issuance of certificates of indebtedness against the reclamation fund to the amount of $30,000,000, payable from future receipts of the fund.

The Elephant Butte dam in New Mexico, the principal structure of the International and interstate Rio Grande irrigation project, was completed by the Reclamation Service on May 13, 1916. It creates the greatest storage reservoir in the world.

It is 318 feet high, 1,674 feet long on top, and weighs a million tons, and took five years to build. It stores 856 billion gallons of water in a lake 45 miles long with an average depth of 65 feet, and when full, will contain enough water to cover Delaware two feet deep.

President Wilson sent the following telegram of congratulations to the Reclamation employes who were in charge of the work:

"The completion of the Elephant Butte Dam is an achievement which arouses the patriotism of all true Americans. It shows what technical and business skill and devoted energy and persistence can accomplish in combat with the forces of nature. The country owes its gratitude and appreciation to the men and the women who have toiled diligently during the five years of constructive effort to produce a result of which the American Nation may well be proud.   WOODROW WILSON."

The dam blocks a canyon of the Rio Grande 120 miles north of El Paso. It is the fifth of the Government's big irrigation projects, and will store the entire flow and flood of the river. It provides a roadway across the canyon sixteen feet wide, and at its base is 235 feet thick.

The following table, prepared by the Census Bureau, shows in detail the statistics for irrigation in the United States in 1910:

Number of farms (1)..............	1,440,822
Approximate land area (1), acres...	1,161,385,600
Land in farms (1), acres........	388,606,991
Improved land in farms (1), acres...	173,433,957
Number of farms irrigated.........	(2) 158,713
Acreage irrigated..................	(2) 13,738,485
Acreage enterprises were capable of irrigating..................	19,334,697
Acreage included in projects.......	31,111,142
Number of enterprises.............	54,700
Total length of ditches, miles.......	125,591
Length of main ditches, miles......	87,529
Length of lateral ditches, miles.....	38,062
Number of reservoirs..............	6,812
Capacity of reservoirs, acre-feet....	12,581,129
Number of pumping plants........	13,906
Capacity of power plants, horsepower..........................	243,435
Cost of irrigation enterprises.......	$307,866,369
Average cost per acre.............	(3) $15.92
Average annual cost of operation and maintenance per acre........	(2) $1.07

(1) Figures relate to entire areas of states included in the inquiry. (2) In 1909. (3) Based on cost to July 1, 1910, and acreage enterprises were capable of irrigating in 1910.

The percentage of increase between 1889 and 1899 in the number of farms irrigated was more than double that during the succeeding decade, but the absolute increases during the two decades were approximately equal. Nebraska showed the largest percentage of increase during the former period and Texas during the latter period, but in neither state is the actual number of irrigated farms large. In Nebraska and South Dakota there were decreases between 1899 and 1909. The largest absolute increase in both decades was in California. In the period 1899 to 1909 the next largest increase was in Colorado, and in the period 1889 to 1899 in Utah.

In total acreage irrigated California ranked first in 1889. Colorado second, and Montana third. In both 1899 and 1909 Colorado reported the largest irrigated acreage, while California and Montana were second and third, respectively. Idaho followed closely in 1909. From 1899 to 1909 California showed the largest absolute increase, followed by Colorado, Idaho, and Montana in the order named. In percentage of increase for this decade, however, Texas ranked first, Washington second, Idaho third, and New Mexico fourth.

Cost of Irrigation.—The total cost of irrigation enterprises up to July 1, 1910, was reported as $307,866,369, which represents an increase of $240,904,094 or 359.8 per cent over the cost reported at the census of 1900. In no state in the arid region was the increase in cost for this period less than 100 per cent, the highest percentage of increase being in North Dakota and the lowest in Oklahoma. With respect to absolute increase California ranked first, Colorado second, Idaho third, and Montana fourth. The year 1910 was in the midst of a period of great activity in the construction of irrigation works, and on July 1, 1910, a large number of works were incomplete. The "estimated final cost" reported, $424,281,186, is the sum of the cost up to July 1, and the estimated cost of completing these unfinished works.

The average cost per acre based on the acreage irrigated in 1909 was $22.41; that based on the acreage enterprises where capable of irrigating in 1910 was $15.92; and that based on the estimated total cost and the acreage included in projects was $13.64.

Value of Irrigated Crops.—The report shows for all crops reported as irrigated an average value per acre of $25.08. The highest average value per acre for crops raised on irrigated land is that for Washington, $49.82, which is followed by that for Texas, $45.43 (exclusive of rice), and that for California, $43.50. Wyoming showed the lowest average value per acre, $12.61. As is to be expected, the average value per acre is highest in the states with large areas of fruits, vegetables, and other specialized crops raised by means of irrigation, while in those where forage crops and grains predominate the average is lower.

(See illustration opposite 7044.)

Irrigation:

Policy of Government regarding, discussed, 5561, 5640, 6657, 6660, 6724, 7047, 7095.

Importance of forest reserves to, 6908.

Storage and use of waters of Rio Grande for, discussed, 5959.

Island No. 10 (Tenn.), Battle of.— About the time of the capture of New Madrid, Mo., Commodore Foote sailed from Cairo, Ill., with a fleet of seven ironclad gunboats, one wooden gunboat, and ten mortar boats to assist Pope in his attack on Island No. 10. March 16, 1862, Foote began a bombardment, which he kept up for many days without effect. Pope in the meantime had dug a canal across the swampy land above New Madrid, so that vessels could pass through to that place without passing the island. Early in April three of the gunboats ran by the batteries of the island under cover of night, and April 7 the Confederates found themselves surrounded by gunboats and transports laden with troops. Nothing remained but to surrender. Three generals, 273 field and company officers, 6,700 privates, 123 heavy guns and 35 field pieces, all of the latest pattern, 7,000 small arms, tents for 12,000 men, immense quantities of provisions and ammunition, hundreds of horses, mules, wagons, harness, etc., were captured. There were no casualties in the Federal army.

Island Pond, Vt., proclamation granting privileges of other ports to, 2859.

Islands. (See Insular Possessions, and the several islands.)

Isthmian Canal. (See Panama Canal.)

Isthmian Canal Commission, work of, 6718, 6806, 6816, 6938.

Italia Irredenta.—(Unredeemed Italy.) That portion of the Southern Tyrol (Trentino) and Trieste, in the hands of Austria, but whose inhabitants for the greater part are Italian in descent and language. Italy has long desired to redeem these provinces from Austria, and that fact was influential in Italy's decision to enter the European War on the side of the Entente.

Italian-American.—An American of Italian birth or descent.

Italian Murder. (See New Orleans Massacre.)

Italy.—Italy is a maritime kingdom of Southern Europe and consists of a peninsula and several islands, the whole being situate between 36° 38′ 30″-46° 40′ 30″ N. latitude and 6° 30′-18° 30′ E. longitude. Of the total area of 110,623 English square miles, 91,277 square miles are mainland and 19,346 islands. The kingdom is bounded on the north by the Alps, on the west and south by the Tyrrhenian Sea (Mediterranean), and on the east by the Adriatic. The greatest length is close on 750 miles, and the distance between the northeastern and northwestern boundaries exceeds 350 miles, although the peninsula is generally less than 150 miles across.

Physical Features.—Northern Italy is encompassed by the Alps, which extend, in an irregular semicircle, from the Austro-Hungarian border in the northeast to the Franco-Italian border in the northwest, the intervening boundary being common to Switzerland and Italy. The northwestern horn extends southward and forms the Apennine Range, which stretches down the center of the peninsula to Cape Spartimento, in the extreme south. West of the southern Apennines is a chain of volcanic heights, including the cone of Vesuvius (4,206 feet), which rises from the Campagna of Naples, near which place stand the ruins of Herculaneum, Pompeii and Stabiae, overwhelmed by an eruption of the volcano in A.D. 79. Between the Alps and the Ligurian-Etruscan Apennines is a great plain, forming the basin of the river Po, and from the center of the plain, at Piacenza, the Via Æmilia (built early in the second century B.C.) runs southeast to Rimini (Ariminium), where it joins the Via Flaminia which leads to Rome. The only great river of Italy is the Po, which rises in the Alps and flows eastward into the Adriatic. The Italian islands number sixty-six, and include the large islands of Sicily and Sardinia, and the smaller island of Elba, with Capraia, Gorgona, Pianosa, Monte Cristo. Sicily contains the highest of European volcanoes in Mount Etna or Mongibello (10,870 feet) in the northeast. The regions of the north have hot summers and cold winters, while central Italy is generally sunny and genial, and the southern districts almost tropical.

Italy is also in temporary occupation of a group of Turkish islands lying between Crete and Asia Minor (Rhodes, Carpathos, Cos, Astropalia, etc.) until such time as the Ottoman troops have been removed from Tripoli and Benghazi.

AREA AND POPULATION

Compartments	Area in English Sq. Miles	Population 1911
Piedmont	11,340	3,424,538
Liguria	2,037	1,196,853
Lombardy	9,386	4,786,907
Venetia	9,476	3,526,655
Emilia	7,967	2,667,510
Tuscany	9,304	2,694,453
Marches	3,763	1,088,875
Umbria	3,748	685,042
Rome	4,663	1,298,142
Abruzzi and Molise	6,380	1,427,642
Campania	6,289	3,347,925
Apulia	7,376	2,128,632
Basilicata	3,845	473,119
Calabria	5,819	1,404,076
Sicily	9,936	3,683,380
Sardinia	9,294	852,934
Total	110,623	34,686,683

History.—The Kingdom of Italy is composed of the former State of Sardinia and the two Sicilies, the Pontifical States, the Lombardo-Venetian provinces of the Austrian Empire, the Grand Duchy of Tuscany, and the Duchies of Parma and Modena, united under the House of Savoy after a heroic struggle between the years 1848 and 1870. Italian unity was completed in 1866, when the Austrians evacuated Lombardy, and in 1870 by the withdrawal of French troops from the Papal States. In 1872 the King (Victor Emmanuel II.) entered Rome, which was declared the capital of Italy. The compartments are subdivided into sixty-nine provinces. The inhabitants, particularly in the south, are derived from a mixture of racial elements, and there is evidence of the diversity of origin in the contrast between the industrious and stable people of the north and center and the less industrious and more excitable southerners.

Government.—The government is that of a constitutional monarchy, founded upon the *Statuto fondamentale del Regno,* granted to his subjects on March 4, 1848, by the King of Sardinia, and since extended to the whole Kingdom of Italy. The crown is hereditary in the male line (by primogeniture) of the House of Savoy, founded in 1032 by Umbertus I. Present ruler : His Majesty Vittorio Emmanuele III., King of Italy. born at Naples, Nov. 11, 1869, son of King Humbert, succeeded to the throne, July 29, 1900.

The Legislature consists of two Houses, the Senate and the Chamber of Deputies. The Senate is composed of Princes of the Blood of full age and of members nominated for life by the Sovereign from twenty-one classes, public service being the principal qualification ; the total member-

ship in 1912 was 370. The Chamber of Deputies contains 508 members, elected for single constituencies, for a maximum of five years, by the direct vote of all male Italians aged twenty-one years who are able to read and write and pay a small amount annually in taxation ; and all illiterate men above thirty, or under that age, provided they have served in the Army or Navy, or pay at least lire 19.80 of direct taxes a year.

The highest courts are the Courts of Cassation at Rome, Naples, Palermo, Turin and Florence, and twenty-four Courts of Appeal throughout the kingdom. Lower courts are the 162 district tribunals, 1,535 mandamenti, and thirteen municipal courts under pretori.

Italy is a member of the Triple Alliance (Germany, Austria-Hungary, Italy) under a treaty signed on May 20, 1882, which provides for mutual support in case of attack by any other nation.

Education.—The law of July, 1904, imposing special disabilities on the illiterate, has afforded a needed stimulus. Prior to that date 49 per cent. of the population over the age of twenty were thus classed. Primary education is maintained by local taxation, with State grants. Private establishments must conform to State curriculum. Universities : Bologna, Cagliari, Catania, Genoa, Macerata, Messina, Modena, Naples, Padua, Palermo, Parma, Pavia, Pisa, Rome, Sassari, Siena, and Turin. Many of these are of very ancient foundation (*e. g.*), Bologna (A. D. 1200), Camerino, Ferrara, Perugia, Urbino.

Production and Industry.—Of the total area cultivated in 1912 18,424,125 acres were under corn crops (wheat 11,888,500 acres, maize 3,983,750 acres), and of the remainder 11,136,000 acres were under vines, 5,781,500 acres under olives, 1,630,000 under chestnuts, and 1,138,000 under potatoes, other crops, including sugar-beet, flax, hemp, melons, tomatoes, citrous fruits and mulberry. The produce of the vines was 133,672,000 cwt. of grapes in 1912; the olive crop was 12,184,000 cwt. in 1912. The Live Stock in 1908 included cattle, sheep, goats, pigs, horses, asses, mules, and buffaloes. The chief minerals are sulphur (the Sicilian mines being one of the principal producing centers of the world), iron, lead, and zinc ; quicksilver and tin are also found, and stone, marble and granite are quarried in large quantities. There are numerous mineral springs from which medicinal waters are obtained.

Manufactures.—The mineral industries (sulphur, iron, steel and salt) give employment to large numbers, and the manufacture of machinery has made great progress. The motor-car industry at Turin (Fabbrica Italiana Automobili Torino) is world-famous. Textiles are increasing in importance, silk, wool, flax and hemp being produced in the country and imported. The condition of the industrial population is improving owing to the sanitary measures undertaken by the State, but the low wages (particularly in agricultural districts) drive the poorer classes to other countries in search of better conditions.

Finances.—The average annual revenue of Italy for five years past was 2,599,000,000 lire and the expenditures averaged 2,535,000,000 lire. The total debt of the country in 1913 was stated at 14,271,607,611 lira. The lira, the standard of value, is equal to $0.19.3, United States money, identical with the franc of France.

Cities.—Capital, Rome, on the River Tiber. Population (1912), 579,285. More than a dozen cities have a population ranging between 100,000 and 700,000.

Railways.—In 1912 there were 10,798 miles of railway open, of which 8,280 miles were State lines. International lines enter Northern Italy from France, from Switzerland, from the Austrian Tirol and from the Adriatic coast of Austria. The northern plain is covered by a network of lines which radiate from Milan, and there are lines down each coast to the extreme south, and a central line runs from Turin, Milan and Venice to Rome.

Trade with the United States.—The value of merchandise imported into Italy from the United States for the year 1913 was $76,285,278 and goods to the value of $54,-107,364 were sent thither—a balance of $22,177,914 in favor of the United States.

ERITREA.—The Italian colony, on the northeast coast of Africa from Ras Kasar, a cape 110 miles south of Suak.n, to Ras Dumeira, in the Strait of Bab-el-Mandeb, a total distance of about 650 miles, extends inland to the borders of the Anglo-Egyptian Sudan Abyssinia and French Somaliland.

ITALIAN SOMALILAND extends on the northeast coast of Africa, from Bandar Ziyada, on the Gulf of Aden, to the eastern horn of Africa at Cape Guardafui, and thence southward to the Juba River in 0° 15' S. latitude. The western boundaries are Abyssinia and British Somaliland, and the southern boundary is British East Africa. The Italian portion of the Juba Valley also contains rich land. Ivory, cattle, coffee, cotton, myrrh, gums and skins are exported; textiles and rice are the principal exports.

TIENTSIN CONCESSION.—After the Boxer movement in China (1900) and the siege and relief of the Foreign Legations, the Italian Government claimed from the Chinese a concession of land, which was accorded by treaty of June 7, 1902. The concession has a total area of twenty square miles fronting the river Peiho on the left bank, with a total population of about 17,000 natives.

LYBIA (TRIPOLI AND CYRENAICA).—In September, 1911, war broke out between Italy and Turkey, after protracted negotiations in connection with the rights and privileges of Italian subjects in Tripoli. An Italian army was landed in the country, and the capital was immediately occupied. On November 5, 1911, the Italian parliament adopted a bill annexing Tripoli to the Kingdom of Italy, the annexation being ratified by Turkey in the Treaty of Ouchy negotiated in October, 1912.

Tripoli is the most easterly of the Barbary States on the northern coast of Africa, between 11° 40-25° 12' E. longitude, with a total area of close on 922,000 English square miles, and a population estimated at 1,000,000. The coast line is about 1,100 miles, and the inland boundary is about 800 miles from the coast. Barley, dates, olives, oranges, lemons and vegetables are produced, and the principal imports are metals, British and other European manufactures, tea, beads, wine and spirits. Tripoli had a population of about 40,000 in 1911; the port of Tripoli is now being built and good progress has been made with the main breakwater, jetties, and quays. Ghadames is the center of a considerable trade in ostrich feathers, skins, ivory and tea, and has a population of about 7,000. The town of Benghazi has a population consisting of Arabs, Greeks, Maltese, and a few Levantines. There are agricultural colonies of Cretan Moslem refugees in the neighborhood of Cyrene and Apollonia. The ancient ruins in Cyrenaica, *i. e.,* at Cyrene, Ptolemais,

and Apollonia, are interesting to explorers, as well as those at Leptis Magna, which is close to Khoms, or seventy miles from the city of Tripoli.

TURKO-ITALIAN WAR.—Sept. 26, 1911. Italy sent an ultimatum to the Turkish government concerning her rights in Tripoli, stating the grievances of Italy against Turkish misrule in that province and characterizing the course of the Porte as hostile to legitimate Italian activity in Tripoli and Cyrenaica; declaring her belief, in the light of past experiences, that further negotiation was useless, and demanding that the Porte give orders permitting Italian occupation of Tripoli and Cyrenaica. The ultimatum demanded an answer within twenty-four hours and the reply of the Porte being considered unsatisfactory, a state of war began Sept. 29, 1911. On that day three Turkish torpedo boats were sunk off Prevesa, on the coast of Epirus, by the Italian squadron commanded by the Duke of the Abruzzi.

Sept. 17, there was fought near Derna, a port on the Mediterranean coast, 140 miles northeast of Bengazi, one of the bloodiest battles of the war. The Italians lost some sixty killed and double that number wounded, and the Turks fled in disorder, leaving more than 800 dead on the field; some reports say a thousand. On the same day it was unofficially announced from Ouchy, Switzerland, that commissioners from the two countries meeting there had tentatively agreed to terms for ending the war. The stipulations were indefinite, but conceded possession of the Tripolitan coast to Italy. The outbreak of the Balkan States put an end to negotiations for a time. The protocol was signed Oct. 15, 1912. (See also Turkey.)

May 23, 1915, Italy plunged into the general European conflict by declaring war against Austria. The Italian offensive, however, proved insignificant.

Italy:

American citizens impressed into service of, and punished by, 5673.

American College at Rome, threatened confiscation of, by, 4801.

American sailor alleged to have been killed in Genoa, 5769.

Annexation of States of the Church to, referred to, 4098.

Claims of, against Colombia and arbitration of President of United States in, 6328.

Claims of United States against Naples, 556, 598, 867, 1109, 1112, 1157.

Extension of time allowed commissioners for settlement of, recommended, 1267.

Confederate envoys sent to Great Britain and France, referred to. (See Mason and Slidell.)

Consular convention with, 3800, 4436, 4448, 4588, 4626.

Expiration of, discussed, 4418.

Consular jurisdiction, treaty respecting, 3896.

Consuls of United States in, interference of, in difficulty in, referred to, 3826.

Copyright privilege extended by proclamation, 5736.

Referred to, 5752.

Diplomatic relations with, discussed, 4715.

Fugitive criminals, convention with, for surrender of, 3828, 3888, 3896, 4806.

Referred to, 5546, 5959.

International meridian conference, invitation to United States to attend, 5546.

Minister of, to United States, title of ambassador conferred upon, 5874.

Minister of United States to Naples, 557.

Minister of United States to, title of ambassador conferred upon, 5874.

Occupation of Rome by King of, referred to, 4085.

Postal convention with, 3775.

Revolution in Papal States of, 2551.

Subjects of, lynched in—

Colorado discussed and recommendations regarding, 6065, 6096.

New Orleans, 5617.

Indemnity for, paid by United States, 5751, 6459, 6461.

Trade-marks, treaty with, regarding, 4789.

Treaty with, transmitted and discussed, 3800, 3828, 3888, 3896, 4082, 4098, 4806.

Vessels of, discriminating duties on, dominions of the Pope suspended, 942, 3022.

Italy, Treaties with.—(For the extradition treaty of 1868, see Extradition Treaties.)—A treaty of commerce and navigation of 1871 provides for freedom of commerce and navigation, liberty to trade and travel, and secures the rights and privileges of the citizens of the one country within the dominions of the other. The importation, exportation and re-exportation of goods is permitted within the countries upon equal terms regardless of the nationality of the carrying vessels, and without the imposition of discriminating, higher, or other duties than those imposed upon other nations. Tonnage, anchorage, and clearance duties shall not be levied upon: Vessels entering and leaving a port in ballast; vessels passing from one to another port of the same country to discharge a part of a cargo, when proof can be furnished that such charges have already been paid at one of the ports; vessels driven to seek shelter in port by stress of weather, and which do not discharge the whole or a part of the cargo. Humane treatment is to be accorded in cases of shipwreck.

The principle that in time of war free ships make free goods, is observed between the nations. In case of the blockading of a port in either country in time of war, a vessel of the other nation shall not be regarded as liable to capture on its first attempt to enter, but shall be if the attempt is persisted in. Articles used in warfare on land and sea, munitions of war, arms, and military equipment are contraband of war. Provision is made for the examination of ship's papers and search with as little detention and embarrassment as possible. Citizens in the dominions of the other have all rights of disposal of property by sale, testament, gift, or otherwise. (For consular convention of 1878, see Consular Conventions.)

In 1900 a reciprocal commercial arrangement was made by which concessions, principally in wines, wine products, and works of art, were made in import duties by the United States; and concessions, principally in cottonseed oil, fish, machinery, etc., were made by Italy, by which lower import duties were imposed for the encouragement of trade in these articles between the two countries. Mutual protection of trade-marks in Morocco and China was agreed to by exchange of notes in 1903 and 1905 respectively. (See also Extradition Treaties.)

Itata, The, seizure of, by United States for violation of neutrality laws discussed, 5618. (See also *Baltimore, The.*)

Iuka (Miss.), Battle of.—The transfer of Gen. Pope to Virginia and Gen. Halleck to Washington in the summer of 1862 left Grant in command of the Army of the Tennessee with headquarters at Corinth, Miss. Halleck ordered most of the Army of the Tennessee to be placed under Buell's command, leaving Grant's force on the defensive and harassed by the Confederates under Van Dorn and Price. Sept. 13, 1862, Price advanced from the south and seized Iuka, a village in northeast Mississippi, twenty-one miles east of Corinth. Van Dorn was then only four days off to the southwest, threatening Corinth. Gen. Rosecrans, with 9,000 men, was ordered to attack Price from the south and Gen. Ord, with 8,000, was to attack from the north. The two armies failed to co-operate, and Price attacked Rosecrans Sept. 19. The latter kept his ground, but lost a battery of artillery, besides 736 men killed and wounded. Darkness put an end to the fight.

I. W. W.   (See Socialism.)

EXTENT OF THE UNITED STATES DURING THE ADMINISTRATION OF PRESIDENT JACKSON, 1829-1837.

(NOT INCLUDING TERRITORIES)

MAINE 1820

VT. 1791

N. H. 1788

MASS. 1788

CONN. 1788

R. I. 1790

N. J. 1787

DEL. 1787

NEW YORK 1788

PENNSYLVANIA 1787

MD. 1788

VIRGINIA 1788

NORTH CAROLINA 1789

SOUTH CAROLINA 1788

GEORGIA 1788

MICHIGAN 1837

OHIO 1803

INDIANA 1816

KENTUCKY 1792

TENNESSEE 1796

ALABAMA 1819

ILLINOIS 1818

MISSISSIPPI 1817

MISSOURI 1821

ARKANSAS 1836

LOUISIANA 1812

FLAG OF 1837

Jackson, Andrew.—1829-1837.

(FIRST TERM, 1829-1833).

Eleventh Administration—Democratic.
Vice-President—John C. Calhoun.
Secretary of State—
Martin Van Buren.
Edward Livingston.
Secretary of the Treasury—
Samuel D. Ingham.
Louis McLane.
Secretary of War—
John H. Eaton.
Lewis Cass.
Secretary of the Navy—
John Branch.
Levi Woodbury.
Attorney-General—
John McP. Berrien.
Roger B. Taney.
Postmaster-General—
William T. Barry.

Nomination.—Andrew Jackson was elected by the Democrats in the election of 1828. In his contest against John Quincy Adams in 1824, Jackson received the plurality of both the popular and electoral votes, and yet failed of election by the House. His friends were much embittered by the result and began to work for his election immediately after the inauguration of President Adams. The candidates were chosen by common consent, the legislatures of the states having made a choice and endorsed the candidates. Jackson's name was presented by the legislature of Tennessee, and Van Buren brought Crawford's friends to Jackson's support. John Quincy Adams was nominated by legislatures and mass-meetings, and he was the candidate of the National Republicans.

Vote.—Twenty-four states took part in the election, which was held Nov. 4. The popular vote gave Jackson 647,231 votes, and Adams 509,097. The electoral vote, counted Feb. 11, 1829, gave Jackson 178 votes, and Adams 83. John C. Calhoun received 171 electoral votes for Vice-President against 83 for Richard Rush.

Opposition.—At its second meeting, at Baltimore, Sept. 26, 1831, the Anti-Masonic party was attended by 112 delegates, who nominated William Wirt for President and Amos Ellmaker for Vice-President. The National Republican Convention met at Baltimore, Dec. 12, 1831, with 157 delegates, and nominated Henry Clay for the Presidency. The Democratic Convention met at Baltimore, March 22, 1832, with 283 delegates, who endorsed Jackson's candidacy unanimously and nominated Martin Van Buren for Vice-President. The two-thirds rule, which has always obtained at Democratic conventions, was adopted at this convention.

(SECOND TERM, 1833-1837).

Twelfth Administration—Democratic.
Vice-President—Martin Van Buren.
Secretary of State—
Louis McLane.
John Forsyth.
Secretary of the Treasury—
Louis McLane.
William J. Duane.
Roger B. Taney.
Levi Woodbury.
Secretary of War—
Lewis Cass.
Secretary of the Navy—
Levi Woodbury.
Mahlon Dickerson.
Postmaster-General—
William T. Barry.
Amos Kendall.
Attorney-General—
Roger B. Taney.
Benjamin F. Butler.

SECOND TERM — Vote. — Twenty-four states took part in the election, which was held Nov. 6, 1832. The popular vote stood: Jackson, 687,502; and Clay, 530,189. The electoral vote, counted Feb. 13, 1833, gave Jackson 219; Clay, 49; Floyd, 11; and Wirt, 7.

Party Affiliation.—Jackson was the single representative to Congress from Tennessee upon its admission in 1796. As a representative he steadfastly opposed Washington's administration and the Federalists. He was one of the twelve who voted against the address to Washington approving of his administration; he opposed the Jay treaty with Great Britain; and Hamilton's financial policy. He was elected as a Democrat and this name was given to the Republican party in 1828 by his followers.

Political Complexion of Congress.—In the Twenty-first Congress (1829-1831) the Senate, of 48 members, was composed of 38 Democrats and 10 Whigs; and the House, of 213 members, was made up of 142 Democrats and 71 Whigs. In the Twenty-second Congress (1831-1833) the Senate, of 48 members, was composed of 35 Democrats and 13 Whigs; and the House, of 213 members, was made up of 130 Democrats and 83 Whigs. In the Twenty-third Congress (1833-1835) the Senate, of 48 members, was composed of 30 Democrats and 18 Whigs; and the House, of 240 members, was made up of 147 Democrats and 93 Whigs. In the Twenty-fourth Congress (1835-1837) the Senate, of 52 members, was composed of 33 Democrats and 19 Whigs; and the House, of 242 members, was made up of 144 Democrats and 98 Whigs.

Civil Service.—In the several administrations which preceded that of Jackson, public office was regarded as a public trust, and not a reward for political or party service. The total number of removals from office between the years 1789 and 1829 were only seventy-four. From March 4, 1829, to March 22, 1830, the changes in the civil service numbered about 2,000. This policy took the name of the "spoils system" from an utterance in the Senate, in 1831, by Senator Marcy of New York, to the effect that "to the victors belong the spoils." In his First Annual Message (page 1012) President Jackson discusses the office-holder and says: "Offices were not established to give support to particular men at the public expense. No individual wrong is, therefore, done by removal. The incumbent became an officer with a view to public benefits, and when these require his removal they are not to be sacrificed to private interests. It is the people, and they alone, who have a right to complain when a bad officer is substituted for a good one. He who is removed has the same means of obtaining a living that are enjoyed by the millions who never held office." In the same message, the President recommends that the tenure of office be limited to four years in a greater number of cases than the law to that effect passed in 1820 covered. One of the most curious effects of this system was the struggle for patronage between Calhoun and Van Buren that followed.

Tariff.—The tariff of 1828, known from its unfairness as the "tariff of abominations," was modified by the tariff act of 1832, which was designed to remedy the injustice of that of 1828. It failed, however, to satisfy the people of the South, and for some time there was talk of nullification. While Jackson was on principle opposed to protective tariffs, he was most determined to preserve the Union. South

Carolina in convention of its citizens at Columbia, Nov. 19, 1832, declared the tariff acts of 1828 and 1832 null and void; officers were sworn to act in accordance with this edict; and threats were made of secession if the Federal authorities attempted to enforce the tariff laws in that state. (See Nullification.) This ordinance was to take effect Feb. 1, 1833, and to be enforced, if necessary, by an appeal to arms. Dec. 16, President Jackson issued his famous nullification message (page 1173) in which he reviews at length the whole question and closes a most forceful exposition of Federal and State Rights with these words: " . . . . and I fervently pray that the Great Ruler of Nations may so guide your deliberations and our joint measures as that they may prove salutary examples not only to the present but to future times, and solemnly proclaim that the Constitution and the laws are supreme and the Union indissoluble." Then followed, Dec. 10, 1832, his equally famous nullification Proclamation in which (page 1206) he says: "I consider then the power to annul a law of the United States assumed by one State, incompatible with the existence of the Union, contradicted expressly by the letter of the Constitution, unauthorized by its spirit, inconsistent with every principle upon which it is founded, and destructive of the great object for which it was formed." South Carolina deferred action; and the tariff act of March 2, 1833, known as the "Clay's Compromise Act," was passed. It provided that in all cases where the tariff on imported goods exceeded twenty per cent of the value of such goods, a gradual reduction should be made of such excess in the following ratio and manner: one-tenth of such excess after Dec. 31, 1833; another tenth after Dec. 31, 1835; another tenth after Dec. 31, 1837; another tenth after Dec. 31, 1839; one-half the residue of such excess after Dec. 31, 1841; and all of the residue of such excess after Dec. 31, 1842. Speaking of the effect of this compromise upon the revenue of the country, the President, in his Fifth Annual Message (page 1247), said: "The changes made in our revenue system by the acts of Congress of 1832 and 1833, and more especially by the former, have swelled the receipts of the present year far beyond the amount to be expected in future years upon the reduced tariff of duties. . . . . I cannot, therefore, recommend to you any alteration in the present tariff of duties; the rate as now fixed by law on the various articles was adopted at the last session of Congress, as a matter of compromises, with unusual unanimity, and unless it is found to produce more than the necessities of the Government call for, there would seem to be no reason at this time to justify a change." In his Eighth Annual Message (page 1459) President Jackson discusses at length the revenue system and the various means of disposing of surplus revenue. "The safest and best mode," he says, "of obviating all of the difficulties which have been mentioned, is to collect only revenue enough to meet the wants of the Government, and let the people keep the balance of their property in their own hands to be used for their own profit."

Public Debt.—The public debt of the United States during the administration of President Jackson stood as follows: Jan. 1, 1830, $48,565,406.50; 1831, $39,-103,191.68; 1832, $24,322,235.18; 1833, $7,001,698.83; 1834. $4,760,082.08; 1835, $37,513.05; 1837, $336,957.83; 1838, $3,-308,124.07.

In his Seventh Annual Message (page 1379) President Jackson said: "Since my last annual communication all the remains of the public debt have been redeemed, or money has been placed in deposit for this purpose whenever the creditors choose to receive it."

Finance.—President Jackson as a strict constructionist was opposed to national banks. In his First Annual Message (page 1025) he began his attack upon the United States Bank, and followed it up most persistently, even to the length of vetoing the bill renewing its charter of 1832. He said: "Both the constitutionality and the expediency of the law creating this bank are well questioned by a large portion of our fellow-citizens, and it must be admitted by all that it has failed in the great end of establishing a uniform and sound currency." The matter was drawn into politics by Clay and it formed an important issue in the election of 1832. In his Fifth Annual Message, the President (page 1250) casts doubts upon the solvency of the bank and suggests the appointment of a committee to investigate. Congress investigated and reported favorably to the bank as a safe repository for Government funds. The President made up his mind that the deposits should be withdrawn. Secretary McLane, of the Treasury, was unwilling to give the order, and he was transferred to the State Department and his place was filled by William J. Duane, who was satisfied that the removal of the funds was neither wise nor necessary, and refused either to give the order or to resign. Duane was removed in September and his place was filled during recess by Roger B. Taney, who ordered that after Oct. 1 deposits should be made in certain State banks and not in the United States Bank. A resolution of censure of the President was, after long debate, carried by Clay in the Senate; but a few weeks before Jackson's retirement from office the resolution was expunged. In the President's Farewell Address (page 1511) he devotes a great deal of attention to the currency, condemning the use of paper money. He says: "The Constitution of the United States unquestionably intended to secure to the people a circulating medium of gold and silver. But the establishment of a national bank by Congress, with the privilege of issuing paper money receivable in the payment of public dues, and the unfortunate course of legislation in the several States upon the same subject, drove from general circulation the constitutional currency and substituted one of paper in its place."

Foreign Policy.—The President expresses the policy of his administration in his Fourth Annual Message (page 1159) in these words: "Our best wishes on all occasions, our good offices when required, will be afforded to promote the domestic tranquillity and foreign peace of all nations with whom we have any intercourse. Any intervention in their affairs further than this, even by the expression of an official opinion, is contrary to our principles of international policy, and will always be avoided." In his Second Inaugural Address (page 1222) he says: "To do justice to all and to submit to wrong from none has been during my administration its governing maxim, and so happy have been its results that we are not only at peace with all the world, but have few cases of controversy, and these of minor importance remaining unadjusted." Great credit was given to the Jackson administration for the enforcement of the French spoliation claims, an account of which is given in the President's Seventh Annual Message (page 1371). European nations found no difficulty in settling their claims against France soon after the peace of 1815; but the claims of the United States were treated with supercilious silence. A treaty was made with France in settlement of these in 1831, by which France obligated herself to pay $5,000,000 in six annual instalments, beginning Feb. 2, 1833. A draft was presented but payment was refused, on the plea that no appropriation had been made. President Jackson, in a message to Congress in December, 1834, advised Congress to direct that French vessels to the value of the amount be captured. The French government threatened war should the President not apologize. Great Britain interposed and advised France to settle quickly, which she did. The moral effect of the course taken by President Jackson was very great in demonstrating that the time had passed when the United States could be insulted with impunity.

Jackson, Andrew:

Annual messages of, 1005, 1063, 1107, 1154, 1238, 1316, 1366, 1455.

Attempted assassination of, illustration, 1455.

Bank of United States discussed by. (See Bank of United States.)

Biographical sketch of, 998.

Cartoons on, 1202, 1456.

Claims against France discussed by. (See France, claims against.)

Conduct of, when entering Florida discussed, 611.

Constitutional amendment relative to mode of election of President and Vice-President, recommended by, 1010, 1081, 1120, 1168, 1253, 1336, 1395, 1478.

Death of—
 Announced and honors to be paid memory of, 2233, 2234.
 Referred to, 2266.

Discretionary power of President over nominations, removals, and other acts discussed by, 1255, 1261, 1272, 1346, 1351.

Executive nominations—
 Authority of Executive regarding, discussed by, 1261, 1272, 1346, 1351.
 Unacted on withdrawn, 1002.

Farewell address of, 1511.

Finances, discussed by, 1014, 1088, 1118, 1159, 1224, 1246, 1326, 1379, 1458.

Fine imposed upon at New Orleans, remission of, recommended, 2062.

Foreign policy discussed by, 1159, 1222, 1324, 1370, 1378, 1456, 1484, 1500.

Home of, tendered Government, 2954.

Inaugural address of—
 First, 999.
 Second, 1222.

Instructions to, relating to treaty with Creek Indians, 886.

Internal improvements discussed by, 1014, 1046, 1071, 1164, 1201.

Lafayette—
 Death of, announced, 1313.
 Orders homage to be paid memory of, 1314.
 Tribute paid memory of, by, 1314.

Lands donated to, by Indians as mark of gratitude, 555.

Large standing army unnecessary in time of peace, 1389.

Madison, James—
 Death of, correspondence with Mrs. Madison on, 1479.
 Writings of, on constitutional convention, correspondence with Mrs. Madison on, 1479, 1481.

Major-general, United States Army, 521, 533, 611.
 Insults offered Spanish officers by, referred to, 709.

Medal offered, in commemoration of delivery of Colombian President from assassins, declined by, 1029.

Medical attendants directed to accompany, home, 1540.

Meeting of Congress, views of, on act fixing day for, 1450.

Military achievements of, in Indian wars, discussed, 521, 533.
 Entrance of, into Florida discussed, 611.

Misunderstanding with Judge Fromentin, referred to, 682.

Nullification message of, 1173.

Nullification proclamation of, 1203.

Oath of office, notifies Congress of time and place of taking, 999.

Our Government supported by ballot box, not musket, 1390.

Pardon granted deserters by, 1062.

Pocket vetoes of, 1071, 1200, 1201, 1275, 1337, 1501.

Portrait of, 997.

Powers of Federal and State Governments discussed by, 1014, 1024, 1046, 1071, 1077, 1082, 1120, 1141, 1201, 1224, 1275, 1288, 1337, 1351, 1395, 1450.

Proclamations of—
 Discriminating duties suspended on vessels of—
  Austria, 1004, 1005.
  Mecklenburg-Schwerin, 1365.
  Oldenburg, 1059.
  Tuscany, 1452.
 Extraordinary session of Senate, 1508.
 Facsimile of, opposite 1041.
 Lands in Louisiana, sale of, 1058.
 Nullification, 1203.
 Ports opened to vessels of Great Britain, 1060.
 Unlawful possession of public lands, 1057, 1106.

Protest of, against, resolutions of Senate, 1258.

Additional statement regarding, 1312.

Public deposits discussed by. (See Banks, State; Deposits, Public.)

Refuses to make further nominations for offices in Mississippi, 1199.

Removals from office, discussed by, 1351.

Revenue laws opposed in South Carolina, discussed by. (See South Carolina.)

Revenue system discussed by, 1459.

Santa Anna, correspondence with, regarding war between Texas and Mexico, 1493.

Signature of, see opposite 1201.

State banks discussed by. (See Banks, State.)

State of Union discussed by, 1005, 1063, 1107, 1154, 1366, 1511.

Surgeon-General of Army directed to accompany, home, 1540.

Surplus revenue discussed by, 1015, 1077, 1459.

Tariff discussed by, 1012, 1086, 1119, 1160, 1247, 1380, 1470.

Texas, relations with, discussed by, (See Texas.)

Treaty with Indians concluded by, 589.

Veto messages of—

　Appointing day for meeting of Congress, 1450.

　Authorizing subscription of stock in Maysville, Washington, Paris, and Lexington Turnpike Road Co., 1046.

　Authorizing subscription of stock in Washington Turnpike Road Co., 1056.

　Compromise of claims against Sicily, 1365.

　Designating and limiting funds receivable for revenue, reasons for applying pocket veto, 1501.

　Extension of charter of Bank of United States, 1139.

　Improvements of rivers and harbors, reasons for applying pocket veto, 1201.

　Light-houses, reasons for applying pocket veto, 1071.

　Louisville and Portland Co., reasons for applying pocket veto, 1071.

　Navigation of Wabash River, reasons for applying pocket veto, 1337.

　Proceeds of land sales, reasons for applying pocket veto, 1275.

　Settlement of State claims, reasons for applying pocket veto, 1200.

War between Texas and Mexico, discussed by. (See Wars, Foreign.)

Warehousing system discussed by, 1015.

Jackson (Miss.), Battle of.—After the engagement at Raymond, McPherson's column proceeded toward Jackson by way of Clinton, where it destroyed a portion of the railroad to prevent the sending of supplies from the east to Vicksburg. Sherman moved along the Raymond road. May 14, 1863, when within two miles of Jackson, both columns met the Confederates whom Gen. Joseph E. Johnston had been collecting in order to reenforce Pemberton at Vicksburg. The combined corps of Sherman and McPherson attacked the small force of Johnston and drove it through Jackson and toward Canton, taking some prisoners. The Union loss was 300. The Confederate loss was 845.

Jails. (See Imprisonment.)

Jamestown and Northern Railroad Co., right of way through Indian reservation, bill for, 4952, 5177.

Jamestown (Va.), Battle of.—Early in 1781 Virginia became the chief theater of the operations of the British and American armies. Benedict Arnold, having turned traitor to his country, was sent by Clinton, with 1,600 men, to the James River with orders to lay waste the country and destroy the stores at Richmond. Washington ordered Lafayette, with 1,200 light infantry, to capture Arnold. Lafayette arrived at Richmond April 29, just in time to witness the burning of the extensive tobacco warehouses at Manchester, on the opposite side of the river, by Gen. Phillips, who had succeeded Arnold. Phillips had 2,000 men. Cornwallis abandoned his unprofitable campaign in the Carolinas and reached Petersburg, Va., May 20, 1781, having nearly 8,000 men. Lafayette, realizing his inability to hold Richmond against this large force, returned northward to the Rappahannock. Here he was joined June 7 by Gen. Wayne with about 800 Continentals. Returning, Lafayette formed a juncture with Steuben June 18, augmenting his force to about 4,000 men. Eluding Tarleton's command, he pursued Cornwallis back toward Richmond, which place the latter evacuated June 20, retiring toward Jamestown. July 6 Lafayette attacked Cornwallis near Green Springs, within a few miles of Jamestown. Lafayette distinguished himself for personal bravery in the fight, but was forced to retire to Malvern Hill. The American casualties were reported as 118 killed, wounded and missing. The British lost 75.

Jamestown, Va., tercentenary of foundation of, 7043, 7095, 7386.

Jamestown Exposition, commended by President Roosevelt, 6913, 7006.

Japan.—"Land of the Rising Sun." An empire of Asia lying in the Pacific Ocean, east of China, Korea, and Siberia. It consists of four principal islands—the main island of Hondo or Nippon, Yezo, Shikoku, Kiu Shiu—and about 4,000 smaller islands, including the Loochoo and Kurile groups and the Island of Formosa, which was acquired from China in 1895.

Physical Features.—The islands of Japan are traversed by a range of mountains with numerous spurs, their general direction being parallel to the coast line. The highest peak is in the main island of Hondo, where are the sacred snow-capped cone of Fuji-yama (12,370 feet), a volcano dormant since 1707, and Asama-yama (8,300 feet), also volcanic and liable to eruption.

The numerous streams, like those of

New Zealand and for the same reason, are short and generally impetuous, rising in the central mountains and flowing to the nearest point of the coast. Slight earthquakes are common in certain districts and the islands are frequently the center of storms or typhoons, especially in September.

History.—Authentic history begins about 500 A. D. The Portuguese traded some with Japan between 1540 and 1638. With the exception of a limited trade with the Dutch, Japan held no commercial relations with the rest of the world till an American expedition under Perry, in 1853, forced a treaty upon her. This was followed by treaty upon her. (See illustration opposite 2708.) This was followed by treaties with other countries. In 1867-68 a revolution transferred the power from the Shogun, the hereditary commander-in-chief of the army, who had held it for 500 years, to the titular Emperor, the Mikado. In 1894, in a war with China, the latter was completely defeated on land and sea. The war ended in 1895 with the payment of indemnity by China, the cession of Formosa, and the independence of Korea.

The estimated population of Japan proper (1913) was 52,985,000. The religion of the Japanese nation is Shintoism and Buddhism, but there is absolute religious freedom. Christianity has not made very great progress.

AREA AND POPULATION

	Area in English Sq. Miles	Population 1908
Japanese Empire—		
Hondo, Central............	36,592	19,044,475
Hondo, Northern..........	30,194	7,480,432
Hondo, Western..........	20,675	10,929,374
Yezo or Hokkaido.........	30,150	1,137,455
Kiu Shiu.................	13,800	7,748,752
Shikoku.................	180	3,288,310
Kurile Islands...........	6,160	4,000
Luchu (Riu-kiu) Islands....	940	460,000
Other Islands............	1,500	......
	140,191	50,052,798
Dependencies—		
Korea (Cho-sen)..........	71,000	13,125,000
Formosa (Tai-wan).......	13,500	3,400,000
Pescadores (Hoko-to).....	85	55,000
Kwangtung...............	1,286	470,000
Sakhalin (Karafuto).......	9,824	40,000
	95,695	17,090,000
Grand Total..........	235,886	67,142,798

Government.—The government is that of a constitutional monarchy, claimed by the Japanese to be hereditary in direct line since the seventh century before the Christian era, and is thus the oldest consecutive government in the world. In the year 1867 the reins of government were reassumed by the Emperor after a lapse of about 600 years of imperial seclusion, during which period the power had been exercised by a Shogun, or Generalissimo, who was *de facto* ruler, although nominally subject to the *de jure* Emperor. In 1871 the Imperial authority was further strengthened by the gradual absorption of the samurai, or sword-bearing warrior class, in the body of the nation. Ruler, His Imperial Majesty Yoshihito, born Aug. 31, 1879; succeeded his father the Emperor Mutsuhito July 30, 1912. The word Mikado is an archaic word seldom heard in Japan, of doubtful etymology, which appears to mean "August Gate," and was used to designate the Emperor, it being thought disrespectful to refer to high personages by name. It is a common custom in Japan to mention persons by places connected with them rather than by name.

The executive power reposes in the Emperor, who is advised by a Cabinet responsible to him, and by a Privy Council of members selected by the Emperor from the nobility and parliamentary or otherwise distinguished persons.

The Imperial Diet consists of two Houses. The Chamber of Peers consists of the Imperial Princes, and Princes and Marquesses of twenty-five years of age; of elected representatives of the remaining ranks of the nobility; of life members appointed by the Emperor; and of representatives elected for seven years by the fifteen principal inhabitants of each of the forty-five administrative districts, a total number in 1912 of 367 members. The Chamber of Representatives consists of 381 members, elected for four years by the direct vote of male resident tax-payers in each electoral district.

The judicial system has been modernized, and consists of district and sub-district courts of first instance and courts of appeal, with judges appointed by the Emperor and irremovable except for misconduct. A court of cassation at Tokyo, similar to that of Paris, is the final appeal court of the Empire.

The official administrative unit is the Prefecture (forty-three in number) under a Prefect who is a civil official appointed by the Emperor and directly responsible to the Home Minister.

Production and Industry.—The area of Japan (exclusive of the Dependencies) is 94,500,000 acres, of which over 54.5 per cent is under forests. The crops are rice, wheat and barley, soy bean, mulberry and millet.

The live stock includes cattle, sheep, goats, pigs, and horses. Gold and silver are found, and iron, copper and manganese are plentiful. Coal is raised in progressive quantities, 17,600,000 tons being won in 1911. Petroleum is being successively exploited and sulphur mines are worked. Iron foundries and ship-building industries are of growing importance. Textiles employ nearly one-half a million persons (mainly women), out of a total of 717,000 factory operatives; besides a large number of workers who are engaged in these industries in their own homes, and paper, matches, earthenware, matting, leatherwork and lacquer ware are produced for the home and foreign trade.

Education.—Primary: Lower grade, compulsory, and free. Age, six to ten. Kindergarten and schools numerous and well attended (82 per cent). Some 55 per cent complete the higher primary course, age ten to fourteen, for which a small monthly fee of thirty to sixty sen is required. Special Schools of industries, commerce, and technics are well attended. State Universities; Tokio, Kyoto, Tohoku, and Kiushiu (Medicine and Engineering only). There are some private institutions of university standing.

The average expenditure for the five years ending with 1914 was 563,960,766 yen, and the receipts for the same time averaged 549,935,010 yen. The budget for 1914 called for an expenditure of 586,807,588 yen. The total debt stated in 1913 was 2,493,970,000 yen, or $1,246,985,000. The yen, the unit of value, is equal to $0.498, United States money.

Railways.—The Japanese railways are almost entirely State-owned. At the beginning of 1913 there were in Japan proper 5,606 miles of railway open. There were also 767 miles open in Korea, while the South Manchurian Railway is under **Japa-**

nese control, the Government being a large shareholder. In 1911 the Antung-Mukden line was opened to broad-gauge traffic, connecting the Korean and South Manchurian systems, and making it possible to proceed from Tokio to Moscow with only eight hours' sea-passage. The cost of construction of the Japanese railway system is estimated at £64,500,000, or about £12,000 per mile. The gross receipts for passengers and goods traffic on all lines in Japan for 1912 was £9,250,000, giving average net earnings per train mile of 1s. 10¼d.

In 1912 there were 7,166 post offices and 4,657 telegraph offices, with 29,500 miles of line. There were also 2,517 telephone offices, with 5,200 miles of line.

Shipping.—The mercantile marine consisted in 1912 of 1,981 steamers over twenty tons, and 1,317 sailing vessels over 100 tons. The principal steamship lines receive a Government subsidy.

Cities.—The capital is Tokio with a population of 2,200,000 (in 1910) and some thirty other cities with a population in excess of 50,000.

Trade with the United States.—The value of merchandise imported into Japan from the United States for the year 1913 was $57,741,815, and goods to the value of $91,633,240 were sent thither—a balance of $33,891,425 in favor of Japan.

CHO-SEN.—The peninsula of Korea, which formed the bone of contention in the Japan-China war of 1894-1895, was surrendered to Japanese influence by the Treaty of Shimonoseki of 1895, the possession being secured after the Russo-Japanese war by the treaty of 1905 and by the Anglo-Japanese agreement of the same year. In 1910 Korea was formally annexed by Japan, the Emperor was deposed, and the name of the country was changed to Cho-sen. It extends southward from Manchuria from 43°-34° 18′ N. latitude, and between 124° 36′-130° 47′ E. longitude, with a total length of about 600 miles, and an extreme breadth of 135 miles. The peninsula is bounded on the east by the Sea of Japan, on the west by the Yellow Sea and the Yalu River, on the north by Manchuria and on the extreme northeast by the Coast Province of Russian Siberia. Round the coast are many islands, the largest being Quelpart, about fifty miles due south of the peninsula (total area about 550 square miles, population 100,000), formerly used as a penal settlement by the Korean government.

The area of Korea is about 71,000 square miles. Population estimated at about 14,-000,000; there are about 210,000 Japanese in the country. The soil is fertile, but mountainous, except in the river valleys. About 4,500,000 acres are under cultivation, the staple agricultural products being rice and other cereals, beans, cotton, tobacco and hemp; the other natural products are chiefly gold and hides. Ginseng, a medicinal root much affected by the Chinese, is largely grown under Government supervision in the province of Pyeng-An, and, being a Government monopoly, forms a rich source of revenue. Gold, copper, coal, iron and other minerals are distributed throughout the country.

Capital, Seoul. Population (1909), 217,-400. Other towns are Chong-ju, 80,000; Phyong-yang, 50,000; Fusan, 50,000; Song-do (Kai-song), 27,000; Chemulpo, 25,000; Wonsan, 17,000.

Trade with the United States.—The value of merchandise imported into Cho-sen (Korea) from the United States for the year 1913 was $1,370,926, and goods to the value of $5,133 were sent thither—a balance of $1,365,793 in favor of the United States.

TAIWAN.—The island of Formosa, between 20° 56′-25° 15′ N. latitude and 120°-122° E. longitude in the West Pacific Ocean, was ceded to Japan by China after the war of 1894-1895. The name was then changed to Taiwan. The area is about 13,500 square miles, with an estimated population of 3,400,000. Formosa is a volcanic island, with the two highest peaks in Mount Morrisson (14,300 feet), now called Nitaka-yama, and Mount Sylvia (12,500 feet), called Setzu-zan. Sugar and rice are grown in large quantities. Very important is camphor, a large proportion of the world's supply coming from this island. Tea is grown, and exported largely to the United States. The administration has been entirely reformed by Japan, and education has been placed upon a scientific footing, while railways, roads and other communications are being developed.

HOKOTO.—The Pescadores (or Fisher Islands)—called by the Japanese Hok-to—are a group of forty-eight islands, of which twenty-one are uninhabited, with a total area of about eighty-five square miles and an estimated population of above 55,000, mainly Chinese, the group having been ceded by China after the war of 1894-1895. The islands are distant about thirty miles west of Formosa in the typhoon-swept area of Formosa Strait.

Japan:

Advancement of, discussed, 5471, 5959, 6065, 7053.

American citizens in, legislation for protection of, 4006.

American citizens selected to serve in offices of importance in Government of, 4099.

American hostility to citizens of, deplored, 7053.

American interests in, measures for protection of, 4006.

American shipmasters warned by proclamation not to anchor at ports of, 3712.

Autonomy and independence, claims of. to, supported by United States, 5086.

Cable communication with, recommended, 4565.

Citizens of, in China, treatment of, and action of United States officers regarding, inquired into, 5992.

Civil war in, neutrality of United States in, 3888.

Proclaimed, 3712.

Claims of United States against, 3446, 4242.

Indemnities received, discussed and recommendations regarding, 3574, 4243, 4520, 4561, 4630, 4692, 4715.

Returned, 4762.

Propriety of applying indemnity to education of youths in Japanese language, submitted, 4243.

Commercial relations with, 2703, 2743, 2769, 4060, 4242, 4448, 6373, 6431.

Constitutional government, establishment of, contemplated by, 4630.

New constitution promulgated by, 5471.

Consular courts and jurisdiction thereof, discussed, 4072, 4630.

Consuls of United States in, claim of, to exercise judicial powers in certain cases, referred to, 3892.

Difficulties of, with China, discussed, 4242.

Fugitive criminals, convention with, for surrender of, 4987, 5086.

Legation of United States in, land for, offered by, recommendations regarding, 4823, 4862, 4923.

Lew Chew Islands, controversy between China and, regarding, 4521.

Minister of, to United States, received, 4718.

Minister of United States to—

Appropriation for support of American youths to serve as part of official family of, recommended, 4101, 4145.

Claim of, for loss of house by fire, 3382.

Correspondence with, referred to, 4004.

Fireproof building for use of legation recommended, 4561.

Naval expedition to, discussed, 2703, 2712, 2743, 2769, 2833.

Successful termination of, 2812.

Neutrality of United States in war with—

Austria-Hungary, 7977.

Germany, 7976.

Postal convention with, 4203.

Questions with, settled, 6264, 6333.

Referred to, 3832, 3836.

Relations with, 2685, 3382, 5959, 6065, 6371.

Ships of war built in United States for, referred to, 3354.

Orders regarding clearance of, 3443, 3444.

Prohibition of departure of, removed, 3539.

Shipwrecked seamen, convention with, for relief of, 4561.

Shipwrecks, convention regarding expenses incurred in consequence of, 4580.

Special provision for naturalizing citizens of, in United States, recommended, 7435.

Subjects of, in Ikisima Island injured by target practice of American vessel, recommendations regarding, 5367, 5386.

Treaty between United States, Great Britain, France, Holland, and, referred to, 3574, 3792.

Treaty of Commerce and Navigation with, 8046.

Treaty with, transmitted and discussed by President—

Buchanan, 3012, 3037, 3061, 3174.

Cleveland, 4987, 5086.

Johnson, 3574, 3722.

Pierce, 2776, 2812.

Revision of, discussed, 4762, 4825, 5086, 5367, 5546.

Convention regarding, 4460, 4520.

Vessels of, discriminating duties on, suspended by proclamation, 4131.

War with China—

Action of United States regarding, 5957, 6059.

Agents of United States requested to protect subjects of contestants, 5957, 6059.

Japan Exposition:

Tokyo, 1912, generous provision for, recommended, 7121.

Postponed to, 1917, 7234.

Japan, Treaties with.—Diplomatic relations with Japan began with the treaty of 1854, which, with several later ones, was superseded by the more comprehensive conventions now in force. The convention for reimbursing shipwreck expenses, concluded in 1880, provided that all expenses incurred by the government of the United States in connection with rescue, clothing, and assisting needy Japanese subjects in cases of shipwreck should be paid by the Japanese government, if the assisted persons be unable to pay them; and reciprocally, the United States government shall be responsible for debts and expenses incurred by Japan in rendering like assistance to United States citizens. This provision shall not extend to expenses incurred in the salvage of the vessels or cargo, which must be a charge against the vessel and goods or the owners. In such claims for reimbursement, the expenses of government, police, and other officials, and the expense of official correspondence is not to be included. (For the extradition provisions of 1886, see Extradition Treaties.)

The treaty of commerce and navigation of 1894 provided for mutual freedom of trade, travel and residence; free access to the courts in pursuit and defense of rights; possession and disposal as well as the succession to property, and the equitable imposition of taxes upon the subjects or citizens of the one country while in the dominions of the other. No discriminating, higher, or other taxes shall be levied upon aliens than upon citizens; nor shall military, naval or other service be imposed upon them. Importation and exportation of goods shall be free from prohibitory or embarrassing restrictions, regardless of the place whence the goods arrive or the nationality of the vessels carrying them; but the usual restrictions of coastwise trade obtain in all cases. The privileges of loading and unloading, and all other privileges of navigation which are enjoyed by national vessels shall be granted without restriction or discrimination to the vessel of the other country. The privileges of visiting two or more ports for the purpose of delivering parts of a cargo are extended to vessels, and in such cases there shall be but one imposition of legitimate charges upon the vessel. Humane treatment is to be extended to vessels of all sorts in distress, and means of assistance and alleviation are to be freely accorded by both nations to the sufferers on vessels of the other. Salvage shall in all cases be conducted and governed according to the laws of the country in which the salvage is made. Goods and merchandise saved from a wreck shall not be liable to customs duties unless cleared for consumption. The usual terms of consular convention are included in this treaty. The treaty was to have endured for a period of twelve years from date of conclusion, with twelve months' privilege of notice of intention to terminate (page 7666). (For Trade-Mark regulations, see Trade-Marks, Conventions.)

In Article VII corporations are dealt with. It permits them to appear in courts subject to the laws of each country, though it is stipulated that the permission to corporations to transact business must remain subject to local laws.

In Article VIII it is provided that there shall be no discrimination between the vessels of the two countries in their right to carry imports without being liable to other or higher charges of duties than national vessels. The same rule is applied to exportation and to the payment of export duties, bounties and drawbacks. Article XIV promises that any trade or navigation privilege extended to another country shall be enjoyed by the signatories to this treaty. Article XV confers protection for patents, trade-marks, and designs. This treaty supersedes the treaty of 1894, and became operative July 17, 1911, and is to remain in force twelve years. At the end of twelve years the treaty also continues operative unless six months' notice to the contrary is given.

Regarding immigration restrictions, the following statement by Y. Uchida, the Japanese Ambassador at Washington, while not a part of the treaty, was made in connection with it:

"In proceeding this day to the signature of the treaty of commerce and navigation between Japan and the United States the undersigned Japanese Ambassador in Washington, duly authorized by his Government, has the honor to declare that the Imperial Japanese Government is fully prepared to maintain with equal effectiveness the limitation and control which it has for the past three years exercised in regulation of the emigration of laborers to the United States."

Japan signed with the United States the general international arbitration treaty in 1908, and conventions protecting trademarks in Korea and China.

Lansing-Ishii Agreement.—On November 2, 1917, the Secretary of State of the United States and Viscount Ishii, special Japanese ambassador, exchanged notes at the Department of State in Washington relative to the policy of the United States and Japan in China. The chief points of the understanding therein arrived at were as follows:

The two governments recognize that territorial propinquity creates special relations between countries, and consequently the Government of the United States recognizes that Japan has special interests in China, particularly in those parts to which Japan's possessions are contiguous.

The territorial sovereignty of China nevertheless remains unimpaired, and Japan's special interests will not discriminate against the trade of other nations or disregard previous commercial treaties between China and other nations. Both governments assert that they will not in any way impair the independence of China and that they will always adhere to the principle of the so-called "open door" policy, or equal opportunity for all trade and commerce.

They declare, moreover, that they are opposed to the acquisition by any Government of any special privileges which would affect the independence of China or deny equal opportunities for commerce in China to the citizens of any country.

The Chinese government, in reply to the above agreement, maintained that China had always treated all nations honorably and justly, that the rights of territorial propinquity have been respected and previously provided for, and that China accordingly would not allow herself to be bound by any agreement entered into by other nations.

Java, The, capture and destruction of, by the *Constitution,* 507.

Jay Treaty.—A treaty of peace and friendship between the United States and Great Britain, negotiated in 1794 by John Jay, on the part of the United States, and Lord Grenville, representing Great Britain. It provided for an evacuation of the British posts to the United States, free commercial intercourse on the American continent, unrestricted navigation of the Mississippi River, indemnity to citizens of each country for damages at the hands of privateers of the other, and a limited trade between this country and the British West Indies. The last-mentioned clause caused the treaty to be very unpopular in America. (See Great Britain, Treaties with.)

Jeannette Polar Expedition:

Failure and abandonment of, 4726.

Remains of members of, removed to United States, 4834.

Services extended in Russia to survivors of, recommendations regarding, 4853.

Testimonials of Congress transmitted to Russian subjects who aided survivors of, 4919, 5088.

Report on, 5120.

Vessels dispatched for relief of, 4726. Recommended, 4586.

Jefferson Manual. (See Manual of Parliamentary Practice.)

Jefferson, Thomas.—1801-1809.

(FIRST TERM, 1801-1805.)

Fourth Administration—Democratic-Republican.

Vice-President—Aaron Burr.

Secretary of State—
James Madison.

Secretary of the Treasury—
Samuel Dexter (continued).
Albert Gallatin, from May 15, 1801.

Secretary of War—
Henry Dearborn.

Secretary of the Navy—
Benjamin Stoddert (continued).
Robert Smith, from Jan. 26, 1802.
Jacob Crowninshield, from March 2, 1805.

Attorney-General—
Levi Lincoln.
Robert Smith, from March 2, 1805.

Postmaster-General—
Joseph Habersham (continued).
Gideon Granger, from Nov. 28, 1801.

Nomination.—There were no conventions or platforms, but the candidates were nominated by a caucus of members of Congress. The Federalists renominated John Adams, and the Democratic-Republicans chose Thomas Jefferson.

Election.—The close race for the Presidency which Jefferson gave Adams in 1796, marked the affection of the people for the man who drew up the Declaration of Independence. The election of Adams in that year, despite his unpopular doctrines, marked the esteem and love which the people had for Washington—for Washington preferred Adams. Jefferson, while Vice-President, was not consulted by Adams in affairs of the administration. His election as the third President of the United States, in 1800, is attributed to the unskillful politics of Hamilton and the political adroitness of Aaron Burr, in New York.

Tripolitan War.—Commodore Dale was sent with three frigates and a sloop of war to protect our commerce on the Barbary coast, and it was found that Tripoli had declared war against the United States.

When the Seventh Congress met Jefferson sent in a written message, establishing the custom which was unbroken until Woodrow Wilson delivered an oral address in 1913.

Vote.—The electoral vote was counted Feb. 11, 1801, and showed Jefferson, 73; Burr, 73; Adams, 65; C. C. Pinckney, 64; and John Jay 1. As no one had received a majority of the votes, the House, on the same day, proceeded to elect a President and a Vice-President. The balloting continued until Tuesday, Feb. 17, 1801, when, on the thirty-sixth ballot, Jefferson was elected President, and Burr, Vice-President. Some of the Federalists, not including Hamilton, tried to elect Burr over Jefferson, and Burr did not discountenance their action.

(SECOND TERM, 1805-1809.)

Fifth Administration — Democratic-Republican.

Vice-President—George Clinton.
Secretary of State—
   James Madison (continued).
Secretary of the Treasury—
   Albert Gallatin (continued).
Secretary of the Navy—
   Jacob Crowninshield, from March 3, 1805.
Secretary of War—
   Henry Dearborn (continued).
Attorney-General—
   Robert Smith, from March 3, 1805.
   John Breckinridge, from Dec. 25, 1805.
   Caesar A. Rodney, from Jan. 20, 1807.
Postmaster-General—
   Gideon Granger (continued).

SECOND TERM—Nomination.—In the election of 1804, candidates were chosen by Congressional caucus for the positions of President and Vice-President, specifically in order to prevent a repetition of the conditions of 1800, when the struggle for President occurred between Jefferson and Burr, and also of the anomalous condition in 1796 when Adams was a Federalist President and Jefferson a Republican Vice-President. Jefferson and George Clinton were the nominees of the Democratic-Republicans. It does not appear, however, that Charles C. Pinckney and Rufus King, the Federalist candidates for these offices, were nominated in a Federal caucus. The strongest party contests occurred in Massachusetts and Connecticut.

Vote.—Jefferson carried Massachusetts against the Federalists led by Adams, but failed to win in Connecticut. The electoral vote was counted Feb. 13, 1805, and was conducted in accordance with the Twelfth Amendment to the Constitution, which went into effect Sept. 25, 1804. Jefferson had 162 votes against 14 for Pinckney. The apportionment following the census of 1800, and the admission of Ohio in 1802, increased the electoral vote to 176 and the number of States participating to 17. Jef-

ferson was victorious in all of the states except Connecticut and Delaware, and in Maryland, where the vote was split 9 to 2.

Party Affiliation.—Prior to his residence in France as United States minister (1784-1789), Jefferson was a Whig of the Revolution. On his return, he was a Republican-Democrat, in deepest sympathy with the French Revolution. He advocated "the will of the majority to be the natural law of every society, and the only sure guardian of the rights of man." The Constitution had been drawn and adopted in his absence, and although on his return he expressed himself against it, he later modified his views regarding it and came to think more favorably of it. His associates in Washington's Cabinet, notably Hamilton and Knox, often expressed themselves in favor of aristocratic or monarchical forms of government, and regarded the Republican form as only a temporary expedient. This was so hateful to Jefferson that he vehemently expressed his grief and astonishment, and ultimately resigned his Cabinet office. He found himself opposed to the whole Federalist policy and, upon his retirement from office in 1796, he and his friends took the name of Republicans. Thus the Democratic party was formed, which in 1800 became the majority party in the United States. It was known as the Republican party until Jackson, in 1824, changed its name to the Democratic party.

Political Complexion of Congress.—In the Seventh Congress (1801-1803) the Senate, of 32 members, was made up of 13 Federalists and 19 Democrats; and the House, of 105 members, was made up of 34 Federalists and 71 Democrats. In the Eighth Congress (1803-1805) the Senate, of 34 members, was made up of 10 Federalists and 24 Democrats; and the House, of 141 members, was made up of 38 Federalists and 103 Democrats. During the second Jefferson administration, in the Ninth Congress (1805-1807) the Senate, of 34 members, was made up of 17 Federalists and 17 Democrats; and the House, of 141 members, was made up of 29 Federalists and 112 Democrats. In the Tenth Congress (1807-1809) the Senate, of 34 members, was made up of 7 Federalists and 27 Democrats; and the House, of 141 members, was made up of 31 Federalists and 110 Democrats.

Acquisition of Territory.—During the year 1800 the territory of Louisiana was learned to have been secretly ceded by Spain to France. Jefferson opened up negotiations with France to acquire a port of deposit at the mouth of the Mississippi. In January, 1803, he sent James Monroe to France to act with Robert R. Livingston, our minister to that country. Napoleon was burdened with debt and threatened with an English war. Livingston and Monroe negotiated a treaty of purchase, agreeing to pay $15,000,000 for the province of Louisiana, which comprised, east of the Mississippi, the territory south of the thirty-first degree of north latitude and as far east as the Perdido River, and, west of the Mississippi River, the whole of the present State of Louisiana, Arkansas, Missouri, Iowa, Nebraska, the Dakotas, Montana, Idaho, Oregon, and Washington, that part of Minnesota west of the Mississippi River, Wyoming and Colorado east of the Rocky Mountains and north of the Arkansas River, and all but a small southwestern section of Kansas, and the narrow northwestern part of Oklahoma. Claims of American citizens against France to the amount of $3,750,000 were turned in on the purchase and the balance was paid in 6 per cent bonds payable in fifteen years. The Federalists claimed the purchase was unwarranted, and Jefferson

18

EXTENT OF THE UNITED STATES DURING THE ADMINISTRATION OF PRESIDENT JEFFERSON, 1801-1809.

(NOT INCLUDING TERRITORIES)

MASSACHUSETTS 1788

N. H. 1788

R. I. 1790

VT. 1791

CONN. 1788

M

N. J. 1787

DEL. 1787

MD. 1788

NEW YORK 1788

PENNSYLVANIA 1787

VIRGINIA 1788

NORTH CAROLINA 1789

SOUTH CAROLINA 1788

GEORGIA 1788

OHIO 1803

KENTUCKY 1792

TENNESSEE 1796

FLAG OF 1809

thought a constitutional amendment necessary. The Senate, however, ratified the treaty Oct. 19, 1803, and the House passed a resolution to carry it into effect by a vote of 90 to 25, the Federalists voting in the minority.

The Louisiana Purchase increased the area of the United States to a total of 1,999,775 square miles. Jefferson was fully alive to the importance of this addition. In his Third Annual Message (page 346) he says: "Whilst the property and sovereignty of the Mississippi and its waters secure an independent outlet for the produce of the western states and an uncontrolled navigation through their whole course, free from collision with other powers and the dangers to our peace from that source, the fertility of the country, its climate and extent, promise in due season important aids to our Treasury, and ample provision for our posterity, and a wide spread for the blessings of freedom and equal laws." Napoleon, in speaking of the sale of the territory, said: "This accession strengthens forever the power of the United States, and I have just given to England a maritime rival that will sooner or later humble her pride." The Lewis and Clark expedition, which formed the basis of the claim of the United States to the northwestern territory, is described in detail by Jefferson in a special message (page 398) and in his Sixth Annual Message (page 396) he says: "It is but justice to say that Messrs. Lewis and Clark and their brave companions have by this arduous service deserved well of their country."

Slavery.—Jefferson's sentiments on this subject are well expressed in his Sixth Annual Message (page 396) in these words: "I congratulate you, fellow-citizens, on the approach of the period at which you may interpose your authority constitutionally to withdraw the citizens of the United States from all further participation in these violations of human rights which have so long continued on the unoffending inhabitants of Africa, and which the morality, the reputation, and the best interests of our country have long been eager to proscribe. Although no law you may pass can take prohibitory effect till the first of the year 1808, yet the intervening period is not too long to prevent by timely notice expeditions which can not be completed before that day."

Tariff.—In his Sixth Annual Message, Jefferson recommended that the duty on salt, a necessary of life, be suppressed. He looks forward to the accumulation of a surplus of revenue, if peace continues, and in discussing the advisability of further reduction of tariff in the future, says (page 397): "Shall we suppress the impost and give the advantage to foreign over domestic manufactures? On a few articles of more general and necessary use the suppression in due season will doubtless be right, but the great mass of the articles on which impost is paid are foreign luxuries, purchased by those only who are rich enough to afford themselves the use of them. Their patriotism would certainly prefer its continuance and application to the great purposes of the public education, roads, rivers, canals, and such other objects of public improvement as it may be thought proper to add to the constitutional enumeration of Federal powers." A tariff act of May 13, 1800, made slight increases in some duties, especially those upon wines. March 27, 1804, there was passed an act "for imposing more specific duties on the importation of certain articles; and also for levying and collecting light money on foreign ships or vessels, and for other purposes." While some duties were increased by this act, it

placed upon the free list rags from cotton, linen, wool, and hemp cloth, regulus of antimony, unwrought clay, unwrought burr stones, and the bark of the cork tree. The act of March 4, 1808, allowed free importation of old copper, saltpeter, and sulphur.

Internal Improvements.—Jefferson was strongly in favor of the application of revenue surplus to internal improvements; but he did not recognize that the Constitution conferred the right of making such upon the Federal Government. In his Sixth Annual Message (page 398) he says, in speaking of such improvements: "I suppose an amendment to the Constitution, by consent of the states, necessary, because the objects now recommended are not among those enumerated by the Constitution, and to which it permits the public money to be applied." In his Eighth Annual Message (page 444) he says: "Shall it (the revenue surplus) lie unproductive in the Public vaults? Shall the revenue be reduced? Or shall it not rather be appropriated to the improvement of roads, canals, rivers, education, and other great foundations of prosperity and union under the powers which Congress may already possess or such amendment of the Constitution, as may be approved by the States?"

Navy.—The navy which had been created during the previous administration for operations against France, was reduced by Jefferson, who put all but six of the vessels out of commission. In his First Annual Message (page 318) he explains that these vessels were laid up in navy yards to reduce expenses. "Whatever annual sum," he says, "beyond that you may think proper to appropriate to naval preparations would perhaps be better employed in providing those articles which may be kept without waste or consumption, and be in readiness when any exigency calls them into use." In his several messages he lays especial stress upon the advisability of preserving the vessels of the navy from decay and injury when not in active use. In a special message of Feb. 10, 1807 (page 407), Jefferson goes fully into the plans for the increase of the navy by the addition of a flotilla of gunboats for the protection of the harbors. Two hundred of these are expected to afford the desired protection, of which number he reports that 73 are built or are building, and that the remaining 127 would cost from $500,000 to $600,000. In his Eighth Annual Message (page 442) he reports that: "Of the gunboats authorized by the act of December last, it has been thought necessary to build only 103 in the present year."

Commerce.—Jefferson did not believe in the paternal fostering of commerce and industries by the Federal Government. In his First Annual Message (page 318) he says: "Agriculture, manufactures, commerce, and navigation, the four pillars of our prosperity, are the most thriving when left most free to individual enterprise. Protection from casual embarrassments, however, may sometimes be seasonably interposed." In speaking of the rapid growth of the country, he says in his First Annual Message (page 314): "I lay before you the result of the census lately taken of our inhabitants, to a conformity with which we are now to reduce the ensuing ratio of representation and taxation. You will perceive that the increase of numbers during the last ten years, proceeding in geometrical ratio, promises a duplication in little more than twenty-two years." The number was 5,308,483 in 1800.

Finance.—Jefferson outlined the financial policy of his administration in his First

Annual Message (page 328) in these words: " . . . there is reasonable ground of confidence that we may now safely dispense with all the internal taxes, comprehending excise, stamps, auctions, licenses, carriages, and refined sugars to which the postage on newspapers may be added, to facilitate the progress of information and that the remaining sources of revenue will be sufficient to provide for the support of Government, to pay the interest on the public debts, and to discharge the principals within shorter periods than the laws or the general expectation had contemplated. War, indeed, and untoward events may change this prospect of things and call for expenses which the imposts could not meet; but sound principles will not justify our taxing the industry of our fellow-citizens to accumulate treasure for wars to happen we know not when, and which might not perhaps happen, but from the temptations offered by that treasure."

Public Debt.—The debt of the United States during the administration of Jefferson stood as follows: Jan. 1, 1802, $86,-712,632.25; 1803, $77,054,686.30; 1804, $86,427,120.88; 1805, $82,312,150.50; 1806, $75,743,270.66; 1807, $69,218,398.64; 1808, $65,196,317.97; 1809, $57,023,192.09.

Foreign Policy.—Of the six vessels which Jefferson retained in commission, he sent four to the Mediterranean to overawe the Barbary pirates who were attacking the merchant vessels of the United States. The brilliance and efficacy of the efforts of Decatur and his brave comrades on that occasion are yet remembered by the American people. In his First Inaugural Address (page 311) he speaks of the country as: "Kindly separated by nature and a wide ocean from the exterminating havoc of one quarter of the globe; too high-minded to endure the degradations of the other." In speaking of the proper attitude of the United States in the long struggle between Napoleon and the allied powers, he says, in his Third Annual Message (page 349): "In the course of this conflict let it be our endeavor, as it is our interest and our desire, to cultivate the friendship of the belligerent nations by every act of justice and of innocent kindness; to receive their armed vessels with hospitality from the distresses of the sea, but to administer the means of annoyance to none; to establish in our harbors such a police as may maintain law and order; to restrain our citizens from embarking individually in a war in which their country takes no part; to punish severely those persons, citizens or alien, who shall usurp the cover of our flag for vessels not entitled to it, infecting thereby with suspicion those of real Americans and committing us into controversies for the redress of wrongs not our own; to exact from every nation the observance toward our vessels and citizens of those principles and practices which all civilized people acknowledge; to merit the character of a just nation, and maintain that of an independent one, preferring every consequence to insult and habitual wrong." Speaking of the attack of the *Leopard* on the American frigate *Chesapeake*, Jefferson wrote in later years: "I had only to open my hand, and let havoc loose." To protect the United States from similar attacks, he issued the embargo of 1807, which continued until the end of his administration: but the conditions were too severe for American commerce to observe, and its frequent violation defeated its purpose. Jefferson always maintained that had the patriotism of the people risen to proper heights, this course would have obviated

the war of 1812, and have secured a recognition of neutral rights. Jefferson himself suffered from the condition of the embargo which forbade the exportation of tobacco, by the loss of fully two-thirds of his income.

Jefferson, Thomas:
Annual messages of, 314, 330, 345, 357, 370, 393, 413, 439.
Biographical sketch of, 307.
Constitutional amendment suggested by, regarding—
Education, 397, 444.
Internal improvements, 397, 444.
Death of, announced and honors to be paid memory of, 913.
Referred to, 930.
Election of, notification of, and reply, 308.
Expedition across continent recommended by, 341, 886.
Extraordinary session of Congress and of the Senate proclaimed, 345, 412, 449.
Foreign policy discussed by, 311, 346, 349.
Inaugural address of—
First, 309.
Second, 366.
Louisiana Purchase discussed by, 346, 348, 350.
Message adopted by, instead of personal address to Congress, 313.
Militia for national defense, 317.
Minister to France, granted permission to return home, 50.
Testimonial of services from King of France, 81.
Oath of office, notifies Congress of time and place of taking, 309.
Pardon granted deserters from Army by, 413.
Portrait of, 306.
Proclamations of—
Attack upon American vessel by British ship, 410.
Collection district of Mobile, 357.
Erection of buildings in Washington, 312.
Extraordinary session of—
Congress, 345, 412.
Senate, 449.
Military expedition against Spanish dominions, 392.
Neutrality; facsimile, opposite, 414.
Pardons to deserters, 413.
Unlawful combinations in Lake Champlain, 438.
Vessels committing depredations in United States, 390.
Retirement of, from office mentioned by, 444.
Secretary of State, 73.
Letters to, from Mr. Otto regarding tonnage, 84, 85.

Spain, military expedition against, 392.

Standing army in time of peace unnecessary, 317.

State of the Union discussed by, 316, 334, 349, 373.

Tariff discussed by, 397.

Jefferson Barracks, Mo., construction of dining rooms, etc., at, referred to, 4660, 4695.

Jemez Forest Reserve, proclaimed, 7346.

Jicarilla Agency, N. Mex., appropriation for Apaches on, recommended, 4692.

Jicarilla Apache Reservation, N. Mex., appropriations to settlers for improvements on, recommended, 4696.

Jingoism.—A political term borrowed from the English and applied to that style of writing or oratory usually known as spread-eagle or braggadocio. The mild oath "by jingo" is a corruption of "by Gingou," i.e., by St. Gingoulph. During the war in Bulgaria between Russia and Turkey in 1877 the British Conservatives under Lord Beaconsfield, the premier, strongly advocated English intervention in behalf of Turkey. The Liberals, under Gladstone, were equally determined to avoid trouble and urged that Turkey be left to herself. Popular interest in the discussion grew to the point where it found expression in the music halls. "Jingo" was soon derisively applied to the war party, and they proudly accepted it. The term has since been commonly applied both in England and America to parties extravagantly enthusiastic in defense of the national honor.

Johanna Island:

Correspondence of Commodore Shufeldt regarding condition of, referred to, 4536.

Treaty with King of, 4536.

John Adams, The, operations of, referred to, 2909.

John Brown's Raid. (See Brown's Insurrection.)

John S. Bryan, The, claim of, against Brazil adjusted, 2116.

Johnson, Andrew.—April 15, 1865-March 3, 1869.

Twentieth Administration—Republican (continued).

Secretary of State—
  William H. Seward (continued).
Secretary of the Treasury—
  Hugh McCulloch (continued).
Secretary of War—
  Edwin M. Stanton (continued).
  U. S. Grant.
  Lorenzo Thomas.
  John M. Schofield.
Secretary of the Navy—
  Gideon Welles.
Secretary of the Interior—
  John P. Usher.
  James Harlan.
  O. H. Browning.
Attorney-General—
  James Speed.
  Henry Stanbery.
  William M. Evarts.
Postmaster-General—
  William Dennison.
  Alex. W. Randall.

Johnson became President on the death of Lincoln, April 15, 1865. He was Lincoln's choice for Vice-President in the latter's second term, for strong political reasons. It was felt that Johnson's election would bring to the support of the party a large body of War Democrats, but especially would it prevent the recognition of the Confederacy by Great Britain and France if a candidate were elected from a reorganized rebellious State (Tennessee) in the heart of the Confederacy.

Party Affiliation.—Johnson's earliest political activity was directed against the aristocratic government by the large landholders of Tennessee; he opposed the so-called "internal improvement" policies, and for a time suffered defeat by reason of this opposition. He was the only ardent supporter of Bell who did not go over to the Whig party. In Congress (1843-1853) he supported Jackson, the annexation of Texas, Polk's administration, and opposed internal improvements. He defended the veto power of the President and supported the compromise measures of 1850. He advocated then and later the homestead bill which the slave-holding power of the South did not favor. He occupied an intermediate position in politics by holding pronounced Union ideas which slave-holders did not appreciate, and by recognizing slavery as an institution guaranteed by the Constitution which made him unpopular with the Republicans. He never believed that any attempt at disruption of the Union would be made; but in 1860 he took positive ground against secession and declared in his speech in Congress on the joint resolution amending the Constitution that he would stand by and act in and under the Constitution. In March, 1861, when speaking of the secessionists, he declared: "I would have them arrested and tried for treason, and, if convicted, by the eternal God, they should suffer the penalty of the law at the hands of the executioner."

Tariff.—The chief revenue acts in the administration of President Johnson were those of July 28, 1866, "to protect the revenue, and for other purposes;" of March 2, 1867, "to provide revenue from imported wool, and for other purposes;" and that of Feb. 3, 1863, "to provide for the exemption of cotton from internal tax." The latter act provided that cotton imported from foreign countries after Nov. 1, 1868, should be exempt from duty. In his Third Annual Message, President Johnson (page 3773) urged a thorough revision of the revenue system. "Our internal revenue laws and impost system," he said, "should be so adjusted as to bear most heavily on articles of luxury, leaving the necessaries of life as free from taxation as may be consistent with the real wants of the Government, economically administered." He advocated a large reduction in the number of articles subject to tax as a means of simplifying and reducing the cost of revenue collection.

Public Debt.—The public debt of the United States during the administration of President Johnson stood as follows: July 1, 1866, $2,636,036,163.84; 1867, $2,508,151,211.69; 1868, $2,480,853,413.23.

In his First Annual Message (page 3563) President Johnson says: "Our debt is doubly secure—first, in the actual wealth and the still greater undeveloped resources of the country, and, next, in the character of our institutions. The most intelligent observers among political economists have not failed to remark that the public debt of a country is safe in proportion as a people are free; that the debt of a republic is safest of all."

EXTENT OF THE UNITED STATES DURING THE ADMINISTRATION OF PRESIDENT JOHNSON, 1865-1869.

(NOT INCLUDING TERRITORIES)

MAINE
1820

N.H.
1788

VT.
1791

MASS.
1788

CONN.
1788   1790

NEW YORK
1788

N.J.
1787

PENNSYLVANIA
1787

DEL.
1787

MD.
1788

WEST
VIRGINIA
1863

VIRGINIA
1788

NORTH CAROLINA
1789

SOUTH
CAROLINA
1788

GEORGIA
1788

FLORIDA
1845

OHIO
1803

MICHIGAN
1837

INDIANA
1816

KENTUCKY
1792

TENNESSEE
1796

ALABAMA
1819

MISSISSIPPI
1817

WISCONSIN
1848

ILLINOIS
1818

IOWA
1846

MISSOURI
1821

ARKANSAS
1836

LOUISIANA
1812

MINNESOTA
1858

NEBRASKA
1867

KANSAS
1861

TEXAS
1845

NEVADA
1864

OREGON
1859

CALIFORNIA
1850

FLAG OF 1869

Civil Service.—In his Third Annual Message (page 3769) President Johnson says: "It is not the theory of this Government that public offices are the property of those who hold them. They are given merely as a trust for the public benefit, sometimes for a fixed period, sometimes during good behavior, but generally they are liable to be terminated at the pleasure of the appointing power, which represents the collective majesty and speaks the will of the people. The forced retention in office of a single dishonest person may work great injury to the public interests."

Johnson, Andrew:
Acquisition of St. John and St. Thomas Islands recomm nded by, 3886.
Act containing provisions depriving of command of Army, protest of, against, 3670.
Repeal of, recommended by, 3871.
Acts to provide for more efficient government of rebel States discussed by. (See Reconstruction.)
Amnesty—
Authority for granting discussed, 3895.
Circular regarding, 3539.
Persons worth more than $20,000 to whom pardons issued referred to, 3583.
Proclamations of, 3508, 3745.
Referred to, 3659, 3669, 3722, 3779.
Annual messages of, 3551, 3643, 3756, 3870.
Biographical sketch of, 3499.
Constitutional amendments recommended by—
Abolition of slavery, 3556.
Ratification of, referred to, 3570, 3644.
Designating officer to succeed President in case of vacancy, 3837, 3889.
Election of President and Vice-President, 3837, 3889.
Election of United States Senators, 3840, 3889.
Tenure of office by judiciary of United States, 3841, 3889.
Correspondence with Gen. Grant regarding vacation of War Office by latter, 3800.
Death of, announced and honors to be paid memory of, 4283.
Death of President Lincoln announced to, 3485.
Dominican Republic discussed by. (See Santo Domingo.)
Executive orders of, 3531, 3637, 3749, 3859.
Exequaturs revoked by. (See Proclamations of, *post.*)
Finances discussed by, 3562, 3648, 3769, 3872.
Foreign policy discussed by, 3564, 3581, 3777, 3886, 3888.

Home of Jackson tendered Government, communication of, regarding, 2954.
Impeachment of—
Articles of, exhibited by House of Representatives, 3907.
Answer of President, 3926.
Replication of House of Representatives, 3951.
Letter of Chief Justice Chase respecting mode of procedure, 3916.
Proceedings of Senate sitting for trial of, 3918.
Verdict of acquittal, 3955.
Inaugural address of, 3503.
Loyal Senators and Representatives denied seats in Congress, discussed by, 3644.
Missouri troops placed on footing with others as to bounties, pocket veto, 3733.
Oath of office administered to, 3486.
Pocket veto of, 3733.
Policy of, toward Confederate States, referred to, 3667.
Portrait of, 3498.
Powers of Federal and State Governments discussed by, 3551, 3570, 3593, 3596, 3603, 3611, 3620, 3643, 3670, 3681, 3687, 3690, 3696, 3729, 3734, 3756, 3766, 3781, 3820, 3837, 3844, 3846, 3848, 3849, 3870, 3889.
Proclamations of—
Admission of Nebraska, 3714.
Amnesty, 3508, 3745, 3853, 3906.
Blockade of Southern ports removed, 3507, 3523.
Commercial restrictions in Southern States removed, 3515, 3524, 3529.
Day of mourning in memory of President Lincoln, 3504.
Postponed, 3504.
Declaring blockade established by Maximilian void, 3631.
Discriminating duties suspended on vessels of—
France, 3711.
Hawaiian Islands, 3713.
Exequaturs revoked—
Consul of—
Chile, 3625.
Frankfort, 3709.
Hanover, 3709.
Hesse, 3709.
Nassau, 3709.
Oldenburg, 3710.
Sweden and Norway, 3626.
Revocation annulled, 3630.
Vice-consul of Sweden and Norway, 3627.
Revocation annulled, 3630.
Extraordinary session of Senate, 3719.
Habeas corpus previously suspended, revoked, 3529, 3531.

Insurgent cruisers, 3506.

Martial law in Kentucky removed, 3529.

Neutrality in war in Japan, 3712.

Obstructions to laws in North and South Carolina, 3743.

Ratification of the fourteenth amendment, 3854, 3855, 3856, 3857, 3858.

Restoration into Union of—
Alabama, 3521.
Florida, 3527.
Georgia, 3516.
Mississippi, 3512.
North Carolina, 3510.
South Carolina, 3524.
Texas, 3519.

Rewards for arrest of instigators of assassination of President Lincoln, 3505.

Termination of insurrection, 3515, 3627, 3632.
Correction in date of, 3747.

Thanksgiving, 3530, 3636, 3748, 3858. (See illustration opposite 3530.)

Protest of, against act depriving, of command of Army, 3670.

Repeal of act recommended by, 3871.

Removals from office discussed by, 3690, 3767, 3820.

Republican form of government discussed by, 3566.

Restoration policy of, discussed by, 3551, 3570, 3593, 3643, 3781, 3870. (See also Provisional Governors; Reconstruction.)

Right of States to representation in Congress, discussed by, 3644.

State of the Union discussed by, 3551, 3570, 3589, 3593, 3643, 3756, 3837, 3871.

Tariff discussed by, 3773.

Thanksgiving proclamations of, 3530, 3636, 3748, 3858.

Veto messages of—
Admission of—
Arkansas, 3846.
Certain Southern States, 3748.
Colorado, 3611, 3681.
Nebraska, 3687.
Amending judiciary act, 3844.
Civil-rights bill, 3603.
Continuation of Freedmen's Bureau, 3620.
Discontinuance of Freedmen's Bureau, 3852.
Duties on imported copper and copper ores, 3903.
Elective franchise in District of Columbia, 3670.
Enabling New York and Montana Iron Mining and Manufacturing Co. to purchase lands, 3614.

Establishing Freedmen's Bureau, 3596.
Exclusion of electoral votes of States lately in rebellion, 3849.
Government of rebel States, 3696, 3743.
Acts supplementary to, 3729, 3734.
Pocket veto of Missouri volunteer bounty bill, 3733.
Surveying district of Montana, 3624.
Tenure of civil offices, 3690.
Trustees of colored schools in Washington and Georgetown, 3903.
War between the States, termination of, proclaimed, 3515, 3627, 3632.
Correction in date of, 3447.

Johnstown Flood. (See illustration opposite 5295, and description on back.)

Joint Resolution.—A resolution passed by both the House of Representatives and the Senate requiring the President's signature to become effective.

Jonathan, or Brother Jonathan.—A term used to denote the typical American. Its origin has been explained in several ways, but the most plausible seems to be that it grew out of Washington's reference to his friend and adviser, Jonathan Trumbull, governor of Connecticut.

Jones, The, sum accruing from sale of, to be paid owners of, 2111.

Jonesboro (Ga.), Battle of.—On the night of Aug. 25, 1864, Gen. Sherman gave up the direct siege of Atlanta and attempted to gain possession of the Macon railroad to the southward. A part of his forces was moved back to the Chattahoochee to the northwest and others pushed southwest. The Army of the Tennessee, under Howard, having destroyed the roads southwest of Atlanta, moved east toward Jonesboro, twenty miles south of Atlanta. Hood, learning of this movement, sent Hardee's corps to defend Jonesboro. When Howard reached the town on the evening of Aug. 30 he found Hardee in possession. The latter attacked Howard on the 31st. After an engagement of two hours the Confederates retired with a loss of 1,400 killed and wounded. During the night Hardee retired to Lovejoy. Seeing his position in Atlanta indefensible, Hood, on Sept. 1, blew up his magazines and evacuated the city, which was occupied by Gen. Slocum with the Twentieth Army Corps.

Jorgen Lorentzen, The, appropriation for seizure of, recommended, 3271.

Josephine, The, referred to, 1030.

Journals of Congress.—The proceedings of Congress from 1774 to 1788 were first published at Philadelphia. They comprised 13 octavo volumes and were completed in 1788. This is the only record of the Continental Congress and that of the Confederation (except the "Secret Journals"), but contains no debates nor laws, that body being without legislative powers, although it adopted many resolutions, ordinances, and recommendations to the states. These journals were reprinted in Washington in 1823 in 4 octavo volumes. "The Journal

Acts, and proceedings of the Convention Assembled at Philadelphia which framed the Constitution of the United States" was published at Boston in 1819. There were also published in Boston in 1821, four volumes of the "Secret Journals of the Acts and Proceedings of Congress from the First meeting thereof to the Dissolution of the Confederation by the adoption of the Constitution of the United States." According to the requirements of the Constitution, the Journals of Congress have been printed each session since its adoption. (See Annals of Congress; Cong., etc.)

Judge Advocate General, Navy Department.—This officer was authorized by act of Congress of June 8, 1880. He is appointed by the President, and must be an officer of either the Navy or the Marine Corps. He holds the title of Captain of the Navy, or, if he be appointed from the Marine Corps, the title of Colonel in the Marine Corps; and he receives the highest pay pertaining to these offices. The judge advocate general is the legal officer of the Navy Department. He acts as prosecuting officer and legal adviser in all courts-martial, and receives, revises, and records all court-martial proceedings. He also investigates the regulations concerning the naval prisons, and renders all other legal aid required by the department. (See Navy Department; Justice Department.)

Judge Advocate General. (See War Department.)

Judge-Advocates, Corps of, recommendation regarding, 4570.

Judges, Circuit:
Increase in number of, recommended, 4453, 4526, 4574, 4939, 5103, 5968.
Inequality in amount of labor assigned each, discussed, 1756.

Judges, District, increase recommended in—
Number of, 4939, 5103.
Salaries of, 5478, 5561, 7589.

Judicial Salaries. (See Salaries, Judicial.)

Judicial Integrity discussed by President Roosevelt, 7521.

Judiciary.—The Federal judiciary system was modeled after that of Great Britain. In the early history of England and of the American colonies the legislative bodies had judicial powers, and the English Parliament is still known as the High Court of Parliament, and the Legislature of Massachusetts as the General Court. Most of these powers, however, were soon transferred to more compact bodies having exclusively judicial functions. Almost the only judicial function retained by legislative bodies is the power of impeachment of high officers. The first step toward a Federal judiciary were the commissions which decided land cases between the states. Commissioners of appeal decided prize cases, and in 1781, under the Articles of Confederation, these were erected into a court. The Constitution of 1787 provided for a Supreme Court and such inferior courts as Congress might establish. By the judiciary act of 1789 circuit and district courts were established. In 1891 the circuit court of appeals was added to this system. The Court of Claims, the Court of

Private Land Claims, and a system of Territorial courts have also been established by Congress. The Judiciary system of the several states is similar in a general way to that of the United States. (See also Courts.)

The Justices of the United States Supreme Court from its establishment to the present are:

(Names of the Chief Justices in italics.)

Name	Service		Born	Died
	Term	yrs		
John Jay, N. Y.	1789–1795	6	1745	1826
John Rutledge, S. C.	1789–1791	2	1739	1800
William Cushing, Mass.	1789–1810	21	1733	1810
James Wilson, Pa.	1789–1798	9	1742	1798
John Blair, Va.	1789–1796	7	1732	1800
Robert H. Harrison, Md.	1789–1790	1	1745	1790
James Iredell, N. C.	1790–1799	9	1751	1799
Thomas Johnson, Md.	1791–1793	2	1732	1819
William Paterson, N. J.	1793–1806	13	1745	1806
John Rutledge, S. C.	1795–1795	..	1739	1800
Samuel Chase, Md.	1796–1811	15	1741	1811
Oliver Ellsworth, Ct.	1796–1800	4	1745	1807
Bushrod Washington, Va.	1798–1829	31	1762	1829
Alfred Moore, N. C.	1799–1804	5	1755	1810
John Marshall, Va.	1801–1835	34	1755	1835
William Johnson, S. C.	1804–1834	30	1771	1834
Brock Livingston, N. Y.	1806–1823	17	1757	1823
Thomas Todd, Ky.	1807–1826	19	1765	1826
Joseph Story, Mass.	1811–1845	34	1779	1845
Gabriel Duval, Md.	1811–1836	25	1752	1844
Smith Thompson, N. Y.	1823–1843	20	1767	1843
Robert Trimble, Ky.	1826–1828	2	1777	1828
John McLean, Ohio	1829–1861	32	1785	1861
Henry Baldwin, Pa.	1830–1844	14	1779	1844
James M. Wayne, Ga.	1835–1867	32	1790	1867
Roger B. Taney, Md.	1836–1864	28	1777	1864
Philip P. Barbour, Va.	1836–1841	5	1783	1841
John Catron, Tenn.	1837–1865	28	1786	1865
John McKinley, Ala.	1837–1852	15	1780	1852
Peter V. Daniel, Va.	1841–1860	19	1785	1860
Samuel Nelson, N. Y.	1845–1872	27	1792	1873
Levi Woodbury, N. H.	1845–1851	6	1789	1851
Robert C. Grier, Pa.	1846–1870	23	1794	1870
Benj. R. Curtis, Mass.	1851–1857	6	1809	1874
John A. Campbell, Ala.	1853–1861	8	1811	1889
Nathan Clifford, Me.	1858–1881	23	1803	1881
Noah H. Swayne, Ohio.	1861–1881	20	1804	1884
Samuel F. Miller, Iowa.	1862–1890	28	1816	1890
David Davis, Ill.	1862–1877	15	1815	1886
Stephen J. Field, Cal.	1863–1897	34	1816	1899
Salmon P. Chase, Ohio.	1864–1873	9	1808	1873
William Strong, Pa.	1870–1880	10	1808	1895
Joseph P. Bradley, N. J.	1870–1892	22	1813	1892
Ward Hunt, N. Y.	1872–1882	10	1811	1886
Morrison R. Waite, Ohio.	1874–1888	14	1816	1888
John M. Harlan, Ky.	1877–1911	34	1833	1911
William B. Woods, Ga.	1880–1887	7	1824	1887
Stanley Matthews, Ohio.	1881–1889	8	1824	1889
Horace Gray, Mass.	1881–1902	21	1828	1902
Samuel Blatchford, N. Y.	1882–1893	11	1820	1893
Lucius Q. C. Lamar, Miss.	1888–1893	5	1825	1893
Melville W. Fuller, Ill.	1888–1910	22	1833	1910
David J. Brewer, Kan.	1889–1910	21	1837	1910
Henry B. Brown, Mich.	1890–1906	16	1836	....
George Shiras, Jr., Pa.	1892–1903	11	1832	....
Howell E. Jackson, Tenn.	1893–1895	2	1832	1895
Edward D. White, La.	1894–1910	16	1845	....
Rufus W. Peckham, N. Y.	1895–1909	14	1838	1909
Joseph McKenna, Cal.	1898–	..	1843	....
Oliver W. Holmes, Mass.	1902–	..	1841	....
William R. Day, Ohio.	1903–	..	1849	....
William H. Moody, Mass.	1906–1910	4	1853	....
Horace H. Lurton, Tenn.	1909–1914	5	1844	1914
Charles E. Hughes, N. Y.	1910–1916	6	1862	....
Willis Van Devanter, Wyo	1910–	..	1859	....
Joseph R. Lamar, Ga.	1910–1916	6	1857	1916
Edward D. White, La.	1910–	..	1845	....
Mahlon Pitney, N. J.	1912–	..	1858	....
Jas. C. McReynolds, Tenn.	1914–	..	1862	....
Louis D. Brandeis, Mass.	1916–	..	1856	....
John H. Clarke, Ohio.	1916–	..	1857	....

Judiciary System (see also Justice, Department of):

Act—

Making appropriation for certain judicial expenses vetoed, 4493.
Regarding judiciary act vetoed, 3844.

Constitutional amendment regarding tenure of office by judiciary of United States, recommended, 3841, 3889.

Extension and revision of, recommended by President—

Adams, John, 279, 296.
Adams, J. Q., 880, 958.
Arthur, 4729.
Cleveland, 4939, 5103, 5879, 5968.
Jackson, 1024, 1121, 1168, 1336, 1396.
Jefferson, 319.
Lincoln, 3250.
Pierce, 2750, 2765, 2825.
Washington, 119, 125, 143.

Judicial districts, increase in, recommended, 4253.

Misdemeanors, trial of, by United States commissioners, recommended, 4939, 5879.

Modifications in, recommended, 3250.

Witnesses' and jurors' fees, referred to, 4730, 4770, 4836.

Jugo-Slavs, National Aspirations of. (See Czecho-Slovaks and Jugo-Slavs.)

Juilliard vs. Greenman.—One of several important legal-tender cases. Juilliard having contracted a sale of cotton for $5,122.90 to Greenman, the latter paid $22.90 in coin (which was accepted) and offered payment of the residue in United States notes. Juilliard refused to accept the notes, demanding gold or silver. The case came before the circuit court for the southern district of New York, which found a verdict for Greenman on the ground that notes issued by the United States are legal tender for payment of any debt. The Supreme Court, March 3, 1884, the case having been appealed to that tribunal on a writ of error, affirmed this judgment, thus establishing the constitutionality of the legal-tender act of March 31, 1862. George F. Edmunds and Benjamin F. Butler appeared as counsel in this case, the former for plaintiff in error, the latter for defendant. Justice Gray, in delivering the opinion, stated that the prohibition in the Constitution of the United States to the several States to coin money, emit bills of credit, or make anything but gold and silver coin a legal tender for debts does not deny to Congress either of these powers. These are powers incident to sovereignty, and the impressing upon Treasury notes the quality of being legal tender in payment of private debts is an appropriate means, conducive and plainly adapted to the execution of the undoubted powers of Congress, consistent with the letter and spirit, and therefore within the meaning, of the Constitution. The wisdom and expediency of such meaning is a political question to be determined by Congress, and not a judicial question to be afterwards passed upon by the courts. Justice Field filed a dissenting opinion.

Jules et Marie, The, collision with United States Steamer *San Jacinto*, appropriation to former recommended, 3343.

Junket.—A word applied to any feast or merry-making, convivial entertainment, or picnic. Politically, any trip, excursion, or entertainment by an official at public expense under the guise of public service.

Jurisdiction.—1. The division or district within which a given court of justice or other body has authority to act. 2. The character of litigation in which a given court has authority to act.

Jurors, fees of, referred to, 4730, 4770, 4836.

Jury.—A certain number of men selected according to law and sworn to inquire into or to determine facts concerning a cause or an accusation submitted to them and to declare the truth according to the evidence adduced. The custom of trying accused persons before a jury as practiced in this country and England is the natural outgrowth of rudimentary forms of trials in vogue among our Anglo-Saxon ancestors. The ancient Romans also had a form of trial before a presiding judge and a body of *judices*. The right of trial by jury is guaranteed by the Constitution in all criminal cases and at common law in cases where the amount in dispute exceeds $20. A petit or trial jury consists of 12 men selected by lot from among all the citizens residing within the jurisdiction of the court. Their duty is to determine questions of fact in accordance with the weight of testimony presented and report their finding to the presiding judge. An impartial jury is assured by the practice of drawing by lot and then giving the accused the right to dismiss a certain number without reason and certain others for good cause. Each of the jurymen must meet certain legal requirements as to capacity in general and fitness for the particular case upon which he is to sit, and must take an oath to decide without prejudice and according to testimony presented. A coroner's jury or jury of inquest is usually composed of from seven to fifteen persons summoned to inquire into the cause of sudden or unexplained deaths. (See also Grand Jury.)

Jury System discussed, 319.

Justice, Department of.—The several colonies, following the custom of England, had their attorneys-general from early times. By the Judiciary Act of Sept. 24, 1789, the first Congress under the Constitution directed the appointment of an Attorney-General who should act as legal adviser to the President and heads of Departments and conduct cases in the Supreme Court in which the United States was concerned. The small salary of $1,500 a year which Congress voted was fixed on the supposition that the Attorney-General would devote only a part of his time to his official duties. Edmund Randolph, however, the first occupant of the office, devoted his entire time to questions which arose in connection with the organization of the courts and their procedure. The salary was gradually increased until, in 1853, it was made $8,000, equal to those of the other members of the Cabinet. No clerical force was provided, however, and

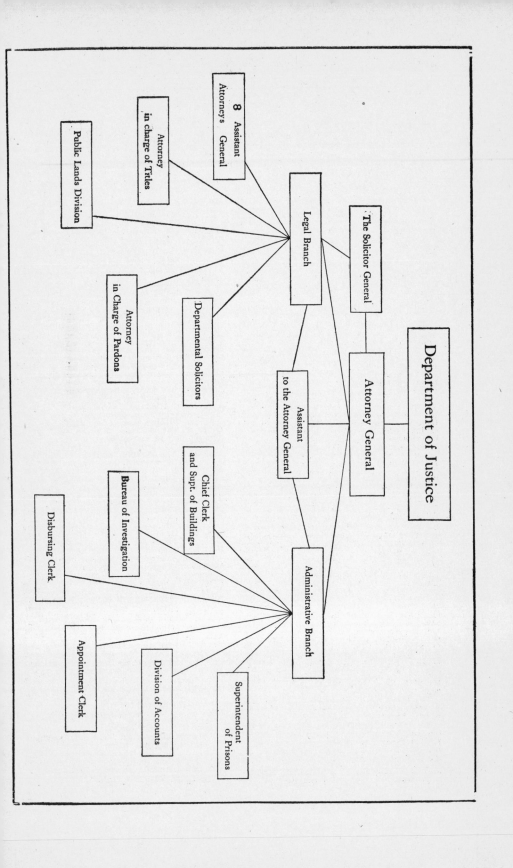

Department of Justice

Attorney General

The Solicitor General

Assistant to the Attorney General

Legal Branch

8 Assistant Attorney's General

Attorney in charge of Titles

Public Lands Division

Attorney in Charge of Pardons

Deparmental Solicitors

Administrative Branch

Chief Clerk and Supt. of Buildings

Bureau of Investigation

Disbursing Clerk

Appointment Clerk

Division of Accounts

Superintendent of Prisons

not until 1818, during the attorney-general-ship of William Wirt, was any appropriation made for clerical hire or office expenses. The clerical force was gradually increased until, in 1855, it consisted of nine employees, but the First Assistant Attorney-General was not appointed until 1859.

A very important step was taken in the organization of the Department in 1861, when the Attorney-General was given control over the various district attorneys.

By an act of Congress of 1870 what had been the Attorney-General's office was formally organized as the Department of Justice. Under this act the office of Solicitor-General was created; two Assistant Attorneys General (since increased to eight) were provided for, and the law officers of the other Departments were placed under the Attorney-General's control. Since its organization the work of the Department and the number of its employees have steadily increased until, at the present time, about two hundred and sixty officers and employees in Washington and nearly thirteen hundred in various parts of the United States are under the control of the Department.

The Attorney-General, the head of the Department, is the chief legal officer of the country. He is and has been from the beginning, a member of the President's Cabinet, and gives his advice and opinions when consulted by the President or heads of Departments. He also supervises the work of the district attorneys and United States marshals. Opinions on Constitutional questions must come from the Attorney-General himself; opinions on other matters may be given by his assistants. Trials in which the Government is interested may be conducted by the Attorney-General or the Solicitor-General, who acts as his assistant and assumes his duties in his absence.

The Assistant to the Attorney-General, an office distinct from those of Assistant Attorneys-General, has special charge of matters arising out of the anti-trust and interstate commerce laws (q. v.).

Eight Assistant Attorneys-General and one Special Assistant aid the Attorney-General and Solicitor-General, some having charge of special lines of business, such as the defense of cases in the Court of Claims (q. v.) and before the Spanish Treaty Claims Commission. The Special Assistant Attorney-General is at the head of the Bureau of Insular and Territorial Affairs. Special attorneys may be appointed when necessary. The Attorney-General also has supervision and control of the law officers connected with the various Departments, that is to say the Assistant Attorneys-General for the Interior and Post Office Departments, the Solicitors of the Departments of State and the Treasury, and the Solicitor of Internal Revenue in the Treasury Department. These act as chief law officers of the Department or office with which they are connected. A General Agent of the Department has charge of United States jails and prisons, and an Accounting Division examines the accounts of United States district attorneys and marshals.

The table in the next column is a list of Attorneys-General and the Presidents under whom they served.

For more detailed information as to the scope and activities of the Department of Justice consult the index references to the Presidents' Messages and Encyclopedic articles under the following headings:

Assistant Attorneys- Assistant to the At-
General. torney-General.

Attorney-General. Courts, Supreme.
Attorney in Charge Customs Court.
of Titles. Judiciary.
Bureau of Investiga- Public Lands Divi-
tion. sion.
Commerce Court. Solicitor-General.
Court of Claims. Solicitors, Depart-
Courts. mental.
Courts-martial.

President	Attorney-General	Appointed
Washington	Edmund Randolph, Virginia...	1789
"	William Bradford, Pennsylvania.	1794
"	Charles Lee, Virginia	1795
Adams....	" "	1797
"	Theophilus Parsons, Mass......	1801
Jefferson...	Levi Lincoln, Massachusetts....	1801
"	...Robert Smith, Maryland......	1805
"	...John Breckinridge, Kentucky..	1805
"	...Cæsar A. Rodney, Delaware....	1807
Madison....	"	1809
"	...William Pinkney, Maryland....	1811
"	...Richard Rush, Pennsylvania....	1814
Monroe....	" "	1817
"	William Wirt, Virginia........	1817
J.Q.Adams.	" "	1825
Jackson....	John McP. Berrien, Georgia....	1829
"	...Roger B. Taney, Maryland....	1831
"	...Benjamin F. Butler, New York..	1833
Van Buren..	" "	1837
"	.Felix Grundy, Tennessee.......	1838
"	Henry D. Gilpin, Pennsylvania..	1840
Harrison...	John J. Crittenden, Kentucky...	1841
Tyler......	"	1841
"	Hugh S. Legare, South Carolina.	1841
"	John Nelson, Maryland.........	1843
Polk......	John Y. Mason, Virginia.......	1845
"	Nathan Clifford, Maine........	1846
"	Isaac Toucey, Connecticut.....	1848
Taylor.....	Reverdy Johnson, Maryland....	1849
Fillmore...	John J. Crittenden, Kentucky...	1850
Pierce.....	Caleb Cushing, Massachusetts..	1850
Buchanan..	Jeremiah S. Black, Pennsylvania.	1856
"	Edwin M. Stanton, Ohio.......	1886
Lincoln....	Edward Bates, Missouri.......	1184
"	Titian J. Coffey, Pennsylvania..	1733
"	James Speed, Kentucky.......	1866
Johnson...	" "	1865
"	Henry Stanbery, Ohio.........	1866
"	William M. Evarts, New York...	1868
Grant.....	Ebenezer R. Hoar, Mass.......	1869
"	Amos T. Ackerman, Georgia....	1870
"	George H. Williams, Oregon....	1871
"	Edwards Pierrepont, New York..	1875
"	Alphonso Taft, Ohio..........	1876
Hayes.....	Charles Devens, Massachusetts..	1877
Garfield...	Wayne MacVeagh, Penn.......	1881
Arthur....	Benjamin H. Brewster, Penn...	1881
Cleveland..	Augustus H. Garland, Arkansas..	1885
B. Harrison	William H. H. Miller, Indiana...	1889
Cleveland..	Richard Olney, Massachusetts...	1893
"	Judson Harmon, Ohio.........	1895
McKinley..	Joseph McKenna, California....	1897
"	John W. Griggs, New Jersey...	1897
"	Philander C. Knox, Penn......	1901
Roosevelt..	Philander C. Knox, Penn......	1901
"	William H. Moody, Mass.......	1904
"	Charles J. Bonaparte, Maryland.	1907
Taft......	Geo. W. Wickersham, New York.	1909
Wilson....	James C. McReynolds, Tenn....	1913
"	T. W. Gregory, Texas..........	1914

Justice, Department of (see also Judiciary System):

Building for, recommended, 6343.

Discussed by President—

Cleveland, 4938, 5578, 5879, 5968.

Grant, 4153.

Harrison, Benj., 5550, 5632, 5755.

Operations of, discussed, 7522.

Reorganization of, 7368.

Kansas.—One of the western group of states; nickname, "The Garden State," "The Sunflower State," etc.; motto, "Ad astra per aspera" ("To the stars through difficulties"). It is situated in the central part of the Union and extends from lat. 37° to 40° north and from long. 94° 38' to 102° west. Kansas is bounded on the north by Nebraska, on the east by Missouri (separated in part by the Missouri River), on the south by Oklahoma and on the west by Colorado, and has an area of 82,158 square miles. It was a part of the Louisiana Purchase and was made a territory in 1854.

The Topeka constitution, prohibiting slavery, was framed in 1855 and the Lecompton constitution, which sanctioned slavery, in 1857. A civil war broke out between the adherents of these two constitutions. (See illustration opposite 2881.) Finally, in 1859, the Wyandotte constitution, forbidding slavery, was adopted. The State was admitted to the Union Jan. 29, 1861.

Statistics of agriculture collected for the last Federal census, place the number of farms in the State at 177,841, comprising 43,384,799 acres, valued with stock and improvements at $2,039,389,910, an increae of $1,175,289,624 over the 1900 report. The average value of farm land per acre was $25.45, as compared with $12.77 in 1900. The value of domestic animals, poultry, etc., was $253,528,577, including 3,079,403 cattle, valued at $80,557,443; 1,147,056 horses, $112,758,108; 208,409 mules, $25,-629,418; 3,050,157 swine, $24,708,885; 272,475 sheep, $1,209,931. The yield and value of field crops for 1911 is given as follows: Corn, 8,700,000 acres, 126,150,-000 bushels, $79,474,000; wheat, 4,810,000 acres, 51,387,000 bushels, $46,762,000; oats, 2,000,000 acres, 30,000,000 bushels, $13,500,000; rye, 18,000 acres, 198,000 bushels, $160,000; potatoes, 80,000 acres, 1,760,000 bushels, $1,866,000; hay, 1,649,-000 acres, 1,402,000 tons, $13,880,000.

The mineral products of the State for 1910 were valued at $28,304,191, consisting of coal, zinc, lead, clay products, petroleum, natural gas, sand, gravel, and stone. The coal production for 1910 was 4,921,451 short tons, valued at $7,914,709, a decrease of more than two million tons from the amount produced the previous year, on account of a strike among the mine-workers. The number of men employed in the mines of the State during 1910 was 12,870, of whom 10,346 were idle more than half time.

Kansas has 8,900 miles of steam railway and 268 miles of electric lines. The population in 1910 was 1,690,949.

The number of manufacturing establishments in Kansas having an annual output valued at $500 or more at the beginning of 1915 was 3,136. The amount of capital invested was $163,790,000, giving employment to 53,032 persons, using material valued at $261,148,000, and turning out finished goods worth $323,234,000. Salaries and wages paid amounted to $34,983,000.

(See also Lecompton Constitution; Topeka Constitution; Wyandotte Constitution.)

Kansas:

Act—

For sale of Indian reservation, 4656.

To provide for sale of New York Indian lands in, vetoed, 5238.

Admission of, into Union discussed, 2980, 3002, 3028.

Recommended, 2893, 3009.

Affairs of, referred to, 2951, 2995, 2996.

Boundary line of, survey of, recommended, 2873.

Chief justice of, functions of, referred to, 2958.

Constitutional convention in, discussed, 3002, 3030.

Disorders and revolutions in, discussed, 2873, 2885, 2915, 2937, 2980, 3002, 3028, 3177.

Proclamation against, 2923.

Election and qualifications for electors discussed, 2885, 2980, 3002, 3028, 3177.

Expenditures for persons called into service of United States in, 2953, 2954.

Fortifications in Lawrence, referred to, 3894.

Government organization in, disturbed, 2885, 2894, 2898, 2937, 2980, 3002, 3028, 3177.

Proclamation against unlawful combinations, 2923.

Indian refugees in, referred to, 3410.

Joint resolution authorizing grant of lands to, for benefit of agriculture, etc., vetoed, 5308.

Meetings in, interfered with by Army, 2915.

Memorial from citizens of, regarding creation of new territory, etc., 3111.

Military forces of United States sent to, referred to, 4013.

Public lands of, 6706.

Relief for suffering people in—

Recommended, 3184.

Referred to, 4272.

Slavery in, discussed, 2962, 2981, 3002, 3028.

Soldiers employed in, to arrest violators of law, referred to, 2908.

Troops of, treatment of, captured by insurgents, referred to, 3398.

Wea trust lands in, referred to, 3400.

Kansas Aid Society.—An organization to aid immigration into Kansas. Under the provisions of the Kansas-Nebraska Act, passed by Congress in May, 1854, the question of slavery in Kansas was left to the residents of the state for settlement, on the principle of local option or "squatter sovereignty." An immigrant aid association, which had been already formed in Massachusetts for the purpose, began sending anti-slavery settlers into the new Territory to forestall its settlement by slaveholders. Similar societies were organized in July, 1854, in New York and Connecticut. The settlers were provided with ample funds and means of defense against the settlers from the slaveholding states of the South. Meantime slavery advocates from Missouri were passing over the line and preempting large tracts of fertile lands. For four years the conflict for supremacy raged between the two parties, the anti-slavery party finally prevailing.

Kansas City, Fort Scott and Gulf Railway Co., act to authorize construction of railway through Indian Territory by, returned, 4986.

Kansas City, Oklahoma and Pacific Railway Co., act authorizing construction and operation of railway by, through Indian reservations vetoed, 6008.

Kansas Indians. (See Indian Tribes.)

Kansas-Nebraska Act.—By the Missouri Compromise of 1820 slavery was prohibited in all the region lying north of lat. 36° 30′ with the exception of that lying in the State of Missouri. As a result of the Mexican War the limits of the United States were extended from the one hundredth meridian westward to the Pacific and southward to lat. 32° 30′ north. By the Kansas-Nebraska Act, passed by Congress in May, 1854, Kansas and Nebraska were separated and organized into two distinct territories, and the question of slavery was left to the people for settlement. As both these states lie north of the line above which slavery was prohibited by the Missouri Compromise, the passage of the bill practically repealed that measure. The status of Nebraska as a free state was soon determined, but the struggle in Kansas was long and bitter. It disrupted the Whig party and led to the establishment of the Republican party, and was an important link in the chain of events that brought on the Civil War.

Kansas-Nebraska Act:

Discussed, 2982.

Referred to, 3030.

Kanso, Straits of, vessels of United States interfered with by British vessels in, referred to, 4068.

Kaskaskia Indians. (See Indian Tribes.)

Ka-ta-ka Indians. (See Indian Tribes.)

Kaw Indians. (See Indian Tribes.)

Kearsarge, The.—A United States corvette built at Portsmouth, N. H., in 1861. She carried 163 officers and men, four 32-pounder and one 28-pounder guns, and two 11-inch rifles. She was commanded by Capt. John A. Winslow. Her greatest service was the sinking of the Confederate cruiser *Alabama*, off Cherbourg, France, June 19, 1864. The *Alabama* had done much damage to United States commerce, and the *Kearsarge* had been sent to sink her. When the *Kearsarge* opened fire her superiority in point of management and gunnery was at once apparent. One of her shells cut off the *Alabama's* mizzenmast, and another exploded, killing half her crew. Feb. 2, 1894, the *Kearsarge* was wrecked on Roncador Reef, in the Caribbean Sea. (See also Alabama Claims.)

Kearsarge, The, destruction of the *Alabama* by, referred to, 3457.

Kenesaw Mountain (Ga.), Battle of.—Between the 1st and 6th of June, 1864, Sherman gradually moved his army so as to envelop Allatoona Pass. This compelled Johnston to withdraw his army from its strongly intrenched positions at New Hope Church and Acworth. Allatoona Pass was then made a depot of supplies, and June 8 Gen. Blair joined Sherman with two divisions of the Seventh Corps and a brigade of cavalry, raising his effective force to its original strength of 98,000. Johnston's force was 62,000. Sherman then advanced toward Kenesaw Mountain, and on June 14 an artillery duel took place in which the Confederate General Polk was killed. On the 15th and 17th of June the Confederates retired from Pine Mountain and Lost Mountain, and thoroughly intrenched themselves on Kenesaw Mountain. June 27 two assaults on the Confederate position were simultaneously made, one by Thomas and the other by McPherson. Both were repulsed. Nothing now remained for Sherman but to turn the position. July 2 the whole army was put in motion toward the Chattahoochee. The Confederates immediately abandoned their position on the mountain and retired to the river. Sherman's loss at the attack on Kenesaw Mountain aggregated 3,000 men including Generals Harker and McCook. The Confederate loss was 630.

Kennebec Purchase.—In 1628 the council for New England granted to William Bradford and other Plymouth colonists a tract of territory along the Kennebec and Cobbiseecontee rivers for fishing purposes. This was sold in 1661 to Tyng and others, and has since been known as the Kennebec Purchase.

Kentucky.—One of the southern group of states; nickname, "The Corn Cracker State;" motto, "United we stand, divided we fall." The name is said to mean in the language of the Indians "Dark and bloody ground." It lies between lat. 36° 30′ and 39° 6′ north and long. 82° and 89° 38′ west. It is bounded on the north by Ohio, Indiana, and Illinois (separated by the Ohio River), on the east by West Virginia (separated by the Big Sandy River) and Virginia, on the south by Tennessee, and on the west by Missouri (separated by the Mississippi River). Area, 40,598 square miles.

A vast tract of land, including what is now Kentucky, was ceded to Great Britain by the Iroquois Indians in 1684. Kentucky was explored by Daniel Boone in 1769, and the first settlement was made at Harrodsburg in 1774. It was made a county of Virginia in 1776 and admitted to the Union June 1, 1792. It took a distinguished part in the War of 1812, the Mexican War, and the Civil War. Although a slave state, Kentucky wished to preserve neutrality in the latter war. Kentucky has abundant natural resources in the shape of coal and iron mines, hard wood forests, fertile soil and great water power facilities. Tobacco, corn and wheat are the chief agricultural products, Louisville being the largest leaf tobacco market in the world.

Statistics of agriculture collected for the last Federal census place the number of farms in the State at 259,185, comprising 22,189,127 acres, valued with stock and improvements at $773,797,880. The average value of farm land was $21.83, as compared with $13.24 in 1900. The value of domestic animals, poultry, etc., was $117,486,662, including 1,000,937 cattle valued at $25,971,-571; 443,034 horses, $44,796,120; 225,043 mules, $26,402,090; 1,491,806 swine, $8,-951,692; 1,363,013 sheep, $5,573,998. The yield and value of field crops for 1911 is given as follows: Corn, 3,600,000 acres, 93,600,000 bushels, $59,968,000; wheat, 780,000 acres, 9,906,000 bushels, $9,114,-000; oats, 170,000 acres, 3,128,000 bushels, $1,564,000; rye, 22,000 acres, 204,000 bushels, $243,000; potatoes, 52,000 acres, 2,028,000 bushels, $2,170,000; hay, 450,000 acres, 428,000 tons, $7,404,000; tobacco, 345,000 acres, 303,600,000 pounds, $23,-377,200.

The principal mineral product of Kentucky is coal, the value of which constitutes about three-fourths of the value of the state's total mineral output. In 1913, according to the United States Geological Survey, the total value of the mineral production of Kentucky was about $27,000,000, of which the coal mines contributed $20,516,749. This is an increase of about $4,500,000 in value of total mineral products over the figures for 1912.

The second industry in importance, clay-working, contributed $2,914,276 in 1913, an increase of $470,536 over 1912. The quarrying industry is third in importance in the state, its products in 1913 being valued at $1,150,205, against $1,282,148 in 1912.

The petroleum production of Kentucky increased from 484,368 barrels in 1912, valued at $424,822, to 524,568 barrels in 1913, valued at $675,748, while the value of the natural gas produced decreased from $522,455 to $509,846.

Kentucky is one of the few states in which fluorspar is produced, and in 1913 the output was nearly double in quantity and value that of 1912. Other mineral products are asphalt, cement, ferro alloys, iron ore, lead, lime, mineral water, oilstones, sand and gravel, sand-lime brick, and zinc.

The receipts for the financial year ending June 30, 1911, were $7,676,588; the disbursements for the same period, $7,013,330; treasury balance, $356,289. The bonded debt of the State at the end of the fiscal year was $2,315,627.

The number of manufacturing establishments in Kentucky having an annual output valued at $500 or more at the beginning of 1915 was 4,184. The amount of capital invested was $193,423,000, giving employment to 77,865 persons, using material valued at $114,829,000, and turning out finished goods worth $230,249,000. Salaries and wages paid amounted to $43,153,000.

The Ohio and Mississippi rivers and their tributaries afford natural means of transit, and 3,432 miles of steam railway and 337 miles of electric lines traverse the State. The population for 1910 was 2,289,905.

Kentucky (see also Louisville):

Admission of, into Union, referred to, 73, 76, 78.

Amendment to Constitution, application to Congress to call convention for proposing, 3194.

Arrests in, referred to, 3278.

Constitution adopted by, referred to, 120, 122, 124.

Constitution, amendment to, application to Congress to call convention for proposing, 3194.

Digest of decisions of Supreme Court asked for, 1496.

Martial law established in, and writ of *habeas corpus* suspended by proclamation, 3420.

Proclamation revoking, 3529.

Militia of, commended for Indian service, 96.

Officers of, attempt to bring Aaron Burr to justice, 403.

Ratification of amendment to Federal Constitution by, referred to, 249, 250.

Kentucky Resolutions.—Nine resolutions prepared by Thomas Jefferson and passed by the Kentucky legislature in 1798. These and the Virginia Resolutions were the outgrowth of a feeling that the Federal party, in passing the alien and sedition laws, was making an illegitimate use of the power granted to the Government by the Constitution. The resolutions declared that the Union was not based on the "principle of unlimited submission to the General Government;" that the Constitution was a compact to which each state was a party as related to its fellow states, and that in all cases not specified in the compact each party had a right to judge for itself, as well of infractions as of the mode and measure of redress. They then proceeded to set forth the unconstitutionality of the alien and sedition laws and invited other states to join in declaring them void. A tenth resolution was passed the following year declaring that nullification of a Federal law by a state was the rightful remedy for Federal usurpation of authority. Upon these resolutions were based in part the doctrines of nullification and secession.

Kernstown (Va.), Battle of. (See Winchester (Va.), Battles of.)

Kettle Creek (Ga.), Battle of.—Feb. 14, 1779, Col. Andrew Pickens, of South Carolina, and Col. Dooley, of Georgia, with 300 men, surprised Col. Boyd's provincials on the north side of Kettle Creek, in Wilkes County, Ga. A short skirmish ensued, in which Boyd's tories were routed with inconsiderable loss on either side.

Keweenaw, The. (See *Baltimore*, The.)

Keystone State.—A nickname for Pennsylvania (q. v.). (See also States.)

Key West, Fla.:

Blockade of port of, having been inadvertently included among those which were not to be opened to commerce, removed by proclamation in April, 1865, 3482.

Fever prevalent at, 782.

Health of squadron at, referred to, 827.

Kickapoo Indians. (See Indian Tribes.)

Kidnapping of American child in Mexico referred to, 3572.

Kiel Canal, encomiums bestowed on American vessels at opening of, 6062.

Kik-ái-llus Indians. (See Indian Tribes.)

Kilbourn vs. Thompson.—A case decided by the Supreme Court in 1880 denying the right of the Senate or House of Representatives to punish anyone except their own members for contempt of their orders. Kilbourn was summoned as a witness before the House in 1876, and required to answer questions as to his private business and to produce certain papers. He refused, whereupon Sergeant-at-Arms Thompson was ordered to imprison him in the jail of the District of Columbia. He remained in prison forty-five days. He was then released on a writ of *habeas corpus*. He brought suit for false imprisonment against Thompson and the members of the committee who caused his arrest. The court decided that the House might punish its own members for disorderly conduct, but that the Constitution did not give either branch of Congress general authority to punish for contempt. It was held, Justice Miller delivering the opinion, that neither House of Congress is a part of any court of general jurisdiction. Judgment was given Kilbourn, which was paid by an appropriation by Congress.

King Philip's War.—Philip, son of Massasoit, sachem of the Wampanoag Indians and a friend to the early settlers of Plymouth, determined to drive away or kill all the European settlers in his territory. His camp was at Mount Hope, R. I., and his first blow was struck at Swansea, Mass., July 4, 1675. The settlers took up arms in defense and drove the Indians to the more remote settlements. Philip was reenforced by other tribes, but the Indians suffered many defeats and were finally subdued. Philip was shot in a swamp by a treacherous Indian and his head was carried in triumph to Plymouth. His son, the last of the line, was sold into slavery and sent to Bermuda.

Kings Mountain (S. C.), Battle of.—Early in October, 1780, Cornwallis sent Colonels Tarleton and Ferguson from Charleston to invade North Carolina, enroll local militia, and compel the allegiance of the people. On the 6th Ferguson, finding himself hotly pursued by the Americans, took up a strong position on Kings Mountain, near the boundary line between North and South Carolina. The next day his army, about 1,500 strong, was attacked by about the same number of American militia under command of Colonels Shelby, Campbell, Cleveland, McDowell, Sevier, and Williams. After a desperate struggle lasting an hour, in which Ferguson was killed, the British force surrendered. The casualties on the British side were 387 killed or so badly wounded as to be left upon the field and about 1,200 taken prisoners. The Americans lost 28 men and 60 wounded. Fifteen hundred muskets and other arms fell into the hands of the Americans.

Kitchen Cabinet.—A name applied to a certain circle of intimate friends of President Andrew Jackson. These friends were said to have more influence with the President than his official Cabinet. The principal member of the Kitchen Cabinet was Duff Green, of St. Louis, who established the newspaper, *The United States Telegraph*, in Washington. This paper was the President's organ until 1831, when Green, siding with Calhoun against Jackson, lost the latter's confidence. *The Globe*, John C. Rives and Francis P. Blair, editors, then became the President's organ, and Blair became a member of his Kitchen Cabinet. Other members were William B. Lewis, of Nashville, who was appointed Second Auditor of the Treasury; Isaac Hill, of New Hampshire, who was made Second Comptroller of the Treasury, and Amos Kendall, of Kentucky, who was made Fourth Auditor of the Treasury and finally in 1835 joined the official Cabinet as Postmaster-General. The term has also been applied to certain advisers of President John Tyler and of President Andrew Johnson, but Jackson's Kitchen Cabinet is meant when the term is used without qualification.

Kittery, Me., dry dock at, 2414.

Klamath Indians. (See Indian Tribes.)

Knights of Columbus.—A fraternal and benevolent order of Catholic men, active in all sections of the United States, Canada, Alaska, Newfoundland, Porto Rico, Philippine Islands, and Cuba. The order performs much charity work, aids educational activities, donates scholarships, provides lectures, organizes recreation, and in many other ways endeavors to increase knowledge of and to aid the functions of the Roman Catholic religion. After the entrance of the United States into the European war, the Knights of Columbus functioned actively in the United States army in providing helpful non-military service, although much of this work was undenominational and non-Catholics were eligible to partake in any of it.

The society was founded in New Haven, Connecticut on February 2, 1882. At first all members were required to participate in the insurance features of the order, but not many years after its organization provision was made for the admission of associate members, who have no part in the insurance features of the order; and at the present time the latter comprise some 75% of the Knights of Columbus membership. In 1915, the membership was 350,-000.

Knights of the Golden Circle.—A secret organization of active Southern sympathizers in some of the Northern States, especially in the Central West, during the Civil War.

Knights of Labor.—A secret order of workingmen, founded by Uriah S. Stevens in Philadelphia in 1869, and formally organized as a national body, with district and local assemblies, in 1871. It was not until 1881 that the name of the order was made public. At that time nearly all the trades were represented. Each trade formed a district, as nearly as possible. The knights are governed by a general executive board, presided over by a general master workman, which has power to order strikes and boycotts. The membership once reached 220,000. They have ordered many strikes among coal miners and railroad operatives. Perhaps the greatest strike ever undertaken by the general assembly of the order was that on the Missouri Pacific system, which failed. A general strike of the district composed of telegraphers also failed. The object of the order is the amelioration of the condition of workingmen. The order has generally been superseded by the Federation of Labor.

Know Nothings. (See American Party.)

Knoxville (Tenn.), Siege of.—Sept. 3, 1863, Gen. Burnside, with the Army of the Ohio, occupied Knoxville, Tenn. Upon his advance the Confederate General Buckner evacuated eastern Tennessee and joined Bragg at Chattanooga. Early in November Longstreet, with 16,000 men, was detached from Bragg's army and sent to regain possession of Knoxville. Burnside, with a force of 12,000, met Longstreet at Campbells Station, Tenn., Nov. 16, and retarded his advance long enough to enable him to concentrate his forces at Knoxville. Longstreet then besieged that town. Nov. 18 and 20 he unsuccessfully assaulted the Federal works. Meantime Grant had defeated Bragg at Chattanooga, and Sherman, with 25,000 men, was sent to the relief of Burnside. Dec. 5, 1863. Longstreet, hearing of the approach of Sherman, raised the siege and retreated toward Virginia. Sherman thereupon returned to the line of the Hiawassee, leaving two divisions under Gen. Granger to sustain Burnside.

Kootenay Indians. (See Indian Tribes.)

Korea. (See Japan, *Chosen*.)

Chemulpo, agreement respecting foreign settlement at, 5391.

Consular courts in, organization of, recommended, 5368, 5471.

Regulations for, 5675.

Diplomatic relations with, discussed, 4761, 4915, 5367.

Legation of United States, at premises for, discussed, 4823.

Military instructors desired by, and recommendations regarding, 4856, 4915.

Minister and party sent to conclude treaty with, treacherously attacked, 4099.

Result of expedition discussed, 4099.

Mission from, received, 5367.

Treaty with, 4698.

Referred to, 4715, 4757, 4761.

War between China and Japan regarding. (See Wars, Foreign.)

Korea, Treaties with.—A treaty of amity, commerce, and navigation was concluded in 1882. It provides for perpetual peace and friendship between the rulers and citizens of both countries. Consular representatives are to be appointed and accredited according to the regulations commonly governing such matters. Humane treatment is to be extended to all vessels in distress, and the customary provisions are made for their relief. United States vessels conducting clandestine trade at a port not open to foreign commerce shall be confiscated. Citizens are to be protected within the dominions of the other country. In cases of controversy between citizens of the one country and subjects of the other, the trial is to be made before a judge of the nationality of the defendant, and all facilities shall extend to the counsel of the plaintiff. This condition shall obtain in Chosen until such time as in the opinion of the United States the judicial conditions and administration of justice in that country shall conform to the standard of the United States; at which time citizens of the United States in Korea shall become subject to the native authorities.

The tariff on all articles of daily use imported into Korea shall never exceed ten per cent. of the value of such goods; articles of luxury, as foreign wines and tobacco, watches and clocks shall be subject to an import duty not to exceed thirty per cent. of the value, and articles of native produce, five per cent., *ad valorem.* The tonnage duties on ships entering harbors or ports in Chosen shall be five mace per ton, payable once every three months. The holding of land, construction of buildings, while freely permitted in any of the ports open to foreigners, is restricted that the property shall always be under the jurisdiction of the authorities of Chosen, and that the only extraterritorial rights in connection with these matters shall be those conferred by this treaty. The trade in Chosen shall be restricted to the open ports and coastwise trade by the citizens of the United States is prohibited. Trade in opium between the two countries is absolutely forbidden. In times of threatened famine in Chosen, the emperor may, at discretion, forbid the export of foodstuffs; the ex-

portation of rice and breadstuffs from the open port of Yin-Chuen is at all times forbidden. Ginseng may not be exported from any port of Chosen. Only the government officials of Chosen may purchase and bring in arms and munitions of war.

Free emigration and immigration between the two countries is permitted to students. A fuller treaty shall be made between the two countries within five years from the date of conclusion of this tentative agreement, the later treaty to be based upon the experience of the two nations on existing conditions. Any privileges which may hereafter be accorded by Chosen to other foreign nations shall accrue to the government of the United States.

The agreement between Japan and Korea of 1905 provides:

"The Government of Japan undertakes to see to the execution of the treaties actually existing between Korea and other powers and the Government of Korea engages not to conclude hereafter any act or engagement having an international character except through the medium of the Government of Japan."

Krebs, Ind. T., miners killed at, 5663.

Ku-Klux Klan.—A secret organization in several of the southern states soon after the Civil War. Its exact origin was never given. It was claimed that a copy of the constitution (prescript, as it was termed) of the order was obtained, from which it was learned that their lodges were called dens; the masters, cyclops; the members, ghouls. A county was called a province and was governed by a grand giant and four goblins. A Congressional district was a dominion, governed by a grand titan and six furies. A state was a realm, governed by a grand dragon and eight hydras. The whole country was the empire, governed by a grand wizard and ten genii. They appeared only at night and carried banners. Their dress was a covering for the head, descending over the body, holes being cut for eyes and mouth, the covering being decorated in any startling or fantastic manner. Its object was to suppress the negro as a factor in politics, by means of intimidation and terrorization, and, for a time, many of the most prominent and respectable citizens of the southern states belonged to it; but later the more respectable element withdrew and the organization outran its original purpose. In many localities gross disorders and crimes were committed by persons in disguise, who were either members of the Klan or who were using the disguise and methods of the order for evil purposes. A Congressional investigation followed, and President Grant in a message asked for legislation to suppress the order, etc. The Ku-Klux act (see Force Bill) was passed in 1871. The same year the president issued proclamations on the subject, and soon thereafter the Klans dispersed and ceased to exist. (See illustration opposite 4104.)

Ku-Klux Klan (see also Rifle Clubs; White Leagues):

Discussed, 4104, 4117.

Proclamations against, 4086, 4088, 4089, 4090, 4093.

La Abra Silver Mining Co., claim of, against Mexico, 4697, 4760, 4982, 4987, 5193, 5502, 6432, 6679.

La Crosse, Wis., bridge over Mississippi River at, 4148.

La Manche, The, appropriation for claims regarding, recommended, 3399.

La Pensee, The, judicial proceedings against, referred to, 706.

La Plata River:

Transactions in region of, affecting political relations with other powers referred to, 3890, 3898, 3899.

Treaties regarding navigation of, 2813.

Labor (see Commerce and Labor, Department of):

Compensated plantation, referred to, 3470.

Discussed by President—

Cleveland, 4979, 5095, 5111, 5359.

Grant, 4255.

Lincoln, 3258.

Roosevelt, 6715, 6786, 6895, 6898, 6973, 6983, 7035, 7089, 7205, 7210, 7213.

Principle of arbitration referred to, 6348, 7089.

Labor Agitator.—Any person who agitates for the improvement of the conditions of the laboring class. Usually used contemptuously to describe the organizers of the American Federation of Labor or of other trade unions (q. v.), the implication of the term in this sense being that such person is endeavoring to make workingmen discontented without improving their condition. (See Agitator.)

Labor, Bureau of, enlargement of, by adding power of arbitration recommended, 4979, 5111.

Work of, discussed, 6898.

Labor, Commission of, establishment of, with power of arbitration recommended, 4979, 5111.

Labor, Commissioner of:

Annual report of, transmitted, 5502, 5569, 5674, 5782, 5909.

Reports of, on—

Building and loan associations, 5909.

Compulsory insurance of working-men in Germany, etc., 5782.

Gothenburg system of regulating liquor traffic, 5785.

Housing of working people, 6001.

Industrial education, 5782.

Slums of cities, 5911.

Labor Day.—The first Monday in September has been made a holiday by thirty-six states and by the United States in the District of Columbia. It was first observed in Colorado in 1887. Meetings for the discussion of labor questions are held. There are usually parades, picnics, and dances. In Europe May 1 is celebrated as a labor festival and there are demonstrations by workingmen.

Labor, Department of.—In response to petitions from labor organizations and trade unions for a department of the government to look after their interests the Bureau of Labor was established in the Interior Department by act of Congress of June 27, 1884. After an existence of four years the bureau was raised to the dignity of a department June 13, 1888, and Carroll D. Wright was placed at its head as Commissioner. He was later succeeded by Charles P. Neill. When Congress established the Department of Commerce and Labor Feb. 14, 1903, the activities in behalf of labor were placed under the jurisdiction of the new secretary. (See Commerce, Department of.)

The Sixty-second Congress, on the last day of its third session, March 4, 1913, separated the Department of Commerce and Labor into the Department of Commerce and the Department of Labor.

The Bureau of Labor Statistics, the Children's Bureau and the Bureaus of Immigration and Naturalization were placed under the new Secretary, with directions to investigate and report to Congress a plan for the co-ordination of the powers of the present bureaus, commissions and departments so far as they relate to labor and its conditions, in order to harmonize and unify them. The new Secretary was charged with the duty of fostering, promoting, and developing the welfare of the wage-earners of the United States, improving their working conditions, and advancing their opportunities for profitable employment. He has power under the law to act as mediator and to appoint commissioners of conciliation in labor disputes whenever in his judgment the interests of industrial peace may require it to be done.

William Bauchop Wilson, member of Congress from Pennsylvania, who had been chairman of the House Committee on Labor, was made the first Secretary.

For more detailed information of the scope of the activities of the Labor Department, consult the Index references to the President's Messages and Encyclopedic articles under the following headings:

Children's Bureau.   Commissioner of
Commissioner of   Naturalization.
Immigration.   Immigration.
Commissioner of
Labor Statistics.

Labor, Hours of:

Referred to, 6348, 6455.

Uniform course regarding, recommended, 1819.

Wages of Government employees not to be affected by reduction in, proclaimed, 3969, 4129.

Labor, International Exposition of, at Barcelona, Spain, discussed, 5177, 5399.

Labor, Knights of. (See Knights of Labor.)

Labor Parties. (See the several parties.)

Labor Question:

Attitude of leaders toward courts, 7210.

Child-labor, 6898, 6980, 6983, 7436.

Discussed by President Roosevelt, 6786, 6895, 6898, 6899, 6980, 6983, 7089, 7205, 7210, 7213.

Hours of railroad employees, 6982, 7035.

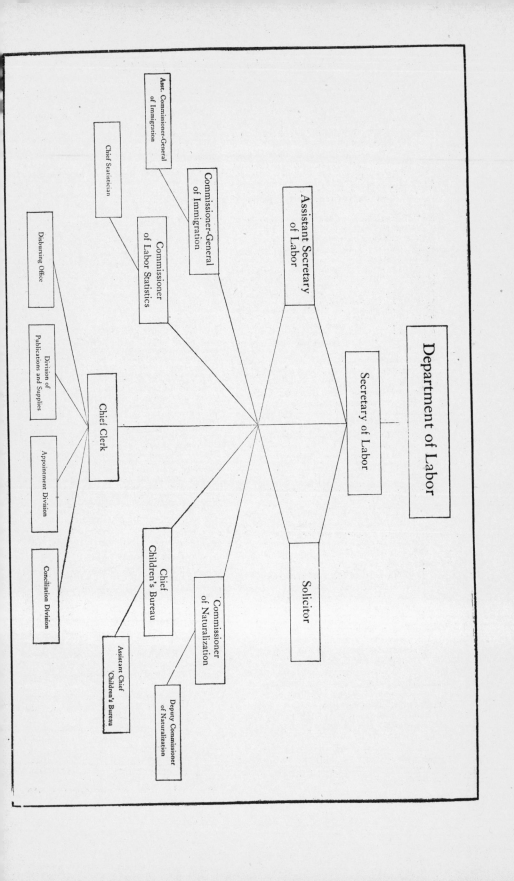

Department of Labor

Secretary of Labor

Assistant Secretary of Labor

Solicitor

Commissioner-General of Immigration

Asst. Commissioner-General of Immigration

Commissioner of Labor Statistics

Chief Statistician

Chief Clerk

Disbursing Office

Division of Publications and Supplies

Appointment Division

Conciliation Division

Chief Children's Bureau

Assistant Chief Children's Bureau

Commissioner of Naturalization

Deputy Commissioner of Naturalization

Power of courts to grant injunctions in labor disputes, 6983.

Relations of National Government to the, 6648, 6715, 6897.

(See also Arbitration, Labor, and Strike Commission.)

Labor Reform Party.—This party was organized in 1872, and in Convention at Columbus, Ohio, placed in nomination David Davis for President, and Joel Parker for Vice President, adopting a platform calling for just distribution of the fruits of labor.

Labor Statistics. (See Commissioner of Labor Statistics.)

Labor Statistics, Bureaus of.—Many states and the United States have bureaus of labor statistics. The first office of the kind was established in Massachusetts by an act of June 23, 1869. Others were established as follows: In Pennsylvania in 1872; Connecticut in 1873 (abolished in 1875 and reestablished in 1885); Ohio in 1877; New Jersey in 1878; Indiana, Missouri and Illinois in 1879; California, Wisconsin, New York, and Michigan in 1883; Maryland and Iowa in 1884. Thirteen states other than those named have organized labor bureaus.

Labor Statistics, Bureau of, act to establish, omissions in, referred to, 4807.

Compilation of labor laws of various States, recommended, 6898.

Exemption from anti-trust law, of organizations of, 7195.

Principle of arbitration referred to, 7036, 7089.

Strikes and lockouts, 7088.

Laborers, Alien, discussed, 6065, 6348, 6455.

Laborers, Government, appointment of, 6707, 6781, 6804.

Lady Franklin Bay Expedition, expedition fitted out for relief of, 4835.

Board to consider expedition to be sent, 4813.

Offer of rewards for rescuers of, discussed, 4795.

Recommended, 4693, 4787.

Vessel presented by Great Britain to United States to aid in, 4791.

Return of, to Great Britain, 4917. Recommended, 4855.

Lafayette, George W., Letters from:

Acknowledging honors to father, 1344.

Transmitting bequest from father to Congress of Declaration of Independence engraved on copper, 1342.

Lafayette, Ind., act for erection of public buildings at, vetoed, 5154.

Lafayette, Marquis de:

Death of, announced, 1273.

Honors ordered paid to memory of, 1313.

Resolutions of Congress on, 1343.

Declaration of Independence engraved on copper bequeathed to Congress by, 1342.

Letters from son of, acknowledging honors paid to, 1344.

Lafitte & Co., memorial from trustees of, presented, 1648.

Laissez-faire. — Meaning "leave alone." The theory that the Government shall not interfere with individual pursuits. In contradistinction to paternalism.

Lake Borgne (La.), Battle of.—The British army, repulsed at Baltimore, retired to the island of Jamaica. Being there reinforced by a sufficient number to make a total of above 7,000 men, it sailed from Jamaica Nov. 26, 1814, in Admiral Cochrane's ships, with the intention of capturing New Orleans, and thus securing possession of the Mississippi River and the Territory of Louisiana. Early in December Daniel T. Patterson, commanding the naval station at New Orleans, sent Lieut. Thomas A. C. Jones with seven small vessels, mounting 23 guns and carrying 182 men, to intercept the British fleet. The British, December 14. 1814, manned sixty barges with 1,200 volunteers from the fleet, under Capt. Lockyer, and sent them out to destroy the American gunboats. The battle took place on Lake Borgne, and lasted almost an hour. Several of the British barges were shattered and sunk and about 300 men killed and wounded. The Americans lost only 6 men killed and 35 wounded. The American gunboats were captured, which gave the British control of Lake Borgne.

Lake Champlain, Battle of.—After arriving at the head of Lake Champlain, Sept. 6, 1814, Governor-General Prevost awaited the co-operation of the British fleet on the lake. Sept. 11 Capt. Downie's squadron rounded Cumberland Head. It consisted of the frigate *Confidence,* brig *Linnet,* sloops *Chub* and *Finch,* and twelve gunboats—in all, sixteen vessels, of about 2.402 tons, with 937 men and a total of ninety-two guns, throwing a broadside of 1,192 pounds. In Cumberland or Plattsburg Bay, awaiting the attack, lay the American squadron, under Capt. Thomas Macdonough, then only 28 years of age. It consisted of the ship *Saratoga,* brig *Eagle,* schooner *Ticonderoga,* sloop *Preble,* and ten gunboats—in all, fourteen vessels, of 2,244 tons and 882 men, with eighty-six guns, throwing a broadside of 1,194 pounds. Kneeling beside his heaviest gun, surrounded by his men, the young captain invoked divine protection and guidance. The first shot from the *Saratoga* was aimed by Macdonough and went entirely through the flagship of the British squadron, demolishing her wheel. The battle raged two hours and twenty minutes, when every British vessel struck her colors. Both squadrons were badly crippled. The British loss was more than 200, including Captain Downie. The American loss was 110, of whom 52 were killed.

Lake Champlain:

Act to authorize construction of bridge across portion of, vetoed, 5060.

Insurgents on, proclamation against authorizing militia officers to dispel by force, 438.

Victory of American squadron on, 534.

Lake Erie, Battle of.—In 1813 the Americans, under great difficulties, constructed a fleet of war vessels at Presque Isle, now Erie, Pa., for service in the lakes. Aug. 12, 1813, the American squadron, consisting of the *Lawrence, Niagara, Caledonia, Ariel, Somers, Tigress, Scorpion, Porcupine, Ohio,* and *Trippe,* manned by less than 400 officers and men, under Capt. Oliver H. Perry, set forth in search of Barclay's British squadron of six vessels, manned by more than 500 men. Sept. 10 Perry's look-out sighted the enemy. At 10 o'clock in the morning the signal for action was run up to the masthead of the *Lawrence.* It bore the words of the dying Capt. Lawrence, of the *Chesapeake*: "Don't give up the ship." During the action the *Lawrence* was disabled and Perry transferred his flag to the *Niagara.* At 3 o'clock in the afternoon the flag of the British flagship was struck. The firing ceased. It was the first time an American fleet had met a British fleet in regular line of battle. The engagement was fairly fought, with the Americans at a disadvantage, and the British fleet surrendered. Perry sent word to Gen. Harrison: "We have met the enemy and they are ours." The British loss in the action was 135, 41 of whom were killed. The Americans lost 123, 27 of whom were killed. (See illustration opposite 489.)

Lake Erie:
Rise of waters of, referred to, 1563.
Victory of American squadron on, 519.

Lake Memphremagog, practicability of connecting Connecticut River with, 873.

Lake Michigan, improvement of harbors and rivers on, 2764.

Lake of the Woods, boundary with Great Britain regarding, referred to, 4141, 4191, 4243, 4356.
Final report of commissioners referred to, 4382.

Lake Ontario, movements of American squadron on, 520.

Lake State.—Alternative nickname for Michigan. (See Wolverine State.)

Lake Superior:
Copper mines on shores of, 764.
Mineral lands on, sale of, recommended, 2304.

Lake-to-the-Gulf Deep Waterway Association.—A representative body of men organized for the development of a deep-water passage between the Great Lakes and the Mississippi and its branches met in Chicago in 1908. In 1909, as result of its activity, the River and Harbor Appropriation Act carried with it the creation of the National Waterways Commission (q. v.). (See Conservation Commission.)

Lake Traverse Reservation:
Agreement with Sioux for purchase of lands in, discussed, 5498.
Opened to settlement by proclamation, 5707.
Right of way for railroad through, 4788, 4954, 5178.

Lakes, Great. (See Great Lakes; the several Lakes.)

Lame-Duck.—A term applied in derision to any legislator who is ineffective; and generally to a politician who has "seen better days," such as one who has failed of re-election to office.

Land Grants.—By this name is known the grant of land to corporations to encourage and aid the construction of railroads in portions of the country in which it would otherwise be unprofitable. These grants are usually made directly to the companies. Before 1862 they were made to the states in order to enable them to extend aid to corporations within their borders. To every state, at its admission, Congress has granted five per cent of the public lands within its limits on condition of the exemption of the remainder from state taxation. In 1850 the first grant for railroad purposes was made. It consisted of about 2,500,000 acres granted to the state of Illinois, and it was used to aid the Illinois Central Railroad. In 1856 about 2,000,000 acres went to Florida, a similar amount was received by Arkansas, while various other states received large tracts all more or less used to encourage railroad building. But the grant of colossal areas began with the construction of the Pacific Railroads. The Union Pacific received 2,000,000; the Kansas Pacific 6,000,000; the Central Pacific (as successor of the Western Pacific) 1,100,000, and on its Oregon Branch 3,000,-000; the Oregon and California 3,500,000; the Southern Pacific 6,000,000; and the Southern Pacific branch line 3,500,000 acres. Among others that received large grants were the Burlington and Missouri River and the Hannibal and St. Joseph. But the most stupendous grants were those of 47,000,000 acres to the Northern Pacific and of 42,000,000 acres to the Atlantic and Pacific. From these generous grants a revulsion has set in, and at every session of Congress bills are now introduced and every effort is made to forfeit such portions of the land as are not earned by a strict compliance with the terms of the grant, thus saving the land for settlement. Bills revoking the grant of lands not as yet earned have been passed; among the principal roads affected are the Atlantic and Pacific, Texas Pacific and Iron Mountain, and over 50,000,000 acres have thus been recovered. (See Subsidies.)

Land of Flowers.—A nickname for Alabama (q. v.) (See also States); sometimes also nicknamed the Cotton State.

Land Office. (See General Land Office.)

Land Offices, Public, act regarding fees of registers and receivers at, vetoed, 6107.

Land Sales. (See Lands, Public.)

Land Titles. (See Lands, Indian; Lands, Public.)

Lands ceded to United States by North Carolina referred to, 64, 105, 167. (See also Franklin.)

Lands, Arid.—The great North American desert possesses all the climatic, geologic and physiographic features of the Desert of Sahara, in Africa, though only about one-third as large. It embraces the vast stretches of country lying between the Sierra Nevada Mountains of California and the eastern ranges of the Rocky Mountains in the United States, and between the Pacific Ocean and the Sierra Madre Mountains, in Mexico, an area of 1,050,000 sq. miles, of which about half lies in Mexico and the other half in the United States, including Nevada, Utah, eastern and southern California, Arizona, New Mexico, and all of Texas west of the Pecos. In general this desert is one of barren, stony mountain ranges, separated by equally barren stretches of desert plain, an aggregation of elongated arid plains and lower mountain ranges. The individual deserts have separate names and each differs from the others in some notable feature. Like the Sahara, the American desert is without water on its surface. Upon its area the average annual rainfall is less than 10 inches—less than falls in two months in the fertile states of the east.

With the aid of the railroad and the mechanical drill American genius and energy have conquered the arid plains of the west, and made them yield double the wealth per capita of any other portion of the United States. Like Sahara, the arid plains of America have an underground supply of water. By the use of the mechanical drill the deep wells on the mesa at El Paso supply 700,000 gallons of water per day, and the flowing well at Benson and those of the Salton Desert afford ample supplies to localities which were formerly hopelessly dry. The sterile soil of the desert is apparently more fertile, when artificially watered, than many regions where rainfall is abundant. In the desert may be seen some of the most skillful and profitable agriculture in the world. Striking examples of this are seen in the wheat fields of Utah and Sonora, the great cotton plantations of Coahuila, Mexico, the alfalfa valleys of the Rio Grande and the orchards of California. The marvelous transformation wrought by irrigation is shown in Southern California, where communities of great wealth and culture have sprung up and where the ideal of perfect conditions of existence seem to have been attained. To the reclamation of these arid lands the attention of Congress has been directed in recent years, and Federal appropriations for irrigation are bringing them more and more each year into a state of productiveness. (See Irrigation.)

Lands, Bounty.—A term applied to the lands in the Northwest Territory belonging to the eastern commonwealths. Sept. 16, 1776, Congress offered bounty lands to volunteers in the Revolution, assessing the money to buy them against the several states. The term Bounty Lands was also applied to the Crown Lands before the Revolution. Lord Dunmore, Governor of Virginia, was empowered to offer bounties in land to all officers and soldiers who served in the French and Indian wars—5,000 acres to each field officer, 3,000 to captains, 200 to subalterns or staff officers, and 50 to private soldiers—up to 200,000 acres, in the King's domain. This was understood by the Americans to refer to the lands of the Northwest Territory, and many of them selected choice tracts west of the Alleghanies. Washington and his land agent, Crawford, had surveyed 70,000 acres and secured patents in his own and other officers' names for 63,000 acres of which his own share was 32,000.

Lands, Bounty:

Appropriation for carrying out laws regarding, referred to, 2840.

Frauds in, discussed and recommendations regarding, 2714.

Grant of, to Mexican War soldiers recommended, 2365.

Granted persons who have been engaged in military service, 555, 2664, 2823.

Recommended, 3387.

Referred to, 1844.

Lands, Crown.—After the treaty of Paris in 1763, by which Great Britain acquired Canada and all the country west of the Mississippi River, a royal proclamation was issued setting aside all the lands west of the colonies and extending to the western limits of the British possessions as Crown lands. These lands were reserved for the use of the Indians and the colonists were forbidden to make settlements in or purchase of them without permission of the home Government. After the Revolution each state laid claim to a portion of the Crown lands.

Lands, Desert.—March 3, 1877, Congress passed the Desert Land law, which it supplemented in 1891, by further legislation, to encourage irrigation by private individuals and associations. It provides that any citizen or any person who declares his intention of becoming a citizen, by paying a registration fee of 25 cents, and declaring his intent to irrigate within three years, may occupy desert land to the extent of one section (640 acres) in any one of a number of specified western states and territories, and if he reclaims it within that time may receive a patent for it upon payment of $1 per acre. He must spend at least $3 per acre in irrigation or securing water rights, and must have secured the rights before making application. Associations may file joint declarations.

Under a recent amendment the settler may take up 320 acres of arid land upon payment of 25 cents per acre; after spending $1 per year in improvements for three years, and proving the ownership of sufficient water to irrigate the entire tract, he may secure full title by payment of $1 per acre to the government. Land so acquired costs about $10 per acre.

Lands, Desert:

Discussed, 5380.

Repeal or modification of laws regarding, recommended, 5107.

Lands, Homestead.—The Federal Homestead laws begin with the act of Congress passed in 1862, now sections 2289-2317, United States Revised Statutes. The object of these homestead land laws is to give portions of the public lands to those who will settle, cultivate, and make permanent homes upon them. Any person who is the head of a family or who is a citizen of the United States, or who has filed his declaration of becoming such, may acquire a tract of unappropriated public land not exceeding 160 acres, on condition of settlement, cultivation and continuous occupancy as a home for himself for a period of five years, and the payment of certain moderate fees. Under the provision of this law more than 85,000,000 acres of unoccupied lands have been transferred to homeseekers. During the year 1901 alone the original homestead entries, final and commuted entries, aggregated 111,390, and covered 15,455,057 acres. Time of service in the United States army, navy, marine corps, during the Rebellion, the Spanish War or the Philippine Insurrection may be deducted from the term of continuous occupancy of a homestead.

The homestead law gives the settler two options: he can settle upon, enter and acquire title to 160 acres of land practically free of cost by maintaining residence thereon for five years; or he may at the end of fourteen months of such continuous residence secure a patent from the government by paying $1.25 per acre.

Lands, Indian.—To quiet the apprehensions of the Indians in the Ohio regions that their lands were to be granted to settlers, a royal proclamation was issued Oct. 7, 1763, forbidding colonial governors from making land grants west of the sources of the rivers flowing into the Atlantic. As the result of treaties, purchase and war, the Indians were eventually transplanted to the country west of the Mississippi, the first territorial reservation set apart for them being June 30, 1834, known as the Indian Territory. Other reservations were subsequently set aside for the exclusive occupation of the Indians, but as the number of Indians decreased and the covetousness of the whites increased these reservations were either bought outright by the Government or exchanged for other territory.

Lands, Indian:

Accounts for advertising Kansas, referred to, 4664.

Act for sale of, vetoed, 4341.
President requests return of bill for his approval, 4342.

Allotment of, in severalty—
Act providing for, etc., 5498.
Discussed, 5381, 5480, 5552, 5637, 5761, 5976.
Recommended, 561, 4528, 4576, 4643, 4730, 4779, 4783, 4955.
Remonstrance against, 4669.
Survey necessary for, 4943.

Cession of, to United States, agreements for, 423, 426, 585, 603, 803, 931, 1257, 1729, 1818, 2501, 5450, 5552, 5638, 5648, 5649, 5671, 5768.
Amount of cession, 5481.
Commission to negotiate for, 5480, 5481, 5508, 5510, 5512, 5514, 5565, 5567. (See also Commissions.)
Report of, discussed, 5496.
Negotiations regarding, 5506.
Proclamation regarding, 5450, 5579, 5591, 5707.
Proposition regarding, 5392.
Opened to settlement. (See Lands, Public.)

Referred to, 167, 256, 331, 335, 360, 362, 375, 422, 425, 890, 1810, 4680.

Sale of, desired by certain tribes, 4075.

Titles to, extinguishment of, referred to, 585, 769, 1716, 2355, 2501, 2769.

Proclaimed, 1538, 5535.

Trespasses upon, discussed and legislation to prevent, recommended, 937, 1099, 4637, 4676, 4742, 4775, 4853, 4953, 5177, 5178.

Lands, Mineral.—Among the classifications of public lands made by the General Land Office is that of Mineral Lands. These vary from placer locations, at $2.50 an acre, to mining rights at $5, not to exceed 1,500 by 600 feet, nor less than 1,500 by 50 feet.

Lands, Mineral (see also California; New Mexico):

Congressional committees to visit, recommended, 4309.

Referred to, 1809, 2218, 2558, 2663, 3330, 3383.

Sale of, recommended, 2304, 2354.

Separation of, from farming lands, recommended, 2493.

System of leasing, unsatisfactory, 2260, 2623.

Lands, Public.—By the treaty of 1783 England relinquished all her lands east of the Mississippi River north of 31° north latitude. So much of this territory as lay east of the Alleghany Mountains was claimed by the original states; and certain of the states claimed lands beyond the Alleghanies based on their crown grants, which extended to the "South Sea" or Pacific Ocean. These grants were indefinite and conflicting and the source of much contention between the states, and the lands were finally (with certain reservations) ceded to the Federal government. The acquisition of more territory from Spain, France, Mexico and Great Britain (through the determination of boundaries) added vast tracts to the public domain, from which states were afterward formed, but with the reservation that the unoccupied lands therein should remain the property of the general government. Only eighteen states thus retained control of the land within their boundaries, and were able to dispose of it as the local governments saw fit. When Texas was admitted to the Union, it retained jurisdiction over its public domain and is administering the same to-day independent of the Federal Land Office. In the other states (formed from the Alaska and Louisiana Purchases, the Mexican Cession, etc.) there yet remain unreserved and unappropriated 290,759,133 acres of public land.

Lands were also purchased by the federal government from the Indians at various times and opened to white settlement. These acquisitions were always advantageous to the government and as President Monroe remarks (page 585), "presumably so to the Indians." But the red men often misunderstood the terms of the trades, and regretted their bargains, and some of the fiercest of Indian wars have been caused by the feeling among the Indians that they had been cheated.

Public lands may be acquired under acts relating to *Lands*—Homestead, Timber and Stone, Desert, Mining, Bounty (q. v.). Abandoned or isolated portions of the public land also are open to purchase from time to time.

Uncle Sam still has considerable land to give to the enterprising citizen, man or woman, who wishes to establish a home. Secretary of the Interior Lane announced August 21, 1916, that more than a quarter of a billion acres of land remain in the public domain, according to official figures, just compiled by the General Land Office. These acres are located in twenty-five different States, extending from California to Michigan, from Florida to Washington. All but 2,290,000 acres of it is in the Far West, with Nevada containing the highest acreage, 55,375,077. An even dozen of the extreme western states alone hold more than 250,000,000 acres. The exact amount of land that is unreserved and unappropriated, according to the official figures, is 254,945,589 acres. Of this amount, approximately 92,000,000 acres are unsurveyed.

Missouri reports the least area of vacant land, having but 952 acres, which are scattered over 16 counties. Alabama has 42,680 acres in 51 counties; Florida 135,237 acres in 45 counties; Mississippi 30,374 acres in 58 counties; and Louisiana 44,804 acres in 57 counties.

In 52 counties of Michigan may be found 90,540 acres, while 30 counties in Wisconsin report 5,872 acres.

Of the Pacific States, California has 20,025,999 acres of vacant land; Oregon 15,337,809, and Washington 1,132,571.

Large areas of vacant land are reported in the Southwestern States as follows: Arizona, 23,597,219; Nevada, 55,375,077; New Mexico, 26,338,379; Utah, 32,968,837.

The land in the Dakotas is rapidly passing into private ownership, only 2,382,588 acres of vacant land being reported in South Dakota, and 381,199 acres in North Dakota.

Of the Northwestern States, Idaho contains 15,510,561 acres of vacant land, of which 6,679,071 acres are unsurveyed; Montana, 16,649,725 acres with 7,420,571 unsurveyed; and Wyoming, 28,528,492 acres with 1,960,752 acres unsurveyed.

Kansas' vacant area is reported as 56,018 acres, while Nebraska contains 146,256 acres.

In Colorado, over two and a quarter million acres were appropriated during the last fiscal year, leaving 14,908,127 acres now vacant. Of this area, over 2,000,000 acres are unsurveyed.

The total area of unappropriated land, surveyed and unsurveyed, in the twenty-five public-land States, is reported as follows:

	ACRES		ACRES
Alabama.....	42,680	Montana.....	16,649,725
Arizona.......	23,597,219	Nebraska......	146,256
Arkansas......	402,219	Nevada.......	55,375,077
California..	20,025,999	New Mexico..	26,338,379
Colorado......	14,908,127	North Dakota...	381,199
Florida........	135,237	Oklahoma.....	55,250
Idaho........	15,510,561	Oregon......	15,337,809
Kansas........	56,018	South Dakota...	2,382,588
Louisiana....	44,804	Utah.......	32,968,837
Michigan.....	90,540	Washington....	1,132,571
Minnesota....	798,804	Wisconsin.....	5,872
Mississippi....	30,374	Wyoming.....	28,528,492
Missouri......	952		
		Total.......	254,945,589

Lands, Public:

Acquired from **Mexico, referred to,** 1275.

Act—

Appropriating proceeds of sales of, reasons for applying pocket veto to, 2108.

Making grant of, to States for benefit of insane persons vetoed. 2780.

To authorize entry of, for gravel pits and reservoir purposes, etc., vetoed, 6002.

To authorize leasing of, for educational purposes in Arizona, vetoed, 6102.

Amount, sales, and expenses of, etc., discussed, 1136.

Appropriations of proceeds of sales of, for educational purposes. (See Education.)

Attempts made to keep down price of, referred to, 1744.

Augmentation in value of, 586.

Ceded to Indians, 108, 1716. (See also Indian Tribes, under Indians.)

Early settlement of ceded lands desired, 2832.

Court for litigated land cases recommended, 5975.

Depredations on. (See Lands, Timber.)

Desert-land laws. (See Lands, Desert.)

Discussed, 586, 5974, 6166, 6346, 6390, 6452.

Disposition of, discussed by President—

Buchanan, 2990.

Cleveland, 4944, 5106, 5379, 5974.

Grant, 4106, 4206, 4309.

Hayes, 4577.

Jackson, 1163.

McKinley, 6345, 6346, 6452.

Roosevelt, 6790, 6800, 7096.

Van Buren, 1601.

Fences, unlawful, removal of, directed by proclamation, 4893.

Discussed, 5107.

Frauds in purchase of, order regarding, 6329.

Fraudulent acquisition of, 6790, 6800.

Fraudulent occupation of, discussed, 5886.

Granted Canadian volunteers, 558.

Granted persons engaged in military service. (See Lands, Bounty.)

Grants of—

In aid of education. (See Education.)

Legislation to remove limitation of time for bringing suits to annul unlawful, recommended, 6092.

Referred to, 4065, 4206, 5974.

To railroads. (See Pacific Railroads; Railroads.)

To States, referred to, 4065, 4206, 5380.

Homestead acts. (See Homestead Laws.)

Instructions to receiving or disbursing officers of land offices, referred to, 1346.

Joint resolution authorizing grant of lands to Kansas, etc., vetoed, 5308.

Laws regarding—

Amendment and change in, recommended, 4944, 5362; 6790, 6800, 6947, 7004, 7096.

Discussed, 5484.

History and codification of, 4581. Recommendations regarding, 4577.

Violations of, referred to, 4743.

Lumber and naval stores taken from, referred to, 4434.

Mineral lands referred to. (See Lands, Mineral.)

Opened to settlement—
Appropriation for, recommended, 5638.
Discussed, 5482, 5637, 5761.
Fraudulent occupation of, discussed, 5886.
Proclaimed, 5450, 5579, 5591, 5707, 5710, 5727, 5838, 6016, 6018, 6020, 6026, 6486, 6506, 6525, 6547, 6553, 6588, 6600, 6603, 6612, 6615, 6616, 6687, 6873, 6875, 6882, 6956.

Patenting of—
In execution of railroad grants discussed, 6166.
To settlers, discussed, 5484, 5552, 5638, 5761.

Payments for, should be made in specie, 1468.

Planting of forests, recommendations regarding, 4158.

Preemption laws discussed. (See Preemption Laws.)

Prices of, should be reduced, 2353, 2407, 2500.

Purchase and cession of, to United States—
Agreements regarding, 146, 167, 182, 203, 256, 347, 360, 375, 422, 426, 431, 585, 603, 803, 887, 931, 957, 1029, 1257, 1729, 1818, 2501, 5450, 5552, 5638, 5648, 5649, 5671, 5768.
Proclamations regarding. (See Opened to settlement, *ante.*)
Proposition regarding, 4892.

Purchasers of—
Indulgence to, recommended, 647, 957, 986.
Patent of, when paid for, cannot be withheld by President, 1098.
Referred to, 79, 80, 100, 105, 113, 127, 128, 474, 586, 591, 599, 957, 1136, 2768.

Revenues derived from sales of. (See Sale of, *post.*)

Russian colony to emigrate to United States discussed, 4207.

Sale of—
Act regarding appropriation of proceeds of—
Reasons for applying pocket veto to, 1275.
Vetoed, 2108.
Discussed by President—
Adams, J. Q., 871, 956.
Buchanan, 2990.
Cleveland, 5974.
Fillmore, 2662, 2708.
Grant, 3995, 4064, 4154, 4206, 4307.
Jackson, 1098, 1163, 1468.
Jefferson, 317.
Johnson, 3651, 3774, 3880.

Lincoln, 3332, 3387, 3451.
McKinley, 6345, 6346, 6452.
Pierce, 2748, 2823, 2873, 2943.
Polk, 2258, 2353, 2366, 2407, 2500, 2506.
Tyler, 2118.
Van Buren, 1601.

Forfeitures for non-payment of purchase money should be remitted, 957.

Frauds in, 1450.

Proclamation of President—
Jackson regarding, 1058.
Monroe regarding lands on Sandusky River, 580.

Referred to, 940, 1136, 1268, 2003.

Revenue derived from, discussed by President—
Adams, J. Q., 599, 986.
Arthur, 4632, 4719, 4763.
Fillmore, 2662.
Grant, 3995, 4064, 4146, 4206, 4307.
Jackson, 1089, 1246, 1381.
Johnson, 3774, 3880.
Lincoln, 3253, 3384, 3451.
McKinley, 6424.
Pierce, 2748, 2823, 2873, 2943.
Tyler, 1895.

Statement of, 1897, 2708, 2990, 6875.

Set apart as public reservation by proclamation of President—
Cleveland, 5859, 5864, 6122, 6205, 6207, 6209, 6211, 6213, 6215, 6216, 6218, 6219, 6221, 6222, 6225, 6227.
Harrison, Benj., 5577, 5590, 5595, 5686, 5695, 5705, 5719, 5722, 5786, 5792, 5795, 5797, 5804, 5810, 5811, 5814, 5815.
McKinley, 6475, 6477, 6482, 6487, 6495, 6497, 6499, 6500, 6504, 6505, 6514, 6516, 6519, 6523, 6536, 6541, 6546, 6549, 6551, 6561, 6566.
Roosevelt, 6697, 6872.
Discussed, 6346.

Set apart for cultivation of vine and olive, 599.

Should be reserved for actual settlers, 2990.

Surveys for, recommendations regarding, 5975.

Timber-culture act. (See Timber-Culture Act.)

Timber on. (See Lands, Timber.)

Title to, referred to, 1605.

Trespasses upon, referred to, 1605, 5177, 5380.

Unlawful inclosures of, proclamation regarding, 4893.
Discussed, 5107.

Unlawful possession of, discussed, 557, 1057, 1106, 5380.
Proclamations regarding, 557, 1057, 1106.

Lands, Swamp.—In 1849 and 1850 Congress passed resolutions granting large tracts of land to the various states for their disposal. Agents of the states selected such lands as were unfit for cultivation, and title to the same was confirmed in the states by an act approved March 3, 1857. At the time of the grant it was estimated from Government surveys that the swamp land would not exceed 21,000,-000 acres. Millions of acres, however, were listed as swamp lands. This led to an investigation, and gross frauds were unearthed. Under the various acts lands have been granted to Alabama, Arkansas, California, Florida, Illinois, Indiana, Iowa, Louisiana, Michigan, Minnesota, Mississippi, Missouri, Ohio, Oregon and Wisconsin. Florida has received the largest share—22,500,000 acres—and Ohio the least—117,-000 acres. In many instances the states have sold the lands to railroad companies.

Lands, Swamp, discussed, 5974.

Lands, Timber and Stone.—Lands which are unfit for cultivation, but are of value for their standing timber or stone, may be had from the Government by individuals to the extent of 160 acres, on payment of $2.50 an acre.

Lands, Timber:

Act for relief of purchasers of stone and, vetoed, 5912.

Agents employed for preservation of, referred to, 2268.

Commission to formulate plans for national forestry system, 6167.

Depredations committed on, and recommendations regarding, 4428, 4456, 4530, 4577, 4954, 5508, 5974.

Discussed, 4309.

Fires upon, carelessly kindled, discussed, 5508.

Memorial regarding preservation of, referred to, 4215, 5495.

Opened to settlement. (See Lands, Public.)

Preservation of, legislation regarding, 5106, 5668, 5886, 5974.

Timber-culture act. (See Timber-Culture Act.)

Las Guasimas (Cuba), Battle of. (See Santiago (Cuba), Battle of.)

Latimer Case.—The first of a series of fugitive-slave trials which took place in Boston. George Latimer was seized in 1842 without a warrant, and kept in the custody of the city jailer awaiting evidence against him. A writ of *habeas corpus* was denied. A writ of personal replevin, asked for under the act of 1837, securing trial by jury, was also denied, this act being declared void. As a consequence of the indignation aroused by this case the legislature in 1843 passed an act forbidding State officers to aid in the capture of fugitive slaves and forbidding the use of State jails for their imprisonment. The sum forfeited for violation was not exceeding $1,-000 or imprisonment not exceeding one year.

Latin American and Mexican Divisions, State Department.—These divisions within the Department of State were organized to control "diplomatic and consular correspondence in matters other than administrative with Mexico, Central America, the Republic of Panama, South America and the West Indies." These divisions fall under the supervision of the second assistant secretary of state (q. v.) (See State Department.)

Latin-American Library, establishment of, at Washington recommended by International American Conference, 5506.

Latin-American Republics, discussed by President Roosevelt, 7231.

Latin Union.—The name given the monetary alliance of Belgium, France, Italy and Switzerland, formed by convention Dec. 23, 1865. Greece joined the union in 1868. The object was the maintenance and regulation of a uniform interchangeable gold and silver coinage based on the French franc. Belgium withdrew from the union in 1885 and adopted the single gold standard.

Latin Union. (See Monetary Convention of Latin Union.)

Latter-Day Saints. (See Mormon Church; Polygamy.)

Lattimer, Pa., claims of Austria-Hungary arising out of conflict between miners and sheriff at, discussed, 6324, 6363.

Law Clerk, State Department.—The Law Bureau in the Department of State was formed in 1870, simply to examine legal questions referred to it. Now the law clerk edits the laws of Congress and prepares them for publication, and attends to other legal matters of importance in the administration of the department. The office of Law Clerk was established in 1903, and his present salary is $2,500. (See State Department; Solicitor, State Department.)

Lawrence, Kans., fortifications at, referred to, 3894.

Laws of United States (see also Revised Statutes):

Newspapers selected to publish, for Congress, referred to, 4116.

Lead Mines. (See Mines.)

League Island, Pa. (situated in the Delaware River, near the junction with the Schuylkill), bill accepting, for naval purposes, referred to, 3649.

Leander, The.—A British war ship, which, while lying off Sandy Hook, April 25, 1806, fired a shot which killed a sailor aboard an American coaster. The citizens of New York in mass meeting denounced the outrage and called upon the President for better protection. President Jefferson issued a proclamation ordering the arrest of the *Leander's* captain if found within the jurisdiction of the United States (See page 390).

Leander, The:

American citizen murdered by shot from, 390.

Ordered from and prohibited from reentering waters of United States, 390.

League to Enforce Peace.—This organization was formed in Philadelphia on June 17, 1915. Its president is William H. Taft, its vice president, Alton B. Parker, and its membership includes a large proporton of the notable men and women of the country. The League takes no attitude towards the present European War, but after the conclusion of the war proposes a league of nations based upon the following proposals:

"1.—All justiciable questions arising between the signatory powers, not settled by negotiation, shall, subject to the limitations of treaties, be submitted to a judicial tribunal for hearing and judgment, both upon the merits and upon any issue as to its jurisdiction of the question.

"2.—All other questions arising between the signatories and not settled by negotiation, shall be submitted to a council of conciliation for hearing, consideration and recommendation.

"3.—The signatory powers shall jointly use, forthwith, their economic forces against any of their number that refuses to submit any question which arises to an international judicial tribunal or council of conciliation before threatening war. They shall follow this by the joint use of their military forces against that nation if it actually proceeds to make war or invades another's territory without first submitting, or offering to submit, its grievance to the court or council aforesaid and awaiting its conclusion.

"4.—Conferences between the signatory powers shall be held from time to time to formulate and codify rules of international law, which, unless some signatory shall signify its dissent within a stated period, shall thereafter govern in the decisions of the judicial tribunal mentioned in article one."

It will be noticed that the League does not propose to end all wars, endeavoring merely at the present stage of human development to make war more difficult. Neither does the League propose "entangling alliances" for the United States, or for any other country, any more than it proposes disarmament. It will be noticed, furthermore, that the League does not propose to enforce the decrees of either Court or Council, but depends upon public opinion in the disputing countries to support such decrees, and upon delay in preventing the final settlement of disputes by resort to arms. The League takes no stand, finally, upon purely domestic revolutions or disorders.

Learning, Institution of. (See Education; Military Academy; National University; Naval Academy; Seminaries of Learning.)

Leather and Shoe Business.—The first American tannery is said to have been established in Virginia as early as 1630, but one or two years later Francis Ingalls established the business in Swampscott near Lynn, Mass., and the center of the trade has hovered about that vicinity ever since. The colonial authorities encouraged the business by forbidding the exportation of hides or unwrought leather. Before the Revolution leather was more plentiful here than in England. In 1790 William Edwards established a tannery in Hampshire, Mass. Out of this grew the Hampshire Leather Manufacturing Company of Massachusetts, incorporated in Boston in 1809 with a capital of $100,000. The tanneries of this company had a capacity for handling 16,000 hides a year. Many other tanneries followed immediately on account of the cheapness of bark, and soon the annual exports reached 350,000 pounds. The value of hides and manufactured skins was stated by the census of 1810 to have been $17,935,477,

though private authorities claimed as high as $20,000,000.

The business increased steadily until in 1840 there were some 8,000 tanneries in the United States, employing about 26,000 hands and a capital of $16,000,000. In 1909 there were 919 establishments reported as engaged primarily in tanning, currying or finishing leather. They gave employment to an average of 67,100 persons, of whom 62,202 were wage-earners. The amount paid in salaries and wages was $38,846,481. The value of products for the year was $327,874,187. The processes of tanning, currying and finishing are comparatively simple and the cost of the materials represents the greater part of the value of the finished goods. The cost of materials in 1909 was $248,278,933, which is equal to 75.7 per cent of the total value of the products. The value added to the materials by manufacture was, therefore, $79,595,254. Pennsylvania is now the leading state in the industry, followed by Massachusetts and New York.

For the fiscal year ending June 30, 1910, the exports of leather were valued at $37,-414,175, and the imports, consisting partly of skins in process of manufacture, were $7,607,923.

There were tanned in the United States during 1914, 138,547,692 hides and skins of all kinds. This number represents a decrease of 5.3 per cent as compared with 1909. The number of cattle hides tanned decreased from 18,613,054 in 1909 to 17,776,558 in 1914, or by 4.5 per cent, while their value increased from $121,266,814 in the earlier year to $151,609,541 in the later, or by 25 per cent. The number of calfskins and kipskins treated decreased from 19,735,-549 in 1909 to 16,067,793 in 1914, or by 18.6 per cent; but during the same period the cost of these skins increased $1,319,450, or 4.1 per cent.

The falling off in the use of goatskins was very marked. There were but 37,755,867 such skins treated in 1914, as against 48,193,848 in 1909, making a decrease of 21.7 per cent. The decrease in cost was $4,011,054, or 14.4 per cent.

On the other hand, sheepskins and lambskins show a large increase over 1909. The number reported for that year was 26,177,-136, whereas the census for 1914 showed 40,364,926, making a gain of 54.2 per cent. The cost increased by $7,069,811, or 57.6 per cent.

In addition to the foregoing, there were tanned in 1914, 1,250,245 horsehides, 1,095,-360 kangaroo skins, 233,180 colt skins, and a number of hog, pig, deer, buck, seal, dog, alligator, shark, elk, moose, and other skins, the total value of which, $8,414,129, represents an increase of $4,611,638, or 121.3 per cent, over the value reported for 1909.

The value of leather produced in 1914 was $348,956,872, representing an increase of $36,385,046, or 11.6 per cent, over the total value, $312,571,826, reported for 1909.

Location of Establishments.—Of the 767 establishments reported for 1914, 130 were located in Massachusetts, 120 in Pennsylvania, 100 in New York, 86 in New Jersey, 30 in Illinois, 29 each in California and Wisconsin, 28 in Ohio, 23 in Michigan, 22 in Virginia, 20 each in Delaware and North Carolina, 18 in West Virginia, 13 in Maine, 11 each in Kentucky and Missouri, 10 each in Indiana and Maryland, 9 in Tennessee, 8 in New Hampshire, 7 each in Connecticut and Georgia, 5 in Oregon, 4 in Minnesota, 3 each in Rhode Island and Washington, 2 each in Iowa, Texas and Vermont, and 1 each in Alabama, Louisiana, Montana, Utah, and Wyoming.

Gloves and Mittens.—In the leather glove and mitten industry there were 377 establishments reported in 1909, which gave employment to 12,950 persons, and paid out $6,019,872 in salaries and wages. They made goods to the value of $23,630,598, utilizing $13,208,001 worth of material. New York is the most important State in the industry, doing more than 60 per cent. of the total business in 1909.

The manufacture of leather gloves and mittens as a factory industry was first carried on in the United States in Fulton County, N. Y., and this locality has ever since been the center of the industry in America. In 1909 41.4 per cent. of the shops in the industry in the United States, and 54.7 per cent. of the value of the goods were reported from this county. Of the persons employed in the industry 48 per cent. are males and 52 per cent. females.

Shoe-Making.—Thomas Beard, the pioneer shoemaker of America, is said to have arrived on the *Mayflower* in 1629, and for his services received a salary of $50 per annum and a grant of fifty acres of land. Seven years later Philip Kertland began the manufacture of shoes in Lynn, and in a few more years Lynn supplied the Boston market.

In 1698 the industry was carried on profitably in Philadelphia and the colonial legislature of Pennsylvania in 1721 passed an act regulating the quality and prices of the output. Most of the shoes worn by the Continental army were made in Massachusetts. In 1795 there were in Lynn 200 master workmen and 600 journeymen, who produced 300,000 pairs of ladies' shoes, and one manufacturer alone turned out 20,000 pairs of men's shoes in seven months of that year. It was the custom of the manufacturer of the time to make weekly trips to Boston with horse and wagon, taking his goods along in baskets and barrels and offering them to the wholesale trade.

It was not until 1845 that machinery came into use in the shoe-making trade. First came the leather-rolling machine, then the leather-splitting machine, peg-making, power-pegging, and the dieing-out machine for cutting soles, taps and heels. In 1860 came the McKay sewing machine, followed by the Goodyear turn-shoe machine. Inventions followed with such rapidity that soon nothing was left for the skilled artisan. Labor in shoe factories today consists chiefly in feeding machines and carrying away the product; and even this is accomplished by mechanical carriers. This has led to the adoption of shoe-making as an occupation for convicts in state prisons. In 1870, before the protests of trade unions began to be heeded, convicts in twenty-six state prisons were employed in shoe-making.

In the boot and shoe industry there were 1,918 establishments reported by the census of 1910. These were capitalized at $222,324,248, gave employment to 215,923 persons, and produced goods to the value of $512,797,642. Establishments engaged chiefly in the manufacture of cut stock formed about one-eighth of the total number, and the value of their products, $44,661,497, represented 8.7 per cent. of the entire industry. Boot and shoe findings formed more than one-sixth of the above total. Very few industries have been more affected by the introduction of machinery than the manufacture of boots and shoes, and to this fact may be attributed the relatively small increase in the number of wage-earners during the thirty years between 1879 and 1909.

The total output of boots and shoes in 1914 amounted to 252,516,603 pairs. Men's boots and shoes numbered 98,031,144 pairs, forming 38.8 per cent. of the total. Women's boots and shoes numbered 80,916,239 pairs, constituting 32 per cent. of the total. Misses' and children's boots and shoes contributed 48,322,395 pairs, or 19.1 per cent. of the total. Boys' and youths' boots and shoes numbered 22,895,719 pairs, representing 9.1 per cent. of the total. Fiber shoes, which were not reported separately in 1909, numbered 2,351,106 pairs and formed nine-tenths of 1 per cent. of the total in 1914.

The number of pairs of slippers, not including infants' slippers and slippers made from felt or other fiber, reported for 1914 was 17,733,689.

In the extent of the boot and shoe business Massachusetts easily ranks first with 850 factories, turning out $236,342,915 worth of goods, 46.1 per cent. of the whole, followed at some distance by Missouri with a production of 9.5 of the whole. The number of women in the boot and shoe industry in Massachusetts in 1909 was 28,922; in New York and Ohio each more than 7,000 and in Missouri 5,800. The number of children under 16 in Massachusetts was 3,335; and in Missouri, 1,392. In all of the factories women formed a considerable proportion of the wage-earners.

Exports of leather boots, shoes, and slippers for the fiscal year ending June 30, 1870, and for each succeeding year to 1910, show a constant increase from $419,612 in the former year to $12,408,575.

Lecompton Constitution.—During the struggle in Kansas over the question of entering the Union as a free or a slave state, the pro-slavery party held a convention at Lecompton Sept. 5, 1857, and adopted a constitution sanctioning slavery and forbidding the enactment of emancipation laws. It was provided that the constitution as a whole should not be submitted to the people of the territory, the vote being taken only on the main question of a constitution with slavery or a constitution without slavery. Free-state advocates refused to vote, and the constitution sanctioning slavery was adopted. Later the Territorial legislature ordered a vote on the constitution as a whole, and, the slave-state settlers abstaining from voting, it failed of adoption. (See also Kansas; Topeka Constitution; Wyandotte Constitution.)

Lecompton Constitution. (See Kansas, Government of.)

Lee, The, demand of Great Britain for surrender of mutineer in, referred to, 1808.

Legal-Tender Acts, modifications in, recommended, 4302.

Legal-Tender Cases.—During the financial emergency caused by the Civil War Congress in 1862 issued $150,000,000 of Treasury notes, the law authorizing their issue making them legal tender for all private debts and public dues except duties on imports and interest on the public debt. The constitutionality of the act authorizing these notes was frequently disputed, especially as to its application to debts contracted prior to its passage, and the Supreme Court was called upon in several cases to decide the question. State courts generally maintained the constitutionality of the law. The Supreme Court in 1869 (Hepburn *vs.* Griswold, q. v.) maintained the validity of the law only in so far as it did not affect contracts made prior to its passage. A year later this decision was overruled, and the constitutionality of the law in its application to pre-existing debts was maintained. The court in the meantime had undergone a change in its membership, two new judges having been appointed. (See also Juilliard *vs.* Greenman.)

Legal-Tender Notes, redemption of, recommended by President—
Grant, 4303, 4379.
Hayes, 4511, 4567.

Legate. (See Ambassador.)

Legation.—The representative, or representatives, sent by one country to the court of another country with authority to act. The legation may be for a specific mission, but the term usually refers to an ambassadorial or consular suite.

Legation Asylum, action of American minister to Chile in harboring criminals discussed, 5867.

Legations:
Military and naval attachés at, recommended, 4923.
Official residences for ambassadors and ministers recommended, 6072, 6155.
Premises for, discussed, 4823, 4825, 4862, 4923.
Appropriation for erection of buildings on, recommended, 5494.
Public documents or libraries in, referred to, 4070.
Secretaries at large, appointment of, recommended, 4923.

Legislature.—The body of men in a state or kingdom invested with power to make and repeal laws. Colonial legislatures were generally modeled after the British Parliament, the Kings, Lords and Commons having their counterparts in the governor, the council appointed by him, and the representatives of the people. Parliamentary procedure was also followed closely. The first representative legislature in America met at Jamestown, Va., in 1619. The first representatives were elected by voters having a property qualification. In 1776 Virginia substituted a senate for its upper council, and other states followed.

Lemhi Reservation, Idaho, agreement with Indians for sale of lands on, 4779.

Leopard, The, attack of, on the *Chesapeake.* (See *Chesapeake,* The.)

Letters, Patent. (See Patents.)

Letters Rogatory, report regarding execution of, transmitted, 5570.

Levees of Mississippi River, preservation of, recommendations regarding, 3652, 4682, 4797.

Lew-Chew Islands:
Compact with, for securing certain privileges to American vessels, 2826.
Good offices of United States tendered China and Japan for settlement of controversy regarding, 4521.

Lew-Chew, Treaties with.—A compact of friendship and commerce was concluded by Commodore Perry for the United States in 1854. Citizens of the United States, seamen, and others are permitted to go ashore on the islands to purchase or sell articles; ships may obtain wood and water on purchase anywhere, but other articles may be bought for them only at Napa. Sailors may go ashore and move freely about without molestation or espionage, so long as their acts are peaceful and legal; for illegal and wrongful acts they are to be arrested by the local authorities and handed over to the captain of the ship to which they belong, for punishment by him. A burial ground for citizens of the United States is established at Tumai. Pilots, appointed by the government of Lew-Chew, shall conduct vessels in and out of Napa for a pilotage fee of $5. Wood is to be supplied to ships at Napa at a selling price of 3,600 copper cash for a thousand catties, and water at the rate of 600 copper cash (forty-three cents) for a thousand catties (six barrels of thirty United States gallons each).

Lewis and Clark Expedition.—A party of citizens and soldiers sent under command of Captains Meriwether Lewis and William Clark, by order of President Jefferson, to explore the country from the Missouri River to the Pacific Ocean. They ascended the Missouri River to its sources, crossed the Rocky Mountains, and, finding the source of the Columbia River, floated down that stream to its mouth. They explored nearly all the territory lying south of the forty-ninth parallel. This expedition is important as forming the basis of our claim to Oregon.

Lewis and Clark Expedition discussed, 386, 396.

Lewis and Clark Centennial Exposition at Portland, Ore., 6798.

Lewiston, N. Y.—Proclamation granting privileges of other ports to, 2319.

Lexington (Mass.), Battle of.—On the night of April 18, 1775, a detachment of 800 British soldiers under Col. Smith left Boston to capture or destroy some military stores which the Americans had collected and stored at Concord. Maj. Pitcairn, who led the advance, was opposed at daybreak at Lexington Green, eleven miles northwest of Boston, by about fifty minute-men under Capt. Parker, who had been summoned by Paul Revere in his midnight ride. Pitcairn's men opened fire and 7 Americans were killed and 9 wounded. This was the first blood shed in the Revolutionary War. The Americans returned the fire and retreated, but rallied and pursued the British toward Concord, capturing 7 prisoners, the first taken in the war. On their return from Concord the British were reenforced at Lexington by 1,200 men under Lord Percy. The Americans had also been reenforced, and kept up a guerrilla fire upon the British, who fled to Boston in disorder. The loss for the day was 93 Americans killed. wounded, and missing. and 273 British. (See also Concord (Mass.), Battle of.)

Lexington (Mo.), Battle of.—Sept. 1, 1861, Col. Mulligan, in command of the "Irish Brigade," stationed at Jefferson City, Mo., was ordered by General Fremont, who had recently been appointed to the command of the Western Department, to proceed up the Missouri River to Lexington, Mo., 160 miles to the northwest, and reenforce the garrison there. Mulligan's brigade reached Lexington Sept. 9, swelling the force to 2,780 men. After the battle of Wilson's Creek (q. v.) the Confederate General Price marched toward the northern part of the State with a constantly increasing force. He arrived in the vicinity of Lexington Sept. 11 with 28,000 men and 13 pieces of artillery. Mulligan's force was well intrenched and was constantly expecting reenforcements from St. Louis. Several unsuccessful efforts were made to dislodge them. The garrison suffered terribly from thirst and many of the horses and cattle perished. On the 20th Price advanced his artillery behind the shelter of bales of hemp, which the men rolled slowly before them as they approached Mulligan's redoubt. When this hempen breastwork was within fifty yards of his lines, no reenforcements having arrived, Mulligan surrendered unconditionally, after a loss of 39 killed and 120 wounded. Two thousand six hundred men, including 500 home guards, laid down their arms. The Confederates lost 1,400 in killed and wounded. Col. Mulligan was twice wounded.

Libby Prison.—A famous Confederate military prison in Richmond, Va., during the war between the states. It was originally a tobacco warehouse and a ship chandlery and was named for its owner. It was taken down in 1888 and carried to Chicago and there set up as a war museum.

Liberal Republican Party.—A defection from the regular Republican organization in 1870-1872. This party was opposed to the strict measures of coercion adopted by the Administration to maintain the newly granted rights to the freedmen, reconstruct the Southern States, and stamp out disorder in the South. Uniting with the Democrats in Missouri in 1870-71, it advocated universal suffrage, universal amnesty, a reform of the tariff, and a "cessation of unconstitutional laws to cure Ku-Klux disorders." At a national convention held in Cincinnati in May, 1872, the Liberal Republicans nominated Horace Greeley for President and B. Gratz Brown, of Missouri, for Vice-President. The ticket was defeated.

Liberator.—1. The name of an anti-slavery paper started in Boston in 1831 by William Lloyd Garrison. 2. A title given, by common consent, to Garrison. 3. The title afterwards applied also to Abraham Lincoln.

Liberia.—The Negro Republic of Liberia is situated on the West Coast of Africa, from French Guinea (8° 25′ N. latitude) southward to the coast and between the British Colony of Sierra Leone and the French Ivory Coast Colony, the eastern boundary being partly marked by the right bank of the Cavalla River. The extreme geographical limits are 11° 32′-7° 33′ W. longitude and 4° 25′-8° 25′ N. latitude. The area is about 40,000 square miles.

Physical Features.—The coastal regions are marked by abrupt hills from 200 to 1,000 feet above sea level, with low-lying land intervening, in which are creeks and swamps; but the interior is generally hilly, and the hinterland is believed to contain mountains exceeding 6,000 feet above sea level.

History.—Liberia was founded towards the end of the first quarter of the nineteenth century by the influx of freed negro slaves from the United States, and in 1847 the colony declared its independence as the Republic of Liberia. After prolonged negotiations it was announced in October, 1910, that a scheme for American financial control has been approved by the United States, Germany, Great Britain and France, whereby the United States assumed responsibility for the internal administration of the country. An American receiver-general was placed in control of the finances, assisted by French, German and British advisers; a frontier police designated by Americans was established to secure the revenues. The first financial measure was the loan of £500,000, secured by a first lien on all import and export customs, or rubber tax and head money.

Ethnography.—The inhabitants consist of about 10,000 descendants of repatriated American negroes included in an indigenous population of about 2,000,000 of various negro tribes. The Americo-Liberian peoples and about 40,000 of the indigenous tribes are civilized and belong to the Protestant Christian faith, but many of the native tribes are Muhammadans, while cannibal rites are practiced by other tribes in the interior. English is the official language of the Republic.

Government.—The government is that of a centralized Republic, with a President and Vice-President, elected for four years. President (Jan. 1, 1912-1916), Daniel Edward Howard. An agreement was arrived at in 1911 between Liberia and the United States (Great Britain, Germany, and France approving), whereby the American Government undertook to reorganize the finances and to develop the agricultural possibilities of the country, while setting on foot a defense force and negotiating the various boundary questions. Under this scheme there is an American Financial Adviser and Receiver General of Customs, with British, French, and German receivers; and officers of the United States are organizing a defense force.

Finance.—Public accounts are kept in United States dollars. The revenue of 1911-1912 was stated to be $471,335 and the expenditure $470,000. The external debt of 1871 of £100,000 has received no interest for many years. The finances of the Republic are being satisfactorily reorganized in accordance with the agreement with the United States.

Production and Trade.—The soil is extraordinarily fertile, but the country is covered with dense forests from a distance of about twenty miles from the coast to the northern boundaries. Occasional clearings have been made, and cocoa, coffee, and cotton are grown. The forest products include rubber and palm-oil. Minerals of great variety are believed to exist, including gold, iron, copper, and zinc. The principal exports are coffee, cocoa, palm-kernels, palm-oil, ivory, piassava, rubber, and camwood; the principal imports are cottons, haberdashery, salt, rice, provisions, arms and ammunition, tobacco, hardware, glass and earthenware, rum, gin, timber, and beads. The total value of the imports in 1911 was about $1,025,000, and of exports $975,000.

Trade with the United States.—The value of merchandise imported into Liberia from the United States for the year 1913 was $96,900, and goods to the value of $2,319 were sent thither—a balance of $94,581 in favor of the United States.

Liberia:

French encroachments upon territory of, action of United States regarding, discussed, 5751, 5870.

Independence of, recognition of, by United States, recommended, 3248.

Loan to ameliorate conditions in, found by American commission, 7669.

Removal of negroes captured on coast of Cuba to, recommended, 3058.

Vessel to, presentation of, recommended, 3445, 5086.

Weakness of, discussed, 5086.

Liberty Bell.—The bell on the Pennsylvania statehouse at Philadelphia, which, according to tradition, was rung on July 4, 1776, to announce the adoption of the Declaration of Independence. It was cast in London and sent to Philadelphia in 1752. The bell was broken up and recast in April, and again in June, of the following year. It was cracked July 8, 1835, while being tolled in memory of Chief Justice Marshall. The Liberty bell was placed on exhibition at the Centennial at Philadelphia in 1876, and at the Columbia Exposition in Chicago in 1893. It bears the motto, "Proclaim liberty throughout the land unto all the inhabitants thereof." It is now in Independence Hall, Philadelphia.

Liberty Loan.—The term applied originally to the $5,000,000,000 of the $7,000,-000,000 first war budget voted by Congress on April 14, 1917, which was to be met outside of taxation. Soon, however, the term was applied to the $2,000,000,000 of the $5,000,000,000 which was offered to popular subscription. The rate of interest is 3½%, with the provision that it will be raised equal to any higher rate of interest which may be paid on later loans. Bearer bonds were offered in amounts of $50, $100, $500, and $1,000; and registered bonds from denominations of $100 to $100,000. The bonds mature in 30 years from the date of issue, June 15, 1917, but are redeemable in whole or in part, at the option of the United States, on or after 15 years, at par and accrued interest. 2% of the amount of the bonds was payable on application, 18% on June 28, 20% July 30, 30% August 15, and 30% August 30. Interest is payable on June 15 and December 15 of each year. Bonds are exempt from all Federal, State and local taxation, excepting estate and inheritance taxes. When subscriptions were closed on June 15, it was found that the loan had been largely over-subscribed.

The Second Liberty Loan campaign occupied most of the month of October, 1917. The details were much the same as those of the First Loan, as described above: but the rate of interest was 4%, thus automatically making the rate of interest for the First Liberty Bonds increase to this rate. The minimum subscription was placed at $3,000,000,000; and it was announced that half of the subscriptions between this sum and $5,000,000,000 would also be issued. Total subscriptions by the public amounted to $4,617,532,300: so that the amount issued became $3,808,766,150. Nine and one-half million persons subscribed.

The Third Liberty Loan campaign was inaugurated on April 6, 1918, the first anniversary of the entrance of the United States into the European War. The campaign closed on the following May 4. The amount of the loan was $3,000,000,000 and oversubscriptions, and the rate of interest was 4¼%, to which the bonds of the First and Second Liberty Loans were as a consequence converted. The bonds were issued to mature in ten years from the date of issue. Five per cent of the amount subscribed for the various bonds was due on subscription, 20% on the following May 28, 35% on the following July 18, and 40% on the following August 15. The lowest denomination of the bonds of the Third Liberty Loan was $50.

The bonds of the Third Liberty Loan were not convertible to any higher rate of interest.

The total subscriptions to the Third Liberty Loan were $4,176,517,550, an oversubscription of 39%, every federal reserve district oversubscribing its quota. The number of subscribers was about 17,000,000, as compared with about 9,500,000 in the Second Loan and 4,500,000 in the first. The record of the Third Loan by federal reserve districts was as follows:

District	Quota	Subscriptions
New York	$900,000,000	$1,115,243,650
Chicago	425,000,000	608,878,600
Cleveland	300,000,000	405,051,150
Philadelphia	250,000,000	361,963,500
Boston	250,000,000	354,537,250
San Francisco	210,000,000	287,975,000
Kansas City	130,000,000	204,092,800
St. Louis	130,000,000	199,835,900
Richmond	130,000,000	186,259,050
Minneapolis	105,000,000	180,892,800
Atlanta	90,000,000	137,649,450
Dallas	80,000,000	116,220,650
U. S. Treasury*		17,915,750

*Subscriptions sent directly to Washington.

Liberty Loan, discussed, 8481.

Liberty Party.—A party organized in 1840 principally for the purpose of opposing slavery. It was the outgrowth of the National Anti-Slavery Society (q. v.), and finally became the Abolition Party (q. v.).

Liberty, Statue of.—A bronze image of a female figure holding aloft a lighted torch, designed by M. Bartholdi for the Franco-American Union in 1874, at an estimated cost of $250,000. It was paid for by popular subscription in France and presented by the French people to the United States as a token of the traditional friendship of the two nations. It was mounted upon a pedestal built by popular subscription in America and erected on Bedloe's Island in New York Harbor, in 1886, at a cost of some $350,000. The lighted torch is maintained by the United States Lighthouse Service.

The height from the water level to the top of the pedestal is 149 feet and 10 inches, and the height of the statue proper is 151 feet 5 inches, making a total height of 301 feet 3 inches. The statue weighs 450,000 pounds. Forty persons may stand within the head, and twelve within the torch.

Liberty Enlightening the World, statue of, erected in New York Harbor, by citizens of France, 4381, 4824, 5083.

Ceremonies of inauguration discussed and recommendations regarding, 4982.

To be placed under superintendence of Light-House Board, 5080.

Libraries. (See Interior Department; Library of Congress; State Department.)

Library, Latin American, establishment of, at Washington, recommended by International American Conference, 5506.

Library of Congress.—When the seat of Government was removed to Washington in 1800, the idea of a Congressional Library was conceived. In December, 1801, John Randolph made a report which formed the basis of an act of Congress of 1802 organizing the library. Some 3,000 books of reference were accumulated, when, in August, 1814, the British army burned the Capitol and the Library was consumed. In 1815 Congress purchased the private library of Thomas Jefferson, consisting of 6,700 volumes, for $23,950. An annual appropriation being made for the purchase of books, the Library continued to grow until in 1851 it numbered 55,000 volumes. Dec. 24th of that year a second conflagration destroyed 35,000 of these volumes. An appropriation of $72,000 was made for repairs, and the Library grew apace. In 1866, 40,000 volumes were transferred from the Smithsonian Institution. The following year Congress purchased for $100,000 the historical collection of Peter Force, very rich in Americana. This library contained nearly 60,000 books, pamphlets and manuscripts. In 1864 President Lincoln appointed Ainsworth R. Spofford to be Librarian, and he was succeeded in 1897 by John Russell Young, who died in 1899, and Herbert Putnam was appointed his successor. One hundred sets of Government publications are at the disposal of the Librarian of Congress for exchange, through the Smithsonian, with foreign Governments, and from this source are received about 12,000 volumes annually.

The collection is now the largest on the Western Hemisphere and the third in the world. It comprised at the end of the fiscal year (June 30, 1913) about 2,128,255 printed books and pamphlets (including the law library of 158,117 volumes, which, while a division of the Library of Congress, still remains at the Capitol), 135,223 maps and charts, 625,098 pieces of music, and 360,494 photographs, prints, engravings and lithographs. It includes various special collections eminent in their respective fields.

The collection of manuscripts, touching every period of American history, includes the papers of nine of the Presidents and the records of the Continental Congress, with numerous other important groups—political, military, naval and commercial.

The Smithsonian deposit is strong in scientific works, and includes the largest assemblage of the transactions of learned societies which exists in this country.

Of the printed books, probably one-sixth are duplicates not in use.

The building containing the Library is an enormous structure in the Italian Renaissance style of architecture, most impressive in its lines and beautiful in its detail. It is in the form of a quadrangle enclosing a central rotunda surmounted by a low gilded dome. The building was begun in 1886 and completed in 1897, at the cost of $6,180,000. It is probably the most ornate and beautiful library building in the world. The public reading room occupies the rotunda. It consists of an octagonal hall one hundred feet in diameter, sumptuously built of soft-tinted Numidian, Sienna and Tennessee marble in variegated hues. In the decorations, some forty painters and sculptors are represented—all American citizens. The floor space is 326,195 sq. feet, or nearly eight acres. The book stacks contain about 56 miles of shelving, affording space for 2,600,000 octavo volumes. The reading desks are arranged in concentric circles about the Librarian's desk in the center, from which easy communication is had to all parts of the fireproof iron book stacks. The Library of Congress has been since 1870 the only office of record for copyrights, and its accessions from that source are very large. (See illustration, frontispiece, Vol. XV.)

Library of Congress:

Arundel manuscripts, copy of, to be placed in, 1445.

Building for, recommended by President—

Arthur, 4651.

Cleveland, 4949.

Hayes, 4431, 4458, 4531, 4579.

Publications presented to, referred to, 3347.

Size of, 6676.

Licenses for Vessels, prohibitory laws in regard to, 480, 504, 508.

Liechtenstein.—Liechtenstein is an independent Principality on the right bank of the Lower Rhine, south of Lake Constance, and between the Swiss cantons of St. Gall and Graubünden and the Voralberg crownland of the Austrian Empire. The western boundary is the Rhine, and the southern boundary runs along the summits of the Naafkopf Falknis and Mittags-Spitze, in the Rhätikon Range. A railway runs from Buchs (Switzerland) to Feldkirch (Austria) with stations at Schaan, Nendeln, and Schaanwald in the Principality. The inhabitants numbered 10,716 in 1911, of German origin and almost all Roman Catholics. Agriculture is the principal industry, corn, wine and turf being produced, together with timber from the forest slopes; textiles and embroidery are locally manufactured. The revenue in 1912 was 860,526 Kronen, and the expenditure 796,036 Kronen (24 Kronen = £1 sterling). There is no debt. The Principality forms part of the Customs Union of Austria and receives a minimum contribution of 50,000 Kronen annually (the payments in 1911 exceeded 100,000 Kronen).

Government. The government is that of a constitutional monarchy, the crown being hereditary (since 1719) in the male line of the house of Liechtenstein. Ruler: His Serene Highness Prince Johann II., Prince of Liechtenstein, Duke of Troppau and of Jägerndorf, born Oct. 5, 1840; succeeded his father Prince Aloysius, Nov. 12, 1858; Member of the Herrenhaus of the Austrian Reichsrat.

There is a Diet of fifteen members (of whom three are appointed by the Prince and twelve elected by indirect vote), meeting annually in October, with a maximum duration of four years. The local courts are subject to a Court of Appeal at Vienna, and the Supreme Court is the Oberlandesgericht at Innsbruck.

History.—From 1719-1806 the Principality formed part of the Holy Roman Empire and from 1806-1815 of the Confederation of the Rhine. From 1815-1866 it was part of the Germanic Confederation under the hegemony of Austria, but since 1866 the Principality has been independent, although closely connected by treaties with the Austrian Empire.

Lieutenant-General.—In the United States Army the rank next below that of general and next above that of major-general. It was first authorized by Congress in 1798 and bestowed upon George Washington. It was abolished in 1799, and was not revived until 1855, when Winfield Scott was brevetted lieutenant-general. At his death it again lapsed. In 1864 it was revived by special act of Congress and conferred upon Ulysses S. Grant, on whose promotion to the grade of general, July 25, 1866, created in his behalf, William T. Sherman became lieutenant-general; and on his succession to the rank of general, March 4, 1869, Philip H. Sheridan was promoted to be lieutenant-general. On the retirement of Sherman, in 1884, the grade of lieutenant-general was discontinued and merged with that of general. By an act of Feb. 5, 1895, it was revived and John M. Schofield appointed, who held it until his retirement, Sept. 29th, of that year. On June 6, 1900, Congress provided that the senior major-general commanding the army should have the rank and pay of the lieutenant-general, the act affecting Major-General Nelson A. Miles, who retired Aug. 8, 1903. On that date Samuel B. M. Young received the commission of lieutenant-general, and on Jan. 9, 1904, it was given to Adna R. Chaffee. He was succeeded by Major-General Arthur MacArthur, and with his retirement June 2, 1909, the rank became extinct.

Life-Saving Medals, government grant of, 6896.

Life-Saving Service.—The ocean and lake coasts of the United States are picketed with the stations of the Life-Saving Service attached to the United States Treasury Department, and there is a corps of inspectors, superintendents, station keepers and crews, extending over the entire coast line, together with a board on life-saving appliances, composed of experts selected from the Life-Saving Service, the Revenue Cutter Service, and the United States Coast and Geodetic Survey and the Army.

At the close of last fiscal year the life-saving establishment embraced 285 stations, 203 being on the Atlantic and Gulf coasts, 62 on the lakes, 19 on the Pacific coast, and 1 at the Falls of the Ohio, Louisville, Ky. In the following table are the important statistics of the service:

	Year Ending June 30, 1913	Since Introduction of Life-Saving System in 1871, to June 30, 1913
Disasters...............	552	26,184
Value property involved.	$14,657,240	$333,893,224
Value property saved....	$12,936,025	$270,088,037
Value property lost......	$1,721,215	$63,805,187
Persons involved........	5,787	168,373
Persons lost............	73	1.417
Shipwrecked persons succored at stations......	437	24,754
Days' succor afforded....	756	55,388
Vessels lost on coasts....	66	......

In addition to the number of disasters shown for 1913, there occurred **1,191** casualties to small craft, such as launches, sailboats, rowboats, etc., on which were 3,254 persons, of whom 14 were lost. The cost of the maintenance of the service during the year was $2,204,074.50. In January, 1915, the Life-Saving Service was combined with the Revenue Cutter Service to form the Coast Guard. (See Coast Guard.)

Life-Saving Service
Discussed, 4931, 6158.
Pensions in, 7013.

Light-House Board:
Referred to, 2747.
Statue of Liberty Enlightening the World to be placed under Superintendence of, 5080.

Light-Houses:
Abaco Island, negotiations with Bahamas for site on, 845.
Act making appropriation for, reasons for applying pocket veto to, 1071.
Cession of, to United States act of New Hampshire legislature for, 102.
Establishment of, and sites for, 182; by an act approved June 17, 1910, reorganized the service and, 678, 873, 955, 960, 1239, 2557.
Lands for—
Designated by proclamation, 1221, 6701, 6702, 6705.
Erection of, negotiations for cession of, 103, 845.
Purchase of, 1733.
On Bahamas, 1239.
On Sandy Hook, 67, 80.
Permanent points for, on coasts of Oregon, Washington, and Alaska, 3902.
Soil and jurisdiction for, complete cession of, required, 142.
System of improvement in, 1683.
Treaty with Morocco concerning maintenance of, on Cape Spartel, 3582.

Light-House Service.—Formerly the management of the light-houses was intrusted to a light-house board, organized in conformity to the act of Congress of Aug. 31, 1852. It consisted of the head of the Treasury Department (later of the Department of Commerce and Labor), three officers of the army, two naval and a civilian member. The head of the department was ex-officio president of the board, and the ranking naval officer was chairman. There were two secretaries, one a naval officer and one an engineer officer of the army. That system involved divided responsibility, and resulted in much friction in administration. Congress, therefore, by an act approved June 17, 1910, recognized the service and abolished the board and created a Bureau of Light-Houses in the Department of Commerce and Labor, with a commissioner in charge directly responsible to the Secretary of Commerce and Labor.

The Bureau is charged with the establishment and maintenance of light-houses, light-vessels, buoys and other aids to navigation on the coasts and rivers of the United States, as authorized by Congress, and with the direction of the officers, depots and tenders required in this work.

Under the old system there were sixteen light-house districts, each in charge of an army or navy officer. The law of 1910 provided that nineteen districts should be created, each in charge of a civilian inspector, but the president was authorized for a period of three years, from July 1, 1910, to assign army and navy officers to act as district inspectors.

In the fiscal year 1910-11 the light-house establishment maintained 2,200 lighted aids to navigation, including sixty-three light-vessels, and about 12,000 unlighted aids and post lights.

For the care and maintenance of these aids there were employed 3,137 keepers, assistant keepers and laborers attending lights, 1,693 officers and seamen on board vessels, 318 employees for construction and repair, also fifty-one light-house tenders.

The amount expended to maintain the light-house establishment in 1910-11 was $5,058,800.

Commissioner, George R. Putnam; Deputy Commissioner, Arthur V. Conover; Chief Constructing Engineer, John S. Conway; Superintendent of Naval Construction, George Warrington.

Light-House Service, transfer of, from Treasury to Navy Department recommended, 4727.

Lillie, The, compensation to owners of, 6730, 6824.

Lincoln, Abraham.—March 4, 1861-April 15, 1865.

(FIRST TERM, 1861-1865.)

Nineteenth Administration—Republican.

Vice-President—Hannibal Hamlin.

Secretary of State—
William H. Seward.

Secretary of the Treasury—
Salmon P. Chase.
William Pitt Fessenden.

Secretary of War—
Simon Cameron.
Edwin M. Stanton.

Secretary of the Navy—
Gideon Welles.

Secretary of the Interior—
Caleb B. Smith.
John P. Usher.

Postmaster-General—
Montgomery Blair.
William Dennison.

Attorney-General—
Edward Bates.
T. J. Coffey.
James Speed.

Nomination and Election.—Lincoln was first elected by the Republican party Nov. 6, 1860. The Republican National Convention met at Chicago, May 16, 1860, and on the third ballot nominated Lincoln over Seward, Cameron, and Chase.

Platform.—The platform condemned disunion; insisted on States Rights; denounced the Democratic administration; censured the reckless extravagance of the Democratic Government; proclaimed the dogma that the Constitution carries slavery into any or all of the territories to be a dangerous heresy; asserted that the Constitution does not countenance slavery nor should Congress give a legal existence to it; insisted upon the admission of Kansas to statehood; recommended tariff for revenue, with encouragement of the industries; protested against selling public lands already occupied by settlers; opposed any change in the naturalization laws; declared river and harbor appropriations to be both desirable and constitutional; and demanded a transcontinental railroad.

Opposition.—The Democratic National Convention met, for the first time in the far South, at Charleston, S. C. After many days of fruitless balloting, the convention divided into two sections. Eventually, the Northern half nominated Douglas and the Southern half declared for Breckinridge. The Constitutional Union Party met in national convention at Baltimore, May 19, 1860, and nominated John Bell, on a plat-

form the basis of which was the recognition of no other political principles than the Constitution, Union, and the enforcement of laws.

Vote.—The popular vote as cast by thirty-three States gave Lincoln, 1,865,913; Breckinridge, 848,404; Douglas, 1,374,664, and Bell, 591,900. The electoral vote, counted Feb. 13, 1861, gave Lincoln, 180; Breckinridge, 72; Bell, 39, and Douglas, 12.

(SECOND TERM, MARCH 4, 1865-APRIL 15, 1865.)

Twentieth Administration—Republican.

Vice-President—Andrew Johnson.

The only change in the cabinet at the beginning of Lincoln's second term was the substitution of Hugh McCulloch, of Indiana, for Secretary of the Treasury to succeed Mr. Fessenden.

SECOND TERM.—In the election of 1864, Lincoln was renominated by the (Regular) Republican National Convention, which met in Baltimore on June 7, 1864.

Platform.—The Republican platform of 1864 pledged the party to preserve the Union; opposed any compromise with the rebels; demanded the utter and complete extirpation of slavery; gratefully acknowledged the services of the Army and the Navy in the war; commended the administration of Lincoln; advocated full and ample protection of the members of the Army and the Navy; encouraged immigration; urged speedy construction of the transcontinental railroad; urged the practice of rigid economy in the expenditure of Government funds; and deprecated European interference or offensive sympathy.

Opposition. — The Radical Republican party, opponents of Lincoln, met at Cleveland May 31 and nominated John C. Frémont; but, before the election, Frémont urged the support of Lincoln and withdrew. The Democratic National Convention at Chicago, Aug. 29, 1864, nominated George B. McClellan on a platform declaring that the Constitution had been violated during the Lincoln administration and urged the cessation of hostilities and the compromise of difficulties; condemned the military interference in some state elections; sympathized with prisoners of war; condemned the exercise of martial law; and expressed sympathy for the suffering soldiers and sailors, to whom future aid and reward was promised.

Vote.—The popular vote cast by twenty-four States gave Lincoln 2,216,067, and McClellan 1,808,725. The electoral vote, counted on Feb. 8, 1865, gave Lincoln 212 and McClellan 21.

Party Affiliation.—After Lincoln's service in the State legislature and his single term in Congress (1846-1848), he became one of the most influential of the Whig leaders in Illinois. The repeal of the Missouri Compromise (1854) brought him back into politics with intense anti-slavery ardor. When the Republican party was formed, Lincoln took his place as the head of that party in his state. Before the Republican Convention in 1858 he said: "A house divided against itself cannot stand. I believe this Government cannot endure half slave and half free. I do not expect the Union to be dissolved; I do not expect the house to fall; but I do expect that it will cease to be divided. It will become all the one thing or all the other. Either the opponents of slavery will arrest the further spread of it and place it where the public mind shall rest in the belief that it is in course of ultimate extinction, or its advocates will push it forward until it shall become alike lawful in all the states, old as well as new, North as well as South."

EXTENT OF THE UNITED STATES DURING THE ADMINISTRATION OF PRESIDENT LINCOLN, 1861-1865.

(NOT INCLUDING TERRITORIES)

CALIFORNIA
1850

OREGON
1859

NEVADA
1864

TEXAS
1845

KANSAS
1861

MINNESOTA
1858

IOWA
1846

MISSOURI
1821

WISCONSIN
1848

ARKANSAS
1836

LOUISIANA
1812

ILLINOIS
1318

INDIANA
1816

MICHIGAN
1837

MISSISSIPPI
1817

ALABAMA
1819

TENNESSEE
1796

KENTUCKY
1792

OHIO
1803

GEORGIA
1768

SOUTH
CAROLINA
1788

NORTH CAROLINA
1789

WEST
VIRGINIA
1863

VIRGINIA
1788

PENNSYLVANIA
1787

NEW YORK
1788

FLORIDA
1845

MD.
1788

DEL.
1787

N.J.
1787

CONN.
1788

R.I.
1790

MASS.
1788

N.H.
1788

VT.
1791

MAINE
1820

Political Complexion of Congress.—In the thirty-seventh Congress (1861-1863), the Senate, of 50 members, was composed of 11 Democrats, 31 Republicans, 7 Americans, and 1 vacancy, and the House, of 178 members, was made up of 42 Democrats, 106 Republicans, 28 Americans, and 2 vacancies. In the Thirty-eighth Congress (1863-1865), the Senate, of 51 members, was composed of 12 Democrats and 39 Republicans; and the House, of 183 members, was made up of 80 Democrats and 103 Republicans. In the Thirty-ninth Congress (1865-1867), the Senate, of 52 members, was composed of 10 Democrats and 42 Republicans; and the House, of 191 members, was made up of 46 Democrats and 145 Republicans. In the Fortieth Congress (1867-1869), the Senate, of 53 members, was composed of 11 Democrats and 42 Republicans; and the House, of 193 members, was made up of 49 Democrats, 143 Republicans, and 1 vacancy.

Foreign Policy.—In speaking of the attitude of foreign nations toward the United States during the war, President Lincoln said in his Second Annual Message (page 3327) that the commercial and social conditions of other nations with whom we have had relations have been disturbed by the war, and adds: "We have attempted no propagandism and acknowledge no revolution. But we have left to every nation the exclusive conduct and management of its own affairs. Our struggle has been, of course, contemplated by foreign nations with reference less to its own merits than to its supposed and often exaggerated effects and consequences resulting to those nations themselves. Nevertheless, complaint on the part of this Government, even if it were just, would certainly be unwise."

Public Debt.—The public debt of the United States during the administration of President Lincoln stood as follows: July 1, 1861, $90,580,873.72; 1862, $524,176,-412.13; 1863, $1,119,772,138.63; 1864, $1,815,784,370.57; 1865, $2,680,647,869.74.

Tariff.—The principal tariff changes in President Lincoln's administration were made by the act of Aug. 5, 1861, "to provide increased revenue from imports, to pay interest on the public debt, and for other purposes." This levied a direct tax on both states and territories and provided for what is believed to be the first income tax ever levied by the general government of the United States. This income tax amounted to three per cent per annum on all income in excess of eight hundred dollars. The act of Dec. 24, 1861, imposed increased duties on tea, coffee, and sugar. That of July 14, 1862, was an act "increasing, temporarily, the duties on imports and for other purposes." The act of March 13, 1863, "to modify existing laws imposing duties on imports, and for other purposes," made slight increases. Duties were further increased by the act of June 30, 1864, and that of March 3, 1865.

Slavery.—In his Inaugural Address (page 3206), President Lincoln sought to assure the people of the Southern states that they had nothing to fear from a Republican administration. He quotes from one of his former speeches: "I have no purpose, directly or indirectly, to interfere with the institution of slavery in the states where it exists. I believe I have no lawful right to do so, and I have no inclination to do so." He holds the Constitution to be clear on the question of surrendering fugitive slaves and states that the difference of opinion rests only on whose authority and how the surrender shall be made. He insists upon the integrity of the Union; that no state has the power to secede lawfully and that the Union is not broken by such declaration of secession on the part of any one state. In urging upon the people not to plunge the country into civil war, he said: "You can have no conflict without being yourselves the aggressors. You have no oath registered in Heaven to destroy the Government, while I shall have the most solemn one to 'preserve, protect, and defend it.'" In the earlier stages of the war, the President was besought by both great parties in the country on the one hand to adopt radical measures to stop slavery and on the other to pursue conservative paths. It was well known that he entertained a deep-rooted hatred of domestic servitude; but so great was his reverence for the law, so careful was he of vested rights and interests, and so desirous of retaining the support and confidence of the people, as an aid for the solution of the great problem, that he followed thus far a moderate course between the two extremes.

Emancipation.—In August, 1861, Congress passed the act confiscating the rights of slave-owners in slaves employed in hostile acts against the Union. Frémont followed with his order to emancipate the slaves in Missouri. Lincoln ordered this declaration to be modified to conform to the orders of Congress and by so doing angered the anti-slavery advocates in Missouri and displeased the more conservative advisers.

On March 6, 1862, the President sent a special message to Congress (page 3269) recommending the passage of a joint resolution bringing about the gradual emancipation of slaves by states, in return for which the states should receive pecuniary aid from the Government. Congress passed the resolution, but public opinion in the states was not ready to grasp this means. In April, Congress freed the slaves in the District of Columbia with compensation to owners—a measure which Lincoln had years before earnestly advocated.

The events of the war during 1862 forced upon Lincoln the conclusion that emancipation was the only means at his command. As early as July, 1862, he began to prepare the proclamation, and though urged by delegations to take the step, he waited until it would be possible to make the order effective and easily operative. Late in August, 1862, the President said: "My paramount object is to save the Union, and not either to save or destroy slavery. If I could save the Union without freeing any slave, I would do it; if I could save it by freeing all the slaves, I would do it; and if I could do it by freeing some and leaving others alone, I would also do that." The defeat of Lee at Antietam and his retreat into Maryland seemed to the President an opportune time to issue his proclamation of emancipation, and his preliminary proclamation was accordingly issued on Sept. 22, 1862 (page 3358).

In his Second Annual Message (page 3335), the President recommended to Congress the passage of a resolution offering "compensated emancipation." But Congress did not act promptly, and Jan. 1, 1863, saw the Proclamation of Emancipation issued (page 3358). There was much speculation as to the President's firmness of anti-slavery convictions, and some suggestions that under some circumstances he might withdraw this proclamation. But in his Fourth Annual Message (page **3456**) he repeated his declaration of the previous year: "While I remain in my present position I shall not attempt to retract or modify the emancipation proclamation, nor shall I return to slavery any person who is free by the terms of that proclamation or by any of the acts of Congress," and he adds: "If the people should, by whatever mode or means, make it an Executive duty to reenslave such persons, another, and not I, must be their instrument to perform it." He concludes the message with the terse paragraph: "In stating a single condition of peace I mean simply to say that the war will cease on the part of the Government whenever it shall have ceased on the part of those who began it." Congress acted promptly on the President's suggestion and on Jan. 31, 1865, prepared and proposed to the states the Thirteenth Amendment to the Constitution abolishing slavery, and this, before the end of the year, was ratified by twenty-seven of the thirty-six states.

Lincoln, Abraham:
Amnesty proclamation of, 3414.
  Discussed, 3390, 3455.
    Persons entitled to benefits of, defined by proclamation, 3419.
    Referred to, 3508.
Annual messages of, 3245, 3327, 3380, 3444.
Assassination of. See Biography of, 3206; Death of, post; Military Commission, etc., post.)
Biographical sketch of, 3204.
Centennial anniversary of birth of, proclaimed a special holiday by Roosevelt, 7344.
Child of, death of, announced by Cabinet, 3266.
Constitutional amendment relative to gradual emancipation of slaves recommended by, 3337.
Death of (see also Military commission, etc., post.)—
  Action of Congress on, 3497.
  Action of Senators and Representatives in Washington on, 3490.
  Announcement of, to Vice-President Johnson, 3485.
  Announcements of, 3485.
  Condolence of Bey of Tunis on, 3565.
  Day of humiliation and mourning in memory of, appointed, 3504.
    Order regarding, 3537.
    Postponed, 3505.
  Funeral announcement and official arrangements for, 3493, 3533.
  Guard of honor, 3496.
  Honors to be paid memory of, 3487.
  Orders regarding, 3491.
  Public offices to be closed in commemoration of, 3638.
  Referred to, 3551.
  Report of George H. Sharpe on assassination of, referred to, 3792.

Reward offered for arrest of alleged instigators of assassination of, 3505.
  Distribution of, referred to, 3577.
Persons claiming, directed to file claims, 3551.
Revoked as to certain persons, 3551.
Scene of, opposite 3485.
Emancipation discussed by. (See Emancipation.)
Emancipation proclamation of, 3358.
Executive orders of, 3218, 3239, 3300, 3360, 3375, 3431, 3474, 3483.
Exequatur issued consul of Belgium revoked by, 3420.
Fasting and prayer, day of, set apart by, 3237, 3365, 3422.
  Referred to, 3437.
Finances discussed by, 3248, 3330, 3350, 3384, 3447.
Foreign policy discussed by, 3248, 3255, 3327, 3444.
Habeas corpus—
  Authority given by, to suspend writ of, 3217, 3218, 3219, 3220, 3240, 3300, 3313, 3322.
    Referred to, 3225.
  Suspension of writ of, by, 3299, 3371, 3420.
    Revoked as to certain States by President Johnson, 3529, 3531.
Inaugural address of—
  First, 3206.
  Second, 3477.
Military commission to try persons implicated in assassination of, to be appointed, 3532.
  Detail for court, 3534.
  Judge-advocate appointed, 3534.
  Order appointing commission, 3533.
  Provost-marshal appointed, 3532.
  Sentence of, approved, 3545.
  Special judge-advocate appointed, 3534.
Pardon granted deserters from Army by, 3364, 3479.
  Act authorizing, 3365.
Pocket veto of, 3471.
Portrait of, 3203.
Powers of Federal and State Governments discussed by, 3206, 3221, 3269, 3274, 3286, 3335.
Proclamations of—
  Absence of soldiers from duty, 3364.
  Admission of—
    Nevada, 3430.
    West Virginia, 3368, and illustration opposite 3389.
  Agreement with Bernard Kock for emigration of negroes, canceled, 3368.

Amnesty, 3414.
Persons entitled to benefits of, 3419.
Anniversary of birth of Washington, 3209.
Blockade of Southern ports, 3215, 3216, 3481.
Removal of, 3290, 3372, 3417, 3431, 3482.
Declaring proclamation of Gen. Hunter void, 3292.
Discriminating duties on vessels of Nicaragua suspended, 3416.
Emancipation, 3358.
Notice of, 3297.
Exequatur issued consul of Belgium revoked, 3420.
Extraordinary session of—
Congress, 3214.
Senate, 3362, 3474.
Fasting and prayer, 3237, 3365, 3422.
Government to be reestablished in Southern States, 3414, 3423.
Habeas corpus, writ of, suspended, 3299, 3371, 3420.
Power to suspend, given, 3217.
Liability of aliens to perform military duty, 3369.
Pardons granted deserters, 3364, 3479.
Persons—
Discouraging enlistments, 3299.
In rebellion, 3214, 3294, 3299.
Supplying Indians with munitions of war, 3480.
Privileges of other ports granted—
Newport, Vt., 3428.
St. Albans, Vt., 3473.
States in insurrection, 3238, 3293, 3366.
Thanksgiving, 3290, 3371, 3373, 3429.
Treatment of American vessels in foreign ports, 3482.
Volunteers called for, 3214, 3216, 3370, 3374, 3427, 3472.
Secession discussed by, 3206, 3221, 3227.
Slavery discussed by, 3206, 3269, 3335.
Special session message of, 3221.
State of the Union discussed by, 3245, 3255, 3334, 3389, 3452.
Thanksgiving order of, 3439.
Thanksgiving/proclamation of, 3290, 3371, 3373, 3429. (See also Fasting and Prayer.)
Order regarding day appointed, 3245.
Tributes of nations to, numbers of copies of, referred to, 4001.
Veto messages of—
Additional medical officers of volunteer service, 3289.
Circulating bank notes in District of Columbia, 3288.
Correction of clerical errors in internal-revenue act, reasons for applying pocket veto to, 3471.
War between the States discussed by, 3221, 3245, 3255, 3278, 3303, 3389, 3452, 3478.
Lincoln Highway. (See Transcontinental Highways.)

Lincoln Memorial University.—This university was established by General O. O. Howard, from the suggestion of Abraham Lincoln himself, on Feb. 10, 1897. The institution is located at Cumberland Gap, Tenn., and exists for the education of the youth of the mountain stock from which Lincoln himself sprang.

Lindesfarne, The, claim by owners of, 6934.

Lindsay & Co. vs. Montana Federation of Labor et al.—Lindsay & Co., wholesale dealers in fruits and vegetables, had been declared "unfair" by the Miners' Union and the Trades Assembly. This action was indorsed by the defendant, the Montana Federation, and a circular issued in which "all laboring men and those in sympathy with organized labor are requested not to patronize Lindsay & Co." The company secured an injunction forbidding this boycott, but the Supreme Court of the State vacated the injunction. It was shown that the plaintiff company's trade had suffered as a result of the boycott. The means of boycott in this case was the publication of the circular as quoted above. The court held that such publication by one person or by an association was perfectly legal, being an exercise of the right of free speech and free press.

The court defined the boycott as "the act of combination, in refusing to have business dealings with another, until he removes or ameliorates conditions which are deemed inimical to the welfare of the members of the combination, or some of them, or grants concessions which are deemed to make for that purpose." A conspiracy was defined as "a combination of two or more persons by some concerted action to accomplish a criminal or unlawful purpose, or to accomplish a purpose, not in itself criminal or unlawful, by criminal or unlawful means." The court held that the company did not have a property right in the trade of any particular person; hence any one person may rightfully withdraw his patronage. The court rejects the doctrine that an act perfectly lawful when done by one person becomes criminal when done by two or more persons acting in concert, and that this concerted action amounts to a conspiracy. If an individual is clothed with a right when acting alone, he does not lose such right merely by acting with others. Hence, if the defendants did not violate any legal right of the plaintiff in withdrawing their patronage, they cannot be enjoined from continuing the boycott in force, so long as the means to make it effective are not illegal.

Linen Industry.—The high prices of linen and of the flax fiber from which linen is made has centered attention on the necessity of establishing a real linen industry in this country, the greatest consumer of linen in the world. There seem to be two big problems which must be solved before success is assured. One is to find some artificial method of preparing the flax straw for the spinner, thus relieving the flax grower of this task, and the other is to convince the American public that American-made linen is as good as any other.

The only country in which the production of flax fiber has increased consistently in recent years is Russia, the report states. In the British Isles and in France the production has decreased in spite of all efforts to keep the industry growing, and in Austria-Hungary, Belgium, and the Netherlands the industry has not been able to hold its own. The American production has never been of importance. Thanks to liberal Government aid and to cheap labor the Russians had gradually been getting a monopoly of the business up to the time the war broke out.

In the United States flax has been raised almost entirely for the seed, which is used to make the well-known linseed oil so necessary for the production of good paints and varnishes. Of some 3,000,000 acres of flax raised in this country in 1915, the Department of Agriculture estimates that only 2,000 acres were devoted to flax for fiber. The bulk of the straw from the seed-bearing plants is burned and used for fertilizer. It should be borne in mind, however, that flax growing for seed and flax growing for fiber are separate and distinct industries. Some flax is grown for both seed and fiber, but a decision must be made as to which is to be the more important product, just as the sheep raiser must decide whether mutton or wool is to be the primary consideration.

In Europe the farmer not only raises the flax, but prepares the fiber for the spinner. This preparation requires several processes, one of which, known as "retting," requires considerable cheap labor and much time and is in addition a most disagreeable process for the workmen. The problem in this country is to find some chemical process of retting that can be carried out at a factory and thus allow the farmer to confine his attention to the agricultural end of the industry. This is the only condition on which the American farmer will take to growing flax for the fiber, Mr. Clark thinks. Some progress is already being made in chemical retting and at least two concerns are now buying flax stalks from the growers for further treatment. Chemical processes have been tried before without much success, but one of the new concerns is now selling chemically retted fiber to Europe and the other is making coarse linens for use in clothing and for curtains.

Even if a good all-American linen is produced in this country, however, there still remains the great problem of finding a market for it. That means that time and effort will be required to persuade the consumer to buy the domestic product instead of the imported. Many people invariably choose the imported article when it is displayed alongside of domestic products, almost regardless of quality. The president of a mill now making dyed and bleached dress linens from American flax has found that, small as is his product, there is difficulty in getting the jobbers and department stores to handle it. The tendency is to assume that, even though it is apparently of excellent quality, it cannot equal the old established linens from abroad. There will never be a better time than the present to popularize the domestic product, for the imported article is scarce and high priced. In normal times our imports of linen goods vary from 25 to 30 million dollars and the demand had been steadily increasing up to the time of the war.

The Bureau's report is entitled "Development of an American Linen Industry," Special Agents Series No. 122, and may be obtained for the nominal price of 5 cents from the Superintendent of Documents, Washington, D. C., or from the nearest district office of the Bureau of Foreign and Domestic Commerce.

There are (1914) 157 establishments in the United States engaged in the manufacture of cordage, twine, jute and linen goods. Only 21 of this number claim to make linen goods. The materials used consist of Manila and New Zealand hemp, Hennequin (sisal from Mexico and Cuba), sisal (from Africa, the Bahamas, Hawaii and Java). The consumption of flax and flax tow was less than 25 million pounds and most of these materials were mixed with cotton.

Liquors—Malt, Vinous and Distilled. —The use of alcoholic liquors in the United States is said to have doubled between the years 1880 and 1900. It was estimated that the per capita consumption in 1902 was 19.48 gallons. The total amount spent for the year was $1,396,098,276. About one-fourth of the population are said to be habitual users of intoxicants. A constitutional amendment providing for nation-wide prohibition of the sale of liquors was defeated in the sixty-third Congress, but many states have general and local laws on the subject. (See Prohibition.) The manufacture of liquors is one of the leading industries of the United States, and the main financial support of the government.

Malt Liquors.—Early New England colonists encouraged the manufacture of malt liquors for the broader market it afforded for grain, and because the supply of a mild beverage promoted temperance and good order among the citizens, who presumably would have indulged in stronger drink if denied ale or beer. In 1795 upward of two million gallons were produced. While, prior to 1795, it does not appear that legislation adverse to the brewing industry was enacted, yet laws favorable to the cheaper distribution of distilled liquors brought these stronger drinks to the fore and held in check the brewing industry. Efforts were made in drawing up the early federal revenue laws to foster malt liquor making, but these were successfully foiled. In 1789 President Madison expressed the hope that the brewing industry would strike deep root in every state in the union, and Thomas Jefferson stated that "no nation is sober where the dearness of fermented drinks substitutes ardent spirits as a common beverage."

In 1810 the domestic production of malt liquors amounted to 5,754,735 gallons. There were 129 breweries in the country, most of them producing ale and porter exclusively. In 1847 the increasing German immigration brought to America not only a demand for their favorite beverage, lager beer, but also a practical knowledge of its manufacture. Before the Civil war the use of strong drink was increasing at an alarming rate. The revenue tax then imposed raised the price of ardent spirits to the consumer, and the Brewers' Association was formed, in 1862, for the purpose of aiding the government in perfecting the law and collecting the tax, as well as to protect its members from unjust discrimination. The patriotism shown by the German-Americans during the war between the States also went a long way toward silencing criticism of them and their national drink. In 1863, there was produced 2,006,625 barrels of beer. The amount steadily increased until 1900, when the production reached 39,330,849 barrels.

The census of 1910 reports the existence of 290 wineries in the country, whose products were valued at $13,120,846. They employed 1,911 wage-earners to whom were paid $971,502.

Whisky.—During the early days of the republic distilling was chiefly conducted by farmers, who made a crude whisky for home consumption. A small kettle and a worm placed alongside his log cabin were almost as essential a part of the farmer's household equipment as the flail to thrash his grain or the plow for his land. In 1791 the first internal revenue tax was imposed on spirits, the rate being nine cents a gallon. It was estimated that about three million gallons were produced. This tax, light as it was, was strongly resisted by the farmers of Western Pennsylvania, and it became necessary to call upon the militia to enforce payment. (See Whisky Rebellion.) From 1802 to 1813 there was no revenue tax on whisky, then a tax on distillers was substituted for a tax on their product. In 1816 the internal revenue tax was reduced one-half, and abolished entirely in 1818. It was not again levied until 1862 when the exigencies of war required more internal revenue. Then a tax of 20 cents a gallon was levied, and this was thrice increased in 1864, until on Dec. 22d of that year the tax was $2 per gallon. After the war successive reductions were made in the tax, but it has always been looked upon as a fruitful source of revenue for the government. In 1874 there was produced about 69,500,000 gallons of spirits upon which the government collected a revenue of $43,000,000.

Census figures published in 1910 place the number of distilleries making whisky, brandy, rum, gin and alcohol at 613 having a yearly output of $500 or more. The Commissioner of Internal Revenue, however, found 1,292 by counting the smaller establishments and those which are engaged primarily in other manufacture, but which report distilled spirits as a by-product. The value of the products is placed by the census at $204,699,412, but this figure includes the revenue tax to be collected when taken out of bond.

Distillers of grain or molasses must, in accordance with government regulations, provide warehouses for their products. These are known as bonded warehouses, and are in charge of bonded officers of the government. All spirits produced from molasses or grain must, before shipment, be placed in warehouses for record, even though they be alcohol, cologne spirits, or other classes that do not require ageing and are immediately marketable. All whiskies that require ageing are allowed by the government to remain in bonded warehouses for a maximum period of eight years and no tax is collected until the goods are withdrawn. There is about $35,-000,000 invested in the industry, and the amount of wages paid in 1909 was $3,074,-395, distributed among 6,430 employees. (See also Distilled Spirits.)

Lisbon, Portugal, International Postal Congress at, discussed, 4938.

Literature should be aided, 58, 60, 61.

Lithuania.—At the time when Lithuania passed into the control of Russia with the dissolution of Poland in 1793, it comprised a country of about 100,000 square miles, bounded on the north by Courland and Livonia, on the south by the Ukraine, on the west by Poland and extending on the east beyond the Dnieper. Under the old Russia, Lithuania comprised the Russian governments of Kovno, Vilna, Grodne, Vitebsk, Mogilev, Minsk, and Suwalka.

The Lithuanians form a distinct race, closely akin to the Letts. They are mostly Roman Catholics. It was estimated that there were in 1910 some 2,000,000 Lithuanians and 1,200,000 Letts. Other inhabitants of Lithuania are the Russians, the Poles and the Jews.

Lithuania consists chiefly of marshes and forests, and the land is generally unproductive. Its unattractive and almost impassable nature rendered it through the Middle Ages both immune from concerted outside attack and from the spread of knowledge and civilization. Indeed, the first definite historical Lithuanian figure does not appear on the pages of history until the thirteenth century, and the country was largely pagan as late as fifteenth century, when Roman Catholicism was established.

From 1375 to 1500 Poland and Lithuania had an alliance recognizing each as an independent government, and from the latter date until 1569 they were under the same ruler. In the latter year, however, Lithuania became incorporated in Poland (q. v.), its autonomy ended, and its later history is the history of Poland.

The tides of the European War swept through Lithuania for many months, but did not succeed in stamping out whatever had existed of a Lithuanian nationalistic movement. After the Russian Revolution in 1917, when the old Russia began to split up into separate nationalities, Lithuania asserted and maintained its right to its previous national independence.

With the military collapse of Russia in the European War, the forces of Germany overran Lithuania without opposition, and the entire country fell definitely under German influence. On December 12, 1917, the Lithuanian Landsrat announced the restoration of Lithuania as an independent state allied to the German power, bound by alliances and military and economic conventions. The independence of the country was officially proclaimed by Germany in May, 1918.

Litigation, measures to prevent delay and unnecessary cost of, 7692.

Little Osage Indians. (See Indian Tribes.)

Lizzie Major, The arrest of, by Spanish frigate, discussed, 3986.

Lizzie Thompson, The, claim arising out of capture of, 3353.

Loans (see also Bonds; Debt, Public):
Authority for making, recommended, 2555.

Contracted with—
Amsterdam, 120.
Antwerp, 120.
Bank of United States, 134.
Holland, 73, 78, 98, 133, 167, 169.
Discussed by President—
Adams, John, 243.
Adams, J. Q., 870, 924.
Johnson, 3264, 3282.
McKinley, 6238.
Madison, 513, 523, 549.
Monroe, 636, 647, 675, 809, 822.
Polk, 2347, 2402.
Tyler, 1934, 1960, 2061.
Washington, 98, 167.

Extraordinary session of Congress convened by President McKinley to obviate, if possible, the necessity of, 6244.

Inability of Government to obtain, discussed, 2061.

Made for defense of States during War of 1812, 809.

Necessary for prosecution of war with Mexico, 2347, 2402.

Obviating the necessity of, by convention of Congress in special session, 6244.

Time of payment of, should be extended, 1934.

Referred to, 1960.

To Mexico, discussed, 3264, 3282.

War-revenue act of 1898, authorizing, 6314.

Loans and Sinking Fund, Commissioner of, office of, should be abolished, 1382.

Lobby.—In political usage, the persons who frequent the halls of Congress or state legislatures—especially the lobbies and committee rooms, for the purpose of meeting legislators and persuading them to support measures desired by the principals employing the lobbyists. Their means of persuasion are usually mere arguments and appeals, but, in isolated instances, money or other valuable considerations are utilized. So long as the lobby confines itself to legitimate arguments, it is not properly objectionable, but is a means of carrying out the American right of petition.

Lobos Islands:

Controversy regarding, referred to, 2696, 2837, 2900.

Sovereignty of Peru over, acknowledged, 2703.

Local Government.—Sometimes written local and self-government. The regulation and administration of the local affairs of a city or district by the people of it, as distinguished from such regulation and administration by authority of the state or nation at large. The state was an institution of the Roman Empire, but the Teutonic tribes or nations developed a local government of their own, and gave the name "town" to language and the idea of "township" to constitutional law. As to whether the first English colonists in America derived the subdivision of the county known in England as town or township from the mother country there was no question until recently, when respectable authority was adduced for the statement that the Plymouth and Massachusetts Bay colonists, especially the former, who came directly from Holland, borrowed their local government system and several other institutions of high value from the Dutch Republic. Certain it is, nevertheless, that when the first settlements were made in this country England had well-developed forms of local government which served as a pattern, beyond doubt, for the Jamestown Colony, Va., and for some other colonies as well. The colony was subdivided into counties, the counties in some cases into hundreds, and the hundreds into parishes or townships. At the time of the colonization the parish of England had generally superseded the township. In the Southern colonies, where the plantation system prevailed and the people were scattered over a large area, the colonists, on their separation from England, retained the county system as being best suited to their population. In the New England Colonies, where population was more compact, the township government was retained. Thus two distinct types of local government prevailed in the United States—the township system in New England and the county system in the South. In the middle colonies a system of local government was instituted which combined the county and township system. This is now generally in use in the Western States.

Local Offices, elimination of, from politics, 7698.

Local Option.—A principle of law established in some of the United States by which the determination as to whether or not any licenses to sell intoxicating liquors shall be granted is submitted to a vote of the people of a town or other minor political community. If the people of any locality decide upon prohibition, it becomes a part of the state law for that community. Local option by states was suggested as a solution of the slavery question, and the Kansas-Nebraska law contained a provision to this effect.

Loco-Focos.—The radical faction of the Democratic party in New York in 1835-1837. The Equal Rights faction was opposed to the granting of bank charters and special privileges to favorites of the Government, and the Tammany men supported the Administration. At a meeting held in Tammany Hall, New York, Oct. 29, 1835, the regular Tammany Democrats tried to gain control, but finding themselves outnumbered they turned out the lights and left the hall. The Equal Rights men produced candles and lighted them by the aid of "loco-foco" matches and continued the meeting. The word, at first used in derision of this faction, was later adopted by the Democratic party as an emblem of promptitude in an emergency, and it was also applied to the party sometimes in derision by their opponents.

Loewe vs. Lawlor et al.—Loewe & Co., hat manufacturers, of Danbury, Conn., brought suit against the United Hatters of North America to restrain the latter from prosecuting a boycott against the plaintiff's hats. The manufacturers had declared an open shop and discarded the use of the union label, whereupon their employees, belonging to the Hatters' Union, induced the latter to institute a boycott throughout the United States. The Supreme Court of the United States, overruling two lower courts, unanimously found in favor of the plaintiff company.

The contention was that the boycott, so called, constituted a combination in restraint of trade, and was, therefore, a violation of the Sherman Anti-Trust Law of 1890. The decision was based on Sec. 1 of that act, which declares "every contract combination in the form of a trust or otherwise, or conspiracy, in restraint of trade" to be illegal, and fixes punishment for violation at not more than $5,000 fine, or imprisonment for one year, or both; and on Sec. 2, which forbids monopoly and fixes similiar punishments; and Sec. 7, which provides that any person who is injured in his business through any act forbidden by this law may sue to recover threefold damages.

The court held that the trade union boycott was a "combination in restraint of trade among the several States" in that it obstructed the free flow of commerce and restricted the right of the plaintiff to engage in business, by trying to compel him to do business only in the way the union imposed. As the plaintiff company was able to show losses aggregating $80,000, as the result of the boycott, it was authorized to sue for $240,000.

Jan. 5, 1915, the Supreme Court for the third time confirmed the decision of the lower courts, granting damages to Loewe & Co. of $252,000, to be paid by the United Hatters.

Log-Cabin and Hard Cider Campaign. —A campaign slogan used by the Whigs during the candidacy of William Henry Harrison for President in 1840,—originated by the fact that a part of his house was originally a log-cabin, and that he served cider on his table instead of wines. This campaign is sometimes referred to as "The Hard Cider Campaign."

Log Rolling.—A term used with reference to legislative bodies where measures become laws as the result of trading votes. That is, where two or more members desire a measure in which no one else is interested, each supports all the measures proposed by the other or others in order to obtain sufficient votes for his own. A noted example of "log rolling" is found in our early history: Hamilton wanted his financing plan approved in Congress, but cared less about the location of the Capitol; Jefferson wanted the Capitol located on the Potomac, but cared less about the financing plan. Each of them threw his support to the other, and each was successful.

Logan Forest Reserve, proclaimed, 6829.

London, England:

Exhibition in, works illustrative of, referred to, 2761.

Industrial exhibition to be held in, in 1862, discussed, 3233, 3254.

Circulars, etc., regarding, 3261.

Vessels to transport American exhibits recommended, 3262.

International Fisheries Exhibition to be held in, 4688.

International Inventions Exhibition to be held in, 4827.

International Penitentiary Congress at, 4162.

Smoke Abatement Exhibit at, 4695.

Lone Star State.—A nickname for Texas (q. v.). (See also States.)

Lookout Mountain (Tenn.), Battle of. —The arrival of the two corps under Hooker and the army of Sherman at Chattanooga increased the strength of Grant's command to 80,000 men. At this critical time Longstreet, with 16,000 men, was detached from the Confederate army and sent to besiege Burnside at Knoxville, leaving Bragg with only about 5,000 men to hold the position. Nov. 24, 1863, to cover Sherman's crossing the Tennessee River and securing a position, Hooker, with 10,000 men, made an attack on the western slope of Lookout Mountain. During a heavy mist he pressed up the mountain side and attacked the position in front and rear, capturing about 1,000 prisoners. The Confederates retired from the mountain to Missionary Ridge.

Loose Constructionist.—The individual or political party construing the Constitution liberally and flexibly; the Federalists and the Whigs and the modern Republicans advocated loose or broad construction of the Constitution. (See Strict Constructionist.)

Lopez Expedition, pardon and release of members of, by Spain, 2678.

Lord Nelson, The, claim of James Crooks against the United States for seizure of, 4975, 5662.

Lorimer Case.—The right of William Lorimer, Republican, of Chicago, to hold his seat in the United States Senate, to which he had been elected by a combination of Democrats and Republicans in the Illinois legislature was challenged Jan. 9, 1911. The Committee on Privileges and Elections reported that the charges were not sustained. Senator Beveridge of the committee made a minority report contending that if only one case of bribery were established it invalidated the whole election. "The testimony is overwhelming," he declared, "not only that four members of the general assembly were bribed, but that three of their fellow members paid them their money. But these seven were not all of the tainted votes cast in the putrid transaction. The testimony shows that at least three additional corrupt votes were cast." After a long debate the Beveridge resolution was lost, March, 1911. The action of the Senate in affirming the legality of Lorimer's election was followed by official protest and public and private criticism from all parts of the country. The Illinois State Senate then made an investigation and found that Lorimer would not have been elected had it not been for bribery and corruption. Senator La Follette, of Wisconsin, reopened the case in the United States Senate April 6, 1911, and another investigation was carried on, both in Washington and Chicago, and Lorimer was expelled from the Senate in the spring of 1912.

Lottery.—The Continental Congress tried to raise money by lottery in 1777. As early as 1612 the Virginia Company was authorized by its charter to hold lotteries for the benefit of its colonization schemes. In the eighteenth century lotteries were extremely popular in America. Legislatures authorized them for building churches, schools and all sorts of public improvements. Faneuil Hall, in Boston, having been destroyed by fire in 1761, was rebuilt by lottery. The Louisiana State Lottery was the last authorized institution of the kind in the United States. Popular opinion has undergone a change regarding lotteries. They were forbidden in 1890 by act of Congress to use the mails. This act resulted in closing the Louisiana Lottery.

Lottery.—Continental Congress recommendations regarding, 5479, 5515.

Passage of act regarding, discussed, 5551.

Louisa, The, proceedings of court regarding, 895.

Louisiana.—One of the southern group of states; nickname, "The Pelican state"; motto, "Union, Justice and Confidence." It extends from the Gulf of Mexico northward to the thirty-third parallel of north latitude and from the eighty-ninth to the ninety-fourth meridian west longitude. It is bounded on the north by Arkansas and Mississippi, on the east by Mississippi (separated by the Mississippi River) and the Gulf of Mexico, on the south by the Gulf of Mexico, and on the west by Texas (separated in part by the Sabine River).

The area of the State is 48,506 square miles. Louisiana is the leading sugar state of the Union, besides which are exported cotton, rice, and corn.

Louisiana was explored by De Soto in 1541, by Marquette in 1673, and by La Salle in 1682. It was settled by the French under Iberville and Bienville about 1700, was ceded by France to Spain in 1763, retroceded to France in 1800, was purchased by the United States in 1803, and was made the Territory of New Orleans in 1804. The portion east of the Mississippi River was annexed in 1810. The State was admitted to the Union in 1812. Jan. 26, 1861, it seceded and joined the Southern Confederacy. It was readmitted by act of Congress June 25, 1868 (3856). (See also Louisiana Purchase.)

Statistics of agriculture collected for the last Federal census place the number of farms in the State at 120,546, comprising 10,439,481 acres, valued, with stock and improvements, at $301,220,988. The average value of farm land per acre was $17.99, as compared with $17.74 in 1900. The value of domestic animals, poultry, etc., was $44,699,485, including 804,795 cattle, valued at $11,605,354; 181,286 horses, $11,-789,695; 131,554 mules, $15,624,962; 1,327,605 swine, $3,824,046; 178,287 sheep, $343,046. The yield and value of field crops for 1911 is given as follows: Corn, 1,800,000 acres, 33,300,000 bushels, $23,-310,000; oats, 40,000 acres, 840,000 bushels, $546,000; rice, 371,200 acres, 11,693,-000 bushels, $9,237,000; potatoes, 22,000 acres, 1,518,000 bushels, $1,518,000; hay, 24,000 acres, 31,000 tons, $372,000; tobacco, 500 acres, 225,000 pounds, $69,750, and 395,000 bales of cotton.

The mineral production of the State in 1910 was valued at $10,119,993, of which petroleum represented $3,574,069, nearly double that of the preceding year, and the production of petroleum for 1911 was near 10,000,000 barrels, exceeding the product of 1910 by three million barrels. New oil wells are frequently being opened.

The industries of the State which give employment to the greatest number of persons are those connected with the lumber and timber products. These industries employ 46,072 persons, and represent an investment of $62,838,000. The business in which the most capital is invested, however, is the manufacture and refinement of sugar and molasses. Industries connected with cotton seed oil and cake have $13,085,-000 invested; the rice industry, $12,529,000; bags other than paper, $5,352,000. There are 86,563 persons engaged in industry, and the total capital invested in 1909 was $221,816,000. The value of finished products was $223,949,000, of which $89,084,-000 was added by manufacture. The population in 1910 was 1,656,388.

Louisiana (see also Confederate States; New Orleans):

Accession of, to United States, discussed and referred to, 346, 348, 350, 669, 853, 929, 957, 3255, 6346.

Effect of, discussed, 2878.

Appropriation for, 382.

Authority to grant or dispose of lands of Spain in, referred to, 651.

Boundaries of, 372, 377, 960.

Branch mint in, referred to, 1383, 1495.

Cession of, to France, referred to, 331, 338.

Colonel-commandant of, commissioned, 364.

Commission to, instruction of President Hayes to, 6341.

Constitution of, referred to, 3831.

Division of, into subordinate districts, 363.

Elections in, and complications growing out of, discussed, 4161, 4166, 4250, 4259.

Federal interference in, discussed, 4259.

Proclamations regarding, 4177, 4230.

Electors in, letter of John Sherman and others regarding canvass of vote of, referred to, 4367.

France, cession of, referred to, 331, 338.

Fourteenth amendment to Constitution ratified by, 3837.

Proclaimed, 3856.

Government of—

Assumed by Governor Claiborne, 355.

Letter regarding, transmitted, 355.

Referred to, 352, 359.

Governor of, letter from, 336.

Indians inhabiting, referred to, 386.

Lands granted to, in aid of railroads, referred to, 3580.

Lands in—

Fraudulent practices of monopolizing, 356.

Proclamation regarding sale of, 1058.

Treaty regarding security of titles to, discussed, 929.

Laws of, referred to, 352, 353, 406.

Lead mines in, 359.

Memorial from purchases of land in, 1029.

Mint at New Orleans seized by authorities of, referred to, 3199.

Possession of, commissioners appointed to receive, 355.

Private land claims in, recommendations regarding, 4691.

Proclamations against unlawful combinations in, 4161, 4166, 4177, 4230, 4250, 4259.

Provisional court established in, order regarding, 3323.

Restoration of, into Union, discussed, 3123, 3452.

Spain, transfer of, to the United States disagreeable to, 376.

Support of, referred to, 382.

Title to, objections to validity of, withdrawn, 358.

Transfer of, to United States disagreeable to Spain, 376.

Unlawful combinations in, discussed and proclamations against, 4161, 4166, 4177, 4230, 4250, 4259.

Louisiana, District of.—That part of the Louisiana Purchase which is not included in the present State of Louisiana. It was erected into a district and the capital was established at St. Louis in 1804. In 1805 it was given a separate government as the Territory of Louisiana. In 1812 the name of the Territory was changed to Missouri.

Louisiana Lottery Co. discussed, 5515.

Louisiana, Province of. (See Louisiana.)

Louisiana Purchase.—A name applied to the territory west of the Mississippi River purchased from France in 1803. It was the most important sale of territory ever executed in favor of the United States. President Jefferson desired the acquisition of New Orleans in order to obtain control of the mouth of the Mississippi and offered to guarantee to Napoleon the territory to the west of the river in exchange. Napoleon, being at that time at war with Great Britain and greatly in need of funds, and being desirous moreover to foil England's aspirations for more territory in the United States, consented to the transfer of the so-called province of Louisiana to the United States for the sum of $15,000,000. The territory thus acquired embraced all the present State of Louisiana lying west of the Mississippi River, together with New Orleans and the adjacent district east, comprising Mississippi and Alabama below the thirty-first parallel; Arkansas, Missouri, Iowa, a portion of Idaho and Minnesota, all of the Dakotas, most of Kansas, all of Nebraska and Indian Territory, part of Colorado, most of Wyoming, and the whole of Montana. In 1904, the Louisiana Purchase Exposition was held at St. Louis, Mo., to commemorate the acquisition of this important territory.

Louisiana Purchase:

Discussed and referred to, 346, 348, 350, 669, 853, 929, 957, 3255.

Effects of, discussed, 2878.

Louisiana Purchase Exposition was held at St. Louis, Mo., between April 30 and Dec. 1, 1904, to celebrate the centennial of the Louisiana Purchase. It was the largest World's Fair ever held, and the third of its kind in America; its grounds covered 1,240 acres, of which 250 acres were roofed over. The total amount expended upon the Exposition by the Exposition Company, the various states, foreign governments, and the concessionaires, amounted to about $44,500,000; while the total receipts came to about $25,000,000; and the Exposition closed free from debt. In point of attendance it fell below the Paris Exposition of 1900 with its 50,000,000 entrances and the World's Fair at Chicago with 27,500,000 entrances, as its attendance only totalled 18,700,000.

Louisiana Purchase Exposition:

Opened by proclamation of President Roosevelt, 6686.

Relations of United States Government to, 6675, 6681, 6729, 6732, 6736, 6740, 6771, 6798, 6825, 6857, 6862, 6865, 6866, 6932.

Louisiana vs. Jumel.—An important Supreme Court case defining the liability of State officers. Jumel held bonds issued under an act of the Louisiana legislature of 1874 and the constitutional amendment adopted in that year. He demanded payment of these bonds in 1880. Payment was refused solely on the ground of obedience to the Louisiana State debt ordinance of the new constitution adopted July 23, 1879, and the law of 1880, carrying out provisions contained in this new constitution. This act, in the language and spirit of the ordinance, recited that coupons of consolidated bonds falling due in January, 1880, were remitted. Suit was brought against officers of the State. The Circuit Court of the State decided for the defendant, and its decision was affirmed by the United States Supreme Court on the ground that relief could not be awarded against officers obeying the supreme power of the State; that the money is the State's property, not held in trust by the officers except in the capacity of her servants. "The political power of the State," said Chief Justice Waite in the opinion of the court, "can not be ousted of its jurisdiction and the judiciary set in its place." Dissenting opinions were rendered by Justices Field and Harlan.

Louisville and Portland Canal Co., act for subscription of stock in, reasons for applying pocket veto to, 1071.

Louisville, Ky., Southern Exposition at, discussed, 4773.

Board on behalf of Executive Departments designated, 4819.

Instructions to, 4820.

Lower Brulé Indians. (See Indian Tribes.)

Loyal Legion, Military Order of.—The Military Order of the Loyal Legion of the United States was organized by officers and ex-officers of the army, navy and marine corps of the United States, who took part in the War of 1861-65. Membership descends to the eldest direct male lineal descendant, according to the rules of primogeniture. There are 21 commanderies, each representing a state, and one commandery representing the District of Columbia. The total membership of the Loyal Legion is 8,880.

Loyalists.—Those of the American colonists who opposed the Revolutionary War and in some instances took up arms against their countrymen in the struggle for independence. They were also called Tories. As early as 1688 parties favorable to the Crown were exerting an influence in all the colonies. As the revolutionary movement grew their opposition to it increased. In no colony was there an overwhelming desire for independence, and in some the advocates of revolution were in the minority. Many of the most respected and eminent men of the middle colonies were loyal to the Crown. During the progress of the war they were treated with great harshness. Their property was confiscated or destroyed: they suffered social ostracism, and some were tarred and feathered. Legislative assemblies banished them from some of the colonies. When the British troops withdrew at the close of the war the Tories found life in the states unendurable and thousands retired to Canada, Nova Scotia, New Brunswick, the Bahamas, and other West Indies. In the treaty of peace in 1783 the British asked to have provision made for recompensating the dispossessed Loyalists, but all they received was a promise to submit the matter to the states, and they refused relief.

Lubeck:

Minister of, received by United States, 949.

Treaty with, 988, 991, 2686, 6294.
Vessels of, discriminating duties on, suspended by proclamation, 642.

Lubeck, Treaty with. (See Hanseatic Republics.)

Luckett and Tyler (assignees of William T. Cheatham), act for relief of, vetoed and reasons assigned, 4334.

Ludlow's Code.—Named for Governor Roger Ludlow, and being a set of laws for the regulation of the New Haven Colony.

Lumber, Lath and Shingles.—(From a report issued by the Census Bureau, August 26, 1913.) A preliminary statement of the output of lumber, lath and shingles in the United States during the calendar years 1912, 1911 and 1910. From data collected in co-operation with the Forest Service of the Department of Agriculture.

The number of active mills contributing to the totals were 29,648 in 1912; 28,107 in 1911, and 31,934 in 1910; while the reported production in these years was, in M feet board measure, 39,158,414, 37,003,-207 and 40,018,282, respectively. The statistics cover the output of practically every commercial mill in operation during the whole or any part of this period. Although the reported cut was slightly less than in 1910, the average yield per mill was 5.3 per cent greater than in that year, while the total production over 1911 was 2,155,207 M feet board measure, or nearly 6 per cent.

STATISTICS OF THE LUMBER INDUSTRY FOR 1914 SHOW:

	Total Saw Mills, Logging Camps, and Independent Planing Mills
Number of establishments	33,060
Persons engaged in manufacture	651,585
Proprietors and firm members	37,471
Salaried employees	38,114
Wage earners (average number)	576,000
Primary horsepower	2,661,759
Capital	$1,183,379,000
Services	351,979,000
Salaries	50,053 000
Wages	301,926,000
Materials	466,179,000
Value of Products	1,022,982,000
Value added by manufacture (value of products less cost of materials)	556,803,000

Waste in the logging industry in the United States amounts to 15 to 20 per cent of the timber cut, or about a billion and a half cubic feet of wood annually. Sawmill waste also amounts to several billion cubic feet of wood, although not all of it is absolute waste.

It was the prodigious waste of American forest resources that led the Bureau of Foreign and Domestic Commerce to plan a thorough study of the methods of utilizing the waste products of the lumber industry, here in the United States and in those European countries that have made the most distinct progress in this line. In the older and more thickly settled countries of the old world necessity led to a careful utilization of the forests many years before the subject was seriously discussed in this country. And in these older countries many methods have been worked out that should be of value in this country now that the old-time wasteful methods have been brought into disrepute.

The annual production of wood pulp in the United States is valued at over $80,000,000. Sulphite-pulp makers are considerably interested in the possible utilization of the sulphite waste liquor for the recovery of sulphur or other profitable utilization. This would result in a lowering of the cost of sulphite pulp. The manufacture of kraft pulp is also becoming well established, and is bringing about the utilization of cheaper wood.

The manufacture of alcohol from sawdust has hardly passed the experimental stage, although technical men are optimistic as to the ultimate success of the process. One of the most interesting possibilities lies in the use of hydrolyzed sawdust as a carbohydrate cattle food. The manufacture of plastics from wood is still enveloped in secrecy, and, like the manufacture of wood flour, has apparently been developed to a much greater extent in European countries.

Claims and controversies over measurements are the disturbing feature of the otherwise satisfactory lumber trade the United States is now doing with Argentina, Uruguay, and Brazil, declares a report on the "Lumber Markets of the East Coast of South America" issued by the Bureau of Foreign and Domestic Commerce, of the Department of Commerce. These disputes arise principally in connection with shipments of southern yellow pine which makes up the bulk of the lumber sold to the east coast of South America. This great district imports annually 565 million board feet of lumber, of which 349 million feet are yellow pine from the United States. The total lumber consumption of the three countries is 735 million board feet.

Argentina and Uruguay, although about 7,000 miles distant from the United States, constitute virtually an addition to our domestic wood-consuming field, so similar are market conditions. For more than 10 years 86 per cent of all lumber going into commerce in the two countries has come from the forests of North America, and nearly 96 per cent of the imports, exclusive of those from other South American countries, is credited to the United States and Canada.

In 1914 the imports of lumber into Argentina amounted to 210,851,000 feet, made up as follows: Yellow pine, 101,200,-000 feet; spruce, 35,600,000 feet; white pine, 30,410,000 feet; Spanish cedar, 11,800,000 feet; South American hardwoods, 15,630,000 feet; oak, 2,445,000 feet; Douglas fir, 3,300,000 feet; ash, 430,000 feet; Parana pine, 9,800,000 feet; walnut, 225,000 feet; mahogany, 11,000 feet. In other words, it is necessary to buy abroad most of the softwoods so necessary in nearly every community. Yellow pine is very generally appreciated and comes almost entirely from our southern ports. Spruce is imported principally from Canada, although important shipments are made from Boston. Until 1911 there was no outside competition with North American spruce, but between that year and the outbreak of the war Austrian spruce became an important factor. Over 80 per cent of imports of white pine comes from Canadian forests, but is shipped mostly from Boston. Shipments from Boston have been the rule for so many years that consignments from other ports are considered inferior. Douglas fir, of course, is imported from our western coast. So far as price is concerned, it competes on about equal terms with southern yellow pine.

In Brazil the lumber situation is rather complicated, writes Mr. Simmons. The virgin forests are unmeasured and contain untold varieties of tall trees of fairly large diameter. Yet Brazil is importing 60 million feet of pine lumber against a domestic production of 45 million feet. One-third of the domestic pine lumber production is exported. As in Argentina and Uruguay, yellow pine from our southern States is the principal lumber imported, but Scotch fir from Sweden has supplanted the North American spruce, which not many years ago found a market in Brazil primarily as a substitute for European pine and fir. On the whole, conditions are not thought to be prejudicial to the sale of American lumber, but they should be carefully studied and watched if the United States is to increase its share in Brazil's lumber trade.

There is a great deal of complaint in Brazil regarding yellow-pine shipments, resulting from the large proportion of overruns. In thickness this overrun will vary from a quarter to three-quarters of an inch, and in length from 4 to 15 inches. The importer is not obliged to pay the American exporter for this overrun, but it is a source of extra expense nevertheless, sometimes amounting to as much as $400 on a single cargo. This results from a Brazilian law that not only provides for the usual duty on parts of cargo not invoiced, but levies a fine equal to the amount of that duty. With the present high duties it does not require much of an overrun on a million-foot cargo for the penalty to run up to a considerable sum. Brokers, exporters, and sawmills interested in Brazilian lumber markets are urged to take immediate steps to relieve the consignees of the burden of this unnecessary expense. The grading of our yellow pine is also unsatisfactory. Three concerns in Rio de Janeiro claim that they are compelled at big expense to maintain representatives in the United States to inspect lumber before shipment. The small dealer can not stand this expense and the large dealer should not have to.

Lumber State.—Alternative nickname for Maine. (See Pine Tree State.)

Lundy's Lane (Canada), Battle of.—After his defeat at Chippewa in 1814 Gen. Riall retired by way of Queenston toward the head of Lake Ontario. He was soon reenforced, and returned to attack the Americans under Brown, who had pursued him as far as Queenston. Hearing of the British reenforcements, Brown retreated to the Chippewa River, and on July 24, 1814, encamped on the south bank, where he had defeated Riall on the 5th. On the 25th Gen. Scott, with about 1,200 men, went forward to reconnoiter and came upon the British army, 4,500 strong, near Niagara Falls, on Lundy's Lane, a road leading from the Falls to the end of Lake Ontario. Soon the entire American force was engaged, the battle lasting from sunset till midnight. The American forces numbered about 2,500 men. During the engagement Gen. Scott and Lieut.-Col. Miller distinguished themselves for daring and efficiency. The British were finally driven back and forced to abandon their artillery, ammunition, and baggage. Both armies claimed the victory, though both left the field. The American loss was 171 killed, 571 wounded, and 110 missing—a total of 852 out of an army of 2,500. The British lost 84 killed, 559 wounded, 193 missing, and 42 prisoners—a total of 878 out of an army of 4,500. Generals Brown and Scott were among the wounded. (See illustration opposite 599.)

Lüneburg, convention with, for acquiring and inheriting property, 2826.

Luquillo Forest Reserve, 6778.

Lusitania, sinking of, 8062.

Luther vs. Borden.—In 1841 a portion of the people of Rhode Island framed a new government and elected Thomas W. Dorr governor in opposition to the charter government. (See Dorr's Rebellion.) Governor King declared the State under martial law and Luther's house was searched, he being implicated in the armed conspiracy against the established government. Luther pleaded the constitutionality of the new government. The circuit court gave judgment against him, and the Supreme Court of the United States affirmed this decision in 1842. It was decided that under martial law suspected persons might legally be subjected to search and arrest by State authority, and that the question of the constitutionality of a State government was one with which Congress rather than the courts should deal.

Luxemburg.—The territory of the Grand Duchy of Luxemburg lies between 49° 27'-50° 18' N. latitude and 5° 45'-6° 30' E. longitude, with a total area of 2,586 square kilometers (998.216 square miles). It is bounded on the west by the Luxemburg Province of Belgium, on the north and east by the Rhine Province of Prussia, and on the south by the German Reichsland of Lorraine and the French Department of the Meuse. The area is about 1,000 square miles.

Physical Features.—The northern districts are crossed in all directions by outrunners of the Belgian Ardennes, and in the south are hills which form part of the plateau of Lorraine; but there are extensive valleys and plains in the north, and the southern districts are mainly low lands in the basin of the Moselle, which forms its southeastern boundary. The only considerable rivers of Luxemburg are the Moselle and its tributary, the Our.

History.—In 1831 the territory known as Luxemburg was divided at the Conference of London into the present Grand Duchy and the Belgian Province of Luxemburg, and from 1831 to 1890 the Grand Duchy was ruled by the Kings of the Netherlands. At the death of King William III. the operation of the Salic law transferred the sovereignty to Adolphus, Duke of Nassau, who was succeeded by his son William. By an amendment of the constitutional law of 1848, the succession was secured to the daughter of the Grand Duke William.

Government.—The government is that of a constitutional monarchy, the territory being declared neutral by the Great Powers of Europe by the Treaty of London (May 11, 1867). The Grand Duchy formed part of the Germanic Confederation, under the hegemony of Austria, from 1815-1866, and the impregnable fortress of Luxemburg was garrisoned by Prussian troops. By the Treaty of London the garrison was withdrawn and the fortress dismantled. The population according to the census of 1910 was 259,891. Present ruler: Her Royal Highness Marie Adelaide, Grand Duchess of Luxemburg, born June 14, 1894; succeeded her father (the Grand Duke William) Feb. 26, 1912, attained her majority and assumed the government June 14, 1912. There is a Council of State (Staatsrat) of fifteen members and a Chamber of Deputies of fifty-three members, elected by direct vote of the Cantons for six years, one-half renewable every three years. All male inhabitants of twenty-five years, who pay ten francs in direct taxes, are voters and eligible for election.

There are courts in each Canton, and District Courts at Luxemburg and Diekirch, with a Supreme Court at the Capital.

There is a gendarmerie of about 180 men, and a volunteer force of 250 men for the preservation of order.

Education and Religion.—Education is compulsory and free, and is widespread, the expenditure in 1912 being 2,310,340 francs. Almost all the inhabitants are Roman Catholics, there being only 4,000 Protestants and 1,300 Jews. The Bishop of Luxemburg is appointed by the See of Rome.

Finance.—The average annual expenditure for five years was 15,408,255 francs and the average revenue 16,345,083 francs. The interest-bearing public debt amounts to 12,000,000 francs, and there is a floating debt, incurred in the construction of railways and public works, of 19,335,674 francs. The franc, the unit of value, is the same as the French franc, and is equivalent to $0.19,3 United States money.

Production and Industry.—The country is rich in iron ore, the output in 1912 being 2,252,229 metric tons. In addition to the iron industry there are tanneries, weaving and glove factories, paper mills, breweries and distilleries, and sugar refineries.

There were 525 kilometers of railway open in 1912, the system being connected with the Belgian, French, and German lines, which converge at the capital.

Luxemburg, fugitive criminals, convention with, for surrender of, 4782.

Luxemburg, Treaty with (see **Extradition Treaties.**)

Lynch Law.—The practice of punishing alleged offenders, generally without trial, by unauthorized persons and without due process of law. Lynch law, it is said, takes its name from Charles Lynch, a Virginia planter and Quaker, and his associates, who during Revolutionary days seized British sympathizers and hanged them by the thumbs till they shouted "Liberty forever."

Lynchings discussed and indemnities voluntarily provided, recommended, 5767, 6248, 6277, 6371, 6430, 6459, 6461, 7029.

Lynn, Mass., act for erection of postoffice building at, vetoed, 5150.

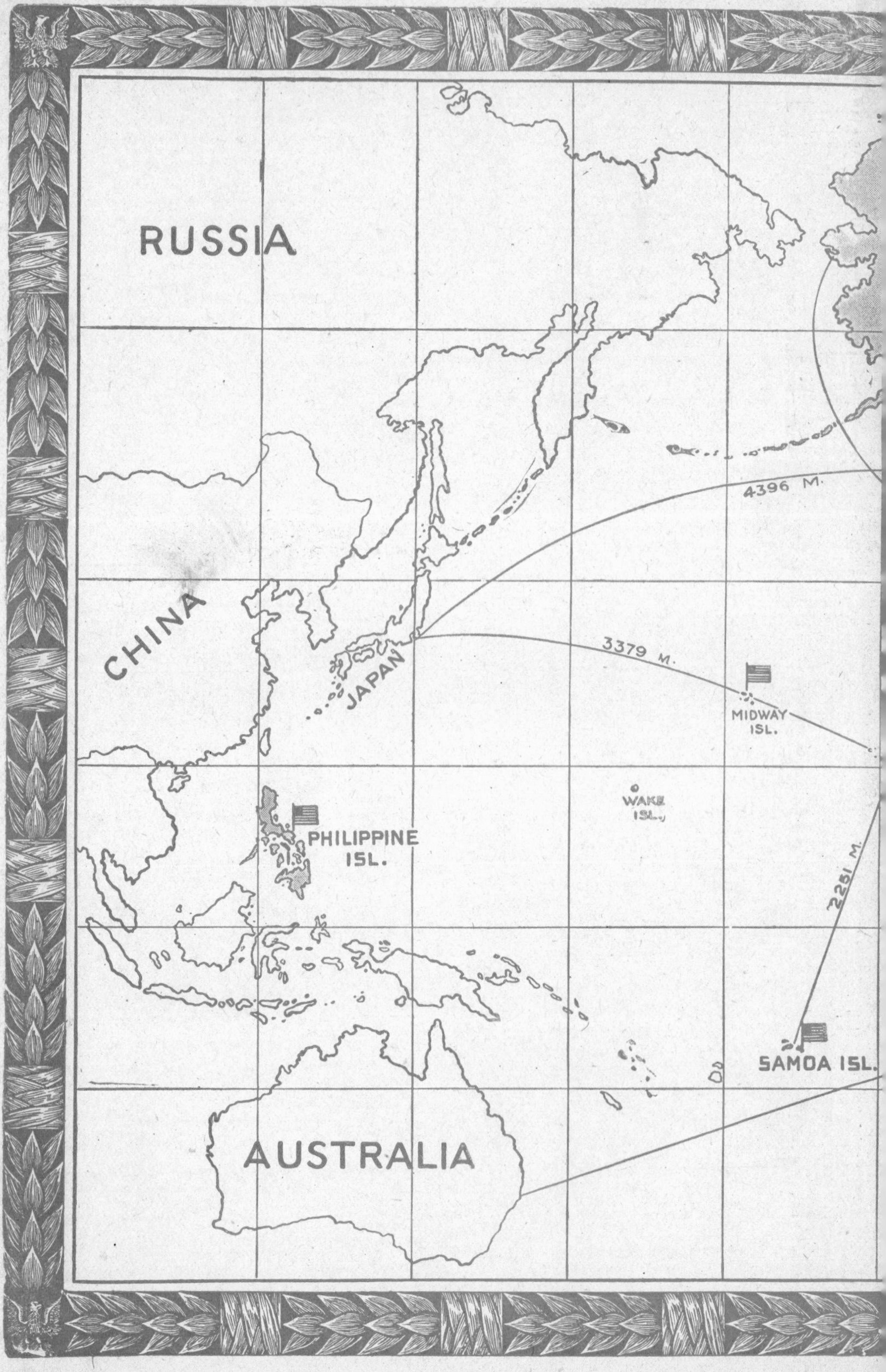

RUSSIA
CHINA
JAPAN
4396 M.
3379 M.
MIDWAY ISL.
WAKE ISL.
PHILIPPINE ISL.
2251 M.
SAMOA ISL.
AUSTRALIA